# Integrating Family Therapy

# Integrating Family Therapy

## HANDBOOK OF FAMILY PSYCHOLOGY AND SYSTEMS THEORY

*Edited by*

Richard H. Mikesell,
Don-David Lusterman,
and Susan H. McDaniel

AMERICAN PSYCHOLOGICAL ASSOCIATION
WASHINGTON, DC

Published by the
American Psychological Association
750 First Street, NE
Washington, DC 20002

Copies may be ordered from
APA Order Department
P.O. Box 2710
Hyattsville, MD 20784

In the United Kingdom and Europe, copies may be ordered from
American Psychological Association
3 Henrietta Street
Covent Garden
London WC2E 8LU
England

Typeset in Berkeley by PRO-Image Corporation, Techna-Type Div., York, PA

Printer: Braun-Brumfield, Inc., Ann Arbor, MI
Cover designer: Supon Design Group, Washington, DC
Technical/production editor: Valerie Montenegro

**Library of Congress Cataloging-in-Publication Data**
Integrating family therapy: handbook of family psychology and systems theory/edited by Richard H. Mikesell, Don-David Lusterman, and Susan H. McDaniel.
    p.    cm.
    Includes bibliographical references and index.
    ISBN 1-55798-280-5 (acid-free paper)
    1. Family psychotherapy.   2. Ecological family therapy.
I. Mikesell, Richard H.   II. Lusterman, Don-David.   III. McDaniel, Susan H.   IV. Title: Systems therapy.
RC488.5.I497  1995
616.89'156—dc20
                                       95-3106
                                          CIP

**British Library Cataloguing-in-Publication Data**
A CIP record is available from the British Library.

*Printed in the United States of America*
*First edition*

For my father, the late H. Orville Mikesell; my mother, Miriam Hess Mikesell; my wife, Susan Gail Mikesell; and my children, Elizabeth Suzanne and Theodore Richard.

*Richard H. Mikesell*
*Washington, DC*

For my wife, Judy; my children, Eliezer, Cheryl, Noam, Stacey, and Gavi; and my grandchildren, Ethan, Ariella, and Talia.

*Don-David Lusterman*
*Baldwin, NY*

For three mentors who taught me to think systems and demonstrated systems principles in their teaching, their collaboration, and their approaches to life: Harold Goolishian, PhD; Lyman C. Wynne, MD, PhD; and C. Glenn Cambor, MD.

*Susan H. McDaniel*
*Rochester, NY*

# Contents

# Preface

Both family psychology and systems therapy represent new perspectives on family therapy and psychology. Family psychology brings to family therapy the research and theory building skills that are the hallmark of psychology as a profession. Systems therapy expands the context of psychological practice to families and other larger systems, such as schools, medical settings, and the broader community in which they are embedded. *Integrating Family Therapy: Handbook of Family Psychology and Systems Theory* integrates these perspectives in both broad and focused areas of application.

With this volume, we hope to reach newcomers to the field as well as those who are already familiar with family psychology and systems therapy. Basic concepts and core techniques of systems assessment and therapy are presented, laying the groundwork for a more focused examination of specific topics. Both neophytes and seasoned family therapists should find useful the integrated application of these core elements to populations such as couples, older persons, and inner-city families; with specific problems such as divorce, domestic violence, and physical illness; and in specific contexts such as schools, hospitals, and community agencies and treatment centers. Special attention is given to life cycle, gender, and ethnic issues affecting families, as well as the ethical, educational, and stress-related factors affecting therapists.

The Division of Family Psychology (Division 43) of the American Psychological Association (APA) played a major role in inspiring this volume and in bringing together leaders in the field. Eleven years old at the time of this writing, the Division was originally created within the APA to provide a "home" within the association for psychologists interested in various aspects of family and systems research and practice. Many psychologists had been involved in this systems work for many years; in 1984 they finally had a distinct organizational home within the APA.

The first and second editors of this book, Richard H. Mikesell and Don-David Lusterman, were cofounders of Division 43 and became close friends and colleagues. Susan H. McDaniel, a pioneer in the evolving field of medical family therapy and also an active member of the Division, subsequently joined them as third editor of this book.

The stimulating context of Division 43 led us as the editing team to bring our individual viewpoints, personal enthusiasm, and unique skills and expertise together to plan a book that we hope you will find to be a creative and stimulating influence on your work. We have selected authors who are leaders in their respective fields and topics that represent key issues in family psychology and systems therapy today. We hope that this synergistic endeavor will serve a variety of readers and that the volume will serve the field by providing a basic framework for the linking of family psychology and systems therapy in a comprehensive and practical way.

A work of this magnitude is not accomplished without the help of a great many people. Gary VandenBos of APA Publications and Communications was a key figure in the instigation of this project. His superb counsel and continual oversight of the book are greatly appreciated and acknowledged. Our contributors all made herculean efforts to product timely, "state-of-the-art" chapters. Richard H. Mikesell is grateful for the excellent word-processing work of Jennifer Arnold, Elizabeth Larson, and Susan Munson. Don-David Lusterman gives thanks to Judy Lusterman for her astute editorial suggestions and to Stacey Lusterman for her consistent and cheerful backup with the many details that must be attended to in such an undertaking. Susan H. McDaniel appreciates Jeanne Klee for her daily support and patient faxing.

Peggy Schlegel, our Development Editor at APA Books, guided the book and authors through the final editorial process with competency, consistency, and clarity. Valerie Montenegro, our Production Editor at APA Books, was superb as she moved the book through its final stages.

Also, we would like to acknowledge, in general, the entire membership of the APA's Division of Family Psychology. While they did not serve a formal role in the project, the membership, and in particular, the Board of Directors and Committee Members of the Division served as our professional extended family. Most critically, we extend our most heartfelt appreciation to our own family members for their forbearance, nurturance, and support during this project. Thank you to Susan, Betsy, and Ted Mikesell; Judy Lusterman; and David, Hanna, and Marisa Siegel.

# Introduction

Family is the primary context of human experience from the cradle to the grave. Psychology, however, first concerned itself with the individual. Only later was the context of the family considered a major focus of the field and then only in a gradual way. For example, if one considers how developmental psychology evolved, the subject of study was initially the child himself or herself, followed by study of the mother–child dyad (Zigler, 1985). Only later was the role of the father, and still later that of the extended family, considered to be of major importance. Moreover, it is just recently that the community and its institutions, the primary contexts of the family, have received the attention they deserve.

## CHANGING CONCEPTS OF THE FAMILY

As these changes have occurred, the understanding of what constitutes the family has undergone radical change. The implicit norm that most therapists and theorists originally posited, the so-called traditional, intact, or nuclear family has given way to a multiplicity of family arrangements. Blended families, single parent families, serial marriages, live-in relationships, gay and lesbian relationships, and "traditional" marriages all demand careful theoretical and therapeutic attention in regard to how they are similar as well as how they are unique.

In line with the debunking of the idea of the family as a monolithic or stereotypical entity, it is now recognized that family norms can vary greatly because of gender, cultural, and ethnic diversity. The last 25 years have seen enormous changes in gender roles; in awareness of culture and ethnic differences; and in the need for sensitivity to these issues in the-

ory, research, and practice. There is no one model of healthy or unhealthy family functioning.

Other differences may also, in special and distinct ways, significantly influence family life. The increasing bifurcation of the population in the United States and in the world at large into two camps—the rich and the poor—provides special challenges and burdens, particularly to women, children, and people of color. The concomitant cacophony of social agencies that are meant to serve families creates still greater stress for them and a field of even greater complexity for the professionals who seek to know and serve them.

## WHAT IS FAMILY PSYCHOLOGY?

Emerging from this evolution in psychology and in society, family psychology represents the matrix of psychological knowledge—theory, research, and practice—involving the contemporary family and its broader contexts. Expanding this definition in the first issue of the *Journal of Family Psychology*, Howard Liddle (1987), its editor, fashioned the following description:

> *Family psychology, using a systemic perspective, broadens psychology's traditional emphasis on the individual, and, while having a primary emphasis on marriage and the family, it uses the systemic view to focus also on the nature and role of individuals in primary relationship structures, as well as, more broadly, the social ecology of the family—those networks in which the family interacts and resides. Individuals*

*and families are thus construed as wholes and parts. (p. 9)*

As mentioned earlier, psychology contributes its research and theory-building skills to family therapy. By the same token, family psychology sensitizes other disciplines of psychology to consider interactions that include the individual, the family, and the societal context.

## WHAT IS SYSTEMS THERAPY?

During the 1950s, an innovative therapeutic paradigm emerged in the matrix of fields concerned with human behavior. Many mental health practitioners became convinced of the critical importance of the present as well as past family to an individual's psychological symptoms and problems and became increasingly convinced that family should become an integral aspect of psychological treatment. For some, for awhile, the initial love affair with family treatment seemed to obscure the usefulness of knowledge about the individual client. As the field matured, most practitioners saw the need to integrate psychological understanding of individual dynamics with this more recent understanding of family dynamics in terms of theory, research, and practice.

During this time, another significant subtheme, the ecosystemic perspective, also gained some prominence. Those with an ecosystemic orientation began to examine individual and family functioning in the context of still larger systems. The ecosystemic approach was at one time considered to be one of several theories influencing research and practice with families. As the 21st century nears, this approach has assumed greater importance, resulting in an actual shift in the field—a metatheoretical shift toward larger systems as a primary influence on the behavior of individuals and families. Thus, the challenge of integration grew to involve not two, but three elements: the individual, the family, and the larger social context.

### Systems Theory

The zeitgeist of systems thinking was not, of course, limited to the behavioral sciences. In fact, Ludwig von Bertalanffy, a biologist with wide-ranging re-search interests, is considered the founder of systems theory. He put forth his theory as early as 1928 and gave it the title General Systems Theory in 1945 (Steinglass, 1978). The theory was fully described in a groundbreaking publication (von Bertalanffy, 1968) and has been a continuing influence not only in the physical sciences, but also the behavioral and social sciences, as well as history and philosophy.

Systems theory is broader than what is usually considered a theory in the behavioral sciences. It has been described as more of a conceptual framework with interdisciplinary applications (Royce, 1981) than a theory. However, the original term *theory* has always been used in descriptions of this framework. In brief, systems theory was designed to move beyond the reductionistic and mechanistic tradition in science that focused on a linear series of cause and event equations. Systems theory framed explanations in the general principles of wholeness, organization, and relationships and simultaneously tracked the significance of interacting variables. Pattern recognition supplanted the deductive reasoning that prevails in reductionism. As Steinglass (1978) has summarized aptly, systems theory is characterized by "attention to organization, to the relationship between parts, to the concentration on patterned rather than on linear relationships, to a consideration of events in the context in which they are occurring rather than an isolation of events from their environmental context" (p. 304).

### Systems Therapy

Systems therapy can to some extent be considered an offshoot of this paradigmatic shift, although as mentioned earlier, this field had its own unique historical lineage, involving psychologists, psychiatrists, social workers, and marriage and family therapists. Because this lineage is well described in several chapters of this book (see, e.g., chaps. 1, 2, 10, 31, and 34), to trace this history here would be redundant. Suffice it to say here that psychology is now training its current generation of systems therapists, and with each succeeding generation, the field has rejected some previous theories, continued to find useful many others, and is generating still more inclusive and integrative models of behavior and behavior change. In addition, the wide range of individuals who have been drawn to systems therapy make it far from a homogenous field.

Although systems therapy can involve family therapy, it is much more encompassing than family therapy per se. As Harlene Anderson writes in chapter 2 of this book, "Family therapy has come to indicate a modality for treating a particular social configuration, while systems therapy is a paradigmatic shift in the concept of family systems and their problems."

In practical terms, *systems therapy,* as we will use the term throughout this book, will be considered the comprehensive set of interventions for treating the family, including individuals, couples, nuclear families, families of origin, medical systems and other larger contexts (such as school and work), and the cultural and ethnic contexts in which all of these are embedded. At any particular time, a unique feature of systems therapy is that it gives the therapist a paradigm from which to view multiple causes and contexts of behavior. Consequently, it provides one of the most comprehensive models for the development of interventions and one of the most promising models for change.

## APPROACH OF THIS BOOK

In this volume, it is our aim to provide a comprehensive perspective of integrated approaches in family psychology and systems therapy pertaining to a wide range of treatment issues. Although the chapter authors explore the growing contribution of family psychologists in the areas of theory, research, and practice, they also emphasize the placement of family systems within larger systems. Techniques from traditional schools of family therapy are integrated to provide the most effective interventive approaches.

Contributors have endeavored to provide the reader with both theoretical insights and practical suggestions to advance the treatment of the ever-changing family. The book is rich with case examples, which are disguised to protect anonymity. Most chapters include important empirical information, but there is a particular emphasis on what the therapist does to bring about change.

Newcomers to the fields of family psychology or systems therapy can gain knowledge of the origins, core concepts, and primary methods of the systems approach to working with families. They will also learn how techniques from schools that were once considered irreconcilable can be usefully integrated in practice.[1] Seasoned researchers and practitioners will deepen and broaden their understanding of systems therapy and will glean up-to-date information in particular interest areas. All of our chapters reflect an integration that should free the practitioner to think in a systemic framework. We are aware that casual eclecticism can make for disjointed and ineffective therapy. To counteract this, the contributors to this volume, like integrative theorists before them (Breunlin, Schwartz, & Karrer, 1992; Weeks, 1989), have woven the theories and ideas that form the basis of their approaches into a coherent tapestry. They show that their eclecticism is not unsystematic, but derives from a deep understanding of multiple recursive influences on the family and a corresponding understanding of the several therapeutic means to the same therapeutic ends.

In like fashion, the chapter authors are united in the belief that the systems therapist is in the most powerful position to facilitate the therapeutic process when he or she has maximum degrees of freedom possible to use the entirety or part(s) of the system for therapeutic change. To use this power, the therapist needs as many sources of data as possible—empirical research about individuals, couples, nuclear families, families of origin, extended family, and social networks, for example, as well as clinical knowledge from therapists, consultants, and supervisors of therapy. The empirical data allow the therapist to construct the best possible map of the situation. The knowledge of skilled therapists can help the practitioner to make clinical decisions as to how best to use that data. Together, they maximize therapeutic leverage in any particular case.

---

[1] In this book, we deliberately have not presented chapters based on specific schools of family therapy, because our purpose is to transcend these divisions for the sake of integration in the field.

*Integrating Family Therapy: Handbook of Family Psychology and Systems Theory* is organized into 10 parts. We have chosen to place Clinical Principles of Systems Therapy first, because that part tells the reader what systems therapists actually do. Some therapists have been privy to demonstrations of family work done by therapists from a particular school of thought. However, most systems therapists, like their individual therapist counterparts, tend to be eclectic. They may leave these demonstrations without knowing how to integrate the useful techniques they have seen into their day-to-day practice. The chapters in this part provide a good introduction to how this is done, from answering the initial phone call from a family member to shaking hands during a last session with the family. These chapters are complemented by a chapter that emphasizes collaboration with the family throughout the therapy.

Just as understanding the life cycle of the individual has contributed to major advances in individual psychology and psychotherapy, so, too, has increasing understanding of life cycles of families as a unit. Part II, Developmental Issues in Families, begins with an overall view of the stages and normative crises of the life cycle and then proceeds to take a more focused look at family development and therapy with stepfamilies, families of the multicrisis poor, and families with an older member. The latter two topics were chosen because, in our view, they are underrepresented in most general books on family therapy. In each of these more focused topic areas, the primary role of family development is stressed.

Although most of the chapters in this book are founded on empirical research, Part III, Assessment and Research in Family Psychology, emphasizes the empirical and quantitative base of family psychology to a greater extent. A chapter describing a multilevel, multifaceted approach to marital and family assessment leads the part, followed by a discussion of the evaluation of family-based psychopathology. A chapter on advances in the field of family therapy research provides a broad overview on this major topic area. The well-respected circumplex model of family systems is updated to integrate ethnic diversity and broader social systems.

Couplehood is the basic building block, birthplace, launching pad, and transition place of family life. Much has been written about couples therapy over the years, so in Part IV, Therapy With Couples, we wanted to focus on areas that have been particularly difficult to work with as well as situations and roles involving dissolution of couples. In these situations, the systems therapist is uniquely positioned to do much preventive work with families. In the challenging areas of sexual therapy and infidelity, the authors show how a systems perspective frees the therapist from a reliance on technique alone and provides a much more useful framework of intimacy to guide therapeutic interventions.

Couples and families are influenced by gender, ethnic, and socioeconomic factors. Family structure, family life cycle, and family processes are each affected in different ways, depending on the family's position vis-à-vis these factors. We have chosen three particularly pertinent topics for Part V, Gender and Ethnic Issues. Lesbian and gay family psychology and the treatment of African American inner-city families are the more specific topics discussed. Broader topics such as ethnic heritage, intergender communication, and gender sensitivity in systems therapy are also represented.

At the most basic level, families consist of individuals whose physical well-being affects and is affected by family functioning. Moreover, physical health problems involve the health care system and its many subsystems. The health care system itself is, of course, undergoing massive changes. Dealing with health issues is perhaps one of the clearest ways of discovering the importance of context: the individual within the family, the family within the medical system, and the medical system within the society. In Part VI, Medical Systems, we have chosen to examine five areas: infertility and pregnancy loss, chronic illness in children, cancer, eating disorders, and patients and families who somatize. Each offers a fresh perspective on working with families and medical systems. For example, the problem of somatization is approached from a narrative perspective involving multiple systems. Most of the principles discussed in each chapter can be generalized to other medical problems and situations.

Work and school are the subsystems and contexts in which families "live by day"; Part VII, Other Larger Systems and Contexts, takes an integrative systems perspective on these two areas. As dual-income families become the norm and school systems become larger and more complex, families are challenged to find balance in their lives and appropriate connections with these systems that claim most of their waking hours. The chapter authors challenge therapists to find ways of thinking about and working with families and systems that is both flexible and realistic. For example, working in a systemic way with families with school-age children may require the therapist to coordinate with school psychologists, counselors, social workers, and teachers and administrators—either directly or indirectly through the family.

Societal problems, such as violence and drug and alcohol abuse all too often impinge on family life. They are also high-risk areas for the family and the systems therapist, the latter of whom must have special skills and expert knowledge. In Part VIII, Coercion and Substance Abuse, chapter authors discuss the basics in working with both violent, coercive processes in the family and coercive processes involved in cults, which leave the family of a cult member feeling both powerless and realistically afraid. Drug and alcohol treatment, from a systems therapy perspective, is also described in a chapter in this part.

Part IX, The Self of the Systems Therapist, focuses on the self of the systems therapist, both as a developing systems therapist and supervisor and as a person faced with significant stressors, particularly in dealing with trauma in families. Inclusion of these chapters is overt recognition that the person and family of the therapist, like the family he or she treats, is vulnerable to stress from work systems. How this stress affects specific roles (e.g., training supervisor), ethical behavior, and the physical and mental well-being of the therapist is discussed.

The book concludes with a single chapter about a model we expect to be dominant in family psychol-

ogy in the future: the psychology of normal family processes, moving from family damage to family challenge and response. Here, the issues of cultural diversity, gender, socioeconomic status, and differing family arrangements are discussed again in the context of normal family process research. Although family dysfunction is the catalyst for families' entering therapy, we believe that researchers studying healthy family functioning may provide the most useful templates for prevention and may also point the way toward highly useful ways of intervening in families and surrounding systems when problems occur.

We hope that readers find this organization as useful as we believe the chapter contents to be and that they experience the excitement we have shared in bringing these authors together to make their unique contributions to the field available to us all.

## References

Breunlin, D. C., Schwartz, R. C., & Karrer, B. M. (1992). *Metaframeworks: Transcending the models of family therapy.* San Francisco: Jossey-Bass.

Liddle, H. (1987). Family psychology: The journal, the field. *Journal of Family Psychology, 1,* 5–22.

Royce, J. R. (1981). A personal portrayal of Ludwig von Bertalanffy (1901–1972): System theorist and interdisciplinary scholar at the University of Alberta. *Journal of the History of the Behavioral Sciences, 17,* 340–342.

Steinglass, P. (1978). *The conceptualization of marriage from a system theory perspective in Paolino & McCrady's* Marriage and marital therapy. New York: Brunner/Mazel.

von Bertalanffy, L. (1968). *General systems theory: Foundations, development, application.* New York: Braziller.

Weeks, G. (1989). *Treating couples: The intersystem model of the Marriage Council of Philadelphia.* New York: Brunner/Mazel.

Zigler, E. (1985). Foreword. In L. L'Abate (Ed.), *The handbook of family psychology and therapy* (pp. v–vii). Homewood, IL: Dorsey Press.

# PART I
# CLINICAL PRINCIPLES OF SYSTEMS THERAPY

# Introduction

In the early stages of the development of family therapy, a number of clearly articulated schools of thought emerged, and many family therapists became disciples of one of these schools. Those not strictly loyal to one school labeled themselves eclectic, attended a variety of workshops, and read widely from all the schools. Based on this and their clinical experiences, they then made intuitive decisions about which approach to use with any given family.

As the field has matured, loyalty to a particular school and decisions made on intuition have given way to serious attempts to develop an integrative framework. This book is based on this integration, and this particular section explores the broad issues that lie at the core of systems therapy: What is the body of techniques on which we can rely? How do we engage families and broader systems? What approach should we take to termination when the model is systemic rather than individual?

Written from this integrative perspective, chapter 1, "Core Techniques in Family Therapy" describes techniques and interventions that most therapists use in practice, regardless of the theoretical orientation they favor. The authors, David Seaburn, Judith Landau-Stanton, and Susan Horwitz, divide these interventions into three categories: here-and-now, transgenerational, and ecosystemic interventions. The authors illustrate how each category of intervention might be applied to a single case example. Then, using the same case, they describe how they would work with this case using a systems approach (the Rochester Model) that integrates these techniques and interventions.

In chapter 2, "Collaborative Language Systems: Toward a Postmodern Therapy," Harlene Anderson describes her work with the late Harry Goolishian as she articulates a therapy informed by social constructionist ideas. This approach emphasizes a participatory partnership between therapist and family (or larger system) and the centrality of language, self-agency, and meaning in the collaborative conversation known as therapy. The challenges of a "not-knowing" stance toward clients are illustrated with several case examples.

To finish therapy well, Timothy Weber and Felise Levine believe, it is critical to begin well. In chapter 3, "Engaging the Family: An Integrative Approach," they interweave the perspectives of object relations theory and transgenerational theory to help the therapist handle the complexities of beginning therapy with a family. Rather than viewing engagement as an initial stage of joining with the family, these authors emphasize engagement as an ongoing process that involves establishing leadership and creating a holding environment. They illustrate these two processes through 11 different phases of the initial engagement—from the thoughts, fantasies, feelings, beliefs, concerns, and motivations that the therapist and family members bring to the initial phone call through the debriefing the therapist should do after the initial session with the family.

The title of chapter 4, "Open-Ended Therapy: Termination in Marital and Family Therapy," may at first appear to be a contradiction in terms. The most widely practiced modes of family therapy today are goal oriented and time limited. How does this relate to the idea of open-ended therapy? Jay Lebow describes an open-ended approach to treatment as one that can be used by the family for brief durations at various times in the life cycle and that involves careful consideration of termination at each of these points. He then outlines 10 tasks that must be accomplished to successfully terminate a treatment period. The author explains how these tasks are derived from various models of family therapy and how they may differ depending on whether the termination is planned or unplanned and client or therapist initiated. Issues involved in terminating successful and unsuccessful treatment are discussed, and recommendations are made for termination under a variety of circumstances.

# CHAPTER 1

# CORE TECHNIQUES IN FAMILY THERAPY

*David Seaburn, Judith Landau-Stanton, and Susan Horwitz*

## INTRODUCTION

The family therapy field is fast approaching a half century of accomplishment. During its evolution, a variety of models have been born and nurtured to maturity (see Guerin, 1976; Gurman & Kniskern, 1981, 1991; Haley & Hoffman, 1968; Nichols, 1984). As with any new discipline establishing its own identity, practitioners and theorists have often held tightly to their perspectives while at the same time trying to maintain a dialogue across their differences. With the emergence of the third and fourth generations of family therapists, the field has progressed to the point of recognizing both our roots and our commonalities. As a result, the current generation of family therapists is trained in multiple orientations and is cognizant of the shared theoretical threads that hold the field together. This change has ushered in a new era marked by the development of integrative models of family therapy. (See especially chap. 31 in this volume.)

Many researchers and theorists have examined and compared various tenets and aspects of family therapy (Figley & Nelson, 1989, 1990; Goldenberg & Goldenberg, 1980; Gurman, 1979; Kaslow, 1987; Madanes & Haley, 1977; Nelson & Figley, 1990; Nelson, Heilbron, & Figley, 1993; Stanton, 1981a; Strupp & Hadley, 1979). In line with their search for understanding, this chapter will focus on what family therapists actually do in therapy. We will identify the techniques or interventions that most family therapists perform in the course of their practice, regardless of the model of family therapy that they espouse. We believe that these core techniques or interventions are related more to a common approach family therapists use than to the model of family therapy or the philosophical position they hold.

If one examines the development of family therapy in context, it becomes apparent that family therapy emerged in parallel with other major changes in society. It arose at a time when industrialization, urbanization, and advances in communication technology were exploding, all accompanied by increased mobility and separation of extended family members. The nature of literature and drama had changed dramatically, and people were living much more in and for the here and now. Two world wars had accelerated the sense of urgency for connectedness in view of the potential fragility of relationships. The advances in communication technology resulted in the replacement of leisurely academic pursuits and the art of letter writing with skills more suited to the less personal expediency of computers.

Family therapy mirrored this process of change closely, with some of the pioneer family therapists holding on to more traditional ideas and others acceding to the pressures of a fast-paced and demanding society. Several of the early family therapists (e.g., Ackerman, 1958, 1966; Bell, 1961, 1975; Boszormenyi-Nagy & Spark, 1973; Bowen, 1978; Framo, 1992), developing an approach to families that grew out of the fields of psychoanalysis and developmental psychology, treated families from a predominantly historical, analytical, or *transgenerational* perspective. The approaches developed by others (e.g., Erickson as cited in Haley, 1973; Epstein, Bishop, & Levin,

1978; Haley, 1963, 1976; Jackson, 1965; Minuchin, 1974; Napier & Whitaker, 1978; Satir, 1967, 1972; Weakland, 1960) mirrored the changing times. These theorists and practitioners attended more to the *here and now*, focusing on current behavior, immediate family experience, interaction, communication, and the needs of the family. Napier and Whitaker (1978) also included in this view the perspective of the person of the therapist. Yet others (e.g., Speck & Attneave, 1973) took a larger systems or more socioanthropological approach, or viewed the behavior of the family from an *ecosystemic* (Auerswald, 1974) perspective, examining the larger context over time to discover events that might have determined present behavior. Many of these early theorists were influenced by the field of cybernetics (Bateson, 1972; von Bertalanffy, 1968) and its applicability to human systems. The early development of the field also saw the beginnings of integration with therapists such as Satir (1967, 1972), who combined historical and here and now interventions in her model of conjoint family therapy, as did Wynne (1958, 1961) and Duhl and Duhl (1981). In addition, clusters of interventions focusing on problem areas or social issues have arisen as family therapists have tapped into their creativity. These types of interventions have made a major impact on the way we do therapy, and frequently their influence extends well beyond the original problem for which they were designed. Two examples of this are bereavement (e.g., Horwitz, in press; Paul, 1986; Paul & Grosser, 1965; Walsh & Mc-Goldrick, 1991) and addiction (Berenson, 1976; Kaufman & Kaufman, 1979; Krestan, 1991; Stanton & Todd, 1982; Steinglass, 1987). These clusters of interventions tend to be adaptations of the core techniques or different combinations of interventions often arising from the early family therapy models. In fact, many of these problem-driven classes of intervention might be regarded as the forerunners of the integrated models.

The therapist's personal perspective and beliefs largely determine how he or she conceives of the change process and therefore influence the approaches used to facilitate change (Kaslow, 1987). Therapists may view family relationships and interactions as primary and superseding the nature of the problem or believe that the particular symptomatol-

ogy or presenting problem is the most important variable. In this way, whether interventions focus on the interaction among family members, the problem being treated, or the context from which the family has come or the problem has emerged appears to depend at least as much, if not more, on the therapist as on the family (Whitaker & Keith, 1980).

Despite differences among therapists and models of family therapy, certain techniques and interventions tend to be applied by most therapists. These classes or clusters of interventions often cross the boundaries of differing schools and may reflect an inherent effort to be integrative in clinical practice. In Part I, we describe these broad classes of core family therapy interventions as we see them and then apply them to a clinical case. In Part II, we describe the case in greater detail and attempt to search for the commonalities between the classes of intervention that have led to the integrative models of family therapy. To illustrate this integration, we apply aspects of transitional family therapy, developed at the University of Rochester, to the family presented in Parts I and II.

## PART I

## Core Family Therapy Interventions

Arising from the schools of family therapy mentioned above, core family therapy interventions can be organized into three broad classes: (a) here and now, (b) transgenerational, and (c) ecosystemic. Elements of each of these classes can be found in almost every school and model of family therapy. In this section we give a simple definition of these intervention classes. We then apply them each to a clinical case in an attempt to illustrate the interventions that form the core of family therapy.

**Here and now interventions.** Here and now interventions emphasize the organization of the family and its process of change as they manifest in the present. Individual problems are conceptualized as reflecting difficulties within the family system as a whole. A dysfunction may be viewed as a current sequence of behavior that originated as an attempt to resolve a problem but subsequently became a repeating problematic pattern. A problem may also be understood as reflecting an ineffectual family structure.

In any case, family problems are seen as both affecting and being affected by how the family interacts as a whole.

Here and now interventions may focus primarily on the family (its structure or its communication or both) or on the specific problem (or solution). Here and now interventions are goal oriented and problem or solution focused (De Shazer, 1980, 1982, 1985). The therapist accepts the responsibility to facilitate change. Consequently, the therapist is active and at times directive, for example, making restructuring moves (Minuchin, 1974). Interventions are designed to alter the family's organization or accepted patterns of relating so that symptoms may be alleviated and problems may be addressed differently in the future (Haley, 1963; Madanes & Haley, 1977).

Family therapy based on here and now interventions is often brief. The emphasis is on behavioral change rather than insight. The therapist may work with the whole family as defined by the family or the therapist. The therapist may also work with subsystems, dyads, and individuals. Interventions may be enacted during the therapy session or directives may be prescribed for the family to accomplish between sessions. In either case, the family is continually encouraged to work on tasks that are designed to facilitate change.

Here and now interventions may be direct or indirect (Stanton, 1984). Direct interventions, such as suggesting that parents work together to set limits with a rebellious adolescent, are compliance based. These interventions assume the cooperation of the family. Indirect interventions, such as prescribing that a couple having sexual problems refrain from intercourse, are noncompliance based. Such interventions are designed to circumvent family reluctance to change by "going with" the resistance. This creates a paradox in which the behavior that is prescribed (sex) is difficult to resist (Watzlawick, Weakland, & Fisch, 1974).

Common examples of here and now interventions include tasks that may be performed both in and outside of the therapy session:

*Reenactment and enactment* (Minuchin & Fishman, 1981). A common in-session task involves instructing the family to reenact a problematic family interaction and then demonstrating an enactment of new

patterns of interaction and communication. In Moreno's psychodrama (Compernolle, 1981), the patient was instructed to experiment with and practice new methods of relating during a simulated interaction. The extension of this technique to use by actual family members (as opposed to fellow patients on a psychiatric ward) served as a major breakthrough in here and now interventions and is applied across many schools and models. For example, the therapist actively engages family members in demonstrating their difficulties, such as arguing. The therapist then directs the family to talk to each other about the changes they would like to make regarding family fights. Finally, the therapist has the family enact, demonstrate, or practice the new behavior in session.

*Reframing/positive connotation/noble ascription and symptom prescription.* These techniques of viewing or framing the problem in a more positive way (Watzlawick et al., 1974) are commonly used when the therapist wants to recognize an individual's or family's positive intention and when resistance to change is high. The attribution of a positive value to an interaction, event, or pattern has been variously called *reframing* (Minuchin & Fishman, 1981), *noble ascription* (Stanton & Todd, 1979, 1982) and *positive connotation* (Selvini-Palazzoli, Boscolo, Cecchin, & Prata, 1978). In the case of symptom prescription (Selvini-Palazzoli et al., 1978), this perspective is taken to its natural conclusion, as the family is not only helped to see the beneficial nature of the symptom or problem but also is asked to do more of the same.

For example, in a hypothetical case, parents may present their child's temper tantrums as an insoluble problem. These parents might disagree on how to approach the problem but also insist that they have "tried everything." They are likely to be angry at each other and at the child and to feel sure that it is the child's problem. The therapist may suggest that far from being a bad child, the child is actually quite loving and is expressing his or her love by behaving in ways that invite the parents to come together and work as a unit. In fact, the child may fear that if he or she cannot keep the parents together they will break apart. The therapist may suggest that the child have a temper tantrum whenever he or she is afraid that the parents may be moving apart.

*Restructuring the family in session.* Restructuring may be facilitated by helping the family identify the repeating patterns on which structures are based (Madanes & Haley, 1977) or by encouraging a change in the physical positioning of family members (Minuchin & Fishman, 1981). The therapist may use nonverbal behavior as much as verbal behavior to alter problematic family interactions and to restructure a family. A common example of this latter technique is changing how a family is seated during a session. For example, in the case of the hypothetical child mentioned above, he or she might be seen as effectively splitting the parents. It would be likely that this child would sit between the parents at the family therapy session. The therapist might ask him or her to move (or ask the parents to have the child move out from between them) and the parents' chairs may be thus brought closer together. Another method by which the system is changed in the here and now is family sculpting, an action (as opposed to verbal) technique that allows for the alteration of how the family occupies and represents its relationships in space (Duhl, Kantor, & Duhl, 1973). A typical sculpting exercise might depict the family structure at various points in time or during a particular situation. The family takes the form of a silent tableau in which people are placed at set distances from one another and in postures that depict their relationships.

*Defining the problem and establishing goals and action plans.* Depending on the orientation of the therapist, these techniques may be seen as two parts of the same whole. The definition of the problem leads to the clarification of goals needed for the development of a solution (Haley, 1976; Landau-Stanton & Stanton, 1985; Watzlawick et al., 1974; see especially chap. 3 in this volume). For example, the parents of the problem child presented above were able to develop an understanding of the repeating pattern that resulted in the child's gaining a position of power vis-à-vis the parents. The child was able to control the parents' behavior by acting out in order to bring them closer together each time they were experiencing conflict. The action plan developed for the purpose of altering this pattern might be for the parents to decide that they will (a) spend time together by going on a date, rather than in response to their

child's bad behavior; (b) not respond to their child's cue of acting out; and (c) define more clearly their mutual goals for their child.

*Family psychoeducation.* These techniques were developed primarily to treat schizophrenia (Anderson, Hogarty, & Reiss, 1986; McFarlane, 1991; see chap. 10 in this volume) but are also used in many other areas, such as substance abuse and chronic medical illness. At the core of this technique is a belief that families can be trained to create a relational context that may compensate for, and in many instances correct, a disability faced by a particular family member. The therapist functions as an educator, teaching members about the disability and training them how to respond and interact differently. Families often meet in multifamily groups that are designed to educate families and provide a setting in which families can support and guide each other.

*Between session homework tasks.* The therapist may devote the end of each session to codesigning tasks with the family that will be done between sessions. These homework tasks are generally clearly linked to the stated family goals for therapy. In the case described above, during the session, the couple may have planned a date or an outing. They might have negotiated the time of the outing and established some of the details. The parents may be encouraged to get a sitter and to block any of their child's efforts to keep them from going out together. The process of designing a task creates different forms of interaction during the session. Carrying out the tasks at home supports the family's sense of competence and accomplishment in reaching their goals for treatment.

*Therapist's use of self with the family* (Satir, 1967; Whitaker & Keith, 1980). The therapist may use self-disclosure, humor, metaphor, and other personal means to increase or decrease energy or anxiety in the therapy session. This active unbalancing of the family is intended to interrupt homeostatic processes and to stimulate new ways of thinking, feeling, and interacting within the family that commence during the therapy session. (See especially chaps. 2, 3, 13, and 20 in this volume.)

These examples should not be considered exhaustive. There are as many here and now interventions possible as the interaction of family and therapist can stimulate. Common elements of here and now interventions are a focus on the identified problem; a perception of family structure, organization, boundaries, and interactional process as central to problem maintenance; active intervention in current family organization and process to resolve problems; and therapist responsibility for facilitating change. (See especially chaps. 6, 17, 18, 20, 25, 27, and 30 in this volume.)

**Transgenerational interventions.** Transgenerational interventions emphasize the evolution of both problems and solutions across many generations of the family. Here and now family interactions are viewed as reflecting patterns that have been developed by and inherited from ancestors. Solutions involve addressing relationship issues in one's family of origin.

The therapist applying a transgenerational perspective believes that families are held together through time by invisible strands of loyalty (Boszormenyi-Nagy & Spark, 1973; see also chap. 3 in this volume). Family members must maintain a delicate balance between how they choose to behave and what is owed to family members (Boszormenyi-Nagy & Spark, 1973). These loyalties transect the genogram in both vertical (e.g., parents and children) and horizontal (e.g., siblings, cousins, and partners) directions. At the intersection of these vertical and horizontal loyalties, the transgenerational projection process is enacted (Bowen, 1976). Unresolved problems from the family's past are bequeathed to the present generations (Bowen, 1976; Framo, 1992; Paul, 1986; Paul & Grosser, 1965; Williamson, 1978).

Transgenerational therapists are attuned to how the family projection process is manifest in the family's current journey through the life cycle (Carter & McGoldrick, 1988; see also chap. 5 in this volume). An assumption of transgenerational therapists is that family difficulties are most likely to emerge during transitional periods from one life cycle phase, such as adolescence, to another, such as leaving home. How families navigate their life cycles is influenced by how each branch of the family has navigated similar stages in previous generations. For example, when an offspring develops problems while preparing to leave home, such as unexplainable failure in school, these difficulties may reflect similar problems

of leaving and self-differentiation in the parent, grandparent, and even great-grandparent generations (Boszormenyi-Nagy & Spark, 1973; Bowen, 1976; Landau, 1982; Landau-Stanton, 1990).

The key that unlocks the door to change in the present is held in the family's past. This is a crucial point when working with families who may be reluctant to explore patterns or problems in the past. Transgenerational issues are directly linked to the current issues facing the family. The efforts of past generations may provide a map for how present generations will traverse their life cycles or tackle their problems. The transgenerational therapist may function as a coach or guide to family members (Bowen, 1976). Although transgenerational patterns are linked to present concerns, the therapist is less likely to focus on interventions that directly address the problem as it exists in the present. Instead, the therapist addresses family of origin issues that are impinging on the present. The therapist may work with the whole family but frequently works with couples or even individuals. The basic assumption is that addressing issues from the past will help the family resolve difficulties in the present.

With child problems, some therapists working from a transgenerational perspective might intervene primarily at the parental level. They might regard the parent generation's capacity to resolve family of origin issues as the key to eliminating these problems in the present. For example, parents who have problems with child rearing might be encouraged to work on their relationships as children to their own parents; couples who argue and cannot communicate may be diverted to work out their unresolved problems with their own opposite-sex parent because these are likely to be influencing their current conflict with their partner. Other transgenerational therapists might work only with the individual. Therapy may include sending him or her "back home again" (Framo, 1976) to resolve earlier issues, or to individuate (Bowen, 1976) from family of origin. In these ways, the patient is helped to work through the problem patterns, relationships, and events.

Transgenerational therapy interventions tend to be less directive than here and now interventions. The responsibility for change in the family is more shared or mutual. The therapist may coach but is less likely to enter the game actively to intervene, other than by offering advice or guiding homework tasks. The patient has greater responsibility for taking action. Transgenerational interventions are more closely tied to the analytical roots of therapy and are more likely to generate insight than are here and now interventions. Insight or understanding of the impact of earlier relationships enables the patient to make decisions and take action.

Common examples of transgenerational interventions (like here and now interventions) include tasks that may be performed both in and outside of the therapy session:

*Genogram development* (Bowen, 1978; McGoldrick & Gerson, 1985). The therapist will usually develop a genogram early in therapy in order to map relationship patterns and transitional conflicts (Landau-Stanton, 1990). It is an effective way to elicit the patient's story and bring absent family members into the room. The therapist will help the patient understand how roles, triangles, losses, transitions, and other family dynamics influence the functioning of current family relationships.

*Trips home* (Bowen, 1976; Framo, 1976). The therapist will use genogram information to help patients develop an understanding of what changes need to occur in their family of origin. It is not enough, though, to identify and understand family of origin issues. Patients often are encouraged to return home to deal directly with those relationships that are contributing to current problems. The goal is to help patients differentiate from their families of origin (Bowen, 1976). Self-differentiation involves maturing sufficiently to relate to members of the family of origin without behaving in an involuntary and emotionally reactive way. Patients who are able to differentiate in this manner are better able to decide for themselves how they will relate to family members. They are less likely to be pulled unwittingly into unhealthy family patterns (Framo, 1992).

*Inviting extended family into therapy.* Transgenerational therapists may involve members of the patient's family of origin in the therapy. In couples therapy, for example, parents of each partner may be included (Framo, 1976). Issues between partners often reflect problems both partners have had in their relationships with their own parents. By including

parents in therapy the couple can work directly on family of origin issues that have an influence on the couple's current relationship. In this way, the therapist brings the family's home into the office, where family patterns can be addressed directly and the wisdom of previous generations can be utilized in solving current problems (e.g., Horwitz, in press; Landau-Stanton, le Roux, Horwitz, Baldwin, & McDaniel, 1991; Whitaker & Keith, 1980).

*Symbolic inclusion of family of origin.* The therapist may bring family of origin into therapy in a variety of other creative ways. The therapist may talk about other family members being present in the room; often these "ghosts" are seen as alive in current family members (Whitaker & Keith, 1980). Or the therapist may have a family member sculpt his or her family of origin (Duhl et al., 1973). The sculpting may entail having current family members represent members of previous generations (Landau-Stanton, 1990) or may employ therapy teams, empty chairs (Duhl et al., 1973), and role play dialogue (Satir, 1967) to manifest the hidden family that is always present. In this way, the family member can return to scenes from the past that are being replicated in the present. By facilitating sculpting of this nature, the therapist can "act as a bridge between generations" (Duhl et al., 1973, p. 62). The opportunity to refashion the past can loosen the logjam that is occurring in the present.

The common elements underlying transgenerational interventions include the following premises: that transgenerational processes across time influence the development of current problems, that these problems often arise during transitional periods such as family life cycle changes, and that solving current problems often involves resolving relationship issues with family members from the past. (See especially chaps. 4, 5, 6, 13, 17, 18, 22, 25, and 26 in this volume.)

**Ecosystemic approaches.** An ecosystemic approach emphasizes the interaction of multiple factors both within the family and beyond the relational bonds of the family (see Imber-Black, 1988). The term *ecosystemic* was coined by Auerswald (1968), who described the balanced interaction of family and larger social systems, which forms an interdependent relational ecology occupying both time and space. For purposes of this chapter we are expanding that original concept to include work by a variety of theorists and therapists who have focused attention on dimensions of the larger ecosystem. Therapists dealing with the ecosystem might consider the immediate social system or extend their hypothesizing to the entire natural and artificial support system as depicted by Lewin (1935), including larger social systems and institutions; political and economic issues; ethnicity, race, culture, religion, gender, language, and social construction; geographical and historic events; the neighborhood; and the immediate and extended family.

Truly ecosystemic interventions are inherently biopsychosocial (Engel, 1977, 1980; see also chaps. 21 and 25 in this volume). Problems develop due to the interaction of multiple factors inside and outside the family (Epstein et al., 1978). The family is seen as one system among many larger systems that influences family and individual functioning. This multisystem, or contextual, perspective has led some ecosystemic therapists to focus on the "problem-determined system" (Anderson & Goolishian, 1988) or the "system of import" (Stanton, 1984) as the unit of treatment. The system of import includes everyone who is involved meaningfully in conversation about the presenting problem. This could include nuclear family members, extended family members, and significant others such as friends, members of families of choice, and representatives of the legal, religious, medical, and social services systems (Berger, Jurkovic, & Associates, 1984; Imber-Black, 1988; Landau-Stanton et al., 1991; Landau-Stanton & Clements, 1993; Mirkin, 1990; Speck & Attneave, 1973; Wynne, McDaniel, & Weber, 1986). Meaningful solutions are co-constructed in the dialogue that occurs among these many participants (Anderson & Goolishian, 1988; Goolishian & Anderson, 1987; Hoffman, 1990; White & Epston, 1990; see especially chap. 21 in this volume).

An ecosystemic approach is inherently collaborative (see especially chaps. 2 and 27 in this volume). The therapist is a partner with the family and other social resources in defining the origin of, and developing solutions to, the family's problems. Depending on the therapist's orientation within an ecosystemic approach, the therapy may have a unique focus. For example, feminist family therapists are particularly attuned to issues of power in relationships (e.g., male/female) and how the unequal distribution of power is supported by social structures and cultural mores (e.g., Goldner, 1988, 1991; Goodrich, Rampage, Ellman, & Halstead, 1988; Hare-Mustin, 1978, 1987; Krestan & Bepko, 1980; McDaniel, 1990; McGoldrick, Anderson, & Walsh, 1989; Reid, McDaniel, Donaldson, & Tollers, 1987; Walters, Carter, Papp, & Silverstein 1988; see especially chaps. 17, 18, and 31 in this volume). A therapist who pays particular attention to ethnicity in a family may explore how ethnic origins (see especially chaps. 19, 20, and 23 in this volume) influence current family values, communication patterns, and problem resolution (e.g., Boyd-Franklin, 1989; Landau, 1982; le Roux, 1992; McGoldrick, Pierce, & Giordano, 1982; Sotomayor, 1991; Sue & Sue, 1990; Szapocznik, Scopetta, Kurtines, & Arenalde, 1978). Such a therapist would also be sensitive to how the family's ethnicity is perceived and influenced by the larger culture.

An ecosystemic approach has few technical interventions that are directly identified with this perspective but tends to include many of the techniques mentioned in both the here and now therapies and the historical approach. Of special note, though, is the use of network sessions developed by Speck and Attneave (1973) as a therapeutic intervention. As they describe, network sessions bring together the important participants and resources to the family problem. Some therapists employ network sessions throughout the course of the therapy. Others call for a network to deal with special issues or when the therapy appears to be stuck. Network sessions may be designed to elevate the family and focus on its own competence (Landau-Stanton, 1986). The therapist works with the family to identify extended family, friends, associates, and professionals who either are currently involved with the problem, have experience with similar problems, or are defined by the family as an important resource to them. Any member of the ecosystem may be called upon for help. Therapists might invite not only extended family members but neighbors and support systems into the therapy session to throw light on some of the problematic patterns (e.g., Landau-Stanton & Clements, 1993; Rueveni, 1975; Speck & Attneave, 1973). Therefore, network sessions may involve large numbers of participants. The group works together to find solutions to the family's problems. This collaboration helps the family break out of its stuck position and move forward. By increasing the diversity of perspectives on the problem and then focusing the network's energy on solutions, the therapist, family, and network co-evolve a new reality. Change occurs because the entire ecosystem has moved together in a new direction.

Common elements in ecosystemic interventions are sensitivity to extrafamilial factors in the development of problems, utilization of larger systems resources in the assessment and treatment process, the therapist's function as more that of orchestrator than that of performer, and the therapist's role as "ecosystemic detective" (Auerswald, 1968). (See especially chaps. 2, 3, 6, 7, 9, 12, 20, 21, 23, 26, and 27 in this volume.)

## The Application of Core Interventions

The three broad classes of intervention that we have described—here and now, transgenerational, and ecosystemic—certainly do not include every possible intervention in family therapy, but they do reflect the broad center of the family therapy field. In order to illustrate techniques from each of these classes, we will present a case that was seen by one of the authors using transitional family therapy.[1] We will then discuss the case hypothetically by demonstrating how therapists using techniques representing each of the intervention classes might approach the case. Later in the chapter we will present the case as it actually was treated.

> *CASE EXAMPLE*
>
> *Louis, age 20, had been hospitalized for depression and suicidality for two months prior to being referred for family therapy. His parents, Angelo and Madeline, with whom Louis lived, wanted to help in any way possible. Louis's parents had felt hope-*

*less about Louis for quite some time. His father did not understand Louis's problems but was willing to do "whatever it takes to get Louis right." Louis's mother told the intake worker at the family clinic that all of Louis's problems stemmed from the death of his maternal grandfather. She contended that Louis felt guilty because of the time he had spent abusing alcohol and drugs with his friends while his grandfather was dying. Louis also had a brother, Mario, 18, who was a dean's list student at a local college and a sister Emily, 10, who was the "apple of her father's eye." Everyone planned to attend the first session.*

**Here and now interventions.** The therapist using here and now interventions helps the family define the problem as clearly and concretely as possible. In the process, the therapist pays close attention to the way family members interact with one another. The therapist attends to such issues as repeating interactional patterns and confused hierarchy. Interventions may be designed to restructure the hierarchy so that boundaries among subsystems are more clear. Alternatively, the therapist might actively alter how family members interact with each other. This might be done by nonverbal methods such as sculpting or rearranging seating. It may also be achieved by directly intervening to alter verbal communication through such methods as blocking, reframing, or noble ascription. A combination of verbal and nonverbal techniques, such as enactment, may be used.

During the initial interview the here and now therapist may notice that Louis and his mother, Madeline, are very close, in fact their chairs are touching. In defining the problem Madeline speaks repeatedly for Louis. Louis sits in silence that his mother defines as depression. Louis's father, Angelo, on the other hand, sits across the room from his wife and son. The seating positions of Emily and Mario further separate their father from Louis and Madeline. Angelo expresses helplessness and confusion about his son, Louis. At this stage a therapist might note

---

[1] Susan H. Horwitz, MS, was the therapist for this family. Some material has been added to further protect anonymity and highlight aspects of the treatment approach.

that whenever Angelo talks he is interrupted not only by his wife but also by Mario and Emily. Angelo seldom completes his sentences and soon withdraws from the conversation. The therapist may also notice that Louis and Angelo often sit in silence, forming mirror images of each other.

The main concern of the family is that since Louis has left the hospital he is silent and withdrawn. He spends little time with the family and seldom goes out. The therapist assesses Louis's suicidality. The family feels Louis is in no immediate danger of committing suicide, but they remain anxious and worried for his safety. Louis agrees that his silence and withdrawal are problems, but he has no solutions. Having clarified the problem and observed the family's interaction, the therapist may proceed in the following manner:

> *The therapist asks the family to change their seating so that Madeline and Angelo can sit together. The therapist feels this will make it easier for the parents to discuss how to approach their son's problem. The therapist then asks the father and mother to discuss ways to address Louis's silence and withdrawal. The other family members are encouraged to listen to their parents and are blocked from interrupting their parents' discussion.*
>
> *The therapist asks Angelo "as Louis's father and as the most experienced man in the family" to share his ideas on what to do. The therapist supports Madeline in listening to her husband because she "has had to carry the responsibility alone too long." Mother and father talk together for the first time about their fears and frustrations. They also decide on a plan of action. Louis, who has not been eating with the family, will be expected to eat dinner with them daily. In order to support Louis in getting out more often, Angelo and Louis will plan an outing to be accomplished before the next therapy session.*
>
> *Since Angelo and Louis are "quiet," the therapist asks Madeline to coach Angelo on talking effectively with his son. The thera-*

> *pist then has Angelo and Madeline brainstorm appropriate and enjoyable outings. Angelo and Louis discuss these options and decide to go to a basketball game. The therapist cautions the family that a whole basketball game may be too much togetherness and suggests staying for half the game. Angelo and Louis, with Madeline's support, say they will decide at half time whether or not to stay longer.*

In this intervention, the therapist maintains a focus on what the family defines as the main problem. The therapist is concerned that the family's structure may be part of the problem and may reflect problems between the mother and father. The therapist actively restructures the hierarchy in the family and alters how communication takes place. Louis has been elevated to peer status with his mother as the central dyad in the family. The family's interaction also reveals a pattern in which the father is either excluded or excludes himself from meaningful involvement in family decisions. The therapist moves quickly to bring mother and father together, thus reestablishing a generational hierarchy. This elevates Angelo, the father, and provides much needed support to Madeline, the mother, and allows Louis to rejoin the sibling generation.

In this example, the therapist addresses the problem in the here and now process of therapy. The therapist intervenes to restructure family interaction and enables the family to enact a different process of communication and decision making. The therapist also adds a restraint-from-change maneuver designed to protect the family from failure and to stimulate their confidence to move ahead. The therapist takes responsibility for creating a context and facilitating a process that helps the family arrive at solutions.

**Transgenerational interventions.** The therapist who approaches the family with transgenerational interventions in mind listens for evidence of transgenerational processes that may influence the family's current functioning. Are there issues of unresolved loss and grief? Have relationship patterns been passed on from one generation to the next? Have other family members faced similar problems in the past when entering the leaving-home phase of development? Does each generation of the family usually have a "sick" member? Are there strands of loyalty to past generations that make it difficult for parents to deal effectively with the current generation? What family legacies may influence the roles family members play in the family now? The therapist may have these and other considerations in mind when meeting with the family.

During the initial interview the transgenerational therapist might be particularly interested in Madeline's explanation of her son's difficulties: All of Louis's problems stem from guilt over the death of his maternal grandfather. The therapist may hypothesize that grief is the central issue not only for Louis but for Madeline and the family as a whole. The guilt Madeline sees in her son may reflect her own guilt and pain. The therapist may want to learn more about other losses on both sides of the family and how the family has dealt with grief traditionally.

> *The therapist listens to Madeline discuss the impact her father's death has had on Louis. Angelo and Louis both confirm Louis's sadness and guilt. The therapist says: "I can see that family ties are very strong in your family and that I will not be able to understand your family well until I understand more about the larger family from which you've come." The therapist then engages Angelo and Madeline in describing members of their families. The therapist constructs a four-generation genogram on an easel. The therapist learns about previous deaths, births, methods of leaving home, and the like. This discussion helps the family recognize that drug and alcohol abuse have been ways some family members have dealt with loss and grief for several generations. The therapist suggests that Louis may not have wanted to neglect his grandfather but that it may have been just too painful for Louis to face his grandfather's death without drugs and alcohol. With this Madeline discusses her own unresolved grief over her father, and Angelo talks movingly about problems he has never resolved with his father who is also*

> *deceased. The therapist then asks what Louis's grandfather would want the family to do at this time. Louis is unsure how to respond. He becomes tearful. Madeline says her father would want them all to "be strong."*

In this session, the therapist's use of the genogram broadens the family's perspective on Louis's problem to include patterns of coping with loss. By expanding the family's view, Louis's substance abuse is presented as a sign of pain and hurt rather than irresponsibility. In addition, the therapist may describe it as a form of grieving that is loyal to the way others in the family have grieved before. The therapist may also feel it is important to understand how men are taught to grieve. By including the father's family of origin the therapist develops an understanding not only of how men grieve but of how they deal with each other's grief. This may be valuable later in therapy if the therapist wants to bring father and son closer together. The therapist then brings the deceased grandfather into the session by asking what he would say to the family. In this way the therapist makes more overt (the grandfather's presence) what has been covert.

From these beginning steps, the therapist may do more extensive work with the patient alone or may work more directly with the parents. The therapist may feel that when the parents have been helped to deal more effectively with loss, they will provide a better model for their son as he deals with loss. The therapist may also believe that by dealing with their own losses, the parents may be saving their son from having to deal not only with his grief but also with the grief of his parents and past generations.

**Ecosystemic approaches.** The therapist who utilizes an ecosystemic perspective with the family is interested not only in intrafamilial relationships but also in relationships with larger systems. The therapist may want to include members of other systems that influence or are influenced by the problem being addressed in the family. The therapist may also be interested in the impact of social currents in the development of the family. These currents may include such considerations as the impact of ethnicity on how the family deals with problems, establishes roles for family members, and maintains its own identity, as well as how gender plays a part in the family's problems and solutions. In these ways, the therapist regards the family as one system in a multiverse of systems that interact and evolve together. Because the therapist sees these larger systems as integral to the family's life and progress, the therapist may actively collaborate with members of other systems in order to treat the family in a comprehensive manner. This collaborative approach may include network sessions in which members of other systems are included in the therapy.

During the initial interview the therapist may be particularly attuned to how members of other systems are an active part of the family's life. The therapist may learn, for example, that Louis was particularly attached to his art therapist while he was an inpatient. The therapist may also learn that the family's priest has been very involved in their lives since the death of Madeline's father. As the therapist learns more about the family's connections to members of other systems, he or she may actively elicit identification of the family's support system. He or she may learn that Angelo's main supports, for example, are friends with whom he socializes at the Sons of Italy hall.

The therapist may also explore the role that being Italian plays in the family's life:

> *The therapist comments on the importance of the Catholic church and organizations that support their identity as Italians. The therapist asks the family to teach him or her about their ethnic identity. Angelo says they have very strong ties to their relatives in Italy even though they do not see them. Both Angelo and Madeline speak Italian but their children do not. As they talk about their relatives, Madeline becomes tearful. She explains, though, that these are not tears of sadness. She simply says, "For us, family is everything." The therapist learns that the family is defined broadly and includes friends and neighbors and members of their parish. The therapist asks the family if it would be valuable to include these important "family members" in*

> *the therapy to help with Louis's problem and to be a support. The family agrees and together they decide who should be invited to the next appointment. They include their priest, two friends, a great aunt and uncle, Louis's godparents, and the art therapist, who they came to see as a member of their family as well.*

The therapist demonstrates respect for the culture of the family by asking the family members, as experts in their own ethnicity, to educate him or her about who they are and how they are connected to their community. The therapist learns how important family is and how broadly family is defined. With that in mind, the therapist asks the family to identify members of the larger ecosystem who might be a help to them. By identifying and mobilizing the larger network the therapist adds diversity (le Roux, 1992) to the family's approach to the problem. No longer alone in their troubles, the nuclear family can draw from the wisdom of professionals, friends, and family whom they have named as resources. The therapist might work with the patient or nuclear family alone or choose to involve other members of the larger system as needed. The therapist using an ecosystemic perspective is inherently confident in the larger system's capacity to work together to resolve the presenting problem.

In this section, we discussed the differences in therapeutic approach that a hypothetical therapist may take with a family depending on the class of intervention he or she chooses. We want to emphasize that each approach can be effective depending on the needs of the family and the skill of the therapist. In the next section we will take the process another step forward by considering an integrative approach to the same case.

## PART II

## Integration

Many, if not most, later generation family therapists apply an amalgam of core techniques as suits the pragmatic needs of the case. Even when they officially espouse a circumscribed family therapy model, we believe that their actual therapy is likely to incorporate core techniques from other models, involving at least two of the categories of intervention described in Part I. A few examples of integrative therapies are structural/strategic family therapy (Stanton, 1981a, 1981b), integrative family therapy (Duhl & Duhl, 1981; Friedman, 1981; Moultrup, 1981, 1986), multimodal therapy (Lazarus, 1971), comprehensive family therapy (Kirschner & Kirschner, 1986), an intersystem model (Weeks, 1989), and metaframeworks (Breunlin, Schwartz, & MacKune-Karrer, 1992).

With all the integrated models, the process of integration results in a larger and more complex entity than just the sum of its parts. To illustrate, we will return to our clinical example and explore how the family was actually treated using transitional family therapy (Horwitz, in press; Landau-Stanton, 1986, 1990; Landau-Stanton et al., 1991; Landau-Stanton & Clements, 1993; Landau-Stanton & Stanton, 1983, 1985; le Roux, 1992; McDaniel, 1990; McDaniel, Hepworth, & Doherty, 1992; McDaniel & Landau-Stanton, 1991, 1992; Seaburn, Gawinski, et al., 1993; Seaburn, Lorenz, & Kaplan, 1993; Stanton, 1981a, 1981b, 1984, 1992; Stanton & Landau-Stanton, 1990; Weber, McKeever, & McDaniel, 1985). We will limit our discussion to one key element of the model, *family competence*, which depends upon an interweaving of here and now, transgenerational, and ecosystemic themes.

Family competence is elicited by assisting the family in exploring their history across multiple generations in order to familiarize them with the strengths and resources that their family has been able to access and utilize (see especially chaps. 6, 8, 9, 20, and 34 in this volume). Interventions are directed toward creating continuity among past, present, and future with careful consideration of the context across time (Landau, 1982). This bridging enables the family to understand its current functioning in terms of both its past and its present relational interactions. A key tenet of this approach is that the therapist does not have secrets from the family, but shares his or her philosophy and hypotheses with them in order to reconstruct the transitional pathway together. The therapist's innate belief that current problem patterns resulted from adaptive and effective solutions from the past allows him or her to engender a sense of competence in the family that en-

hances their solutions and interactions in the here and now. This transgenerational perspective encourages an examination of relationships across the genogram, how transitions have been completed in the past, and how this impacts relationships in the current extended family system.

In assessing aspects of the context from an ecosystemic perspective, the therapist may discover events from the past (such as losses from war and migration that had an impact on Louis's family) that are being played out again in the present. By construction of a transitional map (Landau-Stanton, 1990) and timeline (Stanton, 1992), the family discovers the "why now" of their current difficulties. It also allows the therapist and family to examine whether and how effectively its resources (within both family and community) are being utilized. In order to understand the context of the presenting problem, the therapist elicits information about family history and life cycle stage, ethnic and cultural background, and the extent to which situational and developmental transitions have been resolved. This information is normalized by the therapist, rephrasing the information in terms of the events and changes the family has experienced. The family is then able to recognize that earlier adaptive solutions to unavoidable events have led to patterns that have become entrenched and problematic.

During this process, the family frequently discovers that their current symptoms result from patterns (repeated over time and multiple generations) that may have worked in the past but no longer are effective. Strategic here and now therapists believe that the problem is a failed solution (Watzlawick et al., 1974). We believe that problems develop from the continuation of patterns that arise from solutions that were once successful but are no longer relevant and therefore become problematic. By gaining an understanding of what was happening in the family and its larger context at the time of onset, the family members are able to perceive the intrinsic health of their multigenerational family.

The discussion of the strengths, resources, patterns, and themes that appear across generations allows the family to realize the inherent assets of their traditions, heritage, and values and how these may have extended across generations. This, in turn, provides an understanding of current events that offers relief from guilt and blame, freeing them to work toward solving their current difficulties (Landau-Stanton, 1986, 1990; Landau-Stanton et al., 1993). The family, aware of its own potential health and competence, is then able to identify both the focus of the therapy and who will be needed to assist in its process.

## Integrative Interventions

The process of therapy is both interactive and evolutionary, with family and therapist constantly revisiting earlier tasks and information and integrating them into new directions and solutions. As this occurs throughout the therapy, family and therapist influence each other and the process of change. The family takes increasing responsibility for change and feels more competent to take charge of resolving their problems.

**The initial phase of treatment.** In the initial phase of therapy, the integrative therapist utilizing transitional family therapy accomplishes several key tasks that will form the foundation of the whole therapy. These include many of the first session tasks that might be accomplished by therapists following here and now, transgenerational, and ecosystemic approaches. In the interest of brevity, only a few of these key interventions will be described below:

*Hypothesizing.* As Louis and his family prepared to engage in the first phase of treatment, the therapist constructed several working hypotheses that, if correct, would provide the foundation upon which she would build the primary interventions. For example, the therapist hypothesized that for Louis, difficulties were related to his and his family's unresolved grief over past losses. While taking into account all the ideas presented in Part I (here and now, transgenerational, ecosystemic), the therapist also used the intake information to develop hypotheses about family strengths, areas of competence, and who might be engaged from the extended family and the larger system. The therapist hypothesized, for example, that the longevity of the couple's marriage, maintained despite considerable pain, reflected strengths, such as loyalty and commitment, that were a part of the value systems of both families of origin.

*Joining and mapping.* The therapist began the therapy by spending time joining with the family, not only to establish rapport, but also to begin mapping the players in the family's system. Joining is a critical factor in the process of successful treatment. Through joining, the therapist communicated sensitivity to a variety of family issues, such as generational hierarchies and gender. Joining also provided an initial opportunity for the therapist to validate family members and highlight the importance of their roles in the family. The tone of the overall therapy was set by communicating respect and affirmation of the individuals, the family as a whole, and its various support systems. Joining was utilized throughout, but it was an especially important intervention at the outset of therapy.

The use of the transitional map constructed during this initial phase had two primary purposes, in addition to providing the transitional perspective mentioned above. First, the mapping process was a natural and comprehensive vehicle through which the therapist continued to join the family. Second, while the family began to relate its history, symptoms, and relationships, the therapist learned the family's "terrain" and was able to assess whether or not her initial hypotheses fit the family's experience over time.

At this stage the mapping process included identifying members of the immediate and extended family, plus the family's natural and professional support systems. The therapist also mapped other issues: the symptoms that had shaped the family's responses to each other, the ways they had protected and cared for each other, and their unique qualities. All of these assisted the therapist in bringing them to a successful resolution of their problems. (See Figure 1).

*Establishing goals for treatment.* Often families come to treatment discouraged and overwhelmed by the longevity and/or repetition of their problems. Setting goals is a way to provide forward movement, direction, and hope for resolution. This family's articulation of goals, fashioned in specific and workable language, gave them a new way of thinking about their problems, offering a clearly defined path to achieve change. Among the family's goals in Louis's case were to help him decrease his depression, elimi-

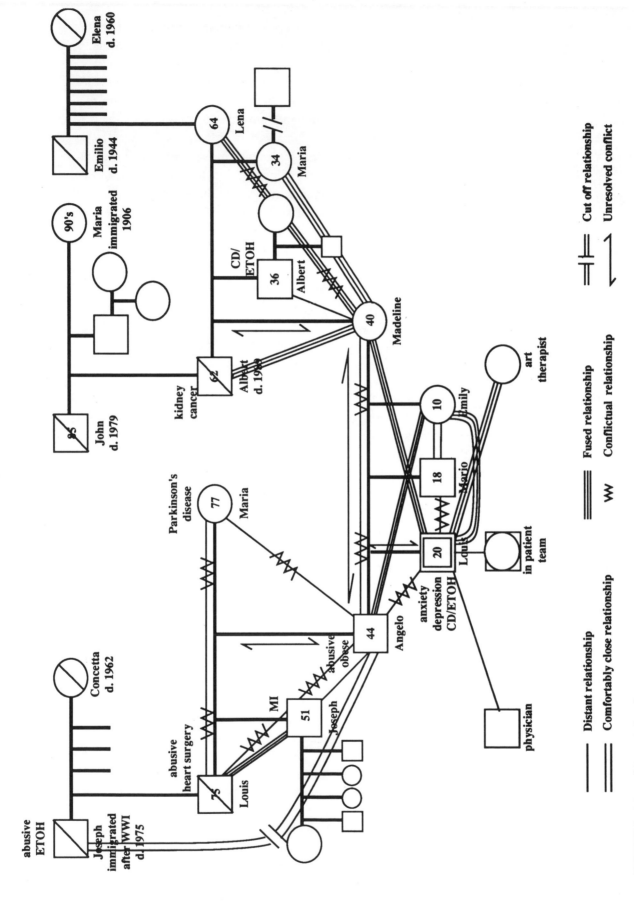

FIGURE 1. Map of Louis's family.

nate substance abuse, grieve his grandfather's death, and move on in his life in a meaningful and productive way. The therapist listened carefully to the family's goals while continuing the mapping process. The therapist ascertained how the family's goals were connected to events and issues that spanned many generations. This process created a context and direction for the family's therapeutic endeavor.

*Assessing family strengths.* The therapist spent a portion of the initial phase helping the family identify and articulate their perception of the family's strengths and resources. This helped family members identify and own their areas of competence and enabled them to plan how they would apply those strengths to the problems they faced.

*Formulating the transitional perspective.* Once the family had traced symptoms and strengths back across three or four generations, they were able to recognize how patterns and events from the past both contributed to current problems and shaped the family's future. A pattern of coping that had been adaptive or appropriate in the past no longer served its original purpose and actually created problems for the family. This family's very traditional family structure may have served them well at the time of immigration. But in the current generation, the same traditional structure was hindering family members who were trying to individuate or leave home. The family did not recognize that they had inherited patterns of interacting that were no longer productive. Consequently, they found themselves stuck in repeating patterns they neither understood nor could change. Therefore, issues related to loss, immigration, and trauma were explored early in the treatment process.

In this way, the therapist and the family began to understand how each family member was connected to the generations before them. They began to appreciate the individual "scripts" they had inherited, as well as the contributions they had made to the continuation of old patterns (Byng-Hall, 1991; Stanton & Landau-Stanton, 1995a, 1995b). The therapist also helped the family focus on the origins of their own strengths and competencies within previous generations. This process helped the family recognize a broader range of options for planning their present and future tasks.

Louis and his family were forthcoming, sincere, and eager to explore their history. They realized that there had been a great deal of love and loss across the generations and that one of the key values and strengths of their family was the willingness to make sacrifices for each other and to protect each other. In concluding the first phase of treatment, the therapist talked about ways in which the family expressed these strengths:

> *I am very impressed with the creative ways in which your family has worked together over these many years to honor the cultural origins of your family and to protect the way in which grandparents have maintained a special place in the family. I can see that both of these issues are of the greatest importance and must be respected throughout our work together*
>
> *The family has taught Louis to be a loving and responsible son and grandson. Somewhere along the line Louis misunderstood his mission and appointed himself sole guardian of the family's pain, so as to free up his loved ones to live, love, and be happy. He has become the reservoir of the family's sadness and grief, centralized among and between all his family members. He is so protective of everyone, he cannot dare to move forward for fear he might not be there if someone needs him.*
>
> *Our job is to find new creative ways to maintain the respect for your Italian heritage and the role of grandfathers in the family while finding a way to lift the depression and overwhelming feeling of total responsibility from Louis's shoulders. In that way he can carry his share without depriving the other men and women of their rights and privileges to membership in the family.*

Through this message to the family, the therapist communicated respect for the family's issues and values and sensitivity to the family's need to maintain and continue those values for future generations. At the same time the therapist framed Louis's behavior as no longer necessary to the survival of the family. The family was now well established in the new country and would not fall apart at the loss of a single member. The family no longer needed to be bound to the grave of the departed in order to prevent splintering and dissolution. In this way the therapist gave both the family and Louis the noble ascription they well deserved, and created a climate of hope and nonthreatening change. She taught the family that they could continue their heritage without sacrificing their son.

**The mid phase of treatment.** The treatment moved into the second phase when clearly defined goals and a working map had been determined, and the family was beginning to take charge of the process. The mid phase was characterized by prioritizing, planning, and working on the goals identified in the initial phase. The strengths and resources of the family were utilized and homework continued the process between sessions. The therapist maintained a focus on the goals established in the earlier phase and developed the theme of the transitional pathway in greater detail. During this mid phase, the therapist expanded the treatment system to include resources identified in the initial phase. This phase continued until both therapist and family believed that the family's work was well under way and that they had established new ways of resolving their problems. Once the initial phase of therapy had been summed up, the therapist invited Louis to share what he had learned through the process:

> Louis painfully disclosed his memories of the excessive physical punishment he remembered receiving throughout his childhood, particularly from ages 7 through 13. In session, he confronted his parents, especially his father, for the lack of judgment and control Angelo had displayed during those years. In an emotionally charged session, Louis expressed his pain; the long-standing poor self-concept he had come to despise, the fear of his father and his father's rage that he carried with him always, and his need for solace, which he believed he could only find in alcohol, drugs, or suicide. Louis expressed his fear that his fa-

> ther could "pop off" at any time and that he felt he needed to "be there" to protect his mother and sister.

> After several sessions of working through the pain, Angelo was coached to embrace his son and to reassure Louis he would work to understand the reason for the long-standing frustration in their family. Both parents made a commitment to him and the other children that they would find a way to correct the problems from the past and renew their relationship with their son using love, rather than rage, as a basis of their future relationship.

At this point, the therapist began to explore rage in the family. The therapist returned to the transitional map to discuss in greater detail the tension-filled environment within which fathers and sons had struggled for several generations. Angelo explained to his family that his father was physically harsh with him as a young boy. This left Angelo angry and confused about what he had done to make his father so angry. When his older brother left home, Angelo's father withdrew all meaningful contact with him, again leaving him confused and deeply saddened. Further investigation led to Angelo's memories of his grandparents, who were his primary source of nurturance. He explained that his paternal grandfather had served in World War I in Italy and had become a highly respected soldier, serving in a special corps. After immigrating to the United States, he had lost his status and had to work in a factory. He began to drink and became the "town drunk," often thrown out of bars onto the streets. This behavior brought much shame to the family and resulted in Angelo's parents' forbidding him from having contact with his grandparents. Angelo explained further that this grandfather had been sent away from his home and family at age 7 because his father was off to war and his mother could not feed all of the children. The grandfather was the oldest child and so it was decided he would go to live with a relative and work on their farm. The family was astounded by the power and sadness of this story, which they were hearing for the first time. The family was able to understand how the issues of father absence, loss of family and status, and alcoholism all contributed to Angelo's rage and Louis's depression.

Angelo's mother was invited to join the therapy to talk about family life when she and her husband were children. She, too, had experienced a sad and deprived childhood. She was able to confirm Angelo's report, and she added valuable information. She also gave Angelo permission to find his grandparents' grave and to visit them as often as he wanted. Angelo agreed to make a trip across country to visit his brother, with whom he had a somewhat strained relationship, to discuss his rage and sadness. Together they were to construct a plan for grieving the past and for finding meaningful ways of staying connected with each other. The therapist shared her thoughts with the family at this juncture:

> *I am very impressed with how courageous you all have been over these many years. Each son, though confused and sad, has suffered in silence and, at some level, has understood the pain of his father. You have all been busy protecting and caring for your families, while taking on the growing burden of grief and sadness. It is no wonder that Louis grieves deeply over the loss of his mother's father, a loving grandfather who understood and nurtured him, much like Angelo's experience with his grandfather. While unfortunate circumstances deprived Angelo of his grandfather, illness and death deprived Louis of his grandfather. Indeed, both Angelo and Louis have much in common. We need to find a way to continue to honor and respect the grandfathers in this family, but first we must find a way to put the grief and sadness in its proper place. With the support of all the family members, I believe we can accomplish this necessary work. Angelo, you will need to lead the way.*

The therapist weaved the transgenerational perspective together with an ecosystemic view of the family's movement over time. The therapist paid close attention to the repeating patterns of father–son conflict and absence, as well as the burden of unresolved grief over the many losses both parents' families had

carried from one generation to another. The transitional map was used to guide the discussion of the family history and to define the points of transitional conflict, namely when sons reach 7 years of age, when fathers go off to war, when families immigrate, when marriages are tension filled, and when sons both prepare to leave home (age 13) and actually leave. The therapist expanded the system by bringing in the extended family to help heal the wounds and to relieve Louis of sole responsibility for protecting his family and grieving their losses. The role of the women in the family was key in this task. For example, Louis's maternal grandmother attended a session in which she helped Madeline grieve her father's death and "let go." Then, Madeline was encouraged by her mother to turn her attention more to her current family. Madeline's example and ongoing support were vital as Louis and his father struggled to forge a new relationship.

Here and now techniques were also included in that Angelo is sent to talk with his older brother. This intervention served to strengthen the sibling subsystem, thereby removing pressure from Louis (the elder son) to be both son and lost brother to Angelo. It also legitimized Louis's symptoms of depression and withdrawal and offered the family a context in which to resolve the etiology of the problems. The transgenerational perspective was weaved into the assignment in that the therapist "sent Angelo home" to do this work with the one other person who was most appropriate.

**The final phase of treatment.** The final phase of treatment was typified by the family being more in charge of the direction of therapy. They felt they were achieving some of the goals they had set in the initial phase; the family also felt confident that they were utilizing their strengths and resources toward planning their future. The primary task of the final phase was to help the family recognize its own capacity to deal with difficulties that may present in the future.

As Louis's family moved toward the end of the mid phase of treatment, they began to see the progress they were making. They had completed many tasks designed to reorganize the family's structure, reconstruct and enact (in and out of session) Louis's and Mario's childhood in the way the parents wished it could have been, and to create safe, productive ways of expressing anger and pain to one another. Because the yarn of tangled family interaction found itself unknotting and smoothly rewinding, several previously unstated issues began to emerge. Convinced Louis was now "safe" from suicide and major depression, Mario expressed his rage at his brother for having treated him in the same way their father had treated Louis, abusively and at times cruelly. The brothers were able to work out their unfinished business to both of their satisfaction. Mario also disclosed that he and his girlfriend were beginning couples therapy at the university's counseling center to work on their chronic conflicts. Emily began to show signs of withdrawal and anxiety similar to those that started Louis on his journey of pain and suffering. The parents quickly stepped in and helped her manage her fears and anxiety in productive ways.

Angelo shared with his family that the depth of his rage was significantly diminished and that even though he could not promise he would never be angry again, he felt certain he would not lose control. In a moving session Angelo and Madeline sat together, holding hands, and told Louis they did not want him to take care of them anymore; they wanted him out of the middle of their marriage and they had decided to engage the therapist for 6 to 8 sessions of marital therapy. Because Louis continued to express a high degree of anxiety, individual time-limited sessions were arranged for him with a co-worker at the clinic. In this way, the overall treatment plan could be coordinated between the two therapists. The separate therapies were critical at this juncture. Drawing an appropriate boundary between the two therapies assisted Louis in differentiating from his parents and their marriage.

The final phase of treatment constituted marital therapy for Angelo and Madeline. This therapy included utilizing extended family members (ecosystemic) to deal with current difficulties (here and now), grief work related to Madeline's father's death (transgenerational), exploration of spousal relationships in both families of origin over multiple generations (transgenerational), and reminiscences and re-enactments of "the good days" of their relationship.

In the course of these discoveries Madeline and Angelo were able to respectfully share both their painful perspectives of the bad times and a newfound ability to hear each other, even though they disagreed about many of the facts. The couple's 25th wedding anniversary served as an incentive for cooperation and forgiveness leading to termination of the marital therapy.

Louis's individual work was slow, but he learned to manage his anxiety through the use of several tasks, one of which was the employment of relaxation techniques (here and now). Even within the context of individual therapy, the therapist utilized transgenerational and larger system techniques by sending Louis to his mother's great-grandmother, still alive in her 90s, who coached Louis to move on with his life and to let her son (his revered grandfather) rest in peace. He became more productive at school and reported greater satisfaction with his limited, but significant, relationships. He began to move away from his former group of friends with whom he had been drinking and began to form new relationships.

Louis became a full-time student in a local college, majored in psychology, and received high grades. He moved in with a girlfriend and they cared for lots of pets. Angelo and Madeline continued "dating," looking forward to getting closer to each other in new ways. Mario graduated from the university with honors. He and his girlfriend were getting along well. He anticipated going on to graduate school in the next academic year. Emily was doing well in school and had lots of friends.

At the time this chapter was written, the family was ready to terminate therapy. They were working on their last assigned task, which was to discuss and agree on the most desirable way to punctuate their progress and their many accomplishments. A follow-up family session was planned to bring proper closure to the therapy.

## CONCLUSION

This case demonstrates that integrating all three classes of intervention—here and now, transgenerational, and ecosystemic—enables the therapist and family to create a working environment in which problems can be resolved effectively. Problem resolution occurs not just within the patient and nuclear family but across the extended family both vertically and horizontally. The therapist's broad and inclusive perspective enhances the family's ability to develop tools to stop ineffectual patterns from repeating across the genogram.

Our discussion of core interventions in family therapy reflects a desire for integration. Integration involves more than borrowing from various models of family therapy—the heart of integration is dialogue. To integrate is first and foremost to facilitate a meaningful exchange between viewpoints that may differ. Such dialogue is much like weaving a fine tapestry. Each strand contributes its own color, texture, and strength. Together all the strands create a fabric that no single strand could have created alone. Exploration of here and now interactions, processes, and structure; inquiry into the evolution of family life and legacies; and curiosity about how families are woven into the larger ecosystem of culture, values, gender, and ethnicity teaches us more about the tapestry of family resilience, competence, and strength than any single strand or perspective could.

Integration is the future of family therapy. Integrative approaches hold the key to a more complete and in-depth understanding of the family. The implications of integration for the field of family therapy are far reaching. As we look at the family through integrative eyes, how we practice, how we train family therapists, and how we do research will surely change and grow.

## References

Ackerman, N. (1958). *The psychodynamics of family life.* New York: Basic Books.

Ackerman, N. (1966). *Treating the troubled family.* New York: Basic Books.

Anderson, C. M., Hogarty, G. E., & Reiss, D. J. (1986). *Schizophrenia and the family.* New York: Guilford Press.

Anderson, H., & Goolishian, H. A. (1988). Human systems as linguistic systems: Preliminary and evolving ideas about the implications for clinical theory. *Family Process, 27,* 371–393.

Auerswald, E. H. (1968). Interdisciplinary versus ecological approach. *Family Process, 7,* 202–215.

Auerswald, E. H. (1974). Thinking about thinking about mental health. In S. Arieti (Ed.), *American handbook of psychiatry* (pp. 316–338). New York: Basic Books.

Bateson, G. (1972). *Steps to an ecology of mind.* New York: Ballantine Books.

Bell, J. E. (1961). *Family group therapy.* Washington, DC: U.S. Government Printing Office.

Bell, J. E. (1975). *Family therapy.* New York: Jason Aronson.

Berenson, D. (1976). Alcohol and the family system. In P. J. Guerin (Ed.), *Family therapy theory and practice* (pp. 284–297). New York: Gardner Press.

Berger, M., Jurkovic, G. J., & Associates. (1984). *Practicing family therapy in diverse settings.* New York: Jossey-Bass.

Boszormenyi-Nagy, I., & Spark, G. (1973). *Invisible loyalties: Reciprocity in intergenerational family therapy.* New York: Harper & Row.

Bowen, M. (1976). Theory in the practice of psychotherapy. In P. J. Guerin (Ed.), *Family therapy: Theory and practice* (pp. 42–90). New York: Jason Aronson.

Bowen, M. (1978). *Family therapy in clinical practice.* New York: Jason Aronson.

Boyd-Franklin, N. (1989). *Black families in therapy: A multisystems approach.* New York: Guilford Press.

Breunlin, D. C., Schwartz, R. C., & MacKune-Karrer, B. (1992). *Metaframeworks: Transcending the models of family therapy.* San Francisco: Jossey-Bass.

Byng-Hall, J. (1991). Family scripts and loss. In F. Walsh & M. McGoldrick (Eds.), *Living beyond loss* (pp. 130–143). New York: Norton.

Carter, B., & McGoldrick, M. (1988). *The changing family life cycle: A framework for family therapy.* New York: Gardner Press.

Compernolle, T. (1981). An unrecognized pioneer of family therapy. *Family Process, 20,* 331–335.

De Shazer, S. (1980). *Clues: Investigating solutions in brief therapy.* New York: Norton.

De Shazer, S. (1982). *Patterns of brief family therapy: An ecosystemic approach.* New York: Guilford Press.

De Shazer, S. (1985). *Keys to solution in brief therapy.* New York: Norton.

Duhl, F. J., Kantor, D. , Duhl, B. S. (1973). Learning, space, and action in family therapy: A primer of sculpture. In D. A. Bloch (Ed.), *Techniques of family psychotherapy: A primer* (pp. 47–63). New York: Grune & Stratton.

Duhl, B., & Duhl, F. (1981). Integrative family therapy. In A. Gurman and D. Kniskern (Eds.), *Handbook of family therapy* (pp. 483–513). New York: Brunner/Mazel.

Engel, G. L. (1977). The need for a new medical model: A challenge for biomedicine. *Science, 196,* 129–136.

Engel, G. L. (1980). The clinical application of the biopsychosocial model. *The American Journal of Psychiatry, 137,* 535–544.

Epstein, N. B., Bishop, D. S., & Levin, S. (1978). The McMaster model of family functioning. *Journal of Marriage and Family Counseling, 4,* 19–31.

Figley, C. R., & Nelson, T. S. (1989). Basic family therapy skills: I. Conceptualization and initial findings. *Journal of Marital and Family Therapy, 15,* 349–365.

Figley, C. R., & Nelson, T. S. (1990). Basic family therapy skills: II. Structural family therapy. *Journal of Family and Marital Therapy, 16,* 225–239.

Framo, J. L. (1976). Family of origin as a therapeutive resource for adults in marital and family therapy: You can and should go home again. *Family Process, 15,* 193–210.

Framo, J. L. (1992). *Family of origin therapy.* New York: Brunner/Mazel.

Friedman, P. H. (1981). Integrative family therapy. *Family Therapy, 8,* 171–178.

Goldenberg, I., & Goldenberg, H. (1980). *Family therapy: An overview.* Monterey, CA: Brooks/Cole.

Goldner, V. (1988). Generation and gender: Normative and covert hierarchies. *Family Process, 27,* 17–31.

Goldner, V. (1991). Sex, power, & gender: A feminist systemic analysis of the politics of passion. *Journal of Feminist Family Therapy, 3,* 63–84.

Goodrich, T. J., Rampage, C., Ellman, B., & Halstead, K. (1988). *Feminist family therapy: A casebook.* New York: Norton.

Goolishian, H., & Anderson, H. (1987). Language systems and therapy: An evolving idea. *Psychotherapy, 24,* 529–538.

Guerin, P. J. (1976). Family therapy: The first twenty-five years. In *Family therapy theory and practice* (pp. 2–22). New York: Gardner Press.

Gurman, A. S. (1979). Dimensions of marital therapy: A comparative analysis. *Journal of Marital and Family Therapy, 5*(1), 5–18.

Gurman, A. S., & Kniskern, D. P. (Eds.). (1981). *Handbook of family therapy.* New York: Brunner/Mazel.

Gurman, A. S., & Kniskern, D. P. (Eds.). (1991). *Handbook of family therapy* (Vol. II). New York: Brunner/Mazel.

Haley, J. (1963). *Strategies of psychotherapy.* New York: Grune & Stratton.

Haley, J. (1973). *Uncommon therapy.* New York: Norton.

Haley, J. (1976). *Problem-solving therapy.* San Francisco: Jossey-Bass.

Haley, J., & Hoffman, L. (Eds.). (1968). *Techniques of family therapy.* New York: Basic Books.

Hare-Mustin, R. (1978). A feminist approach to family therapy. *Family Process, 17,* 181–194.

Hare-Mustin, R. (1987). The problem of gender in family therapy theory. *Family Process, 26,* 15–28.

Hoffman, L. (1990). Constructing realities: An art of lenses. *Family Process, 29,* 1–12.

Horwitz, S. (in press). Trauma due to unresolved grief and its effects on the family. In C. Figley (Ed.), *Death and trauma.* New York: Brunner/Mazel.

Imber-Black, E. (1988). *Families and larger systems: A family therapist's guide through the labyrinth.* New York: Guilford Press.

Jackson, D. D. (1965). Family rules: Marital quid pro quo. *Archives of General Psychiatry, 12,* 589–594.

Kaslow, F. W. (1987). Marital and family therapy. In M. B. Sussman & S. K. Steinmetz (Eds.), *Handbook of marriage and the family* (pp. 835–859). New York: Plenum.

Kaufmann, E., & Kaufmann, P. (Eds.). (1979). *Family therapy of drug and alcohol abuse.* New York: Gardner Press.

Kirschner, D. A., & Kirschner, S. (1986). *Comprehensive family therapy.* New York: Brunner/Mazel.

Krestan, J. (1991). The baby and the bathwater. *Journal of Feminist Family Therapy, 3,* 181–184.

Krestan, J., & Bepko, C. (1980). The problem of fusion in the lesbian relationship. *Family Process, 19,* 277–290.

Landau, J. (1982). Therapy with families in cultural transition. In M. McGoldrick, J. K. Pierce, & J. Giordano (Eds.), *Ethnicity and family therapy* (pp. 552–572). New York: Guilford Press.

Landau-Stanton, J. (1986). Competence, impermanence, and transitional mapping. In L. C. Wynne, S. McDaniel, & T. T. Weber (Eds.), *Systems consultation: A new perspective for family therapy* (pp. 253–269). New York: Guilford Press.

Landau-Stanton, J. (1990). Issues and methods of treatment for families in cultural transition. In M. P. Mirkin (Ed.), *The social and political contexts of family therapy* (pp. 251–275). Needham Heights, MA: Allyn & Bacon.

Landau-Stanton, J., & Clements, C. D. (with Associates). (1993). *AIDS, health and mental health: A primary source book.* New York: Brunner/Mazel.

Landau-Stanton, J., le Roux, P., Horwitz, S., Baldwin, S., & McDaniel, S. (1991). "Grandma, come help." In T.

S. Nelson & T. S. Trepper (Eds.), *101 Favorite family therapy interventions* (pp. 372–279). Binghamton, NY: Haworth Press.

Landau-Stanton, J., & Stanton, M. D. (1983). Aspects of supervision with the "Pick-a-Dali Circus" model. *Journal of Strategic and Systematic Therapies, 2*(2), 31–39.

Landau-Stanton, J., & Stanton, M. D. (1985). Treating suicidal adolescents and their families. In M. P. Mirkin & S. L. Korman (Eds.), *Handbook of adolescents and family therapy* (pp. 309–328). New York: Gardner Press.

Lazarus, A. (1971). *Behavior therapy and beyond.* New York: McGraw-Hill.

le Roux, P. (1992). Diversity and dialogue: The healing narrative. In J. Mason, J. Rubenstein, & S. Shuda (Eds.), *From diversity to healing* (pp. 36–48). Durban: South African Institute of Marital and Family Therapy.

Lewin, K. (1935). *A dynamic theory of personality: Selected papers by Kurt Lewin* (1st ed., D. K. Adams & K. E. Zener, Trans.). New York and London: McGraw-Hill.

Madanes, C., & Haley J. (1977). Dimensions of family therapy. *Journal of Mental and Nervous Disease, 165*(2), 88–98.

McDaniel, S. H. (1990). Marital therapy and the resolution of gender role conflict. *Journal of Family Psychotherapy, 1*(3), 39–49.

McDaniel, S. H., Hepworth, J., Doherty, W. J. (1992). *Medical family therapy.* New York: Basic Books.

McDaniel, S. H., & Landau-Stanton, J. (1991). Family of origin work and family therapy skills training: Both and. *Family Process, 30,* 459–471.

McDaniel, S. H., & Landau-Stanton, J. (1992). The University of Rochester Family Therapy Training Program. *American Journal of Family Therapy, 20,* 361–365.

McFarlane, W. R. (1991). Family psychoeducational treatment. In A. S. Gurman & D. P. Kniskern (Eds.), *Handbook of family therapy* (Vol. II; pp. 363–395). New York: Brunner/Mazel.

McGoldrick, M., Anderson, C., & Walsh, F. (Eds.). (1989). *Women in families: A framework for family therapy.* New York: Norton.

McGoldrick, M., & Gerson, R. (1985). *Genograms in family assessment.* New York: Norton.

McGoldrick, M., Pierce, J. K., & Giordano J. (Eds.). (1982). *Ethnicity and family therapy.* New York: Guilford Press.

Minuchin, S. (1974). *Families and family therapy.* Cambridge, MA: Harvard University Press.

Minuchin, S., & Fishman, H. (1981). *Family therapy techniques.* Cambridge, MA: Harvard University Press.

Mirkin, M. P. (1990). *The social and political context of family therapy.* Needham Heights, MA: Allyn and Bacon.

Moultrup, D. (1981). Toward an integrated model of family therapy. *Journal of Clinical Social Work, 9,* 111–125.

Moultrup, D. (1986). Integration: A coming of age. *Contemporary Family Therapy, 8,* 157–167.

Napier, A. Y., & Whitaker, C. (1978). *The family crucible.* New York: Harper & Row.

Nelson, T. S., & Figley, C. R. (1990). Basic family therapy skills: III. Brief and strategic schools of family therapy. *Journal of Family Psychology, 4,* 49–62.

Nelson, T. S., Heilbron, G., & Figley, C. R. (1993). Basic family therapy skills: IV. Transgenerational theories of family therapy. *Journal of Marital and Family Therapy, 19,* 253–266.

Nichols, M. (1984). *Family therapy: Concepts and methods.* New York: Gardner Press.

Paul, N. L. (1986). The paradoxical nature of the grief experience. *Contemporary Family Therapy, 8,* 5–19.

Paul, N. L., & Grosser, G. (1965). Operational mourning and its role in conjoint family therapy. *Community Mental Health Journal, 1,* 339–345.

Reid, E., McDaniel, S. H., Donaldson, C., & Tollers, M. (1987). Taking it personally: Issues of personal authority and competence for the female in family therapy training. *Journal of Marital and Family Therapy, 13,* 157–165.

Rueveni, U. (1975). Network intervention with a family in crisis. *Family Process, 14,* 193–203.

Satir, V. (1967). *Conjoint family therapy.* Palo Alto, CA: Science and Behavior Books.

Satir, V. (1972). *Peoplemaking.* Palo Alto, CA: Science and Behavior Books.

Seaburn, D. B., Gawinski, B. A., Harp, J., McDaniel, S. M., Waxman, D., & Shields, C. (1993). Family systems therapy in a primary care medical setting: The Rochester experience. *Journal of Marital and Family Therapy, 19,* 177–190.

Seaburn, D. B., Lorenz, H., & Kaplan, D. (1993). The transgenerational development of chronic illness meanings. *Family Systems Medicine, 10,* 385–394.

Selvini-Palazzoli, M., Boscolo, L., Cecchin, G. F., & Prata, G. (1978). *Paradox and counterparadox: A new model in the therapy of the family in schizophrenic transaction.* New York: Jason Aronson.

Sotomayor, M. (Ed.). (1991). *Empowering Hispanic families: A critical issue for the '90s.* Milwaukee, WI: Family Service America.

Speck, R. V., & Attneave, C. (1973). *Family networks: Retribalization and healing.* New York: Pantheon.

Stanton, M. D. (1981a). An integrated structural/strategic approach to family and marital therapy. *Journal of Marital and Family Therapy, 7*, 427–440.

Stanton, M. D. (1981b). Marital therapy from a structural/strategic viewpoint. In G. P. Sholevar (Ed.), *The handbook of marriage and marital therapy* (pp. 303–334). Jamaica, NY: S. P. Medical and Scientific Books (Division of Spectrum Publications).

Stanton, M. D. (1984). Fusion, compression, diversion and workings of paradox: A theory of therapeutic/systemic change. *Family Process, 23*, 135–167.

Stanton, M. D. (1992). The time line and the "why now?" question: A technique and rationale for therapy, training, organizational consultation and research. *Journal of Marital and Family Therapy, 18*, 331–343.

Stanton, M. D., & Landau-Stanton, J. (1990). Therapy with families of adolescent substance abusers. In H. B. Milkman & L. I. Sederer (Eds.), *Treatment choices for alcoholism and substance abuse* (pp. 329–359). Lexington, MA: Lexington Books (Div. of D. C. Heath and Company).

Stanton, M. D., & Landau-Stanton, J. (1995a). The role of ancestors in family life and nonshared environments: I. Family themes, balance, and generation skipping. Manuscript in preparation.

Stanton, M. D., & Landau-Stanton, J. (1995b). The role of ancestors in family life and nonshared environments: II. Family scripts and replacement. Manuscript in preparation.

Stanton, M. D., & Todd, T. C. (1979). Structural family therapy with drug addicts. In E. Kaufman & P. Kaufmann (Eds.), *Family therapy of drug and alcohol abuse* (pp. 55–69). New York: Gardner Press.

Stanton M. D., & Todd T. C. (1982). *The family therapy of drug abuse and addiction.* New York: Guilford Press.

Steinglass, P. (1987). *The alcoholic family.* New York: Basic Books.

Strupp, H. H., & Hadley, S. W. (1979). Specific vs nonspecific factors in psychotherapy: A controlled study of outcome. *Archives of General Psychiatry, 36*, 1125–1136.

Sue, D. W., & Sue, D. (1990). *Counseling the culturally different: Theory and practice.* New York: Wiley.

Szapocznik, J., Scopetta, M. A., Kurtines, W., Arenalde, M. A. (1978). Theory and measurement of acculturation. *Interamerican Journal of Psychology, 12,* 113–130.

von Bertalanffy, L. (1968). *General system theory: Foundations, development, application.* New York: Braziller.

Walsh, F., & McGoldrick, M. (Eds.). (1991). *Living beyond loss.* New York: Norton.

Walters, M., Carter, B., Papp, P., & Silverstein, D. (1988). *The invisible web: Gender patterns in family relationships.* New York: Guilford Press.

Watzlawick, P., Weakland, J., & Fisch, R. (1974). *Change—Principles of problem formation and problem resolution.* New York: Norton.

Weakland, J. H. (1960). The "double bind" hypothesis of schizophrenia and three-party interaction. In D. D. Jackson (Ed.), *The etiology of schizophrenia* (pp. 373–378). New York: Basic Books.

Weber, T., McKeever, J. E., & McDaniel, S. H. (1985). A beginner's guide to the problem-oriented first family interview. *Family Process, 24*, 357–364.

Weeks, G. (1989). An intersystem approach to treatment. In G. Weeks (Ed.), *Treating couples: The intersystem model of the Marriage Council of Philadelphia* (pp. 317–340). New York: Brunner/Mazel.

Whitaker, C. A., & Keith, D. V. (1980). Symbolic-experiential family therapy. In A. S. Gurman, & D. S. Kniskern (Eds.), *Handbook of family therapy* (pp. 187–225). New York: Brunner/Mazel.

White, M., & Epston, D. (1990). *Narrative means to therapeutic ends.* New York: Norton.

Williamson, D. S. (1978, January). New life at the graveyard: A method of therapy for individuation from a dead former parent. *Journal of Marriage and Family Counseling*, 73–101.

Wynne, L. C. (1961). The study of intrafamilial alignments and splits in exploratory family therapy. In N. W. Ackerman, F. L. Beatman, & S. N. Sherman (Eds.), *Exploring the base for family therapy* (pp. 95–111). New York: Family Services Association.

Wynne, L. C., McDaniel, S., Weber, T. T. (Eds.). (1986). *Systems consultation: A new perspective for family therapy.* New York: Guilford Press.

Wynne, L. C., Ryckoff, I., Day, J., & Hirsch, S. (1958). Pseudomutuality in the family relations of schizophrenia. *Psychiatry, 21*, 205–220.

# Chapter 2

# COLLABORATIVE LANGUAGE SYSTEMS: TOWARD A POSTMODERN THERAPY

*Harlene D. Anderson*

The emergence of a postmodern narrative in the human sciences (Berger & Luckman, 1967; Gergen, 1982, 1985a; Harre, 1983; Shotter, 1990, 1991, 1993; Vygotsky, 1934/1986) challenged the modernist perspective of seeing and thinking about the world and our experiences in it. The modernist view is that knowledge is objective and fixed, and the knower and knowledge are independent—presupposing universal truths and objective reality. Postmodernism refers not to an era but to a different, discontinuous theoretical direction: Knowledge is socially constructed and generative, and knowledge and the knower are interdependent—presupposing the interrelationship of context, culture, language, experience, and understanding (Lyotard, 1984; Madison, 1990). Postmodernism offers alternatives to many of the long-held modernism-based assumptions and enshrined traditions of psychotherapy theory and practice, including problems and symptoms as dysfunction, language as representational, the therapist as the knower and curer, the client as an independent object, the notions of a core self and a reflective mind, and the education of therapists.

This chapter reflects my collaborative work, mainly during the past two decades, with my colleague and friend Harry Goolishian and the extensions of this work since his death in 1991. Our journey toward postmodernism, and consequently toward contemporary hermeneutics and social con-

structionism as the centerpoint of the conceptual underpinnings of my clinical theory and practice, began in the early 1970s at the University of Texas Medical Branch and continued at the Houston Galveston Institute (formerly the Galveston Family Institute). These two professional settings have commonalities critical to the generation of our clinical practice and theory: a primary interest in exploring the frontiers of new theoretical paradigms; the opportunity to work with people, including individuals, families, larger systems, and organizations, that represented a broad range of socioeconomic, cultural, and ethnic backgrounds; the opportunity to work with a variety of "problems,"[1] and a teaching context in which we also learned. These combined to influence both our clinical practice and our theory which, as a consequence, constantly evolved, and in which client–therapist collaboration emerged as the core of our work.

## LANGUAGE IN OUR CHANGING PRACTICE AND THEORY

During these years we participated in therapy conversations and conversations about therapy as we tried to describe and explain our therapy experiences to ourselves and others. As we listened to clients' stories about successful as well as unsuccessful therapy, we kept returning to language and conversation as the central parts of therapy (Anderson, 1990). Al-

---

[1] I often place "problem" in quotation marks for several reasons. I do not want to imply that there is such a thing as one problem. There are as many descriptions and explanations of the problem as there are members of the system. Nor do I want to focus on "problem" and deemphasize "solution," which I also place in quotation marks. I do not believe "problems" are solved: problems dissolve.

though the therapeutic landscape has changed over the years, our interest in language dates back to the influence of the Multiple Impact Therapy (MIT) research project in the 1950s (MacGregor et al., 1964).

Our early focus was on speaking the clients' language (metaphorically and literally) to learn about their values and worldviews and to learn their words and phrases. We paid careful attention to our own language, and, like chameleons, we adapted to the client's point of view. Our aim was to work in the clients' language and to use their language as a strategic tool of therapy, a technique to invite cooperation with change. The client's language gave the therapist clues to developing problem definitions and interventions—to revise faulty beliefs, for example, or to correct futile attempts at solution. We believed that if the therapist's diagnosis and intervention (whatever form it might take) was in the client's language, the client and therapy would fit better, the client would be more amenable to the therapist's diagnosis and intervention, and resistance would be less likely to occur.

What we experienced over time, however, was an awareness of several interrelated shifts in our therapy as we carefully tried to learn, work in, and use the client's language in this manner. We realized we were finding ourselves fully engrossed in the clients' unique stories and earnestly inquisitive about their views of life and their problems. Our therapy descriptions and explanations of clients were in the clients' words; that is, when we talked with our colleagues and trainees about clients, we used the clients' descriptions and explanations, their words, and their phrases, and not our professional vocabulary. When we talked about our cases, we shared the clients' self-told stories. We found that telling the clients' stories (or fragments of them) as they had told them to us captured more of each client's uniqueness, the interest of each client's situation, and the essence of the way each client viewed him- or herself.

We have always disliked professional-therapist language and never labeled our clients in professional jargon. In our experience, for instance, presentations at weekly hospital staff meetings in which professional descriptions, explanations, and diagnoses were used produced sterile, lifeless look-alikes. Each

client looked like any other "borderline," "schizophrenic," or "overprotective mother." Clients came alive when you told a story about them and used words and terms of significance for them—like the turkey-leg family, the lawn-mower husband, the Kentucky dancing sisters.

We noticed that rather than learning the family's language, we were learning the particular language of each member of the family system. We were working with multiple descriptions of the problem and its solution, as well as multiple descriptions of the family and of therapy. We were fascinated by the differences in the clients' experiences and explanations of the same event, and we somehow sensed that these differences were valuable and could be fruitful. We no longer wanted to negotiate, blur, or strive for consensus (that is, in problem definitions) but wanted to maintain the richness of differences.

As we immersed ourselves in the clients' language and meanings, our own agendas about such things as outcome, how families ought to be, and in- or end-of-session interventions dissolved. Our once flashy, entertaining, designer intervention therapy began to look somewhat parsimonious, ordinary, and boring to others. To us, however, it became more exciting. When we examined what we thought were novel, carefully strategized, and individually tailored therapist-designed interventions, we discovered that they were not interventions at all in the usual sense of being unilaterally therapist designed (sometimes even outside the therapy room) or driven by the therapist's agenda. That is, although we thought we were doing interventions, we were not. The ideas and actions we now called interventions emerged from therapy conversations and were logical to the family and its members and coherent with the immediate or local conversations.

Family became a restricting concept for us. It implied a priori who should be seen and why, without regard to the unique situation and the individuals communicating with each other and with us about the "problem." The persons we saw in the therapy room and those with whom we had telephone conversations were determined by who was talking with whom about the "problem," and not by their social role and place in the family structure as parents, couples, or siblings. We became less and less inclined, therefore, to see whole families. Much of our work was done with individuals, parts of families, and members of the larger system in which the problem occurred. Those present in each session also shifted. We began to think of problem systems with shifting memberships.

For example, a frightened mother called concerned that her 16-year-old son seemed depressed and was skipping school. She was convinced his behaviors had to do with something that was bothering him that he would not tell her or his father. Worried about teenage suicide, she wanted him to have therapy immediately. The therapist invited the mother, father, and son to come in for the first session. The mother, however, concerned that he would not talk with his parents present, insisted that only the son needed to be seen. The therapist agreed to meet with the son. At the end of the session, the therapist suggested to the boy that she would like to meet with his parents and with him if he would agree to join them. The boy agreed and the parents agreed. During the second session, the therapist learned the boy had been talking with his coach, and the idea evolved that perhaps the therapist, the boy, and the coach could meet together. The conversation of each session informed the membership of the next.

In parallel with these practices, we realized that for many therapists the concept *family therapy* had come to indicate a modality for treating a particular social configuration rather than a paradigmatic shift in the conception of human systems and their problems. The concept risked obscuring the broader applicability of a systems model to human associations other than families—for example, individuals, work groups, age groups, and larger social systems.

We found terms such as *therapy* and *therapeutic* contradictory to our attempts to move away from a medical model, from the implications of such concepts as pathology and normalcy, and from the idea of the therapist as expert on how others should live. Our efforts were in the direction of nonpathology and client expertise. In attempts to deal with the contradictions, we referred to ourselves at times as consultants or described what we did as just talking with people. When Harry Goolishian was asked about his work, he often replied, "I'm an Armenian storyteller." I still have difficulty choosing adequate words to describe my work and to distinguish it from what others do. For instance, I pay careful attention to the meanings words have developed in the mental health field and try to choose words that, for me, best portray the essence I intend. For example, I am often asked why I choose to use the word *collaborative* rather than *cooperative*. *Cooperative* has come to mean, in both the mental heath and general medical arena, to cooperate with or to comply with. That is, the patient conforms to or obeys what the doctor wants him or her to do. Patients who cooperate are good patients; patients who do not are bad patients. I want to stress a participatory partnership.

Our awareness about these distinguishing features was, to a large extent, triggered by trainees' comments and questions as they forced us to try to think about and explain our work. They often commented on the positive way we spoke about our clients. They described our manner and attitude as respectful and humble. They were amazed at our excitement about each case and astonished that we actually seemed to like our clients, even those who might be deemed socially detestable by others. They were surprised by how many of our mandated referrals not only came to the first session but continued coming to therapy. In an effort to describe our approach to therapy, a trainee once commented, "If I was observing and did not know you were the therapist, I do not know if I could identify the therapist."

## A CONCEPTUAL COLLAGE

Coinciding with these shifting clinical experiences was our dissatisfaction with the inadequacy of clinical theories that could make our experiences intelligible. Searching outside the available psychotherapy literature, we explored and sometimes serendipitously bumped into postmodern theories of biology, physics, anthropology, and philosophy. We found ourselves drawn to the notions of chaos theory, randomness, and evolutionary systems (Prigogine & Stengers, 1984); constructivism (Goodman, 1984; von Foerster, 1984; von Glasersfeld, 1984; Watzlawick, 1984); structure determinism and autopoiesis (Maturana, 1978; Maturana & Varela, 1980); language domains, narrative theory, and meaning (Braten, 1984, 1986; Bruner, 1990; Geertz, 1983a,

1983b; Polkinghorne, 1988; Schafer, 1981; Spence, 1984); postmodern feminist perspectives (Flax, 1990; Jordon, 1991; Kitzinger, 1987; Nicholson, 1990); hermeneutics (Gadamer, 1975; Messer, Sass, & Woolfolk, 1988; Rorty, 1979; Wacherhauser, 1986); and social constructionism (Berger & Luckmann, 1967; Gergen, 1982, 1985a; Harre, 1986; Shotter, 1991; Shotter & Gergen, 1989). A description of any one of these theories would be exhausting; the assumptions we adopted, however, shared a challenge to such modernist concepts as observer-independent objectivity, empirical knowledge, and universal truths.

From these fragments we constructed a conceptual collage, ever in motion, that gave us a framework for our shifting experiences (Anderson & Goolishian, 1986, 1988, 1991, 1992; Anderson, Goolishian, Pulliam, & Winderman, 1986; Anderson, Goolishian, & Winderman, 1986a, 1986b; Dell & Goolishian, 1981; Goolishian & Anderson, 1981, 1987a, 1990; Goolishian & Kivell, 1981). More recently, the concepts of contemporary hermeneutics and social constructionism, both interpretive perspectives, became the centerpoint of our conceptual underpinnings. In brief, hermeneutics concerns itself with understanding the meaning of a text or discourse and with understanding as a process that is influenced by the beliefs, assumptions, and intentions of the interpreter. Thus one can never reach a true understanding—the truth is not revealed. There is no one right account of an event, no one right interpretation. Each account, each interpretation, is only one version of the truth. Truth is constructed through the interaction of the participants and it is contextual. In this theory of human understanding, "language and history are always both conditions and limits of understanding" (Wacherhauser, 1986, p. 6). Social constructionism "views discourse about the world not as a reflection or map of the world but as an artifact of communal interchange" (Gergen, 1985a, p. 266). From this perspective ideas, truths, or self-identities, for example, are the products of human relationships. This is a move away from the notion of individual authorship to multiple authorship. That is, everything is authored in a community of persons and relationships.

## Language and Knowledge

Combined, these concepts of hermeneutics and social constructionism influenced our move away from language as representational, as depicting an accurate picture of reality, and our move away from knowledge as objective and fixed—a one-way street in which knowledge is independent of the knower. We moved away, therefore, from universal, grand, overarching psychotherapy narratives. We found ourselves captured, instead, by a postmodern perspective of language and knowledge: people generate meaning with each other through language—by the words, sounds, gestures, signs, and other forms of speech used to communicate. Language is reality. It gives order and meaning to our lives and our world. As Wittgenstein (1953) said, "The limits of language . . . mean the limits of my world."

Knowledge, accordingly, is linguistically and socially constructed. Knowledge and the knower are interdependent; the knower is a contributor. What we know (knowledge, feelings, emotions, thoughts, and perceptions) is known through our constructions and is communicated in language. Language creates. Knowledge, therefore, is not cumulative. In therapy, for instance, finding more fragments does not give the therapist a meaningful whole. The therapist does not fill in the missing pieces with the therapist's knowledge. Client and therapist do this together by joining in language with one another.

As we embraced these ideas about language and knowledge as the central elements of therapy, we moved away from thinking of family systems and family therapy. We disagreed with the dominant view of social systems as rooted in cybernetic mechanical systems metaphors and in order-imposing, layered social systems (Anderson, Goolishian, & Winderman, 1986a, 1986b). We moved toward thinking of human systems as language- and meaning-generating systems (Anderson & Goolishian, 1988, 1989a, 1990a, 1991a, 1992; Goolishian & Anderson, 1987a, 1990) and began to refer to our work as a "collaborative language systems approach to therapy" (Anderson & Goolishian, 1988, 1990b).

## Self-Identity

The events and experiences in our lives, including self-identity, are intersubjective phenomena generated by persons in conversation and action with one another and with themselves, and the experiences are always open to a variety of explications. These socially constructed narrative realities give meaning and organization to the events and experiences and to our self-identities. This is similar to what Bruner (1990) referred to as "meaning making."

Our self-identities, who we believe ourselves to be, are a function of the socially constructed stories we are always narrating to ourselves and others. These stories are set in a history because without it, changes in people's lives would be unintelligible. This view of self emphasizes our capacity to create meaning through language and dialogue. In this view, the self becomes a narrative self and, at best, a coauthored self: a manifestation of changing human action, the action of speaking about oneself with others and with oneself. Self, therefore, is always engaged in conversational becoming, constructed and reconstructed through continuous interactions (Goolishian & Anderson, in press). Thus one's self-identity is what Kenneth Gergen referred to as a "relational self" (Gergen, 1985b) that is subject to shifting definitions as the social interaction shifts. One's individual narratives are always influenced by both the local narratives and the narratives of the sociopolitical context.

## Self-Agency and Change

Our self-identities permit us to do or hinder us from doing what we need or want to do, or they allow us to feel we could act if we so chose (Goolishian, 1989; Goolishian & Anderson, in press). We think of this as having self-agency: the ability to act, feel, and think in a way that is liberating, that opens up new possibilities or simply allows us to see that new possibilities exist. When I think of self-agency, I think of the *freedom* (Anderson, 1992).

This aspect of human agency is embodied in language. From a meaning-generating perspective, change is inherent in dialogue: change is the telling and retelling of familiar stories. It is the redescriptions that accrue through conversation. The concept of agency can be likened to having a voice and being

free to use that voice or not. It is also the telling of a new history that is more tolerable, coherent, and continuous with present intention and agency. Change becomes developing future selves.

This kind of change is similar to what John Shotter, the social psychologist, meant when he wrote about providing "new and empowering accounts of ourselves instead of disabling ones" (Shotter, 1988, p. 5). It is like the British oral historian Ronald Frazier's response to his analyst's question, "What exactly are you hoping for?" Frazier said, "To find, to recreate a past with a certain certainty that I can put it behind me and go on with my life" (Shotter, 1988, p. 7). Both Shotter and Frazier referred to a sense of agency, a sense of freedom.

In therapy we meet people whose "problems" can be thought of as emanating from social narratives and self-definitions or self-stories that do not yield an effective agency for the tasks defined. Women who are either self-labeled or labeled by others as adult survivors of childhood incest, for example, can develop narratives that fix a self-identity that is inherently self-limiting (Anderson, 1992). Such labels risk keeping the past alive in a way that maintains the woman's identity as victim or survivor and forms an obstacle to more viable and liberating self-definitions.

I am reminded of Rita,[2] who grew up in an incestuous family, and who was in anguish for years as she tried to live with "the Rita others saw and liked" and "the Rita I saw and didn't like." Reflecting on her experience in therapy, she said, "I now feel free to get on with my life. When I realized that I could be both of those people, I'm still me. I'm still both of those people, but I like me now." In other words, through therapy Rita developed a new identity that included among other things two previously conflicting identities, freeing her from her anguish and allowing her to get on with her life. The business of therapy is to help people create and gain access to self-identities that are freeing—that allow them to develop understanding of their lives and its events, that permit self-agency or simply a sense of self-agency.

---

[2] Rita is the name I give to a woman in a family Arlene Katz and I worked with.

## THERAPEUTIC CONVERSATION
## AND CHANGE

The philosopher Hans Lipps (1938) believed that any linguistic account contains a "circle of the unexpressed." Gadamer (1975) later called this the "infinity of the unsaid." No communicative account—no word—is complete, clear, and univocal. All communications carry unspoken meanings and possible new interpretations that require expression. This is not to imply that all original linguistic accounts are deficient but to indicate that all communicative actions are an infinite resource for new expression and meaning. Thus, the subject and content of all discourse are open to evolutionary change in meaning. All knowledge advances through this process of looking for the "unsaid."

The realization of change requires communicative action and dialogue. This resource for change, the not-yet-said, is not in the unconscious or any other psychic structure. It is not in the cell or the biological structure, nor is it in a social structure like the family. This resource is in the "circle of the unexpressed." The capacity for change is in the ability people have to be in language with one another and in language always to develop new themes and new stories. It is a resource that resides totally in the inventive and creative aspects of language and narrative. Through this linguistic process people cocreate and codevelop the systemic realities that have meaning for them and through which they continually reorganize their mutual living and self-descriptions. From this view, psychotherapy is a process of expanding and saying the unsaid—the development, through dialogue, of new themes and narratives—from which new meanings may arise and, in turn, new histories may be created that actually give rise to change.

## He Believed Me

A frustrated yet competent and creative psychiatrist colleague requested a consultation for a troublesome case.[3] His client, Lars, a Norwegian merchant seaman, believed he had a chronic disease and was infecting others, even killing them. Although Lars talked of some difficulties in his marriage and his current inability to work, his attention was riveted on the disease. He was distraught because of the harm and destruction he thought he was causing.

During the interview, Harry Goolishian asked Lars, "How long have you *had* this disease?" Looking astonished, and after a long pause, Lars told how it all began, including numerous attempts by doctors and psychiatrists to relieve his growing fear and conviction about his contagious disease.

As Harry showed interest in Lars's dilemma and let him tell his story the way he wanted to, Lars began visibly to relax, even to become somewhat animated, and he began to join in Harry's curiosity. Harry's intent was not to challenge Lars's reality or story or to talk or manipulate him out of his delusion. Harry wanted to learn about it and be sensitive to it.

Colleagues observing the interview were critical of Harry's question, "How long have you *had* this disease?" They feared that the question reinforced the man's "hypochondriacal delusion." A safer, more neutral question, they suggested, would have been, "How long have you *thought* you've had this disease?" The not-knowing position, however, precluded the stance that Lars's story was delusional. Lars said he was sick. Thus, Harry wanted to learn more about his sickness. To do this required not-knowing questions.

Trying to understand Lars was an essential step in a continuous process of establishing and continuing a dialogue. It meant moving with the narrative truth of this client's story, rather than challenging it and assigning meaning to it (i.e., labeling it as delusional). Moving with the client's narrative involved a mutual process and was, therefore, not the same as reifying the delusion. By not-knowing, Harry made room for the story to be retold in a way that allowed for new meaning and new narrative to emerge, and it provided a starting point for dialogue and open conversational space.

Asking a safer question such as, "How long have you thought you've had this disease?" would have served to impose a predetermined, knowing view that the disease was a figment of the client's imagina-

---

[3] A previous article also deals with this client (see Anderson & Goolishian, 1992).

tion, a distortion in need of correction. In response to such a question, the suspicious client would have been left to act according to his own preconceived ideas and expectations of the consultant. Harry would then have been one more in a lineup of professionals who did not believe Lars, who knew better, and who asked knowing or conditional questions. Once again, he would have felt misunderstood and alienated.

The psychiatrist reported that when he asked Lars about the interview with Harry Goolishian, Lars said, "You know, that son-of-a-bitch believed me!" Six months later, the psychiatrist described the continuing effect the interview had on himself and Lars. The psychiatrist said, "I felt freed from having to prove that his fear was an irrational delusion." Therapy sessions now seemed less difficult. Lars's life situation was much better, and whether or not he was infected was no longer an issue. Lars was now working steadily and dealing with his marriage, and he had a beautiful new daughter. Harry's not-knowing had created a starting point for a dialogic exchange between Lars and himself, between the psychiatrist and himself, and between the psychiatrist and Lars. About 2 years after this interview, Lars returned to the psychiatrist and learned from him that Harry had died. He reacted very strongly, saying, "Harry was a wonderful man." The psychiatrist reported Lars felt Harry had made a big change in his life. Surprised by this strong reaction, the psychiatrist asked him what impressed him most, and Lars said, "He believed me. But, you know, something that made all the difference—after telling him about my struggle and what I did; Harry said, 'As a man you did what a man had to do.' That made all the difference in the world, and I see him ever so often in front of me saying that" (I. Hartviksen, personal communication, 1992).

I do not suggest that this or any one not-knowing question can produce a miracle cure, nor that other questions would have begotten a further therapeutic impasse. No one question can influence a dialogic or nondialogic space or occasion. The question itself does not cause someone to shift meaning, to give up an idea, or to have a new idea. But each question, each comment, represents the overall therapeutic posture: not-knowing, not understanding too quickly,

not determining a frame for the dialogue. Each question is an element of the overall conversational process.

## Problems

From an interpretive perspective, a therapy system is simply one kind of meaning-generating system, one kind of linguistic conversational system in which people have gathered in relevant discourse. The particular relevance of the discourse is usually an event or a person someone else is concerned or alarmed about and wants to change. This, usually, is considered the "problem." Using a language systems metaphor, Goolishian and I took the position that social systems—individuals, families, professionals, communities, or any combination—are a product of social communication. Using language (in the way I have described) in the domain of a problem makes a social system. We called that social unit a problem system. Moving away from a social-structure domain to a linguistic domain, as a way of describing and understanding problems, we moved away from the notion of empirical objectivity and representational language. In the narrative and semantic view, each observation and understanding, each problem description and imagined solution, is one of many possibilities.

I enclose "problems" in quotation marks because I do not believe there is such a thing as a "problem," that is, consensus around a definition that reflects an objective pathology. Problems are linguistic events or positions, which are often interpreted and described in conflicting ways. As many problem definitions may exist as there are members of a problem system. Each observation and understanding, each problem description and imagined solution, is one of many possibilities. Each problem is conceived as a unique set of events that has meaning only in the context of the social exchange in which it happened. Each person involved in a dilemma has his or her own story about how the dilemma evolved, what it is about, whose fault it is, and what should be done. This includes the therapist. Both the client and the therapist bring to the therapy arena a framework or ideological base that influences the construction of their view of the problem and its solution as well as the picture they have of each other.

If a problem is no more than what the people involved in the communicative actions are calling a problem, then the traditional diagnostic processes and categories are of little use. I believe it is a mistake to assume that problems in any category (e.g., psychosis, alcoholism, sexual abuse) are univariate and that these pluralistic syndromes have single explanations. This is in contrast to the more common theoretical assumption that there is *a* problem that exists in some kind of common pattern associated with particular categories of problems. It is with this view that clinicians are trained to search for, to recognize, and to diagnose. As Goolishian and I wrote (Anderson & Goolishian, 1988): "It is our belief . . . that, in the end, we arrive only at *our* own descriptions and explanations of the problem. That is, the therapist reaches a diagnosis based on his or her private observations and experiences of the client's behaviors" (p. 386).

## Therapy as Generative Conversation

So, what is therapy? Therapy is a linguistic activity in which conversation, or shared inquiry, about a problem generates the development of new meanings—different ways of understanding, making sense of, or punctuating one's lived experiences that lead to self-agency and problem dissolution.

The process of therapy is what I refer to as a *generative conversation*. This is a conversation in which people create meaning with each other and are engaged in a process together in which they talk *with* each other instead of *to* each other. This dialogue is a two-way conversation in which there is a shared inquiry—a mutual search for understanding of the problem and a mutual exploration of its relevance. The conversation is the mechanism by which the therapist and client coexplore the familiar (i.e., the client's story, view of the problem, and meanings) and codevelop the new (i.e., meanings, realities, and narratives). This kind of conversational process produces something new for both the client and the therapist. It opens the door to multiple possibilities for making a different sense of things and for changing behaviors and feelings. During this process, other descriptions and meanings will emerge that are no longer labeled as a "problem."

Such a conversation is not idle chitchat that leads nowhere or further solidifies preconceptions (held by either client or therapist). It is a purposeful conversation toward restoring dialogue. Dialogue requires that there be room for familiar views, confusing ambiguities, and vigorous attitudes to exist side by side.

How do you achieve this kind of dialogue, this kind of generative conversation, in a therapy that is collaborative and egalitarian, and one in which the client is the expert? And, if the client is the expert, what kind of expertise does the therapist contribute to the process? Furthermore, how can dialogue or newness make any difference at all, for instance, to a single, African American mother whose son is involved with the juvenile system, if she does not have the status or expertise (which the therapist may have) to negotiate with the court and the school in behalf of her son?

Critical to such therapy is the therapist's posture—the attitudes and actions that serve as a backdrop for the conversation. Although several interrelated ingredients combine to influence the therapist's posture, a core ingredient is not-knowing. "I value my ignorance of what is to come," as Commander Sisko of *Star Trek: Deep Space Nine* said.

## NOT-KNOWING

*Not-knowing* refers to the attitude and belief that the therapist does not have access to privileged information, can never fully understand another person, and always needs to learn more about what has been said or not said. T. S. Eliot reflected what I mean by not-knowing when he wrote: "In order to arrive at what you do not know you must go by the way which is the way of ignorance." Not-knowing means the therapist is humble about what she or he knows. Understanding is always developing, and the therapist is continually being informed by the client. In effect it means the therapist is more interested in learning what the client has to say than in preselecting what she or he wants to hear, telling what she or he knows, validating or promoting what she or he knows, or leading the client to a therapist-predetermined replacement story. For example, I would not think of a mother who is afraid for her 11-year-old boy to walk to school by himself or to spend the night with a friend as overprotective. I would not try to lead her, for instance, toward how I believe she should parent, feel, or think. Rather, I would talk with her in a way so that we coexplore and codevelop options for acting, feeling, and thinking that are unique to her beliefs and her life circumstances.

To create this kind of dialogic space and process, the therapist's dominant professional and personal discourse is subordinated. The therapist avoids premature understanding, knowing, and assumption. This gives clients center stage, to lead with their stories as they want to tell them without being guided by what the therapist thinks is important and preselects to hear. In not-knowing the therapist joins the clients in the natural unfolding of their stories. The therapist talks with clients about their concerns, learns about their views, and tries to understand their perceptions. The therapist genuinely wants to learn how the client makes sense of things, to grasp the current story—not to determine its cause, but to learn what the client thinks is its significance. Not to allow the client to be the center of the action is to risk interfering with listening and hearing, and therefore with learning the full meaning of the client's experience. It is also to risk relying on across-the-board assumptions, categorizations, and generalities that have more to do with verifying the therapist's beliefs than with learning about the client's reality.

## Respectful Listening

Not-knowing involves *respectful listening*—listening in an active and responsive way. The therapist listens in a way that shows the client to have something worth hearing. Having an authentic commitment to being open to the other person's story is critical to dialogue.

Recently I watched a therapist, Klaus Deissler, talk with Hans, a 43-year-old man diagnosed as a chronic schizophrenic, and his exasperated, older aunt and uncle who raised him. The staff of the halfway house who referred Hans said they were "forced to discharge Hans prematurely because of his irresponsible behavior." The aunt and uncle were not so much worried about where Hans would now live as they were desperately anxious about Hans's future after their deaths if these kinds of crises kept reoccur-

ring as they had over the last 20-plus years. Hans's self-diagnosis was "I'm confused about who I am." Referring to the halfway house, Hans said, "They kicked me out. They got mad at me because I overslept and didn't get to work on time." Hans went on to say, "They don't understand me." Klaus replied, "Does anyone understand you?" "My aunt," Hans replied. Turning to the aunt Klaus asked, "What do you do to make him feel you understand?" "I take what he says seriously," she said. Hans nodded his head in agreement.

The protagonist in Anne Rice's novel *Interview with the Vampire* captured the essence of respectful listening:

> *I was at a loss suddenly; but conscious all the while of how Armand listened; that he listened in the way that we dream of others listening, his face seeming to reflect on everything I said. He did not start forward to seize on my slightest pause, to assert an understanding of something before the thought was finished, or to argue with a swift, irresistible impulse — he did not do the things which often make dialogue impossible. (pp. 283–284)*

## Shared Inquiry

I refer to the immersion in and being led by the client's story as maintaining coherence. Maintaining coherence is more than honoring the client's reality. It relies on the continuing analysis of experience as it occurs in context and as it is related by the client. It is also being in sync with the client's rhythm. Critical to maintaining coherence is the therapist's authentic commitment to being open to the other person's story. Harry Goolishian, for example, maintained coherence with Lars when he asked, "How long have you had this disease?"

Maintaining coherence is not drowning in a problem, nor is it, wittingly or unwittingly, overtly or covertly, reifying the problem. Talking, for example, within the spouse abuser's or substance abuser's story is not the same as participating in denial, condoning culturally defined inhumanity, or abdicating social and ethical responsibility. It does not perpetuate the problem. Quite the opposite: Maintaining coherence is an important step toward dialogue.

The therapist's involvement in learning about another person's reality in an earnest manner begins to pique the other person's curiosity as well. It invites that person to join the therapist in a shared inquiry into the issues at hand. As the therapist begins to learn about and tries to understand the client's view, the therapist's learning process naturally shifts to a mutually puzzling process in which therapist and client become engaged in conversation with each other in coexploring the familiar in a manner that leads to codevelopment of the new. This is similar to a notion attributed to Gregory Bateson: To entertain new and novel ideas, there has to be room for the familiar. It is also similar to what Tom Andersen (1990) aims for: "We want to talk with people in a way they have not talked with themselves or with each other before."

Shared inquiry is the essence of the therapist—client conversation. It becomes a give-and-take process, an exchange, a discussion, and a crisscrossing of ideas, opinions, and questions. It is not idle, superficial, or goalless conversation that leads nowhere or further solidifies preconceptions held by either client or therapist. Rather, the dialogue is an interpretive process of which the natural, spontaneous consequence is change, a process in which both client and therapist risk change. As Lorraine Code (1988) suggested, "In genuine dialogue, as contrasted both with polite conversation and with adversarial confrontation, both of the participants are changed" (p. 188).

A not-knowing position does not mean the therapist does not know anything or that the therapist throws away or does not use what she or he already knows. It does not mean the therapist just sits back and does nothing or cannot offer an opinion. We each bring who we are and all that entails—life experiences, professional experiences, values, prejudices, and strong opinions—with us into the therapy room. Not-knowing does not mean that prejudices are bad. Letting the client lead does not require patience, nor does it imply that the therapist is a blank screen, knows nothing, or does not use what she or he knows. It does mean, however, that the therapist's contributions, whether they are questions, opinions,

speculations, or suggestions, are presented in a manner that conveys a tentative posture and portrays respect for and openness to the other and to newness.

## HEROIC FEELINGS

### Conditional Questions

I am reminded of the words of Ralph, a 30-year-old man labeled as a treatment failure who had been hospitalized several times for psychosis and who had been unable to work for years. During his recent therapy, Ralph had improved and had resumed his career as a computer programmer. He insisted that his current therapist, Harry Goolishian, was different from the others. Ralph said he now felt more capable of managing his life and that he experienced more self-agency. This conversational context influenced Harry Goolishian to ask, "What, if anything, could your previous therapists have done differently that would have been more useful to you?" Ralph's answer refers to not-knowing:

> That is an interesting and complicated question. If a person like you had found a way to talk with me when I was first going crazy . . . at all the times of my delusion that I was a grand military figure . . . I knew that this was a way that I was trying to tell myself that I could overcome my panic and fear. . . . Rather than talk with me about this, my doctors would always ask me what I call conditional questions.

Harry asked, "What are conditional questions?"

> You (the professionals) were always checking me out . . . checking me out to see if I knew what you knew rather than find a way to talk with me. You would ask 'Is this an ashtray?' to see if I knew or not. It was as if you knew and wanted to see if I could . . . that only made me more frightened. If you could have talked with the me that knew how scared I was . . . we could have handled that crazy general.

A not-knowing position reduces the opportunity for what Ralph called conditional questions and instead leads the therapist to ask conversational questions that help the therapist to learn and to understand the "said" and the "not-yet-said." They invite the client to talk with the therapist. They invite the client into a shared inquiry. In turn, each question leads to an elaboration of descriptions and explanations. Each question leads to another question in a process of continuing questioning. Questions come from the conversation.

## You Have to Ask the Right Question

At a workshop a woman introduced herself to me by saying, "I know you don't remember me, but I'm Anna. You interviewed me one time and the first thing I told you was, 'You have to ask the right questions.' " Hearing this, I remembered her instantly, although she looked remarkably different from the woman I had met several years ago. Anna was a nurse whom I had seen in a consultation interview because her therapist was worried about her chronic suicidal tendencies.

Anna then told me about her experience of the interview and of the dramatic changes in her life since that time.[4] She told me how, when we first met, she did not want to talk with me.

> *I was like a person without a mimic and body language—in a deep sadness. I did not want to be alive. But I tried to make it possible to have a new life—to be independent. To eat and walk for my own. To see colors and flowers. Sun and summer. But inside it was dark. For years and months I longed for death. I sat like a clown with a smile outside and inside it was dark. I wanted death.*
>
> *You had to ask the right questions because I had a secret to hide. I could not talk with you about all the problems. I had to hide. You asked and I told you about my independence and my new life without my daughter. I was worried about her and we talked a lot about that part of the problem.*

> *When you interviewed me I became sure to be in life and try struggling against death. You let me find out that I had to eat for my own sake, go for a walk.*

Some months after our chance meeting I received a letter from Anna in which she said our recent conversation had "awakened more thoughts." As she looked back she was glad to be alive. Most significant was the talking, she wrote. Referring to talking with her therapist, Anna said, "He helped me out of sadness by talking and talking and he gave me responsibility for my own life." The way I talked with her also had a profound impact on her own professional work with patients, she wrote, continuing:

> *Now I can see all my meetings with people are ruled by the responsibility everyone has for his or her own life. The respect for people's meanings and feelings! To say how I feel, to be glad, sorry, or angry. Now today I can stand in my feelings and I try to be a hero of them. I can stand in the situation without running to death. Ask questions, of yourself, of others. I do not know about the future but I feel good in the present.*

She ended her letter with the words "Ask questions!" Anna's conversations with the therapist led her to have new conversations with herself. She, like Lars, composed a new self-narrative through which she became free from her suicidal prison and became the hero of her own story, not one written, edited, or guided by the therapist. Lars was no longer a prisoner of a chronic disease but was a hero of his life. Heroic feelings yield a sense of possibilities.

## Facilitation of Conversational Space and Process

Ivar Hartviksen, a Norwegian psychiatrist, captured the essence of questions from a not-knowing position: "The question is the only tool I have in my work. It is the only way that I have of *wondering*, of *participating* in the patient's life" (comments made

---

[4] English is not Anna's first language, which accounts for what I think of as the poetry of her words. I have tried to use her words and phrases and not lose her meanings.

during a discussion at the Melbu Conference in Melbu, Vesteralen, Norway, 1990). I add Anna's challenge to this: Ask the right questions. They are the ones that come from being immersed in the client's world, letting the client lead, and knowing you do not know.

I do not suggest that any one not-knowing question can produce a miracle cure, nor that other questions would beget a therapeutic impasse. No one question can influence a dialogic or nondialogic space or occasion. The question itself does not cause someone to shift meaning, to give up an idea, or to have a new idea. But each question, each comment, represents the overall therapeutic posture: not-knowing, not understanding too quickly, not determining a frame for the dialogue. Each question is an element of the overall conversational process.

As a facilitator of conversational space and process, the therapist is only "a part of a circular interactive system" (Gadamer, 1975, p. 361). The therapist does not control the interview by moving the conversation in a particular direction of content or outcome, nor is the therapist responsible for the direction of change. Braten (1984) described the process as intersubjective, a dialogue in which all participants can make room for one another's creativity and consciousness.

The not-knowing stance is a spontaneous, natural way of interacting and being in relationship with the client. In this relational process, the client is the expert on his or her lived experiences and the therapist is the expert on inviting the client into and creating a meaning-generating conversational process. It is a relationship in which the expertise of the client and the expertise of the therapist are combined. It is a process characterized by connecting, collaborating, and constructing—or what I have referred to as *C* therapy (Anderson, 1992). The relationship of therapist and client and their conversational interactions are similar to what Kathy Weingarten (1991) called intimacy or to what Judith Jordon (1991) referred to as mutuality.

The depth, power, and excitement of the client's and the therapist's experiences in this process are dif-ficult to describe and explain. I want to emphasize that the position flows naturally from the philosophical stance; it is not deliberate or manipulative, as thinking about it cognitively might suggest. The following gives a glimpse of this conversational process:

### CASE EXAMPLE: CONSULTATION AND THE SENSE OF GROUNDING

A therapist requested consultation on what she called her "uphill and downhill" case, referring to the oscillation of progress and crises during therapy with 13-year-old Anna and her mother, Dorothy. The interview occurred during a workshop the therapist was attending.[5]

**Harlene:** Hi, I'm Harlene Anderson. Please feel free to call me Harlene. Let me introduce the two of you to the folks who are behind the mirror, via the video. This is Dorothy, who is the mother in this family, and this is Anna. And [to Anna] you're fifteen—

**Anna:** Thirteen.

**Harlene:** Oh, thirteen. I just aged you a couple of years, you're thirteen. Okay. Nikki was sharing with me and our colleagues . . . a little bit about the two of you and a little bit about the work that the three of you have been doing together . . . and kind of in a nutshell what she was saying—[addressing Nikki] add what you think I'm leaving out.

I summarized what I had learned about them from Nikki and how they had been referred by the youth worker at school. Anna corrected me.

**Harlene:** Through probation, okay. And there were some concerns about *you* [to Anna], that you were running away, for one, and the possibility of some other kind of things . . . and Nikki said that her experience was that things in the session would seem like things were okay, and then she would find out later that something else had happened, and it was kind of uphill and downhill, uphill—

**Dorothy:** Like a roller coaster.

---

[5] I have talked about this interview elsewhere (see Anderson, 1993).

**Harlene:** Oh, like a roller coaster, okay. And she felt that all of you had really been sincerely, sort of, putting your shoulder to the wheel and working really hard at this and trying to get a handle on this, but somehow nothing seemed to really work in the long run.

**Nikki:** That was for a long period of time.

**Harlene:** And in talking with Harry Goolishian, the idea was, well maybe we can just look at some of the things *you folks* are concerned about, some of the talking that *you all* have been doing, and see where to go from here. But I would be interested in *your* sharing with *us* kind of what *you* currently see as things that *you all* are concerned about or that *you* see as problematic, and maybe where things are now compared to when you first met Nikki, as a way of trying to get a handle on things, and where to go from here.

I shared what I had learned about the family members before their arrival. My misunderstandings were open for correction. I did not begin the conversation with a preconceived idea concerning the family, the therapist, or their work together. Instead, I made clear that *I*, *we*, were to learn what *they* thought *we* should know. I showed my interest in and invited each viewpoint, making room for their stories, their familiar experiences.

Setting the stage for collaboration, I used collective, nonhierarchical language. I used the words *us* and *we*—saying to the therapist, for example, "Tell *us* what *you* think that *we* need to know"). I included myself with the workshop participants. Using *you*, I referred to the individuals and to the collective group (mother, daughter, therapist) as a working group. I also acknowledged that others have participated in the conversations (the supervision group). I used words such as *talking*, not therapy.

The mother began her story. "We still have problems . . . Anna is trying but still wants to determine what she can do and what she can't do." The mother described the problems at home between herself and Anna, conflicts between Anna and her sister, and Anna's temper. She described herself as "a very opinionated person—just do it my way. I'm a dictator type." She talked about tempers flaring when strong wills

clashed. Referring to Anna, she added, "She's got things against her." I commented that they were "a family with two women with very strong opinions and minds of their own." The therapist told about an event the mother had described in a recent telephone conversation. The mother joined in and retold the story of the night the lights went out during a storm. She described a "fantastic" candlelit evening by the fireside where she and Anna talked and felt closer.

Wanting to make room for and validate all views and be what I call multipartial, I turned to Anna.

**Harlene:** Anna, where are you with all of this? How would you describe what's happening now and—

**Anna:** Confusion.

**Harlene:** Confusion, okay. About . . .

Unfinished sentences and hanging words invite the client to finish the thought.

**Anna:** I'm just real confused about all of this. I mean about the home fighting and then I only get to see my friends for weekends, talking to them for the last few days, and my personal life and my family life. There's a lot of things that are confusing.

**Dorothy:** This is like an old cliché, but when I was your age if I were to pull the things that you could pull I wouldn't even be seeing my friends on weekends.

**Anna:** But, I'm not you.

**Dorothy:** So you've got a lot of different—

**Anna:** I'm not you.

**Dorothy:** You've got a lot of different things happening for you.

**Anna:** I know, but I'm not you.

**Harlene** [to Anna]: Well, let me ask about the, you said confusion about the fighting at home, things happening at home. Can you say a little bit more about that—fighting between whom, and about what?

Here I asked about something (the confusion) that Anna mentioned earlier. The therapeutic conversation involves learning a little about one thing and then becoming curious about something else. It is a touching on this and that, never staying with any one thing too long, and not wanting to give the impression that I believe that one thing is more important than another—not wanting to find myself on a narrow path.

Many possible stories could have been evoked in this session. Choices of questions, comments, or other utterances influence the story. I want to make choices that widen both my and the client's room for new possibilities, not narrow it. I want to demonstrate a not-knowing position: listening respectfully to what the clients think is important and maintaining coherence with their story as they want to tell it. My aim is not to gather, for example, information to sort out on my therapist's template, a map that then would inform me about the problem (diagnosis) and guide my actions (strategies and interventions). Nor is it my aim to validate or nullify a hypothesis.

In summary, I heard both Anna's and her mother's views on running away, problems at school, and fights with her sister Christy and her mother at home. They told stories about fights between Anna and Christy over a ring and over chocolate candy. Strong, discrepant opinions emerged quickly; Anna and her mother repeatedly interrupted and corrected each other. Anna was in tears. The therapist said, "This is similar to what usually happens." I then turned to the mother and asked her about something she had said earlier—that she thought Anna was afraid of something.

The mother told how Anna is afraid of school and of "finding out that she's all right . . . she doesn't want to be sick." She described the details of Anna's medical problem and the difficulty of obtaining a diagnosis: ruling out lupus, leukemia, and AIDS. The mother said that she believes Anna's medical problem may be part of, or causing, her other problems. There are still a lot of unknowns, she said, emphasizing that the doctors advised Anna not to use drugs.

Anna interrupted and wanted to finish a story she had begun earlier about blacking out during a fight with her mother.

**Anna:** One of these days I'm afraid that I'm going to get so bad that I'm going to try to kill her [the

mother]. When I black out, I can do anything because my temper gets so high and I get so mad that I don't know what I'm going to do. I see guns all around, her body lying there, and I had a knife in my hand.

**Nikki:** This kind of brings up the point as to why they are here [referring back to her concern that she shared with the group that someone in the family might get hurt].

**Harlene:** Let me tell you about an idea that I have. I was just thinking that since we are all [referring to myself, the family, the therapist, and the workshop participants] gathered here, maybe we could take advantage of what we can take advantage of. I'm wondering about Dorothy and me staying in here and talking some and having you and Anna behind the mirror. Would that be agreeable?

I often use what I think of as more cooperative, softening, indefinite, and tentative words and phrases such as *wondering, kind of,* and *maybe.* Such words and phrases invite dialogue and the coexploration of issues. They show more interest in the other's view and less interest in a therapist-held view.

Anna, her mother, and the therapist agreed with my suggestion. Had anyone not, however, I would have talked with them about their concerns and been willing to take back the suggestion. Talking with the mother and daughter separately while each observed the other, along with the therapist, was not preplanned. The idea emerged from the immediate conversational process. Anna and her mother had become heavily engaged in correcting and interrupting each other. Absorbed in their dueling monologic views, neither was able to listen undefensively to the other. To be able to listen undefensively is an important step toward both internal and external dialogic processes.

Continuing, I talked with the mother first while Anna and the therapist listened and watched behind a one-way mirror.

**Harlene:** Let's start over with *your* story. Can I back up just a little bit. I feel that this sounds like such a complicated situation and sounds like it has certainly escalated recently—

This was not a strategy. I was genuinely interested in what was on her mind.

**Dorothy:** No, it hasn't been recently.

**Harlene:** It hasn't been recently. So this is what I was wondering, this is something that's been going on for a long, long time in terms of your concerns about Anna, and you're sort of experiencing her as a very headstrong child with a mind of her own. Sort of fill me in on when your concerns began, and sort of a real shift. When did those shifts start occurring?

The mother began to tell her story. After I talked with the mother, I talked with Anna while the mother and the therapist observed. I then met with all three of them briefly and suggested they might want to meet again and continue talking about our talk today.

It is difficult to capture the richness of the conversations and the evolution of newness for the daughter, mother, and therapist. At the end of the session the therapist commented on her new experience with the family:

**Therapist:** Well . . . it's come to me. It's almost like watching and listening to this family was like starting at the middle of the book. Now it's like it's in a sequence, and things being said are not information; that is different. I heard a lot of this before, but watching and listening and being here in the room this way, it's very different, it's very sequential. The story is much more organized.

**Harlene:** You have more a sense of grounding just in terms of who these folks are and what's happening with them, is that fair?

**Therapist:** Yes. It's not so much who they are. I felt like I had that before—more grounded, well yes, more a sense of who they are. The pieces fit together to make more sense.

The therapist now had a different family to work with and had a renewed sense of agency.

## IMPLICATIONS AND CONCERNS ABOUT POSTMODERN THERAPY

I am frequently asked about the political implications of our view. Does it favor some descriptions and marginalize others? How do I deal with issues of power? How do I avoid implying that the victim participates in her victimization? How can you not intervene? Aren't you responsible for being—expected to be—the expert? Isn't this what therapists do anyway?

There is no such thing as an innocent therapy. Therapy begins with power differentials, and therapists are always using influence. Therapists must be sensitive to society's, their profession's, and their own personal dominant discourses. They must ensure that the dominant discourse does not fill the whole space. They must be sensitive to the marginal discourse, be it one of gender, poverty, race, therapist-in-training, a single, African American mother with a son involved in the juvenile system, or a merchant seaman who believes he is contaminating others.

I want to create room for and learn about the marginal voice. I do not want to deconstruct or instruct the marginal voice toward what the therapist knows it should be. I believe it is the therapist's responsibility to minimize power differentials. I also believe that therapist intentionality plays a major role in creating, maintaining, and taking advantage of power differentials. My work, however, is the product of an interpretive (as in hermeneutics, not analysis) stance rather than an interventive stance.

Therapists often ask, Isn't it nihilistic to say you're not an expert? Isn't therapy hierarchical? After all, what is the client paying you for? Yes, the client is paying for something. The client is paying for help with a "problem." I am offering an interpersonal experience in which the client and I through a shared inquiry coexplore the familiar and cocreate new meanings and new stories about the client's life. This leads to a sense of self-agency and freedom and problem dissolution. In summary, a collaborative language systems approach to therapy represents the edge of a controversial shift in psychotherapy—a shift from language as a function, as a rhetoric-like tool, to language as generative, as the essence of dialogue and therefore the essence of the therapeutic process. In this conception of language, the therapist is no longer the expert editor of the client's narrative, who uses language as an editing tool. The therapist is more like a coauthor, whose expertise is in a process. This implies a locally coconstructed therapeutic reality in which the client's and therapist's expertise are combined to create a collaborative therapy, one that is less hierarchical, more egalitarian, more mutual, more respectful, more human—and usually briefer. This therapy, I find, does not work with or create dysfunctional categories or people. It discovers, or allows both the client and the therapist to discover, in Anna's words, heroic feelings.

# References

Andersen, T. (1990, June). *Construction, language, and meaning: In research and clinical practice.* Seminar presented at the Melbu Conference, Melbu, Vesteralen, Norway.

Anderson, H. (1990). Then and now: From knowing to not-knowing. *Contemporary Family Therapy Journal, 12,* 193–198.

Anderson, H. (1992, Winter). C therapy and the F word. *American Family Therapy Association Newsletter, 50,* 19–22.

Anderson, H. (1993). On a roller coaster: A collaborative language systems approach to therapy. In S. Friedman (Ed.), *The new language of change* (pp. 323–344). New York: Guilford Press.

Anderson, H., & Goolishian, H. (1986). Systems consultation to agencies dealing with domestic violence. In L. Wynne, S. McDaniel, & T. Weber (Eds.), *The family therapist as systems consultant* (pp. 284–299). New York: Guilford Press.

Anderson, H., & Goolishian, H. (1988). Human systems as linguistic systems: Evolving ideas about the implications for theory and practice. *Family Process, 27,* 371–393.

Anderson, H., & Goolishian, H. (1989a, Spring). Conversations at Sulitjelma: A description and reflection. *American Family Therapy Association Newsletter, 35,* 31–36.

Anderson, H., & Goolishian, H. (1989b). *Questions in therapy.* Unpublished manuscript.

Anderson, H., & Goolishian, H. (1990a). Beyond cybernetics: Comments on Atkinson and Heath's "Further thoughts on second-order family therapy." *Family Process, 29,* 157–163.

Anderson, H., & Goolishian, H. (1990b). Supervision as collaborative conversation: Questions and reflections. In H. Brandau (Ed.), *Von der supervision zur systemischen vision* [From supervision to systemic supervision]. Salzburg: Otto Müller Verlag.

Anderson, H., & Goolishian, H. (1991a). Revisiting history. *Australian-New Zealand Journal of Family Therapy, 12,* iii.

Anderson, H., & Goolishian, H. (1991b). Thinking about multi-agency work with substance abusers and their families. *Journal of Strategic and Systemic Therapies, 10,* 20–35.

Anderson, H., & Goolishian, H. (1992). The client is the expert: A not-knowing approach to therapy. In S. McNamee & K. Gergen (Eds.), *Social construction and the therapeutic process* (pp. 25–39). Newbury Park, CA: Sage.

Anderson, H., Goolishian, H., Pulliam, G., & Winderman, L. (1986). The Galveston Family Institute: A personal and historical perspective. In D. Efron (Ed.), *Journeys: Expansions of the strategic-systemic therapies* (pp. 97–124). New York: Brunner/Mazel.

Anderson, H., Goolishian, H., & Winderman, L. (1986a). Beyond family therapy. *Journal of Strategic and Systemic Therapies, 5,* i–iii.

Anderson, H., Goolishian, H., & Winderman, L. (1986b). Problem determined systems: Towards transformation in family therapy. *Journal of Strategic and Systemic Therapies, 5,* 1–13.

Berger, P. L., & Luckmann, T. (1967). *The social construction of reality: A treatise in the sociology of knowledge.* New York: Anchor Books.

Braten, S. (1984). The third position: Beyond artificial and autopoietic reduction. In F. Geyer & J. van der Zouwen (Eds.), *Sociocybernetic paradoxes* (pp. 193–205). London: Sage.

Braten, S. (1986). Paradigms of autonomy: Dialogical or monological? In G. Teubner (Ed.), *Autopoiesis in law and society* (pp. 42–61). New York: De Gruyter.

Bruner, J. (1990). *Acts of meaning.* Cambridge, MA: Harvard University Press.

Code, L. (1988). Experiences, knowledge and responsibility. In M. Griffiths & M. Whitford (Eds.), *Feminist perspectives in philosophy* (pp. 187–204). Bloomington: Indiana University Press.

Dell, P. F., & Goolishian, H. A. (1981, July). Order through fluctuation: An evolving epistemology for human systems. *Australian Journal of Family Therapy,* 175–184.

Flax, J. (1990). *Thinking fragments: Psychoanalysis, feminism, & postmodernism in the contemporary west.* Berkeley: University of California Press.

Gadamer, H. G. (1975). *Truth and method* (G. Burden & J. Cumming, Trans.). New York: Seabury Press.

Geertz, C. (1983a). Blurred genres: The refiguration of social thought. *American Scholar, 49,* 165–179.

Geertz, C. (1983b). *Local knowledge.* New York: Basic Books.

Gergen, K. J. (1982). *Toward transformation in social knowledge.* New York: Springer-Verlag.

Gergen, K. J. (1985a). The social constructionist movement in modern psychology. *American Psychologist, 40*, 266–275.

Gergen, K. J. (1985b). Theory of the self: Impasses and evolution. In L. Berkowitz (Ed.), *Advances in experimental social psychology* (Vol. 17; pp. 49–115). New York: Academic Press.

Goodman, N. (1984). *Of mind and other matters.* Cambridge, MA: Harvard University Press.

Goolishian, H. (1989). *The self: Some thoughts from a postmodern perspective on the intersubjectivity of mind.* Unpublished manuscript.

Goolishian, H., & Anderson, H. (1981). Including non-blood-related persons in family therapy. In A. Gurman (Ed.), *Questions and answers in the practice of family therapy* (pp. 75–79). New York: Brunner/Mazel.

Goolishian, H., & Anderson, H. (1987a). Language systems and therapy: An evolving idea. *Psychotherapy, 24/3S,* 529–538.

Goolishian, H., & Anderson, H. (1987b). De la thérapie familiale à la thérapie systemique et au-delà [From family to systemic therapy and beyond]. In F. Ladame, P. Gutton, & M. Kalogerakis (Eds.), *Psychoses et adolescence. Annales internationales de psychiatrie de l'adolescence* [Psychosis and adolescence. International annals of adolescent psychiatry] (pp. 160–173). Paris: Masson.

Goolishian, H., & Anderson, H. (1990). Understanding the therapeutic process: From individuals and families to systems in language. In F. Kaslow (Ed.), *Voices in family psychology* (pp. 91–113). Newbury Park, CA: Sage.

Goolishian, H., & Anderson, H. (1992a). Some afterthoughts on reading Duncan and Held. *Journal of Marital and Family Therapy, 18,* 35–38.

Goolishian, H., & Anderson, H. (1992b). Strategy and intervention versus nonintervention: A matter of theory? *Journal of Marital and Family Therapy, 18,* 5–15.

Goolishian, H., & Anderson, H. (in press). Narrative and self: Some postmodern dilemmas of psychotherapy. *Sistemas Familiares.*

Goolishian, H., & Kivell, H. (1981). Planning therapeutic interventions so as to include non-blood related family members in the therapeutic goals. In A. S. Gurman (Ed.), *Questions and answers in the practice of family therapy* (pp. 75–79). New York: Brunner/Mazel.

Harre, R. (1983). Personal being: A theory for individual psychology. Oxford, England: Basil Blackwell.

Harre, R. (1986). *The social construction of emotions.* Oxford, England: Basil Blackwell.

Jordon, J. (1991). The meaning of mutuality. In J. V. Jordan, A. G. Kaplan, J. B. Miller, I. P. Stiver, & J. L. Surrey (Eds.), *Women's growth in connection* (pp. 81–96). New York: Guilford Press.

Kitzinger, C. (1987). *The social construction of lesbianism.* London: Sage.

Lipps, H. (1938). *Untersuchunsen zu einer hermeneutischen logik* [Inquiry into hermeneutic logic]. Frankfurt: Klosterman.

Lyotard, J. F. (1984). *The postmodern condition: A report on knowledge.* Manchester, England: Manchester University Press.

MacGregor, R., Ritchie, A., Serrano, A., Schuster, F., McDanald, E., & Goolishian, H. (1964). *Multiple impact therapy.* New York: McGraw-Hill.

Madison, G. G. (1990). *The hermeneutics of postmodernity.* Bloomington: Indiana University Press.

Maturana, H. R. (1978). Biology of language: Epistemology of reality. In G. Miller & E. Lenneberg (Eds.), *Psychology and biology of language and thought* (pp. 112–123). New York: Academic Press.

Maturana, H., & Varela, F. (1980). *Autopoiesis and cognition: The realization of the living.* Boston: Reidel.

Messer, S. B., Sass, L. A., & Woolfolk, R. L. (1988). *Hermeneutics and psychological theory: Interpretive perspectives on personality, psychotherapy, and psychopathology.* New Brunswick, NJ: Rutgers University Press.

Nicholson, L. (1990). *Feminism and postmodernism.* New York: Routledge.

Polkinghorne, D. (1988). *Narrative knowing and the human sciences.* Albany, NY: State University of New York Press.

Prigogine, I., & Stengers, I. (1984). *Order out of chaos: Man's new dialogue with nature.* New York: Bantam Books.

Rice, A. (1976). *Interview with the vampire.* New York: Ballantine Books.

Rorty, R. (1979). *Philosophy and the mirror of nature.* Princeton, NJ: Princeton University Press.

Schafer, R. (1980). Narration in the psychoanalytic dialogue. *Critical Inquiry, 7,* 29–53.

Shotter, J. (1988). *Red and counterfeit constructions in interpersonal relations.* Paper presented at the Don Bannister Memorial Conference: Metaphors in Life and Psychotherapy, Institute of Group Analysis, London, England.

Shotter, J. (1991, May). *Consultant re-authoring: The 'making' and 'finding' of narrative constructions.* Paper presented at the Houston Galveston Institute Narrative and Psychotherapy Conference, Houston, TX.

Shotter, J. (1993). *Conversational realities*. London: Sage.

Shotter, J., & Gergen, K. J. (1989). *Texts of identity*. London: Sage.

Spence, D. (1984). *Narrative truth and historical truth: Meaning and interpretation in psychoanalysis*. New York: Norton.

von Foerster, H. (1984). On constructing a reality. In P. Watzlawick (Ed.), *The invented reality* (pp. 41–61). New York: Norton.

von Glasersfeld, E. (1984). An introduction to radical constructivism. In P. Watzlawick (Ed.), *The invented reality* (pp. 13–40). New York: Norton.

Vygotsky, L. S. (1986). Thought and language (rev. ed., A. Kozulin, Trans.). Cambridge, MA: MIT Press. (Original work published 1934)

Wacherhauser, B. R. (1986). *Hermeneutics and modern philosophy*. New York: State University of New York Press.

Watzlawick, P. (1984). *The invented reality*. New York: Norton.

Weingarten, K. (1991). The discourse of intimacy: Adding a social constructionist and feminist view. *Family Process, 30,* 285–306.

Wittgentstein, L. (1953). *Philosophical investigations*. Oxford, England: Blackwell.

# CHAPTER 3

# ENGAGING THE FAMILY: AN INTEGRATIVE APPROACH

*Timothy Weber and Felise Levine*

*The beginning is the most important part
of the work.*

*Plato*

At the core of all the diverse orientations in the field of family therapy lies one fundamental goal: Therapy must finish well and result in some kind of healing benefit to the family members. To finish well, however, it is critical that it begin well. How a therapist begins or engages with a family significantly shapes the entire course and outcome of psychotherapy.

The process of engaging families in treatment goes well beyond the bounds of what might be called client recruitment and retention. Engaging the family includes, but goes beyond, what Minuchin (1974) called *joining* and *accommodating*, initially accepting the family's organization and style and blending with them. In our view, engaging the family in treatment is akin to a therapeutic overture. In this overture, all the primary themes of the therapist and the family are played in some way, leadership is defined, and the therapist–family system is created so that the necessary conditions for therapeutic change are primed. This process is essential regardless of whether the treatment is brief or lengthy. In this chapter, we discuss what we believe to be core components of engaging families throughout the therapeutic process; these range from pretherapy to posttherapy phases. Although our focus is on engaging families in treatment, these principles also apply to engaging couples and individuals from a systems-oriented perspective.

Engaging families extends beyond the first meeting and has no fixed number of sessions, although we typically view this beginning phase of engaging continuing from one to three sessions. However, the studies on psychotherapy suggest that, regardless of the therapist's orientation and intent, therapists have a limited time in which to work with families. Most clients stay in treatment for only 6 to 10 sessions (Garfield, 1978; Gurman, 1981; Koss, 1979). Moreover, the mandate of managed health care suggests that longer-term treatment will be increasingly more of an exception. Consequently, this process of engaging families is more likely to be compressed than extended. It should also be viewed not simply as assessment or a precursor to treatment, but also as a circular process in which gathering information affords opportunities for change, intervening gathers new information, and so on. We do not engage families for treatment; engagement is treatment.

The literature on engaging the family in treatment includes a variety of approaches on how to conduct the first interview (De Shazer, 1982; Framo, 1980; Haley, 1987; Stierlin, Rucker-Embden, Wetzel, & Wirsching, 1980; Weber, McKeever, & McDaniel,

We gratefully acknowledge Jim Framo for his consultation in preparing this chapter. We also acknowledge the clerical support of Jeanette Cookson and Debi Vogel of The Leadership Institute of Seattle/Bastyr University.

1985) and how to engage with families (Trotzer, 1982; Wells, 1980; Zuk, 1972, 1974). There also has been a particular emphasis on how to recruit and retain reluctant fathers in treatment (Berg & Rosenblum, 1977; Forrest, 1969; L'Abate, 1975), as well as resistant or therapy-refusing families (Shapiro & Budman, 1973; Slipp, Ellis, & Kressel, 1974; Stanton & Todd, 1982). When families fail to be recruited and retained, a host of reasons—some beyond the therapist's control—may be involved. In this chapter, we examine typical problems in the engagement process and offer suggestions on how to meet those challenges.

The strategies and techniques proffered in this chapter reflect our commitment to an intergenerational perspective as background for our focus on current interactions, a blending of the intrapsychic and interpersonal views, and an emphasis on the self of the therapist—in our view the most critical tool of therapeutic change. We also include references to organizational development and business consultation because there is a wealth of untapped, rich collaboration between the fields of family therapy and organizational consulting.

## CORE COMPONENTS OF ENGAGING FAMILIES

What are the core components of engaging families in treatment? What are the basic conditions aimed for in establishing a healthy therapeutic system? We believe two core components lie at the heart of engaging families: establishing leadership and creating a holding environment.

## Establishing Leadership

A therapeutic system, or for that matter any living organism, cannot be established without a leader (Friedman, 1985). Leadership functions include a host of clinical tasks such as accommodating to the family's style, guiding and directing the interview, managing administrative matters (time, fee, scheduling, consultants, forms, etc.), establishing norms, giving directives, generating hypotheses, and restructuring interactions within the family. However, leadership is much more than conducting the interview or managing the therapeutic process. Leader-

ship has less to do with task and more to do with self. This "leadership of the self" is the core of establishing therapeutic leadership. In addition, there are two other dimensions of establishing leadership in engaging the family in treatment—fostering distributed leadership in the family and crafting a learning organization.

*Establishing leadership of the self.* Since the early days of psychotherapy, the training of therapists generally has emphasized both the technical skill of conducting psychotherapy and the person of the therapist. Analytic training has sought to decontaminate the therapist's countertransference reactions to the patient by having the therapist work through unresolved conflicts in psychoanalysis. Family therapists, most notably Bowen (1978), have also underscored the personal work of the therapist, especially the therapist's family of origin. This work promotes self-knowledge, deepens the capacity to form relationships, opens interpersonal awareness, increases the range of cognitive and affective capacity, and strengthens personal authority—all fundamental competencies in the leadership of the self (Framo, 1992; Williamson, 1992). The use of the self to deepen the encounter with the family and augment technical interventions is an emphasis in some schools of family therapy (Aponte, 1992).

Strength, personal authority, and differentiation of the self are essential to both engagement and therapeutic change. Therapists, like competent leaders, must "walk the empowerment tightrope" (Crosby, 1992, p. 1) and maintain authority while being open to influence. Minuchin (1974) likewise believes that "when a therapist joins the family, he has two main tasks. He must accommodate to the family, but he must also maintain himself in a position of leadership with the therapeutic unit" (p. 139).

Families will not follow a leader who lacks personal authority. They may tag along and pretend, but they will not engage. If they change, it will be in spite of this therapist, not because of this therapist. Authority is central for leadership. Fisch, Weakland, and Segal (1982) also emphasize the importance of therapist maneuverability. They believe that clients may, for a variety of reasons, block the therapist's effort to conduct treatment. To be effective, the therapist must stay free "to take purposeful action despite fluctuating obstacles or restrictions. A therapist needs to keep his options open as therapy progresses, shifting as needed during the course of treatment" (p. 22).

Whitaker and Keith discuss this same aspect of therapeutic leadership as the "battle for structure . . . basically our demand that the family capitulate to the therapist's mode of operating" (Whitaker & Keith, 1981, p. 198). Whitaker and Keith believe that therapy always begins with a "battle for structure," which essentially is a fight between the therapist and the family about who is in charge of the structure of therapy. This battle begins early on, even before the first telephone conversation, and is especially manifest in the beginning sessions as a result of issues such as who should attend the meetings, who decides how the therapy hour is to proceed, whether taping will be allowed, whether there will be a co-therapist or a team, and so on. For the family to engage in therapy, the therapist must win this battle for structure—taking command, staying in charge, being clear about his or her nonnegotiables, and being open to change in the negotiable areas.

Winning this battle is not a matter of defending the therapist's ego or outmaneuvering the family, but is at the core an issue of establishing a trustworthy therapeutic relationship. Trust in therapy can only be built on the strength of the therapist. Families enter therapy with ambivalent feelings—hurting and wanting help, yet also afraid of what change might demand out of them. They begin to unfold the guts of their lives in the presence of a stranger. There is much at stake for families as they enter therapy. If they sense weakness and lack of leadership in the therapist as the therapist caves into the whims and demands of family members, why should they trust that therapist with their lives? Therefore, families will test whether the therapist has the authority to withstand their diversions and challenges. If the therapist survives these tests, the therapist will be seen as someone who can handle what really matters in the family, and an umbrella of trust will invite the family into the process of change.

We believe that the core of therapeutic leadership is found in the concept of "differentiated leadership" as defined by Friedman (1985), drawing from Bowen's "differentiation of self" (Kerr and Bowen, 1988).

The differentiated therapist is not so much in a battle with the family as he or she is focused on self-definition. This process involves (a) staying in touch and connecting personally with family members; (b) articulating a vision of the therapeutic process and how it is to proceed; (c) taking nonreactive, clearly defined "I" positions; and (d) maintaining a nonanxious presence in the midst of the family's anxiety. The therapist continues on course, without forgetting the goals and purpose of therapy, while assuming at times a more playful spin with the family (Friedman, 1985, pp. 229–230).

*Fostering distributed leadership.* Fostering distributed leadership in the family means establishing a partnership with the family with respect to goal setting, determining the direction of therapy, and crafting the most useful methods of working together. This is the other half of "walking the empowerment tightrope": the leader is open to the influence of others in the organization (Crosby, 1992). As much as we emphasize the therapist's authority, we also believe that a spirit of collaboration and partnership is critical for engaging the family. To facilitate this posture, we define ourselves as "systems consultants" (Wynne, McDaniel, & Weber, 1986) who will work collaboratively with the family. Families engage in treatment more productively when they feel valued and respected, when their input is heard and used by the therapist, and when they feel some ownership in coshaping the process.

Fostering distributed leadership is also supporting leadership within the family as family members assume more responsibility for their own lives because of an increasing sense of competency. Cohen and Smith (1976), writing about the stages of group development from an organizational perspective, discuss "distributed leadership" as including a sense of "integrated autonomy" where group members assert their individuality within a context of group solidarity. As distributed leadership unfolds, the leader becomes less central and is seen as more of a person. Members become more willing to assume functions and responsibilities typically accomplished only by the leader. Family members take more responsibility for their difficulties and also for what happens to them in the group. The group increasingly recognizes resources within the group and not simply in the leader. Therapists have emphasized the importance of clients assuming responsibility for their lives as a correlate of successful psychotherapy. This is the basis for a working alliance.

Yalom (1989) notes that "the crucial first step in therapy is the patient's assumption of responsibility for his or her life predicament" (p. 8). Whitaker and Keith (1981) refer to this process as the "battle for initiative," which addresses who will do the work and who is in charge of the clients' lives. The family must win the battle for initiative. If the therapist wins this battle, he or she is overfunctioning and overly responsible for the family, and the family will not engage productively in therapy. The therapist not only delegates the responsibility for change to the family, but also, as Friedman (1985) notes, "delegates the anxiety." It is not difficult to delegate responsibility by telling someone what you want him or her to do. It is much more difficult to delegate anxiety, to assume a nonanxious presence in the midst of a family that lays blames or becomes dependent when it is in the midst of a crisis.

The final dimension of fostering distributed leadership is the continual amplification of competencies, strengths, assets, capabilities, and resources within the family. Boszormenyi-Nagy and Krasner (1986) emphasize the importance of searching for untapped resources within the family and discovering the humanity of every participant, even the family's most "monstrous member." Not surprising, people feel more engaged in relationships and encouraged to embark on a path of wellness and change if they see themselves as more competent and able. Wolin and Wolin (1993) have challenged therapists to shift from the dysfunctional family model to a resiliency based one. Therapists will be able to see strengths in all families if their eyes and ears are turned in that direction. Despair or hope is as much a function of what the therapist sees as it is what is resident within the family. Especially in the beginning of therapy, but also throughout the course of working with the family, we underscore, explicitly, the micro-strengths within the family—strengths that are barely perceptible and that could "fly under the radar" of the family's ability to notice. The courage to change and take leadership comes from believing in oneself

more hopefully. It is the therapist's responsibility to foster this hope by helping the family build a system that notices these strengths.

*Crafting a learning organization.* The third dimension of establishing leadership is crafting a "learning organization"—a community of learners, both therapist and family members, who are in the process of learning from their experience with each other. The concept of a learning organization is more endemic to the world of organizational development than family therapy (Senge, 1990). Learning organizations, said Senge, are "organizations where people continually expand their capacity to create the results they truly desire, where new and expansive patterns of thinking are nurtured, where collective aspiration is set free, and where people are continually learning how to learn together" (p. 3).

Central to the building of a learning organization is the notion of "collective learning." Not only the family but also the therapist is in the position to learn, explore, and discover. Collective learning keeps therapists and families involved, creative, and alive. We believe therapists are more effective if they are learning for themselves and learning from the family. In addition, families are strengthened and engaged in the process of therapy if they think they can teach the therapist something about the guts of life.

The ancient concept of *hospitality* is helpful in understanding the engagement between the therapist and the family. The "host" or "hostess" in other cultures was hospitable not only by giving to the guest, but also in receiving from the guest or stranger. On the basis of this principle, therapy is not dishing out help to guests. Rather, therapy built on hospitality is a form of exchange or collaboration and of cocreation. It is interesting to note that "guest" and "host" were once the same word, as were "give" and "receive" (Dooling, 1990). The therapist–family collaborative process facilitates change and models the collaboration we hope the family will develop among its members.

## Creating the Holding Environment
Another aspect of the engagement process is the creation of a holding environment—a safe, reliable,

therapeutic space within which change and growth can occur. Psychoanalysts have long attended to the relationship between patient and therapist in terms of the intersubjective field (Stolorow, Brandchaft, & Atwood, 1987), establishing a working alliance or rapport (Alexander & French, 1946; Langs, 1992), or working through transference and countertransference issues (Freud, 1938; Kernberg, 1965; Ogden, 1989; Searles, 1968). However, family therapists have traditionally downplayed the family's relationship with the therapist and emphasized instead relationships among family members. Of the original family therapists, primarily those with a psychodynamic, object-relations, or intergenerational perspective (Ackerman, 1966; Boszormenyi-Nagy & Krasner, 1986; Framo, 1968, 1970, 1972; Napier & Whitaker, 1978; Skynner, 1981) have paid attention to the transference relationship between therapist and family. Within the last decade, family therapists influenced by contemporary psychoanalytic theories, such as object relations and self psychology, have contributed to an understanding of transference and countertransference phenomena within marital therapy (Lachkar, 1992; Lansky, 1981) and family therapy (Scharff & Scharff, 1987; Slipp, 1984). With the addition of constructivist and social constructivist thinking (Goolishian & Anderson, 1992; Hoffman, 1990; Watzlawick, 1984), family therapy has rediscovered the importance of the therapeutic relationship.

In contrast to the therapeutic relationship in individual psychotherapy, family therapy takes place in a complex relational matrix that includes the internal worlds or object relations of each family member and of the therapist, the transactional patterns between family members, and the relationship or co-created space between the family and the therapist. This space is the holding environment where safety, trust, appreciation, fairness, and a sense of inclusion create a place for family members and the therapist to be open with their thoughts and feelings, to risk new behaviors, to play and be imaginative, and to be themselves in the presence of one another. When this occurs, engagement is accomplished and therapeutic change can occur. We believe that creating a holding environment involves several factors such as providing emotional containment, establishing rapport or joining others, listening to self, modeling relational ethics, attending to inclusion, using play and imagination, and claiming a right to a private existence.

*Emotional containment.* Framo (1992) describes the role of the therapist as offering "support, protection and control that will contain the emotional charges, underground irrationality, fantasies, secrets, fears that every family member brings to the session" (p. 120). In a similar vein, Ackerman (1982) believes that one of the therapist's functions is to fulfill temporarily the role of a parent figure, to control danger, and to be a source of emotional support. In such a parental role, the therapist determines the pacing and timing of family emotionality, slowing down or accelerating the expression of affect so that the family feels safe and trusts the therapist to regulate the emotional flow within the family.

Winnicott's (1965) idea of the good-enough mother and Bion's (1961) concept of containment are also applicable to understanding the role of emotional containment within the family therapy process. The "good-enough family therapist" is emotionally attuned to family members. The therapist holds, labels, and integrates the rage, love, hate, envy, despair, fear, emptiness, and split-off parts of family members without losing himself or herself; most important, as the emotional container, the therapist is able to do so without defensively retaliating, withdrawing, rejecting, criticizing, or colluding with family scapegoating. In this way, the therapist holds the family so that the family can learn to hold its members. The message to the family is that in this room, in this space, nothing is too dangerous or too frightening for discussion. This creates an atmosphere where painful and unintegrated affects can be integrated, so that understanding and reparation can occur within the family.

*Rapport and joining others.* The establishment of rapport has been linked to therapist empathy, understanding, and supportiveness. Several family therapists have emphasized the importance of the therapist's accommodating to the family's style and entering the system by being congruent with the rules and language of the family (Aponte & Van Deusen, 1981; Minuchin, 1974; Minuchin & Fishman, 1981).

In one of his early writings, Ackerman (1966) described establishing a useful rapport; the therapist "feels the way toward the idiosyncratic language of the family—how members talk, what they choose to talk about, what they avoid" (p. 412). He suggested that rapport was a special combination and fit between the sounds of family members and talents of the therapist. The emphasis of these family therapists has been primarily unidirectional—the therapist accommodates to, tracks, and joins with the family.

However, family members also make efforts to accommodate to, track, and join with the therapist. There are many strangers in the therapy room. Family members are not only strangers to the therapist, but they are also sometimes strangers to themselves; each needs to learn something about the other's rules, expectations, language, and meanings. Thus, we believe that building rapport and joining is not unidirectional, from therapist to family, and it is not just reciprocal between the therapist and the family. Rather, this process is multilateral, where therapist and family members must join one another in understanding personal meanings, accommodating to rules, and creating a language of shared meanings so that a healing atmosphere and learning community is created.

*Listening to self.* Whereas building rapport and joining requires listening to others on their own terms, creating a holding environment also requires listening to oneself. Within the family therapy literature, listening to oneself is usually discussed in terms of a therapist's use of self and countertransference experiences (Ackerman, 1966; Aponte, 1992; Framo, 1968; Scharff & Scharff, 1987; Skynner, 1981). The therapist's own feelings and free associations are seen as a diagnostic barometer for what is happening in the family therapy session and are reflective of a deep stream of feeling moving within the family. Just as family therapists have hypothesized about how one member's voice or symptoms may speak for other family members, therapists themselves become part of the system and may have thoughts and feelings not only about but also of members of the family group (Bion, 1961). The therapist wonders, "Why am I feeling this now? I wonder if there is anyone else in the room who feels this too?" Being able to listen to and hold one's experience can be helpful in

understanding a family member's experience and provide a window for viewing family group process.

*Modeling relational ethics.* In considering relational ethics as a component of the holding environment, we have been influenced by the thinking of Boszormenyi-Nagy and associates (Boszormenyi-Nagy & Krasner, 1986; Boszormenyi-Nagy & Spark, 1984). The therapist promotes an atmosphere of trustworthiness by modeling an ethical stance with the family and balancing the give and take within relationships. In expecting family members to be accountable for their behavior, the therapist first takes responsibility for his or her actions by being accountable to everyone who is potentially affected by his or her interventions. Boszormenyi-Nagy and Krasner emphasize that reciprocal accountability includes future, as well as current, generations within a family. By using multidirected partiality, the therapist shows a willingness to care about past injustices and their consequences for current and future relationships. Modeling relational ethics involves respecting family members' attitudes about therapy and change and informing them about the therapy process. For example, Papp (1983) discusses the dilemma of change with a family by asking members what the price will be for change and who will pay it. By listening to cautionary stories about therapy (Ogden, 1989) and raising the question about the possible repercussions of change throughout the family system (Papp, 1983), therapists engage in ethical conversations with family members and build a sense of fairness, concern, and trustworthiness about the therapeutic relationship. It is within this holding environment that family members can learn to give and take (Boszormenyi-Nagy & Krasner, 1986) and to behave and believe in the ethical trustworthiness of their own relationships.

*Attending to inclusion.* Family therapy is unique in that several points of view of intimately related people are included in the treatment process. Boszormenyi-Nagy and Krasner (1986) call the inclusion process "healing through meeting." In hearing all points of view in an appreciative and validating manner, the family therapist creates an atmosphere for meeting and a setting for family reconnection through a multilateral exchange. When the therapist can be multipartial, sequentially siding with each member, all perspectives are included in the picture.

Thus, in the holding environment, the therapist holds multiple realities while family members learn to include and incorporate multiple stories into the family story. As with most processes of engagement, we see inclusion as reciprocal and multidimensional. If the therapeutic relationship is to be effective, family members must also include elements of the therapist's story, ideals, impressions, feelings, and interventions into their system.

*Play and imagination.* The process of being playful, of being imaginative, is different from the content of play and imagination (Winnicott, 1971). It is about spontaneous self-expression, feeling vital, alive, and experiencing mutual pleasure in an encounter. Ackerman (1982) wrote that when a hearty laugh occurs, "the family is reaching me and I am reached by the family. I feel a deep zest in the closeness of the connection. It does my heart good" (p. 286). Ackerman, who was known for "tickling the family's defenses," reminded therapists that he sought to enjoy the interview and have the family enjoy it with him. Napier and Whitaker (1978) also address the importance of playing, staying alive, and being imaginative. Family members play with one another and with the therapist; they act as if the rules are real but know that they are not. It is only when therapists and family members let go of assuming that knowledge is truth (Goolishian & Anderson, 1992), when they dare to not know, that they become open to imagine. Thus, within the holding environment, family therapist and family members learn to reexamine assumptions and imagine other realities, wonder how others are feeling or thinking, and play with one another through playing with problems and imagining solutions.

*Claiming a right to a private existence.* A private existence refers to the therapist's and individual family member's abilities to pursue their own happiness and personal relationships. Thus, the family therapist must be clear about personal and professional boundaries. As Napier and Whitaker (1978) warn, therapists are the pretend, not the real, parents to the family. Having a private existence also extends to the family. Too often, therapists and family members assume that when a family enters treatment, they inadvertently give up their right to a private existence. Sometimes the therapist and even family members

believe that the family is accountable to the therapist for its actions and that all aspects of family life are open to scrutiny, hypothesis, and intervention. We have heard family members say, "we hope you won't be mad at us, but we didn't do the assignment you gave us"; "you probably think we're terrible patients because we fought so much this week"; or "do we have to discuss this? We don't think it's relevant to our problem." We recognize the challenge of differentiating what is private and what is secret information directly related to the presenting complaint. However, families, like therapists, have a right to their private existence, and seeking a consultation or therapy does not mean that the therapist has a passport to explore all regions of the family's life. Therapists must control their own voyeuristic, controlling, and rescuing impulses. We believe that when the therapist is respectful of the family's boundaries, is clear about his or her own boundaries, and claims a private existence from the family, it sets the tone for the family to balance the forces of togetherness and separateness within the family and tolerate the individuation of its members.

## STAGES OF ENGAGING

The two core components of engaging—establishing leadership and creating the holding environment—permeate our 11 stages of engaging, which include presession, in-session, and postsession processes and tasks in the beginning sessions (see Exhibit 1). We reluctantly use the word *stage* to describe a process that is more fluid and open. Although we do subscribe to some relatively ordered protocol in engaging with families, we view therapy as more art than order and, thus, modify our way of working by frequently depending on the people and the stories we encounter.

## PRESESSION

### Stage 1: Prelude to the Therapeutic Encounter

The family therapy literature typically describes stages of family engagement as beginning with the initial phone call or with contact with the referral source (Anderson & Stewart, 1983; Framo, 1980; Franklin & Prosky, 1973; Haley, 1987; Napier &

Whitaker, 1978; Weber, McKeever, & McDaniel, 1985). However, little has been written about the preexisting conditions that influence both the therapist and family members, factors that affect the outcome of the initial phone call. We believe these preexisting factors make up an early stage in the engagement process, one that we call prelude to the therapeutic encounter.

The prelude stage consists of the inner dialogues of thoughts and fantasies, feelings and beliefs, and concerns and motivations that the therapist and family members bring to the initial phone call and to the therapy process. The therapist considers: "Will I be able to help this family? Will they like and trust me? The family considers: Will this therapist think we're sick? Can we afford to go to therapy or can we afford not to go? What will my friends think when I tell them we had to see a counselor?" These inner dialogues of fears, needs, and preconceived biases make up a kind of personal checklist for each person, and they form the building blocks or potential barriers to the evolving therapeutic system and the possibility of the therapist and the family engaging each other.

For the therapist, the interface between personal and professional needs colors the palette that is extended to the family. Such factors as caseload and current life issues influence how flexible the therapist is about deciding appointment hours, accepting new clients, or deciding the types of clinical situations he or she wants to work with at a particular time.

Focusing on these issues and listening to inner dialogues help therapists become clearer about the personal impact of working with certain kinds of family problems: "Are there any types of family situations or clinical issues that I would prefer referring to colleagues? What is going on in my own life, in my family of origin, or in my intimate relationships that I need to be aware of when I accept new clients?" For instance, a therapist who as a parent is struggling with his adolescent son may decide to limit the number of families with adolescent life cycle issues. A therapist going through a difficult divorce may prefer referring divorce cases to other family therapists. If a therapist has had unresolved or recent losses, he or she might find it difficult to deal with families where death is the major theme. Framo (1968) describes how working with other people's families brings therapists' own families into the treatment room and affects therapists' overresponsiveness or underresponsiveness to the family.

The therapist also thinks about personal as well as professional strengths and limitations. This assessment enables the therapist to be prepared to respond nondefensively to family members' challenges to the therapist's experience, competence, and training. For example, a therapist who looks younger than his or her age and is comfortable with this may react with light-hearted humor when a family member comments on his or her "youth." A male–female cotherapy team who have worked through their own gender biases are less likely to be threatened by or to collude with family members' gender stereotypes. A beginning therapist may be thrown off balance when his or her experience is questioned. When therapists are unaware of personal limitations or preferences, or unprepared to address inevitable challenges, the potential for countertransference entanglements is high.

When therapists do not appropriately take care of their own needs, they may project them and inadvertently collude with one family member against another or overidentify with perceived family victims. When therapists get stuck in overgiving, they get tri-

---

### EXHIBIT 1

**Stages of Engaging With the Family**

*The Presession*
1. Prelude to the therapeutic encounter
2. The initial phone call
3. Generating hypotheses

*The Session*
4. The greeting
5. The orientation
6. Exploring the background (history)
7. Exploring the foreground (problems and attempted solutions)
8. Defining goals
9. The prompt
10. The contract

*The Postsession*
11. Debriefing

angled; they adopt families, lose their own boundaries, and generally want more for their clients than the clients want for themselves. Poor therapist boundaries lead to feeling taken advantage of and resentment, and it increases inappropriate compliance, dependency, and entitlement in the family. Napier and Whitaker (1978) state that therapists must be clear about their boundaries to set the ground rules for family therapy and to win the battle for structure. The therapist cannot win the battle for structure unless he or she is clear about expectations and boundaries before the initial phone contact with a family member. Without this preparation, the therapist will sound unsure about who should attend the first session, will be too rigid or too accommodating when scheduling appointments, or will be vague about the reasons for recommending a family consultation.

When a family is referred for family therapy, the information provided by the referral source affects the presession process. On the basis of what he or she has been told, the therapist begins to construct a story about the family system, the family + referral source system, and the potential family + therapist system. For example, one referral source reported that a family was particularly difficult and would probably be impossible to treat. We were aware of preparing to do battle with people we had not yet met. Other referral sources have minimized problems, and we were unprepared for a difficult first session. Although we prefer to postpone gathering detailed information from the referral source until after we have had the opportunity to form our own impressions about the family, other family therapists believe this contact is important. Framo (1980) stresses that he does not take at face value the school's, the family's, the court's, or another mental health professional's definition of the problem (especially if they do not think systemically), which reminds us that a family is never as sick as its case history. This speaks to our belief that the therapist must be able to remain open and curious while holding multiple stories about the family.

When the referral is made by another professional, it is important for the therapist to know about the relationship between the referral source and the family, as well as to clarify the reasons for the referral. We cannot always assume that a referral

is for treatment; it may be a request for a consultation or assessment. At times, the referring professional is "dumping the family," out of his or her own frustration in working with the family. The covert agenda is, "You work with them, I've had it! They'll defeat you just like they defeated me." In addition to the covert and overt agendas, we also want to know about the referral source's ongoing role with the family (i.e., will the referral source be part of the therapeutic system?) and the expectations for communication, such as sending reports, treatment updates, or participation at staff meetings or case conferences.

Like therapists, family members have their own inner dialogues before an initial phone call and first session. They wonder about whether the therapist will understand them, be fair, side with their side of the story, blame, or humiliate them. Family members are also influenced by who makes the referral and how it was made. For example, sometimes families are referred by former clients who had a positive experience in therapy. Although the family may not understand or fully believe in a family consultation, on the basis of their friend's experience, they are willing to schedule an initial appointment. Attitudes about participating in family therapy are also affected by whether the decision is voluntary ("Our daughter is using drugs and we'll do anything to make things right"), involuntary ("The court ordered us to come so we can get our children back"), or an ultimatum ("If you don't go to therapy with me, I'm leaving you"). Family members may vary considerably in their level of motivation for therapy. Some family members are eager to schedule appointments, informed about family therapy, and motivated and cooperative. Other family members are angry, resentful, distrustful of family therapy, or anxious about coming in. Frustrating encounters with difficult registration procedures, uncooperative staff, or insurance or managed care representatives and prior negative experiences with therapy can create negative mindsets in the family. Before they even speak with the therapist, they expect an unpleasant interaction, and they are prepared to challenge the therapist and make it difficult to schedule an appointment.

Family of origin issues such as dependency needs; sense of entitlement or unentitlement; and reality-based issues of socioeconomic-, ethnic-, or gender-based concerns also influence the presession engagement process and attitudes toward therapy. Some individuals have already decided they want to work with a therapist of a particular ethnic group, religion, age, or gender before contacting the potential therapist. Other family members may be concerned about degrees and professional affiliations, such as wanting to work with a psychologist, a psychiatrist, social worker, or marriage and family counselor. We have heard about other inner dialogues that family members have, such as: "All therapists have too many problems of their own"; "Therapy will make things worse"; Outsiders can't understand our family"; and "Only sick people go to family therapy." Some people think that the therapist will have a magic, one-session cure that will take away all of the family problems. Thus, positive and negative biases toward therapist and therapy influence the potential for engagement even before actual contact occurs between the family and the therapist.

## Stage 2: The Initial Phone Call

The goal of the initial phone call is to make contact with the family, to get preliminary information, and to arrange the first interview (Weber, McKeever, & McDaniel, 1985). We also believe that the first telephone contact offers the family an orientation to a systems approach and provides a window through which both the therapist and family representative can view attitudes about the family system and about therapy. It is during the telephone conversation that a meta-conversation begins. Anderson and Stewart (1983) describe the conversation of the initial phone call as a screening interview during which the family representative presents the family story and assesses the therapist's response. Napier and Whitaker (1978) compare this conversation to arranging a blind date.

Whitaker firmly believes that therapists must take charge of the initial phone call because it is the first battle for structure. In negotiating when to meet, who should come, what type of treatment, if any will be offered, and what it will cost, the therapist establishes the terms for how to proceed. Most therapists have had the experience of resistant or anxious couples or families who cannot seem to find a spare hour to come in for a consultation. We have heard such statements as: "We can't come in then"; "The

children have volleyball practice"; and "We both work—we are too tired to come in after hours, on Saturdays we spend time with our friends, do you see clients on Sundays?" Although for some couples and families work schedules and transportation difficulties are realities, for other families these are tests of initiative and reflective of resistance. Alternatively, the therapist should avoid the rigid judgment that every reason given is an excuse.

Issues of trust and reliability are behind many challenges to the therapist. If the therapist is ambiguous about appointment times, fees, or family member attendance at the first session, the family representative loses confidence in the therapist. The unconscious concern is: "How can I depend on this therapist to protect me, or take care of my family, when the therapist cannot adequately deal with my unreasonable demands?" The therapist is a role model and as such needs to model appropriate boundaries.

We are also curious about how a family member gets designated as the family representative for making the initial phone call. This selection may be voluntary, as in the case of the father who is worried about his teenage daughter and recognizes that their relationship is part of the problem. Other family members are assigned the task to call, such as in the case of a husband requesting an appointment because his wife threatens to end the marriage otherwise. Unless the caller is coerced or attending compulsory therapy (i.e., prompted by mandates from social service agencies or the courts), we assume that the one who makes the initial phone call is the most interested in change and may be the most open to engaging in therapy.

During the initial phone call, family therapists will typically suggest that all family members attend the first meeting. Prospective clients often do not share this perspective. For example, questions we are often asked include: "Why does my husband need to come in? The problem is with our daughter"; "Why can't you see me first and then my wife will come in for marital therapy in a few weeks?"; "I'm not part of the problem, why should I be there?" If the therapist is to engage with the family, yet win this battle for structure, he or she must be able to address the client's concerns respectfully and directly while maintaining strong leadership: "I know it is hard for you to understand why you, your husband, and the other children should come in, but it's been my experience that the more I can hear about each person's perspective and how your family life is affected, the more I'll be able to be helpful to you and your daughter." Presenting the need for family involvement in finding solutions, rather than in assigning blame, facilitates engagement.

Triangulation can occur quickly during the initial phone call. Some family members are so eager to tell their side of the story on the telephone, that the therapist must interrupt and defer the story for the first meeting when all family members are present. At other times, triangulation takes the form of a request for individual therapy when there is a marital problem (see chap. 32 in this volume). One spouse may want to win the therapist as an ally before bringing in a partner for marital therapy. In this situation, we have found it helpful to acknowledge the client's need to be understood, but we explain that it is more difficult to switch from individual to couple therapy because the partner would, in our experience, come in as a guest to the individual therapy. Some therapists agree to see the individual but make it clear that a referral will be made to another therapist for the couple's therapy. Still others see the individual at the outset but are clear that they regard the client as part of a larger system.

During the initial phone call, family representatives sometimes ask personal questions about the therapist's age, religion, or marital status. For instance, we have been asked such questions as: Do you have children? (*The covert questions: Do you have any life experience? Are you mature enough?*) Have you ever been divorced? (*The covert questions: Are you too screwed up to deal with us? Will you be a good role model?*) Are you a Christian (Jewish, Muslim)? (*The covert question: Will you understand and be respectful of our religious and spiritual beliefs?*) What do you think about abortion? (*The covert question: Are your values similar to ours?*) How do you feel about working with homosexuals? (*The covert questions: Will you pathologize us? Will you try to impose your politics on us?*) Often these questions reflect a family's real life experiences as well as transference issues and high anxiety about whether we are experienced enough, or will

understand the family's experiences given our age, ethnicity, gender, religious beliefs, or sexual orientation. We think it is important for the therapist to establish a safe container by responding nondefensively and with appropriate boundaries, by balancing the client's right to know and the therapist's need for privacy: "I can appreciate your anxiety about coming in and your wanting to know something about me. This is normal for many clients and I think that after our meeting you will have a better sense about how comfortable you and your family (or partner) will feel about our working together."

For clients asking about an assessment over the phone, or for a precise length of treatment, the therapist can state that those questions are best answered after meeting the family and having more information. We do believe that clients have a right to know therapist's fees, credentials, theoretical orientation, office policies and procedures, and methods of therapy. We have also found that brief answers to these questions can be given on the phone and that longer, more detailed explanations are better offered during the first session so that all members are equally informed. There is a consensus in the field of family therapy that the initial phone call be brief so that triangulation can be minimized, unless the phone call is for crisis intervention. To determine who should attend the first session, we ask the client if this is an individual or a relationship problem, a problem with a marriage or with a child. In divorce situations, such as when a mother phones about her substance-abusing daughter, we typically ask about the availability of the exhusband and suggest that both parents come in if possible. Even when the client identifies the problem as an individual one, we ask about who else in the family lives at home or who else is affected by the problem. Often we find out the problem includes a child or a partner, and our questions set the tone for bringing the family in.

In some clinical settings, receptionists and secretaries have the initial phone contact with the client. They may obtain preliminary intake information and answer questions about fees and office procedures, schedule appointments, or provide directions to the office. Although this procedure may streamline the intake process and save therapist time, we prefer to have the first phone contact with the family member.

This maximizes the likelihood of presenting a family approach for the initial appointment and gives the therapist some firsthand data to generate tentative hypotheses.

## Stage 3: Generating Hypotheses

On the basis of information from the referral source, the family member, a beginning genogram, and the tone and tenor of the initial phone call, we try to develop some preliminary hypotheses about the urgency of the problem, possible developmental or family life cycle issues and the requisite tasks that the family may be struggling with, and roles of other systems or helpers. Even with limited information, generating hypotheses (individual, developmental, systemic) clarifies our thinking and helps structure the initial interview. Of course, information given on the phone by one family member can be unreliable. Families often look very different when you meet them.

After the initial phone call, the family representative also develops some hypotheses about the therapist and the potential helpfulness of therapy. The family member may report back to the rest of the family: "She sounded nice"; "She was friendly"; "He seemed to understand our problem"; "She sure sounded confused"; "He forgot to give us directions to the office"; "It took him two days to return our call"; and "What would happen if we really need her?" And so the stories unfold. It is the task of family members and the therapist to test the accuracy of their respective assumptions beginning with the initial session.

## THE SESSION

## Stage 4: The Greeting

Family members come to the therapist's office in a variety of emotional states. One of the tasks of beginning with a family is to be able to ascertain and connect with the emotional state of the family system and the diversity of moods among the family members. Some families enter the office as if they were coming to a nuclear arms negotiation. Other families are more jocular and playful. One family member may look confident and businesslike, whereas an-

other family member may be passively shy. Effective therapists "play a lot of notes on the emotional keyboard" by skillfully engaging the diversity of emotions presented. These skills are especially useful in the opening moments of the greeting stage when the family meets the therapist for the first time. The therapist introduces himself or herself, shakes hands with each family member, and invites the family into the therapy room.

We presume that regardless of how they seem, family members generally are anxious as they enter the therapist's office. They are on foreign turf with a stranger—albeit a professional—and are about to reveal what is likely to be a painful, embarrassing, or exasperating story without any guarantee that this stranger will be of help to them. Family members may have a host of fantasies of what will happen once they pass over the threshold of the therapist's office: "He'll put all of us on couches and ask us about our dreams"; "She'll certainly go after Mom. It's about time somebody did! Maybe I can hide." The family may be gauging their fear of the therapist on the basis of how many books and degrees are displayed in the room.

Therapists are like a host at this point with the goal of helping family members settle in as new guests at a home. We introduce ourselves, greet each family member, and ask their names and inquire about what they would like to be called. We ask each family member about his or her name to underscore the value of individuation, even though the family spokesperson may begin to introduce everyone in the family. The therapist must work to establish a bridge to each family member. It is also important to attend to simple environmental features such as bathroom location, temperature, lighting, and seating. If children are present, it is important to have sufficient play materials available such as crayons, paper, puppets, dolls, and toys so they also feel welcome. Parents also feel more attended to and relaxed if the therapist respects children's interests and curiosities.

The presence and absence of certain family members at the first session provides valuable information about the family's organization and the direction of treatment. For example, if a mother appears for the initial interview with her son, while both father and daughter are absent, this suggests a cross-gender, intergenerational coalition in the family, with a weakened parental hierarchy and marital subsystem. Family members are invited to sit where they wish. Seating patterns, along with dress, language, emotional style, interactional patterns, and nonverbal behaviors, are pertinent data that we use to both formulate our hypotheses and help build bridges with family members.

Noting and using the language of family members is particularly important in building bridges to the family. Weaving in the family's language with the therapist's discourse will help the family feel understood. For example, in one family the word *grind* was used to describe distress: "When my wife ignored me, boy, it was grinding on me." The therapist incorporated this expression by asking: "I wonder how well you can hear each other's grinding? Can you hear the grinding or do you have to guess?" The use of the family's language reveals to them that you are listening.

The therapist may also ask conversational questions such as: "Did you find your way here OK?" and "How was the registration process downstairs?" We also increase contact with each family member by fleshing out the demographic identity of each person and asking about ages, school, work, and so on. We make special effort to engage those in the family who are distant, especially the parent who did not make the initial contact. We try to find something in each person that is interesting to us, something that begins to evoke our curiosity and imagination—such as wondering how three left-handed children were spawned from two right-handed parents or how the straightlaced adolescent got mixed up with these acting-out, misguided parents. These initial curiosities may give birth to new learnings for the therapist. The family will also be more interested in engaging with a therapist who is alive and curious rather than one who simply wants to be a manager and help the family put out the fires of its symptoms. Engagement evolves when there are the beginnings of bilateral learning in these early moments—the therapist is curious about the family, and the family is curious about the therapist.

## Stage 5: The Orientation

The goal of the orientation stage is to introduce the family to the format of the first session, gather information on how the family decided to enter therapy, and begin to clarify the family expectations of the therapist and the therapist's expectations of the family.

The first step in this stage is to orient the family to the room and the format of the session. The therapist should explain the purpose and use of any video or audio taping equipment, telephones, observation mirrors, other observers or participants, and procedures such as session breaks or possible telephone interruptions. Family members should be given an opportunity to comment and question, and their written consent for any recording should be gathered. Although some family members may be appraised of these procedures prior to this first meeting, others in the family may be taken by surprise. Patiently attending to any concerns engages and builds trust.

We believe that one of the most effective means of orienting people is to inquire about their immediate experience: "What is it like for you to be here right now, at this appointment?" The question may unleash a host of concerns and consistently helps link the therapist with family members. We emphasize the reporting of immediate experiences, especially feelings, as one of the core values (here and now awareness, reporting immediate experience, congruency) that we use repeatedly throughout therapy. Listening to each member's story underscores the diversity of family experience. Through this conversation, we tease out degrees of hesitation within the family and positively connote hesitation as understandable in most new experiences, especially during the first therapy session with a stranger.

We then ask about how the decision was made to come to therapy. "Who took the initiative to set up the meeting?" "When did you first think about coming in?" "Who told you about coming to this meeting?" "When did you find out?" (e.g., "I thought we were going out to eat and instead they brought me here!") "How were you told about coming?" "What were your reactions to being told about the meeting?" Sometimes the word *meeting* instead of *session* or *therapy* demystifies the process. During this inquiry, therapists begin to get a sense of who carries the initiative for this work in the family; what the family's patterns of communication, control, and influence are; and what the realistic obstacles and frustrations along the way to this first session are.

Understandable frustration can turn into resistance when the therapist bypasses this inquiry about the journey to the office (Anderson and Stewart, 1983). As the discussion about entering treatment proceeds, family members will unravel their expectations about therapy based on their collective fantasies; how therapy is portrayed in the media; previous experiences, especially with the mental health and medical systems; the referral process; and their previous history in any form of psychotherapy. Unmet expectations may lead to disappointment, anger, or confusion and may prevent therapy from even getting off the ground. Therefore, it is imperative to discern expectations for therapy and work toward clarity in building the therapist–family team.

In discerning the family's beliefs and expectations about therapy, one of the most critical targets of inquiry is the referral process (Weber, McDaniel, & Wynne, 1987). Many families who enter treatment do so because they have been sent by someone—an attorney, schoolteacher, the court, community agency, pastor, physician, grandmother, friend, individual therapist, and so on. Family members may have widely differing notions about treatment that were generated during the referral process on the basis of what was conveyed to the family. The therapist should investigate the family's understandings and feelings about the purpose of the referral, the referring person's explanation of the purpose and process of treatment, and their reaction to this explanation. This is at least a two-part inquiry: "What is your understanding of why you were referred, and how do you feel about the referral process?"

A factor in many situations is what Haley (1987) calls "compulsory therapy"—involuntary therapy that occurs, for example, when a judge tells someone to go to therapy (or go to jail) or when a family member is brought in under duress (parents dragging in adolescents, spouses dragging in spouses). The overall goal is to attempt to change the therapy to a more hopeful, voluntary state by framing therapy as

an opportunity for family members to get something out of the work, resolve whatever they might want to resolve ("as long as we're in this together"), and eventually terminate treatment. The therapist must not present as an agent of some outside system, but as someone on the side of the family, who is joining with the family's or a family member's predicament. It is also important for the therapist to align with the family without attacking the outside system. Beginning to do this means exploring reluctance, hesitation, confusion, and anger with compassion while not attempting to persuade the family of the benefits of treatment.

Another matter that may arise during the orientation discussion is the list, sometimes a long list, of diagnostic labels attached to family members that solidify, stick, and become roadblocks to treatment. Family members may understand the problem to be a child who is "delinquent" or who has "attention deficit disorder," an adult who is an "alcoholic," or parents who are characterized by a "dominating mother and passive father" (Haley, 1987). Sometimes labels in the diagnostic–referral process convey pejorative, negative connotations that increase defensiveness and blame.

However, it is important to empathically listen to the family's experiences of this labeling process. Listening is one of the beginning steps in moving from the more individual and pathological labels to a more interactional view with a focus on strengths and competencies. Sometimes labels for the problem may be relieving, such as when biological realities affect family relationships. Bulldozing prized family labels is disrespectful and engenders resistance. Slowly widening the circle of understanding from an individual view to an interactional view while allowing the diagnosis to "tag along" is one of the arts of family therapy. It is useful to move from the abstract label to more behavioral, concrete, and interactional descriptions. For example, when presented with an "anorectic," we might say, "Oh, so you don't want to eat?" We nudge family members from abstractions to behavior specifics.

Another task in assessing the family's beliefs about therapy is to conduct what we call a *therapy of origin* check, a review of the family's history with mental health providers. We ask questions like "Has this family or anyone in the family ever been in counseling?" "When and how long did you go?" "Tell me something about your experience—what was it like for you, what worked, what didn't work?" In this inquiry we get a sense of how the family perceives counselors and the process of therapy. The family also may identify specific procedures that have been useful in helping them solve problems.

In this inquiry, the goal is to engage the family while maintaining strong leadership. The therapist is leader, but the family also has a "leader," that one person who can facilitate or sabotage the therapy. That leader may be influenced by an outside leader (e.g., physician, friend, or pastor). Obtaining clear sponsorship from the leaders is critical to the effectiveness of the project (Crosby, 1992) in both organizations and in therapy.

We conclude the orientation stage by establishing a rationale and agenda for this first meeting and the beginning phase of therapy. Often family members are perplexed, possibly irritated, at having to be present at a family meeting when the problem "has nothing to do with me." We clearly state our position with a stance similar to the following: "My typical procedure is to spend two or three sessions gathering information about the situation so that we will know how to proceed. And in evaluating the situations of people I work with, I have found over the years that it is most helpful for me to invite other family members to these meetings so I can get a more complete picture. You can be very helpful to me and to each other. After these evaluation meetings I will be able to give you my views on how we should proceed, and I will also be interested in all of your opinions at that time."

## Stage 6: Exploring the Background (History)

Within the family therapy field, there has been considerable discussion and disagreement about the relevance of historical information about the family versus immediate, direct attention to the presenting problem and the interactions that maintain the problem (Jordan, 1982; Sluzki, 1981). Our approach is integrative, bringing together family of origin backgrounds, a historical perspective, and immediate attention to interactions in the moment. To engage families and help develop competence and mastery, it

is imperative to attend to the client's presenting problems and available solutions. This is what we would call the *microfocus*. At the same time, there is a higher yield in building resiliency and lowering the risk for further complaints by helping clients to understand and shift certain intergenerational patterns. We call this the *macrofocus*. Alternating between the microfocus and the macrofocus throughout treatment depends on the client's situation and expectations and the therapist's judgment as to what might be most useful. For example, some families are highly reactive and polarized around the presenting problem but may be more responsive and engaged if the therapist begins by gathering historical information. Other families may be focused on "getting down to business" or may be at a crisis point where starting with the current problem is more prudent. With these families, gathering historical information may be perceived as irrelevant and a "waste of time." However, sometimes using a genogram in a crisis situation can infuse the system with a more reflective spirit and a new perspective and can interrupt a spiraling escalation (Perlmutter & Jones, 1986).

Generally, in the initial interview we gather some minimal information about family background: "It is important for me to have some basic information about your family and some sense of your history for me to better understand what brings you here." We then change our lens; move from the macrofocus to the microfocus; and examine the presenting problem, its context, and attempted solutions.

A more complete picture of the family story is explored during the first several interviews and is added to throughout the course of therapy. We prefer to have as many members of the immediate family present for gathering this information in these sessions. Because family members typically tell different stories about the same events, reliability of the information is increased with multiple perspectives and, at the same time, as the different views are expressed reactions between family members can be observed directly. Soliciting and appreciating multiple perspectives within the family can powerfully engage family members with one another. Often this is the first time some stories have ever been shared in the family. As information is elicited through the therapist's questions, themes and patterns may begin to emerge that can help the family connect the current difficulty with a broader and deeper perspective. These connections can begin to lower reactivity and engender a more empathic, reflective spirit that enhances engagement.

While exploring this information, we construct three "family maps" that orient us to the background information of the family: (a) a three-generational genogram, (b) a family chronology, and (c) an ecosystemic map. These maps are informally constructed as the therapeutic conversation evolves during the first several sessions and are expanded throughout the course of therapy.

*Genograms.* Initial genogram information centers on the vital data and basic facts for the three generations (dates of birth, marriage, separation, divorce, death and cause of death, living arrangements, gender, names, ages, sibling position, occupation, education, geographical locations, ethnic and religious background, and basic health–disease information; see Exhibit 2). In addition, we gather relationship information about family members across the generations—closeness, distance, cutoffs, fusion, and conflict. We gather data about family roles (e.g., strong, weak, successful, clown, mediator, or hero), patterns, themes, beliefs, rituals, norms, rules, and traditions that make up the core of the family's unique culture. Throughout the process of interviewing the family, we intentionally underscore the assets and strengths within the family, strengths that often have been masked by difficulties. (More exhaustive discussions about the theory, methodology, and procedures in using the genogram can be found in McGoldrick & Gerson, 1985).

*Family chronology.* The second map we construct is the family chronology (Stanton, 1992), a horizontal time line of significant events in the family's life cycle that includes vertical notations of both developmental stress points (predictable, developmental changes within the family life cycle, such as marriage, birth, adolescence, middle adulthood, and retirement) and situational stress points (events that are not developmentally predictable, such as moves, illness, divorce, and job changes; see Figure 1). We note stress and change not only in the immediate family's life cycle, but also within the multigenerational extended family system that significantly has

an impact on the family (Guerin, Fay, Burden, & Kautto, 1987). More macro changes (economic, political, and cultural shifts) within the surrounding culture may also be noted.

The family chronology is useful in several ways. First, it helps the therapist assess the family, generate hypotheses, and answer the "why now" question—what has changed in this family that contributes to the family's seeking help at this time. Second, like the genogram, it also serves as a vehicle for engaging the family. Third, the therapist joins the family as a coinvestigator, noting patterns across the family life cycle. This kind of process of mutual discovery stimulates feelings of empowerment and authority within the family. Often family members are surprised to see how stress has clustered within their history or how they have displayed marvelous resiliency in the face of continuing challenges. Families then become more engaged in treatment with hope and confidence. Finally, this process tends to reduce blame and normalizes symptoms as signs of attempting to cope with the extenuating circumstances of life.

*Ecosystemic map.* The ecosystemic map is a graphic display of the family's relationship with other professionals (e.g., attorney, physician, clergy, or teacher), organizations (e.g., school, social service agencies, or institutions), and significant friends (Attneave, 1976; Hartman, 1979; Sherman & Fredman, 1986; see Figure 2). Patterns of emotional support, conflict, cutoff, fusion, alliances, and so on are noted. Mapping this information in the initial interview with a family is consistent with our view of beginning with the family as a "systems consultant" (Wynne et al., 1986) with a meta-picture of the family's situation and relationships with the surrounding context.

This process may identify sources of conflict that make it difficult for the family to engage in treatment (Weber et al., 1987). For example, strong ties with a religious system may impede the family's openness to secular psychology. Or conflict with the school system that has referred the family may result in the family's obstinacy to family therapy or distrust toward the therapist. Alternatively, identifying individuals and organizations that are sources of support for the family and including them (e.g., inviting a pastor for a session) or, minimally, consulting with them

## EXHIBIT 2

### Genogram Format

A. Symbols to describe basic family membership and structure (include on genogram significant others who lived with or cared for family members—place them on the right side of the genogram with a notation about who they are).

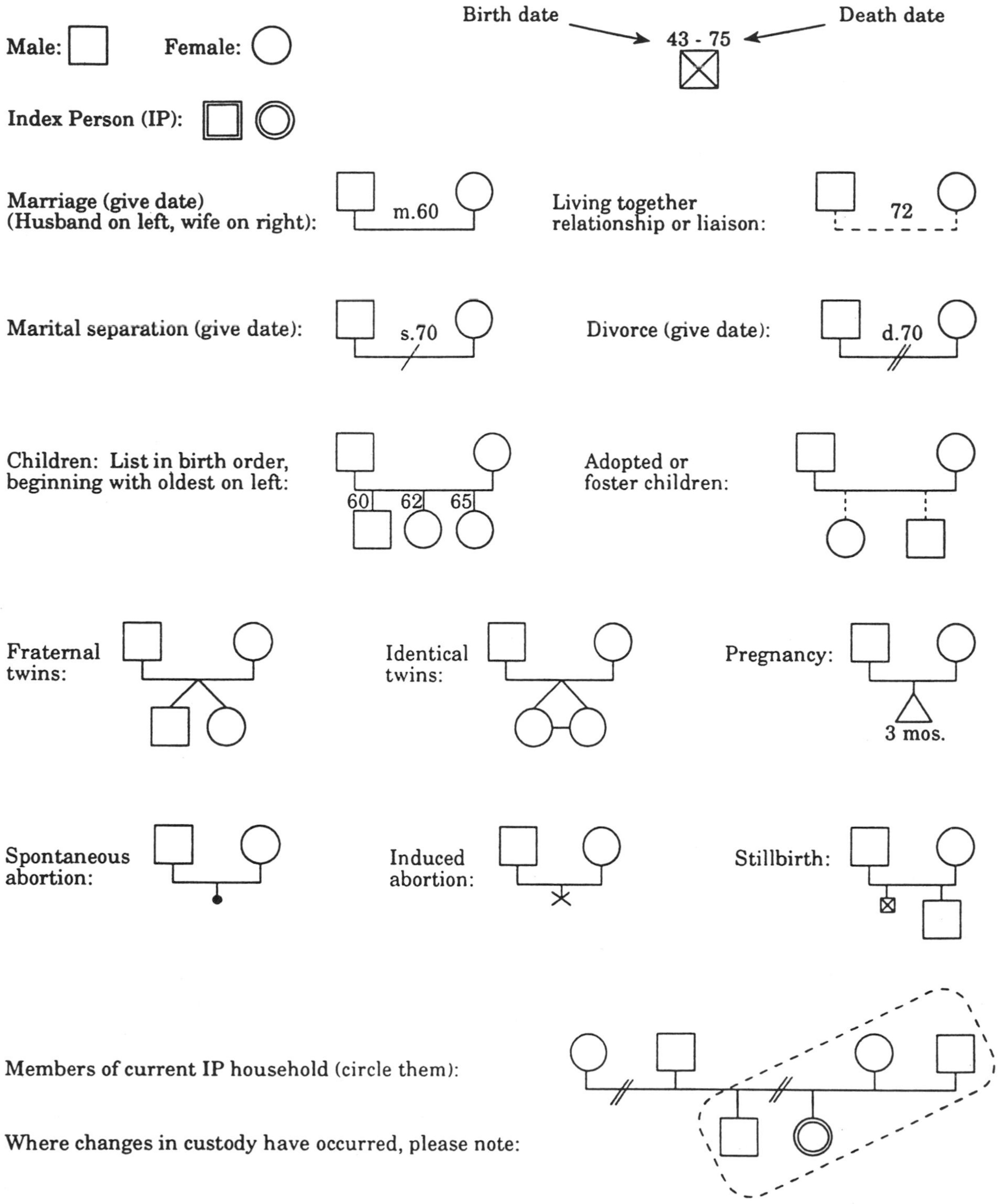

Birth date → 43 - 75 ← Death date

**Male:** ☐  **Female:** ○

**Index Person (IP):** ▣ ◎

**Marriage (give date) (Husband on left, wife on right):** m.60

**Living together relationship or liaison:** 72

**Marital separation (give date):** s.70

**Divorce (give date):** d.70

**Children: List in birth order, beginning with oldest on left:** 60 62 65

**Adopted or foster children:**

**Fraternal twins:**

**Identical twins:**

**Pregnancy:** 3 mos.

**Spontaneous abortion:**

**Induced abortion:**

**Stillbirth:**

**Members of current IP household (circle them):**

**Where changes in custody have occurred, please note:**

*(continues)*

---

**EXHIBIT 2 (Continued)**

B. Family interaction patterns. The following symbols are optional. The clinician may prefer to note them on a separate sheet. They are among the least precise information on the genogram, but may be key indicators of relationship patterns the clinician wants to remember:

---

**Very close relationship:** (symbol: square connected to circle with three parallel lines)

**Conflictual relationship:** (symbol: square connected to circle with jagged line)

**Distant relationship:** (symbol: square connected to circle with dashed line)

**Estrangement or cutoff (give date if possible):** (symbol: square and circle with cutoff marks) Cutoff 62 - 78

**Very close relationship:** (symbol: square connected to circle with zigzag band)

---

C. **Medical history. Since the genogram is meant to be an orienting map of the family, there is room to indicate only the most important factors. Thus, list only major or chronic illnesses and problems. Include dates in parentheses where feasible or applicable. Use** *DSM-III* categories or recognized abbreviations where available (e.g., cancer: CA; stroke: CVA).

D. Other family information of special importance may also be noted on the genogram:
    1) Ethnic background and migration date
    2) Religion or religious change
    3) Education
    4) Occupation or unemployment
    5) Military service
    6) Retirement
    7) Trouble with law
    8) Physical abuse or incest
    9) Obesity
    10) Smoking
    11) Dates when family members left home: LH '74
    12) Current location of family members
    It is useful to have a space at the bottom of the genogram for notes on *other key information*: This would include critical events, changes in the family structure since the genogram was made, hypotheses, and other notations of major family issues or changes. These notations should always be dated and should be kept to a minimum, since every extra piece of information on a genogram complicates it and therefore diminishes its readability.

---

IP = index person; *DSM* = *Diagnostic and Statistical Manual of Mental Disorders*. From *Genograms in Family Assessment* (pp. 154–155), by M. McGoldrick and R. Gerson, 1985, New York: Norton. Copyright 1985 by Monica McGoldrick and Randy Gerson. Reprinted with permission.

during the early phase of family therapy may significantly enhance the family's engagement in therapy.

## Stage 7: Exploring the Foreground (Problems and Attempted Solutions)

As we explore foreground information, we are assessing not only the content of what is said, but also the process in the room—who speaks first, who hesitates, who talks to whom, what emotional and behavioral impacts occur in response to what is said, who seems open and who seems closed, where the alliances and coalitions are, what the family hierarchy is, and so on. Interactional difficulties between family members are not simply discussed, but are displayed in the therapy room as the family drama is enacted.

Generally, we begin this process not by asking about the problem, but by asking more neutrally, "What has brought you here?" This question is a simple but nonetheless critical piece in the overall fabric of relating to the family in a depathologizing manner. Then to underscore our value of individuation in the family, we add, "I realize that you all may have different views as to what brings you here and what has happened. It is important for me to hear from each one of you." This value may be challenged by family members in the ensuing process as some family members are interrupted, others retreat in intimidation, or disagreements arise as to which is the "correct" view of reality. We model multipartiality (Boszormenyi-Nagy & Krasner, 1986) and a norm of individuation by affirming each member's contributions, listening attentively, blocking interruptions, and reframing and normalizing disagreements as "differences." At this point we do not offer advice, interpretations, or solutions even if asked.

The question, "What brings you here?" is posed to the family, but to whom in the family? We permit the family to decide who will speak first and use this information to assess family hierarchy and interactional patterns. We want to engage those family members who seem more peripheral to the problem. We briefly note that we already have spoken to a specific family member on the phone when the appointment was made, only received minimal information, and now want to get a more complete picture. We want to dispel any beliefs about a secret alliance between the therapist and the caller.

We emphasize concrete, behavioral specificity in gathering this information, and we communicate this value to the family: "*who* is doing what that presents a problem, to *whom*, and *how* does such behavior constitute a problem?" (Fisch et al., 1982, p. 70). We may say, "I'm an outsider to your family, and so it is important for me to get as clear of a picture as possible as to what you are describing, almost like a videotape of your story."

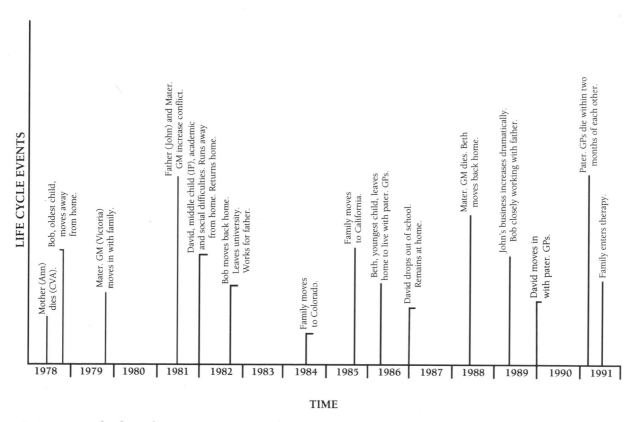

FIGURE 1. Family chronology. mater. = maternal; pater. = paternal; GM = grandmother; GP = grandparent; IP = index person.

We are interested in how each family member would describe the interactions of other family members around the problem: "Tom, when you are fighting with your mother, what does your father do?" We gather observations, rankings ("Rank family members from most concerned to least concerned about the problem"), and fantasies ("Who do you imagine would be the first to jump in if you and your brother got into a fight?"), using methods of inquiry such as those suggested in circular interviewing (Selvini-Palazzoli, Boscolo, Cecchin, & Prata, 1982). Eliciting descriptions about exceptions to the problem is also important (O'Hanlon & Weiner-Davis, 1989): Where does the problem not occur?" "When is the problem most likely or least likely to occur (time of year, season, month, week, day)?" Family members may be surprised by a question that seeks

to elicit examples of competency, ability, strength, and resources. Despite the drive of family members to keep talking about how bad things are, we stay on track in this stage of the inquiry in an effort to establish the norm of searching for strengths (see chap. 34 in this volume). To assess the "why now" question, we ask "When do you think the problem began?" In addition, we ask how serious each family member regards the problem: "How serious do you think this problem is on a scale of 0 to 10?" and "How is this a problem for you?"

Another area of inquiry is to assess each family member's beliefs about why the problem exists. We listen to what family members say—words, symbols, metaphors, phrases, values, notions of causality beliefs, and assumptions. We incorporate the language of these positions in our therapeutic conversation as

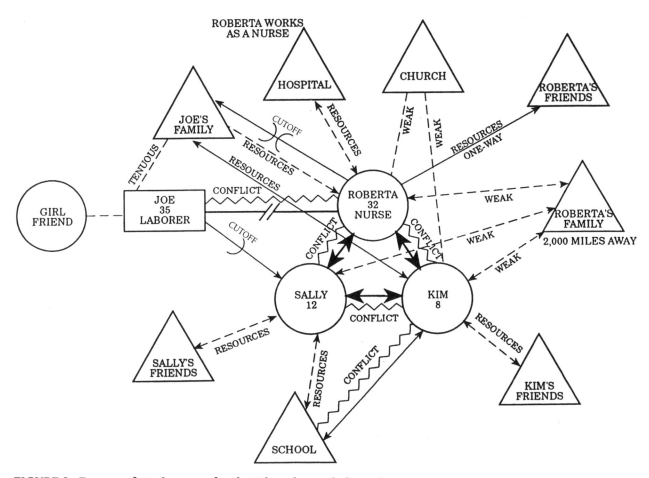

FIGURE 2. Ecomap of single-parent family. When the symbols are known it is not necessary to write in the words for the symbols. They are included in this example to help the reader use the map. From *Handbook of Structured Techniques in Marriage and Family Therapy* (p. 100), by R. Sherman and N. Fredman, 1986, New York: Brunner/Mazel. Copyright 1986 by Robert Sherman and Norman Fredman. Adapted with permission.

we assign tasks and craft interventions. Finally, we ask about attempted solutions—what specific efforts family members have made in trying to solve the problem. Some therapists believe that these attempted solutions are precisely what maintains the problem (Fisch et al., 1982). Suggesting more of the same in the current therapy is not only likely to be unhelpful, but it may also irritate family members who silently or not so silently moan, "I've heard this before. So what is new?" Engaging family members in treatment is enhanced by knowing what not to suggest and moving instead toward widening perspectives, coinventing new solutions, and sparking more imagination and novelty. This inquiry of attempted solutions also alerts the therapist to the possible resources within the larger system that the family has not used.

## Stage 8: Defining Goals

Defining goals for the work in therapy is a process of clarifying what outcomes are realistically possible. As Haley (1987) notes, "If therapy is to end properly, it must begin properly—by negotiating a solvable problem and discovering the social situation that makes the problem necessary" (p. 9). Therapy that proceeds with no goals or goals that are too ambitious or vague invariably leads to confusion, disappointment, anger, or drifting. Alternatively, if the targeted goals are clear, specific, realistic, and positive, an expectancy set of hope and mastery is established that can lead to healing outcomes.

In our continuing effort to support individuation, we ask each family member to state what he or she would like to see changed, using positive behaviors ("I want to spend some time with Dad alone") rather than negative behaviors ("I want my brother to stop fighting"). We also may ask each family member, "In your mind, picture what would be happening in your family if this problem were to go away. Now tell me what you see in that picture." Family members may report similar or different goals. We link the goals as much as possible and begin to establish priorities.

Families and therapists alike may become discouraged in therapy when realistic goals have not been set. In helping family members identify realistic goals, we may ask, "What would be a small sign that would show you're on the right track toward your goal?" These small signs are more possible to achieve and, thus, more likely to engender hope and engage the family in treatment. It is the therapist's responsibility to amplify or acknowledge these competencies, these small signs when they appear in family meetings: "Did you notice how you listened to your son just then without becoming defensive? That seemed like you were moving in the direction you wanted to go."

To underscore the norm of personal responsibility and initiative in the family, we ask family members, "What do you think you can begin to do to move toward this goal?" People tend to be experts in defining what others can do, but they often have no idea about what they personally can do to help bring about change. Boszormenyi-Nagy and Spark (1984) emphasize how delegating responsibility for change is critical to building a therapeutic alliance:

> Unless the family therapists can help a family to accept themselves as the change agents, a therapeutic alliance is not formed. If a family consistently projects its problems and solutions outside themselves, they may bring themselves to the sessions, but there is no commitment to a therapeutic process of growth. (p. 196)

The therapist's task here and throughout therapy is to shift responsibility for change from the therapist to the family and to self–responsibility in the family away from other–blame.

## Stage 9: The Prompt

Defining goals leads naturally to giving the prompt. We use the word *prompt* rather than *homework assignment* because it more accurately conveys our intention to suggest and bring forth something different in the family by inviting rather than directing. Through the prompt, we invite the family to observe, think about, discuss, or even experiment with their interactions. The prompt between sessions is intended to establish a more collaborative relationship between the therapist and the family, to increase family involvement with the therapist between the meetings, and to create therapeutic echoes in the family's ongoing life during the week. The prompt also gives several implicit messages: the therapist will guide and structure the therapy and will use specific plans and procedures; the family will do the work of change; and, most important, therapy is not about therapy, it is about life. The prompt, by directing attention outside of therapy, is the early way that the therapist says good-bye to the family.

The responses of family members to prompts indicate the varying levels of engagement in treatment, the capacity of family members to make use of therapy, and the diversity of learning and response styles in the family. If family members respond to the prompts by avoiding, modifying, challenging, forgetting, or doing the opposite, we view these responses as sources of information about how family members will or will not work with us.

Prompts given at the conclusion of the initial interview usually are not elaborate and are not intended to stimulate significant change. In fact, often these prompts are intended to slow down an impulse to change or an escalation in crisis. Our initial prompts intend to (a) build on the conversation in the initial interview, (b) incorporate the language and symbols of the family, (c) engage all family members, and (d) emphasize observation and reflection. Prompts at this stage are usually straightforward, not paradoxical. However, they also can be playful and imaginative, increasing a sense of curiosity and imagination within the family and countering the deadening spirit of absoluteness that often keeps families stuck. We may preface our prompts with "I'd like you to try an experiment." This preface underscores the value of adventure and discovery and encourages a "see what happens" attitude that moves away from doing "more of the same."

For example, if family members disagree on an issue, we may suggest, "Think about or list your feelings about the issue and let's discuss them at the next meeting. But before you note areas of disagreement with others in the family, note any small, barely noticeable areas of agreement that you might have about this issue." Or a restraining prompt may be given such as, "Instead of working on change, I would like you to take a break and reflect on what you don't want to see changed. There may be some things in your family that you like and want to keep." To accent personal responsibility, we may ask: "Would you be willing to write down or think about one specific thing that you could change in your relationship with each family member to make things better for the family?" We prefer to keep the prompts general or open-ended so that family members can create their own rituals for participation and change. We find it useful to give prompts at the conclusion of most sessions.

## Stage 10: The Contract

The session concludes with the stage of commitments and contracting. We state our position that we see therapy as a partnership between the therapist and the family and that from time to time we will want to reexamine the goals we have set together and how we are proceeding toward those goals. We state that it is important for us to receive feedback from the family and that periodically we will take time for "stock taking"—assessing not only whether the therapy is on track, but also how we are working together (what's working, what's not working, how we should modify our goals and process). This periodic stock taking has been enormously useful in our work. Families practice developing the critical skill of giving and receiving feedback during these discussions. Furthermore, the stock-taking dialogue has been useful in helping us to stay engaged with the family. We have found that unless we initiate discussions to assess our working relationship, this useful information may remain latent or will be acted out covertly. We want to craft with the family the commitment of mutual responsibility for therapy and the commitment of attending to this responsibility with directness and openness.

We then begin to sharpen specific commitments and contracts regarding the structure of therapy, office policies, time, fees, cancellations, confidentiality, scheduling, disclosure statements, releases, and consent forms. Many therapists give clients documents that describe these business policies of practice. At the conclusion of the first meeting, therapists have the greatest leverage to establish their policies and procedures with the family. How the therapist negotiates the business side of psychotherapy influences how the family perceives the strength and leadership of the therapist and, more important, how the therapist can be trusted.

The crafting of this beginning contract with the family will set the theme for the entire therapeutic process. Lack of clarity between the therapist and family is one of the primary reasons therapy drifts or engenders resistance. Furthermore, how the therapist takes leadership in this new organization can have a powerful impact on shaping new norms in the family system. Thus, the therapist will want to take strong positions on healthy, organizational norms: clarity about how decisions are made (unilateral consultative, consensual, etc.), who makes the decisions, roles and jobs, "by-whens" (by when a task will be completed), and "single-point accountability" (who specifically is responsible for the task) priorities. These and other "high performance factors" in healthy organizations (Crosby, 1992) can be established especially at this contracting stage and throughout the work of therapy. Not only are people more engaged in an organization that is functioning in this healthy manner, but the emotional relationships in the system also become founded on "trustworthiness" (Boszormenyi-Nagy & Spark, 1984).

The initial interview concludes by setting the next appointment and clarifying who will attend the meeting. Before parting, we ask the family if they have any questions. Sometimes we are asked questions about our background, experience, our goals in therapy, and so on. We attempt to answer these questions in a straightforward, brief manner. Often we simply reiterate that we see ourselves as consultants to the family and it will take a few meetings for us to get a sense of the family and its life. We refrain from making any elegant observations or interpretations and strive to give a benediction to the family that will send them on their way like "I think this was a good beginning. I'll see you next week."

## THE POSTSESSION

### Stage 11: Debriefing

The therapist's debriefing conversation may be an individual process or may include colleagues, consultants, supervisors, or other professionals on the treatment team. There are three tasks within this debriefing stage: (a) process reflection, (b) self-assessment, and (c) revising hypotheses.

*Process reflection.* Our purpose is to assess the extent to which we have met our goals for the initial interview (Weber et al., 1985). Some of the questions we ask ourselves include the following: Did I:

1. Contact each family member and help him or her feel as comfortable as possible?
2. Establish leadership by clearly structuring the interview?
3. Develop a working relationship with the family without being either too professional or too personal?
4. Recognize and report strengths in the family and in family members?
5. Maintain an empathic position by supporting family members and avoiding blaming or criticizing?
6. Underscore the family's responsibility to take initiative to change?
7. Identify the specific problems and attempted solutions?
8. Begin to understand the family's culture (symbols, rituals, values, language, and beliefs) and each family member's unique language, style, and perspective?
9. Get a sense of the family's structure and repetitive interactions around the problem?
10. Generate some maps about the family's intergenerational story and the larger, systemic context (friends, other professionals, and organizations) in which the family lives?
11. Negotiate a clear contract with the family that includes mutually acceptable goals and commitments for proceeding?
12. Ascertain any legal or ethical issues I need to address (e.g., confidentiality and reporting obligations)?

The therapist should follow through on any commitments to the family to contact the referral person and other consultants.

*Self-assessment.* The second task is to assess the impact of this encounter on ourselves. The risk of not asking this question explicitly is that we are more likely to fall into the trap of reactivity, losing our perspective, and acting out our fantasies with family members as players in our personal drama. "How do I feel with this family?" "Do I have something to learn from working with these people?" "Do I think I have anything to offer this family?" "What draws me to this family?" "What pushes me back from this family?" "Who in the family does what to me?" These questions may touch a wealth of fantasies from experiences in our own history, with our own families (Framo, 1968), that may enrich the therapeutic experience or contribute to transference–countertransference snags. For example, the therapist may passionately attempt to get a father to give to his children like his or her own father never gave to him or her. Or a therapist may withdraw from a volatile mother like he or she withdrew or retreated from his or her own mother.

This self-assessment affords an opportunity to deepen our engagement with the family and alerts us to potential pitfalls and opportunities. Therapy is not different from most of life; we tend to engage with those who we feel comfortable with or who challenge us in some way. How we answer these questions has much to do with the ongoing energy and commitment we bring to our work and the implicit signal we send to the family. Therapists do not have to like families to be helpful, but finding something to like in the family can spark greater imagination and creativity in both the therapist and the family.

*Hypotheses.* Hypotheses about the family generated before the initial interview are now revised on the basis of data ranging from the biological to the macrosystemic levels. The multiple levels of information that together constitute the "system" help generate an interactional assessment and, more important, targets of intervention as the treatment plan is crafted. We continue to revise these hypotheses throughout treatment.

We have found it helpful to organize our thinking around nine categories of data:

1. *Individual*: contains information about the cast of characters in the family (age, work, school grade, etc.); psychodynamic impressions; risk factors, such as suicidality; interests, talents, and strengths; nodal events in individual development; issues and concerns; and the "patient position" of each member (worldview, assumptions, beliefs, language, symbols, etc.).

2. *Health*: includes information and attitudes about medical history and current problems, health and wellness concerns, prescription and nonprescription medications, chemical abuse and dependency history, and beliefs and practices in health care.

3. *Development*: includes family life cycle issues, developmental tasks and concerns associated with current life cycle transitions in both the immediate and extended family systems, and vertical and horizontal stressors.

4. *Structural*: includes information about roles, rules, boundaries, coalitions, alliances, hierarchy, subsystems, conflicts, cutoffs, closeness and distance, redundant sequences of behavior, and patterns of family communication.

5. *Intergenerational*: includes information about family themes across the generations, invisible or split loyalties, family projections, scapegoating, unfinished ledgers, unresolved losses, birth order and inherited legacies, family beliefs and traditions passed on from generation to generation, and the role of the extended family.

6. *Ethnicity*: includes information about the ethnic, economic, religious, racial, and cultural factors influencing the family.

7. *Spirituality*: includes information about how the individual and collective spiritual beliefs and values influence their experiences.

8. *Ecosystemic*: includes information about the political–socioeconomic ecology of the family and other systems that the family is or has been connected with, such as work, school, legal, social services, medical, religious, and other community-based systems.

9. *Family resources*: highlights available strengths and resources within the family and in the family's extended network or community.

## CONCLUSION

To end well, therapy must begin well. In an evolving process, the therapist and family members must engage one another and stay vital and involved in the therapeutic system. We believe that establishing leadership of the self of the therapist, facilitating distributed leadership within the family, crafting a learning organization, and creating a holding environment are essential components of the engagement process. Engagement is the "goodness of fit" between what the therapist and family members bring to the therapy experience. Engagement does not represent a moment in time, a goal in itself, or a means to an end. Rather, engagement is therapy, and as such, is an ongoing process that evolves in stages throughout the therapeutic encounter. Within this framework, we emphasize that therapy is a transitional relationship crafted in the hopes of improving family relationships not only in the office, but also, and especially, in real life. Thus, the hope of engaging well is to disengage well, with families more on a path toward health and wellness and the therapist more imaginative and alive.

# References

Ackerman, N. (1966). Family psychotherapy: Theory and practice. *American Journal of Psychotherapy, 20*(3), 409–414.

Ackerman, N. (1982). The art of family therapy. In D. Bloch and R. Simon (Eds.), *The strengths of family therapy: Selected papers of Nathan W. Ackerman* (pp. 284–286). New York: Brunner/Mazel.

Alexander, F., & French, T. (1946). *Psychoanalytic therapy.* New York: The Ronald Press.

Anderson, C., & Stewart, S. (1983). *Mastering resistance: A practical guide to family therapy.* New York: Guilford Press.

Aponte, H. (1992). Training the person of the therapist in structural family therapy. *Journal of Marital and Family Therapy, 18*(3), 269–281.

Aponte, H., & Van Deusen, J. (1981). Structural family therapy. In A. Gurman and D. Kniskern (Eds.), *Handbook of Family Therapy* (Vol. 1; pp. 310–360). New York: Brunner/Mazel.

Attneave, C. (1976). Social networks as the unit of intervention. In P. J. Guerin (Ed.), *Family therapy theory and practice* (pp. 220–232). New York: Gardner Press.

Berg, B., & Rosenblum, N. (1977). Fathers in family therapy: A survey of family therapists. *Journal of Marriage and Family Counseling, 3*, 85–91.

Bion, W. R. (1961). *Experiences in group.* New York: Basic Books.

Boszormenyi-Nagy, I., & Krasner, B. (1986). *Between give and take: A clinical guide to contextual therapy.* New York: Brunner/Mazel.

Boszormenyi-Nagy, I., & Spark, G. (1984). *Invisible loyalties.* New York: Brunner/Mazel.

Bowen, M. (1978). *Family therapy in clinical practice.* Northvale, NJ: Jason Aronson.

Cohen, A. M., & Smith, R. O. (1976). *The critical incident in growth groups: Theory and technique.* San Diego, CA: University Associates.

Crosby, R. P. (1992). *Walking the empowerment tightrope.* King of Prussia: Pennsylvania Organization Design and Development, Inc.

De Shazer, S. (1982). *Patterns of brief family therapy: An ecosystemic approach.* New York: Guilford Press.

Dooling, D. M. (1990). Focus. *Parabola, 15*, 2–3.

Fisch, R., Weakland, J., & Segal, L. (1982). *The tactics of change: Doing therapy briefly.* San Francisco: Jossey-Bass.

Forrest, T. (1969). Treatment of the father in family therapy. *Family Process, 8*, 106–108.

Framo, J. (1968). My families, my family. In J. Framo, *Explorations in marital and family therapy. Selected papers of James L. Framo* (pp. 282–292). New York: Springer.

Framo, J. (1970). Symptoms from a family transactional viewpoint. In J. Framo, *Explorations in marital and family therapy: Selected papers of James L. Framo* (pp. 11–57). New York: Springer.

Framo, J. (1975). Personal reflections of a family therapist. In J. Framo, *Explorations in marital and family therapy: Selected papers of James L. Framo* (pp. 243–258). New York: Springer.

Framo, J. (1980). Marriage and marital therapy: Issues and initial interview techniques. In J. Framo, *Explorations in marital and family therapy: Selected papers of James L. Framo* (pp. 123–140). New York: Springer.

Framo, J. (1992). *Family of origin therapy: An intergenerational approach.* New York: Brunner/Mazel.

Franklin, P., & Prosky, P. (1973). A standard initial interview. In Don Bloch (Ed.), *Techniques of family psychotherapy: A primer* (pp. 29–37). New York: Grune & Stratton.

Freud, S. (1938). *A general introduction to psychoanalysis.* New York: Garden City.

Friedman, E. H. (1985). *Generation to generation: Family process in church and synagogue.* New York: Guilford Press.

Garfield, S. (1978). Research on client variables in psychotherapy. In S. L. Garfield and A. E. Bergin (Eds.), *Handbook of psychotherapy and behavior change: An empirical analysis* (pp. 271–298). New York: Wiley.

Goolishian, H., & Anderson, H. (1992). Strategy and intervention versus nonintervention: A matter of theory? *Journal of Marital and Family Therapy, 18*(1), 5–15.

Guerin, P. J., Fay, L., Burden, S. L., & Kautto, J. G. (1987). *The evaluation and treatment of marital conflict.* New York: Basic Books.

Gurman, A. (1981). Integrative marital therapy: Toward the development of an interpersonal approach. In S. Budman (Ed.), *Forms of brief therapy.* New York: Guilford Press.

Haley, J. (1987). *Problem solving therapy* (2nd ed.). San Francisco: Jossey-Bass.

Hartman, A. (1979). *Finding families an ecological approach to family assessment in adoption.* Beverly Hills, CA: Sage.

Hoffman, L. (1990). Constructing realities. *Family Process, 29,* 1–12.

Jordan, J. R. (1982). The use of history in family therapy: A brief rejoinder to Sluzki. *Journal of Marital and Family Therapy, 8,* 393–398.

Kernberg, O. (1965). Notes on countertransference. *Journal of the American Psychoanalytic Association, 35,* 38–56.

Kerr, M., & Bowen, M. (1988). *Family evaluation.* New York: Norton.

Koss, M. (1979). Length of psychotherapy for clients seen in private practice. *Journal of Consulting and Clinical Psychology, 47,* 210–212.

L'Abate, L. (1975). Pathogenic role rigidity in fathers: Some observations. *Journal of Marriage and Family Counseling, 1,* 69–79.

Lachkar, J. (1992). *The narcissistic/borderline couple: A psychoanalytic perspective on marital treatment.* New York: Brunner/Mazel.

Langs, R. (1992). *The listening process.* Northvale, NJ: Jason Aronson.

Lansky, M. (1981). *Family therapy and major psychopathology.* New York: Grune & Stratton.

McGoldrick, M., & Gerson, R. (1985). *Genograms in family assessment.* New York: Norton.

Minuchin, S. (1974). *Families and family therapy.* Cambridge, MA: Harvard University Press.

Minuchin, S., & Fishman, C. (1981). *Family therapy techniques.* Cambridge, MA: Harvard University Press.

Napier, A. Y., & Whitaker, C. (1978). *The family crucible.* New York: Harper & Row.

Ogden, T. (1989). *The primitive edge of experience.* Northvale, NJ: Jason Aronson.

O'Hanlon, W. H., & Weiner-Davis, M. (1989). *In search of solutions: A new direction in psychotherapy.* New York: Norton.

Papp, P. (1983). *The Process of Change.* New York: Guilford Press.

Perlmutter, R. A., & Jones, J. E. (1986). Consultation in psychiatric contexts: Psychiatric emergency programs. In L. C. Wynne, S. H. McDaniel, and T. T. Weber (Eds.), *Systems consultation* (pp. 115–131). New York: Guilford Press.

Piaget, J. (1954). *The construction of reality in the child.* New York: Basic Books.

Scharff, D., & Scharff, J. (1987). *Object relations family therapy.* Northvale, NJ: Jason Aronson.

Searles, H. (1968). *Collected papers on schizophrenia and related subjects.* London: Hogarth.

Selvini-Palazzoli, M., Boscolo, L., Cecchin, G., & Prata, G. (1982). Hypothesizing-circularity-neutrality: Three guidelines for the conductor of the session. *Family Process, 19,* 3–13.

Senge, P. M. (1990). *The fifth discipline.* New York: Doubleday.

Shapiro, R. J., & Budman, S. H. (1973). Defection, termination and continuation in family and individual therapy. *Family Process, 12,* 55–67.

Sherman, R., & Fredman, N. (1986). *Handbook of structural techniques in marriage and family therapy.* New York: Brunner/Mazel.

Skynner, R. (1981). An open-systems group analytic approach to family therapy. In A. Gurman & D. Kniskern (Eds.), *Handbook of family therapy* (Vol. 1; pp. 39–84). New York: Brunner/Mazel.

Slipp, S. (1984). *Object relations: A dynamic bridge between individual and family therapy.* Northvale, NJ: Jason Aronson.

Slipp, S., Ellis, S., & Kressel, K. (1974). Factors associated with engagement in family therapy. *Family Process, 13,* 413–427.

Sluzki, C. E. (1981). Process of symptom production and patterns of symptom maintenance. *Journal of Marital and Family Therapy, 7,* 273–280.

Stanton, M. D. (1992). The timeline and the "why now?" question: A technique and rationale for therapy, training, organizational consultation and research. *Journal of Marital and Family Therapy, 18*(4), 331–343.

Stanton, M. D., & Todd, T. (Eds.). (1982). *The family therapy of drug abuse and addiction.* New York: Guilford Press.

Stierlin, H., Rucker-Embden, I., Wetzel, N., & Wirsching, M. (1980). *The first interview with the family.* New York: Brunner/Mazel.

Stolorow, R., Brandchaft, B., & Atwood, G. (1987). *Psychoanalytic treatment: An intersubjective approach.* Hillsdale, NJ: The Analytic Press.

Trotzer, J. P. (1982). Engaging families in therapy: A pilot study. *International Journal of Family Therapy, 4,* 4–19.

Watzlawick, P. (1984). *The invented reality: How do we know what we believe we know.* New York: Norton.

Weber, T., McDaniel, S., & Wynne, L. (1987). Helping more by helping less: Family therapy and systems consultation. *Psychotherapy, 24*(3), 615–620.

Weber, T., McKeever, J., & McDaniel, S. (1985). A beginner's guide to the problem-oriented first family interview. *Family Process, 24,* 357–364.

Wells, R. A. (1980). Engagement technique in family therapy. *International Journal of Family Therapy, 2,* 75–94.

Whitaker, C., & Keith, D. (1981). Symbolic-experiential family therapy. In A. Gurman & D. Kniskern (Eds.), *Handbook of family therapy* (pp. 187–225). New York: Brunner/Mazel.

Williamson, D. (1992). *The intimacy paradox.* New York: Guilford Press.

Winnicott, D. W. (1965). *The maturational process and the facilitating environment.* Madison, CT: International Universities Press.

Winnicott, D. W. (1971). *Playing and reality.* New York: Basic Books.

Wolin, S. J., & Wolin, S. (1993). *The resilient self: How survivors in troubled families rise above adversity.* New York: Villard Books.

Wynne, L. C., McDaniel, S. H., & Weber, T. T. (1986). *Systems consultation: A new perspective for family therapy.* New York: Guilford Press.

Yalom, I. D. (1989). *Love's executioner.* New York: Harper.

Zuk, G. H. (1972). Engagement and termination: The critical reference points in family therapy. *American Journal of Orthopsychiatry, 42,* 323–324.

Zuk, G. H. (1974). Engagement and termination in family therapy. In I. R. Wolberg & M. L. Aronson (Eds.), *Group therapy.* New York: Stratton.

CHAPTER 4

# OPEN-ENDED THERAPY: TERMINATION IN MARITAL AND FAMILY THERAPY

*Jay Lebow*

Endings are generally a difficult subject in most human enterprises and, therefore, are frequently avoided. Marital and family therapy is no exception. The ending of treatment is often belatedly considered by clients and therapist, which leaves many endings unplanned and less than optimal. Consider these cases:

## CASE VIGNETTES

*Mary and Tom had been in marital therapy for 10 sessions. They sought therapy because of a high level of conflict manifested in frequent arguments. Over the past two weeks they had not had any fights. They left a message on the therapist's voice mail stating that they were doing well and were not going to pursue treatment further. The therapist, who had felt positive about the progress in the treatment, was dumbfounded and felt hurt and angry about the clients' way of informing her about their decision.*

◆ ◆ ◆

*The Smith family presented concerned with the behavior of Tony, age 16, who had been frequently truant from school. After the sixth session, Tony adamantly told his family he would not return to therapy. The family called the therapist to say that the therapy had been unsuccessful and they would not be returning. The therapist told the parents he understood and suggested they call again if Tony agreed to further help.*

◆ ◆ ◆

*Sue and Tom had been in marital therapy for 3 years. Although they presented with major issues in communication and different views about the division of tasks in the home, these issues had long been resolved. They had moved from a low to a high degree of marital satisfaction. Sessions continued with little accomplishment. The therapist felt bored much of the time. The clients remained uncertain of how they would do without the therapy, and the therapist did not want to risk the possibility that they might feel rejected. No one raised the idea of ending, and treatment continued.*

Each of these situations represents a failure to deal with issues concerning the ending of treatment. Although these examples may be extreme, difficulties around the handling of termination are hardly rare. The ending of treatment is often shunted to a corner of the field of therapy where it receives little or no attention. Given the number and range of difficulties surrounding termination that occur in family therapy, the discussion of methods for handling termination may well represent the most significant gap in the marital and family therapy literature. The subject of termination is generally approached as an afterthought and assigned a chapter or brief section at the end of discussions. Articles and presentations specifically centered on the topic are rarely encountered, although there have been exceptions (Combrinck-Graham, 1981; Heath, 1985; Kramer, 1980; Minuchin & Fishman, 1981; Treacher, 1989; Wetchler & Ofte-Atha, 1993).

## THE IMPORTANCE OF TERMINATION IN MARITAL AND FAMILY THERAPY

The existence of this hole in the marital and family literature is quite puzzling. There are several compelling reasons that make a clear argument for well thought out termination in marital and family therapy vitally important. First, marital and family therapy is almost invariably short-term therapy in which the end always remains within sight.[1] All of the specific aspects of the treatment must be considered through the lens of an ending that may come soon after beginning.

Second, the most widely practiced models of family therapy are highly goal oriented and therefore move toward some clear end point where the success of reaching goals is reviewed and evaluated. From this pragmatic stance, termination is a point toward which treatment clearly and purposefully moves.

Third, sudden patient-initiated termination is an all-too-frequent fact of life in marital and family therapy (Bischoff & Sprenkle, 1993; Talmon, 1990). In contrast to the slow, evolving stable alliances that are frequently described in individual therapy (which, given high levels of client dropout, represent a myth even in individual treatment), alliances in marital and family therapy are often precarious. Sessions are frequently difficult and anxiety provoking because partners or family members raise powerful complaints about one another. Not only must one face one's own most difficult behavior (a common factor in most psychotherapies), but one must also face other members of the family who are often more than willing to highlight one's failings. Compensating factors such as the ability to deepen personal attachments, to become intimate within the context of our most natural grouping—the family—and to alter significant problems can make for a strong alliance to one's marital and family therapist. However, the possibilities of difficult anxiety-provoking material being

raised and conflict emerging remain so great that marital and family therapy are modes that many clients look to as necessary stressors in their lives. Therefore, they are prepared to end therapy sessions as soon as possible. Furthermore, a family therapy approach involves multiple clients, any one of whom can withdraw from the treatment and some of whom usually never share in the original idea of entering treatment. There always remains the possibility that some outbreak of bad feeling either toward the therapist or between family members will result in a rupture in the therapeutic relationship and that therapy will end suddenly.

The problem is compounded in marital and family therapy where individuals are considering whether they wish to remain together or in contact with each other. Here, the decision of a partner to leave the relationship or of a member to distance from the family is almost invariably also a decision to leave the therapy (see chap. 15 in this volume). Once this occurs, there is an almost inevitable break in the therapist–client bond.

The central place of the systemic perspective in marital and family therapy also has vast repercussions for termination. The systemic paradigm represents a leap from other ways of thinking because it puts events in perspective, delineates feedback loops in causal chains, and emphasizes context. There are hopes that treatment will have continuing effects even after sessions have ended. Although treatment may end, the family goes on, carrying with it the learning that has occurred in the therapy. Thus, the end of treatment is transformed from a break between clients and therapist into a continuity in the lives of the family members, and "termination" becomes yet another punctuation mark that can be applied to relationships.

Through the lens of the life cycle framework of family development shared by most family therapists (Carter & McGoldrick, 1989; see chap. 5 in this volume), it becomes natural to alter the frame for viewing therapy from a special once-in-a-lifetime attempt

---

[1] There are, of course, long-term family therapies such as Bowen therapy, but the long-term practice of marital and family therapy remains a small percentage of the total number of cases.

to resolve all present and future difficulties. Instead, we may view the alliance built with the family therapist as a resource that can be used again and again as new issues emerge. Family therapy thereby becomes analogous to the treatment of a physical problem by a family physician, where the contract between provider and patients assumes that the skills discovered in therapy may well be used again when a new problem emerges or the old one returns.

What emerges is a distinctly different view of termination in family therapy, a view in which termination is not envisioned as a distinct set of sessions marking the finality of ending but as a process for dealing with the issues of ending over the course of treatment that in part helps build a foundation for further use of the therapeutic relationship. This view of treatment, used by a wide range of family therapists and crossing many scholastic boundaries, I term "open-ended family therapy."

## OPEN-ENDED FAMILY THERAPY

In an open-ended approach, the family therapist thinks in terms of building a vehicle for treatment that can be used over time. Families are viewed as making use of treatments usually of brief duration at various times in the life cycle. Themes may extend across time, but they may also vary considerably because of powerful differences in the problems and skills needed at different points in the life of the family. The optimistic expectation that one set of meetings will permanently end difficulties is replaced with the more realistic frame that it is part of the human condition for problems to emerge at various times and that family therapy is a resource that can be enlisted in resolving these difficulties. Families are also viewed as capable and interested in mastering different aspects of their experience at varying points in time. To paraphrase Carl Whitaker (Napier & Whitaker, 1978), sometimes therapists teach the notes, sometimes the scales, sometimes the tunes, and sometimes symphonies. The distinction between treatment and posttreatment also blurs. New processes are established during the treatment that families are expected to continue to use after treatment ends. At this point the therapist is available as a re-

source if these family-based processes do not prove sufficient.

Such a life cycle perspective is augmented by recent data (Jacobson, Schmaling, & Holtzworth-Monroe, 1987) that calls attention to the distinct possibility for deterioration in improvement over the succeeding years after marital and family therapy. These data suggest that even in quite effective treatments the durability of change may be limited, and there may be efforts to anticipate, ward off, and respond to the return of difficulties.

An open-ended approach has vast pragmatic implications for practice. Therapists explicitly present themselves as available throughout the life cycle to build a relationship that clients can draw on in the future. The end of a set of sessions is not labeled as a final contact, but instead as an ending that may prove brief or last a lifetime.

Dealing with ending actually begins at the beginning of therapy. It helps for therapists to clearly label goals and develop a set of criteria for success that can serve as a measure of what ultimately is achieved and how effective treatment has been. Usually these goals will be in the form of a reduction in the level of the presenting problem (e.g., marital dissatisfaction). As treatment progresses, other mediating goals may be highlighted and targeted (e.g., communication or resolved feelings toward family of origin) that help achieve the ultimate goals (Gurman, 1978), and other ultimate goals may develop. The framework of goals provides an anchor for decisions about ending. When is it appropriate to end? What level of change will suggest that it is time? What are appropriate ways of ending? All these questions should be considered from the beginning of treatment.

Early in treatment, the therapist should present a model of how to finish that includes a description of the open-ended viewpoint. The therapist should highlight the benefits of a planned termination: gaining closure, showing the best respect for a meaningful relationship, and providing an opportunity to anticipate the future. Emphasis should be placed on the value of ending with a session rather than a phone call.

It is my practice to provide these thoughts in writing as well as verbally. The last thing clients are thinking about as they enter treatment is the termination process. A written review of expectations about ending that is part of a statement that summarizes procedures that a therapist follows can serve to help clients focus on this information. The therapist should also understand that this view of ending may vary considerably from client expectations, which may have their foundation in other types of relationship where a telephone call suffices as a satisfactory end.

The issues that are typically discussed at termination are then interwoven into the fabric of the entire treatment. The end of treatment is best approached with a generic set of templates that apply to a range of common situations. These templates can be adapted and evolve within the context of specific cases. The therapist must ask both "What does an appropriate ending look like?" and "How is ending affected by particular specific sets of circumstances and the place of this family in its life development?"

It should be highlighted that although "soft termination" is the norm among many family therapists, it is not invariably so. A range of therapists from psychoanalytic to strategic view such methods not only as unnecessary but also as furthering dependency in a way that is harmful. These groups adhere to a more inflexible traditional view of termination. One of the major goals is to wrap up treatment in a way that will minimize the risk that the family will return to treatment and will instead be able to work on their problems among themselves independent of the therapist.

## THE TASKS OF TERMINATION

The 10 tasks that are central to ending most family therapy are considered below. They are not necessarily sequential tasks in a distinct phase of therapy but may be better conceptualized as an agenda over the entire course.

1. *Tracking progress in therapy to determine the appropriateness of ending.* Termination begins with a decision to stop treatment. The task of evaluating where the family is in the process of change extends over the entire course of the treatment. It begins with defining goals and setting criteria for goal attainment early in treatment and marking the progress

sought by the time of a decision to end. It continues when clients ask about their progress or about when treatment might be completed. These matters come to a head when the client, the therapist, or the payer decides the time has come to end treatment.

In work with families, issues of gender and culture must always remain in focus (see chaps. 17, 18, 19, and 20 in this volume). This is no less true in considering termination. In some cultural groups, the idea of a planned, well-discussed termination may be especially foreign. In others, a complete cutoff from the therapist may make especially little sense. For others still the fears about ongoing dependency may be great. Technique needs to be adapted to the population at hand while an attempt is made to serve the completion of the tasks of termination. In a similar vein, men and women often bring different agendas to endings, with men accenting the instrumental tasks and women the affective bonds. Elders, young adults, adolescents, and children may also bring differences in vantage points. Sensitivity to such differences is an essential ingredient in marital and family therapy.

The task then becomes for clients and therapist to collaborate in assessing the plan to end and discussing its ramifications. The therapist should engage the clients in a direct discussion of their respective viewpoints about where they are in the treatment and on the ramifications of ending. In most situations, control over ending resides with the clients (the exceptions lie in court-ordered or inpatient settings where therapists can take action to mandate further treatment). The therapist's primary task is to provide guidance. The therapist must remain wary of the simplistic notion that more therapy is necessarily better. How does ending at this point compare with the gains made by other cases like this one that have continued longer? How much more therapy would be needed to move understanding, feelings, or behavior to another level? If the therapist believes this is a reasonable point for termination, then the other tasks of termination are brought into central focus over a few sessions. If not, then the therapist first attempts to help the clients understand why more sessions would be advisable and, if the effort to continue treatment proves unsuccessful, focuses on the tasks of termination.

2. *Reviewing the course of treatment.* The therapist should help the family to review treatment. What were the major events in the treatment? What were the actions, thoughts, and feelings of the various participants? How have they felt toward each other at various points in treatment? A portion of this review should focus on the accomplishment of goals. Have all goals been accomplished? Which ones have been accomplished? Which goals have not been accomplished? What has made goal attainment difficult in the areas in which change has been slow? What has contributed to the changes that have occurred?

The therapist should encourage family members to review the process of therapy from their own perspective and to examine in the course of the termination process their narrative about what the treatment has been like and what has mattered in the change process. What have they found helpful? What have they found a hindrance? How did change occur? This approach need not suggest that all change will be transparent to the clients. The goal is not to push insights on the family but to help them understand what has occurred as best they can so change can have the greatest likelihood of proving durable over time.

In the review process, therapists should also recognize their own feelings. There is much evidence that the narratives of clients and therapists about treatment often differ considerably from one another. The therapist should use termination to examine both intervention strategy with this case and countertransference and then share what he or she believes will be therapeutic.

3. *Emphasizing the gains made and the client's role in these gains.* Clients often do not fully comprehend the extent of the change that has occurred and their contributions to the change process. Frequently, clients passively see change as the result of the treatment of the therapist. The therapist should actively work to alter such attributions by highlighting the change that has occurred and the clients' role in this change. A greater sense of competence and confidence can be built by mapping the route of the change and specific client behaviors that have allowed for this journey. Statements such as, "It just happened" or "We changed because of you" should be actively questioned to flush out the contribution

of the family in the process. It is often helpful here to contrast these clients to other families that have failed to resolve their difficulties. The family should be helped to grasp what they have done and the special nature of what they have achieved.

4. *Abstracting what has been learned from the treatment and how it may be applied later.* Marital and family therapy is most effective when it leads to clear learning about how to do something, whether it is building a behavioral skill such as communicating, an affective skill such as facing loss, or a psychodynamic skill such as working with one's understanding about self. The therapist should emphasize the competencies that have been built and develop with the family a plan for the maintenance of these skills.

Both client and therapist perspectives about the nature of these skills need to be explored. Which skills have the clients found most valuable? How does each individual most effectively use these skills? How do the family or couple most effectively use them as a unit? What do they believe the most important learning has been over the course of the treatment? What do they see as the most difficult hurdles in maintaining these skills and not falling back into old patterns? Similarly, therapists should share their vantage point about which skills have grown, which competencies have been most important in the change process, and how these skills can best be used in the future.

A plan can then be generated for the maintenance of these skills. The therapist should emphasize that skills built in treatment often erode without practice. An active program to maintain change is needed. This program for the maintenance of change is best presented as both the responsibility of each individual and of the family as a whole.

Much of the learning involves an improved understanding of family process. How can family members observe and talk about the family process without the therapist? What will the vehicle be to carry the change process further? Often, the simple directive to find a weekly time to communicate can make the difference between successful and unsuccessful maintenance of change. This directive becomes useful at whatever point in the treatment the family can successfully communicate without the therapist in a way that does more good than harm.

Circumstances that predict the likelihood of difficulties also should be highlighted. The tendency to return to earlier and more dysfunctional patterns should be presented in a way that suggests the likelihood that some problems will return but that these problems can be anticipated and dealt with when they occur. The therapist may predict the regression with the intent of helping create a paradoxical state of psychological reactivity that moves the clients away from the regression. More frequently, the therapist works to build clients' skills for recognizing regression as it occurs and dealing with it through communication about how to best approach the problem. The therapist helps the family recognize the early warning signs of the kind of difficulties they had been experiencing and to generate action to resolve these problems. Most particularly, the therapist helps the family plan how they will plan for resolving difficulties.

5. *Internalizing the therapist.* The therapist has been an active part of the family's life and has become part of the system over the time of treatment. One goal of termination is for the therapist to remain with the family, not as an active participant, however, but as internalized in the family process. Family members naturally will often speak of what the therapist would do in an inner dialogue or in conversation among themselves. Families should be encouraged to actively develop these skills by imagining what the therapist would do. What would have happened if they had a session with the therapist? How would they work to do the therapist's job? Of course, these suggestions can only hint at the importance of maintaining the sense of a holding environment that is so important to the success of family therapy, which the family must find a way to incorporate into its own experience away from the therapist. The therapist works to build a family's sense of confidence in its ability to remain empathically connected, handle developmental issues, and solve problems.

6. *Considering the ending through the lens of other endings in life.* Endings are powerful and provocative. Each person has a unique history of endings. The termination should be explored in the wake of these issues in the histories of clients. Does the clients' history make it more difficult to end? Does it make it harder to return? Such considerations should be carefully examined in light of genogram information that has emerged in the treatment.

7. *Saying good-bye, with an opportunity to express gratitude and exchange feelings.* This is, after all, a parting and for most an important one. Part of the task is for both clients and therapist to acknowledge the attachment and for the family to express appreciation for the help they have received. Although it remains important to highlight the family strengths and achievements, a therapist must remain genuine by accepting that which is given back in the way of gratitude. Clients all have their special ways of saying good-bye. The therapist should work to understand what are typical ways these clients say good-bye and how the ending in this process may best fit with these ways. At times, this may mean helping the family to end in a different way from old patterns. At other times, this may mean accepting a rapid distancing. The therapist's job remains to end in a positive way that models a constructive way of relating, maximizes the ongoing effectiveness of the treatment, and enables reconnection when it is appropriate.

Affectively, this can prove to be among the most difficult tasks for therapists. The ending of treatment is in some ways more abrupt for the therapist than for the family. In almost all cases, the family continues with one another and, in most situations, regulates the time of ending. In contrast, the therapist is often confronted abruptly with the clients' message that it is time to end the therapy process. Families, who the therapist has invested in and values, are replaced with new clients that are unknown and with whom the therapist has to begin to build a relationship. It remains tempting to continue to keep clients engaged even after the point of maximum benefit. Acceptance of clients' ways of ending, particularly when they are less than optimal ways, therefore can present a difficult issue for therapists. The therapist must work with his or her feelings. What do varying kinds of endings mean for the therapist? What is stirred up? How can the therapist find a therapeutic position even in the wake of what looks like dysfunctional behavior? The therapist must be able to evaluate the treatment in the light of experience and understand and constructively work with a wide range of endings.

Therapists must also consider their own professional history with regard to termination that may influence their termination with a particular family. Therapists must experience, understand, and work with these feelings to help the client with the next task. When treatment is successful, both a sense of accomplishment and loss are likely to be present. With the positive feelings of success come the sad feelings that go with parting. When treatment is unsuccessful, the feelings can become even more complex. The therapist may experience regret about the process or countertransference reactions to the disappointment or anger of the family about not reaching hoped for goals. The therapist must work with these feelings to allow for a useful termination process whatever the outcome. Termination is a point where clients particularly need therapists who can move beyond their own feelings.

Some feelings are particularly difficult. Endings with clients whom the therapist enjoys may lead to great senses of loss and can prompt efforts by the therapist to reengage. With some others, there may be a great level of relief in the end of the struggle and a sense of premature abandonment. In many settings, the end of treatment marks a financial or workload change for the therapist with a range of feelings elicited. Other cases may present ways of leaving that were highly problematic in the therapist's own family of origin. At times, the method by which clients bring information about termination comes as a surprise and sours the reaction of the therapist to the clients. It becomes essential for the therapist to understand the dynamic in the interface between clients and therapist and to work with it as the ending occurs. For example, those with powerful dependency needs often leave therapy suddenly despite what appears to be a strong alliance with the therapist because this is the only way they can envision leaving. The therapist needs to understand this process, work with his or her own feelings about it, and attempt to help the family understand and find better alternatives to their process.

8. *Discussing the conditions for returning.* Decisions about when to enter or reenter therapy are difficult for families. Often decisions to return after termination are made on the basis of the family's own script that may move them to wait until a situation has de-teriorated far beyond the point it might or alternately to return at the first suggestion of difficulty, which maintains an unnecessary dependency. As part of the process of termination, the therapist should help set guidelines for returning. Under what conditions should the family work on their own, and when should they return? The therapist should clearly indicate the natural tendency for problems to reemerge as therapy ends, given the natural anxiety about proceeding without the safety net of therapy. The therapist should help the family to form a plan to address difficulties, with a clear understanding of some time frame or number of efforts to resolve difficulty before consulting the therapist. The possibility of exceptional circumstances that might cause the need for immediate consultation should also be discussed, but with clear parameters for the degree of difficulty that might be entailed in an exceptional circumstance. In the open-ended context of most family therapy, the therapist's goal is to set a framework for the family's efforts to resolve issues on their own, but that leaves the door open if problems prove too difficult or novel. It is a fine line between a regressive use of therapy that reengages the therapist in problems that could be resolved by the family and the appropriate use of the therapeutic process.

At termination, a preplanned set of conditions is laid out for returning. The trigger may be the passage of a particular amount of time (e.g., a return in 6 months) or the emergence of a particular set of possible warning signs for difficulty (e.g., less communication and more frequent arguments). Booster sessions and brief reengagement may be used as methods for maintaining therapeutic gains. Booster sessions are sessions scheduled at the ending of treatment, generally for returns at 3- or 6-month intervals. In the booster sessions, the therapist works to renew old skills and insights, reintroduces the practice of needed behavioral patterns, and directly works to reinstill hope and optimism. The booster session also can serve as a minievaluation for signs that further treatment is advisable; typically, however, the reengagement is limited to a session or two. Whether booster sessions are planned or not, the message is clearly conveyed that returning is an appropriate action to take under a particular set of circumstances.

9. *Referring.* In a small number of cases, the end of one treatment leads to the beginning of another. A set of issues outside of the purview of this treatment may be addressed in another. For example, an individual in a couple seen in marital therapy who are divorcing may be referred to a therapist for work alone on their emerging postdivorce life (see chaps. 15 and 33 in this volume). In a more common variant, a referral may be made to a self-help group for an individual or even the whole family to help stabilize changes after the end of treatment.

10. *Defining posttreatment availability.* The therapist should make clear when and under what terms he or she will be available. The model of open-ended therapy suggests a lifetime commitment to clients to be available as needed. Exceptions to this should be clearly noted, especially to the extent that schedules may be full or as time passes. For most therapists, a commitment to be available, although not necessarily at the same time or under the same circumstances, is a fairly safe one. The ramifications of preferred provider organizations (PPOs) and health maintenance organizations (HMOs) should be clearly stated to the extent that such issues have relevance. It may be that the therapist will be available but not a member of a panel, so that insurance will not pay for service.

Occasionally clients will call after the end of treatment to discuss a particular situation without scheduling a session. To the extent that a phone call can be used as a brief booster session, this form of availability may help and be offered by the therapist without fee as an extension of the earlier work. However, given the pragmatics of practice in any context, the therapist will only be able to allocate brief amounts of time to this task without needing to suggest another appointment.

An increasingly common means of follow-up is scheduling a checkup 3 months to 1 year after the last session. This method, akin to booster sessions to help maintain change, can be effective with many clients, particularly those well-engaged and cooperative. It may be more difficult with those who fear being drawn into greater dependency and further sessions. Convincing these clients that this will truly be a checkup and not a lure toward further treatment is instrumental in gaining cooperation. Sometimes, cli-

ents may not attend the checkup but call instead. This brief checkup may serve the same purpose as a session.

*Exceptions to these procedures.* Within the various schools of family therapy there are a few that take a special view of termination and would take exception at some of the suggestions made in these 10 tasks. For example, therapies that are strategic in focus often accent a clearly marked ending, assignment of responsibility for change entirely to the clients, and even a move toward a rupture in the therapeutic alliance at the end of treatment (Watzlawick, Weakland, & Fisch, 1974). In such therapies, termination is simply about ending and avoiding regression in the form of a return to earlier modes of organization, slipping into longer term involvement with the therapist is seen as a danger, and insight and planning for the future is assigned no importance. Within such models, methods for dealing with termination are therefore quite different, accenting paradox and a clear crisp break with the therapist. However, it should be highlighted that these methods only make sense within the conventions of these specific forms of family therapy and probably have minimal relevance to typical practice that assigns a much more important role to learning, insight, and attachment.

Methods also must be modified in work with families that lack the requisite skills to function on their own. Although such families are rare, they are encountered. Blanket statements highlighting health and coping may not fit well with these families. Many of these families can function much better with an ongoing set of relationships that help contain the feeling in the family and reward problem-solving behavior. The level of required intervention may be minimal with sessions at monthly intervals, but the difference between some intervention and none in these families is monumental. Ongoing therapy provides a forum for problem solving and planning. It may provide the only place where constructive communication occurs. The treatment and therapist may provide the kind of holding environment that a family needs to function. In particular, when there are members of the family who carry individual diagnoses that suggest borderline or psychotic functioning or profound difficulties in the ability to relate, such a holding environment may be crucial. We clearly can accept the notion of chronic ongoing treatment for diabetes or heart disease but may fail to recognize the similar benefits in unending treatment of some family disorders in the psychological realm.

## VARIATIONS ON ENDING

I have itemized common threads in the tasks of termination that transcend particular cases. However, there also are differences that emerge across cases that vastly affect the termination process and how it is handled. Endings vary along a number of dimensions. Termination can be therapist initiated, client initiated, or mutually agreed on by clients and the therapist. Termination ranges from carefully planned to totally unplanned and from cases that are completely successful to those that are unsuccessful. Terminations may be agreed on by all family members or there may be differences among family members about whether to terminate. Each of these variations may necessitate a different approach to termination.

## Who Initiates the Termination

**Therapist-initiated ending.** Although most couples and families initiate termination as soon as goals are met, some remain in treatment well beyond this point and use the therapist to help solve problems that the family could solve itself. When the therapist believes that the goals of treatment have been met and the family desires to continue in treatment, the task falls to the therapist to clearly label the success of the treatment in meeting the original goals and to raise the question of whether termination may be appropriate. The family then can assess whether new goals should be formulated or whether the treatment should end.

After finding a source of problem resolution and family harmony in the therapy, a family can have difficulties parting with the therapist. The therapist's task in such an instance is to help launch the family much as a good parent would launch a child. This should not be a jarring cutoff but a planned approach that allows the family to consider the nature of its reaction to the therapist and to move on.

The therapist, however, should allow the family sufficient time to raise the issue of ending. If they do not do so, the therapist should directly label the difficulty with ending treatment and center particular attention on helping build the confidence of the family in its ability to cope. The therapist should also explore the possibility that the initiation of ending may be seen as rejection, although politeness may be on the surface in this situation. Vehicles for preserving parts of the change process that can become alternatives to treatment, such as weekly meetings without the therapist, should be developed, along with a plan for ending treatment. Most clients will in the long run value the therapist for moving to end therapy at an appropriate time rather than allowing it to continue beyond a point of being helpful. Such an intervention may actually enable a family to return later to explore other problems.

**Client-initiated ending.** Most family therapy ends when clients self-terminate. This may be because they regard their goals as accomplished or because they think there will be no resolution. In most cases, this decision makes sense given the level of goal attainment, and the therapist merely needs to wrap up the various tasks of termination.

The therapist must always be sensitive to the viewpoint of the family. Families are often ready to finish the business of therapy long before therapists, and the therapist must examine the decision from this vantage point. Do the clients have enough skills to move on? It may well be that the full unfolding of the change process will not occur until after the end of the treatment. However, client-initiated termination is sometimes premature by any standard. It is typical for clients to raise the idea of possible termination even in successful family therapies soon after change begins to occur and before a stable period of problem-free behavior occurs. When clients raise the concept of terminating before the therapist believes the time is optimal, the therapist's first task is to ask questions about the stability of change and provide feedback to the family about where he or she envisions the clients as being in the process of change. It may be that with such simple feedback the clients will place their gains in perspective and continue until termination is deemed appropriate by the therapist. Some alterations in the scheduling of appointments, such as reducing the frequency of meetings and helping them to see an end point, may at this point help the family.

For others, these interventions will have little impact and the decision to end will be acted on. The therapist then needs to complete the tasks of termination to as great an extent as possible (see the discussion of unplanned termination below).

**Mutual therapist and client decision.** In the optimal case, therapist and clients decide together about the ending of treatment. The end point unfolds in a natural way, with goals accomplished, a winding down of the intensity of discussions, and a movement to a natural finish. When this happens, the end of the work is apparent, and a stopping point clearly emerges. Sessions often become boring both for clients and the therapist. However, in marital and family therapy, such a clearly agreed on stopping point occurs only in a minority of cases, and therapists must avoid falling prey to the myth that all successful treatments have such a termination.

**Third-party intervention.** It should be noted that with the advent of new forms of third-party payment, termination often is initiated not by clients or therapists but by the payer. When such a decision is made in opposition to the wishes of family and therapist, the therapist is placed in a particularly difficult situation. If the failure to approve further treatment is particularly inappropriate, it remains the therapist's task to bring pressure to bear on the payer, and this failing to consider one's ethical responsibility toward the case regardless of the payment issues. In most instances, the payer's decision must ultimately be accepted, and the therapist is left to address with the family the unmet goals and the work that remains to be done.

One way to deal with the third-party payer issues in a private practice is by working on a fee-for-service basis (Mikesell, 1994). At the beginning of treatment, therapy is presented much like other professional services (i.e., "pay as you go"). Mikesell frames

third-party payment as "nice if you can get any" but not as a necessary factor in the treatment process. The expectation is that the family pays for treatment, and third-party payer influences on ending are bypassed.

## Methods for Handling Planned and Unplanned Endings

Ideal treatment involves a carefully planned ending, marked by a decision to terminate based on the completion of goals and time for a careful discussion of the termination process with completion of the tasks of termination. However, the reality of marital and family therapy is that families often are not amenable to this sort of ending. When goals are met or when discouragement occurs, families may promptly decide to end treatment. The therapist's task becomes twofold: to raise issues around the ending of treatment early enough so that the tasks of termination can largely be completed whatever the family's behavior and to deal with whatever form the termination takes. The therapist must understand the commonly encountered scenarios and remain flexible in approaching termination.

The best method for creating an environment in which the tasks of termination will be accomplished is to deal with them throughout the therapy process. A review at the end of each session of what has been accomplished in that session can be particularly helpful in building a foundation that can readily be recapitulated.

When families suddenly announce that the present session will be their last or when they merely stop attending, the therapist should find some vehicle to recapitulate and complete the tasks of termination as thoroughly as possible. The first effort is to use joining interventions to gain at least enough time to deal with these tasks. Failing this, the plan moves to running through these tasks in an abbreviated way.

If clients attempt to end therapy by phone, in a tape message, in a letter, or by simply not attending, the therapist should present the best case for returning on the phone to the members of the family most likely to reengage and most likely to have power over others' returning. The proximate goal becomes holding a session to discuss the treatment and leaving open the possibility to reconsider the ending. The task is difficult given that many clients desire to slip quietly away, given the feeling shared by many clients that returning for another session means opening the door to further undesired sessions, and given that the therapist is proposing continuing a service for which a fee will be charged. The therapist's best possibilities lie in drawing on the strength of the therapeutic alliance, reassuring the clients that they can end after the next session, and highlighting the value of discussing the ending in a way that will prompt greater understanding.

A letter may be substituted for the phone call if needed. However, letters allow for only limited communication and provide little of the warmth that human contact engages. Letters are preferable only for those who clearly present with a need for privacy and respond better to the possibility for control over communication offered by a letter. Letters are more useful when there is no response to a call or when the efforts in a call fail. Final letters can communicate the vital information that the door remains open; they occasionally can enable the return of clients later even when there is a unilateral ending.

When the therapist can arrange a final meeting, intervention in the session consists of some combination of listening to the point of view of those who wish to terminate, joining with them in what can be agreed on, and attempting to set some workable contract that reengages those who drive the decision to end treatment. The therapist tries to help the family understand the value of having treatment continue. If the family holds to its decision, a substantial amount of time should be reserved in the session for the tasks of termination.

## Methods for Handling Endings in Successful and Unsuccessful Cases

The termination process also varies considerably along the continuum between those who have fully accomplished the goals of therapy and those who have not. If goals are accomplished, whatever the ending, the feeling is generally positive; if not, the feeling most often is down and dejected. In the former case, the tasks of termination can be readily ac-

complished, building a sense of future growth and movement.

When the goals have not been accomplished, termination is quite different. The family must face not having accomplished their goals. The therapist must work much harder to find a frame that can help wrap up the treatment and convey a sense of what has been accomplished. Often, when the central goal of treatment is not achieved (e.g., a change in behavior in an adolescent), process goals have been completed (e.g., parents working together) that can suggest to the family that they have accomplished something of worth that they can use in the future. In other instances, the therapist may have some insight that can be shared about what might make for more success in the future. Such messages can assume great importance as the family moves forward.

When goals are not accomplished, discussion of future plans becomes even more important. What will the family's strategy be in the future? What does the failure to accomplish goals mean to the family and its future plans? Often in families such failures parallel clear splits within the family. How will these be dealt with? What alternatives does the family have in mind? How readily might the family use therapy with this therapist or another in the future? Such issues need to be discussed.

## Dealing With Differences Within the Family About Whether to End Treatment

As opposed to individual therapy where there is a single client and, therefore, only one client termination, marital and family therapies almost invariably involve the presence of multiple individuals who may have varying vantage points on ending treatment and may even end treatment at different times. Sometimes members of the couple or family end treatment when others do not (see chap. 32 in this volume). Sometimes a therapist is told by one family member about the termination of another. Numerous dilemmas are thus created for the therapist. Should the therapist continue with the remainder of the family and work on the salient issues? Should the therapist regard the absent member as still part of the system to be treated and continue to actively try to engage that member? A systemic approach suggests an ongoing concern for these individuals even if they are no longer attending, but how far should concern go in terms of active behavior to involve those who no longer want treatment? Should there be a formal process of termination with those leaving? Should everyone be terminated if everyone will not attend?

There has been a considerable change in the view of most family therapists about how to handle such situations. The first two decades of family therapy emphasized the need for the entire system to be in treatment and efforts to use pressure on the remaining members of the system to keep the recalcitrant members in treatment until the problem was resolved. Thus, Napier & Whitaker (1978) describe a case in which the family would be terminated by the therapist if they could not get everyone to continue treatment. In present practice therapists mostly emphasize efforts to work with remaining members of the family system and thus to alter the systemic issues. In particular, the work of Bowen (1978) has moved family therapists to extend efforts to affect the system when there only remains one family member in treatment.

What pragmatically is to be done with the family in which some members desire to terminate and others do not? Clearly, the process varies with the location of the family in the course of treatment. If initial problems have yet to be resolved and if the intervention has not been offered at a dosage that would be likely to test whether change can occur, almost all family therapists would work with the recalcitrant family members to augment an alliance with them, engage their sense of open-mindedness about the treatment, hear about their complaints and attempt to deal with them, and attempt to reengage them in the treatment process. The therapist may call the terminating members to discuss their decision with them. Phone calls should be handled much like those with entire families that fail to return for sessions with the proximate goal being an additional session.

In other situations, the desire of some to end treatment while others do not does not necessarily imply that it would be better to continue. The initial goals of the treatment may be completed, but other goals may have emerged; some may see the initial

goals as completed, whereas others do not. The individuals who believe treatment has been completed may have a valid position or it may even be that continuing treatment would only serve to limit the family's coping on its own. In this territory, the therapist's tasks are to lead a discussion about these varying viewpoints without prejudice, to remain relatively free of serving his or her own agenda, to offer the best professional vantage point on the matter, and to determine whether some mutually agreeable agenda is possible. The experienced therapist has the advantage here of knowing what purposes either continuing or ending might serve for such a family and can share the respective advantages and disadvantages so that the family can make an informed decision. The task here is not so different than that at the beginning of therapy of helping bring disparate views together into some working plan.

If some members of the family do terminate and others do not, this need not be the worst of circumstances. Different members of families have varying needs, and there are times when the most productive process lies in refocusing on a subsystem or individual motivated toward change. When some members terminate, the therapist is faced with how to gain closure on the ending of those who are leaving. If treatment is to continue with part of the family, there first should be closure on the treatment with the larger system before moving to the smaller unit.

A problem in discussing termination in family therapy is that so many family therapies have become fluid in their constituents over time. The therapy may begin with the treatment of the whole family focused on the behavior problem of a child, may then enter a phase of marital therapy with the parents, and then return to family therapy focused around some other issue. Passages and alterations in participation in the treatment need to be clearly acknowledged and processed. The therapist needs to understand what such changes in membership and focus mean to the participants, and the goal of any segment should always remain clearly in focus. In some situations, it will be most prudent to attempt to reinvolve the family members who have left because the new information or issues that have been raised suggest that they should be consulted. In such a fluid therapy, ethical concerns should also remain always in focus, and every time the constituency of the treatment changes, such matters as guidelines for maintaining confidentiality and secrets must be reexamined (see chap. 32 in this volume).

## TRAJECTORIES IN TERMINATION

There are a variety of trajectories for ending treatment. Brief therapy may be structured as a 100-yard dash with intensive intervention followed by a very brief period of disengagement and a quick end. In longer-term treatment, the therapist may envision a long period of launching that may go on for several months with sessions spaced over longer periods. As a rule of thumb, the length of the termination should be in proportion to the length of treatment: Longer treatments require longer periods of termination.

At one end of the spectrum is the single therapy session. Talmon (1990) advocates that most goals can be accomplished in one session. He suggests that sessions be treated as if they were the last because in any practice there is a high percentage of single sessions, whether planned or not (i.e., the client drops out after one session).

When there is time for a more planned and gradual termination, more flexibility is permitted. For most family therapists, the movement to termination is gradually engaged by a spacing of sessions at increasingly distant intervals. Sessions may go from weekly to biweekly to monthly before the scheduling of a final session. This method allows clients to experiment with time away from therapy and build a sense of functioning without the help of the therapist.

## CONCLUSION

Endings are nearly always significant. Termination is a special experience and a vitally important aspect of family therapy. Perhaps because of the strong feelings about it, ending receives insufficient attention in practice and in the family therapy literature. However, a unique family therapy approach to ending has quietly emerged: open-ended therapy. The systemic context makes for a quite different view of ending than in individual therapy. Without much writing or discussion of the subject, many family therapists

have moved to a view of endings that includes a continuous processing of the experience of treatment as sessions progress and an open-ended view toward returning after the end of treatment when other issues emerge or problems return. Family therapy is seen not as a panacea forever ending all problems but as a resource that may be of value at various times over the life cycle.

Each family therapist should have a clearly articulated view of ending (Lebow, 1984, 1987a, 1987b). The therapist cannot control how and when termination will occur but can bring an informed attitude to the endeavor. The therapist does best to have a generic template for ending that can be adapted to the wide-ranging sets of circumstances that may present. This template should include a plan for completing the essential tasks at ending and a set of contingencies for what to do in various circumstances. At the same time, the therapist must remain a feeling individual, involved in the very human experience of parting. The therapist's thoughts, feelings, and attitudes about ending require careful self-examination. With such an informed view of termination, treatment can end better, have more durable effects, and enable timely use of therapy in the future.

## References

Bischoff, R., & Sprenkle, D. (1993). Dropping out of marital and family therapy: A critical review of research. *Family Process, 32,* 353–376.

Bowen, M. (1978). *Family therapy in clinical practice.* Northvale, NJ: Jason Aronson.

Carter, B., & McGoldrick, M. (1989). *The changing family life cycle.* Needham Heights, MA: Allyn & Bacon.

Combrinck-Graham, L. (1981). Termination in family therapy. In A. S. Gurman (Ed.), *Questions and answers in the practice of family therapy* (pp. 505–509). New York: Brunner/Mazel.

Gurman, A. S. (1978). Contemporary marital therapies. In T. Paolino & B. McCrady (Eds.), *Marriage and marital therapy* (pp. 445–566). New York: Brunner/Mazel.

Gurman, A. S. (1981). Integrative marital therapy: Toward the development of an interpersonal approach. In S. Budman (Ed.), *Forms of brief therapy* (pp. 415–460). New York: Guilford Press.

Gurman, A. S., Kniskern, D., & Pinsof, W. (1978). Research in marital therapy. In S. Garfield & A. Bergin (Eds.), *Handbook of psychotherapy and behavior change* (2nd ed.; pp. 565–624). New York: Wiley.

Heath, A. (1985). Ending family therapy. *Family Therapy Collections, 14*, 33–40.

Hoffman, L. (1982). *Foundations of family therapy*. New York: Basic Books.

Jacobson, N. (1991). Toward enhancing the efficacy of marital therapy and marital therapy research. *Journal of Family Psychology, 4*, 373–393.

Kramer, C. (1980). *Becoming a family therapist*. New York: Human Sciences Press.

Lebow, J. L. (1984). On the value of integrating approaches to family therapy. *Journal of Marital and Family Therapy, 10*, 127–138.

Lebow, J. L. (1987a). Developing a personal integration in family therapy: Principles for model construction and practice. *Journal of Marital and Family Therapy, 13*, 1–14.

Lebow, J. L. (1987b). Integrative family therapy: An overview of major issues. *Psychotherapy, 40*, 584–594.

Mikesell, R. H. (1994, August). *Surviving managed care with a fee for service practice*. Paper presented at the annual convention of the American Psychological Association, Los Angeles, CA.

Minuchin, S., & Fishman, C. (1981). *Family therapy techniques*. Cambridge, MA: Harvard University Press.

Napier, A. Y., & Whitaker, C. A. (1978). *The family crucible*. New York: Harper & Row.

Pinsof, W. M. (1983). Integrative problem-centered therapy: Toward the synthesis of family and individual psychotherapies. *Journal of Marital and Family Therapy, 9*, 19–35.

Talmon, M. (1990). *Single session therapy*. San Francisco: Jossey-Bass.

Treacher, A. (1989). Termination in family therapy. *Journal of Family Therapy, 11*, 135–147.

Watzlawick, P., Weakland, J., & Fisch, R. (1974). *Change: Principles of problem formation and problem resolution*. New York: Norton.

Wetchler, J. L., & Ofte-Atha, G. R. (1993). Empowering families at termination. *Journal of Family Psychotherapy, 4*, 33–44.

Wynne, L., McDaniel, S., & Weber, T. (1986). *Systems consultation: A new perspective for family therapy*. New York: Guilford Press.

# PART II
# DEVELOPMENTAL ISSUES IN FAMILIES

# Introduction

For those involved in studying families, there seems to be an orderly quality about the study of individual human development that is somehow harder to come by in family development. It seems as if developmental theories of the individual, such as those of Piaget and Erikson, have us marching through our lives, one developmental sequence following the other in a neat and invariant sequence. Not so for the theories issuing from the study of family development.

In the early years of the family therapy movement, therapists tended to believe there was a "normal" family and that we would eventually be able to define the normal stages such a family would go through. Our ideas of what constituted this normal family seem now, with the wisdom of hindsight, more a product of our unintentional cultural biases than the reality of families' lives. Even now, every time we think we are developing a perspective on how families develop, we become more aware of the wide variance in contemporary families.

The issues this awareness of diversity raises are many. In this section we will explore: How does family development and family therapy differ when working with the multicrisis poor? With stepfamilies? With later life families? In Parts V, VI, and X, other issues related to diversity in families are taken up, but here we want to stress a life cycle approach more systematically in this regard.

The section begins with a chapter presenting a model that will help to organize our thoughts about how families grow and develop in general, laying the groundwork for chapters to follow. In "The Family Life Cycle: Phases, Stages, and Crises," Randy Gerson illustrates in broad strokes the ways in which people couple, how families expand, and how, eventually, they contract. Given this rhythm of family development, the author focuses on general life cycle stages; the practical, emotional, and relational challenges of each stage; and, finally, the potential crises inherent in each.

Patricia Minuchin, in "Children and Family Therapy: Mainstream Approaches and the Special Case of the Multicrisis Poor," alerts us to the importance of directly observing children as we treat families, rather than the reliance on parental report alone. She reexamines the issues of hierarchy and boundaries in light of current theoretical challenges and the diverse family forms the therapist is likely to encounter in working with the poor. She reminds us that families frequently come into therapy with "stage-specific problems rooted in their inability to manage particular developmental issues." Then, she relates these issues to the special problems imposed by poverty, which often results in families that move from crisis to crisis and from agency to agency, caught in a maze of systems that many times hinder rather than help. Finally, she provides rich clinical data and a wide range of treatment suggestions.

Stepfamilies are now so commonplace as to be normative, and yet they are still surrounded by myths. In "Systems-Oriented Therapy With Stepfamilies," James Bray dispels some of those myths before exploring the diverse structures these families take. On the basis of his longitudinal study of stepfamilies during the first 10 years after remarriage, he describes the predictable developmental stages and tasks associated with stepfamily life. Examining additional research, he begins to tease out the characteristics that distinguish functional stepfamilies from those that require interventions. Finally, using a case example, Bray illustrates how psychoeducational and strategic interventions can be used to help stepfamilies adjust.

Older persons are both the fastest-growing segment of the population and the least-examined group with regard to systems-oriented therapy. Cleveland Shields, Deborah King, and Lyman Wynne begin to rectify this situation in "Interventions With Later Life Families." The authors use a strength–vulnerability model, which looks at strength factors, vulnerability factors, health factors, and risk factors arising from the individual and family life cycle. Using this model, they examine how to assess the elderly and their families from a life cycle and process-oriented perspective and describe a five-level biopsychosocial model of intervention. This model, richly illustrated with case examples, stresses intervention for problems in problem solving, communication, and attachment–caregiving.

# CHAPTER 5

# THE FAMILY LIFE CYCLE: PHASES, STAGES, AND CRISES

*Randy Gerson*

*All the world's a stage,*
*And all the men and women merely*
  *players:*
*They have their exits and their entrances;*
*And one man in his time plays many*
  *parts,*
*His acts being seven ages.*

> *William Shakespeare*
> As You Like It, *Act II, Scene 7*

All families change over time. Many of these changes are obvious and typical: A family is formed; children are born; and they grow up, go to school, and eventually leave home to form their own families. Others, such as divorce and remarriage, are not as predictable but still common in modern family life. Each transition requires the family to change, to reset priorities, and to reorganize to meet the challenges of the new life cycle stage. Therapists can learn much about a family and how it is coping and functioning by assessing how that family meets the challenges of each life cycle transition.

Systemic theorists describe the family as an organized, interdependent system, regulated by a set of norms and rules. The question arises: Organized for what? The not very useful usual answer is homeostasis or survival. Less globally, the family can be seen to organize itself to meet the demands of each stage of the family life cycle. Family assessments should include an evaluation of how well families are man-

aging the organizational tasks at their point in the life cycle.

Family crises often arise during times of major life cycle transitions. These can be particularly stressful times for families. Most of the critical family life cycle transitions (marriage, pregnancy, gaining a new family member, beginning school, child leaving home, and retirement) are listed by Holmes and Rahe (1967) as typical major life stressors and are some of the most salient events remembered decades later (Hurwicz, Durham, Boyd-Davis, Gatz, & Bengtson, 1992). An important advantage of the family life cycle perspective is its normalizing approach to viewing family and individual problems. One of the most significant insights of systemic thinking is the recognition that how we think about personal difficulties greatly influences our ability to be helpful in ameliorating them. The very act of labeling or "pathologizing" behavior can have a tremendous negative impact on a family. The family life cycle framework allows us to describe family crises in a less pathological way that is easily understood and accepted by family members.

The family life cycle is more a conceptual tool for understanding family development than an empirical classification scheme for research purposes. The transitions from one stage to another are rarely clear-cut and may occur over a number of years. Life cycle stages tend to merge into one another, often sharing variations of the same issues and challenges. There is not even the invariant sequence so common in most models of individual developmental stages. Family researchers have often found it more useful to focus on easily quantifiable variables such as years of marriage or the absence or presence of children (Anderson, Russell, & Schumm, 1983; Nock, 1979; Rhyne, 1981; Spanier, Sauer, & Larzelere, 1979). Unfortunately, much of the richness and clinical use of the family life cycle concept is lost in the process.

## FAMILY LIFE CYCLE MODELS

Family researchers have been describing family life cycle stages for decades. As early as the 1950s, sociologist Duvall (1977) had divided the life cycle into eight stages depicting the nodal events of a normal family. Rodgers (1960) expanded Duvall's schema to include 24 separate stages, an unwieldy number for anyone but the most dedicated researcher. Solomon (1973) was one of the first clinicians to use the family life cycle perspective. He proposed a five-stage model of the family life cycle to be used as a basis for deciding the type of changes that needed to be made in family therapy.

Haley popularized the use of the family life cycle in family therapy. In his influential book, *Uncommon Therapy*, on Milton Erikson's work, Haley (1973) pointed out how major transitions during a family's development can lead to increased stress and, thus, be a time when symptoms are most likely to appear in a family. Symptoms are seen as a signal that the family is "stuck" and having difficulty moving on to the next stage of development, and family therapy is the process by which normal family development can continue. Since this critical insight, almost all models of family functioning have included a family life cycle perspective.

The most comprehensive and clinically demonstrated family life cycle model is that developed by Carter and McGoldrick (1980, 1988). This chapter will borrow heavily from their excellent books on the subject. They divided the family life cycle into six distinct stages: (a) the launching of the single young adult, (b) the joining of families through marriage, (c) families with young children, (d) families with adolescents, (e) launching children and moving on, and (f) families in later life. Carter and McGoldrick describe the emotional and organizational challenges for each life cycle stage. In their edited books on the subject, separate chapters are devoted to each life cycle stage and describe the issues, challenges, and common clinical situations for that stage. In addition, Carter and McGoldrick were the first to insist that divorce and remarriage are normal, although sometimes problematic, alternative routes along the family life cycle and should be treated as such.

Carter and McGoldrick emphasized the multigenerational nature of the family life cycle and did not view the family's influence as restricted to one particular household or a particular nuclear family branch. Recognizing the typical American pattern of separately domiciled nuclear family units, they insisted on considering each family unit as an emotional subsystem, "reacting to past, present, and anticipated future relationships within the larger three-generational family system" (McGoldrick & Carter, 1988, p. 168). It is important to maintain this larger multigenerational perspective as we describe the normal transitions of a particular family. The parents of one family are children in another family, each in a different stage in their family life cycle. A family is not isolated in time. What has gone on in the past affects the present and the future.

## UNIVERSALITY

One must be wary of creating a normative straitjacket for the family. After all, each family is different, and there is a range of developmental possibilities for families. Carter and McGoldrick (1980, 1988) are careful to point out they are describing "normal" family development in traditional middle-class America near the end of the 20th century, which may vary significantly across different times and cultures. Equally important, we would not want to give families the idea that there is a "right" way to develop and that their movement through the life cycle is problematic if it deviates from rigid cultural norms.

Carter and McGoldrick (1980, 1988) have paid particular attention to the changes occurring to the modern family, especially for women. It is clear that specifics of family life have changed continuously throughout history and across cultures and dramatically over the past few decades in America. The impact of industrialization, the intermingling of multiple ethnic groups, and most important, the changing roles of women in our society cannot be underestimated. All these influences must be included in a comprehensive understanding of family life and change.

Nevertheless, if we take a broad enough perspective, there are general patterns of change that seem universal to all families. All families must organize to cope with multiple entrances (births) and exits (deaths) of its members. People have been coupling, having families, growing up in families, and leaving families to start their own families since the beginning of recorded history. There is a natural rhythm to this process. It begins with a coupling or a decision to join together and form a new family. Then there is a period of expansion where the family grows in number, influence, and its boundary with the outside world. Finally, there is a phase of contraction where the family shrinks in number, direct influence, and boundary. But even as one family unit is contracting, it is sending its offspring to couple and begin the process all over again.

## FAMILY GROWTH PHASES

In broad strokes, I will describe the family developmental process as three distinct phases of growth: coupling, expansion, and contraction. Later, I will describe specific transitional stages within each phase.

## Coupling

Before a new family can begin, there must be a coupling (i.e., two people coming together to create a family; see Figure 1). This usually involves marriage, but a same-sex couple may form a family unit without a formal or legal marriage. Modern reproductive technology even allows such couples to produce offspring. In some cases, as with single parent families, one parent may depart after the coupling and leave the other parent and child to constitute the new family. Nevertheless, the initial coupling is usually a necessary prerequisite in the formation of a family. Single people without children living communally may call themselves a "family," but they show few of the predictable transitions described in this chapter.

Often, there is a preliminary time, ranging from years to decades, for each partner to prepare for coupling. They are unattached young adults. During such time, the future partner separates from family of origin and learns to develop and maintain self in work and other social networks. A portion of this period is usually spent in searching for a suitable partner: meeting, dating, courting, and learning to establish a lasting relationship.

Most people see the decision to couple as simply a joint choice of two people deciding to commit to one another. However, from a family systems perspective, marriage is more than just the union of two people who love each other. It is the merger of two family branches to create a new family unit that will perpetuate many of the antecedent patterns and traditions. Loyalty conflict is endemic in this situation because each partner represents to some extent the survival of his or her family history. Most people are unaware of their role in this intergenerational process (Bowen, 1978).

Once the coupling is accomplished, the challenge is to form a stable relationship as a foundation for further family growth. This involves both commitment and the establishment of a boundary around their relationship that defines them as a couple. Partners must move from dependence or independence to interdependence. They must learn to negotiate their different needs. In modern times, this has been made more difficult by the concept of romantic love, which suggests there should not be such differences. This has been particularly problematic for women whose status has not benefited by the traditional marital status quo (McGoldrick, 1988).

Further complications involve the loyalty ties to each partner's family of origin. On the one hand, excessive allegiance to the original family can prevent the stabilization of the new coupling. On the other hand, a cutoff or negative overreaction to the family

Unattached young adults    Meeting and courtship    Commitment boundary around relationship

FIGURE 1. **Coupling phase of the family life cycle.**

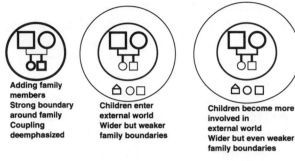

**Adding family members**
**Strong boundary around family**
**Coupling deemphasized**

**Children enter external world**
**Wider but weaker family boundaries**

**Children become more involved in external world**
**Wider but even weaker family boundaries**

FIGURE 2. **Expansion phase of the family life cycle.**

of origin can break the support of generational continuity and perpetuate unresolved emotional issues. The challenge is for the couple to see themselves as a couple while maintaining ties to their families of origin.

## Expansion

With the birth of children, the family begins to expand rapidly (see Figure 2). The addition of new family members requires the couple to make major adjustments. With increased caretaking responsibilities and minimal social support, parents may feel overburdened. The coupling may suffer. One or both parents may even resist the changes necessary to become effective parents.

Initially, there is a strong boundary around the family. The parents are protective of the children and monitor carefully their contact with those outside the family. As the expansion continues, the children begin to interact increasingly outside the immediate family unit. Children attend school and develop peer friendships. Parents interact with schools and other

children and their parents. Concurrently as the family boundary becomes wider, it becomes more permeable as parents have less control over the nature of these interactions.

The challenge for the parents is to balance the children's need for continued support with the development of autonomy and self-reliance. Widening the boundaries too quickly creates insecurity for the child, whereas overprotectiveness and overcontrol inhibit the natural growth process.

## Contraction

Eventually, the children expand into a social world into which the parents cannot follow. This is usually the beginning of adolescence. At this point, children are caught halfway between the family and the external world. As the last child enters this period, the family begins to contract (see Figure 3). A more permeable boundary is needed to allow the child to move freely between the family and the ever-beckoning outside world. Adolescence is a time for children to prepare to leave the family. At the same time, the parents must prepare for the contraction in their relational world and often must attend to both their individual needs and needs as a couple for the first time in many years.

The family contracts further as the first and eventually the last child is launched. Finally, the boundary has contracted so much that only the couple remains. The outcome can be a depressing sense of an "empty nest" or the "golden years," depending on how the couple reconstitute their coupling. The challenge of the contraction phase is the successful preparation and launching of the children and rediscovery of the coupling relationship. When this is not done well, a child may be caught in the contraction phase and may sacrifice his or her functioning to remain with the family orbit (Haley, 1980).

Figure 3 overemphasizes the contraction process for illustrative purposes. In fact, as children leave home and start their own families, they never completely leave the orbits of their family of origin. In addition, even as their caretaking responsibilities may decrease in relation to their children, they often increase in relation to their aging parents. A more accurate depiction would show children at all ages within the boundaries of their extended family. This

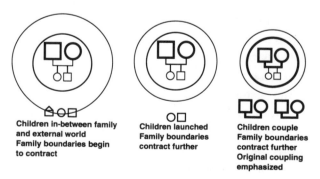

**Children in-between family and external world**
**Family boundaries begin to contract**

**Children launched**
**Family boundaries contract further**

**Children couple**
**Family boundaries contract further**
**Original coupling emphasized**

FIGURE 3. **Contraction phase of the family life cycle.**

is illustrated in Figure 4, which shows a number of nuclear families in different phases of coupling, expansion, and contraction, all enclosed within the dotted boundary of the larger extended family. This again emphasizes the importance of looking at the family life cycle in its multigenerational context.

## FAMILY LIFE CYCLE STAGES

Having broadly tracked the different phases of family growth, we will now delineate the specific transitions or stages occurring during each phase and use the stages outlined by Carter and McGoldrick (1988). The practical, emotional, and relational challenges at each stage will be examined (see Table 1). It is im-

portant to remember that the details of each stage are specific to the particular class, culture, and historical period in which they occur (i.e., late 20th-century middle-class America).

## Unattached Young Adult

The first stage marks the beginning of the coupling phase. In this stage the practical challenge for the unattached young adult is to establish some level of financial independence and the ability to live on his or her own. The extent of independence expected has varied widely historically and across gender. In the past, men have been expected to be more economically autonomous than women. In the first half

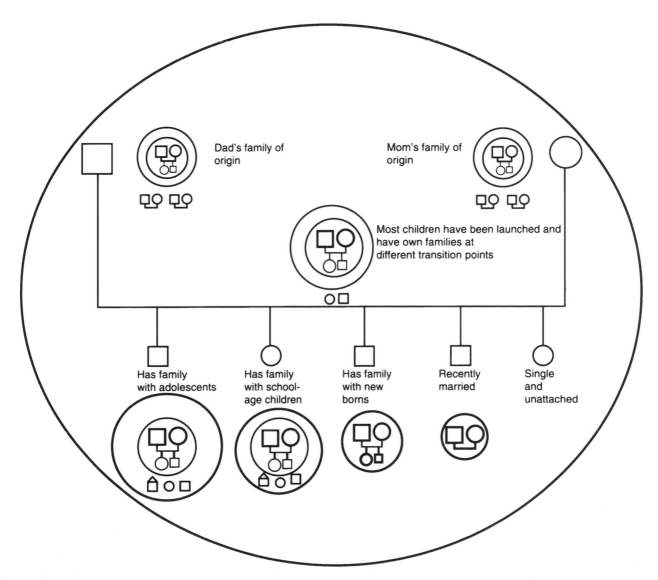

**FIGURE 4. Multiple family life cycles in the multigenerational family.**

of this century, both men and women frequently lived with their families until they married. More recently, both sexes during this stage are likely to develop livelihoods and often establish their own domiciles separate from their families.

The emotional challenge for the young adult is to develop a strong and secure sense of self. This is described by Erikson (1959/1980) as identity formation, a perception of who one is and how one fits into society, and by Bowen (1978) as the development of a "solid self" (i.e., a sense of one's own beliefs and convictions that are not simply adaptive to others). The young adult at this stage should develop the emotional resources to function on his or her own.

The relational challenge is differentiation from one's family of origin. Bowen (1978) describes this as the ability to maintain a sense of self while also maintaining connection with emotionally significant others, usually one's family of origin. Much of the psychological literature has described the relational process at this stage in terms of separation, individuation, and autonomy. Gilligan (1982) and others have rightly pointed out that this emphasis reflects a

## TABLE 1

### Family Life Cycle Phases, Stages, and Crises

| Phases | Family life cycle stage | Practical challenges | Emotional challenges | Relational challenges | Potential crises |
|--------|------------------------|---------------------|---------------------|----------------------|------------------|
| Coupling | Unattached young adult | Financial independence<br>Caretaking of self | Secure sense of self<br>Feelings of competency | Differentiation of self from family of origin | Failure to grow up |
| | Family formation through coupling | Finding potential mate<br>Economic partnership<br>Domestic cooperation<br>Compatibility of interests | Commitment<br>Balancing needs and expectations of self and partner | Form stable marital unit<br>Shifting allegiances from family of origin to new family | Failure to find a mate or commit<br>End of "honeymoon"<br>In-law conflict |
| Expansion | Family with young children | Financial obligations<br>Organizing household for raising children | Accepting new members<br>Nurturance<br>Parental responsibilities | Maintaining marital unit<br>Integrating grandparents and other relatives | Marital dissatisfaction<br>School and behavior problems |
| Contraction | Family with adolescents | Less predictable routines and schedules<br>Adolescent unavailability | Flexibility with change<br>Sense of irrelevance<br>Loss of control | Maintaining contact between parents and adolescent<br>Caring for elderly parents | Adolescent rebellion |
| | Launching children and moving on | Financial burdens (college, weddings, etc.)<br>New financial resources<br>Refocus on work | Loss of family life with children<br>Aging and death of parents | Reestablishing primacy of marriage<br>Adult relationships with children | "Empty nest"<br>Children returning home |
| | Family in later life | Uncertainties of old age: economic insecurities<br>Medical care | Coping with loss<br>Maintaining dignity despite decline | Maintaining adequate support systems<br>Reconciliation | Retirement<br>Illness and death |

male bias toward individuality and ignores the equally important values of relatedness and family connectedness. Finding the balance between what Bowen calls the forces of "togetherness" and "individuality" is a major task at this stage.

## Family Formation Through Coupling

Coupling is established in the second stage. The practical challenge is the formation of a viable, workable partnership. Whatever else marriage may be, it is an economic partnership and usually a shared residential arrangement. Additionally, the couple must agree on their allocation of leisure time and their degree of companionship.

The emotional challenge of long-term coupling is for each partner to adjust his or her needs and wants to the demands of the relationship. This requires a commitment to the relationship beyond one's own immediate needs. This can be particularly difficult because the expectations and hopes at the beginning of a relationship are often so elevated. In the flush of early love, everything seems possible. Inevitably, differences become apparent, and the disappointment that each partner will not get everything he or she wants emerges. Coming to terms with this disappointment and negotiating an equitable, relatively mutually satisfying arrangement is the task at hand, beginning in courtship and continuing throughout the relationship.

The relational challenge is the shifting of allegiances of each partner from their families of origin to the new family unit while at the same time maintaining the earlier emotional ties. A clear boundary around the couple is necessary to form a stable marital unit. However, cutting off from families of origin disrupts generational continuity and can lead to fusion and dysfunction in the isolated nuclear family (Bowen, 1978).

## Family With Young Children

The expansion phase officially begins when the first child is born or adopted into the family. The practical challenge of this stage involves the financial obligations and the organizational tasks of raising children. The expense and effort are often underestimated, and parents who are not prepared to make the necessary economic and career sacrifices will often feel overburdened.

The emotional challenge for families with young children is the acceptance of new members into the family. A couple who, before children, is used to privacy and abundant time for intimacy suddenly can become overwhelmed with the demands of a totally dependent creature. Raising children requires a tremendous giving of self (i.e., the willingness to subjugate one's own needs to the needs of a dependent). Fortunately, the bonds of love and attachment make this relatively easy for most parents, although judging by the incidence of abuse and neglect, the stress of such self-sacrifice can be too much at times for some. To compound the issue, parents have, beginning almost at birth, the responsibility of preparing their children for becoming responsible, competent adults in society. As the child becomes increasingly autonomous, this task becomes especially challenging.

The relational challenge particular to this stage is maintaining the quality of the couple's relationship in the midst of the demands of parenting, work, and the multitude of other external demands. With so many responsibilities, the needs of both the individuals and, in particular, the couple are often ignored. The relationship accordingly suffers. Also, at this stage, the respective families of origin must again be integrated and allowed access to their grandchildren. Young parents may expect guidance on rearing children from their parents. In addition, parents who are quite willing to leave newlyweds alone become more interested when grandchildren are involved. After all, the next generation determines the survival of family traditions and patterns.

## Family With Adolescents

The family with adolescents includes both the end of the expansion phase and the beginning of the contraction phase of the family life cycle. As can be seen in Table 1, the transition between expansion and contraction usually occurs sometime in the middle of this stage. Rarely is there a sudden, dramatic turnabout; more likely, sometime after the last child enters adolescence there is a gradual, imperceptible transition from a family whose boundaries are growing to one whose boundaries are shrinking. Puberty signals the phase of adolescent transition (Hopkins, 1983). This seems to be occurring earlier in families as there is a modern trend for both genders toward earlier sexual maturity.

The practical challenge for the family at this stage is to maintain a "loose" day-to-day routine that allows the adolescent to move easily between family, peers, and school. The adolescent's need to be more independent and explore the world outside the family can be very disruptive to family life. Often, adolescents would rather be on their own or with friends than attend family functions. Teenagers may prefer not even to go on family vacations. Busy high-school schedules can be highly detrimental to regular family meals or bedtimes. In early adolescence, parents may feel they are little more than glorified chauffeurs who are finally relieved when the adolescent gets a driver's license. The family routine is constantly changing during this stage.

The emotional challenge during this stage is to remain flexible during a period of intense change. The parents usually cannot help feeling a loss of importance. As the adolescent world is expanding, the parent's influence is shrinking. This is particularly frightening in a world that seems increasingly dangerous to children's coming-of-age. Nevertheless, parents must find the right balance between the expectation of an adolescent's family participation and responsible behavior and the empowerment that comes from doing things independently while learning from mistakes.

The relational challenge is to maintain meaningful contact between parents and adolescents despite rapid changes and different emotional agendas. There may be a good deal of conflict. Parents may resent their adolescent moving emotionally away from the family and fear they will lose their special bond with them. Sometimes parents have to struggle with their own sexual feelings concomitant with their increasing awareness of the child's developing sexuality (Preto, 1988). Parents may have high expectations for their adolescent that lead to blame, criticism, and overcontrol when they fear disappointment. Alternatively, adolescents are seeking more control over their lives and may be contemptuous of parental wisdom or may simply see adults as irrelevant. All these factors

provide a volatile mix of feelings during this period of family life. Also at this time in the life cycle, parents may find it necessary to take increasing responsibility for their aging parents. The middle generation may feel sandwiched in between needy parents and independence-seeking adolescents while trying to maintain responsible positions with both.

## Launching Children and Moving On

This stage is a time of contraction. Family size is reduced as the children one by one are launched into their own lives and families. With parents living longer, the duration of this stage from the first child leaving home until the later years has increased dramatically over the last century.

The practical challenge is a new utilization of resources and focus of energies. Early in this stage of launching, parents may be financially strained to provide their children a good start towards economic self-sufficiency, usually by providing monetary support for college or job preparation. Fortunately, for many parents this often occurs during the peak of their earning capacity. However, following the launching, parents may find themselves in an unanticipated position. For the first time in years, they have money to spend on themselves. They may also feel they have the freedom to pursue new activities, a new career, or focus more intensely on their work life.

The emotional challenge comes from dealing with the loss of ongoing family life with children. Although the family has been contracting for years, the changes are so gradual that often parents are not emotionally confronted with the reality until the last child leaves home. Then, the loss may be devastating as exhibited in the empty nest syndrome. However, launching is rarely a single event process. Children may go off to college and then return home before marrying or getting their first job. The challenge for the entire family system is to tolerate the disruption of comings and goings while maintaining a supportive atmosphere for the dramatic and ongoing changes in the family. Parents are often having to deal with the illnesses and deaths of their own parents. The loss of both children and parents can be a tremendous emotional strain for someone in midlife.

The relational challenge is to reestablish the primacy of the marriage. For some couples after many years of benign neglect of their relationship, they have the opportunity to rediscover each other. Other couples who have been staying together primarily for the children may find married life without children even more difficult. In either case, there will be a refocusing on the couple. Another challenge will be for parents to establish adult relationships with their children. Both parents and children, who have become accustomed to many years in a dependent relationship, may find this adjustment uncomfortable. As the children get married and have children of their own, parents and grandparents often get to know each other as individuals for the first time.

## Family in Later Life

At this point, the family is entering the final stage of its existence. The family has contracted to the original couple. First, one will die, and then the other. Of course, when there are children, the family does live on as the children couple and begin the life cycle again.

The practical challenge is to deal with the uncertainties of old age. These include the vicissitudes of economic security and medical care. Many people look forward to their later years as a time they can retire and enjoy life, free from the pressures of earning a living. Those who save for their later years may actually fare pretty well as long as they have their health. Unfortunately, with inadequate social security and financial planning and the erosion of savings through inflation, many couples face their later years with few financial resources. Children often shoulder much of the economic burden for their parents. The situation is even more problematic when it comes to the decline of physical health. With the ever-rising cost of medical care, families often have to make hard choices about institutionalization and the provision of dwindling resources to sustain dying family members.

The emotional challenge is to cope with loss and physical decline. This is true both for parents and their children and grandchildren. People who have known their parents all their lives as forceful and capable now often find they have to become the caretakers for their parents. For some, it is only in old age that the parents become life-size and not such an overwhelming emotional presence in their lives. The situation is also difficult for the aging parent. People who they have known for years are dying around them. One difficulty with retirement is a loss of a sense of importance. After spending years as a vital contributor to others, some people find the golden years empty and themselves as irrelevant. This can be doubly difficult if failing health also requires an older person to become economically or physically dependent on later generations. As Erikson (1959/1980) points out, the individual life cycle task at the final stage of life is to face impending death with dignity rather than despair.

The relational challenge is to maintain an adequate support system despite the attrition of significant others. One spouse may survive the other for many years. Those years can be lonely unless the survivor finds other significant relationships. Remarriage is not uncommon. Family relationships with siblings and children are particularly important throughout later life. If relationships between the generations are strained, this can be a time for reconciliation. Parents need their children both practically and emotionally, and the children need some resolution in their feelings toward these two important figures in their lives.

## CRISES

When a family has difficulty meeting the challenges of a particular life cycle stage or moving on to the next stage, there may be a crisis. This was what Haley meant when he pointed out how families become "stuck" at a stage of the life cycle. A number of investigators have found some relationship between symptom onset in families and family developmental crises (Hadley, Jacob, Milliones, Caplan, & Spitz, 1974; McGoldrick, 1977; Thomas & Duszynski, 1974; Walsh, 1978). Unfortunately, there has been little research in this area. This is probably due to the problems of measuring life cycle crises and the difficulties of longitudinal research. Clearly, more systemic study is direly needed.

Erikson (1963) proposed an "epigenetic principle" for understanding psychosocial crises in individual human development. His model has eight psychosocial stages. At each stage, the individual is challenged with a specific set of issues (trust vs. mistrust, autonomy vs. shame, etc.). These issues exist for the individual at all stages of development, but each issue comes into play at a stage-specific time when it is most critical that it be resolved. However, because each stage builds on the accomplishments of the last, if the issues of one stage are not resolved, it is more difficult for the issues of later stages to be resolved. Thus, we see the source of developmental snags. This principle applies equally well to family life cycle stages. The challenges of each stage can be seen in some form in every other stage. For example, the challenge of forming stable relationships is present at each stage of the life cycle. At the unattached young adult stage, it is in the young adult's efforts to have friends. The young couple during the coupling stage must form a new domestic unit. The parents in the stages of family with children and adolescents must maintain their relationship despite challenges of raising children. In the launching stage, the couple must readjust their relationship to the new situation of no children in the household. Finally, at the stage of family in later life, forming meaningful relationships is critical for combating the losses and isolation of later life. In other words, the failure to meet the challenges at an earlier stage will have repercussions throughout the family life cycle. The unattached young adult who has difficulty in maintaining a stable relationship will have difficulty finding a mate or staying married. The couple who does not have a stable mutually satisfying relationship will have difficulties parenting together and adjusting to the children leaving home and old age. The unresolved issues of earlier stages of the life cycle make the challenges of the later stage even more difficult to resolve.

We must also look at family life cycle crises in historical context. Bowen (1978) has pioneered a multigenerational approach to understanding family dysfunction. He developed a clinical method of tracking family patterns over several generations and focused particularly on transition points over the life cycle to understand current family problems. Thus, a family's vulnerability to the challenges of each stage of the life cycle is influenced by the family's difficul-

ties at previous stages in both the current and previous generations. Carter and McGoldrick (1988) have illustrated this process by viewing the flow of anxiety in families as moving along both vertical and horizontal paths. The horizontal flow of anxiety includes all the contemporaneous stresses that impinge on people's lives, both the predictable developmental stresses in face of life cycle challenges and those unpredictable events that so often interrupt life (untimely deaths, unemployment, etc.). The vertical flow of anxiety includes patterns of functioning and relating that are passed down the generations: the family's outlook, attitudes, taboos, expectations, labels, and all the unresolved issues of the previous generations.

In summary, to understand a family's current adaptation to life cycle crises, we must examine: (a) the challenges of the current family life cycle stage, (b) the unresolved issues from previous life cycle stages, and (c) the unresolved issues of previous generations. The last two points often come together because families who have difficulty moving on from one stage to the next may be repeating a similar pattern from the last generation.

We will now look at some typical family life crises. This list does not claim to be comprehensive. Admittedly, there are multiple psychological and situational factors related to each of these types of crises, but I will focus here exclusively on the perspective of the family life cycle, examining some, but not all, of the family life cycle snags that may contribute to each type of crisis. In focusing on crises, we run the risk of emphasizing the more difficult aspects of family life. It is important to remember that despite the growing pains of the life cycle, most families feel it is well worth it. In fact, many feel that it is the most worthwhile process that life has to offer.

## Failure to "Grow Up"

### CASE VIGNETTE

*Peter was 35 years old but barely capable of supporting himself. He would hold a job for a short time and then lose it because of some tempestuous outburst. When he became really destitute, he would go back to live with his parents, but they would eventually become unable to tolerate his demands and slovenliness and ask him to leave. Peter did not seem unhappy with his life. He enjoyed his freedom and felt that his parents and married friends were trapped by their "ties."*

Sometimes a family member is unable or unwilling to "grow up" and take on the responsibilities of adulthood. Like Peter Pan, they seem determined to stay in the Never-Never Land of childhood or adolescence. This is a crisis that is rooted in the unattached young adult stage where the young adult has difficulty meeting the challenges of financial independence, taking care of self, developing a sense of competency and a secure self, and differentiating from family of origin. Although this may or may not be a personal crisis for the immature family member, it is usually a crisis for the family as a whole. The family cannot move onto the next life cycle stage if children do not couple. That branch of the family ceases to exist. The parents may tire of caring for children who should be taking care of themselves. Even if children who refuse to grow up do couple, perhaps to find partners who will take care of them, problems resulting from this failure to develop into adult selves will appear throughout the life cycle.

From a family life cycle perspective, the failure to grow up can be seen as an unresolved issue left over from the previous life cycle stage (i.e., that person's family of origin). Perhaps the child is modeling an immature parent who also refused to grow up. Or perhaps the unwillingness to enter the adult world is a reaction to observing parents who often fought and did not seem to enjoy themselves as responsible adults. Or a child unable to function in the adult world may serve to block launching (i.e., keeping the child in the family nest and allowing the family not to move onto the next stage).

## Failure to Find a Mate or Commit

### CASE VIGNETTE

*Sue worried that she would be an old maid. She was 30 years old and still not married. Sue had many boyfriends. She had even been engaged twice. But at the last minute, she would call it off. She always had nagging doubts about whether they were the "right" man for her. She was very selective. If she was going to make a commitment to a man for the rest of her life, she better be sure he was the "right" one. Her parents would always support her in her decisions not to go through with it. In fact, she often had the impression that they did not approve of the men that she dated. Sue would remind herself that it was she who was looking for a life partner, not them.*

Sometimes, mature, responsible children still have difficulty in finding or committing to a mate. They seem unable to find someone to whom they are willing to make a lifelong commitment or who will commit to them. This is a crisis of the family formation through coupling stage. The person seeking a mate is having difficulty meeting the challenges of finding a suitable partner, committing, and shifting allegiances from the family of origin to a new family. Although there is no right time to mate, families may become anxious if the children reach a certain age and are not beginning their own families. There may be pressure for the child to find someone. Alternatively, there may be subtle or not so subtle disapproval of any person the child threatens to bring into the family.

From the family life cycle perspective, it is important to assess whether unresolved family issues are influencing the children's ability to find a partner and commit. As we have seen, someone having difficulty assuming adulthood may not be ready for coupling. Again, we can also go back to previous life cycles. Perhaps the parents felt they had made a mistake in their coupling choices and the children are being careful not to make the same mistake. Children may be particularly anxious about making the right choice if their parent's marriage ended in separation or divorce. Alternatively, the family may be stuck at the stage of launching. Rather than start their own families, children may feel obligated not to desert their family of origin. In some families, there will be one child, often the youngest, whose family role is to remain uncoupled and take care of the aging parents.

## End of "Honeymoon"

*CASE VIGNETTE*

*Bill and Nancy just could not understand why they were always fighting. It seemed that they would argue over the smallest matters. It had not been that way the first year of their marriage. They had been so much in love. But then they started to notice little things about the other that really irritated them. What they had once appreciated in the other had become an annoyance. Nancy used to see Bill's reticence as quiet strength but now viewed it as withholding and stubborn. Bill used to see Nancy's outgoingness as a sweet interest in others but now viewed it as pandering. To make things worse, Nancy began to feel that she was contributing more than her share to the relationship. All she asked was that Bill clean up after himself, but more times than not, it was she who had to pick up his messes. Bill was beginning to doubt Nancy's commitment to the relationship. She seemed more interested in their friends and her family than spending time together with him. The honeymoon was definitely over!*

It is not uncommon that at some point early in a coupling relationship, one or both partners start to wonder whether they have made a mistake. After the blinders of "love" come off, they begin to notice the differences between them. Their doubts about their compatibility may lead to conflict, separation, and even divorce. This is a crisis of the family formation through coupling stage that occurs after the commitment has been made. The couple are often having difficulty forming a stable marital unit and meeting the challenges of economic partnership, domestic cooperation, and compatibility of interests; balancing opposing needs; and coping with each other's families. This crisis can be particularly difficult because of the idealization of each other earlier in the relationship. Often, a partner may feel the other has changed when they are actually seeing that person accurately for the first time. However, each partner may have only showed the parts of himself or herself that he

or she knew would be liked by the other. There is also evidence that men and women often want very different things from marriage (Rhyne, 1981).

Seen from the family life cycle perspective, this crisis seems almost inevitable. After all, each partner comes from two different families with different sets of values, beliefs, and traditions. In addition, unresolved issues from previous life cycle stages can exacerbate this crisis and make it more difficult for each partner to come to terms with the limitations of the other. As with the decision to commit, the decision to stay in a less than perfect relationship can be influenced by similar decisions made by the parents in the previous generation. Children with parents who divorced may find this a more palatable solution than others. There may also be unresolved issues from the launching stage. Children who have not been well-launched from their family of origin may return as soon as it becomes difficult in their coupling. Alternatively, those who cut off from their family of origin, perhaps marrying against the parents' wishes, may see their eventual marital difficulties as proof that their parents were right and an excuse to return to the bosom of the family.

## Marital Dissatisfaction Following Birth of Children

*CASE VIGNETTE*

*The infant was crying, demanding to be fed in the middle of the night. Awakened for the third time, Mary was on the verge of exhaustion. She tried to arouse John, but to no avail. She wondered how he could sleep with a baby crying in the next room. She fumed that she was the one who always had to get up, even though they were now using the bottle. As she stumbled into the next room and fed the baby, she thought about how difficult the last few weeks had been. They were both always so tired. Each had a full-time job, but taking care of a child was also a full-time job. Most of the burden seemed to fall on Mary. And she knew that their relationship was changing. They never had time to talk with each other. Sex was out of the question.*

*John complained that she seemed totally preoccupied with the baby. But, she thought, it was he who wanted a child in the first place. And if he would help more with the baby's care, then maybe she could have some time for herself.*

One of the most satisfying experiences in family life is the birth of a child. Nevertheless, having a child is itself a crisis that makes tremendous demands on the parents. Most parents are probably aware of this but are nevertheless surprised with the demanding reality of adjusting to a newborn. What they usually do not anticipate is the potential for a crisis of marital dissatisfaction. A number of studies have shown that marital quality goes down after the birth of children (Belsky, Perry-Jenkins, & Crouter, 1985; Finkel & Hansen, 1992). This is a crisis of the family with young children stage. In the face of the many challenges of this family life cycle stage of incorporating new family members, including financial obligations, parental responsibilities, nurturing and loving, and integrating the extended family, the coupling relationship often suffers. In addition, new strains often appear in the relationship because of gender roles and in-laws. Gender-specific stereotypes become particularly obvious when it comes to raising young children. Although working mothers are now the norm (Bradt, 1988), mothers are often expected to do most of the parenting with minimal help from fathers. At the same time, husbands may feel neglected by their preoccupied wives. Also, in-laws often become more involved when grandchildren are born. They have an emotional investment in the outcome of the next generation. They may put additional pressure on the parents, particularly the mother, to raise the children according to the family's values and traditions.

From a life cycle perspective, the marital crisis following the birth of children may be the product of both the inherent stresses of caring for demanding children and unresolved issues from previous life cycle stages. If the coupling had been unstable from the start (difficulties at the family formation through coupling stage), then having children, contrary to the popular belief that children can bring a couple together, will probably add further strain to the relationship. Parents who felt their parents' parenting

was inadequate (unresolved issues from the family with young children stage in the previous generation) may feel additional pressure to be good parents themselves, which leads to criticalness of both self and spouse. Parents who have not emotionally separated from their own parents (unresolved issues from the launching stage) may feel obligated to raise their children according to the family tradition and ignore or criticize the input of the other parent.

## School or Behavior Problems

*CASE VIGNETTE*

*Johnny was not doing well in the first grade. This was the second note sent home by the teacher in the same week. He would not stay in his seat and do his classwork and was constantly caught teasing other children. Mother was very upset. How could this be that her "little angel" was getting into so much trouble? He was not much trouble at home. Oh sure, he would get into things at times, but for the most part, they had a very close relationship. She knew how to engage his attention. She planned to talk to his teacher. She wondered if he really understood her child's special needs. The father was more sanguine. After all, boys will be boys. He felt that his child's misbehavior was nothing more than what a little "good" discipline could tame. He just hoped that the teacher would not "baby" his son the way his wife did.*

This is a crisis at the family with young children stage (see also chap. 6 in this volume). The expansion phase of the life cycle reaches a critical point when the first child goes off to school. How the parents are meeting the challenge of their parental responsibilities is now open to public scrutiny. A crisis occurs when the child is reported by teachers or other adults to have behavior or school problems. Parents often hear this as an indication of their deficient parenting. In fact, if the household is poorly organized or the children receive little guidance or support for appropriate behavior, school performance may suffer. The parents may react by harshly disciplining the child or seeking professional help. Alternatively, they may question or blame the teacher or other accusers and become an advocate for the child against an unfair hostile world.

There are multiple reasons why children have difficulties in school, not all because of parental irresponsibility. However, we will focus solely on the family life cycle perspective and how families respond to this crisis. School and behavior problems can be an indication of a family's difficulty in making the transition from an insular unit to one that must interact with the outside world. When a family dreads or resists this transition, children may have difficulty coping with their new environment. If the parents' relationship has been unstable (because of issues not resolved at the coupling stage), the child may resist going to school (school phobia) or be preoccupied at school with what is happening at home. If the parents had similar problems at school (similar crisis of previous generation), they may expect similar problems or overfocus on the school performance of their child. If parents' attachment to the child is overintense because of unresolved issues with their parents (unresolved separation issues left over from their launching), then a child leaving home for long periods of time may be emotionally painful. Finally if education has been the escape route from difficult family circumstances in the past (launching crises of previous generations), then poor school performance may be a particularly charged issue for the family.

## Adolescent Rebellion

*CASE VIGNETTE*

*The parents liked to look back and remember what a nice girl their child used to be. That is, before she became a teenager. Those days were gone. Now, they had to tolerate her loud music, outrageous clothing and hairstyles, and a tone in her voice that always verged on the disrespectful. It was as if they no longer served a purpose in her life. She thought every word they uttered was ridiculous or, at best, irrelevant. They worried incessantly that she might be involved in sex, drugs, or something worse that they couldn't even imagine. Once they*

*had tried to totally restrict her behavior and not allow her to spend any time with her friends, but she had made their lives so miserable that eventually they gave in. After all, they couldn't restrict her for the rest of her life. And then there were the rare times when she let down her guard and for a few brief moments became their little girl again.*

This crisis of rebellion during the adolescence stage is a common scenario in American life. For many families, it is a rite of passage that signals the transition from childhood to adulthood. Theorists have viewed it as necessary for some children to develop a sense of identity and autonomy (Erikson, 1959/1980; Montemayor, 1986). The course of this crisis can be highly influenced by how the parents meet the challenges of the family with adolescents stage: maintaining flexibility with change and coping with a sense of irrelevance and loss of control. Inflexible parents who are overprotective may actually exacerbate the rebellion (Kelly & Goodwin, 1983; Pardeck & Pardeck, 1990; Peterson, Rollins, & Thomas, 1985). Alternatively, frustrated or preoccupied parents who totally abdicate responsibility and provide little support or guidance may abandon their children when they need protection from making irreversible mistakes. Parents must maintain some contact with their adolescent if they are to be there for the adolescent when their child really needs them. Finding the balance between parental tolerance and guidance is the major challenge of this crisis.

From a life cycle perspective, the severity of this crisis may be influenced by unresolved issues of earlier life cycle stages. Parents who were never able to manage their children's behavior when they were younger (behavior crisis of family with young children) will find their unruly teenager even more difficult to handle. Estranged or battling parents (because of issues not resolved at the family formation through coupling stage) may have difficulty cooperating or showing unity with adolescents who are often skillful at playing one parent off another. The parents' experiences during their own adolescence (family with adolescents stage of the previous generation) may also play a role in the crisis. Those parents who were compliant as teenagers may have difficulty understanding their child's desire for freedom and self-expression. Alternatively, parents who saw themselves as floundering or self-destructive in their teenage rebellion may especially fear the consequences of their children's behavior. Such parents may determine their children will avoid all their mistakes rather than learn from their own experiences.

## Empty Nest

*CASE VIGNETTE*

*The house seemed deserted. Their youngest child had left home last fall. A home that had always seemed too small now seemed too large. Mom found herself sometimes sitting alone in a now uncluttered bedroom of her "baby," reminiscing about happier times. The couple spent little time together. There seemed little to talk about now that there were no children to worry about on a day-to-day basis. Nevertheless, each was very busy. Mom was preparing to go back to school. Dad buried himself in his work, now finally free to pursue his career without distractions. He did not notice that his wife was distant and preoccupied. He would have never guessed that she was depressed.*

The empty nest feeling is a crisis of the launching stage. At this stage, the challenge is to cope with loss of family life with children and reestablish the primacy of the marital relationship. Couples who have invested all their energies in their children at the expense of their own relationship may find this difficult to do. They may try to hang on to their children or lead solitary, parallel lives. One or both partners may be at high risk for anxiety or depression during this crisis.

Many couples quickly adapt to the loss of the children and go on with their lives (Harkins, 1978; Schram, 1979). After all, with lengthening life spans, most couples have many good years left after the launching of the children. However, unresolved family life cycle issues are particularly likely to become noticeable at this stage and may potentially exacerbate the empty nest crisis. Partners who did not establish a stable couples unit (issues not resolved at the family formation through coupling stage) and continued to struggle with each other in raising children and then adolescents may finally decide to separate or divorce now that the children have left home. Parents who were not able to accept the gradual movement of their children into the outside world (overprotectiveness in the earlier stage of family with young children and adolescent) may now have to face that reality for the first time. Their children may even feel that they have to cut off from their overbearing parent. Those parents willing to accept autonomy in their children are less likely to experience their own midlife crisis (Silverberg & Steinberg, 1987). Finally, parents who had difficulties in their own launching (unresolved separation issues left over from the launching stage of the previous generation) may feel abandoned by their children.

One variation of this crisis is when children return home for brief periods of time. When children are failing or experiencing difficult economic times, they may have to return home for shelter. Couples who are over the empty nest crisis may resent this intrusion. Alternatively, children returning home may prolong the crisis and interfere with the parents' resolution of loss and transition to renewed couplehood. In some cases, children continue to fail and return home, which acts to stabilize the family by short-circuiting the empty nest crisis.

## Retirement

*CASE VIGNETTE*

*It was supposed to be the "golden" years. They would retire and enjoy themselves. They had not anticipated that their savings would be worth so little or that their health would prohibit what they could do. Bob's health started to decline as soon as he stopped going to the office. Always full of home projects he wanted to do when he was working, he now seemed disinterested. He just watched TV and was inactive, bored, and irritable. The change was even more difficult for June. Used to often having the house for her own, she felt that her irksome husband was always getting in the way. Continuing her part-time job, she was often enraged when she came home and the house was a mess, and Bob, idle all day, had not made any effort to maintain a livable home. Often, she found herself wishing he would go back to work.*

Retirement can be a crisis for the family in later life. What is supposed to be a welcome break from the rigors of employment can be a crisis for the family, particularly if the couple is economically unprepared or begins to decline in physical health. Especially vulnerable are those who have obtained most of their sense of worth from their occupations and have not developed other hobbies or interests. Wives in traditional marriages often have a more difficult adjustment with their husband's retirement than the husband (Heyman, 1970).

Again, unresolved issues from previous life stages can have a tremendous impact on this crisis. If the couple's relationship has not been intimate in many years (because of crises in the previous stages), then they may be little comfort or companionship to each other in later years. If the launching of their children led to cutoff or a strained relationship, there may be limited or only superficial contact with the children, which also increases a sense of isolation. Also important may be how the parents of the previous generation adjusted to retirement in later life. With previous generations often not reaching this point in the life cycle, couples may have few models for growing old together.

## Caretaking of Older Persons

### CASE VIGNETTE

*Rick never thought he would have to institutionalize his father. Their relationship had been rocky earlier in life, but in recent years, before his father's decline, they had become friends. He wanted to do right by his father. Dad had always been so adamant against going to a "home." When his father had become so feeble that he could not care for himself, Rick brought him to his house. He hired a part-time nurse to take care of his father during the day. But*

*even this did not work out. Dad's health was deteriorating, and he needed more constant medical attention. Finally, Rick's wife convinced him that putting his father in a home was the best thing he could do. He visited his father almost every day. Still, he felt pangs of guilt.*

Health crises are inevitable at the family in later life stage (see chap. 8 in this volume). The challenge for older persons is to maintain their sense of integrity and dignity despite multiple losses and inevitable physical decline. The challenge for their children is to provide adequate support during this final family life cycle stage. Family relationships continue to be important throughout later life. Older people (over the age of 65) live in multigenerational households in far greater numbers (38%) than is usually realized (Beland, 1987). Only 5% of those over 65 are institutionalized. Eighty-six percent of all older adults have chronic health problems that require increasing hospitalization, medical expenditures, and daily caretaking (Cantor, 1983).

The quality of the relationship between the generations is critical at this point in the life cycle. If the children are unattached (perhaps because of perceived deficiencies in parenting during the childhood and adolescence stages) or cut off (perhaps because of unresolved issues during the launching stage) from their aging parents, then they may refuse to care for their parents or the caretaking relationship may be strained. Abuse of older persons is not uncommon. Alternatively, the children may be at a difficult stage in their own family life cycle (family with children or adolescence or launching their own children) and may feel overwhelmed and sandwiched between two generations with different needs. There does seem to be a need for many adult children to come to terms with their parents before they die, sometimes leading to late-life reconciliations and improvements in the relationship.

## Loss

### CASE VIGNETTE

*What Sally remembered most about growing up was the death of her mother.*

*She was only 12 years old. Her mother had been sick for about a year. At that point, everything seemed to change in the family. Sally always felt so alone. Her father seemed preoccupied with his own grief and worries. Sally was expected to care for the younger children. But there was no one there to care for her. Sally always felt she did not have a normal family life after her mother died. She was determined to have her own family one day to make up for what she had lost. But now that she was her mother's age, she wondered if she would always be around to care for her little girl.*

Illness and death can occur at any point in the family life cycle. The timing of the loss can be critical in determining its impact on the family (McGoldrick & Walsh, 1991). Untimely, sudden, unexpected losses are often the most difficult for a family to absorb. There may be prolonged mourning and survivor guilt. Particularly painful are suicide and the death of a child. It is not unusual for symptoms to occur in other family members during times of illness and death. Posttraumatic responses and unresolved mourning may continue long after the loss and affect later family life cycle stages and generations.

For tracking the relationship between family losses and life cycle events in the family, the genogram is a particularly useful tool (Gerson, 1986; Gerson & McGoldrick, 1986; McGoldrick & Gerson, 1985, 1988). The coincidence of losses and other life cycle crises may overload a family and may make it difficult to meet the challenges of the family's particular life cycle stage. For example, parents coping with the loss of a parent may find it difficult to meet the nurturing needs of young children or the guidance needs of adolescents. Alternatively, a child born near the time of an important family loss may come to serve a special replacement function and receive the intense focus of the grieving parent. (This overattachment can become problematic at adolescence or at the stage of launching.) Studies by Walsh (1978) and McGoldrick (1977) suggest that the death of a grandparent within two years of the birth of the

child may be related to later emotional problems of that child.

From a systemic perspective, so-called coincidences of losses and other life cycle events may not be completely coincidental. The members of a family system may be reacting to crises in other parts of the family and at other times in the family's history. For example, someone may marry or have children shortly after the death of a parent. Although this may complicate the bereavement process, the person may feel compelled or unleashed by the loss to move onto the next stage of the life cycle. Particularly interesting are transgenerational anniversary reactions. This is the tendency to repeat the life cycle patterns of the previous generation. For example, if a loss or tragedy occurred in the previous generation, there may be an expectation, often subconscious, that something terrible will happen when the next generation reaches that same point in the life cycle. A person may fear having a heart attack at the same age his father had a heart attack (Engel, 1977).

The type and timing of the loss in the family life cycle can influence how a family copes with later life cycle crises. A major loss can fixate a family at a particular point in the life cycle. For example, the loss of a young child may make it difficult for the parents to allow the other children to grow up (leading to overprotection in the adolescence stage and potential problems at launching). Or the loss of a parent may result in curtailed parenting and a lost childhood (with unresolved issues about parenting in the next generation). Sometimes, only after a family experiences the unresolved grief of losses long past can they be free to move on in the life cycle.

## Divorce

Divorce can occur at any point in the family life cycle. Divorce is a crisis that disrupts and then propels the family life cycle onto a different course. With divorce and redivorce rates higher than 50% of all marriages, it is no longer proper to see divorce as an anomaly, but rather a variation of the life cycle (Carter & McGoldrick, 1988). Divorce is thus a crisis and then becomes a stage of the family life cycle.

Divorce will be discussed extensively in two other chapters of this book (see chaps. 15 and 16 in this volume). Our focus here will be its role in the family life cycle. Carter and McGoldrick (1988) have described four new stages in the life cycle following a divorce: the decision to divorce, the plan to break up the system, separation, and the divorce. It takes one to three years for the family to restabilize.

The family life cycle continues, but in two separate households, when both parents are involved. Most of the same challenges are still present. The parents still have the responsibilities of raising children. The children still develop, expanding their contacts into the external world, and making increasing demands on the flexibility of the family's boundaries. It may seem that the parents' jobs are even easier because they no longer have to balance the needs of the marital relationship against the demands and rewards of parenting. Unfortunately, this is rarely the case. Bitterness about the marriage and its breakup, unresolved issues that have always plagued the relationship, and the inevitable competition for the children's affections often lead to intense emotional triangles that include the parents and their children (Peck & Manocherian, 1988).

Of critical importance is when the divorce occurs in the family life cycle (Ahrons & Rodgers, 1987; Wallerstein & Kelley, 1980). Obviously, there is relatively minimal impact when there are no children, although a sense of failure may reverberate throughout the extended families. It is families with young children who are at most risk when there is a divorce. Overburdened parents may not be emotionally available, and there is a danger of fathers' losing their connection with their children. Children in elementary school going through divorce seem to have a particularly difficult time and often are very sensitive to the loyalty issues between the parents. Adolescents may be equally sensitive to the demands of divorce and may feel added pressure to grow up quickly. Divorce occurring when children are being launched, as when parents stay together for the children, may delay the process. However, even after children have left home, they may find themselves having to choose sides when their parents split.

In fact, divorce itself can be seen as the failure to resolve earlier issues in the family life cycle. Partners who cannot differentiate from their families of origin

may have a hard time committing to a new family. When a couple does not form a committed, mutually satisfying relationship, it may founder when it faces the many challenges of the family life cycle: parental responsibilities, developing and demanding children, the children leaving home, and old age. In addition, if divorce was an acceptable way for earlier generations to reroute their family path, it is even more likely to be used by the current generation (Mott & Moore, 1979). Divorce is often a failure of the coupling to endure the challenges of the family life cycle, even when divorce may be advantageous for the family and the individuals involved in the long run.

## Remarriage

With the breakup of the original coupling, there is the possibility of a new coupling for one or both parents, which again creates a crisis that shifts the course of the family life cycle. More than half of all who divorce will remarry (McGoldrick & Carter, 1988). With this coupling comes a whole new type of family, what has been variably called stepfamilies, reconstituted families, blended families, and binuclear families. The remarried family is nothing if not extremely complex. Again, the focus will be solely on its role in the family life cycle.

The key challenge of this crisis is the participation of the children in multiple family structures at various stages of the family life cycle (see also chap. 7 in this volume). Children may have two or more sets of parents and possibly stepsiblings and stepgrandparents. A family in the stage of family with adolescents may suddenly become also a family at the stage of family formation through coupling and then a family with young children. The steady progression through the life cycle is no longer unilinear. The multiple allegiances and the varying life cycle challenges across the different family households make the situation ripe for competition, loyalty conflicts, and triangles (McGoldrick & Carter, 1988). The unresolved issues from the divorce and all the earlier family life cycle stages can exacerbate the crisis.

Remarried families can be disruptive for both families with young children and those with adolescents. Remarried families with children are twice as likely to divorce as those without children (White & Booth, 1985). Children with stepparents are more likely to change residence or leave home early than those with both biological parents. Nevertheless, many remarried families do successfully raise children. The key seems to be patience, clear lines of responsibility, and easy access across family boundaries. It takes three to five years for children to develop a sense of belonging to a remarried family (Dahl, Cowgill, & Smundsson, 1987). Adolescents may take even longer. Remarried families seem to function best when biological parents take primary responsibility and allow the stepparenting relationship to develop over time (Anderson & White, 1986; Stern, 1978). This can be a problem when rigid gender stereotypes require the woman to be the primary caretaker even when she is a stepparent. Finally, it is important that children are allowed easy movement across the different family boundaries (McGoldrick & Carter, 1988). Unfortunately, there is a tendency for remarriage of either mother or father to decrease children's contact with their father (Furstenberg & Spanier, 1984).

## THE FUTURE OF THE FAMILY LIFE CYCLE

The more things change, they more they stay the same. There have been dramatic changes in the family over the last century that have accelerated in the last few decades. The industrialization and urbanization of society, increases in the incidence of divorce, the changing roles of women, and alternative family structures have all had their impact on the family. Nevertheless, the general outline of the family life cycle promises to remain the same over the generations. People will couple, families will expand and eventually contract, all in a natural flow and rhythm. As Shakespeare so elegantly said over 500 years ago, family members will always have their "entrances" into and "exits" from the family stage, and each one in their time will play many parts. And for each "act," there will be predictable challenges. Understanding these challenges for each particular age and culture can help us maintain a sense of perspective and continuity and connect our current crises with those of previous generations.

## References

Ahrons, C. R., & Rodgers, R. H. (1987). *Divorced families: A multi-disciplinary developmental view*. New York: Norton.

Anderson, J. Z., & White, G. D. (1986). Dysfunctional intact families and step-children. *Family Process, 25*, 407–423.

Anderson, S. A., Russell, C. S., & Schumm, W. R. (1983). Perceived marital quality and family life-cycle categories: A further analysis. *Journal of Marriage and the Family, 45*, 127–139.

Beland, F. (1987). Multigenerational households in a contemporary perspective. *International Journal of Aging and Human Development, 25*, 147–165.

Belsky, J., Perry-Jenkins, M., & Crouter, A. (1985). The work-family interface and marital change across the transition to parenthood. *Journal of Family Issues, 6*, 185–204.

Bowen, M. (1978). *Family therapy in clinical practice*. Northvale, NJ: Jason Aronson.

Bradt, J. O. (1988). Becoming parents: Families with young children. In E. A. Carter & M. McGoldrick (Eds.), *The changing family life cycle: A frame work for family therapy* (2nd ed.; pp. 235–254). New York: Gardner Press.

Cantor, M. (1983). Strain among caregivers: A study of experience in the United States. *Gerontologist, 23*, 597–604.

Carter, E. A., & McGoldrick, M. (Eds.). (1980). *The family life cycle: A frame work for family therapy*. New York: Gardner.

Carter, E. A., & McGoldrick, M. (1988). Overview: The changing family life cycle: A framework for family therapy. In E. A. Carter & M. McGoldrick (Eds.), *The changing family life cycle: A framework for family therapy* (2nd ed.; pp. 3–28). New York: Gardner Press.

Dahl, A. S., Cowgill, K. M., & Smundsson, R. (1987). Life in remarriage families. *Social Work, 32*, 40–44.

Duvall, E. M. (1977). *Marriage and family development* (5th ed.). Philadelphia: Lippincott.

Engel, G. (1977). The death of a twin: Mourning and anniversary reactions: Fragments of 10 years of self-analysis. *International Journal of Psychoanalysis, 56*, 23–40.

Erikson, E. H. (1963). *Childhood and society* (2nd ed.). New York: Norton. (Original work published 1950)

Erikson, E. H. (1980). *Identity and the life cycle*. New York: Norton. (Original work published 1959)

Furstenberg, F., & Spanier, G. (1984). *Recycling the family*. Beverly Hills, CA: Sage.

Finkel, J. S., & Hansen, F. J. (1992). Correlates of retrospective marital satisfaction in long-lived marriages: A social constructivist perspective. *Family Therapy, 19,* 1–15.

Gerson, R. (1986). *Genogram-Maker, a computer program for constructing genograms.* Atlanta: Humanware, 2908 Nancy Creek Rd. N.W., Atlanta, GA 30327.

Gerson, R., & McGoldrick, M. (1986). Constructing and interpreting genograms: The example of Sigmund Freud's family. In P. Keller & L. Ritt (Eds.), *Innovations in clinical practice* (Vol. 5; pp. 203–220). Sarasota, FL: Professional Resource Exchange.

Gilligan, C. (1982). *In a different voice.* Cambridge, MA: Harvard University Press.

Goodrich, W., Ruder, R. G., & Raush, H. L. Patterns of newlywed marriage. *Journal of Marriage and the Family, 30,* 383–390.

Hadley, T., Jacob, T., Milliones, J., Caplan, J., & Spitz, D. (1974). The relationship between family developmental crises and the appearance in symptoms in a family member. *Family Process, 13,* 207–214.

Haley, J. (1973). *Leaving home: The therapy of disturbed young people.* New York: Norton.

Haley, J. (1980). The family life cycle. In J. Haley, *Uncommon therapy: The psychiatric techniques of Milton Erikson, M.D.* (pp. 41–64). New York: McGraw-Hill.

Harkins, E. (1978). Effects of the empty nest transition: A self-report of psychological well-being. *Journal of Marriage and the Family, 40,* 549–556.

Heyman, D. (1970). Does a wife retire? *Gerontologist, 10,* 54–56.

Holmes, T. H., & Rahe, R. H. (1967). The social readjustment rating scale. *Journal of Psychometric Research, 2,* 213–228.

Hopkins, J. R. (1983). *Adolescence: The transitional years.* New York: Academic Press.

Hurwicz, M. L., Durham, C. C., Boyd-Davis, S. L., Gatz, M., Bengston, V. L. (1992). Salient life events in three generation families. *Journal of Gerontology, 47,* 11–13.

Kelly, C., & Goodwin, G. (1983). Adolescents' perception of three styles of parental control. *Adolescence, 18,* 567–571.

McGoldrick-Orfinidis, M. (1977, October). Some data on death and cancer in schizophrenic families. Paper presented at Georgetown Presymposium, Washington, D.C.

McGoldrick, M. (1988). Women and the family life cycle. In E. A. Carter & M. McGoldrick (Eds.), *The changing family life cycle: A frame work for family therapy* (2nd ed.; pp. 29–68). New York: Gardner Press.

McGoldrick, M., & Carter, B. (1988). Forming a remarried family. In E. A. Carter & M. McGoldrick (Eds.), *The changing family life cycle: A framework for family therapy* (2nd ed.; pp. 399–429). New York: Gardner Press.

McGoldrick, M., & Gerson, R. (1985). *Genograms in family assessment.* New York: Norton.

McGoldrick, M., & Gerson, R. (1988). Genograms and the family life cycle. In E. A. Carter & M. McGoldrick (Eds.), *The changing family life cycle: A frame work for family therapy* (2nd ed.; pp. 164–189). New York: Gardner Press.

McGoldrick, M., & Walsh, F. (1991). A time to mourn, Death and the family life cycle. In F. Walsh & M. McGoldrick (Eds.), *Living beyond loss: Death in the family* (pp. 30–49). New York: Norton.

Montemayor, R. (1986). Family variation in parent-adolescent storm and stress. *Journal of Adolescent Research, 10,* 15–31.

Mott, F. J., & Moore, S. F. (1979). The causes of marital disruption among young American women: An interdisciplinary perspective. *Journal of Marriage and the Family, 41,* 355–365.

Nock, S. L. (1979). The family life cycle: Empirical or conceptual tool. *Journal of Marriage and the Family, 41,* 15–26.

Pardeck, J. A., & Pardeck, J. T. (1990). Family factors related to adolescent autonomy. *Adolescence, 25,* 311–319.

Peck, J. S., & Manocherian, J. R. (1988). Divorce in the changing family life cycle. In E. A. Carter & M. McGoldrick (Eds.), *The changing family life cycle: A frame work for family therapy* (2nd ed.; pp. 335–370). New York: Gardner Press.

Peterson, G. W., Rollins, B. C., & Thomas, D. L. (1985). Parental influence and adolescent conformity: Compliance and internalization. *Youth and Society, 16,* 397–430.

Preto, N. G. (1988). Transformation of the family system in adolescence. In E. A. Carter & M. McGoldrick (Eds.), *The changing family life cycle: A framework for family therapy* (2nd ed.; pp. 255–283). New York: Gardner Press.

Rhyne, D. (1981). Bases of marital satisfaction among men and women. *Journal of Marriage and the Family, 43,* 271–292.

Rodgers, R. (1960, June). *Proposed modifications of Duvall's family life cycle stages.* Paper presented at the annual meeting of the American Sociological Association, New York.

Schram, R. (1979). Marital satisfaction over the life cycle: A critique and proposal. *Journal of Marriage and the Family, 41,* 7–12.

Silverberg, B., & Steinberg, L. (1987). Adolescent autonomy, parent-adolescent conflict, and parental well-being. *Journal of Youth and Adolescence, 16,* 293–311.

Solomon, M. (1973). A developmental conceptual premise for family therapy. *Family Process, 12,* 179–188.

Spanier, G., Sauer, W., & Larzelere, R. (1979). An empirical evaluation of the family life cycle. *Journal of Marriage and the Family, 41,* 27–38.

Stern, P. N. (1978). Step-father families: Integration around child discipline. *Issues in Mental Health Nursing, 1,* 50–56.

Thomas, C. G., & Duszynski, D. R. (1974). Closeness to parents and the family constellation in a prospective study of five disease states: Suicide, mental illness, malignant tumor, hypertension, and coronary heart disease. *Johns Hopkins Medical Journal, 134,* 251–270.

Wallerstein, J., & Kelley, J. B. (1980). *Surviving the Breakup: How children and parents cope with divorce.* New York: Basic Books.

Walsh, F. (1978). Concurrent grandparent death and the birth of a schizophrenic offspring: An intriguing finding. *Family Process, 17,* 457–463.

White, L., & Booth, A. (1985). Remarriage: A family developmental process. *Journal of Marital and Family Therapy, 8,* 59–68.

# CHAPTER 6

# CHILDREN AND FAMILY THERAPY: MAINSTREAM APPROACHES AND THE SPECIAL CASE OF THE MULTICRISIS POOR

*Patricia Minuchin*

*Arielle, age 4, is rough with her young brother, has frequent tantrums, and pays little attention to demands or requests; her parents feel helpless and bewildered. Andrew, age 9, the only child of a single mother, is dreamy and withdrawn in the classroom, has no friends, and does not keep up with his schoolwork; the teacher feels he is disturbed but cannot reach him. Paul, age 11, a juvenile diabetic, is smaller and more fragile than his 9-year-old sister, but he is increasingly interested in participating in sports; his parents are alarmed about his health and safety. Marge and Jarvis, in their 30s, have embarked on what is a second marriage for each, creating a household that includes his son and her daughter; they are happy with each other but find themselves tense and competitive when handling the children of their first marriages.*

Families with children come to family therapy in large numbers. Sometimes the children are the center of the presenting problem: Arielle's behavior, Andrew's emotional withdrawal, or Paul's physical vulnerability. In other cases—divorce, remarriage, substance abuse, or domestic violence—the problems are located elsewhere in the family but are assumed to involve and affect the children. Even if the family approaches therapy with an identified patient and a focused description, family therapists think about context. They are concerned with patterns, alliances, the self in the system, the family story, and the relationships across generations. So Paul's parents are invited to come in with Paul, his sister, and the paternal grandmother, who is part of their daily lives and who grew up with a diabetic brother who died young.

Some therapists, of course, do not include children in their sessions at all, even if the presenting problem concerns a child. That stance often reflects a lack of experience and comfort in working with children, as well as a conviction that child behavior is a function of family patterns and that therapeutic work with the adults is sufficient. As Combrinck-Graham (1989) has noted, however, failure to probe a child's input in the family's patterns or to take account of the child's distress misses an essential tool for understanding and intervention.

In this chapter, I will discuss family therapy with children as it relates to theory and practice in the field at large. I will review concepts that are particularly relevant and describe some of the ways that therapists work with families when children are included. I will then consider the special case of poor, multicrisis families, using the foster-care system to illustrate some of the issues, and will describe some basic principles that govern constructive interventions.

# A FRAMEWORK FOR FAMILY THERAPY WITH CHILDREN

Therapy for families with children shares the general systemic orientation that has marked the field from the beginning, as well as the divergence of approach and the controversies about theory and technique that are currently active. Therapists who work with families, with or without children, carry the marks of their training and beliefs. However, some issues require particular consideration when children are involved, and therapists must adapt their work accordingly. For one thing, the current move toward a "narrative" emphasis in therapy (White & Epston, 1990; Zimmerman & Dickerson, 1994) has limitations in such situations. Young children are multimodal in the way that they think and express themselves, and adult–child interchange is not always verbal. A concern for the behavioral patterns of interaction in families with young children is always crucial for understanding dysfunction and facilitating constructive change. In addition, therapists must deal with two issues that are primary in work with young families: (a) conceptions of power, hierarchy, and boundaries within the family; and (b) the implications of developmental stages, as these define the needs and capacities of children and the realities with which a family must cope.

## Power, Hierarchy, and Boundaries

Whether consciously or not, therapists working with children and their families must take a position concerning the nature of power and hierarchy in the family. The issue is interesting because it is controversial. Systems thinking has generated a clash between some basic concepts of systemic theory and what many perceive as the realities of family life and of society.

System concepts, such as circularity and complementarity, have replaced linear formulations about cause and effect and have proven productive for understanding and treating families. With systems theory as rationale, therapists have brought an extended cast of characters into treatment, expanded the focus of attention beyond the identified patient, lifted blame from targeted members, and emphasized the organization of family life as a source for dysfunctional patterns. However, certain principles have been strongly challenged, including the idea that all parts of a system are equally influential. Haley (1976) pointed out two decades ago that systems theory does not deal with hierarchy and unequal power and thereby loses some of its applicability to human systems. In the current literature, the issue is most frequently discussed in terms of gender and ethnicity. Writers point to the expression of a male-dominated society in the usual organization of the family (Goldner, 1985; Walters, Carter, Papp, & Silverstein, 1988) and to the dominant discourse of a culture that "marginalizes" the less powerful parts of the population (White & Epston, 1990). The issue has equal relevance, however, for families with children.

How does one balance the principles of mutuality and complementarity with the realities of parental role in relation to nurturance, socialization, and control? Therapists do not usually articulate their theories in these terms, but therapeutic practice carries implicit positions. When therapists work exclusively with the adults in a family, for instance, they are assuming that the power for change resides in the adults and that the input from the children is not significant. That linear viewpoint is no longer considered tenable, even in the field of child development, where adult-to-child influence was the dominant orientation for many decades. Theories have shifted to a complex view of bidirectional influence. They take into account child temperament and the cycle of interaction between children and adults, as these factors shape behavior, developmental change, the effect of parenting, and even the arousal of abusive behavior (Maccoby & Martin, 1983; P. Minuchin, 1985, 1992; Thomas, Chess, & Birch, 1968). Therapists who work with young families cannot sensibly avoid recognizing their own beliefs about power and hierarchy in the family or evaluating the ways in which they handle the implications for change.

In the same way that power has become a point of contention, so too has the assumption that normality and deviation can be defined or can serve as a framework for therapeutic work. Critics claim that perceptions of dysfunction and interventions to improve family functioning often impose the therapist's values on the family. They propose a therapy of neutrality or nonintervention, in which the family can produce its own version of constructive reorganization (Goolishian & Anderson, 1992; Selvini-Palazzoli, Boscolo, Cecchin, & Prata, 1980). Whatever the merits of this orientation or the countercharge that therapy can never be neutral in practice, the issues are, again, particularly relevant for families with children. When Arielle's family comes into treatment, it would be a rare, and probably ineffective, therapist who has no preconceptions about what behavior would normally be expected of a 4-year-old or what level of parental control would generally be appropriate. Therapists who work with young families can hardly avoid some framework concerning "good-enough" patterns of parenting or the development of therapeutic practices that take into account the implication of norms.

Therapists must also consider the nature of boundaries in the family, including the permeability of boundaries around generational subsystems. How does a family balance the intervention of parents to guide or discipline their offspring with the goal of granting autonomy to the child or sibling group? How does it assure the ready access of children to parents while maintaining privacy for the adults as a couple or as individuals? And how does it maintain the integrity of the parent–child unit while allowing fluidity across the three generations that include grandparents? The balance varies widely, from one family to another, but in well-functioning families the boundaries also change, as children move from their earliest years to and through adolescence. It is precisely because some families cannot shift customary patterns, as the children grow older, that they enter therapy.

## Developmental Issues and Adaptations

Developmental psychology describes stages of child development and periods of transition when the child must reorganize behavior in response to changing realities and needs. A growing literature on the family life cycle also notes the issues that are preeminent for a family at particular stages and the pressure to reorganize at points of transition (Carter & Mc-

Goldrick, 1988; Falicov, 1988; Walsh, 1993; chap. 5 in this volume). The growth of children, logically enough, is a major source of changing realities. Families often come to therapy with stage-specific problems that are rooted in their inability to manage particular developmental issues, even if they have lived comfortably with the pleasures and pains of earlier stages. They may not know how to negotiate change, as a child moves from infancy to toddlerhood or from the focused behavior of a competent 12-year-old to the wifty, unavailable, boundary-pushing behavior of the young adolescent.

With young babies, the developmental issue is attachment and nurturance, the establishment of a mutual, secure, dependable flow between infants and caregivers. Early bonding can be a major issue, but the birth of a baby may precipitate problems that do not directly involve the child. Therapists may deal, rather, with the fallout that accompanies the necessary reorganization of relationships and activities. The challenge to the life trajectory of each adult and the style of nurturance, bred in the bone of each parent and often differing between them, become immediate factors of daily life. They must be newly negotiated, no matter how thorough any prior discussion. In addition, the presence of other family members, such as grandparents, may be helpful but supervisory and may register differently with the two parents. Studies document that the marriage may become less satisfactory, at least for a time, and that the disruption may be felt unequally by the two partners (Cowan & Cowan, 1992).

With preschool children, families must find a balance between autonomy and control, between the encouragement of the child's enthusiastic exploration of the universe and the necessary limitations that ensure safety and acceptable behavior in the family and with playmates. What adults usually find most difficult is the establishment of controls, and the family may come to therapy because the child seems unmanageable. In other professional hands, the child may be treated through play therapy or medication, but the family therapist is apt to focus on interactive patterns in the family. The therapist looks for ways in which the adults undermine each other's authority, the child escalates unacceptable behavior, and the cycle repeats itself, so that the adults feel increasingly angry and helpless, and the child makes little progress toward the acceptance of limits.

For children in the middle years, from about age 6 to age 12, the world generally expands. The child moves toward a different role in the family, with a larger voice in family decisions and more responsibility for daily chores. Peers become influential, as the child balances the opinions of contemporaries with those of the family, and the school brings the family a new, external perspective on the qualities and behavior of their child. Families may come to therapy because of behavioral difficulties at home, but they may also come because the school reports problems in learning or behavior, and the family does not cope effectively.

All family therapists see the major issues of adolescent development played out in the family, a reorganization of autonomy and control in every area of life, from clothing and music to value systems, sex, drugs, and school. Few families get it right with ease, but some families come to therapy because the arguments have become repetitive, the anger has risen, and the inability to resolve conflict has become a major fact of daily life. The adults cannot agree on how to handle the issues and the adolescent is, by now, a skillful adversary with an accurate fix on parental vulnerabilities. In some cases, of course, the issues have a life-and-death quality, involving drug dependency, suicide attempts, or delinquent behavior.

It would be simplistic to suggest that families exist at a single developmental stage, defined by the age of the child. At the least, there is a dynamic tension between the needs and capacities of the child and those of the adults, who may be dealing with job issues or the care of aging grandparents while they cope with changes in the children. Most families have more than one child, which requires attention to a mix of developmental needs. Parents concerned about the school behavior of their 8-year-old are also aware of the drug culture that flourishes around their teenager. As the children grow, the organization of the sibling group also changes. The siblings may have had a clear leader in the 13-year-old girl and a close alliance between this girl and her 11-year-old sister, until the former developed new interests and

abandoned her sister to the companionship of their 8-year-old brother, whom both girls consider a brat. When a family of five comes into therapy because some problem has gotten beyond them, there is no developmental formula relevant to treatment. To understand what a family is inevitably coping with, however, gives the therapist a framework. More important, it normalizes the therapist's perception. Many families are not pathological, in the sense of an explosion waiting to happen. They are often just stuck, unable to manage the complexities and sense of crisis that comes with transitions, including those that are fundamentally developmental. It is a helpful tool for the therapist, and by extension the family, to see the developmental issues as normal and to work with these as the focus.

## THERAPEUTIC ADAPTATIONS

No two therapists approach a family in exactly the same way. Some never see the children at all, and most vary their contacts by seeing the whole family for some sessions and subgroups or children alone for others. Some send the children for individual therapy, whereas others assume that dysfunction is in the system of interaction and must be treated in that context. The differences are theoretical, and sometimes the stakes are high. In a situation where a 10-year-old boy talked about suicide, agency personnel were alarmed and wanted individual therapy for the boy. The family therapist judged his behavior as not dangerous and was concerned that individual therapy would work at cross-purposes with the family sessions. Judgment, professional competence, and collaboration are crucial, in such situations, whatever the issues.

Given the variety of approaches to working with children and their families, it seems most useful to offer examples of the techniques used in what might be called "child-inclusive" family therapy.

### Child-Inclusive Family Therapy
Special adaptations in therapy that take account of the children apply basically to preadolescents. Teenagers are usually incorporated into family sessions much as adults are. Their verbal skills, cognitive or-

ganization, and ability to sit still are considered to be well developed, although therapists may have particular ways of handling adolescent withdrawal or challenge and may schedule individual sessions that honor privacy, once the family has been seen together.

Most adaptations in family therapy focus on the particular needs of younger children. Chasin and White (1989) offer suggestions concerning the appropriate use of space and toys and note that family drawings, storytelling, and child play are useful, although the purpose of children's play differs from that of traditional play therapy. The latter is usually open-ended and projective to foster the expression of inner fantasies. In family therapy it is usually more productive to set up structured situations that use puppets, stories, and role play to explore perceptions of the real people and behavior in the family.

Chasin and White (1989) emphasize the use of language that all participants can understand, and Cooklin (1993) has described a framework for maintaining a "dialectic" relationship between therapist and child. He notes that it is useful for the therapist to express an opinion as long as children can challenge it. This provides a model for family debates that are not destructive. He asks young children what they understand, keeping track meanwhile of who is in charge, so that family patterns are not undermined ("Do you think mommy and daddy will let you answer alone, or should we ask their permission?"). He suggests mixing humor and serious talk, handling noncommittal shrugs by phrasing questions with two alternatives, and setting up some verbal games, such as asking children to describe a family member ("You know who's sitting next to you? Tell me about her").

Salvador Minuchin has no formula for incorporating children into family therapy, but he has a variety of recognizable procedures (S. Minuchin & Fishman, 1981). If a family comes in with a young child they find unmanageable, he sits back while the adults manage the initial settling down, or he may set up a simple management task: "I want Brian not to touch the microphone during this hour we'll be together." The "enactment" is a way of bringing typical family patterns into the session and allowing therapist and family to work on the implications of this shared experience.

Minuchin uses metaphors that are meaningful to children; for instance, about age and size: "You're 12, but when you kick your teacher, you're 4." It is a metaphor that is easily caught. It is uncomfortable for the child, but implies the child would of course rather be 12 than 4 and allows for recognition of the moments when his behavior is age appropriate rather than immature. The comment "You're 10, but sometimes you're 50; are you your mother's mother?" picks up the "parent-watching" behavior that is burdensome for the child and intrudes on the domain of the adults. Size comparisons, emphasized by asking child and parent to stand up together, are graphic in the same way: "Oh, I see! You're not so very big. So if you're stronger than your mother, you must be standing on somebody's shoulders."

With younger children, Minuchin may have parents play with the child, which broadens the focus from the tension and defeat that are dominating the relationship. Play reinforces the sense of pleasure that is an important part of parenting and clarifies the distinction between areas where the children can have power and those where the adults must be in charge.

In keeping with structural ideas, Minuchin often organizes discussions in subsystems that are not part of the typical family pattern; for instance, having the mother and daughter talk together, while the father and older sister are to remain atypically silent. Or the siblings may be asked to discuss their perceptions and complaints, while the parents are restrained from entering to support or blame. These procedures are partly diagnostic and partly an impetus toward changing the patterns that are typical and dysfunctional. A developmental framework is always implicit, in that sessions with young families generally explore the nature of age-appropriate controls, whereas sessions with adolescents often deal with negotiations about autonomy and letting go vis-à-vis interdependence and the responsibility to family. The whole family is always present at the beginning, but the particular mix of people, as the session goes on or in subsequent sessions, depends on the judgment of what is useful.

In the case of an 11-year-old girl with a hysterical paralysis of one leg, Minuchin worked with three generations and shifted personnel and focus through the month of treatment. Part of the work concerned the permeable boundaries between grandparents and the younger generations, and part concerned the hidden estrangement in the marriage. Both are familiar foci in family therapy and were here regarded as framework for the child's problems. Direct work with the child took many forms. Accustomed to leaning literally on her mother, she was asked to lean on her more distant father instead. She was instructed to teach her father how to limp, so he could later help her walk straight—an absurd piece of theater that made the child the expert, had the dignified father tramping around with pants rolled up, and filled the session with laughter. Finally, the therapist arranged for the construction of a special crutch, and the crutch became a metaphor with multiple meanings: parent substitute, parent catcher, and parent preserver. It was also a bond between therapist and child. It established a medium for playful contact and served as a marker for progress and success in the therapy (see S. Minuchin & Nichols, 1993).

## Treating Specific Problems: Child Sexual Abuse

The field of family therapy has moved toward specialization, focusing on situations of divorce, remarriage, illness, substance abuse, and so forth. There are specific problems involving children, in such situations. Divorce and remarriage bring issues of divided loyalty, multiple authority, and children's search for new roles in the sibling group. The reality of a chronically ill or handicapped child means that the family must balance protection and autonomy for this child, pay adequate attention to the siblings, and maintain time and energy for adult relationships. Such situations do not inevitably demand treatment, but families may come to therapy because they cannot cope with the difficulties. The compendium of Combrinck-Graham (1989) describes family therapy in a number of these specialized areas.

Family-oriented approaches to child sexual abuse offer a useful illustration. In most programs of this nature, it is a basic premise that the treatment for child sexual abuse must always involve the family.

Family members are often the offenders, and other members are usually implicated in that they did not or could not protect the child. The family is also the essential resource for positive change, once the abuse has come to light.

All programs share the assumption that the abuse is maintained by secrecy in the family and that this must be dispelled, but their methods and emphases differ. Bentovim (1992) conceptualizes these families as "trauma-organized systems," in which action has been predominant and much of the "narrative" suppressed. With careful steps that protect the child and move the abuser toward open admission of guilt, he and his colleagues are intent on helping child and family to externalize the story of the abuse and to work toward a shared and more constructive narrative.

The approach of Madanes (1990) is interesting, for our purposes, because she works not only with the family but also with male juvenile offenders, who are often older siblings. Her procedures move through a structured sequence of 16 steps. Concrete rituals for the offender include begging forgiveness on his knees and negotiating long-term "reparations" to the victim. Work with the young female victim concentrates on dispelling blame, on her own part and by others, and on connecting her to the more positive and spiritual elements of her life. There is also an emphasis on establishing a long-term "protector" within the family, although Madanes asserts that this should be a member of the extended family rather than the mother, who has proven ineffective. In reorienting the male juvenile offender toward normal life and sexuality, she sets up a particular connection to the father, as a resource for sexual information and discussion, and emphasizes the reestablishment of love and forgiveness with the mother, as well as the development of a normal protective relationship to younger siblings.

Sheinberg and her colleagues (Sheinberg, True, & Fraenkel, 1994) focus on helping the family develop a more realistic perception of the events and on moving the abused child from a powerless, self-blaming stance to a more positive sense of self. This multimodal approach sets up a variety of family, group, and individual settings for the exploration of the abuse and is described as "recursive," in that material arising in one context, such as the child group, transfers and evolves in others, such as the parent–child sessions. Work with the children includes an array of techniques that provide protective distance and are appealing to the young: puppets, stories, and role play. In one case, Sheinberg used puppets to explore the child's (accurate) sense that her father's mother supported her son and blamed the girl. With the child playing the grandmother, the therapist puppet asked why the grandmother thought the father should not be blamed ("Because he's young; he never had a child before; he didn't know it was wrong") and helped the child to clarify the situation and to form a plan for talking with the father, who reassured the girl.

Like Madanes, Sheinberg and her colleagues look for a trustworthy family adult to support the child. Unlike Madanes, they generally connect mother and child, if the mother is the nonoffending parent, and help them to deal with the child's distrust and the mother's sense of guilt. Both programs recognize that therapy cannot innoculate a child against anxiety and other future problems. The child's view of sexuality and relationships will change, as she (or he) grows, and it will be necessary to revisit memories, fears, and questions from the perspective of new developmental stages. That is best done with the help of family members who are perceived as trustworthy.

An important issue, in this area, is the validity of child reports. Therapists are intent on bringing sexual abuse into the open, but the research of Ceci and Bruck (1993) points to the suggestibility of young children. Their preschool subjects modified their stories, with repeated questioning, from denial to "recall" of events that were described by adults but, in fact, never occurred. The finding is consistent with the established developmental reality, known since the work of Piaget, that young children do not distinguish well between deliberate lies and things that are not so or between fantasies and actual events. The dilemma is very real. It is important to explore sexual abuse openly and to clarify blame, but a narrative of abuse that has been coconstructed by professionals and the child is destructive, places parents on the defensive, and raises the specter of judicial actions that split the family and traumatize relationships. It will be useful for therapists to be guided by

psychological research, although in the end it is the community of helpers that must balance the dangers of false positives against those of false negatives.

In treating sexual abuse, as in other areas, developmental stage is an important factor. Adolescents and adults can entertain multiple perspectives; middle-years children are more literal and rigid; and preschool children are more playful and suggestible. Therapists do not usually specify their adaptations, although it is often implicit in their techniques. In the puppet play with "grandmother," for instance, Sheinberg asks why the father didn't know what he did was wrong: Was he on drugs? Did he have some damage to his brain? The 8-year-old understood; a 4-year-old would not have gotten the point. Future clinical research is needed to further specify the adaptations therapists make to developmental stage.

## CHILDREN IN POOR, MULTICRISIS FAMILIES: A DIFFERENT REALITY

Poor, multicrisis families with children present a challenge to the mental health profession, which has been little involved with their welfare. They have generally been served by the large institutions of society, which follow social and judicial mandates, and there has been little understanding of psychological complexities. Although social concern has centered on the young, procedures to save the children have often backfired, compounding the trauma and damage they are designed to alleviate.

When considering the needs of this population, it is not possible to directly apply the ideas and procedures discussed earlier. Family therapists generally deal with middle-class families: coherent entities with discernible boundaries, even when they are complex and troubled. Their children start life in a small society that guides experience, stimulation, and the expansion of contact with kin and strangers. When there are problems, it is reasonable to demarcate the family as the crucial unit for therapy, assuming that dysfunctional patterns are located here and that beneficial change can take place within these borders. Not so for the multicrisis poor. This is not the experience of their children, and this is not usually the sufficient unit for intervention.

To understand these families, we must see them in the context of the disorganized, often violent neighborhoods in which they are frequently embedded and in relation to the social institutions that intervene to monitor and offer help (see also chap. 20 in this volume). The amorphous nature of boundaries around families is one of the basic facts of life. Their stories are coconstructed with the many representatives of society's larger systems, and the official record may have little of the family's own understanding of what has happened to them and what they need.

When family therapists enter such situations, they need to understand that they are entering a system much more complex than the family. In these circumstances, questions of power, hierarchy, boundaries, and developmental stage take on new meaning. In the following sections, I will revisit these topics and focus on the situation of foster care.

## Children and Families in Foster Care[1]

Children from all levels of society may be placed in foster care, but the majority come from poor, multicrisis families, and they are often from minority, ethnically diverse backgrounds.

The foster-care system varies by state and region. However, certain features are typical, particularly in areas where protective services are understaffed and overworked and where there are a large number of troubled and disorganized families. The basic purpose of foster care, presumably, is to offer respite to a family during a period of difficulty, so that problems can be dealt with, the family can be reunited, and the children can be safely cared for at home. In fact, the process often works against that outcome, starting with the first investigative procedures and continuing through the period of placement.

When protective services are informed that children are being neglected or abused, an investigator goes to the home. The case may be dismissed or other services provided, but the decision is often made to remove the children from the family. That

decision may be essential for the protection of the children. However, it is sometimes guided by a reaction to poverty in the living conditions, by inadequate information about family members as resources, and by a system-wide sensitivity to media crusades. The trauma of separation for child and family is not generally understood or dealt with. Once the child is placed, the biological family may not know where the child lives, may have only biweekly visiting times on agency premises, and may have little or no contact with the foster family. The child may move from one placement to another and may stay in foster care for months or years.

Whatever the rationale for these procedures, there are psychological byproducts that do not command sufficient attention: the confusion and trauma of abrupt separations for the child, the depowering effect on parents who are already overwhelmed and disorganized, and the missed opportunity to work constructively with the newly created system of foster and biological families. The recent trend toward family preservation and reunification is a positive development, but it has not been accompanied by a sufficiently complex understanding of the need for procedures that reduce trauma and build family competence.

## Power, Hierarchy, and Boundaries Revisited

The issues of family power discussed earlier are not primary here. Children born into poor, multicrisis families grow up with a different understanding of authority and family boundaries. They do not share the evolutionary experience described in the child-development literature, whereby young children see their parents as all-powerful and reliable, until those perceptions are gradually modified. In these families, authority and hierarchy are often erratic; the behavior of adults fluctuates as a function of drugs, unmanageable problems, and a context of violence. In addition, the children learn early that these adults are not in charge. Official helpers and inspectors enter the family, often unbidden, or are sought out as

---

[1] The material in this section is based on the work of Family Studies, Inc., a New York training center, which has been involved with public agencies and the foster-care system of New York City for several years.

the pathway to housing, health care, and other necessities. The children absorb the fact that the family is not self-contained; and when they wait long hours in clinics or watch the paralysis of their parents when the workers come to investigate, they understand that their parents have little power and do not make the important decisions. In the growing literature on family-based services for the poor, *empowerment* is the most important concept and goal.

The foster-care situation compounds the problem. As the process unfolds, children see a hierarchy of power, in which family adults are at the bottom. When the caseworker comes to the house, accompanied by a policeman, to take the infant, the 4-year-old, and the 14-year-old son, the mother's power resides solely in persuading the angry adolescent, who is refusing to go, that it's best if he complies and in telling the policeman that Anthony is a good boy and there's no need to threaten him with handcuffs.

Once the children are placed, the hierarchy of foster over biological family is evident. Society has judged one family fit to raise children and the other less so; both foster and biological parents take in the message. When the two families are brought together, the foster parents generally manage the children and maintain order, while the biological parents sit passively, making abortive attempts at contact (P. Minuchin, 1995). Inevitably, the children are confused. To whom do they owe loyalty and affection? Who is in charge, and who must be obeyed? How do these families fit together? The boundaries around the biological families may be amorphous, but the boundaries between biological and foster families are usually impenetrable. It is up to the children to make sense of unconnected life settings, in which they must relate to the members of old and new families, function acceptably, and resolve their anxieties and anger.

In this situation, the morass of authority and relationships is a constant, but it is experienced differently by children of different ages. Infants and 10-year-olds have different histories of attachments, have been differently incorporated into the patterns of their natural families, and have different capacities to understand separation and cope with placement. The matter of developmental stage, therefore, is a crucial

factor in understanding the situation and working professionally in the system.

## Developmental Issues Revisited

The first connections between infants and adults are basic for psychological security. The child-development literature is replete with theory about the importance of early bonding and research on adequate patterns of attachment (Ainsworth, Blehar, Waters, & Wall, 1978). Underlying such studies is the assumption that relationships are predictable and parent and child work out a form of attachment that can be reliably assessed for style and adequacy.

The reality of the multicrisis family is, again, different. Living in chaotic situations and poorly equipped to deal with multiple problems, these parents often have an erratic relationship with their infants: sometimes close and nurturant, and sometimes neglectful or angry. From experience with these families, we know that most of the adults love their babies and that parent and child usually become attached, but neglect or abuse may occur when pressures become unmanageable.

When infants are placed in foster care, questions of bonding become complex: Who is the primary caretaker? Can mother and child relate successfully if they have been separated for many months? Babies who are placed in foster care bond to the foster parents, who become attached in turn, and visits with the natural parents are often confusing and discouraging. When Wilma visited her 10-month-old son, who had been in foster care for 8 months, the child cried desperately, resisted her attempts to soothe him, and reached for the foster mother. In time, he calmed down and responded to both women. If the goal is to reunite mother and child, it is necessary to assume that children can become attached to more than one person. It is also necessary to provide for frequent contact between mother and child, for support in the face of discouraging rejections, and for the willing participation of foster families in facilitating the involvement of biological parents. A model with this framework is described below in the section on intervention.

For preschool children, the developmental issue concerns control and socialization. It is the family's task to shape behavior, deal with challenge, and help the child to accept limits. Consistency and patience are useful assets, along with a sense of confidence in the measured use of authority. This is a difficult prescription for adults who do not feel much control over their own lives and who may have harsh or ineffective models of parenting from their own childhood. Home-based family therapy with these families often concentrates on issues of appropriate hierarchy and control.

When children in this age group are placed, parents and children lose the daily contact through which a family explores workable patterns of control and compliance. The children learn the rules in a different family, and when the biological family is reunited, they are apt to flounder over the small incidents of daily life. Parents and children have different expectations, and the parents may have little credibility with the children for establishing rules.

School-age children who are placed in foster care already have a substantial history in their own family. They are part of the family's patterns; they have established roles and loyalties, differentiated relationships with siblings, and experience in school. When they are placed, they may have difficulty accepting the rules and fitting into the structure of this new system—for instance, as the youngest rather than the oldest child. If they remain any length of time, they and the members of their natural family grow and change; when they return home, children and parents may seem strange to each other. The parents will also have lost touch with the child's experience in school. School systems seldom make adequate contact with parents in poor, disorganized neighborhoods, and they do little to help children adjust to new placements or the return home.

By the time adolescents are removed from the home, they are often victims or survivors of society's major problems; they have dealt with or succumbed to drugs, violent gangs, and the possible concomitants of sexual activity, such as disease or pregnancy. The particular impact of placement depends on the age and characteristics of the adolescent, the nature of the family, and the participation of this youngster in family patterns. In most situations, however, the

developmental challenge of belonging and separating exists, in some form, and foster placement complicates the challenge. A 14-year-old who is placed in a foster home must relate to a new family, not of his or her choosing, at a time when the impulse is to move out and establish more distance from home base, rather than work on family connections. At the same time, the separation from the biological family may be more abrupt and dramatic than is comfortable. For instance, it may not allow for the protective relationship of a particular teenager to an abused mother or for his or her function as role model and streetwise educator for younger siblings. With this dismemberment, as well, the family may have lost the adolescent's practical functions, which jeopardizes further their precarious ability to mobilize resources and cope with life.

## INTERVENTION WITH POOR, MULTICRISIS FAMILIES

Professional work with poor, multiproblem families is best thought of as intervention, rather than therapy. Effective help is necessarily multifaceted. Direct therapeutic work with families may be a part, but it is often ineffective if basic needs are not met and if damaging policies and procedures at the level of larger systems do not change.

When family therapists trained in systemic concepts enter such situations, they carry useful tools. They know that the relevant system is always larger than it seems, and they understand that the relations between subsystems may embody power struggles, even while they provide resources. The skills of family treatment are also potentially useful: the ability to join, manage varied groupings, and search for strength in the system. However, the context is different, and the analogy is partial. Large systems have features of their own. In such situations, it is necessary to focus on system policies that affect the families, as well as on the training of professional staff. An ecological model developed for work in the foster-care system offers an example.

During the 1980s, Salvador Minuchin developed a system-oriented approach to foster care, and his staff at Family Studies, Inc., embarked on a training project with foster-care agencies.[2] The focus of the model was on connections, rather than on fragmentation; on empowerment and involvement of the child's biological family; and on an expansion of roles for professional staff and foster parents. The premise was that separation and placement create a new, triadic system, comprising agency, foster family, and biological family. This network has no history or established patterns. It is in formation, and the way it develops affects the experience of the child and the possibility of family reunification (see P. Minuchin, 1995).

The goal of the model was to create a collaborative system, in which the two families would keep contact and share information. They would function as a kind of extended kinship system, in which the members are united not by blood but by their mutual concern for the children. Such systems are a familiar resource in many cultures and offer informal support and backup child care in periods of difficulty.

During this project, the training staff worked with agency administrators on the revisions of intake procedure, visiting policies, and case management that would allow for more family involvement. They also worked with professional staff and foster parents, facilitating their contact with biological families and highlighting certain attitudes and skills (e.g., an orientation toward family empowerment, techniques for eliciting family strength, an understanding of developmental stage as it affects the child's experience of foster care, and procedures for involving the biological family in planning and care for the children). A *Training Manual for Foster Parents* was subsequently prepared for use by agencies interested in this approach (P. Minuchin et al., 1990).

It is notable that we did not work primarily with the children. Creating change in large, complex systems is difficult and slow. We needed to work first with the adults, from administrators and caseworkers to foster and biological parents; establish basic principles about the importance of continuity in the disrupted lives of the children; and offer our expertise

on how to construct and maintain a collaborative system. The details of contacting and including children in family sessions could not be the primary task.

Is conventional family therapy ever relevant for poor, multicrisis families, or in the foster-care situation? Yes, if it is seen as part of a repertoire or as the natural tool of particular circumstances. In kinship foster care, for instance, family therapy is the treatment of choice. When children are placed with relatives, the shock of separation for family and child is minimized, thereby obviating one of the worst features of foster placement; kinship foster care, however, is not without problems. The extended family already has established patterns, and these may be conflictual as well as supportive. Generational tensions and coalitions that block effective parenting are familiar to therapists who work with families, and treatment may follow conventional lines, clarifying boundaries and functions, encouraging the emergence of members who have been disqualified, and engaging the children. In these situations, issues and techniques discussed in the earlier section on therapy are applicable, although it is never possible to ignore the impact of the courts, child protective services, and the foster-care system on the lives and functioning of the multicrisis poor.

## THE FUTURE

There is a general framework for systems therapy with children and their families, and there are some creative clinical adaptations, but there is also considerable unfinished business. Future efforts in this area will need to use both sharper close-ups and wider lenses. A survey of mainstream approaches highlights the gaps in therapeutic work with young families, especially the failure to deal with the psychological complexity of growing organisms and the need for families to adapt continuously to changing developmental realities. The incorporation of developmental knowledge into therapy is erratic, and it is often implicit rather than articulated, so that adaptations are

---

[2] The project was supported by the Edna McConnell Clark Foundation.

not easily available for study or for the training of therapists.

A consideration of poor, multicrisis families suggests that family therapists must move in a different direction: toward context, rather than toward the elaboration of internal family characteristics. It highlights the complexity of the social forces that interact with family life and reminds us that efforts to combine social interventions with psychological realities are at an early stage. Therapists who work in this arena need to have the ability to intervene in complex systems as well as basic skills for treating families.

In the end, of course, all families should be approached with a specific awareness of their developmental realities, and all families should be understood in the context of their times and their society. The difference in professional tasks, in relation to mainstream and poor, multicrisis families, is simply a matter of priority.

# References

Ainsworth, M., Blehar, M., Waters, E., & Wall, S. (1978). *Patterns of attachment: A psychological study of the Strange Situation.* Hillsdale, NJ: Erlbaum.

Bentovim, A. (1992). *Trauma-organized systems: Physical and sexual abuse in families.* London: Karnac Books.

Carter, B., & McGoldrick, M. (Eds.). (1988). *The changing family life cycle: A framework for family therapy* (2nd ed.). New York: Gardner Press.

Ceci, S., & Bruck, M. (1993). Suggestibility of the child witness: A historical review and synthesis. *Psychological Bulletin, 113,* 403–439.

Chasin, R., & White, T. (1989). The child in family therapy: Guidelines for active engagement across the age span. In L. Combrinck-Graham (Ed.), *Children in family contexts: Perspectives on treatment* (pp. 5–25). New York: Guilford.

Combrinck-Graham, L. (Ed.). (1989). *Children in family contexts: Perspectives on treatment.* New York: Guilford.

Cooklin, A. (1993, May). *Being seen and heard: Engaging children in the family therapeutic process.* Workshop presented at the 5th World Family Therapy Congress, Amsterdam, The Netherlands.

Cowan, C., & Cowan, P. (1992). *When partners become parents: The big life change for couples.* New York: Basic Books.

Falicov, C. (Ed.). (1988). *Family transitions: Continuity and change over the life cycle.* New York: Guilford.

Goldner, V. (1985). Feminism and family therapy. *Family Process, 24,* 31–47.

Goolishian, H. A., & Anderson, H. (1992). Strategy and intervention versus nonintervention: A matter of theory? *Journal of Marital and Family Therapy, 18,* 5–15.

Haley, J. (1976). *Problem-solving therapy: New strategies for effective family therapy.* San Francisco: Jossey-Bass.

Maccoby, E., & Martin, J. (Eds.). (1983). Socialization in the context of the family: Parent-child interaction. In E. M. Hetherington (Ed.), P. H. Mussen (Series Ed.), *Handbook of child psychology. Vol. 4: Socialization, personality, and social development* (pp. 1–101). New York: Wiley.

Madanes, C. (1990). *Sex, love, and violence: Strategies for transformation.* New York: Norton.

Minuchin, P. (1985). Families and individual development: Provocations from the field of family therapy. *Child Development, 56,* 289–302.

Minuchin, P. (1992). Conflict and child maltreatment. In C. U. Shantz & W. W. Hartup (Eds.), *Conflict in child and adolescent development* (pp. 380–401). Cambridge, England: Cambridge University Press.

Minuchin, P. (1995). Foster and natural families: Forming a cooperative network. In L. Combrinck-Graham (Ed.), *Children in families at risk: Maintaining the connections* (pp. 251–274). New York: Guilford Press.

Minuchin, P., Brooks, A., Colapinto, J., Genijovich, E., Minuchin, D., & Minuchin, S. (1990). *Training manual for foster parents.* New York: Family Studies, Inc.

Minuchin, S., & Fishman, H. C. (1981). *Family therapy techniques.* Cambridge, MA: Harvard University Press.

Minuchin, S., & Nichols, M. (1993). *Family healing.* New York: The Free Press.

Selvini-Palazzoli, M., Boscolo, L., Cecchin, G., & Prata, G. (1980). Hypothesizing-circularity-neutrality: Three guidelines for the conductor of the session. *Family Process, 19,* 3–12.

Sheinberg, M., True, F., & Fraenkel, P. (1994). Treating the sexually abused child: A recursive multimodal program. *Family Process, 33,* 263–276.

Thomas, A., Chess, S., & Birch, H. (1968). *Temperament and behavior disorders in children.* New York: New York University Press.

Walsh, F. (Ed.). (1993). *Normal family processes* (2nd ed.). New York: Guilford.

Walters, M., Carter, B., Papp, P., & Silverstein, O. (1988). *The invisible web: Gender patterns in family relationships.* New York: Guilford.

White, M., & Epston, D. (1990). *Narrative means to therapeutic ends.* New York: Norton.

Zimmerman, J. L., & Dickerson, V. C. (1994). Using a narrative metaphor: Implications for theory and clinical practice. *Family Process, 33,* 233–245.

# CHAPTER 7

# SYSTEMS-ORIENTED THERAPY WITH STEPFAMILIES

*James H. Bray*

Over 33% of all children in the United States are expected to live in a stepfamily before they reach age 18 (Glick, 1989). Stepfamilies are more common family structures than in previous generations. It is estimated that there are over 11 million remarried families in the United States and there are over 4 million stepfamilies with stepchildren in residence (Glick, 1988, 1989). The social revolution that began in the 1960s in the United States and contributed to the increase in divorce, remarriage, and single parenting will probably continue through the 1990s making remarried families a normative family form. Given that children and adults from divorced families and stepfamilies have a higher risk of developing behavioral and emotional problems (Hetherington, Arnett, & Hollier, 1988; Zill & Schoenborn, 1990), these demographic trends clearly suggest that psychologists will see more of these families in their future practices.

The name *stepfamily* originated in England and was applied to families in which a parent had died. The prefix *step* is from an Anglo-Saxon word that means to bereave or to make orphan. A steprelationship was established because of loss through death. Historically, the death was most often the mother, thus, most stepfamilies were stepmother families. In modern society it is far more common that a stepfamily is a stepfather family and is established be-cause of the death of a marriage through divorce rather than the death of a parent.

A stepfamily is formed when a man or woman who was previously married and has children from that relationship marries again. The new spouse may or may not have been previously married and may or may not have children from that marriage. A remarried family is one in which at least one partner has been previously married and may or may not have children. Thus, all stepfamilies are remarried families, but not all remarried families are stepfamilies.

More specifically, stepfamilies may be stepfather families, in which a man (who may or may not have been previously married) marries a woman who has children from a previous marriage living with her. The stepfather in this case may or may not have children, but if he does, the children do not reside with him on a full-time basis. A simple stepfather family exists when a stepfather does not have children from a previous relationship. A complex stepfamily includes a stepfather with children from a previous relationship. Stepmother families are the converse of stepfather families. When two adults marry and bring children from previous marriages to live together the stepfamily is referred to as a blended or dual stepfamily. There is no standard term for stepfamilies who have a child in the remar-

This chapter is based in part on a paper presented at the Annual Convention of the American Psychological Association, San Francisco, CA. Preparation of this paper was supported in part by grant RO1 HD22642 from the National Institute of Child Health and Human Development to James H. Bray.

Address correspondence regarding this chapter to James H. Bray, PhD, Associate Professor, Department of Family Medicine, Baylor College of Medicine, 5510 Greenbriar, Houston, TX 77005, (713) 798-7751.

riage. We call children born in stepfamilies "ours babies"—as in his, hers, and ours—or half-siblings because of their biological connection to the existing children in the family. These types of families may be created following the death of a spouse, divorce, or abandonment by a spouse. In addition, there are also nonresidential stepfamilies in which a parent, usually a father, has nonresidential children who visit. In this case the stepparent is a nonresidential, part-time parent. Overall, stepfather families formed following the divorce of the mother are the most common type of stepfamily (Glick, 1988). Stepfather families have the highest incidence because women are awarded custody of the children 85% to 90% of the time following divorce.

Stepfamilies include many different family structures, and they also are referred to by various names. Common names for stepfamilies include blended families, remarried families, reconstituted families, REM families, binuclear families, and second families. Each of these names carries positive and negative connotations. To illustrate, according to Patricia Papernow (1993), a stepfamily scholar, if you have a blended family, then someone must "get creamed," or if you have a reconstituted family, then the family must have been dismembered, split apart, and in need of putting back together. Because of the prevailing myths and stories about stepfamilies, family members—and particularly children—often enter a remarriage with fears and anxieties that are unconsciously reinforced by our descriptions and names for stepfamilies. As therapists we need to consider how the implications of our language, our own biases about families, and our labeling may affect family members.

The term *stepchild* or *stepparent* continues to have a negative or pejorative connotation (Coleman & Ganong, 1990). The familiar folk stories and fairy tales about the "wicked stepparent" persist in our society. The history of stepfamilies explains why there are so many stories and fables about the wicked stepmother and relatively few about wicked stepfathers. Images and fantasies of stepfamilies develop during early childhood as children are exposed to popular fables and stories, such as Cinderella, or unrealistic depictions of stepfamily life through television and movies. These perspectives are reinforced through our everyday language. Referring to the biological parents as *natural* parents implies that stepparents are somehow *unnatural*. Referring to firstmarriage nuclear families as *regular* or *normal* families implies that stepfamilies are *irregular* or *abnormal*. It is important to consider these negative overtones or implications and the impact they may have on the therapy process and life in a stepfamily.

## DEVELOPMENTAL-SYSTEMS FRAMEWORK FOR STEPFAMILIES

It is useful to view stepfamilies as an evolving interactional family system. Research and clinical observation suggests that there are unique normative issues and tasks that occur during the stepfamily life cycle (Bray & Berger, 1992, 1993a; Bray, Berger, Silverblatt, & Hollier, 1987; McGoldrick & Carter, 1980; Whiteside, 1982). Relationships in stepfamilies change over time and are affected by previous individual and family experiences, developmental issues within the stepfamily, and developmental issues for individual family members. Marital and family experiences during the first marriage, separation, and divorce may have a great impact on the functioning of the stepfamily (Bray & Berger, 1993a; Hetherington, Cox, & Cox, 1982). Thus, the multiple developmental trajectories of family members and the stepfamily life cycle are important to consider in understanding the functioning of stepfamilies.

Forming a stepfamily with young children is likely to be different than forming a stepfamily with young adolescents because of the differing developmental needs of children and adolescents. The stepfamily life cycle and individual developmental issues may be congruent, as in the case of a new stepfamily with young children, or may be quite divergent, as in the case of a new stepfamily with adolescents (see Figure 1). The developmental issues are congruent in new stepfamilies with young children because both the children and stepfamily need close, cohesive family relationships. The centripetal forces of stepfamily formation coincide with the need that young children have for affective involvement and structure. In the latter case, the stepfamily is moving to develop a

**A**

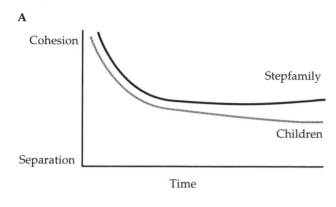

**B**

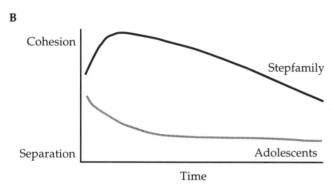

FIGURE 1. **Developmental trajectories of stepfamilies with (A) young children; (B) adolescents.**

remarried family system comprises the current residential stepfamily and also includes links to the nonresidential parent's extended family system and the stepparent's extended family system. In addition, relevant issues from the previous marital and divorce experiences, particularly unresolved emotional problems and attachments, and issues from the family of origin are central concerns. The context is defined as family members' interactional patterns and styles, the expectations of family relationships, and the attributions or understanding that they make about family relationships and patterns. Differentiating the unique issues encountered by stepfamilies from the expectations based on a "nuclear family model" is a frequent part of the normalization process in psychoeducation. In addition, it is useful to educate family members about developmental issues and sequences for all children so that the problems are not labeled as created by the stepfamily. Strategic–intergenerational interventions are also used to facilitate change in family patterns, interactions, expectations, and meanings (Williamson & Bray, 1988). These interventions are designed to consider the interactions between the life cycle tasks of the stepfamily and the individual family members. Throughout this chapter specific interventions are suggested and illustrated through case examples.

cohesive unit, whereas the adolescents are moving to separate from the family. Adolescents want to be less cohesive and more separate from the family unit as they struggle with identity formation and separation from the family of origin. In this case the developmental needs of the adolescent are at odds with the developmental push of the new stepfamily for closeness and bonding. Stepfamilies are usually less cohesive than first-marriage nuclear families, although their ideal levels of cohesion are usually similar to nuclear families (Bray, 1988a; Bray & Berger, 1993b; Pink & Wampler, 1985).

## Systems Approach to Treating Stepfamilies

A useful approach for working with stepfamilies is based on the developmental-systems model described above. Helping family members understand the context of stepfamily life through psychoeducation about divorce and remarriage is an effective intervention to normalize the experiences of family members. The

## Developmental Issues and Tasks for Stepfamilies

Research on remarriage and stepfamilies suggests many factors and tasks that have direct relevance for family therapy. This chapter draws from the Developmental Issues in StepFamilies (DIS) Research Project (Bray, 1988b) and its applications to therapy with stepfamilies. The DIS Research Project is a longitudinal study of stepfather families during the first 10 years after remarriage. The project investigated developmental issues for stepfamilies, the impact of divorce and remarriage on children's and adults' psychosocial adjustment and development, and family relationships in stepfather families and first-marriage nuclear families. This chapter focuses on seven major issues for stepfamilies identified from the DIS Research Project: planning for remarriage, marital relationships, parenting in stepfamilies, stepparent–child relationships, nonresidential parent issues, developing a stepfamily identity, and differences between functional and dysfunctional stepfamilies.

## Planning for Remarriage

There are at least three central issues for families to consider as they plan for remarriage. These include preparing for the financial and living arrangements for the family, resolving feelings and concerns about the previous marriage, and planning for changes in parenting the children. Many couples who plan to remarry address these issues before marriage, but unfortunately many do not. Stepfamilies in the DIS Research Project reported a variation of ways that they prepared their children for the remarriage. Some couples discussed the remarriage with their children and included them in their plans, whereas in some families the children did not know about the wedding until after it had occurred.

The adults have to decide where they will live and how they will share money. In general, adults report that it is advantageous to move to a new residence, so that it becomes "their home." Living in the home of one of the adults, particularly if it was the home of the previous marriage, makes it more difficult to establish a new family identity. Families generally decide to share all of their funds and be a "one-pot family" or they decide to keep separate funds and be a "two-pot family." Both methods can work, although couples that use a one-pot method generally report higher family satisfaction than couples that use a two-pot method.

The remarriage may resurrect old, unresolved feelings, such as anger and hurt, from the previous marriage. In addition, because stepfamilies are born out of loss, any unresolved grief over the first marriage needs to be resolved (Visher & Visher, 1988). New conflict between former spouses may suddenly arise as plans for remarriage are announced. Furthermore, children may respond to the announcement with mixed or negative feelings because their fantasies that their parents will reconcile are laid to rest. This process can be reframed as "perfect timing" and part of the "final emotional divorce" to help the new couple clear the way for a new beginning. Involving the children in the planning, especially if they are adolescents, is a way to get them ready for the re-

marriage. In addition, it is important for parents to allow their children to grieve the loss of their dream of family reconciliation.

Anticipating and preparing for changes in parenting following remarriage is a central task. Discussions about the role of the stepparent, changes in household rules, and parenting for the children are useful topics to address. Even if the couple has cohabited before marriage or the stepparent has been around the children, the children are likely to respond to the stepparent differently after the remarriage because the stepparent is now in an official parental role and both adults and children view their relationships differently. This issue will be discussed more fully in a later section.

## Marital Relationships in Stepfamilies

Because stepfamilies are "instant" families with children present from the beginning, marital relations are somewhat different in stepfamilies than in first marriages or remarriages without children. The marital relationship serves as the foundation for the stepfamily and facilitates other aspects of family functioning, particularly parenting of children. The "honeymoon" period after remarriage is either short-lived or nonexistent, probably because of the presence of children from the beginning (Bray & Berger, 1993b; Hetherington, 1993; Hetherington & Clingempeel, 1992). Many couples report that their children accompany them on their honeymoons and, because of the demands of childrearing, they spend little time without the children. Thus, the period during early marriage in which a newly wed couple normally spends time alone and builds a strong marital bond and loyalty to the marriage is compromised and complicated by the children's presence. Young children may feel a sense of abandonment or competition as their parent devotes more time and energy toward the new spouse. Adolescents have a heightened sensitivity to expression of affection and sexuality and are often disturbed by the active romance between the remarried couple (Hetherington & Clingempeel, 1992). Thus, remarried parents may feel guilty about their children's reactions and ignore their marriage in response to their children's demands. Educating the couple about the need to build a strong marital bond and the ultimate benefit for the children sets the stage for changes in the marriage. Suggesting that the couple have regular dates or trips without the children can be a beneficial intervention to support the marriage.

The marital subsystem appears to affect other family subsystems differently in stepfamilies than in first-marriage families (Bray, 1988a; Bray & Berger, 1993b). During early remarriage, marital adjustment and satisfaction have little impact on children's behavior (Bray, 1988a; Hetherington & Clingempeel, 1992). This is in contrast to first-marriage families in which marital relationships are usually predictive of more adjustment difficulties for children (Emery, 1982). After several years in a stepfamily, marital relationships have more impact on children's adjustment and parent–child interactions, similar to first-marriage families (Bray & Berger, 1993b; Hetherington & Clingempeel, 1992).

Another factor that contributes to conflict between the couple relates to jealous feelings the stepparent may have about the former spouse (Ahrons & Wallisch, 1987; Visher & Visher, 1988). In this situation the stepparent believes that his or her new spouse is too involved with the former spouse, beyond the needs of coparenting. A joint meeting with the remarried couple and ex-spouse to explicitly address coparenting issues can be used to clarify these issues. The meeting is only to discuss the coparenting issues; the divorce and the ex-spouses' relationship is off-limits for discussion during this meeting. During the session, it is useful to negotiate an arrangement between the parents and stepparent as specific and workable as possible to reduce the need for future discussion between former spouses. It is also important to negotiate how the parents will communicate when coparenting issues arise to short circuit potential problems. Common issues include how the parents will handle sudden problems of the child, changes in visitation arrangements, or sharing school information. If appropriate, it may be useful to address emotional attachments between ex-spouses, loyalty concerns of the new spouse, or triangulation between the parties. Reframing these issues can facilitate changes in their relationships. For example, if there is jealousy by the new spouse and there are unresolved emotional attachments between the former spouses, reframing their behavior as "your new husband unconsciously realizes that you have

some unresolved issues with your ex-spouse and he is trying to help you work them out," can open the door for change in their interactions. This may be the time for former spouses to settle any unresolved issues from the divorce.

## Parenting in Stepfamilies

Parenting and stepparenting are the most difficult and stressful aspects of stepfamily life, both during early remarriage and in longer-term stepfamilies (Bray, 1988a, 1988b; Bray & Berger, 1992). During the early months of remarriage, the stepparent may have difficulty playing a parental role. Functioning as a friend or "camp counselor," rather than a parent, can facilitate the children's acceptance of the stepparent (Bray, 1988a; Visher & Visher, 1988). Children are more likely to accept the stepparent when he or she first attempts to form a relationship with the children instead of actively trying to discipline or control the children. A caveat to this perspective is in order. In a very few cases, the custodial parent may be an incompetent parent, whereas the stepparent is competent and provides the needed parenting for the children. In these cases it may be temporarily useful for the stepparent to play the major parental role, even during early remarriage, until the custodial parent can improve his or her parenting.

The development of a parenting coalition is facilitated by a strong marital bond and the minimization of conflict between stepparent and custodial parent over parental authority issues. Even when a stepparent is overtly invited by the custodial parent to play a parental role, the biological parent may unconsciously respond to the stepparent's attempt to discipline by undermining the stepparent out of loyalty to the children. A useful approach is to have the custodial parent remain primarily responsible for control and discipline of the children during early remarriage. This approach allows time for a relationship and bond to develop between the stepparent and children. Encouraging the stepparent to actively monitor and be aware of the children's behavior and activities is a beneficial role that facilitates children's adjustment during both early and later remarriage (Bray, 1988b; Hetherington, 1987; Hetherington & Clingempeel, 1992).More active parenting by the stepparent can follow after a relationship has been established. Boys seem to respond more quickly to this process than girls in stepfather families (Bray, 1988b; Hetherington & Clingempeel, 1992). This sequence is important for short-term adjustment of children and is also predictive of better adjustment during later remarriage (Bray, Berger, Pacey, & Boethel, 1991; Hetherington & Clingempeel, 1992).

Older adolescents are more independent from the family and usually have more peer relationships and outside sources of support and interests (Baumrind, 1991; Bray & Berger, 1992; Marcia, 1980). Older adolescents are focusing on leaving the family of origin and developing their lives outside of the family. They may welcome their custodial parent's remarriage because it may attenuate their sense of responsibility for their parent. Thus, for a stepparent to move in too strongly with either authority or closeness can be particularly problematic for older adolescents. Recent research suggests that younger adolescents may have more difficulty adjusting to a stepfamily, whereas older adolescents and younger preadolescent children may adjust easier to a remarriage (Bray 1988b; Hetherington, 1993; Hetherington & Clingempeel, 1992). This is probably due to developmental differences in the children. Older adolescents need less parenting than younger children and may have less investment in the stepfamily, whereas younger children are usually more accepting of a new adult in the family, particularly when the adult has a positive influence. In contrast, young adolescents are dealing with identity formation issues, tend to be rather oppositional, and are particularly sensitive to expressions of affection between parent and stepparent (Baumrind, 1991; Hetherington, 1993). These factors make it more difficult for young adolescents to accept a stepparent.

Rules and discipline within the family are likely to change after remarriage. Adjusting to a new stepparent and changes in household rules and roles after remarriage takes time, usually from two to four years (Bray, 1988b; Hetherington & Clingempeel, 1992). Specific, enforceable rules are needed. An exercise to develop rules is a useful intervention if there are problems in parent–child relationships over household rules (Visher & Visher, 1988). The following intervention is one method of developing rules within a stepfamily. During a session with the cou-

ple, suggest a homework assignment for them to each develop a personal list of important household rules. In the next session with the couple negotiate the basic three to five rules that will be implemented immediately in the family. It is important to keep the number of rules below five to promote interparental agreement. After there is a consensus on the rules, have the couple negotiate the discipline and rewards that will be imposed for violating and following the rules. Both the rules and discipline need to be clearly specified to minimize disagreements over violations. In the next session, have the couple negotiate the rules and discipline with the children in the family. With adolescents, more negotiation is usually required to support their compliance and sense of independence. Suggest that the family post the rules and discipline in a visible place in the home. This process generates parental consensus and decreases interparental conflict. In addition, constructive problem-solving and communication skills are modeled and developed. By having the rules explicit, the stepparent is detriangulated from the custodial parent and stepchildren, and the stepparent is less likely to be viewed as "the heavy" and placed in the role of disciplinarian for the family.

## Stepparent–Child Relationships

Stepparent–child relationships in stepfamilies are likely to be more conflictual, involve more coalitions and triangles, and be more distant and negative than those in nuclear families (Anderson & White, 1986; Bray, 1988b; Bray & Berger, 1993b; Hetherington & Clingempeel, 1992; Perkins & Kahan, 1979; Santrock, Warshak, Lindberg, & Meadows, 1982). Therefore, stepfamilies are at risk for developing problems with parent–child relationships that require professional intervention. Normalizing these differences can help stepfamilies adjust and can counter the nuclear family myth, expectation for instant love, and notion that stepparent–child relationships will be just like parent–child relationships.

It is useful for stepparents to balance their desire to quickly form a close relationship with their stepchildren with the children's readiness and developmental status. Younger children seem to accept a stepparent more quickly than young adolescents.

Boys appear to accept a stepfather faster than girls. Coming on too strong, even in positive and otherwise reasonable ways, may result in the children withdrawing from or rebuking the stepparent. This may result in the stepparent disengaging from the children (Hetherington, 1987). In addition, children may view affection and bonding differently than adults. For example, in the DIS Research Project stepfathers' reports of expression of affection toward their stepchildren, especially girls, were related to more adjustment problems for the children, whereas the children's reports of the stepfathers' expression of affection were related to fewer adjustment problems for the children. To understand this apparently contradictory finding we reinterviewed the children and stepparents and found that they defined affection in different ways. Stepfathers indicated that they attempted to show affection through physical contact, such as embraces or hugs. The children, and especially the girls, were quite uncomfortable with such attempts. Children in stepfamilies stated that they liked verbal affection, such as praises or compliments, and this was related to better adjustment.

When focusing on issues concerning parent–child and stepparent–child relationships, it is important to set a context for change during the beginning of the therapy process. Frequently, there is a conflict between custodial parent and stepparent about loyalty and love of the children (Carter, 1989). The stepparent may overtly or covertly ask: Is the custodial parent more loyal to me or the children? This attitude creates an inappropriate triangle involving the children, custodial parent, and stepparent. This is a problem-generating question because it presumes that the stepparent and children are at the same hierarchical level within the family. Adults and children are in different categories, and this question is like comparing apples and oranges. Making this distinction explicit can detriangulate this situation and set a context for relationships within the family.

A useful context is for family members to agree to treat one another with courtesy. It is important to differentiate between courtesy and respect or love. Respect cannot be demanded, it is earned. It is suggested that the custodial parent tell the children to treat "my husband" (not your parent or stepparent)

with courtesy. The language is important. By not referring to the new spouse as a stepparent, the expectations about parental roles are subtly addressed. In addition, it is recommended that the custodial parent tell the stepparent to treat "my children" (not our children) with courtesy. This process detriangulates relationships and sets the stage for resolution of other problems.

## Nonresidential Parent Issues

After a divorce, more contact and a better relationship between nonresidential parents and children is usually related to better adjustment for children and adolescents (Hetherington, 1993; Hetherington et al., 1982; Wallerstein & Kelly, 1980). This is not necessarily the case for children after parental remarriage (Bray & Berger, 1990, 1993a). During early remarriage, more contact and a better relationship between nonresidential parents and children is associated with better behavioral adjustment for boys and girls but lower self-esteem for boys. During later years of remarriage, the nonresidential parent–child relationship has few effects on children's adjustment. Enduring anger and animosity from the divorce may reemerge after remarriage. Some type of resolution is necessary to have a successful integration of both families. Any remaining fantasies or desires that the original couple will reunite are usually dealt a final blow after the remarriage. However, even years after the remarriage, some children still want their divorced parents to reunite (Bray & Berger, 1992). After the remarriage some children may begin to treat the stepparent with animosity and hostility, despite a good relationship before the remarriage. These changes indicate that the emotional divorce has not been resolved completely (see chap. 5 in this volume).

Children may act more distant toward the stepparent and have more behavior problems after a visit with the nonresidential parent. This reaction may reflect a loyalty conflict involving their biological parent and stepparent. The custodial parent or stepparent may assume that the nonresidential parent is actively interfering with their relationship, which is occasionally true. However, more often children may act differently after a visit because of the loyalty bonds they have to their biological parent or because

of the effects of adjusting to different rules and expectations in separate family systems (Bray & Berger,
1992, 1993a).

Even several years after a divorce and remarriage,
conflict and hostility between parents and stepparents can have adverse effects on the children. When
there are high levels of interparental conflict involving the children, contact between nonresidential parents and children may be detrimental for the children (Hetherington, 1993; Johnston, Kline, &
Tschann, 1989). The more children are exposed to
this type of enmity and strife, the more injurious the
effects on their adjustment. Although it may be a difficult task, it is clearly in the children's best interest
for parents to work together or, at a minimum, not
to expose their children to continued conflict and
hostility.

After divorce and remarriage, nonresidential parents often decrease their contact with their children
or maintain stable, but low levels, of contact with
their children (Bray & Berger, 1990, 1993a; Furstenberg, Nord, Peterson, & Zill, 1983). Children may
feel abandoned as the nonresidential parent reduces
visitation after remarriage or as the custodial parent
focuses on the new spouse and directs less attention
toward the children. A useful intervention is to encourage reinvolvement between the children and parents and reassure the children about the process. An
adolescent boy complained that since his father had
remarried, he never went fishing with him anymore.
The father defensively countered, "That's not true,
you, me, and Jane [the stepmother] have been fishing several times." The boy countered with, "That
doesn't count cause you spend all of your attention
on her." Developing special activities or continuing
activities that involve only the child and parent promotes a positive relationship and decreases feelings
of abandonment.

The following case illustrates common issues with
nonresidential parents.

### CASE EXAMPLE

*Ms. Obledo and her second husband
brought her 12-year-old son, Marcus, for
therapy because of his behavior problems
and difficulties in getting along with other
family members. The couple had been
married for about 3 years. The mother
stated that the onset of the problems was
about 3 months ago, although the boy had
been difficult for her to manage since her
divorce from Marcus's father 5 years ago.
On inquiring about what had changed in
the past 3 months, the couple noted few
changes, except that Marcus's father had
"suddenly" appeared again and wanted to
visit with Marcus after a several-year absence. Ms. Obledo had filed a lawsuit to
collect back child support, and this had apparently brought the father back into the
picture. The mother continued with a long
explanation about how the father was "no
good," "had lots of problems," had abandoned her and Marcus, and did not pay
his child support. The stepfather supported
his wife's viewpoints by adding brief derogatory comments. Ms. Obledo stated that
she could not understand why Marcus
wanted to see his father when he had disappeared and would not support them.
Marcus appeared quite uneasy as his
mother overtly criticized his father. Marcus
was asked about his feelings for his father.
He angrily stated that his mother had
"driven" his dad away and that she would
not let him visit with his dad. He also de-
fended his father against his mother's and
stepfather's accusations.*

*It was affirmed with the mother that she
"loved her son and wanted the best for
him." She agreed and stated that she was
afraid that Marcus would turn out "bad"
like his father. Ms. Obledo was then asked,
"Do you realize that you are criticizing
Marcus when you speak negatively about
his father?" She looked puzzled and replied,
"No." It was then suggested that because
"Marcus was at least 50% his father," any
criticism of the father was an implicit criticism of Marcus. Therefore, Marcus was not
only defending his father but also himself.
The mother appeared moved by this new
perspective and apologized to Marcus. She
told Marcus that, "I didn't mean to talk
bad about you. I'm only trying to protect*

*you from more hurt." Marcus's tone also appeared to soften, and the family discussed their concerns about Marcus's involvement with his father in a more rational and empathic manner.*

As illustrated in this case, negative statements about the nonresidential parent made by parents or stepparents can create problems for the children. Parents may need interventions, including education, about this issue because no matter how true their allegations against the former spouse, blaming or undermining their child's parent will only make the child feel anger, shame, or sadness, and deepen the loyalty conflict. Denigration of the nonresidential father can result in poor self-esteem for boys (Bray & Berger, 1990). Emphasize to the custodial parent that criticizing the nonresidential parent implicitly criticizes the child, because the child is 50% the biological product of the nonresidential parent. This suggestion is often an eye-opener for the parent because they usually do not realize that criticizing the nonresidential parent implicitly criticizes their child. If the custodial parent relinquishes the denigration, this may decrease conflict between the child and custodial parent or stepparent because the need to exonerate the nonresidential parent no longer exists.

## Developing a Family Identity

Developing a family identity for a stepfamily is a long-term process that occurs through the development of family rituals, roles for family members, and stable relationship patterns within the family. The family identity is complicated by the binuclear nature of stepfamilies and the multiple demands from nonresidential family members. Even when there is limited or no contact with nonresidential parents and their family, children often keep that part of the family alive through their memories and desires for contact with the nonresidential family.

Accepting continual change appears to be a basic tenet of life in a stepfamily (Visher & Visher, 1988). Because the stepfamily is linked to another family, over which they have limited control, stepfamily members' lives are often influenced in unexpected ways. The remarried couple may plan for a weekend without the children only to be informed at the last

minute that the nonresidential parent has changed plans and cannot take the children. One stepfamily commented that they realized that they had "made it" as a family when they had alternative plans and backup in case their original plans did not go as scheduled.

Developing family rituals is important in forming a cohesive family identity. Rituals range from minor issues such as who takes a shower first in the morning to major functions such as how to celebrate holidays. For many families the major holidays are important times when families gather and celebrate together. Thus, developing a workable and satisfactory holiday ritual can have a major impact on the development of a family identity. The following case exemplifies how this process can work.

### CASE EXAMPLE

*A stepfather family came for therapy because of conflict over the children and concerns about one child's school performance and behavior. Although the family had been together for almost 3 years, many of the basic issues about parenting and dealing with the nonresidential parent had not been worked out. The stepfather complained that the family did not "come together well" and there was not a sense of family cohesion and identity. He was even more concerned because the Christmas holidays were approaching and the past two Christmases had been "disasters." I inquired about how they spent their Christmas and what type of traditions they had developed. They stated that they really did not have their own traditions but tried to keep things the same as before the divorce, for the sake of the children.*

*This year the children would be with the couple for Christmas day. I asked them how they celebrated this holiday. The woman answered that the tradition in their house was to open presents on Christmas morning and then gather in the afternoon with other family members for Christmas dinner. On Christmas morning they handed out the presents to each family member, and one family member opened one present while the rest of the family watched. Then another family member opened a present, and so on, until all of the presents were open. She stated that this often took several hours, but she continued to do this "for the children." I asked why they opened their presents in this manner, and she stated that this was the way that her ex-husband's family had always done it; she had just kept doing it that way after the divorce because she thought that was the way the children wanted to celebrate Christmas. I turned to the children and asked them what they thought about this tradition, and they stated that they hated it because it took so long to see what presents they had received. The mother was shocked and stated that she had no idea that they felt that way. This created the opportunity for the family to design a new ritual for Christmas and to include the stepfather and his family's traditions into the celebration. After the holidays, the family reported that Christmas had been great and the family members felt closer than ever before. The stepfather stated that he finally felt like they had a family because the ex-spouse was out of the middle of the family, and he felt he could have a better relationship with the children. He further stated that this had freed the couple to examine other aspects of the family and redesign how they handled things.*

## Functional and Dysfunctional Stepfamilies

What characteristics distinguish functional stepfamilies from those that require clinical interventions? Because there are few established norms for stepfamilies, the family processes that contribute to problem formation are also lacking (Bray, 1991). Clinicians have speculated about problematic aspects of remarriage (cf. Sager et al., 1983, Visher & Visher, 1988); however, there has been little empirical research that investigated functional and dysfunctional stepfamilies (Bray, 1991).

In a controlled study, Anderson and White (1986) evaluated functional and dysfunctional stepfamilies and first-marriage families with adolescents. They found that there was less involvement between stepfathers and their stepchildren and stronger tendencies toward the development of parent–child coalitions in both clinical and nonclinical stepfamilies in comparison to first-marriage families. Parent–child coalitions were even more extreme in dysfunctional stepfamilies than other families and were related to more problematic family processes. This is a common clinical problem in which the stepparent is excluded while the biological parent and children side together against the stepparent. In addition, functional stepfamily members reported better marital adjustment, more reciprocal positive involvement of stepchild and stepfather, and less exclusion of the stepfather than in dysfunctional stepfamilies. A surprising finding by Anderson and White was that marital adjustment was better in both functional and dysfunctional stepfamilies than in either functional or dysfunctional intact families. While there is often a strong association between marital problems and children's problems in first-marriage families, as mentioned earlier, it appears that the marriage in stepfamilies functions somewhat independently from parent–child relations.

Brown, Green, and Druckman (1990) investigated stepfamilies that entered therapy for a child-focused problem and stepfamilies that were not in therapy. Members of nonclinical stepfamilies reported more role reciprocity by the stepchild in response to the stepparent's initiatives and more satisfaction with the stepparent's role than members of clinic stepfamilies. In addition, clinical stepfamilies reported more conflict and less emotional expressiveness than members of nonclinical stepfamilies. Similar to Anderson and White, this study found that couples' communication and conflict resolution in both types of stepfamilies were higher than that of couples in a nondivorced normative sample.

In a recent study (Bray, 1992), we compared marital and family processes and children's behavioral adjustment in clinical and nonclinical stepfather families and investigated the relationship of family processes to children's behavioral adjustment. Clinical stepfamilies reported less-effective problem solving, less spousal individuation, poorer marital adjustment, and more negative and less positive child–parent interactions than nonclinical stepfamilies. In addition, children in clinical stepfamilies had more behavior problems and were rated by trained observers as less prosocial and more shy and withdrawn than children in nonclinical stepfamilies. More negative (i.e., more hostility, coercion, conflict) and less positive (i.e., warmth, assertiveness, self-disclosure) child-to-parent interactions, less effective problem solving, and less spousal individuation correlated with more behavior problems and less prosocial behavior of children. Marital satisfaction and adjustment were not related to children's behavior problems.

These studies address the quantitative differences between clinical and nonclinical stepfamilies. However, the presence or absence of quantitative differences does not inform us about the qualitative characteristics and issues that have an impact on stepfamily functioning and problem formation (Bray, 1991). Both first-marriage families and stepfamilies may seek treatment because of increased conflict and communication problems; however, the kinds of conflict and issues that affect communication are likely to be quite different in the two family types. Stepfamilies may have conflict over the parental authority of the stepparent or over loyalties to the noncustodial parent, but first-marriage families may have conflict about parenting practices or marital problems. Similarly, children's problems with emotional bonding and responsiveness in stepfamilies may be related to expectations of "instant love" and loyalty issues, but similar processes in first-marriage families may be due to rebellion or anger at parents. The quantitative differences often help clinicians in an assessment of the problem, whereas qualitative differences often direct the focus of treatment with stepfamilies.

It is important to note two issues. First, this research indicates that not all stepfamilies have problems or need treatment. Second, none of these studies examined longitudinal changes or compared specific interventions. Thus, the causal sequence of family relationships and problem formation has not been clearly delineated. It appears that problem formation may differ as children go through developmental cycles and interact with the developing and changing stepfamily. Future research needs to investigate the causal links between family processes and children's behavior problems to clarify these relationships and to identify the patterns of family interactions that lead to specific types of problems.

The following case exemplifies how psychoeducation and strategic interventions can be used to help stepfamilies adjust. The case also demonstrates the interconnected nature of the issues described earlier. Attempting to change one part of the system, such as the marriage, may not be possible until other issues are resolved.

### CASE EXAMPLE

*A blended family came for therapy because of conflict between the parents over parenting issues and conflict between the residential stepsiblings. The couple had been remarried about 8 months. The woman had two sons, age 9 and 7, from her first marriage. Her former spouse had regular contact and visitation with the boys, and there were few problems expressed about her previous marriage or divorce. The man had a daughter, age 8, from his first marriage. The man described his previous marriage as "highly conflictual and difficult." He stated that he could not talk with his ex-spouse because they always got into an argument. Although his former spouse had custody of the daughter during the separation and divorce, he reported that his daughter was very close to him, and she had always spent a lot of time with him before and after the divorce. The daughter moved in with the remarried couple about a month after they married. According to the woman, the family had not planned on having the girl live with them. According to the man, he had wanted his daughter to live with him from the beginning but had not pushed the issue because of his wife's concern about his daughter. The daughter was sent to live with her father by the daughter's mother because of* parent–child conflict and behavioral problems. The man was very happy that his daughter was able to live with him, but he felt very guilty and responsible about his child's problems. The couple reported that before the marriage that they had had an excellent relationship. They frequently had dates by themselves and took short trips without the children. The woman reported that since the day of the marriage she and her new husband had had virtually no time away from the children. All of the children were present at the wedding and went on the honeymoon with the couple. To build a strong family the parents included the children in all of their activities. Because the woman's children had a different visitation schedule than the man's daughter, there was always at least one child present in the home.

The couple had many disagreements about how to discipline the children. The woman claimed that her new husband treated his daughter differently than her children. In addition, she stated that he was too lax and easy with the children, especially his daughter. As a result, she felt that her children were also beginning to have behavioral problems. The man acknowledged that he was easy on his daughter because he felt guilty about her problems. This guilt was also stimulated by angry accusations from his ex-spouse that he had ruined their daughter because of the divorce. The woman complained that "his daughter would not mind her." The daughter had stated several times that she did not have to listen to the stepmother because, "her mother told her she [the stepmother] was not her real parent."

At the end of the session, the family was complimented for being on target and struggling with important developmental issues. Common developmental issues were discussed with the family, and questions were answered about appropriate expectations for the family. The daughter's behav-

ior toward the stepmother was reframed as a normal reaction to a new stepfamily, and she was complimented for her loyalty to her own mother. This seemed to reduce the tension between the family members. The family was asked not to change anything during the next week and take notes on family disagreements for the next session. They were asked to write down how family disagreements started, what was said, and how they ended. The purpose of this intervention was twofold. First, it served as a form of symptom prescription, given the reframe of the family problems as normative. Second, the notes would provide more detailed descriptions on the problems in interactions within the family.

At the next session, the adults reported that things had improved and there had been only a couple of arguments. The first part of the session was spent discussing these issues and suggesting different ways of handling disagreements. The evolution of this discussion was that the parents did not have any clear and consistent rules for the children. Rather, the woman was continuing with the rules and pattern of discipline she had used before the remarriage, and the man did likewise. They had never really discussed their expectations for the children, other than to want things to go well. The remainder of the session was spent discussing family rules and expectations for parenting the children. The couple was given the rule-development assignment discussed earlier. It was also suggested that the couple have at least one date without the children before the next session. The woman seemed very happy about this idea, whereas the man reluctantly agreed, "if they could find a good baby-sitter." Only the couple was invited back for the next session.

The next couple of sessions were spent helping the couple develop a set of basic rules for the household. As it became difficult to reach a consensus between the couple, it was apparent that the husband needed to resolve his guilt over his divorce and the potential impact this had on his daughter. The daughter's problem behavior had escalated during the past week, and this was reframed as his daughter's sacrifice to help her father resolve his feelings about the divorce. After directly addressing this issue, the woman was better able to understand her husband's behavior and feelings about his daughter, and the couple was able to agree on a basic set of household rules. The couple decided to present the rules and negotiate any changes on their own at home with the children.

The family returned a couple of weeks later. The parents and children reported that they had agreed on the rules and that things had been better for a few days. However, after a couple of days the parents had trouble agreeing and working together to enforce the rules. There seemed to be a great deal of tension between the couple. On inquiry, the husband stated that they had been planning their summer vacation. He announced that the entire family was going to California for 2 weeks and tour the southern part of the state and visit various sights and amusement parks. The husband seemed quite pleased with the plans. The wife appeared very angry. I asked her if she was excited about the vacation plans, and she stated, "not about his plans." She wanted to take one week of vacation just for herself and her husband, without the children. She wanted the children to join them after their week of vacation and spend another week as a family. I asked the man what he thought about this plan. He initially stated that he did not realize his wife wanted a different vacation; however, he was very concerned about how his daughter would react to spending a week away from him. The daughter stated that it would be all right, especially if she could stay with her mother. The father was very reluctant to call his former spouse to ask

for his daughter to stay with her because he felt that his ex-spouse would lecture him on abandoning his daughter in favor of his new wife. In addition, he was afraid that she might try to regain custody of the daughter. The man was encouraged to call his former spouse and "tentatively" check out the possibility of her keeping the daughter. It was suggested that he start the conversation with his ex-spouse by telling her that this was his new wife's idea, but he was not sure that it was a very good one. Thus, if his ex-wife balked, he could just agree with her that it was a bad idea and drop it. The family was sent home with the additional assignment of coming up with another alternative so that the couple could spend some part of the vacation alone.

During the next session, the man reported that he had called his former spouse as suggested and, to his surprise, she thought that taking a vacation was an excellent idea and this would give her extra time to be with her daughter. So the couple agreed to spend one week of vacation alone and the second week with their children.

The family returned 3 weeks later and the mood was quite different. They stated that the vacation had been wonderful and the best ever. I inquired about what made it go so well. The man stated, "You know you were right, we needed some time alone, just me and my wife. I think that I have been worrying too much about my daughter and ex-wife." The adults stated that the week alone had given them an opportunity to renew their marital bonds and meet their adults needs, which facilitated working together concerning the children. The woman reported that her husband had supported her and agreed with her about dealing with the children. The children, especially his daughter, had responded with better behavior. I warned them of the possibility of a relapse in the near future, and we agreed to meet in a couple of weeks.

*They canceled their next appointment and returned in about a month. In this session they stated that things had been going much better, although there had been a couple of incidents. In one case, the man's daughter had gotten upset with him and threatened to call her mother on him. He told his daughter that it was a good idea to let her mother know about her bad behavior. He followed this by telling his daughter that he had resolved his issues with her mother and he didn't need her help anymore to remind him about it. He said his daughter gave him a funny look and did what he asked. The couple stated that they felt they were on the right track and could probably handle their issues on their own.*

This case demonstrates several significant issues about working with stepfamilies. First, this case highlights the importance of people resolving their feelings about previous family transitions and the impact this can have on their children. Second, the need to develop a strong marital bond to work together as parents is further illustrated. If adults can not support each other in their marriage, it makes it much more difficult to work together for the benefit of their children. Third, developing a parenting coalition and acceptable rules for children is an essential step in stepfamily functioning.

## SUMMARY AND CONCLUSIONS

Providing therapy for stepfamilies can present a unique challenge to psychologists and other mental health professionals. A systems orientation to stepfamilies is useful to understand the multiple family systems involved in the stepfamily suprasystem and the interactional processes that produce both positive outcomes and problems. The interaction between the rapid developmental changes of the stepfamily and the distinctive and stressful aspects of remarriage coalesce to produce a complex web of family relationships that require specialized knowledge and clinical skills. Given the large numbers of stepfamilies, and their overrepresentation in clinical settings, it is clear that mental health professionals will encounter these types of families in therapy, and it is imperative for

clinicians to familiarize themselves with basic issues prior to working with stepfamilies. Working with stepfamilies also requires that clinicians examine their own family models so that they do not attempt to consciously or unconsciously mold and model stepfamilies into a first-marriage, nuclear family.

With the increased attention on stepfamilies in the media, many of the "basic and easy" problems encountered by stepfamilies are handled through self-help, bibliotherapy, and support groups. Thus, psychologists are likely to encounter more difficult presenting problems in working with stepfamilies. Often these problems do not present as stepfamily issues. Families may present with adolescent alcohol or drug abuse, sexual abuse, or runaway children that are embedded in the stepfamily context. At first, the link between stepfamily relationships and these presenting problems may not be readily apparent. However, in most cases the interactional patterns within the stepfamily create or contribute to the individual pathology, and solutions to these difficulties lie in understanding the stepfamily functioning.

Knowledge about ethical and legal requirements are also important in working with stepfamilies. In most states stepparents have no legal rights concerning their stepchildren. Therefore, stepparents cannot consent for their stepchildren to enter therapy, be hospitalized, or to release confidential records. However, stepparents are usually legally responsible for their stepchildren, so that if the children get into trouble with the law or destroy property, then a stepparent can be held liable and responsible for the acts of the stepchildren. This position of responsibility with no rights creates an uneasy tension for stepparents.

Finally, current and ongoing research on the divorce and remarriage process can inform clinicians about the normative and atypical tasks and issues for stepfamilies. There are a number of large-scale longitudinal studies underway (cf. Bray & Hetherington, 1993) that are providing valuable information about stepfamily functioning and that have major implications for clinical practice with stepfamilies. A systems-oriented approach is useful for integrating the findings, facilitating a better understanding of stepfamilies, and providing insights into new interventions for these families.

# References

Ahrons, C. R., & Wallisch, L. (1987). Parenting in the binuclear family: Relationships between biological and stepparents. In K. Pasley & M. Ihinger-Tallman (Eds.), *Remarriage and stepparenting: Current research and theory* (pp. 225–256). New York: Guilford.

Anderson, J. Z., & White, G. D. (1986). An empirical investigation of interactional and relationship patterns in functional and dysfunctional nuclear and stepfamilies. *Family Process, 25,* 407–422.

Baumrind, D. (1991). Effective parenting during the early adolescent transition. In P. A. Cowan & E. M. Hetherington (Eds.), *Family transitions* (pp. 111–164). Hillsdale, NJ: Erlbaum.

Bray, J. H. (1988a). Children's development during early remarriage. In E. M. Hetherington & J. Arasteh (Eds.), *The impact of divorce, single-parenting and step-parenting on children* (pp. 279–298). Hillsdale, NJ: Erlbaum.

Bray, J. H. (1988b). *Developmental Issues in StepFamilies Research Project: Final Report (Grant Number RO1 HD18025).* Bethesda, MD: National Institute of Child Health and Human Development.

Bray, J. H. (1991). Families in transition: Clinical and nonclinical stepfamilies. *The Family Psychologist, 7*(4), 37–38.

Bray, J. H. (1992). Family relationships and children's adjustment in clinical and nonclinical stepfather families. *Journal of Family Psychology, 6,* 60–68.

Bray, J. H., & Berger, S. H. (1990). Noncustodial parent and grandparent relationships in stepfamilies. *Family Relations, 39,* 414–419.

Bray, J. H., & Berger, S. H. (1992). Stepfamilies. In M. E. Procidano & C. B. Fisher (Eds.), *Contemporary families: A handbook for school professional* (pp. 57–79). New York: Teachers College Press.

Bray, J. H., & Berger, S. H. (1993a). Nonresidential family-child relationships following divorce and remarriage. In C. E. Depner & J. H. Bray (Eds.), *Noncustodial parents: New vistas in family living* (pp. 156–181). Newbury Park, CA: Sage.

Bray, J. H., & Berger, S. H. (1993b). Developmental issues in stepfamilies research project: Family relationships and parent-child interactions. *Journal of Family Psychology, 7,* 76–90.

Bray, J. H., & Hetherington, E. M. (1993). Families in transition: Introduction and overview. *Journal of Family Psychology, 7,* 3–8.

Bray, J. H., Berger, S. H., Pacey, K., & Boethel, C. L. (1991, April). *Longitudinal predictors of children's adjustment to divorce and remarriage.* Paper presented at the biennial meetings of the Society for Research in Child Development, Seattle, WA.

Bray, J. H., Berger, S. H., Silverblatt, A., & Hollier, A. (1987). Family process and organization during early remarriage: A preliminary analysis. In J. P. Vincent (Ed.), *Advances in family intervention, assessment and theory* (Vol. 4, pp. 253–280). Greenwich, CT: JAI.

Brown, A. C., Green, R. J., & Druckman, J. (1990). A comparison of stepfamilies with and without child-focused problems. *American Journal of Orthopsychiatry, 60,* 556–566.

Carter, E. A. (1989, October). *Working with the remarried family.* Workshop presented at the American Association for Marriage and Family Therapy, San Francisco, CA.

Coleman, M., & Ganong, L. H. (1990). Remarriage and stepfamily research in the 1980s: Increased interest in an old family form. *Journal of Marriage and the Family, 52,* 925–940.

Emery, R. E. (1982). Interparental conflict and the children of discord and divorce. *Psychological Bulletin, 92,* 310–330.

Furstenberg, F. F., Jr., Nord, C. W., Peterson, J. L., & Zill, N. (1983). The life course of children of divorce: Marital disruption and parental contact. *American Sociological Review, 48,* 656–668.

Glick, P. C. (1988). The role of divorce in the changing family structure: Trends and variations. In S. A. Wolchik & P. Karoly (Eds.), *Children of divorce: Empirical perspectives on adjustment* (pp. 3–34). New York: Gardner Press.

Glick, P. C. (1989). Remarried families, stepfamilies, and stepchildren: A brief demographic profile. *Family Relations, 38,* 24–27.

Hetherington, E. M. (1987). Family relations six years after divorce. In K. Pasley & M. Ihinger-Tallman (Eds.), *Remarriage and stepparenting today: Current research and theory* (pp. 185–205). New York: Guilford Press.

Hetherington, E. M. (1993). An overview of the Virginia longitudinal study of divorce and remarriage. *Journal of Family Psychology, 7,* 39–56.

Hetherington, E. M., & Clingempeel, W. G. (1992). Coping with marital transitions: A family systems perspective. *Monographs of the Society for Research in Child Development, 57*(2–3, Serial No. 227).

Hetherington, E. M., Arnett, J. D., & Hollier, E. A. (1988). Adjustment of parents and children to remarriage. In S. A. Wolchik & P. Karoly (Eds.), *Children of divorce: Empirical perspectives on adjustment* (pp. 67–110). New York: Gardner Press.

Hetherington, E. M., Cox, M., & Cox, R. (1982). Effects of divorce on parents and children. In M. E. Lamb (Ed.), *Nontraditional families: Parenting and child development* (pp. 233–288). Hillsdale, NJ: Erlbaum.

Johnston, J. R., Kline, M., & Tschann, J. M. (1989). Ongoing postdivorce conflict: Effects on children of joint custody and frequent access. *American Journal of Orthopsychiatry, 59,* 1–17.

Marcia, J. (1980). Identity in adolescence. In J. Adelson (Ed.), *Handbook of adolescent psychology* (pp. 159–187). New York: Wiley.

McGoldrick, M., & Carter, E. A. (1980). Forming a remarried family. In E. A. Carter & M. McGoldrick (Eds.), *The family life cycle* (pp. 265–294). New York: Gardner.

Papernow, P. L. (1993). *Becoming a stepfamily.* San Francisco: Jossey-Bass.

Perkins, T. F., & Kahan, J. P. (1979). An empirical comparison of natural-father and stepfather systems. *Family Process, 18,* 175–183.

Pink, J. T., & Wampler, K. S. (1985). Problem areas in stepfamilies: Cohesion, adaptability, and the stepfather adolescent relationship. *Family Relations, 34,* 327–335.

Sager, C. J., Brown, H., Crohn, H., Engel, T., Rodstein, E., & Walker, L. (1983). *Treating the remarried family.* New York: Brunner/Mazel.

Santrock, J. W., Warshak, R. A., Lindberg, C., & Meadows, L. (1982). Children's and parent's observed social behavior in stepfather families. *Child Development, 53,* 472–480.

Visher, E. B., & Visher, J. S. (1988). *Old loyalties, new ties: Therapeutic strategies with stepfamilies.* New York: Brunner/Mazel.

Wallerstein, J. S., & Kelly, J. (1980). *Surviving the breakup: How children and parents cope with divorce.* New York: Basic Books.

Whiteside, M. F. (1982). Remarriage: A family developmental process. *Journal of Marital and Family Therapy, 4,* 59–68.

Williamson, D. S., & Bray, J. H. (1988). Family development and change across the generations: An intergenerational perspective. In C. J. Falicov (Ed.), *Family transitions: Continuity and change over the life cycle* (pp. 357–384). New York: Guilford.

Zill, N., & Schoenborn, C. A. (1990). Developmental, learning, and emotional problems: Health of our Nation's children, United States, 1988. *Advance data from vital and health statistics; no 190.* Hyattsville, MD: National Center for Health Statistics.

# CHAPTER 8

# INTERVENTIONS WITH LATER LIFE FAMILIES

*Cleveland G. Shields, Deborah A. King, and Lyman C. Wynne*

Becoming older is a condition all of us hope someday to reach. Older persons make up the fastest growing segment of the population. If only for this reason, the field of family therapy must confront the concerns of aging and develop new models for understanding and intervening in later life families. Intentionally focusing on aging not only will benefit older persons in therapy but also will add a richness to family therapy theory and to the lives of therapists who choose to work with older persons.

The model proposed in this chapter was developed from our own work and was influenced by the work of other family therapists (Hargrave & Anderson, 1992; Herr & Weakland, 1979; Hughston, Christopherson, & Bonjean, 1989; Knight, 1986; Walsh, 1988). We also wish to note that any family therapist working with geriatric clients must be familiar with normal age-related changes in health, cognition, and psychosocial roles as well as with medical and serious mental illnesses common in later life (see Albert & Moss, 1988; Birren & Schaie, 1990; Birren, Sloane, & Cohen, 1992; Butler, Lewis, & Sunderland, 1991; Carstensen & Edelstein, 1987).

## LIVING LONGER AND DEMANDING MORE FROM OUR FAMILIES

Our society is undergoing a demographic revolution as more and more people live longer and longer. Life expectancy has risen dramatically since 1900. These changes in life expectancy indicate that the percentage of older people in our population has risen from 4% in 1900 to 11.3% in 1980, and it is projected to rise to 21.8% in 2030 (U.S. Department of Health and Human Services, 1991). On the average, men are living 25 years longer and women 30 years longer now than in 1900.

Not only is the demographic structure of our society changing in terms of aging, but so is the structure of families. It is as if an extra generation has been added to the life of every family. Butler et al. (1991) characterized this as a shift from the horizontal to the vertical family. As couples have fewer children, individuals in upcoming generations will have fewer siblings and cousins (horizontal dimension) and more relatives in the older generations (vertical dimension). People in later life themselves may have complex family structures. Divorces and remarriages by children may multiply the vertical lines of the family. Some older persons may remain in contact with their former inlaws. This is not only a way to keep in touch with grandchildren, but also a sign of the genuine affection that developed when their offspring were married. Many older persons will themselves remarry, complicating and possibly enriching their family structure even further. Most older people who have children maintain some kind of regular contact with them, no matter how far away they may live. Shanas (1980) refers to this as "intimacy at a distance." Regardless of individual perspectives, family relationships are likely to remain the most important relationships for people throughout their lives.

Several shifts are taking place that make attention to later life concerns imperative for the field of family therapy. First, there are simply more older people living who will suffer depression and other mental illnesses, marital conflict, and family conflict. As the baby boomer generation ages, many of them will seek therapy because they have grown up in a culture that more and more accepts therapy as a valid form of help. Second, the longer people live, the more likely they are to contract debilitating illnesses. Family members, especially spouses and adult offspring, function as the primary support persons for older people who are ill and may suffer from depression and anxiety related to the caregiving role (Gallagher, Rose, Rivera, Lovett, & Thompson, 1989). Many of these people will seek therapy to help them cope. Finally, with the change from horizontal to vertical family structures, intergenerational family relationships will become more common and potentially more important than ever. It is likely that these factors will lead more families to seek help for problems related to aging and family relationships.

## THE STRENGTH–VULNERABILITY MODEL

The strength–vulnerability (SV) model of mental health and illness in older people is an extension of vulnerability–stress models that have informed much of the research on psychopathology in children and young adults (Rolf, Masten, Cicchetti, Nuechterlein, & Weintraub, 1990). Shields and Wynne (in press) have taken the concepts of the vulnerability–stress literature, reorganized and renamed many of them, and applied them to the life cycle issues of older persons to produce what we call the SV model.

The SV model posits four major sets of factors: strength factors, vulnerability factors, health-enhancing factors, and risk factors (see Figure 1). These factors arise from family and individual life cycle factors and interact across the life span, producing healthy functioning individuals within families or producing individuals who function poorly because of psychological symptoms. *Strengths* are internal processes based on personality or personal history that individuals bring to bear against mental illness, and they foster healthy functioning. *Vulnerabilities* are internal processes that increase the likelihood of developing psychopathology. These are characteristics of the individual that have been acquired through life experience or that are genetically endowed.

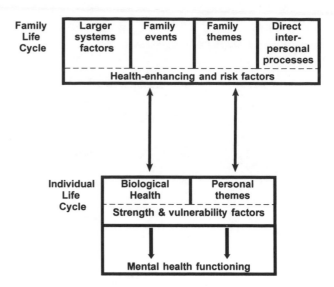

FIGURE 1. The strength–vulnerability model of mental health and illness.

*Health-enhancing factors* are external or environmental processes that protect against psychopathology, such as effective family problem solving, positive family emotional support, or the larger social and family network. *Risks* are external, environmental hazards that increase the likelihood (when interacting with vulnerabilities) that the individual will develop psychopathology. These risks include, for example, a marital environment dominated by cricitism, poor marital problem-solving skills, or economic problems. Internal strengths or vulnerabilities may shape or evoke environmental health-enhancing and risk factors. The SV model postulates that it is the interaction of these processes that determines the mental health or illness of individuals across the life cycle.

Family therapy has traditionally overlooked individual assessment, especially biological factors. With the development of medical family therapy (McDaniel, Hepworth, & Doherty, 1992), there is a greater appreciation for biological processes in the individual. The focus now is on a biopsychosocial family systems model that appreciates the effects of biology on individual and family functioning, as well as the effects of family functioning on individual psychological and biological health.

## ASSESSMENT OF LATER LIFE FAMILIES FROM A LIFE CYCLE PERSPECTIVE

Both the client and the family need to be assessed from a developmental framework. (See chap. 5 in this volume.) This is especially important in working with older persons because there are so many negative preconceptions about normal aging processes in our culture and in the families with whom we work (Schaie, 1993). It is important to understand their ideas about aging, to understand how aging has historically been dealt with in their families, and to examine the interaction between older clients' ideas about aging and their family members' ideas about aging.

## Individual Life Cycle

We propose two prominent factors that influence the strengths and vulnerabilities that the individual older client brings to bear to solve problems: *biological health* and *personal themes*. We need to recognize that there is tremendous variability in the biological health of older persons. Some older people may be quite healthy, with no illnesses and no disabilities. Others may have several chronic illnesses yet still function independently, and still others may have chronic illnesses that greatly reduce their functioning. Finally, some older people may be coping with impending death from fatal illnesses, and fatal illnesses may or may not automatically diminish their functioning. Any of these changes may require enhanced coping and psychological flexibility.

It is essential for family therapists to have a clear understanding of the health of their older clients from the multiple perspectives of the person, the family, and the family's health care providers. Often these points of view can be radically different, and this fact in itself may be a focus of intervention for the family therapist (Wynne, Shields, & Sirkin, 1992; Wynne, Sirkin, & Shields, 1992). Thorough medical evaluation and a close working relationship with the client's providers are indispensable components of family therapy with older people.

*Personal themes* evolve from a person's life history, ethnicity, developmental life cycle crises, personality structure, and psychological problems. What are clients' personal and cultural histories? What have been the major successes in their lives? What events in their lives do they see as defeats? Are they still haunted by them? Have they experienced major traumas such as the depression, violence, and war? Therapists have to take time to learn their clients' histo-

ries in order to enhance understanding and facilitate the therapeutic alliance. This aspect of assessment lets clients know that the therapist is interested in them. It sets the stage for the therapist and client to join more effectively. Therapists and clients are often of different generations, so therapists need to take the initiative to find information in the clients' history that will help them identify and emotionally connect with them.

Many older people have strong ethnic identifications (Gelfand, 1982; McGoldrick, Pearce, & Giordano, 1982). (See also chap. 19 in this volume.) They or their parents may have immigrated to the United States. Older people may maintain strong ties to their cultural heritage and its institutions such as the church or the tribe. Ethnicity and cultural factors affect patterns of communication and decision-making styles. Awareness of ethnicity and cultural factors and appreciation of the client's loyalties aid in making the client comfortable with the therapist and help define acceptable approaches or goals in therapy.

An understanding of older clients' mastery of individual developmental challenges lays the groundwork for supporting existing strengths while promoting enhanced coping with vulnerabilities. Erikson's eight stages of development can be viewed as a continuum of adaptive versus maladaptive coping (Erikson, 1950; Erikson, 1968; Erikson, Erikson, & Kivnick, 1986). The therapist can use these to assess the client's preparedness for mastering the challenges of later life. In doing so, the therapist must consider all of the stages, not simply those thought to reemerge later in the life cycle, because the earlier themes are recycled in the context of the challenges of aging. For example, trust versus mistrust, an early conflict thought to lay the foundation of a sense of hope about people and one's world, later becomes a fortifying sense of faith about future generations. The earlier conflict of autonomy versus shame may surface later in life as the elder struggles to accept the help and support of younger generations, especially in the face of debilitating illness. Earlier resolution of intimacy versus isolation lays the groundwork for a sense of one's "lovableness" later in life, even in the face of multiple losses.

Generativity versus stagnation is another normative conflict that is often potent in the lives of older persons. Do clients feel that they are contributing to their families, their work, or their community? Do they have a sense of commitment or connection to a purpose that is greater than themselves? Or do they feel they have no contribution to make and are merely existing or waiting to die? Often times older parents, mothers or fathers, will think that they are no longer needed in their families. Their children are on their own and they (the parents) are no longer needed in the same way in their adult offsprings' lives. As well, older clients may feel that their usefulness at work or in their local community has ended.

Older persons face the challenge of integrity versus despair when they begin assessing their lives. As people age they are faced with the prospect of making sense of the whole span of their living. It is an opportunity to face with honesty their successes and failures and to develop a consistent life story that can be handed down to their family with integrity. For some older people this is a time of despair, when they are unable to construct a consistent story that integrates their life experience into a meaningful whole. For others, this evaluation or "summing up" process culminates with a sense of ego integrity, a strong sense of personal identity, and a conviction that one has lived the life that was meant to be.

Central to the assessment of older clients is the evaluation of strengths and opportunities for growth. In what areas of the clients' lives can therapists engender a sense of hope, a sense that things can be better, a sense that change is at hand, and a belief that such change is good? Creative family therapists attempt to find strengths in their older clients that can be harnessed to build energy for change in therapy even while acknowledging and dealing with their client's vulnerabilities.

## Family Life Cycle

Health-enhancing and risk factors arise from the family life cycle (See chap. 5 in this volume). We describe the family life cycle as consisting of four major components: *larger systems, family events, family*

*themes,* and *direct interpersonal processes.* By *larger systems,* we mean societal issues that impact the family. Health care, social security and retirement income, housing, the economy, and societal attitudes toward aging are all issues in the larger society that impact the later life family. For example, because of inadequacies in the U.S. health care system younger family members may have ongoing caregiving responsibilities for their own children and limited time or money to provide care for their parents. Poverty or near poverty are further stressors.

Later life *family events* are the predictable and unpredictable gains and losses that take place during the life cycle, but especially during later life. These include marriages of children, births of grandchildren, deaths of older parents, deaths of other family members, death of spouse, divorces, remarriages, retirement, illness, and disability. Events that happen "in-phase," such as the birth of child to a married son or daughter or the death of an older parent may be easier to cope with than an "out of phase" event, such as the birth of a child to a teenager or the serious illness or death of a young child (Carter & McGoldrick, 1988).

*Family themes* are the issues confronted by family members as a group throughout the life cycle. Steinglass, Bennett, Wolin, and Reiss (1987) described the family life cycle in terms of the themes family members must confront and resolve in each of three phases: early, middle, and late. In the early phase of the family life cycle, the newly formed family unit must forge its own identity and establish boundaries. In the late-phase family the issue of identity reemerges with a focus on the future rather than the present. As children[1] leave home, marry, or have their own children, later phase family members are challenged to condense and define the essential elements of their family's identity so that they can convey and entrust it to the newly forming family unit. Therefore, the early-phase family works to develop both a family *identity* and *boundaries.* The midphase family has *commitments* and the *stability* to fulfill them. The late-phase family seeks to *clarify* the essential ingredients of the family *legacy* and to pass

---

[1] This includes not only a person's own children, but any children in the family (e.g., nieces, nephews, cousins).

this on to newly forming units of the family. According to Steinglass et al.'s (1987) model, these phases can apply to the life cycle of any family unit no matter what their ages. Family members may participate in more than one phase at a time. Older family members who remarry will experience early-phase themes of boundary making and identity formation, while also experiencing late-phase issues of clarification and transmission of their legacy to their newly married children, nieces, or nephews.

*Direct interpersonal processes* refers to the underlying processes of relational development posited by Wynne (1984). *Attachment/caregiving* is the affectional bond in a relationship. *Communication* is the ability to develop shared meaning between people. *Problem solving* is the ability to develop solutions to problems and carry them out cooperatively. *Mutuality* is the long-term commitment to the relationship and the ability to reinvent the relationship in the face of major life cyle events or changes. These processes are sequential, that is, some attachment/caregiving is necessary before communication can take place. Good communication is necessary for effective problem solving, and effective problem solving is a prerequisite to sustaining relationships through periods of crisis and life change.

Family relationships change over the life span. As children become adults, the balance of attachment and caregiving between offspring and parents necessarily changes. As offspring reach adulthood, the relationship begins to shift from a bond based on caregiving of parent to child to an adult to adult bond of affection and interest. Parents grow to see their adult offspring as persons who are separate and responsible for their own lives. At the same time, adult offspring must surrender the often unacknowledged fantasy that their parents will "be there" forever to care for and counsel them.

This developmental transition can be more difficult when neurological, mental, or any illness renders elders incapable of making their own decisions and grown children are called upon to make decisions for their parents for the first time. If the requisite shift from parent–child to adult–adult relationship has not yet occurred, the family may become paralyzed and temporarily unable to execute decision making. Other factors, such as a history of insuffi-

cient nurturance in the parent–child relationship, will make this crisis even harder to negotiate (King, Bonnacci, & Wynne, 1990). An extreme, but not uncommon, example of this problem is when a previously abused child becomes the primary caretaker for the abusive parent and repeats the cycle of attachment/caregiving failure by abusing or neglecting the elder (Henton, Cate, & Emery, 1984; Steuer & Austin, 1980). Demonstrating the importance of this developmental shift in dependency, Pillemer and Finkeher (1989) found that the adult offspring most at risk for abusing their older parents are those who have remained the most dependent on their parents throughout their adult lives.

The goal in assessing developmental issues for the later life family is to build upon health enhancing aspects of family life while minimizing, reducing, or eliminating the effects of risk factors. It is important to know about risk factors, but it is equally important to help family members tell the story of the family in such a way that hope is built and change seems possible. Therapists can build hope by underscoring health-enhancing aspects of families, accomplishment, positive emotional bonds, good communications, and problem solving.

## Interaction of Individual and Family Life Cycles

Changes over the life cycle are not always smooth. Sometimes an individual's life cycle stage or family life cycle stage will conflict with the life cycle needs of another family member or another part of the family (Carter & McGoldrick, 1988). These are conflicts that can call forth either creative responses or stalls in growth for family members. For example, the retirement of older parents may free them up for spending more time with their children at the same time that the children are starting new marriages and wish to keep themselves a little distant in order to develop an identity as a couple (Steinglass et al., 1987).

Therapists working with later life families must consider the ways the individual and family life cycles mesh and the ways they clash. The task is to find a way for each life cycle stage to enhance the others. How can the needs of the individual client be addressed in ways that are also helpful to the family, or in ways that at least take into account the needs of the family? How can the needs of the family be met while taking into account the needs of the individuals? This is a balancing act, but the art for the therapist is to convince the family that new ideas and new ways can be found that provide solutions to old problems.

## ATTENDING TO FAMILY OF ORIGIN ISSUES OF THE THERAPIST

We think it is essential for therapists to be aware of the role older persons played in their lives and how their own family history shapes their reactions to client families. Therapists should give considerable thought to the assumptions they bring to therapy about the role of older people in families and family members' responsibilities toward them. Therapists whose childhood included daily contact with grandparents will have an outlook on the role of grandparents different from that of therapists who saw their grandparents or other older relatives only on holidays. In Exhibit 1 we have listed a series of questions about the role of older persons in one's family of origin.

It is also important to be aware of how client families might view the therapist. Does the therapist represent the good son or daughter that older clients wish their own children would be? Is the therapist the warm parent or grandparent for whom their clients long? How does the therapist's own life cycle stage match up with or conflict with the life cycle stages of the later life families? Does the therapist identify more with older people, with the adult offspring, or with the grandchild generation? In what ways does the therapist's own stage of life cycle development influence his or her therapy?

*DON'T DO THAT TO YOUR (MY?) GRANDMOTHER*

*A young therapist was struggling to help a family decide whether or not the grandmother of the family needed to be placed in a nursing home. Medical evaluation suggested Mrs. Fleming needed a high level of nursing care best provided in a nursing*

*home environment. Her adult offspring were in agreement; they were exhausted from trying to maintain their mother in her own home. However, Mrs. Fleming was resisting the idea of placement. The supervisor of the case was puzzled when the therapist suddenly began siding with Mrs. Fleming, underscoring issues such as her right to maintain her independence and the family's responsibility to help her stay at home. After the session the therapist was surprised to find that her supervisor was puzzled by her championing of Mrs. Fleming's refusal to go to the nursing home. Af-*

---

### EXHIBIT 1

**Questions on the Role of Older Persons in One's Family of Origin**

1. Did you grow up in close contact with grandparents, great aunts and uncles, or other older relatives?
2. What was the role of these older relatives in the family?
3. What was the relationship between your parents/guardians and these older relatives?
4. How emotionally close were you to your various older relatives?
   To whom were you the closest?
   Did any of your older relatives have a caregiving role with you?
5. How do you or your family members remember family members who have died?
6. To what ages did your grandparents (and your parents' grandparents) live?
7. How did your grandparents (or your parents) live or are they living their final years?
   Did they live independently and disability-free up until their deaths, or were they disabled and in need of care?
   Who cared for them?
   If they were placed in institutions, how was the decision made? How did people in the family respond to that decision?

*ter gentle, but insistent, questioning from the supervisor the therapist revealed that her own grandmother had recently been placed in a nursing home. She felt strongly that her grandmother had been placed against her will and now felt guilty about it. She had to work to hold back tears as she talked about her grandmother's impending death and the fact that she was not able to visit her very often. Discussing these issues with her supervisor helped her disentangle her own family issues from the Flemings' family issues and again join with the whole family, so that she could work with Mrs. Fleming to look more realistically at her needs and support the family to make the difficult decisions facing them.*

Many personal issues can sidetrack therapists in working with later life families. Young therapists' personal focus on autonomy and achievement can cause avoidance of dependency needs in older people. Therapists' own striving for filial maturity (adult to adult relationships with their own parents) can lead to over involvement with certain cases because of their desire to befriend their own older parents. Therapists' or physicians' denial of mortality issues may increase likelihood of excessive medical treatments and tests and avoidance of preparation for death. Family therapists working with older persons should strive to be mindful of their own family of origin issues and personal developmental conflicts so that they can remain as open and flexible as possible in helping their older client families.

## DEFINING THE PROBLEM AND THE GOALS FROM MULTIPLE VIEWPOINTS

It is important to solicit the viewpoints of as many people as possible when defining the presenting problems of older clients and their families. Older persons who have begun to have problems that impair their functioning may have many people involved in or concerned about their welfare. Spouses, adult offspring, siblings, friends, physicians, nurses, clergy, social workers, apartment house managers, or

other professionals may have valuable information and be useful resources for working with older clients and their families. For example, if an older person is in the early stages of dementia, some family members may see the problem clearly while others may be unable or unwilling to face such a difficult diagnosis.

*STRENGTH IN NUMBERS*

*Mrs. Jones was concerned about her husband, who had gotten lost several times when driving home from the grocery store and from church. She spoke to her children, who chastised her for being alarmist about their father. She arranged an assessment for her husband at a memory disorders clinic, but the children took the father's side in opposing the appointment. Finally, through the family physician, a family meeting was called with a family therapist consulting. The therapist arranged for the family physician, the apartment manager, the pastor, and an old family friend to attend in addition to the couple's children. Only after hearing the pastor, the apartment manager, and the family friend express concern about their father's forgetfulness were the adult offspring able to support their mother and agree to their father's receiving a complete dementia workup.*

Each individual and family situation is different. In some cases it may take several sessions before an older client will allow a therapist to contact other family members. In other cases, adult offspring may come in seeking help with their older parents. Either way, the family therapist's goal should be to expand the network from which information can be garnered and from which support for change can be obtained.

Treatment goals should not only be described in a language of change (Haley, 1976) and oriented toward solutions (De Shazer, 1985), but also be informed by the biomedical or neurological realities. It is possible for older clients or family members to have either unnecessarily low or unrealistically high expectations for change in therapy. Hence we stress a complete assessment of the system, which includes the perspective of the primary care physician and other persons who may have long-term relationships with the client and may be especially sensitive to changes in functioning over time.

## FIVE-LEVEL MODEL OF INTERVENTION

On the basis of Wynne's epigenetic model (1984), we developed a model of the intervention process with later life families that consists of five sequential levels. Each of these levels represents intervention in deeper strata of the family's direct interpersonal processes (see Table 1).

These five levels of intervention are not a static prescription for treatment. Rather they indicate that certain family problems must be addressed before others. During the initial consultation the therapist assesses both the presenting problems and the family's direct interpersonal processes. Difficulties in family problem solving, communication, or attachment/caregiving may be disruptive to the process of therapy and lead to early termination of the session or refusal to engage in or return to treatment. Family therapists need to intervene immediately to control or eliminate conflict resulting from difficulties in these areas. For example, there may be very negative feelings between an older mother and her adult son and daughter. So negative, in fact, that there is little chance that they can learn to communicate effectively unless more positive feelings can be created. The therapist may choose to intervene at Level 5, seeking to create a more positive attachment between this woman and her offspring. Only after more positive feelings between mother and offspring are engendered does the therapist encourage them to communicate more openly. Only after they have mastered the art of active listening and speaking in noncritical ways to each other are they ready to try to solve the pressing problems that brought them to treatment in the first place. In this case, the therapist and family would have started at Level 5 and worked their way back up to Level 1, in which the therapist would be consulting with a family now capable of solving its own problems. The problem remains, however, that some presenting problems of older persons may not wait for family members to work through long-

standing difficulties in their relationships so that they can effectively solve problems together. Some family members may not want or be able to work to resolve the long-standing difficulties that exist in their families. It is this complexity of historical problems and urgent present problems that makes family therapy with older people both challenging and rewarding.

## Level 1 Interventions—Consultation

These are families that have positive and balanced attachment/caregiving, positive and clear communication, and effective problem-solving skills. These families come to see a family therapist not to change their families but for professional guidance and reassurance; what Wynne, McDaniel, and Weber (1986, 1987) have termed "family consultation." These families are often capable of solving their own problems, but they need additional information, support, and the perspective of an outsider to help them sort through their options and choose how they wish to deal with the problems facing them. There are many reasons families or professionals seek consultations for problems concerning older people. Physicians may request a consultation for help in managing a patient with chronic illness or help in dealing with a family who has become overwhelmed by the burdens of caring for the ill elder. Family members inundated with advice from physicians, clergy, friends, and others may need help in sorting through their options. A family coping with a crisis may seek a consultation to determine if they need therapy or if they have the resources to manage the problem on their own. As a consultant, the professional can establish collaborative relationships with other professionals. Such relationships are especially important in working with older persons, since many problems require multidisciplinary approaches to management.

The following case illustrates how the family therapist as consultant was able to elucidate the family's strengths and enable them to have the courage to make difficult decisions.

### WE JUST WANT TO TALK THIS OVER WITH SOMEONE

*Mrs. Williams arranged a consultation with a family therapist because her husband was dying of cancer and her daughter*

| | | TABLE 1 | | |
|---|---|---|---|---|

## The Five-Level Model of Intervention

| | Assessment | | | |
|---|---|---|---|---|
| | **Attachment/ Caregiving** | **Communication** | **Problem solving** | **Interventions** |
| Level 1 | Positive, balanced | Positive, clear | Effective | a. Education<br>b. Information<br>c. Referral<br>d. Support |
| Level 2 | Positive, balanced | Positive, clear | Temporarily overwhelmed by the situation | a. Liberal emotional support<br>b. Active problem solving<br>c. Minimum structuring of communication |
| Level 3 | Positive, balanced | Negative | Ineffective | a. Active structuring of communication<br>b. Teaching of communication skills |
| Level 4 | Positive, unbalanced, hierarchical | Negative | Ineffective | a. Family life review focused on establishing the adult status of the offspring and adult-to-adult relationships between elderly parents and adult offspring<br>b. Boundary setting<br>c. Active challenging of family members' nonadult perceptions of each other |
| Level 5 | Negative, weak, or ambivalent | Negative, unengaged, and lacking in depth | Ineffective | a. Family life review<br>b. Active challenging of family members' negative perceptions (and lack of positive perceptions) of each other<br>c. Inducing empathy for the positions of other family members<br>d. Creation of emotionally positive exchanges between elderly and adult offsping<br>e. Blocking of any and all attempts to communicate about or problem solve the serious issues facing the family until substantial progress has been made in building a positive attachment |

*and son-in-law were not allowing their 10-year-old son to visit his grandfather. The grandfather and grandson had been especially close and Mr. Williams had told his wife, the physician, and his daughter that he wanted to see his grandson. The family gathered in the physician's office with Mrs. Williams and her daughter and son-in-law in attendance. They talked at length about Mr. William's desire to see his grandson. They each cried as they talked about how difficult Mr. William's illness was for them. The daughter and her husband stated how bad they felt for their son because they did not lose their own grandparents until they were in their twenties. They had both been away at college when their grandparents had died and they felt that they had had the privilege of long relationships with their grandparents that their son was now losing. They had not had to deal with death when they were children and they were now afraid of traumatizing their son if they made a mistake in dealing with his grandfather's impending death. The therapist lavished praise on the boy's parents for their insight, for their commitment to their family relationships, and for their desire to do the right thing for their son and for their father. After much reassurance that they had the wisdom and sensitivity to help their son deal with his feelings about seeing his grandfather, they decided it was time to let their son and grandfather visit. They knew the situation would be difficult emotionally, but with reassurance from the therapist, they now knew that they were capable of supporting their son and felt confident that they were making the right decision.*

In this consultation the therapist listened to the family's problems and underscored their strengths. The therapist was able to reassure the family members of their ability to cope with the emotions that would arise from a visit of the grandson with the grandfather. Because it was a novel situation for the family

members, they were not certain of their abilities to cope with it. Reassurance and support was all the intervention they needed.

## Level 2 Interventions for Problems in Problem Solving

Many families function well and competently handle most crises that come their way but seek therapy when these usually successful problem-solving methods are not enough to manage their current difficulties. These are families whose members have positive attachments toward each other, communicate well, and have a history of successfully working out their problems. Because these are families that have traditionally solved problems well, intervention can focus on supporting the family members' traditional methods of problem solving. This is done by supplying liberal amounts of emotional support to the family while actively helping family members come up with ideas to solve their problems. These families have become overwhelmed and may have lost confidence in their ability to cope and lost hope that they can solve the current dilemma. In these families, members are able successfully to communicate their ideas and listen respectfully to each other's opinions with minimal structuring of communication by therapists.

*WE JUST HAVEN'T SAT DOWN AND TALKED ABOUT IT*

*Mr. Kaplan called the therapist and asked for an appointment. He told the therapist that his son and daughter and their spouses were fighting and unable to cooperate. He said he needed his offsprings' help so that he could take care of his wife, who was demented and bedridden after suffering several strokes. Mr. Kaplan, his son and daughter, and their spouses came to the first session. Within minutes of the session's beginning, the son and daughter were arguing with each other about the need for the other person to contribute more to their parents welfare. It turns out that over the years the two sides of the family had gotten along fairly well, but during the last 3 years their parents' failing health had resulted in tension between brother and sister. At the therapist's prompting the family members told stories of happier times before their parents' health diminished. The therapist used this information to create a verbal picture of solid and loving family overwhelmed by circumstances that would tear many families apart, but "Here you are trying to work together because you care so much. Because you, Mr. Kaplan, with your wife, set the stage so long ago for a family that sticks together. You all have so much going for you as a family that I am confident that with a little help, you will all be able to work together to help your father take care of your mother." Using this verbal picture as backdrop, the therapist began carefully structuring family problem-solving discussions about caregiving.*

It turned out that not only was the mother disabled, but the father was on renal dialysis and had severe heart failure. It took five sessions before the son and daughter were able to discuss family problems together without the discussion disintegrating. By building a positive verbal picture of the family and describing the problems facing the family as external to the family itself (White & Epston, 1990; Wynne et al., 1992), the family members were able to begin working together to solve their own problems without need for therapy. They did, however, need to link up with community health care agencies and visiting nurse services and place their mother on the waiting list for a nursing home. The therapist and primary care physician collaborated to guide them in getting the extra help they needed to support in-home care for the mother and father and aid them in preparing for the future when their parents might no longer be able to be cared for in their own home.

## Level 3 Interventions for Problems in Communication

These are families who lapse into chaos when confronted by major problems, even though in noncrisis times they manage to maintain more or less smooth relationships with each other. They care about each other and maintain regular contact, but they do little to communicate about serious issues facing their family. Generally, there is a history of arguments and bad feelings related to times of crisis. When confronted with a crisis such as depression or other illness of an older family member, these families are unable to develop a common understanding of the problem and are thus unable to do even rudimentary problem solving. These families are said to have positive and balanced attachment/caregiving but negative communication and ineffective problem solving.

Families with communication problems need active structuring of their conversation during therapy sessions. Often they are in the habit of arguing rather than listening, assuming rather than wondering and checking, accusing rather than expressing their own feelings and asking for clarification. Frequently, communication training, similar to that advocated by Guerney (1977), presents a model for changing the way family members talk with each other. We teach family members to do active listening, which we define as carefully listening to another family member and actively responding with comments that demonstrate listening to the other.

Structuring the sessions in this manner has the benefit of slowing down or stopping the escalation of conflict many of these families experience in their interactions. Therapy should be a different experience—it should be a change from the way they normally relate. Communication training allows clients to express their views, hurts, and disappointments to each other, but in a controlled manner that sets the stage for each party to actively listen and respond respectfully to the other.

*MY SISTER (MY BROTHER) IS
AN IDIOT
    Dr. Moore felt annoyed as she read another phone message from Sandy, the daughter of one of his older patients, Mrs. Peak. Sandy and her brother George called Dr. Moore two to three times a week requesting help or complaining about her care of their mother. Sandy and George also complained about each other to Dr. Moore, and Dr. Moore was beginning to feel caught in the middle. Mrs. Peak had*

*Alzheimer's disease, and Dr. Moore was concerned that unless Sandy and George started working together, Mrs. Peak would not receive the care she needed. Dr. Moore arranged a family meeting with Sandy, George, and a family therapist. Within minutes of starting Sandy and George were arguing, pressing charge and countercharge against each other, and calling each other names. The therapist immediately intervened, stopped each one from interrupting the other, and began to insist that they take turns talking and listening to the other. If one person made highly critical statements to the other, the therapist insisted that he or she rephrase the statement. The therapist gained leverage to structure the session in this manner by heavily connoting the underlying positive feelings of Sandy and George for each other. "I know that there are problems now, but I can tell that deep down you both care deeply about your mother and you also care about each other. This is a family that has always cared for each other, and I know you two wish to continue that tradition. With all this stress of your mother's illness, it has been hard for you two to find ways to work together, but I am confident that you can again find ways to talk over your problems, understand each other, and eventually decide upon good solutions for your mother and yourselves." The therapist placed communication first (i.e., "find ways to talk over your problems") before he suggested that Sandy and George try to solve their problems. For the next four sessions Sandy and George learned to communicate again. Their therapist insisted they slow down, actively listen to each other, and demonstrate that they understood the other as they talked. Only after they had developed the new habit of active listening were they encouraged to try to generate solutions and to begin making decisions together about their mother's care.*

Sandy and George were positively attached to each other and to their mother. The therapist was able to build on that positive attachment to help them change their communication style. After Level 3 interventions changed their communication patterns, the therapist guided them through problem-solving activities, helping them generate possible solutions and make joint decisions about goals for their mother's care (Level 2 interventions). Finally, the therapist consulted with them about possible solutions and referred them to appropriate agencies in the community that could aid in caring for their mother (Level 1 interventions).

## Level 4 Interventions for Problems in Attachment/Caregiving (Unbalanced and Hierarchical)

Level 4 interventions are required when hierarchy and lack of balance in attachment/caregiving thwart needed communication and problem solving regarding problems of older family members. In these families there are positive feelings toward the parents from the adult offspring but there has never been a shift in the role of the adult offspring in the family. Earlier in this chapter we discussed how important it is for adult offspring to develop adult-to-adult relationships with their parents. When this does not happen, adult offspring are often unable to take on responsibility for decisions or care that older family members may need. In these families the older parents still hold the decision-making power in the family (hierarchy) and maintain at least the illusion that they are still responsible to care for their adult offspring (unbalanced caregiving). These problems in attachment/caregiving usually mean that communication and problem solving are precluded from being positive and effective.

There are three general types of interventions that can help change the balance and hierarchy of attachment/caregiving: (a) family life review—focused on establishing the adult status of the offspring and adult-to-adult relationships between older parents and adult offspring, (b) boundary setting, and (c) active challenge of family members' nonadult perceptions of each other. These interventions can be used independently of each other, or boundary making and challenging perceptions can be used in conjunction with life review.

*Life review* refers to a technique first described by Butler (1963) and expanded to family therapy by Hargrave and Anderson (1992). Butler described life review as a developmental task of aging. He stated that many older people engage in the act of reminiscence and suggested that reminiscence itself might be a mental process of particular meaning and importance to older persons. He hypothesized that the outcome of this life review could be candor, serenity, and wisdom or despair and depression, depending on the conclusions that older people draw from reviewing their life. He proposed that psychotherapy with older people ought to take advantage of this natural tendency of older people to review their lives and build at least part of the therapy process around this review. In order to intervene in family relationships, we propose a family life review in which family members engage in reviewing their lives together and evaluating how they want to construct their future together. In Level 4 and Level 5 we discuss two distinct uses of family life review. In Level 4 the purpose is to impact the caregiving balance and hierarchy of the attachment/caregiving bond by helping to develop adult-to-adult relationships between the generations. In Level 5 the purpose is to change negative attachment between parents and adult offspring to a neutral or preferably positive bond.

Family life review takes place by having the family members tell the story of their family. Using the genogram as a start, parents can be prompted to tell their offspring about their own parents and their own childhood. Parents can tell the story of their courtship and marriage, pregnancies, births, miscarriages, and the stories of the early lives of their children. Family life review is much like family of origin therapy except that it is motivated by the needs of the older client, not the needs of a young or middle aged adult. Most family therapy literature on family of origin therapy focuses on the problems and needs of the younger generation to differentiate from or be empowered within their relationships with their parents (Bowen, 1978; Framo, 1992; Williamson, 1991). Life review focuses on changing relationships in the family from the top down.

Family life review directly impacts the attachment/caregiving balance by helping family members develop new views of each other. As parents and their offspring review their life together, each can be encouraged to develop a more realistic view of the other. Parents can be reminded of their struggles with their own parents and recall their need to develop their own authority in their family system. They in turn can be persuaded to encourage the development of personal authority in their own children based on how important they know it was for themselves. Often this may involve boundary setting and direct challenges to parents' adult offsprings' perceptions of each other.

Boundary setting is an important intervention in intergenerational family therapy. At times during life reviews in families with hierarchical intergenerational relationships and unbalanced caregiving, parents will feel free to comment negatively and intrusively on their children's lives. Therapists may need to step in to block such comments or to encourage the adult offspring to respond appropriately, telling their parents that such advice is neither desired nor appreciated. Because these families are typically negative in their communication or lack depth in their communication and are unable to talk about negative emotions, it may be best to channel communication through the therapist until the family is ready to work directly on communication issues. The therapist can do this by asking the adult offspring how they feel about what their parents just said and then reframing and conveying that information in boundary-setting ways to the parents. If the adult offspring ask their parents for advice or help in ways that maintain their nonadult status, then therapists need to block those interactions by teaching the parents to set limits on what is appropriate for them to give to their adult offspring, or again channel communication from parents to offspring to help set these boundaries.

As the family story unfolds, the therapist constantly looks for instances or aspects of the story that can be highlighted to underscore the adult status of the offspring and the "normal person" status of the parents. Parents in a hierarchical relationship with their adult offspring may have a hard time recognizing the achievements or competence of their off-spring. Offspring in a one-down position to their parents may have a difficult time recognizing their own competence and the fact that their parents are "regular people" who make mistakes and have needs just like anyone else. The difference between these families and those at Level 5 is that at Level 4 the therapist can consistently build upon the fact that these family members do care about each other. Underlying their relationships are positive feelings and a reasonably positive family history. The idea is that they started out feeling positive about each other, but the relational development was stunted. The children were not encouraged, for whatever reason, to become adults in the eyes of their parents and thus in their own minds too. This delayed development forestalls the formation of open communication and effective problem solving, which are the reasons these families end up in a therapist's office.

### MY HUSBAND IS SICK AND I NEED HELP WITH MY DAUGHTER

*Mrs. Schirmer called the therapist for help in coping with her husband's illness—he was undergoing radiation therapy for prostate cancer. The problem she stated was that she and her daughter were constantly getting into arguments that ended with her daughter breaking down and crying. She was at her wits' end, since she really needed her daughter's help. Mrs. Schirmer made an appointment for herself and her husband, promising to bring her daughter and son-in-law. However, the couple arrived for the appointment without their daughter. They both stated that they thought therapy would be too upsetting for their daughter because she had been hospitalized twice for suicide attempts and had suffered with depression throughout her life. They also reported that they spent a great deal of time and money supporting their daughter and son-in-law, who they considered to be irreponsible with money and not completely attentive to their children.*

*The therapist was able to convince Mrs. and Mrs. Schirmer that including their daughter in therapy was essential if this problem was to be improved and that resolving this conflict would decrease stress and tension on their daughter. The therapist called their daughter, Mrs. Martin, during the session to invite her and Mr. Martin to the next session.*

*The Schirmers and the Martins both came to the next session. As the therapist began joining with the Martins and they talked about their children, he underscored their concern for their children and their closeness as a family. At this point, Mrs. Schirmer interrupted to criticize her daugther and son-in-law for the way they handled money. The therapist immediately began to structure the session and worked to draw out each person's perception of the conflict between mother and daughter. After listening to the pain the family members felt about being stuck in this conflict (the men wanted it to end, Mrs. Martin felt her mother was overbearing, and Mrs. Schirmer was afraid for her daughter yet felt she was irresponsible) the therapist suggested that working together in therapy might help them find a way to work together better during this crisis of Mr. Schirmer's illness. He described them as a family who cared a great deal about each other, but because of these arguments they were not able to deal with this new crisis.*

*Therapy proceeded with a family life review starting with the Schirmers. They were encouraged to tell the story of their relationship, during which the therapist underscored both their strengths and struggles, seeking to paint a realistic picture of Mr. and Mrs. Schirmer to help their adult offspring see them as more human, and less as the all-powerful and all-knowing parents. As the story of Mrs. Martin's childhood and adolescence was told, the therapist took every opportunity to underscore Mrs. Martin's strengths and to praise her parents for fostering them. When the story moved to Mr. and Mrs. Martin's courtship,*

the therapist consistently drew parallels between Mr. and Mrs. Schirmer's early relationship and Mr. and Mrs. Martin's early
years as a couple.

*During this life review the therapist
used similarities between these couples of
two different generations to indirectly and
directly challenge their views of each other.
The parents were challenged to see that
their daughter and her husband often did
as good a job in managing their lives as
they themselves did in managing theirs.
Also, the parents were prompted to praise
Mr. and Mrs. Martin for their successes
and to verbally acknowledge their competencies. In turn, Mr. and Mrs Martin were
encouraged to ask their parents questions
about their struggles and failures, which
helped equalize the sense of power and
mastery in their relationships.*

*With the establishment of adult-to-adult
relationships between the generations, this
family was able to begin talking about
their current dilemma, sharing their concerns and fears about the future. Eventually they were able to develop plans for
Mr. and Mrs. Schirmer to continue to be a
source of support for their daughter and
son-in-law, and the Martins were able to
find ways to provide Mrs. Martin's parents
with extra help during the time when her
father was ill and receiving intensive treatment for cancer.*

## Level 5 Interventions for Problems in Attachment/Caregiving (Negative, Weak, or Ambivalent Attachment)

The most difficult families to work with are those
with negative, weak, or ambivalent attachment bonds
between the generations (Doane, Hill, & Diamond,
1991). These families often have a history of conflict
and marginal functioning during the time when the
adult offspring were being raised. The problems of
these families can seem overwhelming and intractable
to family therapists because therapists must manage
two levels of behavior during therapy: attachment
and communication. The critical and negative com-

munication of the family members toward each other
and toward the older client keeps the emotional atmosphere of therapy sessions on edge, which makes
progress in reconstructing attachment bonds difficult
and threatens the continuation of therapy. Therapists
have to be vigilant to actively suppress negative communication and criticism during therapy sessions
while trying to rebuild or develop positive feelings
between the generations.

We have found two typical constellations of attachment and communication: disturbed attachment
with neutral or unengaged communication and disturbed attachment with highly critical communication. Each of these constellations presents its own
unique treatment challenges.

Families with disturbed attachment and neutral or
unengaged communication present a unique set of
treatment issues. In these families there is often a
distinct lack of depth or emotional connection. These
families run the continuum from polite disengagement to complete emotional cutoff. Therapists may
be confused by those family members who do attend
therapy sessions. They will be polite and listen in-
tently to the problems their elders are facing, but
they offer no assistance or express unwillingness to
be involved in helping to deal with the problems.
They will state that they do not have time or that
their elder's problems are not their problems, occasionally expounding a philosophy of individualism
over family ties. Rather than vigilance, these families
require patience and extreme circumspection as therapists attempt to create more positive attachments.
Adult offspring have dealt with the pain and disappointment of their negative, weak, or ambivalent attachments by disengaging and cutting off from their
elders. These offspring may flee therapy if therapists'
attempts to change the nature of the attachment
bond are too overt. Often the adult offspring can be
engaged in therapy for the purpose of "helping or
consulting with the therapist who is helping their elder." If therapists can show respect for and honor
the need of the adult offspring to remain safely disengaged or cut off from their older parents in the
face of disappointing attachment bonds with them,
they may be able to engage the adult offspring in an
exploration of those bonds both for their sake and
for the sake of their older parents.

Therapy with families with disturbed attachment and highly critical communication requires a high-wire balancing act for therapists. In these families, negative feelings toward family members are openly displayed, and this negativity in communication can reinforce the negative attachment family members have for one another. Therapists have to control the negative communication so that it does not cause family members to quit participating in therapy; yet therapists must remain respectful of the story, often including many negative incidents, that family members may feel compelled to tell about their life together.

The basic method of reconstructing attachment bonds between the generations is the process of family life review described in Level 4. The difference is one of emphasis: here the goal is to establish a positive emotional bond where a negative, weak, or ambivalent bond currently exists. The following case illustrates how empathy for the elder's position can be induced in an angry and blaming son. In this case, there were positive benefits for both the son and the mother.

### MY MOTHER ALLOWED MY FATHER TO ABUSE ME

Mrs. Potter, a 67-year-old woman, suffering with depression, was cut off from her 35-year-old son, Mark, and his children. Mrs. Potter's husband was an alcoholic and had physically and verbally abused her and her oldest son, Mark. She felt that Mark blamed her for the abuse he received from his father. Mark had drinking problems of his own, was raising several children with limited help from their mother, and had managed to complete a bachelor's degree in social work. Mark agreed to attend one session, explaining to the therapist that this would be a chance to tell his mother why he wants nothing to do with her. During the session Mrs. Potter was encouraged to describe how she met her husband, their early years of marriage, and Mr. Potter's drinking and violence toward her and Mark. Several times during this story the therapist had to block very negative com-

ments from Mark toward his mother. The therapist asked Mark his opinion as a social worker: What would he do if a woman came into his office requesting help with an alcoholic and violent husband? He talked about safety issues, lining up shelter, orders of protection, and keeping the children out of harm's way. Then they discussed the status of women and the availability of such external supports in the 1950s, when his mother was living with his father and raising their children: There were few if any shelters for battered women. Her family told her it was her fault that her husband beat her; thus she had no support for standing up to or for leaving her husband.

This information was used to induce empathy for his mother's position. Mark was encouraged to see that his mother was stuck; she had few options and no support for using those options that did exist. His mother told how terrible she felt about the abuse Mark experienced and how helpless she had been to stop it. Mark stated that he understood all that, but that he still felt very angry and did not know if he could ever forgive her for what he went through. The session ended with Mark stating that he might be willing to come back for another session in the future, but not right away. Five months later Mark checked himself into an alcohol treatment program and initiated contact with his mother. He wrote her a letter stating that he now realized it was not her fault and that he had been compounding her difficulties by blaming her. After he left treatment they began seeing each other on a more regular basis and she began to develop a stronger relationship with the grandchildren.

If there is a medical or mental health crisis, it may not wait for the family to resolve its difficulties before solutions are found. These crises may need to be managed through hospitalization, day care, day treatment, visiting nurse services, or health aid service. The services may need to be arranged through the intervention of the primary care physician, medical social workers, adult protective workers, or other professionals.

## CONCLUSION

The problems facing older persons and their family members will only increase in the coming years. The growth of the older population is dramatic evidence that there will be more and more need for family therapists with expertise in working with older people and their families. More family therapists need to accept the challenge of working with older persons, which includes working with the intergenerational and health complexities that accompany therapy with later life families. Just as family therapists working with children need to be schooled in developmental disabilities, attention deficit disorders, and learning disabilities, family therapists working with older people need to be knowledgeable about chronic illnesses, the neuropsychology of aging, and the cognitive and emotional side effects of medications.

We hope to see a substantial increase in family therapy publications about aging in the future. Family therapy with older persons is particularly challenging and invigorating because it requires a knowledge of the entire life cycle, the ability to work with family members of all ages (older clients, their great-great grandchildren, and the generations in between), a knowledge of medical issues, and the ability to work collaboratively with other health care providers. We encourage others to join us in this challenge.

## References

Albert, M. S., & Moss, M. B. (1988). *Geriatric neuropsychology*. New York: Guilford Press.

Birren, J. E., & Schaie, K. W. (1990). *Handbook of the psychology of aging*. San Diego: Academic Press.

Birren, J. E., Sloane, R. B., & Cohen, G. D. (1992). *Handbook of mental health and aging*. San Diego: Academic Press.

Bowen, M. (1978). *Family therapy in clinical practice*. New York: Aronson.

Butler, R. N. (1963). The life review: An interpretation of reminiscence in the aged. *Psychiatry Journal for the Study of Interpersonal Processes, 26*, 65–76.

Butler, R. N., Lewis, M., & Sunderland, T. (1991). *Aging and mental health: Positive psychosocial and biomedical approaches*. New York: MacMillan.

Carstensen, L. L., & Edelstein, B. A. (1987). *Handbook of clinical gerontology*. New York: Pergamon Press.

Carter, B., & McGoldrick, M. (Eds. ). (1988). *The changing family life cycle: A framework for family therapy*. New York: Gardner Press.

De Shazer, S. (1985). *Keys to solution in brief therapy*. New York: Norton.

Doane, J. A., Hill, L. W., & Diamond, D. (1991). A developmental view of therapeutic bonding in the family: Treatment of the disconnected family. *Family Process, 30*, 155–175.

Erikson, E. H. (1950). *Childhood and society*. New York: Norton.

Erikson, E. H. (1968). *Identity, youth and crisis*. New York: Norton.

Erikson, E. H., Erikson, J. M., & Kivnick, H. Q. (1986). *Vital involvement in old age: The experience of old age in our time*. New York: Norton.

Framo, J. L. (1992). *Family of origin therapy: An intergenerational approach*. New York: Brunner/Mazel

Gallagher, D., Rose, J., Rivera, P., Lovett, S., & Thompson, L. W. (1989). Prevalence of depression in family caregivers. *Gerontologist, 29*, 449–456.

Gelfand, E. G. (1982). *Aging: The ethnic factor*. Boston: Little, Brown.

Guerney, B. G. (1977). *Relationship enhancement*. San Francisco: Jossey-Bass.

Haley, J. (1976). *Problem-solving therapy*. San Francisco: Jossey-Bass.

Hargrave, T. D., & Anderson, W. T. (1992). *Finishing well: Aging and reparation in the intergenerational family*. New York: Brunner/Mazel.

Henton, J., Cate, R., & Emery, B. (1984). The dependent elderly: Targets for abuse. In W. H. Quinn & G. A. Hughston (Eds. ), *Independent aging: Family and social systems perspectives*. Rockville, MD: Aspen.

Herr, J. J., & Weakland, J. H. (1979). *Counseling elders and their families*. New York: Springer.

Hughston, G. A., Christopherson, V. A., & Bonjean, M. J. (1989). *Aging and family therapy: Practitioner perspectives on golden pond*. New York: Haworth.

King, D. A., Bonnacci, D. D., & Wynne, L. C. (1990). Families of cognitively impaired elders: Helping adult children confront the filial crisis. *Clinical Gerontologist, 10*, 3–15.

Knight, B. (1986). *Psychotherapy with older adults*. Newbury Park, CA: Sage.

McDaniel, S. H., Hepworth, J., & Doherty, W. J. (1992). *Medical family therapy: A biopsychosocial approach to families with health problems*. New York: Basic Books.

McGoldrick, M., Pearce, J. K., & Giordano, J. (1982). *Ethnicity and family therapy*. New York: Guilford Press.

Pillemer, K., & Finkeher, D. (1989). Causes of elder abuse: Caregiver stress versus problem relationships. *American Journal of Orthopsychiatry, 59,* 179–187.

Rolf, J., Masten, A. S., Cicchetti, D., Nuechterlein, K. H., & Weintraub, S. (1990). *Risk and protective factors in the development of psychopathology*. New York: Cambridge University Press.

Schaie, K. W. (1993). Ageist language in psychological research. *American Psychologist, 48,* 49–51.

Shanas, E. (1980). Older people and their families: The new pioneers. *Journal of Marriage and the Family, 42,* 12.

Shields, C. G., & Wynne, L. C. (in press). The strength—vulnerability model of mental health and illness in the elderly. In T. Hargrave & S. Hanna (Eds.), *Between generations: Handbook of family therapy and later life*. New York: Brunner/Mazel.

Steinglass, P., Bennett, L. A, Wolin, S. J., & Reiss, D. (1987). *The alcoholic family*. New York: Basic Books.

Steuer, J., & Austin, E. (1980). Family abuse of the elderly. *Journal of the American Geriatrics Society 28,* 372–376.

U.S. Department of Health and Human Services. (1991). *Aging America: Trends and projections*. Washington, DC: Health and Human Services.

Walsh, F. (1988). The family in later life. In B. Carter & M. McGoldrick, (Eds. ), *The changing family life cycle* (pp. 312—327). New York: Gardner Press.

White, M., & Epston, D. (1990). *Narrative means to therapeutic ends*. New York: Norton.

Williamson, D. (1991). *The intimacy paradox*. New York: Guilford Press.

Wynne, L. C. (1984). The epigenesis of relational systems: A model for understanding family development. *Family Process, 23,* 297–318.

Wynne, L. C., McDaniel, S. H., & Weber, T. T. (1986). *Systems consultation: A new perspective for family therapy*. New York: Guilford Press.

Wynne, L. C., McDaniel, S. H., & Weber, T. T. (1987). Professional politics and the concepts of family therapy, family consultation, and systems consultation. *Family Process, 26,* 153–166.

Wynne, L. C., Shields, C. G., & Sirkin, M. (1992). Illness, family theory and family therapy: I. Conceptual issues. *Family Process, 31,* 3–18.

Wynne, L. C., Sirkin, M., & Shields, C. G. (in press). Illness, family theory and family therapy: II. Clinical issues. *Family Process*.

# PART III

# ASSESSMENT AND RESEARCH IN FAMILY PSYCHOLOGY

# Introduction

As is evident in most of the chapters in this book, family psychology brings to the field of systems therapy a strong concern with empirical research. Observation, one aspect of such research, has been a strong focus of the family therapy movement from the beginning. From the outset, many schools of family therapy encouraged observation of treatment through one-way mirrors and videotaping. Thus, it is "in the bones" of family psychologists and family therapists to consider the evaluation and assessment of the family—as well as of individuals—and the act of therapy itself through of process of direct observation and empirical research.

We want this process to tell us about the strengths, the weaknesses, and the unique perceptions of the family and its individual members. We also want to learn about the relationship between individual psychopathology and family disturbance. And we of course want to know when, where, how, and with whom family therapy is effective. The chapters in this section provide both a theoretical and an applied perspective on such issues.

In "Marital and Family Assessment: A Multifaceted, Multilevel Approach," Douglas Snyder, Timothy Cavell, Robert Heffner, and Laurel Mangrum present an evaluative schema that helps the therapist to clearly articulate the family's difficulties on several systems levels: the individuals, the dyads, the nuclear family, the extended family, the community, and the larger culture. Assessment in these realms is described along five dimensions: cognitive; affective, communication and interpersonal; structural and developmental; and control, sanctions, and related be-

havioral domains. The authors remind us that the evaluative process is an ongoing and recursive process and should be guided by sophisticated theory based on a solid empirical foundation.

In chapter 10, "The Evolution of Family-Based Psychopathology," David Miklowitz explores the association between individual psychopathology and family disturbance. He carefully dissects the complex controvery around this issue from both a historical and a theoretical perspective and pays particular attention to the development of theories about the etiology and treatment of schizophrenia. He presents evidence to uphold the position that schizophrenia has genetic and neurobiological bases and that the family is a risk or protective factor that may augment or diminish the likelihood that the disorder will become full blown. Reviewing the literature on family interventions in severe psychopathology, Miklowitz examines psychoeducational family interventions in schizophrenia and in mood disorders, and he presents a case study of behavioral family management for bipolar disorder.

In "Family Therapy Research," James Alexander and Cole Barton focus on research about clinically meaningful processes and clinical populations. They remind us of the myriad complexities that face the researcher in a dynamic field that operates in larger sociopolitical, economic, and moral and ethical contexts. Taking the position that we must read the literature for a "preponderance of evidence" and then draw reasonable conclusions, they develop a comparative analysis of different types of marital and family therapy. Next, they explore the effectiveness of the different types of marital and family therapy with specific problems, such as alcoholism, schizophrenia, depression, anxiety, and behavior disorders in children and adolescents. Discussing current trends and future directions in family therapy research, they describe how some traditions in marital treatment are being challenged. They note that research supports the wisdom of the blurring of definitional boundaries that is occurring today in the field of both marital and family therapy. However, they stress that tensions between approaches can be positive and that alternative voices can help prevent complacency in established intervention models.

In "Circumplex Model of Family Systems: Integrating Ethnic Diversity and Other Social Systems," Dean Gorall and David Olson review the history and recent refinements in the circumplex model of family functioning, developed more than 15 years ago by Olson and his associates. This model is of particular interest because it provides us not only with a theory of family functioning, but also with a means of assessment and therapeutic intervention. In addition to describing the latest conceptualization and evaluative instruments that are based on the model, the authors pay particular attention to its use with populations other than those that were used in the original research. For example, the authors describe how their model has now been used to study ethnically diverse families, single parent and blended families, and lesbian relationships. They conclude by discussing ecosystemic applications of the circumplex model to other systems, such as school–family and family-business systems.

CHAPTER 9

# MARITAL AND FAMILY ASSESSMENT: A MULTIFACETED, MULTILEVEL APPROACH

*Douglas K. Snyder, Timothy A. Cavell, Robert W. Heffer,*

*and Laurel F. Mangrum*

*Amy and Mike Brewer's distress was clearly etched on their faces as they sat down on their therapist's couch and began to describe their current difficulties. The couple had been referred by a child psychologist at the local health-care clinic for treatment of acute marital distress precipitated by Amy's sexual involvement with a co-worker and Mike's physical aggression toward his wife. Both parents reported conflict regarding care of their two young sons, the older of whom had repeatedly been in trouble at school for disruptive and aggressive behavior toward his classmates.*

How should the therapist go about acquiring an understanding of this family's difficulties? What aspects of family functioning should be assessed? What levels of the family system should be targeted for initial evaluation—individual, couple, or family—and from whom should information be obtained? What assessment approaches would facilitate collection of the necessary information, and what methods should be used for organizing these data and incorporating them in treatment?

Although many of the overall objectives of marital and family assessment overlap with those of traditional individual assessment strategies, the task of evaluating and understanding couples and families is both qualitatively and quantitatively far more com-

plex. Essential to this endeavor is a conceptual framework for organizing both the process and outcome of family systems assessment.

This chapter presents underlying assumptions and overarching objectives directing the family assessment process. We delineate multiple levels at which couples and family assessment proceeds and, within each level, describe conceptual domains critical to effective intervention from a variety of theoretical perspectives. A clinical case study highlights principal assessment constructs. Finally, both the strengths and limitations of various evaluation strategies are discussed.

## PRINCIPLES AND GUIDING ASSUMPTIONS

## Marital and Family Assessment Is Both Qualitatively and Quantitatively Distinct From the Assessment of Individuals

Marital and family therapy differs from most individual therapy in important ways affecting the assessment process. First, whereas participants in individual therapy acknowledge on at least some level their own responsibility for bringing about change, participants in couples and family therapy typically focus initially on the need for other members of the family to change. Second, in contrast to individual therapy, marital and family therapy offers the unique opportunity to observe directly the problematic interpersonal exchanges of clients and to contrast these with subjective appraisals of these events. Third, the sheer number of participants in family therapy tends to increase both the complexity and pace of within-session exchanges; it also affects the nature of the therapist–client relationship. Finally, the level of hostility expressed directly within couples and family therapy typically exceeds that experienced in individual therapy and influences both the pacing and nature of assessment and intervention strategies.

## Assessment Is Vital to Effective Intervention

Couples and families vary, and without adequate assessment even structured therapeutic approaches can be misapplied. Marital and family therapists must use assessment techniques that quickly target therapeutic issues and avoid evaluation strategies that do not influence treatment.

## Assessment Should Be Guided by Theory

Theoretical differences in how a therapist conceptualizes the marital or family system lead to significant differences in decisions concerning what facets to assess and how to link findings to clinical intervention (Barnett & Zucker, 1990; Jacob & Tennenbaum, 1988). Although we favor an informed eclectic or pluralistic approach that draws selectively on theoretical constructs and clinical procedures bearing greatest relevance to a given couple or family, we also concur with Filsinger (1983b) that "most assessment techniques are . . . linked, to some degree, to specific theoretical orientations and may do a better job of measuring some concepts than others" (p. 19).

## Assessment Must Occur on Multiple Levels

The importance of multilevel assessment in marital and family therapy has been cited extensively (Cromwell & Peterson, 1981; Filsinger, 1983b; Grotevant & Carlson, 1989; Jacob & Tennenbaum, 1988; Schumm, 1990). We find it useful to conceptualize the following levels of assessment: (a) individuals, (b) dyads, (c) nuclear families, (d) extended family systems and related systems interfacing with the immediate family, and (e) community and cultural systems. Our clinical experience directs us typically to begin at an intermediate level of analysis—delineat-

ing distress at the couple or family level—and then moving in both directions toward the individual level and broader systemic levels.

## Assessment Must Proceed From Multiple Perspectives

The importance of both "insider" and "outsider" perspectives in couples and family assessment was initially noted by Olson (1977) and has subsequently been expanded to include both subjective and behavioral self-reports as well as subjective and behavioral observer reports. Both self-report and observational approaches contain inherent strengths and limitations that complement one another when they are used in a comprehensive assessment strategy.

## Assessment Is an Ongoing, Recursive Process

Assessment and intervention processes should reflect a continuous, iterative interweaving of evaluation, hypothesis formulation, intervention, and observation of effects—conducted across domains and across system levels. As a collaborative effort comprising interpretation and corrective feedback from both therapist and family members, the assessment process has itself been framed as a therapeutic intervention (Selvini, Boscolo, Cecchin, & Prata, 1980; Tomm, 1988).

## Assessment Should Be Based on an Empirical Foundation

Although we recognize the contributions that so-called new epistemologists have made in broadening our views of family systems, we are not yet ready to suspend our belief that families can be understood in both an objective and benign manner (cf. Cavell & Snyder, 1991). Within the positivist tradition, our theoretical leanings are diverse but driven primarily by empirically based research, although our experience as marital and family therapists undoubtedly influences our views on assessment as well.

Representative assessment techniques available to marital and family therapists are noted later in this chapter (see Table 1). However, selection of specific techniques must be guided by an integrative conceptual model addressing both multiple facets and levels of family systems.

## A CONCEPTUAL MODEL

Marital and family assessment is facilitated by an integrative conceptual model that considers multiple assessment techniques to gather information across distinct but overlapping domains at each system level. We have elected to organize assessment along five dimensions similar to those identified by both Grotevant and Carlson (1989) and Jacob and Tennenbaum (1988) in their reviews of family assessment models, namely: (a) cognitive; (b) affective; (c) communication and interpersonal; (d) structural and developmental; and (e) control, sanctions, and related behavioral domains. A graphic presentation of our conceptual model is provided in Figure 1. From a systems perspective, the nuclear family system comprises two or more individuals involved in one or more dyadic relationships. Each dyad is influenced, in part, by members' dyadic relationships with others. The nuclear family system lies embedded in an extended system including parents' respective families of origin as well as close relationships with others from work, school, or the neighborhood. Similarly, the extended system operates within a broader community or cultural context. Individuals' roles vary across system levels; for example, parents of the nuclear system function as children in their respective families of origin.

Each system level may be assessed across the five domains identified earlier. Consider, for example, the cognitive domain. At the individual level cognitive considerations include intelligence, aptitude, capacity for self-reflection and insight, and self-view. At both the dyadic and nuclear system levels, important cognitive factors include assumptions and standards regarding the relationship, expectancies, selective attention, and attributions regarding the causes for relationship events (Baucom, Epstein, Sayers, & Sher, 1989). Values and expectations of significant others outside the nuclear family, as well as community standards and subcultural norms, constitute additional cognitive elements at these extended system levels.

Inconsistencies in these cognitive components across system levels bear particular relevance to mar-

ital and family therapy. For example, relationship distress frequently derives from differences in expectations between husband and wife or between parent and teenage son or daughter. Inconsistencies at broader system levels may assume prominence in a family where members at one generational level strive to blend in with peers adopting a predominant or mainstream culture, while members of an older generation in the same home labor to preserve the distinguishing customs reflecting their ethnic heritage.

Information across domains may be gathered using multiple assessment strategies, including both formal and informal self-report and observational techniques. Clearly the most common evaluation strategy involves informal assessment of family members' self-reports and observation of their interactions during the clinical interview or therapy session. For some domains at some system levels, more formal techniques may complement informal assessment; however, the availability of formal or structured assessment techniques varies considerably across both domains and system levels. For example, structured self-report measures of dyadic affect abound, as do self- and other-reports of individual personality or psychopathology. Similarly, highly detailed observational systems for coding couples' and families' interactions have also been developed. By contrast, formal techniques for assessing constructs at the extended system or community/cultural system levels are virtually nonexistent.

This conceptual model is not intended to be necessarily exhaustive or prescriptive. Rigid adherence to a checklist approach both detracts from the interactive process of clinical assessment and neglects differential relevance of domains for any given couple or family. We liken the initial phases of assessment to scanning through television channels without a program, obtaining an initial impression of the offerings, and then returning to more salient material one selection at a time.

## Assessing Individual Members

The chapter began with a brief description of a couple referred to marital therapy for whom childrearing was a significant component of relationship distress. What strengths and limitations do these individuals

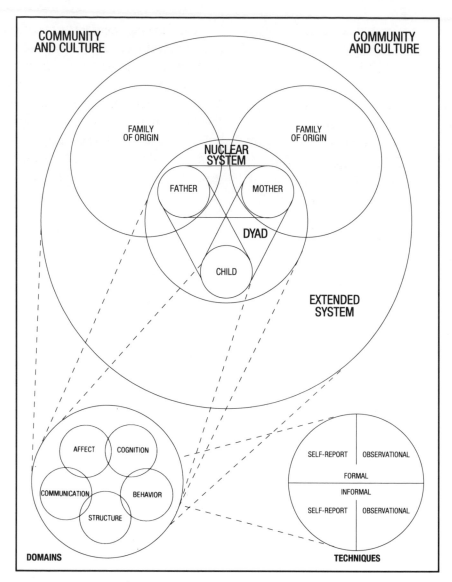

**FIGURE 1. Conceptual model for assessing families from a systems perspective. The model presents five system levels including: (a) individuals, (b) dyads, (c) the nuclear family, (d) the extended family system, and (e) the community and cultural systems. Each system level may be assessed across five overlapping domains: (a) cognitive; (b) affective; (c) communication and interpersonal; (d) structural and developmental; and (e) control, sanctions, and related behavioral domains. Information across domains may be gathered using multiple assessment strategies, including both formal and informal self-report and observational techniques.**

bring to their marriage? What capacity do they have for self-reflection and for adopting each other's perspectives? How motivated and able are they to modify their own behavior in order to bring about relationship change? What emotional or behavioral difficulties characterize the two young boys in this family, and to what extent may these result from or contribute to the parents' marital distress? How does each family member's current situation relate to his

or her own level of development and previous life experiences?

Addressing these questions requires consideration of unique resources and liabilities characterizing each member of the family system. For example, the therapist needs to assess each individual's ability to understand psychological or behavioral concepts and his or her capacity for self-reflection and insight, because alternative intervention modalities differ in the extent to which they require these abilities. School-related difficulties for children or adolescents may warrant assessment of basic intellectual ability and academic achievement using classroom observations or traditional measures of individual cognitive abilities. Educational and occupational attainment are relevant for adult members. Cognitive style, attitudes, and distortions should also be considered—particularly if this last element extends beyond irrational beliefs to a more serious thought disorder.

The content, intensity, and mutability of each individual's affect may also constrain the person's responsiveness to both the therapist and other family members. Anxiety constricts and immobilizes; the highly anxious person defends against both intra- and interpersonal stress and avoids risking new behaviors with uncertain outcomes. Depression generally suppresses level of response. One reason why depressive symptoms have consistently been found to predict poorer response to marital therapy may be the reduced energy and hopelessness that depressed partners bring to efforts toward relationship change (cf. Snyder, Mangrum, & Wills, 1993). Similarly, anger and hostility may exert a suppressive effect on other members' willingness to engage in collaborative exchange. The ability to relate warmly to others and to engage in goal-directed negotiation are critical elements of each individual's interpersonal style (Beavers, Hampson, & Hulgus, 1985; Grotevant & Carlson, 1989).

Capacity for behavioral self-control determines the extent to which individuals can defer immediate impulses toward self-gratification either for the sake of other persons' benefit or for preferred delayed rewards for oneself. Problems associated with individual deficits in self-control, especially those involving substance abuse or physical aggression, have impacts on the marital and family system well beyond the individual. Medical conditions or other health-related concerns may also have an impact on individuals' affect and capacity for self-control. (See Part VI of this volume.)

Developmental considerations are also of central importance. For example, from a psychosocial perspective, the successful resolution of identity issues necessarily precedes attainment of genuine intimacy (Erikson, 1968). Evaluating the developmental context looms prominently in family therapy with children and adolescents; as Jacob and Tennenbaum (1988) note, "Without this context, ideally derived from both theory and normative data, it is extremely difficult to anticipate whether the behavior is likely to change, over what period of time, to what degree, and in what direction" (p. 7). However, developmental context is no less important for adults (Levinson, 1986). For example, extramarital sexual behaviors of a 65-year-old grandfather in a marriage of 40 years might be presumed to have different antecedents and consequences than the same behavior in a 19-year-old who recently felt compelled to marry his girlfriend after she became pregnant.

Finally, assessment of individuals across these domains may warrant a formal diagnosis according to the *Diagnostic and Statistical Manual of Mental Disorders*, fourth edition (*DSM-IV*; American Psychiatric Association, 1994) reflecting individual symptomatology, level of adjustment, and degree of stress. In some cases, individual issues or difficulties may warrant referral of that spouse or family member to individual therapy as a complement to couples or family work. We recognize that this position conflicts with a purely systemic perspective in which individual symptoms are viewed not as problems to be vanquished but rather as mechanisms functioning to stabilize the marital or family system. However, to assume that symptoms serve only functional goals is empirically unfounded, unnecessarily limiting conceptually, and potentially damaging to the client–therapist relationship. As Nichols and Schwartz (1991) have observed, "The emphasis on functionalism too often has turned therapists into pathology detectives, hunting for clues to the underlying function and suspicious that the family's reports about their problems are attempts to mislead or obfuscate" (p. 156).

*CASE STUDY*

*How did assessment of individual domains provide important information relevant to treatment of Mike and Amy Brewer? Amy was a 40-year-old senior lecturer in physics at a large state university. Her professional status had been attained despite a long history of psychological diffi-*

culties. Her parents had been divorced when she was five, and Amy lived most of her childhood and adolescence with her alcoholic mother and younger brother. She described both neglect from her mother and physical abuse over several years from a stepfather and tearfully recalled spending hours as a toddler screaming from her crib while her mother drank and passed out. Amy suffered from recurrent depression and had been hospitalized for several months 10 years earlier following two suicide attempts. She had been physically dependent on alcohol and addicted to cocaine for a period spanning 7 years, but she had suspended all substance abuse other than occasional use of marijuana since becoming pregnant with her 6-year-old son, Johnny.

Mike was a 35-year-old semiskilled plumber's apprentice who had dropped out of school and left home to escape a physically abusive father. He too had a long history of alcohol and cocaine addictions and continued to use alcohol and marijuana daily. He had been unable to maintain steady employment over the past 2 years. Mike also acknowledged losing control of his anger, engaging in a variety of physically aggressive behaviors toward his wife and children, and, at one point, breaking the stock of a shotgun over his wife's head. His demeanor during conjoint therapy sessions was more one of perplexity than hostility, feeling generally overwhelmed by his inability to gain control over any substantive area of his life.

Although both Johnny and his 4-year-old brother Andrew presented their parents with challenges in behavior management, Johnny was identified by both as the more problematic youngster. His first-grade teacher reported chronic inattention and disruptive behavior in addition to physical aggression against other children. At home he threw tantrums and bit or kicked his mother when she tried to restrain him. Further inquiry revealed that 2 years earlier, Johnny had been sexually abused by a boy several years older at day care and on several occasions had been forced by this youngster to perform oral sex. Independent assessment of Johnny's cognitive functioning suggested an attention-deficit disorder, and school behavior improved somewhat in response to pharmacologic interventions.

## Assessing Dyads

What patterns of interaction characterize Amy and Mike's marriage and their relationships with their two children? How do they describe relationship conflicts within the family? What do they view as the causes of their distress, what efforts have they undertaken to resolve conflicts, and to what extent have these efforts been successful? How do Amy and Mike and their two sons feel toward each other? Were there times in the past when this family felt more cohesive? To what extent do Amy or Mike attempt to form coalitions with their sons to gain additional influence over their spouse?

Communication difficulties rank first among reasons couples give for entering marital therapy (Geiss & O'Leary, 1981); they also rank high among families entering therapy, along with complaints regarding children's lack of behavioral control. A variety of self-report and observational techniques have been developed for evaluating communication at the dyadic level (cf. Filsinger, 1983a; Robin & Weiss, 1980; Snyder, 1982). Most frequently studied among dyads is the ability to resolve conflicts and negotiate mutually acceptable solutions. Elements of problem-solving communication include problem identification, problem clarification, solution generation, implementation, and evaluation. Straus (1979) distinguishes among three primary tactics in couples' approaches to conflict: use of reasoning, verbal aggression, and physical aggression.

Separate from problem-solving communication is the expression and experience of each individual's affect. To what extent do persons in a relationship share their thoughts and feelings with one another in the absence of conflict? To what extent do they feel understood and cared for by the other? Affective communication proceeds on both verbal and nonverbal levels and may range from support and empathy to intrusive concern to hostile rejection. Some research data suggest that, among couples, nonverbal expression of negative affect is a particularly powerful indicator of overall relationship accord (Gottman, 1979).

Several affective domains emerge in a review of the relationship literature. The first—labeled "cohesion" by Olson, Sprenkle, and Russell (1979)—refers to the level and quality of emotional bonding between two individuals, similar to the concept of attachment in the developmental literature (Ainsworth, Blehar, Waters, & Wall, 1979). (An elaboration of Olson et al.'s circumplex model is presented in chap. 12 in this volume.) The distinction of cohesion from emotional expressiveness can be observed in the comparison of hostile-dependent with hostile-detached relationships.

Relationship satisfaction is the most widely measured and researched dimension of intimate dyads. As a construct of comfort or contentment, it is distinct from either closeness (cohesion) or emotional expressiveness. (Indeed, as therapists we are often struck by individuals satisfied with what we perceive as disengaged and nonresponsive relationships.) Unlike other dyadic dimensions of affect, relationship satisfaction is almost entirely a subjective phenomenon and does not lend itself to observer ratings. A variety of measures have been developed for assessing relationship satisfaction; some attempt to assess relationship satisfaction along specific dimensions of interaction (e.g., leisure time together, sexual interaction, or childrearing).

Commitment is an additional component of relationship affect. Independent of relationship satisfaction, what is each person's degree of intent or pledge to remain in the relationship? Given the decision to remain, what is each person's commitment to relationship change? Although commitment overlaps with cognitive elements and may be inferred on a behavioral level (e.g., failure of a spouse to pursue divorce; willingness of an adolescent to engage with a parent in relationship dialogue), our clinical impression is that commitment is both perceived and experienced on an affective level.

Recent literature has also begun to address the construct of "acceptance" in spousal relationships and "tolerance" in parenting—a recognition of relationship conflicts and an ability to suspend the hurt or anger associated with these conflicts (Jacobson, 1992). We perceive the construct of acceptance or letting go of anger as similar to the construct of "forgiveness" (Smedes, 1984; Sofield, Juliano, & Hammett, 1990)—although scholarly treatments of this term in the clinical or research literature are sparse.

Baucom et al. (1989) proposed five categories of cognitions moderating intimate relationships, including *assumptions* and *standards* about how relationships work, *selective attention* to relationship events and *attributions* regarding their causes, and *expectancies* for the relationship. For example, considerable evidence indicates that couples tend to accentuate the positive in nondistressed relationships and the negative in distressed relationships. Equally important are spouses' differences in assumptions and standards for their relationship and their tolerance of these differences.

Among structural considerations at the dyadic level, the one most frequently cited involves what Olson et al. (1979) have labeled "adaptability," roughly akin to flexibility and effectiveness in responding to demands both internal and external to the relationship. Related constructs from systems theory include entropy (i.e., disorder and chaos) and negentropy (i.e., organization and structure). Adaptive relationships require an optimal balance of organization and flexibility; imbalance toward either extreme (chaos or rigidity) impairs the relationship's capacity to grow and respond effectively to change.

Another structural consideration in relationships involves the distribution of power (Huston, 1983). The means by which two persons each struggle to exert influence on the other (positive versus negative; verbal versus nonverbal) and the models adopted for decision making (unilateral versus collaborative) are key dimensions in a dyadic relationship. A prominent pattern of interpersonal control labeled "coercion" (Patterson, 1982) involves the exchange of negative for positive reinforcement (i.e., the termination of aversive behavior by one individual contingent on the execution of positive [preferred] behavior by the other) and characterizes parent–child as well as spousal relationships.

Finally, developmental context applies to dyads as well. Independent of the individuals' ages, both the likelihood of specific conflicts and their interpretation and impact may vary as a function of the stage of the relationship's development. For example, parental conflict over privileges and responsibilities of teenage children has a different meaning for a couple married 20 years than for a couple of the same age married 6 months and dealing with one partner's children from a previous marriage.

*What dyadic considerations were important to therapy with the Brewer family? Amy and Mike Brewer had been married 5 years and lived together for 3 years before that. During the first 2 years of their relationship, the two interacted in large part around their respective cocaine abuse. Amy's comorbid depressive disorder contributed to her adopting a predominantly passive and submissive role in the marriage. As her substance abuse abated and she experienced growing success in her physics career, Mike's position of dominance in the home was increasingly threatened. His efforts to maintain control became progressively more violent, and Amy increasingly sought interpersonal rewards outside her marriage.*

*Both spouses reported extensive dissatisfaction with their marriage. Amy's level of discontent suggested wavering commitment to their relationship, and she acknowledged that she was considering divorce in order to escape this marriage and pursue a more satisfying relationship with her lover. Mike expressed strong desires for their marriage*

*to continue, but also indicated his belief that responsibility for change rested with Amy. Their lack of cohesion and persistent anger contributed to negative attributions regarding each other's behavior. Mike consistently viewed Amy's behaviors involving either the children or work as efforts to retreat from him, and she viewed his approaches as efforts to constrain and control her.*

*Mike's relationship with the boys was frequently punitive and occasionally aggressive. Within the past year Johnny had increasingly become more openly defiant toward his father, while Andrew remained quiet and withdrawn. Although Johnny was frequently intolerant of his younger brother, he had tried to protect him from his father's angry outbursts. Both boys often sought consolation from their mother, but Amy rarely experienced an emotional surplus with which to nurture them adequately. At times she perceived the boys as "clinging," and she wished to retreat from them but feared leaving them with their father. Neither parent reported many satisfying moments with their sons.*

*The Brewers' scores on the Marital Satisfaction Inventory (MSI; Snyder, 1979, 1981; Snyder & Costin, 1994; Snyder, Lachar, Freiman, & Hoover, 1991) confirmed high levels of relationship distress across several dimensions for both spouses (see Figure 2). The computer-based interpretive report (Snyder & Lachar, 1986) for the couple's profiles emphasized serious difficulties in communication, particularly in negotiating conflict.[1] Amy's level of discontent was significantly higher than Mike's in several areas, including global distress and disagreement about finances; both spouses*

[1] The *Marital Satisfaction Inventory* (including materials for administration and either hand or computer scoring and interpretation) is published and distributed by Western Psychological Services, 12031 Wilshire Boulevard, Los Angeles, CA 90025.

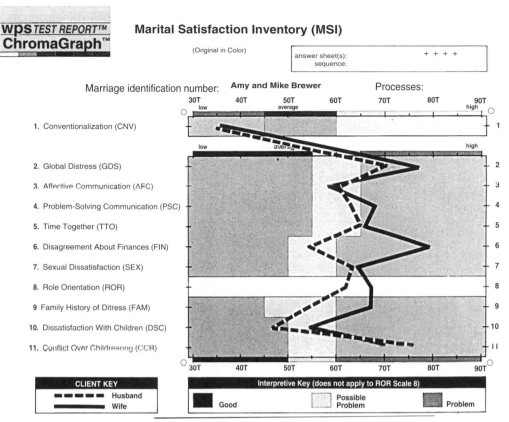

**FIGURE 2.** *Marital Satisfaction Inventory* (MSI) ChromaGraph™ profiles for Amy and Mike Brewer obtained at the beginning of marital therapy. MSI ChromaGraph™ copyright 1988 by Western Psychological Services. Reprinted with permission of the publisher, Western Psychological Services, 12031 Wilshire Boulevard, Los Angeles, CA 90025.

*reported extensive conflict over childrearing and additional distress involving the quality of shared leisure time and their sexual relationship. Although both Amy and Mike espoused a nontraditional approach to marital and parental roles, Mike's self-reports in this regard contrasted sharply with his efforts in the home to reestablish a pattern of patriarchal authority.*

## Assessing Nuclear Systems

Most if not all of the constructs identified as relevant to dyads apply to assessing nuclear systems, as well. Family systems are made up, in part, by a network of interlocking dyadic relationships. However, family structure can be viewed only by simultaneous observation of all members of the nuclear system.

Functional family systems must possess both flexibility and hierarchy. Family routines provide an organization and predictability to family life that en-

hance security and efficiency. How do different family members describe a typical day during the week or weekend? Most families develop both implicit and explicit conventions regarding household chores, management of meals and bedtime preparations, transportation, facilitation of schoolwork, and so on. The goal of balancing organization with modification of routines to meet situational stressors is a fundamental challenge of family life.

Family hierarchy refers to the differential allocation of authority, responsibilities, and privileges across family members. In dysfunctional families parents sometimes seek emotional ties with their children in exaggerated and inappropriate ways in response to their own inability to address these needs with other adults; other parents experience tremendous inadequacy in their parental role and retreat from setting limits or implementing consequences for fear of eliciting their children's anger. Who do family members turn to in time of crisis? Do parents share a relationship with each other that is qualitatively distinct from their relationships with the children? Does either parent pursue or facilitate a relationship with one or more children that excludes or undermines the authority or nurturing behaviors of their spouse?

Consideration of developmental context is critical in evaluating family structure. For example, Hill and Mattessich (1979) have argued that families share enough commonality to chart development across the life span in predictable stages. Changes in family development are marked by the emergence and alteration over time of norms, roles, and other family characteristics necessary for the persistence of the family as a social system. The interrelatedness of members within a family necessitates that changes in roles for one member lead to changes in roles for all family positions.

The process by which families allocate and execute authority may be evaluated across two domains: (a) models of family decision making, and (b) parents' approaches to discipline. In a unilateral model of decision making, each member functions without seeking input from others; decisions may be enforced autocratically or, at the other extreme, may be ignored due to the relative lack of power held by the decision maker. In a consultative model, family members' input is sought by one or more members (e.g., parents), but decisions remain within the purview of those seeking input. A collaborative model goes beyond consultation in providing each family member with some degree of power, although the distribution of power may be unequal across different members (e.g., organized along generational lines). Finally, a democratic model imparts roughly equal power to all family members. Families may employ different decision-making models across different domains of family life or across different subsystems within the family. For example, parents may adopt a consultative model regarding curfew for their teenage children, but use a collaborative or democratic model for decisions regarding family leisure time. Conflicts over power and control often emerge when parents resist their children's efforts to acquire a greater proportion of decision-making power. In what ways do a family's decision-making models fa-

cilitate or hinder conflict resolution in areas of distress?

In addition to differences in decision-making models, families differ in the means they adopt to enforce these decisions. Differences in parental disciplinary style have received considerable attention particularly in the developmental literature (cf. Baumrind, 1971). Common patterns of discipline include: (a) authoritarian parenting based on efforts to control children's behavior in accordance with rigid values and standards of conduct in the absence of a warm, nurturing relationship; (b) authoritative parenting emphasizing directiveness combined with warmth and acceptance within specified limits; and (c) permissive parenting involving a nonpunitive and accepting environment with few expectations regarding household responsibilities or orderly conduct. Extending across patterns of discipline are issues of (a) degree of parental concurrence on standards and methods of discipline; (b) degree of consistency by one or both parents across situations and time; and (c) the affective tone of discipline (e.g., control by anxiety, guilt, positive affect, or punishment; Roberts, Block, & Block, 1984). Related to hierarchy is the structure of affective relationships within the family system. Are relationships among siblings ones of companionship or competition? Affection or antagonism? Are patterns of attachment organized along generational dimensions, gender, or personality style? The strength of affective bonds within the family and their intensity relative to individuals' relationships outside the family contribute in part to the identity of the family as a distinct, vital system by its members. Higher levels of cohesion lead to clearer boundaries (implicit understandings regarding who does or does not belong to the system, with attendant expectations regarding the nature of members' interactions outside the nuclear system). Families often convey a collective mood or tone that may vary along dimensions of optimism, contentment, anger, worry, guilt, or despair.

*The Brewer family exhibited continuous disorganization. The parents' marital hostility precluded collaborative efforts to establish or implement agreements regarding be-*

*havioral limits for their two children. Amy advocated family values of achievement and intellectual pursuit, while Mike experienced physical activity and recreation as the preferred medium for interacting with his sons. The parents' mistrust of each other prohibited their tolerating or benefitting from these differences; instead, each tried to align the children with them in a manner that excluded the other. Decisions regarding children's privileges and responsibilities were made by each parent unilaterally, and discipline was exercised inconsistently and primarily using threats of physical punishment. Both Johnny and his younger brother responded to their parents' dissension by threatening to align with one parent against the other in order to avoid negative consequences for their misbehavior.*

*There were few viable routines in the Brewer family. Both Amy and Mike frequently left home to avoid each other, and there was little structure to parenting. Affective relationships within the family were weak and functioned almost exclusively along vertical (intergenerational) rather than horizontal (intragenerational) pathways. Among the children the expression of negative affect was suppressed; among parents it was uncontained. The sense of family identity was weak, and family pride was absent; antagonism prevailed over companionship.*

## Assessing Extended Systems

To what extent are Amy and Mike's relationship distress and difficulties with their children either exacerbated or ameliorated by extended systems outside the nuclear family? How much support is provided by their friends and by their respective families of origin? Do significant others outside the extended family reinforce or undermine the integrity of the family unit?

It is useful to distinguish between extended systems in which family members interact on an affective basis with individuals outside the nuclear family

and broader social systems at the community or cultural levels. Among extended systems we would emphasize three common classes: (a) relationships with extended families including family of origin or families by a previous marriage; (b) friendships or other central social support networks (e.g., at work or church); and (c) sexual relationships outside the marriage. The extent to which extended systems play a critical role in either contributing to or reducing a family's distress varies considerably across families.

The family should be asked, "Who are the other key players who have an important role in the quality of your individual and family life?" Extended family systems provide vital sources of emotional support that may buffer relationship distress and enrich the quality of interactions within the nuclear family. From a systemic perspective, closed systems gradually deteriorate from an inability to draw on external resources. Social support is a vital resource for family as well as individual functioning.

However, extended systems may also function as sources of conflict and stress (Figley, 1989). For example, assumptions within the family of origin regarding appropriate childrearing practices may conflict with emerging values or practices within the family of procreation, generating anxiety, guilt, resentments, or conflict between spouses or sets of in-laws. An important developmental task of family life involves balancing the need to differentiate from extended systems with the ability to draw upon the support functions of those systems.

Extended systems exhibit the same potential for coalitions with members of the nuclear family and with each other as do elements within the nuclear system. An extreme case involves the extramarital sexual partner, who commonly joins with the family member in blaming marital difficulties on the uninvolved spouse. Other common coalitions occur in family members' relationships with in-laws, and in friendships sought by one family member but rejected by another. The structural relationships between the nuclear family and elements of the extended system may serve to either strengthen or undermine the priority members place on preserving the nuclear system.

Finally, the therapist must recognize that he or she constitutes an important element in the couple's or family's extended system. The therapist's responses to family members' expectations, congruence or divergence of values, nature of attachment to different family members, consistency of self-presentation, and efforts to exert (and resist) influence all warrant careful assessment throughout the course of therapy.

> *Amy and Mike Brewer differed considerably in their degree of involvement with elements of an extended system. Mike was generally isolated, with no close friends and limited contact with his family of origin out of state. His isolation increased his feelings of emotional vulnerability and resentment of Amy's time away from home. Mike had maintained almost no contact with his 12-year-old daughter from his first marriage over the previous 10 years, and this contributed to his fears of losing involvement with his two sons should he and Amy get divorced. One month into therapy Mike's daughter unexpectedly initiated contact with him, and they began to correspond by letters. He was able to pursue some friendships of limited quality, but he regarded his therapist as his most reliable source of social support—-despite the intensity of some of his therapist's challenges and confrontations regarding Mike's substance abuse and physical aggressiveness.*
>
> *The most salient element of Amy's extended system involved her lover of 1 year's duration—an English professor at the university who himself was unhappily married and in individual therapy. She had just recently developed strong friendships with two women in the community who advocated Amy's taking any measures necessary to protect herself and her children from Mike's physical aggression. Amy had also found social support at a small community church. During the course of therapy Amy initiated contact with her biological father, with whom she had not interacted for nearly 15 years. He and his*
>
> *second wife welcomed her into their home, and Amy began to draw conceptual linkages between her current interpersonal struggles and early childhood and adolescent experiences.*

## Assessing Community and Cultural Systems

To what extent do formal and informal systems within the local community offer Mike and Amy support? How able are they to draw on these resources? What control does the community exert over their behavior? What influences do Mike's and Amy's respective cultures continue to have on their family values and their expectations regarding roles in and outside the home?

Community and cultural values often play an important role in a family's decision to enter therapy. For example, referrals may be precipitated by children's interactions within their schools or by family members' involvement with the legal or medical communities. A battered wife's presentation at the emergency room of the community hospital may lead to involvement of law-enforcement personnel, legal proceedings against the husband, or court-mandated psychological services for the husband or the couple.

Family members' assumptions and attributions regarding the community system also require careful assessment. What knowledge do family members possess regarding community resources? What expectations do they have regarding the availability and potential helpfulness of these resources? What biases exist within the larger social system that may mediate the offering of services or other responses of the community to this family?

Cultural expectations also contribute to patterns of interaction within the family regarding expression of feelings, distribution of authority, gender roles, childrearing practices, values placed on achievement and independence, and related constructs (Boyd-Franklin, 1989; Hansen & Falicov, 1983; McGoldrick, Pearce, & Giordano, 1982; Slonim, 1991). To what extent does this couple or family exhibit beliefs or behaviors specific to their cultural heritage? To what degree do individual members display similar levels of influence from cultural factors? What conflicts arise from differences in subcultural expectations and those of the larger social community?

Control at the community level occurs on both formal and informal levels. Examples of the latter involve the degree of influence and acceptance afforded to family members on the basis of their conformance with social norms or their economic or political status. For example, ethnic minority members may find it more difficult to elicit support or effect change in traditional societal institutions. Some families may experience stigmatization by other families in their neighborhood if they fail to follow local conventions regarding social behavior.

Control at a formal level involves explicit negative or positive consequences implemented by elements of one system contingent on the behaviors of another. For example, repeated failure of an adolescent to comply with school policies regarding conduct may lead to formal actions to dismiss the youngster from school, and this may require parental involvement. Conversely, failure of a school to provide resources for a child with special educational needs may lead to a lawsuit by the family to force the school's compliance with legal statutes mandating special educational services.

*Amy and Mike initially pursued psychological services for their son, Johnny, after the school threatened to remove the first-grader from his classroom due to repeated disruptive behavior and physical aggression. The child therapist with whom they consulted indicated after several months of unsuccessful treatment that she would not continue to work with Johnny unless Amy and Mike sought help for their own issues of substance abuse and physical aggression in the home.*

*After 2 months of couples therapy Amy made explicit her wish to pursue divorce. By this time, some stability had been brought to the home environment and both spouses had made moderate gains in social support outside the family; although Mike's*

*threats of physical aggression continued, the actual incidence of abuse diminished considerably. The couple were able to use marital therapy to work out pragmatic details of their separation and to discuss their respective wishes for collaborative parenting following divorce. Legal custody was awarded to Amy, with Mike given visitation rights every other weekend contingent on his restraint from physical aggression and abuse of alcohol or other substances.*

*Following their separation Amy continued in individual therapy to address relationship issues and her continuing vulnerability to depression; opportunities for individual therapy were offered to Mike as well, but he initially declined these. Two months later Mike's abuse of alcohol reached acute levels, and he called the therapist desperate for help. Despite the severe shortage of community resources, the therapist was able to draw on his close relationships with staff at the local community mental health center to arrange for detoxification and short-term residential treatment at a nearby facility. During this same period, Johnny received additional psychotherapy addressing his social interactions and lingering sexual anxieties resulting from his abuse by an older boy at a day-care center 2 years earlier.*

*Mike and Amy's divorce proceeded reasonably amicably considering their long history of marital hostilities. Amy worked diligently to mobilize the support of Johnny's school teacher and counselor and to implement more organization and tranquility in their home. In response to his own treatment and gradual adjustment to the separation and divorce, Mike's substance abuse abated and his generalized anxiety diminished. His interactions with Amy around parenting issues became more collaborative, and she described him as inter-*

*acting with the boys in a more consistent and less punitive manner.*

## SELECTION OF ASSESSMENT STRATEGIES

Table 1 summarizes modal conceptual issues and lists some of the more established assessment techniques available at various system levels. Apparent from this table is the broad range of formal assessment techniques developed at the individual and dyadic levels, in contrast to fewer techniques at the extended family or community system levels. At the individual level we have noted relatively broad-band multidimensional measures varying in the levels of functioning they are intended to assess (cf. the NEO Personality Inventory—Revised [Costa & McCrae, 1992] vs. the Minnesota Multiphasic Personality Inventory—2 [Butcher, Dahlstrom, Graham, Tellegen, & Kaemmer, 1989]). Both self-report and formal observational techniques can be found at dyadic and family system levels; among the latter, Table 1 cites more global coding systems better suited to clinical settings. At the extended family and community/culture levels, formal assessment techniques are lacking almost entirely in some domains (e.g., standards or expectations among the extended family or community regarding family behaviors); semistructured techniques (e.g., the genogram or ecomap) may complement more formal assessment instruments. At all system levels, the clinical interview and informal observations likely remain the dominant sources of assessment data.

In considering these assessment alternatives, both clinicians and researchers need to consider the strengths and limitations of both self-report and observational methodologies. Self-report measures (and ratings by significant others) represent the most commonly used clinical and research measurement strategy for the study of human relationships, following the clinical interview (Grotevant & Carlson, 1989). Advantages to the self-report approach are that such measures (a) are convenient and relatively easy to administer, obtaining a wealth of information across a broad range of issues germane to the initial assessment process; (b) lend themselves to collection of large normative samples; (c) allow disclosure about events and subjective experiences about which re-

spondents may initially be reluctant to discuss in an interview; and (d) provide important data concerning internal phenomena opaque to observational approaches, including values and attitudes, expectations and attributions, and satisfaction and commitment.

However, self-report strategies suffer from a variety of limitations in that they (a) exhibit susceptibility to both deliberate and unconscious efforts to bias self- and other-presentation in either a favorable or unfavorable manner; (b) are vulnerable to individual differences in stimulus interpretation and errors in recollection of objective events; (c) may inadvertently influence respondents' nontest behavior in unintended ways; and (d) typically provide few fine-grained details concerning moment-to-moment interactions (Jacob & Tennenbaum, 1988).

By contrast, observational techniques present inverse advantages and disadvantages. Based on a "sample" as opposed to a "sign" approach (cf. Snyder, 1982), observational strategies provide data regarding actual exchanges among family members directly relevant to empirically driven systems of clinical intervention. Observational data are less susceptible to respondent bias, particularly if sampled from natural as opposed to laboratory or analog settings. However, formal observational strategies at the microanalytic level are typically costly and labor intensive, and both the meaningfulness of behavioral codes and their relevance to nonbehavioral treatment approaches may be obfuscated.

We suspect that most clinicians may find a small subset of self-report techniques useful in planning and evaluating marital or family therapy, particularly if these measures were developed specifically for use with couples or families and lend themselves to an array of theoretical modalities. Given the number and breadth of measures available, it is critical that the therapist select those techniques most likely to facilitate differential diagnosis and target specific interventions having greatest relevance for that couple or family. We also believe that familiarity with specific observational strategies increases clinicians' awareness and response to subtle nuances of family members' verbal and nonverbal exchanges; toward this end, we would encourage all family therapists to videotape or audiotape at least one complete therapy session and subject data from this session to the rig-

## TABLE I

### Modal Conceptual Issues and Formal Assessment Techniques Across Family System Levels

| Modal conceptual issues | Formal assessment techniques |
| --- | --- |
| **Individual** | |
| How may cognitive style or abilities influence family members' response to therapy or each other? | Short-form Wechsler administrations (Silverstein, 1990) <br> Peabody Picture Vocabulary Test–Revised (Dunn & Dunn, 1981) <br> Attributional Style Questionnaire (Peterson & Villanova, 1988) <br> Children's Attributional Style Questionnaire (Fielstein et al., 1985) |
| What dimensions of individual emotional or behavioral functioning influence family interaction? Which of these, if any, warrant separate treatment? Which reflect strengths? | Minnesota Multiphasic Personality Inventory-2 (Butcher, Dahlstrom, Graham, Tellegen, & Kaemmer, 1989) <br> Millon Clinical Multiaxial Inventory-II (Millon, 1987) <br> NEO Personality Inventory–Revised (Costa & McCrae, 1992) <br> Schedule for Affective Disorders and Schizophrenia (Endicott & Spitzer, 1978) |
| How should current issues be viewed from a developmental perspective? | Child Behavior Checklist (Achenbach & Edelbrock, 1983) <br> Personality Inventory for Children (Wirt, Lachar, Klinedinst, & Seat, 1984) <br> Kiddie-Schedule for Affective Disorders and Schizophrenia (Puig-Antich & Chambers, 1978) |
| **Dyad** | |
| What are the sources and levels of distress or satisfaction in the marriage? In the parent–child relationships? | Marital Satisfaction Inventory (Snyder, 1981) <br> Sexual Functioning Inventory (Derogatis, 1975) <br> Parenting Stress Index (Abidin, 1986) |
| What patterns of communication typify these relationships? | Marital Interaction Coding System–Global (Weiss & Tolman, 1990) <br> Rapid Couples Interaction Scoring System (Krokoff, Gottman, & Hass, 1989) <br> Parent–Adolescent Interaction Coding System (Robin & Weiss, 1980) |
| How consistent and functional are relationship expectations? How do members view each other's behavior or motives? | Relationship Brief Inventory (Eidelson & Epstein, 1982) <br> Relationship Attribution Measure (Fincham & Bradbury, 1992) <br> Child's Report of Parental Behavior Inventory (Burger & Armentrout, 1971) |
| **Nuclear family** | |
| How close do family members feel to each other? How effective is the family in responding to daily challenges and crises? | Family Environment Scale (Moos & Moos, 1986) <br> Children's Version–Family Environment Scale (Pino, Simons, & Slawinowski, 1984) <br> Family Assessment Measure-III (Skinner, Steinhauer, & Santa-Barbera, 1984) <br> Family Adaptability and Cohesion Evaluation Scales III (Olson, Portner, & Lavee, 1985) |
| How is the family organized along dimensions of affect, authority, and control? What strategies do family members use to influence each other? | Child-Rearing Practices Report (Block, Block, & Morrison, 1981) <br> Family Behavior Interview (Robin & Foster, 1989) <br> Family Interaction Coding System (Reid, 1978) |
| **Extended system** | |
| To what extent do relationships with extended family, friends, or co-workers serve as sources of support or stress? | Genogram (McGoldrick & Gerson, 1985) <br> Interpersonal Support Evaluation List (Cohen, Mermelstein, Kamarck, & Hoberman, 1985) <br> Survey of Children's Social Support (Dubow & Ullman, 1989) <br> My Family and Friends (Reid, Landesman, Treder, & Jaccard, 1989) |

*(continues)*

| TABLE 1 (Continued) | |
| --- | --- |

**Modal Conceptual Issues and Formal Assessment Techniques Across Family System Levels**

| Modal conceptual issues | Formal assessment techniques |
| --- | --- |
| How do family members vary in their sources of external stress or support? How are these shared in the marriage or nuclear family? | |
| Community and culture | |
| What community resources are available to this family? Are these resources used? How does the community contribute to this family's distress or survival? | Mothers' Activities Checklist (Kelley & Carper, 1988) Community Interaction Checklist (Wahler, 1980) Eco-Map (Hartman, 1979) |
| To what extent do family members identify with a particular ethnic heritage? | Behavioral Acculturation Scale (Szapocznik, Kurtines, & Fernandez, 1980) |

ors of at least one highly developed observational coding system. In our own experience and the experience of our students, we have become better clinicians after conducting this exercise.

Finally, we would strongly urge the clinician or researcher to consider, prior to adopting any specific measurement strategy, previously identified criteria for evaluating outcome assessment instruments (American Psychological Association, 1985; Newman & Ciarlo, 1994). Specifically, selection criteria for a measure should include: (a) relevance to presenting complaints; (b) availability and appropriateness of norms, including consideration of both developmental issues and contextual elements of both the client (e.g., cultural background) and treatment setting (e.g., forensic, medical, or psychological); (c) inclusion of multiple informants (family members or outsiders); (d) traditional psychometric properties including both reliability (particularly temporal stability) and criterion-related validity; (e) cost of administration, scoring, and interpretation relative to treatment utility (c.f., Hayes, Nelson, & Jarrett, 1987); (f) social validity, including acceptability and understandability to the couple or family; (g) linkage to theory; and (h) above all, usefulness in planning, implementing, and evaluating specific clinical interventions.

## INTEGRATION OF CLINICAL FINDINGS

Our discussion of marital and family assessment would not be complete if it did not address method-

ological and conceptual issues in the integration of clinical findings. In their text concerning the personal and social assessment of children, Barnett and Zucker (1990) address common limitations of clinicians' problem-solving models. Citing research by Payne (1982) they note the following: (a) increasing the amount of information available to clinicians increases the variability of their responses, decreases the quality of their choices, but also increases their confidence in their decisions; (b) when too much information is available, the apparent completeness can blind the clinician to information that is missing or bias a decision without corresponding awareness of the bias; and (c) when time pressures are introduced, there is a normal tendency to emphasize negative information and to search for confirming rather than disconfirming evidence.

These limitations contribute to several caveats in integrating clinical findings in the assessment of couples and families. First, the better informed we are about the psychology of couples and families—both empirically and conceptually—the better our ability to assess a particular couple or family. Complex family behaviors are likely to be multiply determined, and the clinician must consider a range of alternative hypotheses addressing recursive cause–effect relationships.

Second, the adequacy of clinical decisions will be restricted by the psychometric soundness of the assessment procedures that generate the data on which the decisions are based. Consequently, differentially greater weight should be assigned to those evaluation procedures with the greatest documented reliability, validity, and usefulness in treatment.

Third, structured approaches to interpreting and integrating data, including use of graphic displays and incorporation of base-rate information, should be used where possible. When available, formal decision rules or actuarial prediction models should be used. As Barnett and Zucker note, "The most effective safeguards for practice at present involve (1) iterative combinations of reflective and empirical strategies . . . and (2) the use of assessment practices related to theory and research on psychosocial change" (p. 186).

Finally, presentation of initial assessment findings to family members should provide the opportunity for clarification and corrections to omissions or misinterpretations of assessment data. The provision of feedback comprises a critical therapeutic intervention. It sets the stage for the initial collaborative alliance between the therapist and the couple or family, as well as among family members themselves. Assessment data should facilitate reframing of relationship difficulties away from attributions that foster anger, pessimism, and blame—and instead toward explanations that promote understanding, tolerance, and hope. The assessment process should clarify not only what has "gone wrong," but also what steps can be undertaken to make things "right." Most importantly, the feedback must constitute an active exchange among therapist and family members in a shared process of discovery. Provision of feedback should proceed as a series of hypotheses, with clients asked to provide their own interpretation of assessment findings. Tentative therapeutic goals and intervention strategies should be outlined at varying levels of confidence and immediacy—some to be pursued early in the therapy, others as potential objectives to explore after some of the initial distress has been alleviated.

## CONCLUSIONS

Assessment of couples and families differs from assessment of individuals in critical ways. Foremost among these are the complexity of relationships that make up the target of clinical intervention, the op-

portunity to observe directly the content and structure of problematic interpersonal exchanges, and the importance of evaluation across multiple levels of system functioning. Guided by theoretical sophistication, armed with the best assessment techniques available, and forewarned of the hazards of reaching firm conclusions from potentially unreliable or incomplete data, clinicians should be reasonably prepared to undertake the challenge of assessment in planning and evaluating interventions with couples and families.

## References

Abidin, R. (1986). *Parenting stress index* (2nd ed.). Richmond, VA: Pediatric Psychology Press.

Achenbach, T. M., & Edelbrock, C. S. (1983). *Manual for the Child Behavior Checklist and Revised Child Behavior Profile*. Burlington: University of Vermont.

Ainsworth, M. D. S., Blehar, M. C., Waters, E., & Wall, S. (1979). *Patterns of attachment: A psychological study of the strange situation*. New York: Halsted.

American Psychiatric Association. (1994). *Diagnostic and statistical manual of mental disorders* (4th ed.). Washington, DC: Author.

American Psychological Association. (1985). *Standards for educational and psychological tests*. Washington, DC: Author.

Barnett, D. W., & Zucker, K. B. (1990). *The personal and social assessment of children*. Boston, MA: Allyn & Bacon.

Baucom, D. H., Epstein, N., Sayers, S., & Sher, T. G. (1989). The role of cognitions in marital relationships: Definitional, methodological, and conceptual issues. *Journal of Consulting and Clinical Psychology, 57,* 31–38.

Baumrind, D. (1971). Current patterns of parental authority. *Developmental Psychology Monographs, 4,* 1–103.

Beavers, W. R., Hampson, R. D., & Hulgus, Y. F. (1985). The Beavers Systems approach to family assessment. *Family Process, 24,* 398–405.

Block, J. H., Block, J., & Morrison, A. (1981). Parental agreement–disagreement on childrearing orientations and gender-related personality correlates in children. *Child Development, 52,* 965–974.

Boyd-Franklin, N. (1989). *Black families in therapy: A multisystems approach*. New York: Guilford Press.

Burger, G. K., & Armentrout, J. A. (1971). A factor analysis of fifth and sixth graders' reports of parental child-rearing behavior. *Developmental Psychology, 4,* 483.

Butcher, J. N., Dahlstrom, W. G., Graham, J. R., Tellegen, A., & Kaemmer, B. (1989). *MMPI-2: Manual for administration and scoring*. Minneapolis: University of Minnesota Press.

Cavell, T. A., & Snyder, D. K. (1991). Iconoclasm versus innovation: Building a science of family therapy—Comment on Moon, Dillon, and Sprenkle. *Journal of Marital and Family Therapy, 17,* 167–171.

Cohen, S., Mermelstein, R., Kamarck, R., & Hoberman, H. M. (1985). Measuring the functional components of social support. In I. G. Sarason & B. R. Sarason (Eds.), *Social support: Theory, research, and applications* (pp. 73–94). Dordrecht, The Netherlands: Martinus Nijhoff.

Costa, P. T., & McCrae, R. R. (1992). *NEO Personality Inventory—Revised manual*. Odessa, FL: Psychological Assessment Resources.

Cromwell, R. E., & Peterson, G. W. (1981). Multisystem–multimethod assessment: A framework. In E. E. Filsinger & R. A. Lewis (Eds.), *Assessing marriage: New behavioral approaches* (pp. 38–54). Newbury Park, CA: Sage.

Derogatis, L. R. (1975). *Preliminary scoring manual: Derogatis sexual functioning inventory, clinical*. Baltimore: Psychometric Research.

Dubow, E. F., & Ullman, D. G. (1989). Assessing social support in elementary school children: The survey of children's social support. *Journal of Clinical Child Psychology, 18,* 52–64.

Dunn, L. M., & Dunn, L. M. (1981). *Peabody Picture Vocabulary Test Revised*. Circle Pines, MN: American Guidance Service.

Eidelson, R. J., & Epstein, N. (1982). Cognition and relationship maladjustment: Development of a measure of dysfunctional relationship beliefs. *Journal of Consulting and Clinical Psychology, 50,* 715–720.

Endicott, J., & Spitzer, R. L. (1978). A diagnostic interview: The schedule for affective disorders and schizophrenia. *Archives of General Psychiatry, 35,* 837–844.

Erikson, E. H. (1968). *Identity, youth, and crisis*. New York: Norton.

Fielstein, E., Klein, M. S., Fischer, M., Hanon, C., Kobuger, P., Schneider, M. J., & Leitenberg, H. (1985). Self-esteem and causal attributions for success and failure in children. *Cognitive Therapy and Research, 9,* 381–398.

Figley, C. R. (1989). *Treating stress in families*. New York: Brunner/Mazel.

Filsinger, E. E. (1983a). Choices among marital observation coding systems. *Family Process, 22,* 317–335.

Filsinger, E. E. (1983b). Assessment: What it is and why it is important. In E. E. Filsinger (Ed.), *Marriage and family assessment: A sourcebook for family therapy* (pp. 11–22). Newbury Park, CA: Sage.

Fincham, F. D., & Bradbury, T. N. (1992). Assessing attributions in marriage: The Relationship Attribution Measure. *Journal of Personality and Social Psychology, 62,* 457–468.

Geiss, S. K., & O'Leary, D. (1981). Therapist ratings of frequency and severity of marital problems: Implications for research. *Journal of Marital and Family Therapy, 7,* 515–520.

Gottman, J. M. (1979). *Marital interaction: Experimental investigations*. New York: Academic Press.

Grotevant, H. D., & Carlson, C. I. (1989). *Family assessment: A guide to methods and measures*. New York: Guilford Press.

Hansen, J. C., & Falicov, C. J. (1983). *Cultural perspectives in family therapy*. Rockville, MD: Aspen.

Hartman, A. (1979). *Finding families: An ecological approach to family assessment in adoption*. Beverly Hills, CA: Sage.

Hayes, S. C., Nelson, R. O., & Jarrett, R. B. (1987). The treatment utility of assessment: A functional approach to evaluating assessment quality. *American Psychologist, 42,* 963–974.

Hill, R., & Mattessich, P. (1979). Family development theory and life-span development. In P. B. Baltes & O. G. Brim (Eds.), *Life-span development and behavior* (Vol. 2, pp. 161–204). New York: Plenum.

Huston, T. L. (1983). Power. In H. H. Kelley, E. Berscheid, A. Christensen, J. H. Harvey, T. L. Huston, G. Levinger, E. McClintock, L. A. Peplau, & D. R. Peterson (Eds.), *Close relationships* (pp. 169–219). New York: Freeman.

Jacob, T., & Tennenbaum, D. L. (1988). *Family assessment: Rationale, methods, and future directions*. New York: Plenum.

Jacobson, N. S. (1992). Behavioral couple therapy: A new beginning. *Behavior Therapy, 23,* 493–506.

Kelley, M. L., & Carper, L. B. (1988). The Mothers' Activity Checklist: An instrument for assessing pleasant and unpleasant events. *Behavioral Assessment, 10,* 331–341.

Krokoff, L. J., Gottman, J. M., & Hass, S. D. (1989). Validation of a global rapid couples interaction scoring system. *Behavioral Assessment, 11,* 65–79.

Levinson, D. J. (1986). A conception of adult development. *American Psychologist, 41,* 3–13.

McGoldrick, M., & Gerson, R. (1985). *Genograms in family assessment*. New York: Norton.

McGoldrick, M., Pearce, J. K., & Giordano, J. (1982). *Ethnicity and family therapy*. New York: Guilford Press.

Millon, T. (1987). *Manual for the Millon Clinical Multiaxial Inventory-II* (2nd ed.). Minneapolis, MN: National Computer Systems.

Moos, R. H., & Moos, B. S. (1986). *Family Environment Scale manual* (rev. ed.). Palo Alto, CA: Consulting Psychologists Press.

Newman, F. L., & Ciarlo, J. A. (1994). Criteria for selecting psychological instruments for treatment outcome assessment. In M. E. Maruish (Ed.), *Use of psychological testing for treatment planning and outcome assessment* (pp. 98 110). Hillsdale, NJ: Erlbaum.

Nichols, M. P., & Schwartz, R. C. (1991). *Family therapy: Concepts and methods* (2nd ed.). Boston, MA: Allyn & Bacon.

Olson, D. H. (1977). Insiders' and outsiders' views of relationships: Research strategies. In G. K. Levinger & H. L. Rausch (Eds.), *Close relationships: Perspectives on the meaning of intimacy* (pp. 115–135). Amherst: University of Massachusetts Press.

Olson, D. H., Portner, J., & Lavee, Y. (1985). *FACES III*. Unpublished manuscript. (Available from Family Social Science, University of Minnesota, St. Paul, MN 55108).

Olson, D. H., Sprenkle, D. H., & Russell, C. S. (1979). Circumplex model of marital and family systems. I: Cohesion and adaptability dimensions, family types, and clinical applications. *Family Process, 18,* 3–28.

Patterson, G. R. (1982). *Coercive family process.* Eugene, OR: Castalia.

Payne, J. W. (1982). Contingent decision behavior. *Psychological Bulletin, 92,* 382–402.

Peterson, C., & Villanova, P. (1988). An expanded attributional style questionnaire. *Journal of Abnormal Psychology, 97,* 87–89.

Pino, C. J., Simons, N., & Slawinowski, M. J. (1984). *Children's version: Family Environment Scale.* Palo Alto, CA: Consulting Psychologists Press.

Puig-Antich, J., & Chambers, W. (1978). *The schedule for affective disorders and schizophrenia for school-age children (Kiddie-SADS).* New York: New York State Psychiatric Association.

Reid, J. B. (Ed.). (1978). *A social learning approach to family intervention: Vol. 2. Observation in home settings.* Eugene, OR: Castalia.

Reid, M., Landesman, S., Treder, R., & Jaccard, J. (1989). My family and friends: Six- to twelve-year-old children's perceptions of social support. *Child Development, 60,* 896–910.

Roberts, G. C., Block, J. H., & Block, J. (1984). Continuity and change in parents' childrearing practices. *Child Development, 55,* 586–597.

Robin, A. L., & Foster, S. L. (1989). *Negotiating parent-adolescent conflict.* New York: Guilford Press.

Robin, A. L., & Weiss, J. G. (1980). Criterion-related validity of behavioral and self-report measures of problem-solving communication skills in distressed and nondistressed parent–adolescent dyads. *Behavioral Assessment, 2,* 339–352.

Schumm, W. R. (1990). Evolution of the family field: Measurement principles and techniques. In J. Touliatos, B. F. Perlmutter, & M. A. Straus (Eds.), *Handbook of family measurement techniques* (pp. 23–36). Newbury Park, CA: Sage.

Selvini, P. M., Boscolo, L., Cecchin, G., & Prata, G. (1980). Hypothesizing—circularity—neutrality: Three guidelines for the conductor of the session. *Family Process, 19,* 3–12.

Silverstein, A. B. (1990). Notes on the reliability of Wechsler short forms. *Journal of Clinical Psychology, 46,* 194–196.

Skinner, H. A., Steinhauer, P. D., & Santa-Barbara, J. (1984). *The Family Assessment Measure: Administration and interpretation guide.* (Available from Addiction Research Foundation, Toronto, Ontario, Canada.)

Slonim, M. (1991). *Children, culture, and ethnicity: Evaluating and understanding the impact.* New York: Garland.

Smedes, L. B. (1984). *Forgive and forget: Healing the hurts we don't deserve.* San Francisco: Harper & Row.

Snyder, D. K. (1979). *Marital Satisfaction Inventory.* Los Angeles: Western Psychological Services.

Snyder, D. K. (1981). *Manual for the Marital Satisfaction Inventory.* Los Angeles: Western Psychological Services.

Snyder, D. K. (1982). Advances in marital assessment: Behavioral, communications, and psychometric approaches. In C. D. Spielberger & J. N. Butcher (Eds.), *Advances in personality assessment* (Vol. 1, pp. 169–201). Hillsdale, NJ: Erlbaum.

Snyder, D. K., & Costin, S. (1994). The Marital Satisfaction Inventory. In M. E. Maruish (Ed.), *Use of psychological testing for treatment planning and outcome assessment* (pp. 322–351). Hillsdale, NJ: Erlbaum.

Snyder, D. K., & Lachar, D. (1986). *A computerized interpretation system for the Marital Satisfaction Inventory.* Los Angeles: Western Psychological Services.

Snyder, D. K., Lachar, D., Freiman, K. E., & Hoover, D. W. (1991). Toward the actuarial assessment of couples' relationships. In J. P. Vincent (Ed.), *Advances in family intervention, assessment, and theory* (Vol. 5, pp. 89–122). London: Kingsley.

Snyder, D. K., Mangrum, L. F., & Wills, R. M. (1993). Predicting couples' response to marital therapy: A comparison of short- and long-term predictors. *Journal of Consulting and Clinical Psychology, 61,* 61–69.

Sofield, L., Juliano, C., & Hammett, R. (1990). *Design for wholeness: Dealing with anger, learning to forgive, building self-esteem.* Notre Dame, IN: Ave Maria Press.

Straus, M. A. (1979). Measuring intrafamily conflict and violence: The Conflict Tactics (CT) scales. *Journal of Marriage and the Family, 41,* 75–88.

Szapocznik, J., Kurtines, W. M., & Fernandez, T. (1980). Bicultural involvement in Hispanic American youths. *International Journal of Intercultural Relations, 4,* 353–365.

Tomm, K. (1988). Interventive interviewing: Part III. In-tending to ask lineal, circular, strategic, or reflexive questions? *Family Process, 27,* 1–15.

Wahler, R. G. (1980). The insular mother: Her problems in parent–child treatment. *Journal of Applied Behavior Analysis, 13,* 273–294.

Weiss, R. L., & Tolman, A. O. (1990). The Marital Interaction Coding System-Global (MICS-G): A global companion to the MICS. *Behavioral Assessment, 12,* 271–294.

Wirt, R. D., Lachar, D., Klinedinst, J. K., & Seat, P. D. (1984). *Multidimensional description of child personality: A manual for the Personality Inventory for Children* (Revision by D. Lachar). Los Angeles: Western Psychological Services.

# CHAPTER 10

# THE EVOLUTION OF FAMILY-BASED PSYCHOPATHOLOGY

*David J. Miklowitz*

The association between family disturbances and individual psychopathology has long been intriguing to clinicians and researchers. Dysfunction in the family has been of interest to those seeking to (a) understand interaction patterns or other family attributes that may be etiologically related to the onset of psychopathology, (b) identify family attributes that predict the longitudinal course of psychological disorders, and (c) design family interventions that modify family dysfunctions and lead to improvements in the course of these disorders.

The family disturbance–individual psychopathology link is fraught with controversy. There are three alternative, although not necessarily mutually exclusive, interpretations of this association: (a) that the family causes psychopathology in individual members (hereafter referred to as the "primary etiological model"); (b) that individual psychopathology stimulates dysfunctional reactions in family members (the "reactivity model"); and (c) that the association is based on yet a third variable, such as genetic predisposition to psychopathology (the "shared vulnerability model"). Each of these interpretations has its problems and sociopolitical implications. For example, the primary etiological model "blames" parents for psychopathology in their offspring, whereas the reactivity model blames psychologically ill persons for the disturbances in their families. Some of these viewpoints have more empirical support than others. However, none of these views is inconsistent with

the goal of designing family interventions for the delay or prevention of episodes of major mental disorder.

This chapter examines the historical roots of our current thinking about the association between the family and individual psychopathology and draws conclusions based on the existing evidence about the role of the family as (a) an etiological factor in the onset of mental disorders (with emphasis on "communication deviance"), (b) a prognostic variable in the course of such disorders (with emphasis on "expressed emotion"), and (c) an agent of change in the psychosocial treatment of severe disorders (with emphasis on psychoeducational approaches to the families of the chronically mentally ill).

The focus of this chapter is on schizophrenia, reflecting the major interest of investigators in this field. However, findings regarding other disorders (often used as comparison groups in studies of schizophrenia) receive some attention, with particular emphasis on the mood disorders. The relative validities of each of the three alternative interpretations of the family–psychopathology link are evaluated, and recommendations for future work are offered.

## THE ROLE OF THE FAMILY IN THE ONSET OF SCHIZOPHRENIA

### Early Clinical Studies

The notion that families contribute to the onset of schizophrenia has a long and rather unfortunate his-

This work was supported in part by National Institute of Mental Health Grants MH43931 and MH42556.

tory. Originally, families were viewed as the primary cause of schizophrenia. For example, Fromm-Reichmann (1950) described mothers of preschizophrenic children as "schizophrenogenic," combining overprotectiveness with subtle signs of rejection. Bateson, Jackson, Haley, and Weakland (1956) believed that mothers made many "double-bind" messages to the preschizophrenic child, who could neither comment on these messages nor escape the situation. These early theories may be the source of much of the blame families of schizophrenic patients feel is cast on them today (e.g., Hatfield, Spaniol, & Zipple, 1987).

The empirical support of these and other theories that arose around the same time (Bowen, 1960; Lidz, Cornelison, Fleck, & Terry, 1957) is scant at best (Hirsch & Leff, 1975). First, these theories were based on observations of families who already had a schizophrenic member, and it was taken for granted that the observed pathological family processes were causally related to the onset of the disorder. Many have assumed the opposite, that living with schizophrenia promotes unclear communication or ineffective coping mechanisms in caretakers (e.g., Fontana, 1966). Second, these observations were made before the appearance of the many studies indicating that schizophrenia is an illness with large genetic and/or biological etiological components (for a review, see Gottesman, 1991). Subsequent studies of the family as a factor in the onset of schizophrenia did consider these alternative models.

## Studies of Communication Deviance

**Definition of the construct and mechanisms.** A common thread in the early clinical observations about families of schizophrenic patients was that family-wide transactions seemed to be unfocused, unclear, and contradictory. Wynne and Singer (1963) described these transactions as characterized by "communication deviance" (CD), or an inability for the family to share a focus of attention. This family-wide communication disturbance was seen as qualitatively different from that in any individual family member (Wynne & Singer, 1963).

Wynne and Singer hypothesized that parents who spoke with high levels of CD created a stressful atmosphere that increased the likelihood of a schizophrenic onset in a child who was already genetically and/or biologically at risk. The child was thought to internalize the parents' deviant ways of thinking, attending, or processing information. Then, when a stressor presented itself in adulthood (e.g., separation from the family of origin), these deviant cognitive processes became activated and were reflected in the core symptoms of schizophrenia (Jones, 1977; Woodward & Goldstein, 1977; Wynne & Singer, 1963).

Singer and Wynne (1965) developed a system for coding CD from Rorschach protocols conducted with individual parents. Jones (1977) developed a similar system for the Thematic Apperception Test (TAT). Examples of communication deviance are contained in Table 1.

**Specificity to schizophrenia.** The first step in identifying factors with etiological significance in any major mental illness is to demonstrate that the factor occurs with higher frequency in those with the disorder than in comparison groups. That high levels of CD occur more frequently in parents of schizophrenics than in parents of nonpsychotic patients or normal persons has been replicated in 12 different studies (for a review, see Miklowitz & Stackman, 1992). Comparison groups have included parents of borderline, autistic, withdrawn, and depressed patients. However, Miklowitz et al. (1991) found no differences in levels of CD when comparing the parents of

---

### TABLE 1

**Examples of Communication Deviance**

| Type | Example |
|---|---|
| Contorted, peculiar language | "This man is in the process in thinking of the process of becoming a doctor." |
| Misperceptions | "This is either a violin or a gun." |
| Closure problems | "These people have nothing to do with each other." |

*Note:* Communication deviance is coded from relatives' responses to projective tests like the Thematic Apperception Test (Jones, 1977).

schizophrenic and bipolar, manic patients. Sass, Gunderson, Singer, and Wynne (1984) found that high levels of CD characterized only the parents of schizophrenic patients with high levels of thought disorder. Furthermore, Wynne, Singer, Bartko, and Toohey (1977) found that amount of CD in parents increased as a monotonic function of the severity of the diagnosis of the offspring (normal, neurotic, borderline, schizophrenic). Thus, CD may not be a marker of schizophrenia as much as of illness severity, with relatives of psychotic patients showing the most speech deviance.

The results of the diagnostic discrimination studies can be explained by any of the three models outlined earlier: CD could be a primary etiological factor, a reaction of parents to illness in an offspring, or a shared vulnerability factor. The next sections will address the viability of these competing models.

**CD as an etiological mechanism.** Only one study has directly evaluated the primary etiological model within a longitudinal, high-risk paradigm. A team based at the University of California, Los Angeles (UCLA; Doane, West, Goldstein, Rodnick, & Jones, 1981; Goldstein, 1987) systematically assessed the families of disturbed, nonpsychotic adolescents who requested treatment at an outpatient clinic. Adolescents were prospectively followed for 15 years to determine who developed schizophrenia or related disorders.

The UCLA team found that certain substyles of parental CD as coded from TAT protocols (Jones, 1977) were strongly prospectively related to the onset of "schizophrenia spectrum disorders" (schizophrenia or schizotypal, paranoid, schizoid, or borderline personality disorder, as identified in the *Diagnostic and Statistical Manual of Mental Disorders*, third edition, *DSM-III*; American Psychiatric Association, 1987) in these adolescents followed into adulthood. Misperceptions of the TAT Stimuli (e.g., seeing the boy in card I as a girl) and Failure to Integrate Closure Problems (e.g., viewing the characters in the cards as bearing no relation to each other) were the predictive measures. Prediction of adolescent outcomes was strongest when these CD measures were combined with a measure of negative (critical and/or intrusive) parent–offspring communication during family problem-solving interactions (termed "negative affective style"; Doane et al., 1981). That is, adolescents with parents who both spoke unclearly and showed high levels of negative affective style in family problem-solving discussions were the most likely to develop schizophrenia spectrum disorders in adulthood (Goldstein, 1987).

Goldstein (1987) also measured family history of psychopathology in these high-risk families. Although parental CD was not directly related to the presence or absence of severe psychopathology in the parents themselves or in other first- or second-degree relatives of the target adolescent, an interaction emerged between parental CD and family history: 86% of the adolescents from families both high in CD and having a positive family history for severe psychopathology developed schizophrenia spectrum disorders at 15-year follow-up, as opposed to only 20% of those from families with high CD and no such history. Thus, as originally hypothesized by Wynne and Singer (1963), parental CD was strongest as a predictor when evaluated in the context of a genetic predisposition to severe psychopathology.

**CD as a reaction to offspring attributes.** In the UCLA high-risk study, the relation between parental CD and the type and severity of the adolescents' initial problems (i.e., internalizing versus externalizing) was relatively weak. However, of greater significance was the finding that baseline adolescent problem type did not predict adult outcomes as well as parental CD did. Of course, other adolescent attributes not measured in this study could have served as eliciting stimuli for parental speech deviance, such as personality disturbance, mood lability, or neurobehavioral or neurocognitive deficits.

Other studies have more directly examined the reactivity hypothesis. Johnston and Holzman (1979) found a direct but rather weak correlation between the degree of speech deviance among parents of schizophrenic patients and that of their affected offspring. In contrast, Glaser (1976) found that parental CD scores were actually lower when parents were interacting with their schizophrenic offspring than when they were interacting with an experimenter.

Thus, parental CD probably reflects more than a reaction to the stress of living with a schizophrenic person, although the issue is unresolved.

**CD as a shared vulnerability mechanism.** Perhaps the co-occurrence of high parental CD with psychotic symptoms in an offspring reflects a shared genetic vulnerability. For example, high CD may reflect a subsyndromal form of schizophrenia in parents that is present in fully syndromal form in the next generation.

Results of studies investigating the relation between CD and psychopathology in parents have not yielded convincing results. Goldstein et al. (1992) found no relation between levels of CD and lifetime diagnosable psychopathology in parents of schizophrenic patients. Two studies using adoption study methodology also found no relation between CD and psychopathology in parents (Wender, Rosenthal, Rainer, Greenhill, & Sarlin, 1977; Wynne, Singer, & Toohey, 1976).

A more promising avenue is to return to the original hypothesis of Wynne and Singer (1963) that CD reflects disturbances in shared foci of attention. Do parents with high CD and their schizophrenic offspring share disordered information processing styles? There are now three studies that suggest an association between parental CD and poor performance by schizophrenic offspring on attentional tests, including tests of vigilance and guided visual search (Nuechterlein, Goldstein, Ventura, Dawson, & Doane, 1989; Wagener, Hogarty, Goldstein, Asarnow, & Browne, 1986) and distractibility (Asarnow, Goldstein, & Ben-Meir, 1988).

Despite the cross-sectional nature of these studies, they do provide support for Wynne and Singer's notion that communication disturbances in parents are linked to information processing anomalies in offspring. The difference, perhaps, is that Wynne and Singer hypothesized that this relation is psychosocially based, whereas the large literature on attentional and information-processing dysfunctions (for a review, see Nuechterlein & Dawson, 1984a) suggests the influence of vulnerable genotypes shared across generations. Thus, family CD, found to be related to the onset of schizophrenia or related disorders, may exert its action directly via psychosocial mechanisms (the primary etiological model) and/or indirectly through shared genetic vulnerabilities.

## Clinical Implications of Communication Deviance Research

Are CD studies merely academic exercises that have little impact on our clinical understanding of these disorders or their care? What does it mean that high levels of family CD are risk factors for the onset of schizophrenia or that they reflect information-processing deficits?

Communication deviance can inform our clinical expertise if we think of it as (a) a way of identifying children at risk for schizophrenia or other psychotic disorders and (b) a family attribute to target for change in early preventive interventions. First, we may benefit in our prevention efforts from knowing that a child presenting with an internalizing disorder who shows evidence of deficient attentional performance, *and* whose parents have high CD, is at greater risk for a schizophrenic onset than, for example, a child with similar clinical features whose parents are low in CD. Second, we may be able via communication skill training (see page 190) to modify existing communication patterns so that they become less confusing and anxiety-provoking for the preschizophrenic child. The question of whether interventions of this sort reduce the likelihood that an at-risk child develops schizophrenia is worthy of investigation in longitudinal studies.

## THE FAMILY AND THE COURSE OF SCHIZOPHRENIA AND OTHER DISORDERS

The sections above focused on various efforts to describe and operationalize family environments that predispose children to develop schizophrenia. Other investigators have been interested in family factors that predict the course of schizophrenia once it is manifest. After all, most clinicians treat patients diagnosed with a mental disorder rather than persons at risk. Which family environments are associated with greater risk for relapses of schizophrenia or other disorders, and which provide protective influences?

## Expressed Emotion Research

The most well-known method of categorizing risk among families of severely mentally ill patients is by the "expressed emotion" method (Brown, Birley, & Wing, 1972; Vaughn & Leff, 1976). This method classifies families as high-EE (high expressed emotion) if relatives (usually parents) show high levels of criticism, hostility, or emotional overinvolvement (overprotectiveness or overconcern) toward their ill relative, and low-EE if not (see Table 2). The source of these ratings is the Camberwell Family Interview (CFI; Vaughn & Leff, 1976). The interview is usually conducted with a parent or spouse of a patient who experiences an episode of mental disorder, and it evaluates the ways in which family members, particularly the responding relative, were affected by this episode.

The following sections describe high- and low-EE families and review data on the prognostic validation of this construct, within the framework of the three competing explanatory models described throughout this chapter.

## Expressed Emotion as a Primary Risk Indicator

Expressed emotion is perhaps the most well-validated risk indicator for relapses of schizophrenia.

---

### TABLE 2

### Examples of Expressed Emotion

| Type | Example |
|---|---|
| Critical statements | "I don't like it when she goes out late at night." |
| | "I resent his unwillingness to take a shower." |
| Hostile statements | "I wish he had never been born." |
| Emotionally overinvolved statements | "I've quit my job and spend all my time at home now in case he ever needs me." |
| | "When I know she hasn't eaten, I can't eat anything myself." |

*Note:* Expressed emotion is coded from relatives' responses to the Camberwell Family Interview (Vaughn & Leff, 1976).

---

There are now 17 independent replications of the finding that hospitalized schizophrenic patients who are discharged to high-EE families are about two to three times more likely to experiences recurrences of schizophrenia at 9-month to 1-year periods of follow-up than those returning to low-EE families (for reviews, see Kavanagh, 1992; Parker & Hadzi-Pavlovic, 1990).[1] There are also about 6 nonreplications of this result, although the methodologies of some of these nonreplication studies have been questioned (Goldstein, Strachan, & Wynne, in press).

Research on EE and illness outcome has extended well beyond schizophrenia to include many other disorders. EE has been linked to relapses of bipolar mood disorder (Miklowitz, Goldstein, Nuechterlein, Snyder, & Mintz, 1988), unipolar depression (Hooley, Orley, & Teasdale, 1986; Vaughn & Leff, 1976), eating disorders (Hodes & Grange, 1993), childhood depression (Asarnow, Goldstein, Tompson, & Guthrie, 1993), and other disorders. Also, among families of schizophrenic patients, the EE–relapse association holds true across African-American, Eastern Indian, and Hispanic cultures. Mean *levels* of EE criticism and emotional overinvolvement do, however, vary across cultures (Jenkins & Karno, 1992).

The association between EE and the short-term outcome of various mental disorders has been conceptualized within a vulnerability–stress framework (Nuechterlein & Dawson, 1984b; Zubin & Spring, 1977). EE may reflect a generalized stressor that interacts with specific vulnerabilities in bringing about relapses of mental disorder. Thus, an individual with a "diathesis" for schizophrenia (for example, a dopamine dysregulation) who experiences a stressful home environment may become physiologically overstimulated by this stress in a way that decreases the threshold for the development of a new psychotic episode. In parallel, a unipolar patient with a "cognitive vulnerability" to depression (Hammen, Marks, Mayol, & deMayo, 1985) who is exposed to high levels of criticism may assimilate the content of these criticisms to the neglect of positive information, such

---

[1] One study (Doane, Falloon, Goldstein, & Mintz, 1985) also found that levels of negative affective style (the aforementioned measure of negative parent-to-patient emotional and verbal behavior—criticism or intrusiveness—in direct family interaction), were prospectively related to 9-month relapse rates in relatively chronic schizophrenic patients. Levels of affective style in parents have been found to be related to their expressed emotion classifications, although not perfectly (Miklowitz, Goldstein, Falloon, & Doane, 1984).

that a new episode of depression is more likely to occur.

## Expressed Emotion as a Reaction to Attributes of the Ill Family Member

The repeated finding that EE is prospectively associated with high rates of relapse in various psychiatric disorders does not prove that it is a *causal* factor. It is possible that attitudes like criticism and overprotectiveness reflect a parent's modes of coping with psychological illness in an offspring in the absence of more clearly effective strategies. These EE attitudes could reflect reactions to disruptive or delusional behaviors in the patient that would be annoying (or anxiety-provoking) to anyone.

To address these possible reactivity explanations, one must outline those patient attributes that might (a) generate high-EE attitudes and (b) in themselves place a patient at a greater risk for relapse. The patient factors that have received the most investigation in this regard are (a) attributes of the illness itself (i.e., symptom status or prior course of illness) and (b) the patient's styles of interacting with relatives.

**Illness attributes as stimuli for negative parental reactions.** Most studies have concluded that levels of parental EE, as well as their longitudinal association with patient outcomes, cannot be accounted for by the patient's baseline symptom severity, medication status, or illness history, whether in schizophrenia (Kavanagh, 1992), depression (Hooley et al., 1986), or bipolar disorder (Miklowitz et al., 1988). It does not appear that relatives become more critical or overinvolved in direct reaction to the severity or overt symptomatic presentation of the patient's disorder.

Fully syndromal symptoms, however, are only part of what relatives are up against. There is also the issue of subsyndromal psychopathology. Rosenfarb, Goldstein, Mintz, and Nuechterlein (1993) examined this issue via detailed analyses of family problem-solving discussions conducted after schizophrenic patients had returned home from the hospital. Patients whose parents were high in EE and primarily critical displayed more evidence of subsyndromal "odd, disruptive behaviors" (i.e., unusual

thought content, irritability, socially inappropriate behavior) during these interactions than patients with low-EE parents. More important was their finding that high-EE parents were more likely than low-EE parents to criticize the patient during interactions if he or she had just expressed an unusual thought (e.g., "I must be able to connect with a higher consciousness before I can work"). Moreover, patients from high-EE families who had been criticized following expression of an unusual thought were more likely to express another unusual thought later in the interaction than those who had not been earlier criticized.

This sequence of patient unusual thought/parent criticism/patient unusual thought may help us to understand how family stress and patient symptoms are interwoven in bidirectional, mutually reciprocal patterns. Unusual thinking or other symptoms may be more likely to be expressed by patients in the face of eliciting stimuli (i.e., criticism) from parents. Likewise, negative parental attitudes or behaviors may be more likely to be expressed when patients show subsyndromal symptoms. The relation between these bidirectional family patterns and longitudinal outcomes in patients deserves study.

**Patients' styles of interacting with relatives.** The Rosenfarb et al. data raise the more general question of how patients verbally interact with their relatives. Could relatives simply be responding to a patient's argumentative or provocative style with criticism, or to his or her needy, dependent style with overinvolvement?

Two studies conducted on a single sample of recent-onset schizophrenics (Hahlweg et al., 1989; Strachan, Feingold, Goldstein, Miklowitz, & Nuechterlein, 1989) suggest that high-EE attitudes should be understood as coming about via bidirectional, recursive processes. Both studies concluded that schizophrenic patients often respond to or elicit criticisms by behaving negatively toward parents (i.e., criticizing the parent, showing avoidant nonverbal responses). In other cases, patients respond with self-critical, intrapunitive statements that may fuel criticism or intrusiveness from parents, as in this example from a high-EE family (from Strachan et al., 1989):

**Mother:** When you get in one of those moods, it makes us very shaky. It's like asking somebody else to carry a thousand-pound load. . . . you should be grateful and thankful for the help you've had. [*Critical and guilt-inducing*]

**Daughter:** I know, but I feel like I don't deserve any part of you guys' help. . . . [interrupted] [*self-denigrating*]

**Mother:** But by my way of thinking, that's just reverting back to the "poor me" attitude. [*Critical*]

In this example, a bidirectional process has been set in motion in which the mother's criticisms may generate self-denigration in the patient, which in turn fuels more criticism from the mother. No one is at fault in this example. In fact, Hahlweg et al. (1989) showed that negative back-and-forth volleys were just as likely to be initiated by schizophrenic patients as by their parents.

What happens in low-EE families that is different? It may be the ability to call "time out." For example, in Hahlweg et al.'s (1989) analysis, members of low-EE parent–patient dyads or triads who became embroiled in negatively escalating cycles were likely to change the subject or refuse to counter with another negative behavior once four or five volleys had occurred. High-EE dyads or triads, in contrast, often permitted as many as 20 volleys to occur.

When we combine this data with the Rosenfarb et al. (1993) data derived from the same sample, a picture begins to emerge of some high-EE families: Parent(s) and schizophrenic offspring are locked into mutually unfulfilling, reciprocal patterns of interaction that are fueled by the parents' underlying attitudes toward the patient, the patient's symptoms, and the patient's attitudes and interactional behaviors toward the parents.

## Expressed Emotion as a Genetic Vulnerability Marker

We have examined the relevance to EE of the first two models that have guided this chapter, and have concluded that (a) EE has significance as a prognostic variable and (b) one cannot determine whether EE is causal or reactive; in fact, it is probably both. But can EE be reduced to a measure of predisposition to psychopathology (the shared vulnerability model)? Do high-EE parents show greater genetic loadings for psychopathology than low-EE parents?

An obvious argument against this view is that EE has been found to predict recurrences of a variety of different mood and thinking disorders, such that the hypothesized vulnerability to high-EE would have to be one that varied from disorder to disorder. Second, EE predicts relapses of depression even when the key relative is a spouse rather than a parent (e.g., Hooley et al., 1986).

One study (Goldstein et al., 1992; Goldstein, 1993) found evidence of a linkage between levels of EE and lifetime psychopathology among parents of schizophrenic patients, but only when combining data from two measures of EE (the CFI and a briefer measure, the Five-Minute Speech Sample [Magaña et al., 1986]). Paradoxically, low-EE parents had higher frequencies of diagnosable affective disorder in their families of origin than did high-EE parents.

Psychopathology in parents may be one factor that decreases the threshold for the expression of critical and/or overinvolved attitudes, but the evidence is not compelling. Of course, there may be other, less obvious genetic and/or biological predispositions—-such as temperamental disturbances or other physiologically based difficulties in coping with stressful situations—-that underly EE attitudes in parents and their association with psychopathology in offspring.

## A Model for Understanding Expressed Emotion in Families

Whatever the nature of the relation between EE and outcome in psychological disorders, it is unlikely to be a simple, univariate one. It is more likely that this relation reflects a series of internal processes in relatives and in patients that are both elicited by and affected by each other and by other environmental contingencies. In fact, the link between parent EE and patient relapse could be conceptualized as a set of interlinked "disposition by situation interactions" (Mischel, 1973). For the patient, there may exist psychological, neurobiological, or cognitive predispositions that are most likely to be expressed as illness in the context of a high-EE environment (the situation).

A low-EE environment may protect against the expression of these "latent traits" in patients. In turn, some relatives may be predisposed to develop high-EE attitudes when facing the stress and burden associated with the patient's developing episode of illness (the situation), and these attitudes may not be evident when the patient is well.[2] In contrast, the low-EE parent may have evolved different styles of coping due to the different circumstances of living with a patient who, for reasons related as well as unrelated to the family, is at lower risk for relapse.

To illustrate this Disposition × Situation interactional model, consider the following extension of Hooley's (1987) EE–attributional theory. Hooley has proposed that high-EE, critical parents are prone to making internal, stable, controllable attributions about schizophrenic behavior (e.g., "He is withdrawn and low in energy because he's lazy"), whereas low-EE parents view the patient's behavior as uncontrollable and a product of his or her illness. These attributional styles in parents may arise in reaction to the prodromal signs of a developing episode of the patient's illness and may disappear once the symptoms have abated. However, the family's reactions, even if state-dependent, may for the patient serve as stressors that augment the expression of underlying biological vulnerabilities to specific disorders (e.g., increased physiological arousal in schizophrenia; Tarrier, Barrowclough, Porceddu, & Watts, 1988a). The stimulation of these biological vulnerabilities may in turn give rise to irritability, thought disturbance, negativism, or self-denigration in the patient, which in family interactions may further fuel high-EE attitudes and specific attributional processes among parents.

When viewed in this light, the association between parental EE and patient relapse becomes less a question of who is at fault than one of understanding the specific emotional relationship between the parents and the ill offspring at a particular point in the course of the disorder. With this understanding, we are in a better position to intervene and attempt to reduce the patient's risk of recurrence and the relatives' level of caretaking burden.

## FAMILY INTERVENTIONS IN SEVERE PSYCHOPATHOLOGY

### Psychoeducational Family Interventions in Schizophrenia

Most of the studies described above have examined family factors that predict the onset and/or course of severe psychopathology. But do these studies tell us how we should go about treating families of schizophrenic or other patients? Can family interventions modify levels of EE or other family attributes, leading to reductions in patient relapse rates and/or improved family functioning?

Stimulated in part by the EE research, a number of controlled clinical trials of family intervention programs have been undertaken. There is now strong evidence that the addition of an outpatient program of family intervention to maintenance medication affords a significant advantage for schizophrenic patients, in terms of relapse reduction, over medication alone (Goldstein, Rodnick, Evans, May, & Steinberg, 1978; Hogarty et al., 1986; Hogarty et al., 1991; Leff, Kuipers, Berkowitz, & Sturgeon, 1985; Tarrier et al., 1988b), or individual therapy (Falloon, Boyd, & McGill, 1984). Table 3 summarizes the efficacy data for various controlled psychoeducational treatment studies.

These treatments were designed for families of schizophrenic patients who are discharged from the hospital to the family's home or community. They share the following assumptions: (a) schizophrenic disorder is a primarily biological illness that must be managed using a combination of pharmacological and psychosocial interventions, (b) the focus of treatment should be on resolving the current episode of psychosis and fostering the patient's reentry into the community, (c) the patient and family should be educated about the nature of schizophrenic disorder, and (d) dysfunctional family interaction patterns and coping mechanisms that have evolved in response to the illness may be modifiable.

Most of these intervention studies have reported treatment-associated reductions in pretreatment levels

---

[2] In support of this hypothesis, approximately 25% to 50% of initially high-EE critical parents are low-EE when retested at a time when the patient is in remission, and the degree of diminution in criticism scores directly parallels the patient's degree of clinical improvement (Brown et al., 1972; Dulz & Hand, 1986; Hogarty et al., 1986).

## TABLE 3

Family Intervention Studies of Schizophrenia

| Study | Follow-up period | Family group: % relapsed | Comparison group: % relapsed | Nature of comparison group |
|---|---|---|---|---|
| Goldstein, Rodnick, Evans, May, & Steinberg, 1978 | 6 months | 0 | 17 | Moderate dose neuroleptic |
| Leff, Kuipers, Berkowitz, & Sturgeon, 1985 | 2 years | 20 | 78 | Routine treatment |
| Leff et al., 1989 | 9 months | 8 | 36 | Education; relatives' groups |
| Falloon, Boyd, & McGill, 1984 | 2 years | 17 | 83 | Family education; supportive individual therapy |
| Hogarty et al., 1991 | 2 years | 29 | 50 | Individual skills training |
| Tarrier et al., 1988b | 2 years | 33 | 59 | Education; routine treatment |

*Note:* All patients in these studies were maintained on phenothiazine medications.

of family EE (or negative affective style), although levels of criticism appear easier to modify than levels of emotional overinvolvement (Doane, Goldstein, Miklowitz, & Falloon, 1986; Hogarty et al., 1986; Tarrier et al., 1988b; Leff, Kuipers, Berkowitz, & Eberlein-Fries, 1982; Leff et al., 1989). Most important, treatment-associated modifications in parental attitudes or interactional behaviors correlate with lower rates of psychotic relapse among schizophrenic patients at follow-up.

## Extension of Psychoeducational Approaches to Mood Disorders

An advantage of the existing psychoeducational approaches is their relatively easy extension to mental disorders other than schizophrenia. In this section, we describe our application of one form of psychoeducational treatment for schizophrenia, behavioral family management (BFM; Falloon et al., 1984) to bipolar affective disorder (see Miklowitz & Goldstein, 1990).

Working with schizophrenic patients receiving standard phenothiazine drug regimes, Falloon et al. (1984) conducted this behavioral treatment in the families' homes in 21 sessions spread over 9 months. Behavioral family management consists of four core components: (a) a functional assessment of the family unit, in which skill assets and deficits are identi-

fied; (b) an educational module, in which the patient and family are taught about the signs and symptoms of schizophrenia and its prognosis and treatment; (c) a communication module, in which family members and patients are taught via role playing and behavioral rehearsal to communicate in more constructive ways; and (d) a problem-solving module, in which the family is encouraged to define and solve fairly circumscribed problems (e.g., how to get the house clean). In Falloon et al.'s (1985) study, relatively chronic schizophrenic patients whose families received BFM had, at a 2-year follow-up, fewer relapses, less behavioral disturbance, better social/occupational adjustment, lower dosages of phenothiazine drugs, and better family relations than patients receiving supportive individual therapy.

In modifying BFM for bipolar disorder, we were able to adhere to Falloon's basic treatment structure but also found it necessary to incorporate certain techniques derived from strategic family therapy. For example, we found that exploring, validating, and reframing resistance to treatment was a necessary step before certain of the educational or communication skill interventions could be implemented with these families (Miklowitz & Goldstein, 1990). The efficacy of this modified treatment for bipolar disorder is currently being evaluated in controlled clinical trials conducted in California (Goldstein & Miklowitz,

1989; NIMH grant 42556) and Colorado (Miklowitz & Frank, 1993).

## CASE STUDY OF BEHAVIORAL FAMILY MANAGEMENT FOR BIPOLAR DISORDER

*Russell, a 30-year-old unemployed fire-fighter, lived with his wife, Julie, and his two school-aged children. He had had several manic episodes. He was approached during a hospitalization for mania about taking part in home-based family treatment. Although he and his wife agreed they needed marital treatment, they preferred not to involve their children. Couples treatment was begun on a weekly basis following discharge by a trained EFM therapist and cotherapist.*

*The initial functional assessment sessions revealed high-EE, critical attitudes in Julie. These attitudes derived from longstanding resentments toward Russell, including anger about his marital infidelities, his irritability, and his unemployment. Russell responded to her requests and criticisms of him with rancor and resentment. For example, her requests for more physical affection were met with angry reproaches centering on his need for "space."*

*The educational sessions about the nature and causes of bipolar disorder were received with mixed emotions. Whereas Julie appreciated being told the facts about Russell's illness and what the future held, Russell became increasingly withdrawn. He began to cancel sessions. In part, his resistance reflected a worsening postmanic depression, but also resentment about being labeled as mentally ill and "reduced to molecules." The therapists validated his concerns with statements such as, "We can understand your feelings about having an illness and having to discuss it in here. You might sometimes feel like you're an 'object of discussion' rather than a person. A question people often have when thinking about these issues is, 'Can I still think of myself*

*as a person with wishes, needs and goals?'" He resonated to these interventions, but had to be readmitted to the hospital due to his worsening depression.*

*Russell was in the hospital for 3 weeks and underwent electroconvulsive therapy. The treatment was successful, and sessions were resumed after he returned home. The therapists modified the education sessions so that they were delivered in a less didactic, more Socratic manner, with less emphasis on imparting scientific facts and more emphasis on affectively laden issues, such as how the illness had affected Russell's family and his life goals. Russell responded more positively to this approach, perhaps in part because of his improved clinical state.*

*The transition to structured communication training led to a much better rapport between the therapists and this couple. The couple participated in regular role plays in which, for example, one member of the pair spoke while the other actively listened, or one member expressed a request of the other to perform a certain task. Julie was instructed to deliver negative feedback in a very specific, succinct manner, such that identifiable behaviors performed by Russell were targeted for change instead of his personality traits. The couple noted an improvement in their marital relationship during this period. In addition, Julie opened a business in which Russell became employed on a part-time basis. Russell continued to express ambivalence about the treatment, but his attendance of and participation in sessions improved.*

*During the final portions of treatment, the couple engaged in problem solving, usually about family problems that affected work or the functioning of the household: When and how to take a vacation, problems in arranging for day care of the children, and household chores. Julie and Russell appeared to appreciate the structure provided by these problem-solving tasks.*

*The marital situation and Russell's illness had stabilized to some degree by the end of the 9 months of treatment. At termination, Julie was again interviewed as to her EE status, and her baseline level of EE criticism had dropped substantially. At a 2-year follow-up, Russell had had no recurrences of mania or depression.*

## Commentary

In this case, it was difficult to implement the BFM treatment "by the book." It was often necessary to use strategic and other psychotherapeutic interventions such as reframing, relabeling, and exploration and interpretation of affect in order to gain a stronger therapeutic alliance with this couple.

Surprisingly, this couple often reported that the treatment was very helpful to them even though they rarely practiced or implemented the prescribed modes of communication between sessions. It appeared that a great deal of therapeutic benefit derived from (a) breaking family taboos against talking about the illness, (b) opening lines of communication and thus restructuring the "balance of power" within the marital relationship, and (c) giving the couple a feeling of mastery and self-efficacy over their life problems. The structure provided by the role-playing and problem-solving exercises decreased the anxiety level of this couple. The education sessions, although often threatening to Russell, may have led in part to the observed reduction in criticisms from Julie as she began to see her husband's behavior as a manifestation of an uncontrollable chemical imbalance rather than of his personality or attitudes. The net result was a reduction in tension in the family, which, directly or indirectly, may have contributed to the improved course of illness seen in this patient at follow-up.

## MENTAL DISORDERS AND THE FAMILY: WHERE ARE WE AND WHERE SHOULD WE GO?

### What Do We Know About Family Risk Indicators?

There are several general conclusions that can be drawn from the existing literature.

1. There are features of the family environment, in the domains of affective attitudes, interactional behaviors, and communication clarity, that increase or decrease the probability that a biologically vulnerable family member will develop an episode of psychosis or mood disorder.

2. Whatever the actual relation between the family environment and individual pathology, it is unlikely to be a linear one. To focus on the behavior of one family member to the exclusion of others is short sighted. Attributes like EE and CD are best thought of as "leading indicators" (Hogarty et al., 1988) of mutually produced, bidirectional processes within the family.

3. The addition of a psychoeducational family intervention to a regular program of outpatient pharmacological maintenance may greatly improve the prognosis of patients with schizophrenia and possibly other disorders, especially if family risk indicators such as EE can be modified via treatment.

## Where Should We Go From Here?

Many suggestions for future research have been made throughout this chapter. However, there are other issues that should be addressed in future studies of severe mental disorders. Much of the current literature deals with family attitudes and communication patterns. Other research has focused on specific traumatic events in the lives of persons with severe disorders. These include intrafamilial experiences of sexual victimization, physical abuse, parental neglect, and loss. There have been few attempts to prospectively link these family variables to the onset of psychotic disorders such as schizophrenia or to assess their covariation with some of the prognostically important family constructs described in this chapter. Using multiple approaches to defining family pathology in single studies may increase the explanatory power of the family as an etiological or prognostic agent.

There is an entirely separate body of literature on the dynamics of marital distress and its associated communication patterns. Can marital and family researchers develop complementary hypotheses and share common methodologies? For example, Holtzworth-Munroe and Jacobson (1985) have reported that, in comparison with members of maritally nondistressed couples, members of distressed couples tend to attribute their partners' negative relationship behaviors to internal, global, stable, and intentional factors. To what extent do bidirectional, negatively escalating cycles of communication between parents and offspring with mental illness reflect distorted patterns of attribution about parent or offspring behavior? Can these attributions be modified via conjoint intervention, as can be done for maritally distressed couples (Baucom & Epstein, 1990)?

## Concluding Comments

Investigators who study family factors in severe mental disorders generally view the family as a system in which one member is expressing psychopathology. However, the empirical work in this field differs from clinical writings about family systems in that it incorporates the well-founded view that these disorders have genetic and neurobiological bases. The family, then, is seen as a risk or protective factor that may augment or diminish the likelihood that underlying genetic and/or biological vulnerabilities in a family member will be expressed as symptoms of a mental disorder. Family interventions are correspondingly viewed as useful adjuncts to pharmacological maintenance because they aim to modify the stress end of the vulnerability–stress equation. This field will evolve further as new methodologies and findings from both psychological and biological lines of inquiry provide a more complete understanding of severe mental disorders within an environmental context.

## References

American Psychiatric Association. (1987). *Diagnostic and statistical manual of mental disorders* (3rd ed.). Washington, DC: Author.

Asarnow, J. R., Goldstein, M. J., & Ben-Meir, S. (1988). Parental communication deviance in childhood onset schizophrenia spectrum and depressive disorders. *Journal of Child Psychology and Psychiatry, 29,* 825–838.

Asarnow, J. R., Goldstein, M. J., Tompson, M., & Guthrie, D. (1993). One-year outcomes of depressive disorders in child psychiatric inpatients: Evaluation of the prognostic power of a brief measure of expressed emotion. *Journal of Child Psychology and Psychiatry, 34,* 129–137.

Bateson, G., Jackson, D., Haley, J., & Weakland, J. (1956). Toward a theory of schizophrenia. *Behavioral Sciences, 1,* 251–264.

Baucom, D. H., & Epstein, N. (1990). *Cognitive–behavioral marital therapy.* New York: Brunner/Mazel.

Bowen, M. (1960). A family concept of schizophrenia. In D. D. Jackson (Ed.), *The etiology of schizophrenia* (pp. 346–372). New York: Basic Books.

Brown, G. W., Birley, J. L. T., & Wing, J. K. (1972). Influence of family life on the course of schizophrenic disorders: A replication. *British Journal of Psychiatry, 121,* 241–258.

Doane, J. A., Falloon, I. R. H., Goldstein, M. J., & Mintz, J. (1985). Parental affective style and the treatment of schizophrenia: Predicting course of illness and social functioning. *Archives of General Psychiatry, 42,* 34–42.

Doane, J. A., Goldstein, M. J., Miklowitz, D. J., & Falloon, I. R. H. (1986). The impact of individual and family treatment on the affective climate of families of schizophrenics. *British Journal of Psychiatry, 148,* 279–287.

Doane, J. A., West, K. L., Goldstein, M. J., Rodnick, E. H., & Jones, J. E. (1981). Parental communication deviance and affective style: Predictors of subsequent schizophrenia-spectrum disorders in vulnerable adolescents. *Archives of General Psychiatry, 38,* 679–685.

Dulz, B., & Hand, I. (1986). Short-term relapse in young schizophrenics. In M. J. Goldstein & K. Hahlweg (Eds.), *Treatment of schizophrenia: Family assessment and intervention* (pp. 59–77). Berlin: Springer-Verlag.

Falloon, I. R. H., Boyd, J. L., & McGill, C. W. (1984). *Family care of schizophrenia.* New York: Guilford Press.

Falloon, I. R. H., Boyd, J. L., McGill, C. W., Williamson, W., Razani, J., Moss, H. B., Gilderman, A. M., & Simpson, G. M. (1985). Family management in the prevention of morbidity of schizophrenia. *Archives of General Psychiatry, 42,* 887–896.

Fontana, A. F. (1966). Family etiology of schizophrenia: Is a scientific methodology possible? In N. L. Corah & E. N. Gale (Eds.), *The origins of abnormal behavior* (pp. 62–73). Reading, MA: Addison-Wesley.

Fromm-Reichmann, F. (1950). *Principles of intensive psychotherapy.* Chicago: University of Chicago Press.

Glaser, R. (1976). *Family, spouse, and individual Rorschach responses of families with and without young adult schizophrenic offspring.* Unpublished doctoral dissertation, University of California, Berkeley.

Goldstein, M. J. (1987). Family interaction patterns that antedate the onset of schizophrenia and related disorders: A further analysis of data from a longitudinal, prospective study. In K. Hahlweg & M. J. Goldstein (Eds.), *Understanding major mental disorder: The contribution of family interaction research* (pp. 11–32). New York: Family Process Press.

Goldstein, M. J. (1993, April). *Transactional processes related to the course and outcome of schizophrenia.* Paper presented at the biannual meeting of the International Congress on Schizophrenia Research, Colorado Springs, CO.

Goldstein, M. J., & Miklowitz, D. J. (1989). *Lithium and family management of bipolar disorder.* Unpublished grant proposal MH42556, National Institute of Mental Health, Bethesda, MD.

Goldstein, M. J., Rodnick, E. H., Evans, J. R., May, P. R. A., & Steinberg, M. (1978). Drug and family therapy in the aftercare of acute schizophrenia. *Archives of General Psychiatry, 35,* 1169–1177.

Goldstein, M. J., Strachan, A. M., & Wynne, L. C. (in press). DSM-IV literature review: Relational problems with high expressed emotion. In T. A. Widiger, A. J., Frances, H. A. Pinkus, W. Davis, & M. First (Eds.), *DSM-IV sourcebook.* Washington, DC: American Psychiatric Press.

Goldstein, M. J., Talovic, S. A., Nuechterlein, K. H., Fogelson, D. L., Subotnik, K. L., & Asarnow, R. F. (1992). Family interaction vs. individual psychopathology: Do they indicate the same processes in the families of schizophrenics? *British Journal of Psychiatry, 161*(Suppl. 18), 97–102.

Gottesman, I. I. (1991). *Schizophrenia genesis: The origins of madness.* New York: Freeman.

Hahlweg, K., Goldstein, M. J., Nuechterlein, K. H., Magana, A. B., Mintz, J., Doane, J. A., Miklowitz, D. J., & Snyder, K. S. (1989). Expressed emotion and patient–relative interaction in families of recent-onset schizophrenics. *Journal of Consulting and Clinical Psychology, 57,* 11–18.

Hammen, C., Marks, T., Mayol, A., & deMayo, R. (1985). Depressive self-schemas, life stress, and vulnerability to depression. *Journal of Abnormal Psychology, 94,* 308–319.

Hatfield, A. B., Spaniol, L., & Zipple, A. M. (1987). Expressed emotion: A family perspective. *Schizophrenia Bulletin, 13,* 221–226.

Hirsch, S. R., & Leff, J. P. (1975). *Abnormalities in parents of schizophrenics.* London: Oxford University Press.

Hodes, M., & Grange, D. L. (1993). Expressed emotion in the investigation of eating disorders: A review. *International Journal of Eating Disorders, 13,* 279–288.

Hogarty, G. E., Anderson, C. M., Reiss, D. J., Kornblith, S. J., Greenwald, D. P., Javna, C. D., Madonia, M. J., & the EPICS Schizophrenia Research Group (1986). Family psychoeducation, social skills training, and

maintenance chemotherapy in the aftercare treatment of schizophrenia. *Archives of General Psychiatry, 43,* 633–642.

Hogarty, G. E., Anderson, C. M., Reiss, D. J., Kornblith, S. J., Greenwald, D. P., Ulrich, R. F., Carter, M., & The EPICS Research Group (1991). Family psychoeducation, social skills training, and maintenace chemotherapy in the aftercare treatment of schizophrenia: II. Two-year effects of a controlled study on relapse and adjustment. *Archives of General Psychiatry, 48,* 340–347.

Hogarty, G. E., McEvoy, J. P., Munetz, M., DiBarry, A. L., Bartone, P., Cather, R., Cooley, S. J., Ulrich, R. F., Carter, M., Madonia, M. J., & the EPICS Research Group (1988). Dose of fluphenazine, familial expressed emotion, and outcome in schizophrenia: Results of a two-year controlled study. *Archives of General Psychiatry, 45,* 797–805.

Holtzworth-Munroe, A., & Jacobson, N. S. (1985). Causal attributions of married couples: When do they search for causes? What do they conclude when they do? *Journal of Personality and Social Psychology, 48,* 1398–1412.

Hooley, J. M. (1987). The nature and origins of expressed emotion. In K. Hahlweg & M. J. Goldstein (Eds.), *Understanding major mental disorder: The contribution of family interaction research* (pp. 176–194). New York: Family Process Press.

Hooley, J. M., Orley, J., & Teasdale, J. D. (1986). Levels of expressed emotion and relapse in depressed patients. *British Journal of Psychiatry, 148,* 642–647.

Jenkins, J. H., & Karno, M. (1992). The meaning of expressed emotion: Theoretical issues raised by cross-cultural research. *American Journal of Psychiatry, 149,* 9–21.

Johnston, M. H., & Holzman, P. S. (1979). *Assessing schizophrenic thinking.* San Francisco: Jossey-Bass.

Jones, J. E. (1977). Patterns of transactional style deviance in the TATs of parents of schizophrenics. *Family Process, 16,* 327–337.

Kavanagh, D. J. (1992). Recent developments in expressed emotion and schizophrenia. *British Journal of Psychiatry, 160,* 601–620.

Leff, J. P., Berkowitz, R., Shavit, N., Strachan, A., Glass, I., & Vaughn, C. (1989). A trial of family therapy: V. A relatives group for schizophrenia. *British Journal of Psychiatry, 154,* 58–66.

Leff, J. P., Kuipers, L., Berkowitz, R., Eberlein-Fries, R., & Sturgeon, D. (1982). A controlled trial of social intervention in the families of schizophrenic patients. *British Journal of Psychiatry, 141,* 121–134.

Leff, J. P., Kuipers, L., Berkowitz, R., & Sturgeon, D. A. (1985). A controlled trial of social intervention in the families of schizophrenic patients: Two year follow-up. *British Journal of Psychiatry, 146*, 594–600.

Lidz, T., Cornelison, A., Fleck, S., & Terry, D. (1957). The intrafamilial environment of schizophrenic patients: II. Marital schism and marital skew. *American Journal of Psychiatry, 114*, 241–248.

Magaña, A. B., Goldstein, M. J., Karno, M., Miklowitz, D. J., Jenkins, J., & Falloon, I. R. H. (1986). A brief method for assessing expressed emotion in relatives of psychiatric patients. *Psychiatry Research, 17*, 203–212.

Miklowitz, D. J., & Frank. E. (1993). *A comparison of family and individual therapy in the outpatient maintenance of bipolar disorder.* Unpublished grant proposal, John D. and Catherine T. MacArthur Depression Network, University of Pittsburgh, PA.

Miklowitz, D. J., & Goldstein, M. J. (1990). Behavioral family treatment for patients with bipolar affective disorder. *Behavior Modification, 14*, 457–489.

Miklowitz, D. J., Goldstein, M. J., Falloon, I. R. H., & Doane, J. A. (1984). Interactional correlates of expressed emotion in the families of schizophrenics. *British Journal of Psychiatry, 144*, 482–487.

Miklowitz, D. J., Goldstein, M. J., Nuechterlein, K. H., Snyder, K. S., & Mintz, J. (1988). Family factors and the course of bipolar affective disorder. *Archives of General Psychiatry, 45*, 225–231.

Miklowitz, D. J., & Stackman, D. (1992). Communication deviance in families of schizophrenic and other psychiatric patients: Current state of the construct. In E. F. Walker, R. H. Dworkin, & B. Cornblatt (Eds.), *Progress in experimental personality and psychopathology research* (Vol. 15, pp. 1–46). New York: Springer.

Miklowitz, D. J., Velligan, D. I., Goldstein, M. J., Nuechterlein, K. H., Gitlin, M. J., Ranlett, G., & Doane, J. A. (1991). Communication deviance in families of schizophrenic and manic patients. *Journal of Abnormal Psychology, 100*, 163–173.

Mischel, W. (1973). Toward a cognitive social learning reconceptualization of personality. *Psychological Review, 80*, 252–283.

Nuechterlein, K. H., & Dawson, M. E. (1984a). Information processing and attentional functioning in the developmental course of schizophrenic disorders. *Schizophrenia Bulletin, 10*, 160–203.

Nuechterlein, K. H., & Dawson, M. E. (1984b). A heuristic vulnerability/stress model of schizophrenic episodes. *Schizophrenia Bulletin, 10*, 300–312.

Nuechterlein, K. H., Goldstein, M. J., Ventura, J., Dawson, M. E., & Doane, J. A. (1989). Patient–environment relationships in schizophrenia: Information processing, communication deviance, autonomic arousal, and stressful life events. *British Journal of Psychiatry, 155*(Suppl. 5), 84–89.

Parker, G., & Hadzi-Pavlovic, D. (1990). Expressed emotion as a predictor of schizophrenia relapse: An analysis of aggregated data. *Psychological Medicine, 20*, 961–965.

Rosenfarb, I. S., Goldstein, M. J., Mintz, J., & Nuechterlein, K. H. (1993). Expressed emotion and subclinical psychopathology observable within the transactions between recent-onset schizophrenics and their families. *Schizophrenia Research, 9*, 271.

Sass, L. A., Gunderson, J. G., Singer, M. T., & Wynne, L. C. (1984). Parental communication deviance and forms of thinking in male schizophrenic offspring. *Journal of Nervous and Mental Disease, 172*, 513–520.

Singer, M., & Wynne, L. (1965). Thought disorder and family relations of schizophrenics: III. Methodology using projective techniques. *Archives of General Psychiatry, 12*, 187–200.

Strachan, A. M., Feingold, D., Goldstein, M. J., Miklowitz, D. J., & Nuechterlein, K. H. (1989). Is expressed emotion an index of a transactional process? II. Patient's coping style. *Family Process, 28*, 169–181.

Tarrier, N., Barrowclough, C., Porceddu, K., & Watts, S. (1988a). The assessment of psychophysiological reactivity to the expressed emotion of the relatives of schizophrenic patients. *British Journal of Psychiatry, 152*, 618–624.

Tarrier, N., Barrowclough, C., Vaughn C., Bamrah, J. S., Porceddu, K., Watts, S., & Freeman, H. (1988b). The community management of schizophrenia. *British Journal of Psychiatry, 153*, 532–542.

Vaughn, C. E., & Leff, J. P. (1976). The influence of family and social factors on the course of psychiatric illness: A comparison of schizophrenic and depressed neurotic patients. *British Journal of Psychiatry, 129*, 125–137.

Wagener, D. K., Hogarty, G. E., Goldstein, M. J., Asarnow, R. F., & Browne, A. (1986). Information processing and communication deviance in schizophrenic patients and their mothers. *Psychiatry Research, 18*, 365–377.

Wender, P. H., Rosenthal, D., Rainer, J. D., Greenhill, L., & Sarlin, M. B. (1977). Schizophrenics' adopting parents: Psychiatric status. *Archives of General Psychiatry, 34*, 777–784.

Woodward, J. A., & Goldstein, M. J. (1977). Communication deviance in the families of schizophrenics: A comment on the misuse of analysis of covariance. *Science, 197*, 1096–1097.

Wynne, L. C., & Singer, M. T. (1963). Thought disorder and family relations of schizophrenics: I. A research strategy. *Archives of General Psychiatry, 9*, 191–198.

Wynne, L., Singer, M., Bartko, J., & Toohey, M. (1977). Schizophrenics and their families: Recent research on parental communication. In J. M. Tanner (Ed.), *De-

*velopments in psychiatric research* (pp. 254–286). London: Hodder & Stoughton.

Wynne, L., Singer, M., & Toohey, M. (1976). Communication of the adoptive parents of schizophrenics. In J. Jorstad & E. Ugelstad (Eds.), *Schizophrenia 75: Psy-*

*chotherapy, family studies, research* (pp. 413–452). Oslo, Norway: Universitetsforlaget.

Zubin, J., & Spring, B. (1977). Vulnerability—-A new view of schizophrenia. *Journal of Abnormal Psychology, 86,* 103–126.

# CHAPTER 11

# FAMILY THERAPY RESEARCH

*James Alexander and Cole Barton*

## INTRODUCTION

Although traditional psychology researchers have been trained to be as objective as possible and hence "free" from contextual bias, it is increasingly recognized that any research is influenced by its context. Methods, theories, and measurements in family therapy process and outcome research have been contextually influenced in many ways, although these influences are often not acknowledged (Alexander, Holtzworth-Munroe, & Jameson, 1993). For systemic marital and family therapists, too, context is the major, if not only, source of clinical meaning. This chapter is written from this framework. We are in a dynamic field that is influencing and being influenced by larger sociopolitical, economic, and moral/ethical forces. In this environment there are few, if any, consensual undeniable truths or incontrovertible findings. Instead we face dilemmas, dialectics, "bottom lines," and "worst case scenarios." We do not have the luxury of waiting for all these issues to be resolved, whether it be by rhetoric, passion, faith, or definitive research. Instead, we arbitrarily adopt a perspective based on the preponderance of evidence and on what seems reasonable to do or conclude with respect to family therapy research.

We emphasise accumulated patterns of evidence, but this is not intended to deny the importance of unique findings, including those that emerge from small sample demonstrations and qualitative investigations. For example, the field-defining work of Minuchin et al. (1975) with brittle diabetic children had a powerful impact on the field, even though it was not replicated for a decade after its initial appearance

(cf. Gurman, Kniskern, & Pinsof, 1986). Numerous similar examples exist of reports and single studies that represent potent sources of new intervention strategies and techniques, of exceptions to the current practices of the day, and of stimulating conceptual and philosophical insights into the complexities of various clinical populations and problems.

However, our center of gravity must be in the preponderance of evidence, the same criterion we demand from other (especially competing) fields. We do not abandon marriage and family approaches just because we are shown single case studies and qualitative descriptions (even with testimonials) of successful alternative treatments such as individually based psychotherapy, religious conversions, or unreplicated drug trials. As family psychologists we demand a more rigorous basis as evidence for important clinical and policy decisions, and we cannot expect others to accept any less from us.

In this chapter we do not attempt to tell family therapy researchers how to do research; others have already done a masterful job at that (e.g., Greenberg, 1991; Gurman et al., 1986; Jacobson, 1991; Jacobson et al., 1984; Pinsof, 1989; Whisman, Jacobson, Fruzetti & Waltz, 1989). We also do not replicate the polemics concerning qualitative versus quantitative research, gender and cultural sensitivity, or developmental and systemic perspectives as they relate to family therapy research. These important topics and issues are reviewed elsewhere (cf. Alexander et al., 1993).

Instead, we will add to the voices that ask that family therapy research focus on clinically meanful processes and clinical populations. As clinicians and researchers we also ask that clinical models address the complexities of family therapy process and not become oversimplified and decontextualized descriptions of major techniques or rhetorical assertions. Many people are doing important work, but at the same time most research accounts have been insufficient and incomplete in description, scope, and/or rigor. The replications necessary to produce consensus regarding family therapy efficacy require many elements: the technical specificity of journal articles, the clinical detail of case studies, and the coherence of well-developed treatment protocols.

Based on the considerations described above, we develop a series of general conclusions based on research that, if not unassailable, is at least based on consistency, replication, and a growing body of evidence. Our conclusions do not require a new review of individual studies; such careful scholarly work has already been accomplished in numerous reviews. Gurman et al. (1986), for example, listed 47 reviews published between the years of 1970 and 1986 and added conclusions of their own. Using that review as a starting point, we examine subsequent major reviews of marital and/or family therapy to discern patterns of conclusions. We also examine major reviews of the treatment literature for specific syndromes that include marital or family therapy. Finally, we add a review of the published meta-analyses that focus on marital and family therapy. These secondary sources (represented in Table 1), combined on occasion with exemplary studies, provide the basis for a series of conclusions that can be made with varying degrees of confidence about research in marital and family therapy. The first two of these conclusions are about overall efficacy. They are important as what might be called "marketing issues," because they influence the placement of family therapy within the larger array of services delivered to distressed individuals, couples, and families.

## THE EFFECTIVENESS OF MARRIAGE AND FAMILY THERAPY

Does marriage and family therapy work? The answer based on outcome research is *yes*—with slight qualifications. Some earlier reviews (e.g., Masten, 1979;

Wells & Dezen, 1978) asserted that there was not sufficient empirical support for concluding that family therapy had beneficial effects, or that it represented a treatment of choice for childhood problems. However, as can be seen in column 3 of Table 1, since the mid 1980s almost all reviewers (on the basis of an increasing volume of studies and careful attention to methodology) have been increasingly confident in asserting positive effects for marital and family therapy. In perhaps the most widely cited review, Gurman et al. (1986) considered marital and family therapy together and concluded that "the practice of marital and family therapy leads to positive outcomes" and "no longer needs to justify its existence on empirical grounds" (p. 570). Subsequent reviews and meta-analyses have consistently supported this optimistic conclusion with respect to marital therapy (e.g., Alexander et al., 1993; Hahlweg & Markman, 1988), family therapy (Alexander et al., 1993; Hazelrigg, Cooper, & Borduin, 1987), parent effectiveness training (Cedar & Levant, 1990), parent management training (Patterson, Dishion, & Chamberlain, 1992), and family enrichment (Giblin, Sprenkle, & Sheehan, 1985).

The most recent and probably most representative meta-analysis including both marital and family therapy (Shadish et al., 1993) examined a much larger data set (including dissertations) than had previous meta-analyses. This produced a sufficient sample size for the investigators to evaluate each domain independently and also to compare one domain with another. Their findings were generally consistent with previous conclusions: Marital and family therapy is associated with improved client outcome when compared with control treatments, and the improvement endures at follow-up (Shadish et al., 1993). Beyond this general conclusion, however, the findings were more complex. Effect sizes for marital therapy were somewhat larger (though not significantly so) than those for family therapy. However, the implication of a possible superiority of marital therapy over family therapy may be confounded by the nature of the two therapies. Shadish et al. suggested that studies of marital therapy, in general, focused on a more restricted range of problems, that the studies generally used dependent measures derived specifically as measures of those problems (such as marital accord),

## TABLE 1

Summary of Meta-analyses and Major Reviews of Marital and Family Therapy Outcomes

| Type of article / Authors and date | Domain or programs reviewed | Overall outcome efficacy concluded | Positive efficacy concluded | Lack of empirical support | Problems treated effectively | Specific intervention models and programs cited |
|---|---|---|---|---|---|---|
| Meta-analysis Giblin, Sprenkle, & Sheehan, 1985 | Family enrichment | Yes: overall EF = .44 | Premarital EF = .526 Marital EF = .419 Family EF = .545 | | Heterogeneous measures | Relationship enhancement (EF = .96) Parent–adolescent relationship development (EF = .96) Couple communication (EF = .42) Marriage encounter (EF = .44) |
| Meta-analysis Hazelrigg, Cooper, & Borduin 1987 | Family therapies | Yes: Overall EF = .45–.50 | Pragmatic[a] family therapies | Aesthetic[b] family therapies (outcome studies not found) | Child & adolescent behavior problems | |
| Meta-analysis Hahlweg & Markman 1988 | Behavioral marital therapies | Yes: Overall EF = .95 | Behavioral marital therapies | Insufficient non-behavioral studies for review | Marital | |
| Meta-analysis Markus, Lange, & Pettigrew 1990 | Family therapy | Yes: Overall EF = .70 | | | Delinquency conduct disorder schizophrenia | Functional family therapy (6 studies, EF = .8) Behavioral (3 studies, EF = 1.05) |
| Meta-analysis Shadish, Montgomery, Wilson, Wilson, Bright, & Okwumabua, 1993 | Marital and family therapies | Yes: Overall Marr Tx EF = .60 Fam Tx EF = .44 | Behavioral & psychoeducation systemic psychodynamic (one study)[c] | Humanistic | Marital dissatisfaction, communication, conduct disorders, phobias, schizophrenic symptoms | |

*(continues)*

TABLE 1 (Continued)

Summary of Meta-analyses and Major Reviews of Marital and Family Therapy Outcomes

| Type of article / Authors and date | Domain or programs reviewed | Overall outcome efficacy concluded | Positive efficacy concluded | Lack of empirical support | Problems treated effectively | Specific intervention models and programs cited |
|---|---|---|---|---|---|---|
| Meta-analysis Cedar & Levant 1990 | Parent effectiveness training | Yes: Overall EF = .33 | | | Heterogeneous child problems | |
| Major review Gurman, Kniskern, & Pinsof, 1986 | Marital and family therapies | Yes | Highly directive approaches | | Childhood conduct, schizophrenic behaviors, marriage conflict, juvenile delinquency, anxiety disorders | Social-learning-based parent management training (PMT) Psychoeducational family therapy Behavioral marital therapy Behavioral family therapy Behavioral spouse-assisted exposure |
| Topical review Gendreaux & Ross 1987 | Rehabilitation of delinquents | Yes | Pragmatic family therapies | | Delinquency | Functional family therapy Social-learning-based parent management training |
| Major review Bednar, Burlingame, & Masters, 1988 | Marital and family therapies | Mixed | Behavioral marriage and behavioral family therapies | Systems-based family therapies | Heterogeneous | Functional family therapy Social-learning-based parent management training Behavioral marital therapy |

| Review | Area | EF | Aesthetic therapies[b] | Pragmatic therapies[a] | Disorder | Effective treatments |
|---|---|---|---|---|---|---|
| Topical review Kazdin, 1993 | Psychotherapy for children and adolescents | | | | Adolescent substance abuse, conduct disorder & delinquency | Structural family therapy Functional family therapy Parent management training |
| Major review: Alexander, Holtzworth-Monroe, & Jameson, 1993 | Marital and family therapies | Yes | Aesthetic family therapies | Pragmatic family therapies and marital therapy | Aggressive children, substance-abusing youth, delinquency | Social-learning-based parent management training Structural family therapy Functional family therapy |
| Topical review Patterson, Dishion, & Chamberlain, 1992 | Antisocial children | Yes | | Parent training (social learning based) | Childhood antisocial problem behaviors | Parent training (behavioral) perhaps in combination with one or more of social skills training, cognitive skills training, and/or family systems therapy |

*Note:* EF = effect size; Cohen (1977) classified EF as small (.2), moderate (.5), and large (.8); Marr Tx = marital therapy; Fam Tx = family therapy.
[a]Pragmatic therapies are those identified by Hazelrigg et al. as being "principally concerned with behavioral outcomes" (p. 426).
[b]Aesthetic therapies "arise from phenomenological, psychodynamic, existential, and systems perspectives" (Hazelrigg et al., 1987, p. 425).
[c] Snyder, Wills, & Grady-Fletcher (1991) is cited as a stark exception to the general serious underrepresentation of psychodynamic marital and family therapies in clinical trials outcome research.

and that the research was dominated by just a few major orientations (behavioral marital therapy and cognitive–behavioral marital therapy in particular). Marital therapy researchers also have tended to study well-defined but somewhat restricted populations.

Family therapy has been applied to a wide range of problems, many of which may represent greater pathology than marital distress (e.g., conduct disorder, substance abuse, schizophrenia, oppositional disorder in children, eating disorders). In addition, family therapy includes more variations and integrations of treatment models. Thus most family therapy models have not received as much programmatic scrutiny as have the behavioral marital therapies. As a result the family therapies have not had the opportunity for as much empirically based refinement and corrective feedback.

Although this explanation might comfort proponents of family therapy, it reflects a more fluid and hence more troublesome context for family process and outcome research. The greater number of variations and integrations of family therapy may reflect a more dynamic and responsive field in the process of refinement. Conversely, it may reflect a field characterized by poorly defined and understood parameters, with refinements based not on empirical validation but on other, less rigorous, processes.

Although the latter conclusion may have some basis in fact, it does not warrant a blanket indictment of the field. Some sections of the family therapy literature show indications of programmatic evolution and empirical support, while still retaining clinical sensitivity (see Table 1). However, other forms of family therapy have not demonstrated evidence for outcome efficacy. In our own research, for example, functional family therapy (FFT) was more effective with delinquents than was no treatment (Alexander & Parsons, 1973; Barton et al., 1985) or individual attention (Alexander & Barton, 1980). However, FFT was also superior to two other *family-based* treatment programs espousing a humanistic or psychodynamic orientation. Data such as these indicate that it is clearly inappropriate to discuss the domain of family therapy as though it represents homogeneous processes or uniform outcome efficacy.

It is useful, therefore, to highlight distinctions between marital and family therapy models. The outcome evidence already described has demonstrated that marital and family therapy are legitimate clinical enterprises. Beyond this, the outcome evidence shows there are important differences between marital and family therapy models. Models vary in (a) the kinds of syndromes/problems with which they have been shown to be effective, (b) the components or ingredients of intervention, and (c) the sustained course of research and development associated with each model. Subsequent portions of this chapter will analyze the differences in these three categories.

## SYNDROMES EFFECTIVELY TREATED BY MARITAL AND FAMILY THERAPY

The 6th column of Table 1 lists specific successfully treated syndromes or problems identified in the various reviews. Note that individual studies exist that have demonstrated a positive treatment effect for specific problems not represented in Table 1. However, the conclusions in that table reflect a whole pattern of positive and replicated results based on exhaustive reviews of most, if not all, available studies in particular domains. The following sections are organized around marital and family therapies, and clinical problem areas are addressed in each section.

### Marital Therapies

As suggested by Alexander et al. (1993) and Shadish et al. (1993), the marital therapy research literature has been relatively focused and programmatic. Although initially developed to intervene in marital problems per se, marital therapies are increasingly being seen as a treatment system that often operates in the context of the larger system of the family. Several reviews detail the comparative and absolute efficacy of marital therapies (Alexander et al., 1993; Gurman et al., 1986).

The ubiquitous outcome measure in marital research is marital satisfaction; a strength of the marital therapy literature is its relatively strong consensus on measures of marital satisfaction (Bersheid & Peplau, 1983; Filsinger, Lewis, & McAvoy, 1981). This consensus contributes substantial empirical strength to the literature and has enabled worthwhile comparisons of intervention models, and even of components of intervention models.

For obvious clinical reasons, these "microsystemic" (Bronfenbrenner, 1977) measures of relationship satisfaction have been studied in relation to traditional measures of the adjustment of individuals within marital relationships. Although some may question such a research strategy on systemic grounds, we prefer the perspective that this research provides support for systemic models in two important ways (Alexander et al., 1993).

First, current research is showing that targeting the marital relationship with a preventive intervention focused on the dyad produces better future adjustment of the individuals in the relationship (Markman, Floyd, Stanley, & Lewis, 1986). Attention to these issues and this kind of promising data have obvious and dramatic implications for the theoretical legitimacy of marital and family approaches.

Second, traditional person-centered, disease-model categories of problem behavior are still important clinical targets. To the extent that managed health care initiatives circumscribe, if not prescribe, the course of clinical treatment, clinicians will increasingly be forced to justify the interventions they use on the basis of evidence that these interventions are effective. Again, we argue that evidence for the efficacy of marital interventions with traditional diagnostic categories does not compromise clinical, ideological, or empirical commitments to systemic therapies. We in fact relish these findings as evidence that relationship-based interventions have an empirical basis of legitimacy.

**Specific diagnostic syndromes and marital therapy.** Gurman et al. (1986) observed that there was evidence for the effectiveness of marital therapies with substance abuse (alcohol) and anxiety disorders. In a more recent review, Alexander et al. (1993) concluded that the majority of research showing the efficacy of marital therapies with traditional disorders has examined depression, agoraphobia, and alcoholism. Some of the earliest paradigmatic premises of systemic models proposed that traditional psychological problems were maintained, if not created, by relationship dysfunction (Riskin & Faunce, 1972). From another direction, contemporary clinical research developments are also converging on that hypothesis, moving progressively toward it from pyra-

miding empirical evidence (Coyne, 1990; O'Leary & Beach, 1990).

**Depression.** Both individual therapy and behavioral marital therapy provide wives with symptomatic relief from depression. Marital therapy also enhances marital satisfaction at termination and a year later (O'Leary & Beach, 1990). It appears, however, that there are couples who have a depressed member who are not dissatisfied with their marriages. Treatment of these couples with behavioral marital therapy is no more effective than other methods of treating depression (Jacobson, Dobson, Fruzzetti, Schmaling, & Salusky, 1991). Marital therapy treatment improves marital satisfaction whether or not the individual members of the couple are distressed. To the extent that it can be concluded that marital satisfaction might mediate depression, marital therapies for depression could also produce longer term maintenance of gains (Alexander et al., 1993).

Additional support for this assertion comes from studies of couples whose presenting problems were marital rather than affective. Sher, Baucom, and Laurus (1990) demonstrated that both partners increased marital satisfaction in response to marital therapy. Although there was residual affective distress in some couples, there were meaningful reductions in depression. Holtzworth-Monroe's analysis of this study noted that other diagnostic symptoms were not changed but that couples decreased negative interaction (Alexander et. al., 1993). In a similar vein, Friedman (1975) showed that both pharmacotherapy and marital therapy were superior to control conditions in treating depression. However, there were no significant differences between the two treatments in depression symptom relief (Friedman, 1975).

In sum, evidence does not support the hypothesis that achieving changes in marital interaction will lead directly to the amelioration of distress. However, there are impressive demonstrations that marital therapies, either alone or in conjunction with other treatments, improve symptoms of depression and create a marital relationship more likely to support gains and not contribute to depression.

**Alcohol abuse.** Earlier reviewers lamented the lack of empirical evidence supporting the efficacy of marital therapies in the treatment of substance abuse (Olson, Russell, & Sprenkle, 1979; Stanton, 1979). Others concluded that conjoint therapies might be the most efficacious treatment for members of alcohol-involved marriages (Gurman & Kniskern, 1978). Some methodologically sound studies offer evidence for these latter claims.

A consistent dictum of systemic therapies is that the proper focus in treating a clinical problem is not the symptom but rather the relationship in which the symptom is embedded (Haley, 1963; Watzlawick, Beavin, & Jackson, 1967). McGrady et al. (1986) cleverly created independent variables to show the comparative efficacy of a behavioral therapy and a relationship approach to therapy with alcohol-involved couples. They grouped patients with alcohol problems into treatment conditions in which they received either behavioral marital therapy, an intervention that focused both the patient and spouse on alcohol, or a treatment with minimal spouse involvement. This study demonstrated that marital therapy may keep the patient and his or her spouse engaged in treatment and also support an interpersonal climate promoting positive changes in drinking. Evidence supporting marital intervention for alcohol problems also comes from another study, showing that alcoholics who had been treated and discharged from an inpatient setting and who received conjoint marital therapy showed more abstinence than patients not receiving marital therapy (Cadogen, 1973).

O'Farrell, Cutter, and Floyd (1985) have sustained research on a cohort of patients originally assigned to behavioral marital therapy, an interactional couples treatment, or a control condition. Immediately after intervention all groups showed improvement in drinking behavior, but the behavioral marital couples were more satisfied with their marriages.

In general, most methodologically sound studies of marital therapies and alcohol abuse show a consistent pattern of findings. Although it can be tentatively concluded that marital therapy enhances alcohol treatment and is more effective than alcohol-focused treatment, the reasons remain elusive (Alexander, et al., 1993). (See also chap. 30 in this volume.)

**Anxiety-related disorders.** In reviewing family and marital therapy approaches with anxiety disorders, Gurman et al. (1986) summarized the confused conceptual underpinnings of this enterprise. First, several clinical researchers pursued the intuitive notion that agoraphobia would negatively influence a marriage or produce symptoms in a spouse, but only mixed results emerged. As a corollary assumption, behavioral clinicians attempted to support the assertion that the inclusion of spouses would enhance the treatment of agoraphobics (Barlow, O'Brien, Last, & Holden, 1983). Although including spouses did seem to produce favorable changes in targeted agoraphobia symptoms, it was not clear that these changes were related to marital intervention. To clarify these issues, researchers included spouses in both treatment and control groups. These studies have generally demonstrated that the inclusion of spouses does enhance the quality of treatment (Jacobson, Holtzworth-Munroe, & Schmaling, 1989).

## Family-Based Approaches

**Antisocial children.** As early as the mid-1960s, Gerald Patterson (cf. Patterson, 1982) and Robert Wahler (Wahler, 1988) published the first of many clinical treatment descriptions and outcome evaluations of parent-based training programs for treating antisocial children. Since that time, parent training therapy (cf. Patterson et al., 1992; also identified as parent management training in several reviews) has repeatedly been demonstrated to be an effective and efficient intervention, especially with younger problem children. Results often are enhanced when traditional parent training is paired with some combination of social skills training, cognitive skills training, and family systems therapy (Patterson et al., 1992). Note in Table 1 the numerous references to successful intervention in child behavior problems for the social-learning-based approach to parent training.

**Adolescent behavior problems.** The developmental changes that occur between childhood and adolescence require changes in therapeutic intervention strategies (Jameson & Alexander, 1994). With adolescent disorders that involve acting out (delinquency, substance abuse, conduct disorder), parent management training must give way to more systemically oriented (but still pragmatic) family-based therapies. These treatments have shown impressive and consistent effects. As reflected in several reviews summarized in Table 1, functional family therapy (FFT) has demonstrated its efficacy for over 20 years (Alexander & Parsons, 1973; Barton, Alexander, & Sanders, 1985; Klein, Alexander, & Parsons, 1976. See also the replication by Gordon, Arbuthnot, Gustafson, & McGreen, 1988, under the title "systems–behavioral" intervention). This model has demonstrated outcome efficacy, and both process and analogue studies have identified possible mechanisms and variables that contribute to the positive changes experienced by families treated by FFT (Kazdin, 1993). These include therapist structuring and relational skills (Alexander, Barton, Schiavo, & Parsons, 1976), therapist reframing of adolescents' negative behaviors (Robbins, Alexander, Newell, & Turner, 1994), therapists' warm humor and antecedent supportive behaviors (Newberry, Alexander, & Liddle, 1988; Newberry, Alexander, & Turner, 1991), family members' changes in negative attributional set (Barton, Alexander, & Turner, 1988), and a shift toward equality of talk time and interruptions (Parsons & Alexander, 1973). The phasic nature of FFT intervention has been conceptualized and articulated, and treatment manuals have been developed (Alexander, Barton, Waldron, & Mas, 1983). The model also emphasizes the clinician's interpersonal sensitivity and responsiveness to family members' value systems, culture, and phenomenological experiences (Alexander, 1992; Alexander et al., 1983; Alexander et al., 1993).

More recently developed models such as multidimensional family therapy (Liddle, 1991), family systems therapy (Joanning, Quinn, Thomas, & Mullen, 1992), and multisystemic therapy, which has a family component (Henggeler, Melton, & Smith, 1992), add to a consistent demonstration of treatment efficacy with youth who are acting out. Although FFT and these newer models are certainly far from perfect, they are consistently superior to any alternative treatments with which they have been compared.

In addition, integrations of empirical rigor, clinical effectiveness, and cultural sensitivity are appearing. With Hispanic youth, José Szapocznik et al. (1988) have demonstrated the absolute and comparative treatment efficacy of strategic structural systems family therapy for substance abuse. They also have also developed and demonstrated a culturally sensitive engagement process that doubles the rate of initial therapeutic participation of family members (Szapocznik et al., 1988). This program thus represents good clinical work, cultural sensitivity, and good science all at the same time.

**Schizophrenic behaviors.** Schizophrenia was an early focal point in the study of family systems. (See chap. 10 in this volume.) Although the original thrust of most of this theorizing was to challenge the biological bases of schizophrenia, the current evidence supports the use of biological and family system treatments together in such a way that family therapy enhances clinical outcomes for schizophrenia. Michael Goldstein and colleagues set the course for successful family intervention with schizophrenia (Goldstein, Rodnick, Evans, May, & Steinberg, 1978). They called for a return to observing family processes in order to understand the context of schizophrenia. They compared patients receiving medication with patients receiving medication plus a program that taught family members stress reduction techniques for dealing with the patient. Patients who received both high doses of medication and the family therapy were less likely to relapse in both the short and long term. Several other research teams have demonstrated that a combination of family intervention and pharmacotherapy reduces relapse rates of schizophrenic patients beyond those obtained with pharmacotherapy alone (Anderson, Reiss, & Hogarty, 1985; Falloon et al., 1982; Leff, Kuipers, Berkowitz, Eberlein-Fries, & Sturgeon, 1982).

Several of the studies are relatively robust. There is evidence that the family component of the intervention was related to changes in the relapse rates of patients and also to changes in family processes. Intervention packages that include medication and family therapy reduce relapse rates of schizophrenics more than medication alone and more than other types of psychotherapy intervention (Falloon, Boyd, & McGill, 1985; Falloon et al., 1982; Leff et al.,

1982). Noting that effective family interventions must be coupled with drug therapies, Carol Anderson's group has produced results showing that psychoeducational family therapies reduce relapse rates more than other forms of group or individual psychotherapy (Anderson, Hogarty, & Reiss, 1980, 1981).

In sum, it seems that today, as in 1986 (Gurman et. al.), effective family interventions with schizophrenia share these features: educating relatives of the patient about the disorder; providing medication for the patient; changing relatives' expectations; and supporting the patient's family.

## COMPARATIVE ANALYSIS OF MARITAL AND FAMILY THERAPY EFFECTIVENESS

Some therapies have received more consistent empirical support than others, and some have received no empirical support at all (see Table 1). Hazelrigg et al. (1987), for example, asserted that "outcome studies from an aesthetic perspective were not found" (p. 430), and Gurman et al. (1986) lamented the "dearth" of traditional research from the aesthetic perspective. In a similar vein Alexander et al. (1993) echoed Beavers' (1991) warning that we can "hurt people" when we "teach absolutes without supportive data and without outcome studies to guide us" (Beavers, 1991, p. 20). Hahlweg and Markman (1988) found sufficient representation only for behavioral marital therapies to allow for meta-analysis of therapy outcomes. Finally, in the most comprehensive analysis to date, Shadish et al. (1993) reported that of the formal schools of family therapy, the psychodynamic therapies again had insufficient representation to be evaluated meaningfully, and the humanistic therapies did not produce effect sizes greater than zero. Of other orientations, the behavioral therapies had greater effect sizes than the systemic therapies.

These findings obviously create dilemmas for family psychologists who want to be accountable, ethical, and effective (Alexander et al., 1993). The consistent conclusions that point to the superior efficacy of some family therapies present a tremendous challenge to therapies that have received less or no empirical support, especially in the current Zeitgeist of accountability and competition for health care funding. At the same time, many persuasive voices have argued that the therapies with demonstrated outcome efficacy are inadequate on grounds such as clinical sensitivity, culture and gender bias, and models of healthy family functioning (Alexander et al., 1993). Unfortunately those making most of these claims have not provided rigorous empirical support for any of the alternatives they espouse (Alexander et al., 1993; Gurman et al., 1986; McFall, 1991). As researchers and responsible clinicians, we argue that although most marital and family therapies are effective, not all variations deserve to be included under the umbrella of efficacious treatment. As a discipline we can no longer avoid taking a critical look at this issue. Certainly we have precedents in such other issues as right to treatment, entry level training, continuing education requirements, and ethical behavior.

## CURRENT TRENDS, FUTURE DIRECTIONS

We need to provide coherence and the potential for growth in an apparently fragmented field. Clearly there is a gulf between empirical evidence and clinical assertions. However, research-informed clinical caveats, as well as programmatic examples of increasing sensitivity to clinical nuance, gender issues, and cultural diversity, are available. Challenging the summary dismissals of some reviews, Shadish et al. (1993) cast a new light on the growing consensus that some therapies, particularly the behaviorally based and other pragmatic therapies, are superior to all others. Specifically, when Shadish et al. adjusted for covariates, the differences between therapy orientations with positive effect sizes disappeared. It appears that the apparent superiority of behavioral approaches might be the result of the fact that, compared with other types of therapy, this therapy orientation (a) focuses on specific problems and processes, (b) reports fewer measures, (c) uses dependent measures that are behavioral (vs. nonbehavioral) and specifically tailored to the problems and processes targeted in therapy, (d) uses more reactive measures and ratings by others rather than self-reports, (e) uses larger sample sizes, (f) has lower attrition, and (g) has more therapy sessions. In other words, the apparent superiority of behavioral approaches may accrue from the fact that behavioral and pragmatically oriented program developers often have better training in (or at least a greater appreciation for) research, and are more efficient at targeting specific processes and behaviors for change. As a result they approach clinical evaluation from a perspective of accountability and rigor.

Several new trends in marital therapy suggest that old traditions may be disappearing. One trend is to evaluate whether the addition of cognitive components to behavioral marital therapies enhances their effectiveness. In general, it appears that adding cognitive components to behavioral marital interventions does not add much to traditional outcomes such as global marital satisfaction or communication skills. However, members of couples, perhaps unsurprisingly, do change their cognitions about the marriage and/or each other (Baucom & Epstein, 1990; Behrens, Sanders, & Halford, 1990; Margolin & Weiss, 1978). There is not yet solid evidence that cognitive factors alone enhance behaviors associated with improvements in marital functioning. The potency of cognitive factors may still be obscured by or already embedded within the techniques of behavioral marital therapy.

Marital treatments based on emotion have also received recent attention with promising results (Alexander et al., 1993). In the most provocative of these studies, Greenberg and Johnson (1988) found that emotion-focused therapy and behavioral marital therapy were both superior to waiting list control conditions. The couples in the emotion-focused marital therapy showed more changes on outcome measures than did couples in the behavioral intervention condition. This provides solid evidence for the efficacy of a marital therapy program that has not had a behavioral genesis. Likewise, in an indisputably sound outcome study, Snyder, Wills, and Grady-Fletcher (1991) produced clinical outcomes for insight-oriented marital therapy comparable to the outcomes of traditional behavioral marital therapies at termination. However, at long-term follow-up (4 years) there was more evidence for deterioration and there were

significantly more divorces in the behavioral marital therapy group than in the insight-oriented marital therapy group. The provocative nature of these findings and the ensuing debate led to a host of interpretations as to what the actual critical ingredients in insight-oriented marital therapy might be (cf. Alexander et al., 1993), including: "affective changes . . . changes accompanied by strong affect" (Gurman, 1991, p. 403); "'insight' into emotional conflicts" (Snyder et al., 1991, p. 433); "'acceptance' of unresolvable conflicts" (Jacobson as cited in Alexander et al., 1993, p. 604); "'cognitive–emotional shifts' and sharing of thoughts and feelings" (Baucom & Epstein, 1991, p. 336); "increased 'emotional engagement' between spouses" (Johnson & Greenberg, 1991, p. 413); and "increased ability to manage and handle negative affect" (Markman, 1991, p. 417). An apparent impetus for the debate was the reaction of prominent behavioral marital therapists, who took the position that what was described as insight-oriented marital therapy was indeed a behavioral marital therapy that coopted the (implicit) therapeutic maneuvers of the adroit behavioral clinician (Alexander et al., 1993).

In sum, then, there is a greater parity in outcome data emerging from the marital therapy literature. As in other areas of the marital and family-therapy literature, however, there is not unequivocal process evidence as to what is actually going on in marital therapy studies, let alone what the crucial ingredients of marital interventions might be.

To the extent that emotion-focused and insight-oriented marital therapies do in fact include theoretical or conceptual variance from behavioral marital therapies, these findings should be taken as evidence that there are other efficacious treatments for marriages. We suggested earlier in this chapter that a strength of the marital literature has been that the relatively common outcome measure of marital satisfaction allows reviewers to compare and contrast marital outcome studies on a common dimension. The comparative efficacy of emotion-focused and insight-oriented marital therapies argues that clinical researchers in the marital area next need to examine the conceptual fits between the topography of marital interventions and the topography of problems experienced by couples. It may be that some problems are more emotion based than behaviorally based. This may well account for some of the emerging utility of marital interventions emphasizing cognitive or emotional experience.

Alternatively, if emotion-focused or insight-oriented marital therapies do in fact have variance that overlaps with the proven behavioral marital therapies, then these findings argue for making these dimensions of marital therapy more explicit and showing which components of therapy might be necessary or sufficient conditions for change. Component studies (e.g., Baucom & Lester, 1986; Baucom, Sayers, & Sher, 1990) can provide clues about whether different styles of intervention represent alternative means to the same clinical ends or are additive in their effects. Historically, behaviorally based clinical researchers have not had clinical evidence of nonbehavioral aspects of therapy that match their own in empirical rigor, nor have they typically claimed that aspects of treatment other than changes in overt behaviors are important. Contemporary findings may indeed blur conceptual distinctions between models and at the same time sharpen the focus on the most important elements of effective marital therapy.

The family therapy domain has experienced a similar blurring of traditional definitional boundaries. For example, the social-learning-based parent training models clearly fall into the category of pragmatic therapy. Specifically targeted dependent variables and well articulated (sometimes to the point where a formal manual has been written) therapeutic techniques and sequences are emphasized. Patterson and his colleagues (e.g., Patterson & Chamberlain, 1992) have broadened their process research focus beyond those techniques that can be described in a manual to study such clinically central phenomena as therapist behaviors that influence parent resistance. The functional family therapy model is likewise highly formalized but includes a focus on relational processes that require contingent clinical sensitivity and responsiveness on the part of the therapist (see the analysis of intervention [AIM] model of Alexander et al. 1983). This clinical ability has been studied in terms of independently evaluated therapist characteristics (Alexander et al., 1976) and direct observations of therapy process (Newberry et al., 1991). Rigorously evaluated

and pragmatically focused models also can be culturally sensitive and adapted as necessary with different populations (cf. Szapocznik et al., 1988). To meet all these objectives, clinical models demonstrating outcome efficacy must also include good process research with an appropriate focus.

Such a focus, according to Pinsof (1989), is on the "interaction between therapist and family systems" (p. 54), which includes both directly and indirectly involved subsystems. For example, indirect subsystems for the therapist may include the supervisor or other team members; for the family, the indirect subsystem includes family members not directly involved in treatment. These systems, subsystems, and individuals must be evaluated at multiple levels and with multiple appropriate measures, and the emphasis must be on the bidirectional effects of interaction. Further, Pinsof (1989) and Greenberg (1991) assert that the traditional "process–outcome" distinction is inappropriate. Instead, family therapy process researchers must examine within session and out of session effects in ways that include their mutual influence and distinguish between immediate influences ("proximal outcomes") and more distant ("distal") outcomes.

Unfortunately, the microanalytic perspective reflected in the framework described above results in a domain of studies and possible variables that is immense. It is no wonder that previous reviewers such as Alexander et al. (1993), Greenberg (1991), Gurman et al. (1986), and Pinsof (1989), as well as the authors of the numerous meta-analyses identified earlier in this review, have avoided summarizing the content of all that has been done in this domain.

At this point it is impossible to extract just a few general conclusions from the myriad process studies (including qualitative analyses and case reports). Studies in the process domain, unlike those in the outcome domain, involve too many different research contexts, designs, focuses, and measures for general conclusions to be made. However, we agree with Greenberg's assertion that we cannot fully understand the process of change or discover the richness and multivariate nature of family therapy if our research limits our perceptions (Greenberg, 1991). We introduce limitations and biases in our research (Alexander et al., 1993) if we (a) artificially focus on only a subset of variables, (b) decontextualize them (Fauber & Long, 1991; Hetherington, 1989), (c) force them into a linear cause–effect framework when the phenomena we are studying are in truth transactional in nature, and (d) code (or otherwise record) them in units that do not correspond to the "chunks" in which clinical meaning occurs (see also Robbins et al., 1994).

Although we agree with these points, we nonetheless take issue with the view that any and all focuses for process research are equally important. We offer a perspective for organizing and perhaps prioritizing the extensive domain of family therapy process research. In light of the contexts (sociopolitical, economic, ethical, professional) within which our research takes place, we assert that process research that is not linked directly to demonstrated outcome efficacy is less relevant than research that links process to clinical outcomes. Most clinical work and outcome research is driven by specific "problems" (symptoms, syndromes, complaints), and the credibility and viability of marital and family therapy depend on the ability to demonstrate amelioration of or at least positive impact on such problems. This suggests that process research that cannot be tied directly to problems—that is, those "final definitive outcomes" discussed by Greenberg and Pinsof (1986)—cannot play the same role as process research that can be tied to clearly identified improvements in problem behaviors.

This conclusion does not imply that clinical richness is less with intervention models that have failed to demonstrate outcome efficacy. We are aware that our perspective reflects a somewhat traditional view of family therapy process research that is consistent with the goals of the pragmatic therapies described above (Alexander et al., 1993; Gurman et al., 1986; Hazelrigg et al., 1987). Although we believe the aesthetic perspective (Hazelrigg et al., 1987) is extremely useful in preventing premature closure at conceptual, clinical, and methodological levels, a pragmatic focus is more appropriate in the context of the numerous forces currently calling for accountability in terms of efficient and demonstrable change on specific problems (Alexander et al., 1993).

In functional family therapy research, for example, rates and sequences of within-family defensive and supportive communication behaviors were found to distinguish between families of delinquent youth and those of nondelinquent youth (Alexander, 1973). These defensive and supportive interactive processes, which are presumed to at least mediate if not produce delinquent behaviors (Barton & Alexander, 1981), represent targets of therapeutic intervention via such techniques as reframing and communication training (Alexander & Parsons, 1982; Barton & Alexander, 1981; Robbins et al., 1994). Such behaviors, and the way they are affected by therapist interventions, have been examined within therapeutic sessions (e.g., Alexander et al., 1976; Newberry et al., 1991), and their relationship to traditional outcome variables such as subsequent delinquent behavior have been evaluated (Alexander et al., 1976). Note that research of this nature does not meet Pinsof's (1989) criterion of comprehensiveness; focusing on defensive and supportive behaviors does not tell us all that is going on in the therapy session. However, such research does extract a clinically relevant and theoretically derived marker of important family and therapist–family relational sequences. The measures can be applied across many intervention models and treatment populations, the process can be operationalized and coded at a level that has immediate clinical relevance for both trainees and experienced clinicians, and the defensive–supportive scheme can tap multiple domains of experience (behavioral, cognitive, and emotional).

Examples of similar research strategies include the previously mentioned work of Patterson et al. (1992) on resistance and the strategic structural systems engagement model of Szapocznik et al. (1988). Such phenomena are linked to family characteristics (including culture), to problem expression, to the process of intervention, and to the nature of outcomes that accrue from this intervention. This research is being buttressed by methodological and statistical advances that have allowed it to become increasingly systemic in its nature (Alexander et al., 1993). Finally, this type of research does not require that we *first* demonstrate outcome efficacy. Many therapeutic approaches need to evolve in a circular and iterative model-building and hypothesis-generating process (Greenberg, 1991).

## CONCLUSION

Very positive processes are operating in family and marital therapy research. In marital therapy the continuing improvement of behaviorally oriented approaches coupled with the emerging success of emotion-focused therapy (Greenberg & Johnson, 1988) and insight-oriented marital therapy (Snyder et al., 1991) suggests positive evolutionary trends in model development. Family therapy, though diverse in its forms and effects, has grown to the point where conflict and diversity are evolving into more of a dialectic in which tension can produce new growth (Alexander et al., 1993). Intervention models have emerged that represent rigorous programmatic, effective, and clinically sensitive interventions. These models are described with clarity sufficient for training and replication, and have been sufficiently disseminated (in workshops, books, etc.) to make them available to the larger community.

Through this specificity and rigorous process research we are learning more and more about the processes that are important to facilitate treatment efficacy. Already established intervention models are changing in response to identified shortcomings, and a "discovery" orientation (Greenberg, 1991) is adding richness to more traditional strengths in the field. In addition, our therapies are desirable because in general they are of shorter duration (currently a powerful economic and political issue) while being equally or more effective than alternative interventions. They also are efficient in that they often ameliorate specific individual symptoms (see the earlier discussion of depression) while simultaneously affecting larger systemic processes.

In sum, family therapy does not represent a homogeneous domain, but much of the work contained therein represents both clinically rich and empirically supported positive effects. The maturity and fundamental health of the field should mean that alternative voices (Alexander et al., 1993) can offer criticism and create positive internal tensions. These tensions in turn can prevent complacency in established intervention models. Concerns and proposed alternative therapeutic strategies relevant to gender and power in families; to culture, ethnicity, and class; to new clinical populations; and to alternative relationship forms generally have not been associated with programmatic demonstrations of outcome efficacy. However, they represent important constituencies and philosophies that must be included in our focus. Our ability to be open to challenge by such voices, while at the same time maintaining a center of gravity in empirically supported efficacious intervention, reflects a positive though not always smooth trajectory.

## References

Alexander, J. F. (1973). Defensive and supportive communications in normal and deviant families. *Journal of Consulting and Clinical Psychology, 40*, 223–231.

Alexander, J. F. (1992). An integrative model for treating the adolescent who is delinquent/acting-out. In W. Snyder & T. Ooms (Ed.), *Empowering families, helping adolescents: Family-centered treatment of adolescents with alcohol, drug abuse, and mental health problems* (pp. 101–110). Rockville, MD: U.S. Department of Health and Human Services.

Alexander, J. F., & Barton, C. (1980). Intervention with delinquents and their families: Clinical, methodological, and conceptual issues. In J. Vincent (Ed.), *Advances in family intervention, assessment and theory* (pp. 53–87). Greenwich, CT: JAI Press.

Alexander, J. F., Barton, C., Schiavo, R. S., & Parsons, B. V. (1976). Behavioral intervention with families of delinquents: Therapist characteristics and outcome. *Journal of Consulting and Clinical Psychology, 44*, 656–664.

Alexander, J. F., Barton, C., Waldron, H., & Mas, C. H. (1983). Beyond the technology of family therapy: The anatomy of intervention model. In K. D. Craig & R. J. McMahon (Eds.), *Advances in clinical behavior therapy* (pp. 48–73). New York: Brunner/Mazel.

Alexander, J. F., Holtzworth-Munroe, A., & Jameson, P. B. (1993). Research on the process and outcome of marriage and family therapy. In A. E. Bergin & S. L. Garfield (Eds.), *Handbook of Psychotherapy and behavior change* (4th ed., pp. 595–630). New York: Wiley.

Alexander, J. F., & Parsons, B. V. (1973). Short term behavioral intervention with delinquent families: Impact on family process and recidivism. *Journal of Abnormal Psychology, 81*, 3, 219–225.

Alexander, J. F., & Parsons, B. V. (1982). *Functional family therapy: Principles and procedures.* Carmel, CA: Brooks/Cole.

Anderson, C. M., Hogarty, G. E., & Reiss, D. J. (1980). Family treatment of adult schizophrenic patients: A psychoeducational approach. *Schizophrenia Bulletin, 6*, 490–505.

Anderson, C. M., Reiss, D. J., & Hogarty, G. E. (1985). *Schizophrenia in the family: A practitioner's guide to psychoeducation and management.* New York: Guilford Press.

Barlow, D. H., O'Brien, G. T., Last, C. G., & Holden, A. E. (1983). Couples treatment of agoraphobia: Initial outcome. In R. Spitzer & J. B. Williams (Eds.), *Psychotherapy research: Where are we, and where should we go?* (pp. 29–45). New York: Guilford Press.

Barton, C., & Alexander, J. F. (1981). Functional Family Therapy. In A. S. Gurman, & D. P. Kniskern (Eds.), *Handbook of family therapy* (pp. 403–443). New York: Brunner/Mazel.

Barton, C., Alexander, J. F., & Sanders, J. D. (1985). Research in family therapy. In L. L'Abate (Ed.), *The handbook of family psychology and therapy* (pp. 1073–1106). Homewood, IL: Dorsey Press.

Barton, C., Alexander, J. F., & Turner, C. W. (1988). Defensive communications in normal and delinquent families—the impact of context and family role. *Journal of Family Psychology, 1,* 390–405.

Baucom, D. H., & Epstein, N. (1990). *Cognitive–behavioral marital therapy.* New York: Brunner/Mazel.

Baucom, D. H., & Epstein, N. (1991). Will the real cognitive–behavioral marital therapy please stand up? *Journal of Family Psychology, 4,* 394–401.

Baucom, D. H., & Lester, G. W. (1986). The usefulness of cognitive restructuring as an adjunct to behavioral marital therapy. *Behavior Therapy, 17,* 385–403.

Baucom, D. H., Sayers, S. L., & Sher, T. G. (1990). Supplementing behavioral marital therapy with cognitive restructuring and emotional expressiveness training: An outcome investigation. *Journal of Consulting and Clinical Psychology, 58,* 636–645.

Beavers, R. (1991, Spring). A personal view of science and family therapy. *AFTA Newsletter, 43,* 19–20.

Behrens, B. C., Sanders, M. R., & Halford, W. K. (1990). Behavioral Marital Therapy: An evaluation of treatment effects across high and low risk settings. *Behavior Therapy, 21,* 423–433.

Berscheid, E., & Peplau, L. A. (1983). The emerging science of relationships. In H. H. Kelley, E. Bersheid, A. Christensen, J. H. Harvey, T. L. Huston, G. Levinger, E. McClintock, L. A. Peplau, and D. R. Peterson (Eds.), *Close relationships* (pp. 1–15). New York: Freeman.

Bronfenbrenner, U. (1977). Toward an experimental ecology of human development. *American Psychologist, 4,* 513–531.

Cadogan, D. A. (1973). Marital group therapy in the treatment of alcoholism. *Quarterly Journal of Studies on Alcohol 34,* 1187–1194.

Cedar, B., & Levant, R. F. (1990). A metaanalysis of the effects of parent effectiveness training. *American Journal of Family Therapy, 18,* 373–384.

Cohen, J. (1977). *Statistical power analysis for the behavioral sciences* (2nd ed.). New York: Academic Press.

Coyne, J. C. (1990). Concepts for understanding marriage and developing techniques of marital therapy: Cognition über alles? *Journal of Family Psychology, 4,* 185–194.

Falloon, I. R. H., Boyd, J. L., & McGill, C. W. (1985). *Family care of schizophrenia.* New York: Guilford Press.

Falloon, I. R. H., Boyd, J. L., McGill, C. W., Razani, J., Moss, H. B., & Gilderman, A. M. (1982). Family management in the prevention of exacerbations of schizophrenia. *New England Journal of Medicine, 306,* 1437–1440.

Fauber, R. L., & Long, N. (1991). Children in context: The role of the family in child psychotherapy. *Journal of Consulting and Clinical Psychology, 59,* 813–820.

Filsinger, E. E., Lewis, A. L., & McAvoy, P. (1981). Introduction: Trends and prospects for observing marriage. In E. E. Filsinger & A. L. Lewis (Eds.), *Assessing marriage: New behavioral approaches* (pp. 9–22). Beverly Hills, CA: Sage

Friedman, A. S. (1975). Interaction of drug therapy with marital therapy in depressive patients. *Archives of General Psychiatry, 32,* 619–637.

Giblin, P., Sprenkle, D. H., & Sheehan, R. (1985). Enrichment outcome research: A meta-analysis of premarital, marital, and family interventions. *Journal of Marital and Family Therapy, 11,* 257–271.

Goldstein, M. J., Rodnick, E. H., Evans, E. R., May, P. R. A., & Steinberg, M. R. (1978). Drug and family therapy in the aftercare of acute schizophrenia. *Archives of General Psychiatry, 35,* 1169–1177.

Gordon, D. A., Arbuthnot, J., Gustafson, K. E., McGreen, P. (1988). Home-based behavioral-systems family therapy with disadvantaged juvenile delinquents. *The American Journal of Family Therapy, 16,* 243–255.

Greenberg, L. S. (1991). Research on the process of change. *Psychotherapy Research, 1,* 14–24.

Greenberg, L. S., & Johnson, S. M. (1988). *Emotionally focused couples therapy.* New York: Guilford Press.

Greenberg, L., & Pinsof, W. (1986). Process research: Current trends and future perspectives. In L. Greenberg, & W. Pinsof (Eds.), *The psychotherapeutic process: A research handbook* (pp. 3–21). New York: Guilford Press.

Goldstein, M. J., Rodnick, E. H., Evans, J. R., May, P. R. A., & Steinberg, M. R. (1978). Drug and family therapy in the aftercare of acute schizophrenia. *Archives of General Psychiatry, 35,* 1169–1177.

Gurman, A. S. (1991). Back to the future, ahead to the past: Is marital therapy going in circles? *Journal of Family Psychology, 4*, 402–406.

Gurman, A. S., & Kniskern, D. P. (1978). Research on marital and family therapy: Progress, perspective, and prospect. In S. L. Garfield & A. E. Bergin (Eds.), *Handbook of psychotherapy and behavior change: An empirical analysis* (2nd ed., pp. 817–901). New York: Wiley.

Gurman, A. S., Kniskern, D. P., & Pinsof, W. M. (1986). Research on the process and outcome of marital and family therapy. In S. L. Garfield & A. E. Bergin (Eds.), *Handbook of psychotherapy and behavior change* (3rd ed., pp. 565–624). New York: Wiley.

Hahlweg, K., & Markman, H. J. (1988). Effectiveness of behavioral marital therapy: Empirical status of behavioral techniques in preventing and alleviating marital distress. *Journal of Consulting and Clinical Psychology, 56*, 440–447.

Haley, J. (1963). *Strategies of psychotherapy.* New York: Grune & Stratton.

Hazelrigg, M. D., Cooper, H. M., & Borduin, C. M. (1987). Evaluating the effectiveness of family therapies: An integrative review and analysis. *Psychological Bulletin, 101*, 428–442.

Heatherington, L. (1989). Toward more meaningful clinical research: Taking context into account in coding psychotherapy interaction. *Psychotherapy, 26*, 436–447.

Henggeler, S. W., Melton, G. B., & Smith, L. A. (1992). Family preservation using multisystemic therapy: An effective alternative to incarcerating serious juvenile offenders. *Journal of Consulting Clinical Psychology, 60*, 953–961.

Jacobson, N. S. (1991). Toward enhancing the efficacy of marital therapy and marital therapy research. *Journal of Family Psychology, 4*, 373–393.

Jacobson, N. S., Dobson, K., Fruzzetti, A. E., Schmaling, K. B., & Salusky, S. (1991). Marital therapy as a treatment for depression. *Journal of Consulting and Clinical Psychology, 59*, 547–557.

Jacobson, N. S., Follette, W. C., Revenstorf, D., Baucom, D. H., Hahlweg, K., & Margolin, G. (1984). Variability in outcome and clinical significance of behavioral marital therapy: A reanalysis of outcome data. *Journal of Consulting and Clinical Psychology, 52*, 497–504.

Jacobson, N. S., Holtzworth-Munroe, A., & Schmaling, K. B. (1989). Marital therapy and spouse involvement in the treatment of depression, agoraphobia, and alcoholism. *Journal of Consulting and Clinical Psychology, 57*, 5–10.

Jameson, P. B., & Alexander, J. F. (1994). Implications of a developmental family systems model for clinical practice. In L. L'Abate (Ed.), *Handbook of developmental family psychology psychopathology* (pp. 392–411). New York: Wiley.

Joanning, H., Quinn, W., Thomas, F., & Mullen, R. (1992). Treating adolescent drug abuse: A comparison of family systems therapy, group therapy, and family drug education. *Journal of Marital and Family Therapy, 18*, 345–356.

Johnson, S. M., & Greenberg, L. S. (1991). There are more things in heaven and earth than dreamed of in BMT: A response to Jacobson. *Journal of Family Psychology, 4*, 407–415.

Kazdin, A. E., (1993). Psychotherapy for children and adolescents: Current progress and future research directions. *American Psychologist, 48*, 644–657.

Klein, N. C., Alexander, J. F., & Parsons, B. V. (1976). Impact of family systems intervention on recidivism and sibling delinquency: A model of primary prevention and program evaluation. *Journal of Consulting and Clinical Psychology, 45*, 469–474.

Leff, J., Kuipers, L., Berkowitz, R., Eberlein-Fries, R., & Sturgeon, D. (1982). A controlled trial of social intervention in the families of schizophrenic patients. *British Journal of Psychiatry, 141*, 121–134.

Liddle, H. A. (1991). A multidimensional model for treating the adolescent drug abuser. In W. Snyder & T. Ooms (Eds.), *Empowerment families: Family centered treatment of adolescents with mental health and substance abuse problems* (pp. 91–100). Rockville, MD: U.S. Department of Health and Human Services.

Margolin, G., & Weiss, R. L. (1978). Comparative evaluation of therapeutic components associated with behavioral marital treatments. *Journal of Consulting and Clinical Psychology, 47*, 743–749.

Markman, H. J. (1991). Constructive marital conflict is not an oxymoron. *Behavioral Assessment, 13*, 83–96.

Markman, H. J., Floyd, F. J., Stanley, S. M., & Lewis, H. C. (1986). Prevention. In N. S. Jacobson & A. S. Gurman (Eds.), *Clinical handbook of marital therapy* (pp. 173–195). New York: Guilford Press.

Masten, A. (1979). Family therapy as a treatment for children: A critical review of outcome research. *Family Process, 18*, 323–335.

McFall, R. M. (1991). Manifesto for a science of clinical psychology. *The Clinical Psychologist, 44*, 75–88.

McGrady, B. S., Noel, N. E., Abrams, D. B., Stout, R. L., Nelson, H. F., & Hay, W. M. (1986). Comparative effectiveness of three types of spouse involvement in outpatient behavioral alcoholism treatment. *Journal of Studies on Alcohol, 47*, 459–467.

Minuchin, S., Baker, L., Rosman, B., Liebman, R., Milman, L., & Todd, T. (1975). A conceptual model of psychosomatic illness in children: Family organization and family therapy. *Archives of General Psychiatry, 32*, 1031–1038.

Newberry, A. M., Alexander, J. F., & Liddle, N. (1988, August). The effects of therapist gender on family therapy process. In James F. Alexander (Chair), *Female and male clients and counselors: Do their differences matter?* Symposium conducted at the meeting of the American Psychological Association, Atlanta, GA.

Newberry, A. M., Alexander, J. F., & Turner, C. W. (1991). Gender as a process variable in family therapy. *Journal of Family Psychology, 5,* 158–175.

O'Farrell, T. J., Cutter, H. S. G., & Floyd, F. J. (1985). Evaluating behavioral marital therapy of male alcoholics: Effects on marital adjustment and communication from before to after treatment. *Behavior Therapy, 16,* 147–167.

O'Leary, K. D., & Beach, R. H. (1990). Marital therapy: A viable treatment for depression and marital discord. *American Journal of Psychiatry, 147,* 183–186.

Olson, D., Russell, C., & Sprenkle, D. (1979). Circumplex model of marital and family systems: I. Cohesion and adaptability dimensions, family types, and clinical applications. *Family Process, 18,* 3–28.

Patterson, G. R. (1982). *Coercive family process.* Eugene, OR: Castalia.

Patterson, G. R., & Chamberlain, P. (1992). A functional analysis of resistance (A neobehavioral perspective). In H. Arkowitz (Ed.), *Why don't people change? New perspectives on resistance and noncompliance* (pp. 53–70). New York: Guilford Press.

Pinsof, W. M. (1989). A conceptual framework and methodological criteria for family therapy process research. *Journal of Consulting and Clinical Psychology, 57,* 53–59.

Riskin, J., & Faunce, E. E. (1972). An evaluative view of family interaction research. *Family Process, 11,* 365–455.

Robbins, M. S., Alexander, J. F., Newell, R. M., & Turner, C. W. (1994, February). The immediate effects of positive reframing on client attitude in the initial session of functional family therapy. In (Chair), *Process research on family-based interventions with adolescents.* Panel session presented at the North American Society for Psychotherapy Research Second Regional Chapter Conference, Santa Fe, NM.

Shadish, W. R., Montgomery, L. M., Wilson, P., Wilson, M. R., Bright, I., & Okwumabua, T. (1993). *The effects of family and marital psychotherapies: A meta-analysis.* Manuscript submitted for publication.

Sher, T. G., Baucom, D. H., & Larus, J. M. (1990). Communication patterns and response to treatment among depressed and nondepressed maritally distressed couples. *Journal of Family Psychology, 4,* 63–79.

Snyder, D. K., Wills, R. M., & Grady-Fletcher, A. (1991). Long-term effectiveness of behavioral versus insight-oriented marital therapy. *Journal of Consulting and Clinical Psychology, 59,* 138–141.

Stanton, M. D. (1979). Family treatment approaches to drug abuse problems: A review. *Family Process, 18,* 251–280.

Szapocznik, J., Perez-Vidal, A., Brickman, A. L., Foote, F. H., Santisteban, D., Hervis, O., & Kurtines, W. M. (1988). Engaging adolescent drug abusers and their families in treatment: A strategic structural systems approach. *Journal of Consulting and Clinical Psychology, 56,* 552–557.

Wahler, R. G. (1988). Skill deficits and uncertainty: An interbehavioral view on the parenting problems of multistressed mothers. In R. Dev. Peters & R. J. McMahon (Eds.), *Social learning and systems approaches to marriage and the family* (pp. 45–71). New York: Brunner/Mazel.

Watzlawick, P., Beavin, J., & Jackson, D. D. (1967). *Pragmatics of human communication.* New York: Norton.

Wells, R., & Dezen, A. (1978). The results of family therapy revisited: The nonbehavioral methods. *Family Process, 17,* 251–273.

Whisman, M. A., Jacobson, N. S., Fruzetti, A. E., & Waltz, J. A. (1989). Methodological issues in marital therapy. *Advances in Behavioral Research and Therapy, 11,* 175–189.

# CHAPTER 12

# CIRCUMPLEX MODEL OF FAMILY SYSTEMS: INTEGRATING ETHNIC DIVERSITY AND OTHER SOCIAL SYSTEMS

*Dean M. Gorall and David H. Olson*

Any theoretical model is a product of its time and social context and is biased by the values and ideas that are prevalent at a given time in a given culture. The Circumplex Model of Marital and Family Systems is part of the Zeitgeist, in that the model is a product of the theoretical thinking and cultural biases of the 1970s and 1980s. It was based on the theoretical ideas of the time and thus reflects the lack of attention to cultural issues and nontraditional types of families that was then prevalent.

This chapter specifically addresses these significant issues by focusing on three major issues in the field of family theorizing and assessment. First, the chapter discusses how the circumplex model deals with issues of cultural diversity, since the model was developed primarily with Caucasian families. Second, the model has been developed and used primarily with intact two-parent families and traditional couples. The chapter addresses how the model applies to various family structures, including single-parent families, stepfamilies, and same-sex couples. Third, this chapter illustrates how the model is increasingly being applied to other social systems such as work, schools, therapy settings, and family businesses.

First, increasing attention is being given to various racially and ethnically diverse families in our society. This is important because family research and clinical work is conducted in these diverse populations. Recent family research and theory reviewed here indicates that, with proper interpretation and cultural considerations, the circumplex model can be used with Mexican American, African American, and Asian American families as well as with Caucasian families (Olson, Russell, & Sprenkle, 1989).

Second, the various family forms to which the circumplex model has been applied are presented. Three of the more traditional family forms to which the model has been applied are premarital, marital, and nuclear intact families. These groups represent the largest number of research studies in which the circumplex model has been used in past years. Three additional family forms are highlighted here that have received greater attention in both the general family literature and literature concerned specifically with the circumplex model in recent years. Studies involving blended families, single parent families, and same-sex couples illustrate the increasingly diverse family forms being described through use of the circumplex model.

Finally, it will be shown that the circumplex model can be used in assessing and understanding larger social systems with which individuals or families may be involved. The larger systems include work, school, therapy, and family business systems. Families seen by clinicians in therapy settings both affect and are affected by these larger systems. If clinicians are to work successfully with families, they must have at their disposal some systemic way of understanding these interactions between systems.

## UPDATE ON THE CIRCUMPLEX MODEL

### Brief Overview of the Model

The Circumplex Model of Marital and Family Systems was originally developed in an attempt to bridge a gap that was found to exist between research, theory, and practice in the family field. The model evolved out of an extensive review of earlier theoretical models of family systems (Olson, 1993). Three basic concepts were found to be common to most other models of family systems. These three concepts were cohesion, flexibility/adaptability, and communication.

*Cohesion* is defined as the degree of emotional bonding or closeness within a family (Olson, Russell, & Sprenkle, 1989). There are four levels to the cohesion dimension of the circumplex model. They are, in order from low to high: *disengaged, separated, connected,* and *enmeshed.*

*Flexibility* is the second dimension of the circumplex model. The revised flexibility dimension is defined as the amount or degree of change in family leadership, role relationships, and relationship rules (Olson, 1993). This dimension was previously termed *adaptability;* the change in terminology has been made to reflect a change in the definition of the dimension. The adaptability dimension was previously defined as the *ability* of a marital or family system to alter its power structure, role relationships, and rules in response to changing demands and expectations within the family or from the environment. The four levels of flexibility are, in order from low to high: *rigid, structured, flexible,* and *chaotic.*

*Communication* is viewed as the facilitating dimension of the circumplex model. *Communication* is defined as the family skill level in listening and speaking with one another (Olson, 1993). Positive communication skills allow families to move from one family type or level of cohesion and/or flexibility to another on the circumplex model. Negative communication skills make movement from one system type to another or to a new level of cohesion and/or flexibility difficult for family systems. The communication dimension has not received as much attention as the cohesion and flexibility dimensions in past research and clinical use of the model. It is our view, however, that because communication is a key to family system change, it is an integral part of the model and needs to be used conjointly with the cohesion and flexibility dimensions for the model's utility to be fully realized.

There are 16 possible family system types in the circumplex model (see Figure 1), and these 16 system types are divided into 3 general system types. If a family is in the moderate range of both the cohesion and flexibility dimensions, the family is said to have a *balanced* system. Four of the 16 possible family types fall into the *balanced* category of the circumplex model. If a family is in the highest or lowest level of either the cohesion or the flexibility dimension and in the moderate range on the other dimension, the family is said to have a *midrange* system. If a family falls into either the highest or lowest level of both the cohesion and flexibility dimensions, then the family system is said to be *unbalanced.*

In the past the term used to refer to the area of the circumplex model referred to here as *unbalanced* was the term *extreme.* Thus families that fell into either the very high or very low ends of both the cohesion and flexibility dimensions were said to have *extreme* family system types. The change in terminology from *extreme* to *unbalanced* has taken place because in the past *extreme* families were thought by some to have negative traits inherent within them due to the negative connotation of the term *extreme.* It is hoped that the term *unbalanced* will be less prejudicial and will leave open the possibility for viewing *unbalanced* families as capable of functioning positively and as capable of change.

There are six main testable hypotheses proposed with the Circumplex Model of Marital and Family Systems (Olson, 1993). They are stated briefly here to illustrate the intended understanding of family systems that the circumplex model entails.

1. Couples or families with *balanced* system types will generally function more adequately across the family life cycle than *unbalanced* couples or families.

2. If the normative expectations of a couple or family system support behaviors at the extreme on one or both of the cohesion and flexibility dimensions, the family will function well as long as all couple or family members accept these expectations.

3. *Balanced* couple or family systems have larger behavioral repertoires than *unbalanced* couple or

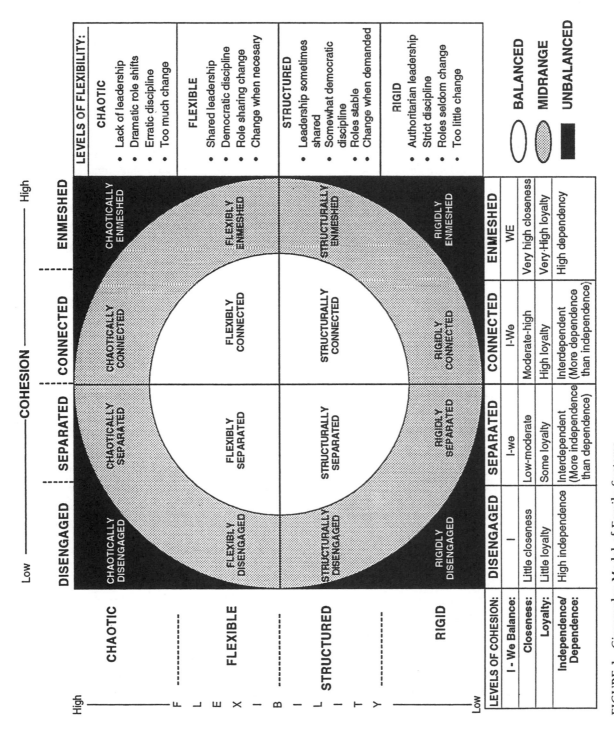

FIGURE 1. Circumplex Model of Family Systems.

family systems and are more able to change than *unbalanced* couple or family systems.

4. *Balanced* couple or family systems will tend to have more positive communication skills than *unbalanced* couple or family systems.

5. Positive communication skills will make it easier for *balanced* couple or family systems to change their cohesion or flexibility levels compared with *unbalanced* systems.

6. In order to deal with situational stress and developmental changes across the family life cycle, *balanced* family systems will change their cohesion and flexibility levels, whereas *unbalanced* systems will tend to resist change over time.

## Recent Critiques and Revisions

There is inherent within the circumplex model and its hypotheses an assumption that the cohesion and flexibility dimensions are curvilinear with respect to family functioning. That is, moderate levels of both cohesion and flexibility are most conducive to adequate family functioning, and very high or very low levels of either cohesion or flexibility are correlated with problematic family functioning. There has been mixed support for this curvilinearity hypothesis in the literature (Beavers, Hampson, & Hulgus, 1985; Fristad, 1989; Green, Kolevzon, & Vosler, 1985a, 1985b; Miller, Epstein, Bishop, & Keitner, 1985; Thomas & Cierpka, 1989), but new research seems to aid in understanding these often contradictory findings.

Most studies using the Family Adaptation and Cohesion Evaluation Scales (FACES; Olson, Portner, & Lavee, 1985) II and III have found a linear relationship between the cohesion and flexibility dimensions of the circumplex model with regard to family functioning. A number of studies compared FACES III (self-report data) with other self-report measures that claim to measure family functioning in a linear way. In these studies (Beavers et al., 1985; Fristad, 1989; Green et al.,1985a, 1985b; Miller et al., 1985; Thomas & Cierpka, 1989) the authors concluded that because FACES II and III correlated linearly with the linear measures they used, the curvilinear hypothesis of the circumplex model was not supported.

Two studies have recently been completed that provide some aid in understanding the sometimes contradictory findings concerning the curvilinear nature of the cohesion and flexibility dimensions of the circumplex model with respect to family functioning. Using the Clinical Rating Scale (CRS; Olson, 1988), the observational measure designed to assess circumplex model dimensions, Thomas and Olson (1993) found the curvilinear hypothesis to be strongly supported by the measure's ability to discriminate between problem and nonproblem families. Families were video taped while they interacted together to solve puzzles and make some decisions. Specifically, control families and families that had a child with Down's syndrome were used as nonproblem families, and families in family therapy or with an emotionally disturbed or behaviorally disordered adolescent were used as problem families. Nonproblem families were found to be significantly more represented in the *balanced* range and to be higher in satisfaction than problem families. Problem families were found to be represented in the *unbalanced* range of the circumplex model significantly more than nonproblem families. Thus the use of the CRS to code family interaction yielded strong support for the curvilinear hypothesis of the circumplex model.

Thomas and Olson (1992) hypothesized that the difficulty may not lie in the curvilinear hypothesis of the circumplex model, but in the self-report method (FACES) used to measure the dimensions of the model. Thomas and Olson (1992) used both the traditional self-report scale of FACES III (Olson et al., 1985) and the CRS to test the curvilinearity hypothesis. They found that the curvilinear hypothesis of the circumplex model with respect to family functioning was supported by observational CRS data, but not by FACES III self-report data, which found a linear relationship.

These findings have led to a revised scoring of FACES that assumes a linear relationship, and this has allowed a re-interpretation of the findings that supports the curvilinear hypothesis. Also, the observational assessment of families using the Clinical Rating Scale has found clear support for the curvilinear hypothesis. FACES IV is now being developed for the purpose of developing a self-report measure that will tap into curvilinearity the way the observational methodology does. For a more complete overview of the circumplex model, including revisions and responses to critiques, readers are directed to a recent chapter by Olson (1993).

## Three-Dimensional Circumplex Model

The three-dimensional (3-D) circumplex model has been developed to accomplish three goals. First, it illustrates the difference between first and second order change. *First order* change is the kind of change that can occur within a system that itself stays relatively unchanged. *Second order* change is change in the system itself. These concepts can be more fully understood as they are applied in the 3-D circumplex model (see Figure 2). In the new 3-D circumplex model, first order change is represented in the flexibility dimension. That is, as a system moves higher on the flexibility dimension, the level of change that occurs within the family type increases. Therefore a rigid family has very little change in its relationship rules, roles, and so on, whereas a chaotic family has a great deal of change occurring in these variables. However, these are not considered first order changes. Second order change, or change in the system type itself, is more characteristic of *balanced* families' reactions in meeting developmental and environmental demands. Conversely, *unbalanced* families are less able to change their system type when necessary and are therefore low on second order change.

Second, the 3-D model makes more clear the distinction between *balanced*, *midrange*, and *unbalanced* family system types. System types at each level are grouped more clearly together so as to graphically represent both the similarities they possess and the distinctions that separate them from the other levels. The two-dimensional model (see Figure 1) is retained to more clearly display the interplay of the cohesion and flexibility dimensions and to make clear the belief that families are capable of change from one system type to another and from one circumplex model level to another.

Third, this revised model provides a way of scoring FACES II and III that more accurately reflects the linear relationship of FACES scores and family functioning. *Balanced* family types have the highest scores and *unbalanced* family types have the lowest scores.

## Clinical Application With Couples and Families

The utility of the circumplex model for clinical application lies in the ability to use the model and its self-report and behavioral measures in all stages of clinical work. The model can be used in assessment, in treatment planning, in ongoing assessment of clinical progress, and as an end measure of clinical outcome. Two studies, though dealing with very different family difficulties, are used here to show the clinical utility of the circumplex model.

Walsh and Olson (1989) offer a model for utilizing the circumplex model with severely dysfunctional family systems. The authors provide a case study of two boys who are involved in severe vandalism. They use this case as an example of the model's utility as treatment moves from stage to stage. The family was assessed with the FACES III self-report instrument and the CRS observational instrument. It was determined through these measures that the family was very high on both the cohesion and flexibility dimensions of the circumplex model, with the family falling into the chaotically enmeshed family type (see Figure 1). Taking the boys' behavior into account, it was determined by the therapist that the family would function better if they moved toward a flexibly connected family system type, lowering their levels of both cohesion and flexibility. This would move the family from an *unbalanced* to a *balanced* family system type. To achieve this change from chaotically enmeshed to flexibly connected, the therapist created space between family members. In an effort to reduce cohesion, the family developed their own sleeping areas, which also added structure to this otherwise chaotic aspect of their lives. In this example the circumplex model offered an assessment of the family at the outset of treatment, a direction for treatment, and an outcome measure during and after treatment.

Trepper and Sprenkle (1989), in an article on intrafamily sexual abuse, offer a similar use of the model. FACES III and the CRS were once again used to assess where families fell on the circumplex model

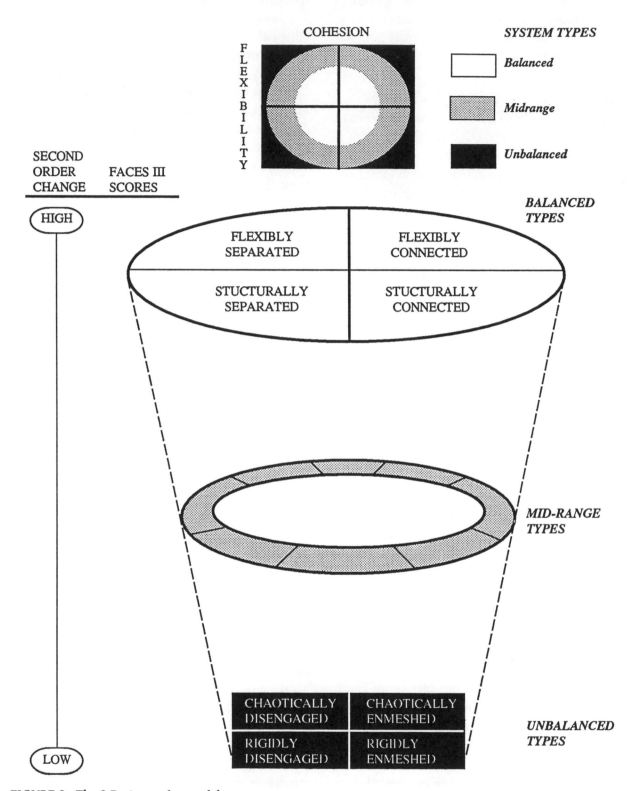

FIGURE 2. The 3-D circumplex model.

at the outset of treatment. The authors offer a variety of scenarios for how a family exhibiting intrafamily sexual abuse may fall into any of the four *unbalanced* quadrants of the circumplex model, with each quadrant having its own particular family dynamics that may be contributing to the abuse.

It is important to note that an overall diagnostic assessment was made combining FACES III, CRS scores, and other relevant information. Trepper and Sprenkle also point out that discrepancies between individual scores on the FACES III inventory can be used to aid in assessing coalitions or alliances that may exist in the family. After determining where on the circumplex model a family falls, efforts are made to move the family slowly toward a more *balanced* family system type. The circumplex model is utilized throughout the treatment process for initial assessment, to monitor progress during treatment, and as a follow-up assessment to make sure system changes are enduring.

Although in both clinical examples cited here the stated goal is to move a family toward a more *balanced* system type, this is not necessarily always the goal of therapy. There may be developmental or situational environmental demands on a family which indicate that a *midrange* or *unbalanced* system type may be the most functional for a given family for a given time frame.

Families may also be under stress or exist within a larger system in which a *midrange* or *unbalanced* family system type may enable families to function more effectively. In other words, in some stressful situations (e.g., a member has a heart attack) a family may move to an unbalanced area (e.g., rigidly enmeshed) to deal with this major stressor. After the crisis has passed, they often move back to a family type similar to (but usually not the same as) what was typical for them before the crisis. Families that live in environments that are continuously stressful may exist as an *unbalanced* family system for long periods of time, with this system type being functional within their larger context.

## ETHNIC DIVERSITY AND THE CIRCUMPLEX MODEL

The racial and ethnic heritage of families has too often been overlooked in the development of theoretical models and related assessment tools. We must consider the consequences of either ignoring ethnic or racial differences or stereotyping ethnic or racial groups. Hare-Mustin and Marecek's (1988) article on the theoretical biases related to gender issues is equally valuable in the consideration of race and ethnicity. They defined ignoring differences as *alpha bias*, and stereotyping as *beta bias*. They concluded that there is no way to eliminate both of these biases but that awareness of the issues can help minimize the problems. Awareness of the issues of stereotyping or ignoring differences is particularly relevant when discussing theoretical models and assessment tools. Thus the comments made here are intended to give direction for possible applications and possible problems in using the circumplex model with the various groups discussed below.

In her theoretical work based on research literature on cultural diversity, Woehrer (1989) also included an intergenerational focus. Woehrer reviewed studies of African American, Chinese American, Italian American, Mexican American, Polish American, and Scandinavian American families. On the basis of her analysis Woehrer makes three main recommendations regarding the use of the circumplex model with these culturally diverse families. First, it is important to determine what is culturally normative for these groups, rather than simply comparing them to white middle class Americans. Second, it is recommended that acculturation be taken into account so that no stereotypes are applied to any ethnic groups. Third, it is recommended that we take into account both nuclear and extended family systems when assessing levels of cohesion and flexibility.

## African American Families

The circumplex model has been used in several studies with African American families; three studies are highlighted here. FACES III was used by Calleja (1989) in a study of 56 single parent, low socioeconomic status, African American families with adolescent sons in an effort to examine the relationship between stress, family functioning, and behavior problems. The author found *balanced* families to have significantly fewer behavioral problems reported than either *midrange* or *unbalanced* family types. Low cohesion was significantly associated with conduct disorders, socialized aggression, and anxiety withdrawal. These findings have implications for clinical families where the goal is to move families toward a more *balanced* family system type.

In research aimed at studying the dynamics of interracial families involving one African American and one Caucasian parent with at least one child, Spivey (1984) used FACES II and the circumplex model with 20 families. The purpose of the study was to examine the relationship between the circumplex model and the adolescent social adjustment of the children within these families. No relationship between family system type and adolescent social adjustment was found. However, Spivey noted that these results must be viewed cautiously, because of the small sample size and exploratory nature of the study.

Fonza (1986) used FACES II and the circumplex model to test the efficacy of both the instrument and the model with middle-class African American families. African American students from fraternities and sororities constituted the sample for the study. The author concluded that the scores achieved by these individuals were not significantly different from the norms established for FACES II, indicating relevance of these norms to African American middle-class families.

## Asian American Families

The circumplex model has been utilized in a relatively small number of studies with Asian American families. The studies that have been done with Asian Americans have focused on Chinese American and Japanese American families, which of course do not represent the vast variety of Asian American families. These studies have supported the use of FACES and the circumplex model with these groups.

So (1990) used FACES III and the circumplex model to study 69 Chinese immigrant families who had been in the United States from 3 to 30 years. There were 34 clinical and 35 nonclinical families within this sample. The author reported a significant difference between *balanced* and *unbalanced* families with respect to family functioning, with *balanced* families reporting significantly higher family functioning. Cohesion was also found to be positively correlated with family functioning. So reported an additional interesting finding: that the real–ideal difference on cohesion and family functioning correlated in a negative manner. That is, the farther away a family was from where they wanted to be on the circumplex dimensions of cohesion and flexibility, the lower their family functioning. The author pointed out that this once again highlights the importance of paying attention to the specific cultural norms when working with families. So concluded that the use of FACES III with Chinese immigrant families is supported by this research.

Hsu et al. (1988; cited in Tseng & Hsu, 1991) used FACES to study Caucasian American, Japanese American, Chinese American, and Hawaiian families. The authors found no differences between these groups on the cohesion and flexibility dimensions in a nonclinical sample. These findings support those of So regarding their support for the use of the FACES instruments with Chinese American, and additionally Japanese American, families.

## Mexican American Families

In a study of 600 Mexican American families, Flores and Sprenkle (1989) used FACES III to examine whether the norms developed for the instrument and model were appropriate for this ethnic group. The Acculturation Rating Scale for Mexican Americans (Cuellar, Harris, & Jasso, 1980) was also used in an attempt to account for acculturation as a variable that may influence the scores on FACES III. There were statistically significantly more *unbalanced* and fewer *balanced* families in this Mexican American sample than would have been predicted by the normative sample. Flores and Sprenkle, however, state that the similarities between the normative sample and the Mexican American sample are still strong enough to allow use of the Caucasian norms because the two groups appear to be "more similar than different" (p. 246; see Figure 3). This similarity was found to hold most strongly if the Mexican American families were not poor and had become acculturated. For poorer, less educated, and less acculturated Mexican American families, new norms need to be developed.

In a study of 294 parents of school-age children, Vega et al. (1986) used FACES II and the circumplex model to determine whether the Caucasian norms

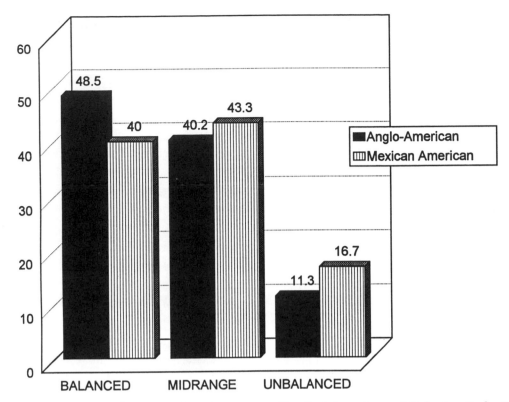

FIGURE 3. Anglo American and Mexican American parents: Family Adaptation and Cohesion Evaluation Scales (FACES) III scores.

were appropriate for Mexican American families. An acculturation measure was also used. The author found that although there were some differences in the distributions of scores among the *balanced*, *mid-range*, and *unbalanced* regions between the Mexican American and the normative Caucasian sample, the differences were small enough to suggest the use of the FACES II measure and the circumplex model with Mexican American Families. Vega et al. found that low-acculturation respondents were more likely to score outside the *balanced* region of the circumplex model, thus supporting the findings of Flores and Sprenkle (1989).

## ASSESSMENT OF DIVERSE FAMILY STRUCTURES

As professionals have become more cognizant of the diverse family structures that exist in our society, it is clear that our research and clinical practices may need to be altered. What in the past was termed the traditional or nuclear family now represents fewer of the families in society. The application of the Cir-

cumplex Model of Marital and Family Systems to these more diverse family forms is discussed in the following sections.

## Couple/Marital Systems

The circumplex model has been utilized extensively with marital systems. As a part of the Enriching Relationship Issues, Communication and Happiness (ENRICH) marital assessment tool, which has been used with over 150,000 couples, the type of marriage is assessed based on a revised version of FACES called MACES (Olson, Fournier, & Druckman, 1992). Another example of this type of application is dissertation work completed by Captain (1988). In this research the circumplex model was used with marital couples in which one member had been diagnosed as an alcoholic. FACES III was used pre- and posttreatment. Most changes for these couples occurred within the flexibility dimension. Couples tended to be low on both flexibility and cohesion before treatment, with their flexibility scores increasing at the posttreatment measurement.

## Family Relationships

The most frequent use of the circumplex model in the past has been with nuclear families where there are two parents, mother and father, and at least one child present. An example of how the model can be used to measure a nuclear family system with clinical implications is research conducted by Volk, Edwards, Lewis, and Sprenkle (1989). In this research the author used FACES III and the circumplex model to study the nuclear family units of drug-abusing teenagers and a control group. The results of the study supported circumplex hypotheses in that the families of drug-abusing teenagers were found to be more disengaged and more *unbalanced* than the control group families. The findings of this study differ from those of previous drug-abuse literature, which would have predicted that the families of drug-abusing teenagers would have been rigidly enmeshed.

## Family of Origin for Premarital Couples

The circumplex model has also been used to examine the families of origin of premarital couples taking the Premarital Personal and Relationship Evaluation (PREPARE) premarital inventory developed by Olson, Fournier, and Druckman (1979, 1992). The inventory covers 11 subject areas found to be of importance in marital relationships. Included within the inventory are shortened versions of the FACES III cohesion and flexibility scales that the premarital couple answer in reference to their families of origin.

Gorall and Fournier (1992) studied over 7,000 couples who completed the PREPARE inventory. They found that couples where both members reported coming from *balanced* families of origin scored significantly higher on 8 of the 11 PREPARE subscales than couples where both members reported coming from *unbalanced* families of origin. The 6 subscales on which there were significant differences between these two groups included communication, conflict resolution, personality, children and parenting, family and friends, and sexual relationship.

The use of the circumplex model within the PREPARE inventory helps premarital couples understand and discuss their families of origin with each other and helps them think about the type of system they would like for their family.

## Extended Family Relationships

Woehrer (1989) hypothesizes that the extended families of various ethnic groups may function differently along the circumplex dimensions than nuclear families. Therefore, assessment of families from various ethnic groups should include both nuclear and extended families. She hypothesizes that rigidly enmeshed extended families may function well when high expectations for togetherness are present. This hypothesis is similar to Hypothesis 2, that if the normative expectations of a couple/family system support behaviors at the extreme on one or both of the cohesion and flexibility dimensions, the family will function well as long as all couple/family members accept these expectations.

However, Woehrer points out that rigidly enmeshed extended family systems may be particularly acceptable to some families due to the unique support functions extended families may serve. Woehrer also advises that extended families of various ethnic groups will likely function differently from traditional normative groups on inventories such as FACES III on the basis of their level of acculturation. This issue is a theme that runs through much of the research and clinical work cited here.

## Blended Family Relationships

Over 20% of families in the United States are blended families, and this group will continue to rise because of the high divorce rate. Thomas and Olson (1993) used the CRS for the circumplex model to compare clinical and nonclinical families from intact, blended, and single parent families. With regard to blended families, Thomas and Olson found that the CRS was able to differentiate between clinical and nonclinical families in both the intact and blended family groups and that the curvilinear hypothesis of the circumplex model was supported in both these groups.

Chollack (1990) compared blended and nuclear families to see if the norms developed for flexibility and cohesion with nuclear families are appropriate for blended families. No differences were found between these groups for flexibility, but parents in the blended families had significantly lower cohesion scores than parents from nuclear families. It is interesting to note that parents from both the nuclear and blended families had a connected level of cohesion as their ideal, thus indicating that parents in blended families desired more cohesion than was actually present in their families. Chollack (1990) advises others using FACES III with blended families to be aware of this possible normative difference in the levels of cohesion for blended and nuclear families.

Kennedy (1985) conducted a study to assess how college students coming from three family forms (intact, single parent, and blended) rated the amount of stress, cohesion, and flexibility in their families of origin. A total of 631 undergraduates were given FACES II. Intact families were significantly higher on cohesion than blended families, but no significant differences were found between the two groups on flexibility. These findings support those of Chollack (1990) cited above. The findings by Kennedy are to be viewed with caution because of the differences in cohesion between blended and intact families being quite small, even though they were significant.

In summary, it would appear, on the basis of the preliminary findings cited here, that it is appropriate to use the FACES III and CRS instruments and the circumplex model with blended families, as long as there is an awareness that blended families may tend to score lower on the cohesion dimension than intact families.

## Single Parent Families

Thomas and Olson (1993) used the CRS to examine clinical and nonclinical "first marriage for mother" and single mother families. They found significant differences between clinical and nonclinical families on the CRS in both the intact and single mother families. Thomas and Olson offer a caution concerning the use of the CRS with single parent families with regard to the wording of the rating items on the CRS. Several of the CRS rating items are focused on marital/adult relationships, which makes the coding of these items for a single parent family inappropriate. The authors offer a way around this difficulty in that the global ratings for cohesion, flexibility, and communication are not sums of the items within these subscales but are separate global ratings arrived at by the raters. This global rating allows the rating

of single parent families on all the circumplex model dimensions.

As was reported previously, Kennedy (1985) compared single parent families with intact and blended families. The results of comparisons between single parent and intact families were quite similar to those between blended and intact families. Intact families were found to have significantly higher cohesion than single parent families, but no significant differences were found between the two groups on flexibility. The same caution regarding small yet significant differences stated for blended and first-marriage families holds true for the single parent families in the Kennedy (1985) study. Researchers and clinicians using the circumplex model with single parent families will need to take into account the possibility that this group of families may have lower cohesion on FACES III than first-marriage families.

## Lesbian Relationships

Although a search of the literature yielded no studies utilizing the circumplex model with gay male relationships, some studies involving the use of the circumplex model with lesbian relationships have been completed. Zacks, Green, and Marrow (1988) used FACES III and the circumplex model to study 52 lesbian couples and found significantly higher levels of cohesion, flexibility, and satisfaction than in normative heterosexual couples. The authors propose several possible explanations for these findings, including the possibility that high levels of cohesion and flexibility may help lesbian couples function more effectively in a predominantly heterosexual world. Also, women's socialization may predispose female couples to form more cohesive and flexible relationships. Zacks et al. (1988) suggest that attention be paid to cultural relativity of norms for all minority groups. In the case of lesbian couples, higher cohesion may place the couple in the *midrange* or *unbalanced* area of the circumplex model, which may be normative for these couples.

In an effort to understand the cultural context of lesbian couples and how it relates to couple dynamics, Meyer (1988) used FACES III to assess couple cohesion and flexibility. Meyer was attempting to delineate the relationship between couple closeness and social support in lesbian couples. Sixty lesbian couples participated, and Meyer found a significant negative relationship between social support from friends and couple closeness, but a significant positive relationship between perceptions of support from family and couple closeness. Possible explanations for these findings are that support from friends precludes the need for as much closeness from one's partner, whereas support from family may allow this closeness to be more complete.

In summary, the studies with diverse structures indicate that the circumplex model can be and has been used with a wide variety of family structures. Findings from the studies with extended family relationships, blended family relationships, single parent families, and lesbian couples indicate, however, that these families may have norms slightly different from traditional intact families.

## ECOSYSTEMIC APPLICATIONS OF THE CIRCUMPLEX MODEL

A systems-oriented approach can be used in settings other than family therapy, with populations other than therapy clients, and with systems other than family systems. Wynne, McDaniel, and Weber (1986) offer an excellent overview of how a therapist knowledgeable of systems can utilize this knowledge with groups and organizations other than family systems. They provided guidelines for systems consultation with groups such as mental health systems, medical systems, community groups, service systems, military systems, and business systems. Use of the circumplex model with multisystems, school–family systems, family therapy systems, and family businesses will be briefly discussed.

### Multisystems Approach

The Multisystem Assessment of Stress and Health (MASH) was developed by Olson and Stewart (1993) as a systemic approach to focus on the interconnections between individuals, couples, families, and work systems. This model is presented as a biopsychosocial approach and as an attempt at providing a more integrative approach to conceptualizing the circular relationship between stress, coping, and adaptation across systems. This ecosystemic context is provided by looking at the interplay between the individual, couple, family, and work systems.

The MASH model utilizes the circumplex variables of cohesion and flexibility, which are assessed at the individual, couple, family, and work system levels. Stress, resources, and level of adaptation are also assessed at all four system levels. The four system levels are not understood as functioning individually, but as systemically influencing one another. A main focus of this work is to provide an understanding of stress and coping across systems. Validation of the importance of multisystem assessment is offered in a study where an understanding of work, family, couple, and individual levels was necessary for understanding the difference between those who did and did not cope well with stress (Stewart & Olson, 1993).

Building on the same MASH model, Weiss (1992) studied the interplay of stress and satisfaction across the four system levels of work, family, couple, and individual. As might be expected, stress and satisfaction had strong negative correlations within each level (−.31 to −.79). A large percentage of the variance, ranging from 18% to 42%, in amount of stress at each level could be accounted for by stress at the other three levels. Thus, to understand stress at one level it is necessary to understand stress at the other three levels. The shared variance between levels of *cohesion* and *flexibility* across the four system levels was much lower, with the understandable exception being couple and family levels, which are the most closely tied system levels. The two studies on the MASH model by Stewart and by Weiss highlight the importance of an ecosystemic focus in working with individuals and families.

### School–Family Systems

There has been increasing attention given recently to the importance of the interplay between school and family systems (see chap. 27 in this volume). A seminar for policy staff titled "The Family School Partnership: A Critical Component of School Reform" was conducted by the Family Impact Seminar—a group sponsored by a consortium of family-focused organizations (Ooms & Hara, 1992). In a report from this seminar, several recommendations for school reform were put forth on the basis of the absolute importance of the systemic ties between school and family. This report calls families the most important allies of educators. It calls for systems of parental involvement with schools tailored to fit each community, neighborhood, school, and family.

Lusterman (1989) developed an ecosystemic evaluation for school and family system levels based on the circumplex model. It is intended for use when a school behavior problem, or any problem with school involvement, is the presenting problem in a therapy situation. School and family systems are both evaluated on the cohesion and flexibility dimensions of the circumplex model. The family system is evaluated with FACES III, and the school is evaluated with an adapted form of the Organizational Styles of Work Groups developed by Lusterman.

Based on the information gathered from each system, an ecosystemic intervention is made to move both the family and the school system toward a more *balanced* system type (see Figure 4). This may involve first moving one or both of these systems to an *unbalanced* system type before moving the system to a *balanced* system type, as is the case with much of the clinical work involving the circumplex model.

The interplay of these two systems is plotted on the circumplex chart before, during, and after treatment. The theory behind this intervention is that individual difficulties do not exist in a vacuum, but within an ecosystemic context. Children's school problems do not exist only within the family, but also within the school system. To think that we can understand a child's problem at school without some understanding of the school system seems inconsistent with systemic thinking.

In an effort to understand the systemic dynamics of the school setting, Fish and Dane (1992) developed a classroom evaluation rating scale based on the FACES inventory. The authors assume that if understanding the family system is important to understanding the behavior problems of children, then so is understanding the school or classroom and the interplay of these systems. The classroom rating scale focuses on classroom cohesion and flexibility. Outside raters are used to rate individual classrooms. The circumplex model provides insights into the systemic interplay between the family and school systems.

## Ecosystemic Therapy and Consulting

Maddock and Lange (1989) have developed a model for studying the effects of ecosystemic consultations on therapeutic systems using the circumplex model and Milan systemic therapy with a consultation team. (For a more complete discussion of Milan systemic therapy see Selvini-Palazzoli, Boscolo, Cecchin, & Prata, 1978, 1980). The authors point out that the consultants in this situation must be cognizant that the addition of a consultation team creates another ecosystemic level that must be monitored. In this consultation model the goal of the consultation team is to balance the family–therapist ecosystem along the cohesion and flexibility dimensions of the circumplex model. Thus the consultation team must first assess and then continue to monitor the ecosystem, utilizing the circumplex model. The Milan systemic component to the therapy is based on the techniques of hypothesizing, circular questioning, neutrality, and session structure.

## Family–Business Systems

Kaslow (1993) has offered a developmental model for how and why family businesses have developed into such a widespread enterprise in the United States. According to her statistics, approximately 80% of the businesses in this country are family-owned enterprises. As with any phenomenon this widespread and involving so many families it was bound to be only a matter of time before the field of family business consultation would emerge. Kaslow offers a model for understanding the dynamics of family businesses by understanding the individual, family, and societal system levels at play in family businesses.

Grant (1982) used the circumplex model with family business systems and focused on the impact on the family system of being involved in a family-run business. Grant (1982) studied individuals involved in family businesses in which the members of the business were second or third generation family members. The author hypothesized that these families would display lower flexibility and higher cohesion than a control sample of similar business people not involved in a family business. FACES I was used as the circumplex measure. Neither of the hypotheses was confirmed. Members of family businesses

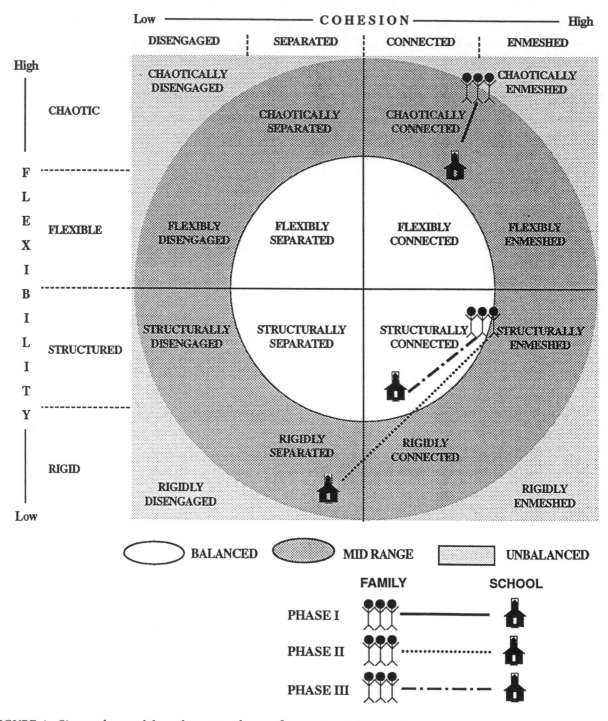

FIGURE 4. Circumplex model used to map phases of ecosystemic intervention.

were not found to differ significantly on cohesion or flexibility from those involved in nonfamily businesses. The circumplex model does provide an opportunity to study the interplay between family and family business.

The circumplex model dimensions of cohesion, flexibility, and communication are incorporated into the MASH model described earlier and the new multisystem assessment called the Coping and Stress Profile (CSP). The CSP is now being used by family business consultants to help them deal with the complexities and conflicts present in family businesses.

## CONCLUSION

This review provides an overview of applications of the circumplex model to a wide range of family systems and other social systems. The use of the model with these diverse systems was supported by much of the literature presented. However, continuing efforts must be made to evaluate the appropriateness of applying both the model and the assessment tools to other situations. More extensive study of the use of the circumplex model and its measures with racially and structurally diverse family forms is under way.

It is important that issues of family structure, racially and ethnically diverse families, and applications to other social systems be dealt with in a sensitive and appropriate manner. Although this model and these measures can be highly useful in both research and clinical practice, and some guidelines have been offered in this chapter, we do suggest caution in utilizing FACES, the Clinical Ratings Scale, and the circumplex model in general with diverse families and other systems. Also, whereas theoretical models and normed assessment devices are highly useful in research and clinical practice, each family must be viewed as a unique system and assessed and treated with regard to its unique conditions and relationships.

## References

Beavers, W. R., Hampson, R. B., & Hulgus, Y. F. (1985). Commentary: The Beavers Systems approach to family assessment. *Family Process, 24*, 398–405.

Calleja, A. C. (1989). Family functioning, stress, and dimensions of adolescent psychopathology. *Dissertation Abstracts International, 50*, 3146–B.

Captain, S. C. (1988). Marital adaptability during recovery from alcoholism. *Dissertation Abstracts International, 48*, 2601–B.

Chollack, H. B. (1990). Stepfamily adaptability and cohesion: A normative study. *Dissertation Abstracts International, 50*, 2789–A.

Cuellar, I., Harris, L., & Jasso, R. (1980). An acculturation scale for Mexican-American normal and clinical populations. *Hispanic Journal of Behavioral Sciences, 2*, 199–217.

Fish, M. C., & Dane, E. (1992, September). *Assessing classrooms using systems constructs: Instrument development.* Paper presented at the meeting of the National Association of School Psychologists, Nashville, TN.

Flores, M. J., & Sprenkle, D. H. (1989). Can therapists use FACES III with Mexican Americans? A preliminary analysis. In D. H. Olson, C. S. Russell, & D. H. Sprenkle (Eds.), *Circumplex model: Systemic assessment and treatment of families.* New York: Haworth.

Fonza, M. (1986). *Family cohesiveness and adaptation in middle-class blacks.* Unpublished master's thesis, Southern Illinois University, Edwardsville.

Fristad, M. A. (1989). A comparison of the McMaster and Circumplex family assessment instruments. *Journal of Marital and Family Therapy, 15*, 259–269.

Gorall, D. M., & Fournier, D. G. (1992). *Use of the modified (3–D) Circumplex Model to assess contrast between the families of origin of premarital couples.* Unpublished master's thesis, Oklahoma State University, Stillwater.

Grant, P. W. (1983). The intergenerational family in business. *Dissertation Abstracts International, 43*, 2803–A.

Green, R. G., Kolevzon, M. S., & Vosler, N. R. (1985a). The Beavers-Timberlawn Model of family assessment and the Circumplex Model of family adaptability and cohesion: Separate but equal? *Family Process, 24*, 385–398.

Green, R. G., Kolevzon, M. S., & Vosler, N. R. (1985b). Rejoinder: Extending the dialogue and the original study. *Family Process, 24*, 405–408.

Hare-Mustin, R. T., & Marecek, J. (1988). The meaning of difference: Gender theory, postmodernism, and psychology. *American Psychologist, 43*, 455–464.

Hsu, J., Tseng, W. S., Lum, K. Y., Lao, L., Vaccaro, J., & Brennan, J. (1988). Cross-ethnic study of normal families in Hawaii. In J. Hssu (Ed.), *Asian family mental health proceedings* (pp. 19–27). Tokyo: Psychiatric Research Institute of Tokyo.

Kaslow, F. (1993). The lore and lure of family business. *American Journal of Family Therapy, 21*, 3–16.

Kennedy, G. E. (1985). Family relationships as perceived by college students from single-parent, blended and intact families. *Family Perspective, 19,* 117–126.

Lusterman, D.-D. (1989). School–family intervention and the Circumplex Model. In D. H. Olson, C. S. Russell, & D. H. Sprenkle (Eds.), *Circumplex Model: Systemic assessment and treatment of families.* New York: Haworth.

Maddock, J. W., & Lange, C. G. (1989). Integrating Milan therapy and the Circumplex Model: Ecosystemic consultation with families and their helpers. In D. H. Olson, C. S. Russell, & D. H. Sprenkle (Eds.), *Circumplex Model: Systemic assessment and treatment of families.* New York Haworth Press.

Meyer, C. J. (1990). Social support and closeness among lesbians. *Dissertation Abstracts International, 50,* 2667–A.

Miller, I. W., Epstein, N. B., Bishop, D. S., & Keitner, G. I. (1985). The McMaster Family Assessment Device: Reliability and validity. *Journal of Marital and Family Therapy, 11,* 345–356.

Olson, D. H. (1988). *Clinical Rating Scale (CRS) for the Circumplex Model of Marital and Family Systems* (rev. ed.). Unpublished manuscript, Department of Family Social Science, University of Minnesota, St. Paul.

Olson, D. H. (1993). Circumplex Model of Marital and Family Systems: Assessing family functioning. In F. Walsh (Ed.), *Normal Family Processes* (2nd ed.). New York: Guilford Press.

Olson, D. H., Fournier, D. G., & Druckman, J. M. (1992). *PREPARE/ENRICH counselors manual* (rev. ed.). Minneapolis, MN: PREPARE/ENRICH.

Olson, D. H., Portner, J., & Lavee, Y. (1985). *FACES III manual.* Unpublished manuscript, Department of Family Social Science, University of Minnesota, St. Paul.

Olson, D. H., Russell, C., & Sprenkle, D. (Eds.). (1989). *Circumplex Model: Systemic assessment and treatment of families* (2nd ed.). New York: Haworth.

Olson, D. H., & Stewart, K. L. (1993). *Multisystem assessment of stress and health (MASH) model and the Coping and Stress Profile (CSP).* Unpublished manuscript.

Ooms, T., & Hara, S. (1992, November). The family–school partnership: A critical component of school reform. In T. Ooms (Chair), *Family Impact Seminar.* Seminar conducted at the American Association of Marriage and Family Therapy, Washington, DC.

Selvini-Palazzoli, M., Boscolo, L., Cecchin, G., & Prata, G. (1978). *Paradox and counterparadox: A new model in the therapy of the family in schizophrenic transaction.* New York: Jason Aaronson.

Selvini-Palazzoli, M., Boscolo, L., Cecchin, G., & Prata, G. (1980). Hypothesizing—circularity—neutrality: Three guidelines for the conductor of the session. *Family Process, 19,* 3–12.

So, D. K. (1990). *Circumplex Model of Marital and Family Systems: Application to Chinese immigrant families in the United States.* Unpublished doctoral dissertation, California Graduate School of Family Psychology, San Francisco.

Spivey, P. (1984). Interracial adolescents: Self-image, racial self-concept, and family process. *Dissertation Abstracts International, 45,* 3632–B.

Stewart, K. L., & Olson, D. H. (1993). *Stress and adaptation: Testing multisystem model of individual, couple, family and work systems.* Unpublished Manuscript.

Thomas, V. K., & Cierpka, M. (1989, October). *FACES III and FAM III: A comparison of family assessment instruments.* Paper presented at the meeting of the National Council on Family Relations, New Orleans.

Thomas, V. K., & Olson, D. H. (1993). Problem families and the Circumplex Model: Observational assessment using the Clinical Rating Scale (CRS). *Journal of Marital and Family Therapy, 19,* 159–175.

Thomas, V. K., & Olson, D. H. (1992). *Circumplex Model: Curvilinearity using Clinical Rating Scale (CRS) and FACES III.* Unpublished manuscript, University of Iowa, Iowa City.

Trepper, T. S., & Sprenkle, D. H. (1989). The clinical use of the Circumplex Model in the assessment and treatment of intrafamily child sexual abuse. In D. H. Olson, C. S. Russell, & D. H. Sprenkle (Eds.), *Circumplex Model: Systemic assessment and treatment of families.* New York: Haworth.

Tseng, W. S., & Hsu, J. (1991). *Culture and family: Problems and therapy.* New York: Haworth.

Vega, W. V., Patterson, T., Sallis, J., Nader, P., Atkins, C., & Abromson, I. (1986). Cohesion and adaptability in Mexican-American and Anglo families. *Journal of Marriage and the Family, 48,* 857–867.

Volk, R. J., Edwards, D. W., Lewis, R. A., & Sprenkle, D. H. (1989). Family systems of adolescent substance abusers. *Family Relations, 38,* 266–272.

Walsh, F., & Olson, D. H. (1989). Utility of the Circumplex Model with severely dysfunctional family systems. In D. H. Olson, C. S. Russell, & D. H. Sprenkle (Eds.), *Circumplex Model: Systemic assessment and treatment of families.* New York: Haworth.

Weiss, J. (1992). *Coping and stress: An international comparison of an American and a German study using the Coping and Stress Profile.* Unpublished manuscript. University of Minnesota, St. Paul.

Woehrer, C. E. (1989). Ethnic families and the Circumplex Model: Integrating nuclear and extended families. In D. H. Olson, C. S. Russell, & D. H. Sprenkle

(Eds.), *Circumplex Model: Systemic assessment and treatment of families*. New York: Haworth.

Wynne, L. C., McDaniel, S. H., & Weber, T. T. (1986). *Systems consultation: A new perspective for family ther-* apy. New York: Guilford Press.

Zacks, E., Green, R. J., & Marrow, J. (1988). Comparing lesbian and heterosexual couples on the Circumplex Model: An initial investigation. *Family Process, 27,* 471–484.

# PART IV

# THERAPY WITH COUPLES

# Introduction

The term *couples therapy* is a relatively recent addition to the vocabulary of the family systems field. Unlike the term *marital therapy*, it reflects the fluid and manifold state of couples relationships in the late 20th century. These include couples ambivalent about their commitment, couples in the midst of courtship, married couples, homosexual couples, and couples who do not contemplate marriage. The issues that we explore in this section include sexuality and intimacy, the impact and treatment of infidelity, the dilemmas facing couples contemplating separation and divorce, and the divorce mediation process.

In chapter 13, "Sex Therapy and Intimacy: A Family Systems Approach," David Schnarch emphasizes the importance of taking the relational context into account as we conceptualize a couple's sexual issues. At the same time, he reminds us that, historically, our training as psychologists and as family therapists has all but ignored sexuality and that we need to develop a knowledge base and a cogent philosophy of treatment. He provides us with "a multi-systemic approach using the concepts of fusion and differentiation as organizing principles in both the exploration and treatment of couples' sexual problems." His approach pays special attention to the need to "develop and maintain eroticism and intimacy in emotionally committed relationships."

In "Treating Marital Infidelity," Don-David Lusterman begins by exploring the impact on both members of the couple of the discovery of a lengthy extramarital affair, and then later extrapolates from the treatment of such affairs to the discussion of one-night stands, sexual relations with prostitutes, and philandering. Using a case example of a lengthy affair, Lusterman likens the issues faced by the couple and the therapist to the issues faced in cases of Post-traumatic Stress Disorder. Using the concept of trauma and a three-stage model of treatment, he shows how to help the couple restore trust, understand what predisposed them to this crisis, and self-disclose, problem-solve, and make decisions about their marriage. Lusterman provides insightful answers to questions every therapist must address in working in this often heated and pain-filled marital crisis.

Florence W. Kaslow, in "The Dynamics of Divorce Therapy," provides a stage model of divorce that enables the therapist to anticipate the issues that people face as they evolve from being a couple to being single individuals again. She takes the reader through the predivorce period, when emotional issues predominate; to the divorce period itself, when legal, custody, and economic issues often become central and social, community, and extended family adjustments become critical; to the final postdivorce period, in which it is hoped that both parties reach a mature acceptance of the marriage's dissolution and achieve a psychic divorce. Using case material to illustrate each stage, she outlines the expected emotional issues and behaviors and appropriate therapeutic interventions to assist the couple and the family to cope most effectively with one of life's most stressful transitions.

To deal with some of the legal aspects of this transition, S. Richard Sauber, Stephen Beiner, and Gail Meddoff recommend a specific form of resolution in their chapter, "Divorce Mediation: A New System for Dealing With Families in Transition." The authors explain the five mediation methods or styles: integrative, structured, therapeutic, negotiatory, and interdisciplinary. To enable therapists to become more informed in working with mediators or in becoming better mediators themselves, the authors analyze and compare each method of mediation. They note that critics of mediation claim that mediated divorce agreements are inequitable to the party with the least amount of power in the relationship, and they attempt to address these power imbalances in a way that offers the benefits of mediation to all of the involved parties to the system.

CHAPTER 13

# A FAMILY SYSTEMS APPROACH
# TO SEX THERAPY
# AND INTIMACY

*David M. Schnarch*

In family or couples therapy, a couple's sexual and intimacy problems often become evident, either at the outset or later in treatment. This chapter presents an approach to these problems that unites systemic treatment and sex therapy as powerful triggers for personal development.

## EARLIER APPROACHES TO SEXUAL THERAPY

Early in the development of sexual therapy, clinicians turned to psychoanalytic formulations of psychosexual development to explain sexual problems (Freud, 1905/1986). The ineffectiveness of this approach led therapists to seek new theoretical bases for treatment. Salter (1949), Lazarus (1965), and Wolpe (1969) used behavioral concepts such as systemic desensitization in treating sexual dysfunctions. Ellis (1962) used cognitive psychology to explore the role of dysfunctional thinking in patients' sexual problems. A synthesis of these elements evolved into a cognitive–behavioral approach for treating couples and some individuals (e.g., Hartman & Fithian, 1972; LoPiccolo & Lobitz, 1972; Masters & Johnson, 1970). Shortly thereafter, psychodynamics were reintegrated into sexual therapy to deal with resistance to the straightforward cognitive–behavioral approach (e.g., Kaplan, 1974). Although ostensibly couples-based, none of these approaches were concerned with the context of the marriage beyond the issue of sexual dysfunction. And although they initially appeared to produce startling rates of success (Masters & Johnson, 1970), subsequent studies showed less benefit and frequent relapse (e.g., DeAmicis, Goldberg, Lo-

Piccolo, Friedman, & Davies, 1985; Kilmann, Boland, Norton, Davidson, & Caid, 1986; Schover & LoPiccolo, 1982).

These approaches were based on the common-sense notion that sex is a natural function that can be restored through disinhibition and/or reeducation. This stance, however, may itself cause new problems. It pressures patients to produce sexual desire, genital response, and orgasm, while at the same time it paradoxically directs the patient not to worry about sexual performance. It likewise focuses the therapist's attention on *dysfunction* and on desire as eagerness to do what is natural, rather than on pursuing the best of human intimacy and eroticism.

Although it sounds enlightened, the concept of natural sexual function can lead both clinician and client to view the absence of presumably automatic function as pathological. This may increase the patient's anxiety because, given this context, failure to improve suggests failure to be normal. Such an approach also locates the "pathology" within the individual—as does the *Diagnostic and Statistical Manual of Mental Disorders*, fourth edition (*DSM-IV*; American Psychiatric Association, 1994), thus ignoring the sexual system that each couple cocreates. Given this, therapy based on the natural-function theory can generate iatrogenic treatment resistance.

## RAISING THE TOPIC OF SEX

Therapists must usually take the initiative to raise the topic of sex, but clients often talk easily enough once the therapist has modeled such behavior. Becoming comfortable discussing details of a couple's sexual interactions requires that the clinician carefully reexamine her or his own ideas, feelings, and attitudes. Enabling clients to feel at ease is important. Nonetheless, one must guard against falling prey to subtle negotiations regarding the level of anxiety at which treatment will operate. Introducing the topic of sex is one thing; colluding in the couple's unwillingness to confront the anxiety inherent in growing sexually is quite another. In reducing the couple's and the clinician's anxiety about broaching the topic, the level of explicitness and anxiety is often set below the level realistically required for the couple to effectively modify entrenched patterns.

## INTERVENING TO ENHANCE DIFFERENTIATION

This chapter illustrates a multisystemic approach using the concepts of fusion and differentiation (Bowen, 1978) as organizing principles in both the exploration and treatment of couples' sexual problems. This approach (which I have referred to elsewhere as the "sexual crucible"; Schnarch, 1991) harnesses natural sexual systemics to develop and maintain eroticism and intimacy in emotionally committed relationships. A second major organizing principle of this chapter is the quantum model of sexual function (Schnarch, 1991), which, like modern physics' quantum theory, studies dynamic variables that specify a system's behavior. Together, the concepts of differentiation, fusion, and the quantum model of sexual function create a framework within which sexuality and relationship can be approached at a contextual level.

Differentiation involves maintaining a clear sense of self in the face of pressure by loved ones to conform. The task in marriage is to find out who you are, with a partner who is usually overeager to tell you. (H. L. Mencken said, "People may be fools and not know it—but not if they're married"; Peter, 1980).

Differentiation differs from childhood individuation (Mahler, 1968) in that the goal is not to get away from or separate from significant others. It is the ability to balance needs for autonomy and togetherness. Developing a clearly defined sense of oneself permits greater involvement with loved ones without the risk of losing oneself in the process or requiring distancing maneuvers.

Even knowing who you are, however, does not keep you from getting really anxious at times if your self-definition is only in relation to your partner. Differentiation—knowing who and what you are, in and of yourself—provides the ability to tolerate anxieties that frequently occur in exploring sexuality. We want stability in our primary relationship and with our partner's (sexual) persona. When we've got it, however, we're bored. Differentiation determines a person's capacity for self-validated intimacy (Schnarch, 1991), which differs from other-validated intimacy in the latter's emphases on reciprocity, empathy, and external validation. Poorly differentiated people's dependence on other-validated intimacy creates sexual boredom and intimacy problems because of the difficulty they have handling the anxiety of their partner's changing or introducing new sexual behaviors. Well-differentiated partners are better able to initiate and innovate sexually—and keep intimacy and sexual interest alive—because they have less of a need to keep each other the same and are less dependent on mutual validation.

Couples enter therapy to find a way to change their partner rather than to risk changing themselves. The therapist, then, must encourage both partners to "hold onto themselves" and not compromise. Without taking a stance as to the accuracy of either person's perceptions, the therapist encourages each to act according to her or his reality (See chap. 2 in this volume). Couples often fear they will separate if both people maintain their selfhood. One or both mates may see the issue as choosing between one's integrity and one's marriage. This is an error. The natural systemics of committed relationships in fact facilitate clearer self-delineation and greater self-validated intimacy. There is a release from the need for external validation and unconditional positive acceptance from one's partner. What develops, instead, is hard-won mutual respect.

Sensate-focus exercises and homework assignments have almost no place in this approach. Nor do communication training or listening skills. The former strategies attempt to force clients' behavior into predetermined shapes rather than letting sex come forward in the couple's own image. The latter ignore the fact that communication is no virtue if you cannot tolerate the message. Together, they promote emotional fusion and undifferentiated other-validated behavior.

## SEXUAL THERAPY COMPARED WITH MARITAL THERAPY

A review of core texts (e.g., Kaplan, 1979; Leiblum & Pervin, 1980; Leiblum & Rosen, 1988) reveals that until recently, sex therapy has focused primarily on changing specifically sexual behavior and has lacked significant systemic emphasis. By contrast, couples therapy, when it deals with sexual issues, tends to operate from the belief that if the couple's relationship improves, then sexual satisfaction will almost automatically follow. A few truly systemically oriented sex therapy strategies have emerged (e.g., Stone Fish, Fish, & Sprenkle, 1984; Verhulst & Heiman, 1979, 1988). More commonly, however, authors have recognized the need to address both cognitive–behavioral and systemic issues without actually providing a systemic model or a clinical approach to forward their goals (e.g., LoPiccolo & Friedman, 1988; Mason, 1991). The result has been more appearance than substance to systemically sophisticated sex therapy.

Ironically, in both sex and marital therapy, when there is a sexual problem, the relationship becomes the patient and treatment is therefore built, for the most part, around the couple. This may direct attention away from the important personal development required of each individual to resolve sexual/intimacy problems—and the powerful growth opportunities these problems present. Spouses often become sexually deadlocked precisely because one spouse begins to perceive the relationship itself to be at the core of a sexual problem, effectively blocking self-confrontation and self-development. Such a person may believe that sexual difficulties indicate that the couple no longer love one another. Thus, a successful sexual–marital therapy must include both the individual *and* the system.

## SEXUALITY IN THE CONTEXT OF RELATIONSHIP

It is important to see the couple's sexual problem in its broader context. Such a contextual awareness takes into account, for example, the developmental stage of the family. Consider for instance, a couple experiencing the inevitable problems of low sexual desire and poor communication as they parent their adolescent son and daughter.

The husband is struggling to maintain his own self-esteem as he realizes his career is not going well. He will never achieve the income or career status of his aspirations. Unable to express his fears and worries, he appears to his wife to be distracted and uninterested. She in turn is dealing with menopausal issues. Her feelings are influenced by her mother's frequently stated view that sexual love ends with menopause and by glances at her own daughter's body.

Both husband and wife are very concerned about the sexual activities of their children. On the one hand, they feel powerless to control what they think may be dangerous risk taking on their children's part. On the other, they have unshared fantasies about the powerful urges and pleasure they imagine their children to be having and contrast them with the current barren state of their own relationship. Everyone in the house is pressured in different ways by the myth that adolescence is the sexual peak of life.

The clinician must take context into account when exploring couples' reports of their sexual relationships and fashioning meaningful interventions. Just as relationship problems can affect sexual interaction, so can sexual problems injure marital intimacy, even when the couple really desire one another. As a sexual problem grows, the symptomatic partner tends to become ever more self-conscious and may try even harder to please (or just withdraw). This often pushes the couple further apart. For this reason, couples with sexual dysfunction often say they are "lonely" during sex.

The clinician should not accept at face value idyllic reports of emotional communion when there are continuing sexual difficulties. Such reports often mask denial and defensiveness in the relationship. They may also suggest that the couple has so little experience with sexual intimacy that they don't know what they are missing.

Partners of mates with a sexual problem may also be caught in a double bind. On the one hand, they want to appear satisfied in order to spare the other's feelings and not make matters worse. On the other, they do not want to encourage denial or avoidance of necessary changes. The result is an increased loss of intimacy during sex, because neither partner wants to be truly known or felt while they are touching.

Several systemic principles, for example, can be delineated about inhibited sexual desire. These observations all relate to the issue of emotional fusion in that the action taken is not a function of the self but of the couple's poorly boundaried interaction. They are examples of the numerous incongruent power hierarchies that permeate sex and stimulate differentiation.

1. The person with the least sexual desire always controls sex. The partner with the higher desire (often seen by the couple as the "sex expert") makes the sexual initiations, and the identified patient (who manifests lower desire) determines when sex will actually occur.
2. The identified patient often has control (and responsibility) for the spouse's sense of adequacy. Knowing that the designated sex expert needs the mate to respond adequately puts the identified patient in the paradoxical position of being less likely to give the desired response because of pressure and expectations. It may also lead the identified patient to fake or withhold orgasm in order to modulate the partner's self-esteem.
3. One partner can always force the other to choose between loyalty to self and loyalty to marriage. This is an example of a *crucible* (i.e., severe test) of committed relationships. Another is that one partner can successfully push the other to *have* sex but cannot force the other to *desire* it. The sex that is granted under these circumstances may produce orgasm but lack both enthusiasm and eroticism.

In these issues, both partners are naturally either driven to a higher level of differentiation in search of resolution or forced to accept the unsatisfying status quo. Given these systemic realities, therapeutic suggestions to "communicate" or "negotiate" around issues of desire are ineffective. When people are emotionally fused, negotiation and communication are useless and may, in fact, further fuel the fusion. The solution, instead, involves helping the couple to differentiate.

Differentiation is a basic life force that propels every living thing to grow and become distinctly itself while remaining part of its species' social unit. In humans it shows up as the ability to maintain a clearly defined sense of yourself in close proximity to significant others, especially when pressured to conform. It involves the ability to soothe your own anxiety and provides resilience to others' anxiety, which permits responses determined by clear thinking and modulated feelings rather than impulsive emotional reactivity. These are necessary characteristics if sexual novelty and intimacy are to flourish in long-term relationships.

It is my experience that most couples do not enter marriage at a high level of differentiation. They have little ability to appreciate the views, values, and priorities of their partner, or they too easily lose their own. In this sense, they are not ready for marriage. Indeed, the normal sexual problems of marriage, handled properly, enable a couple to reach higher levels of differentiation and thereby become capable of a deeply intimate and erotic relationship.

## UNDERSTANDING SEXUAL FUNCTION: THE QUANTUM MODEL

It was mentioned earlier that the "sex is a normal function" paradigm led sex therapy to focus on dysfunction and to evolve pathologic explanations to explain the absence of what this paradigm says should be automatic sexual performance. With few notable exceptions (e.g., Apfelbaum, 1977), therapists rarely consider what makes people function in ways we deem "normal." (See chap. 34 in this volume.)

Quantum theory, as mentioned earlier, studies dynamic variables that specify a system's behavior. Everyday events are understood as sophisticated interactions of small energy sources, which undergo abrupt changes when the system achieves a specified condition or level. The quantum model of sexual function offers a multisystemic view of sexual functioning that focuses on helping people achieve more than utilitarian genital function. It considers many dimensions of sexual experience, including depth of involvement and profoundness of sex, intimacy, and sexual style. At the limits of their sexual potential, humans are capable of bringing high meaning and profound intimacy to sex and of integrating sexuality and spirituality in mutually enhancing ways. In short, the quantum model integrates humans' most unique capacities into sexual functioning and experience.

For all our apparent interest in intimacy and rejection of orgasm as the focus of sexual union, orgasm is still at the heart of contemporary models of sexual response. An integrative model must both treat sexual dysfunctions and help people to explore the limits of their sexual potential. Such a paradigm transcends the popular four-stage sexual response model proposed by Masters and Johnson (1966) and later reformulated into the "triphasic model" by Kaplan (1979), which many clinicians unquestioningly accept as physical fact.

At one level, genital response and orgasm can be considered reflexes, similar to the knee-jerk patella reflex. They occur in healthy people when sufficient stimulation triggers them. When the level of sexual energy (physical and psychological stimulation) exceeds the individual's response threshold, the anticipated genital changes (i.e., vaginal lubrication in women; initial erection in men) and subsequent orgasm occur. We refer to these reflexive responses as "normal" or "natural" sexual functioning. But human sexuality is infinitely more complex and cannot be reduced to such a simplistic formula.

As human beings evolved sexually over time, we developed unique abilities and problems. As a species, we became capable of engaging in intercourse while facing one another and of experiencing nonreproductive sexual desire. We became conscious of subtle interpersonal signals of sexual interest, commonly referred to as "sexual chemistry" or "vibes." Most significantly, we developed the capacity to experience intimacy during sex as well as at other times.

However, in trading programmed regularity and hormonally driven sexual interest for the ability to attach high meaning to sex, we became more susceptible to sexual dysfunctions and inhibited sexual de-

sire. Intimacy or self-preoccupation during sex are made possible by similar self-reflective processes. In developing the cognitive capacity to modulate biological drives, we effectively transcended the biological drive model of human sexual desire embraced in the *DSM-IV* (American Psychiatric Association, 1994) and the sexual anorexia model of inhibited sexual desire described by Kaplan (1979).

Sexual stimulation in humans consists of more than sensory excitation. People's subjective evaluations of their sensations are even larger determinants of overall level of sexual arousal (and genital function and orgasm) than is tactile stimulation itself. (Note that this negates common notions of "giving someone an orgasm" or "making someone come.") *Total level of stimulation* is composed of tactile input and the receiver's emotional processes. When total level of stimulation (and not just physical touch) reach the response threshold (e.g., lubrication/erection or orgasm), the expected response occurs.

Physical stimulation and the receiver's emotional processes are interactive variables that can potentiate, mitigate, or debilitate each other. Deficits in one dimension can be compensated for by particularly good stimulation in the other. For example, poor technique in the right circumstances can lead to orgasm, but the same technique in other circumstances may not. Consider, for example, a woman who finds her new boyfriend's shy and clumsy attempts to stimulate her clitoris refreshing and endearing. Several years into their marriage, the same physical technique creates continued anger and frustration instead of sexual pleasure. Before marriage she reaches orgasm with her partner; once the honeymoon is over, she no longer does.

At its most basic level, repairing sexual dysfunctions involves increasing the total level of stimulation. This is accomplished by optimizing both the receiver's internal processes and the tactile stimulation he or she receives. This in turn increases the likelihood of achieving response threshold levels and is therefore the key to functional genital response.

Unfortunately, there is often a difficulty in one dimension or the other. Many people achieve little more than the degree of arousal required for reflexive functioning. Their sexuality remains perpetually vulnerable to minor variations in both touch and meaning, which can reduce total stimulation below threshold levels and create sexual dysfunction.

It is possible in some instances to raise total stimulation to threshold levels by improving only one dimension. It is more readily (and enjoyably) accomplished when all dimensions are addressed. This can be accomplished in a variety of ways. The first two that follow are among the most common (and quickest) approaches:

1. Optimize stimulus transmission. Anything that interferes with the transmission of stimulation (from peripheral nerve receptors to the central nervous system and back to the genitals) can limit sexual function. Intervention involves ruling out deficits caused by diseases, injuries, or prescription or recreational drugs. Vascular, neurological, and hormonal problems secondary to common syndromes (e.g., alcoholism, diabetes, multiple sclerosis, renal failure) must also be ruled out. Lists of medications and physical conditions that require evaluation are available elsewhere (e.g., Kaplan, 1983).

2. Optimize physical stimulation. This includes increasing the duration and intensity of pleasuring received during sex. Improved communication about sexual preferences leads to better stimulation between some partners.

   It is not uncommon, however, for people to experience better erections/lubrication when they are ostensibly giving their partner stimulation than when they are receiving. Such responses highlight how emotional stimulation (and the absence of negative emotions like guilt about receiving or the feeling that your genitals ought to respond because your partner is touching you) is often a more powerful determinant of genital function than is tactile stimulation.

3. Raise or lower threshold. People's response thresholds differ. It is also quite normal for thresholds to vary for a given individual over time. The natural slowing of response associated with aging, which requires increasing amounts of physical stimulation to trigger sexual function, is one common example. The tendency for men to develop more ejaculatory control as they age is another.

Thresholds for sexual response are subject to conditioning, like many other physiological processes once considered to be outside of conscious control (e.g., peripheral vasodilation, which can be modified through biofeedback training; alpha wave conditioning). This conditioning process is fairly long term. As a treatment strategy for rapid ejaculation, for instance, one can either help a man keep total stimulation below his threshold or help him raise the threshold. It is easier in the short run (although less adaptive for long-term functioning or satisfaction) to control ejaculation through stimulation-lowering methods such as "stop–start" (Semans, 1956) or inhibiting the reflex through the "squeeze technique" (Masters & Johnson, 1970). It is possible, in contrast, to raise a man's orgasmic threshold by repeated exposure to extremely dense stimulation while not attempting to control his ejaculation. This method is often counterintuitive to men who commonly attempt to delay their ejaculation by reducing their pleasure or trying to hold back. Obviously, raising the threshold requires reshaping the couple's behavior repertoire and emotional system surrounding sex, and this often demands—and produces—increased differentiation. This is the point of a differentiation-based approach to sex and intimacy.

4. Optimize the receiver's internal process. People's involvement during sex varies anywhere from ineffectively superficial contact, to a level of involvement minimally utilitarian for achieving orgasm, to profound engagement and transcendent spirituality. Tone and depth of involvement potentiates (or debilitates) the impact of concurrent physical stimulation in reaching thresholds for genital response and orgasm.

   Critically watching one's own performance from an emotionally remote perspective (spectatoring) or getting caught up in worries about sexual adequacy and genital function (performance anxiety) are examples of phenomena that inhibit ardently deep involvement. Someone panicking about pleasing his or her partner during sex out of fears of sexual inadequacy is not really *with* the partner during those times.

## TRADITIONAL SEX THERAPY VERSUS AN INTIMACY-BASED APPROACH

Even contemporary sex therapy approaches often unwittingly undermine intimacy. For example, common interventions such as "sensate focus" assignments (Masters & Johnson, 1970) encourage people to take turns focusing on their own kinesthetic sensations and to basically ignore their partner (except for "giving feedback" and "telling your partner what you want"). This style of sexual interaction often causes people to feel ignored and used by their partner—even when it is prescribed by a therapist. Such an approach is of little help in regaining the passionate sex that many couples only dimly remember but greatly desire. Likewise, Kaplan's (1974) directive to use fantasies to overlook untoward feelings about one's partner ("bypassing") is also antithetic to sexual intimacy. Many partners of people who spontaneously adapt this strategy indeed *experience* low sexual desire—as do those who dislike sex with partners they have to ignore.

As a final example, consider the "squeeze technique" (Masters & Johnson, 1970), long regarded as a principle method of treating rapid ejaculation. Although somewhat effective in stopping ejaculation, it stops intimacy cold too: Imagine a man whipping his penis from his partner's body as orgasm approaches and squeezing its corona! Long before that he has stopped focusing on his partner, attending instead to the proper moment to perform the sexual Heimlich maneuver. Common preoccupation with genital performance has kept clinicians from recognizing that our cures often are not much better than the problem itself and that they may, in fact, be worse in the long run.

It is possible, however, to develop a highly effective erotic mindset that facilitates intimacy and opens the door for profound sexual union. An intimacy-based approach grounded in differentiation helps people explore the limits of their sexual potential and maximize physical and emotional stimulation. At the same time, it alleviates sexual dysfunction and addresses problems of low or disparate sexual desire. This is accomplished by shifting the focus of therapy away from fixing defects and toward eroticism and intimacy. Specifically, this involves:

- deepening the emotional in-the-moment involvement;
- broadening the sexual repertoire of behaviors, techniques, and tones, thereby increasing the range of styles in which profound partner engagement and involvement of core self can occur;
- increasing the level of intimacy, intimacy tolerance, and meaningfulness of encounters;
- expanding the psychic energy exchange through investment in eroticism and exchange of sexual vibes;
- removing pleasure-antagonistic anxiety, while increasing pleasure-facilitating anxiety (novelty);
- reducing situational distractions;
- optimizing the emotional tone of sexual interactions by decreasing interfering marital dynamics;
- resolving object-relations transference storms; and
- enhancing anxiety tolerance and ability to self-soothe one's own frustrations and disappointments (differentiation).

All these elements come under the heading of optimizing the receiver's internal processes. It is part of helping people develop the ability to achieve orgasm without destroying intimacy. Interestingly, at times this may include looking into their partner's eyes. Many people have to close their eyes and tune out their partner in order to make their bodies function. Yet, the ability to have face-to-face sex is part of our earlier mentioned human evolution, and with this comes the ability to look *into* one another. The suggestion to explore making love with eyes open—and even have eyes-open orgasms—is but one example of an intimacy-based approach designed to help people to explore their sexual potential. Realizing that you cannot or will not do this is another example of a sexual crucible; others are presented in the illustrative case material that follows.

## COMMON CLINICAL DISORDERS AND ILLUSTRATIVE VIGNETTES

Many therapists approach different sexual dysfunctions as discrete disorders having discrete etiologies that require discrete treatments. By contrast, the model presented here utilizes a unified and holistic approach to both etiology and treatment.

## Primary Anorgasmia

### CASE VIGNETTE

Patty was a single 24-year-old woman who had never had an orgasm. She suggested that the therapist, a specialist in sexuality, teach her how to masturbate. Instead, the therapist asked her, "How do you know when to stop?" Patty reported that she gave up when it seemed that nothing was going to happen. Actual duration of clitoral stimulation was about 5 minutes. With some hesitancy, she reported further details of her masturbatory style.

From this information, the therapist pointed out that (a) her approach to masturbation was orgasm-focused, work-oriented, and all-or-nothing; (b) she was self-rejecting while she was supposedly self-pleasuring, with little emphasis on truly experiencing pleasure; (c) this was as much an issue of self-acceptance as it was of orgasms; (d) any other sexual partner she treated similarly probably would not orgasm either; and (e) she would probably still feel inadequate after learning to orgasm, because it perpetuated her belief she needed an orgasm to be adequate.

The therapist then asked if (and why) she felt that she was only worth 5 minutes of stimulation? How did she decide this was the right amount of time in which to orgasm? Did she have the nerve to give herself pleasure when she was not measuring up? Rather than use the common clinical ploy of calling masturbation "self-pleasuring," the therapist pointed out that there was no self-pleasuring in her masturbation. Instead the therapist referred to it as self-pushing.

The therapist refused either to teach Patty how to masturbate or to suggest any books. Rather, he suggested that the problem was that she was not willing to be the expert about her own body and sexuality. All she needed to do was pay attention to what felt good to her and do more of it. The situation was redefined as an opportunity to watch herself play out her issues of self-acceptance and as a way she could increase her self-worth and her relationship with her self—not by having an orgasm, but by noting how she maintained herself in the face of her inner dialogue.

The therapist took the stance that not having an orgasm just was not the worst thing in the world, particularly if one was withholding from oneself. What was much more important, noted the therapist, was how one treated oneself.

What ensued for Patty (in and out of the next several sessions) was an intense period of self-confrontation and life review. This mirrored concomitant changes in her behavioral style and mental processes during masturbation. After 3 weeks, she became orgasmic.

Patty continued the process begun in therapy. She became increasingly resilient and self-directed in her struggles with her controlling and jealous boyfriend. Eventually, she demonstrated her new ability by stimulating herself during intercourse. This threatened his sense of mastery and security. His critical remarks triggered further self-confrontation for Patty, which resulted in further self-acceptance. She eventually terminated the relationship. In working through the breakup, Patty began to deal more effectively with her domineering and infantilizing parents.

By structuring treatment in this manner, the therapist made masturbation the stage upon which Patty's dramas of self-definition and differentiation played out. Masturbation was used to stimulate personal growth in the relationship with self inherent in sex. In this instance, we see a systemic formulation in the treatment of an individual indirectly impacting the broader system.

The following case describes conjoint treatment of secondary anorgasmia.

## Secondary Anorgasmia

*CASE VIGNETTE*

Monica had been able to attain orgasm in almost every sexual encounter with her husband, Ted. This had become less consistent as they increasingly fought over his submission to his ailing mother's demands. Monica became consistently anorgasmic with Ted around the time her mother-in-law moved into their home, taking the bedroom next to theirs. However, she remained orgasmic during masturbation.

Diverse etiological factors in this situational anorgasmia (difficulty reaching orgasmic threshold) involved Monica's fear of being overheard by her mother-in-law during sex and her mental turf war with Ted's mother for control of her own home. These, and her anger at Ted for inviting his mother to move in against her objections, competed for Monica's attention to pleasurable sensations during sex. She also felt less desire for Ted, whom she now saw as weak and immature. In addition, Ted's touch became increasingly tentative and careless due to both his fear of her anger and his passive-aggressive withholding. And whereas noncoital sex had lasted for as much as 20 or 30 minutes in the past, their encounters rapidly moved into orgasm-focused coitus after Ted's mother's arrival. Now faced with multiple frustrations herself, Monica enjoyed having Ted feel incompetent to satisfy her sexually.

In their initial session, Monica, in anger and disappointment, accused Ted of "having no balls." Ted complained he was "caught between two women." The therapist suggested that if Ted was going to turn himself over to anyone, it did not matter which woman he chose. The problem, actually, was that he refused to define himself, to "hold onto himself."

Approaching this positively, the therapist suggested that Ted might be in the process of "growing a penis of his own"—the part of his own masculinity that he missed and Monica craved. This aspect of his sexual aggression and eroticism could not be gotten from either woman, only from one particular man—himself. The therapist asked whether Ted could move his mother into a smaller bedroom located farther down the hall. The therapist avoided being too helpful or supportive so that if Ted "made his move," he would be sure he was standing on his own two feet and using himself his own way. The question was not "would Ted and Monica divorce?" but rather, "would they grow enough to get married more deeply than ever before?" One way or another, they were at a turning point.

Ted moved his mother down the hall, not because he "caved in," but as an act of personal heroism and self-definition (differentiation). Monica became more respectful of Ted, not only because he was standing up to his mother, but also because he had begun to do the same with her. She began to see him in a more desirable light. Ted became more sexually aggressive, pushing the norms of their repertoire into behaviors that Monica had always wanted to try but was unwilling to initiate because she considered them "wicked." More importantly, the tone of their interactions, both sexual and nonsexual, became more mature. He finally stopped trying to please his wife and started being with her when they made love. The frequency and duration of their sexual encounters increased, reflecting their growing mutual satisfaction and Monica's pleasure in seeing the change in her marriage and reclaiming her home.

In their second sexual encounter after Ted's mother's relocation to the other end of the house, Monica reached orgasm. Within 3 months, their relationship was in better shape than it had been in all the years past. They continued in treatment, pursuing their own individual development and seeing how good their sex and intimacy could get.

## Dyspareunia

Although painful intercourse (dyspareunia) can occur in men (e.g., as a result of Peyronie's disease or prostate inflammation), it is more common in women (e.g., resulting from endometriosis, tipped uterus, micro-inflammation of secreting glands in the vaginal walls, or pelvic inflammatory disease). Treatment requires urological/gynecological examination, resolution of contributory physical conditions, and help for the individual/couple in rebuilding a sexual ambiance focused on relaxed pleasure rather than anticipated pain. Modification of sexual technique is often involved.

### CASE VIGNETTE

Mary's dyspareunia had the most frequent cause: Her husband Joe rushed her into intercourse before she was sufficiently aroused. Rejecting condescending advice from her obstetrician-gynecologist to "have a few drinks before sex," she sought treatment from a sex therapist. Initial evaluation revealed why Mary's requests for Joe to "slow down" went unheeded: As is often the case, Joe pushed for rapid penetration as a solution to his own problem with rapid ejaculation. In their relationship in general, Joe decided when things happened. He was defensive about his own sexual competency and somewhat resistant to treatment.

The therapist began by pointing out that their pattern was extremely common and brought forward the differentiation issues being played out sexually by both partners. Mary "didn't have an answer" as to why she had not taken control of her own body and refused coitus until she was ready. The problem was framed as her needing to decide whether or not she was willing to stop turning herself over to Joe and claim ownership of her vagina (and her life). One way or another, she would find out the an-

swer to her "unanswered question," and/or stop having pain during intercourse.

To maintain a similar (balanced) alliance with Joe, the therapist encouraged him to do what he thought was in his own best interest: to pressure Mary for intercourse or to learn to control himself (sexually and otherwise) so that he did not have to control her. Instead of trying to feel adequate by becoming an expert on vaginas (which, of course, he could never be), Joe was offered help in becoming an expert on developing prolonged ejaculatory control.

The therapist talked with awe about the complex changes that occur as women become aroused ("tenting" of the vagina, rising of the cervix to avoid contact with the penis, lubrication starting at the back of the vagina rather than at introitus), and how men's common attempts to delay ejaculation by reducing pleasure can lead to erectile problems. This increased the clients' appreciation of the need to respect their own processes and created curiosity where only anxiety had been.

Creating room for both spouses to increase their expertise and status, both in bed and in therapy, made them more eager for treatment and changed the tone of their sexual engagements. Their genital function, sexual satisfaction, and length and density of physical stimulation during sex all increased, as did their self-esteem and self-concept. Power hierarchies between them were rebalanced, both in and out of bed.

## Vaginismus

Vaginismus involves involuntary spasm and contraction of the sphincter surrounding the opening to the vagina, making penetration painful and difficult (or impossible). In severe cases, vaginismus occurs globally (e.g., during gynecologic exams and tampon insertion); more commonly, it is specific to intercourse.

Vaginismus is a conditioned response to real or anticipated pain, often occurring in response to rape, repeated dyspareunia, and sexual abuse. Antisexual indoctrination can contribute to vaginismus through horror stories of painful intercourse, sex guilt (diminishing arousal and lubrication), and ineffective sexual technique. Relationship hostility is a common result and subsequent sustaining factor of vaginismus.

Theories of unconscious causation (e.g., hatred of men, penis envy, desire to castrate) lack empirical validity. The first effective treatments, developed in the 1960s and 1970s, were behavioral therapies acting directly on the vaginal sphincter by the self-insertion of dildos of increasing size into the vagina (see Kaplan, 1974; or Kolodny, Masters, & Johnson, 1979). Treatment success was often reported higher than 90% (e.g., Kolodny et al., 1979; Masters & Johnson, 1970), although this is not supported by many clinicians' experience (e.g., Leiblum, Pervin, & Campbell, 1989).

### CASE VIGNETTE

*Mary had already been unsuccessful with her prior therapist, who recommended the common dilator program. Instructions to go on to the next larger dilator when she could insert the current one without discomfort sometimes felt like "self-rape" to Mary. It seemed that treatment was for her partner's benefit—stretching her vagina so his penis could be inserted. She resented her husband Richard's attitude that her vagina should be available to him upon demand, which seemed consistent with the therapist's program.*

*Her next therapist, instead, reaffirmed Mary's right to have nothing in her vagina she did not want, regardless of the consequences. Taking the stance of supporting each partner's prerogatives, and "refusing to sell out one spouse's option to the other," the therapist also helped Mary confront the reality that although Richard did not have the right to push her into having intercourse, that did not mean he had to wait around forever. As a result, Mary was less focused on Richard's expectations and more motivated to make progress for her own reasons.*

*Like many women, Mary was uncomfortable and embarrassed about her vagina. Although she did not like Richard's acting as if it belonged to him, she was not sure she wanted ownership and responsibility for it herself. Mary was offered help learning to extract pleasure from her own body.*

*During solitary sex, Mary began with genital self-examination using a mirror and learned to masturbate to orgasm with clitoral stimulation. With a growing sense of self-mastery and sexual maturity, Mary experimented by adding insertion of one, two, and then three fingers into her vagina during masturbation. Fingers were recommended over dildos for increased sensory control and for confronting herself to accept her own vagina. Most importantly, Mary stopped focusing on pain or on inserting things into her vagina without pain. She started focusing on how she could make her vagina feel as good as possible. As she became adept at this, her frame of reference shifted from anticipated pain to foreseen pleasure.*

*Throughout this period, the therapist carefully monitored the reported ambiance of the interactions. At the outset, the couple focused on noninsertive forms of stimulation during mutual contact such as oral sex (to which both were regularly orgasmic). Mary was challenged to maintain the same delicious sense of self-control she had during masturbation even when Richard had his penis inside her. Mary, and not Richard, determined the pace, depth, and duration in which coitus was gradually introduced. Richard feared losing Mary's sexual interest and access to her vagina if she became proficient at masturbation. His fears were soothed by Mary's becoming willing to masturbate in front of him, which they both found to be "daring" and highly erotic. He was somewhat in awe of Mary's progress and noted she was more willing to "stick with him" in their arguments. As she be-*

came more interested in prolonged intercourse, he requested help with developing increased ejaculatory control.

## Erectile Dysfunction

Commonly referred to as "impotence" (the equally pejorative counterpart to "frigidity" for women), erectile dysfunction (ED) can be primary (i.e., lifelong, and never permitting completion of sexual intercourse), or secondary (i.e., intercourse has been completed on previous occasions). Primary ED in adult men is usually due to organic conditions and/or very severe personality disorders. Secondary ED, like secondary anorgasmia for women, is a near universal experience for men, and the two share similar etiological possibilities.

Men are often vague in reporting their sexual difficulty. Given this, the clinician must conduct a very explicit interview to achieve a clear diagnosis. When a patient complains of not getting an erection it may mean (a) no degree of tumescence occurs at any point during sex, which is suggestive of organic etiology; (b) becoming flaccid after some degree of erection; or (c) maintaining a semihard erection throughout the encounter. Causes of the latter two patterns can be organic (e.g., vascular leakage in the penis, diabetes, alcoholism), and/or psychogenic (i.e., insufficient ongoing stimulation, increased distraction and anxiety at start of intercourse). *Intermittent* secondary ED is more suggestive of situational and psychological involvement.

### CASE VIGNETTE

Steve felt obliged to "satisfy" his wife—which, to their way of thinking, meant bringing her to orgasm with his penis during intercourse. He had no difficulty with erections while receiving oral sex but almost invariably did during coitus. Usually it happened at the moment of insertion or shortly thereafter—the most common time for a man to loose his erection.

Gail interpreted this as Steve's being interested only in his own pleasure. Over years of repeated sexual frustration, they were alienated and constantly defensive with each other. Although each blamed the other in their frequent fights, both secretly felt increasingly inept, undesirable, and undesired.

In response to his wife's pressure, Steve tried to insert his penis as soon as he was erect, hoping to bring his wife to orgasm before he lost his erection. During oral sex, which occurred less and less often, Steve could focus on his own sensations and relax. This was "for him." Intercourse gradually became defined as "for Gail," and accordingly, Steve tried to move his penis "for her" the moment he inserted it. His sole focus was "keeping it up until she's done."

In presenting the issue as emotional growth and differentiation, the therapist clarified Steve's choice between inserting his penis when his wife "expected" it and doing so when he was ready. It was also suggested that they use female superior position so he could lie back and not have to awkwardly balance himself and attempt insertion at the same moment. Gail was somewhat uncomfortable about being on top and claimed this was his responsibility. It took some time for Steve to master himself in the face of Gail's pressure, but when confronted with his steadfast refusal to mount her, Gail eventually addressed her own sexual discomforts about "taking the lead during sex."

Treatment involved increasing length and intensity of stimulation prior to penetration and open communication about readiness for coitus during each sexual encounter. The therapist pointed out that the couple lost emotional contact with each other during intercourse. They were encouraged to do only those things that permitted them to maintain their sense of intimacy and connection during sex. Gradually, they mastered a variety of sexual positions and techniques, finally adding intercourse to the list.

In the course of treatment, Steve revealed that his father was pressuring him to quit his job in order to join the father's business. Steve's mother emphasized that his father needed Steve so he could avoid bringing outsiders into executive positions and intimated that Steve's inheritance from them would be greatly reduced if he "did not see what needs to be done and do it." Using the same sexual metaphor from earlier in treatment, Steve decided that he needed to use himself "his way" and "not plug myself into somebody else's empty space just because they want the use of me."

## Delayed Ejaculation

Although delayed ejaculation (inhibited male orgasm), like rapid ejaculation, is an almost universal occasional experience, chronic versions of rapid ejaculation are about four times more common than difficulty ejaculating at all. Sometimes referred to by the derogatory labels "retarded ejaculation" or "ejaculatory incompetence," delayed ejaculation refers to a man's difficulty in reaching orgasmic threshold. Primary (i.e., lifelong) inability to ejaculate is extremely rare. More frequently, delayed ejaculation is a situational or intermittent problem. It generally appears as difficulty reaching orgasm during extended, and often arduous, intercourse (although it can occur during other behaviors). Penile thrusting often becomes mechanical, solely focused on reaching orgasm and avoiding "failure." Some men with this difficulty try to reframe it as "great staying power," but intercourse is often so pleasureless that many begin to avoid sexual encounters.

In delayed ejaculation, anxiety appears to be a critical interference with reaching orgasmic threshold. Why this same anxiety appears to cause rapid ejaculation in other men is not known. In rare individuals, the two problems may alternate. Treatment generally involves increasing anxiety tolerance, reducing anxiety, increasing effective stimulation, and increasing emotional connection. Men with delayed ejaculation are often "off in another world during sex," cut off from their partner by silent ruminations and monitoring the clock. A gay male couple, Phillip and Glenn, were treated as follows.

### CASE VIGNETTE

Phillip was often sore and found sex painful by the time Glenn was sometimes able to reach orgasm. About half the time Glenn thrust to the point of exhaustion without success. After a while, both partners began to anticipate Glenn's pattern. He often could ejaculate within about 5 minutes of coitus or oral sex without difficulty. If it went longer than about 10 minutes, both became increasingly convinced (and anxious) he would not achieve orgasm at all. At that point, Glenn would begin to thrust faster and harder, thinking that more friction would produce enough stimulation to trigger his orgasm. Phillip began to recognize this movement as an act of desperation, and would lose all interest. He lay passive, allowing Glenn to bring himself to orgasm inside him if he could. Glenn could sense Phillip's lack of involvement, which only added to his mounting pressure to "get it over with." With each repetition, Glenn became more concerned that Phillip would leave him for another man.

The therapist showed Glenn how his request that Phillip make a commitment not to leave, despite its apparent logic, would make him only more dependent on Phillip and more insecure. Instead, the therapist suggested that Glenn stop focusing on his feelings of inadequacy and stop trying to prove himself with his penis. Capitalizing on Glenn's prior success in coming out to his parents after years of fearing their disappointment about his sexuality (by being gay), the therapist suggested that the current issue of apologizing for himself for not being able to ejaculate was much the same. Glenn began to approach their sexual interactions as matters of self-respect and self-acceptance. Phillip resonated with this viewpoint and became a more willing and involved partner.

The connection between them during sex became the focus. This involved decreasing *distractions, increasing stimulation by slow thrusting, and having Phillip take Glenn's face in his hands and talk to him while methodical movement produced the sense of being "in synch."*

## Desire Disorders

Shortly after Lief (1977) coined the term *inhibited sexual desire*, Kaplan (1979) introduced the concepts of a "desire phase" and desire-phase disorders. Although this model was a major advance in recognizing issues of sexual desire, it presents significant clinical problems. Its major deficit is that it views sexual desire as a biological drive, assumed to be present unless suppressed by pathology of one sort or another. In this drive-reduction model, the need for sex is compared to the need for food and water, and inhibited sexual desire is described as a kind of "sexual anorexia." Aside from subtly pressuring people to want sex, the model focuses on impersonal sexual desire rather than desire for one's partner—both of which unfortunately create low sexual desire in many couples. Moreover, the notion of a desire *phase* encourages therapists to conceptualize desire solely as eagerness to start having sex (a view perpetuated in *DSM-III-R* and *DSM-IV*; American Psychiatric Association, 1987, 1994) and blocks consideration of desire as passion throughout the encounter.

The quantum model, by contrast, considers desire and intimacy *during* sex. To do this, it is necessary to go beyond conceptualizing desire disorders as nothing more than the inhibition of an impersonal biological drive to seek sex, and to recognize the strength (differentiation) required to love and *want* your partner.

*CASE VIGNETTE*

*Bill and Jeanne, a couple in their late 30s, sought treatment for his lack of sexual desire. They had been married for approximately 5 years, during which time he demonstrated progressively declining interest in sex with her. They had not had sex in the last 4 months, and had done so only three times in the preceding year. During this time both masturbated privately. Although*

*each knew that the other was masturbating, they avoided talking about it.*

*This was Jeanne's first marriage, and Bill's second. His first marriage ended when he discovered his wife's affair with his best friend. The fact that she was often sexually indifferent and uninspired in bed with Bill made the affair even harder to endure.*

*Just before meeting Jeanne, Bill became involved with a married woman, who eventually terminated the affair in an abrupt and crude manner. He had become totally obsessed with her and had bowed to her requests that he terminate other dating relationships. He had a robust sexual relationship with this woman, far beyond anything he'd experienced before. Although he had qualms about interfering in another family, they were far weaker than this burning passion.*

*Bill met Jeanne on the rebound 2 months after the breakup. She supported him through his depression, and they married 6 months later. She had little relationship experience with other men and was grateful for Bill's acceptance and trust. He was also by far her best sexual partner to date. Bill enjoyed the way she thrilled to his touch and the adoration she showered on him.*

*However, their estrangement had grown in the last year to the point that divorce was increasingly likely. Jeanne pushed for an explanation of his seeming indifference and irritability with her, but Bill had "nothing to say." During an argument, he finally announced he had lost all sexual desire for her but had not told her in an effort to "spare her feelings." Eventually they agreed to seek treatment to determine whether their marriage could be saved.*

*At the outset of the evaluation, Bill claimed no understanding about why he did not want sex with his wife. Inquiry about circumstances at the time they met disclosed his first divorce and his unhappy* affair. In response to Bill's statement that the problem was his lack of sexual feelings for Jeanne, the therapist noted that although it could be seen as the problem, it could also be seen as his failed attempt to reach a personal solution. Dumbfounded, curious, and wary, Bill asked what the therapist meant.

The therapist suggested the "problem" might be a fundamental dynamic of their relationship. Was Bill's selection of his wife, in part, an attempt to pick a partner he did not find extremely sexually appealing, and who would not stimulate a desire so strong that he might "lose himself," as he had done previously?

The therapist then raised the question of "who really chose whom?" Jeanne felt that Bill had never really chosen her. She chose him, and he married her because he did not have to choose and thus become vulnerable again. She remembered how he had kept her wondering if he would really marry her. After a brief display of interest immediately preceding their engagement, Bill had become increasingly withdrawn as the wedding approached. Her realization that she had never been "picked" validated her intuitive experience, but the ensuing self-confrontation was painful and sobering. Jeanne finally reached a decisive turning point in her life: She could not settle for "second class status" and keep her integrity. Being "accepted" was not enough. She wanted someone who wanted her.

Bill did not really want Jeanne, but he did not want to be without her either. Confronting herself as much as her spouse, she announced she was not going to beg him to want her. She was temporarily willing to continue their relationship, but she was not willing to seduce him or take responsibility for motivating him. "Wishing" that he wanted her because it would make her happy and stabilize things was not enough. Bill would have to want her for herself,

and he would have to want her because he wanted to want her.

Bill expected the therapist to try to make him want her, which the therapist explicitly declined to do. Instead, the therapist pointed out that Bill's "not wanting to want" made sense, given his experiences with his first wife's affair, his own disastrous affair, and his mother's death during his early adolescence. "Not wanting to want" was an understandable response, but not one that would allow him to stay married. The therapist maintained that Bill had a right not to want his wife, just as she had a right to be with someone who really wanted her.

The imminent possibility of a separation seemed to shake Bill. In conjoint sessions, he talked about his mother's death and his disappointment in his father, who quickly "disappeared" into a subsequent marriage to a younger woman. The therapist suggested that Bill had firsthand knowledge of the pain of really desiring someone and the strength it takes to love.

Jeanne and Bill's relationship appeared to improve for the next 2 months, and separation seemed less likely. The breakthrough that seemed imminent, however, failed to materialize. They become emotionally closer, but not much more sexually active. Bill had passively gone along in one or two sexual encounters. Jeanne indicated this was no longer enough for her, although she did appreciate their improved communication out of bed. He admitted he found her more interesting since her recent displays of autonomy, but he thought their sex was always bland. He had not had the nerve to reveal that he secretly worried that staying together would condemn him to a life of sexual frustration and that his low sexual desire was his passport out of the marriage.

The therapist then asked Bill whether he could have sex with his wife the way he *really wanted to. Jeanne said that she did not think of it as having sex and much preferred the phrase "making love." Bill sheepishly acknowledged that he knew what the therapist was talking about, and said he could not "do that with her," although it was what really turned him on in his prior affair. Bill then revealed to Jeanne a previously hidden aspect of his eroticism: his enjoyment of "doing someone" and "being done." It was hard for him to share that with someone he believed was so proper and conventional. Jeanne then disclosed that she too wanted their encounters to be a little more experimental and "rambunctious," but had always deferred to the sexual tone he set. Shocked to hear that she was interested in the "hard-core sex" he secretly craved, Bill was also surprised to see his own resistance when she was willing to give it a try. Now it was his own holding back that prevented it from happening.*

*Subsequent treatment shifted to two interlocking individual questions: Could Bill "put his heart where he put his penis" (rather than "learning to want his wife")? This involved developing a mature acceptance of both his own and Jeanne's eroticism and integrating it with his needs for both nurturance (expressed by him as "being done") and autonomy (expressed as "doing"). It also confronted him with his fear of loss and of becoming as dependent on women as his father had been. For Jeanne, the question became, "If I become the person I think I could be, will it end my marriage?"*

*The style of their subsequent sexual encounters changed markedly over the next year of treatment. Sex became increasingly athletic and adventurous. At one point, they experimented with taking turns gently but firmly tying up and "doing" one another. In the course of increasingly deeply engaged sexual encounters, Jeanne was surprised to discover her own hips moving automatically during intercourse while on top*

*of Bill. Their intense emotional connection was such that her pelvis just moved in concert with their union. Bill felt challenged to keep pace with her sexual growth and responded with a productive sense of competitiveness and aggression. The result fueled both their sexual interest and their self-esteem.*

## ENHANCING DIFFERENTIATION AND ANXIETY TOLERANCE

Not all cases flow as neatly as the foregoing examples might suggest. Dealing with people, and not just their genitals, is complex, and the journey to sexual maturity is difficult. The effectiveness of the approach outlined here lies in its multidimensional impact. This approach differs from traditional sexual therapy in its focus on enhancing anxiety tolerance and personal growth rather than anxiety reduction. Although it may take longer than traditional sex therapy, it must be remembered that its goal is broad, second-order change in the couple's intimacy system.

If we examine each of the case histories cited, we can see how various aspects of differentiation permeate sexuality and intimacy in long-term relationships. Differentiation was part of the problem in each case, shaped the intervention strategy, and was the natural outcome of resolving the presenting sexual difficulties. Enhancing differentiation involves more than critical self-reflection and insight. It involves *doing* something.

The demonstrated multisystemic approach harnesses the processes that drive marital systems, thereby helping people use their sexuality to grow to the point where they are truly capable of loving. In other words, this health-based (vs. pathology-based) approach employs the natural, but at times unpleasant, developmental process of marriage. Intimacy problems and sexual boredom are inevitable when spouses' level of differentiation does not keep pace with the ever-growing importance of the partner. Such common marital complaints are both the stimulus and the vehicle for enhancing differentiation.

Following is a list of strategies that, although frequently employed, may lead to an impasse in sexual–marital therapy because they do not enhance differentiation and may unintentionally trigger increased fusion:

- contracting
- bans on intercourse
- constructed paradoxical suggestions
- alignment with "the relationship" or "the marriage" as client
- aligning with the therapy-positive spouse to counterbalance a partner reluctant for therapy
- empathizing or commiserating with clients' pain, particularly when they're in an emotional regression
- pacing therapy so clients do not become "nervous," and thus ultimately letting the least-differentiated partner control the therapy through his or her anxiety (as that partner has done in their marriage)
- encouraging negotiation and compromise over disparate sexual frequency or preferences and/or marital disputes

Although widely accepted, these stratagems often involve an undifferentiated therapeutic stance and encourage emotional fusion in poorly differentiated clients. It is no coincidence that traditional treatment is often antithetical to differentiation, because differentiation (like systemics and intimacy) has generally been outside the purview of sex therapy.

By contrast, increased differentiation has the following impacts:

- Self-soothing one's own anxieties optimizes the receiver's internal processes during sex, reducing the likelihood of distractions and dysfunctions.
- Partners are better able to recover from disappointments and occasional dysfunctions with only minor residual impact.
- Spouses are less affected by their partner's anxiety and pressure to conform; they are more able to push the boundaries of sexual norms in their relationship, increasing self-disclosure through display of eroticism, decreasing sexual boredom, and facilitating more depth of involvement in sex (greater tolerance for intimacy).
- There is increased shift from other-validated to self-validated intimacy; less dependence on lock-

step mutuality and acceptance from one's partner; and less susceptibility to manipulation, threats, and withholding.

- Decisions about sexual behavior are more likely to be based on reason and well-modulated feelings rather than emotional reactivity or the need to reduce anxiety; the relationship is steered by partners' unique strengths rather than their lowest common denominator.

Differentiation also allows people to want or to choose their partner, conveying a uniqueness that makes oneself vulnerable to the threat of loss from emotional extortion or life's illnesses and accidents.

## THE THERAPIST'S LEVEL OF DIFFERENTIATION

Clinicians are no better equipped to have wonderful relationships than are others. Almost nothing in professional training provides therapists with greater knowledge of or capacity for intense intimacy or eroticism than the people they treat. Lacking this, the therapeutic tendency to avoid explicit sexual topics and the realities of profound intimacy is common. Unfortunately, treating couples' systemic issues to the exclusion of their sexual content is unlikely to produce the desired change. The multisystemic approach requires that the therapist be extremely sensitive to his or her own sexual values system and address unresolved differentiation issues in his or her sexual/intimate relationship.

A major part of the therapist's differentiation involves risking standing apart from many contemporary practices. The therapist's level of differentiation also plays a more direct role in treatment. Couples have to get to "critical mass" in order for personal metamorphosis (differentiation) to occur. Often, the threat of separation or divorce is omnipresent. Clearly facing this threat helps to keep couples from endless and cyclical impasses. As a cycle is broken, intense anxiety is often generated. The therapist must be able to stand the emotional heat as this occurs.

A therapist cannot bring clients to a higher level of differentiation than he or she has reached. When the therapist's level of anxiety tolerance and emotional nonreactivity is exceeded, interventions may be more determined by the therapist's anxiety rather than well-thought-out solutions.

## A FINAL WORD

It is an awesome experience to witness couples' integrity and courage to love one another on life's own terms. It is something that professional training rarely prepares therapists for. The stretching they experience as therapists is one of the blessings and trials of helping couples reach their potential, both sexual and otherwise—and helps them reach their own.

## References

American Psychiatric Association. (1987). *Diagnostic and statistical manual of mental disorders* (3rd ed.). Washington, DC: Author.

American Psychiatric Association. (1994). *Diagnostic and statistical manual of mental disorders* (4th ed.). Washington, DC: Author.

Apfelbaum, B. (1977). On the etiology of sexual dysfunction. *Journal of Sex and Marital Therapy, 3*(1), 50–62.

Bowen, M. (1978). Family therapy in clinical practice. New York: Jason Aronson.

DeAmicis, L. A., Goldberg, D. C., LoPiccolo, J., Friedman, J., & Davies, L. (1985). Clinical follow-up of couples treated for sexual dysfunction. *Archives of Sexual Behavior, 14*, 467–489.

Ellis, A. (1962). *Reason and emotion in psychotherapy.* New York: Stuart.

Freud, S. (1986). Three essays on the theory of sexuality. In A. Freud (Ed.) and J. Strachey (Trans.), *The essentials of psycho-analysis.* London: Hogarth Press and The Institute of Psycho-Analysis. (Original work published 1905)

Hartman, W. E., & Fithian, M. A. (1972). *Treatment of sexual dysfunction.* Long Beach, CA: Center for Marital and Sexual Studies.

Kaplan, H. S. (1974). *The new sex therapy.* New York: Brunner/Mazel.

Kaplan, H. S. (1979). *Disorders of sexual desire and other new concepts and techniques in sex therapy.* New York: Brunner/Mazel.

Kaplan, H. S. (1983). *The evaluation of sexual disorders: Psychological and medical aspects.* New York: Brunner/Mazel.

Kilmann, P. R., Boland, J. P., Norton, S. P., Davidson, E., & Caid, C. (1986). Perspectives on sex therapy outcome: A survey of AASECT providers. *Journal of Sex and Marital Therapy, 12*, 116–138.

Kolodny, R. C., Masters, W. H., & Johnson, V. E. (1979). *Textbook of sexual medicine.* Boston: Little, Brown.

Lazarus, A. A. (1965). The treatment of a sexually inadequate man. In L. P. Ullmann & L. Krasner (Eds.), *Case studies in behavior modification.* New York: Holt Rinehart.

Leiblum, S. R., & Pervin, L. A. (Eds.). (1980). *Principles and practice of sex therapy.* New York: Guilford Press.

Leiblum, S. R., Pervin, L. A., & Campbell, E. H. (1989). The treatment of vaginismus: Success and failure. In S. R. Leiblum & R. C. Rosen (Eds.), *Principles and practice of sex therapy* (2nd ed., pp. 113–138). New York: Guilford Press.

Leiblum, S. R., & Rosen, R. C. (Eds.). (1988). *Sexual desire disorders.* New York: Guilford Press.

Lief, H. (1977). What's new in sex research? Inhibited sexual desire. *Medical Aspects of Human Sexuality, 7*, 94–95.

LoPiccolo, J., & Friedman, J. (1988). Broad-spectrum treatment of low sexual desire: Integration of cognitive, behavioral, and systemic therapy. In S. R. Leiblum & R. C. Rosen (Eds.), *Sexual desire disorders* (pp. 107–144). New York: Guilford Press.

LoPiccolo, J., & Lobitz, W. C. (1972). The role of masturbation in the treatment of orgasmic dysfunction. *Archives of Sexual Behavior, 2*(2), 163–171.

Mahler, M. S. (1968). *On human symbiosis and the vicissitudes of individuation.* New York: International Universities Press.

Mason, M. J. (1991). Family therapy as the emerging context for sex therapy. In A. S. Gurman & D. P. Kniskern (Eds.), *Handbook of family therapy* (Vol. 2, pp. 478–507). New York: Brunner/Mazel.

Masters, W. H., & Johnson V. E. (1966). *Human sexual response.* Boston: Little, Brown.

Masters, W. H., & Johnson, V. E. (1970). *Human sexual inadequacy.* New York: Little, Brown.

Peter, L. J. (1980). *Peter's quotations: Ideas for our time.* New York: Bantam Books.

Salter, A. (1949). *Conditioned reflex therapy.* New York: Creative Age Press.

Schnarch, D. M. (1991). *Constructing the sexual crucible: An integration of sexual and marital therapy.* New York: Norton.

Schover, L., & LoPiccolo, J. (1982). Effectiveness of treatment for dysfunctions of sex desire. *Journal of Sex and Marital Therapy, 8*(3), 179–197.

Semans, J. H. (1956). Premature ejaculation: A new approach. *Southern Medical Journal, 49*, 353–357.

Stone Fish, L., Fish, R. C., & Sprenkle, D. H. (1984). Treating inhibited sexual desire: A marital therapy approach. *The American Journal of Family Therapy, 12*, 3–12.

Verhulst, J., & Heiman, J. R. (1979). An interactional approach to sexual dysfunctions. *The American Journal of Family Therapy, 7,* 19–36.

Verhulst, J., & Heiman, J. R. (1988). A systems perspective on sexual desire. In S. R. Leiblum & R. C. Rosen (Eds.), *Sexual desire disorders.* New York: Guilford Press.

Wolpe, J. (1969). *The practice of behavior therapy.* New York: Pergamon.

# CHAPTER 14

# TREATING MARITAL INFIDELITY

*Don-David Lusterman*

Extramarital affairs have captured the public imagination for centuries. Literature, theater, opera, and film abound with tales of the compelling excitement and the destructive power of such liaisons.

It is my belief that a good understanding of the dynamics of lengthy extramarital affairs (Lusterman, 1989) enables the skilled couples therapist to extrapolate to other related types of extramarital issues. For this reason, I begin by examining the treatment of protracted marital infidelity and then describe the traumatic effects of its discovery. I suggest an intervention model that enables both members of the couple to move beyond the trauma of discovery so the ground can be prepared to explore the marital relationship and its potential for change. I then discuss the clinician's role in the treatment of undiscovered infidelity.

A lengthy extramarital affair causes a remarkable degree of trauma for the discoverer, and often for the other involved parties. The initial therapeutic session with a couple following discovery is typically painful and dramatic. The rage expressed by the mate who has discovered the infidelity seems to suffuse the room. The profound sense of betrayal is both enraging and debilitating for the discoverer. It is not unusual to see a rapid succession of conflicting emotions. At one moment the discoverer may jump out of the chair, ready to strike the offending mate. At another, he or she may sob disconsolately. The mate who has been involved in the affair appears little more comfortable. She or he is by turns apologetic, defensive, and angry. Frequently there is a plea to continue the marriage, but often it is coupled with a demand that there be no further mention of the affair. The affair-involved mate may attempt to justify the affair by describing the problems in the marriage. This generally serves to further upset the mate who has discovered the affair, because it is seen as an attempt to justify the betrayal. To understand more fully the trauma of discovery, it is useful to place marital infidelity into its larger social context.

## THE FREQUENCY OF MARITAL INFIDELITY

Some authorities hold that, given the supposed frequency with which extramarital sex (EMS) occurs, it is hard to understand why its discovery causes such strong emotions (Finzi, 1989). There is indeed an abundance of estimates over the course of many years indicating a high degree of EMS, a notion that supports the public imagination. However, the figures cited by various authorities vary widely. This may be a result of sampling differences, or there may be some fluctuation over the course of time as societal values and mores shift and change. Kinsey and his colleagues (1948) estimated that 50% of husbands and 26% of wives (Kinsey, Pomeroy, Martin, & Gebhard, 1953) have engaged in EMS at some point in their marriage. Glass and Wright (1992) compared categories, which they named *primarily sexual, primarily emotional,* and *combined-type involvement.* They found that, for both men and women, combined-type involvement is correlated with the lowest marital satisfaction scores. They found that 44% of husbands and 25% of wives have engaged in at least one EMS experience. There are still lower estimates. Greeley (1991) estimates that fewer than 10% of marriage partners have been unfaithful. The General Social Surveys of The National Opinion Research Center (Smith, 1993) conducts an annual full-proba-bility survey. Over the past 5 years, it has included a self-completion form on sexual behavior, with an an-nual sample of more than 1,200 respondents. This study found that roughly 15% of individuals married at the time of the survey or ever married had sexual relations with a person other than their spouse while married. This included 21% of men and 12% of women. Because this finding has been replicated nu-merous times over a 5-year period, it appears to be particularly robust. Although the overall percentage of any sort of EMS reported in this survey is remark-ably low, there is reason to believe that it is a valid estimate.

Almost all surveys report that men are considera-bly more likely than women to engage in extramari-tal sex of any sort. One conjecture is that many of the married men's experiences may have been with prostitutes. Because one prostitute may see many cli-ents per day, the number of men engaging in EMS increases accordingly. Additionally, it is well estab-lished that many fewer women than men engage in EMS with prostitutes. Therapists are likely to find themselves treating more couples in which men are accused of cheating by their wives than the reverse. This may be because many men will simply leave the marriage rather than work through the problem, whereas many more women, for a variety of reasons, are likely to attempt to salvage the marriage. This may be a function of the power differential between men and women, or it may be because women often feel that they are more responsible for relationship issues than are men. (See chap. 17 in this volume.)

There appears to be no research in which the length and intensity of EMS has been systematically studied. The term itself is misleading, since it en-compasses many types of behavior. A single experi-ment with a prostitute, a one-night stand on a busi-ness trip, and an extramarital affair that has lasted as long as or even longer than the marriage itself would all be considered examples of EMS. It is my conten-tion that these events are not on a continuum and in fact represent very different marital issues. To cite but a few instances, a person may experiment with prostitution out of curiosity, or engage in a one-night stand or a brief fling while away at a conference un-der different social rules, often including sanctions for increased indulgence in alcohol or other drugs. A lengthy affair, in contrast, is intense and includes a heavy emotional involvement. It is safe to assume that such a relationship at the very least fills some perceived lacuna in the marital relationship.

Our present surveys do not differentiate among types of EMS, so there is no way of accurately esti-mating the portion that is accounted for by any spe-cific subtype. Given the current findings that EMS in general is a relatively rare event, the oft-heard state-ment that protracted marital infidelity is a very com-mon event seems unfounded.

## PROTRACTED MARITAL INFIDELITY

A number of authors have devised interesting typolo-gies of EMS (Brown, 1991; Charny, 1992; Humphrey, 1982; Lawson, 1988; Moultrup, 1990; Pittman, 1989). They describe a range of behaviors: brief sex-ual encounters; lengthy relationships that may be emotionally intense and erotically charged, but are not necessarily sexual; and lengthy affairs that are both emotionally and sexually charged.

The person engaged in what I term *protracted marital infidelity* (PMI) is obsessed with the object of his or her infatuation and quickly becomes involved in an ever-widening web of deception that, over time, inevitably increases the emotional distance with the mate. The mate is often unaware of the affair at first, although it may be increasingly evident to oth-ers. Persistent questioning and insistent denial only increase the outpouring of rage following discovery.

The therapist's first contact after the discovery may be with only one mate or with the couple. I am limiting my description at this point to *discovered* in-fidelity, although the phenomenon that I am describ-ing has important treatment implications for the therapist struggling with *undiscovered* infidelity, which is discussed later. It should be noted that the inten-sity of the extramarital relationship and the necessity for persistent deception produce particularly vexing problems for husband, wife, and therapist. The fear-some rage exhibited by the discoverer derives not only from the breach of intimacy inherent in PMI, but even more from the persistent lying that is its inevitable accompaniment.

To understand the rage, we need to place the discovery in its context. An examination of almost any marriage ceremony, at least within Western culture, reveals that the issue of trust and fidelity is at the heart of the marital contract. Indeed, the marriage begins with a legal, public, and often religious declaration of this fidelity, usually in the presence of family and friends. Kaslow and Hammerschmidt (1992) surveyed a sample of "good" marriages and reported that among the factors that such couples considered most important were "trust in each other that includes fidelity, integrity and feeling 'safe'," and "permanent commitment to the marriage" (p. 35). There is little reason to believe that most couples undertaking a commitment to marriage expect any less. Yet, in the case of PMI, one party has proceeded on the assumption that the relationship is founded on mutual trust, while the other has consistently violated that trust over a considerable period of time.

A person who has been betrayed feels an overwhelming sense of hurt because someone else has gotten what is rightfully that person's, and thus feels appropriately aggrieved, angry, and deprived. There is also the sense that something has been taken away and can never be retrieved, whether it be time, the sharing of intimate secrets, or enjoyment—in fact, the sum of all of the shared experience of marriage. Many people report a sense of shame, feeling that they have come up wanting in the eyes of their mate and a third party, or that many other people have become aware of the affair. These are all issues relating to the proprietary nature of marriage, which may be defined as the acceptance by both parties of the idea that, together, they "own" their marriage and share certain "secrets" to which others are not privy. The normative assumption is that this is a history that belongs to the couple and can only be shared by the couple. In this sense, part of the hurt of the affair is the breaking of the bond and boundary that every couple establishes as part of its definition of its own, unique couplehood.

## Choice of Terminology

Not every EMS fits the description of PMI. For example, two people may agree that their marriage is bereft of emotional and/or sexual satisfaction and accept extramarital relationships as part of a new con-

tract. If we mean by *fidelity* faithfulness to the marital contract, then such "arrangements" (Pittman, 1989) do not qualify as PMI because there is no deception. Nor does a single, brief "fling" that ends quickly and is *never* repeated. Such flings often end immediately because of guilt about betraying the mate. Humphrey (1987) categorizes types of EMS by the following criteria:

- Time
- Degree of emotional involvement
- Sexual intercourse or abstinence
- Secret or not
- Single or bilateral EMS
- Heterosexual or homosexual

This is a useful schema. I would suggest an additional criterion: the number of EMS partners. Using these criteria, for example, a philanderer might be described as having sexual intercourse with many partners, usually with the absence of emotional involvement. Generally speaking, the time for each encounter is brief, and the philandering may or may not be secret.

The discovery that a mate is a philanderer, if it has been well concealed, may produce much the same shock as the discovery of PMI, because it too is protected by a web of lies. It is the protraction and the concatenation of lies that appear to create so much pain. The philanderer, unlike the mate involved in PMI, generally avoids intimacy with any partner and appears to be primarily interested in power over the other person (Pittman, 1993).

A one night stand, by these criteria, would include sexual intercourse, little time, and no emotional involvement and might be either secret or revealed. By comparison, PMI is long term, includes an intense emotional involvement, includes intercourse, and is secret. It may also be either heterosexual or homosexual. (See chap. 18 in this volume.) I choose the term *infidelity* as opposed to the more general term EMS because it conveys the breach-of-faith aspect. For the same reason I call the affair-involved mate the *infidel*, since this term focuses attention on the breaking of faith. Finally, I use the word *victim* to describe the discoverer of infidelity (Lusterman, 1989). This powerful word is chosen because it vividly portrays the experience of the discoverer. It is not intended to deny the many systemic issues that predict the PMI, but to reify the immediate reality of the situation in which the couple finds itself, and to help the couple, or the individual members of the couple, to face what has happened and why it is the cause of so much immediate, and often enduring, pain. The purpose of this labeling is not to keep the discoverer in the victim position, but rather to help the couple to deal with and transcend the traumatic effects of the discovery.

## The Impact of Discovery

As painful as is the moment of discovery, the sequelae are frequently devastating, both to the victim and to the infidel. For example, here is a description of a 60-year-old man who attended therapy with his wife 6 months after he had discovered her infidelity. Immediately upon the discovery, he was treated by a therapist who saw his reaction as one of "pathological jealousy." The patient and his wife were subsequently referred to couples therapy because his "jealous" rages were increasing and his wife feared for her life.

*CASE EXAMPLE*

*Bob Sloane and his wife Rita sought treatment because he felt he could not stop ruminating about her affair. His feelings of suspicion and rage were frightening to both of them. After 3 years of consistent denial, during which she frequently told him he was crazy to have such suspicions, he began to check her behavior on an hour-to-hour basis, and had begun to think of tapping the telephone and hiring a private detective. As he made plans to do so, he discovered some evidence that she had left around, and confronted her once again. This was the first time that she admitted that his fears were correct. He was frightened by the intensity of his own reaction, and felt that his entire world was crashing around him. He felt like a fool because he had continued to believe her protestations of innocence, and questioned whether he could ever trust or love her again, despite her insistence that the affair had ended,*

*and that, more than anything else, she wanted the incident forgotten, and to move ahead with the marriage.*

*Bob was plagued by persistent thoughts about every aspect of her unfaithfulness, constantly discovering more of the lies that had protected the affair. Each new discovery intensified his hurt and rage. Any event that reminded him of any aspect of the affair triggered extreme stress. He walked out of a movie that dealt with the subject. He had to excuse himself from a conversation in which another couple's affair was being discussed because he began to cry. He experienced many dreams, flashbacks to the moment of discovery, and constant intrusive thoughts. He was irritable, had difficulty with sleep, and his concentration was so impaired that it interfered with his work. Above all, he felt that he was in a constant state of hypervigilance. He alternated between a desperate desire to maintain the marriage and constant threats to divorce. He was frequently physically menacing, and a tender exchange could suddenly erupt into an angry outburst.*

## Is the Response Based on Jealousy?

The reaction described above is quite familiar to the clinician who has met with such a patient. Some therapists erroneously label this as jealous behavior. Teisman (1979, 1982) describes this type of patient as the "Jealous Person," and the affair-involved mate as the "Affair Person." He reminds us that these are systemic labels, and reframes both the affair and the jealous behavior as acts that "mask the real pain of longing for an elusive intimacy" (1979). Although one occasionally confronts a marriage in which the issue of pathological jealousy has always played a role, this presents a very different clinical picture and history than the reaction described above. A "pathologically jealous" mate has a long history of unprovoked jealous outbursts, usually tracing back to adolescence. Further investigation often reveals that jealousy was an issue for the jealous partner in previous adult relationships as well. It is probably related to a low level of self-esteem and the consequent fear of loss.

Couples presenting with PMI may occasionally report a prior history of pathological jealousy, which then requires separate treatment for the pathologically jealous mate, concurrent with the marital therapy. In the absence of such a history, we can assume that the victim of PMI is in the throes of a traumatic reaction, which may, understandably, include some "reactive" jealousy. The issue is one of trait versus state. The pathologically jealous mate exemplifies a kind of paranoid personality disorder, whereas the victim's suspicion and jealousy is reactive. In order to understand better the effect of this particular trauma, we will now turn our attention to studies of trauma and Posttraumatic Stress Disorder (PTSD).

## The Psychology of Trauma

PTSD (see chap. 33 in this volume) was first recognized as a diagnostic category in 1980, with the publication of the *Diagnostic and Statistical Manual of Mental Disorders,* third edition (*DSM-III;* American Psychiatric Association, 1980). The fourth edition (American Psychiatric Association, 1994) states, in part:

> *The person has been exposed to a traumatic event in which both of the following were present:*
>
> *(1) the person has experienced, witnessed, or was confronted with an event or events that involved actual or threatened death or serious injury, or a threat to the physical integrity of oneself or others*
>
> *(2) the person's response involved intense fear, helplessness, or horror (pp. 427– 428)*

Additional criteria require that the event be persistently reexperienced and that there be persistent avoidance of stimuli associated with the trauma. Further, there are symptoms of increased arousal and impairment of function.

There has been considerable debate concerning precisely which stressors and what subjective reactions justify the diagnosis of PTSD (March, 1993). Janoff-Bulman (1992) has, over the past 15 years, studied the issue of trauma and its effects. She re-

ports that "regardless of population . . . we have found remarkable similarities across different victim populations. The basis for these similarities is apparent in the words and responses of survivors: The traumatic event has had a profound impact on their fundamental assumptions about the world" (p. 51). She further points out that such a disorder may strike "psychologically healthy individuals" and is not necessarily associated with prior pathology. She reminds us that well-functioning individuals are able to maintain an illusion of invulnerability and that "core assumptions are shattered by the traumatic experience" (p. 52).

The fact that one lives at the edge of a volcano does not prepare one for the psychological impact of its eruption. When our illusions of stability are shattered, we enter the volcano's abyss and are confronted with our own fragility.

Walker (1901) documented the characteristic symptoms of battered women and noted a considerable overlap with PTSD. These symptoms include intrusive memories and flashbacks, dissociative experiences, cognitive disturbances, avoidance behaviors, depression and high arousal (anxiety, phobias, sleeping and eating disorder, sexual dysfunction, and hypervigilance to cues of danger).

It is probable that each type of trauma produces its own unique fingerprint and that each posttraumatic reaction is uniquely related to the trauma that produced it. It is also evident that chronic trauma, such as childhood abuse by a family member, has different consequences (see chap. 28 in this volume) than sudden and acute trauma, such as rape by a stranger. We may also make a distinction between *current* and *post* traumatic reactions. This is often an important issue in the treatment of infidelity, in that persons who experience the trauma of discovery often remain in a chronic state in which they are not sure whether or not the infidelity is ongoing. This uncertainty potentiates the effects of the original and traumatic discovery. It is not surprising, given the nature of the trauma, that the primary reaction appears to be hypervigilance, rather than numbing, although, as a rule, both are present.

A poignant complication in the treatment of the victims of infidelity and their spouses is that, for the most part, the victim does not immediately leave the marriage. Thus, he or she lives day in and day out with persistent stimuli associated with the trauma. These include daily contact with the mate, social contact (in some instances) with the third party, the discovery of new bits of information about the deception, and community gossip. Even in couples who reunite and seem to survive a PMI successfully, it is not unusual for small reminders of the infidel's behavior, such as unexpected lateness in returning home from work, to produce renewed fear on the part of the former victim throughout the course of the marriage. Anniversary phenomena also are frequently found.

Based upon clinical observation, I suggest the following tentative description of the traumatic reaction following the discovery of PMI. This is not meant to suggest a formal diagnosis of PTSD. From a standpoint of a diagnosable condition for third-party payment, a symptom-based diagnosis such as dysthymia, anxiety reaction, or adjustment disorder with mixed features will suffice. Nonetheless, it is useful for both the clinician and patient to be able to name and to describe the events that often follow discovery, and for this reason I have followed the *DSM* format to describe the reaction to discovered infidelity.

*A: The stressor is the discovery of protracted marital infidelity when the "victim" believes that a monogamous contract still obtains.*

*B: The traumatic event is persistently reexperienced in at least one of the following ways:*

*(1) recurrent and intrusive distressing recollections of the event and the many lies that the victim begins to realize preceded the moment of discovery;*

*(2) recurrent distressing dreams;*

*(3) sudden acting or feeling as if the traumatic event were recurring, with particular emphasis on the lying that preceded discovery.*

*C: Obsessive rumination about the affair, its discovery, and the antecedents of the affair, combined with attempts to stop the obsessive ruminations. It is also characterized by an alternating sense of estrangement*

*from the mate, followed by bursts of great need for closeness and reassurance. There is generally a sense of foreboding that the marriage will end, often despite assurances to the contrary.*

*D: Persistent symptoms of increased arousal (not present before the trauma), as indicated by at least two of the following:*

*(1) difficulty falling or staying asleep;*

*(2) irritability or outbursts of anger;*

*(3) difficulty concentrating;*

*(4) hypervigilance;*

*(5) exaggerated startle response;*

*(6) physiologic reactivity upon exposure to events that symbolize or resemble an aspect of the traumatic event (e.g., being unable to watch a TV show or movie about infidelity).*

## TREATMENT ISSUES

### Orienting Couples About the Therapy

I find that it is most useful to educate both the victim and the infidel about this normal and *nonpathological* reaction to discovered infidelity. In fact, most couples find it very reassuring to understand what is happening to them, and this knowledge makes it infinitely easier to begin to restore meaningful communication.

I begin by helping them to understand the nature of the trauma. I then explain that the first task is to begin to heal this wound and that this may be a very difficult process. I indicate to the couple that the purpose of our work will be to help them to change their relationship, and that this may mean moving toward a better marriage *or* toward a better divorce. I define a better divorce as one in which both members of the couple maturely accept responsibility for the failure of the marriage. I explain that this enables the couple to move toward better subsequent relations (postdivorce) with one another and with potential new mates. Such a resolution also reduces the likelihood of destructive litigation and of trapping the children in endless parental anger (see chaps. 15 and 16 in this volume). I also state that there may be a time at which I wish to see one or both of them alone, and should this occur, I will consider the contents of such meetings (although not the fact that they have occurred) to be confidential.

## How Confidentiality Forwards Treatment

The assurance of confidentiality is useful for several reasons. It provides an opportunity to determine whether meetings between the infidel and the third party have ceased. If they have not, I stress that this is necessary in order to refocus his or her emotional energy on the exploration of the marriage. It also enables me to help the infidel to explore his or her own guilt and shame, sadness, feelings about the loss of the affair, and possible depression. I also attempt to clarify whether the infidel has already decided to terminate the marriage. In this case I urge that the mate be informed, and indicate that to fail to do so will only cause later difficulties.

Should the infidel refuse a moratorium on the affair, I exercise the already agreed-upon therapeutic contract to continue to see the couple separately, while maintaining confidentiality for the individual meetings. This often serves to mobilize the anxiety of both members of the couple, and helps to break the conspiracy of silence, either because the infidel decides to reveal the issue, or because the person in denial becomes aroused and challenges the infidel directly. Should the victim ask why the couple is now being seen separately, I remind him or her about the promise of confidentiality. I suggest that while the infidel works on his or her issues, it would be worthwhile that he or she also continue in parallel individual meetings. The infidel may also become very anxious about my refusal to see the couple conjointly and ask whether I will reveal the infidelity to the partner. I assure him or her that I will not, but that if the mate begins to ask whether an affair is taking place, I will encourage him or her to "check things out," just as I would do for any other patient who suspected an affair.

Individual sessions have other advantages. The victim may welcome the opportunity to explore his or her personal feelings about the further viability of the marriage, feelings that she or he may feel unsafe disclosing at this point in therapy in the presence of the mate. The victim may also have decided to terminate the marriage. Should this be the case, I urge that this be revealed.

## How Defining Trauma Forwards Treatment

Let us return to the earlier case example. We now examine interventions that help to move the couple beyond the immediate crisis, which is the inevitable trauma upon discovery.

*At the first session, Rita frequently arose from her seat and paced around the room. "I can't stand his constant accusations, his jealousy, his suspiciousness. He's always watching me. Every time I walk into the house, I get a grilling from him." "You're damned right," he replied, "You act like a damn whore behind my back for ten years, and now you suddenly expect me to believe you?" After a few exchanges of this nature, I stopped them and thanked them for demonstrating for me what each was experiencing. I explained that each was having a response to the discovery that was normal and predictable.*

*Rita expressed amazement that even 6 months later, and even though she had had no further contact with the other man, Bob was still so punitive toward her. I pointed out that his response was very usual. First of all, he had always believed that whatever problems they had, they both accepted that marriage was, as he said, "for keeps." I asked her to put herself in Bob's shoes, and imagine how she would have felt had she discovered that Bob was having a lengthy affair. The reason for doing this is that it sometimes begins to break the impasse by encouraging an empathic reconnection between husband and wife. Before she had a chance to respond, Bob was up and out of his seat, nervously pacing and moving toward her in a menacing way. "Didn't I tell you when we were going together, that the last person hurt me so deeply, and that this is the worst thing you could ever do, and you did it!"*

*Rita turned to me and said, "See, if this was at home, this is when we would get into a big fight, and I would have to run out of the house to feel safe, and then he* says I'm abandoning him. I don't know what it is he wants." I asked Bob if he could sit down, collect his thoughts for a moment, and report what he was feeling to her, rather than emoting it to her, as he had been doing. He calmed down, and said, "Rita, I want you to know that I do love you, and I really don't want the marriage to end. It's just that every time I think about it, I feel scared and angry again, and maybe . . . ." I asked, "Maybe what?" but he said nothing, although his eyes began to tear. I turned to both of them and said, "Perhaps he feels he keeps the anger alive to protect himself against the fear of still more hurt and loss." (The purpose of such an interpretation is to emphasize the functional nature of suspiciousness as a protection against anticipated additional trauma.)

Bob nodded in agreement, and Rita said, "But even if that's so, what can I do about it?" I said, "You can try to tell Bob what you're hearing him say, so that he knows that you at least hear him." She says, "I think you're blaming me for everything that went wrong. It's not fair."

He reacts angrily, and she cannot understand why. I point out that he is trying to tell her what is going on inside of himself, his hurt, fear, and loss, and she is accepting it as blame of her, so she is defending against it. After several attempts, she is finally able to repeat to him what he has said, without defending herself. He looks a bit more at ease. Now I again ask her to tell him how she might feel if she were in his shoes, and she replies, "About the same—sad, angry, hurt, suspicious, but still wanting to try again."

## Moving Beyond the Crisis Phase

The early focus on the trauma of discovery is a necessary first step in treating discovered infidelity. It was mentioned earlier that the powerful word *victim* was chosen to name and validate the immediate experience of the discoverer of the infidelity. This inter-

vention enables the victim to feel that he or she is being heard and that the pain of betrayal can be accepted and understood by the mate. Its purpose is not to cast blame on the infidel, but to help the couple to transcend the discovery and move on to deal with other marital issues in a nonblaming and problem-solving manner. Most importantly, it gives the infidel something to do to help the situation, rather than to remain stuck in the role of defender of her or his past actions.

The most frequent questions posed by the infidel are, "What can I really do to get my mate to calm down?" and "How can I defend myself when my mate is attacking me?" The therapist must help the infidel to understand that one answer serves both questions: *The mate in the victim position requires reassurance that suspicion and fear are understandable, and that the situation may be talked about as much as is necessary.*

This is often very difficult for the infidel, because each time that the issue arises, his or her own feelings of defensiveness and self-justification once again obtrude. To the degree that the mate continues to justify the affair, the victim's anxiety remains very high. The infidel needs to acknowledge the hurt that was imposed by the lying and deceit and avoid justifying the affair because of the marital issues that preceded it. Further, as the victim makes more discoveries, it is very important for the infidel to be supportive and honest as these new discoveries are reviewed. For the most part, simply admitting what has occurred is not sufficient for the victim. It is also necessary that the infidel express remorse for the constant lying, and an understanding of the impact of the lying on the mate. *In the absence of expressions of remorse, the prognosis for an improved marriage diminishes, and the possibility for an acrimonious divorce increases.*

When the offending mate expresses remorse, an interesting shift occurs as the victim senses that the mate is now empathic with his or her pain. At this point, the infidel is *also* able to express feelings of shame, disappointment in his or her own behavior, and, not infrequently, sadness and mourning about the loss of the other relationship. Probably one of the more touching experiences for the therapist is to see the victim now begin to develop empathy for the mate, and even to offer support as the mate experiences his or her own depression. Despite the fact that the original suspicion and rage may continue to surface from time to time, it is this growing empathic field between the two that enables therapy to progress and that increases the probability of a favorable outcome. It is important to remember, however, that a better marriage *or* a better divorce is a good outcome.

## PHASES OF TREATMENT

The treatment of infidelity may be thought of as occurring in three phases (Lusterman, 1989):

*I. Restoring Trust*

*In this phase, the initial trauma of the betrayal of trust is explored, and the infidel is encouraged to validate and support the victim. The purpose of this phase is to restore trust, and thereby help the victim to transcend the "victim position," so that the couple can begin to examine the factors that may have predisposed the couple to the infidelity. The restoration of trust is a lengthy and often complex process. Periods of trust often increase the victim's feelings of vulnerability. He or she often defends against the sense of vulnerability with a renewed hypervigilance. This in turn may elevate the infidel's defensiveness. As described below, this issue persists well into the second phase, and even beyond.*

*II. Examination of Predisposing Factors*

*As the initial rage and mistrust diminishes, the therapist is able to help the couple review the marriage as it existed prior to the infidelity. This work is familiar to any experienced systems-oriented therapist. It should be noted, however, that because of the posttraumatic tendency to remain hyperalert and to continue searching for a possible recurrence, it is important that the therapist immediately return to Phase I interventions should such a regression occur. Failure to so do frequently results in a premature termination of therapy.*

*III. Rapprochement*

*The emphasis here is on enabling the couple to build skills of self-disclosure and problem-solving. The couple has by now, it is hoped, transcended the blaming position that characterizes Phase I. At this point, they need to consider whether they can continue with a successful marriage, or whether they need to move toward separation and ultimate divorce.*

## UNDISCOVERED INFIDELITY

As clinicians, we are often confronted with a range of problems relating to *undiscovered* EMS and infidelity. For example, an individual may request a consultation because of conflict about whether or not to break off an affair, to discuss the suspicion that a mate is involved in an affair, or to seek advice following guilt or fear about a "one-night stand." (It should be noted that it is important for the therapist to inquire whether "safe sex" has been practiced, and to make a medical referral where necessary.) A therapist may also begin to suspect that an affair is in progress in a couple under treatment, and that it is keeping the marriage in a "stuck" position.

Each of these problems presents particular challenges for the systems-oriented practitioner. Their solution lies not in a cookbook approach, but in a clear understanding of systems theory and in the particular dynamics of PMI. For example, should the therapist who begins by seeing one patient alone, particularly one who presents the therapist with a secret, later engage both members of the couple in treatment? If the therapist begins to suspect that one of the mates is engaged in an affair and that it is maintaining the couple in a stuck position, is there a responsibility to raise the issue? What are the issues of possible breach of confidentiality? (See chap. 32 in this volume.) Should the therapist decide to intervene, will it be construed as a therapeutically responsible act, or as an imposition of the therapist's values system on the lives of patients?

As a systems-oriented practitioner, one never views a presenting problem as existing solely within the psyche of the presenting patient. Given this, I usually inform the person coming alone that I will always be aware that there are other people who are, in some sense, "in the room" with us, and that I will try to frame the therapeutic issues in a way that includes them. I also explain at the outset that, although we are beginning therapy alone, at some point the mate and perhaps others may join us. I then proceed to provide information cited earlier in the section Orienting Couples About the Therapy. Finally, I clearly describe how I will deal with confidentiality. "Anything that is discussed in an individual session will be regarded as confidential. If you wish to discuss it with others, you may, but I will not."

These actions create an informed consent situation, in which the patient is free to examine the therapist's approach and to ask relevant questions. This also permits patients to make a decision to terminate with the present therapist because they fear the possible consequences. It is important to be very clear at the outset about the therapist's intentions. For example, I always point out to a person who consults because of concern about an ongoing affair that I will refuse conjoint treatment until there is a moratorium on the affair. By the same token, I refuse to meet with the third party. Sometimes the person will refuse the moratorium but come for a number of sessions to review his or her ambivalence both about the affair and about the marriage. During this time I indicate that, for the most part, the third party turns out to be a "transitional object" in the person's life, and that the purpose of the affair is to find out whether the marriage can be improved, or will end. The person may have the illusion that there will simply be a "shift of mates," but this is seldom the case. At that point it is also possible to examine the effects of the patient's devious (although not yet discovered) behavior on the mate. The purpose of this is to help the person to see that his or her present behavior is exacerbating marital problems, which, if worked on, might help either to create a stronger and healthier marriage or to pave the way for a more healing separation and possible divorce. Because an extramarital affair is certainly a possibility in a troubled marriage, it is wise to schedule at least one individual session for each member of the couple very early in therapy, after both mates are reminded of the rules concerning confidentiality. During this meeting, the therapist

should directly ask whether the person is currently involved in an affair or has ever been involved in one. The person should also be asked whether they either know or suspect that the mate is or has been involved in an affair. If an affair is in progress, it is important to determine whether it is an "arrangement" or a secret. If it is a secret, it is usually necessary to schedule additional individual meetings. The person's confusion and ambivalence, the impact on the mate of continued lying, and other related issues require exploration. The person may ask whether this information will be revealed in individual meetings with the mate. The person is assured that no direct information will be revealed, but that if the mate voices his or her own suspicions, the therapist will explore those suspicions, as would be done with any patient suspecting an infidelity. It has been my experience that most people accept this information and continue in therapy. Usually after a few such meetings, couples therapy resumes, often with increased energy and focus.

## CONCLUSION

This chapter has described an approach to the treatment of marital infidelity, with particular attention to the shattered assumptions of the discoverer and the resultant trauma. It is important to understand that once the issue of trauma has been dealt with, it is possible for the clinician to go on using already established skills to explore and facilitate marital change and growth. Patients are extremely relieved to hear information about marital infidelity and other types of EMS that help them to place these events into an understandable context. For example, many patients find it comforting to know that PMI is a relatively rare event and that the frequent advice simply to accept it as a "norm" is poorly founded.

There is a great need for well-designed research that will help us to attain more knowledge about the incidence of various types of EMS. To clump all the information under one undifferentiated and poorly defined classification does relatively little to advance knowledge. Such studies need to also take into account differences that are a function of gender (see chap. 17 in this volume) and ethnicity (see chap. 19

in this volume). A clearer understanding of various patterns of EMS will enable us to build better models for treatment.

## References

American Psychiatric Association. (1980). *Diagnostic and statistical manual of mental disorders* (3rd ed.). Washington, DC: Author.

American Psychiatric Association. (1994). *Diagnostic and statistical manual of mental disorders* (4th ed.). Washington, DC: Author.

Brown, E. (1991). *Patterns of infidelity and their treatment.* New York: Brunner/Mazel.

Charny, I. (1992). *Existential/dialectical marital therapy: Breaking the secret code of marriage.* New York: Brunner/Mazel.

Finzi, S. (1989, May/June) Cosi fan tutti. *The Family Networker, 13,* 31–33.

Glass, S., & Wright, T. (1992). Justifications for extramarital relationships: The association between attitudes, behaviors and gender. *The Journal of Sex Research, 29,* 361–387.

Greeley, A. (1991). *Faithful attraction: Discovering intimacy, love and fidelity in American marriage.* New York: Tor.

Humphrey, F. (1987). Treating extramarital sexual relationships in sex and couples therapy. In G. Weeks & L. Hof (Eds.), *Integrating sex and marital therapy: A clinical guide* (pp. 149–170). New York: Brunner/Mazel.

Janoff-Bulman, R. (1992). *Shattered assumptions: Towards a new psychology of trauma.* New York: Free Press.

Kaslow, F., & Hammerschmidt, H. (1992). Long-term "good marriages": The seemingly essential ingredients. *Journal of Couples Therapy, 3*(2/3), 15–38.

Kinsey, A. C., Pomeroy, W. B., & Martin, C. E. (1948). *Sexual behavior in the human male.* Philadelphia: W. B. Saunders.

Kinsey, A. C., Pomeroy, W. B., Martin, C. E., & Gebhard, P. H. (1953). *Sexual behavior in the human female.* Philadelphia: W. B. Saunders.

Lawson, A. (1988). *Adultery: An analysis of love and betrayal.* New York: Basic Books.

Lusterman, D.-D. (1989, May/June). Marriage at the turning point. *The Family Networker, 13,* 44–51.

March, J. (1993). What constitutes a stressor? The "Criterion A" issue. In J. Davidson & E. Foa (Eds.), *Post-traumatic Stress Disorder: DSM-IV and beyond* (pp. 37–54). Washington, DC: American Psychiatric Press.

Moultrup, D. (1990). *Husbands, wives, and lovers: The emotional system of the extramarital affair.* New York: Guilford Press.

Pittman, F. (1989). *Private lies: Infidelity and the betrayal of intimacy.* New York: Norton.

Pittman, F. (1993). *Man enough: Fathers, sons and the search for masculinity.* New York: Putnam.

Smith, T. (1993). *American sexual behavior: Trends, socio-demographic differences, and risk behavior* (Version 1.2). Chicago: National Opinion Research Center, University of Chicago.

Teismann, M. (1979). Jealousy: Systematic, problem-solving therapy with couples. *Family Process, 18,* 151–160.

Teismann, M. (1982). Persistent jealousy following the termination of an affair: A strategic approach. In A. Gurman (Ed.), *Questions and answers in the practice of family therapy* (Vol. 2., pp. 89–104). New York: Brunner/Mazel.

Walker, L. (1984). *The battered woman.* New York: Harper and Row.

# CHAPTER 15

# THE DYNAMICS OF DIVORCE THERAPY

*Florence W. Kaslow*

A legal divorce marks the culmination of a painful process that began earlier in the marriage and has numerous sequelae in the postdivorce period. Bohannon (1970) developed a six-stage model of divorce, which he termed "the stations of divorce." I have incorporated the ideas of others (Kessler, 1975; Turner, 1980) as well as my own into the model to make it more comprehensive (Kaslow, 1981b, 1984, 1987) and have added another stage (Kaslow, 1990, 1994; Kaslow & Schwartz, 1987a).

## THE DIVORCE PROCESS: A DIACLECTIC MODEL OF STAGE THEORIES

The "diaclectic" model of the divorce process integrates theories of human growth and development, marital dissolution, and family systems. The invented term *diaclectic* combines the concepts *eclectic* (selective) and *dialectic* (seeking a synthesis that continues to emerge as new data come forth) to encompass numerous theories of behavior dynamics and humanistic–existential ideas (Kaslow, 1981a, 1981b, Kaslow & Schwartz, 1987b).

The stages described below do not necessarily occur in sequence, nor do all individuals go through every stage. Rather, the stages provide a broad overview that helps to sensitize both therapist and patient to the issues and to suggest useful strategies.

The very high divorce rate might suggest that there is a growing acceptance of divorce on the part of some segments of society. For most individuals faced with divorce, however, the event appears at first to be catastrophic. The therapist must help the family to get beyond this crisis and to develop new skills to meet this intense, even if transitional, situation.

The accompanying chart (Table 1) summarizes the stage model of divorce.

## PRE DIVORCE

### Stage 1: The Emotional Divorce

The *emotional divorce* (Bohannon, 1970), which can be brief or prolonged, happens as the pair become aware of their discontent. One partner may sense this dissatisfaction before the other and convey it to the mate. This usually evokes some kind of emotional response.

Some marriages fare well for many years. I believe that people select a mate because of the "fit" that each perceives with the other. As people grow and change, however, their needs may also change, and they may think that their mate is no longer the appropriate choice. Often, a couple may manage a seemingly adequate marriage only to find, when a major crisis occurs, that their resources are too depleted to meet it.

The intense anxiety raised by a possible breakup may motivate the couple to enter therapy. Couples are more apt to be able to resolve their marital conflicts if they enter treatment conjointly than if one or both enter individual therapy (Whitaker & Miller, 1969). Couples therapy at this stage often deals with such issues as conflict resolution, exploration of anger, improved communication, and marital enrichment. Where children are involved, the therapist can sensitize the couple to the disruption in the lives of

TABLE 1

Diaclectic Model of Stages in the Divorce Process

| Phase | Stage | Feelings | Behaviors | Therapeutic approaches | Mediation issues |
|---|---|---|---|---|---|
| Pre divorce: A time of deliberation and despair | 1. Emotional divorce | Disillusionment Dissatisfaction Alienation Anxiety Disbelief | Avoiding the issue Sulking and/or crying Confronting partner Quarreling | Marital therapy (one couple) Couples group therapy | |
| | | Despair Dread Anguish Ambivalence Shock Emptiness Anger Chaos Inadequacy Low self-esteem Loss Depression Detachment | Denial Withdrawal (physical and emotional) Pretending all is fine Attempting to win back affection Asking friends, family, clergy for advice | Marital therapy (one couple) Divorce therapy Couples group therapy | |
| During divorce: A time of legal involvement | 2. Legal divorce | Self-pity Helplessness | Bargaining Screaming Threatening Attempting suicide Consulting an attorney or mediator | Family therapy Individual adult therapy Child therapy | Set the stage for mediation-orientation session Ascertain parties' understanding of the process and its appropriateness for them |
| | 3. Economic divorce | Confusion Fury Sadness, loneliness Relief Vindictiveness | Separating physically Filing for legal divorce Considering financial settlement Deciding on custody/visitation schedule | Children of divorce group therapy Child therapy Adult therapy | Define the rules of mediation Identify the issues and separate therapeutic issues from mediation issues Focus on parental strengths, children's needs, and formulating best possible coparenting and residential arrangement |

| Stage | Feelings | Actions/Tasks | Therapeutic interventions | Mediation interventions |
|---|---|---|---|---|
| 4. Coparental divorce and the problems of custody | Concern for children<br>Ambivalence<br>Numbness<br>Uncertainty | Grieving and mourning<br>Telling relatives and friends<br>Reentering work world (unemployed woman)<br>Feeling empowered to make choices | Same as above, plus family therapy | Negotiate and process the issues and choices<br>Reach agreement<br>Analyze & formalize agreement |
| 5. Community divorce | Indecisiveness<br>Optimism<br>Resignation<br>Excitement<br>Curiosity<br>Regret<br>Sadness | Finalizing divorce<br>Reaching out to new friends<br>Undertaking new activities<br>Stabilizing new lifestyle and daily routine for children<br>Exploring new interests and possibly taking new job | Adults<br>Individual therapy<br>Singles group therapy<br>Children<br>Child play therapy<br>Children's group therapy | |
| 6. Religious divorce | Self-doubt<br>Desire for church approval<br>Fear of God's displeasure or wrath | Gaining church acceptance<br>Having a religious divorce ceremony administered<br>Making peace with spiritual self | Divorce ceremony for total family<br>Adult therapy<br>Pastoral counseling | |
| 7. Psychic divorce | Acceptance<br>Self-confidence<br>Energy<br>Self-worth<br>Wholeness<br>Exhilaration<br>Independence<br>Autonomy | Resynthesis of identity<br>Completing psychic divorce<br>Seeking new love objective and making a commitment to some permanency<br>Becoming comfortable with new lifestyle and friends<br>Helping children accept finality of parents' divorce and their continuing relationship with both parents | Parent–child therapy<br>Family therapy<br>Group therapies<br>Children's activity group therapy | |
| Post divorce: A time of exploration and reequilibration | | | | Return to mediation when changed circumstances require a renegotiation of the agreement |

*Note:* From "Divorce Mediation and Its Emotional Impact on the Couple and Their Children," by F. W. Kaslow, 1984, *American Journal of Family Therapy*, 12(3), pp. 60–61. Copyright 1984 by F. W. Kaslow. Adapted with permission of the author.

their children that is likely to come with divorce. The couple will also face pain as parents in the event of a divorce. It is also useful to recommend books for both parents and children, such as Gardner's *The Parent's Book About Divorce* (1977) or Ricci's *Mom's House, Dad's House* (1980), which provide a clear view of life for divorcing and/or divorced parents and their children.

In some cases, couples who have been helped in therapy to explore their feelings of anger and disillusionment are able to renew their commitment and rebuild their marriage on a new footing. This is possible primarily when the couple still profess love and caring, despite continuing conflict.

An alternative approach to single-couple therapy is short-term psychodynamic group therapy for couples (Kadis & Markowitz, 1972; Kaslow, 1982; Kaslow & Lieberman, 1981). Because this is time-limited therapy and has a focal theme, most couples in the group are able to decide within 10 to 12 weeks whether they wish to stay together. Group members support, mirror, and confront one another, thus intensifying the impact of the therapy.

Rarely is there anything anyone can do to dissuade a spouse who is determined to sever the marital ties. Nonetheless, the rejected spouse may be able to coerce the mate into staying temporarily by becoming depressed or physically ill or by threatening or attempting suicide or homicide. In such instances, the therapist should attempt to guide the couple in exploring the probable implications of remaining married versus getting divorced. The therapist may suggest a trial separation, which can serve as a cooling-off period during which to make more rational choices. Clearly, the choice must be the couple's and not the therapist's. The couple may no longer be willing to attend conjoint sessions. Either one or both of them may then decide to enter individual or group therapy in order to explore their feelings. Issues common to the rejected mate are desertion, loss, fury, and failure. For the departing spouse, guilt and sadness may be explored. One or both may stay in treatment with the original therapist or continue with a different one. The advantage of staying with the original therapist is that she or he is already familiar with the situation. If occasional conjoint ses-

sions are needed—for example, around parenting and visitation—these are easily arrangeable. It is advisable to leave the choice to the patients. If both trust the therapist, splitting maneuvers can be avoided.

When working with couples in conflict who are apt to pursue divorce, the therapist should express an unwillingness to shift roles from therapist to expert witness at a later point and should establish an agreement about this as part of an initial therapeutic contract. However, records should be kept in such a way that the therapist is prepared if a subpoena arrives. Should this occur, the therapist should acquire a written release from both parties. If this is not forthcoming, the therapist's options include (a) asking the attorney of the unwilling patient to have the subpoena quashed or to have a protective order issued; (b) contacting the judge and indicating why, on ethical grounds, he or she is reluctant to testify; (c) explaining to the attorney of the patient who requests the testimony why it might not be in the patient's best interests.

Once the choice of divorce has been made, the therapist's role may shift to helping the spouse who feels deserted to take charge of reconstructing his or her future and urging the couple to make the divorce process a constructive, growth-oriented experience. Sometimes it is appropriate to suggest that the patient consider mediation rather than litigation, as it is more conducive to a constructive divorce and more consistent with the goals of holistic and humanistic therapy (Gold, 1992; Kaslow & Schwartz, 1987a; Marlow, 1992; see chap. 16 in this volume). Couples who enter mediation may find that continuation of therapy, concurrent with but separate from mediation, provides for the continued resolution of highly charged emotional issues. (The reader is referred to the "divorce mediation" chapter in this volume [chap. 16] for an explanation and comparative analysis of different models of divorce mediation.)

### CASE EXAMPLE: THE BONNERS

*Joe and Corinne married when he was 24 years old and just starting his career as an engineer. Corinne was then 20 and a junior in college. Joe was the quieter and* better organized of the two; Corinne was lively and gregarious. During her senior year, Corinne discovered that she was pregnant. She had hoped to work several years before having a baby. Nonetheless, the couple decided against an abortion, and Danny was born 2 months after her graduation. They soon had a second child, Janine. By then they had purchased a home. Corinne planned to work when Janine entered kindergarten. A year after Janine's birth, Corinne's father was diagnosed with cancer. Shortly thereafter, Corinne found that she was pregnant again. Despite some ambivalence, she decided to continue the pregnancy. Her father's death was imminent and she wanted to insure that the family would expand. She also felt that a new baby would help her and her mother to recuperate from the loss to come.

However, Joe was opposed. He had added consultation to his responsibilities and was traveling a great deal. His horizons were broadening. He felt that Corinne was becoming too family oriented and that her interests had narrowed. He hoped that after his father-in-law died, Janine would enter nursery school and Corinne would "do something" in the field she had studied. He was feeling bored at home and wanted his wife to be a stimulating and fun companion again. Corinne found Joe increasingly detached from family issues and occasionally commented to her mother about his insensitivity to the high level of family stress. When she refused his request that she have an abortion, he accused her of selfishness. The tension mounted, but Corinne did not deal with it. She was overburdened by caring for the two children, her father's failing health, her own and her mother's grief, and her more difficult pregnancy.

When Billy was born, Corinne went into a moderate postpartum depression. Joe was unsympathetic, feeling that his advice

against a third child had been ignored. Following Corrine's father's death, her mother moved into their house to take care of her daughter and to help with the grandchildren until the crisis passed. Both women believed Corinne would get the marriage back on a positive track as soon as she felt better and Joe acclimated to their expanded family.

Although Corinne soon rebounded from her depression, Joe remained busy and aloof. Six months later, they took a week's vacation, returning refreshed and more attuned to one another than they had been in years. Yet Joe was still reserved with the children.

Corinne began noticing that Billy did not seem "quite right." Joe belittled her fears, but her pediatrician referred her to a neurologist, who gave a tentative diagnosis of seizure disorder. Corinne was overwhelmed and depressed by her child's abnormality, which added to the burden of her responsibilities.

Joe was infuriated by her preoccupation with the children, detested coming home, and involved himself increasingly in his work. He often spent evenings and weekends away. Through work, he met Tracy, an attractive, single attorney. They soon began an affair, and Joe found the stimulation and admiration he craved. He was happy to live in an adult rather than a child-centered world. He enjoyed Tracy's brilliance and wit. She respected his competence, shrewdness, and ambition. Ultimately, Joe decided that his marriage was no longer viable, and he asked Corinne for a divorce. Corinne was stunned as Joe accused her of neglecting him and their relationship in favor of the children. Angrily he added, "You rarely have energy to make love—and I no longer find you desirable." But faced with a desperate and sobbing Corinne, Joe agreed to go with her for marital therapy.

## Case Analysis and Treatment Interventions

**Session 1.** *When the couple came for couples therapy, they had been married for 9 years. Joe and Corinne were dealing with different aspects of the emotional stage of divorce. Joe was close to complete disengagement while Corinne was still in a degree of denial. In the first meeting with the therapist, Joe agreed to give the marriage "one more shot." The therapist suspected that this was more an appeasement than a genuine commitment.*

**Session 2.** *Corinne came in optimistic and attractively groomed. But Joe had already decided to see a lawyer and then revealed his ongoing affair. Corinne felt betrayed and disillusioned.*

*The therapist reserved a few minutes at the end of the session to speak with Corinne alone and to give her a chance to calm down. She was told she could call the therapist at any time and was encouraged to seek the support of her mother and friends. Joe and Corinne had moved from the emotional divorce to the next stage, the legal divorce.*

## DURING DIVORCE

### Stage 2: The Legal Aspects

This period encompasses the *legal, economic, and coparental/child custody stations of divorce* (Bohannon, 1970). It begins when either the husband, the wife, or both initiate legal action. Until recently, this caused the parties to become legal adversaries. The American Bar Association's Canon of Ethics (1981) holds that an attorney is ethically bound to represent *only* his or her client. Although many states rewrote their divorce laws in the 1970s and 1980s to reflect a shift from fault to no-fault, from sole custody to shared parental responsibility, and from contested to noncontested divorce actions, there are still some bitter, long-drawn-out adversarial proceedings.

The mid-1970s witnessed the evolution of divorce mediation after the publication of Coogler's seminal book (1978). The rapid expansion of mediation theory and practice during the 1980s and early 1990s

(Erickson & McKnight-Erickson, 1988; Folberg & Milne, 1988; Haynes, 1981, 1982; Marlow & Sauber, 1990; see chap. 16 in this volume) has enabled couples to participate directly in key decisions about parenting, child support, and property distribution. Mediation often prevents the need for costly and contentious litigation and stresses empowerment, concern for the best interests of *all* family members, cooperative problem solving, and equitable distribution of assets. Striving to evolve a mutually acceptable agreement while minimizing anguish enhances one's sense of self-worth (see chap. 16 in this volume).

Nonetheless, mediation is not a panacea. A great power differential in a relationship may mean an attorney's services are needed for the couple to secure a fair settlement. Also, when parting spouses are so enraged that fairness is the opposite of what they desire, they may need to battle ferociously as a way of working through their wrath en route to letting go of the relationship and healing psychologically. One mate's dishonesty or need for vengeance may also necessitate an adversarial process.

Although mediation is frequently successful, it is not invariably so, and it may not be the couple's choice. Whatever course is taken by the couple, however, the job of the clinician during divorce therapy is to help them reach a level where they have grieved sufficiently to be able to cooperate in reaching a divorce agreement. The therapist who is successful in helping the couple to proceed in a nonadversarial problem-solving manner may continue to play a significant role over many years. The couple may return as coparents to deal with various developmental issues in the lives of their children. The therapist may then meet with the original couple as coparents, or with a parent and new mate in a stepfamily situation, or with both parents and their new mates. Such an approach is consonant with the growing interest in larger systems interventions that are at the cutting edge of systems theory.

**Sessions 3 through 10.** *Joe announced that he had rented an apartment and planned to move that weekend. The therapist rehearsed with the couple what and how they would tell the children, what*

*their reactions were likely to be, and how to reassure them of the continuing love and support of both parents. The choice of mediation was broached, and information about it was given to the couple (Ferstenberg, 1992; Kaslow, 1988, 1994).*

*By Session 4, the children had been told of the impending divorce, and the couple agreed that it had been well handled, although it was extremely painful for all. There was particular difficulty with Billy, who had begun to show his upset by biting and kicking. The parents were advised to bring all the children in for therapy sessions. Initially Joe balked at the suggestion, but he later agreed. The couple had decided to attempt mediation.*

*In Sessions 5 and 6, Corinne came in alone to ventilate her feelings of rage, despair, and personal failure. She felt overwhelmed at being a single parent, with no surcease from obligations or any outlets available for herself. During these sessions, she was reassured about her role as wife and mother in the past and given concrete suggestions about how to alleviate her stressful home situation and how to provide more freedom for herself.*

*During Sessions 7 through 10, the children spent the opening and closing 10 or so minutes with either Joe or Corinne present, discussing their feelings and evaluating the visitation schedule. During the middle half-hour, the children were seen in sibling therapy (Bank & Kahn, 1982), where play and art therapy were used. The parents were encouraged to read books about children living in two households. They discussed with the therapist what age-related behaviors they might anticipate from each child, as well as coping strategies.*

## Stage 3: The Economic Divorce

Fears about economic survival may cause people to cling to an unsuccessful marriage. For those who decide to divorce, it is ironic that at the very time they are under the greatest emotional stress, they must also deal with knotty financial issues. These include the discharge of debts, the division of assets, and child and spousal support. When there is little property to be divided, the process is simpler, but everyone is apt to emerge with much less than they need. Women and children tend to fare worse than men, and they often become downwardly mobile (Weitzman, 1985).

Several different kinds of alimony exist, ranging from temporary through longer term rehabilitative alimony to permanent alimony. The tax consequences of different kinds of settlement packages must be addressed. What is divisible may hinge on what is determined to be premarital versus marital property and whether or not there was a prenuptial agreement (Kaslow, 1991). Other couples issues stem from legal rulings about pension and profit-sharing plans, the rights of one spouse to a share of the other's professional practice or business, claims against future earnings, and the like.

Most states have child-support guidelines, and there are numerous statutes for enforcing payment and garnishing wages. Still, many people evade payment, and myriad children continue to be exposed to the worst sequelae of divorce.

Therapists treating individuals going through divorce can assist by being empathic with their rage, sense of betrayal, and desire to retaliate. Having validated their feelings, they can then guide them toward seeing each other's real needs and toward engaging in fair, nondestructive negotiating. They can help interpret the complex economic issues, if they are knowledgeable, while encouraging them to request clarification from their lawyer, accountant, or mediator. They can stress the importance of clarity and long-range planning because the marital separation agreement (MSA) becomes the map for their financial futures. It is critical to note that the economic divorce is not coterminous with the legal divorce but ends with the final transfer of funds from the payor spouse to the recipient spouse. If permanent alimony is ordered, the couple is bound together until one spouse dies. Thus, the financial settlement has long-term consequences that will impact heavily on the future of all family members.

**Sessions 11 through 14.** *The couple had reached a mediated settlement which* *provided that Joe would pay the maximum child support recommended and Corinne would receive 10 years of rehabilitative alimony. An equitable distribution of assets was arranged with a minimum of strife. They had evolved a plan to meet Billy's special needs, while providing Corinne with time to train to resume a part-time career.*

*During an emotional session, Joe apologized for the hurt he had caused Corinne, and assured her that he would remain an involved parent.*

## Stage 4: Coparenting and Child Custody Issues

The lives of children are changed drastically when their parents end their marriage (Ahrons, 1981; Ahrons & Rodgers, 1987). In order to ease this painful transition for their children, parents should:

- explain, preferably together, that they are divorcing and assure the children that it is not their fault, and there is nothing the children can do to get them back together;
- decide on a primary residence based on the best interest of the child and not on their own wishes;
- reassure the children that each parent will continue to love them and remain actively involved in their lives;
- refrain from deprecating the other parent and his or her family of origin;
- refrain from placing children in loyalty conflicts;
- arrange adequate financial support for the children;
- work out a cooperative parenting schedule based on children's needs, activities, and preferences;
- make as few changes as possible in the child's life.

If rapid changes are unavoidable (i.e., relocation, change of schools, or rapid remarriage), parents should explain what is happening and why it is essential and work to cushion the added upheaval as best they can.

Older children of divorce also experience trauma when their parents divorce. Their loyalties are challenged, and they may feel angry and alienated from one parent. If they have children, they worry about

the loss of contact with grandparents. In some states grandparents have rights to visitation, which are written into the divorce laws. However, rarely are they accorded the right to enjoin someone from moving out of state. The loss of nurturing grandparents is a sad one for the children, already beset by other major losses and disruptions. Grandparents often provide a sense of stability, unconditional love, and approval. Cutting grandparents off from grandchildren is often experienced by the children as cruel and devastating. Except in the event that the grandparents have been abusive, the relationship should be fostered by therapist and parents alike.

Important family events and holidays are often a source of conflict and difficult decision making. Those assembled may have to deal with a parent's new mate, or with knotty questions such as inheritance or future care of an aging parent (Kaslow & Schwartz, 1987b). The therapist may schedule a session of anticipatory rehearsal to prepare for such events.

Therapists working with children of divorce should have a firm grasp of individual and family development and both the typical and idiosyncratic responses to divorce of children and adolescents. The therapist may be the only one in the child's life at this time who can listen sensitively and attentively to the child's story. Treatment of choice may be play or art therapy; individual psychotherapy; sibling group therapy to strengthen the bonds and diminish the rivalries; or groups for children of divorce. The latter have proven quite effective in lessening alienation and the sense of being alone, promoting problem-solving skills, and reframing and normalizing the experience (Kessler & Bostwick, 1977; Roizblatt, Garcia, Maida, & Moya, 1990).

How children survive the breakup (Wallerstein & Kelly, 1980) is to some extent correlated with the degree of conflict during and post divorce. Other factors include the child's personal resilience and the parents' degree of emotional recovery. Longitudinal research (Wallerstein & Blakeslee, 1989) indicates that effects may be long lasting and that sometimes repressed feelings resurface years later. This so-called "sleeper effect" may become visible in the reluctance of an adult child of divorce to make a commitment to a permanent relationship in order to avoid another divorce experience. Thus, therapy that occurs close to the time of the original trauma or when it is first evident that a child is deeply troubled is most likely to avert future distress and dysfunction.

## Stage 5: The Community, Social, and Extended Family Aspects

One's extended family, friends, colleagues, and neighbors can provide a much-needed support network during and after divorce. Being there to listen, to care, and to validate the disillusioned individual is extremely helpful. Wallerstein and Kelly indicated (1980) that women with a strong support system that can provide financial help, temporary housing, and child care during the crisis and transition fared much better than their counterparts who were lonely and alienated. Being the recipient of understanding in the workplace for the adults and in school for the children can make a major difference in whether one feels valued by others or experiences the world as a hostile, nonresponsive place.

For men who move out of the family home and perceive that they have lost the daily experience of family life, the support system may be more amorphous. It may be their parents and siblings. Some maintain contact with both single and married friends either by telephone or socially. If not, or perhaps in addition, they may seek solace in alcohol or drugs, or seek companionship at a singles bar. Some turn toward working excessive hours to fill the emptiness, and others increase their recreational time. Some ask friends to introduce them to available women, and others find themselves pursued by women. Often what is lacking, and for a long time, is someone to talk with who really cares.

Stage 5 begins during divorce, and like the economic and coparenting phases, continues beyond the legal divorce. Those who are censured by significant others are likely to have the greatest difficulty forgiving themselves and the former mate for the decision to divorce. Those who are invited warmly to participate in activities by others will find their path made smoother. The divorced person should request that friends and relatives not push them to date or, on the other hand, restrain them from "too much" socializing; they need to find their own rhythm. It will

take a while to become comfortable in the singles world and adjust to current psychosexual mores.

At this stage, individual therapy often constitutes the treatment of choice. Some conjoint parent–child sessions may also be necessary to keep lines of communication open and to ensure that children's needs are being met. A divorce therapy group can also be beneficial. Members can share their issues and receive reflective feedback, both critical and supportive. Self-help groups for single parents provide a forum for addressing and normalizing mutual problems. Group meetings become a place to socialize, acquire new friends, and plan activities that may involve the post divorce family as a unit.

**Sessions 15 through 20.** *These were held monthly; a week before each session we determined who should attend. This phasing-out took the family through to about 7 months post legal divorce. Everyone had begun to stabilize in this binuclear family (Ahrons & Rodgers, 1987). Corinne was dating occasionally and taking a graduate course. Joe had decided not to rush into a live-in situation until the children's well-being seemed solidified, and he often saw them without his lover present. The two older children had been in a children-of-divorce group, as well as in some sibling and family therapy, and were adapting reasonably well to living in two households. The carefully chosen nursery provided a good choice for Billy, and between the quality tutelage he received there, proper medication, and the separate attention he was finally getting from his father, he was learning and behaving much better. Corinne's mother had gone back to work and had resumed a personal social life, yet was still available to baby-sit once a week, or just to visit with her daughter and grandchildren.*

*During Session 20, the case was put "on hold," with the family asking if they could call and return periodically as needed. They were assured that they could, and their progress to date was affirmed by the therapist.*

## Stage 6: The Religious Aspects

Many patients reveal that their sense of alienation can be overwhelming. They long for community approval to mitigate their shame and sense of failure. Many people who originally were married in a religious ceremony indicate that they also want to be divorced through one. It seems best if this occurs in church or synagogue, as this may signify being in a state of grace, receiving a blessing from God through His emissary on earth, or being welcome in the congregation as a divorced person. In some religions, such as Orthodox Judaism, it is essential to have a religious divorce before a rabbinic tribunal or one cannot be remarried. In Catholicism, annulment may be suggested, although it introduces many complexities and ambiguities regarding the children of a union that has thus been declared null and void. Nonetheless, annulment is required in addition to civil divorce if a new Catholic marriage is to be contemplated. Given the fact that religion is important to so many people, it is surprising that it has received such scant attention in the mental-health literature on divorce.

If the church's policy does not include the possibility of a divorce ritual or if the officiating clergyperson is opposed to such a ceremony, this type of ritual can be conducted in a different context, fulfilling a similar need. I have devised and revised a quasi-spiritual divorce ritual over the past decade and a half. This ceremony enables the divorced spouses to reclaim and acknowledge the happier early portion of their marriage and their original love for one another, to let the children know that they were conceived in love and are free to relate to each parent without interference, and to apologize genuinely for hurts inflicted. For the children it provides an often missing opportunity to tell the parents how they felt about the divorce and what they need from each of their parents now and in the future. Typically, many tears are shed during the ceremony; upon its closure, there are often spontaneous embraces as the family says a different goodbye. This is rarely possible until several years after the legal divorce, because much of the hurt and anger have to abate before acceptance and forgiveness can occur. (For the complete ceremony, see Kaslow & Schwartz, 1987a; Kaslow, 1993.)

## POST DIVORCE

## Stage 7: The Psychic Divorce

Many individuals who have gone through a divorce experience liken it to being on a roller coaster. It appears to take from 2 to 4 years for even reasonably well-balanced people to re-equilibrate. The length of time depends on numerous factors, including: (a) who initiated the divorce and who was the rejected party, (b) whether one party was still struggling to save the marriage, (c) the length of the pre divorce separation, (d) whether the grief work was well under way before the physical breakup, (e) resiliency of personality, (f) financial resources, (g) age, (h) gender, (i) strength of support network, (j) level of self-confidence and optimism versus pessimism about the future, and (k) the larger family constellation.

When individuals have been moderately to extremely dysfunctional prior to the breakup, the recuperation is apt to be slower and accompanied by more acrimony. For them, divorce becomes the critical life incident that colors their entire future; the former spouse continues to be seen as a villain who caused all of their problems, and resentment can continue to govern many of their actions. From this group come the patients who try to keep the children (of all ages) engaged in post divorce battles about money, visitation issues, and emotional loyalties. Those who cannot relinquish and mourn the now-dead marriage are destined to remain locked in their own hurt and anger. They are not free to go on and form a new and more productive relationship.

The post divorce period can be one of challenges and opportunities, at least for those who have the enthusiasm, time, and money to create and utilize new pathways or to reactivate former friendships and activities. However, during the early post divorce period, there are many who experience acute anxiety or depression. Their adjustment may be more difficult because they lack time (because they are working harder), enthusiasm (because their future appears bleak), and money (either women, who bear the financial brunt of a divorce, or men whose formerly modest income becomes insufficient after child support and alimony payments are made).

It is useful to ask the adults and children what they might gain following divorce. Answers may include (a) freedom from abuse; (b) no longer fearing embarrassment from partner's alcoholism, drug abuse, or humiliating comments and behavior; (c) diminution of arguments and nagging, and a more peaceful household; (d) space to think one's own thoughts and be one's own person; (e) freedom to make one's own choices and be in charge of one's own life. The therapist is then in a position to emphasize that the gains may outweigh the losses. This in turn enables the therapist to help patients to see the strengths and resiliency that they bring to a post divorce adjustment.

Some patients enter post divorce therapy in an angry, distressed, pessimistic, vituperative, and hurt state. They are apt still to be denigrating their former spouse and trying to turn children and friends against him or her and to be engulfed in self-pity. When this is the case, individual or group therapy should focus on decreasing the rage and toward examining the patient's own role in provoking and sustaining the marital conflict beyond the divorce. They should be helped to diminish their negativism and sense of helplessness and to release their children from a "parentified" role and from an overly enmeshed relationship with them that is detrimental to the children's ability to individuate (Kaslow, 1988).

Unless this is achieved, one cannot reach closure on the psychic divorce. Evidence of closure can be seen in a return of optimism, willingness to enter into a relationship and to trust again (if a relationship is something the person wants), a diminution of anger, and the ability to let go of the past and think productively about the future.

## AN OPTIMISTIC SYNTHESIS

It is essential for the therapist to be aware of the various phases of the divorce process. The turmoil and upheaval is experienced differently by each member of the nuclear family. There is also an impact on

many members of the couple's families of origin, on extended families, and on friends as well.

This chapter has tried to describe the factors that can influence a family's ability to cope successfully. Those mentioned include: age and developmental level, gender, religion, mental and physical health, financial resources, and social support system. Other important variables include education and occupation, race and ethnicity, personality, and sense of self.

It is imperative that the clinician assess accurately at what point in the transitional process from marriage to divorce each member of the family stands. This is true both at the inception of therapy and throughout the therapeutic process. A family systems perspective should be maintained because changes in one family member will affect other family members. Consideration of the two new familial subsystems—mother and children and father and children—also require sensitive attention. Interventions should be age and stage appropriate and should be modified as patients move from stage to stage.

The therapist will need to be concerned not only with the family constellation, but with multisystemic issues as well. There is often the need to cooperate with other professionals—attorneys, mediators, physicians, clergy, and school personnel, for example. Such team cooperation enhances the benefits of professional guidance and can minimize conflict. In times of conflict and confusion, patients do not need a replication of their own dissension among their professional helpers. The therapist is usually in a pivotal position (with patients' permission) to establish contact with other involved professionals and to evolve a cooperative spirit. At times it is valuable to request that several, or, if possible, all involved professionals meet together to avoid splitting, working in opposition to each other, and duplication of services. Such a meeting is analogous to a hospital-staff team meeting. The skilled professional should decide when it is advisable or contraindicated to include the patient.

A comprehensive (Kirschner & Kirschner, 1986) and multisystemic approach to divorce, such as the diaclectic model, which has been described in this chapter, provides a theoretical frame of the family members' feelings and coping strategies, as well as flexibility of choice in treatment approaches. In the case example in this chapter, the case formulation utilized a combination of psychodynamic, life cycle, and family systems constructs, and interventions incorporated structural, strategic, psychodynamic, intergenerational, problem-solving, and cognitive–behavioral approaches.

Divorce therapy is most successful when treatment is provided close to the inception of the traumatic event. Letting patients know that achieving resolution may take several years helps them accept their ambivalence, delays in taking action, and occasional emotional outbursts or withdrawals, and enhances their patience with their own progress.

Therapy for children is preventive in that the resolution of current despair can preclude delayed reactions such as bitterness, fear of commitment, inability to achieve emotional intimacy, and prolonged anger over abandonment and the sense that divorce has been an unforgivable disruption to their lives. Therapy can help to normalize, interpret, and ease the painful divorce process for children, parents, and grandparents.

# References

Ahrons, C. R. (1981). The continuing coparental relationship between spouses. *American Journal of Orthopsychiatry, 51*(3), 415–428.

Ahrons, C. R., & Rodgers, R. H. (1987). *Divorced families: A multidisciplinary developmental view.* New York: Norton.

American Bar Association. (1981). *Model code of professional responsibility.* Chicago: National Center for Professional Responsibility.

Bank, S. R., & Kahn, M. D. (1982). *The sibling bond.* New York: Basic Books.

Bohannon, P. (1970). The six stations of divorce. In P. Bohannon (Ed.), *Divorce and after: An analysis of the emotional and social problems of divorce* (pp. 29–55). New York: Doubleday.

Coogler, O. J. (1978). *Structured mediation in divorce settlement.* Lexington, MA: Heath.

Erickson, S., & McKnight-Erickson, M. (1988). *Mediation casebook.* New York: Brunner/Mazel.

Ferstenberg, R. L. (1992). Mediation vs. litigation in divorce and why a litigator becomes a mediator. *American Journal of Family Therapy, 20*(3), 266–273.

Folberg, J., & Milne, A. (1988). *Divorce mediation.* New York: Guilford Press.

Gardner, L. A. (1977). *The parent's book about divorce.* New York: Bantam Books.

Gold, L. (1992). *Between love and hate: A guide to civilized divorce.* New York: Plenum.

Haynes, J. M. (1981). *Divorce mediation.* New York: Springer.

Haynes, J. M. (1982). A conceptual model of the process of family mediation: Implications for training. *American Journal of Family Therapy, 10*(4), 5–16.

Kadis, A., & Markowitz, M. (1972). Short term analytic treatment of married couples in a group by a therapist couple. In C. Sager & H. S. Kaplan (Eds.), *Progress in group and family therapy* (pp. 463–482). New York: Brunner/Mazel.

Kaslow, F. W. (1981a). A diaclectic approach to family therapy and practice: Selectivity and synthesis. *Journal of Marital and Family Therapy, 7*(3), 345–351.

Kaslow, F. W. (1981b). Divorce and divorce therapy. In A. Gurman & D. Kniskern (Eds.), *Handbook of Family Therapy* (pp. 662–696). New York: Brunner/Mazel.

Kaslow, F. W. (1982). Group therapy with couples in conflict. *Australian Journal of Family Therapy, 3*(4), 199–204.

Kaslow, F. W. (1984). Divorce mediation and its emotional impact on the couple and their children. *American Journal of Family Therapy, 12*(3), 58–66.

Kaslow, F. W. (1987). Stages in the divorce process: Dynamics and treatment. In F. W. Kaslow & L. L. Schwartz (Eds.), *The dynamics of divorce: A life cycle perspective* (pp. 23–37). New York: Brunner/Mazel.

Kaslow, F. W. (1988). The psychological dimension of divorce mediation. In J. Folberg & A. Milne (Eds.), *Divorce mediation: Theory and practice* (pp. 83–108). New York: Guilford Press.

Kaslow, F. W. (1990). Divorce therapy and mediation for better custody. *Japanese Journal of Family Psychology, 4,* 19–37.

Kaslow, F. W. (1991). Enter the prenuptial: A prelude to marriage or remarriage. *Behavioral Sciences and the Law, 9,* 375–386.

Kaslow, F. W. (1993). The divorce ceremony: A healing strategy. In T. Nelson & T. Trepper (Eds.), *101 Favorite family therapy interventions* (pp. 341–345). New York: Haworth.

Kaslow, F. W. (1994). Painful partings: Providing therapeutic guidance. In L. L. Schwartz (Ed.), *Mid life divorce counseling* (pp. 67–82). Alexandria, VA: American Counseling Association.

Kaslow, F. W., & Lieberman, E. J. (1981). Couples group therapy: Rationale, dynamics and process. In G. P. Sholevar (Ed.), *The handbook of marriage and marital therapy* (pp. 347–362). New York: SP Medical and Scientific Books.

Kaslow, F. W., & Schwartz, L. L. (1987a). *Dynamics of divorce: A life cycle perspective.* New York: Brunner/Mazel.

Kaslow, F. W., & Schwartz, L. L. (1987b). Older children of divorce: A neglected family segment. In J. Vincent (Ed.), *Advances in family intervention* (pp. 99–120). Greenwich, CT: JAI Press.

Kessler, S. (1975). *The American way of divorce: Prescription for change.* Chicago: Nelson Hall.

Kessler, S., & Bostwick, S. (1977). Beyond divorce. Coping skills for children. *Journal of Clinical Child Psychology, 6,* 38–41.

Kirschner, D. A., & Kirschner, S. (1986). *Comprehensive family therapy.* New York: Brunner/Mazel.

Marlow, L. (1992). *Divorce and the myth of lawyers.* Garden City, NY: Harlan Press.

Marlow, L., & Sauber, S. R. (1990). *The handbook of divorce mediation.* New York: Plenum.

McGoldrick, M., & Gerson, R. (1985). *Genograms in family assessment.* New York: Norton.

Ricci, I. (1980). *Mom's house, dad's house: Making shared custody work.* New York: Macmillan.

Roizblatt, A., Garcia, P., Maida, A. M., & Moya, G. (1990). Is Valentine still doubtful? A workshop model for children of divorce. *Contemporary Family Therapy, 12,* 299–310.

Turner, N. W. (1980). Divorce in mid life: Clinical implications and applications. In W. H. Norman & T. J. Scaramella (Eds.), *Mid life: Developmental and clinical issues* (pp. 149–177). New York: Brunner/Mazel.

Wallerstein, J., & Blakeslee, S. (1989). *Second chances: Men, women and children a decade after divorce.* New York: Ticknor & Fields.

Wallerstein, J. S., & Kelly, J. B. (1980). *Surviving the breakup: How children and parents cope with divorce.* New York: Basic Books.

Weitzman, L. J. (1985). *The divorce revolution: The unexpected social and economic consequences for women and children in America.* New York: Free Press.

Whitaker, C. A., & Miller, M. H. (1969). A re-evaluation of psychiatric help when divorce impends. *American Journal of Psychiatry, 126,* 57–64.

# CHAPTER 16

# DIVORCE MEDIATION: A NEW SYSTEM FOR DEALING WITH THE FAMILY IN TRANSITION

*S. Richard Sauber, Stephen F. Beiner, and Gail S. Meddoff*

To combat the trauma of adversarial divorce, a growing number of family therapists and attorneys are using divorce mediation as an alternative dispute resolution process. Approximately half of all marriages today end in divorce. Most of the marriages are dissolved through the adversarial system, in which combating attorneys represent husband and wife, and the couple are often pitted against each other in a win–lose situation. Such prolonged battles often leave emotional scars on the spouses and their children long after the divorce is final (Wallerstein, 1989).

Divorce is now considered a normal part of the family life cycle (see Kaslow & Schwartz, 1987; see also chap. 15 in this volume). Because family psychologists have knowledge of family systems, child development, problem solving, and conflict resolution, divorce mediation is a natural outgrowth of their expertise. Integrating these skills within a financial and legal framework is the main challenge for the family psychologist who wishes to function as a mediator.

As an alternative to the emotionally and financially draining adversarial approach, divorce mediation is more humane. It also offers practice opportunities to psychologists. It bypasses the constraints of managed health care and insurance companies because it is a necessary human service not covered by third-party health insurance carriers.

## WHAT IS DIVORCE MEDIATION?

Divorce mediation is an intervention in the lives of each family member involved in the marital dissolution. It has been shown to reduce conflict, minimize loyalty struggles, enhance the adjustment phase and communication style, and stabilize the family unit while the marital bonds are severed (Slyck, Newland, & Stern, 1992).

The purpose of divorce mediation is to help couples resolve conflicts and to make their own decisions concerning child custody and visitation, division of property, child support, and spousal support. To achieve this goal, the mediator acts as a neutral third party who helps the divorcing spouses reach a mutually acceptable agreement on these issues. If the couple is not yet separated, the mediator will help them to develop a separation agreement that specifies temporary financial and living arrangements for the spouses and their children. At other times, the mediator may enter the system after the actual separation has occurred. In this case, a separation agreement may or may not already have been developed. Individual attorneys may already be involved. It is imperative for the mediator to assess the system and intervene to promote future cooperation of the couple. Mediation examines the system context of the impending divorce. It examines the roles played by others significant to the couple, including in-laws and grandparents. A consulting accountant may provide information as to the tax consequences of the various alternatives. The agreement is first put in writing in a mediation agreement, sometimes called a *memorandum of understanding*. An attorney then drafts a legally binding contract, usually called a *separation agreement* or a *property settlement agreement,* which includes the terms and provisions agreed on by the parties at mediation, and which is ultimately incorporated by the judge in the courts order of divorce.

Unlike arbitration, where the parties agree in advance to be bound by the decisions of a third party, mediation is the process whereby the spouses work out their own agreement with the help of a facilitator.

## FACTORS IN MEDIATION

The success of mediation depends on a number of factors: the skill and style of the mediator, the family systems involved, the complexity of the issues, and the intensity of the conflict.

Proponents of mediation insist that mediation saves time and money for both the litigants and the courts, compared with the traditional adversarial approach. There may be additional benefits to the children and spouses: lessened hostility, greater emotional stability, improved self-esteem, and an increased chance that there will be full performance of the terms in the final decree. When spouses reach a mutually agreeable settlement, they are less likely to renege on support and visitation arrangements.

Opponents to mediation contend that male–female power imbalances can result in unjust settlements. They argue that an overbearing or financially sophisticated spouse—frequently the husband—can manipulate negotiations in his favor. By not having a separate attorney represent her interests, they contend, a divorcing wife may not get her fair share.

## FRAMEWORK OF THIS CHAPTER

This chapter provides an analysis of the five different methods of mediation and addresses the major criticism of mediation. The analysis is designed to enable practitioners to evaluate which system is best suited to their own practice, their clients, and the family system with which they are dealing. This will enable therapists to become better educated consumers of mediation services and better mediators themselves.

The five mediation methods are (a) integrative (the most recently developed methodology), (b) structured, (c) therapeutic, (d) negotiatory, and (e) interdisciplinary (see Exhibit 1). These five styles differ greatly. The integrative approach is more laissez-faire, whereas structured mediation is more authoritarian.

Therapeutic mediation is emotion oriented, whereas the negotiation approach is more business oriented. The interdisciplinary approach attempts to harness the strengths of each of the other approaches.

The second part of the chapter considers a major criticism of mediation, the so-called power imbalance between the genders. It addresses several crucial questions: Is there, in fact, a power imbalance? If so, what are the factors affecting the family system and the interpersonal power dynamics of the divorcing couple? How can mediators recognize and deal with abuses of power? Is interdisciplinary mediation—the fifth mediation method—a viable solution in such situations?

## ANALYSIS OF FOUR MEDIATION METHODOLOGIES

### Method One: Integrative Mediation

Integrative mediation radically departs from many of the practices of traditional divorce mediators, who simply use an alternative dispute resolution methodology to determine the couple's respective legal rights and obligations. The integrative approach avoids assumptions about divorce as a legal event (Marlow & Sauber, 1990). Developed collaboratively by a divorce attorney (Marlow) and a family psychologist (Sauber), this method views divorce not as a *legal* problem in a couple's lives, but as a serious *personal* problem—a personal family crisis to be resolved by the divorcing parties. This distinction is crucial because it changes the focus and goal of mediation.

Marlow and Sauber maintain that viewing divorce mediation as a personal, rather than a legal, event enables the couple to achieve a psychological as well as a legal divorce. It empowers the couple to make self-determined decisions based around a new partnership and its future effects on the family. They contend that integrative mediation encourages the divorcing couple to deal with their emotional and practical problems in a way that encourages the participants to find adaptive solutions to life after the crisis of divorce has passed. The focus is on future plans rather than on past hurts; on common interests rather than on conflicting ones; and on emotional closure and redefinition of the couple's relationship rather than on righting past wrongs.

**Legal myths.** The underlying premise of integrative mediation is the identification of several assumptions, or legal myths, as listed here (Marlow & Sauber, 1990):

- Divorce is solely a legal event.
- Justice is guaranteed by protecting each person's legal rights.
- A divorce agreement must be fair.

Marlow (1992) further expands upon, and punctures, other legal myths:

- The sole issue in a couple's separation and divorce is the determination of their legal rights and obligations.
- If separating and divorcing couples do not look to the law and to legal rules, they run the risk of making a mistake and getting it wrong.
- Separating and divorcing couples are best protected by retaining separate lawyers.
- The divorce is usually caused by one of the parties and the law's function is to punish that party for his or her misconduct.

---

## EXHIBIT 1

**Characteristics of Divorce Mediation Approaches**

Integrative mediation
- Laid-back, laissez-faire approach
- Divorce viewed as personal, rather than legal, problem
- Collaboration by psychologist and attorney mediators
- No formalized or standardized set of rules
- Single financial data sheet instead of separate budgets
- Emphasis on solution of mutual problems

Structured mediation
- Authoritarian approach
- Rigid rules and timetable specified in mediation contract
- Goal-oriented system geared to quick resolution of issues
- Rigid structure may help equalization of power

Therapeutic mediation
- Emotion-oriented approach requiring active listening
- Resolution of emotional issues before substantive issues
- Concentration on family system and familial relationships
- Crisis therapy where children may be included in sessions
- Approach most familiar to those in mental health field

Negotiatory mediation
- Business-oriented approach
- Emphasis on leaving both parties in best financial position
- Separate negotiating sessions to break impasses
- Emotional conflicts resolved quickly or referred to therapist
- Approach used in labor and international negotiations

Interdisciplinary mediation
- Therapist–attorney team approach
- Mediators follow rigid role definitions of their professions
- Collaborating approach has mediators use one another as referrals
- Conjoint approach uses joint sessions of mediators and spouses
- Dual mediators of opposite sexes may prevent triangling and bias

---

- Adversarial legal proceedings are designed to protect the best interests of children.
- Adversarial proceedings may not be perfect but there is no better way.
- Separating and divorcing couples get exactly what they deserve.

These legal myths are avoided as assumptions in mediation. Most mediators help draft an agreement that resembles what the parties would have received had they gone to court. One problem with using a legal yardstick is that so-called fairness is often determined by outside circumstances unrelated to the couple's situation.

What is legally fair, for example, may depend on where the person happens to live at the time of his or her divorce, because dissolution statutes differ from state to state. Some states obligate parents to support their children until they reach the age of 18; others require parental support until the age of 21. A wife who is found guilty of fault may be awarded support in one state but precluded from receiving alimony in another. An inheritance or gift given to one spouse during the marriage is considered marital property to be divided at the time of divorce in some states, but not in all. What is considered fair also depends on the mediator's own life experiences, gender, and prejudices.

Integrative mediation defines fairness differently. It bases fairness not on what a third party or the legal system deems to be just, but on what the parties are willing to accept and believe they can live with.

**Application of integrative mediation.** Because of its philosophical differences from other mediation methodologies, integrative mediation differs from other methods in its approach. A psychotherapist and an attorney form a collaborative relationship, sharing the responsibility for helping the couple in conflict. In integrative mediation, there are no rigid role definitions. For instance, a psychologist-mediator may handle the financial aspects of mediation, and the attorney-mediator may help resolve a child's visitation schedule. The attorney and psychologist often have some joint sessions with the clients as well as each seeing the clients alone. Once the couple reaches a tentative agreement, it is stated in a formal document called a *memorandum of understanding* prepared by either the attorney-mediator or an outside attorney of the couple's choice.

In other methods of mediation, especially structured mediation, it is common practice for mediators to enter into a formal written agreement with the couple prior to the commencement of mediation setting forth the agreed-upon rules that will govern the mediation sessions. Integrative mediators, however, contend that such rule agreements are counterproductive. They believe the rules and conditions of the mediation are best left to the parties to formulate themselves.

Unlike in other forms of mediation, in integrative mediation the parties are not instructed to prepare budgets for themselves. Integrative mediators view separately drawn budgets as adversarial weapons used in the game of attempting to extract as much as one can while giving as little as possible. By concentrating on their differing views of what each wants to give and to get, the couple underscore their conflict.

Instead, the couple together fill out one financial data sheet listing their income, assets, and liabilities. Each then documents and confirms the data and accuracy of the information. The financial analysis focuses on what each of the spouses presently earns or is capable of earning and on their joint and separate assets. The question posed to the participants is not how much each party wants, but how the available dollars should be divided between them.

Although the mediator can help the parties divide the marital pie, he or she cannot guarantee that each of the parties will have enough to eat (Marlow & Sauber, 1990). It is the mediator's role to explore ways that additional monies can be found or earned to expand the pie before dividing it. Obviously, this is not always possible. At all times, the ideas and suggestions should flow from the couple to the mediator. For instance, the husband may agree to pay the wife's living expenses and tuition for schooling while she learns employable skills. This approach differs from imposing rehabilitative alimony on the parties because the law requires it. Instead, the emphasis is on how the couple can solve a mutual problem to make both of their lives more manageable.

**Integrative mediation's facilitative style.** Because integrative mediation is based on the premise that divorce is a personal problem, the mediators do not automatically take charge each time the mediation veers off course. Instead, they wait to see how the parties resolve an area of contention through their own discussions. This tends to result in a rather nondirective style. The mediator takes the responsibility for establishing the structure of the mediation but allows the participants to take the initiative in resolving areas of contention. This is often referred to as the battle for structure versus the battle for initiative (Neill & Kniskern, 1982, pp. 292–293).

For example, while the couple was still happily married, their discussions revolved around whether their son would enjoy going to camp, what type of camp, how long he should go, and how much they could afford to spend. Now that the couple has separated, the camp discussion should not be permitted to shift to such questions as: Is the husband legally obligated to pay to send his son to camp? If so, is the wife legally obligated to contribute? Does she have the legal right to child support while their son is at camp? Integrative mediators maintain that the issue of summer camp should be treated as consistently as possible with the preseparation, predivorce period. The focus should remain on what camp arrangement is best for their child and how the couple can cooperatively accomplish it.

## Method Two: Structured Mediation
Structured mediation requires adherence to a set of 40 rules and a strict timetable. In contrast to integrative mediation's laissez-faire approach, structured mediation has a fairly rigid format.

Structured mediation was developed by the attorney O. J. Coogler, who is often referred to as the father of divorce mediation. After 20 years in practice, Coogler experienced a bitter divorce himself. Convinced there was a more civilized way of dissolving a marriage, he sought to find an alternative to the adversarial divorce. The result was a system of highly structured negotiating guidelines and procedural rules, which he described in *Structured Mediation in Divorce Settlement* (Coogler, 1978).

The process detailed in this first professional mediation text is designed to reduce the emotional pain and suffering involved in divorce. This goal-oriented system focuses on cooperative negotiations based on open communication, trust, and self-determination. The detailed rules equalize the balance of power necessary for the spouses to reach a victimless settlement.

**Structured mediation's contract of commitment.** As they enter structured mediation, the couple are asked to sign a contract titled Marital Mediation Rules, which itemizes the mediation method in great detail. The participants agree to abide by the rules and to help enforce them. Included in the 40 rules set forth by Coogler and the Family Mediation Association[1] are the following:

- The spouses are required to deposit with the mediator an amount of money sufficient to cover 10 mediation sessions.
- They agree that if they are unable to resolve an issue through negotiation, they will submit that issue to arbitration, which will result in a binding decision.
- They agree to attend mediation sessions at least once weekly.
- They agree to provide a full disclosure of their finances.
- They agree not to communicate with mediators and advisory attorneys concerning matters in mediation except in the presence of each other during a mediation session.

Almost everything the couple discusses is detailed in the rules, including guidelines for division of property, spousal maintenance, child support, custody, rights of custodial and noncustodial parents, and the use of an advisory attorney. In the event mediation fails and litigation is sought, the rules preclude the representation of either party by the mediator or the advisory attorney, if one is used.

---

[1] The Family Mediation Association is now called the Academy of Family Mediators. For a listing of resource organizations, see the appendix to this chapter.

The mediator attempts to help the couple reach an interim support agreement during the first session. Designed to be in effect only for the duration of the mediation, this interim agreement attempts to alleviate immediate financial concerns and demonstrates to the couple that they can cooperate (Coogler, 1978). The interim agreement provides for temporary support for the minor children, temporary support for the spouse seeking maintenance, attorney's fees, and the cost of mediation and arbitration.

The rules provide mediators and their clients with a structured formula for dealing with the issues of divorce. Unlike other systems, individual counseling sessions are prohibited because they are considered to be counterproductive to the continuing neutrality and trust of the mediator. The mediator discusses issues only when the couple is together, so neither party feels that anything is being decided without his or her input and cooperation.

**Active involvement in structured mediation.** During the initial meeting, the spouses are assigned homework. They are required to prepare budgets, provide income tax returns, and fill out financial information and income statements. They may also be asked to provide a monthly expense budget and an analysis of family expenses and anticipated future expenditures. By preparing such materials the participants are encouraged to consider the relevant issues. Having the figures available also accelerates the mediation process by providing information necessary in the resolution of a settlement.

Adherents of structured mediation believe that although the detailed agreement may at first be intimidating to the couple, the rigid rules serve several valuable purposes. They provide structure to lives that have been thrown into chaos. By promoting openness, the rules lessen misunderstanding, provide a framework for discussion, and establish a time frame for resolution. The rules help spouses who are not serious about, or ready for, mediation enter into the proper negotiating mind-set. Much of the financial information required in structured mediation is also required by independent attorneys in an adversarial divorce proceeding.

A major advantage of structured mediation is the equalization of power at the onset of negotiations.

Delineated rules, roles, and cooperative problem solving serve to prevent either spouse from maintaining a position of immovable power. Thus, the rules help the untrained spouse/negotiator hold his or her own against a more experienced and forceful spouse.

Structured mediation is a goal-oriented system. It is useful in the resolution of property division issues, particularly when emotional issues have been resolved and the spouses are equally motivated to obtain a divorce. However, as is often the case, if emotional issues are a primary problem that must be resolved first, the couple is encouraged to see a family therapist who specializes in the therapeutic mediation approach.

## Method Three: Therapeutic Mediation

This is the method that is most familiar to those in the mental health field. In therapeutic mediation, the couple resolves emotional traumas before dealing with substantive issues. For instance, before a couple negotiates child custody and visitation issues, they seek at least some resolution of the emotional problems related to the marital conflict, separation, and impending divorce. A wife may seek to retaliate for a husband's indiscretion with another woman by refusing him visitation rights. A husband may lie about his wife's fitness as a parent because she has asked for a divorce. The focus of therapeutic mediation is to minimize the impact of emotional issues on child custody and visitation, child support, division of property, and spousal support.

Therapeutic mediators utilize a family therapist's therapeutic skills rather than an attorney's analytic skills in resolving child-related issues. Mediation concentrates on the family system and the consequent familial relationships. Actions by one family member invariably result in compensating reactions by other family members (Irving, 1980) and are dealt with accordingly.

Therefore, when divorce threatens to disrupt the natural balance between family members, the mediator must find a way to restore that balance. The mediator restores natural harmony to the family by containing the damage caused by divorce and helping the parents establish an atmosphere that is as conflict free as possible for the children. This belief in balance and harmony is compatible with several ancient mediation traditions—precursors to modern-day divorce mediation. For instance, Japanese and Confucian mediation methods use persuasion and compromise, emphasizing compassion over retaliation. This philosophy is also consistent with the work of the Jewish Conciliation Boards of Justice (Folberg, 1983).

The therapeutic mediator spends the first few sessions actively listening to the spouses, encouraging them to vent their feelings. The mediator tries to diffuse their anger and helps them change their focus from past pain and injustices to future plans and growth. The mediator also encourages them to trust and cooperate with each other in formulating a plan. While listening to the spouses, the mediator analyzes their conflict management skills, their emotional stages in the divorce process, and their interactional power balance (Haynes, 1981; Kelly, 1983).

Because children are often at the core of therapeutic mediation, they are sometimes invited into the sessions to demonstrate the effect the conflict is having on them. This may capture the attention of parents who are at an impasse on a major issue or may help them modify their destructive behavior. This type of crisis therapy can also be used to reform relationships and restore familial balance.

Mediators with therapeutic training are skilled in active listening. They are able to reframe questions in noninflammatory language and summarize the motivations and concerns of the spouses in nonthreatening ways. However, some therapeutic techniques that are successful in most therapy may not be helpful in mediation, such as open-ended questions (Vanderkooi & Pearson, 1983). According to the principles of therapeutic mediation, anger and hostility must be diffused before the spouses can approach any meaningful communication and negotiation.

## Method Four: Negotiatory Mediation

Negotiatory mediation is the model of mediation most familiar to the public. It is the form of mediation most of us use in our everyday interpersonal relationships and transactions (Bahr, 1981). Negotiatory mediation, on a more formal level, has long been used to resolve international and labor–management disputes. Unlike therapeutic mediation, which concentrates on emotions and family relations, the negotiatory approach to divorce focuses on reaching

a final contract that leaves both parties in the best possible *financial* position.

Negotiatory mediation uses fairly frequent changes of format. Utilizing negotiating skills and techniques, the mediator may work with the disputing parties in separate rooms and in separate sessions. Each side individually develops offers and counteroffers with the mediator. Divorce mediators employ this caucusing technique when the couple reach an impasse or an issue becomes too emotionally charged to resolve in a conjoint session. Agreements are later finalized in group meetings.

For example, the couple may disagree over how their two cars should be allocated. The husband rigidly adheres to his position that he is going to keep their new large luxury car, even though he knows the two-door sports coupe is not adequate for the needs of his wife and children. He also refuses to help pay for a new family car for her. Any joint discussions lead to nonproductive shouting. Although the husband knows he is being unreasonable, he refuses to back down.

By meeting with the spouses separately, the mediator may be able to position the husband to be more reasonable or to enable the wife to explore additional alternatives. This may be more readily accomplished because each warring spouse does not have to back down in front of the other and can save face.

Following the negotiatory framework, the divorce mediator often utilizes the tool of nonreversible concessions to prevent the bargaining process from backsliding. For instance, once Fred agrees to give Gwen the computer, he cannot later change his mind.

Another negotiatory technique utilized is that all areas of dispute—custody/visitation, support, property division—are tossed onto the bargaining table and bartered like trading cards. Individual areas of dispute are not finalized until all negotiations are finished. In other words, the spouses trade off items between and within issue areas until they reach agreement on the final package (Haynes, 1981). For instance, Fred might agree to a concession in spousal support if Gwen agrees to let the children spend summer vacation with him.

The labor-based method starts with the premise that couples seeking mediation, rather than litigation, are ready to cooperate. If the spouses get so embroiled in emotional conflicts that they are unable to negotiate substantive matters, negotiations cease. The mediator will refer the couple to a therapist or try to diffuse the anger or hostility in order to get the mediation back on course.

## CHOOSING A MEDIATION SYSTEM

Because of their backgrounds, many mental health professionals naturally gravitate toward the therapeutic or integrative approach. Attorneys generally tend to favor the negotiatory or structured methods. Each mediator has to choose the style that is most compatible with his or her own personality and training.

Even though the four systems use different techniques, their goals and solutions often overlap. Different systems work best with different couples and different issues. For example, if child custody is an issue and the spouses are immersed in bitterness and anger, therapeutic mediation may help diffuse their hostility and shield their children from the bitter fray. It is also valuable when spouses are at different emotional stages of the divorce process.

Alternatively, if there are a large number of conflicting issues to be resolved in a relatively short time frame, a structured approach may be most effective. In negotiatory mediation, a fair financial settlement is the primary goal. In integrative mediation, self-determination and the creation of a future working relationship with the former spouse are chief motivators.

It is important to consider both the advantages and disadvantages of individual sessions with each spouse, as advocated in the negotiatory mediation approach. There are advantages to the individual session approach. It enables the mediator to learn about underlying emotional issues and fears the spouse may not want to disclose in joint sessions. By targeting the areas of agreement and disagreement, the mediator can better structure the sessions and narrow the issues to be resolved.

Individual sessions may be particularly successful when spouses cannot be together in the same room without suffering great emotional distress or intimidation. This is true, for instance, when one spouse is overbearing and abusive. The mediator can try to

reach a consensus by shuttling back and forth between the parties, thereby neutralizing the power imbalance.

Conversely, there are major disadvantages to the individual session format. Individual sessions may result in triangulation by creating suspicion in the mind of the excluded party. For instance, one or both spouses may believe the other spouse is plotting secretly with the mediator or is lying to get the mediator on his or her side. Each spouse may fear the mediator has become biased or has developed a closer relationship with the other spouse.

Another drawback to individual sessions is that one spouse may divulge an essential confidence that should be a part of the negotiations. However, that spouse may refuse to divulge the information to the other spouse. For instance, the wife might confide during a private session that she managed to hide thousands of dollars during her 20-year marriage but balk at telling her husband. The mediator should have an agreement with the couple that there are to be no secrets that would hinder the mediation process.

## DEALING WITH A POWER IMBALANCE

Whichever divorce mediation method one chooses—integrative, structured, therapeutic, or negotiatory—most mediators are forced to confront the issue of potential power imbalance. More specifically stated, critics of mediation claim that unequal negotiating powers between the parties render mediated divorce settlements inequitable to the financially weaker or more submissive party. Typically this party is the woman.

### Is There a Gender-Based Power Imbalance?
Opponents of mediation contend that after much pressuring by feminists for enactment of equitable distribution statutes, women are seeing their hard-won gains lost in mediation. According to Lefcourt (1984), women's advocates view the trend toward the use of divorce mediation with justified skepticism and suspicion. They believe that most women are not equal to their husbands in bargaining power, negotiation experience, or financial resources. This of-

ten results in women's agreement to joint rather than sole custody and to large economic concessions (Fineman, 1988).

Joanne Schulman (1983) also advises women against the use of mediation. Several factors she believes give men power over women in divorce negotiations are greater knowledge of family finances, larger income, higher career mobility, greater experience at bargaining, a stronger belief that the earnings and assets are one's own, and more familiarity with the use of control and power tactics.

However, integrative mediators disagree with these assertions. They contend that the concept of power imbalance is based on the old stereotype of the astute, financially sophisticated, domineering husband and the ignorant, unsophisticated, submissive housewife (Marlow & Sauber, 1990). Although the wife today is not necessarily weaker, it has been established that women now often lose financially and get poorer access to the children or lose meaningful time with them. Good mediation needs to deal with these problems. In fact, the probability of increased compliance with the final agreement between the parties is maximized when these issues are properly dealt with. This must be openly acknowledged with both parties.

Integrative mediators contend that even with traditional couples, mediation changes the marital power dynamics in a positive way. They believe that mediation is empowering. For instance, wives unhappy with financial arrangements during marriage have little recourse because courts are reluctant to interfere with marital privacy. However, in mediation, a husband knows his wife is free to reject his offer and to go to court to seek greater financial relief. Mediation helps equalize power. The only alternative is adversarial divorce, which typically removes power from the spouses and places it in the hands of the attorneys.

## What Are the Power Factors?

Power can be considered control of or access to those emotional, economic, or physical resources desired by the other person (Haynes, 1988). Power is relational and situational and shifts with changes in circumstances.

There are several factors affecting the power dynamics of the couple during the divorce process (Neumann, 1992). Power may be gained by the spouse who:

- Wants the divorce.
- Does not want the divorce, and is willing to pay, emotionally and financially, to slow or stop the divorce.
- Has legitimate power, defined as each person's moral and cultural perception of who should have the power.
- Has legal favor, meaning that divorce laws would probably favor that gender in terms of custody and visitation, division of property, and child and spousal support.
- Feels guilt concerning the termination of the marriage. This usually applies to the party initiating the divorce and/or having an affair.
- Makes promises or threats that the other spouse believes. The promise or threat can be about an issue outside of the settlement.
- Develops the divorce settlement proposals or options.
- Has a strong representative, such as an attorney, or supportive people in his or her life.

In addition to these power factors, there may be additional elements that were present during the marriage and that gain added significance during negotiations. A party may additionally gain an advantage if he or she has the larger income and financial assets, has the greater knowledge of financial issues, or has used physical force or violence (Neumann, 1992).

## How to Recognize and Deal With Abuses of Power

Divorce mediators have to recognize the degree of power held by each spouse, assess the effect of the imbalance of power upon the negotiations, and utilize techniques to equalize the balance of power to effectuate an equitable settlement (Neumann, 1992).

However, when mediators are faced with the expression of power—or with the expression of stubbornness, selfishness, insensitivity, or unrealistic expectations—it is not productive for the mediator to counterbalance the scales with equal expressions of power, stubbornness, selfishness, insensitivity, or unrealistic expectations. Instead, the mediator should view these as existential realities which must be dealt with and perhaps circumvented in order to successfully conclude an agreement between the parties (Marlow & Sauber, 1990, p. 117).

Mediation offers clients the best opportunity to become empowered, but mediation provides no guarantees. According to Neumann (1992), empowerment is immensely valuable for a divorcing individual, because it is the sense of competency and the ability to take control of one's own life during the process of divorce that enables each person to successfully move ahead with his or her life.

However, although mediation is empowering and gives parties a forum for expressing their feelings, it is important for mediators to interrupt intimidating negotiating patterns (Davis & Salem, 1984). Mediators should not tolerate patterns of humiliation or domination. It is also necessary to insure that both parties have full information to make informed decisions; to be alert that one spouse does not settle out of fear of retaliation or violence; and to not press an unwilling party to settle or to leave key issues unsettled in order to finish mediation quickly.

An essential element in dealing with unequal bargaining power is to have the parties sign a contract stipulating full and open disclosure of all financial matters. Mediators should strongly encourage the parties to have their potential agreement reviewed by outside counsel and an accountant before they sign a binding document. To achieve a more balanced negotiation, dominant and passive spouses can be allotted equal talking and listening time in joint sessions. Negotiation sessions should be stopped whenever one party resorts to name calling, threats, or ridicule. When necessary, separate negotiating sessions may help reduce a dominant spouse's physical intimidation and verbal abuse of his passive partner.

## Are All Dispute Resolution Forums Equal?

In a study to determine which dispute resolution forum delivers the most equitable separation and divorce settlements for women, Jessica Pearson found

that mediation does not exacerbate a woman's financial woes (Pearson, 1991). Nor does mediation do a better job than other forums in protecting women from prolonged and severe financial dislocations.

The overall findings of Pearson's (1991) research revealed there are few differences in the substantive terms of divorce agreements generated in various forums regarding child custody and visitation, child support, division of property, and spousal support. However, mediated child-support agreements achieved through mediation are more likely to include a college-payment plan. Although the settlements reached through mediation and litigation were substantively similar, attitudes toward the agreement were very different. Satisfaction and fairness ratings were highest in mediation forums. Postdivorce compliance with the agreement was also higher for those agreements achieved through mediation.

Pearson's study, prepared under a grant from the State Justice Institute, included structured telephone interviews with 302 divorced individuals. Those interviewed had used various methods to resolve the issues involved in their divorce. These methods included mediation, adversarial attorney negotiation, autonomous negotiation (i.e., issue resolution on the couple's own without a third party), and judicial assistance.

Two types of mediation had been used: public and private. In public mediation, the mediation is typically court ordered. The spouses frequently each have an attorney but they have reached an impasse. The mediation confronts a particular issue, such as child custody or child visitation. It is at no cost or at a reduced cost. In private mediation, the couple engages the services of a mediator to help them formulate their own divorce agreement. Individual attorneys are used as consultants or to write the final draft of the agreement.

According to Pearson (1991), a pattern worth noting was that although mediated clients in most public sectors were represented by attorneys, few reported that their attorneys substantially changed the mediated agreements. These responses underscore both the importance of the mediator role and the danger of assuming that attorneys or judges will critically review and alter mediated agreements.

## METHOD FIVE: INTERDISCIPLINARY MEDIATION

In order to deal adequately with both the emotional and financial issues of divorce and to confront the power imbalance criticism, many mediators are turning toward an interdisciplinary approach to mediation. In interdisciplinary mediation, an attorney defines the issues and provides the technical, financial, and legal information, and a mental health professional provides communication and conflict reduction skills (Gold, 1984).

There are major distinctions between integrative mediation, which also utilizes the services of a therapist and attorney, and the interdisciplinary approach. In integrative mediation, the two professionals meet with the couple separately on an as-needed collaborative basis. There are no clear-cut role definitions.

In interdisciplinary mediation, the attorney–therapist approach is structured in one of two ways. In the collaborating approach (Wiseman & Fiske, 1980), sometimes referred to as *tandem mediation,* the attorney and therapist see the couple in separate sessions dealing with their individual areas of expertise. The therapist refers clients to the attorney for legal and financial matters. The attorney refers clients to the therapist for emotionally charged issues, such as child custody. They do not meet with the couple in joint sessions.

In the *conjoint* approach, also referred to as *joint mediation* or *co-mediation,* the attorney and therapist meet as a team with the couple in joint sessions. Occasionally each will meet separately with the couple when specific issues render the role of the other unnecessary. For instance, the explanation of complex financial matters may be handled by the attorney alone.

## Issues in the Interdisciplinary Mediation Approach

Mediators need to be cautious about their comments on the prevailing law so as not to be construed as interpreting the law or giving legal advice. Commenting on the law is outside of the function of the mediator and makes the mediator vulnerable to attorneys hostile to the mediation process.

A male–female team is frequently used in interdisciplinary mediation. It has the advantage of reducing the dangers of triangling and mediator bias. For example, John and Mary were involved in mediation with a sole female practitioner. They were stalemated on several major issues, including spousal support and the listing of John's pension as a marital asset. John interpreted the mediator's suggestions as biased toward his wife. "It's always two against one," he complained. "You women always stick together." Dual mediators of opposite sexes can help prevent problems of triangling and bias.

In addition to minimizing bias, a male–female team aids communication. One mediator can be a calming influence or the voice of reason when the other fails to relate. Gender balancing provides each spouse with the feeling that he or she is understood. Opposite-sex mediators also serve a role model function, demonstrating by example how to calmly discuss issues and brainstorm solutions.

Two facilitators are also more likely to be successful in equalizing unequal bargaining powers (Gold, 1984). These power inequities may be strategic, emotional, or knowledge based. The lawyer and the therapist who work as a team may help to deter legal or psychological manipulation because of each professional's implicit monitoring functions. Spouses are less likely to take advantage of each other when knowledgeable authorities are so close at hand.

For example, one mediator can act as consultant to the less-informed spouse to make bargaining more equitable. The attorney-mediator explains the spouses' rights and options, and the therapist-mediator helps them understand their reasons for making the underlying decisions.

### Dealing With the Issues

Experts such as tax attorneys, accountants, and financial planners can provide valuable assistance to couples resolving issues in mediation. Whichever method of mediation is used, the issues to be resolved remain the same, although the order of resolution may differ.

When there are minor children, the major issues to be dealt with prior to divorce include

- child custody and visitation arrangements;

- child support;
- division of marital property;
- spousal support.

In structured mediation, couples are required to resolve the issues in a prescribed order: first custody and visitation, next division of property, and finally child and spousal support. In order to determine what amount of support is equitable and adequate, it is necessary first to settle custody and division of property issues. In structured mediation, once an issue is resolved, it cannot be reopened unless the mediator deems it to be necessary.

In integrative, therapeutic, negotiatory, and interdisciplinary mediation, the four issues may be worked on simultaneously or in any order. First, the mediator determines the areas of agreement. Then negotiating begins on problem areas. Each area of contention can be bartered and traded. Because no issues are closed in negotiatory mediation until final resolution, bargaining and compromising continue until the end.

In selecting the order of issues, some mediators, except structural mediators, prefer to focus on the easiest issues first to bolster the couple's confidence and trust in the system, in the mediator, and in each other. Others prefer to confront the most difficult issue first. Just as family therapy is often viewed as open-ended (see chap. 4 in this volume), mediation needs to retain that element. This is true as children enter new development phases and visitation or custody needs to be reexamined as to what is in the best interest of the child.

## CONCLUSION

Divorce mediation requires great skill and finesse. Next to the death of a loved one, divorce is viewed as the most devastating event a person experiences. In fact, from some perspectives, divorce is the more complex and devastating event, especially when children are involved, because death has a finality, but children link a couple forever. Divorce mediators must proceed delicately at certain times and boldly at other points in the process. They must know when to remain quiet and when to intercede.

Mediation has a dynamic quality—a life that often lasts long after the agreement has been signed. As children grow older, couples may want, or need, to return to mediation to deal with changing issues. These issues may include a dramatic increase or decrease in the income of one or both spouses or may involve the special needs of a child.

With approximately one out of every two marriages ending in divorce, mediation is a growing field and a viable alternative to adversarial divorce. The five different methods of mediation—integrative, structural, therapeutic, negotiatory, and interdisciplinary—have all been used successfully. Interdisciplinary mediation, utilizing the expertise of both attorneys and mental health professionals in a team approach, often provides clients with the best outcome.

By being cognizant of how the family system functioned during marriage and the power factors affecting divorce, mediators can address power imbalances that may exist. Successful mediation is a matter of creating the correct blend of mediator, clients, and system. Divorce mediation offers the family psychologist a broad range of therapeutic interventions for families experiencing divorce that have a preventive, as well as a rehabilitative, impact on each of the family members and on future generations.

## References

Bahr, S. J. (1981). An evaluation of court mediation. *Journal of Family Issues, 2*, 39–60.

Coogler, O. J. (1978). *Structured mediation in divorce settlements: A handbook for marital mediators.* Lexington, MA: Heath.

Davis, A., & Salem, R. (1984). Dealing with power imbalances in the mediation of interpersonal disputes. *Mediation Quarterly, 6*, 17–26.

Fineman, M. (1988). Dominion and discourse: Professional language and legal change in child custody decision making. *Harvard Law Review, 101*, 727.

Folberg, J. (1983). A mediation overview: History and dimensions of practice. *Mediation Quarterly, 1*, 3–14.

Gold, L. (1984). Interdisciplinary team mediation. *Mediation Quarterly, 6*, 27–45.

Haynes, J. (1981). *Divorce mediation: A practical guide for therapists and counselors.* New York: Springer.

Haynes, J. (1988). Power balancing. In *Divorce mediation: Theory and practice* (pp. 277–296). New York: Guilford Press.

Irving, H. H. (1980). *Divorce mediation: A rational alternative to the adversary system.* New York: Universe Books.

Kaslow, F. W., & Schwartz, L. L. (1987). *The dynamics of divorce: A life cycle perspective.* New York: Brunner/Mazel.

Kelly, J. B. (1983). Mediation and psychotherapy: Distinguishing the differences. *Mediation Quarterly, 1,* 33–45.

Lefcourt, C. H. (1984). *Women and the law.* New York: Clark Boardman.

Marlow, L. (1992). *Divorce and the myth of lawyers.* New York: Harlan Press.

Marlow, L., & Sauber, S. R. (1990). *The handbook of divorce mediation.* New York: Plenum.

Neill, J. R., & Kniskern, D. (1982). *From psychic to system: The evolving therapy of care.* New York: Guilford Press.

Neumann, D. (1992). How mediation can effectively address the male–female power imbalance in divorce. *Mediation Quarterly, 9,* 227–239.

Pearson, J. (1991). The equity of mediated divorce agreements. *Mediation Quarterly, 9,* 179–197.

Slyck, M. R., Newland, L. M., & Stern, M. (1992). Parent–child mediation: Integrating theory, research, and practice. *Mediation Quarterly, 10,* 193–208.

Vanderkooi, L., & Pearson, J. (1983). Mediating divorce disputes: Mediator behaviors, styles and roles. *Family Relations, 12,* 557–566.

Wallerstein, J. S., & Blakeslee, S. (1989). *Second chances: Men, women, & children a decade after divorce.* New York: Ticknor & Fields.

Wiseman, J. M., & Fiske, J. A. (1980). A lawyer–therapist team as mediator in marital crisis. *Social Work, 25*(6), 442–445.

# Resource Organizations

For further information regarding training, professional standards, and certification, the following organizations will be helpful:

Academy of Family Mediators, 355 Tyrol West, 1500 S. Highway 100, Golden Valley, MN 55416. Tel: (612) 525-8670; 1-800 859-8699

American Arbitration Association, 140 West 51st Street, New York, NY 10020-1203.

Society of Professionals in Dispute Resolution, 815 15th Street, NW, Suite 530, Washington, DC 20005. Tel: (202) 787-7277

# PART V
# GENDER AND ETHNIC ISSUES

# Introduction

Americans have always lived in a world of ethnic, racial, and gender diversity. Because of a growing consciousness of the patriarchal and White middle-class ethos that has dominated the social sciences, as it has in other areas of Western culture, family therapists now find themselves reconsidering and reevaluating the rich and diverse "real world" of cultural difference. In this section, contributors examine gender, lesbian and gay relationship development, ethnicity, and therapy with African American inner-city families.

In "Intergender Communication and Gender-Sensitive Family Therapy," Carol Philpot and Gary Brooks examine the ways in which traditional gender socialization contributes to a breakdown in communication between the sexes and how this has been exacerbated unintentionally by the cultural processes involved in gender-based movements. They invite readers to consider alternative models, among them their own, that sensitize therapists and families to gender-relevant issues of power, values, roles, and communication. A case example from each of the author's models illustrates these concepts in day-to-day practice and shows how interventions can be used to enhance the freedom of all members of the family.

As the visibility of gay men and lesbians increases, family therapists, including those of a heterosexual orientation, are increasingly called on to work with them on specific problems regarding their sexual identity as well as on issues related to couple and family formation. In their chapter, "Lesbian and Gay Family Psychology," Roy Scrivner and Natalie Eldridge describe both individual and systemic perspective on the development of lesbians and gay men as individuals and as couples. Emotional intimacy, sexuality, and power between couples are explored, as well as family of origin reactions to sexual orientation. The challenges facing gay male and lesbian parents and their children and the crisis of AIDS are discussed, and specific suggestions are made for therapists regarding awareness of bias, use of gender-free language, the need for understanding specific developmental issues facing gay male and lesbian clients, the usefulness of local support networks to these clients, and the appropriate use of consultation and referral.

In the next chapter, Joe Giordano and Mary Ann Carini-Giordano use their personal history and clinical experience to describe "Ethnic Dimensions in Family Treatment." They consider ethnic affiliation as fulfilling a "deep psychological need for identity, security, and historical continuity." As they explore how ethnicity operates in the family treatment process, they highlight interventions used with a Jewish American family, an Irish American family, and an intermarried couple of Argentinean and German descent. They urge the therapist to be aware of and to correct for cultural biases and lack of knowledge, to assess the importance of ethnicity in every family they treat, to validate ethnic identity, and to learn to be a "cultural broker."

In "The Treatment of African American Inner-City Families," Nancy Boyd-Franklin begins by orienting the therapist to frequent responses of this "culture" to therapy and to the importance of the therapist's use of self. She describes the multiple family structures prevalent in this population and the implications for intervention depending on the structure of the family. She emphasizes spirituality as a strength that can be drawn on frequently in working with these families, but she also notes that it is important for the therapist to keep in mind more negative influences on these families, such as effects of racism on gender roles, the impact of drugs, and the intrusion of outside systems. Using an extensive case study to illustrate her method of working, she presents a six-step model that is useful in organizing assessment and treatment that attends to diverse family structure and contextual stress and resources.

# CHAPTER 17

# INTERGENDER COMMUNICATION AND GENDER-SENSITIVE FAMILY THERAPY

*Carol L. Philpot and Gary Brooks*

Some have claimed that the problems couples bring to marital therapists can be reduced to women wanting more time in the living room (conversation), and men wanting more time in the bedroom (sexual activity). Although this gender stereotype is simplistic and insulting to both genders, it is, nevertheless, well enough accepted to illustrate that men and women recognize that they live in different gender worlds, with each poorly understanding life in the other world much of the time. In many ways, traditional gender socialization promotes gender segregation and polarization, resulting in intergender relationships characterized by partial knowledge, fantasized truths, and misunderstanding.

In this chapter, we first describe the most common intergender communication problems encountered in our practices. Although communication differences impact intergender communication in the workplace, in schools, in political arenas, and in many other social contexts, this chapter focuses on communication between spouses and significant others within families. We will look at how the field of family therapy has not responded adequately to gender issues, as well as how feminism and men's studies have recently emerged to provide invaluable constructive criticism to practitioners and theorists. In the remainder of the chapter, we will describe qualities of gender-sensitive family therapists and provide two family therapy models emphasizing intergender communication. Finally, we offer techniques found useful by other practitioners.

## INTERGENDER COMMUNICATION PROBLEMS

### Communication and Intimacy

A common complaint of women therapy patients is that the men in their lives do not talk to them. Men often deny this, however, and are puzzled as to exactly what women want them to talk about. If they have something to say, they say it. What women mean, of course, is that men do not generally talk about intimate matters, such as their feelings, doubts, concerns, and worries, or the details of daily experience. These are the matters that create intimacy between women—the sharing of struggles and the daily progress report. Women use verbal communication of this sort to bond with each other and wish to do the same thing with men.

Most men use communication to share information, provide advice, establish their credibility, and impress others. Often, they feel that home should be a protected environment where they can relax, free of pressures to talk or be on stage. They tend to minimize the value of rehashing the so-called trivialities of the day. They may feel that talking about problems will put them in the one-down positions that they struggle vigorously to avoid. Spouses' requests for "troubles talk"—what Tannen (1990) refers to as talk about problems and concerns—make men feel pressured and vulnerable, since men are trained to always appear competent, self-sufficient, an "un-needy." Therefore, unless they have specific information to share, or a specific problem to solve, they are likely to remain silent. Men are more likely to seek closeness through shared activities, such as sports, hobbies, or mutual interests (Wright, 1982) or to seek intimacy through sexual activity. When women seek greater intimacy outside these narrow areas, problems commonly ensue.

This difference is highlighted in sexual interactions between husbands and wives. Women frequently complain that they cannot jump into bed with their husbands and have passionate, uninhibited sex without feeling intimately connected to their partner. To enjoy lovemaking, women commonly need the connection that comes from verbal communication about emotions and about the relationship. For many men, the lovemaking itself can create enough intimacy. Although they may engage in the foreplay of lovetalk to further things, they usually do not feel an intense need for such communication. In fact, some men view lovetalk as romantic nonsense that gets in the way of lovemaking. When women partners experience a man's participation in foreplay as mechanical and insincere, their romantic ardor is likely to cool markedly, creating significant frustration for both parties.

Women also frequently complain that men do not really listen to them or understand what they are saying. When they want to talk out a problem, men may offer quick solutions that seem to simultaneously negate the importance of the issue while implying that the woman is inadequate because she could not find the answer herself. Frequently, what a woman wants at that time is validation and commiseration, which she does not ask for directly because she assumes the man knows this. However, action-oriented men feel the need to supply a solution, which they often view as a challenge or a test. This puts them in a one-up position and makes them feel competent, but at the expense of their spouses' egos. This is particularly the case if the woman actually acts on the solution, which does not usually occur, because what she really wanted was empathy, not answers. The man becomes frustrated because he feels invalidated and worthless when the woman will not do as he suggests, and the woman feels invalidated because the man will not simply listen and show sympathy. In fact, one of the ways men try to help each other is by minimizing the problem, a tactic that merely infuriates most women. In short, many

times the genders appear at cross purposes with each other.

## Communication and Conflict

Both genders wish to be seen as strong and competent. Both genders can enjoy emotional and physical intimacy. However, each gender has been indoctrinated into value systems that affect how these values will be prioritized in the face of conflict. Women, in general, prioritize connection, whereas men, in general, prioritize individuation. Therefore, women may be more comfortable than their spouses in making the changes in their behavior that their spouses might request, because preservation of the relationship is more important than establishing their individuality. Additionally, women have been socialized to monitor the health of their relationship and examine how they might bring about positive change, often feeling guilty if the relationship fails, as though they were to blame. On the other hand, traditional masculinity shapes men to view relationships hierarchically, making it more important for them to be "right." They are especially troubled by the need to acknowledge errors or a need to change established patterns. Often, even among those enlightened couples in which the man would never openly state that he believes women should be submissive, one finds a resistance to requests for change made by the woman.

Criticism, suggestions, and offers of help and sympathy are rebuffed by the man, because, to him, these communications imply that he has failed at being a man. This kind of man has a psychological need to maintain his position near the top of the hierarchy, which makes it difficult for him to make changes requested by his spouse if they are perceived as demands or orders. Indeed, he may even see her criticism as an expression of imminent abandonment and overreact by taking control and dramatically suggesting that she leave him, if he is not good enough. This mindset puts his spouse at a disadvantage if she feels she must confront him on issues. His tendency is to resist change unless the idea to change comes from within himself. In this way he can preserve his unconscious perception that he is dominant and, therefore, manly. This leaves the woman in this type of relationship with a choice between being indirect and even manipulative in getting her needs met or being clear and direct in her requests but risking passive-aggressive noncompliance, outright rejection, or the physical or emotional withdrawal of her spouse. For the woman whose priority is to be intimate and connected with a significant other, conflict and withdrawal can be frightening states, because they threaten the relationship. She is placed in the double-bind, no-win situation of enduring the relationship the way it is or risking its loss. What she might not understand is that when he withdraws, the self-reliant man is often attempting to find his own solution to the problem, retreating into his cave. His answer might be some form of self-designed action, rather than communication, since he needs to preserve his highly-prized sense of independence and autonomy.

## Gender Role Stereotypes and Self-Disclosure

The capacity for genuineness has repeatedly been shown to be a critical determinant of success in a variety of interpersonal interactions. Simply stated, people are better able to communicate with people they feel they know and understand, people who are authentic. Another well-established principle is that appropriate self-disclosure generally enhances interpersonal communication. It would seem logical then that communication between men and women should be characterized by abundant sharing about differences in backgrounds and experiences, as well as by efforts to describe accurately gender-based reactions to all situations.

Unfortunately, this is nearly the opposite of what actually takes place. Men and women often hide their private lives from each other, wear gender masks, and demand parallel role-playing from their partner in the relationship tableau. This takes place because gender role pressures are so restrictive and unforgiving (Cahill, 1986). Perhaps, this is because gender role pressures, until recently, were relatively invisible, faithfully obeyed, yet rarely discussed. Whatever the cause, participants in the gender drama have encountered major obstacles in dropping their gender masks. There is considerable value when a person's awareness of membership in a gender world provides a better sense of individual identity. How-

ever, this process creates new problems when the norms of this world are kept secret from members of the other gender world and when it prevents authenticity and self-disclosure. For example, a man faced with a devastating personal loss, trained that masculinity requires a stoic facade, will neither communicate his pain to his partner, nor be able to explain why he is emotionally constricted. Likewise, a woman who sees nurturing, caretaking, and self-sacrifice as an integral part of her femininity will have great difficulty acknowledging the part of herself that is enraged by the need to care for her husband who has a disabling illness such as Alzheimer's disease. To the extent that men and women are insecure about how well they are meeting their role mandates, or feel compelled to rigidly adhere to all aspects of their gender role programming, they will frequently be constrained from achieving interpersonal communication that is fully authentic and genuine.

## Toward Resolution: Empathy and Compassion Between the Genders

Empathy, the ability to understand the experiential world of another without actually being a member of that world, allows for greater trust in and commitment to relationships. People who understand the struggles of others are more likely to approach them from an accepting, less hostile, framework. People who deeply fear altering customary patterns are more confident about experimenting with new patterns if they feel that their stresses are understood. People who appreciate the experiential world of their partner are more capable of experiencing greater interpersonal warmth.

There was a time when men and women believed the opposite sex was mysterious and unpredictable and did not even try to understand each other. Then, for a while, a movement was afoot that endorsed androgny as the ultimate goal, suggesting that men and women should have the same values, the same goals, the same needs, and therefore the same patterns of communication and interaction. As Hare-Mustin and Maracek (1988) said, both an exaggeration of differences or a denial of them are errors of bias. The research clearly shows that differences exist, whether due to socialization or biology or both (Belenky, Clinchy, Goldberger, & Tarule, 1986;

Fausto-Sterling, 1985; Gilligan, 1982; Tannen, 1990). But there is also a great deal of overlap. There is common ground for understanding and accepting one another without blame and criticism.

Unfortunately, however, intergender empathy and understanding have been slow in arriving. Although there has been a recognition that gender is a "fundamental category" (Avis, 1988) and a "central organizing principle in society and in everyday social interactions" (Cook, 1990), there has been minimal progress in helping men and women understand each other's experiential worlds. To help remedy this, of late a number of experiential workshops have been developed to promote fuller understanding of differing gender experiences (Bergman & Surrey, 1992; Roberts, 1991). Table 1 offers a synopsis of the major stereotypical differences in communication styles.

## THERAPY AND GENDER BIAS

Although gender is a most basic ecosystem, until recently, the mental health field has largely ignored its ramifications. For centuries, the average woman has held a near-universally inferior position to her male counterpart in economic, political, legal, and physical arenas. That reality has been well documented and does not need reiteration here. Here, however, we will focus on the manner in which mental health professions, including family therapy, have perpetuated this oppression.

Because the early psychological theorists were predominantly male, theories have been produced through men's experiences and value systems, with no recognition that women's experiences might be radically different. Therefore, that which deviated from typical male experience was thought to be pathological or, at least, deficient. Whereas the healthy feminine personality was characterized as sensitive, nurturing, emotional, conforming, compliant, cooperative, dependent, and passive, men have typically valued and rewarded the masculine characteristics of competitiveness, aggression, dominance, control, rationality, and logic. Hence, women with masculine characteristics were considered to be unfeminine, and those with feminine characteristics were considered to be inferior (Broverman, Brover-

man, Clarkson, Rosenkrantz, & Vogel, 1970), a double-bind position that many still do not recognize. Only since the most recent feminist movement have some (men included) come to recognize that feminine values are equally important and absolutely necessary to living a fulfilling, balanced life.

Today, phenomenological and existential psychologists and constructionists (see Anderson, 1993) promulgate the concept that reality is always colored by the eye of the beholder and, therefore, the social context of any theorist of psychology or psychotherapist will have a major impact on what is thought of as normal or healthy. However, in earlier times, men-

| TABLE 1 |
| :-- |

### Stereotypical Differences in Communication Styles

| Female | Male |
| --- | --- |
| Provide understanding | Give advice |
| Commiserate | Provide solutions |
| Validate problems and experiences | Dismiss problems as unimportant |
| Give praise | Give information |
| Make communication accessible to help | Obscure communication to impress |
| Use personal experience to support, illustrate | Use research, surveys to support, illustrate |
| Wait to be asked | Compete for the floor |
| Listen to be supportive | Interrupt to change subject |
| Support others' position | Challenge others' position |
| Avoid conflict/threat to intimacy | See conflict as contest |
| Indirect | Direct |
| Tentative, qualified | Assertive, firm |
| Self-deprecating/downplays abilities | Boasts of accomplishments/ impresses with credentials |
| Low volume, high-pitched voice | High volume, low-pitched voice |
| Eye contact when personal talk; avert eyes, look down in public | Eye contact in public; avert eyes in private talk |
| Rapport talk | Report talk |
| Talk to connect with others | Talk to provide information |
| Private speaking/freedom to speak without judgment | Public speaking/freedom to remain silent in private |
| Share insignificant details to connect | Engage in mutual activities to connect |
| Rule by consensus (in business) | Direct rule (in business) |

*Note:* Summary of findings in Tannen (1990).

tal health professionals acted as agents of a society that was oppressive toward women, without being aware that their theories were affected by their social content. Because women were the major consumers of a mental health system dominated by male therapists, female patients received a large dosage of misguided and uninformed treatment that was based on a male perspective. Women who did not fit into the mold of happy and compliant wife and obedient servant of a dominant husband were accused of having a strange disease called "penis envy" and consequently of castrating their husbands. Women were continually encouraged to live through their husbands and children and deny any strivings of their own. Any anger expressed about this clearly unfair arrangement was another indication of mental illness, a rather subtle way of taming the shrew. Thus many women repressed their anger, turned it inward, guiltily blamed themselves for not being able to be happy as a woman, suffering further emotional damage in the form of depression.

In 1990, McGrath, Keita, Strickland, and Russo reported that women's risk for depression exceeds that of men by two to one worldwide. This higher risk is believed to be related to a number of factors including (a) the socially endorsed passive, dependent cognitive and personality style of women; (b) the high rate (an estimated 37% of all women) of sexual and physical abuse; (c) the inequity in marriage that protects men, but asks women to put their children and husband first (in fact, women in unhappy marriages are three times as likely to be depressed than are married men or single women); and (d) poverty (75% of people who make less than $5,776 annually are women). By not addressing the very real economic, social, physical, and political issues that contribute to women's depression, the field of mental health essentially ignored women's reality and acted as an agent of social control.

Another case in point is the prevalent feminine diagnosis of histrionic personality disorder. Previously this disorder was labeled *hysterical personality disorder* or *wandering uterus*. Many of the symptoms of histrionic personality disorder are merely exaggerations of socially prescribed ideals of feminine behavior (i.e., being sexually seductive in appearance or behavior and being overly concerned with physical

attractiveness). Others are typical responses of people in powerless positions, such as a need for reassurance, approval, or praise or the use of manipulative rather than direct means of meeting one's needs. For male therapists who have not experienced total economic dependence on a significant other except in childhood, such behavior may appear to be immature and disagreeable. For women who know that, without their husband's income, they and their children will barely survive at the subsistence level, manipulative behavior becomes more understandable, even smart.

Similarly, many therapists failed to recognize society's failure to provide a living wage to women or its inadequate provision of child care resources. Such therapists were frequently quick to mislabel as masochistic a woman who chose to remain in an abusive relationship. Sometimes, they assumed that since the woman did not leave, she must either take pleasure from the abuse, or, at least take some role in its provocation. The undesirable social and economic alternatives to abuse were often not considered by her naive therapist, often a man who had a very different gender experience. Furthermore, he had no paradigm through which to understand the socially prescribed feminine value system that requires the prioritizing of the family's needs above one's own and assuming responsibility for the success of the relationship. According to this value system, termination of the relationship is clear proof of failure and cause for self-loathing (Caplan & Hall-McCorquodale, 1985).

## Pioneers of Family Therapy

Family therapists, with their emphasis on the interpersonal and multisystemic context of an individual's identity, problems, growth, and change, would seem to be naturally bent toward a recognition of gender as a primary dimension in understanding behavior. However, although early family systems theorists introduced a revolutionary new concept by considering the family context in which a patient developed and maintained his or her symptoms, they were as blind to the larger gender ecosystem as previous individual theorists had been. The pioneers of family systems were mostly male, except for Virginia Satir, and they were products of their time, as were the originators of individual and group therapies.

In the 1950s, when family systems theories were developing, the typical middle-class American family consisted of a mother who was a homemaker, a father who worked outside the home, and two or three children. The fact that this particular family type was relatively new and occupied only a nanosecond of the history of humankind was ignored. Systems concepts were developed from a Western, middle-class male value system based on the family of the 1950s, with virtual disregard for historical, cultural, or gender differences.

Luepnitz (1988) provided a provocative and thoughtful critique of several approaches to family therapy as well as the theoretical formulations of the pioneers who have come to represent them. Avis (1988); McGoldrick, Anderson, and Walsh (1989); and Goodrich (1991) have also identified several ways in which the pioneers' male construction of reality conflicts with the feminist view. Table 2 summarizes Luepnitz's analyses of family pioneers in this regard.

## TABLE 2

### Pioneers' Male Construction of Reality Conflict With the Feminist View

| Family theory pioneer | Gender issues[a] |
|---|---|
| Ackerman | Devaluation of women; assumption of male supremacy; assumes family dysfunction caused by disruption of complementary pattern of dominant male and submissive female. |
| Bowen | Male value system that includes autonomy, rationality, and self-sufficiency is elevated above a female value system of emotion, relatedness, and caring for others in his definition of a differentiated adult. Failed to recognize that a capitalistic and separatist society that sends men away to work all day while leaving women responsible for child rearing sets women up to be "overinvested" in their children. |
| Satir | Devaluation by male colleagues due to stereotypical feminine qualities of assessibility and nurturance. Due to her humanistic approach, she fails to recognize the need for global political change, believing that change within each human is sufficient. |
| Minuchin | Tendency to mother-blame and unbalance the system by bringing in competent father to show incompetent mother how to control children rather than to empower her. The Functionalist foundations emphasize a concern for the parts (each individual) adapting to the whole (family) without considering the possibility that one part (the mother) might be sacrificed for the whole. Research indicated that the institution of marriage in a patriarchal society is generally protective of men and detrimental to women. |
| Strategic (Haley) | Emphasis on a struggle for power *over* the family rather than using a cooperative approach (Haley, 1984). The indirect prescriptions for change used by strategic therapists unaccompanied by insight or debriefing. |
| Systemic theorists | Belief that therapy should be conducted apolitically, conforming to their three-part definition of neutrality (i.e., neutral with regard to each individual's position in the family, to value systems endorsed by the family, and to whether or not the family changes in any way), a view that many consider to be impossible to achieve. The systemic definition of circularity that fails to take into consideration power differentials between genders and the larger cultural system, thus providing a theoretical means for blaming the victim. |
| Cybernetic (Bateson) | Failure to address the inequality of the socially legitimized power of the man in the family system compared to the weaker of influence held by the woman. The failure of several pioneers (Whitaker, Nagy, Satir) to address the larger issue of sexual politics in a consistent manner despite their support of or theoretical compatibility with feminist views regarding role flexibility, equity, and stereotypical feminine values. |

[a]Data derived from an analysis by Luepnitz (1988).

## Power Differentials and Communication

An essential element in feminist critiques of family systems therapy is that it has been highly influenced by an emphasis on circularity, reciprocity, and shared responsibility for problems, and far too little concerned with the sweeping effects of the power differences between women and men. Feminist therapists have attempted to correct for this oversight by insisting that these power differences receive major emphasis in all conceptualizations of family and marital dynamics (Goodrich, 1991).

Communication issues are especially vulnerable to this type of analysis, and in this area, pioneers of family therapy helped lay some of the groundwork. For example, Watzlawick, Beavin, and Jackson (1967) exhaustively described the differences in communication between "equals" (symmetrical interactions) and communication between "non-equals" (complementary interactions). Although these authors did not attend to the larger sociocultural context in which their communicants functioned (i.e., the patriarchy), they did break ground in discussing how power differences are played out in interpersonal communication. They described how healthy relationships are those in which the participants are able to move freely between complementary and symmetrical interactions, depending on the demands of the situation. For example, each marital partner should be able to nurture the other during times of adversity. Neither should be frozen into a protector or savior posture, or a protected or saved posture. Likewise, when legitimate differences of interest occur, each partner should feel comfortable entering into negotiations with the other. The unhealthy relationship then is one in which healthy conflict is not possible.

Using this framework, it can be seen that rigid socialization, which differentially imbues men and women with power, sets the stage for unhealthy communication patterns between genders. Traditionally, men have had far greater political, socioeconomic, and physical power. Women have usually had more power in terms of relationship and communication skills. When there are extreme cases of these power imbalances, major communication problems ensue. Obviously, a woman who fears physical or financial retaliation will be reluctant to engage in symmetrical interactions (i.e., to push her position too far). Instead, she might be likely to resort to more indirect communications. Men, who are socialized to view dominance and leadership as an entitlement (and a man's responsibility), will be distressed when women interact symmetrically (i.e., get too pushy) and may feel the need to keep a woman in her place.

Women's greater affective communication skills and relationship power may also create asymmetrical relations between the genders. In situations requiring interpersonal relationship skills (e.g., nurturing children, dealing with extended family, and interacting with friends), men typically defer to women, putting themselves in one-down position. In the critical area of relationship maintenance, men commonly are highly threatened by women's greater verbal skills and ability to identify affective states. As a result, men frequently avoid emotional conflict as long as possible, or, in all too many cases, may try to suppress the communication pressures by exerting their superior physical and financial assets.

## Intergender Communication and Contemporary Family Therapy

Poor communication is often stated as the most common presenting problem of couples entering therapy. An extensive body of research on human communication has been developed and has provided the basis for a number of different psychoeducational, behavioral, marital enrichment, and relationship enhancement therapies that target improved communication as a major therapeutic focus. Unfortunately, interest in the gender dimension of communication is very recent development (Tannen, 1990).

Recently, however, the field of gender studies has improved the situation by adding interpersonal communication to the growing list of human endeavors mediated by gender socialization. Instead of studying how people communicate, it is now becoming possible to study how *men* communicate and how *women* communicate. Recognition of key differences promises to enrich this area of study, as well as provide insights into common relationship difficulties.

Contemporary family therapists have developed gender-sensitive training models for family therapy trainees that also have application for couples in treatment (Roberts, 1991). Each of these models has, as a common denominator, the insight that comes from understanding that gender messages are universally transmitted across generations and are part of a larger culture. This realization creates greater empathy for the other sex and can be the genesis for a dialogue about how to change those messages that appear to be detrimental to either spouse. Most of these models incorporate a number of stimuli such as cartoons, quotes, newspaper articles, television shows, songs, and movies that can stimulate discussion around gender issues.

Many family therapists, however, are insufficiently informed about the critiques of the culture's gender socialization offered by feminism and by its elaboration in men's studies.

## THE FEMINIST CRITIQUE AND THE MEN'S MOVEMENT

### The Feminist Critique

Feminist scholars such as Dinnerstein (1976) and Chodorow (1978) have attempted to explain the development and perpetuation of patterns that are destructive to both genders. In each of these theories, the conventional allocation of child care responsibilities to women in a capitalistic society causes women to have different value systems, different relational capacities, different patterns of communication, and different experiences of power, based solely on gender identification.

For example, Dinnerstein has argued that misogyny is rooted in irrational infantile fears of the engulfing power of the female caretaker. This unconscious and exaggerated fear is contrasted to a more realistic appraisal of the father's role in discipline formed through the eyes of the older child. Chodorow suggested that girls can form their sexual identity while relating closely to and modeling themselves after their mothers, but that boys must identify themselves as different and separate from the mother. Because boys often do not have a father present with whom they can relate closely, they develop a value system based on separation, autonomy, and abstract principles. Boys form their identity not through modeling, but by defining themselves as different from mother.

By so doing, they reduce their capacity for intimacy and emotional expressivity. Girls, on the other hand, place a high priority on relatedness, connectedness, and caring for others as modeled by their mothers. By identifying with a mother who sacrifices herself for her family, however, girls reduce their capacity for autonomy and independence.

As children leave their homes and start school, society places expectations on both genders that merely serve to promote and augment these early value systems. Communication patterns, then, reflect these different value systems. Male communication is designed to establish independence and a favored position within a hierarchy, whereas female communication is meant to provide connection and support. The result, at its best, is a complementary communication pattern that leaves women in a one-down position. At its worst, both genders feel frustrated, misunderstood, and helpless.

Theorists such as Miller (1986), Gilligan (1982), and Belenky et al. (1986) have proposed developmental models of mental health based on feminine values of affiliation and relationship rather than the traditional masculine values of autonomy and separation. Feminist scholars are arguing for a revalorization of female values. Interestingly, the recent men's movement is beginning to publicly recognize the validity of the feminist arguments in their search for a more fulfilling and balanced definition of manhood.

Well-educated, White, middle-class women without young children in Western capitalistic societies have come a long way in the last three decades. They sign leases, obtain loans, buy houses, run for congress, govern cities, serve as ministers and psychologists, are brokers on Wall Street, run Fortune 500 businesses, publish magazines, and so on. Compared to women in less advanced nations or to minority women within the same culture, these women have it made. But even these apparent success stories have their problems. The glass ceiling that keeps women from rising to the top is still unbroken. Women still make only 75 cents on the dollar, compared with men's wages for doing the same job. Many women find themselves having to adopt the male value system of competition, power, and control in order to survive in male-dominated businesses and are beginning to suffer higher rates of alcoholism, strokes, and heart attacks. Many women, who, like their male counterparts, wish to have it all—career, family, and home—find they need a "wife" to run the home and take care of children, something only the very wealthy can afford. Given that women have been trained for centuries to believe they should take primary responsibility for raising the children and nurturing a marriage, even when they can afford help, these women suffer pangs of guilt and periods of conflict regarding the amount of time and energy their career takes away from family. These women are the lucky ones.

The majority of women work double shifts—one in the Pink Ghetto (holding dead-end, low-paying jobs like sales clerks and secretaries) and one at home, cooking, cleaning, doing the laundry, and providing child care. Sixty-eight percent of all women with children now work outside the home (Morgan, 1991), many in occupations and professions that are populated by women and therefore command lower salaries and prestige. Typically, those with spouses find that they maintain executive responsibility for the running of the home and child care, even if their husbands are willing "to lend a hand" (Hochschild, 1989). Many men find "women's work" degrading and refuse to participate; after all, housework and child care within a home is not rewarded financially and does not contribute to the GNP.

Single women with children make up 75% of the poor in this country (McGrath et al., 1990). No-fault divorce laws have removed the protection once afforded the woman who sacrificed her own education and career for her husband and family, so she is often unable to provide for her children at more than subsistence level (Weitzman, 1985). Add to this the vulnerability of women to sexual and physical abuse (McGrath et al., 1990; Walker, 1985); the recent political trend toward conservatism that threatens to take away hard-earned rights, such as the right to abortion; and the subtle eroding of women's belief in themselves (Faludi, 1991), and it is clear that even in an enlightened society, women are suffering. What is so ironic about this is that men, who have traditionally been looked upon as the oppressors, are suffering as well, in different ways. It is the public recognition of this fact by leaders and participants in the recent men's movement that provides hope for a uniting of the genders against an oppressive societal structure.

## The Men's Movement

Although some men have supported the women's movement for decades (Kimmel & Mosmiller, 1992), until recently, many more men viewed feminism with suspicion, hostility, indifference, or bewilderment (O'Neil, 1982; Solomon, 1982). Of late, however, some have recognized that the feminist agenda may be vital not only for women but also offers critical opportunities for men—the chance to examine how rigid gender-role socialization produces profound constraints in men's lives. Within professional circles, there is increasing general agreement that the feminist critique has focused much-needed attention on the abuses experienced by women in many sociocultural relationships, including psychotherapy. Men's studies that extend feminist scholarship to the study of men's lives and role restrictions have a less obvious mandate. Given the historically advantaged position of men in a patriarchal culture, it has been more difficult to accept the idea that men may experience distress from gender role socialization. Furthermore, because men have been the normative or benchmark gender (Kimmel, 1987), it may seem absurd to propose increased study of masculinity. Many men's studies scholars have responded that this new field is necessary, not as a repetition of traditional androcentric scholarship, but as an extension of women's studies, an attempt to "emasculate patriarchal ideology's masquerade as knowledge" (Brod, 1987) independent of the cultural context.

The men's movement is, of course, an outgrowth of feminism and the gay liberation movement. Less obviously, it is also a product of the 20th-century shift from an agricultural economy to an industrial and technological economy, and then to a service-delivery economy (Brod, 1984; Pleck & Pleck, 1980). These recent sociocultural shifts have undercut the male breadwinner role (Bernard 1981) and lessened demand for the valued aspects of traditional masculinity—physical strength, endurance, and emotional stoicism. New behaviors more consistent with a modern male role (Pleck, 1981) are esteemed—sensitivity, empathy, and interpersonal communication skills. The cumulative effect of these social forces has been to produce a situation in which contemporary men experience substantial gender role strain (O'Neil, 1982), which is best described as a deep sense of confusion and insecurity about the meaning of masculinity. Men's studies, and the men's movement, have been responses to the gender-role strain of contemporary men.

Just as there are critical differences between boys and girls in the expected outcome of gender socialization, there are also important gender-based differences in the socialization process itself. Each gender is encouraged to adopt certain characteristics and reject certain others, a seemingly innocuous process. Unfortunately, this differential role assignment takes place in a culture that has been shown to be patriarchal and sexist, in which the world of women is deemed to be of lower value (Bullough, 1973). Women, as a group, are grossly disadvantaged. Men, as a group, are grossly advantaged. Ironically, this environment of privilege for men as a group, the product of the differential status of the genders, may create special problems for many men as individuals. Although masculinity, as the preferred gender role, may come with certain entitlements (Gilbert & Scher, 1987), these benefits are not automatically granted to all men. They must be earned, through proof of masculinity. The benefits are accorded only to so-called real men. After extensive cross-cultural surveys, Gilmore (1990) reported that in nearly all cultures, masculinity is an achieved status, acquired through numerous rites of passage.

Furthermore, boys are socialized somewhat differently than girls. Developmental research has shown that deviation from the prescribed gender role is more severely punished when displayed by boys (O'Leary & Donahue, 1978). Girls who experiment with other-gender behavior are usually encouraged, ignored, or only mildly rebuked. Boys who experiment with even the mildest forms of feminine behavior are subject to harsh sanctions. Fathers traditionally invest greater energy in enforcing role stereotypes in their children, whereas women tend to be more neutral (Lamb, Owen, & Chase-Lansdale, 1978).

It seems that men are socialized to live in a hierarchical world, preoccupied with performance, continually wondering if (or for how long) they will measure up. They cannot relax their need to compete with others for affirmation of masculinity. They feel envy for those above them in their hierarchies, contempt for those below. They may eventually wield considerable political, economic, or interpersonal power, yet few ever feel truly powerful (Farrell, 1987). Especially relevant here is the notion that although most men are highly desirous of the entitlements of manhood, they are highly anxious that they will not be able to meet the duties of masculinity—to prove themselves to be real men.

We can see that socialization into masculinity creates a double-edged sword for men. It has offered a set of advantages that can be experienced only when there is a complementary set of lower-order values (the feminine) against which to be juxtaposed. As a result men greatly fear any evidence of femininity in themselves (O'Donovan, 1988; O'Neil, 1982). This creates a powerfully restrictive situation for men—obsession with performance in one gender world, coupled with minimal tolerance for experimentation in the other gender world. The principal activity of men's studies has been the investigation of the costs of masculinity. Because many authors have already delineated the key elements of the male role (David & Brannon, 1976; Doyle, 1989; Goldberg, 1976; O'Neil, 1982), this topic will be only touched on here.

Perhaps the most dramatic consequence of men's socialization is its health-diminishing, life-threatening effects. Men live shorter lives, have a higher incidence of stress-related physical disorders, are more likely to engage in high-risk behaviors, are more likely to ignore the health-maintenance needs of their bodies, and are more likely to be victims of homicide (Nathanson, 1977; Skord & Schumacher, 1982; Verbrugge, 1985; Waldron, 1976). Socialization also harms men's mental health: it limits men's stress-reduction repertoires and overemphasizes physical activity, violence, cognitive distraction, and substance abuse (Eisler & Blalock, 1991; Nolen-Hoeksema, 1990). Sociopathy and alcoholism can be considered principle mental health sequelae of role socialization.

Masculine role socialization provides men with confusing and contradictory messages about women and about appropriate male–female relations. Men are taught that women are highly desirable as emotional caretakers, sexual partners, nurturers of children, organizers of households, and validators of masculinity (Pleck, 1981; Williams, 1977). Yet men are raised in a patriarchal society that fosters misogynistic attitudes as well—that women are inferior, unpredictable, unreliable, overly emotional, and impossible to please. They are taught that in their intergender relationships they should maintain control and provide leadership (O'Neil, 1982).

Although increasingly more men are adopting new roles, particularly as fathers, the traditional breadwinner role maintains great saliency for many men. Many factors have been cited as contributing to men's resistance to change. Bronstein and Cowan (1988) cited culture-wide institutional resistance. Balswick (1988) explored men's emotional inexpressiveness as another factor compromising interpersonal relationships. Levant and Kelley (1989) have implicated men's limited parenting skills and experiences. A general lack of nurturing opportunities in adolescence (such as babysitting) and men's fears of raising soft children (especially sons) creates an environment in which many fathers limit their parenting to imbuing children with emotional stoicism, interpersonal toughness, and compulsive competitiveness. Although dual-earner families are now far more common than the older model of father/breadwinner and mother/homemaker (Gilbert, 1988), men continue to define themselves according to the demands of the good provider role (Bernard, 1981). Unable to appreciate the value of any family contributions except those of the worker–provider, men are especially vulnerable to disruptions to that role, such as those caused by unemployment, disability, and retirement.

In general, it has been argued that despite the many obvious benefits men receive as a result of gender socialization, there are many less visible negative consequences. Given the hierarchical and competitive nature of men's socialization, few men are deeply secure in their masculinity and are easily provoked to prove its continued presence. Furthermore, we are living in a changing culture, one that places emphasis on role flexibility, that is, the ability to in-

corporate both masculine and feminine characteristics. Unfortunately, many men, socialized to fear femininity, are usually handicapped in this area and are particularly vulnerable to gender role strain. Finally, in a culture experiencing substantial cultural ambiguity, men continue to be exposed to an abundance of mixed messages about what is expected of them as men and as relationship partners.

The heightened level of consciousness about the constraints of masculinity has been expressed in a number of different academic, political, psychological, social, and spiritual avenues, sometimes referred to collectively as the men's movement. There are several branches of this movement, consisting of (a) mythopoetic men who emphasize spiritual activities to help men reclaim "deep masculinity," (b) pro-feminist men who see themselves as a logical sociopolitical extension of the women's movement, and (c) men's rights groups that focus on claims of sexism against men. Despite major philosophical differences, all of these perspectives share the belief that collective action by men is necessary to broaden antiquated definitions of masculinity and to facilitate men's "gender role journey" (O'Neil & Roberts Carroll, 1988). For a description of these perspectives, see Brooks (1991a) and Clatterbaugh (1990).

## GENDER-SENSITIVE APPROACHES TO FAMILY THERAPY: A BRIDGE BETWEEN MEN'S AND WOMEN'S LIVES

The escalation of the battle of the sexes in the wake of the feminist movement can be viewed as *schizmogenesis*, a polarization between the sexes on issues, whereby each side becomes so invested in converting the other to the right way that any hope for resolution appears to be lost. A second-order change is required to release couples from their entrenched positions and enrich their cognitive maps enough to offer a two-winner approach. The instrument of second-order change suggested here is an expanded version of gender-sensitive psychotherapy. New gender-sensitive psychotherapy generally refers to therapy that is conducted from the perspective that men and women encounter different life experiences.

Like their individually-oriented counterparts, systemically defined, gender-sensitive therapists are knowledgeable about the differing perception of reality for men and women that grows out of biological differences, male/female developmental theory, socialization in a capitalist/patriarchal society, value systems, levels of moral development, role definitions, and power differentials in the political, economic, and legal arenas. They are current on the implications of the latest literature in women's studies, men's studies, and gender-difference research.

Such therapists are familiar with the theoretical bases for understanding gender differences and are aware of the uses and limitations of their theories. They impose no limits on the roles to be played by men or women and impose no limits on the potential for growth by either sex. They view the often predictable dichotomies of distancer/pursuer, expressive/instrumental, logic/emotion, and function/form as inevitable, but perhaps exaggerated, results of socialization, rather than as intrapsychic pathology. And, to the extent possible, given the limitations of their own gender, they approach therapy from an androgynous perspective and maintain an awareness of the special needs of men and women and of the techniques that will best facilitate treatment for each.

If one is willing to stretch the cross-cultural counseling concept to the separate gender worlds of men and women, then it becomes evident that all family therapy is a type of therapy with culturally different persons. A primary theme in cross-cultural counseling (Sue & Sue, 1990) is that initiating changes, without appreciation of a client's ecosystem, devalues the client's integrity and risks a form of cultural imperialism. Rather than assuming that therapy clients, and therapists themselves, have identical world views, we must devote greater efforts to recognizing gender-based value differences. The therapist who is unaware of gender blindness cannot serve as a culture broker. That therapist, instead of promoting greater understanding between family members, is prone to be drawn into gender-based triangulations.

The family therapist's job is that of the interpreter and diplomat, one who negotiates between the genders, teaching cultural differences to the clients so that they can learn to interact in a manner that results in satisfaction rather than frustration and conflict for both. In the case where two cultures occupy the same territory with mutual acceptance and re-spect, each culture incorporates that which they find valuable from the other culture. In this way each culture is enriched, expanded, and transformed. Ideally, when couples grow to understand and accept the gender culture of the other, a similar growth will occur, which can only be beneficial to both sexes.

However, the gender-sensitive family therapist is also aware of the ways in which the dysfunctional patterns between the genders are reproduced by the very structure of the family itself. Equipped with the knowledge that inflexibility in expectations for either gender results in destructive consequences for both, the family therapist can educate the couple as therapy progresses so that they can design a family structure and communication patterns that can serve as a new paradigm for their children to model. It is true that children will encounter strong influences from their peers to revert to old gender stereotypical roles and behaviors, but the family can work to change this. Although there was a time lag in response, the media did begin to depict the working mother, the single-parent family, the career woman who chose not to marry, the sensitive and involved father, the confusing inner world of the adolescent male, and the vibrant older woman when society became populated by these persons or groups. By modeling what previous generations have done and what they see in the world around them, men and women automatically place gendered expectations on one another and either subtly or overtly discourage that which does not fit the model.

If the therapist can educate the couple to comprehend the negative results of rigid gender socialization on their relationship, to themselves as individuals, and to the legacy for their children, the couple will have the motivation to forge new ground. Instead of acting in blind collusion with the values of the gender ecosystem, we family therapists can, at the very least, arm our clients with the awareness that gender socialization has an enduring negative impact on our physical and mental health and let them decide what to do about it. If, once armed with such knowledge, they choose to maintain the same patterns of behavior, the therapist can simply point out that "If you always do what you've always done, you'll always get what you've always gotten!"

## A Nonblaming, Systemic Approach to Gender Relations

This whole process, however, hinges on the therapist's ability to facilitate intergender communication. Much of the success at doing so will depend more on the attitude of the therapist than on any particular technique. As is always the case, the therapist's value system and relationship with clients will determine the course that therapy takes.

For therapists who are willing to work on their own gender biases, models of gender-sensitive family therapy can be useful. In the remainder of this chapter we discuss two models developed by the authors, each of which is illustrated by a case example. We also describe techniques that we have borrowed from others that are valuable in various phases of this work.

## Philpot's Psychoeducational Approach

Philpot (1991) has developed a psychoeducational approach to gender-sensitive family therapy that essentially unites the couple against a common scapegoat—a society that socializes them into rigid roles that are detrimental to both genders. The goal of therapy with a couple who has become entrenched in polarized positions over gender issues is depolarization through expansion of their cognitive maps. Most often, when they reach the therapist's office both spouses are locked into a repetitive, dysfunctional set in which each partner tries desperately to convince the spouse that his or her way is the right way. They have become submerged in an either/or, right/wrong, black/white dichotomous manner of thinking, in which one perspective must defeat the other. To this end, they will attempt to triangulate the therapist as judge, each hoping to form a coalition with the expert in order to validate his or her position. It is at this point that the therapist can begin the depolarization process, which consists of four steps.

The first step is simply reflection with some tentative amplification—that is, merely restating what both husband and wife have expressed individually, sensitively restating the emotional stance and thought processes of each. When the therapist is thoroughly familiar with the issues and the couple's gender perspectives, he or she can follow the client's lead and

with a high degree of accuracy predict the feelings and rationale that will follow. The correct and empathic statement by the therapist of positions that the spouses have not yet verbalized fully but recognize as resonating with deep-felt emotions, has the validating, bonding effect that creates the therapeutic magic. Both sexes feel heard, understood, and supported at once.

The second step is psychoeducational and somewhat didactic. The fact that the therapist simultaneously agrees with what the clients view as dichotomous and incompatible positions is disconcerting and stimulates curiosity. At this point the therapist can teach the clients about the construction of reality along gender lines and the attitudes and values that can be expected to result from the socialization process. The educational component can be kept simple or made sophisticated, depending on the client's education and intelligence. It is important for the therapist to connect with the negative aspects of gender socialization for both genders, so that motivation for change is mutual. This step has the effect of enriching the cognitive map and opening new possibilities for perception. Additionally, by normalizing the male and female positions, therapists can show that some problems are actually a byproduct of gender socialization and not deliberate efforts to undermine another person's worth.

Step three is confrontation with reality. It consists essentially of a short speech that points out that gender differences will exist between all men and women to some degree and must be accepted. The following is an example of such a speech.

> *Therapist (following a discussion of Chodorow): Well, now that you understand where each other is coming from, we need to find a way to communicate so that you can meet each other's needs. Because there is one thing I can guarantee you, if either one of you imposes your perception or value system on the other, you kill the relationship. Whenever one person dominates the other, both suffer, and eventually the relationship becomes bitter and unrewarding. And since you both tell me, by your very presence here, that this relationship is valu-*

*able to you, we need to start working on a two-winner approach to resolving these issues. It should also be clear by now that changing spouses (if either of you has fantasized that solution) is probably not going to help too much with a lot of these issues either, because most men and women will have been socialized in the same way. Women will be like women, and men like men, whether we like it or not. I'm reminded of Rex Harrison's lament in* My Fair Lady, *"Why can't a woman be more like a man?" But then that would probably be boring as the devil. Anyway, what I would like for you to do right now is to think of yourselves as speaking two different languages, say French and Spanish, because there are similarities in your thinking, but also differences. And for the last few sessions I've acted as an interpreter. Which is okay, but I don't plan to move in with you, so it would be much more efficient for me to teach you how to speak each other's language. Then you can communicate and work on solutions.*

The fourth step consists of brainstorming for solutions. Each partner states his or her position, not with the purpose of converting the partner, but in order to inform his or her spouse about feelings and needs. Partners learn to listen to the experience of the other without feeling the need to defend or impose his or her own view. The therapist helps them clarify the most important underlying needs that must be met for the relationship to be satisfying to both. Creative two-winner solutions to problems emerge from the clients themselves. These solutions may require the therapist to do some skills training such as active listening or behavioral contracting. Or the therapist may need to offer a ritual prescription, simply reframing or employing any one of the many therapeutic techniques at his or her disposal in order to facilitate the clients' accomplishing their goal.

When such issues arise during the course of therapy, the therapist will continue to offer systemic interpretations. The therapist, while treating both male and female positions as valid, will move clients through the steps of reflection, education, normaliza-

tion, depersonalizing, and brainstorming. (It must be emphasized that no form of violence or intimidation is ever tolerated.) The most important element of this approach is its nonblaming viewpoint, which unites the couple against a common enemy—gender socialization—in an effort to save their relationship. Couples develop creative teamwork to defeat this problem that is bigger than both of them.

The following case, using Philpot's psychoeducational approach, illustrates the dramatic affective changes that can occur when a couple begins to recognize that the problems they are experiencing are not due to defects in the personality of either party but are instead a result of gender socialization and rigid role definition.

### CASE EXAMPLE

*Kay, a 37-year-old former nurse and mother of three, who has not worked outside the home since the birth of her first child, now 12, and her husband, Carl, a city planner, came to the initial session at the recommendation of a child psychologist who felt the separation anxiety experienced by their youngest child, Sam, 5, was due to marital difficulties between the parents. As is so often the case, Carl reported that he had been unaware of his wife's marital dissatisfaction, despite her claim that she had been signaling unhappiness for more than 10 years. Carl was shocked, hurt, and angry when Kay, in the presence of the child psychologist, rated the marriage a "5" on a 1 to 10 scale. After that session, the couple lived in an emotional atmosphere that was usually frigid, yet sometimes punctuated by intense outbursts of anger. Carl wanted Kay to be his best friend, but Kay continued to feel emotionally isolated and unable to share her feelings with Carl. She considered seeking a divorce. Carl was adamantly opposed to a divorce, partially because in his teenage years his mother divorced Carl's alcoholic father. Carl adopted an emotional stance of "justified outrage." Both partners were distraught and confused.*

During the first half hour of the initial session, Carl played a dominant role, dogmatically describing his frustrated efforts to improve his wife's problems with self-esteem. He detailed his multiple contributions as provider, occasional babysitter, and sexual partner, as well as his feelings of being unappreciated. In addition, he felt undermined in his attempts to parent because Kay intervened on behalf of the children when he attempted to administer discipline. He angrily pointed out Kay's unrealistic expectations and clearly had no understanding of her unhappiness as a housewife and mother. Kay sat quietly weeping and looked to the therapist for understanding. Whenever she tried to speak, Carl interrupted with defensive comments.

When it became clear that Kay would not be able to express her position until Carl felt truly understood, the therapist stated, "Here we go again! Another couple falling victim to society's prescribed roles without any understanding of how they got there. This is a very common problem, Carl, and you're right, it's not your fault! (At this point, Carl leans forward, feeling validated and ready to listen.) Neither is it Kay's. You didn't make the rules! Our society teaches men and women to play certain roles that are absolutely doomed to dissatisfaction, unhappiness, and failure, if we blindly follow them as though they were law. You were taught that a real man should provide for his family, lay down the law, discipline his children, and solve all the problems family members raise. You've done your best, and because Kay is still unhappy, you think you've failed, and you're hurt. (Carl feels understood and connects more with the therapist.) But what you were taught is wrong! Kay doesn't want you to solve her problems. She needs to solve her own problems. What she wants is your support in helping her do that. Before marriage, Kay was a competent nurse, very bright and independent. You have al-

ready pointed that out. Unfortunately for both of you, our society requires that women give up their careers for their husbands and children. It's drummed into their heads. Not that you particularly wanted her to do that, but the larger society out there tells women almost from birth that, even if they want a career, their children and relationships must come first. So women stay home, take care of their husbands and children, and then lose confidence in their ability to work outside the home. That wouldn't be so bad if our society didn't place a much higher value on making money than raising children. But in our society, power is money and position. You know that! Look at your own business. So women who stay home for an extended period of time feel incompetent, unimportant, and powerless. No wonder Kay got depressed! So would you if you were in that position! (Kay looks relieved, nods her head vigorously and also leans forward, connecting with the therapist.) But again, that's not your fault. You've both done what society expects of you. The result is you are both unhappy. Kay, because she feels worthless, and you, because Kay is so miserable that your life is also miserable. You will only be happy when Kay is happy, and Kay will only be happy when she feels good about herself again. Your diagnosis was correct, Carl (Carl looks satisfied, validated). But your solutions fell short of the mark because you tried to fix things in a typical masculine way, and Kay is a woman. (Carl looks puzzled; Kay nods vigorously again.) Since you are a man, I wouldn't have expected you to do anything differently. However, when you understand better what a woman needs, you will be able to support her in a way that is more effective."

The therapist then followed up with a brief discussion of gender differences in communication and relieved Carl of having to provide a solution to Kay's difficulties. Then, reminding Carl that he was not at fault for what Kay was experiencing, the therapist asked Kay to express her feelings about herself, her position in life, her concerns regarding her marriage and her future. The therapist coached Carl in listening nondefensively and reflecting rather than attempting to provide solutions. At first, it was necessary to stop Carl frequently from getting on his soapbox, and this was done in a somewhat lively and humorous fashion. The therapist would intervene frequently with, "Commiserate, Carl, don't solve. Don't try to minimize to make her feel better. That's what a man wants. Not a woman. C-o-m-m-i-s-e-r-a-t-e! Share her frustration. Tell her what you hear her saying without editorializing. Even if it feels artificial and worthless. Or just say nothing and listen."

By the end of the first session, both spouses began to feel more understood and validated, as well as relieved of blame. The therapist assigned bibliotherapy (either Deborah Tannen's [1990] You Just Don't Understand or John Gray's [1992] Men Are from Mars and Women Are from Venus are good suggestions) and set an appointment for one week. By the second session, the atmosphere of blame and anger had begun to dissipate. Both partners felt good about the other and predicted a positive prognosis for their marriage. Both were motivated to begin the work of learning the other's culture and negotiating solutions to their problems. Within 10 sessions, Kay was enrolled in refresher nursing courses and very excited about the new goals she and her husband had set for themselves. Carl was supportive in helping to babysit the children and willing to have Kay's mother help with the housework. (His dislike for housework was used to help him gain empathy for the work his wife had

done for over 12 years and engendered further emotional support for helping Kay relaunch her career with the goal of hiring someone to do the work neither liked to do). They had come to a workable compromise regarding the disciplining of their children. As Kay began to feel more power and control over her own life, she felt less need to win the children over as allies and backed off from intervening in her husband's disciplining of the children. His frustration level went down, and he became a more effective disciplinarian. As the atmosphere at home warmed up, their youngest child seemed to relax and began to enjoy kindergarten. The couple continued to practice cross-cultural communication skills, with the knowledge of the specific styles and value systems of their respective gender worlds.

In this case example, breakthrough change came very early, with the affective change being brought about when the spouses saw each other as victims of a rigid socialization process, rather than the enemy. Once the partners felt positive about one another again, the intergender communication learning process was easily achieved and they were able as a team to solve their problems effectively.

## Brooks' Intergender Translating and Reframing Approach

Brooks (1991b) has described his efforts to improve communication in couples stressed by disequilibrium in traditional gender role alignments. This approach is largely a product of his work as a psychologist at a Veteran's Administration hospital. He found that many of his patients were men with a highly traditional gender-role orientation and great resistance to relationship change. Because the impetus for change typically comes from the newly empowered woman, this approach places extensive emphasis on the therapist as political agent of change. This perspective holds that no in-session techniques are likely to be effective unless three things occur: The political context of the relationship is managed, pro-change pressures have been supported, and the anti-change pressures have been neutralized. Only when that has been accomplished can the therapist move to the next phase—the estimable task of promoting compassion and understanding between the partners, serving as intergender translator and reframer.

The basic premise of Brooks' approach is that in traditional relationships (those in which both partners began the relationship with traditional gender role expectations of each other), a common precipitant to therapy is the poor fit between traditional marital roles and contemporary pressures on men and women. Typically, the partner who seeks help is the woman; the partner resisting change is the man. Given that the husband generally has more physical, financial, or political power, change potential is dependent on a woman's empowerment. Brooks (1991b) suggested a six-stage treatment model for this situation: (1) the therapist becomes knowledgeable of the gender-role pressures and socialization of each partner; (2) the therapist maintains therapeutic leverage by perpetuating homeostatic imbalance (i.e., resisting premature reconciliation); (3) the woman's empowerment is supported; (4) encouragement is given to the man for willingness to consider change; (5) consciousness-raising activities are provided to the man; and (6) the therapist monitors the situation regarding possible conjoint therapy for reconciliation.

Brooks' approach also places special emphasis on the need for the therapist to make connections with each marital partner, to convey deep appreciation concerning their unique adaptations to gender role pressures. Although this sometimes can be done in conjoint sessions, separate sessions are often necessary, usually because the woman has been thinking about the relationship issues for a longer period of time. It is not uncommon, for example, for the man to see the problems as coming out of the blue or to feel blindsided.

The sessions with the woman are usually easier, because of the woman's interest in therapy as a mechanism for change. Although the woman may be distrustful of her husband, she is likely to view the therapist as a potential ally. This will be especially true if the therapist validates her distress with traditional role arrangements and supports her demands for greater equality in her marital relationship. Primary issues in these sessions are reinforcement of her empowerment and education about possible anti-change tactics from her husband.

Sessions with the man are initially far more stressful. Typically distrustful of psychotherapy, the man commonly enters the sessions with a variety of negative postures—hostility, resentment, fear, embarrassment, or shame. He may view therapy as a necessary price to pay to reestablish the marital relationship, or he may see it as a mechanism for manipulating his spouse. Whatever the posture, the therapist's task is to defuse the man's negative expectations, to demonstrate that his gender-based distress is recognized, and to generate hope that therapy offers potential benefits to both partners. An informed therapist usually has little difficulty helping a man discover formerly unrecognized areas of emotional pain. Education about the changing culture and the pressures of masculinity offer new avenues of exploration for men, as well as alternative explanations for role failures.

For example, even the most well-defended and argumentative man may be relieved to find a therapist who does not begin from a critical stance, but begins from a posture of validating the man's best intentions. In this more comfortable atmosphere, the male client is likely to be engaged by inquiries about his work (or inability to work), his social isolation or estrangement from his children's lives, his sexual disappointments or dissatisfactions, his need to ignore his physical discomfort and emotional distress, and his anxiety about his ability to maintain a stoic masculine facade.

When the previous treatment stages have been completed, and the marital partners seem confident that the therapist appreciates their respective positions, conjoint sessions are helpful. In these sessions the therapist may do well to be more active than usual in facilitating communication. Much as the language interpreter occupies a central position in international negotiations, the therapist may find it helpful to serve as a communication mediator, a translator of separate languages of the genders. After receiving input from one partner, the therapist decodes the message by placing it in the context of that person's value system and, before sending it to the intended receiver, reframes it in terms of that person's efforts to enhance the overall relationship (according to the logic of the first person's gender world). Once the receiver of the input recognizes the positive intent of the message, he or she can then respond as to how well that behavior meshes with his or her needs. The process continues with the therapist helping the partners see how traditional role patterns create problems and helping them negotiate new arrangements that more closely meet each other's needs.

In general, Brooks' approach is quite similar to most couples therapy approaches, except that it places major emphasis on how gender-based differences in communication style affect therapy. It differs in terms of (a) its preoccupation with power and relational politics and (b) the initially high degree of centrality of the therapist.

In this second case example, using Brooks' approach, gender role reversal proved to be devastating to the couple's relationship until both partners were able to recognize and overcome their own discomfort with a nontraditional gender role.

### CASE EXAMPLE

*Alice called to make the appointment for herself and her husband Robert, saying that she was depressed, frustrated, and somewhat hopeless about the relationship. She and Robert had been together 12 years, with two daughters, ages 10 and 5. The older daughter (Melanie) had suffered a severe brain injury at birth that left her bedridden and profoundly retarded. The younger daughter (Meredith) was healthy and intellectually above average. Alice worked as a bank loan officer. Robert had not worked in several months, following a layoff from his job as a hardware store clerk. This work arrangement was not considered a major problem because Robert's unemployment allowed him to remain in the home and provide care to the children. Alice was able to make a far higher salary than Robert. Care of Melanie was a con-*

*siderable issue because of her extensive needs (Alice's parents pressured her to place Melanie in an institution). Alice's primary complaints were that Robert had stopped providing high-quality care to Melanie, frequently not changing her for many hours. Alice also suspected that Robert had returned to his earlier habits of marijuana use, had begun collecting pornographic magazines, and, perhaps, even had a girlfriend he would leave the house to see.*

*In the first session, Robert was quiet and sullen; Alice was tentatively outspoken and unhappy. Whenever she voiced complaints, she became tearful, whereas Robert became defensive, irritable, and verbally aggressive. Alice would then back off, as communication would end. The therapy room filled with gloom and a sense of futility. After a rather unproductive conjoint session, separate sessions were scheduled for Alice and Robert.*

*In Alice's first individual session, she described a lengthy series of dissatisfactions about Robert's failure to contribute as a father, worker, or partner. She recounted her own history of overfunctioning as parental child in her family of origin. In fact, she admitted that one possible motive for her relationship with Robert was an effort to escape a difficult home environment. She painfully described her "dilemma." She felt that she was dependent on Robert to provide care for Melanie but was deeply dissatisfied with the variability of that care, as well as with his unappreciative and generally hostile attitude toward her. She saw herself as "trapped."*

*In his separate session, Robert came with expectations that he would be "scolded" for his irresponsibility and generally inadequate performance as a husband, breadwinner, and father. Although he admitted to marijuana use and guilt about daily masturbation with pornographic mag-*

azines, he denied any extramarital relationships. He made no significant protest to Alice's portrayal of him as a relatively low-functioning person. Furthermore, he initially expressed no specific complaints about Alice. Essentially, he seemed to buy into the presenting picture—Alice as responsible worker, knowledgeable parent, and frustrated wife; Robert as unmotivated worker, inadequate babysitter, and disappointing husband.

The therapist devoted substantial effort to developing a respectful relationship with Robert, one in which his strengths were validated and his points of view were valued. Working from this agenda, the therapist learned that Robert had competencies and noteworthy perspective on the relationship. He was found to be a reasonably skillful handyman and carpenter, with an abundance of useful and practical information. Furthermore, he had well-developed common sense and the capacity to put issues in perspective. He had a sensible low-key approach to many matters, including the raising of children, that could serve as a welcome counterpoint to Alice's seriousness and obsessiveness. Once he developed confidence in the therapy relationship, he began acknowledging areas of dissatisfaction—Alice's need to always be right; to prevail in all household decisions; and to always be too depressed, tired, or upset to engage in sexual activity. He even admitted that he sometimes coped with her "superiority" and greater verbal fluency with emotional and physical withdrawal, marijuana use, and semi-intentional "screwing-up." He ultimately recognized that therapy could be a big help to him if it made Alice appreciate him more and helped improve their sexual relationship.

Once connections had been established with both Alice and Robert, conjoint sessions were resumed. Working through the therapist as interpreter of their concerns,

each partner detailed difficulties with the nontraditional role arrangements—Alice as breadwinner, Robert as home manager and caretaker of children. Alice's "criticism" of Robert's performance was framed as one method for her to deal with discomfort caused by "abandoning" her traditional duties, and a way for her to feel like a contributor in that area. Robert's withdrawal, passive–aggressive behavior, and anger outbursts were framed as reactions to his feeling "unmasculine," as well as his method of demonstrating that he was not a "wife-dominated wimp" (thereby unworthy of her respect).

Over several subsequent sessions, Alice and Robert negotiated possible new approaches to their quandary. As Robert and Alice became more comfortable with their nontraditional roles (thanks, in part, to liberal exposure to adjunctive consciousness-raising activities for each, such as readings, films, and attendance at consciousness-raising group experiences), they developed more confidence in Robert's judgments as a primary caretaker of children. Additionally, they developed creative avenues for each to fulfill traditional aspects of their identities. Robert began part-time work with the volunteer fire department. Arrangements were made for Alice to have relaxing quality time with Melanie and Meredith.

Both this and the previous case example serve to illustrate the liberating effect of understanding the genesis of, and choosing to alter traditional messages absorbed during, gender socialization. Once men and women understand the gender ecosystem of the other, creative solutions can be generated to resolve what once appeared to be insurmountable difficulties.

## OTHER USEFUL TECHNIQUES IN GENDER-SENSITIVE FAMILY THERAPY
### Empathy and Communication Skills
In order to really empathize and connect with others, it is often necessary to, as the saying goes, walk

a mile in their shoes. Lusterman's (1989) interview technique makes it possible for a couple to do just that. Essentially what Lusterman does is to teach the couple Interviewing Skills 101, coaching them in asking open-ended questions, active listening skills, reflecting what they hear, avoiding interruptions and defensive responses, and validating the needs, concerns, and hopes of the other partner. This experience interrupts the reflexive patterns of accusation and defense that so often occur between couples who automatically interpret any unhappiness of the partner as a criticism or deficiency within themselves. It then allows the couple to design solutions that can meet the needs of both partners. Even if the behaviors themselves do not change that much, often the very act of validation changes the emotional atmosphere so that what once was felt as an imposition becomes the opportunity to offer a gift.

Scarf (1988) described a similar exercise in her book, *Intimate Partners*. Couples are asked to set aside an hour for intimacy time each week. For the first 30 minutes, the partner whose turn it is to go first this week is to talk about him- or herself, discussing, for example, hopes, dreams, fears, concerns, plans, and worries. The other partner is to listen only and not respond. For the second 30 minutes, the other partner will talk about her- or himself in the same manner. Neither partner is to respond to the other about anything that is said or to talk about the exercise except in the therapist's office. The opportunity to talk about oneself uninterrupted and uncontested is validating and helpful in making sense out of one's life. The opportunity to listen to one's partner without responding allows one to put aside defensive and angry responses and really get to know one's spouse as if he or she were a stranger again. The result is greater intimacy and an understanding of the world of the other. Marital enrichment programs utilize similar exercises.

To improve couples' communication, Stuart (1980) has emphasized the importance of focusing on the positive aspects of one's partner. Therefore, he proposed the "positive-change principle"—the idea that change is more likely if one places less emphasis on another's failing and more emphasis on positive changes that would replace the offensive behaviors. In areas involving modifying gender roles, this em-

phasis on positive change is particularly important, because most people now seeking therapy are already fearful of being labeled as sexist or as unfeminine feminists.

## Gender Messages and the Family of Origin

Also highly relevant to gender-sensitive family therapy are the questions about gender messages coming from one's family of origin and, in particular, reflexive circular questions (Tomm, 1988) that give clients the possibility of making the choice to be different. Examples of such questions can be seen in Exhibit 1. The purpose of these questions is threefold. First, they teach, through personal example, that the gender ecosystem is at the core of many of the misunderstandings and dissatisfactions that spouses are ex-

---

### EXHIBIT 1

**Gender Message Questions**

1. Who in your family of origin taught you the most about being a girl/woman? boy/man? What did they teach you? How?
2. Did your parents teach you similar or different things about gender roles?
3. What did your parents model for you about gender relationships in their interactions?
4. When you were younger and cried, what did your parents do?
5. Who would touch whom in your family of origin?
6. Who would be most likely to withdraw from a disagreement in your family of origin? Who would want to talk it out?
7. How did you see men/women, boys/girls acting differently in your family of origin?
8. How do the gender messages you received work for you in your present relationship? How do they fail you?
9. If you were to change any gender messages, what would they be? Why?
10. What gender messages do you want to pass on to your children?

*Derived from Roberts (1991).*

periencing and therefore depersonalize much of the conflict between spouses. Second, they demonstrate how the sexes influence and mold one another within the family of origin and pass on similar destructive messages to future generations. Third, they expand cognitive maps and offer the possibility of change in the present to bring about change in future generations.

## CONCLUSION

For many centuries sex roles have remained rigidly delineated. Now, however, dramatic changes are unfolding, profoundly altering the respective worlds of women and men and the nature of the interactions among them. A number of fundamental cultural shifts have contributed to the creation of an atmosphere conducive to reshaping gender relationships. These forces include, among others, the feminist movement, the men's movement, and the dramatically altered 20th-century workplace.

Because of profound alterations in the expectations of men and women and the unsettled nature of relations between them, a state of considerable disequilibrium now exists. For example, although changes in the legal system regarding sexual harassment in the workplace have had positive results for both genders, they have also resulted in an upsurge of distrust between the sexes. In the home, although women and men clamor for "new" male–female relationships, it is clear that they need more than superficial changes in roles. They need transforming changes in the customary nature of relations between the sexes. With the help of gender-sensitive family systems therapists, intergender relations can move beyond insecure relationships between half-persons and become enhancing relationships between full persons. Family psychologists who are thoroughly familiar with the gender ecosystems of men and women can serve as bridges between the separate worlds and promote relationships based on the shared experiences of equals.

By focusing on systems, rather than individuals, as units of intervention, a family systems orientation makes it possible to broaden the conceptual focus as far as necessary to include all relevant sociocultural ecosystems. Just as family systems therapy "emerged

from the myopia of the intrapsychic view," it has begun to be understood that "family behavior itself makes sense only in the larger context of culture" (McGoldrick et al., 1989, p. xv). Family systems therapists are now likely to consider ethnic, social class, and gender "macrosystems" (Schwartzman, 1985) in their case conceptualizations. With this broadened focus, family systems therapists are in an ideal position to serve as "culture brokers" (Pittman, 1985), that is, to help family members negotiate complex gender role value issues during times of significant cultural transition and to suggest practical strategies so that women and men can replace heavily scripted patterns with ones that are less rigid, and more authentic.

## References

Anderson, H. (1993). On a roller coaster: A collaborative language systems approach to therapy. In S. Friedman (Ed.), *The new language of change* (pp. 323–344). New York: Guilford Press.

Avis, J. (1988). Deepening awareness: A private study guide to feminism and family therapy. *Journal of Psychotherapy & the Family, 3*.

Balswick, J. O. (1988). *The inexpressive male.* Lexington, MA: Lexington Books.

Belenky, M., Clinchy, B., Goldberger, N., & Tarule, J. (1986). *Women's ways of knowing: The development of self, voice, and mind.* New York: Basic Books.

Bernard, J. (1981). The good provider role. Its rise and fall. *American Psychologist, 36*, 1–12.

Bergman, S. J., & Surrey, J. (1992). The woman–man relationship: Impasses and possibilities (Stone Center Document #55). Wellesley, MA: Stone Center.

Brod, H. (1984). Work clothes and leisure suits: The class basis and bias of the men's movement. *Gentle Men for Gender Justice, 11*, 10–12.

Brod, H. (1987). A case for men's studies. In M. S. Kimmel (Ed.), *Changing men: New directions in research on men and masculinity* (pp. 263–277). Newbury Park, CA: Sage.

Bronstein, P., & Cowan, C. (Eds). (1988). *Fatherhood today: Men's changing role in the family.* New York: Wiley.

Brooks, G. R. (1991a). Men's studies and psychotherapy: A current perspective on the status of the men's movement. *The Psychotherapy Bulletin, 26*, 19–22.

Brooks, G. R. (1991b). Traditional men in marital and family therapy. In M. Bograd (Ed.), *Feminist approaches for men in family therapy* (pp. 51–74). New York: Haworth Press.

Broverman, I. K., Broverman, D. M., Clarkson, F. E., Rosenkrantz, V., & Vogel, S. R. (1970). Sex-role stereotypes and clinical judgement of mental health. *Journal of Consulting Psychology, 34,* 1–7.

Bullough, V. (1973). *The subordinate sex: A history of attitudes toward women.* Athens, GA: University of Georgia Press.

Cahill, S. (1986). Language practices and self-definition: The case of gender identity acquisition. *The Sociological Quarterly, 27,* 295–311.

Caplan, P., & Hall-McCorquodale, I. (1985). Mother-blaming in major clinical journals. *American Journal of Orthopsychiatry, 55*(3), 345–353.

Chodorow, N. (1978). *The reproduction of mothering.* Berkeley: University of California Press.

Clatterbaugh, K. (1990). *Contemporary perspectives on masculinity: Men, women, and politics in modern society.* Boulder, CO: Westview Press.

Cook, E. P. (1990). Gender and psychological distress. *Journal of Counseling and Development, 68,* 371–375.

David, D. S., & Brannon, R. (1976). *The forty-nine percent majority: The male sex role.* Reading, MA: Addison-Wesley.

Dinnerstein, D. (1976). *The mermaid and the minotaur: Sexual arrangements and the human malaise.* New York: Harper & Row.

Doyle, J. A. (1989). *The male experience* (2nd ed.). Dubuque, IA: William C. Brown.

Eisler, R. M., & Blalock, J. A. (1991). Masculine gender role stress: Implications for the assessment of men. *Clinical Psychology Review, 11,* 45–60.

Faludi, S. (1991). *Backlash: The undeclared war against American women.* New York: Crown Publishers.

Farrell, W. T. (1987). *Why men are the way they are.* New York: McGraw-Hill.

Fausto-Sterling, A. (1985). *Myths of gender: Biological theories about women and men.* New York: Basic Books.

Gilbert, L. A. (1988). *Sharing it all: The rewards and struggles of two-career families.* New York: Plenum.

Gilbert, L. A., & Scher, M. (1987). The power of an unconscious belief: Male entitlement and sexual intimacy with clients. *Professional Practice of Psychology, 8,* 94–108.

Gilligan, C. (1982). *In a different voice.* Cambridge, MA: Harvard University Press.

Gilmore, D. (1990). *Manhood in the making: Cultural concepts of masculinity.* New Haven, CT: Yale University Press.

Goldberg, H. (1976). *The hazards of being male.* New York: New American Library.

Goodrich, T. J. (1991). *Women and power: Perspectives for family therapy.* New York: Norton.

Gray, J. (1992). *Men are from Mars, Women are from Venus: A practical guide for improving communication and getting what you want in your relationships.* New York: Harper Collins.

Haley, J. (1984). *Ordeal therapy.* San Francisco: Jossey-Bass.

Hare-Mustin, R., & Marecek, J. (1988). The meaning of difference: Gender theory, postmodernism, and psychology. *American Psychologist, 43*(6), 455–464.

Hochschild, A. (1989). *The second shift: Working parents and the revolution at home.* New York: Viking Penguin.

Kimmel, M. (1987). Rethinking masculinity: New directions in research. In M. Kimmel (Ed.), *Changing men: New directions in research on men and masculinity* (pp. 9–24). Newbury Park, CA: Sage.

Kimmel, M., & Mosmiller, T. (1992). *Against the tide: Profeminist men in the United States 1776–1990.* New York: Beacon Press.

Kohlberg, L. (1969). Stage and sequence: The cognitive-development approach to socialization. In D. A. Goslin (Ed.), *Handbook of socialization and research* (pp. 347–480). Chicago: Rand McNally.

Lamb, M. E., Owen, M. J., & Chase-Lansdale, L. (1978). The father–daughter relationship: Past, present, future. In C. B. Knopp & M. Kirkpatrick (Eds.), *Becoming female* (pp. 145–160). New York: Plenum.

Levant, R., & Kelley, J. (1989). *Between father and child.* New York: Viking Press.

Luepnitz, D. (1988). *The family interpreted.* New York: Basic Books.

Lusterman, D. (1989, August). Empathic interviewing. In G. Brooks (Chair), *Men and women relating: The carrot or the stick?* Symposium conducted at the meeting of the American Association of Marriage and Family Therapists, San Francisco, CA.

McGoldrick, M., Anderson, C., & Walsh, F. (Eds.). (1989). Women in families: A framework for family therapy. New York: Norton.

McGrath, E., Keita, G., Strickland, B., & Russo, N. (1990). *Women and depression: Risk factors and treatment issues* (Final Report of the American Psychological Association's National Task Force on Women and Depression). Washington, DC: American Psychological Association.

Miller, J. B. (1986). *Toward a new psychology of women* (2nd ed.). Boston: Beacon Press.

Morgan, L. (1991). *After marriage ends: Economic consequences for midlife women.* Newbury Park, CA: Sage.

Nathanson, C. A. (1977). Sex roles as variables in preventive health behavior. *Journal of Community Health, 3,* 142–155.

Nolen-Hoeksema, S. (1990). *Sex differences in depression.* Stanford, CA: Stanford University Press.

O'Donovan, D. (1988). Femiphobia: Unseen enemy of intellectual freedom. *Men's Studies Review, 5,* 14–16.

O'Leary, V. E., & Donahue, J. M. (1978). Latitudes of masculinity: Reactions to sex-role deviance in men. *Journal of Social Issues, 34,* 17–28.

O'Neil, J. M. (1982). Gender-role conflict and strain in men's lives. In K. Solomon & N. Levy (Eds.), *Men in transition: Theory and therapy* (pp. 5–44). New York: Plenum Press.

O'Neil, J. M., & Roberts Carroll, M. (1988). A gender role journey. *Journal of Counseling and Development, 67,* 193–197.

Philpot, C. L. (1991). Gender-sensitive couples' therapy: A systemic definition. *Journal of Family Psychotherapy, 2*(3), 19–40.

Pittman, F. (1985). Gender myths: When does gender become pathology? *Family Therapy Networker, 9,* 24–33.

Pleck, E. H., & Pleck, J. H. (1980). *The American man.* Englewood Cliffs, NJ: Prentice Hall.

Pleck, J. H. (1981). The myth of masculinity. Cambridge, MA: MIT Press.

Roberts, J. M. (1991). Sugar and spice toads and mice: Gender issues in family therapy training. *Journal of Marital and Family Therapy, 17*(2), 121–132.

Scarf, M. (1988). *Intimate partners.* New York: Random House.

Schwartzman, J. (Ed.). (1985). *Families and other systems: The macrosystemic contest of family therapy.* New York: Plenum Press.

Skord, K. G., & Schumacher, B. (1982). Masculinity as handicapping condition. *Rehabilitation Literature, 43*(9–10), 284–289.

Solomon, K. (1982). The masculine gender role: Description. In K. Solomon & N. B. Levy (Eds.), *Men in transition: Theory and therapy* (pp. 45–76). New York: Plenum.

Stuart, R. (1980). *Helping couples change: A social learning approach to marital therapy.* New York: Guilford Press.

Sue, D. W., & Sue, D. (1990). *Counseling the culturally different: Theory and practice.* New York: Wiley.

Tannen, D. (1990). *You just don't understand: Women and men in conversation.* New York: Ballantine Books.

Tomm, K. (1988). Interventive interviewing: Part 3. Intending to ask lineal, circular, strategic, or reflexive questions? *Family Process, 27,* 1–15.

Verbrugge, L. M. (1985). Gender and health: An update on hypothesis and evidence. *Journal of Health and Social Behavior, 26,* 156–182.

Waldron, I. (1976). Why do women live longer than men? *Journal of Human Stress, 2,* 1–13.

Walker, L. (1985). *The battered woman.* New York: Harper & Row.

Watzlawick, P., Beavin, J. H., & Jackson, D. D. (1967). *Pragmatics of human communication.* New York: Norton.

Weitzman, L. J. (1985). *The divorce revolution: The unexpected social and economic consequences for women and children in America.* New York: Free Press.

Williams, J. (1977). *The psychology of women: Behavior in a biosocial context.* New York: Norton.

Wright, P. (1982). Men's friendships—women's friendships and the alleged inferiority of the latter. *Sex Roles, 8,* 1–20.

# CHAPTER 18

# LESBIAN AND GAY FAMILY PSYCHOLOGY

*Roy Scrivner and Natalie S. Eldridge*

As lesbian and gay populations become more visible, family therapists are being asked to provide specialized services to these families and to help families of origin deal with their frequently ambivalent or hostile responses to gay or lesbian family members. New family structures have been created by lesbians and gays who are raising children from previous heterosexual marriages, whereas other structures are being created through adoption, donor insemination, or surrogacy.

This chapter is about people and the relationships they form, people who exist within a society that stigmatizes them as a deviant minority group. Lesbians and gays are uniquely different from ethnic and other stigmatized groups. Unlike people of color, gays and lesbians are usually "invisible," assumed to be heterosexual members of their cultural group. Unlike children of ethnic minority parents, lesbian and gay children rarely have a lesbian or gay parent who can help them to understand their particular minority status in the dominant culture. Lesbian and gay parents usually raise heterosexual children, who will not replicate a same-sex family form. Lesbians and gay men seldom enjoy the rootedness of a multigenerational family, in which certain experiences are passed down by one generation and reflected in the next. Sometimes multigenerational lesbian and gay families with nonbiologically related extended lesbian and gay family members may be found in churches and other settings. A final way that gay and lesbian individuals differ from members of many other stigmatized groups has to do with how gender role socialization impacts the intimate relationships they

form. Although norms of heterosexual relating may differ from one cultural group to another, the process of reaching across gender lines to form intimacy is a commonality. In forming same-sex relationships, however, gender plays a very different role in the dynamics of intimacy for lesbian and gay couples. What are these gay and lesbian family dynamics and structures like?

This chapter will answer this question by providing both individual and systemic perspectives on lesbian and gay family psychology. An integration of several models of lesbian/gay identity development is described, followed by widely used models of gay and lesbian couple development. The stage models summarized here are not intended to be prescriptive of developmental sequences for all. Rather, they are useful in describing particular behaviors or conflicts that an individual or couple might present in therapy and in locating these within a larger context of developmental processes. Space limitations preclude an adequate discussion of the challenging issues of bisexuality. Readers are referred to Fox (1995) and Weinberg, Williams, and Pryor (1994) for a comprehensive review of these concerns. Much of the theoretical work presented here has been based on studies of Caucasian individuals. However, research and theoretical constructs drawn from the experiences of individuals of other racial groups are included when available. The chapter concludes with a discussion of various clinical issues that may arise, as well as some specific suggestions for therapists for increasing sensitivity and effectiveness.

We emphasize that the terms *lesbian* and *gay* are much preferred to the term *homosexual*, which has been associated with a mental disorder and does not differentiate between men and women. Also, we use the term *gay* in this chapter to refer exclusively to men, whereas the term *lesbian* is used solely in reference to women. The term *homosexual* also contributes to an overemphasis on gay and lesbian sexuality, rather than portraying sexuality in the context of many other dynamics within the individual's lifestyle. Like most of the large dominant nations of the world, America is a sex-negative culture (Smith, 1975). Sex-negative cultures have a stigma against many kinds of heterosexual sexual expressions and against same-sex sexual relations. In an empirical study of sex-negative and sex-positive individuals, Berry and Marks (1969) found that sex-negative persons see lesbians and gays less positively than do sex-positive individuals. Sex-negative views in America contribute to the stigma against lesbians and gays. In lieu of referring to *sexual orientation,* many prefer the term *affectional orientation,* which designates from which gender one selects a love object.

In this chapter, we will focus on the affectional relationships between lesbians and between gays. We will also note their caring relationships with their children, members of their extended nonbiologically related families of choice, and members of their families of origin. The frequently overlooked negative effects of the stigma against lesbians and gays on all of these family members will be addressed.

## INDIVIDUAL DEVELOPMENT

We live in a culture that assumes heterosexuality for all and provides little support for and many deterrents to the expression of alternative identities. It is remarkable that so many individuals have found a path for the expression and development of positive lesbian or gay identities. Others, however, find themselves stuck between their emotional and sexual yearnings and their internalized negative cultural values about gays and lesbians. Conflicts are often expressed in symptoms of anxiety, depression, substance abuse, sexual dysfunction, and the entire array of psychological concerns. As psychology has moved away from a pathological view of homosexuality and

a focus on etiology, greater attention has been paid to the impact of societal stigma and to the factors that encourage healthy identity development in lesbians and gays. Models of stages in the development of lesbian and gay identities have been presented by Plummer (1975), Troiden (1979), Cass (1979), and Coleman (1982). An integration of these models (Scrivner, 1984) is summarized in Table 1.

Morales (1989) proposed a model of identity formation that incorporates the doubly stigmatized status of being from a nondominant racial or ethnic background and being lesbian or gay. This model is summarized in Table 2. He noted the tasks that may be the focus of therapy for individuals in the various stages and suggested that movement through the stages decreases anxiety and tension. An individual in Stage 3, for example, may need help in recognizing the need to establish priorities of allegiance, at least temporarily, in order to ensure adequate social support and a decrease in isolation. An individual in Stage 5, however, may work in therapy on how to personalize a multicultural identity and integrate his or her connection to various communities. This usually needs to be a creative process, calling on a commitment of the individual's energy, personal interests, and values.

## FORMATION AND DEVELOPMENT OF LESBIAN AND GAY COUPLES

Lesbians and gay men are more like heterosexual women and men than they are different from them. Analogously, the development of relationships among same-sex pairs have much in common with the development of heterosexual relationships. Variations among lesbian, gay, and heterosexual couple paradigms reflect broad ecosystemic influences such as cultural biases against gays and lesbians. These cultural biases often result in invisibility. However, researchers have been able to overcome this invisibility barrier and identify some of the characteristics of these couples.

### A Model of Gay Couple Development
McWhirter and Mattison (1984) conducted a 5-year study of 156 gay couples living together from 1 to 37 years and found six stages of couple develop-

## TABLE 1

Stages in the Development of Lesbian and Gay Identities

| Stage | Characteristics | Therapy notes |
|---|---|---|
| 1. Sensitization | Individuals gain experiences that later may serve as sources for interpreting their feelings as being gay or lesbian. There may be gender confusion, feelings of differentness, or acts that seem not intrinsically sexual or affectional, but that can later be defined as such. Children may introject ecosystemic stigma against homosexuality even before they become aware of same-sex attractions. | This stage is quite universal, and may have more to do with the growing awareness of sexuality than with sexual orientation, per se. Therapists can work with client's fears about sexuality, and the development of self-esteem, encouraging the client to remain open as to eventual orientation. This stage may begin as early as preschool and only be identified retrospectively. It may occur later, even in late adulthood. |
| 2. Identity confusion | Individuals begin this stage thinking of themselves as heterosexual and knowing what the word *homosexual* means. Confusion begins when the individual has feelings, thoughts, or behaviors that can be defined as "homosexual."[a] Retroactive interpretation, the reinterpretation of past events as related to having a lesbian or gay identity, may begin in this stage. | How individuals deal with their confusion depends on how they perceive the thoughts, feelings, or behaviors that precipitated this stage. Perception is affected by the socialization absorbed from the environment about diversity in general, and homosexuality in particular. Denial and repression will lead to identity foreclosure. Acknowledging confusion moves the client toward the next stage. |
| 3. Identity comparison | The individual realizes that all the guidelines for a heterosexual identity are no longer relevant for her or him. Alienation, feeling "in a void," is common. Suicide is most likely in this stage, especially among adolescents. Any grief work related to giving up a heterosexual identity may begin in this stage. | Movement into this stage is likely to increase conflict for the individual. It is useful to provide support and encourage the client to decrease isolation by exploring the lesbian and gay subculture through reading, attending meetings, or cultural events. Finding role models and other positive aspects of the lesbian/gay lifestyle needs to be encouraged. |
| 4. Identity tolerance | This stage is reflected by greater commitment to the thought, "I probably am gay or lesbian." Some gays and lesbians may temporarily describe themselves as bisexual, whereas others may continue to develop an integrated bisexual identity.[b] Once labeling themselves as "probably gay or lesbian," contacting others in the lesbian and gay culture is viewed as something that has to be done in order to counter isolation and alienation. Support is not typically sought from heterosexuals, including family of origin members. | In this stage, a client may actively seek a lesbian or gay therapist referred by other members of the lesbian or gay community. Referrals to such therapists might be considered. Issues of trust and acceptance will be raised in the therapy relationship, even for long-standing therapeutic alliances. Alternatively, the client may rely on the therapist as the only source for information on how to enter the lesbian or gay community in a safe way. Knowledge of the local community and consultation may be important tools for the therapist. |

*(continues)*

## TABLE 1 (Continued)

### Stages in the Development of Lesbian and Gay Identities

| Stage | Characteristics | Therapy notes |
|---|---|---|
| 5. Identity acceptance | This stage is characterized by continued and increasing contact with other gays or lesbians. The person feels the impact of those features of the subculture that validate and normalize having a gay or lesbian identity. Introjected stigma and inaccurate information from the ecosystem must be confronted and changed.[c] The individual may experience a "gay adolescence" that occurs after their chronological adolescence. There is increasing need to learn to relate socially to lesbians and/or gays. | This stage usually marks a major life transition, and clients often experiment with new behaviors, experience more intense emotions, or make outer changes in clothing style, career, and so on. Otherwise very mature and successful lesbian or gay adults might find themselves becoming easily infatuated with others. Therapy can provide grounding support and promote safety, as with any major life transition or change. The words *gay* and *lesbian* may begin to be used more by clients in this stage to focus on a social identity, while the word *homosexual* is seen as a negative diagnostic label. |
| 6. First relationships | This stage is marked by the developmental task of learning how to function in a same-sex affectional relationship. It will be affected by the individual's overall experience in intimate relationships. First same-sex affectional relationships are often characterized by intensity, possessiveness, and lack of trust. The absence of role models and a failure to negotiate earlier stages (not accepting gay or lesbian identity) make these first relationships more difficult. | Family therapists skilled in couple therapy with heterosexuals need to learn about roles of stigma and gender in same-sex couples and how these couples are uniquely different from one another and from heterosexual couples. Heterosexist bias can cause harm in therapy by reinforcing internalized stigma within these relationships. Therapists may be in the role of the only "public" recognition of the couple. |
| 7. Identity commitment and pride | Commitment to an identity presupposes a reluctance to abandon the identity, even if given the chance to do so. In this stage a person may divide the world between the subculture of lesbians and gays, and the "straight" world of heterosexuals, devaluing the latter. Pride leads to increased candor about one's gay or lesbian identity with heterosexuals. | Growing pride in negotiating a positive lesbian or gay identity in the face of adversity may be accompanied by intense anger at the straight world, or those considered to be the oppressors. Therapists may want to help clients differentiate between those who are supportive and who may collaborate with them, versus other nonsupportive heterosexuals, for whom confrontation may be appropriate. How others, especially heterosexuals, respond to the client's openness about being gay or lesbian may influence whether the client can move into next stage. |
| 8. Identity synthesis | Feelings of pride are still present, but the "them" versus "us" philosophy is not. One's lesbian or gay identity is seen as only one aspect of one's overall identity. | Clients rarely bring in issues of a gay or lesbian identity as a presenting problem, unless focused on handling external discrimination or harassment. |

[a]Coleman (1987) is recommended for working with those who are confused about their sexual orientation.
[b]See Fox (1995) for a discussion of bisexuality.
[c]Helminiak (1994) is recommended for those who have religious beliefs that conflict with an acceptance of lesbians and gays.
[d]Savin-Williams (1995) discusses lesbian, gay, and bisexual male and female adolescents.

## TABLE 2

## Individual Development of Ethnic Minority Gays and Lesbians

| Stage | Characteristics | Therapy issues |
|---|---|---|
| 1. | Denial of conflicts is prevalent. Individuals minimize the discrimination against their ethnic group. There may or may not be identification as lesbian or gay. If so, they experience their sexual orientation as having limited significance. | The focus of therapy is on an increased awareness of the stigma they experience as both a member of a nondominant ethnic group and as a gay or lesbian person. The positive aspects of such a multiple identity are important to explore. |
| 2. | Some ethnic lesbians and gays prefer to identify themselves as bisexual in an effort to maintain support in both worlds. The lesbian and gay communities may be perceived as White communities, and identification with these communities could be perceived as a betrayal of allegiance to ethnic community. | Therapy may focus on the continuing conflicts between the two identities and the ecosystemic stigma against both. The specific label or language used (e.g., *gay, bisexual*) is less important than the exploration of the conflict between inner awareness and the impact of social roles and expectations. |
| 3. | Conflicts in allegiances deepen. Loyalty conflicts between one's ethnic group and the lesbian and gay community are intensified. | Therapy may focus on the need to develop priorities, rather than choose sides, in an effort to reduce conflict. Examining supportive aspects of each community tends to encourage a shift from a monocultural to a multicultural perspective. |
| 4. | Establishing priorities in allegiances begins. Priority is often given to the ethnic group first. There may be anger and resentment toward this group for lack of acceptance as a gay or lesbian person, as well as anger toward the lesbian and gay community for discrimination against one's ethnic groups. | Therapy can focus on an examination of the anger and rage at each community and on the development of a proactive perspective, rather than a reactive one, in their relationships and allegiances. |
| 5. | Integration of the various communities is the task of this stage. The development of a multicultural perspective is the outcome. Limited options for supports integrating both ethnic and lesbian/gay identity may be a source of anxiety or contribute to alienation and isolation. | Normalizing the conflicts can be reassuring at this point. Ways to reduce isolation can be explored such as social[a] and political organizations for lesbians and gays of the client's ethnicity. |

*Note:* The following are recommended for a further understanding of lesbians and gays from specific ethnic groups: Greene (1994), Peterson (1992), Lockman (1984), Whitman and Mathy (1985), Balka and Rose (1989), and Tafoya and Rowell (1988). See also Morales (1989).
[a]See Jackson (1993) for addresses and meetings of groups for gays and lesbians of specific ethnic backgrounds.

ment. The stages of the McWhirter and Mattison model are based on research that was conducted on White gay couples prior to the AIDS epidemic. Later, Mattison and McWhirter (1990) conducted a study of gay couples where either one or both partners developed AIDS. For some couples in the early stages of development, the AIDS crisis propelled them through subsequent stages rapidly until they reached Stage 6. Couples in dissatisfying relationships often terminated the relationship in response to this crisis. Stages identified by Mattison and McWhirter (1984) are summarized in Table 3; a case example depicting some of the stages follows.

*CASE EXAMPLE: ROGER AND JAY*
*Roger and Jay had been together about a year when they entered couples therapy. Roger complained that Jay, a computer analyst, was becoming excessively angry at him. Jay complained that Roger, an attorney, used his courtroom skills to intimidate Jay and win arguments. In the past, they had often tried to deal with their differences nonverbally during sex, but the frequency of sexual relations had diminished, and both were afraid the relationship was breaking up.*

The therapist made an assessment of the identity development of each as a gay man, and of the stage of their couple relationship. The assessment indicated that each was in Stage 6 (see Table 1) of their individual development and in Stage 1 of their development as a couple (see Table 3). Both men had been in previous gay relationships and reported that the quality and commitment in their current relationship was much higher than in the previous relationships. Each had some lesbian and gay friends, but none in their local area, as each had recently moved to the area about the same time. The therapist suggested that part of their compatibility was due to each being at the same stage in their development of a positive identity as a gay man. Their relationship appeared to be at the end of the Blending Stage. Some of their concerns (e.g., reduced frequency of sex) were described as typical for couples after the first year of a relationship. The arguments were identified as being distancing maneuvers, and general issues of closeness

and distance were discussed. Subsequently, Jay and Roger were better able to identify when they wanted to be alone and to do that without the other feeling rejected. The frequency of arguments decreased.

Through a focus on family of origin work, the couple came to realize how much of their conflict reflected unresolved issues with their families. Jay was able to identify how he sometimes misplaced his anger toward his abusive parents onto Roger. Furthermore, he was jealous of and threatened by Roger's very close-knit and accepting family. Roger, on the other hand, began to recognize how he sacrificed his own time in running family business ventures, while his brother did nothing. He had been able to displace some of his anger toward his brother during courtroom trials, but in his new job he had less opportunity for this. He recognized that he had been taking his anger at his brother out on Jay. As the couple began to work on these family of origin issues in therapy, they argued far less and became increasingly committed to the relationship. They began devoting more time and resources to furnishing their joint apartment, marking their entrance into the Nesting Stage (see Table 3, Stage 2).

## A Model of Lesbian Couple Development

Clunis and Green (1988) developed a six-stage model of lesbian couple development based on both the McWhirter and Mattison (1984) model for gay relationships and the Campbell (1980) model for male–female relationship development. Stages of the Clunis and Green model are presented in Table 4; a case example depicting some of these stages follows.

*CASE EXAMPLE: KAY AND BARBARA*
*Kay and Barbara came to therapy for help in making a decision about parenting a second child. They already had a 6-year-old daughter, Kelly, who had entered the first grade and was doing very well. Barbara gave birth to Kelly during the third year of marriage to an alcoholic man and went through a difficult divorce during Kelly's first year. Barbara and Kay began dating then, moving through the pre-relationship and romance stages (see Table 4,*

## TABLE 3

### Gay Male Couple Formation and Development

| Stage | Characteristics |
|---|---|
| 1. Blending | Blending refers to an intensity of togetherness, where similarities bind the couple and differences are mutually overlooked. The couple does everything together, often to the exclusion of others. There is a feeling of being "in love with love" and a shared attitude of equality. Sexual activity varies but usually includes several encounters weekly and defacto sexual exclusivity. |
| 2. Nesting | In the second year, attention to surroundings takes the form of homemaking activities; decorating a new home, rearranging an old one. Couples in this stage also tend to see each other's shortcomings and discover or create complementariness that enhances compatibility. The partners' desire in being "in love with love" is usually not simultaneous and is often a cause for worry and concern. This decline and lack of compatibility may lead to ambivalence. |
| 3. Maintaining | Maintaining the relationship depends upon establishing balances between individualization and togetherness, conflict and its resolution, autonomy and dependence, confusion and understanding. A reemergence of individual differences (individualization) occurs. This is accompanied by some necessary risk taking, whether in outside sexual liaisons[a], more time apart, greater self-disclosure, or new separate friendships. These risks often result in conflicts that are dealt with either by confrontation and resolution or by avoidance. Another characteristic is relying on the relationship as if it possessed certain dependable qualities, such as steadfastness, comfort, and familiarity. Recognition and support of the relationship by family and friends often begins only after a couple has been together 3 years. |
| 4. Collaborating | Couples in stage four may unwittingly collaborate to aid the development of boredom and feelings of entrapment. After 5 years together, couples experience a new sense of security and a decreasing need to process their interactions. On the one hand, this decline in communication frequently gives rise to making unverified assumptions about each other. On the other hand, their collaborative adjustments often lead to effective complementarity. This complementarity, combined with the coping mechanisms for dealing with conflict and boredom, yields new energy which may lead to mutual as well as individual productivity of a visible nature, such as business partnerships, financial dealings, estate building, or achieving personal gains in professional or academic worlds. |
| 5. Trusting | Trust develops gradually for most people. As the years pass, and as they gain experience, gay couples trust each other with greater conviction. The trust of stage five includes a mutual lack of possessiveness and a strong positive regard for each other. A merger of money and possessions may be a manifestation of this trust. In the latter half of stage five, there may occur an isolation from the self as manifested by lack of feelings and inattention to personal needs, isolation from the partner by withdrawal and lack of communication and, sometimes, isolation from friends in the same ways. This type of constriction may be a result of the men's ages. The attitude of taking the relationship for granted develops as a result of the other characteristics of this stage. |
| 6. Repartnering | The 20th anniversary appears to be a special milestone for gay male couples. Couples report a renewal of their relationship after being together for 20 years or more. Goals of financial security often have been met. Other goals reached may include business, professional, and academic success. Couples in this stage assume that they will be together until separated by death. There are personal concerns, such as for health and security, fear of loneliness, and death of partner or self. Most are struck by the passage of time and reminisce about their years together. |

*Note:* See McWhirter and Mattison (1984) for elaboration of this material.
[a]Outside sexual liaisons are much less common now; see the section on AIDS, this chapter.

TABLE 4

## Lesbian Couple Formation and Development

| Stage | Characteristics | Tasks | Therapy issues |
|---|---|---|---|
| 1. Prerelationship | Dating, spending time. Stage often relatively brief for lesbians due to ambiguity of defining relationship, and gender role socialization encouraging women to link sexuality with love and commitment. | Getting to know each other. Deciding whether to invest more time and energy. Deciding whether or when to be sexual. | Partners bring different sets of expectations and assumptions. If women find asking for what they want or clarifying their expectations uncomfortable or unacceptable, disappointments and misunderstandings may arise. |
| 2. Romance | Merger, fusion, and sexuality. Partners tend to neglect their friends and focus on relationship. | Developing a sexual relationship. | Partners may minimize difficulties that could arise between them. Absence of clear rituals (e.g., dating, engagement, marriage) may augment the meaning given to beginning a sexual relationship or moving in together. |
| 3. Conflict | Differences in partners' needs or expectations emerge, demanding attention. | Learning to negotiate conflict. Developing couple decision-making processes, conflict resolution styles, communication channels, and relationship goals. Understanding the expectations and desires of the partner. | How conflict is negotiated is based in part on how well each partner made choices in the prerelationship stage, based on knowledge of the other person. If this stage was too rushed or skipped altogether, differences now emerging may be irreconcilable. |
| 4. Acceptance | Increasing stability. | Gaining confidence in relationship through experience in recognizing conflict and negotiating solutions. Viewing the partner more realistically, accepting the strengths and flaws they see. | Help each partner identify how she contributes to their particular conflict patterns. Bring in the perspective of past experiences, former relationships, and family of origin to understand each partner's responses to the current relationship. |
| 5. Commitment | Defined as "the decision to make choices about the relationship and be responsible for them" (p. 23). Must be preceded by the power struggle of the conflict stage and the clarity about the differentiation between the individual and the couple that evolves in the acceptance stage. | Coming to terms with opposing needs such as the needs to be separate and to be together, or needs for freedom and for security. Commitment to the relationship becomes a commitment to continually negotiate the changing needs of the individuals and the outside environment. | Support couple in the establishment of negotiation styles and, often, in considering or planning a public ceremony or recognition of their commitment. Several religious groups now make a formal commitment ceremony or marriage available through their structures; no legal recognition yet exists. |
| 6. Collaboration | Examples of collaborative processes: working toward a political cause together, raising a child or children collaboratively, starting a joint business, sharing their relationship experience and rituals with other lesbians. | Focusing on something beyond their relationship to share with the rest of the world. | As the couple embarks on their new project together, they may reexperience aspects of the former relationship stages. However, their history of survival and acceptance generally lends greater resiliency to the reworking of the stage. |

*Note:* See Clunis and Green (1988) for elaboration of this material.

*Stages 1 and 2). Kay felt ready to live with Barbara after 18 months, but they did not begin living together until Barbara was convinced that her ex-husband would not bring a custody suit against her because of her lesbian relationship. Barbara's reticence was a source of much conflict for the couple (see Table 4, Stage 3). Kelly was almost 3 when Kay moved in with them, and establishing a blended family was difficult over the first 18 months. In the last year, the relationship stabilized and deepened (see Table 4, Stage 4), and Kay and Barbara bought a house together, which neither of them could have afforded on their own. This move has provided an excellent school district for Kelly.*

Therapy focused on clarifying and reframing the impasse between Barbara's desire to have a second child and Kay's ambivalence. Barbara had always wanted at least two children and was now approaching 40. Kay was very committed to raising children with Barbara but felt resentful about how hard she has had to work to become part of Barbara's biological family. Her main concern seemed to be the lack of recognition by Barbara's family of origin that Kay was now a co-parent to Kelly. Kelly accepted her "two mommies," even bragging about this to friends, but learned not to talk about Kay when she was at Barbara's parents' home. Kay's parents, on the other hand, completely accepted Kelly as their granddaughter, and Kelly often visited with Kay's sister and brother-in-law, who lived nearby and had a son about Kelly's age. Kay feared that having another child would increase Barbara's family's involvement with them, and thus increase Kay's invisibility and further invalidate her role in the family.

The therapist assessed that the couple was in the commitment stage (see Table 4, Stage 5) based on their decisions to buy a home together and to enter therapy. After consultation with colleagues, the therapist identified a support group for lesbian parents in a nearby city and suggested that Kay and Barbara attend together to supplement their work in therapy. The group experience stimulated their creative thinking about possibilities and provided invaluable support for both Barbara's and Kay's perspectives.

In therapy, the couple identified conflicts stemming from different expectations and family of origin experiences. Barbara realized that she was colluding with her parents by allowing Kay's invisibility. Even though the family knew Kay, they would never ask about her or would change the subject when Barbara or Kelly talked about her. Kay, on the other hand, came to understand that her "second-class status" stirred up past history with her younger sister, who Kay felt always got more attention from family and the outside world. Particular relevant examples were the sister's glamorous marriage and the excitement surrounding her having the first grandchild.

As Kay and Barbara recognized the dimensions of their conflicts and felt the support and understanding of other lesbian couples raising children, a new direction emerged. Kay and Barbara were exploring the possibility of Kay's being the biological mother to their second child, and they both realized that this would fortify her place in the family in the eyes of the outside world, especially within Barbara's family. Kelly was already very excited about having a sibling and had been asking about this as a result of her experience with other children in school. Barbara and Kay felt new possibilities that would strengthen their family commitment and had resources through their group experience to explore in terms of pregnancy through donor insemination. The therapist affirmed the collaborative process in which they were making decisions for the family's future (see Table 4, Stage 6). As they began the process of Kay's insemination, the couple ended therapy. The financial drain of the insemination process contributed to their decision, but they also felt they had overcome the impasse that brought them into therapy.

## Lesbian and Gay Couples From a Life Cycle Perspective

Slater and Mencher (1991) stressed the importance of viewing the lesbian family from a life cycle perspective and of considering the myriad systems involved. These systems include (a) the lesbian family system created by a couple (with or without children); (b) the family of origin of each family member; (c) the lesbian community within which the family is embedded; and (d) the mainstream community in which the family must function. This comprehensive view of the context of systems for lesbian family development (Slater, in press) will be broadened here to elaborate on the importance of these various overlapping systems in understanding both lesbian and gay families.

For some gay or lesbian couples, families of origin may play a positive and significant role. For others, familial rejection produces a painful void. Members of the family of origin of one partner may never acknowledge the family created and view their son or daughter as being single or a single parent, or they may not accept their offspring's partner's biological child as their kin. How a couple manages this invisibility is extremely significant and is influenced by the couple's acknowledgment in each of the other three systems.

There are myriad ways in which a lesbian or gay family might connect with the wider gay and lesbian community, ranging from fear and disavowal of any association, to friendship and work environments that are exclusively lesbian or exclusively gay. Many families are isolated from other gay or lesbian families because of the invisibility required for survival. In some geographic areas, a sense of community is strong, evidenced by social networks, gay and lesbian cultural events, and openly identified lesbian or gay leaders in politics and the professions. There, family members have access to role models, and community participation provides the lesbian or gay family with a source of positive public and social identity. Often friendships with members of the lesbian and gay community, ex-lovers, and other supportive figures may be more significant than family of origin members to family functioning (D'Augelli & Garnets, 1995; Weston, 1991).

A gay or lesbian couple's relationship with the mainstream community around it will vary according to the couple's individual and family stage of comfort with their sexual identity, the degree of risk in the community in being open about the relationship (e.g., risk of job loss or potential loss of custody of children), and the family's interests and needs. Career advances, age of children, and leisure interests may affect the family's level of contact with the main-

stream community. As couples reach the collaborative stage, political and social justice commitments or spiritual pursuits may bring them into closer contact with predominantly heterosexual organizations and subgroups. Aging lesbians or gays may be forced to depend on mainstream services for survival and community (e.g., nursing homes). The additional challenges faced by interracial couples involved in various racial and ethnic support networks are discussed by Peterson (1992); Lockman (1984); Garcia, Kennedy, Pearlman, and Perez (1987); and Smith (1983).

A developmental understanding of lesbian and gay families over time is in its infancy, but useful models do exist on which to build appropriate research paradigms, expand theoretical ideas, and inform clinical practice. Family therapists must begin to identify the similarities and differences among various family forms to be effective in treatment. Issues of heterosexual bias (Morin & Charles, 1983), stigma (Herek, 1995), health (Shernoff & Scott, 1988), and legal status of gay and lesbian parenting (Curry & Clifford, 1991) are all crucial to adequate treatment of lesbian and gay families.

## EFFECTS OF GENDER ROLE SOCIALIZATION ON LESBIAN AND GAY COUPLES

Gender role socialization is reflected in certain observed differences between gay and lesbian couples. Differences in emotional intimacy, sexuality, and power are highlighted here. As traditional gender roles are challenged and broadened, gender-related differences in same-sex couples are expected to diminish. Although there are these gender-related differences in lesbian and gay couples, there are few differences in overall relationship satisfaction (Kurdek, 1995).

### Emotional Intimacy

Lesbian couples have reported significantly higher levels of cohesion, adaptability, and satisfaction than have heterosexual couples (Zacks, Green, & Marrow, 1988). Peplau (1991) found that, regardless of affectional orientation, women were more likely than men to value emotional expressiveness and a similarity of attitudes between partners. Initial reports on lesbian fusion pathologized the intimacy in lesbian relationships because of its deviation from norms generated from research on heterosexual couples. However, recent theorists have seen the capacity for fusion in lesbian relationships as a strength (Burch, 1993; Mencher, 1990). It may be that intense intimacy is normative in lesbian relationships, just as enmeshment can be considered normative in Jewish and other families (Herz & Rosen, 1982). Lesbians with high ego development have consistently reported experiencing of blurred boundaries in the context of their relationships and valued this favorably (Carroll & Gilroy, 1993; Mencher, 1990). Of course, when ego development is low, fusion can become rigidified and problematic for any couple. Rohrbaugh (1992) suggested that temporary fusion may be a healthy component of all close female relationships.

As was noted previously, whereas women are socialized to value and maintain relationships, focusing their energies on the care and nurturance of others, men are socialized to value autonomy, separation, and differentiation (Elise, 1986; Pollack, 1990) and to focus on their work identities through competition and achievement. Elise (1986) noted that a common response of gay couples to systemic pressures is reactive distance rather than fusion. Because the maintenance of the relationship must be done by men in gay couples, and because many men rely on sexual contact as a vehicle for emotional intimacy, sexual relations are a significant component of gay relationships. Bergman (1991) proposed a concept of a male self that includes a focus on relationships, rather than solely on autonomy and differentiation. His concept appears to be more characteristic of gay and heterosexual men who reflect less traditional gender role socialization. As was discussed in Pollack (1990), Kohut also argued for a male "self-with-others." Chodorow (1994) argued for more attention to the development of love and passion in gays and lesbians.

## Sexuality
Men are typically socialized to express sexual feelings before emotional intimacy, whereas women often are socialized to prefer affectional relationships before expressing sexual feelings (Forstein, 1986). Such social-

ization is reflected in the gay culture, where relating sexually often occurs at the beginning of a relationship (Klinkenberg & Rose, 1994). On the other hand, lesbians often form friendships or affectional commitments prior to sexual relationships (Eldridge, 1987). Burch (1993) reported that sexuality is much more likely to be inseparable from relational desires for women than for men.

Other results of gender role socialization were reported by Kurdek (1995), who found that gay couples have sex more frequently than heterosexual couples, whereas lesbian couples have sex less frequently than heterosexual couples. Gay men also have more sexual partners than lesbians, and the forms of gay sex are more diverse than those of lesbians and heterosexuals. Multiple sex partners are relatively common among men in the gay community. Gay extramarital sex is often casual, brief, and recreational rather than emotionally intense and may not threaten the primary affectional commitment between two men. It appears that agreement among partners on whether the relationship will be open or closed is a critical factor, and agreement on this dimension tends to increase as the length of relationship increases (Eldridge, 1987).

Both gay and heterosexual men may be more likely than women to use sex as a nonverbal means of communication. Lesbian couples may have a higher level of verbal communication and less of a need to use sex for nonverbal communication. Thus, socialization may explain a significant portion of the reported differences in frequency of sexual contact between partners in lesbian and gay couples.

## Power
Peplau (1991) found that, regardless of sexual orientation, women were more likely than men to value equality between partners in an intimate relationship. Kurdek (1995) reported that lesbian couples are more likely than either gay or heterosexual couples to follow an ethic of equality. For example, when lesbians perceive a power differential in their relationship, even the most powerful partner tends to be less satisfied with the relationship than when the power is equally shared (Eldridge & Gilbert, 1990). Gender differences in egalitarian values are similarly reflected in some gay and lesbian organizations, where men

tend to value formal structure and hierarchy, and women often value informal networking and equality of power. Feminist values and consciousness are more common in the lesbian community, although they are beginning to emerge in some segments of the gay culture.

## LESBIAN AND GAY PARENTS AND THEIR CHILDREN

The structure of gay and lesbian families includes many variations. A primary couple relationship between two women or two men is generally defined. Sometimes a larger unit of three or four may define the primary system, which can challenge heterosexual assumptions that stable relationships are dyadic, that friendship should be asexual and distinct from a primary relationship, and that monogamy is preferable to any of its alternatives (Goodrich, Rampage, Ellman, & Halstead, 1988).

If the gay or lesbian family includes children, there are various formations to consider. A blended family includes a lesbian or a gay man who has children from a previous relationship, that individual's children, and her or his partner, who may or may not also have children. Some lesbian or gay families involve a single parent and her or his children. In the past 10 years, there has been a great increase in the number of lesbian couples who are choosing to have children together, using a variety of sources for sperm donation (Patterson, 1995). These families may include a noncustodial father if the donor is known, or a father with joint custody. Gays have created families through adoption and surrogacy (Martin, 1993), the latter allowing a biological link between father and child.

To understand the context of any particular gay or lesbian family, it is important to understand its developmental history as well as the current structure of the family. Historically, most lesbians and gays have become parents during a heterosexual marriage. These marriages may end when the lesbian or gay spouse develops a strong same-sex affectional relationship with which the benefits of the heterosexual marriage can no longer compete (Buxton, 1994). If the sexual orientation of a gay father or lesbian mother is revealed during divorce proceedings, that parent is highly unlikely to be awarded custody of any children. Visitation rights may be denied. Because they fear losing custody, lesbian and gay parents with custody of their children tend to build strong boundaries for their families and allow few outsiders into their system. This is an example of how social stigma reinforces invisibility. Such invisibility decreases the opportunity for role modeling for other gay and lesbian families raising children and contributes to the negative stereotyping in the general population that gays and lesbians are not good parents.

Green and Bozett (1991) reported that children of lesbian and gay parents are no different than children of heterosexual parents on a variety of dimensions, including the children's sexual orientation. They also found no evidence that children experience long-term problems related to learning about the sexual orientation of their parents. Patterson (1995) reported that children of donor-inseminated lesbians are as psychologically healthy as the general population. McPherson (1994) reported that gay couples experience more satisfaction with parenting arrangements than do heterosexual parents. Martin (1993) has provided information about organizations and readings for lesbian and gay families, donor insemination programs, surrogate motherhood, and adoption by gay and lesbian parents.

## THE FAMILY OF ORIGIN

Many family members have difficulties accepting a gay son or lesbian daughter, and temporary or permanent estrangement after disclosure is not uncommon. Robinson, Walters, and Sheen (1989) have documented a five-stage grief process (shock, denial, guilt, anger, and acceptance) that parents often go through in coming to accept a gay son or lesbian daughter. Specific challenges facing the family of origin include the following: (a) internalized stereotypes and dehumanizing attitudes toward lesbians and gays, and the process of replacing these with more accurate information about lesbian and gay lives (Hammersmith, 1987; Strommen, 1989); (b) fears related to the lack of civil rights protection for their children; (c) fears related to their children's being a target of hate crimes; (d) fears that their sons may die of AIDS; (e) the stigma in the ecosystem against those sons with AIDS; and (f) the stigma of having a gay son or lesbian daughter and the shame and guilt associated with this stigma.

In working with family members who resist accepting a gay son or lesbian daughter, it is important to assess how much of the resistance is due to the son or daughter's affectional orientation and how much is a function of the child's attempt to separate and differentiate from the family (Devine, 1984). Family members are faced with lifelong choices as to whom they will disclose that they have a lesbian or gay family member. Local groups of Parents, Families, and Friends of Lesbians and Gays (PFLAG) can be useful for families that are struggling to accept a gay son or lesbian daughter. Also, PFLAG has established a support group for heterosexual spouses married or formerly married to a gay man or lesbian. Support is also provided for children of gay and lesbian parents. (See the Appendix to this chapter for the address and phone number of PFLAG.)

## AIDS

Research clearly documents that since the AIDS epidemic began, gay men have adopted safer sex practices with a resulting decrease in all types of sexually transmitted diseases and reduced use of drugs (Paul, Hays, & Coates, 1995). Many gay couples no longer have sex outside their relationships. Single gays are increasingly limiting their sexual relationships to one partner and giving increased consideration to establishing committed relationships (Carl, 1986). Some couples may commit prematurely or stay in dissatisfying relationships because of the fear of AIDS (Forstein, 1986). When a partner is diagnosed with HIV or AIDS, the couple relationship is transformed, and it may either be terminated or strengthened. Some family members may learn of a son being gay at the same time they learn that he is HIV-positive or has AIDS and may die. Many gays and lesbians are dealing with a different type of grief—a grief related to multiple deaths of significant others in their extended family network.

Family therapists need to be aware of the massive impact of AIDS in the gay community, as well as the fears and shame in the family of origin in discovering a gay family member. The therapist must effectively work with both the extended gay family and the biological family members of a person with AIDS in order to help both systems deal with the extensive emotional and physical caretaking demands of the situation (Lovejoy, 1990; Tunnell, 1993). In working with a couple in which one partner is diagnosed as HIV+, the family therapist must help each partner to understand the meaning of this in their lives and assist the couple in renegotiating sexual, emotional, financial, and other aspects of the relationship. Guidance for working with AIDS in various ethnic communities has been provided by the National Commission on AIDS (1992).

## RECOMMENDATIONS FOR THERAPY

Lesbian and gay individuals and couples enter therapy for the same reasons others do, that is, for depression, anxiety, alcoholism (Shernoff & Finnegan, 1991), conflicts in intimate relationships, and dysfunctional families of origin (Isenee, 1991). Their concerns are frequently intertwined with issues specific to gays and lesbians such as concerns about disclosure, lack of role models or guiding rituals, discrimination, and anti-gay violence (Herek, 1995). The therapist needs to assess the extent to which the presenting problems are related to a gay or lesbian identity. In working with individuals, it is useful to assess the stages of lesbian/gay identity development and how this intersects with other aspects of identity development (e.g., ethnic/cultural, religious, or professional), the degree of connection or support the client can draw from the lesbian and gay community, and the degree of real or feared discrimination in job, housing, or neighborhood safety. Additional considerations in working with couples include assessing the impact of the lack of social validation of the relationship, the need for positive role models, exploring effects of gender role socialization and current relationship expectations of each partner, and assessing differences between the two partners in acceptance of a gay or lesbian identity and degree of disclosure to others. All of this must be done within an environment of recognition and validation for the hurdles clients currently face and those that have been overcome. A few specific recommendations follow.

**1. Be aware of heterosexism.** An essential aspect of understanding stereotyping and prejudice is examining one's own biases. Cultural heterosexism, like institutional racism and sexism, is pervasive in societal customs and institutions. Psychological heterosexism is the manifestation of cultural heterosexism in the individual, as "reflected in feelings of personal disgust, hostility or condemnation of homosexuality and of lesbians and gay men" (Herek, 1995, p. 322). We are less challenged in our biases about things when we have little information about or exposure to them.

Therapists may be uncomfortable discussing lesbian and gay sexuality. In addition, therapists who have introjected negative ecosystemic values about multiple sex partners may need to reexamine those beliefs. Therapists trained to believe that extramarital sex is always a reflection of problems in a primary relationship need to be sensitive to research (Kurdek, 1995) indicating that such perspectives are not necessarily valid for lesbian and gay couples. Reexamining one's beliefs about sexuality often takes courage and support.

**2. Use gender-free language.** A useful technique for consciousness-raising about our own heterosexist bias is developing the habit of using gender-free language when exploring relationships with any client. (For example: "You indicated you were involved with someone in college, tell me about this person;" "In understanding your current marital relationship, it will be helpful for each of you to describe your experience with former romantic relationships.") Rather than assume that someone is heterosexual, or that you will know if someone is struggling with sexual identity, leave open the possibility that any client or family member may have some feelings or experiences related to same-sex relationships. There is ample evidence that therapists' premature assumptions of heterosexuality have prevented many clients from disclosing same-sex attractions or relationships (Garnets, Hancock, Cochran, Goodchilds, & Peplau, 1991). Using gender-neutral language when asking about relationships provides a message to all family members that the therapist is aware that intimacies can exist between members of the same sex and, furthermore, that the therapist is open to receive information about these relationships or feelings.

**3. Educate yourself and your clients about lesbian and gay experience.** This would include becoming familiar with models of lesbian and gay identity formation and couple development such as those presented in this chapter. These models, an essential foundation for affirmative work with lesbians and gays, address the following: (a) the process by which an individual comes to develop a positive, integrated lesbian or gay identity, (b) stages in the development of lesbian and gay couple relationships, and (c) the unique characteristics of these relationships. Therapists need to appreciate differences between lesbians, gays, and bisexual men or women, and to have some understanding of the vast diversity within each community. The specific cultural context of each client regarding attitudes toward sexuality and sexual identity development can then be considered against this knowledge base. A psychoeducational approach is often indicated as part of working with lesbian and gay clients as well as their families of origin.

**4. Identify and use a consultant.** A colleague with more experience with gay or lesbian clients can provide clinical consultation. Discussions with a friend who is familiar with the gay or lesbian communities might provide useful consciousness raising. Many professional associations now have formal or informal groups of members interested in the concerns of lesbians and gays. Our clients are our best consultants concerning their own experiences, but it is often counterproductive to rely solely on our clients to provide us with broad perspectives about their experiences.

**5. Learn about local support networks.** Networks for lesbians may be totally different from those for gays, and networks for bisexual men and women different still. Are lesbians welcome at certain gay events? Where is child care for gay families available? Therapists who are knowledgeable about differences between various resources can encourage clients to become involved in appropriate support networks. Finding positive lesbian or gay role models can be a powerful tool for enhancing self-esteem and allaying fears and stereotypes that are based on misinformation or lack of information.

**6. Become aware of relevant ethical issues.** Therapists practicing lesbian and gay family psychology need to be aware of ethical issues common to family psychology—for example, confidentiality, impact of the therapist's values, determining who the client is in family therapy, and so on (Patten, Barnett, & Houlihan, 1991). Dworkin (1992) discussed issues of beneficence, autonomy, diagnosis, confidentiality, privilege, transference and countertransference, dual relationships, and boundary violations in providing therapy to lesbians and gay men. Common bias in therapy with gays and lesbians have been reported by the Committee on Lesbian and Gay Concerns (1990).

**7. Use genograms.** Genograms (McGoldrick & Gerson, 1985) are useful tools in family therapy and help the therapist and client to understand the family context intergenerationally. In sketching a genogram with a lesbian or gay individual or couple, it is critical to ask who belongs on the genogram and how close the connection should be. Spouses and children from any former heterosexual marriages may be important parts of the genogram (Buxton, 1994). If gay and lesbian clients do not identify extended nonbiological family members, it is recommended that the therapist raise the possibility of defining *family* beyond biological and marital kinship.

**8. Use bibliotherapy.** You do not need to be the sole source of information for clients, even if they are very closeted about their sexual orientation. Guiding clients to the excellent literature now available, in both fiction and nonfiction forms, can help them discover the variety of experiences for lesbians, gays, and bisexual men and women (see, e.g., Berzon, 1993; Clark, 1990; Fairchild & Hayward, 1989). Their choice of readings and responses to the content can be useful material for therapy.

**9. Consider referral when appropriate.** We believe that all therapists who sensitize themselves to the concerns of gay and lesbian people can do effective work with these clients. Yet, there are times when referring clients to others is an appropriate choice. Perhaps a client is at a stage in the development of his or her identity where working with a gay or lesbian therapist would be optimal. Perhaps you have worked so well with other gay clients that your caseload is becoming too homogeneous. Working within a small town or with members of the therapist's own culture (e.g., gay, religious, ethnic) may also necessitate referrals to avoid dual relation-

ships (Eldridge, Mencher, & Slater, 1993). If you work with a lot of clients with AIDS or those who have lost lovers and friends to HIV-related illness, you may feel too drained to accept new clients with these concerns for awhile. In such cases, referral to other professionals seems ethical and wise.

Therapists need to be aware of local attorneys, physicians, dentists, and other health care professionals who are competent in addressing lesbian and gay issues in their respective fields. Some clients will not be familiar with these resources.

## CONCLUSION

There are negative ecosystemic factors that contribute to the high divorce rate among heterosexuals, and some of these factors are a source of stress for lesbian and gay couples as well. Negotiating these sources of stress without the benefit of legal boundaries and protection is evidence for the strength of lesbian and gay couple relationships. Although the longevity of a relationship is not necessarily an indicator of relationship quality, it is notable that some lesbian and gay couples remain together for more than 50 years, and relationships of 20 years or more are common in the studies that include older gay and lesbian cohorts (Peplau, 1991).

In this chapter, we have addressed important aspects of lesbian and gay family psychology in an effort to make the hidden more visible and to assist clinicians in affirmative work with a range of families that include lesbian and gay members. The discussion of gender role socialization contributes to an understanding of the impact of gender on all family forms, as well as the significant differences that are found between gay and lesbian relationships. We hope that the greater knowledge about lesbian and gay families will bring an appreciation for the similarity of issues and struggles across all family systems and for the diversity of creative responses that are available to all of us in the human family.

## References

Balka, C., & Rose, A. (1989). *Twice blessed: On being lesbian, gay and Jewish.* Boston: Beacon Press.

Bergman, S. J. (1991). Men's psychological development: A relational perspective. *Work in Progress, No. 48.*

(Stone Center Working Paper Series). Wellesley, MA: Stone Center.

Bernstein, F. (Ed.). (1993, Spring). *The PFLAGpole: Newsletter of Parents, Families and Friends of Lesbians and Gays.* Washington, DC: Parents, Families and Friends of Lesbians and Gays.

Berry, D. V., & Marks, P. A. (1969). Antihomosexual prejudice as a function of attitude toward own sexuality. *Proceedings, 77th annual convention, American Psychological Association,* 573–574.

Berzon, B. (Ed.). (1993). *Positively gay.* Berkeley, CA: Celestial Arts.

Burch, B. (1993). *On intimate terms: The psychology of difference in lesbian relationships.* Chicago: University of Illinois Press.

Buxton, A. (1994). *The other side of the closet: The coming-out crisis for straight spouses and families.* New York: Wiley.

Campbell, S. M. (1980). *The couple's journey: Intimacy as a path to wholeness.* San Luis Obispo, CA: Impact.

Carl, D. (1986). Acquired immune deficiency syndrome: A preliminary examination of the effects of gay couples and coupling. *Journal of Marital and Family Therapy, 12*(3), 241–247.

Carroll, L., & Gilroy, P. (1993, August). *Study of merger in lesbian couples.* Paper presented at the meeting of the American Psychological Association, Toronto, Canada.

Cass, V. C. (1979). Homosexual identity formation: A theoretical model. *Journal of Homosexuality, 4,* 219–253.

Chodorow, N. J. (1994). *Femininities, masculinities, sexualities.* Lexington, KY: The University Press of Kentucky.

Clark, D. (1990). *Loving someone gay.* Berkeley, CA: Celestial Arts.

Clunis, D. M., & Green, G. D. (1988). *Lesbian couples.* Seattle, WA: Seal Press.

Coleman, E. (1982). Developmental stages of the coming out process. *Journal of Homosexuality, 7*(2/3), 31–44.

Coleman, E. (1987). Assessment of sexual orientation. *Journal of Homosexuality, 14*(1/2), 1–8.

Committee on Lesbian and Gay Concerns, American Psychological Association. (1990). *Final report of the Task Force on Bias in Psychotherapy with Lesbians and Gay Men.* Washington, DC: Author.

Curry, H., & Clifford, D. (1991). *A legal guide for lesbian and gay couples.* Berkeley, CA: Nolo Press.

D'Augelli, A. R., & Garnets, L. D. (1995). Lesbian, gay and bisexual communities. In A. R. D'Augelli & C. J. Patterson (Eds.), *Lesbian and gay identities over the lifespan: Psychological perspectives on personal, relational, and community processes* (pp. 293–320). New York: Oxford University Press.

Devine, J. (1984). A systemic inspection of affectional preference orientation and the family of origin. In R. Schoenberg & R. S. Goldberg (Eds.), *Homosexuality and social work* (pp. 9–17). New York: Haworth.

Dworkin, S. H. (1992). Some ethical considerations when counseling gay, lesbian, and bisexual clients. In S. H. Dworkin & F. J. Gutierrez (Eds.), *Counseling gay men and lesbians: Journey to the end of the rainbow* (pp. 325–334). Alexandria, VA: American Association for Counseling and Development.

Eldridge, N. S. (1987). Gender issues in counseling same-sex couples. *Professional Psychology, 18,* 567–572.

Eldridge, N. S., & Gilbert, L. A. (1990). Relationship satisfaction in lesbian couples. *Psychology of Women Quarterly, 14,* 43–62.

Eldridge, N. S., Mencher, J., & Slater, S. (1993). The conundrum of mutuality in psychotherapy: A lesbian perspective. *Work in Progress, No. 48.* (Stone Center Working Paper Series). Wellesley, MA: Stone Center.

Elise, D. (1986). Lesbian couples: The implications of sex differences in separation-individuation. *Psychotherapy, 23*(2), 305–310.

Fairchild, B., & Hayward, N. (1989). *Now that you know: What every parent should know about homosexuality.* New York: Harvest/HBJ.

Forstein, M. (1986). Psychodynamic therapy with gay male couples. In R. S. Stein & C. J. Cohen (Eds.), *Contemporary perspectives on psychotherapy with lesbians and gay men* (pp. 103–137). New York: Plenum.

Fox, R. C. (1995). Bisexual identities. In A. R. D'Augelli & C. J. Patterson (Eds.), *Lesbian and gay identities over the lifespan: Psychological perspectives on personal, relational, and community processes* (pp. 48–86). New York: Oxford University Press.

Garcia, N., Kennedy, C., Pearlman, S., & Perez, J. (1987). The impact of race and culture differences: Challenges to intimacy in lesbian relationships. In the Boston Lesbian Psychologies Collective (Ed.), *Lesbian psychologies* (pp. 142–160). Chicago: University of Illinois Press.

Garnets, L., Hancock, K. A., Cochran, S. D., Goodchilds, J., & Peplau, L. A. (1991). Issues in psychotherapy with lesbian and gay men: A survey of psychologists. *American Psychologist, 46,* 964–972.

Goodrich, T. J., Rampage, C., Ellman, B., & Halstead, K. (1988). *Feminist family therapy: A casebook.* New York: Norton.

Greene, B. (1994). Ethnic-minority lesbians and gay men: mental health and treatment issues. *Journal of Consulting and Clinical Psychology, 62*(2), 243–251.

Green, G. D., & Bozett, F. W. (1991). Lesbian mothers and gay fathers. In J. C. Gonsiorek & J. D. Weinrich (Eds.), *Homosexuality: Research implications for public policy* (pp. 197–229). Newbury Park, CA: Sage.

Hammersmith, S. (1987). A sociological approach to counseling homosexual clients and their families. *Journal of Homosexuality, 14*(1/2), 173–190.

Helminiak, D. (1994). *What the Bible really says about homosexuality.* San Francisco: Alamo Square Press.

Herek, G. M. (1995). Psychological heterosexism in the United States. In A. R. D'Augelli & C. J. Patterson (Eds.), *Lesbian and gay identities over the lifespan: Psychological perspectives on personal, relational, and community processes* (pp. 321–346). New York: Oxford University Press.

Herz, F. M., & Rosen, E. J. (1982). Jewish families. In M. McGoldrick, J. K. Pearce, & J. Giordano (Eds.), *Ethnicity and family therapy* (pp. 364–392). New York: Guilford Press.

Isensee, R. (1991). *Growing up gay in a dysfunctional family: A guide for gay men reclaiming their lives.* New York: Simon & Schuster.

Jackson, L. (1993). *Colorlife: The lesbian, gay, twospirit & bisexual people of color magazine* (pp. 21–23). 2840 Broadway, Suite 287, New York, New York 10025.

Klinkenberg, D., & Rose, S. (1994). Dating scripts of gay men and lesbians. *Journal of Homosexuality, 26*(4), 23–35.

Kurdek, L. A. (1995). Lesbian and gay male close relationships. In A. R. D'Augelli & C. J. Patterson (Eds.), *Lesbian and gay identities over the lifespan: Psychological perspectives on personal, relational, and community processes* (pp. 243–261). New York: Oxford University Press.

Lockman, P. (1984). Ebony and ivory: The interracial gay male couple. *Lifestyles, 7*(1), 44–55.

Lovejoy, N. C. (1990). AIDS: Impact on the gay man's homosexual and heterosexual families. In F. W. Bozett & M. B. Sussman (Eds.), *Homosexuality and family relations* (pp. 285–316). New York: Harrington Park.

Martin, A. (1993). *The lesbian and gay parenting handbook: Creating and raising our families.* New York: Harper Collins.

Mattison, A. M., & McWhirter, D. P. (1990). Emotional impact of AIDS; Male couples and their families. In B. Voeller, J. M. Reinisch, & M. Gottlieb (Eds.), *AIDS and sex* (pp. 401–419). New York: Oxford University Press.

McGoldrick, M., & Gerson, R. (1985). *Genograms in family assessment.* New York: Norton.

McPherson, D. (1994, August). *Gay parenting couples: Same gender parents raising children.* Paper presented at the meeting of the American Psychological Association, Los Angeles, CA.

McWhirter, D. P., & Mattison, A. M. (1984). *The male couple: How relationships develop.* Englewood Cliffs, NJ: Prentice-Hall.

Mencher, J. (1990). Intimacy in lesbian relationships: A critical re-examination of fusion. *Work in Progress, No. 42.* (Stone Center Working Papers Series). Wellesley, MA: Stone Center.

Morales, E. (1989). Ethnic minority families and minority gays and lesbians. *Marriage and Family Review, 14,* 217–239.

Morin, S. F., & Charles, K. A. (1983). Heterosexual bias in psychotherapy. In J. Murray & P. R. Abramson (Eds.), *Bias in psychotherapy* (pp. 309–338). New York: Praeger.

National Commission on AIDS. (1992). *The challenge of HIV/AIDS in communities of color.* Washington, DC: Author.

Patten, C., Barnett, T., & Houlihan, O. (1991). Ethics in marital and family therapy: A review of the literature. *Professional Psychology, 22,* 174–176.

Patterson, C. J. (1995). Lesbian mothers, gay fathers, and their children. In A. R. D'Augelli & C. J. Patterson (Eds.), *Lesbian and gay identities across the lifespan: Psychological perspectives on personal, relational, and community processes* (pp. 262–290). New York: Oxford University Press.

Paul, J. P., Hays, R. B., & Coates, T. J. (1995). The impact of the HIV epidemic on U.S. gay male communities. In A. R. D'Augelli & C. J. Patterson (Eds.), *Lesbian and gay identities over the lifespan: Psychological perspectives on personal, relational, and community processes* (pp. 347–397). New York: Oxford University Press.

Peplau, L. A. (1991). Lesbian and gay relationships. In J. C. Gonsiorek & J. D. Weinrich (Eds.), *Homosexuality: Research implications for public policy* (pp. 177–196). Newbury Park, CA: Sage.

Peterson, J. L. (1992). Black men and their same-sex desires and behaviors. In G. Herdt (Ed.), *Gay culture in America* (pp. 147–164). Boston: Beacon Press.

Plummer, K. (1975). *Sexual stigma: An interactionist account.* London: Routledge and Kegan Paul.

Pollack, W. S. (1990). Men's development and psychotherapy. *Psychotherapy, 27*(3), 316–321.

Robinson, B. E., Walters, L. S., & Sheen, P. (1989). Response of parents to learning that their child is homosexual and concerns over AIDS. *Journal of Homosexuality, 18*(1/2), 59–80.

Rohrbaugh, J. B. (1992). Lesbian families: Clinical issues and theoretical implications. *Professional Psychology, 23,* 467–473.

Savin-Williams, R. C. (1995). Lesbian, gay, and bisexual adolescents. In A. R. D'Augelli & C. J. Patterson (Eds.), *Lesbian, gay, and bisexual identities across the lifespan: Psychological perspectives on personal, relational, and community processes* (pp. 165–189). New York: Oxford University Press.

Scrivner, R. W. (1984, August). *A model for the development of lesbian and gay identities*. Paper presented at the meeting of the American Association for Marriage and Family Therapy, San Francisco, CA.

Shernoff, M., & Finnegan, D. (1991). Family treatment with chemically dependent gay men and lesbians. *Journal of Chemical Dependency Treatment, 4*(1), 125–135.

Shernoff, M., & Scott, W. A. (1988). *The sourcebook on lesbian/gay health care*. Washington, DC: The National Lesbian and Gay Health Foundation.

Slater, S. (in press). *The lesbian family life cycle*. New York: Free Press.

Slater, S., & Mencher, J. (1991). The lesbian family life cycle: A contextual approach. *American Journal of Orthopsychiatry, 61*(3),. 372–382.

Smith, M. J. (Ed.). (1983). *Black men/white men*. San Francisco: Gay Sunshine Press.

Smith, R. W. (1975). Why are many societies sex negative? A social-functionist theory. *Counseling Psychologist, 5*(1), 84–89.

Strommen, E. (1989). Hidden branches and growing pains: Homosexuality and the family tree. *Marriage and Family Review, 14*(3/4), 9–34.

Tafoya, T., & Rowell, R. (1988). Counseling gay and lesbian Native Americans. In M. Shernoff & W. A. Scott (Eds.), *The sourcebook on lesbian/gay health care* (pp. 63–67). Washington, DC: The National Lesbian/Gay Health Foundation.

Troiden, R. R. (1979). Becoming homosexual: A model of gay identity acquisition. *Psychiatry, 42*, 362–392.

Tunnell, G. (1993, August). *Couples therapy with gay males: The challenges of HIV and AIDS*. Paper presented at the meeting of the American Psychological Association, Toronto, Canada.

Weinberg, M. S., Williams, C. J., & Pryor, D. W. (1994). *Dual attraction*. New York: Oxford University Press.

Weston, K. (1991). *Families we choose*. Boston: Alyson.

Whitman, F. L., & Mathy, R. M. (1985). *Homosexuality in four societies: Brazil, Guatemala, the Philippines, and the United States*. New York: Praeger.

Zacks, E., Green, R., & Marrow, J. (1988). Comparing lesbian and heterosexual couples on the circumplex model: An initial investigation. *Family Process, 27*, 472–484.

APPENDIX

# Resources for Lesbian and Gay Families

## Publications

Barrett, R. L., & Robinson, B. E. (1990). *Gay fathers.* Lexington, MA: Lexington Books.

Bor, R., Miller, R., & Goldman, E. (1993). *Theory and practice of HIV counseling: A systemic approach.* New York: Norton.

Carl, D. (1990). *Counseling same-sex couples.* New York: Norton.

Gay and Lesbian Parents Coalition International (1993). *Books for children of lesbian and gay parents.* Washington, DC: Gay and Lesbian Parents Coalition International.

Graham, D. L., Rawlings, E. I., Halpern, H. S., & Hermes, J. (1984). Therapists' needs for training in counseling lesbians and gay men. *Professional Psychology: Research and Practice, 15,* 482–496.

*In the Family,* 7302 Hilton Av., Takoma Park, MD 20912 (professional magazine).

Kimmel, D. C., & Sang, B. E. (1995). Lesbians and gay men in midlife. In A. R. D'Augelli & C. J. Patterson (Eds.), *Lesbian and gay identities across the lifespan: Psychological perspectives on personal, relational, and community processes* (pp. 190–214). New York: Oxford University Press.

Quan, J. D. (Ed.). (1994). *Outward.* (Quarterly newsletter of the Lesbian and Gay Aging Issues Network of the American Society on Aging, 833 Market St., Suite 511, San Francisco, CA 94103-1824).

Reid, J. D. (1995). Development in late life: Older lesbian and gay lives. In A. R. D'Augelli & C. J. Patterson (Eds.), *Lesbian and gay identities across the lifespan: Psychological perspectives on personal, relational, and community processes* (pp. 215–240). New York: Oxford University Press.

Roth, S. (1985). Psychotherapy with lesbian couples: Individual issues, female socialization, and the social context. *Journal of Marital and Family Therapy, 11,* 273–286.

Walker, G. (1991). *In the midst of winter: Systemic therapy with families, couples, and individuals with AIDS infection.* New York: Norton.

*Youth Magazine,* P.O. Box 34215, Washington, DC 20043. Tel: (202) 234-3562 (for lesbian and gay youth).

## Organizations

Children of Lesbians and Gays Everywhere (COLAGE), 3023 North Clark, Box 121, Chicago, IL 60657. Tel: (202) 583-8029.

Gay and Lesbian Parents Coalition International (GLPCI), P.O. Box 50360, Washington, DC 20091. Tel: (202) 583-8029.

Parents, Families, and Friends of Lesbians and Gays (PFLAG), P.O. Box 96519, Washington, DC, 20090-6519. Tel: (202) 638-4200.

345

# CHAPTER 19

# ETHNIC DIMENSIONS IN FAMILY TREATMENT

*Joe Giordano and Mary Ann Carini-Giordano*

*You can change your name. You can change your spouse. You can't change your grandparents. You are stuck with an ethnic identity.*

Ethnicity is a powerful but little-understood concept in therapy. During the past 25 years, research and clinical practice have demonstrated that ethnic values and beliefs are retained for many generations. They play a significant role in the development of our individual and group identities. They also influence the way we define problems and arrive at solutions and often determine to whom we turn for help (Boyd-Franklin, 1989; Giordano, 1973; Greeley, 1974; Ho, 1987; Klein, 1980; Kleinman, 1988; Mc-Goldrick, Pearce, & Giordano, 1982; Papajohn & Spiegel, 1975; Pinderhughes, 1989). One expanded definition of the concept of ethnicity reads as follows:

> *From a clinical perspective, ethnicity is more than distinctiveness defined by race, religion, national origin, or geography. It involves conscious and unconscious processes that fulfill a deep psychological need for identity, security, and historical continuity. It is transmitted in an emotional language within the family and reinforced by social and institutional networks within the community and the larger society. (Giordano, 1973, p. 11)*

## THE THERAPIST'S CULTURAL FILTERS

How we as therapists assess, treat, and communicate with a family will be screened through both our professional knowledge and training, and our own cultural filters. At times, the latter may create distortions and inaccuracies in evaluating patient's behavior. There is a significant body of knowledge to indicate that patients often are misdiagnosed and receive inappropriate treatment because the therapist did not understand their culture (Comas-Diaz & Griffith, 1988; Giordano & Giordano, 1981; Kleinman, 1988; Pinderhughes, 1989).

Cultural dissonance may be a serious issue for patient and therapist alike. For example, during the 1960s, as young family therapists, we were well-equipped with a wide range of psychological terms like *blocked*, *non-motivated*, and *inappropriate therapy patients*, to describe many families' resistance to treatment. We soon discovered, however, that our patients' resistance was not always related to psychological issues, but to cultural values, attitudes, and behaviors that were part of their ethnic group heritage as transmitted by their families of origin.

We also came to realize that, as well-trained as we were, our own ethnic backgrounds (Joe is from a Catholic, working-class, Italian American family, and Mary Ann is from a Catholic, Irish American family) still were powerful influences on who we were and how we related to others. At the time, we had little awareness of our own cultural baggage. There also was little in the literature about ethno-cultural factors and less in our graduate training.

When Joe first began to work with Jewish families, he found them exciting. They talked! They not only told him what their prolems were, but also how to solve them.

At times, Joe felt insecure because many of his patients had been in therapy for a number of years; some had read more Freud than he. But although Joe would hear important insights articulated session after session, he would observe very little change in family patterns. There was lots of talk, but no action. In other families, an aptitude for seeking out and expounding underlying meaning was effectively used as a "cultural defense" against changing dysfunctional behavior.

With Irish families, he experienced the opposite. Joe's questions were met with little response and even silence. At other times, these families would be very talkative and humorous, spinning convoluted stories that left him confused as to their meaning. Many families had difficulty talking about their feelings or sharing marital conflicts in front of their children. At staff conferences, many Irish American patients and their families would be labeled "not good therapy cases."

When working with families that came from Joe's own Italian American background, he sometimes would overidentify or collude, thus totally missing appropriate and necessary interventions. There were other families whose behaviors mirrored back to him his own unresolved negative feelings about his Italian American identity. With African American families, we found that our ideological commitment to civil rights and the War on Poverty tended to make us view their family problems almost exclusively in terms of racism and deprivation. This overemphasis on larger societal issues often hindered our clinical assessment of what was troubling these families.

When Joe first shared these clinical observations, as well as his research on ethnic families with colleagues, he was cautioned that these are stereotypes, and we cannot label a patient because he or she is a member of an ethnic group. Such caution was, and continues to be, valid. Ethnic generalizations about an individual's behavior can be as harmful as "compressing" a patient's behavior into a one-dimensional diagnostic category. Each individual must be viewed and understood in the context of his or her unique history and personality.

However, it is vital to know ethnic groups' histories, values, beliefs, and expressive styles, as well as what they identify as problems and how they seek help. Such knowledge can provide a more accurate context for understanding the meaning of the family system and behavior. It can also provide the therapist with insight into the nature of resistance that may be related to cultural distortions. Today, although there is greater awareness and knowledge about the significance of ethno-cultural factors, we still lack a more precise theory and treatment approach. Thus, we must turn to our own clinical experience to discover how ethnicity operates in the treatment process. In the following sections, we describe two experiences treating ethnic families.

### CASE EXAMPLE: THE SCHWARTZES, A JEWISH AMERICAN FAMILY

*Sylvia Schwartz insisted that her family needed therapy because of her son David's verbally abusive and acting-out behavior. She and her husband, Harry, were very experienced in using therapy; they had logged over 20 years in psychoanalysis. David, 16, had been in analysis since age 5, and his sister Debbie, 12, was currently receiving supportive therapy for her newly diagnosed diabetic condition.*

*Sylvia and Harry were successful professionals. He was a law professor and she was an advertising executive. Neither had siblings, and both had experienced familial conflict and alienation with their own parents. Intelligent and articulate, they extensively interviewed us as to our approach and experience in working with similar families. They liked the idea that we would be co-therapists. Sylvia thought this was innovative and would be different from the previous therapy they had experienced (it did not hurt that Mary Ann was a graduate of a well-known psychoanalytic institute).*

*During the first session Sylvia remarked: "David was tough to deal with right from the beginning. Life always seems to revolve around his repeated temper tantrums and it's destroying our family relationships."* David's hostility was particularly directed at his mother. A well-built young man, David towered over his shorter parents and younger sister. Although he was not physically abusive with any family member, his mother feared that he might hurt her if sufficiently angry.

Whereas David had always created havoc at home, he had only recently begun to act out in school. He attended a prestigious boys school and was considered a gifted student. However, he was doing poorly academically and was in danger of being expelled because of his bullying and other disruptive behaviors. Sylvia and Harry were very upset that he was not fulfilling his potential.

David also was a performer who insisted on taking center stage and not allowing anyone to divert attention from him. Although his parents often felt beaten down by his loquaciousness and verbally domineering manner, they usually applauded his ability to perform and be humorous. Sylvia felt helpless in trying to limit her son. She was angry with her husband for withdrawing—Harry would go off and play his piano when David was on a rampage. Shortly into the first session, David's rage and verbal abuse burst forth at his mother. Debbie began to cry, Sylvia became silent, and Harry sat passively.

Clearly, the Schwartzes could not contain David's aggressiveness. They simply did not know how to parent an adolescent who desperately wanted them to channel his boundless energy. They needed to deal with unresolved issues involving their own parents, but Sylvia and Harry also were affected by deeply held values that evolved out of their Jewish American background, which had contributed to their professional success but may well have hampered their ability to help David.

The Schwartzes were highly acculturated, nonobservant Jewish Americans who placed great emphasis on achievement and success. In the Jewish tradition, these values are deeply rooted in studying the Torah. As assimilated Jews, secular educational achievement had supplanted religious study but was equally revered.

Herz and Rosen (1982) pointed out that "success is so vitally important to the Jewish family ethos that you cannot understand the family without understanding the place of success for men and more recently for women" (p. 368). They indicate that the Jewish definition of success is measured by intellectual achievement. This ethos is so strong that, in some Jewish families, no matter how much they accomplish, children report feelings of failure if they do not do well educationally. In extreme cases, this can lead to unhealthy competition among siblings, as well as a deemphasis on family intimacy. In the Schwartz family, the parental pressure to succeed also created intense and hurtful sibling rivalry. David often would cruelly taunt Debbie, who, unlike her brother, was excelling in school.

Because David was extremely intelligent, talented, and highly verbal, the Schwartzes found it difficult to place any limits on his expression, even when it was destructive. They tended to view such appropriate parental discipline as restricting their son's ability to express his talents. One moment they would applaud his expression of hostile humor as clever, another, they would tell him how destructive it was. One of our main treatment goals was to help the parents understand that setting limits to David's behavior would not harm his ability to excel.

From working with many Jewish American families, we have learned that it is not easy to focus on a single issue about which they need to act. The Schwartz family, which was well-versed in the intricacies of therapy and which had an overintellectual approach to problem solving, repeatedly wished to engage in exploring the reasons for and meaning of what they were experiencing. Consequently, we frequently found ourselves becoming entangled and thus diverted from the goal of helping them set limits and learn new ways to parent their children.

Our approach in working with the Schwartzes was to teach them parenting strategies that would enhance family boundaries and develop limits. Both Sylvia and Harry had unresolved conflicts with their own parents. It was important to help Sylvia understand that her unresolved anger toward her father was immobilizing her to react appropriately to David's expression of anger. Family of origin work with both parents was significant in helping them to separate the experience with their parents from their experience with David's current behavior.

In coaching the parents, the emphasis was to get them to act rather than to intellectualize. David immediately became more responsive and less reactive to the limit-setting. We encouraged Harry to take a more active role in parenting, and this shifted the rigid, negative interactive patterns between mother and son. Within a year, David's acting-out behavior diminished, and he was succeeding in school.

In contrast to the highly verbal and expressive Schwartzes, the Fitzgeralds, a third-generation Irish American family, were nonexpressive, keeping their emotions tightly under control.

### CASE EXAMPLE: THE FITZGERALDS, AN IRISH AMERICAN FAMILY

*The Fitzgeralds entered therapy because the oldest child, Mary, was failing out of her Catholic high school. John, the father and a widower, could not hide under his tough exterior a deep sense of shame that Mary's school recommended therapy for his family. He also feared that, if expelled, Mary might be forced to attend a public school. Although education was an important value in this family (Mary's deceased mother, Kathleen, had been a principal), there was greater concern that the learning be in a Catholic setting "where the right moral messages would be taught."*

*Mary was an attractive, mature 14-year-old who had been a high-achieving student until her mother's death a year earlier. Kathleen had been strict but nurturing, and their relationship had been close. Mary's father viewed her behavior as "rebellious and mischievous."*

*In sessions, John also reported that Mary was "disobedient and lazy." He had little understanding of an adolescent's needs and behavior. He would ridicule and shame Mary about the way she dressed, the music she enjoyed, and her general messiness. In the early sessions, Mary said little, crying when attempting to respond to her father. John would not allow the expression of feeling. Crying was perceived by him as a sign of weakness. With a sense of pride, he related how he went to work, and the children to school, the day after his wife was buried. The family system "shut out" any discussion of Kathleen's death or the accompanying feelings of loss. Our attempts to raise them were dismissed by John as irrelevant. "That is over and done with. She is in heaven. Life goes on," he responded.*

*At times, the sessions resembled a confessional, with John telling his sins and asking forgiveness. At other times, John presented himself as a helpless parent informing the therapists how bad his child was and expecting the authorities (the therapists) to instruct the child to behave.*

The family's inexpressiveness, their being out of touch with their feelings and couching their anger under the guise of wit, ridicule, sarcasm, and silence, could be interpreted as resistance or pathological repression. However, such behavior is culturally normative for many Irish Americans. McGoldrick (1982), pointed out that the belief that people are "bad" and suffer deservedly for their wrong deeds, a belief related to the concept of original sin, is basic to the Irish character. Thus, no matter how hard one tries to be good, he or she will fail, because human nature is weak and "life is a vale of tears." She added that the Irish tend to view people as good or bad, strong or weak, villain or victim. Irish families often designate one child as good and another as bad.

Although John did not say so directly, he nevertheless communicated that Mary was the bad child. His other two children, Julie, 12, and John, Jr., 10, were seen as the good ones—high-achieving, obedient, and religious. No matter how much Mary tried to be the good child, she could not succeed. She was the family's black sheep.

The same values and behaviors that shaped the Fitzgeralds' sense of identity, and which had guided them through other family life transitions, now were constraining them as they tried to cope with the loss of Kathleen and the ensuing family changes.

It was evident that if we were to engage this family in a working relationship, we needed to develop strategies and interventions that fit their cultural context. We had to accept the father's limited goals for therapy and involvement. Any attempt to deal with emotional issues would create greater anxiety for John, who probably would end therapy.

We prescribed tasks for the father and children, which they followed unquestioningly. Mary Ann saw Mary separately, allowing her to begin to face the emotional issues related to her mother's death and her heavy caretaking responsibilities for the younger children. By utilizing the Fitzgeralds' strengths—their religion, internal loyalty, responsibility, and humor—and by focusing on the presenting problem of Mary's school and home behavior, we were able to build trust and engage them in treatment.

Ethno-cultural factors were extremely important in these two cases. Understanding and being sensitive to the Schwartzes' and the Fitzgeralds' ethnic backgrounds helped us to modify and adapt family treatment interventions to make them compatible with their value systems, family roles, and communication styles. Drawing on our clinical practice and research, in the next section we offer some suggestions and guidelines for incorporating ethno-cultural factors into family treatment.

## SOME RECOMMENDATIONS FOR ETHNO-SENSITIVE FAMILY THERAPY

### Assess the Importance of Ethnicity

Therapists, whatever their orientation, tend to universalize conceptions of dysfunctional and healthy behavior. Consequently, they may be unaware of or insensitive to cultural differences, thereby impairing the quality of treatment. In the initial phase of contact with a family, the therapist should consider the extent to which its members identify with their ethnic background and ascertain the part that ethnic issues may play in the presenting problem.

Once the therapist raises this issue, many other questions follow. Are family members' behaviors reflective of the norms of their ethnic or religious background? Are they dysfunctional within this context? To what extent is the problem related to internal or external cultural conflict in values? To what extent is it due to personality and characterological factors?

The therapist not only must evaluate the dysfunctional or pathological individual behavior and family patterns, but also must understand the meaning of the family's behavior within its own culture. For example, what may appear to the therapist as an enmeshed relationship in an Italian or Puerto Rican family may be perceived by family members as close and loving. Conversely, for Italian and Puerto Rican families that emphasize close family relationships, isolation or distance among family members may be a more serious problem than it would be for families whose cultural values stress independence.

In assessing ethno-religious factors affecting the family, clinicians also must consider other diverse contextual influences such as class, educational level, degree of acculturation, and gender. With the increasing influx of new immigrants and refugees (some 600,000 annually), special issues related to migration and stress of adjusting to a new country also may affect family dynamics. Pinderhughes (1989) cautioned therapists who are treating new immigrants to avoid "confusing a patient's appropriate cultural response to stress (cultural shock) with serious pathology" (p. 150). She provided the example of a 15-year-old Puerto Rican boy who was misdiagnosed as schizophrenic by a Caucasian clinician because he talked of "seeing the devil, who tried to get him to do bad things." The recommended treatment called for powerful tranquilizers and hospitalization.

Fortunately, a second therapist evaluated the case and found that the patient, who recently had arrived in the United States, was experiencing a serious emotional reaction to the separation from his family and difficulty in adjusting to a crime-ridden neighborhood. The change in diagnosis from psychosis to stress reaction (adjustment disorder with mixed emotional features), rescued the youngster from treatment that might have compounded his emotional problems.

Pinderhughes (1989) pointed out that "to use diagnostic thinking that transcends stereotypes" (p. 162), the clinician must not only be flexible and appreciate cultural differences, but also must explore his or her own values and beliefs.

## Know Thyself

Therapists are vigilant about not allowing their own emotional issues to become an impediment in treatment. For more analytically oriented clinicians, this issue usually is identified as countertransference. However, this heightened awareness usually has not included the impact of the therapist's own ethnic identity. This neglect may be due to the personal ambivalence, if not antipathy, toward ethnicity that seems evident among upwardly mobile, middle-class professionals who have embraced universalist lifestyles and value systems. This blind spot may become a serious stumbling block in the treatment relationship, leading at times to inappropriate interventions (Gottesfeld, 1978; Spiegel, 1976).

For example, we learned how our own cultural perceptions and personal feelings, as colored by our ethnic backgrounds, affected our responses while working with the Levines, another Jewish American family.

*CASE EXAMPLE: THE LEVINES*

*In contrast to the Schwartzes, the Levines were a working-class family: Sam was a cab driver, his wife Edith, a bookkeeper. Their son, Josh, an only child born late in their lives, had been seeing an analyst for three years. Josh, 20, had dropped out of an Ivy League college. Totally dependent on his parents, he also experienced tremendous anger toward them. Yet Josh could not separate from Sam and Edith, with whom he fought constantly.*

*At times, all three family members seemed to enjoy these expressions of hostility. When they were in conflict or under stress, the volume and drama would escalate. During one session, the Levines*

*reached truly operatic heights in the volume and the violence of their expression toward one another.*

Joe had a high tolerance for shouting and expressions of anger because he had grown up in a working-class family that was expressive and dramatic in verbal exchanges. He also had worked with hundreds of Jewish American families and knew that carping, complaining, nagging, criticism, and other forms of verbal jousting were a group norm. Although the Levines went well beyond the norm, he did not intervene.

Mary Ann was experiencing something quite different. She had grown up in a middle-class, Irish American family where emotional expressions of anger were avoided at all costs. Such conflicts were dealt with by family members pulling back and separating. So in the middle of this heated exchange between Josh and his parents, Mary Ann stood up, walked to open the office door and exclaimed, "That's it! If you can't stop this screeching, you must leave!"

Joe sank in his chair. He thought to himself, "She blew it. She let her own feelings get in the way." The Levines seemed startled. But Mary Ann's gut reaction to them produced a desired result—they quieted down and vowed they would control themselves.

When we evaluated the session, it was evident that we *both* had "lost it." Whereas Joe came to realize that he had overidentified with the Levines, permitting them to act out in a destructive way toward each other, Mary Ann became aware that the Levines' intense and loud expression of anger was a toxic issue for her. It is important to note that cultural transference can occur with families when they are of the *same* or *different* ethnic or racial background as that of the therapist.

## Validate Ethnic Identity

Ethnic identity is anything but homogenous. Greeley (1969) posited six stages between immigration and full acculturation: (a) culture shock, (b) the organization and emergence of self-consciousness, (c) assimilation of an elite, (d) group militancy, (e) self-hatred and antimilitancy and anti-adjustment, and (f) emerging adjustment. In her research on the psychological nature of Jewish American identity, Klein (1980), building on the work of Cobbs (1972), described three types of ethnic identification:

- The *positive identifier* attributes many personal traits to his/her allegiance to the community and is able to integrate them into a single, healthy self-concept.
- The *ambivalent identifier* also identifies good and bad characteristics with his/her group identity, but cannot achieve a positive self-image that integrates both.
- The *negative identifier* sees only the group failings and thus distances him/herself from it as much as possible.

Klein (1980) found that individuals with unidentified or ambivalent ethnic images often have lower self-esteem as well as problems in their social relationships. Her conclusions were echoed in studies of Polish Americans (Sandberg, 1974) and Italian Americans (Sirey, Patti, & Mann, 1985). If ambivalent and negative feelings about an individual's group are not worked through, he or she may feel uprooted. At their worst, negative feelings about one's own group may result in self-hatred. Whether transmitted from the larger society or from within a family, negative ethnic stereotypes often are internalized and induce feelings of inferiority, shame, and low self-image, as the following example illustrates.

### CASE EXAMPLE: THE EVANSES, AN AFRICAN AMERICAN FAMILY

*Bill Evans was a light-skinned African American. He entered therapy feeling anxious about not being able to establish meaningful relationships with women and sensing that his life was disorganized. Although he was a successful radio commentator, he had refused numerous lucrative offers to do television, stating that he was "not comfortable in that medium." Listening to his voice on radio, there was no indication that he was an African American. On television, his race would be obvious. He had been born into an upper-middle-class, genteel Southern family. We learned*

*that Bill's maternal grandparents had not approved of his mother marrying a dark-skinned man, although he was of the same economic status.*

Boyd-Franklin (1989) pointed out that skin color is a very charged issue for many African American families, and it sometimes impels family myths and secrets. So it was for the Evans family. Bill's confusion about his African American identity prevented him from advancing his career in television because he felt he would "not look good." It also affected his relationships with Caucasian and African American women.

*Bill's father left his wife shortly after Bill was born and never had any contact with his son. The father's abandonment caused the family a great deal of shame. His mother refused to speak about his father, and, although Bill loved his mother, he also had a great deal of animosity toward her for the secrets she continued to keep. As he began to express anger toward his parents, Bill also began to deal with his feelings of being an African American. When his mother participated in a few sessions, we were able to help "open" the family system and enable the family to piece together its story and its secrets. Bill began expressing greater pride in his African American identity and also was able to express negative feelings about it. We coached him to differentiate his feelings about his ethnic and racial identity from those toward his parents and other family members.*

Although Bill had many unresolved issues concerning his parents, he became more comfortable about his identity as an African American. He also began to find a way to make contact with his father and accepted an important television assignment. Bill's getting in touch with both what he took pride in and what he felt shame about in his heritage helped him to feel better about himself. It also freed up psychic energy that previously was spent on repressing his ethnic and racial identity.

## Learn to Be a Cultural Broker

When therapists work with families of multicultural backgrounds, they must be especially aware of the impact of cultural differences. Such differences often contribute to or exacerbate problems for which the family originally sought help. In working with ethnically intermarried couples, we found that their initial attraction to each other is often directly related to their cultural differences. However, that which is originally experienced as attractive often becomes a major source of conflict as the marriage evolves.

For example, a British American/Italian American couple may experience conflict because the British American takes literally the dramatic expressiveness of the Italian American, who in turn finds intolerable the British American's emotional distancing. In the heat of a serious disagreement, what may earlier have seemed a desired cultural difference now is labeled as emotionally injurious. Thus, the British American husband calls his Italian American wife "hysterical" and she labels him "unfeeling and rejecting." Couples and family therapists must help their clients to deal with and resolve these cultural conflicts or they will occupy center stage, creating an obstacle in the treatment process. The therapist's role in these situations is that of an intercultural mediator, clarifying the meaning of behaviors and, perhaps above all, promoting the idea that cultural differences exist and must be negotiated and compromised.

The case of the Steiners exemplifies how a couple's cultural differences can become the focal point of their marital conflict, while also serving as smoke screen for more serious issues and feelings that often are too painful to confront.

*CASE EXAMPLE: LOLA AND STEVEN,*
*AN INTERMARRIED COUPLE*

*Lola and Steven Steiner had been married for 7 years and had a 4-year-old daughter, Angela. They entered therapy because they felt that their marriage was coming to an end. Lola had been in individual analytical therapy for several years but was unable to resolve feelings of being "stifled and suffocated" in her relationship with Steven, feelings she had begun to experience after the birth of their daughter.*

*Although she expressed love for her husband, she repeatedly threatened to leave him.*

*Steven in turn was bewildered and confused by his wife's behavior. She had been born in Argentina and gone to college in Miami, where she had met him. Lola yearned to return there, "where it was warm and friendly" and the Hispanic culture was familiar to her, as opposed to living in New York, which she found "dirty, cold, and unfriendly." About Miami, Lola often would say, "I feel comfortable there; it feels like family." But Steven would not think of going to Florida because he recently had started a publishing business and needed the contacts he had in New York.*

*Lola was attractive, energetic, sociable, and expressive. Steven, a German American, was deliberate, reserved, and prone to solitude. When they argued, she would become aggressive, and he would sink into silence. As their fighting increased, their expressive differences became the focal point of each session.*

We knew that we needed to diffuse the conflict around these expressive differences in order to attend to underlying emotional issues. We worked on having each talk about the different family value systems in which each had grown up. As they got in touch with the traditions and values that were still important to them, Lola and Steven began to listen to each other with greater understanding and tolerance. One turning point revolved around Angela's fourth birthday party, to which family, friends, and neighbors were invited.

*Lola, who was working full-time as a college instructor, asked Steven to pick up cold cuts and salads. When he inquired, "How much?" she responded, "Get enough for 20 people." When she returned home minutes before people were to arrive, Lola became furious upon seeing the small amount of food Steven had purchased, and they proceeded to have a huge fight.*

During the next session, we asked each to talk about attitudes toward food and celebrations. Lola expansively and joyfully recalled large groups of people indulging in vast amounts of food and drink, and dancing. For Steven, although memories about family gatherings were generally pleasant, the presentation and focus on eating and other kinds of celebrations were not nearly as important. Moderation and frugality, having enough and not wasting, were important values in his family. When Steven counted slices of ham and cheese per person, he felt he was doing the right thing. For Lola, however, it was inconceivable to present guests with anything less than a lavish display of food. As they listened to each other and began to understand the source of their differences, they were able to dispel their immediate reaction that the other had acted out of anger or a desire to control, and to appreciate their cultural differences. There were many similar incidents. As each was painstakingly reviewed, we were able not only to reduce polarization and anger, but also to contribute to positive and caring interactions between the spouses.

> *Both had experienced abuse and neglect while growing up. Lola's father, a charismatic fundamentalist preacher who traveled throughout South America, had sexually abused her. Her mother lived in her own world, providing little care to Lola and her sister. Steven's father was an alcoholic and a gambler. Although he identified with his caring mother, he felt insecure and feared abandonment.*

Although Lola and Steve knew each other's basic history prior to entering therapy, after recounting in therapy painful events in their lives, they began to develop a deeper empathy for each other. Eventually Lola also began to get in touch with her feelings around the birth of her daughter and realized that, unconsciously, she had developed a deep-seated fear that she, too, would be an abusive parent like her father. We believe that dealing with these cultural differences was the key to opening the family system and to offering Lola an opportunity to feel safe enough to explore the underlying emotional issues that were being acted out in their marital conflict.

One final note. Although different cultural values may be deeply held and be at the core of serious conflicts between spouses and or among family members, they also may provide a convenient way of rationalizing and displacing anger arising from other conscious or unconscious family problems. Therapists should be alert to such "cultural subterfuge." For example, a person who claims, "I'm late for our session because I'm on 'Italian time'" or "I don't think you understand me because of your different ethnic or racial or religious background," may be trying to deflect attention from dealing with a difficult issue.

## CONCLUSION

Ethnicity and family life are so intertwined that one cannot reflect on one without considering the other. As therapists, we have a responsibility to become culturally competent in assessing and treating families. In developing that ability, it is crucial for us therapists to explore our own ethnic identities. Only when we can get in touch with previously conscious or unconscious feelings of pride, shame, and or ambivalence about our own ethnicity can we begin to understand, and intervene effectively in, complex family systems.

Ethnicity and race, however, are not the only social realities that will demand that the therapist be more culturally competent as we enter the 21st century. Gender, religion, class, immigrant status, age, sexuality, and disabilities are also powerful identity issues that are increasingly pervading our clinical work. Add to this reality the changing nature of family life, and it becomes evident that more than ever we need to reexamine our treatment approaches in a larger multicultural context. This is our challenge in the new century.

## References

Boyd-Franklin, N. (1989). *Black families in therapy: A multisystems approach.* New York: Guilford Press.

Cobbs, P. (1972). Ethnotherapy in groups. In L. Solomon & Berzon (Eds.), *New perspectives on encounter groups* (pp. 383–403). San Francisco: Jossey-Bass.

Comas-Diaz, L., & Griffith, E. (Eds.). (1988). *Cross-cultural mental health.* New York: Wiley.

Giordano, J. (1973). *Ethnicity and mental health: Research and recommendations.* New York: National Project on Ethnic America of the American Jewish Committee.

Giordano, J., & Giordano, G. (1981). *The ethno-cultural factor in mental health: A literature review and bibliography.* New York: Institute for American Pluralism, American Jewish Committee.

Gottesfeld, M. (1978). Countertransference and ethnic similarity. *Bulletin of the Menninger Clinic, 1 42 1,* 32–34.

Greeley, A. (1969). *Why can't they be like us?* New York: Institute for Human Relations, American Jewish Committee.

Greeley, A. (1974). *Ethnicity in the United States: A preliminary reconnaissance.* New York: Wiley.

Herz, F., & Rosen, E. (1982). Jewish families. In M. McGoldrick, J. Pearce, & J. Giordano (Eds.), *Ethnicity and family therapy* (pp. 364–392). New York: Guilford Press.

Ho, Man Keung. (1987). *Family therapy with ethnic minorities.* Newbury Park, CA: Sage.

Klein, J. (1980). *Jewish identity and self-esteem.* New York: Institute for American Pluralism, American Jewish Committee.

Kleinman, A. (1988). *Rethinking psychiatry: From cultural category to personal experience.* New York: Free Press.

McGoldrick, M. (1982). Irish families. In M. McGoldrick, J. Pearce, & J. Giordano (Eds.), *Ethnicity and family therapy* (pp. 310–339). New York: Guilford Press.

McGoldrick, M., Pearce, J., & Giordano, J. (Eds.). (1982). *Ethnicity and family therapy.* New York: Guilford Press.

Papajohn, J., & Spiegel, J. (1975). *Transactions in families.* San Francisco: Jossey-Bass.

Pinderhughes, E. (1989). *Understanding race, ethnicity and power: The key to efficacy in clinical practice.* New York: Free Press.

Sandberg, N. (1974). *Ethnic identity and assimilation: The Polish-American community.* New York: Praeger.

Sirey, A., Patti, A., & Mann, L. (1985). *Ethnotherapy: An exploration of Italian-American identity.* New York: National Institute for the Psychotherapies.

Spiegel, J. (1976). Cultural aspects of transference and countertransference revisited. *Journal of American Academy of Psychoanalysis, 41,* 447–467.

# CHAPTER 20

# THERAPY WITH AFRICAN AMERICAN INNER-CITY FAMILIES

*Nancy Boyd-Franklin*

The treatment of African American inner-city families is a critical component in family psychology. Clinical training programs, however, frequently do not train students to work with these families. This chapter presents key areas that family psychologists must address in order to provide effective treatment.

Although families of African descent come from many different countries and backgrounds, such as Afro-Caribbean, Haitian, African, and Afro-Latino, the emphasis here will be on African American families whose ancestors were brought to this country as slaves. This chapter will highlight the treatment issues for African American families living in poverty, even though many similarities exist with middle-class African American families.

In the first half of this chapter, a background for therapists working with poor, inner-city, African American families is provided. The class-not-race myth, the opinions many of these families have of therapy, and the importance of the therapist's use of self are emphasized. Some of the multiple family structures often found within these families are described, and the importance of spirituality to this population is stressed. Next the effects of racism on gender roles are examined, and treatment-relevant issues related to poverty are highlighted. In each of these areas, implications for practice are described.

In the second part of the chapter a multisystem intervention model for working with these families is introduced. Multisystemic issues, tools to assess multisystems, and use of the model to organize treatment are explained. To see the model in action, an extended case example of work with an African American extended family, living in poverty in the inner city, is provided. The chapter concludes by examining some of the implications of this model for training and supervising professionals.

## INITIAL CULTURAL AND THERAPEUTIC CONSIDERATIONS

To understand the complex therapeutic relationships that family psychologists may encounter in the treatment of African Americans, professionals first need to be cautioned against stereotyping, to realize the shortcomings of the class-not-race theory, to comprehend the expected responses of African American families to therapy, and to understand the importance of the therapist's use of self with these families.

There is tremendous variability among African American families in terms of geographic region, spiritual or religious orientation, class and socioeconomic level, education, skin color, and family structure. The material in this chapter should be used as a cultural lens through which African American inner-city families can be viewed, or as a set of guidelines that must be readjusted and sometimes discarded, depending on the particular family with which the therapist is working.

To understand fully the complex interplay of issues affecting African American families, one must consider both social class and racial issues (Boyd-Franklin, 1989). Poor African American families are affected daily by unemployment, violence, crime, drugs, and homelessness. Furthermore, the intrusiveness of outside systems, such as the welfare department, child protective services, and various agencies, clinics, and hospitals engenders a profound suspicion. In addition, unlike other ethnic groups, they must cope with the burdens of racism, discrimination, and oppression as a consequence of the legacy of slavery in the United States.

There is a tendency on the part of some clinicians to dismiss racial differences. Many Caucasian clinicians tend to minimize these differences as "class-not-race" issues (Boyd, 1977). This dismissal is unfortunate because the issues of race and racism persist even as the individual and family rises to middle class and a higher income and educational level. Therapists must be aware of the complex interplay of racial, cultural, and class themes in order to work effectively with these clients.

The clinician needs to understand the suspicion toward therapy that exists in many African American communities, which derives from the class and race issues just discussed. Grier and Cobbs (1968) have called this "healthy cultural paranoia." I prefer "healthy cultural suspicion," because of the pejorative nature of the word *paranoia*.

Therapy is also viewed by many African Americans as being appropriate only for others—sick, crazy, or weak people, or for Caucasians. African Americans may also distrust therapy because they see it as being anti-spiritual. Because of these unfavorable predispositions, family psychologists must first take the time to join with all family members and to build trust. This is particularly important with clients who feel coerced into therapy, as is common with inner-city African American families. Too often, African American clients are mislabeled as "resistant" and may be dismissed by therapists because many training programs prepare clinicians to work only with clients who want therapy. However, the majority of these families can and do benefit from therapy once their fears and concerns are addressed. This process will be discussed in more detail later in the chapter.

The most important component in the treatment of inner-city African American families is the therapist's use of self. Indeed, this is the most important part of the therapeutic process with any family. It is particularly crucial in work with African American families because of the healthy cultural suspicion

with which they may approach therapy. Therapists must especially take the time to connect with these families and help them understand the process of therapy.

Because of the legacy of racism and discrimination in this country, African Americans are particularly sensitive to the way in which they are approached by therapists. This is not only an issue in cross-racial therapy. A therapist who is of the same race as the family may still be perceived by family members as different—either as a result of social class or because the therapist is identified as being part of the system.

African Americans are very conscious of "vibes"—verbal and nonverbal clues that indicate whether the therapist respects them, is judgmental of their lives or family circumstances, and is "for real" (Boyd-Franklin, 1989). It is very important during supervisory sessions that therapists be helped to be themselves and to take the time to connect as people with each family member. It is often very helpful, for example, for the therapist in a cross-racial therapeutic situation to ask the family how they feel about working with a Caucasian therapist. This gives a message that even the difficult subject of race can be raised in therapy. This should not be done in the first session but should be raised only at points where the therapist is encountering resistance from the family.

## MULTIPLE FAMILY STRUCTURES

Although the stereotype in the literature is of single-parent families (Deutsch & Brown, 1964; Moynihan, 1965), many family structures are represented within African American inner-city communities. Families may be traditional two-parent nuclear families, they may consist of a single parent and a boyfriend or girlfriend, or they may form a complex extended family that includes members from both inside and outside the household, as well as blood and non-blood relatives (Billingsley, 1968; Boyd-Franklin, 1989; Hill, 1972, 1977). Clinicians must be aware of this diversity because African American families who are suspicious about therapy may send in an "expeditionary force" to "check out" the therapist.

As was just mentioned, African American families may include complex extended family kinship systems. Stack (1974) discussed the reciprocity inherent in these systems in which very poor family members assist each other with child care, finances, emotional support, housing, counseling, and so forth, particularly in times of trouble or stress. Blood family members might include mothers, fathers, grandmothers, grandfathers, aunts, uncles, cousins, or siblings. In addition, African American families, particularly when moving to new communities, may create bonds with nonblood relatives, such as neighbors, babysitters, friends, ministers, ministers' wives, and church family, that are as strong as those with family members (Boyd-Franklin, 1989; Billingsley, 1968; Hill, 1972, 1977; Hines & Boyd-Franklin, 1982; McAdoo, 1981; McAdoo & McAdoo, 1985).

In addition, because of the legacy of slavery in which family systems were pulled apart, and the segregated nature of child welfare and adoption systems prior to 1950, African Americans have developed their own informal systems to take in children (and sometimes the elderly) in times of loss, separation, or crisis—a process called *informal adoption* by Hill (1977). This concept, often confusing for family psychologists when first encountered, is also complicated by the reluctance of African Americans to air family business in public (Boyd-Franklin, 1989; Hines & Boyd-Franklin, 1982). Also, because of a cultural admonition not to discuss these issues with children (irrespective of age), family secrets may result. The exploration of such secrets requires a great deal of sensitivity and timing on the part of the therapist (Boyd-Franklin, 1989).

When family systems are very complex, therapists may spend hours treating the "wrong" family or a small subsystem of the family (e.g., mothers and children). Far too often powerful family members—blood as well as nonblood—are overlooked because they are not the initial patients. However, these members can undermine or sabotage treatment if they are not engaged.

Families may not reveal the true, complex nature of the family support system to the therapist until trust is established. As trust develops, constructing a genogram may be of great help. Because of the family's potential suspicion, therapists are cautioned against using a genogram in a first session (Boyd-

Franklin, 1989). The process of gathering this information should evolve over time: As trust in the therapist grows, more family members will be revealed.

Although many family psychologists have been trained to expect a family to come in for treatment, effective therapy with African Americans often involves outreach in the form of home visits, letters, or phone calls. Fathers or boyfriends are often particularly difficult to engage. The following is an example of a letter that might be sent to a father in order to reach out to him initially. This direct communication in a letter or a phone call is often more effective than working through mothers:

> *Dear _____ :*
>
> *My name is _____, and I am working with your son Johnny in family counseling to try to resolve his school problems. As you know, things are very serious right now, and the school has threatened to leave him back if his behavior does not improve. Your wife and I have been working with him on doing his homework after school, but we need your help. Can you give me a call at (telephone number) so that I can get your ideas on how best to help him? You are a very important person is his life, and I would not treat your son without asking for your input and advice.*
>
> *We have been meeting on Wednesday nights at 7:00 p.m. If you can join us next week, it would be very helpful. Let me know if the time is a problem and we can reschedule.*
>
> *Sincerely yours,*
>
> _____

The extended family kinship system is a cultural legacy and testament to the survival skills of those of African heritage. However, therapists must distinguish between functional kinship networks and conflictual support systems. In functional systems, there is a great deal of reciprocity between extended family members; in conflictual systems there often tends to be one central (Aponte, 1976a, 1976b), overburdened family member—typically a grandmother, mother, or aunt—who constantly provides support to others but receives little in return. This person has been termed a "switchboard" by Boyd-Franklin (1989), because all communication runs through her.

Whereas such a style of family organization may be very rewarding for the switchboard, it is also a prescription for burnout. Often grandmothers or great-aunts, who may have held this role for generations, must be helped to ask for support from other family members and to delegate tasks. This is not easy for African American women who have been given cultural messages to be strong. An extended family system that is functioning well may deteriorate when key family supports die or move away.

Lindblad-Goldberg and Dukes (1985), Lindblad-Goldberg et al. (1988), and Boyd-Franklin (1989) have explored the differences between functional and conflictual support systems in single-parent African American families, and provide models of functional extended family interactions that can be utilized by family psychologists to restructure and reframe extended family involvement.

Families with conflictual supports often lack structure, suffer from "underorganization" (Aponte, 1976b), and are particularly susceptible to boundary and role confusion. Reframing and clarifying roles is often necessary when extended family members give diverse and confusing mixed messages to children (Boyd-Franklin, 1989). Family psychologists must be trained to identify the key members of the extended family and to involve them in the process of boundary and role clarification. This is particularly important when different family members are involved in discipline and child rearing.

In addition to overcentralization, some families are also very susceptible to isolation. Individuals and family subsystems who become cut off or isolated are particularly vulnerable to mental health problems. Patients often experience isolation either through cut-offs that are due to drug and alcohol histories or chronic mental illness or through deaths, losses, diseases such as HIV/AIDS, homelessness, and relocation. Isolation can also, ironically, be the result of upward mobility.

Therapists can often help those in isolated situations to reconstruct their original family genogram and heal cutoffs (Bowen, 1976; Carter & Orfanides-McGoldrick, 1976). It was pointed out earlier that

when functional African American families move to a new community, they build a nonblood family network of friends, neighbors, and church family members. Therapists must empower their clients to build these networks also. When this is not possible, families can be helped to form "families of choice" by becoming involved in multiple family groups (Boyd-Franklin, Steiner, & Boland, in press).

## SPIRITUALITY

Another extremely important strength derived from the African heritage of African American families is that of spirituality. In some families, this may mean a formal expression of religious orientation and church membership; in others, it is part of a pervasive belief system that is more spiritual than religious.

Many African Americans, particularly older ones, describe "psychological" pain in spiritual terms. For example, a grandmother, when asked how she had tried to change her grandson's behavior, responded that she had "prayed to the Lord." Without training, therapists mislabel or misdiagnose such expressions as evidence of religiosity or grandiosity. This, in turn, gives rise to the suspicion by African Americans that therapy is antispiritual. Therapists must be trained to inquire further and explore the person's actual belief system. For example, an adolescent may express rebellion through conflict with familial religious values.

Unresolved mourning issues, related to complex cultural and spiritual belief systems, can also be a source of psychological and spiritual pain for African American families. The ritual of the funeral assumes special significance in African American families (Hines, as cited in McGoldrick et al., 1991 & Boyd-Franklin et al., in press). For many religious groups, the *whole* family comes together at a funeral, so it is often postponed for a week after the death to give extended family members time to travel from distant areas. Because the funeral is a time when deep emotions can be expressed, it is not uncommon to see tears, weeping, moaning, and fainting. The problem, however, is that these emotions are expected to "seal over" after the spiritual and emotional release of the funeral. Family members are expected to be strong, and tears subsequent to the funeral may be viewed as a sign of weakness.

When therapists are attuned to these beliefs they can help African American families with serious losses to share their grief and complete the mourning process. Therapists working with inner-city families should also be aware of the repercussions of violent deaths and losses on the family. This is often expressed through acting-out behavior in children and adolescents, depression in one or more family members, and/or increased somatic complaints, particularly in older adults.

It is important for therapists to inquire with care and sensitivity about losses that may have occurred at the time that symptoms began to appear. These may include deaths or anticipated losses of, for example, a terminally ill family member. Losses frequently are not fully processed or discussed with the children and can inadvertently become secrets in the family (Boyd-Franklin, 1993).

## THE EFFECTS OF RACISM ON GENDER ROLES

### The Invisibility Syndrome and African American Men

One of the most misunderstood areas in the treatment of African Americans is the impact of racism on gender roles and male–female relationships. This complex interplay requires therapists to be familiar with the concept of the "invisibility syndrome" and its impact on African American men (Franklin, 1993).

Invisibility is both a racial and cultural paradox. High skin color visibility, as well as the fears and guilt associated with slavery and continuing experiences of racism, have caused American society to treat African American men as if they are invisible. African American children (particularly males) are overrepresented in special education programs and are frequently subject to the expectation of teachers that they will fail (Kunjufu, 1985; Rosenthal & Jacobson, 1968).

Media images have ingrained a stereotype of violent African American men in the psyche of many Americans, so that when African American male children grow taller and stronger they are often responded to with fear. The welfare system has also contributed to the invisibility of Black men because

the mother's representation as a single parent is often a condition for the family's ability to receive benefits. Because researchers have often used intactness (a two-parent nuclear family) as a measure of family strength (Moynihan, 1965), family therapists may play into the invisibility myth by dismissing a boyfriend in an African American family because he is not married to the mother.

African American mothers have responded with fear to the legacy of racism (and often violence) in society against their male children and often compensate for the invisibility syndrome in their socialization and child-rearing practices. For example, a commonly held cultural belief is that many African Americans "raise their daughters but love their sons." African American mothers are in a dilemma: They struggle with the desire to raise strong, assertive children, but they fear society will punish their children for this assertiveness, particularly if they are male.

### Double Jeopardy for African American Women

African American women experience the double burdens of racism and sexism in society, the workplace, and the family. As a survival mechanism they have learned to be strong. However, this strength can become a burden in some families when African American women are able to find jobs when African American men are not. This has often created power struggles for African American couples. The dilemma for therapists treating such families and couples is that they are often confused when clients conceptualize these issues in terms of racism. Therapists are often surprised at the degree of rage they experience in African American couples when this issue is discussed, but it is important for therapists to accept this formulation and not attempt to impose gender role expectations based on a Caucasian middle-class orientation (Boyd-Franklin, 1989).

A very helpful reframe with couples such as these, who may be experiencing intense conflicts around the husband or boyfriend's job loss, can be to help them in their struggle against a common enemy, such as racism, unemployment, discrimination, or last hired, first fired practices. It should be noted, however, that this reframe should be applied only if it is appropriate to the situation. Contrary to many popularly held stereotypes (Moynihan, 1965), even chronically unemployed African Americans want to work (Hill, 1972) and feel defeated by their inability to gain and keep employment (Wilson, 1987).

## ISSUES RELATED TO POVERTY

When issues surrounding the extreme poverty in which many African American and other minority families live in this country are not explored in training programs, psychologists are often unprepared for and overwhelmed by these realities. One staff member at the Community Mental Health Center in Newark, NJ on a school visit discovered that the ground outside the building was littered with crack vials and exposed needles. He was horrified that children played in an area that had served as a shooting gallery and crack den the night before.

Inner-city families may live in housing projects or tenements in which rats and roaches are everywhere and where hallways and elevators can be the scene of violent crimes. Because of the incidence of drug traffic there, children have frequently experienced random violence against close friends and family. The development of psychiatric symptoms in a child, adolescent, or family member can often be traced to a chronic posttraumatic stress disorder following experiences of violence.

Many parents struggle desperately to protect their children and raise them right against tremendous odds. A "60 Minutes" episode on television depicted a school in inner-city Los Angeles in which kindergarten children had found a dead body in the yard outside their classroom. The program portrayed the therapeutic support and group intervention for these children and their families created by the principal, the school psychologist, and the social worker.

African American inner-city families may be victims of arson, eviction, or homelessness. It is not uncommon to see families huddled together in a shelter or "welfare motel" or an abandoned building. These families are confronted with basic issues of survival: hunger and illness and lack of housing, resources, and money. Faced with chronic unemployment, they struggle to survive with the barest necessities of life. Often these are the first psychological issues that they want to address in therapy.

It is incorrect to assume that all African Americans living in the inner city are on welfare. These areas contain many families considered working-class or the working poor. Such families may be overlooked because of the stereotypes with which the mental health profession has often approached poor families (Parnell & Vanderkloot, 1989).

The status of these working families, however, is tenuous. If the key provider is laid off or becomes sick, the family often has no choice but to seek public assistance, because minimum-wage jobs frequently do not offer health benefits. Family members may also work "off the books" but choose not to inform their therapists for fear of being reported to the welfare department.

In many inner-city, poor African American neighborhoods, the impact of the drug culture is profound. In African American poor communities, parents frequently fear that they are fighting a losing battle against the lure of drugs. Parents are afraid not only that their children will use drugs, but also that they will begin dealing drugs at a young age or become runners for drug dealers. Injecting drug use has exacerbated the spread of HIV/AIDS in African American communities, and the crack epidemic has resulted in many more reports of violent drug reactions.

Inner-city African American parents are eager to help their children. In fact, the education of children is one of the issues that will bring an African American family into treatment. These families need therapists who will work with them to "take their children back from the streets"—a very powerful reframe with African Americans.

Pervasive fear of the drug culture has led many African American families to resist placing children or adolescents or adults on medication (e.g., ritalin or psychotropic drugs). For example, at a pediatric AIDS unit in a large inner-city area, medical staff had to build a great deal of trust with families before they would even consider the use of AZT (a drug used in treating AIDS). These families need therapists who understand and are realistic about the survival issues they face and who are willing to address these issues in treatment.

Inner-city, poor families are often vulnerable to the intrusion of outside systems and agencies, such as schools, hospitals, mental health clinics, courts, police, juvenile authorities, welfare departments, housing authorities, and child protective services. For example, when there is a report of neglect or abuse, child protective services is far more likely to remove a child from an inner-city home than from a more affluent home. Paradoxically, clinicians who work with African American inner-city families have also found it more difficult to get systems to intervene in truly dangerous situations because the current economic situation has caused agencies to lay off personnel.

Poor families may have a welfare case worker, a child protective worker, teachers, a school social worker, hospital and medical staff, and a probation officer involved with them, so that a therapist may be viewed as just one more intrusive person or agency. Family psychologists thus need to distinguish themselves from other agencies and to explain the concept of confidentiality because of families' concerns that the therapist will "tell their business" to another agency. These fears must be addressed early in treatment.

## A MULTISYSTEM INTERVENTION MODEL

As was discussed in the last section, outside agencies have a tremendous amount of power in the lives of poor families. Child protective services has the power to remove a child, the welfare department can take away the family's livelihood, the family can be evicted from public housing, and so on. Many family psychologists, however, have been trained to consider problems with agencies to be the province of the agencies' social workers. This is unfortunate because these issues often bring families into treatment and provide the entree into a family and the means of joining and building therapeutic credibility.

Discussing multisystems issues with a family allows communication between family members to be explored and facilitated, and it gives a therapist a means of joining and an initial vehicle for exploring the family's structure, resiliency, executive or parental system, and the important "powerful figures" in the family. Empowerment must be a very important theme in therapy. The therapist's role is to mobilize the strengths and the strong individuals in the family

and extended family to work together efficiently to solve their problems.

In order to work effectively with the complex issues and problems facing these families, the therapist must take into account different systems levels, including the individual, family and extended family, nonblood kin and friend supports, church and community services, social service agencies, and outside systems. Boyd-Franklin (1989) and Boyd-Franklin and Shenouda (1990) described in detail and gave case examples to illustrate the utility of such a multisystem model.

Hartman and Laird (1983) provided another tool known as the ecomap (see Figure 2), which allows the therapist to depict the family at the center of a complex system and to diagram through a series of circles the outside agencies that are involved. The therapist can then work with the family to prioritize each problem and to identify the agencies needed to be involved or disengaged from overinvolvement. A genogram or family tree (see Figure 1) can also be constructed to help diagram the family structure (Carter & Orfanidis-McGoldrick, 1976; McGoldrick & Gerson, 1985; McGoldrick, Pearce, & Giordano, 1982).

By empowering the family to decide on their own priorities and by facilitating rather than helping, the therapist can begin to put the adults in the family in charge of these interventions. For example, it is not unusual for these families to have workers and case managers in different systems working at cross-purposes. The therapist may empower a family to call a meeting of these key agency representatives and facilitate discussion and problem resolution.

Family therapists often find working with such complex systems to be overwhelming. A clear model helps the therapist to structure useful interventions. The problem-solving focus that has evolved from the structural school of family systems theory is helpful (Haley, 1976; Minuchin & Fishman, 1981; Minuchin, 1974). Axis 1 of the multisystems model incorporates these guidelines. The treatment process involves the following steps:

> *Step 1. Joining and engaging new family members and subsystems*
> *Step 2. Initial assessment*

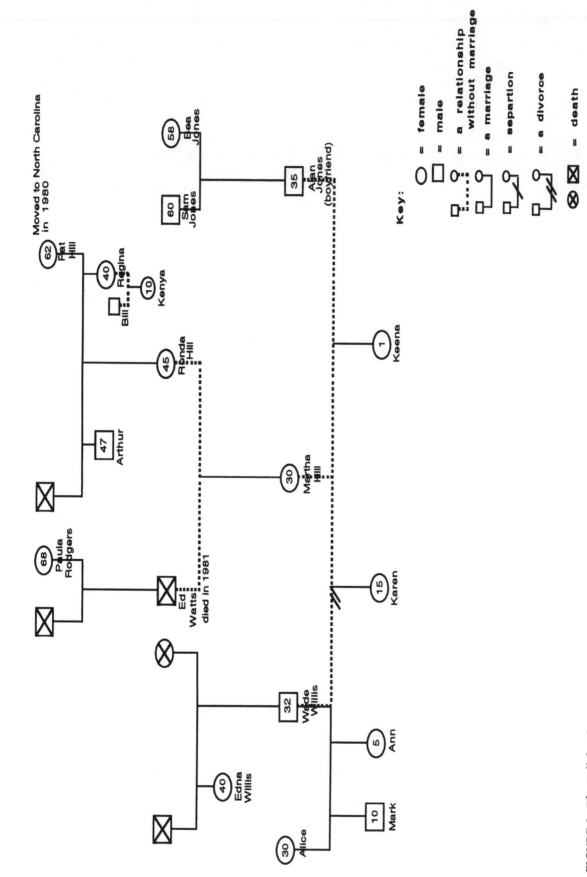

FIGURE 1. The Hill family genogram.

Step 3. *Problem solving (establishing credibility)*

Step 4. *Use of family enactment prescriptions and tasks*

Step 5. *Information gathering: the genogram*

Step 6. *Restructuring the family and the multisystems*

(Boyd-Franklin, 1989, p. 35)

The following case illustrates these processes, as well as the involvement of multisystems including an extended family member (the grandmother), the mother's boyfriend, the school, Planned Parenthood, and the church family.

*CASE EXAMPLE: THE HILL FAMILY*

*The Hill family was referred for therapy by the high school counselor, who was concerned about the behavior of Karen (15). The initial call to my office was made by Ronda Hill (45), her grandmother. On the day of the first interview, Karen, her grandmother, and her mother, Martha Hill (30), arrived for the session.*

*In the first session, I joined with each member of the family and learned that Karen's mother, Martha Hill, had given birth to Karen when she was 15 and Karen's grandmother, Ronda Hill, and her great-grandmother, Pat Hill (62), had raised her when she was very young. Pat Hill, the great-grandmother, subsequently moved in 1980 to North Carolina to live with her extended family. The mother, Martha Hill, returned to high school and lived as a sibling with her daughter in the grandmother's house. There had been no contact since Karen's birth with her father or his family. When Karen was 10 years old, her mother had become involved in a relationship with a boyfriend, moved out of her mother's house, and went on public assistance (welfare, ADC benefits). Approximately one year later, Martha was reported to the child protective agency by a neighbor for "neglecting" Karen and leaving her alone in the apartment. The child protec-*

*tive agency then made a kinship placement to the grandmother.*

*Subsequently, Martha became pregnant by her boyfriend (Alan, age 35) and had a second child Keena (now 1). She then returned to live in Ronda Hill's home. The Hill family household then consisted of the grandmother, Martha, Karen, and Keena. Both Karen's grandmother and mother were very concerned about her acting out behavior. She had been a very good student when she was younger but had become "boy crazy" (by her grandmother's description) in the past year and was now failing two subjects in school. She had also stayed out late and returned home after her curfew on a number of occasions. After joining with this family and learning their concerns, we began to discuss these issues further.*

*In the problem stage of the first session, it was clear that Ronda Hill, the grandmother, was the spokesperson for the family and appeared to be very much in charge. However, when each family member was asked what they thought the problems were in the family, the grandmother stated that she felt that Karen's mother was "too easy on her." Karen defiantly mumbled that she felt that her grandmother was "too hard on her." Martha Hill agreed with her daughter and appeared to be in a cross-generational alliance with her against the grandmother.*

*In an attempt to further explore the mother–daughter relationship, I asked Martha to talk to Karen about her behavior in missing curfew. As mother and daughter began to talk, the grandmother interrupted a number of times. Finally, I asked her to please sit near me so that we could observe the daughter and granddaughter's interaction and give them some suggestions for improving their communication.*

*From the discussion, it was obvious that Martha had not set limits for her daughter and was often inconsistent about consequences for her daughter's misbehavior. Af-*

ter a short period of interaction, it became clear that a large part of the problem was related to arguments between the grandmother and mother regarding how Karen should be raised. The grandmother attempted to interrupt a number of times to point out how incompetent Martha was as a mother.

Therefore, I asked the mother and grandmother to talk to each other about the issue of Karen's curfew and to come to some agreement on the time they would expect her in this Saturday night. After a number of false starts in which they each attempted to talk to me instead of each other and each assured me that they could never agree, they decided that she had to be home by 11:00 p.m. I asked them to discuss the consequences if she arrived home later than the designated time. They agreed that she would be "grounded" for the following week and would not be allowed to go out with her friends on the next Saturday.

Because the family was new to the concept of therapy, I explained that we would need to meet once per week to work on these issues with the family. At the end of the session, I gave the family a task and asked the mother and grandmother to discuss Karen's curfew with her when she arrived home on Saturday. If she was on time, they were to praise her; if not, they were to ground her for the week. Grandmother, mother, and Karen all agreed to try this plan and to let me know in the next session how things had gone.

In the second session, mother and grandmother reported that Karen had acted out and come in late on Saturday and that they had grounded her for that week. She therefore had to come straight home from school and would not be able to go out with her friends the following Saturday night. Karen came into the second session very angry and refused to speak. I praised the teamwork of the mother and grand-

mother and asked if Karen had talked to them about how she would begin to earn back her privileges. Karen immediately sat up in her chair, and all three family members looked very surprised: The concept of earning or returning privileges was a new one for them. Karen reported that in the past, her grandmother would punish her "for life," and her mother would let her off in a day or so. I asked the three members of the family to discuss what would happen after the following Saturday. After some initial arguments about Karen's misbehavior in the past, her mother proposed that if Karen came straight home every day after school this week and stayed in on Saturday, that she could start over on Sunday and earn the right to go out the next Saturday. I asked the mother to discuss this idea with the grandmother, who raised the question of "What if she messes up one day?" She and the mother were able to agree that they would "tighten up" on Karen and not let her off if she misbehaved. I turned to Karen and asked if she thought that her mother or her grandmother would really be able to "tighten up" on her, or did she think, "they'd let her off"? Karen replied that she thought they would be able to keep to the plan.

In the third session, Karen had kept to the after-school rules and had stayed home on Saturday and was working on earning the right to go out the next Saturday. I asked the family to continue the task for the next week. In this third session, I also felt that I had a strong enough relationship with the family to help them to construct a family genogram (see Figure 1) and find out more of the details of their history. We also constructed an ecomap (Hartman & Laird, 1983) to explore the family's support systems with other systems and agencies (see Figure 2).

The genogram revealed that there was a multigenerational pattern of teenage pregnancy in this family. Both mother and grandmother had become pregnant and had had a child at 15, and the great grandmother had had her first child at 17. This is a common pattern in many inner-city African American families. This created two multigenerational transmission processes (Bowen, 1976) in this family: (1) the "nonevolved grandmother" (Hines, 1988), and (2) the increased anxiety within the family and concerns about teenage pregnancy as the adolescent approaches the age at which her mother first became pregnant.

Ronda (at age 45) was in fact a nonevolved grandmother (Hines, 1988). When she had become pregnant at 15 and given birth to Martha, her mother Pat had raised Martha. Ronda, therefore, had never had an opportunity to be a mother. When Martha also became pregnant at 15 and had Karen, Ronda technically became a grand-

mother but, in fact, had her first opportunity to actually mother a child. Therefore, her investment in Karen was really that of a mother. However, she was very ambivalent about this and gave Martha very mixed messages about her mothering role.

As Karen had entered adolescence, her family had become very anxious about the fear of her repeating the family pattern of teenage pregnancy. They had never discussed this openly. Her grandmother became preoccupied with her boy crazy behavior and had tightened up on her because, as she said, she did not want her to "have a baby before she was grown." When this happens with no explanation, adolescents typically act out even more. In some cases, acting out and teenage pregnancy become a self-fulfilling prophecy. I therefore decided to use this pattern and to

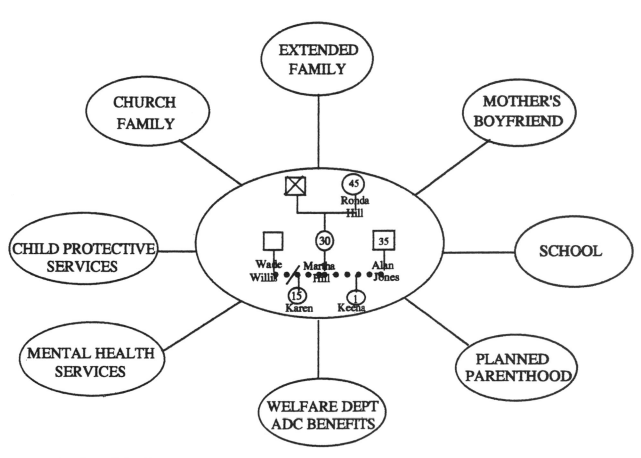

FIGURE 2. The Hill family ecomap.

discuss it openly with the family. Although on some level, the issue of multigenerational teenage pregnancy was known in this family, it had become a "toxic secret" that was never discussed.

I shared with the family that I sensed that they were all concerned about Karen becoming sexually active and that they were worried about the possibility of her becoming pregnant. Both grandmother and mother agreed. Karen seemed surprised. I asked her why, and she told me that no one had ever discussed this with her before. I told Karen that I had a feeling that her mother and her grandmother had both had a very difficult time with their mothers when they were adolescents. She was intrigued by this idea and asked each of them. Both told a very similar tale of family members who had tightened up but been inconsistent with them in adolescence and described situations that led to more staying out late with boyfriends.

I told the mother and grandmother that I felt that they had discovered a very important factor, and I asked the grandmother if she would support her daughter in explaining to Karen why they were concerned about her staying out late and becoming involved with boys, and their concerns about pregnancy. Martha explained that her whole life had changed when she had Karen. She loved her, but she could not go out with her friends any more because she had to stay home and help out with her care, and she reported that she began to resent the additional responsibility. The grandmother added that they both wanted more for Karen than they had had. I asked her to tell her granddaughter what their hopes and dreams were for her. She told Karen that no one in the family had evern gone to college and they hoped that she would go. I asked the grandmother to check that out with Martha also. They both agreed, and Karen stated that she wanted to go to college. The dream of an education

for their children is often expressed by African American families.

As I underscored how important that goal was, I used that opportunity to help the grandmother and the mother see that they had to work together if they were going to break the cycle of acting out and teenage pregnancy in their family and help Karen to succeed and go on to college. For the next five sessions, this issue was focused on in many different ways. One of these sessions was a subsystem meeting with just the mother and grandmother to discuss their issues with each other, particularly Martha's anger at her mother for allowing her grandmother to raise her. This allowed an opening for me to empower Martha to tell her mother that she wanted more of a role in raising her daughter. Although the grandmother agreed, this was a very difficult process for her.

Karen provided them with a crisis at school in which to test their fragile alliance. After a period of good school behavior and better grades, she had been cutting classes and was again in danger of failing one of her classes. I spoke with the mother and the grandmother and Karen together and asked the grandmother if she would be willing to allow the mother to call the school herself this time and arrange for a family session at the school. They both agreed. Martha called and made the appointment. At the school meeting, both the mother and the grandmother were able to express their concerns about Karen. The school counselor supported their plans to tighten up on Karen and offered to check in with her teachers regularly and let them know how she was doing. She talked with Karen about arranging regular meetings with her at the school. I underscored the theme of teamwork between the mother and grandmother as a parenting team and their teamwork with the school and their support of Karen. This multisystems intervention at the school was another important turning point.

This theme of teamwork and clarifying roles continued over the next 3 months. In one session, a visit by Karen and her mother to Planned Parenthood to obtain birth control information was discussed. The grandmother objected at first on religious grounds, but was able to understand the mother, Martha's, pragmatic concerns about pregnancy. By the end of the session, the grandmother encouraged the mother to take Karen to the local Planned Parenthood office. Increasingly, I also discussed the need for both the mother and the grandmother to have a life of their own.

About 2 months later, Martha reported that she and her boyfriend, Alan, wanted to move out and "become a family" with Karen and Keena. The grandmother at first was very opposed. Although she worked as a teacher's aide, I sensed that their moving would leave a large void in her life. I said as much to her in a family session and began to discuss with her the idea that she was still a young woman who was entitled also to a life of her own. She seemed surprised until I shared with her that she and I were close to the same age. This seemed to make the concept more acceptable to her. Martha and Karen encouraged Ronda to, as they put it, "get a life." This was actually a surprisingly light and humorous session, which occurred about a year into the therapy. In subsequent sessions, we discussed many different facets of Ronda's life. It was clear that she was a very spiritual person and that her church was a very important part of her world. Although she was a regular churchgoer, she reported that she had "never had time" to get more involved. Over the next few months, she discussed more and more involvement. She had joined the senior choir and had gotten very involved in a parenting project for teenage mothers.

She was finally able to let Martha, Karen, and Keena go, and they moved into their own apartment in September. A session was held with the mother, her boyfriend, Karen, Keena, and the grandmother. At the end, Martha and her boyfriend were seen alone briefly to draw a boundary around their relationship and to encourage and support their couple bond. The following December, after a year and a half, they completed treatment. Karen was doing well in school, and she, Martha, and Keena maintained close contact with the grandmother through regular visits.

## SUPERVISION AND TRAINING

Supervision, within the multisystems model, requires a very active, hands-on approach. Trainees need the opportunity to work with African American inner-city families during their training. The supervisor must provide a supportive environment that is easily accessed by the supervisee. This is especially true during crisis intervention periods, when therapists must feel their supervisors are available to them, at least by phone. Furthermore, the supervisory process provides trainees with the opportunity to develop their most important therapeutic tool—*themselves*. It can become a time when the therapist's countertransference issues with African American families living in poverty can be discussed (Hunt, 1987). Because this is very demanding work, supervision can become a lifeline and an important antidote to staff burnout.

Training in the area of racial and cultural diversity requires two levels of intervention: increasing awareness and developing sensitivity. The first level requires concrete knowledge about different racial, cultural, and class groups that include African Americans. Students who have never experienced these cultures need a starting point. Once again, caution must be applied to avoid using this material in a stereotypical manner. Movies, videotapes of interviews with families from different cultural backgrounds, and the inclusion of faculty and students of diverse cultural backgrounds into the training program can all facilitate the level of cultural diversity and awareness within a program.

The most important issue in training, however, is the development of cultural sensitivity. Paradoxically, the most profound and powerful way to learn about the culture of others is to start with one's own. The most significant part of any course on cultural diversity must involve students sharing their own family genograms and cultural backgrounds, as well as their own experiences of feeling different and the things they like and do not like about their own cultural group(s). This is often a very moving experience for students and promotes a degree of sharing and sensitivity that can become the true basis for the exploration of families from another culture.

In conclusion, as clinicians become more sensitive to the issues facing African American inner-city families, the quality of psychotherapeutic and family therapy services will become more effective. This chapter has addressed how a culturally sensitive multisystems model can meet the needs of this population.

# References

Aponte, H. (1976a). The family-school interview: An ecostructural approach. *Family Process, 15*(3), 303–311.

Aponte, H. (1976b). Underorganization in the poor family. In P. J. Guerin (Ed.), *Family therapy: Theory and practice* (pp. 432–448). New York: Gardner Press.

Billingsley, A. (1968). *Black families in white America.* Englewood Cliffs, NJ: Prentice-Hall.

Bowen, M. (1976). Theory in the practice of psychotherapy. In P. J. Guerin (Ed.), *Family therapy: Theory and practice* (pp. 42–90). New York: Gardner Press.

Boyd, N. (1977). *Clinicians' perceptions of Black families in therapy.* Unpublished doctoral dissertation, Teachers College, Columbia University, New York.

Boyd-Franklin, N. (1989). *Black families in therapy: A multisystems approach.* New York: Guilford Press.

Boyd-Franklin, N. (1993). Racism, secret-keeping, and African-American families. In E. Imber-Black (Ed.), *Secrets in families and family therapy* (pp. 331–354). New York: Norton.

Boyd-Franklin, N., & Shenouda, N. (1990). A multisystems approach to the treatment of a Black family with a schizophrenic mother. *American Journal of Orthopsychiatry, 60*(2), 186–195.

Boyd-Franklin, N., Steiner, G., & Boland, M. (in press). *Children, families and AIDS/HIV: Psychosocial and psychotherapeutic issues.* New York: Guilford Press.

Carter, E., & Orfandis-McGoldrick, M. (1976). Family therapy with one person and the family therapist's own family. In P. J. Guerin (Ed.), *Family therapy: Theory and practice* (pp. 193–219). New York: Gardner Press.

Deutsch, M., & Brown, B. (1964). Social influences in Negro–white intellectual differences. *Social Issues, 27–36.*

Franklin, A. J. (1993, July/August). The invisibility syndrome. *Family Therapy Networker, 33–39.*

Grier, W., & Cobbs, P. (1968). *Black rage.* New York: Basic Books.

Hartman, A., & Laird, J. (1983). *Family centered social work practice.* New York: Free Press.

Haley, J. (1976). *Problem-solving therapy.* San Francisco: Jossey-Bass.

Hill, R. (1972). *The strengths of black families.* New York: Emerson-Hall.

Hill, R. (1977). *Informal adoption among Black families.* Washington, DC: National Urban League Research Department.

Hines, P. M. (1988). The family life cycle of poor Black families. In B. Carter & M. McGoldrick (Eds.), *The changing family cycle: A framework for family therapy* (2nd ed., pp. 513–542). New York: Gardner Press.

Hines, P. M., & Boyd-Franklin, N. (1982). Black families. In M. McGoldrick, J. K. Pearce, & J. Giordano (Eds.), *Ethnicity and family therapy* (pp. 84–107). New York: Guilford Press.

Hunt, P. (1987). Black clients: Implications for supervision of trainees. *Psychotherapy, 24*(1), 114–119.

Kunjufu, J. (1985). *Countering the conspiracy to destroy Black boys* (Vol. 1). Chicago: African-American Images.

Lindblad-Goldberg, M., & Dukes, J. (1985). Social support in black, low-income, single-parent families: Normative and dysfunctional patterns. *American Journal of Orthopsychiatry, 55*, 42–58.

Lindblad-Goldberg, M., Dukes, J., & Lasley, J. (1988). Stress in Black, low-income, single-parent families: Normative and dysfunctional patterns. *American Journal of Orthopsychiatry, 58*(1), 104–120.

McAdoo, H. P. (Ed.). (1981). *Black families.* Beverly Hills, CA: Sage.

McAdoo, H. P., & McAdoo, J. L. (Eds.). (1985). *Black children: Social, educational and parental environments.* Beverly Hills, CA: Sage.

McGoldrick, M., & Gerson, R. (1985). *Genograms in family assessment.* New York: Norton.

McGoldrick, M., Moore Hines, P., Garcia-Preto, N., Almeida, R., Rosen, E., & Lee, E. (1991). Mourning in different cultures. In F. Walsh & M. McGoldrick

(Eds.) *Living beyond loss: Death in the family* (pp. 176–206). New York: Norton.

McGoldrick, M., Pearce, J., & Giordano, J. (Eds.). (1982). *Ethnicity and family therapy.* New York: Guilford Press.

Minuchin, S. (1974). *Families and family therapy.* Cambridge, MA: Harvard University Press.

Minuchin, S., & Fishman, C. (1981). *Family therapy techniques.* Cambridge, MA: Harvard University Press.

Moynihan, D. P. (1965). *The Negro family: The case for national action.* Washington, DC: U.S. Department of Labor, Office of Policy Planning and Research.

Parnell, M., & Vanderkloot, J. (1989). Ghetto children. In L. Combrinck-Graham (Ed.), *Children in family contexts: Perspectives on treatment* (pp. 437–462). New York: Beacon Press.

Rosenthal, R., & Jacobson, L. (1968). *Pygmalion in the classroom: Teacher expectation and pupil intellectual development.* New York: Holt, Rinehart & Winston.

Stack, C. (1974). *All our kin: Strategies for survival in a black community.* New York: Harper & Row.

Wilson, W. (1987). *The truly disadvantaged: The inner city, the underclass and public policy.* Chicago: The University of Chicago Press.

# Part VI

# MEDICAL SYSTEMS

# Introduction

Health problems have a significant impact on individuals and their families. The biopsychosocial approach to health care provides a new medical model that is consistent with and complements systems theory. In collaboration with other health-care providers, medical family therapy works to counteract the mind–body split. With health-care reform, it is vitally important for psychologists to participate fully as members of the health-care team in providing comprehensive care for patients and families in the 21st century.

This section considers the timely questions involved with the psychosocial care of patients and their families challenged by a wide range of illnesses: What kind of collaboration with families and other health-care professionals can benefit patients with somatization disorder? Are the psychosocial demands of different types of cancer different? Given the range of approaches to anorexia and bulimia, which ones work and how can they be integrated? How can we be helpful to the many couples who experience the invisible losses associated with infertility and infertility treatment? What are the special problems experienced by families when children are diagnosed with chronic illness?

Somatization is a disorder at the boundary of the mind–body split. "Medical Family Therapy With Somatizing Patients: The Co-creation of Therapeutic Stories" (chap. 21) describes the individual, family, and cultural processes that support the development and maintenance of this common problem. Susan McDaniel, Jeri Hepworth, and William Doherty provide a useful explanation of the genesis and goals of medical family therapy and the usefulness of this kind of treatment for somatizing patients, who are typically described as poor candidates for traditional individual psychotherapy. The authors examine the language and experience of the patient, the family, and the medical providers. Negotiating a mutually agreeable understanding of the problem on the basis of shared language is seen as the key to successful intervention. The logistics of work with somatizing patients in the medical setting, the typical phases of treatment, and useful interventions at each stage are described and illustrated with case examples. The authors advocate for close collaboration of the therapist with nurses and physicians to help patients increase their sense of agency and communion and develop healthier physical and emotional lives.

In "A Family Systems Approach to Coping With Cancer," David Wellisch reviews key themes in working with families of cancer patients. He uses extended case examples of families of varying compositions dealing with different kinds of cancer at different developmental stages to illustrate the differing psychosocial demands made on families. In each case, he describes the medical, psychological, and family-functioning information needed to design treatment goals and the most effective interventions to reach them. Clinical strategies are presented to help the family deal with the grief and interpersonal strife that often results from the uncertainty and loss associated with cancer.

"A Customized Approach to the Treatment of Anorexia and Bulimia" explains how William Friedrich departed from the conventional protocol for treating

eating-disordered patients. He discovered that the characteristics of many of the families with whom he consulted failed to fit commonly accepted family theories, particularly structural theory, and failed to respond to "family therapy." In the context of the literature on family theory and family therapy regarding anorexia and bulimia, including efficacy studies, he concludes that the families of eating-disordered patients are much more heterogeneous than previously thought. He challenges therapists to keep an open mind with regard to treatment strategies and includes the idea that family therapy may not, in some cases, be the most appropriate treatment.

Couples struggling with infertility and with pregnancy loss often experience an overwhelming sense of helplessness. They are often faced with difficult and controversial choices of available reproductive technology. In "Infertility and Pregnancy Loss: The Role of the Family Consultant," Susan Mikesell and Margaret Stohner use family systems concepts of the family life cycle, chronic anxiety, emotional maturity, and triangles to describe assessment and intervention of couples experiencing these particular forms of stress. They describe a consultation model for use in the medical setting and describe typical intervention foci such as psychoeducation, anxiety self-management, decision making, and grief and loss.

For parents, one of their greatest fears is that their child may become seriously ill or incapacitated in some way. "A Developmental Biospsychosocial Approach to the Treatment of Chronic Illness in Children" describes the interaction between the developmental issues of children and families and the demands of a child's chronic illness. In this chapter, Beatrice Wood uses the structural family model's construct of boundary as a multilevel conceptual tool to organize assessment and intervention. She presents an extended case example of a 13-year-old boy with severe combined immunodeficiency syndrome to illustrate how the boundary dimensions of proximity, hierarchy, and responsivity help the therapist to understand and intervene with the family. The author provides a useful reference list for systems-oriented interventions in other chronic disorders and provides checklists of questions and tasks for assessment and for establishing adaptive interactions among family, school, peer group, and health-care systems.

# CHAPTER 21

# MEDICAL FAMILY THERAPY WITH SOMATIZING PATIENTS: THE CO-CREATION OF THERAPEUTIC STORIES

*Susan H. McDaniel, Jeri Hepworth, and William Doherty*

Medical family therapy is a systems approach to psychotherapy with patients and families experiencing a medical illness, trauma, or disability (McDaniel, Hepworth, & Doherty, 1992). This approach assumes that no biomedical event occurs without psychosocial repercussions, and that no psychosocial event occurs without some biological feature (see chaps. 22–25 in this volume for other examples of therapy for families with health problems). Nowhere is this more evident than in the treatment of somatizing patients and their families. These patients, who carry one of the *Diagnostic and Statistical Manual of Mental Disorders* (*DSM*) diagnoses of Somatoform Disorder, are people with difficult life situations who present not with anxiety, depression, or relationship problems but with numerous physical symptoms.

Some of these patients have a medical illness; for others no disease process can be identified. In either case, they are somatically fixated (Van Eijk et al., 1983). The language they use to construct their problems, their solutions, their identities, their relationships, and their lives is a language of the body. Rather than using emotional language to express emotional distress, they use somatic language to describe all difficulties, whether physical or emotional. These patients typically experience multiple power struggles with helping professionals—both physicians and psychologists—who insist they use emotional language to express their distress.

Here is an example of the kind of exchange common with these patients:

Mrs. Thomas: I can barely get out of bed in the morning. My back aches. My head is throbbing. And I can't eat because my throat is closed up. I finally get going to do the chores to keep the farm running. Then I fall back into bed exhausted by lunchtime. I wonder if I have a tumor, my head hurts so badly. Is this possible?

Therapist: I understand that you are exhausted and very uncomfortable today, Mrs. Thomas. I know your physician does not currently believe you have a tumor, but you should discuss any new symptoms with her. She mentioned to me that your husband works very hard every day and expects you to do the same. Can you tell me some more about your marriage?

Mrs. Thomas: Of course we both work hard. What does my back pain have to do with my husband? Leave him out of this! Farming is extremely difficult work, day after day, and someone has to keep it going. I had to be hospitalized a year ago because my back was killing me. I had surgery on a disc in my back. It's never really been right since. I haven't been able to work like I did before, so naturally my husband gets frustrated. Do you think that new medicine that's in the paper today might help me?[1]

---

[1] Aspects of this case were first described in Taplin, McDaniel, & Naumburg, 1987.

In this complex situation, the therapist was pushing an agenda and a language that was vastly different than that of the patient. No matter how accurate the hypothesis that marital problems might be intensifying the stress and pain for this patient and the timing and manner in which it was communicated, the question resulted in little information for the therapist, further somatization by the patient, and threatened polarization of the positions of both patient and therapist. The art of medical family therapy with somatizing patients and families involves collaborative negotiation and co-creation of therapeutic stories that are mutually acceptable to the patient, the family, the therapist, and the medical provider.

## MEDICAL FAMILY THERAPY

Medical family therapy uses biopsychosocial systems theory (Doherty, Baird, & Becker, 1987) to interweave the biomedical and psychosocial, with collaboration between medical providers and family therapists as a centerpiece of the approach. Close attention is paid to medical illness and the role that illness plays in the emotional life of the patient and the interpersonal dynamics of the family. The roots of medical family therapy are intertwined with the origins of the family therapy field. Pioneer psychiatrists such as Auerswald (1968), Bowen (1976), Minuchin (1975), Whitaker (1953), and Wynne (1978) foresaw the use of family therapy for problems of both mental and physical health. However, this initial interest in family treatment from a biopsychosocial perspective did not become widespread among family therapists.

Much of the avoidance of biological aspects of problems by family therapists was related to the rejection of the traditional medical model in favor of a systems model. However, since 1977 and the publication of Engel's (1977) biopsychosocial medical model, health care practitioners have had a medical model available that is compatible with systems theory. With the growth of the specialty of family medicine and the development of the field of family systems medicine (Bloch, 1983), medical providers and family therapists have been exploring the application of systems theory to medical practice (Doherty & Baird, 1983; McDaniel, Campbell, & Seaburn, 1990). The potential for collaborative practice between these physicians and family therapists has grown and been realized by some (McDaniel, 1995; Seaburn, 1995).

The biopsychosocial systems model, although not yet the dominant model in medicine or psychotherapy, allows clinicians to avoid the traps of "somatic fixation" that can be as prevalent among physicians as it is among patients and "psychosocial fixation" that is equally common in psychotherapy (McDaniel, Campbell, & Seaburn, 1989). Either kind of fixation reduces a complex problem to either its physical or its emotional component exclusively. Although this Cartesian mind–body split still dominates Western culture, biopsychosocial theory reaches toward an integration consistent with the tenets of systems theory.

Medical family therapy is the psychotherapy that has emerged from this comprehensive theory. The goal of medical family therapy is not the cure of an illness, for that usually falls in the domain of medicine. Goals for medical family therapy often take the form of better coping with a chronic illness, less conflict about managing medication, better communication with medical providers, more acceptance of a medical problem that cannot be cured, or help making a lifestyle change. With somatization, for example, goals might include acceptance of medical uncertainty about the source of the patient's pain, decreased expectations of a cure for the illness, less conflict with medical providers, lower medical bills, and increased pleasure with life for the patient and the family.

The cornerstone objectives of all medical family therapy are to promote agency and communion.[2] Increasing agency means increasing a patient's and family's sense of effectiveness in managing the illness and other aspects of their lives. Communion refers to the need to attend to the communication and emotional bonds that can be frayed by the challenges of pain and illness. With somatizing patients the clash of languages and health beliefs among patients, families, physicians, and sometimes therapists frequently causes breakdowns in communication. The rest of

---

[2] These terms were first used in a discussion of theology and psychology by D. Bakan (1969).

this chapter will describe the experiences of the somatizing patient, the family, the medical provider, and the medical family therapist and the process by which therapeutic stories can be developed to enhance agency and communion for these families.

## THE LANGUAGE AND EXPERIENCE OF THE SOMATIZING PATIENT AND FAMILY

The language of somatization is part of a lifelong coping style that functions like a chronic illness; it ebbs and flows, depending on other physical and emotional stresses and strains. For example, Mrs. Thomas, the patient mentioned earlier, experienced a ruptured disc soon after the death of her mother, with whom she had a very close relationship based in part on their both experiencing the father's physical abuse. Mrs. Thomas's illness, like that of many somatizing patients, was complex and affected by multiple biological, psychological, and social factors. The farm placed tremendous physical demands on her back and her body. In addition, the emotional components of her problem played a significant role in her length of disability and her inability to recuperate fully.

Somatizing patients can range from the "worried well"—those without disease process who are sensitive to and worry about bodily cues—to those with an injury or disease who obsess about their symptoms—such as Mrs. Thomas—to those with somatic delusions—such as a patient with pseudocyesis (McDaniel, Campbell, & Seaburn, 1990). Somatizing patients frequently seek medical attention, but their physical symptoms either do not make physiologic sense or are grossly in excess of what would be expected from physical findings. Typically somatizing patients like Mrs. Thomas strongly deny the legitimacy of any emotional language to describe their problems.

Kellner and Sheffield (1973) found that 60% to 80% of healthy people experience some somatic symptoms in any one week. However, most of them do not perceive their symptoms as requiring diagnosis and treatment by the medical system. Individuals' perceptions of a symptom are quite variable. Several studies have shown that the same amount of tissue pathology produces varying degrees of functional im-

pairment and subjective distress in different individuals (Eisenberg, 1979). Those who are sensitive to bodily cues and experience greater impairment and distress are more likely to label their symptoms as problems in need of medical treatment. Coryell (1981) found that the life span of somatizing patients is no shorter than that of the general population. However, the life of these patients and families can be dominated by physical symptoms, interpersonal struggles, and an excess of medical treatments.

Kellner (1986) hypothesizes that, in the beginning, these patients have some somatic symptoms at times of anxiety or depression; these elements become linked in a vicious cycle, and the pairing becomes predictable. For example, perhaps a patient's stomach tightens and churns when he or she is stressed. The patient labels his problems as an illness rather than an anxiety and then becomes "sick" each time he feels emotionally upset. For patients who have been abused like Mrs. Thomas, the pairing of emotional physical pain happens very early in life. The coincidence of grief and a back injury resulted in a flood of somatic symptoms for this woman. It is not difficult to imagine how family members and medical providers in such a situation might reinforce somatizing behavior.

Some family cultures lack any language for emotional experience. The adults may be alexithymic and allow only language about physical experience. Children in these families receive attention for physical pain but not for emotional pain. This approach conditions children to experience any need or problem as physical, and physical symptoms become their language for a range of experiences. Several studies have uncovered a relationship between severe somatizing behavior and early deprivation, physical or sexual abuse, or trauma (Katon, 1985). For patients like Mrs. Thomas, early emotional trauma has a significant physical component.

Families with severely somatizing members share patterns of interaction that seek to avoid or anesthetize emotional pain. Not surprisingly, a significant number of somatizing adults are married to other somatizing adults. These couples speak the language of bodily discomfort. Other somatizing adults seek out and marry caregiving partners. These caregivers may not themselves be ill, but they, too, privilege communication about physical events and deny most emotional experience (McDaniel, Hepworth, & Doherty, 1992).

Somatic fixation is embedded in our cultural language and belief systems that dichotomize the constructs labeled *mind* and *body*.[3] Cartesian dualism pervades the language and the meanings used to describe illness experiences. The notion that a physical symptom must have a primarily organic cause, or that an emotional feeling is primarily determined by psychological experience, is widely accepted in our society. The idea that mind and body are an integrated, related, communicating whole has only recently and tentatively been considered by mainstream Western society. The complex disorder of somatization symbolizes our culture's struggle to recognize the integration and interdependence of physical and emotional aspects of life (McDaniel, Hepworth, & Doherty, 1992).

Our culture also struggles with the relationship between individual responsibility and illness. Again the dichotomy: We tend to hold people responsible for their emotional problems, although believing on the whole that they are not responsible for disease or illness (McDaniel, Hepworth, & Doherty, 1992). Framing a problem as physical, as is true for somatizing patients, allows for a passive–dependent patient role that is socially acceptable. Medical anthropologist Kleinman (1986) described somatization as "culturally authorized, socially useful, and personally availing" (p. 151). Psychologist Adams (1992) wrote: "Somatization and the somatoform disorders are not a defense against depression. They are merely a means of gaining treatment without risking the rejection inherent in acknowledging psychological limitations" (p. 17). A medical family therapy approach does not demand a choice be made between a psychological and a social explanation for these problems; somatization is often multifactorial, but clearly the social and cultural components are significant in this disorder.

The fields of medicine and psychotherapy also struggle with the mind–body dichotomy. Medicine's worship of biomedicine, with its specificity and high-tech approach to treatment, seduces physicians and patients alike into becoming somatically fixated and concluding that biomedicine is all of medicine rather than only one important component of the diagnosis and treatment of a patient. Exclusive application of the biomedical model to somatizing behavior is likely to escalate the symptoms, frustrate both patient and physician, and increase the utilization and expense of medical services. In the psychotherapy field, likewise, exclusive focus on psychosocial issues often results in rejection of psychotherapy and the language of emotions by the somatizing patient and rejection of the patient by the therapist.

Traditional psychotherapy has not been helpful with these patients. Psychodynamic theory defines somatization as part of the patient's character structure that defends against frightening, traumatic, or depressing emotional experiences. Somatization is seen as deeply rooted, and somatizing patients are believed to be some of the most difficult with whom to establish a working alliance. These patients are widely described as "poor candidates for psychotherapy" (Greenson, 1967).

Consider Mr. Berzansky, a somatizing patient who also had asthma and a panic disorder that he treated with a large amount of alcohol. (Few of these patients only have one problem, and alcoholism or a family history of alcoholism occurs frequently in conjunction with somatization.) Mr. Berzansky agreed to the referral by his internist for psychotherapy because of family pressure; however, he scheduled sessions infrequently and came only about 50% of the time. After 8 months of treatment when he had not come to therapy for 10 weeks, the patient showed up in his internist's office disheveled and suicidal. The psychological nature of his symptoms was undeniable and gave the therapist entry that had been previously resisted by the patient. However, it

---

[3] Somatization occurs in all cultures, but its prevalence varies depending the culture's belief systems. For example, Asian cultures are even less tolerant of psychosocial explanations for distress. These groups have a higher incidence of somatization than the West (Bhatt, Tomenson, & Benjamin, 1989). It also appears that first-generation Asian immigrants to the United States have a very high prevalence of somatization disorder (Moore & Boehnlein, 1991).

was very difficult to convince the psychiatric hospital to admit him because of his somatization disorder and his alcohol abuse.

After almost a week of negotiations with the hospital, he was admitted for detoxification, alcohol treatment, and psychiatric assessment. He was then placed on an antidepressant, which helped his depression and his panic disorder. At this point, he agreed to regular individual and family sessions with the family psychologist. Somewhat surprisingly, given that he had been a loner all his life, this patient especially liked group therapy during his hospitalization. When he was discharged, it took 8 months to find a group that would accept him, even with his high motivation, because one group leader after another was unwilling to accept his somatizing language, his alcoholic history, or both.

Primary care physicians frequently are desperate for help with these patients that many mental health professionals believe are "hopeless" and not worthy of their time. Somatizing people are challenging patients who offer a window into those cultural health beliefs that are not functional for this widespread problem. These patients live at the center of the mind–body split. They are people in distress whose major problem is that we don't understand them.

## THE LANGUAGE AND EXPERIENCE OF THE MEDICAL PROVIDER

In many ways, the medical profession has done no better. They end up with huge headaches and enormous costs from expensive procedures and overutilization of medical services as a result of not being able to connect successfully with these patients. The following is a poem titled "Second Thoughts," written by a family physician, Tillman Farley. Dr. Farley's poem captures the way many physicians feel when faced with somatizing patients:

*Second Thoughts*

*It's five o' five
day's almost done.
All the patients seen
but one.*

*I stand outside
the exam room door,
read the nurse's note
with horror.*

*"New patient says
teeth itch at night,
stomach aches when shoes
too tight.*

*"Numbness starting
in the knee,
dizziness
since '63.*

*"Food goes up
instead of down,
always tired,
lies around. . . ."*

*Tears start to fall
I just can't hide 'em.
The note goes on
ad infinitum:*

*". . . Climbing stairs
causes gas,
no sense of smell
when driving fast.*

*"Left hand hurts
and right hand's weak,
sneeze sends pain
from hands to feet.*

*"Last week had
a pain in the chest. . . ."
Stop! No more!
Can't read the rest!*

*I think business school
would have been wiser,
'cause they don't have
somaticizers.*

(Tillman Farley, MD, in McDaniel, Hepworth, & Doherty, 1992, p. 131. Reprinted with permission of the author.)

Empathy with the physician's dilemma is an important part of any psychological consultation involving a somatizing patient. Somatizing patients are extremely common in the offices of primary care physicians like Dr. Farley. Cummings and VandenBos (1981) found that as many as 60% of all primary care patients present with somatic complaints that are an expression of psychosocial distress. These patients require some reassurance and time from medical providers, but it is the small group of patients with serious somatizing disorders that most challenge the technical skills of physicians. DeGruy, Columbia, and Dickinson (1987) found that patients with somatization disorder had a 50% higher rate of office visits, 50% higher charges, charts 200% as thick as the average chart, and significantly more diagnoses than control-group patients. These patients may undergo expensive, potentially dangerous, and unnecessary procedures, including surgery and hospitalization (Zoccolillo & Cloninger, 1986). With the sensitivity over skyrocketing medical costs in the United States, it is important to note the estimates that one fifth of the medical budget is spent on somatizing patients (Kellner, 1990). The potential exists for family psychologists working in collaboration with primary care physicians to deliver more effective and considerably less expensive care. In a pilot study Huygens (1982), a Dutch family physician, found that employing family therapists in his office resulted in significantly decreased costs for medical visits.

Quill (1985), a general internist, has termed somatization disorder as medicine's *blind spot*. In large part, this is due to miscommunication and lack of shared language between the patient and the medical provider. Many physicians misunderstand the indirect communication conveyed by somatizing language and use a biomedical approach to understand and attempt treatment of the complaint. Figure 1 illustrates the somatic fixation cycle that can commonly occur between physician and patient. The patient experiences symptoms, the physician orders tests and prescribes medications, the tests are negative, and the physician is relieved. At this point physicians reassure the patients and tell them they are healthy or give them a benign diagnosis. These patients then feel misunderstood and react with anger and persistent complaints and demands. Physicians

become irritated and withdraw or refer the patient to a specialist, where the cycle can start all over again. At best, patients walk away feeling physicians are inept and unhelpful. Physicians place the patient in a category with alcoholics and other demanding patients for whom they feel there is no hope.

The alternative to this cycle is for physicians to undertake a biopsychosocial approach with patients: interspersing biomedical and psychosocial questions from the beginning, establishing a collaborative rather than authoritarian relationship with the patient and family, tolerating uncertainty, establishing limited goals, setting limits on costly tests and procedures, and attempting to understand patients' experience and language from their unique point of view (McDaniel, Campbell, & Seaburn, 1990). With very difficult patients, physicians may ask a family psychologist to join the treatment team.

## CO-CREATING A THERAPEUTIC LANGUAGE WITH SOMATIZING PATIENTS

Psychotherapy with somatizing patients involves negotiation of a therapeutic language with the patient, the family, and the medical providers (see also chap. 2 in this volume). Exhibit 1 summarizes clinical strategies that are helpful in the development of therapeutic stories with somatizing patients. The difficulties about language begin at the time of referral. In many ways, for somatizing patients to accept a mental health referral they have to change radically their perspective and definition of their problems as medical. Yet if they could do this, they would not need the referral in the first place! Some patients will accept a therapy referral because of the stress associated with having an undiagnosable illness. Others, like Mr. Berzansky, yield to family pressure. A significant number, however, hear such a referral as a rejection by the physician of them and their view of the problem.

Therefore, it is often useful for the family psychologist to have at least the first meeting at the physician's office. This allows the family therapist to accept, for the moment, the patient's definition of the problem. It allows the therapist to meet the patient and family with the physician, to receive the physician's blessing, and to demystify the therapy so that trust can begin to develop. It also provides the patient and family with an integrated experience that can counteract their polarization of mind and body. Symbolically the joint session validates both physical and psychological experience as important and related to each other. These sessions may be used for referral at times of difficulty in the medical or psychological treatment and at termination when the patient will continue with the physician. With the most severe cases, it may be necessary to have sessions with patients and their physician throughout the treatment. (See the case described in chap. 16 of McDaniel, Campbell, & Seaburn, 1990.) The "stereoscopic vision" (Bloch, 1988) offered by both psychologist and medical provider is a powerful treatment approach for somatization.

In any session, with or without the physician, the patient's language and definition of his or her prob-lem are the tools used to facilitate changes desired by the patient. If the therapist insists that a somatizing patient understand and speak psychological language, patients will feel invalidated, insulted, and may fulfill the prophesy that he or she is "not a good candidate for psychotherapy." However, the most useful approach is for therapists to use an ecosystemic approach in which the language of treatment evolves as a collaboration between the relevant parties, like the therapy advocated by Goolishian and Anderson (1987, see also chap. 2 in this volume). With an ecosystemic approach, these patients do not have to be ruled out and a power struggle over language (i.e., whether their problems are physical or psychological) does not occur. Instead, the therapist may treat each patient, family, and situation as unique, speak the patient's (rather than the therapist's) language, ask questions to understand better the pa-

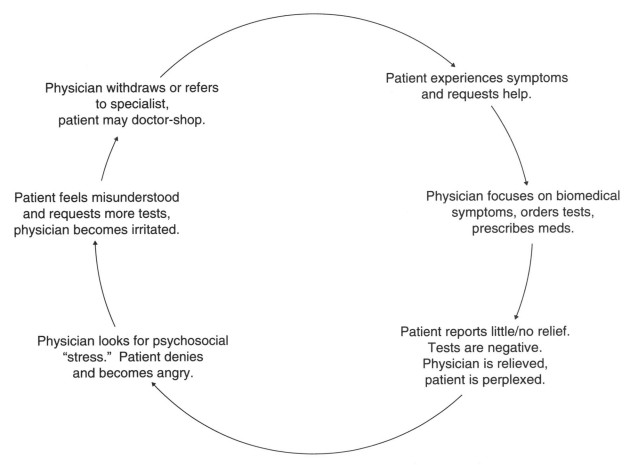

FIGURE 1. **Somatically fixated physician–patient interaction. From *Family-Oriented Primary Care* (p. 252), by S. H. McDaniel, T. Campbell, & D. Seaburn, 1990, New York: Springer-Verlag. Copyright 1990 by Springer-Verlag. Adapted with permission.**

---

**EXHIBIT 1**

**Strategies for Treating Somatizing Patients and Their Families**

*Referral*

1. Empathize with the physician.
2. Suggest an integrated treatment approach in which physician and psychologist have regular and continued involvement with the patient and the family.
3. Ask the physician to explicitly support the referral and the psychotherapy process.
4. For patients who are highly resistant to psychotherapy, offer to meet first with the physician at his or her office.

*Early Phase*

1. Focus on symptoms, ask about the family's "diagnosis," and listen for metaphors of emotional pain.
2. Elicit all relevant details of the illness story.
3. Discuss the patient's and family's strengths and areas of competence.
4. Take a genogram to help understand any transgenerational meanings for the symptoms. Ask, "Has anyone else in the family had an illness that in any way resembles this one?"
5. Listen for how the symptoms may have changed the typical roles or balance of power in the family.
6. Use medical language and medical-style interventions in this phase, such as symptom diaries, desensitization tapes, and attention to diet, exercise, and sleep.
7. Refrain from emotional language and in-depth emotional exploration until the family demonstrates its willingness to discuss these issues.
8. Tolerate and recognize the uncertainty involved in the patient's symptoms. Collaborate with the patient and family, and engage them in experiments to see what helps and what does not.

*Middle Phase*

1. Work toward a definition of the problem that is mutually acceptable to the patient, family, medical providers, and therapist. Use words that bridge physical, emotional, and interpersonal experience. Use this definition in both medical and psychotherapeutic settings.
2. Maintain curiosity about the patient and family's experiences.
3. Introduce emotional language slowly, until very gradually sessions are more balanced and include language about biological, psychological, and social experiences.
4. Reinforce attempts by the patient at higher levels of activity. Encourage the family to reinforce these attempts as well. Withhold reinforcement for symptomatic behavior.
5. Avoid psychosocial fixation. Remain open to the possibility of biological problems that remit with biomedical intervention.

*Late Phase*

1. Predict setbacks as symptoms decrease in frequency.
2. Write a "prescription for illness" with the family, detailing what each would have to do to make the symptoms worse.
3. Terminate softly.

---

*This exhibit is derived from ideas first presented in McDaniel, Hepworth, and Doherty (1992).*

tient's experience, and always maintain a position of "not knowing" rather than making assumptions about others' experience.

Speaking the patient's language with somatizing patients means eliciting their symptoms rather than trying to move them quickly from a biological to a psychological framework. It is easy to be intimidated, bored, or annoyed by their numerous symptoms if the therapist does not recognize the symptoms as a unique form of communication. It is important in the joining phase to understand the patient and family's experience and "diagnosis" of the problem. Strategies to facilitate this process include listing symptoms on poster paper and asking patients to describe them in detail, asking patients to draw the organ or the part of the body involved, and asking patients and family members with close involvement to keep symptom diaries formatted with physical symptoms on the left side of the page and life events and emotional reactions on the right (McDaniel, Campbell, & Seaburn, 1990). This exercise indirectly begins the process of examining the relationship between the physical and the emotional for that person. Questions about diagnosis and prognosis, and any theories about what kind of treatment might be helpful, inform the therapist about the health beliefs and language of the family.

Symptoms can have both biological and psychological or interpersonal meaning, and all symptoms deserve assessment by a medical provider. However, it is also useful for the therapist to listen to symptoms for any symbolism or metaphor of emotional pain particularly meaningful to the patient and family (Seaburn, 1995). Mrs. Thomas with back pain, for example, was not only carrying heavy loads around her farm but she was also carrying a heavy emotional burden in her current family and her family of origin. The emotional burdens were not spoken, except through the language of physical pain. For instance, many patients who have never spoken of their sexual abuse present to their physician with abdominal pain.

The details of the patient and family's illness story—when the symptoms began, how they were experienced, how they have changed, how the family has reacted, and how the medical system has responded to the symptoms—inform the therapist about their experiences and elaborate any emotional metaphors. The meaning of the symptoms for each person may be related to his or her own or others' previous illness experiences. For Mr. Berzansky, who had difficulty getting hospitalized and then finding an out-patient therapy group, his symptoms symbolized since childhood a feeling of being different and misunderstood—by this family, his peers, and also by the medical system.

A genogram with a family medical history may help to uncover transgenerational meanings of a symptom. One patient with headaches discovered that her mother, who died when the patient was 11, also had headaches. Her mother attributed her headaches to frequent destructive arguments with her husband, the patient's father. That patient remembered her parents' arguments but not the headaches. In her own marriage, she had vowed not to argue with her husband "like her parents had." When this couple learned to argue productively, the patient's headaches decreased drastically in frequency. Genograms also allow for questions about how the illness has changed the typical roles or balance of power in the family.

Much of the first phase of treatment, which can be extended, is medically focused, with the therapist and the physician showing the family that it is possible to tolerate the uncertainty that they all feel about the cause of the patient's symptoms.[4] The somatizing patient often expresses the family's fears of dying, fears of incompetence or disability, and general unease with uncertainty of any kind (McDaniel, Hepworth, & Doherty, 1992). However, any in-depth emotional exploration is premature until the patient and family signal their readiness. Medical language and physical interventions, such as relaxation tapes and attention to diet, sleep, and exercise, are also

---

[4] From an existential point of view, tolerating this uncertainty is a metaphor for tolerating the uncertainty that we all have about life in general.

useful in this phase. Many of these interventions can be family projects. Eliciting patient and family strengths helps to balance the assessment, provide support, and identify resources that will be useful in further treatment.

With the family, the therapist explores the unknown, mysterious aspects of the patient's illness, aspects that have eluded treatment by the medical system. The patient and family can begin to notice the factors that seem to produce even small improvements and the factors that seem to make the symptoms worse.

In the middle phase of treatment, the definition of the problem has begun to be more complex, sometimes including emotionally based reasons for the exacerbation of symptoms. Words that bridge physical and emotional experience such as *stress*, *scarring*, and *pain* may be used or accepted by patients as the sessions gradually become less somatically fixated (McDaniel, Campbell, & Seaburn, 1990). These bridging terms open conversations to the patient's emotional reactions (e.g., what stresses you most while you are coping with this illness?). These terms may also be of use to the physician as he or she seeks common ground with these patients.

Medical interventions can be used in the service of psychotherapy during this phase. For example, Mr. Resin, a patient with chronic and severe somatization disorder, had not been able to discuss the deaths of his children without provoking a stream of somatic complaints. He and his wife were finally able to speak openly when their physician joined a therapy session and read the babies' death certificates line by line, stopping to explain the medical significance of each term and answer their questions. With the physician remaining, an emotional and therapeutic story emerged about the couple's grief and what these losses had meant to each of them and to their family (McDaniel, Campbell, & Seaburn, 1990).

Similar to many other medical family therapy patients, the goal of treatment with somatizing patients is not to become symptom-free, as this is likely unrealistic, but for the patient to function significantly better at home, at work, and with the family. Occasionally, patients' symptoms do diminish drastically. More frequently, they continue at some low level but

no longer dominate or interfere with work or relationships. These patients experience a much improved quality of life. They may feel some greater sense of effectiveness, or agency, and may feel more in charge of their symptoms. Communion between the patient and family, and often the medical providers, has increased significantly. Therapy sessions can move from flat, sterile, biological discussions to warm, humorous, and expressive exchanges.

Termination occurs when patients, families, therapist and physican become more comfortable with the patient's symptoms, either because of decrease in severity or frequency or because all understand that the symptoms no longer represent medical crises. This is a new awareness, which may be maintained with increasing intervals throughout the lengthy termination period. One of our patients benefited from "reality inoculations," monthly for about eight months. These reality inoculations helped her state her fears, discuss again how symptoms were related to stress in her life, and support her increasing sense of agency. She often made gentle jokes about her concerns, such as "Last week I knew I had a brain tumor, but fortunately that went away, and this week I only fear a muscle spasm in my back."

A helpful technique during termination is a collaboratively composed "prescription for illness" that details what the patient and each family member has to do to bring back or exacerbate the patient's symptoms (McDaniel, Hepworth, & Doherty, 1992). Sometimes medical providers also wish to add comments about their own behavior to these prescriptions (e.g., "I'd have to not listen carefully to Mrs. Thomas or try to understand how hard this has been for her"). Although this tends to be a playful exercise, it also reveals the complexity with which the family now views the illness, including its physical, psychological, and social components. Illness stories shift, and there often is a sense of connection among the family against the illness, rather than a feeling of the illness coming in between the patient and other family members.

A joint session with the physician at the end of treatment can summarize the patient's and family's successes and mark their return to the exclusive care of the physician when a problem arises. A "soft termination" (see chap. 4 in this volume) allows for the physician, patient, or family to request further consultation at any later date.

Although working with somatizing patients and their families is complex, it is also intellectually stimulating and personally rewarding. Medical family therapy often requires knowledge and skill beyond generic family therapy or family psychology training. This challenging work occurs precisely at the interface of our struggles to understand the constructs we lable *mind* and *body*. It is poignant to experience the patient and the family as they begin to develop new stories and consider new language that allows them to process and respond directly to emotional events. As the therapy helps families, it also helps family psychologists and medical providers to understand and better appreciate the interdependency of body and mind. This is careful work, often long-term, that helps move the health-care system to recognize the ambiguity in people's lives and the limits of traditional medical treatment.

Medical family therapy with somatizing patients provides an exciting arena for collaborative thinking and patient care. It offers family psychologists the opportunity to participate in much-needed health-care reform. A collaborative approach with the family and the medical system can result in comprehensive biopsychosocial treatment and offer relief for many patients who otherwise would continue to suffer.

# References

Adams, D. B. (1992). Somatoform disorders: Physiological and socially sanctioned pathology. *The Psychotherapy Bulletin, 27,* 16–17.

American Psychiatric Association. (1994). *Diagnostic and statistical manual of mental disorders* (4th ed.). Washington, DC: Author.

Auerswald, E. (1968). Interdisciplinary versus ecological approach. *Family Process, 7,* 202–215.

Bakan, D. (1969). *The duality of human existence.* Chicago: Rand McNally.

Bhatt, A., Romenson, B., & Benjamin, S. (1989). Transcultural patterns of somatization in primary care: A preliminary report. *Journal of Psychosomatic Research, 33,* 671–680.

Bloch, D. (1988). The partnership of Dr. Biomedicine and Dr. Psychosocial. *Family Systems Medicine, 6*(1), 2–4.

Bloch, D. (1983). Family systems medicine: The field and the journal. *Family Systems Medicine, 1,* 3–11.

Bowen, M. (1976). Theory in the practice of psychotherapy. In P. Guerin (Ed.), *Family therapy: Theory and practice* (pp. 42–90). New York: Gardner Press.

Coryell, W. (1981). Diagnosis-specific mortality: Primary unipolar depression and Briquet's sundrome (somatization disorder). *Archives of General Psychiatry, 38,* 939–942.

Cummings, N., & VandenBos, G. (1981). The twenty-year Kaiser-Permanente experience with psychotherapy and medical utilization: Implications for national health policy and national health insurance. *Health Policy Quarterly, 1,* 159–175.

deGruy, F., Columbia, L., & Dickinson, P. (1987). Somatization disorder in a family practice. *Journal of Family Practice, 25,* 45–51.

Doherty, W. J., & Baird, M. (1983). *Family therapy and family medicine: Toward the primary care of families.* New York: Guilford.

Doherty, W. J., Baird, M., & Becker, L. (1987). Family medicine and the biopsychosocial model: The road toward integration. *Marriage and Family Review, 10,* 51–70.

Eisenberg, L. (1979). Interfaces between medicine and psychiatry. *Comprehensive Review, 10,* 51–70.

Engel, G. L. (1977). The need for a new medical model: A challenge for biomedicine. *Science, 196,* 129–136.

Goolishian, H., & Anderson, H. (1987). Language systems and therapy: An evolving idea. *Psychotherapy, 24,* 529–538.

Greenson, R. (1967). The working alliance and the transference neuroses. *Psychoanalytic Quarterlies, 34,* 155–181.

Huygen, F. J. (1982). *Family medicine: The medical life history of families.* New York: Brunner/Mazel.

Katon, W. (1985). Somatization in primary care. *Journal of Family Practice, 21,* 257–258.

Kellner, R. (1986). *Somatization and hypochondriasis.* New York: Praeger-Greenwood.

Kellner, R. (1990). Somatization: Theories and research. *Journal of Nervous and Mental Disease, 78,* 150–159.

Kellner, R., & Sheffield, B. (1973). The one-week prevalence of symptoms in neurotic patients and normals. *American Journal of Psychiatry, 130,* 102–105.

Kleinman, A. (1986). *Social origins of distress and disease.* New Haven, CT: Yale University Press.

McDaniel, S. H. (1995). Collaboration between family psychologists and physicians: Opportunities to implement the biopsychosocial model. *Professional Psychology.*

McDaniel, S. H., Campbell, T. L., & Seaburn, D. B. (1989). Somatic fixation in patients and physicians: A biopsychosocial approach. *Family Systems Medicine, 7,* 5–16.

McDaniel, S. H., Campbell, T. L., & Seaburn, D. B. (1990). *Family-oriented primary care: A manual for medical providers.* New York: Springer-Verlag.

McDaniel, S. H., Hepworth, J., & Doherty, W. (1992). *Medical family therapy: A biopsychosocial approach to families with health problems.* New York: Basic Books.

Minuchin, S., Baker, L., Rosman, B., Liehman, R., Milman, L., & Todd, T. (1975). A conceptual model of psychosomatic illness in children: Family organization and family therapy. *Archives of General Psychiatry, 32,* 1031–1038.

Moore, L. J., & Boehnlein, J. K. (1991). Posttraumatic stress disorder, depression, and somatic symptoms. *Journal of Nervous and Mental Disease, 179,* 728–733.

Quill, T. (1985). Somatization: One of medicine's blind spots. *Journal of the American Medical Association, 254,* 3075–3079.

Seaburn, D. B. (1995). Language, silence, and somatic fixation. In S. McDaniel (Ed.), *Counseling families with chronic illness.* Baltimore: American Counseling Association.

Taplin, S., McDaniel, S., & Naumburg, E. (1987). A case of pain. In W. Doherty & M. Baird (Eds.), *Family-centered medical care: A clinical casebook.* New York: Guilford Press.

Van Eijk, J., Grop, R., Huygen, F., Mesker, P., Mesker-Niestan, J., van Mierlo, G., Mokkink, H., & Santo, A. (1983). The family doctor and the prevention of somatic fixation. *Family Systems Medicine, 1,* 5–15.

Whitaker, C., & Malone, T. (1953). *The roots of psychotherapy.* New York: Blakiston.

Wynne, L., Cromwell, R., & Matthysse, S. (1978). *The nature of schizophrenia: New approaches to research and treatment.* New York: Wiley.

Zoccolillo, M., & Cloninger, C. (1986). Somatization disorder: Psychologic symptoms, social disability and diagnosis. *Comprehensive Psychiatry, 27,* 65–73.

# CHAPTER 22

# A FAMILY SYSTEMS APPROACH TO COPING WITH CANCER

*David K. Wellisch*

Cancer is a widespread phenomenon in American society. Approximately one out of four Americans can expect a diagnosis of cancer in their lifetimes, and three out of four families will at some point have a member with cancer. These experiences will not necessarily be brief because about 40% of those diagnosed will live five years beyond their diagnoses (American Cancer Society, 1991). Given the extensiveness of these demographics, it is almost certain that cancer-generated family stresses, fears, and traumatic memories will find their way to the consulting room of the family therapist. This offers opportunity as well as crisis for these families. The opportunity is that cancer provides a motivational stimulus for families to bond, support, and relate as never before. The family therapist can become a catalyst in this process with the family in a state of receptivity for change that is probably unprecedented in their history. As an old Chinese proverb reflects, danger contains the twin elements of crisis and opportunity. The family and family therapist can truly capitalize on these two themes with the presence of cancer.

## LITERATURE REVIEW

A modest literature on family themes in dealing with cancer exists, including discussion of some key themes and issues that I will mention.

Families prefer to share responsibility in decision making. Families almost universally desire information about the cancer they face and wish that provision of such information could be more routine (Derdarian, 1986). In addition, it has been found that one of the most crucial elements in family satis-

faction with medical treatment is sense of involvement in decision making (Chesler & Barbarin, 1984).

Family stresses occur in phases corresponding to developments in the biologic illness (Rait & Lederberg, 1989). These include the acute phase where family members are presented with a frightening crisis and can react in a number of ways, largely on the basis of previous patterns of responding (Koocher, 1986). One possible direction this may take is a "conspiracy of silence," which is an attempt to manage and reduce anxiety through reduction of communication (Bluebond-Langner, 1978).

In the chronic phase families attempt to cope with and adapt to lengthy treatment courses and declines in physical functioning because of the ineffectiveness of treatments. Families in this phase may often find themselves isolated from support. It has been reported that only 33% of families in this phase make use of supports they knew about in spite of self-acknowledged needs (Hinds, 1985). In this phase there has been found to be a positive correlation between length and severity of illness and measures of dysfunction in family members (Cancer Care Inc. & National Cancer Foundation, 1977; Koocher & O'Malley, 1981). Such dysfunction is not inevitable, as many families learn to cope and adapt (Rait & Lederberg, 1989).

Resolution–bereavement is the last phase in the trilogy. Resolution is different for families whose members survive versus those who die from cancer. Resolution for families whose member survives may be affected by the Damocles Syndrome where recurrence fears are chronically present (Koocher & O'Malley, 1981). Chochinov and Holland (1989) describe the complexities of bereavement in cancer as starting with anticipatory grief and often leading to families' questioning themselves in the postdeath period along the lines of "Did we do everything?" and "Could it have been prevented?"

There are many circumstances and variables that result in families that are differentially affected by the illness. These include: (a) spouses of patients who may feel protective (Sabo, Brown, & Smith, 1986) or vulnerable and helpless (Vachon, 1977); (b) parents of children with cancer (see Lansky, Cairns, Hassanein, Wehr, & Lowman, 1978); (c) children of cancer patients, which represents a small literature about a large and potentially high-risk group (Nir, Pynoos, & Holland, 1981; Rosenheim & Reicher, 1985; Wellisch, 1979); and (d) siblings of cancer patients who also tend to be a neglected group with a mixed set of outcomes in the existing literature (Bank & Kahn, 1982; Koocher & O'Malley, 1981; Sourkes, 1980).

Families with a cancer patient must relate to and interface with the health care system. An intense relationship develops between families and staff, with medical caregivers becoming endowed with enormous significance (Cassileth, 1979). Families may be intimidated by the health-care delivery team and may be confused and anxious over conflicting reports from different professionals (Imber-Coopersmith, 1985).

This brief review is not meant to be exhaustive of the psychological literature around family issues in cancer but instead is meant to focus on a few key themes. The remainder of the chapter attempts to present the experiences of families living with cancer.

## CLINICAL EXPERIENCES OF THREE FAMILIES

This chapter will describe the experiences of three families facing cancer in a family member. Each family situation will be described in terms of four basic issues:

1. The medical situation at hand. It will become apparent that the term *cancer* is in no sense an all-inclusive label; it is more realistically a general label under which many different diseases exist, each with radically different implications for the patient and his or her family members. The following three case examples of family scenarios have been selected to reflect this important point.

2. Composition of each family unit. The diversity of family systems is reflected in important ways with cancer experiences. The wide differences in composition, lifestyle, developmental stage, and patterns of interaction of three family scenarios will illustrate this reality.

3. The impacts of the illnesses on family functioning. The three case examples range along a spectrum of illnesses that are acute–curable, chronic–containable, and terminal–uncontainable. The impacts of these illnesses on the families in relation to the seriousness of the prognoses and severity of treatment bear some similarities and some significant differences.

4. The therapeutic interventions made with different families. These scenarios express the different therapeutic solutions on the basis of the nature, complexity of treatment, side effects of treatment, and outcome of these illnesses with these families.

Table 1 depicts the combination of basic issues for families dealing with cancer, along with intervention possibilities.

Technology in cancer treatments is now greatly complex and enveloping of patients and families no matter how treatable or curable the form of cancer. As a result, the family system of the cancer patient becomes subsumed into the health-care delivery system. The family therapist, therefore, must contend with the patient and family in the context of the oncology office, outpatient clinic, home setting, and hospital ward. All of these places have different "people systems" that differentially affect the patient and family. To not consider the family dealing with cancer in the context of these multiple systems would be tantamount to ignoring the family reality.

*CASE EXAMPLE: FAMILY ONE*
**Medical situation.** *Mr. J., a 73-year-old retired executive, was found by his internist at his yearly physical exam to have a hard nodule on his prostate (see Table 1). The*

## TABLE 1

**Basic Issues of Three Families Dealing With Cancer**

| Client | Medical status | Family unit | Impact on family | Intervention |
|---|---|---|---|---|
| Family One: Mr. J. | Acute–curable (prostate) | Older couple with separate adult children | Sexual disability<br><br>Social anxiety–disruption of social life<br><br>Recurrence fears | Couple-based stress reduction<br><br>Referral to community support groups<br><br>Facilitation of blocked communication |
| Family Two: Ms. B. | Chronic–containable (Hodgkins) | Young adult with separate nuclear family | Reactivation of sibling (childhood) roles and conflicts<br><br>Labeling of one member as identified patient<br><br>Symbiosis of family because of medical procedures | Functional involvement of family in patient's care<br><br>Reframing labeling of identified patient |
| Family Three: Mr. A. | Terminal–uncontainable (glioblastoma) | Nuclear family with dependent child | Loss of family income<br><br>Acting out by patient's child<br><br>Role shifts in marriage and parent–child | Facilitation of family grief<br><br>Facilitation of shift from family somatizing to family verbalizing<br><br>Emphasis on continuity of family rules during illness |

internist was immediately suspicious of prostate cancer, and the patient was sent to his local urologist for further evaluation. Mr. J., accompanied by his wife, began the work up with the local urologist, which consisted of a digital rectal examination; a biopsy; chemical studies; examination of urine and prostatic fluid; and imaging scans, including bone scans, computed tomography (CT), and magnetic resonance imagery (MRI; Lind & Nakao, 1990). The tests took about a week to complete.

The urologist presented Mr. J. with two important conclusions. Mr. J. did have prostatic cancer, which was in stage B in a system ranging from stages A through D. A stage B tumor is confined to the prostate with no metastases (spreading) to other organs or bones (Hanks, 1988). Mr. J. was told that this stage tumor would require either radiation treatment or surgery. Mr. J.

asked for a second opinion before deciding and was referred to a large university medical center 60 miles from his home where a national authority on prostatic cancer was located. This was arranged, and Mr. J., accompanied by his wife, daughter (a nurse), and son-in-law, saw this urologist within one week.

At the consultation, two key decisions were made: Surgery in the form of radical prostatectomy would be performed, and the consulting urologist would perform the surgery. Mr. J. was told that radical prostatectomy would almost certainly cure his cancer and that no follow-up treatment would be required. He also learned that an impotency rate of 90% has been reported following this procedure, but with newer, nerve-sparing surgical techniques, the rate of impotence could be as low as 14% (Lue, 1991). Mr. J. was informed about another medical consequence of this surgery, which was transitory problems in urinary continence likely to last for about 6 months postsurgery (Steiner, Morton, & Walsh, 1991).

**Composition of family unit.** The J. family had four members. Mr. and Mrs. J. had been married for 48 years by the time of his diagnosis. Mr. J. was a retired executive and Mrs. J. was a housewife. They had two children, a 45-year-old daughter, who was an office nurse who lived one-hour away in Southern California, and a 43-year-old son who lived in a different state and was an engineer. The daughter, initially quite upset by her father's diagnosis, was calmed by the urologist's explanation of prostate cancer and its curability in the early stages. She had initially thought that prostate cancer becomes metastatic and inevitably leads to a lingering and painful death. The son mainly received information through his parents and sister. The couple, therefore, became the unit of focus in the family interventions. An important aspect of the couple's life and recovery was their life-style and living arrangement. They lived in a retirement community where they were in a network of older couples; many of the men had prostate cancer. They came to learn and focus on the reality that about 70% of American men over age 70 have some form of prostatic malignancy (Ross, Pagnanini-Hill, & Henderson, 1988). Thus, their social network aided in the normalization of this problem.

**Impacts of the illness on family functioning.** Mr. J. was referred for psychological help by his urologist at a 3-month clinic follow-up visit. The urologist was concerned about two problems: Mr. J. seemed hesitant to get back into life with friends and colleagues and seemed to have a sense of shame about which he could not articulate but seemed evident. Mr. J. did accept the referral; on the phone, however, the therapist suggested that his wife might

accompany him. This was troubling to him, and he requested that the first visit be him alone. He presented in that visit as "every inch the executive" dressed in white shirt, conservative blue suit, and black brogan business shoes. At one level he was in control, in charge, polished, and organized. However, the expected results of the surgery had, in fact, come to be true, and he was experiencing subsequent loss of control of important and crucial aspects of his life. Although urinary continence was improving, he still experienced an inability to exercise absolute control and needed to wear a diaper. He found himself living in fear of a return of his illness and feared return visits to the urology clinic, especially for repeat scans some months in the future. He could not control any of these things, much to his chagrin. These were the multiple bases of the shame that the urologist was sensitively perceiving.

An additional concern was that he could not protect his wife from the stress of all this and that she was seeing some of his fears. He related that he never wanted his family to be afraid and that "a man's duty is to protect his family from fears." He accepted the recommendation that his wife be included in future visits, given that some of these issues directly involved her and that he was making some assumptions on how she felt in her absence. Mr. J. presented his wife as having changed in the course of his diagnosis, treatment, and recovery. The main change was her 25-pound weight gain in 5 months. He observed her to be frightened, withdrawn, and increasingly preoccupied with her own physical problems.

**Interventions with the J. family.** Mrs. J. presented as an anxious, very overweight, and overly dependent woman who seemed pleased to be included in the sessions. The couple contracted for short-term work because of the over 120-mile round-trips each visit required. This seemed reasonable given that they were faced with some acute problems and adjustments to longer term realities. We developed a plan for a ten-session course of work. I viewed the structure and boundaries of this as anxiety reducing for both of them. Neither was opting for relationship restructuring or personality change in our work.

My plan was to perform a set of interventions modeled after those developed in the Fawzy study group with melanoma patients (Fawzy et al., 1990). The key foci and goals in that very successful intervention program centered around education, generation of support, problem solving, and relaxation training.

It quickly became evident that this couple had fallen into a lack-of-communication pattern about his illness and treatment on the basis of a mutual wish to "protect" the other from anxiety and stress. This is very typical of families where a member has cancer (Wellisch, 1981). Our first task was to break through this mutual projective and protective process so communication could occur. Mrs. J. was most willing to begin and presented her key concerns. She indicated little sense of remorse over the loss of sexual intercourse but great sadness over the loss of affection and was experiencing Mr. J. as withdrawn and avoidant. Her key issue was the fear that his illness would recur and she would be left widowed in old age. She also viewed Mr. J. as increasingly socially isolated and depressed. She was puzzled by his unwillingness to even see his male friends, play golf, and go to the daytime social events, meetings, and lunches he ordinarily enjoyed. She felt isolated and agitated and viewed her dramatic escalation in eating as her form of "friend and tranquilizer."

Mr. J., as Mrs. J. broke the ice, seemed pulled into the therapy and revealed many pent-up feelings in response to Mrs. J's issues. He felt immense shame over his loss of erectile function, so much so that he felt "pushed into the corner" by his own feelings. He was stunned by his wife's acceptance over the loss of intercourse. He had felt that to be affectionate would only have led to frustration for her. It was interesting for him to see that her key concerns meshed with his: fear of recurrence of his illness and loss of life. This was a joint concern that each agreed hung heavy in the air but could not be discussed previously. He talked at length about his shame over the urinary incontinence and the fears he would have an accident in public, especially with his male friends. The image of himself as "an old man peeing in his pants" was fearful and distasteful to him to an extreme degree. Thus, the three concerns of urinary incontinence, erectile dysfunction, and recurrence of illness were foremost for Mr. J., with Mrs. J. coming to understand his first two fears but only sharing and fearing recurrence as a primary fear.

These concerns became the foci of educational efforts that were to be presented to the urologist at the follow-up. Some practice of the framing of these questions was done in our sessions. In addition, the couple was taught relaxation skills to be used to counter fearful thoughts about recurrence and for Mr. J. when facing repeat scans. The couple eagerly learned and later practiced these exercises.

Mr. J. saw the urologist sooner than planned, with Mrs. J. joining the visit to discuss these issues. They learned that 75% of men resolve urinary incontinence by six months, and 89% at 12 months postsurgery (Steiner, Morton & Walsh, 1991). They learned he had the options of either an inflatable or semirigid penile prosthesis, both of which they jointly rejected as undesirable. The elected not to hear exact percentages of recurrence of his illness but accepted the notion that his chances for surviving the next 5 years were excellent. The actual 5-year relative survival rate for patients whose tumors are diagnosed while still localized (like Mr. J.) is 88% (De-Kernion, 1985). When this is considered relative to his age, it is unlikely this malignancy would actually shorten his expected life span.

Given this information, the key problems we focused on were how to encourage affection in the absence of sexual intercourse; how to have a social life in the face of his incontinence fears; and how to live with the fact that his mortality had been threatened and that they must accept recurrence as a possibility while continuing to live a life of some quality.

They felt that "getting their signals clear" about affection being mutually desirable was most helpful to their relationship. He agreed to wear double diapers when going out socially and was calmed by the clear discussion with the urologist. This was a "light at the end of the tunnel" for him. He found out about a support group of men who were prostate survivors ("Men for Men") near his home and felt he would benefit by attending. He wished to see others "in the same boat" and to see others where the urinary incontinence had improved. Mrs. J. felt she could also use such a group and resolved to approach the wives of the men in "Men for Men." If no group could be organized, she would attend a general support group for family members of cancer patients near her home.

The couple left at the end of the 10 sessions having communicated about difficult issues previously blocked; made several decisions, the most important of which was no penile prosthesis for him; learned answers and information about pressing issues; learned techniques to help them in the face of acute stress; and made plans for future support.

## CASE EXAMPLE: FAMILY TWO

**Medical situation.** Ms. B., a 28-year-old midlevel business executive, had been diagnosed with Hodgkins Disease (lymphoma) at age 22 (see Table 1). This is a relatively uncommon cancer of the lymphatic system representing 1% of all cancers, with about 7,400 new cases in the United States each year (Yarbro, 1990). However, the first "peak" in its incidence comes in the second and third decades of life, exactly when Ms. B. was diagnosed. It is, therefore, a not-infrequent cancer of young adulthood.

Ms. B., by the time she was seen by me, had been ill for 6 years, mostly without a significant remission or disease-free interval. She had initially been treated with radiation, but the disease recurred. She then was treated with the usual four-drug chemotherapy protocol for later-stage Hodgkins Disease. This too proved ineffective, and the disease recurred. She then was treated with a different, more toxic four-drug regimen of chemotherapy. The disease recurred, and only one viable intervention was left, a bone marrow transplant (BMT). Ms. B. was not always cooperative with treatment, had changed oncologists several times in the 6 years, and had done off conventional treatments altogether for periods up to a year to try unproven and unconventional treatments. It is fair to say, however, that conventional treatments up to that time had not cured her or even given her a significant remission. She had experienced much toxicity, hair loss, and debility with conventional treatment. She had been ambivalent about many of her treatments and approached BMT with severe ambivalence. The medical oncologist in charge of BMT wanted both an intensive psychological evaluation and a plan for psychological management before BMT was to be considered.

Ms. B. was to have an allogenic BMT where she would need a bone marrow donor with a properly matching human leukocyte antigen (HLA). The best match is an HLA-identical sibling. There is about a

*25% chance for every patient to be HLA-matched with a sibling (Hansen, Clift & Thomas, 1979). Ms. B.'s two siblings were matched, and her older brother, age 32, turned out to be a perfect (6-point) match.*

*The medical steps for BMT in extremely abbreviated form for Ms. B. involved identification and matching of the HLA compatible marrow donor; admission to the hospital for an expected stay of at least 40 days; administration of ultrahigh-dose chemotherapy and irradiation to eradicate the malignant cells in the bone marrow and peripheral blood system; transplantation of the donor sibling's marrow, after its "harvest" from the donor-sibling; engraftment, with the management of acute complications such as infections, graft versus host disease, fevers, delirium, and pain; and discharge to outpatient care once the white blood cell count rises to a level sufficient to permit survival outside the protective hospital environment (Buchsel, 1990).*

**Composition of family unit.** *The B. family had five members. Ms. B. had two married parents who lived in the next county, 70 miles from the University of California, Los Angeles (UCLA) Medical Center. She had two siblings, a married younger sister, age 26, who had children and lived in Northern California. She was an infrequent visitor during the BMT. Her brother, age 32, was an unmarried graduate student in biological science who took a leave of absence during the BMT. He and the mother were relatively continually present, whereas the younger sister and father were relatively absent, during the BMT process.*

**Impacts of the illness on family functioning.** *Ms. B. was referred for BMT by her outside oncologist and clearly labeled as a high-risk patient in terms of compliance and psychological integration. It quickly became clear that she was viewed as an eccentric and unstable "identified patient" by her family also. Ms. B. had been essentially individuated from her family for several years and reported the family to be a "dysfunctional, abusive place" in childhood. Her illness had a semicohesive effect on at least part of the family with the brother and mother becoming closely involved. The brother's views of the early family history, predictably and interestingly, were very different from Ms. B.'s. He viewed her as the stimulus for much disruption and conflict, perhaps more so than the parents.*

*The brother, by dint of his crucial, life-saving role as the histocompatible HLA-matched donor, was drawn into a biopsychological symbiosis with his sister. He was wary of her and served careful warning to the health-care team of doctors, nurses, and mental health professionals to also be careful with her and to be careful of her. He was willing to take a leave of absence from school to be extremely involved with his sister's BMT but lacked a true ability to choose whether he would or would not be involved. His withholding of his HLA-matched bone marrow would condemn her to a certain death. At one level he had a choice, and at another he did not.[1]*

*The mother, as with so many parents of young adults who are ill, was faced with a dilemma. How could she be with her young daughter in such a way that she could be functionally involved and yet not intrude or threaten her daughter's need to be separate and an adult in her own right? She was*

---

[1] In the early era of kidney transplantation, when sibling-to-sibling donorship was common, the stresses and ethical complexities of this were so intense that psychiatric opinion was to stop such donations and move to cadaveric (nonrelated kidney from deceased persons) donations. This, in fact, was done (Cramond, 1968). The BMT arena cannot permit such a shift, given the HLA compatibility issue that comes mainly from siblings. Thus, historical issues of sibling relatedness, sibling rivalry, and the black sheep–white sheep role of siblings in families all become potentially revived and enlivened in the BMT situation (Futterman & Wellisch, 1990).

profoundly stressed by the seriousness of the illness and knew, as did the rest of the family, that if BMT was not successful, death would be the certain outcome.

**Interventions.** I took two basic positions with planning for Ms. B.'s BMT. First, I chose to hear the referring oncologist and also her brother but to not participate in labeling Ms. B. as the identified patient or deviant in her family of origin system. Second, I saw the BMT as the ultimate crisis that might disrupt the B. family's homeostasis enough to reprogram their interactions and create a new, possibly different relatedness post-BMT. I felt that BMT is such a biologically and psychologically regressive experience that fundamental change could occur.

The interventions had two foci. First was to work with the BMT staff to increase the likelihood that their relationship with Ms. B. remained intact and functional during the long hospitalization. Second was to functionally involve the mother and brother in her care and support. With the staff this involved consistency of people and routines—the same staff doing the same things as much as possible. Ms. B. seemed to need this and requested this more than anything in pre-BMT consultations.

I and the rest of the BMT team agreed to help Ms. B. keep her level of anxiety down to a minimum during the BMT. She took a high and steady level of antianxiety medication (Ativan), and a member of our psychiatric consultation–liaison service saw her daily, 7 days per week, throughout the transplant process. The best sign of success with the staff was that they never saw her as anything but a "regular patient."

The mother and brother received a great deal of attention. They attended the weekly family support group on the BMT unit and were seen twice weekly separately for family supportive therapy. They were carefully integrated into Ms. B.'s care plan after negotiations between them, our consultation–

liaison service, and the staff. The mother–daughter interaction was closely monitored, with the mother being open and receptive to feedback about her anxiety and tendency to be controlling and intrusive. She was loving and supportive with her daughter. It was the most successful series of interactions they had ever had together. The key was how much the mother wanted things to work and tried to see herself in the interactional process as it unfolded. Here was an example of a family rising to the challenges of the BMT situation to relate more supportively and functionally than ever before.

The brother–sister interactions were as successful, if not more so, than the mother–daughter ones. The brother found, not renewed, a fundamental respect for his sister's tolerance of the rigors of BMT. She was so uncomfortable and afraid at times that there were tears in her eyes, but she never complained or acted out in the ways he predicted. They too became a loving, functional unit. He stayed beyond marrow donation to give other essential blood products, especially platelets that guard against bleeding. His were most able to be biologically absorbed by her, but others could donate. Ms. B. survived her BMT.

The relapse rate of patients with her profile is about 60%, and the 5-year survival rate is not clearly known but not likely to be above 30% (Buchsel, 1990). She and her brother attend the post-BMT support group at UCLA. In the first few months after her discharge, she returned to her parents' home, and then she returned to her own apartment. Her prognosis is guarded, but her self-esteem and relationship with her family of origin is more robust than previously in her life.

CASE EXAMPLE: FAMILY THREE
**Medical situation.** One day, Mr. A., a 46-year-old computer scientist, lost his visual depth perception on the tennis court (see Table 1). He then in rapid succession

had an episode of expressive aphasia where he had trouble verbalizing his thoughts and had two partial complex seizures. A neurological work up was done, including a CT scan, with inconclusive results. The neurologist suspected a small stroke in the temporal occipital region of his brain. The couple wished for no more tests at that time, although more could have been performed. He got better. He and his wife celebrated and tried to put it behind them, as did their 14-year-old son.

At a party 4 months later, he developed peripheral vision problems that led to double vision. Again, the neurologist was puzzled. An MRI was performed. This time, a highly significant and disturbing result was found. Mr. A. was diagnosed with a brain tumor, glioblastoma multiforme. This had invaded his frontal lobes, but cells had migrated to other areas of his brain, which accounted for his visual, speech, and perceptual–motor problems. Glioblastoma multiforme has four stages, with prognosis becoming graver with each higher stage. Mr. A. was stage 4, with a terminal prognosis. The 1-year survival rates for this stage range from a low of 5% to a high of 40% from several studies (Batzdorf & Selch, 1985). The 2-year survival rate ranges from 0% to a high of 18% (Batzdorf & Selch, 1985). Mr. A. was offered the possibility of surgery followed by radiation to his entire brain, but no assurances were made that either procedure would prolong his life, and solid assurances were made that both would create severe side effects and negative sequelae.

Mr. and Mrs. A. consulted the premiere expert on this tumor, also located in Los Angeles, who was using a new technique called stereotactic radiosurgery with a gamma knife. This is a technique that crossfires an intracranial target (tumor-mass site) with multiple beams of ionizing radiation (Lunsford & Flickinger, 1989). This center is one of the few in the United States where this is done. Unfortunately, the consultant felt that the tumor mass was too large for this to be effective; there was the likelihood that the negative effects would outweigh the possible positive effects.

The couple returned to their internist, a person they felt particularly close to, for more consultation. He advised two things. One was for Mr. A. to have full brain irradiation because to do nothing seemed impossible for Mr. A. to bear. Given the attachment and anxiety the internist felt for the couple, it is possible he also could not bear doing nothing. Second was for the family to begin family counseling after the radiation was under way. They agreed to both procedures. Mr. A. underwent a course of radiation therapy to his total brain that lasted 8 weeks. He went 5 days per week for a total of 40 treatments. He and his wife were carefully warned that this procedure had many side effects including total and permanent hair loss; chronic cerebral edema (swelling of the brain), which required a steroid medication (Decadron) in high doses to counter; necrosis of good brain tissue along with malignant cells, which would create unknown and unpredictable problems; possible seizures; and certain weakness. Several of these are also created by the disease itself (Wegmann & Hakius, 1990). The family presented for therapy in the 5th week of the radiation-treatment course.

**Composition of the family unit.** The family was composed of Mr. A., a computer scientist, his wife, Mrs. A., a business executive, and their 14-year-old son. This was a second marriage for Mr. A. and a first for Mrs. A. They had been happily married for 16 years. Both spouses had parents and siblings, but none of them lived in Los Angeles. Mrs. A. had an elderly aunt who did live locally.

**Impacts of the illness on the family unit.** By the time the family presented for therapy, the impacts of the illness on the family were multiple and enormous. Mr. A. was unable to work because of exhaustion, inability to concentrate, and vulnerability to seizures that were difficult to control. Mrs. A. was essentially spending full time at home caring for Mr. A. but still trying to "keep her foot in the door" at work. Their son, Zack, was into a new school year (grade 9), but not with "both feet on the ground," in his mother's words. He was never a model student but now was increasingly angry, sullen, unable to concentrate, and interestingly, developing headaches that kept him home from school at times.

Mr. A. had been trying to write a computer manual that now became his full-time focus. He was constantly hungry and gained almost 30 pounds in the first few weeks of the treatment. Mr. A. had taken to listening to one song, "It's a Wonderful World" by Louis Armstrong, in an obsessional manner. Mrs. A. related that if left to his own devices he would play and replay it literally all day long, perhaps 100 times in a row. Several of these issues framed the interventions that we deemed essential to our work in family sessions.

**Interventions.** Five key issues became foci for the family counseling sessions. These sessions lasted almost exactly a year up to Mr. A's death and then continued for 4 months after his death with Mrs. A and her son together. The five key issues were: family grief, which was powerfully present but largely unexpressed in the family interactions; the son's school problems, which seemed to be a sector where he could express and act out feelings that were not possible to express at home; the son's developmentally appropriate needs to separate and individuate in the face of pulls to have him spend more time at home with his parents; the son's, and later the wife's somatic expressions of stress, and; the confusion in the family around the continuity of

usual family rules, especially with regard to Mr. A.

Family grief was the most constant factor in the family experience. A serious complicating factor was the fact that Mr. A. had become labile and childlike in his personality style, almost certainly reflective of an organic personality disorder. The combination of his tumor, the radiation, and the high-dose steroid (Decadron) created this effect. In addition, his affect was significantly flattened at times so that his responses were often not congruent to what was being discussed. In a sense, the adult Mr. A. was already gone. Thus, grief work directly with him was not particularly productive.

Mrs. A. and Zack seemed to need permission, support, and modeling from me in the beginning to express grief. Zack had two responses to any expression of these feelings early in therapy. One was to try to "protect" his mother by angry denials that she was facing the terminality of Mr. A. and would become a widow. A poignant example was her description of getting dressed to attend a party alone and her dread of this. I heard her saying in a subtle fashion, "I already feel like a widow," and "this is a trial run of what it will be like when my husband dies and I am really alone." Zack, furious at my articulation of these unstated feelings, said angrily, "Don't you dare take our hope away!" We then, and many times thereafter, discussed why we were doing the therapy, how pregrieving the loss might help the postdeath grief process, and how we differed on our definition of hope. He and I discovered we had different goals. He hoped his father would not die; I hoped our work and that of the other doctors might make Mr. A.'s dying process easier and less painful for all concerned.

Zack also felt greatly shamed and threatened in the early visits when his tears began to flow. I shared with him the fact *that both of my parents died of cancer and that I too had often wept. I also shared that, although I still miss them at times, it does not hurt anymore that they died. This seemed to help him along with the safe containment of his feelings in our sessions. At first he struggled with staying in the room when he felt or actually was tearful; gradually, he was able to stay seated throughout. Neither I nor Mrs. A. ever attempted to bring him back in the room when he felt the need to flee in the earlier sessions.*

*With great difficulty, Zack was slowly able to engage with his father in sessions and home. His father was too ill and debilitated to attend the majority of sessions, but Zack was able to tell him in a session how sad he felt that he was ill and gave him neck rubs from time to time at home. I felt strongly that his bouts of rage and irritation at me in the sessions represented, in part, a transference-based displacement of his rage at his father for getting sick. This notion was slowly and carefully presented to Zack. He was horrified at the thought of being angry at his ill and severely weakened father. However, in this period his headaches began to improve, which I will discuss later.*

*Mrs. A. also had trouble, as most devoted spouses do, accepting the inevitably ambivalent feelings toward an ill partner. The sense of feeling angry, trapped, and resentful provokes so much guilt that these feelings are then deeply submerged (Vachon et al., 1977). A predictable pattern is that these feelings are neutralized by an overdevoted, almost obsessional attention to the needs of the ill family member. If this continues unabated, the family will promote infantalization, regression, and overdependence in the ill member. The end result is an overwhelming sense of burden on the family and early "burnout" in their ability to care for the ill member.*

*Zack's school problems took the form of angry defiance and inability to concentrate on work. The defiance at school seemed fueled by two things. One was the unexpressed and submerged anger at his father for being ill, and the other was the sense that it was necessary to be "perfect" at home. As discussed, we dealt in an increasingly direct fashion with the legitimacy of anger in combination with grief and sadness toward his father. We also began to deal with the need to be "perfect" at home. Zack worried that any slip would upset his father with catastrophic consequences and that additional upset for his mother was also unbearable. We tried to normalize the interactions and reduce everyone's sense of "walking on eggshells," as Zack expressed it. The bottom line was if anger, frustration, or affection was felt, family members were supported in expressing such a feeling.*

*Zack was less angry and defiant at school, but concentration problems continued episodically throughout his father's illness. In a previous study almost half the spouses of breast cancer patients were noted to have episodic concentration difficulties at work, so Zack's pattern was to be expected (Wellisch, Jamison & Pasnau, 1978). Mrs. A. met with his teachers and counselor at school and kept them periodically informed of Mr. A.'s deteriorating condition. (See also chap. 27 in this volume.)*

*A frequent problem in families where a parent has cancer and adolescents are involved is a pull toward reversal of the normal adolescent separation and individuation developmental pattern (Wellisch, 1979). This was present in the A. family. Mrs. A., without meaning to, found herself confiding in, leaning on, and restricting Zack. She preferred that he stay home on Saturday nights "just in case something happened." This was a subtle but persistent pattern that Zack complied with but, I felt, acted out against at school. This acting out* forced Mrs. A. to be his mother rather than his pseudospouse. It also served to remind her that he was still a relatively immature adolescent and not a seemingly mature young adult. We took several steps to deal with this crucial issue. First was to face the issue of Zack's need to continue the normal process of separation and individuation. To thwart this process was to invite increased symptomatology and acting out (Wellisch, 1979). This meant facilitating his needs to see friends on weekends.

Second was to network Mrs. A. into a supportive matrix. This took the form of hiring a helper–companion for Mr. A. Mrs. A. also felt able to confide in and talk to this woman, and she felt freer to go out if she wished. She also sought out a support group of spouses in her situation that had a "buddy system." Instead of confiding in Zack, she called up her buddy for support. She also used the therapy as a focused place for adult-to-adult support. Zack's life returned to a semblance of normality. Mrs. A. built a matrix of support that would endure well into the period of mourning beyond Mr. A.'s death.

Zack's headaches were an ominous sign. When a child or adolescent develops somatic symptoms that mimic the parent's problems, this becomes a psychosomatically lethal form of empathy, identification, and grief expression. This has the potential to become a way of life if left untouched as the adolescent grows into an adult with unresolved mourning and "somatopsychic" symptoms that are very resistant to change in later adult life (Engle, 1975). When the headaches became manifest, my goal as the family therapist was to facilitate in Zack the channels of grief to flow emotionally rather than somatically. The challenge here was to encourage grief expression in such a way that Zack did not feel the intense vulnerability and shame so characteristic of boys in this developmental phase. I felt that strategic self-revelation about my own par-

ents' deaths and my own grief was an important avenue toward this goal. With this "joining," we could be two men who could both tolerate and experience grief emotionally (Minuchin, Rosman, & Baker, 1978).

Mrs. A. presented serious problems of her own in this same regard. She tended to be stoic in her emotional stance. She related her sisters as having had histories of spinal disc disease and surgeries, but she commented she had none of her own yet. One day after a couples' session, I watched Mrs. A. guide Mr. A. down the hall. It was akin to the image of a tugboat with an ocean liner, this scene of a huge and overweight man and tiny, birdlike woman. I had the fantasy that he would crush her, possibly emotionally but more directly physically. I promptly forgot this fantasy. Shortly after Mr. A.'s death a few months later, Mrs. A. developed intense back pain and then downgoing numbness in her legs. A full spinal–back work up was performed, and the results were chillingly reminiscent of my fantasy. Virtually all of her cervical-spinal discs had disintegrated, and she needed massive surgery to fuse as many discs as possible. The maximal number possible was three, and the surgery took place within 3 months of Mr. A.'s death. Two pounds of titanium were placed in her back to facilitate the spinal fusion. Therapy ended before her recovery from the surgery. She visited for a follow-up a year later with the metal from her back in a jar. It was possible to remove it when her spine fused. This serves as an ultimate reminder of the "weight" a spouse or partner bears and carries when a spouse or partner is chronically or terminally ill. It truly can be a crushing burden.

A final issue in our work was around the continuity of family rules during Mr. A.'s illness. His obsessional attachment to the recording "It's a Wonderful World" became an ideal place to deal with this issue. She was hesitant to confront him on this, even *though it drove her crazy. "How can I put limits on a dying man?" she asked. This led to many vigorous discussions of how different everything had become since Mr. A.'s illness. Our task, we came to agree, was how to keep things somewhat the same when everything was changing. Expecting Mr. A. to be aware of others' needs as he had always done, even though he was sick, fit into this goal. Mrs. A. was encouraged to keep up her family routines that included cooking dinner at night with the expectation that everyone, including Mr. A., would sit down together. Zack was expected to attend school faithfully and to work productively, even though he was severely preoccupied. This continuity of sameness in family interactional structure is a small but potent way of binding anxiety. Structure offers continuity that produces security. In families of cancer patients, changing the rules so that ill members get to abuse others, be irresponsible, stop parenting, be passive-dependent, or stop supporting their spouse is almost never helpful. For well members, changing the rules so they get to stop being productive in work or school, stop being sexual partners to their mates, stop treating ill mates like adults, or stop being able to fight or be joyous with their ill kids or spouses is also rarely, if ever, functional.*

## CONCLUSIONS

These cases raise several points that serve to sensitize the therapist. The family therapist can feel like a "stranger in a strange land" where cancer is a family concern. Family therapists can become so intimidated by the disease, the hospital setting, and the necessary interface with the medical team that they can minimize or forget their own potential contribution on the basis of their family therapy training. The family of the cancer patient can benefit immensely from the training and skills of the family therapist.

The family therapist must realize that cancer is really a set of diseases and not one disease. This be-

ing true, knowledge of the disease, its treatment, and the expected outcome is essential to anticipate proper planning and interventions for the family. These three cases reflect the wide variance between three different cancers for the families involved.

Communication remains the bedrock of effective family work in cancer. The natural tendency for families will be to "protect" members in a veil of silence, fear, and denial. The family therapist must model, not order, such communication.

Oncology staffs vary from setting to setting. All are pivotal to the care of families with cancer. They must be identified and drawn into alliances with the family therapist.

As this chapter has shown, family therapy can be a potent and crucial intervention when cancer is present. In the short term it can be the bridge that enables the family to traverse the many chasms and pitfalls of the disease. In the long term it can lead to more intimate family relatedness after the cancer, regardless of the outcome of the disease.

## References

American Cancer Society. (1991). *1991 Cancer facts and figures*. Atlanta: Author.

Bank, S. P., & Kahn, M. D. (1982). Siblings as survivors: Bond beyond the grave. In S. P. Bank & M. D. Kahn (Eds.), *The sibling bond* (pp. 271–295). New York: Basic Books.

Batzdorf, U., & Selch, M. T. (1985). Brain tumors. In C. Haskell (Ed.), *Cancer treatment* (2nd ed., pp. 653–687). Philadelphia: W. B. Saunders.

Bluebond-Langner, M. (1978). *The private world of dying children*. Princeton, NJ: Princeton University Press.

Buchsel, P. C. (1990). Bone marrow transplantation. In S. Groenwald, M. H. Frogge, M. Goodman, & C. H. Yarbro (Eds.), *Cancer nursing* (2nd ed., pp. 307–337). Boston: Jones & Bartlett.

Cassileth, B. R. (Ed.). (1979). *The cancer patient: Social and medical aspects of care*. Philadelphia: Lea & Fibiger.

Cancer Care, Inc., & National Cancer Foundation. (1977). *Listen to the children: A study of the impact on the mental health of children of a parent's catastrophic illness*. New York: Author.

Chesler, M. A., & Barbarin, O. A. (1984). Relating to the medical staff: How parents of children with cancer see the issues. *Health Social Work, 9*, 49–65.

Cochinov, H., & Holland, J. C. (1989). Bereavement: A special issue in oncology. In J. Rowland & J. C. Holland (Eds.), *Handbook of psychooncology* (pp. 612–627). New York: Oxford University Press.

Cramond, W. A. (1968). Medical, moral and legal aspects of organ transplantation and long-term resuscitative measures: Psychological, social and community aspects. *Medical Journal of Australia, 2,* 622–625.

DeKernion, J. B. (1985). Cancer of the prostate. In C. Haskell (Ed.), *Cancer treatment* (2nd ed., pp. 352–365). Philadelphia: W. B. Saunders.

Derdarian, A. (1986). Informational needs of recently diagnosed cancer patients. *Nursing Research, 35,* 276–281.

Engle, G. L. (1975). Psychological aspects of gastrointestinal disorders. In S. Arieti (Ed.), *American handbook of psychiatry Vol. IV Organic disorders and psychosomatic medicine* (pp. 653–692). New York: Basic Books.

Fawzy, F. I., Cousins, N., Fawzy, N. W., Kemeny, M. E., Glashoff, R., & Morton, D. (1990). A structured intervention for cancer patients: I. Changes over time in methods of coping and affective disturbance. *Archives of General Psychiatry, 47,* 720–725.

Futterman, A. D., & Wellisch, D. K. (1990). Psychodynamic themes of bone marrow transplantation: When I becomes thou. *Hematology/Oncology Clinics of North America, 4*(3), 699–710.

Hanks, G. E. (1988). Radical prostatectomy or radiation therapy for early prostate cancer. *Cancer, 61,* 2153–2160.

Hansen, J. A., Clift, R. A., Thomas, E. D., Buckner, C. D., Mickelson, E. M., & Storb, R. (1979). Histocompatibility and marrow transplantation. *Transplantation Proceedings, 11,* 1924–1929.

Hinds, C. (1985). The needs of families who care for patients with cancer at home: Are we meeting them? *Journal of Advances in Nursing, 10,* 575–581.

Imber-Coopersmith, E. (1985). Families and multiple helpers. In D. Campbell & R. Draper (Eds.), *Applications of Systemic Family Therapy: The Milan Approach* (pp. 203–212). London: Grune & Stratton.

Koocher, G. P. (1986). Psychosocial issues during the acute treatment of pediatric cancer. *Cancer, 58,* 568–572.

Koocher, G. P., & O'Malley, J. (1981). *The Damocles Syndrome: Psychological consequences of surviving childhood cancer.* New York: McGraw-Hill.

Lansky, S. B., Cairns, N. U., Hassanein, R., Wehr, J., & Lowman, J. T. (1978). Childhood cancer: Parental discord and divorce. *Pediatrics, 62*(2), 184–188.

Lind, J. M., & Nakao, S. L. (1990). Urologic and male genital cancers. In S. Groenwald, M. H. Frogge, M. Goodman, & C. H. Yarbro (Eds.), *Cancer nursing* (2nd ed., pp. 1026–1073). Boston: Jones & Bartlett.

Lue, T. F. (1991). Impotence after radical pelvic surgery: Physiology and management. *Urology International, 46,* 259–265.

Lunsford, L. D., & Flickinger, J. C. (1989). Stereotactic radiosurgery using the gamma knife: An alternative to microsurgical removal. *Proceedings of the 30th Annual Meeting of the American Society of Radiation Oncologists,* Abstract 78, 156.

Minuchin, S., Rosman, B. L., & Baker, R. L. (1978). *Psychosomatic families.* Cambridge, MA: Harvard University Press.

Nir, Y., Pynoos, R., & Holland, J. C. (1981). Cancer in a parent: The impact on mother and child. *General Hospital Psychiatry, 3,* 331–342.

Rait, D., & Lederberg, M. (1989). The family of the cancer patient. In J. Rowland & J. C. Holland (Eds.), *Handbook of psychooncology* (pp. 585–597). New York: Oxford University Press.

Rosenheim, E., & Reicher, R. (1985). Informing children about a parent's terminal illness. *Journal of Child Psychology and Psychiatry, 26,* 995–998.

Ross, R. K., Paganini-Hill, A., & Henderson, B. (1988). Epidemiology of prostatic cancer. In D. Skinner & G. Lieskousky (Eds.), *Diagnosis and management of genitourinary cancer* (pp. 40–45). Philadelphia: W. B. Saunders.

Sabo, D., Brown, J., & Smith, C. (1986). The male role and mastectomy: Support groups and men's adjustment. *Journal of Psychosocial Oncology, 4*(1/2), 19–31.

Sourkes, B. (1980). Siblings of the pediatric cancer patient. In J. Kellerman (Ed.), *Psychological aspects of childhood cancer* (pp. 47–69). Springfield, IL: Charles C Thomas.

Steiner, M. S., Morton, R. A., & Walsh, P. C. (1991). Impact of anatomical radical prostatectomy on urinary continence. *Journal of Urology, 145,* 512–515.

Vachon, M. L., Freedman, K., Formo, A., Rogers, J., Lyall, W., & Freeman, S. (1977). The final illness in cancer: The widow's perspective. *Canadian Medical Association Journal, 117,* 1151–1153.

Wegmann, J., & Hakius, P. (1990). Central nervous system cancers. In S. Groenwald, M. H. Frogge, M. Goodman, & C. H. Yarbro (Eds.), *Cancer nursing* (2nd ed., 751–773). Boston: Jones & Bartlett.

Wellisch, D. K. (1979). Adolescent acting-out when a parent has cancer. *International Journal of Family Therapy, 1,* 230–241.

Wellisch, D. K. (1981). On stabilizing families with an unstable illness: Helping disturbed families cope with cancer. In M. Lansky (Ed.), *Family therapy and major psychopathology* (pp. 281–300). New York: Grune and Stratton.

Wellisch, D. K., Jamison, K. R., & Pasnau, R. O. (1978). Psychosocial aspects of mastectomy: II. The man's perspective. *American Journal of Psychiatry, 135*(5), 543–551.

Yarbro, C. H. (1990). Lymphomas. In S. Groenwald, M. H. Frogge, M. Goodman, & C. H. Yarbro (Eds.), *Cancer nursing* (2nd ed., pp. 975–989). Boston: Jones & Bartlett.

CHAPTER 23

# A CUSTOMIZED APPROACH TO THE TREATMENT OF ANOREXIA AND BULIMIA

*William N. Friedrich*

I look for similarities among families, but sometimes the outliers teach me the most. Consider the Smiths, a family of four:

*CASE EXAMPLE: THE SMITHS*
    *The father had had three heart attacks by the age of 40 and was still working at a demanding job. The mother, moderately overweight, was a sales representative and out of the home 3 to 4 days a week. The older daughter, Julie, was 17, overweight, an underachiever in school, and, as we discovered later, a binge drinker. Jackie was 13, severely underweight for the past year, an average student, and had been sporadically attending individual counseling for the previous 6 months. They came to my attention after Jackie fainted in the school hallway and was hospitalized with a diagnosis of anorexia nervosa.*
    *During my first interview with the Smiths, I found none of the supposed cardinal features of anorectic families (Minuchin, Rosman, & Baker, 1978). The parents were not overprotective; they had no rules or curfews and often did not know where either girl was in the evening. Julie had started to date at 13. The parents did not enmesh their daughters; neither girl was in a parental role or a confidant to either parent. They exhibited no triangulation; both parents denied relaying messages to the other through either daughter or allying*

*with one child against the other. There was no lack of conflict resolution; the parents were in open conflict, as opposed to the more common "hidden conflict" in anorectic families, but there was no resolution. There was also no rigidity; this was a family with no rules. In fact, both parents seemed overtly rejecting of the parental role, and both girls had learned to fend for themselves. Halfway through the first session, I caught myself looking again at Jackie to see if she was truly anorectic. She certainly appeared to be.*
    *What did emerge in the course of 37 sessions, over a 14-month period, were two compelling issues. The first was the unspoken fear of Mr. Smith's sudden death. Each parent had lost one or both parents prior to age 18; the discomfort when this came up reflected an unresolved loss. The second issue was the role of food in the family. Despite being on constant diets, Mrs. Smith and Julie openly binged during times of conflict. Jackie described a scene in an early session where her mother was yelling at her, in between bites of cake, and how she needed to eat more. Mr. Smith made several comments in early sessions about the "skinny girl I married," which resulted each time in Mrs. Smith looking hurt. Rather than a compelling argument for psychosomatic features, the Smiths' issues*

*related to unresolved loss as well as ambivalence regarding food and weight.*

*Rather than schedule a family lunch session for our second or third session, a usual practice for me at that time in my clinical practice, I gave in to my own curiosity about what drove this father to work himself to death. I found myself becoming quite anxious around him, and I noticed that he took his pulse two to three times that first session. I started asking him questions about his parents' deaths, whether there was a genetic predisposition, and whether he was doomed to the same fate. The other family members became much more anxious when I raised these questions, with Jackie swinging her legs, Julie looking away, and Mrs. Smith digging in her purse. I asked each member what they felt about his working, whether they worried about him dying, and whether they noticed him checking his pulse.*

*More typically, anorectic families usually greeted my blunt questions with smiles and deflections. Not the Smiths. They seemed to enjoy telling on each other. Mrs. Smith and her daughters were angry at Mr. Smith because he had no life insurance. Mr. Smith and his daughters were angry at Mrs. Smith for being a slob at home and for being on the road so much. Mrs. Smith responded to the latter accusation by asking me, "If you had to look at him every day, and worry about him dying, would you want to be around?" At that point, she began to cry, and every family member turned away from one another. Even though she could state her fear so directly, their lack of connection made resolution of the fear impossible.*

This case illustrates several points that are critical to this chapter. These include that structural family theory about anorectic families may be insufficient, eating-disordered families are heterogenous and most likely cluster into several different groups, and there

likely is no one approach to family-based therapy with eating-disordered families.

## FOCUS OF THE CHAPTER

After the first few anorectic families I saw, I envisioned that my future practice with eating-disordered families would consist of numerous family lunch sessions with 14- to 18-year-old overachieving, smiling, impenetrable anorectics and their families. That has not been the case, and I have had to broaden the scope of my thinking from a focus on the external structure of the family to a consideration of sociocultural influences on women (an absolute must for male family therapists) and even to a consideration of the individual within her larger interpersonal world.

For family theorists, the initial focus on the external features of the family, such as enmeshment and difficulty with conflict resolution, was in apparent reaction to the intrapsychic focus of earlier theories about anorexia nervosa. As the literature on eating disorders has evolved, a greater appreciation of cultural expectations regarding body image and appearances has also developed (Root, Fallon, & Friedrich, 1986). Included in this sociocultural perspective is the feminist perspective on the conflicting expectations of women in our culture, which is an important additional perspective with particular relevance to the etiology and continuation of eating disorders. As Luepnitz (1988) has said, "men do not define themselves in terms of their appearance nearly so much as women do" (p. 224).

As family therapy has evolved, a reconsideration of the individual has also occurred. Nonfamily therapists tend to use traditional psychodynamic or cognitive–behavioral approaches with eating disorders. For family therapists, however, the approach is more likely to be either an appreciation of the internal family system (Schwartz, 1987) or actually working directly with the individual to make changes in their family (Selvini-Palazzoli & Viaro, 1988).

Three perspectives will be examined in this chapter, including the sociocultural perspective, the family systems perspective, and finally, the internal family systems level. In addition, relevant family therapy outcome research will be reviewed for both anorexia nervosa and bulimia nervosa.

## DEFINITIONS

Anorexia nervosa is characterized by the refusal to maintain body weight over a minimal normal weight for age and height; intense fear of gaining weight or becoming fat even though underweight; a distorted body image; and, in women, amenorrhea (*Diagnostic and Statistical Manual of Mental Disorders*—4th ed., *DSM–IV*, American Psychiatric Association, 1994). Changes in the diagnostic criteria for anorexia nervosa from the *Diagnostic and Statistical Manual of Mental Disorders* (*DSM–III–R*; 3rd ed., rev., American Psychiatric Association, 1987) to *DSM–IV* are the inclusion of bulimic and nonbulimic subtypes of anorexia nervosa.

The 1980s will probably be known in the history of eating disorders for the recognition of the "new" syndrome of bulimia (Vanderlinden & Vandereycken, 1987). Bulimia nervosa is a syndrome characterized by recurrent episodes of binge eating, a feeling of lack of control over eating behavior during the eating binges; self-induced vomiting; use of laxatives or diuretics; strict dieting, fasting, or vigorous exercise to prevent weight gain; and persistent overconcern with body shape and weight (American Psychiatric Association, 1994). *DSM–IV* (American Psychiatric Association, 1994) includes several changes from *DSM–III–R* (American Psychiatric Association, 1987), and discusses purging and nonpurging (fasting and vigorous exercise) subtypes. In addition, the Eating Disorders Working Group is considering a new diagnostic category, Binge Eating Disorder, which describes individuals not meeting the complete criteria for bulimia nervosa (Wilson & Walsh, 1991).

## SOCIOCULTURAL PERSPECTIVE

Families are ecosystems within a larger ecological level pertaining to the institutionalized attitudinal patterns of the culture and subculture (Bronfenbrenner, 1979). For example, Western culture has evolved to a thinner body ideal (Garner, Garfinkel, Schwartz, & Thompson, 1980). This evolution is associated with increasing pressures on women to diet.

It is now widely recognized that sociocultural factors play an important role in the increasing prevalence of eating disorders in contemporary Western society.

Gordon (1990) has conceptualized eating disorders as "culture-bound syndromes." For a given disorder to qualify as a syndrome, its characteristics include the disorder's prevalence in the culture, the continuity of the disorder's symptoms with normal behaviors and attitudes that are typically highly valued in the culture, and its function as an acceptable vehicle for the individual to be deviant. Gordon argues that anorexia nervosa and bulimia nervosa both express core cultural conflicts that are pervasive for women.

Sterner-Adair (1986) points out that, in the same way that hysterical behavior in 19th-century women was related to that era's cultural imperative, certain 20th-century sociocultural influences make eating disorders an adaptive response to the demands of growing up a woman. The author describes a "developmental double-bind" (p. 99) in which the adolescent woman is unable to value characteristics of herself, like her focus on relationships, that society is now teaching her to devalue.

To be clinically relevant, the concept of a culture-bound syndrome should also provide a mechanism whereby sociocultural factors transmit eating-disordered symptoms (Gordon, 1990). These transmission mechanisms include modeling by prestigious and socially influential individuals or peers who are reinforced for symptomatic behavior, the glamorization of thin body ideals, and the actual modeling of eating-disordered symptomatology (e.g., diets that promote severe caloric restriction).

Culture-bound syndromes may symbolize the attempts of individuals who are considered inferior to protest against or escape oppression. For example, contemporary women with eating disorders may be struggling for power and control within the sociocultural milieu in which they feel inferior. Not surprisingly, issues of power and control are frequently mentioned in the clinical discussion of eating-disordered individuals.

Women with anorexia nervosa may initially evoke admiration because of their emulation of slenderness, control, and competition. However, because they have refused to cooperate with normative social expectations (i.e., by being thin but not too thin), they eventually evoke negative reactions. Gordon (1990) concludes that, until body shape is no longer an indication of women's worth, eating-disorder symptoms will persist.

Feminists have added to the sociocultural perspective on eating disorders. They suggest that the patriarchal nature of Western culture is reflected in the majority of therapy approaches designed to be used with families. This shows up as focusing on the symptom, blaming the mother, and eschewing the importance of relationships. In fact, a key principle of a feminist approach to therapy is to understand the social genesis for problems that occur very frequently among women, such as eating disorders (Luepnitz, 1988). Feminist therapy reflects an attitude or perspective and not a collection of techniques (Goodrich, Rampage, Ellman, & Halstead, 1988).

The sociocultural perspective is also related to one of several typologies that have been developed for the families of bulimia nervosa patients (Schwartz, Barrett, & Saba, 1984). These authors describe three types of families with a daughter with bulimia nervosa. The type depends on the degree to which the family holds a strong ethnic identity or is "Americanized." The three types of families are all-American, ethnic, and mixed. One of the features of the all-American family is an extreme emphasis on appearing stylishly attractive and inordinately successful at all times and at any cost. The ethnic family, alternatively, provides extreme pressure on the young woman to maintain traditional ethnic roles, with all of her behavior being a reflection on the family. Finally, the mixed family emerges when each parent advocates a different set of values, American versus ethnic, which results in a situation in which profound sociocultural roles and expectations, which conflict with each other, are expected to be successfully played out by the young woman.

Two seemingly different eating-disordered families whom I have treated capture the struggle that families have when transitioning between cultures. The first is a more overt example, a Southeast Asian girl with anorexia. Her family had been in the United States less than 10 years but was struggling with how strictly to adhere to their cultural mores, which emphasized loyalty and parental authority. An older brother was Americanized and a disappointment to the family. The youngest daughter was overtly more loyal to the family but had spoken to the school counselor about her strict parents. Her anorexia brought the family to the attention of Western medicine, and in this way she obtained an audience for her distress that opened up her family.

The second family was Caucasian. The father was the only successful professional in his family, and his wife was the only college graduate in her family of origin. Obesity represented the previous generation's illiteracy and poverty to both parents, and they therefore both idealized thinness. Their only daughter developed early-onset anorexia.

In summary, family theories and therapy approaches that do not appreciate such issues as sociocultural pressures for thinness, or role pressures in families transitioning from one culture to the next, will be insufficient. In addition, the therapist needs to be sensitive to how traditional cultural perspectives about the role of father and mother quite likely contribute to the etiology of culture-bound syndromes such as eating disorders.

## FAMILY SYSTEMS AND ANOREXIA NERVOSA

Early family systems theorizing reflected a remarkable consensus regarding the families of patients with anorexia nervosa. Bruch (1973) commented on how self-expression and antonomy were discouraged, and Selvini-Palazzoli (1978) described such features as covert coalitions between parent and child, the sacrifice of autonomy in favor of a cohesive family, permeability of generational boundaries, and the denial of overt conflict. These sound very much like the features described by Minuchin et al. (1978): enmeshment, overprotectiveness, rigidity, lack of conflict resolution, and involvement of the child in parental conflict.

Do these features describe family characteristics that contribute to the eating disorder, or are they features of a family that has organized around and is reacting to the eating disorder? Only a few data-based studies have examined the specific features named above in anorexic families.

Empirical research has not confirmed the universality of Minuchin's structural family features. An early study with ten families of anorectics by Kog and her colleagues (Kog, Vandereycken, & Vertommen, 1985) found that "the variability of these families is striking" (p. 536).

A larger study that uses both observation and questionnaires examined the families of 55 eating-disordered patients, the majority meeting the criteria for anorexia nervosa (Kog, Vertommen, & Vandereycken, 1987). Several types of families were identified, some similar to Minuchin's model, but others showing less extreme and even opposite kinds of interaction. Families most similar to those on which Minuchin built his model (e.g., young, restrictive anorectic patients) varied over several family types. Empirical evidence existed for the concepts of boundaries, adaptability, and conflict but not for overprotectiveness.

Studying a sample of 55 families with children suffering from a number of psychosomatic disorders, including eating disorders, Stierlin and his colleagues found that only about half fit Minuchin's model (Stierlin & Weber, 1989). In addition, major similarities applied to both anorectic families and families with high blood pressure, bronchial asthma, migraine, and ulcerative colitis.

Stierlin and Weber (1989) suggested that the most important difference between anorectic families and other psychosomatic families was that "at the beginning of anorexia nervosa we find an act of will, the decision of a family member to reduce food intake, the decision not to eat" (p. 55). This decision creates a dramatic quality for the anorectic family, unlike the apathetic quality of the generic psychosomatic family. From their perspective, this dramatic quality allowed more room for therapeutic movement and change. This is a positive connotation about the anorectic family's "dramatic quality" and is reflective of the strategic therapy perspective of these researchers (Stierlin & Weber, 1989).

Pediatric psychologists have also failed to validate either the physiologic responses reported by Minu-

chin et al. (1978) or differences in family interaction across groups of diabetics in terms of control (Delmater et al., 1988). This is similar to research on the families of children with gastrointestinal disorders, including ulcerative colitis, Crohn's disease, and recurrent abdominal pain (Wood et al., 1989). The authors partially validated several features of the psychosomatic model but stated that "the actual influence of these particular family patterns on disease activity has not been established" (p. 412). Families whose members have eating disorders and other "psychosomatic" disorders seem similar to each other, but yet there also appears to be clear diversity among these families.

Luepnitz (1988) also criticized Minuchin's structural model, but for clinical reasons, including that a structural approach takes too little account of the family's personal history; it treats problems as they appear in the present; and it fails to address the issue of patriarchy in the family. In fact, Minuchin's tendency to unbalance the family through the mother is quite pervasive in his clinical work, particularly around enmeshment. This phenomenon, representing a breach of the parent–child hierarchy, has been used to implicate maternal overinvolvement with the anorectic daughter. However, overinvolvement is not solely with the mother (Selvini-Palazzoli & Viaro, 1988).

Because anorectic families are more diverse than originally stated, no single theory or approach has emerged as applying to all of them. Although Minuchin's theory had been useful in helping me think about some families, and then knowing how to proceed once in therapy with them, I felt on uncharted territory with the Smiths. The end result was that I was freed to adopt other approaches.

## FAMILY SYSTEMS AND BULIMIA NERVOSA

Heterogeneity has also been reported with families of bulimia nervosa patients. Two three-part, clinically derived typologies have emerged. The first, developed by Schwartz et al. (1984), articulated the previously mentioned all-American, ethnic, and mixed types. These types were defined earlier and reflect the degree to which the young woman has identified with either the cultural ideals of thinness and achievement or the intrafamilial ideals of the ethnic family (e.g., life revolving around the family).

The second typology is organized on symptom presentation and family functioning (Root et al., 1986) and includes three types: overprotective, perfect, and chaotic. Overprotective families promote dependency and a lack of autonomy in their daughters, and they have less emphasis on achievement. Perfect families emphasize achievement, physical appearance, and the reduction and avoidance of conflict. Chaotic families are characterized by more antisocial behavior, family dislocation, chemical dependency, and overt rejection.

Issues of food, autonomy, and intimacy have been reported to be multigenerational across the three bulimic family types (Friedrich & Fallon, 1987). For example, the single mother of a bulimic adolescent could not understand her daughter feeling lonely and misunderstood because the grandmother, mother, and adolescent "worked out" together five to six times per week at the health club. Treatment included finding new ways for the mother and daughter to feel connected.

The Structural Analysis of Social Behavior (SASB; Benjamin, 1974) has been used in several studies to differentiate bulimic and anorectic families from control families. The SASB rates both interpersonal relationships and intrapsychic representations along dimensions of affiliation (attack–loving attachment) and interdependence (independence–enmeshment). The SASB is not entirely congruent with any specific family theory on eating disorders.

Humphrey (1986) found few differences between bulimic and anorectic women in the SASB. Only deficits in perceived nurturance were specific to bulimia. In a separate study, Humphrey and her colleagues (Humphrey, Apple, & Kirschenbaum, 1986) suggested that the frequent use of negativistic, complex, and contradictory communications may be important in both the development and the maintenance of bulimia–anorexia. In a later study, Humphrey (1988) found that anorectic families denied problems with neglect, rejection, and blame, whereas bulimic families reported greater neglect, rejection, and blame.

A cluster–analytic study that used the SASB with families with an anorectic child contrasted with matched-control families emphasized the heterogeneity of eating-disordered families (Griff, Friesin, & Sheppy, 1989). Seven distinct family groups were identified: (a) the harmonious transitional family (i.e., friendly and consistent, the majority of which belong to the control group); (b) the perfect family (i.e., friendly, caring, with no conflict); (c) the marginal transitional family, which emphasizes control and authority; (d) the discordant–distancing family, with marital discord (composed entirely of the families with an anorectic daughter); (e) the hostile–conflicted family, with a hostile father and warm mother (all families had an anorectic daughter with recent bulimic behavior); (f) the mistaken family, with confused mixture of warmth and distance (all families had an anorectic daughter); and (g) the ambivalently differentiated family (i.e., warm, but with a distant father and a caring mother). An overlap between the anorectic and control families occurred unless mentioned. The validity of SASB studies has been questioned by a recent article by Wonderlich and Swift (1990) on the grounds that when level of mood disturbance was controlled statistically, no significant differences in parent ratings among restricting anorectics, bulimic–anorectics, bulimics, and normal control subjects were demonstrated.

Stierlin and Weber (1989) describe the clinical differences between anorectic and bulimic families as anorectic girls being younger on the average than bulimic patients and bulimic patients tending to display greater emotional instability and a more marked tendency to show negative feelings openly. The parents of the bulimic are also more commonly separated or divorced, and sexual issues (e.g., sexual acting out by parents or children) are more likely.

I agree with Stierlin and Weber's (1989) impression about differences between anorectic and bulimic families. The more overt emotional instability and fewer restrictions about displaying negative feelings make the bulimic families easier for me to treat. The overt distress provides an avenue for connection. I have found that even with an emaciated daughter present in the room, anorectic families can talk for session after session as if there were no problem.

The Smiths, cited at the beginning of the chapter, were a "transition" family. Jackie regained weight and left the hospital but began to use binging and purging as a way to maintain a reduced weight. The fact that they were more openly conflictual in the first session was actually more like the usual presentation of a bulimic family. This exemplifies the difficulty of conceptualizing anorexia and bulimia as an "either/ or" diagnosis.

Depression in first-degree relatives and extended family members of eating-disordered patients is another relatively consistent finding. This has led to the conclusion that eating disorders are a depressive equivalent. The validity of this assertion has been questioned by a number of psychiatrists (Altshuler & Weiner, 1985), who report no greater incidence of affective disorders in relatives of eating-disordered patients than relatives of patients with other psychiatric disorders.

The conflict about eating disorders as a depressive equivalent illustrates a well-known finding in the family-interaction literature (Jacob, 1975). The few differences in family characteristics that do emerge often cannot be replicated, are not explained by theory, and often can be accounted for by other variables. In fact, family interaction is so complex and difficult to quantify that any differences that do emerge are rare. It may well be that the clinician needs a wide acquaintance with the many conceptualizations of eating disorder, so that a good fit between a particular conceptualization and a given case can be further explored and put to good clinical use.

## INTERNAL FAMILY SYSTEMS LEVEL

The internal family systems level is the last ecological level to be examined in this chapter. Schwartz (1987) wrote that discussion with his patients regarding their internal experience just prior to a binge–purge episode led him to the view that their internal experience suggested conflicting parties in a family struggle. He applied systems concepts to the internal family that eating-disordered patients carried within themselves. He wrote that "the power that human systems—especially families—exert upon us comes from their ability to evoke particular subidentities within us" (p. 27).

The internal family systems level is in striking contrast to the external family systems level that assumes that the most effective therapeutic leverage is found within the interpersonal context of people's lives. External family systems practitioners have historically shown little interest in issues of the self, with the exception of Bowen theory (Bowen, 1978). Schwartz's (1987) clinical experience suggests that internal relationships are highly related to external family relationships. For example, a bulimic adult reported a negative–critical–rejecting internal family systems member that paralleled her father's relationship with her. Binging–purging was temporally related to criticism from her internal family system member, and therapy focused on reminding her that how she dealt with her father would work for her internal self as well.

Watanage-Hammond (1987) has developed an apparently related internal family systems approach that she labels "cast of characters" (p. 54). Her therapeutic work relies on accepting and accounting for the various behaviors of each person's characters and the search for a more functional arrangement between them.

Although no empirical validation of the internal family systems model has been demonstrated, in many ways this approach is a potentially very powerful therapeutic mechanism to recast cognitive therapy into a family systems model. The majority of eating-disorder patients are treated from a cognitive–behavioral perspective on an outpatient basis. The cognitive approach, while examining the various messages and thoughts with which eating-disordered patients bombard themselves, does not appreciate the fact that these thoughts may arise from an internal family system that in turn lends itself to a systems-based treatment approach.

Breunlin, Schwartz, and MacKune-Karrer (1992) propose that an internal family systems model reduces rather than compounds the complexity facing the family therapist. They believe it is easier to choose a focus, either external or internal, when the therapist understands the different characteristics of each family member that is involved in the family's stereotypic and unproductive interactions. This would come about from a careful interview not only of the external family but also of the internal family. Given that this work emerged in Schwartz's (1987) early therapeutic interactions with eating-disordered patients, the applicability of an internal family systems approach to the eating-disorders treatment field clearly warrants further examination by family therapists.

In summary, three ecological levels—sociocultural, external family systems, and internal family systems—appear to have both heuristic and clinical relevance in understanding and treating anorexia nervosa and bulimia nervosa. Each level is also part of a much larger system representing the combined influences on the emergence of eating-disordered behavior.

## FAMILY THERAPY APPROACHES

Several common treatment approaches will be briefly presented. These include the structural approach of Minuchin (Minuchin et al., 1978), the structural–strategic approach of Stierlin (Stierlin & Weber, 1989), and the invariant prescription approach of Selvini-Palazzoli (Selvini-Palazzoli & Viaro, 1988). This overview will focus on the outpatient portion of the treatment, which is often preceded by an inpatient hospitalization. As Russell and his colleagues write, "It is relatively easy to restore a malnourished anorectic patient to her normal weight in the course of inpatient treatment. Unfortunately many of these patients lose weight again on discharge from hospital" (Russell, Szmukler, Dare, & Eisler, 1987, p. 1047).

After the intense, usually short-term inpatient phase in which family therapy begins, usually around lunch sessions, the outpatient portion of structural family treatment focuses on four processes (Minuchin et al., 1978). The first process, along with stimulating weight gain, is to shift the family's focus from the daughter's refusal to eat to an awareness that she is "refusing to grow up" or "being stubborn." This prevents the family from focusing on the patient's symptoms to detour or avoid family conflict. The enmeshment and overprotectiveness that maintains the patient's symptom is addressed second. Often this involves greater involvement by the father, especially if he has been distant, and a withdrawal by the

mother. The third focus emphasizes change in the functioning of the family system so as to prevent the appearance of a new symptom. Parents are expected to work together more harmoniously, address conflict directly, and not triangulate the daughter. Usually the end of the family therapy is marked by a fourth focus with the parents' continuing in marital therapy and the anorectic patient's continuing in individual therapy aimed at preventing relapses. The structural approach uses tasks designed to establish generational boundaries. Often the structural therapist engenders intensity in the family to create therapeutic movement because the prevailing perspective is that the anorectic family is strongly resistant to change.

The structural–strategic approach suggested by Stierlin & Weber (1989) is designed to place the responsibility for change squarely within the family. This is very different from the more directive and task-oriented structural approach. Therapy ranges from 1 to 10 sessions at intervals of 4 to 8 weeks. The most crucial task of this approach is to initiate individuation among family members with circular questioning. This technique helps family members elaborate on the simultaneous fears of separation and loss and their positive evaluation of the status quo; it also creates a sense of power in the daughter by talking about her decision to hold a "hunger strike" (Stierlin & Weber, p. 85). The first interview has the family remembering the period in which the anorexia had not yet manifested itself. In my experience, this can create a sense of hopefulness in the parents for the first time in months or years.

In my work with the Smiths, after they seemed to have made some steps in dealing with the premature deaths of their parents, we spent some time talking about their "hoped-for family," and they were able to remember a period of time, before Mr. Smith's first heart attack, when they felt harmonious. We talked about why at 12 years of age, Jackie chose to restrict her food intake. Mrs. Smith blamed her attitudes toward food for some of this, and the family accepted my suggestion that Jackie was scared about her family and felt as if it was falling apart.

Selvini-Palazzoli and Viaro (1988) suggest a typology of anorectics, Type A and Type B, with the former growing up more closely involved with the mother and the latter with the father. Her six-stage model for how anorexia develops makes for fascinating reading and also guides her therapy. Briefly summarized, each stage differs for each typology, but Stage 1 involves a parental game of provocation–no response; Stage 2 marks the first involvement by the anorectic-to-be in the parent's game. Stage 3 begins in adolescence and reflects a shift in the girl's relationship with her father, marking Stage 4, where relational distress and the "diet ploy" come onto the scene. Stage 5 marks a further father–daughter split, with Stage 6 being the final stage, which is characterized by a solidification of the anorectic symptoms. Why a "diet ploy" is chosen for some families and not others is not discussed, but I believe it pertains to how food and body are viewed in the family.

Two preliminary sessions are held prior to drawing up a therapeutic contract. During these first two sessions, the therapist's task is to identify the "family game" at the moment of presentation into therapy. Therapy is then held on the average of once a month, and the therapist is very explicit about his or her hypotheses regarding the family and the interventions and strategies he or she wishes to use. The patient is expected to modify her behavior outside of the therapy session in such a way that the validity of the various hypotheses presented by the therapist can be checked. Some of these hypotheses result in specific tasks that the patient might use, including detriangulating from family conflict. Therapeutic rapport is reported to be more critical than the specific interventions made.

In the latter two approaches—the structural–strategic approach and the invariant prescription approach—therapists are less directive and structuring than Minuchin and colleagues (Minuchin et al., 1978). Selvini-Palazzoli's (1978) emphasis on rapport and straightforward communications is striking. Stierlin & Weber's (1989) model appears dialogue-based, and limits the number of total sessions, with the sessions spread out in frequency. In addition, Selvini-Palazzoli, having come full circle in her own practice, works primarily with the individual.

I have used these three models over the years in working with eating-disordered individuals and families. My interpretation of the structural approach, and my efforts at imitating Minuchin, characterized my first stage of clinical development. I was active,

confrontational, anxiety-generating, and focused on empowering parents to get their daughter to eat. At times I felt "assaultive" with my direct, repetitive confrontation. As I began to see older patients, no longer living at home, or worked with bulimics in group therapy, I realized that I needed additional methods. I didn't like being as "assaultive" as I felt, and I had some success with several families where we talked about the meaning of their daughter's behaviors, addressed marital issues, and dealt with unresolved loss. The Smiths are a good example:

> Both parents spent time sorrowfully reminiscing about their deceased parents and what they had missed out on with their absence. This seemed to help Mr. Smith begin to work at a more sane pace, and the parents and children were spending more time together. Jackie had gained enough weight to be out of danger and several family sessions focused on what the three women in the family had learned about food and body image from their families and society.
>
> In keeping with the openness suggested by the invariant prescription approach, I generated several hypotheses in front of the family. These were related to the effect Mr. Smith's subtle criticism about weight had on his wife and daughters. For example, I predicted that his criticism would trigger maladaptive food-related behavior (e.g., dieting and self-criticism about body) from his wife and daughter. This proved to be correct and illustrated to everyone how family dynamics affected them. Mr. Smith was forced to be more sensitive about weight and became less critical.
>
> At this point, we became aware of Jackie's binging–purging, which prompted a crisis, and a combination of marital sessions as well as individual sessions with Jackie that focused on countering leftover criticism from herself and mother. Two sessions with her mother also seemed important to Jackie. They ended therapy with the expectation that in a few years they would likely

*need some more treatment, but they were functioning better for the time being.*

My current position is that the longer I work with eating-disordered families, the more heterogeneity I appreciate. This means I can recommend no single approach; I now believe that most of these families need a customized approach, one that fits their circumstances as well as the therapist's style.

## FAMILY THERAPY OUTCOME RESEARCH: ANOREXIA NERVOSA

The efficacy of family therapy with anorexia nervosa has not been demonstrated, despite the influence of Minuchin's (Minuchin et al., 1978) and Selvini-Palazzoli's writings (Selvini-Palazzoli, 1978). The treatment that each group of patients (Minuchin, N = 53; Selvini-Palazzoli, N = 22) received was not systematically delivered and was neither controlled nor followed up on systematically.

The patients described by Selvini-Palazzoli (1978) received a hybrid treatment approach that increasingly involved family components as Selvini-Palazzoli evolved in her therapeutic perspective; they began, however, at a time when she was using a more individually oriented approach. Her follow-up mechanism appeared to be relatively informal, and the length of follow-up has not been described. Follow-up with the 1978 Minuchin sample ranged from 1.5 to 7.0 years (mean follow-up = 2.7 years), but whether it was systematically obtained was not clearly indicated. At the very least, a 4- to 5-year follow-up is recommended with anorexia nervosa (Russell et al., 1987).

The first controlled trial of family therapy with anorexia nervosa was published by Russell and colleagues (Russell et al., 1987). It included 80 patients, 57 with anorexia nervosa and 23 with bulimia nervosa. They were randomly assigned, at the end of an inpatient hospitalization aimed at "refeeding," to one of two modalities, family therapy or individual therapy. At the end of one year, their progress was reassessed on several dimensions (e.g., weight gain for anorexia nervosa patients and frequency of binging–purging for bulimia nervosa patients, menstrual function, psychosexual adjustments, socioeconomic status, and mental state). Four groups of patients

were developed: Subgroup 1, adolescent onset, illness duration less than 3 years; Subgroup 2, adolescent onset, illness duration more than 3 years; Subgroup 3, adult onset; Subgroup 4, bulimia nervosa patients.

Family therapy appeared to work best with Subgroup 1, the younger, less chronic patients. Nine of 10 patients receiving family therapy in this category had an intermediate to good outcome, whereas 9 of 11 patients receiving individual therapy in this category had a poor outcome. No other significant, between-treatment findings were reported. Interestingly, Minuchin and his colleagues (Minuchin et al., 1978) report an 86% recovery rate for their patient group, the majority of whom were adolescent (only 2 of 53 had a symptom onset after age 18).

Russell and colleagues examined different aspects of their treatment with regard to treatment dropouts (Dare, Eisler, Russell, & Szmukler, 1990; Szmukler, Eisler, Russell, & Dare, 1985). The strongest association with treatment dropout was a parental variable related to expressed emotion (i.e., the number of critical comments made by the parent about the patient in the course of an initial family interview). The authors suggest that in conflict-avoidant families, the emergence of high levels of critical comments can be quite threatening, even intolerable, leading to flight from therapy. In fact, expressed emotion was not related to dropping out if individual therapy was the treatment modality (Szmukler & Dare, 1991). Although many anorectic patients are hospitalized as part of their treatment, these authors report that they have evidence from two partially controlled retrospective surveys that family therapy is as effective as inpatient treatment for early-onset, short-history anorexia nervosa (Dare & Szmukler, 1991).

A second controlled study, which used outpatient family therapy as a treatment component, examined 90 patients with severe anorexia nervosa who were randomly assigned to one of four treatment options (inpatient treatment, outpatient individual and family therapy, outpatient group therapy in which parents and patients were in separate groups, and no treatment; Crisp et al., 1991). At 1-year follow-up, there were no different levels of effectiveness between the treatment groups, all of which were more effective than no treatment. Only 12 sessions were offered as part of the family therapy condition, and the authors did not see this as a good test of family therapy. They report that "ideally . . . therapy needs to continue for about two years . . . involving both the core patient and the family" (p. 332).

In a more systematic fashion than earlier clinical studies like Minuchin et al. (1978), Stierlin and Weber (1989) provided a standard treatment (6 sessions) to 42 families. All but one of the families received no more than 14 sessions. Eighty-six percent of the families changed in the direction of greater functionality, twelve percent did not show any movement at all, and two percent showed a deterioration. A follow-up interview that supported sustained change was conducted at least 2 to 3 years after the end of treatment.

My clinical experience supports Crisp et al.'s (1991) contention that longer (1–2 years) therapy is needed for real change. The few families that I have treated with Stierlin and Weber's approach were more stable after 8 to 10 sessions, but marital and young adult–parent interaction had not changed as much.

In summary, only three studies met the criteria of random assignment to contrasting modalities or the use of a relatively standard treatment approach. Tentative findings suggest a differential effectiveness for family therapy favoring the younger, less acute anorectic, but with clinical improvement reported in the majority of those receiving treatment.

## FAMILY THERAPY OUTCOME RESEARCH: BULIMIA NERVOSA

The Russell et al. (1987) study is the only report of the effectiveness of family therapy in a controlled fashion for bulimia nervosa patients. Patients were offered either family or individual therapy. At 1-year follow-up (23 began, 4 dropouts), there was no significant difference between either therapy modality. In fact, 79% of the bulimic patients were in the poor outcome category. These results paralleled the poor success rate for family therapy with older anorexia nervosa patients.

The success rate for a behavioral approach has been reported to be much higher than Russell et al.'s (1987) results (Pyle, Mitchell, Eckert, Hatsukami, &

Goff, 1984), and so the literature is still unclear as to the relative efficacy of family therapy with bulimia nervosa patients. Although bulimia tends to have an average age of onset later than anorexia nervosa, this does not preclude a family therapy, or family-oriented approach. At this point, however, no well-designed family-treatment study has demonstrated its effectiveness when contrasted with either a waiting-list or other individual-treatment comparison groups.

## THE ROLE OF TRAUMA IN EATING DISORDERS

Victimization experiences are rarely addressed in studies of eating-disordered families. Incest and physical abuse are not even mentioned in the index of such classic books as Minuchin et al. (1978), Garner and Garfinkel (1984), Stierlin and Weber (1989), and Selvini-Palazzoli (1978). This issue is not mentioned in studies of family patterns (Humphrey, 1986) and therapy outcome (Russell et al., 1987). However, sexual abuse appears associated with the development of eating disorders, including bulimia nervosa (Root, Fallon, & Friedrich, 1986) and anorexia nervosa (Palmer, Oppenheimer, Dignon, Challener, & Howell, 1990).

A review of the literature on childhood sexual abuse as a risk factor for bulimia nervosa concluded that the available evidence does not support child sexual abuse as a risk factor for bulimia nervosa (Pope & Hudson, 1992). However, the authors discounted postadolescent victimization, they failed to consider the percentage of patients who "forget" their victimization history, and they failed to appreciate that patients may be less likely to disclose. In addition, I have worked with several families in which sexual abuse was denied, but subtle boundary violations and sexual talk between parent and child appeared to be very unsettling to the eating-disordered daughter and were probably part of the eating disorder's etiology.

Current models of psychopathology usually consider a variety of predisposing and protective factors because a direct linear relationship between a psychosocial variable (e.g., sexual abuse history) and a diagnosis is rarely found. For example, it remains to be empirically determined whether sexual abuse severity, in the studies reviewed by Pope and Hudson (1992), is related to symptom severity, or whether it is moderated by familial factors (e.g., support and low levels of expressed emotion). In addition, clinical observations have suggested that in the overprotective bulimic type of family (Root et al., 1986), a significant percentage of the mothers in these families have a victimization experience themselves, which the authors believed was transmitted directly or indirectly to the daughter and resulted in greater fear of growing up.

Luepnitz (1988) presents a family therapy case of a 15-year-old anorectic girl and her parents that highlights these contentions. Luepnitz originally viewed the family as "a classic case of an overinvolved father and an underinvolved mother" (p. 205). She then altered her conceptualization when she became aware that the father had fondled his daughter for 1 year on a weekly basis, approximately 7 to 8 years earlier. The family did not volunteer the information. Rather than creating distance between the mother and the daughter, as a structural approach would suggest, Luepnitz restored their relationship with a number of mother–daughter sessions.

It is my belief that whether or not sexual abuse and other forms of maltreatment are related to the etiology of eating disorders remains to be determined. Part of the difficulty involves the definition of sexual abuse. Several anorectic or bulimic families that corresponded closely to Selvini-Palazzoli's (Selvini-Palazzoli & Viaro, 1988) Type B families exhibited extreme father–daughter closeness that appeared subincestuous to me, but sexual abuse was denied by all parties.

## CONCLUSIONS

Although family therapists have been writing about the successful treatment of anorectic families since the early 1970s, the few empirical outcome studies in existence that used a comparison group or delivered a reasonably standard therapy to the patients have demonstrated the effectiveness of family therapy over other treatments only with a subset of families. One of the few sound outcome studies conducted relatively few sessions, and although the authors limited themselves to 12 sessions by design, they stated

in their discussion that this was less than the majority the families needed (Crisp et al., 1991). Clearly, research examining the relative and selective efficacy of family therapy in this area is very much needed.

Another problematic area is the fact that all of the studies that have examined the family-interaction patterns of anorexia nervosa or bulimia nervosa patients have been cross-sectional in nature. The results may not be that relevant to etiology. Although Selvini-Palazzoli (Selvini-Palazzoli & Viaro, 1988) have suggested a fascinating six-stage etiological model for the development of anorexia nervosa, only a prospective study of a large number of female children from childhood into early adulthood could tease out the numerous etiological mechanisms that contribute to the development of eating disorders. In the only prospective study of any size to date, eating-behavior problems of one sort or another in girls age 1 to 10 were related to later diagnoses of eating disorders (Marchi & Cohen, 1990). This suggests that research that focuses only on family variables, and does not examine sociocultural permeability and food-related issues, will not be as comprehensive a study as needed.

The etiology of eating disorders is likely to be very complex, and the Pope and Hudson (1992) article that rules out trauma as a contributing factor is extremely premature. However, it is not just trauma that is understudied. The majority of etiological studies completely ignore larger sociocultural issues and continue to focus on the pathological mechanisms of family interaction as the primary contributors.

It is also extremely important to consider treatment techniques that are developmentally appropriate. The family lunch session (Minuchin et al., 1978), which is reported to be very useful with anorectic families, may not be very useful with older adolescent or adult anorectic patients, particularly not the portion of the lunch session in which one or both of the parents uses their status to force the patient to begin to eat. With older anorectics, parental authority is less the issue.

Another important question has to do with what constitutes a family. It may be that a family-oriented perspective is the most critical, rather than family therapy per se (Vandereycken & Meerman, 1984). The Selvini-Palazzoli invariant prescription model

(Selvini-Palazzoli & Viaro, 1988) allows single family members to engage the therapist to learn new ways to interrupt the family game. In addition, to date, the most effective therapy for bulimia nervosa is intensive outpatient group therapy focused on relationships (Mitchell et al., 1990).

Future treatment outcome studies must wrestle with appropriate treatment outcome variables. Although there are a number of overt symptoms that are potential outcome variables, Luepnitz (1988) suggests that therapists should aim for more than simply symptom relief. If changes in complex patterns of family interaction become the outcome measure of choice, it is likely that a range of potential changes in family-interaction patterns would need to be targeted given the heterogeneity of eating-disordered families.

What does a therapist do in light of the ambiguity outlined above? Begin by appreciating the heterogeneity in eating-disordered families and responding flexibly, but with a clear focus on making sense of the symptom at this stage in the woman's life and activating an appropriate family response. Alternate resources, such as hospitalization for refeeding, is also critical and can serve to open the family up to new possibilities of relating.

In summary, eating-disordered individuals are far more heterogeneous than originally thought, and the early publication of a compelling theoretical model, although extremely helpful clinically, obscured that fact to some degree. Only recently, and far too slowly, have alternative treatment approaches been suggested for syndromes that have proven to be relatively difficult to treat. Family therapy clearly has yet to be identified as the most appropriate treatment of a wide range of eating-disordered patients. Family psychologists have the opportunity to be instrumental in helping expand a field that is still developing.

# References

Altshuler, K. Z., & Weiner, M. F. (1985). Anorexia nervosa and depression: A dissenting view. *American Journal of Psychiatry, 142,* 328–332.

American Psychiatric Association. (1987). *Diagnostic and Statistical Manual of Mental Disorders* (3rd ed., rev.). Washington, DC: Author.

American Psychiatric Association. (1994). *Diagnostic and statistical manual of mental disorders* (4th ed.). Washington, DC: Author.

Benjamin, L. S. (1974). Structural analysis of social behavior. *Psychological Review, 81,* 392–425.

Bowen, M. (1978). *Family therapy in clinical practice.* Northvale, NJ: Jason Aronson.

Breunlin, G., Schwartz, R., & MacKune-Karrer, A. (1992). *Metaframeworks: Transcending the models of family therapy.* San Francisco: Jossey-Bass.

Bronfenbrenner, U. (1979). *The ecology of human development: Experiments by nature and design.* Cambridge, MA: Harvard University Press.

Bruch, H. (1973). *Eating disorders: Obesity, anorexia nervosa, and the person within.* New York: Basic Books.

Crisp, A. H., Norton, K., Gowers, S., Halek, C., Bowyer, C., Yeldham, D., Levett, G., & Bhat, A. (1991). A controlled study of the effect of therapies aimed at adolescent and family psychopathology in anorexia nervosa. *British Journal of Psychiatry, 159,* 325–333.

Dare, C., Eisler, I., Russell, G. F. M., & Szmukler, G. I. (1990). The clinical and theoretical impact of a control trial of family therapy in anorexia nervosa. *Journal of Marital and Family Therapy, 16,* 39–57.

Dare, C., & Szmukler, G. (1991). Family therapy of early-onset, short-history anorexia nervosa. In D. B. Woodside & L. Shekter-Wolfson (Eds.), *Family approaches in treatment of eating disorders* (pp. 23–47). Washington, DC: American Psychiatric Press.

Delmater, A. H., Bubb, J., Kurtz, S. M., Kuntze, J., Smith, J. A., White, N. H., & Santiago, J. V. (1988). Physiologic responses to acute psychological stress in adolescents with Type 1 Diabetes mellitus. *Journal of Pediatric Psychology, 13,* 69–86.

Friedrich, W. N., & Fallon, M. P. (1987, October). Multigenerational issues in bulimic family types. Paper presented at the Annual Conference of the American Association of Marriage and Family Therapy, Chicago, IL.

Garner, D. M., & Garfinkel, P. E. (Eds.). (1984). *Handbook of psychotherapy for anorexia nervosa and bulimia.* New York: Guilford Press.

Garner, D. M., Garfinkel, P. E., Schwartz, D., & Thompson, M. (1980). Cultural expectations of thinness in women. *Psychological Reports, 47,* 483–491.

Goodrich, T. J., Rampage, C., Ellman, B., & Halstead, K. (1988). *Feminist family therapy: A casebook.* New York: Norton.

Gordon, R. A. (1990). *Anorexia and bulimia: Anatomy of a social epidemic.* Oxford, England: Basil Blackwell.

Grigg, D. N., Friesen, J. D., & Sheppy, N. I. (1989). Family patterns associated with anorexia nervosa. *Journal of Marital and Family Therapy, 15,* 29–42.

Humphrey, L. L. (1986). Structural analysis of parent-child relationships in eating disorders. *Journal of Abnormal Psychology, 95*, 395–402.

Humphrey, L. L. (1988). Relationships within subtypes of anorexic, bulimic, and normal families. *Journal of the American Academy of Child and Adolescent Psychiatry, 27*, 544–551.

Humphrey, L. L., Apple, R. F., & Kirschenbaum, D. S. (1986). Differentiating bulimic-anorexic from normal families using interpersonal and behavioral observational systems. *Journal of Consulting and Clinical Psychology, 54*, 190–195.

Jacob, T. (1975). Family interaction in disturbed and normal families: A methodological and substantive review. *Psychological Bulletin, 82*, 33–65.

Kog, E., Vandereycken, W., & Vertommen, H. (1985). Towards a verification of the psychosomatic family model: A pilot study of ten families with an anorexia/bulimia nervosa patient. *International Journal of Eating Disorders, 4*, 525–538.

Kog, E., Vertommen, H., & Vandereycken, W. (1987). Minuchin's psychosomatic family model revised: A concept-validation study using a multi-trait-multi-method approach. *Family Process, 26*, 235–253.

Luepnitz, D. A. (1988). *The family interpreted.* New York: Basic Books.

Marchi, M., & Cohen, P. (1990). Early childhood eating behaviors and adolescent eating disorders. *Journal of the American Academy of Child and Adolescent Psychiatry, 29*, 112–117.

Minuchin, S., Rosman, B. L., & Baker, L. (1978). *Psychosomatic families: Anorexia nervosa in context.* Cambridge, MA: Harvard University Press.

Mitchell, J. E., Pyle, R. L., Eckert, E. D., Hatsukami, D., Pomeroy, C., & Zimmerman, R. A comparison study of antidepressants and structured intensive group psychotherapy in the treatment of bulimia nervosa. *Archives of General Psychiatry, 47*, 149–157.

Palmer, R. L., Oppenheimer, R., Dignon, A., Challener, D. A., Howell, K. (1990). Childhood sexual experiences with adults reported by women with eating disorders: An extended series. *British Journal of Psychiatry, 156*, 699–703.

Pope, H. G., & Hudson, J. I. (1992). Is childhood sexual abuse a risk factor for bulimia nervosa? *American Journal of Psychiatry, 149*, 455–463.

Pyle, R. L., Mitchell, J. E., Eckert, E. D., Hatsukami, D. K., & Goff, G. (1984). The interruption of bulimic behaviors: A review of three treatment programs. *Psychiatric Clinics of North America, 7*, 275–286.

Root, M. P. P., Fallon, M. P., & Friedrich, W. N. (1986). *Bulimia: A systems approach to treatment.* New York: Norton.

Russell, G. F. M., Szmukler, G. I., Dare, C., & Eisler, I. (1987). An evaluation of family therapy in anorexia nervosa and bulimia nervosa. *Archives of General Psychiatry, 44*, 1047–1056.

Schwartz, R. (1987). Our multiple selves: Applying systems thinking through the inner family. *Family Therapy Networker, 11*, 25–31, 80–83.

Schwartz, R., Barrett, M. J., & Saba, G. (1984). Family therapy for bulimia. In D. M. Garner & P. E. Garfinkel (Eds.), *Handbook of psychotherapy for anorexia nervosa and bulimia* (pp. 280–307). New York: Guilford Press.

Selvini-Palazzoli, M. (1978). *Self-starvation.* Northvale, NJ: Jason Aronson.

Selvini-Palazzoli, M., & Viaro, M. (1988). The anorectic process in the family: A six-stage model as guide for individual therapy. *Family Process, 27*, 129–148.

Sterner-Adair, C. (1986). The body politic: Normal female adolescent development and the development of eating disorders. *Journal of the American Academy of Psychoanalysis, 14*, 95–114.

Stierlin, H., & Weber, G. (1989). *Unlocking the family door: A systemic approach to the understanding and treatment of anorexia nervosa.* New York: Brunner/Mazel.

Szmukler, G. I., & Dare, C. (1991). The Mandsley Hospital Study of family therapy in anorexia nervosa and bulimia nervosa. In D. B. Woodside & L. Shekter-Wolfson (Eds.), *Family approaches in treatment of eating disorders* (pp. 1–21). Washington, DC: American Psychiatric Press.

Szmukler, G. I., Eisler, I., Russell, G. F. M., & Dare, C. (1985). Anorexia nervosa, parental expressed emotion and dropping out of treatment. *British Journal of Psychiatry, 147*, 265–271.

Vandereycken, W., & Meerman, R. (1984). *Anorexia nervosa: A clinician's guide to treatment.* New York: Walter de Gruyter.

Vanderlinden, J., & Vandereycken, W. (1987, May). *Family therapy in bulimia nervosa.* Paper presented at the International Symposium on Eating Disorders in Adolescents and Young Adults, Jerusalem.

Watanage-Hammond, S. (1987). The many faces of Paul and Dora. *Family Therapy Networker, 11*, 54–55, 87–89.

Wilson, G. T., & Walsh, B. T. (1991). Eating disorders in the *DSM-IV. Journal of Abnormal Psychology, 100,* 362–365.

Wonderlich, S. A., & Swift, W. J. (1990). Perceptions of parental relationships in the eating disorders: The relevance of depressed mood. *Journal of Abnormal Psychology, 99,* 353–360.

Wood, B., Watkins, J. B., Boyle, J. T., Nogueira, J., Zimand, E., & Carroll, L. (1989). The "psychosomatic family" mode: An empirical and theoretical analysis. *Family Process, 28,* 399–417.

# CHAPTER 24

# INFERTILITY AND PREGNANCY LOSS: THE ROLE OF THE FAMILY CONSULTANT

*Susan G. Mikesell and Margaret Stohner*

When most couples marry, they expect to decide if and when they will have children. However, one in every six couples of child-bearing age have their plans challenged when they are unable to conceive a child or carry one to term (Menning, 1988). If their attempts remain unsuccessful for longer than a year, the couple meets criteria for an infertility diagnosis (U.S. Congress, Office of Technology Assessment [OTA], 1988). Only 50% of all couples who come into a fertility specialist's office within 2 to 3 years will leave with a baby. Of those couples, 5% will become pregnant spontaneously; 45% will submit to treatments that run from a few hundred to tens of thousands of dollars and will eventually have their much desired child. The other 50% will have spent as much or more time and money and end up going home without a child. Pregnancy loss will be part of many of these couples' experiences. Miscarriage or an ectopic pregnancy will bring couples in for consultation with the reproductive endocrinologist who is the medical infertility specialist; sometimes, such problems may be the result of one of the treatments. The couple's medical history could reveal the pregnancy loss of an elective abortion prior to the infertility experience in this relationship. When pregnancy loss occurs in the second or third trimester or in the neonatal period, without a previous history of infertility, the couple is catapulted from a normal developmental experience of pregnancy and birth to the crisis of inadequacy in their reproductive attempt.

With the advancement of medical diagnoses, 90% of infertile couples find an identifiable cause such as tubal factors, cervical factors, anovulation, luteal phase defects, male factors, or some combination of these (Sadler & Syrop, 1987). Depending on the type of pregnancy loss, some couples will ultimately experience the birth of a healthy child. Even though a cause of infertility may be identified, there is not always a treatment or procedure available that will provide these couples with the guarantee that they will have a birth child to raise. The assault on the reproductive functions of the couple being assessed and treated for infertility and pregnancy loss sets the stage for a range of emotional responses in the individual partners and in the relationship (Nachtigall, Becker, & Wozny, 1992).

This chapter will provide a basic understanding of the couple's emotional experience as they proceed through the medical maze toward building a new family. The special vulnerabilities of the infertile couple and those who experience pregnancy loss will be discussed in relation to the Bowen family systems concepts of the family life cycle, chronic anxiety, emotional maturity, and triangulation (Bowen, 1978). The medical system will be considered as a target for both collaboration and intervention. Various therapeutic approaches will be described, including a consultation model and psychoeducational groups.

## INFERTILITY

Historically, psychogenic factors were regarded as possible etiological determinants of infertility (Benedek, 1952; Deutsch, 1945; Fischer, 1953; Rothman, Kaplan, & Nettles, 1962). During the 1970s, women in Boston who were experiencing infertility gathered to talk about the stress that accompanied their treatment. This led to the development of the self-help organization Resolve[1] and the writing of the first book describing the emotional impact of infertility on couples, *Infertility: A Guide for the Childless Couple* (Menning, 1977). In the early 1980s, the professional community began to recognize that the symptoms used to suggest a psychogenic *cause* of infertility were more likely a *result* of the infertility experience (Seibel & Taymor, 1982). This recognition led to the development of the Psychological Special Interest Group of the American Fertility Society,[2] a collaborative effort between medicine and psychology. Most mental health professionals now focus on the psychological reactions to infertility.

## Typical Emotional Responses

Clinical studies have identified typical patterns of response to infertility that differ somewhat for men, women, and the couple as a unit. It is important to understand these differential gender responses as a preliminary to clinical intervention.

**Women's emotional responses.** Women generally experience infertility as a problem of great significance and show higher distress than men, particularly on measures of anxiety, depression, cognitive disturbances, and stress (Freeman, Boxer, Rickels, Tureck, & Mastrioanni, 1985; Griel, Leikko, & Porter, 1988; Wright et al., 1991). For wives more than husbands, infertility stress results in low self-esteem and general well-being (Andrews, Abbey, & Halman, 1992; Lalos, Lalos, Jacobsson, & Von Schoulta, 1985). Women are likely to display the same pattern of distress whether the infertility is theirs or their partner's (Nachtigall et al., 1992).

The monthly menstrual cycle triggers characteristic emotional patterns when a woman is attempting conception. She begins each cycle with the anticipation of success. Perhaps she is trying a new treatment or has learned something new about the timing of sexual intercourse. As the middle of the cycle approaches and the estrogen levels rise, so does her op-

timism. The fantasy that pregnancy has been achieved may be abruptly shattered when her temperature drops or when she experiences signs of an impending period. She is flooded with disappointment, depression, and despair. As this cycle repeats itself, the woman has more and more sadness to address, which can erode hope and impede goal-directed behavior (Domar & Seibel, 1990).

With the repeated disappointments of infertility, a woman can be overwhelmed with sadness or depression over her many losses. Loss experiences during infertility include loss of relationship, real or imagined; loss of health; loss of status; loss of self-esteem; loss of confidence; loss of security; and loss of hope (Mahlstedt, 1985). Guilt can be present from past sexual experiences, a history of sexually transmitted disease, or a previous elective abortion. This can increase the depression or bring on a feeling of being punished by the infertility and its treatment. A sense of depersonalization often occurs with the use of noncoital reproductive technologies.

Infertility poses a challenge to what many have come to know and expect as a legitimate role expectation for an adult woman. Some women may feel less feminine and worry about disappointing others, particularly a spouse or parents. Relationships with friends often become strained and less satisfying as peers move into the "motherhood club" (Mahlstedt, 1985). If after many attempts pregnancy does not occur, the woman has to redefine her adult role, grieve the lost hope of her own biological child, and decide whether to pursue adoption or define herself as a child-free adult.

**Men's emotional responses.** It frequently takes up to 3 years of infertility experience for a man to begin feeling the same level of emotional distress as his wife (MacNab, 1984). Men carry culturally defined scripts that perpetuate such patterns as not demonstrating weakness, displaying little or no emotional expression beyond courage or anger, and being the steady "shoulder to cry on" when the menstrual pe-

[1] Resolve is a self-help organization for infertile persons based in Boston with 50 chapters nationwide. For information, contact Resolve, Inc., 1310 Broadway, Somerville, MA 02144-1731.

[2] Information about the Psychological Professional Group of the American Society of Reproductive Medicine can be obtained by writing to the American Society of Reproductive Medicine, 1209 Montgomery Highway, Birmingham, AL 35216-3809.

riod begins each month (Zoldbrod, 1993). The man often remains eternally optimistic about "next month." When the man himself is diagnosed with the infertility problem, his distress is similar to the infertile woman's in terms of stigmatization, perception of loss, and challenge to self-esteem. This sense of role failure is present for both men and women, independent of the diagnosis (Nachtigall et al., 1992). Shame is a response that is likely to occur for both men and women, but because the production of children is frequently associated with virility many infertile men seem more vulnerable to this response. Kaufman (1985) describes three responses to the experience of shame: (a) feeling unexpectedly and self-consciously exposed; (b) feeling fundamentally different from other human beings; and (c) feeling a sense of impotence or helplessness about changing the situation. All are present for the man experiencing infertility.

The emotional distress for an infertile man is greatest when he carries the diagnosis and feels responsible for the problem. He may find himself being supportive of a partner about her pain and loss while suppressing his own emotional needs. Alternatively, the fertile man may feel angry toward his infertile wife as the obstacle to his role of purveyor of the family name (Baran & Pannor, 1993). He may even have fantasies of wanting to be with another woman of known fertility. These feelings can elicit guilt even if never expressed. Regardless of the source of the fertility problem, the man may experience growing resentment at having to organize his sexuality around a schedule.

**Emotional and behavioral responses for the couple.** By the time infertile couples meet the criteria for an infertility diagnosis they are in a state of chronic stress from their year of monthly hope–loss cycles. When the diagnosis is male infertility or the couple has to go through a prolonged process to determine the cause of their infertility, they experience more emotional distress, an increase in negative feelings toward their partners, and a trend toward marital deterioration (Connolly, Edelmann, & Cooke, 1987; Lalos et al., 1985). Ten percent of all infertile couples remain undiagnosed, making them more susceptible to functioning in a chronic crisis state.

Each couple develops a pattern for reacting to a crisis. This pattern may be known to the couple if they have had to address previous crises, or they may be discovering it for the first time with the infertility. Berk and Shapiro (1984) suggested infertile couples that pull together will feel a strengthening of the marriage, with empathy, caring, and support expressed openly by both spouses. Some couples address the infertility crisis by increasing conflict or distancing. This may threaten the marital bond and increase the isolation for the partner who feels the pain and disappointment. Kraft and his colleagues (Kraft et al., 1980) suggests that these couples are more likely to divorce. If there is a differential desire for children, the infertile couple is more likely to divorce if the husband wants a child and the wife does not (Lorber, 1987). The following case illustrates how a couple can move from cooperation to conflict under the strain of infertility.

### CASE VIGNETTE

*Two years prior to beginning infertility treatment, Jane and Tom had to deal with the crisis of the illness and death of Jane's father. Tom was fond of Jane's father and had much empathy for her when she would have crying spells after a visit. He was willing to take on some of the regular family chores so she could make more frequent visits to see her father. He openly told her how much he admired her ability to help in her father's care, work with her siblings and mother to make family decisions, and continue to function at her job. She felt extremely close to him and made a point of thanking him in special ways for all his caring and understanding.*

*When this couple hit the crisis of infertility they expected that the same would occur. Early attempts to find the cause of the infertility were unsuccessful. Tom's sperm count was on the low side of normal, Jane had a slight case of endometriosis (uterine lining tissue found outside of the uterus). When she cried, she expected Tom to be supportive similar to his response when her father was dying. When he was feeling*

423

*frustrated and angry at the ambiguity of the diagnostic and treatment process, he became less attentive to her. They began to distance from each other. She stopped letting him know how upset she was each month. He felt unable to share his feelings because they seemed to burden her.*

In this example, both individuals were unaware of the impact of their own responses to the infertility on their relationship. Eventually, the couple needs to find a way to join together to deal with the loss to make the decisions needed to redefine family building.

A couple often considers infertility a private matter. Their invisible problem makes them vulnerable to painful inquiry by family and friends. A birth announcement of a classmate in another city can set off a depression. An advertisement for diapers can evoke an angry outburst. The couple depends mainly on each other to handle these stresses. Meeting other people who are infertile, sharing the struggle with family, or telling a close friend the anguish may reduce the stress the couple carries.

*Sexuality.* Any sexual relationship can suffer from the "on-demand" scheduling of infertility intervention. Integrating into one's sex life daily temperature taking and ovulation prediction leaves little room for spontaneity. Hertz (1982) suggests that sexual insecurities can be reinforced by infertility treatment.

Many couples have difficulty making the transition from a rigidly proscribed sexual regimen during ovulation times to their "normal" sexual pattern. Both desire and performance can suffer throughout the cycle.

Some men in infertile couples develop midcycle erectile dysfunction, ejaculatory difficulty, and changes in sexual frequency and desire (Berger, 1977, 1980; Seibel & Taymor, 1982). Sabatelli, Meth, and Gavazzi (1988) report that women's sexuality also may be significantly affected by infertility. More than half of the respondents in this study reported a decrease in the frequency of intercourse and sexual satisfaction after the diagnosis of infertility.

Erectile dysfunction, vaginismus (tightening or spasms of the vagina), dyspareunia (painful intercourse), and infrequency of intercourse because of lack of desire can directly contribute to infertility. Fagan et al. (1986) found that couples with the diagnosis of unexplained infertility are more likely to have a sexual dysfunction.

*Decision making.* The need to make important decisions is an added stressor while absorbing the pain and disappointment inherent in the realization that there is a fertility problem. The couple must learn how to educate themselves about the diagnosis and the options available to them for treatment. Decisions include which specialist to see, who attends which medical appointments, how to pace the intervention efforts, which option to choose, and how far to pursue each option before shifting gears or stopping (see Exhibit 1). The financial demand of many treatment options complicates the joint decision making (see Table 1).[3]

Decisions about career, particularly for the women, become agonizingly difficult in this ambiguous period of infertility treatment. It is not unusual for a female infertility patient to report staying in an unsatisfactory job longer than intended to have flexibility for time-consuming medical appointments or to keep insurance or maternity-leave benefits. Decisions for men and women about buying homes, planning vacations, and attending family gatherings are often held in abeyance.

## Family Systems Concepts
**Family life cycle framework.** The family life cycle framework defines a series of stages with expectable time lines that most people imagine as their predictable life course (Carter & McGoldrick, 1980). To decide to have children and to implement that decision is an implicit part of most marital contracts. The couple who is struggling with infertility is stuck indefinitely in the "couple" stage. They must adapt to ambiguity in the marriage because neither can be certain if reproduction will someday be possible. Some couples find that the prolonged couple stage

---

[3] For example, in 1994 one month's supply of Perganol (the ovulation-enhancing drug) cost from $500 to $2,500. One in vitro treatment costs between $6,500 and $10,000.

makes it more difficult to define boundaries between the couple and their families of origin. Couples with infertility problems may respond with rigid boundaries between themselves and their families of origin and friends in an attempt to protect themselves from intrusive questions about reproduction. This attempt to create a necessary boundary can backfire and further isolate the couple. Alternatively, infertility may cause a loss of necessary boundaries. For example, an infertile woman may find her mother or sister more sensitive to the problem than she believes her husband can be. Any support can be quite helpful

---

## EXHIBIT 1

**Infertility Medical Evaluation**

Initial visit with reproductive endocrinologist[a]
    Meet with couple for a general interview
        obtain detailed reproductive history including previous pregnancies, when birth control stopped, previous testing from gynecologist or urologist
    Sexual history (done together and separately)
        frequency of intercourse, exposure to sexually transmitted diseases
    Medical history and physical exam for both
        includes gynecological exam for woman and genital exam for man
    Instructions in charting basal temperature to determine ovulation pattern
        if known menstrual abnormalities, schedule blood tests of ovarian hormones (estrogen, progesterone, testosterone) and pituitary hormones (follicle-stimulating hormone, FSH, and luteinizing hormone, LH)
    Semen analysis scheduled
Diagnostic testing for male factor
    Repeat semen analysis if not within normal limits
    Postcoital test (examination of sperm taken from vagina within two hours of intercourse) with follow-up autosperm antibody test if abnormal
    Examination of scrotum for varicocele (may include ultrasound or venogram)
    Hormone levels (testosterone, FSH, LH)
    Sperm penetration assay (hamster egg test)
Diagnostic testing for female factor
    Ovulatory functioning
        basal body temperature
        preovulatory urine testing for LH (necessary for ovulation)
        serum progesterone levels and endometrial biopsy to determine ovarian and postovulatory preparation of the uterus
    Cervical mucus
        postcoital test
        mucus quality and sperm mucus interaction measured
    Uterus and fallopian tubes
        hysterosalpingogram (HSG) inflation of uterus and tubes for X-ray exam
        laporoscopy and hysteroscopy (invasive surgical procedure for direct examination of uterus, tubes, and the abdominal cavity for endometriosis and adhesions)

[a]*Although it is suggested that this comprehensive medical workup be done by a reproductive endocrinologist, frequently the woman's gynecologist will have done many of these diagnostic procedures. However, the specialist is likely to repeat them.*

## TABLE 1

### Medical Treatments for Infertility

| Diagnosis | Treatments |
|-----------|------------|
| Male factor | Sperm washing, concentrated sample, interuterine insemination (IUI; prepared sperm inserted directly into uterine cavity) |
| | In vitro fertilization (IVF) (prepared sperm fertilization of retrieved egg in petri dish returned to uterus) |
| | Variations of IVF |
| | Donor sperm with IUI |
| Female factor | Ovulation-stimulating drugs |
| | Clomid (oral) |
| | Pergonal (injection) and sonograph monitoring with IUI |
| | IVF |
| | Gamete interfallopian transfer (GIFT; eggs retrieved from ovaries returned to tubes with sperm) |
| | Zygote interfallopian transfer (ZIFT; fertilized retrieved eggs returned to tubes) |
| | Donor egg |
| Either | Adoption |

and only becomes a problem if a pattern develops in which the emotional communication is directed exclusively to the extended family member to the exclusion of her husband. In-law relationships may also become more strained when a couple is unexpectedly delayed in childbearing. The arrival of grandchildren is usually the point at which these relationships begin to mellow and become more meaningful (Carter & McGoldrick, 1980).

**Unbalancing family relationships.** The stress of infertility can unbalance family relationships and increase the tendency for triangulation. A triangle reduces anxiety in one relationship by focusing on a third party. Perhaps the most common triangle in infertility is the focus of the couple on the fantasy child or on the infertility process itself. Problems in the marriage may be ignored or attributed to the infertility problem with the belief that "if only we could have a baby, everything would be fine." There is some evidence that this rigid triangle translates into an unhealthy focus on the child when the couple becomes parents. Burns (1990), in one of the first studies on parenting after infertility, reports that

infertility-treated parents were more likely to rate their parenting as overprotective, child-centered, or abusive and neglectful than parents without a history of infertility.

Occasionally cross-generational coalitions stabilize under the stress of infertility and have an impact on the flexibility of the marital relationship. The earlier example of mother–daughter closeness around the reproductive issue is not unusual. Such coalitions are particularly likely to rigidify if the marital relationship is distant and the reproductive issue has special significance in the family of origin. When an infertility patient is an only child (perhaps signaling unresolved infertility issues in the previous generation) or has siblings who are cut off from the parents or have no plans to have children, she may feel additional pressure to produce a grandchild. Family losses, such as a premature sibling death or the death of a parent, can also contribute to intensified reproductive anxiety. Infertility and pregnancy losses in the previous generation can also increase the anxiety around the issue for the couple. Sometimes these issues have been buried for years in the family of origin but resurface with a remarkable intensity when a child is experiencing infertility.

Sibling rivalry issues can intensify with the stress of infertility. Some patients find it particularly painful when a younger sibling, especially a sister, becomes pregnant. The resulting envy and tension can undermine years of progress in resolving childhood rivalry.

**Maturity level of the couple.** Although predictable patterns of response exist for all infertile couples, great variations occur in the intensity of emotional reaction and consequent impact on the marriage. Kerr (1988) described the average level of chronic anxiety of individuals as parallel to the basic level of differentiation of the individuals and the couple. A well-functioning couple with few other stressors may be able to adapt quite well in the face of an initial encounter with infertility. The genogram illustrated in Figure 1 depicts an emotionally mature couple facing infertility.

*CASE VIGNETTE*

*Andrew, a 30-year-old MBA, was on a satisfying career path. Charlotte, his 29-year-old wife, worked long hours as an at-*

torney but planned to work part time after the birth of their child. They both maintained regular contact with their respective families of origin. Their complementary birth orders have contributed to their ability to make effective decisions about their infertility. The couple developed a treatment plan in consultation with a trusted fertility specialist. After failures with Clomid and Pergonal (see Table 1), they decided to attempt in vitro fertilization (IVF), costing over $7000, and used the savings they had set aside for the down payment on a new home.

Andrew and Charlotte increasingly avoided old friends who had babies. Joining a support group decreased the isolation and helped them make new friends. When sex became routinized they adapted by taking three months off from treatment to rejuvenate. To counter their stereotypical responses (Andrew the supporter and Charlotte the expressor), they scheduled time each week to allow each person to openly discuss the stress each was experiencing.

This couple met with the psychologist in the in vitro program for one session. They learned the normal reactions to infertility and received acknowledgment and support for the strategies they had already used to cope with the emotional stress of infertility.

The emotional maturity of this couple allowed them to adapt even in the face of the increasing stress of the infertility. A less emotionally mature couple with a higher level of chronic anxiety may appear quite different even in the early diagnostic stages of infertility. A thwarted pregnancy can disturb the balance of a relationship, and an immature couple may respond with rigidity. The second genogram (see Figure 2) depicts the marriage of two youngest children, each of whom is still overly involved with problems in his or her family of origin.

*CASE VIGNETTE*
The marriage followed shortly after the death of Jack's father, with whom he had an intensely conflictual relationship. Nancy is the caretaker of an alcoholic mother. Each has had a disruptive career path.

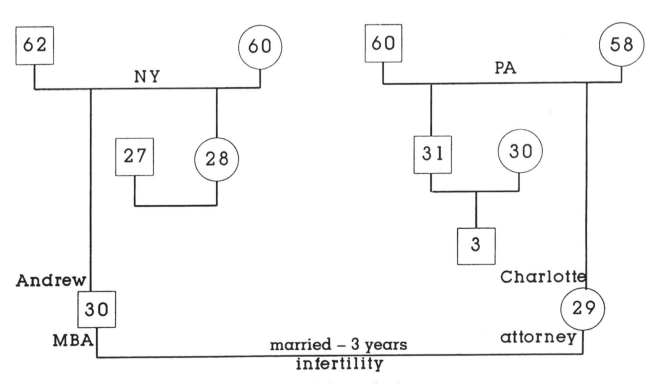

**FIGURE 1. The family of an emotionally mature couple facing infertility.**

Jack has a daughter from a previous marriage.

This couple struggled ineffectively with the decisions demanded by infertility. When options were presented, each avoided communication that would allow them to move forward. Nancy found it easier to communicate with her older sister than to confront Jack's denial. This pattern increased Nancy's disappointment and anger with Jack and led to distance in the relationship. Nancy secretly believed that Jack didn't want any more children.

Jack and Nancy often avoided sex, even at midcycle, because the polarization had created such unexpressed anger between them. Their inability to share the emotions triggered by infertility made them feel isolated from their long-standing friends. Financial issues also increased their anxiety, but the couple was paralyzed and unable to prioritize or construct a financial plan. It is hard to imagine progress for this couple without mental health intervention.

## Therapeutic Interventions

It is clear that the stress of infertility puts a significant strain on a marriage. It begins before diagnosis and is exacerbated by treatment processes, failures, and ongoing cycles of hope and disappointment. Often, however, the emotional side of infertility is ignored or misunderstood by both the patient and the medical system. Referrals to mental health professionals to aid in coping with infertility can be ex-

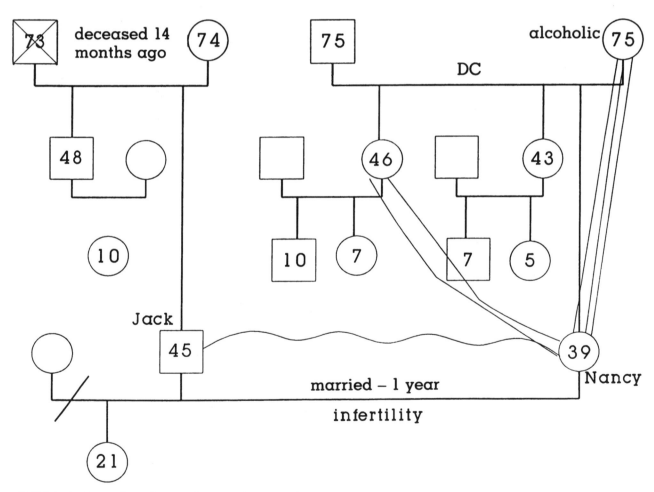

FIGURE 2. A couple with marital strain and infertility.

tremely helpful to a couple facing painful procedures and difficult decisions (McDaniel, Hepworth, & Doherty, 1992).

**Consultation model in a medical setting.** Infertility offers a unique opportunity for collaborative efforts between medical providers and family therapists to maximize biopsychosocial services to patients. Daniluk (1988) found that 53% of men and 72% of women beginning infertility treatment reported they would have participated in counseling if it were available.

Ideally, a patient and spouse are offered a routine session with a family consultant (Wynne, McDaniel, & Weber, 1986) as part of an assessment in the beginning stage of infertility treatment. A single session can address some of the anxieties common at this stage and help the couple identify and assess their coping strategies. It provides a forum for beginning open communication between partners about their reactions to the infertility issues. Support networks and family of origin relationships are assessed to increase the couple's awareness of any rigid or dysfunctional patterns. The inclusion of a family consultant as a routine part of the medical team helps to decrease the resistance that is often encountered to an outside mental health referral (Mandelbaum 1984).

Covington (1990), the director of counseling for a private infertility practice in Rockville, Maryland, described a team philosophy that treats the medical and emotional aspects of infertility as interdependent problems, each influencing the progression of the other. A psychosocial evaluation is done to assess the couple's functioning in relation to their fertility problems. The onsite counselor communicates to the medical staff the psychosocial issues unique to particular patients and helps the patients to understand the medical terminology, evaluation, and treatment process. This "bridge" role can be used whenever necessary during the treatment process.

The psychologist can also be an outside consultant to staff and patients. The first author developed such a model for direct services to patients. The initial component of the model is a psychoeducational group for patients early in treatment. Individual consultation for couples can be initiated as needed after

the group. Couples making the decision to use an expensive assisted approach for the first time and couples deciding if they should stop treatment are frequently the best candidates for this single consultation.

**Psychoeducational groups.** Psychoeducational programs for groups of infertile patients are composed of no more than 10 couples. The educational pieces describe typical emotional responses and coping styles in dealing with infertility, including reactions to assisted reproductive technologies (i.e., IVF, gamete interfallopian transfer [GIFT], and donor gametes). One or two physicians, nurses, and laboratory staff may attend this group to become more knowledgeable about the emotional reactions of patients and to understand the coping mechanisms of particular patients. These groups serve a preventive function by educating patients and teaching them skills for stress management. Information can help normalize the couple's distress in the face of infertility and contribute to a sense of increasing emotional mastery. Another value of a psychoeducational group is the opportunity to come together in a nonthreatening environment with other couples who are experiencing infertility. A couple often can recognize the importance of putting infertility "in its place" (Gonzalez, Steinglass, & Reiss, 1989) more easily if they can observe others' struggle for balance. They begin to understand how the dominant focus on infertility may be compromising other aspects of their identity as individuals and as a family. The structured format of a psychoeducational group offered routinely in collaboration with the medical provider is a much easier step for most couples than following through on an outside referral.

**Anxiety self-management techniques.** Both physiological and emotional reactivity are heightened in a situation of chronic stress. The highly stressed infertile couple may have difficulty developing the self-focus that is needed to address this situation objectively. Anxiety self-management techniques—such as relaxation training, biofeedback, and self-hypnosis—provide skills for physiological self-regulation during painful and invasive infertility-treatment techniques. This behavioral training complements other interventions. As self-focus increases for each member of the couple, automatic emotional behavior that interferes with decision making and general feelings of well-being decreases (Guerin, Fay, Burden, & Kautto, 1987).

**General psychosocial evaluation.** It is important to rule out chronic depression or an anxiety syndrome not related to the infertility that may need traditional intervention. These symptoms, which can be identified in a thorough history, can be exacerbated by the stress of the infertility and its treatment. The use of a tool like the Comprehensive Psychosocial History of Infertility (CPHI), which provides the medical team with a "comprehensive outline of the psychological and social issues of infertility" (Burns, 1993), can help differentiate couples who need psychological intervention from those that need supportive or educational counseling.

**Grief and loss work.** Loss is a pervasive theme in the infertility process and must be recognized and dealt with directly. The therapist will sometimes help a couple develop rituals for coping with the emotion of each new menstrual cycle or an actual pregnancy loss. These rituals provide a forum for conjoint mourning. Some couples may find it important to find a quiet space and sit silently with each other or each spend time alone and return with a special shared meal. Acknowledging the losses is an integral step in helping a couple to move on to the next level of intervention. When the time comes, the couple will need to develop their own ritual for letting go of the wished-for child and accepting the childfree choice or welcoming in the child that comes to them through intervention or adoption.

Once pregnancy is achieved, the infertile couple frequently is in a state of resolution. The immediate grief response from previous unsuccessful cycles feels terminated. The couple has worked hard to conceive and is less aware of the possibilities of additional hazards. The experience of infertility identifies the pregnancy as high risk, setting the stage for a possible pregnancy loss.

## PREGNANCY LOSS

The loss of a pregnancy is a relatively common event in the course of a couple's reproductive life. It is more prevalent than one might suspect. The most common form of pregnancy loss, miscarriage, usually occurs in the first trimester but can happen up to the 20th week of pregnancy. Approximately 15% to 20% of all recognized pregnancies, as many as 900,000 per year in the United States, may end in miscarriage. When the embryo develops outside of the uterus, the pregnancy is called ectopic. These pregnancies are potentially life threatening for the mother and fatal to the embryo. Two percent of pregnancies, about 70,000 per year, end as ectopic pregnancies. Elective abortions in this first trimester are also considered pregnancy losses and should be identified in an infertile couple's history.

The identification of abnormalities in the fetus through prenatal testing results in unwanted elective abortions in the second trimester. Less than 5% of all amniocenteses result in identification of abnormalities. Of those couples, 95% choose to abort. Stillbirth and fetal death in utero occur between week 20 and the delivery. About 30,000 babies per year, 1 in 123, are affected. Neonatal deaths occurring in the first 28 days of life comprise 1 in 144 infant births (Borg & Lasker, 1989). The medical systems through the years have underemphasized the emotional side of these pregnancy losses.

Each of these loss experiences creates a crisis for the couple. Clinical experience has demonstrated that many factors affect the severity of this emotional crisis, including the circumstances of this specific loss, the history of infertility or previous pregnancy loss, the mother's age, the preexistence of marital problems, the availability of emotional support, and any other major stressors that have occurred in the couple's life during the past year or two.

## Affects of Gestational Age and Stages of Attachment

The experience of pregnancy involves the mother traversing three psychological stages of attachment to her growing child (Furman, 1978). The achieved stage of the pregnancy will influence the experience of loss. The first stage is the confirmation of pregnancy. The mother and the developing fetus at this stage are often experienced as one, with no distinct separation. A miscarriage or ectopic pregnancy for a woman at this time can be dominated with feelings of loss of some aspect of the self. The man may focus on the well-being of his wife but feel little if any attachment to the fetus.

The second stage involves recognizing the child as an individual entity still unable to survive separately from the mother. When technology like chorionic villae sampling (CVS)[4] or sonography[5] provides couples with the sex of their child and a glimpse at the heart beating, attachment begins. At this stage the loss of a potential baby is mixed with a sense of loss of self. From our clinical experience, it appears that the husband's level of attachment is higher at this stage if he has been present for the sonogram.

The third and final stage occurs when the viability of the baby is confirmed at some time prior to delivery. The death of a child at this point is experienced as a loss of a potential person who has already acquired an identity from his or her 9-month journey from conception to birth (Leon, 1986).

Golbach, Dunn, Toedter, and Lasker (1991) have shown that gestational age is a particularly important factor in the determination of parental grief after a pregnancy loss. Those experiencing a late loss, late in the second or in the third trimester, experienced more grief than those experiencing an early loss. This same group shows more chronic expressions of grief when measured after 2 years. The following case will illustrate how these factors intertwine.

### CASE VIGNETTE

*Sharon and Tom were practicing attorneys in a large metropolitan area. They decided to delay childbearing until their careers were established. Sharon was then 40 years old, and Tom was 44 years old. They anticipated the likelihood that it would take them somewhat longer to conceive than their younger counterparts. After 18 months of trying, they decided to consult an infertility specialist who prescribed diagnostic testing and interventions. When Sharon conceived on her second round of*

*treatment with Pergonal (fertility-enhancement hormones), they held their breath for the first 3 months, knowing that her chances of miscarriage were substantially higher than for the woman under forty.*

*After the confirmation with amniocentesis that they had a healthy baby boy, the remaining months of pregnancy were uneventful. Sharon had minimal discomfort. She was so excited about becoming a mother that she decided to leave her job She spent her time at home decorating the nursery and reading all the books she could find on the care of a newborn. With natural childbirth classes under their belt Sharon and Tom felt fully prepared for the challenge of their new profession, parenthood, when her due date arrived.*

*That morning before her regular visit to the doctor Sharon noticed something different about the movement of the baby. He was considerably less active. She knew he was a large baby, and she thought that maybe he was just getting cramped. By the time she got to the doctor's office, she wasn't sure if there was any movement at all. The doctor had a difficult time getting a heartbeat and immediately sent her to the hospital to be placed on a fetal monitor. They were preparing to do an emergency cesarean-section. By the time they got to the hospital, 15 minutes later, Sharon knew that her son had stopped moving completely. When the nurses strapped on the fetal monitor, the silence was deafening. The surgery was cancelled. Their doctor told them that he was sorry but there was no need to put her through unnecessary surgery because the baby had died. He also told her that it would be better for her to allow her body to deliver "the fetus" natu-*

---

[4] CVS is a procedure done around the 10th week of pregnancy. A small portion of tissue that makes up the placenta is removed and examined under a microscope to determine genetic defects and the sex of the child.

[5] Sonography is a procedure that uses sound waves to view the developing fetus within the uterus. The initial sonogram, when a heartbeat is visible, can occur as early as 8 weeks of pregnancy.

*rally. Although the contractions were already beginning she was sent home. It took three agonizing days and the use of induction drugs that made her uterus contract more intensely for Sharon to deliver her perfectly formed dead son. Sharon and Tom now had to prepare for an experience they never anticipated, the funeral of their baby boy.*

## Gender Differences

The physical experience is unique for the mother in a pregnancy loss in that after the child has died her body maintains responses that are graphic reminders of the incompleteness. Beside the bleeding that always accompanies these losses, there can be soreness in the breasts or milk production that leave the woman intensely aware of her absent child.

The expression of grief at the loss of a baby differs for men and women, with mothers more open with their depression and withdrawal and fathers more stoical, coping primarily with denial (Benfield, Leib, & Vollman, 1978; Helmrath & Steinitz, 1978; Peppers & Knapp, 1988). This difference may have more to do with social norms that provide mothers with opportunities and support for these expressions that are not similarly provided for fathers. Goldbach et al. (1991) found that the overall grief expressed by men and women following pregnancy loss only differed significantly prior to the first anniversary. Thereafter, up to 29 months, there are few differences in overall grief. Rollins (1988) found that anger changed inversely for men and women over the 2-year period after the loss of a child of any age. Women's anger decreased over time, and men's increased. These gender differences in grief expression can create marital tension and inhibit open communication in the couple at a time when mutual support and understanding are critical.

## Inhibitors to Resolution of Pregnancy Loss

A miscarriage or perinatal death is always painful. A couple who has suffered years of infertility will be more vulnerable to incomplete mourning of this loss. Leon (1986) argues that perinatal death might be more difficult to resolve than other losses. There are six aspects of this loss that make it unique: (a) The loss is experienced as a narcissistic wound; (b) the bereaved mother overwhelmingly blames herself for the loss; (c) the child and the loss are experienced as less real because of the lack of concrete objects; (d) the death cannot be anticipated; (e) there is mourning of fantasies of future interactions; and, (f) the lack of social support and understanding by the medical profession and the community at large.

Some of these issues overlap with experiences of the infertile couple, particularly those couples who fail with the new reproductive technologies. Approximately 8 out of 10 attempts with IVF lead to a pregnancy loss (OTA, 1988). The IVF procedure involves removing eggs from a woman's stimulated ovaries, fertilizing them in a petri dish with her husband's sperm, incubating them for a day or two and then returning the fertilized and dividing embryos to the woman's uterus. When fertilized embryos are transferred, the woman can feel pregnant and subsequently experience failure of the procedure as a first-stage pregnancy loss.

As with other grief experiences, therapists are now learning that resolution of a pregnancy loss is fixed neither by time nor by the subsequent birth of a child. Peppers and Knapp (1980) describe a particular type of grief that appears to be unique to pregnancy loss, called "shadow grief." This experience comes from both the desire of the parents to never forget the baby and the lack of appropriate expression of these feelings to others. Shadow grief is always present in a dull sense that intensifies at anniversaries of conception, due dates, death dates, and holidays.

## Interventions

Increasing awareness of the emotional crisis of pregnancy loss is evidenced by many medical systems and providers incorporating immediate interventions that promote the beginning resolution of the grief of bereaved parents. The manner in which pregnancy loss is handled, either at home or in the hospital, will forever be part of the internal videotape permanently associated with this pregnancy loss. Sensitivity to hospital room assignments can prevent unknowing blunders by staff. If it is necessary to place a woman who has experienced a pregnancy loss on a maternity unit, marking the door to indicate to unknowing staff that a loss has occurred can alert them to respond appropriately. Four particular efforts have been identified as useful in facilitating a positive resolution (Chez, Flood, Lamb, & Davidson, 1982): (a) Find ways to make the loss real and tangible (e.g., viewing the dead child or the fetal remains, giving pictures of the baby, providing mementos, or naming the baby); (b) find ways to acknowledge the loss (e.g., funeral or some other ritual to share the loss with others); (c) find ways to facilitate emotional expressiveness about the loss for both parents (e.g., give permission to cry by talking about the details of the loss); and (d) find ways to restore self-esteem and self-image (e.g., share medical information and autopsy results to cut down on the guilt and self-blame).

The experience of pregnancy loss, like infertility, presents an emotional challenge to the couple and to the mental health professional. A family consultant can provide effective short-term intervention at the time of the pregnancy loss. Schreiner, Gresham, and Green (1979) found that a single phone call of 15 to 45 minutes within 10 days of the death that reviews the grieving process and addresses parental concerns significantly reduces parental guilt and depression several months later. Klaus and Kennell (1976) proposed a three-meeting model spread out over 6 months for couples experiencing pregnancy loss. The first occurs immediately after the loss. The second occurs later in the first week, and the third is within 6 months of the pregnancy loss. The meetings should be partly psychoeducational, focusing on the importance of the rituals of grieving, normalizing the emotional process, stressing the importance of obtaining, and integrating medical information about the loss and sharing resources such as the value of meeting with other parents in a support group organized around pregnancy loss.

If and when a new pregnancy occurs, the bereaved couple can benefit from meeting with the family consultant, especially at the time during the pregnancy when the first loss occurred. The intervention helps them recognize and focus on the differences between this pregnancy and the last one.

The couple may also be aware of the disappointment of the extended family who have been "robbed" of the anticipated new roles as grandparents and

have their own grieving to do. This generation may also feel guilt about the loss because of genetic factors or history of pregnancy losses themselves. Sharing these reactions is sometimes inhibited in an effort to "protect" the bereaved parents (Borg & Lasker, 1989) and may need to be encouraged by a family consultant.

As with infertility and other losses, pregnancy loss can pose a strain on the couple's communication and relationship. The chronic anxiety following such a loss can increase anger and emotional distance in a couple. Blame of one's partner sometimes occurs in an effort to find some explanation for the loss. Sexual distance is common. Polarization is not unusual where one partner is sad and depressed and the other tries to be cheerful and avoid discussion of the loss to "help" the other. Sometimes a designated period each day, even 10 minutes, to discuss the loss and share shattered fantasies can help keep communication open for the couple (Borg & Lasker, 1989).

## CONCLUSION

The therapeutic interventions most often used by infertile persons or those who experience a pregnancy loss are consultation and psychoeducation. Services offered within the medical setting provide an easier opportunity for referral and reduce the resistance to mental health intervention. A thorough psychosocial assessment, including relationships with families of origin, will provide clues to the vulnerability level of the couple entering these difficult experiences.

For the mental health provider to be effective with infertile couples and be taken seriously by medical practitioners, it is important to have a thorough understanding of medical systems and the specific procedures involved in infertility treatment in order to ask knowledgeable questions. The effective consultant has an expertise in family systems and an understanding of the typical emotional-response patterns stimulated by the infertility procedures. The unique position of the mental health professional allows him or her to bridge communication and understanding between the couple and the medical system.

The work of the family consultant with the infertile couple is to help the couple rebalance their perspectives on having children. Family building is only one component of anyone's life script. Every couple entering treatment should have the opportunity to explore feelings about alternatives, including child-free living. It is especially true because many couples eventually leave their physicians' care without a biological child. Educating couples about the intense fluctuating emotional responses and gender differences typical with infertility and pregnancy loss allows them to develop more effective coping styles at times of crisis and over the long term.

The validation of infertility as legitimate stress for every couple can "improve the emotional climate of a marriage by allowing the spouses to view the marriage as suffering from stress rather than as intrinsically bad" (Guerin et al., 1987, p. 150). Normalizing changes in the sexual behavior of the couple during planned sex helps couples to resume their former sexual relationship once the infertility treatment is not actively being pursued.

During treatment, decision making is challenged in every area. Medical decisions are predicated on financial, career, and time issues. However, the emotional impact of losing the option to produce a "child of one's own" can create an intense, emotionally reactive context that impedes decision making. Understanding the reality and impact of the chronic stress and learning skills for anxiety management are key to developing assistance models for infertile couples. Pregnancy loss also demands that a couple understands the emotional and the physical aspects of the situation. These couples have accomplished the goal of pregnancy but now are forced to change their criteria for success. Unanswerable questions often remain when a pregnancy fails. The mental health provider in a hospital setting has the unique opportunity and responsibility to ensure that the grief work allows the couple to reach closure about this loss.

With health-care reform, some medical systems are coming to understand the importance of treating the whole person and even the whole family. The stress of infertility diagnosis and treatment and pregnancy loss are problems where family psychologists can collaborate with other health-care professionals to provide integrated biopsychosocial care to patients.

# References

Andrews, F. M., Abbey, A., & Halman, L. J. (1992). Is fertility-problem stress different? The dynamics of stress in fertile and infertile couples. *Fertility and Sterility,* 57, 1247–1251.

Baran A., & Pannor, R. (1993). *Lethal secrets: The psychology of donor insemination.* New York: Amistad.

Benedek, T. (1952). Infertility as a psychosomatic defense. *Fertility and Sterility,* 3, 527–537.

Benfield, D. G., Lieb, S. A., & Vollman, J. H. (1978). Grief response of parents to neonatal death and parent participation in deciding care. *Pediatrics,* 62, 171–177.

Berger, D. M. (1977). The role of the psychiatrist in a reproductive biology clinic. *Fertility and Sterility,* 28, 141–145.

Berger, D. M. (1980). Infertility: A psychiatrist's perspective. *Canadian Journal of Psychiatry,* 25, 553–559.

Berk, A., & Shapiro, J. L. (1984). Some implications of infertility on marital therapy. *Family Therapy,* 11, 37–47.

Borg, S., & Lasker, J. (1989). *When pregnancy fails: Families coping with miscarriage, ectopic pregnancy, stillbirth, and infant death.* New York: Bantam.

Bowen, M. (1978). *Family therapy in clinical practices.* Northvale, NJ: Jason Aronson.

Burns, L. H. (1990). An exploratory study of perceptions of parenting after infertility. *Family Systems Medicine,* 8, 177–189.

Burns, L. H. (1993). An overview of psychological infertility. *Infertility and Reproductive Medicine Clinics of North America,* 4(3), 433–454.

Carter, E., & McGoldrick, M. (1980). *The family life cycle.* New York: Gardner.

Chez, R., Flood, B., Lamb, J. M., & Davidson, G. (1982). Helping patients and doctors cope with prenatal death. *Contemporary OB/GYN,* 20, 98–134.

Connolly, K. J., Edelmann, R. J., & Cooke, I. D. (1987). Distress and marital problems associated with infertility. *Journal of Reproductive and Infant Psychology,* 5, 49–57.

Covington, S. (1990, October). *The psychosocial evaluation of the infertile couple within the medical context.* Paper presented at the annual meeting of the American Fertility Society, Washington, DC.

Daniluk, J. C. (1988). Infertility: Intrapersonal and interpersonal impact. *Fertility and Sterility,* 49, 982–990.

Deutsch, H. (1945). *Psychology of women: Vol. 2. Motherhood.* New York: Grune & Stratton.

Domar, A. D., & Seibel, M. M. (1990). Emotional aspects of infertility. In M. M. Seibel (Ed.), *Infertility: A comprehensive text.* (pp. 23–35). East Norwalk, CT: Appleton & Lange.

Fagan, J. P., Schmidt, C. W., Rock, J. A., Damewood, M. D., Halle, E., & Wise, T. N. (1986). Sexual functioning and psychological evaluation of in vitro fertilization couples. *Fertility and Sterility, 46,* 668–672.

Fischer, I. C. (1953). Psychogenic aspects of sterility. *Fertility and Sterility, 4,* 466–470.

Freeman, E. W., Boxer, A. S., Rickels, K., Tureck, R., & Mastrioanni, L. (1985). Psychological evaluation and support in a program of in vitro fertilization and embryo transfer. *Fertility and Sterility, 43,* 48–53.

Furman, E. (1978). The death of the newborn: Care of parents. *Birth and the Family Journal, 5,* 214–218.

Golbach, K., Dunn, D., Toedter, L., & Lasker, J. (1991). The effects of gestational age and gender on grief after pregnancy loss. *American Journal of Orthopsychiatry, 6*(3), 461–467.

Gonzalez, S., Steinglass, P., & Reiss, D. (1989). Putting the illness in its place: Discussion groups for families with chronic medical illnesses. *Family Process, 28,* 69–87.

Greil, A. L., Leitko, T. A., & Porter, K. L. (1988). Infertility: His and hers. *Gender and Society, 2,* 172–199.

Guerin, P., Jr., Fay, L., Burden, S., & Kautto, J. G. (1987). *The evaluation and treatment of marital conflict.* New York: Basic Books.

Helmrath, T. A., & Steinitz, E. M. (1978). Death of an infant: Parental grieving and the failure of social support. *Journal of Family Practice, 6,* 785–790.

Hertz, D. G. (1982). Infertility and the physician-patient relationship: A biopsychosocial challenge. *General Hospital Psychiatry, 4,* 95–101.

Kaufman, G. (1985). *Shame: The power of caring.* Rochester, VT: Schenkman Books.

Kerr, M. (1988, September). Chronic anxiety and defining a self. *Atlantic Monthly,* pp. 35–48.

Klaus, M., & Kennell, J. (1976). *Maternal–infant bonding.* St. Louis, MO: Mosby.

Kraft, A., Palombo, J., Mitchell, D., Dean, C., Meyers, S., & Schmidt, A. (1980). The psychological dimensions of infertility. *American Journal of Orthopsychiatry, 50,* 618–628.

Lalos, A., Lalos, O., Jacobsson, L., & Von Schoulta, B. (1985). Psychological reactions to the medical investigation and surgical treatment of infertility. *Gynecological and Obstetric Investigation, 20,* 209–217.

Leon, I. (1986). Psychodynamics of prenatal loss. *Psychiatry, 49,* 312–324.

Lorber, J. (1987). In vitro fertilization and gender politics. *Women and Health, 13*(1–2), 117–133.

MacNab, R. T. (1984). Infertility and men: A study of change and adaptive choices in the lives of involuntary childless men. *Dissertation Abstracts International, 47,* 774–778.

Mahlstedt, P. P. (1985). Psychological components of infertility. *Fertility and Sterility, 43,* 335–346.

Mandelbaum, E. K. (1984). Family medicine consultant: Reframing the contribution of medical social work. *Family Systems Medicine, 2*(3), 309–319.

McDaniel, S., Hepworth, J., & Doherty, W. (1992). Pregnancy loss, infertility and reproductive technology. In S. McDaniel, J. Hepworth, & W. Doherty (Eds.), *Medical family therapy* (pp. 152–183). New York: Basic Books.

Menning, B. E. (1977). *Infertility: A guide for the childless couple.* Englewood Cliffs, NJ: Prentice-Hall.

Menning, B. E. (1988). *Infertility: A guide for the childless couple* (2nd ed.). Englewood Cliffs, NJ: Prentice-Hall.

Nachtigall, R. D., Becker, G., & Wozny, M. (1992). The effects of gender specific diagnosis on men's and women's response to infertility. *Fertility and Sterility, 57,* 113–121.

Peppers, L., & Knapp, R. (1988). *How to go on living after the death of a baby.* Atlanta: Peachtree.

Rollins, J. (1988, August). *Longitudinal grief responses of husbands and wives following the death of a child.* Paper presented at the Society for the Study of Social Problems, Atlanta, GA.

Rothman, D., Kaplan, A. H., & Nettles, E. (1962). Psychosomatic infertility. *American Journal of Obstetrics and Gynecology, 83,* 373–381.

Sabatelli, R., Meth, R., & Gavazzi, S. (1988). Factors mediating the adjustment to involuntary childlessness. *Family Relations, 37,* 338–343.

Sadler, A. G., & Syrop, C. H. (1987). The stress of infertility: Recommendations for assessment and intervention. *Family Therapy Collections, 22,* 1–17.

Schreiner, R., Gresham, E., & Green, M. (1979). Physician's responsibility to parents after death of an infant. *American Journal of Diseases of Children, 133,* 723–726.

Seibel, M., & Taymor, M. (1982). Emotional aspects of infertility. *Fertility and Sterility, 37,* 137–145.

U.S. Congress, Office of Technology Assessment. (1988). *Infertility: Medical and social choices* (OTA-BA-358). Washington, DC: Author.

Wright, J., Bissonnette, F., Duchesne, C., Benoit, J., Sabourin, S., & Girard, Y. (1991). Psychological distress and infertility: Men and women respond differently. *Fertility and Sterility, 55,* 100–108.

Wynne, L. C., McDaniel, S. H., & Weber, T. (1986). *Systems consultation: A new perspective for family therapy.* New York: Guilford Press.

Zoldbrod, A. (1993). *Men, women, and infertility.* New York: Lexington.

# CHAPTER 25

# A DEVELOPMENTAL BIOPSYCHOSOCIAL APPROACH TO THE TREATMENT OF CHRONIC ILLNESS IN CHILDREN AND ADOLESCENTS

*Beatrice L. Wood*

Childhood chronic illness challenges the human spirit. The seriously ill child is faced with life and death concerns well beyond his or her years, and for parents there is nothing more heartbreaking than having their child compromised by severe illness or disability, just when children should be most care-free. The courage and perseverance these families bring to bear on this devastating life circumstance is a source of inspiration, which makes it a privilege to participate in their care. Nonetheless, there are times when health caregivers suffer from demoralization, particularly when children and families are mired in apparently endless patterns of psychosocial and physical dysfunction and developmental arrest.

There is a valuable role for the systems therapist to play in promoting the well-being of these children, families, and health caregivers. Early intervention can promote successful multisystem (child, family, health caregiver, school, and peer) accommodation to chronic illness, thus preventing maladaptive response patterns. This chapter provides a developmental biopsychosocial framework to guide such intervention toward the following goals:

1. to minimize the impact of the disease on the physical and emotional development and functioning of the child and family;
2. to achieve a dynamic balance between disease management and quality of life for the patient and family; and
3. to facilitate the integrated functioning of the chronically ill child with his or her psychosocial surroundings.

The assumptions underlying this approach will be outlined; the overarching goal of treatment will be described as *biopsychosocial balance*. The structural family model's construct of *boundary* will be introduced as a multilevel conceptual tool to organize assessment and intervention. Boundary will then be differentiated into proximity, hierarchy, and responsivity to provide greater precision in application to individual, intrafamily, and social system levels of function. A case will be presented to illustrate the application of these concepts and demonstrate the therapeutic approach to restoring biospsychosocial balance for a chonically ill adolescent. Finally, guidelines for early assessment, preventive intervention, and restoration of biopsychosocial balance will be presented.

## CHILDREN'S HEALTH PROBLEMS

Children's health problems are among the most pressing concerns of this decade. They encompass infant mortality; low birth weight; neuropsychiatric compromise from maternal addiction; malnutrition; failure of immunization; substance abuse; teenage pregnancy; sexually transmitted disease, including AIDS; and accidental injury (Children's Defense Fund [CDF], 1991, 1992). Furthermore, despite improvements in children's mortality rates, chronic illness remains a significant health problem with an estimated 31% of children under the age of 18 having at least one chronic health condition (Adams & Hardy, 1989; National Center for Health Statistics, 1990; Newacheck & Taylor, 1992). These illnesses dramatically affect the psychosocial functioning and development of children and their families (Cadman, Boyle, Szatmari, & Offord, 1987; Hobbs, Perrin, & Ireys, 1985). To complicate matters further, stressful psychosocial factors have negative consequences for health by directly influencing the disease process and by interfering with disease management (CDF, 1991; Weiner, 1992). These bidirectional influences indicate the need for a multilevel treatment approach to chronic illness. However, one impediment to such comprehensive treatment is an obsolete "either–or" mind-set regarding the nature of disease.

## BEYOND THE PSYCHOSOMATIC–ORGANIC ILLNESS DICHOTOMY: A BIOBEHAVIORAL CONTINUUM OF ILLNESS

The organic–psychosomatic dichotomy is rendered obsolete by recent scientific advances in the realm of psychoneuroimmunology and behavioral medicine (Ader, Felton, & Cohen, 1991; Weiner, 1992). A more useful approach is a systems paradigm that assumes mutual influence of social, psychological, and physical factors in all aspects of health and illness. Within this systems framework one could construct a continuum of disorder that varies according to the relative proportions of psychological and physical influence on the disease (see Figure 1). At one extreme would be disorders with relatively strong psychosocial influence, such as functional abdominal pain. At the other extreme would be disorders such as neuromuscular disease. Diseases such as asthma or diabetes might range anywhere in between, depending on the relative contribution of psychosocial and physical factors in the course of illness for a particular patient.

Recent advances in biological psychiatry demonstrating the physiological underpinnings of diseases that previously have been considered emotional or mental illnesses (e.g., bipolar affective disorder, schizophrenia, autism) indicate a comparable appreciation of the convergence of the psychological and biological aspects of illness. Thus, physical and emotional

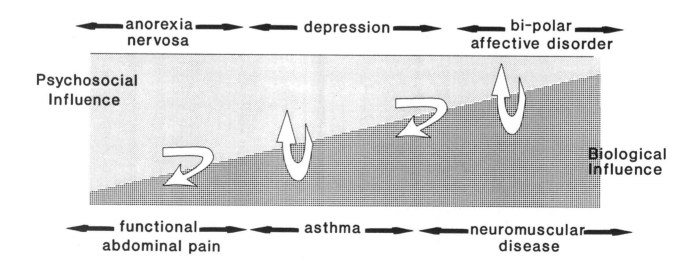

**Psychosocially Manifested Disease**

**Physically Manifested Disease**

FIGURE 1. A biobehavioral continuum of disease.

illnesses can be represented on the same biobehavioral continuum (see Figure 1).

The advantage of conceptualizing disease in this manner is that it permits a general but integrated biopsychosocial approach to assessment and treatment of both physically and psychosocially manifested aspects of illness. The term *biobehavioral* was chosen to characterize this continuum because this concept emphasizes the unity of biological and behavioral processes and avoids unidirectional psychic causal connotations suggested by the term *psychosomatic*. Other chapters in this handbook will cover the behaviorally, psychologically, and emotionally manifested domains of dysfunction. Hence, this chapter will concentrate on disorders that manifest themselves physically.

## BIOPSYCHOSOCIAL BALANCE

Each illness has its own particular psychosocial and developmental challenges and sequelae, whether episodic or chronic, progressive or life threatening (see Rolland, 1984, for a psychosocial typology of illness). Table 1 has been provided as a guide to publications with a systemic approach to specific diseases in children. (Where publications were not available for particular diseases in children, a general or adult-oriented article was substituted.)

Despite the unique characteristics of each disease, there are developmental and biopsychosocial features that childhood illnesses have in common (Hobbs, Perrin, & Ireys, 1985), which provide the basis for a general integrated treatment model. Indeed many of the same issues hold true for chronic mental and emotional, as well as physical, illness, and the model presented herein can be applied to them as well (see Anderson, Reiss, & Hogarty, 1986). Issues include, but are not limited to: (a) the tendency of chronic illness to impede psychosocial well-being and development of the patient; (b) the emotional and financial stress and time demands on the family or caregiver system; (c) the necessity for the family and social structure to change to accommodate to the demands of the chronic illness; (d) the tendency for maladaptive family or caregiver patterns to interfere with disease management, either through poor coordination with medical care or by direct influence on

the disease process through stress-mediating psychophysiological pathways (Gottman & Fainsilber Katz, 1989; Wood, Watkins, Nogueira, Zimand, & Carroll, 1989); and (e) the tendency for chronic illness to disrupt school and peer functioning.

The developmental biopsychosocial approach presented herein assumes that the well-being of the patient depends on a dynamic balance among three levels of functioning—individual physical functioning, individual psychological functioning, and family–social functioning—which at times may be in

| TABLE 1 | |
|---|---|

**Systems-Oriented Intervention for Physically Manifested Disorders**

| Physical Manifestation Disorder | Reference |
|---|---|
| AIDS | Landau-Stanton & Clements, 1993 |
| Asthma | Masterson, 1985 |
| | Meyerstein, 1992 |
| | Miller & Wood, 1991 |
| Cancer | Noeker, Petermann, & Bode, 1990 |
| Cystic fibrosis | Patterson, Budd, Goetz, & Warwick, 1993 |
| Diabetes | Sargent & Baker, 1983 |
| Epilepsy | Jan, Ziegler, & Erba, 1991 |
| | Griffith & Griffith, 1992 |
| Gastrointestinal disorders | Wood, 1991 |
| Juvenile rheumatoid arthritis | Vandvik, Hoyeraal, & Fagertun, 1989 |
| Nonorganic failure to thrive | Drotar & Sturm, 1988 |
| Sickle cell disease | Nevergold, 1987 |
| Somatization | Campo & Fritsch, 1994 |
| | McDaniel, Campbell, & Seaburn, 1990 |
| **General chronic illness sequelae** | |
| Pain | Covelman, Scott, Buchanan, & Rosman, 1990 |
| | Shapiro, Cohen, Covelman, Howe, & Scott, 1991 |
| Disabilities | Patterson, 1991 |
| Terminal illness and death | Koocher & MacDonald, 1992 |
| | McDaniel, Campbell, & Seaburn, 1990 |
| | Rolland, 1991 |
| | Walsh & McGoldrick, 1991 |

competition (see Figure 2). This balance is relevant for health and illness at all ages but is particularly critical during childhood and adolescence when biopsychosocial imbalances can arrest or delay development and thus have dramatic and far-reaching consequences. Imbalance can occur in several ways.

One kind of imbalance can occur when particular family (or other social context) patterns optimize medical management of physical well-being, while seriously undermining the child's psychosocial functioning and development. For example, frequent monitoring of blood glucose for a diabetic child may optimally control the disease but may also constrict the child's peer and social interaction, thus impairing development in this domain.

Another common imbalance occurs if emotional development and psychosocial functioning of the child patient proceeds to the detriment of physical well-being when, for example, medical treatments are chronically neglected in favor of academic or social functions.

From the perspective of the family, patterns that optimize the child's medical management and psychosocial functioning may severely impair aspects of the family functioning. For example, a marriage can be neglected, or even sacrificed, to provide intensive caretaking for the ill child or siblings' needs may remain unappreciated and unaddressed. Alternatively, failure of family patterns to accommodate to the child's illness may support ongoing family functioning but medically or psychosocially endanger the child. The developmental biobehavioral systems framework presented in the following section can support the therapist in attending to this dynamic interplay of processes while guiding assessment and intervention.

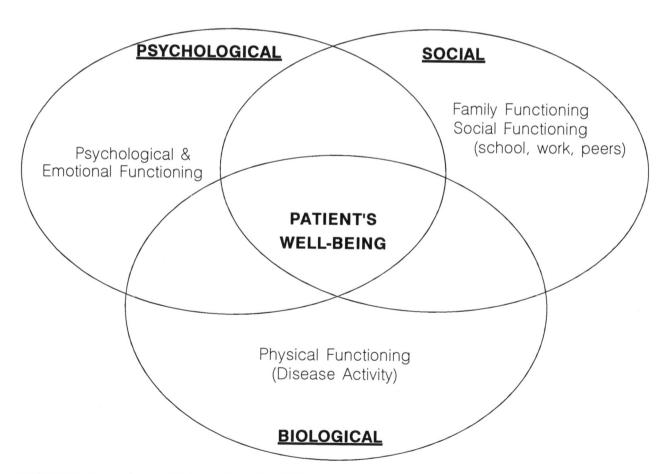

**FIGURE 2. Biopsychosocial balance of quality of life.**

## THE FAMILY IS PIVOTAL IN ACHIEVING BIOPSYCHOSOCIAL BALANCE

The family is indisputably one of the most influential contexts determining the child's physical and psychosocial well-being and development and achieving biospsychosocial balance. Current cultural evolution and diversity of caregiving systems requires a redefinition of the term *family*. This chapter considers family to be a nexus of people, living together or in close contact, who take care of one another and provide guidance for the dependent members of the group. Because of its pivotal role in biospsychosocial balance, the family can be a powerful ally to the health care provider in assisting the child to respond to illness in adaptive and creative ways. Unfortunately, chronic illness can compromise family functioning, which, in turn, can impair the child's physical and psychosocial well-being. Early systemic intervention guided by a biopsychosocial model can help prevent such sequelae. The structural family model (Minuchin, 1974) is uniquely well-suited to address these developmental biopsychosocial issues.

## BOUNDARY: A MULTILEVEL CONCEPTUAL TOOL

The central construct around which structural family theory evolved is the concept of boundary, defined as the "rules defining who participates and how" (Minuchin, 1974, p. 53). The metaphor of boundary is applicable at the individual level, intrafamily level, and social system level. Change in boundaries is a fundamental aspect of the developmental process, and boundaries also change in response to important life challenges, such as chronic illness. Thus, understanding how boundaries normatively develop and how they may be compromised by chronic illness provides a powerful conceptual approach to assessment and treatment of chronically ill children in their natural surroundings.

### Individual and Intrafamily Boundaries

Two aspects of boundaries are particularly relevant to the development of the child in the context of the family: self-concept and personal identity and the degree of interpersonal involvement.

At the beginning of childhood the infant's self is merged with the caregiver's in a high degree of interpersonal involvement, and distinctions between the self and interpersonal aspects of boundary have not yet emerged. Individuation, which entails the progressive differentiation of boundaries, is a critical process of psychosocial and emotional development (Mahler, 1968). As a child individuates and forms firmer boundaries between self and other, he or she is developing a self-concept (Eder & Mangelsdorf, in press) and ultimately an identity. A child with diffuse self-boundaries is unclear about identity and proper roles, whereas a child with rigid self-boundaries may be inflexible when faced with developmental or environmental requirements for change in behavior. The developing child is also learning to achieve a balanced boundary between autonomy and interpersonal involvement. An isolated child may be described as having rigid boundaries, whereas a child who is unremittingly involved with family members may be described as having diffuse boundaries.

Flexible self–identity boundaries and interpersonal boundaries facilitate adaptive psychosocial interaction. Unfortunately, severe acute or chronic childhood illness can compromise the normative development of these two boundary processes. In the care and treatment of illness, the child's physical and emotional boundaries are necessarily rendered more permeable to family and medical caregivers. To the extent that children must surrender sovereignty over their own bodies, their psychosocial competency and development of autonomy (increased interpersonal boundaries) may be impeded. Over a period of time this process can also influence self-concept, and identity confusion can occur, with children thinking of themselves and identifying themselves to others as "an asthmatic" or "a diabetic," rather than according to other normative ethnic or cultural identifiers.

Similar boundary diffusion can occur in other family members and in the family at large. For example, boundaries articulating parental roles as opposed to health caregiver roles can become blurred, with parents abdicating parental rights and responsibilities in their attempt to protect the child from recurrences or worsening of the illness. This blurring of role boundaries may result in the neglect of the child's developmental need to assume responsibility for his physical and psychosocial well-being. For example, it is tempting for parents of children with diabetes to take complete charge of monitoring the child's blood glucose. Although this degree of parental involvement may maximize medical safety in the short run, it fails to support the development of self-care skills that the child needs and deprives the child of the sense of mastery that is necessary to psychosocial and emotional development.

Subsystem boundaries can become blurred, with siblings acting as parents, thus depriving both the patient and the siblings from the developmental benefits of normal sibling relationships, including negotiation of conflict. Siblings sometimes suffer from undetected influences of having a chronically ill brother or sister (Wood et al., 1988). They may experience compelling conflict between guilt over being healthy and anger over having less attention. Indeed, some real needs may have been neglected because of the apparent or actual need to prioritize attention and resources for the ill child. Caring for a child with chronic illness can impair the family's identity. Family therapy has unwittingly fostered this impairment by conceptualizing and referring to families as "diabetic families," "anorexic families," and so on. This labeling results in the alienation of families from their normal sociocultural contexts, which compromises healthy functioning.

The degree of interpersonal attention and support required in families of chronically ill children may increase intrafamily involvement to the detriment of a healthy balance between autonomy and belonging (diffuse intrafamily boundaries). Family members and the family as a whole may also become isolated from social systems outside the family (rigid boundaries), which would serve not only as support for them, but also as healthy stimulation to psychosocial growth and development.

## Social Systems Boundaries

The physical and psychosocial development of the chronically ill child proceeds in four critical social systems: the family, the school, the peer group, and the health care system (Figure 3). The illness of the child influences the interaction of these systems with the child and with one another. In turn, the way in which these systems respond to the ill child either enhances physical and psychosocial functioning and development or undermines it (Miller & Wood, 1991). Adaptive coordination among these larger social systems is critical to the child's and family's physical and psychosocial well-being. As will be fully discussed later in this chapter, the construct of boundary is a powerful conceptual tool for characterizing and intervening with patterns of relationship among these social systems.

## THE ONTOGENY OF INDIVIDUAL AND INTRAFAMILY BOUNDARIES IN CHILDHOOD CHRONIC ILLNESS

The developmental aspect of interpersonal and systems boundaries throughout the family life cycle is crucial to considerations of childhood chronic illness. First, particular stages in development have specific implications for the balance of psychosocial developmental needs and disease management. Second, there is a normative developmental shift that needs to take place with the patient becoming increasingly responsible for the management of his or her disease and its psychosocial sequelae (increasingly articulated personal boundaries). Third, differentiation of identity (development of self-boundaries) apart from the illness needs to be fostered by the family, school, peers, and the health-care system.

## Preschool Children

Some childhood chronic illnesses occur early in a child's life. These young children are normatively quite vulnerable and may require more extensive and frequent medical management, both at home and in the doctor's office. At the same time, it is important for even young children to become active participants in managing their illness. For example, young children with asthma can be taught to notice when breathing is easy and when it is strained, and medicine or respiratory treatments can be self-administered with close parental observation and supervision. Active participation will help these children to begin to achieve mastery over their illness and their bodies (strengthening personal boundaries). A balance must be struck, even at an early age, between family management and the self-care of chronic illness. This is essential groundwork for the developmentally synchronized increase in children's active responsibility in the management of and adaptation to chronic illness.

## Elementary School Children

With entry into school, chronically ill children must assume a more active and responsible role in the assessment and management of their illness. They must be able to recognize symptom states, express their needs in this regard, and effect treatment. To do so, they will need to interact and negotiate directly with school personnel without the assistance and protection of their parents. This key transition necessitates increasing autonomy or personal boundaries of the chronically ill child, as well as permeable boundaries with school personnel, caretakers, and peers, who will need to be educated about the disease.

## Adolescence

The shift toward self-management of chronic illnesses picks up momentum during adolescence. However, the transition to full responsibility for the management of the medical and psychosocial aspects of a child's illness will be smoother if it is part of a gradual shift toward independent self-care that has been taking place all along. Again balance in boundary permeability is key in this process. Sometimes families and health care providers retain too much responsibility for the disease and thus maintain diffuse boundaries. Alternatively, they may abdicate responsibility to the adolescent prematurely and thus maintain impermeable boundaries.

Not infrequently, adolescents will demand this control as part of their general attempt to take charge of their destiny. This is not in itself inappropriate. However, a common error is to hand over responsibility to adolescents because of their chrono-

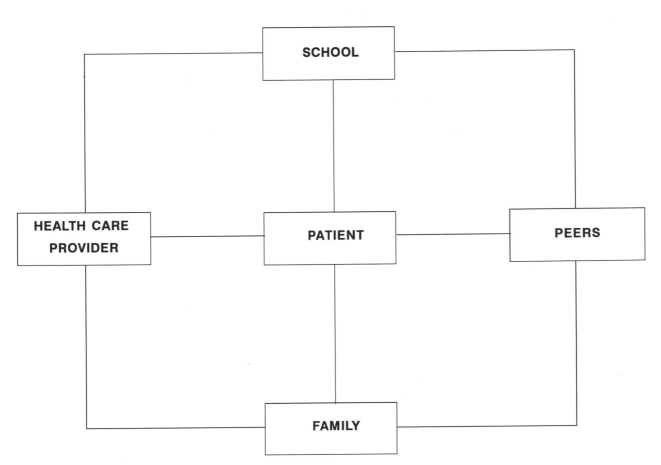

**FIGURE 3. Critical elements in the social surround of the chronically ill child.**

logic age or in response to the intensity of their demands for control. This is not wise. Adolescents must demonstrate through their behavior, not through argument, that they can manage their illness responsibly. But to do so, adolescents need to have some aspects of self-care given over to them to demonstrate their mastery. At times, disease management can become the focus around which adolescents attempt to rebel during the process of individuation. Usually, this can be prevented if the process of increasing self-care has been part of the ongoing treatment.

Establishing a new balance of autonomy and belonging in the family requires movement in the direction of firmer boundaries and increased independence for adolescents. This is understandably difficult for chronically ill adolescents and families to negotiate. These families are accustomed to a great deal of involvement and diffuse boundaries and thus may lack confidence that their adolescents will be able to manage their illness on their own. This may eventuate in an intense struggle between the adolescent and his or her parents, which can be eased by supportive intervention of the primary health-care provider or the systems therapist.

Occasionally, parent–adolescent struggle over the illness is part of other dysfunction in the family or is indicative of emotional disorder in the adolescent or other family members. If this appears to be the case, prompt and intensive intervention is warranted, as this can be a very dangerous situation for a medically ill child. (See Boxer, Carson, & Miller, 1988).

Adolescence is a particularly crucial stage for chronically ill youngsters because this is the time when identity formation is a primary task. Care must be taken to encourage the adolescent to develop a firm boundary between the disease and his or her self-identity. *The child or adolescent should neither be referred to nor think of himself or herself as an "asthmatic" or "diabetic," but rather as a person who has asthma or diabetes.* Parents, health-care providers, and school personnel can assist healthy identity formation by striking a balance between firm limit setting and nurturance, while expecting the chronically ill adolescent to function as normally as possible.

The systems therapist can monitor these changes in boundary function and intervene as necessary so

as to facilitate the dynamic balance and pacing of the reorganization of intrasystem and intersystem boundaries.

## INTRAFAMILY BOUNDARIES: PROXIMITY, HIERARCHY, AND RESPONSIVITY

The differentiation of the concept of boundary into three dimensions adds precision to this developmental biopsychosocial framework. Wood divided the concept of boundary into two component dimensions: proximity (interpersonal boundaries) and generational hierarchy (one type of subsystem boundary; Wood, 1985; Wood & Talmon, 1983). Subsequently a third boundary-relevant dimension was introduced: responsivity, defined as the degree or intensity with which individuals in the family respond to emotionally charged events and to one another (Wood, 1993).

Proximity refers to the extent to which various domains of interaction are shared by family members. Four important domains of proximity are personal space, private information, emotions, and decisions. Families vary in the extent to which they share interaction in these domains: Families who share much interaction would be characterized as having high proximity, and families who share little would have low proximity. Level of proximity does not indicate function or dysfunction. It is the way patterns of proximity interact with other family and individual patterns and needs that determines whether particular levels of proximity are adaptive or maladaptive. (This will be elucidated later with case material.)

Generational hierarchy is defined as the extent to which parents are in charge of their children by providing them with nurturance and limits through a strong parental alliance. The absence of parent–child coalitions against the other parent supports functional generational hierarchy. Again, families range widely with respect to strength of generational hierarchy, and the adaptiveness of these patterns is jointly determined by other family and individual patterns and needs.

*Responsivity* is a notion that has frequently been used to characterize certain aspects of family process. Bowen described a similar phenomenon that he termed *reactivity,* conceptualized as being linked to the degree of "differentiation of self" and the degree of anxiety at the individual and family levels (Kerr & Bowen, 1988). Responsivity encompasses Bowen's reactivity but emphasizes normative aspects of functioning by explicitly including different kinds and origins of responsivity, such as temperament or psychophysiologic reactivity (see Boyce, Barr, & Zeltzer, 1992).

The extent to which individual family members are responsive will partially determine the amount and quality of family responsivity. High levels of responsivity will tend to yield highly resonant interactions, which may have positive or negative effects on family functioning, depending on the quality of the affect and other contextual factors. Resonance can be beneficial to the family, especially when the emotions are positive ones. Resonance can be detrimental if the emotions are primarily negative or if contextual factors make such resonance a risk factor. Chronic physical or emotional illnesses that are influenced by psychological factors give rise to situations in which extremely high or low responsivity may be a risk factor (see Wood, 1993, for a relevant heuristic model).

Responsivity is also important in the child and family's psychosocial functioning and development. If family members are too responsive, they may stress one another emotionally or overfunction for one another, impairing emotional well-being and the development of autonomy and identity. Alternatively, minimal levels of interpersonal responsivity may be insufficient to support emotional and caretaking functions of families.

## The Interaction of Proximity, Hierarchy, and Responsivity

The boundary dimensions of proximity and hierarchy are shaped by and either enhance or modulate responsivity in families. A family stucture of moderate proximity and moderately strong generational hierarchy modulates levels of responsivity. A highly proximal family with extremely strong or weak generational boundaries will likely escalate high responsivity (see the next case example). Thus, the way in which these three characteristics interact may influence disease activity or the psychosocial well-being of the child and family members. The following case illustrates the interaction of boundaries in a family

with a seriously chronically ill child. This case was chosen because it exemplifies the confluence of patterns, many of which were maladaptive for the family's and child's developmental stage. Chronic illness tends to organize families in some of these ways, but families differ widely in their proximity, hierarchy, and responsivity configurations. No particular configuration should be assumed to be maladaptive or dysfunctional unless the individuals in the family are having difficulties that are clearly related to aspects of the configuration. However, the Biobehavioral Family Model (BBFM) predicts that high proximity, weak hierarchy, high responsivity, triangulation, and parental dischord will undermine physical and psychosocial well-being (Wood, 1993).

### CASE EXAMPLE
*Tony, a 13-year-old son of second-generation Italian parents, was born with severe combined immunodeficiency syndrome (SCIDS), which is a disorder of both T and B cell function. This disease renders patients highly susceptible to runaway infections, and early death is common. The cause and cure are unknown. Tony, his parents, and his 18-year-old brother are a highly emotionally and behaviorally responsive family. Throughout the years of medical care, Tony and his mother had become very close, sharing many private thoughts, crying together about the illness, spending much time together in great physical closeness (high proximity). The father worked double shifts to support the medical expenses and therefore was less available, so that most of the family decisions were left to the mother, who frequently deferred to Tony's desires and wants (weak generational hierarchy). This highly attentive care and division of labor no doubt played a crucial role in Tony's survival. Tony's family, with the support of their pediatrician, attempted to balance quality of life and disease management and allow Tony to take medical risks if psychosocial needs prevailed. For example, Tony was permitted to attend children's birthday parties,*

despite the risk of contagion that could be life threatening. However, the family and health care system did not facilitate a developmentally synchronized shift in medical self-care and psychosocial autonomy.

This shortcoming contributed to the crisis that brought the family into treatment. Their pediatrician insisted that Tony was ready to resume regular schooling, after having homebound tutoring for years. However, each August, when school opening approached, Tony would be admitted to the hospital with a severe infection (stress-induced disease activity). Furthermore, each morning when it was time to go to school, he became physically ill, with abdominal pain and excessive stooling through his ostomy (which was necessitated by surgical removal of a section of massively infected colon). It became clear over the course of treatment that Tony's illness was stimulated by anxiety that was escalated in interaction with his mother's anxiety over his returning to school (interpersonal responsivity).

**Responsivity and triangulation of the chronically ill child.** Triangulation is a serious hierarchy problem in which generational boundaries are breached by either cross-generational coalitions of the child with one parent against the other or by conflict detouring through attention to the child or his illness. Triangulation stresses the child and thus is likely to activate psychophysiological pathways that influence the disease process (see Gottman & Fainsilber Katz, 1989, and Wood et al., 1989, for empirical support). High responsivity and triangulation potentiate one another because responsivity catalyzes such relationship patterns.

Tony was triangulated with his parents. The more his mother became worried about the physical and emotional consequences of sending Tony to school, the more his father worried about Tony's social isolation and delay in socioemotional development. When the father would push Tony to go to school, his mother would get scared, and Tony, being highly resonant with his mother (high responsivity), would have his fears activated, which stimulated his stooling (disease activity). When he was with both parents, he would alternately side with his father against his mother in criticizing her for her "nerves" and with his mother against his dad by criticizing him for being too harsh and unavailable (cross-generational coalition/weak generational hierarchy). When his mother and father disagreed in sessions, Tony would divert them by talking about his disease or his fears about school (triangulation). His parents would immediately respond with intense worry, and Tony's confidence would spiral downward (high responsivity).

**Dysfunctional parental relationships.** A troubled parental relationship is empirically associated with greater disease activity and triangulation processes (Wood et al., 1989) and with stress-related physiological arousal in the parent (Levenson & Gottman, 1983) and the child (Gottman and Fainsilber Katz, 1989). Dysfunctional parental relations and triangulation interact recursively. In addition, high responsivity accelerates these processes. (See Wood, 1993.)

Tony's parents were quite distant from each other. Although they avoided conflict, it was apparent that the father was frustrated with the mother's high degree of involvement and protection of his son, which the father thought was not good for him. The father also admitted feeling isolated from his wife, and the mother felt undermined by her husband's criticism of her "nerves" in front of Tony. When discomfort increased in sessions around these disclosures, Tony would step in and mediate or draw attention to himself (triangulation). The family's intense responsivity caused these interactions to occur rapidly and automatically, yielding ingrained patterns of high proximity, weak generational hierarchy, triangula-

*tion, parental-relationship dysfunction, and exacerbated disease activity.*

**Intervention.** *The family therapist intervened in these patterns with a father-son session in which Tony described his despair and fears to his father, who listened and shared his sorrow on behalf of his son. This increased father–son proximity and decreased mother–son proximity. The therapist supported the mother during this difficult rebalancing of interpersonal proximity by underlining her success in keeping Tony alive and well during the dangerous years and emphasizing her courage in beginning to allow her son more independence. In addition, Tony's mother and father were assisted in rediscovering the playful side of their relationship (increased proximity). Furthermore, parental teamwork was developed through their planning and executing a strategy for Tony's gradual resumption of school and for handling his daily reluctance (strengthened parental relationship). Attempts to include Tony in the discussion were blocked (preventing triangulation thus strengthening generational hierarchy). The therapist set an optimistic, confident, and humorous tone in most sessions to modulate the level of anxiety and decrease intense responsivity of negative emotions. This allowed more fluid reorganization of proximity, generational hierarchy, and parental relationship.*

*The parents' relationship improved through their successful teamwork and through a couple's session in which they resolved some issues and rediscovered their affection for one another. Tony, the pediatrician, the therapist, and the family developed a plan by which Tony would gradually assume responsibility for self-care, including hooking up his daily supplemental nutritional apparatus, monitoring his own symptoms, and re-*

*porting them directly to his doctor. In addition, Tony discussed directly with the doctor his prognosis and the expectations for future medical interventions.*

## SOCIAL SYSTEMS BOUNDARIES: PROXIMITY, HIERARCHY, AND RESPONSIVITY OF THE PSYCHOSOCIAL CONTEXTS

Family, school, peers, and the health care system encompass the natural surroundings of the chronically ill child. The degree of proximity and hierarchy of the relevant authorities and the responsivity of the systems to one another are all shaped by and in turn influence the physical and psychosocial well-being of the child. Furthermore, each of these systems is embedded in ethnocultural contexts that may vary from system to system and shape each systems' response to the child's illness. (See Elizur & Minuchin, 1989; Pachter & Weller, 1993; Patterson & Blum, 1993.)

If the boundaries among these systems are not in balance, risk to the child's physical and psychosocial well-being may ensue. Imbalance can result from too little sharing of basic information about the illness and the requirements for care (too little proximity). It also can come from insufficient assumption of responsibility by the responsible adults in each situation (weak hierarchy). A general lethargy or understaffing (nonresponsiveness) of the systems themselves can impair adaptive response to chronic illness in students.

Alternatively, these systems can become overly involved with the child's illness (too much proximity), which in a process analogous to what occurs within families, can result in impairment of psychosocial functioning in favor of focus on the disease and its management. Schools may also overreact to the illness, take too much control, and unduly restrict the child, thus treating him or her as an invalid (overly strong hierarchy). Discomfort of peer groups with the illness can manifest in rejection and ignoring of the child (underresponsivity), or in undue fascination and concentration on the disease (overresponsivity).

At times, even the health care system can be overly responsive and overmedicate, make too many changes in disease management, or manage the disease so tightly that it interferes with normal psychosocial development. Furthermore, if the health care team carries too much responsibility for the disease management (too much proximity and too strong hierarchy), this can impair the normal shift toward the child's and family's self-management of the medical and socioemotional aspects of the illness. Alternatively, if health care systems are underresponsive, the child may be placed at medical risk and the family exposed to unnecessary emotional stress.

A further complication arises when the child or family becomes triangulated between the school and health care systems, with each system making incompatible demands. For example, the physician may expect the chronically ill child to return to school, but the school may resist the child's reentry because of the potential liability issues or because of lack of information regarding reentry plans. The systems therapist can monitor the balance in boundary function within and among these systems and intervene as necessary so as to facilitate adaptive coordination.

> *Tony's school system had provided him with homebound tutoring; they were uninformed as to the family and pediatrician's determination that Tony was medically prepared to resume school (insufficient proximity between family, health-care provider, and school). Furthermore, no one at school was assuming responsibility for organizing Tony's reentry (weak hierarchy), and indeed the school was passively resisting Tony's reentry. In addition, the tutor was fueling Tony's anxiety with his own worry about Tony's medical safety at school (too responsive). Thus, Tony was torn between the family and pediatrician's expectation that Tony attend school and the school's resistance to his reentry (triangulation).*
>
> *The therapist had the pediatrician update the school and tutor regarding Tony's current stable medical status. The family informed the school that they were committed to balancing quality of life (psychosocial*

*well-being and development) with adequate disease management. The school was assured that they could contact the family and pediatrician should they become concerned about Tony's physical or emotional well-being (increased school–health system proximity). This lowered the school's anxiety and thus minimized the likelihood of maladaptive responsivity on the part of school personnel.*

> *Tony also needed to reenter the peer system (increase proximity). Italian American culture expects certain style and behavior from young men, with which the therapist, a Jewish woman, was unfamiliar. So Tony was coached by his father and his pediatrician (a man), who suggested a nonembarrassing way that Tony could describe his illness to friends.*
>
> **Follow-up.** *Tony has been regularly attending school, has not had any preschool hospitalizations, and in general has been physically healthier. His mother has a part-time job, and Tony's older brother is coming to terms with his previously undiagnosed depression, with the assistance of his family in therapy. The patient, family, and their psychosocial surroundings are well on the road to reestablishing biopsychosocial balance and age-appropriate developmental process.*

## EARLY PROMOTION OF BIOPSYCHOSOCIAL BALANCE

Biopsychosocial balance and an age-appropriate developmental process is best promoted and sustained by preventative intervention. Exhibit 1 presents guidelines for establishing functional boundaries among the systems in the chronically ill child's natural surroundings. The systems therapist can guide the health care team and family in ways to achieve adaptive interactions among these domains (see Exhibit 1).

---

**EXHIBIT 1**

**Establishing Adaptive Interactions Among Family, School, Peer Group, and Health-Care Systems**

**Step 1. Open channels of communication:**

*Family*: Encourage both parents to come to appointments; if divorced, obtain permission to keep non-custodial parent involved if possible.

*School*: Identify one school person to coordinate communication with family and health-care provider.

*Peers*: Have parents communicate with parents of patient's friends and have patient or parents (depending on age of patient) communicate with peers regarding the illness.

**Step 2. Provide education regarding the illness:**

*Family*: Provide initial information about the illness to all parental figures and to siblings; assist and encourage family to share information with extended family members.

*School*: Have initial meeting at school with parents, patient, and relevant school personnel (e.g., nurse, homeroom teacher, gym teacher, bus driver). Outline the characteristics of the illness, specific for that child. Devise a written plan for medical treatment and for what to do in the event of an emergency.

*Peers*: Have family educate peers and their parents as to the nature of the patient's illness.

**Step 3. Emphasize the importance of balance between medical management of the disease and quality of life and developmental demands:**

*Family*: Assist family to overcome the tendency to neglect the psychosocial and developmental needs in favor of the child's physical well-being and development.

*School*: Assist the school in achieving balanced expectations of the child with regard to disease management and participation in academics and extracurricular activities.

*Peers*: Encourage patient to be involved with informal neighborhood peer activities. Emphasize to parents the critical nature of peer relationships for psychosocial development.

**Step 4. Initiate age-appropriate self-care and facilitate increases in self-care in accordance with the child's development:**

*Family*: Guide the family in home-care routines that maximize the patient's active participation in management of the illness and its psychosocial concomitants.

*School*: Prepare the child for self-care activities at school and obtain the school's coordination.

*Peers*: Encourage the family to inform peers and their parents as to the care the patient will need to provide for himself and the assistance he might need from adults.

## ASSESSING BIOPSYCHOSOCIAL BALANCE

The developmental biopsychosocial framework suggests three diagnostic criteria for assessing biopsychosocial balance:

1. physical well being, including acceptable disease activity levels;
2. adequacy of the psychosocial and emotional functioning, including meeting appropriate developmental milestones; and
3. a balance between 1 and 2.

These criteria are applied not only to the patient, but also to the other family members, under the assumption that the well-being of family members is mutually interactive.

Failure to meet the criteria of physical and psychosocial well-being and balance in family members will signal that the aspects of family and social system boundaries described earlier should be assessed to consider whether they are organized in adaptive versus maladaptive ways (see Exhibit 2). For example, repeated asthmatic episodes in school may indicate rigid boundaries between the health care system or the family and the school, which may result in the lack of a preventative treatment plan. Or, psychosocial delay may reflect parental overinvolvement in the child's self-care (too much proximity), which has impeded the shift towards self-management of the disease and its psychosocial aspects.

## DEVELOPMENTAL BIOPSYCHOSOCIAL INTERVENTION

A biopsychosocial assessment may indicate the need for intervention. Intervention will be most effective when it is collaborative (with the health care, school, and peer systems), preventative (part of ongoing medical care of chronically or acutely ill children), pragmatic, and brief. It is important for the therapist to know and assess the whole family and to have at least some family sessions. However, it is not necessary for the whole family to be present for the therapist to carry out effective systems therapy (see chap. 6 in this volume). It is more crucial for the model guiding the systems therapist to be comprehensive and systemic and include biological, psychological, and social considerations and for the therapist to be

flexible in finding multiple strategies to meet the treatment goals. Furthermore, chronically ill children and adolescents and family members benefit greatly from brief individual interventions from time to time, even if they do not have any psychosocial or developmental difficulties. The systems therapist should provide opportunities for individual family members to explore and understand concerns and feelings they have about the illness and its psychosocial concomitants. Couples sessions may also be invaluable.

One essential component to successful treatment of chronically ill children and their families is an ongoing collaborative relationship of mutual trust between the systems therapist and primary health care provider. Critical aspects of this trust include mutual loyalty, respect for each other's profession, and a sense of humor (see Wood & Miller, in press, for a description of the evolution of such a collaboration).

## COMMON CHALLENGES TO FAMILY WELL-BEING

Because of the family's pivotal role in biopsychosocial balance it is important to identify the most common challenges to family well-being.

### Family Illness Identity

Families in which the child and the disease are the primary focus may develop a family identity that has become confused with the disease entity. These families are at risk for developing maladaptive interlocking patterns of functioning that in turn may influence the disease process (Wood, 1993). For example, one parent may become intensely involved and protective of the sick child and shelter him or her from appropriate discipline from the other parent. This can cause marital discord, which in turn may stress the sick child and siblings. If the family believes that stress can affect the sick child's illness (many families do), family members may adopt a strategy of conflict avoidance, which then prevents resolution of normal and illness-related disagreements. Such nonresolution of conflict is not only detrimental to marital and family relations, but it also can undermine adequate management of the disease. These patterns call for intervention from a systems therapist to decrease proximity and responsivity and to support generational hierarchy.

## The Underinvolved Family

Some families are so threatened by the chronic illness, or are so preoccupied by other severe physical or emotional illnesses and by overwhelming life situations, that they have difficulty acknowledging and managing the child's illness. The patient's medical and psychosocial well-being may then be neglected through missed appointments and failure to monitor the child's symptoms and medication. When families underfunction in these ways, they require intensive

---

and consistent psychosocial outreach and intervention that can be provided by the systems therapist.

## Family Economic Stress

The health care provider and the systems therapist must maintain a perspective on the economic issues for a family with a chronically ill child. The financial drain of health care may produce severe stress that disrupts family well-being. It can raise the level of parental anxiety and depression, which tends to exaggerate maladaptive family patterns of functioning.

## The Extended Family

Extended family members can be a source of support and guidance for the nuclear family, or they can be a hindrance. Information regarding the disease and the issue of balance between medical management and psychosocial development will help them be valuable resources for the child and family. The systems therapist can facilitate this process by encouraging the family to directly inform extended family members about the disease and related psychosocial issues. Alternatively, extended family members can be included in relevant discussions with a health care provider. Sometimes previous or current experience with illness has shaped belief systems and experience in ways that impair the parents' and extended family's ability to respond adaptively to the chronically ill child and family. These issues may need to be addressed to facilitate more adaptive family support (see Seaburn, Lorenz, & Kaplan, 1993, for therapeutic strategies).

## Separated, Divorced, and Remarried Families

Treating patients with separated, divorced, or remarried parents is a common experience and one that requires special attention with respect to the level of involvement of the noncustodial parent in the child's life (see chap. 7 in this volume). Both parents and their respective families should be educated about the medical and psychosocial aspects of their child's illness. It is not always prudent to rely on the custodial parent to transmit this information to the other parent. The health care provider should consider requesting permission to inform the noncustodial par-

ent as to the child's illness and progress. This is becoming increasingly important as joint custody becomes more prevalent. The noncustodial or joint custodial parent or step-parent should be involved in the medical, school, and peer contextual interactions as appropriate, depending on the level of this parent's involvement with the child. If conflict between the divorced parents is affecting the patient, the health care provider must intervene vigorously and probably repeatedly with both parents and the child (not necessarily together) to minimize the negative effect on the child and his or her illness. This kind of intervention is often very challenging, and a strong therapist–physician team intervention may be required to achieve the necessary outcome. Again, early communication with all responsible parents can prevent conflicts that impair the child's physical and emotional well-being and complicate medical management.

## Developmental and Life Stressors

It is important to anticipate potential difficulty at times of developmental or family stress (e.g., loss through death or divorce, economic hardship, and the birth of a sibling) or at times of natural transitions (e.g., beginning, moving, or changing schools). Intervening at the psychosocial level can avert potential problems in disease management. The systems therapist in close collaboration with the health care team may provide special expertise identifying opportunities for preventative intervention.

## Death Is a Developmental Biopsychosocial Process

Terminal illness and death are among the most neglected areas of systemic psychosocial intervention. Yet they are developmental transitions that all families undergo. Furthermore, they are events that powerfully affect all the systems in the child's psychosocial surround: family, school, peers, and health caregivers. The responses of each system to the child's terminal illness and death affects the other systems and influences their level of adaptive functioning. It is thus abundantly clear that death is a biopsychosocial process and needs to be addressed as such in the treatment of the chronically ill child.

For the child, death has different meanings, depending on the child's developmental stage. When children in infancy and early childhood are dying, they are most frightened about the separation aspect of death. They need extra physical contact and comfort from their parents, sometimes including sleeping with them. Occasionally, parents, overwhelmed by anxiety and grief, defer basic care to the nursing staff. Fathers may be particularly vulnerable in this way. Parents need support and encouragement to remain in close contact with their dying child. Older children who are dying may react most strongly to the threat to their competence. They may worry about falling behind in school, and they may become markedly depressed and anxious. At times they may regress to much younger behavior and need to be cared for at that level rather than being encouraged to "be brave." Giving them choices about minor decisions in their care can relieve some of their overwhelming helplessness. The dying adolescent suffers intensely from the anticipatory loss of life, actual loss of autonomy, and from whatever withdrawal they might experience from family and friends who can not face their own or the adolescent's emotional pain. Adolescents may become uncharacteristically clinging. Or they may become angry, depressed, and alienated from those around them. These latter teenagers need to be persistently sought after and their emotions accepted as understandable.

Parents, siblings, family members, and friends are devastated by the dying and death of their relative and friend. Siblings need to be assisted according to their developmental stage, and parents may need couples intervention to help them remain in supportive contact with each other. Intervention with peers and school personnel to help them come to terms with this child's dying and eventual death may be much appreciated and can help these systems to be supportive to the child and family. Families as a whole may need assistance in maintaining open communication, providing one another with support, maintaining some control over the medical process, and in preparing for the care of the child and themselves during the child's dying and death.

The biopsychosocial balance of quality of life becomes an acute need during the terminal phases of a child's illness. Families may need assistance in making decisions about life support, about medical interventions, and about hospitalization versus home care. They may need the systems therapist to be a strong advocate with them in negotiating these issues with the health-care system.

After the death of a child, the family needs an opportunity for follow-up visits with both the health caregivers and the therapist. They need to come to terms with and resolve whatever medical and emotional issues remain. They also need to come to a healing closure with the people who have become so important to them in providing care throughout their child's illness.

The systems therapist can aid the child and family during this process by remaining involved and assisting members of the health-care system (especially the primary-care physician) to do so as well. Several excellent publications are available to guide the therapist in navigating this challenging life-cycle transition (Koocher and MacDonald, 1992; McDaniel, Doherty, & Hepworth, 1992; Rolland, 1991; Walsh & McGoldrick, 1991).

## HEALTH CARE OF THE FUTURE?

Family systems medicine proposes ongoing treatment partnership between family therapists and primary-care physicians. Unfortunately, these liaisons frequently falter. One reason for this may be the lack of unifying models of illness and intervention that can bridge medical and psychosocial diagnosis and treatment. Family therapy models emphasize the mutual influence of family patterns of functioning and illness in individual family members. They often neglect or underappreciate individual psychological and developmental factors. Medical models focus on individual aspects of health and disorder but usually do not provide the framework for understanding family and sociocultural aspects of illness. The language and ways of thinking in these two paradigms are quite different, yet not necessarily incompatible, if some integrating model were brought to bear.

The developmental biopsychosocial framework described in this chapter may serve such a function for interdisciplinary collaboration and training. There are many useful biopsychosocial models consistent with this framework, any one of which may facilitate collaboration and training. (See Jacobs, 1992; Mc-Daniel, Doherty, & Hepworth, 1992; Patterson, 1988; Wood, 1991).

It is my expectation that ongoing clinical, training, and research collaboration between psychosocial and medical professionals holds the key to health care reform. The exigencies of such collaborations force these professionals to question and understand each other's models. If they trust one another and want to learn, they may develop innovative biopsychosocial models that will serve as bridges between the medical and mental health systems, thus beginning an evolution toward integrated, cost-effective and humane health care.

# References

Adams, P. F., & Hardy, A. M. (1989). *Current estimates from the National Health Interview Survey: United States, 1988. Vital and Health Statistics (advance data)*. Series No. 188. Hyattsville, MD: National Center for Health Statistics.

Ader, R., Felton, D. L., & Cohen, N. (Eds.). (1991). *Psychoneuroimmunology* (2nd ed.). San Diego, CA: Academic Press.

Anderson, C. M., Reiss, D. J., & Hogarty, G. E. (1986). *Schizophrenia and the family: A practitioner's guide to psychoeducation and management.* New York: Guilford Press.

Boxer, G. H., Carson, J., & Miller, B. D. (1988). Neglect contributing to tertiary hospitalization in childhood asthma. *Child Abuse and Neglect, 12,* 491–501.

Boyce, W. T., Barr, R. G., & Zeltzer, L. K. (1992). Temperament and the psychobiology of childhood stress. *Pediatrics, 90,* 483–486.

Burlew, A. K., Evans, R., & Oler, C. (1989). The impact of the child with sickle cell disease on family dynamics. In C. F. Whitten & J. F. Bertles (Eds.), *Sickle cell disease.* New York: New York Academy of Sciences.

Cadman, D., Boyle, M., Szatmari, P., & Offord, D. R. (1987). Chronic illness, disability and mental and social well-being: Findings of the Ontario child health study. *Pediatrics, 79,* 805–813.

Campo, J. V., & Fritsch, S. L. Somatization in children and adolescents. *Journal of the American Academy of Child and Adolescent Psychiatry, 33,* 1223–1235.

Children's Defense Fund. (1991). *The health of America's children.* Washington, DC: Author.

Children's Defense Fund. (1992). *The state of America's children.* Washington, DC: Author.

Covelman, K., Scott, S., Buchanan, B., & Rosman, B. (1990). Pediatric pain control: A family systems model. *Advances in Pain Research Therapy, 15,* 225–236.

Drotar, D. D., & Sturm, L. (1988). Parent–practitioner communication in the management of nonorganic failure to thrive. *Family Systems Medicine, 6,* 42–53.

Eder, R. A., & Mangelsdorf, S. C. (in press). The emotional basis of early personality development: Implications for the emergent self-concept. In S. Briggs, R. Hogan, & W. Jones (Eds.), *Handbook of personality psychology.* San Diego, CA: Academic Press.

Elizur, J., & Minuchin, S. (1989). *Institutionalizing madness: Families, therapy and society.* New York: Basic Books.

Gottman, J. M., & Fainsilber Katz, L. (1989). Effects of marital discord on young children's peer interaction and health. *Developmental Psychology, 25,* 373–381.

Griffith, J. L., & Griffith, M. E. (1992). Speaking the unspeakable: Use of the reflecting position in therapies for somatic symptoms. *Family Systems Medicine, 10,* 41–51.

Hobbs, N., Perrin, J. M., & Ireys, H. T. (Eds.). (1985). *Chronically ill children and their families.* San Francisco: Jossey-Bass.

Jacobs, J. (1992). Understanding family factors that shape the impact of chronic illness. In T. J. Akamatsu, M. A. Parris Stephens, S. E. Hobfoll, & J. H. Crowther (Eds.), *Family health psychology* (pp. 111–127). Washington, DC: Hemisphere.

Jan, J. E., Ziegler, R. G., & Erba, G. (1991). *Does your child have epilepsy?* (2nd ed.). Austin, TX: Pro-ed.

Kerr, M. E., & Bowen, M. (1988). *Family evaluation.* New York: Norton.

Koocher, G. P., & MacDonald, B. L. (1992). Preventative intervention and family coping with a child's life-threatening or terminal illness. In T. J. Akamatsu, M. A. Parris Stephens, S. E. Hobfoll, & J. H. Crowther (Eds.), *Family health psychology.* Washington, DC: Hemisphere.

Landau-Stanton, J., & Clements, C. D. (1993). *AIDS, health and mental health: A primary sourcebook.* New York: Brunner/Mazel.

Levenson, R. W., & Gottman, J. M. (1983). Marital interaction: Physiological linkage and affective exchange. *Journal of Personality and Social Psychology, 45,* 587–597.

Mahler, M. S. (1968). *On human symbiosis and the vicissitudes of individuation.* Madison, CT: International Universities Press.

Masterson, J. (1985). Family assessment of the child with intractable asthma. *Developmental and Behavioral Pediatrics, 6,* 244–251.

McDaniel, S., Campbell, T. L., & Seaburn, D. B. (1990). *Family-oriented primary care: A manual for medical providers.* New York: Springer-Verlag.

McDaniel, S. H., Doherty, W. J., & Hepworth, J. (1992). *Medical family therapy: A biopsychosocial approach to families with health problems.* New York: Basic Books.

Meyerstein, I. (1992). Creating a network of volunteer resources in a psychoeducational family asthma program. *Family Systems Medicine, 10,* 99–110.

Miller, B. D., & Wood, B. L. (1991). Childhood asthma in interaction with family, school and peer systems: A developmental model for primary care. *Journal of Asthma, 28*(6), 405–411.

Minuchin, S. (1974). *Families and family therapy.* Cambridge, MA: Harvard University Press.

Minuchin, S., Baker, L., Rosman, B. L., Liebman, R., Milmam, L., & Todd, T. C. A. (1975). A conceptual model of psychosomatic illness in children: Family organization and family therapy. *Archives of General Psychiatry, 32,* 1031–1038.

National Center for Health Statistics. (1990). *Prevention profile. Health, United States, 1989.* Hyattsville, MD: Public Health Service.

Nevergold, B. S. (1987). Therapy with families of children with sickle cell disease. *Family Therapy Collections, 22,* 67–79.

Newacheck, P. W., & Taylor, W. R. (1992, March). Childhood chronic illness: Prevalence, severity, and impact. *American Journal of Public Health* (82)3, 364–371.

Noeker, M., Petermann, F., & Bode, U. (1990). Family counseling in childhood cancer: Conceptualization and empirical results. In L. R. Schmidt, P. Schwenkmezger, J. Weinman, & S. Maes (Eds.), *Theoretical and applied aspects of health psychology.* London: Harwood Academic.

Pachter, L. M., & Weller, S. C. (1993). Acculturation and compliance with medical therapy. *Developmental and Behavioral Pediatrics, 14,* 163–168.

Patterson, J. M. (1988). A family stress model: The family adjustment and adaptation response. In C. N. Ramsey (Ed.), *Family systems in medicine.* New York: Guilford Press.

Patterson, J. M. (1991). A family systems perspective for working with youth with disability. *Pediatrician, 18,* 129–141.

Patterson, J. M., & Blum, R. W. (1993). A conference on culture and chronic illness in childhood: Conference summary. *Pediatrics, 91, Supplement,* 1025–1030.

Patterson, J. M., Budd, J., Goetz, D., & Warwick, W. J. (1993). Family correlates of a 10-year pulmonary health trend in cystic fibrosis. *Pediatrics, 91,* 383–389.

Rolland, J. S. (1984). Toward a psychosocial typology of chronic and life threatening illness. *Family Systems Medicine, 2,* 245–262.

Rolland, J. S. (1991). Helping families with anticipatory loss. In F. Walsh & M. McGoldrick (Eds.), *Living beyond loss: Death in the family* (pp. 144–163). New York: Norton.

Sargent, J., & Baker, L. (1983). Behavior and diabetes care. *Primary Care, 10,* 83–594.

Seaburn, D. B., Lorenz, A., & Kaplan, D. (1993). The transgenerational development of chronic illness meanings. *Family Systems Medicine, 10,* 385–394.

Shapiro, B. S., Cohen D. E., Covelman, K. W., Howe, C. J., & Scott, S. M. (1991). Experience of an interdisciplinary pediatric pain service. *Pediatrics, 88,* 1226–1232.

Vandvik, I. H., Hoyeraal, H. M., & Fagertun, H. (1989). Chronic family difficulties and stressful life events in recent onset juvenile arthritis. *Journal of Rheumatology, 16,* 1088–1092.

Walsh, F., & McGoldrick, M. (Eds.). (1991). *Living beyond loss: Death in the family.* New York: Norton.

Weiner, H. (1992). *Perturbing the organism: The biology of stressful experience.* Chicago: University of Chicago Press.

Wood, B. (1985). Proximity and hierarchy: Orthogonal dimensions of family interconnectedness. *Family Process, 24,* 487–507.

Wood, B. L. (1993). Beyond the "psychosomatic family": A biobehavioral family model of pediatric illness. *Family Process, 32,* 261–278.

Wood, B., Boyle, J. T., Watkins, J. B., Nogueira, J., Zimand, E., & Carroll, L. (1988). Sibling psychological status and style as related to the disease of their chronically ill brothers and sisters: Implications for models of biopsychosocial interaction. *Journal of Developmental and Behavioral Pediatrics, 9*(2), 66–72.

Wood, B., & Miller, B. D. (in press). Biopsychosocial care. In W. A. Walker, P. R. Durie, J. R. Hamilton, J. A. Walker-Smith, & J. B. Watkins (Eds.), *Pediatric gastrointestinal disease: Pathophysiology, diagnosis, management* (2nd ed.). St. Louis: Mosby.

Wood, B., & Talmon, M. (1983). Family boundaries in transition: A search for alternatives. *Family Process, 22,* 347–357.

Wood, B., Watkins, J. B., Nogueira, J., Zimand, E., & Carroll, L. (1989). The "psychosomatic family": A theoretical and empirical analysis. *Family Process, 28,* 399–417.

# Part VII

# OTHER LARGER SYSTEMS
# AND CONTEXTS

# Introduction

Both the workplace and the schools have massive impact on families. These two large contexts are environments in which family members spend time away from one another, and each places special demands on families. Systems therapists take into account these organizations, directly and indirectly, in their work with families. They also at times work directly with these groups, for example, through consultation and training.

In "The Changing Family–Work System," Sylvia Shellenberger and Sandra Hoffman begin by examining the recent, major changes in these systems, including the expansion of women's work roles, the increase in dual-earner families, the increasing diversity in family forms, and the changing work environment. Stressors associated with each of these changes are illustrated with case examples, showing how the marital relationship and parenting responsibilities are affected. Workplace values, such as competition, may exacerbate this stress, whereas increased flexibility in workplace schedules can help ameliorate it. The authors consider how family therapists can help families negotiate roles, values, and traditions; advocate for family support in the workplace; and act as consultants to organizations around system dysfunction.

Marvin Fine takes an applied approach to the child's "workplace" in his chapter "Family–School Intervention." Exploring the intersection of these systems from an ecosystemic perspective, he conceives the systems therapist as a liaison–consultant, whose primary job is to facilitate a process of collaborative decision making when it comes to the child's best interests. He uses case examples to illustrate systemic and ecological concepts and strategies he has found most useful in his work with schools and families. Trends in schools with regard to services for students with special needs are also described.

# CHAPTER 26

# THE CHANGING FAMILY– WORK SYSTEM

*Sylvia Shellenberger and Sandra S. Hoffman*

Once upon a time 200 years ago, men and women knew what they were supposed to do. Men tilled the fields or worked in the mines, mills, or factories and struggled to provide for their families. Women cooked and sewed, reared children, and nurtured their families. It was usually a practical partnership, sometimes arranged by the respective families. A marital choice was usually made for a lifetime. The man was the master of the house, and the wife and children accommodated. All knew their places.

We have come a long way since those simpler times. Some would say too far. Even granted our nostalgic idealization of the past, few would argue that things have dramatically changed over the past two centuries. Few people work on farms anymore. In fact, since the early 19th century when statistics were first recorded, the percentage of workers in farm occupations has decreased from 71.8% in 1820 to just 2.4% in 1990 (Hoffman, Foley, & McGuire, 1993). Women are no longer tied to the hearth but are often climbing the corporate and professional ladder. Men may mind the children while women are tending the store. "Till death do us part" has become "until we can't stand each other any more." Children often grow up in multiple configurations, from single parent households to extensively blended families. As the pace of change accelerates, everyone is trying to figure out how they will fit into the total picture. Men defend their dwindling prerogatives.

Women worry about how they can do it all. And the children wonder about who will take care of them.

As family psychologists, we see the changes around us everyday in our practices. Families are struggling to survive in an increasingly complex and bewildering world. Families are falling apart as the forces of personal striving and marital dissatisfaction are pulling at their seams. With more choices than they can consider, people are struggling to find the right balance among work, play, love, and family responsibility. As family therapists and researchers, we not only witness but also try to understand the forces that shape the family, both our own and those we see. Whether working with families in any number of formats or consulting with larger organizations, a systemic understanding of change is essential to successful intervention.

A basic assumption of systemic thinking is that the impact of changes can be understood only in the context of the multiple systems in which they occur. This is particularly true in examining the interaction of family and work systems. Changes in the family must be understood in terms of what is happening at work and vice versa. Furthermore, changes in both family and work systems must be seen in the larger contexts in which they are embedded: historical trends, shifts in societal norms, and multigenerational family patterns. In this chapter we will look at a number of societal trends that have greatly influ-

The authors would like to acknowledge Randy Gerson for his suggestions regarding the conceptual framework and elaboration of this chapter.

enced the interaction between family and work. We will use our understanding of systems to track how both the family and work systems react and adapt to the ever-increasing pace of change in our society.

## FAMILY–WORK SOCIETAL TRENDS

### The Expansion of Women's Work Roles

One of the most dramatic changes in our society has been the expansion of women's work roles. In fact, whereas in 1960 only 36% of all American women were employed outside the home, that figure jumped to 53% in 1988 (U.S. Department of Labor, 1989a). Although women have always worked for economic reasons, almost 90% of women, as well as men, cite work as a source of identity and self-worth (Louis Harris and Associates, Inc., 1981).

An important factor in this change has been the advent of easily obtainable birth control, allowing women more independence and choice, including if and when to work. Couples can now delay fertility and choose to have fewer children. Interestingly, women's choice to work has an effect on the total number of children they plan to have (Bianchi & Spain, 1986). Growing numbers of women are deciding to remain single or to delay marriage, which results in a pattern of employment early in women's lives (Moen, 1992). Many married couples are opting not to have children to focus on work goals (Bianchi & Spain, 1986; Louis Harris and Associates, 1981) or to have them later to extend their careers (Louis Harris and Associates, 1981).

Also critical for women's changing status in the workplace has been increasing educational opportunities. The percentage of bachelor's degrees awarded to women has risen from 38% in 1961 to an estimated 54% in 1991; the percentage of graduate and professional degrees awarded to women has risen from 24% to an estimated 50% (U.S. Department of Education, 1992). Changing government policies related to civil rights and the women's movement have led to enhanced opportunities for women at every level of education. For example, Title IX of the 1972 Education Amendment legislation requires that women have equal opportunities in school settings.

## Dual-Earner Families

Not surprisingly, given the growing presence of women in the workplace, there has been a dramatic rise in the number of dual-earner families. Economic survival and the expectations of a higher standard of living leave many families dependent on more than one income. The steady decline in real earnings has rendered men's wages, which have traditionally been regarded as families' wages, insufficient to maintain a satisfactory standard of living for most contemporary families in the United States. Tripling in number from 1950 to 1990, 29 million, or 58% of all married women, were employed outside the home (Moen, 1992). These women represent employed women across race and ethnic groups, including large numbers of mothers who are employed outside the home. Of the working women in 1990, 55% said they were working to support themselves and their families, up from 46% in 1980 (Moen, 1992).

The preservation of two incomes sometimes requires changes in living arrangements, including moving for a job, long-distance commuting, or establishing separate residences. Transfers, a common phenomenon in corporate America, may be seen by many families as broadening their perspective and development. However, the burden of these changes have often been on women who were responsible for the logistics of relocation and who frequently lost seniority in their jobs. Thus, these women became more strongly tied to the family as homemaker and mother (Seidenberg, 1973). Families who move for a job may regret the loss of family and other social supports and depend on the work system to replace these contacts. Although long-distance commuting or commuting between residences is physically wearing and limits the amount of time that spouses have together, couples in these arrangements may do amazingly well, especially when there are no young children at home (Busch, 1992). Couples in these commuter arrangements who perceive their relationships as good maintain their relationships over the telephone and by making their time together special and exclusive. Conflicted couples report their lifestyles further complicate their relationships. Women find their lifestyles empowering and liberating and like the arrangement more than men do (Busch, 1992).

## Diverse Family Structures

The two parent family is no longer the statistical norm. Among other family structures, single parent families, parents living alone, couples, stepfamilies, and families with older relatives at home have replaced these two parent families. With 67% of first marriages ending in divorce (Martin & Bumpass, 1989), the high divorce rate often leads to both parents' functioning on their own instead of in partnership. In fact, in 1988, 20% of children lived in homes headed by single parent mothers (U.S. Department of Labor, 1989b). For women, divorce may necessitate going to or returning to work, sometimes without the requisite skills, experience, and education. As a result, many women and their families fall into poverty (Bergman & Roberts, 1987). Although men's standards of living may improve economically when they divorce (Weitzman, 1985), they often suffer emotionally from lack of family involvement (Ahrons & Rodgers, 1987). Changes in women's roles may have increased the likelihood of divorce, whereas the higher risk of divorce makes it even more important for women to be able to support themselves.

Another common family arrangement includes aging relatives living in the home while the heads of the household work. What has changed is the difficulty of caring for the elderly when they become infirm because the caretakers are often working. In 1980, approximately 10% of workers reported they were responsible for aging relatives; that figure doubled to 20% by 1992 (Shellenberger, 1992) and is expected to climb even higher with the aging of America's workforce (The Conference Board, 1992). The responsibility of maintaining a job, raising children, and caring for older family members can be overwhelming. Employees who are responsible for elderly relatives are twice as likely to report somatic symptoms and nearly three times as likely to report frequent anxiety or depression (Wagner, 1987). At the same time, many individuals report positive benefits to caregiving for dependent elderly such as an

increase in a sense of self-worth and life satisfaction (Moss, Lawton, Dean, Goodman, & Schneider, 1989).

Other modern family structures include remarried households and same-sex partnerships. In remarried households with stepchildren, the parents may feel like they are working for two different families. There may be competition around the resources of time, money, and responsibility for accomplishment of household and child-care tasks. In families with same-sex partners, traditional work-related stereotypes no longer apply. Nevertheless, issues of economic dependence and the balancing of family and work lives may still become a source of strife.

## Changing Work Environment

In its own gradual way, the work environment is also changing. The civil rights movement, the women's movement, and the changing needs of employees with families have forced many businesses to attend to the changes around them. According to a survey of 645 work organizations (Towers Perrin & Hudson Institute, 1990), companies are concerned about the changing nature of their work environments and are making plans to address these changes. They report that half of their workforces are women and a quarter are minorities. Cultural diversity in the workplace is a primary focus for management in hiring and promoting minority employees. There is growing recognition that changes at work require a new style of management, one that places as much emphasis on human resources as on financial or other resources. To that end, the workplace has responded by experimenting with such incentives as child care, flexiplace, job sharing, and alternative schedules (U.S. Merit Systems Protection Board, 1991).

However, the changes are not all for the better for families. Today's work world is in a constant state of flux. Our technologically changing, fast-paced economy often requires periodic job shifts and reeducation. Many jobs require extensive travel and frequent relocations. Constant business turnovers make it unlikely that family members will remain in one employment environment throughout their lifetimes. An unstable economic environment places great strain on families and their sense of economic security, particularly when steady employment is threatened. For those with few skills, education, or opportunities, unemployment or underemployment may be a way of life.

## THE RESPONSE OF THE FAMILY SYSTEM

Family systems respond and react to the societal systems in which they are embedded. Family psychologists and others in the field have participated in an ongoing dialogue regarding whether families are more a force against basic societal change (reaction or homeostasis) or the mediator of societal change (evolution or second-order change). As we shall see, there are forces in the family that both discourage and encourage the trends described above.

## Family of Origin Patterns

The intergenerational nature of family patterns is a source of continuity in families and may lead family members to expect that previous roles, traditions, and values be perpetuated. Families are, after all, transmitters of dominant cultural values. Traditional values for some families include the notion that employment for women is not compatible with family life (Etaugh & Nekolny, 1990) or simply that women should not work outside the home (Ratcliff & Bogdan, 1988). Alternatively, men are often seen as defined by their work and the primary breadwinners for their families (Sekaran, 1986). Similarly, there may be a tradition in some families that divorce is seen as a source of great shame. Choices that contradict these time-honored family norms can be a source of tension. For example, family members may criticize mothers who divorce or work outside the home. They may belittle men who choose nontraditional roles such as househusband or part-time employee. Families may have strong emotional reactions and intensely resist deviations from the basic family pattern. The strain between the generations may be even greater in immigrant or first-generation families where other cultural norms conflict with the values so common in American families.

From the perspective of the family of origin, basic changes in the family tradition are frequently seen as acts of disloyalty. Family members may express alarm for the family members involved, voicing concern for the marriage or the children. However, the underly-

ing issue is usually one of loyalty and family cohesion. It is only by addressing this issue, either overtly or covertly, that the family adapts to the changes perceived as threatening to its security and stability.

*CASE EXAMPLE:*
*A TRANSITIONAL COUPLE*

*Martha and her husband, Jacob, were at great odds. Tradition in their farm families held that women should not work but instead should rear children. Jacob prided himself on providing adequately for his family, even with the small parcel of land that was his share of their family farm. But the tobacco crop had not done well this year, and they were having great difficulty even keeping the children clothed. Both Martha's and Jacob's parents volunteered to help financially to see them through poor times. Martha's pride was too great to accept handouts, and having been reared with a strong work ethic, she accepted a job as a clerk in a bookstore at the town shopping mall, without consulting Jacob. Jacob took her action as a personal affront. Both sets of parents were so distraught that they were barely speaking to Martha. In fact, Jacob's parents were so disturbed they refused to look after the children for the few hours after school before Martha returned from work. They firmly believed the children would suffer. They saw the role of women as remaining in the home, rearing children, keeping the house, and helping on the farm as needed.*

*Referred by a new friend on her job, Martha came willingly to conjoint marital therapy. Jacob came with much reluctance. There was a very cold tension between them. Jacob preferred not to reveal their family problems to an outsider. Martha believed this was their only chance to bring the family back together. In efforts to build a therapeutic alliance and create an atmosphere where it was safe to reveal feelings, the therapist acknowledged Jacob's hesitations to come to therapy and validated his reasons for reluctance; likewise, the therapist reflected understanding of Martha's belief that therapy was their only hope of reuniting the family (see chap. 5 on building the therapeutic alliance). The next task of therapy was to explore the differences between the couple. Guided by the therapist in a very structured mirroring dialogue that helped the couple to feel safe with each other, Jacob admitted he blamed the group of farm women, of which Martha was a member, for influencing her decision to go to work. He saw her involvement as disloyal to him and disrespectful of what he was trying to do for the family. Martha argued that it was only the desperate financial situation that propelled her to go against Jacob's will. Eventually, she disclosed that she was not satisfied with staying home and had often yearned for work outside the home. Using the genogram as a tool, the therapist explored family-of-origin issues with the couple. Jacob revealed the shame he felt for not sufficiently providing for the family and the resentment he harbored toward his father for giving up much of their family land for development rather than preserving it for succeeding generations. With improved communication, the couple became more accepting of each other, and Jacob began to acknowledge how Martha's income benefited the family.*

*Next, the couple was coached in talking to their respective families. They felt the need to convince their families that employment for Martha was best for their family. The therapist guided them in presenting their newly found common perspective to both families. As Jacob's parents began to see their son as a willing participant in the new arrangement and even proud of Martha's work, they were able to discuss the guilt they had been feeling for not having more land to give Jacob and become less protective of him. Martha's family was less accepting but nevertheless acknowledged the couple's right to their own decision.*

Families of origin can also be a force toward change and adjustment to new societal realities. Female children who have watched their families fall into poverty as a result of divorce and experienced the struggle their mothers endured to find employment may be driven to seek educational opportunities or a career so as to be self-supporting. In fact, mothers may be increasingly giving their daughters, overtly or covertly, the message of the importance of self-sufficiency on the basis of their own experiences of dependency. In families where divorce or single-parenting has become the norm, young women may envision a life of providing for themselves and their families on their own. Even in families with traditional work values, the next generation's emotional reactions to what they have seen in their parents' lives can actually lead to change. For example, men who have grown up rarely seeing their fathers because of long work hours may seek a more balanced life, including time for leisure and family. Women who have seen their mothers either not work or work at part-time or low-paying jobs may become determined that they will achieve higher status or better-paying work opportunities. Men, having observed their mothers' work dilemmas, may embrace a work ethic for women, including their wives and daughters. Young women may adopt this value even when the primary focus of ambition is for the sons in the family. When there are no sons, daughters may receive an even more powerful message about the importance of career. Researchers studying highly successful women in business found not a single woman in the sample of 25 had a brother (Hennig & Jardim, 1977).

## The Marital Relationship

It is probably in the marital relationship that the changes in work and family structure are most clearly realized. When wives work there is a shift in balance of power in the marital relationship, a shift that requires a redefinition of marital roles. It is adaptation to these changes that will determine the quality of family life and sometimes even the survival of the relationship.

It is not unusual for couples to continually struggle over work-related issues. After all, we learn from our families of origin specific, usually gender-based, norms and values. Even couples who say they are trying to have an "equal" relationship may have their resolve sorely tested when balancing different work and family roles. For example, men who fully appreciate the additional income that their wives bring home may still expect their spouses to maintain their domestic tasks as well. Women often complain of fatigue because they carry the larger share of the family responsibility (Bianchi & Spain, 1986; Hochschild, 1989; Pleck, Staines, & Lang, 1980). Hochschild (1989) has coined the term *second shift*, which refers to the shift women work at home when they return from their day in the workplace. Under this stress, the marital relationship may deteriorate.

The number and intensity of different roles for both men and women have multiplied and expanded, demanding flexibility from everyone involved. For example, men have increasing demands on them to take on additional roles related to home and child care. At the same time, women are asking men for an increase in intimacy and for emotional support of their new work roles. Men, alternatively, are more expectant of women sharing the financial responsibility for the family. These new role strains may tax or stretch the balance in the family and lead to resentments between the spouses with each blaming the other for not making sufficient contributions. Furthermore, both men and women may experience role overload where the demands of the family compete with the requirements of work.

In some families, the husband may have a difficult time adjusting to these new demands for role flexibility. He may question his whole identity as a man. Identity dilemmas occur when beliefs related to long-standing, gender-based roles and values conflict with contemporary roles that are being established. For example, a husband who is asked by his wife to fix dinner because she has to stay late at the office may have a difficult time accommodating her need. This dilemma may intensify if the request is overheard by his friends who may judge him as "henpecked" or feel threatened by similar changes in their own marriages. Although the husband may indeed desire to change his role into a more egalitarian one, he may also be pulled into old feelings and behaviors because of discomfort with his changing sense

of self. In fact, Burke and Weir (1976) conclude that husbands of employed wives may suffer from more severe identity problems than their spouses. The researchers further show that men whose wives work experience poorer psychological and physical health in part because they lose some of their support system and a special status in the family.

As a result, many men are faced with resolving issues for which they have no role models. They may be reluctant to forego some of the benefits of the traditional marriage because they do not perceive sufficient benefits to do so. Husbands with working wives are more likely to evaluate marriages negatively (Burke & Weir, 1976) and report more mental health problems (Kessler & McRae, 1982). Interestingly, this is less true when the wife works out of choice instead of economic necessity (Orden & Bradburn, 1969). Perhaps men feel less like a failure as a provider when their wives are choosing, not having, to work.

Women also are sometimes ambivalent about their changing roles. Some women may cling to the traditional view of women and resent their husbands when economic circumstances force them into the workplace. This is particularly true when the workplace neither respects nor validates the woman's worth in that setting. The wife may blame her husband for not providing well for her family and forcing her to work. Sometimes, it is the husband, for economic reasons, who promotes the value of work equality, often showing little sympathy for the difficulties of women in the workplace. Even women who have adopted a more feminist perspective may find old attitudes resurfacing when they least expect it. For example, a woman who demands equal pay for equal work may still feel uncomfortable when her husband makes less money than she does. After all, a message in the socialization of many women is that the man should be "taking care" of them. As a result of their ambivalence, women may communicate mixed messages to their husbands. For example, wives who have agreed to support their husbands through more education or retirement may find themselves panicked about their abilities to provide or resentful about carrying the primary or sole financial burden for the family.

Marriages may also be threatened by the evolving norm of men and women working in teams and in many cases traveling together. The workplace may be seen as fertile ground for the office affair. Men who have historically traded stories about workplace affairs may now find themselves suspicious when their wives work late or do not call home when traveling on business. Women, responding to the multiple stressors of the family–work demands and to what they believe to be a double standard of men having affairs in the workplace, may in some instances choose to express their resentment by engaging in affairs at the office.

Despite these difficulties, couples may actually benefit when both partners are working. Most obvious are the economic gains resulting from two incomes. Less apparent are the mental health advantages. Women report a sense of well-being (Birnbaum, 1971; Burke & Weir, 1976; Feld, 1963; Kessler & McRae, 1982), greater self-esteem and self-confidence (Birnbaum, 1971; Ohlbaum, 1971), and good physical health (Burke & Weir, 1976; Feld, 1963). Men may benefit by having happier wives. The mental health of men has been found to improve as their wives' incomes increase (Kessler & McRae, 1982), which suggests that men may be receiving relief from the role as sole breadwinner. Many men have welcomed the expansion of their roles in egalitarian marriages. For example, men who in earlier decades have been reluctant to prepare meals may find themselves enjoying creative cooking. In summary, researchers studying dual-career couples (Epstein, 1971; Goldscheider & Waite, 1991; Hopkins & White, 1978; Rapoport & Rapoport, 1972) believe that this family–work structure creates a greater potential for enhanced marital communication and a greater sense of purpose within the marital relationship. These couples may experience increased intellectual and emotional benefits from feelings of heightened expressiveness, competence, and self-worth associated with their work and their collegial partnership (Sekaran, 1986). Many dual-career couples believe that the excitement and challenge they experience generally outweighs the exhaustion, time limits, and diminished social interaction that they encounter (Rice, 1979).

## CASE EXAMPLE: MARRIAGE AND THE SECOND SHIFT

*Regina is a 30-year-old married woman who came into therapy on referral from her gynecologist with complaints of depression and fatigue. Regina is a secretary at an insurance company; her husband, Thomas, is a salesman for plumbing products. They had been married for 2 years and were beginning to plan for a family. Regina could not understand why she was so unhappy. After all, she had waited all her life for the day when they would finally be married and in a financial position to have a family. They had a very satisfying courtship and early marriage, but things began to change after about 6 months. It was at this point they began to fight, mostly about "stupid, little silly things."*

*Regina was the oldest daughter in a family of four children. Regina had grown up with the responsibility for the younger children and the household chores. Her parents had a traditional marriage, her father a traveling salesman and her mother a homemaker. Regina did not want to quit working, even if she and Thomas were successful in their plans for pregnancy. Regina had been employed since completing a business college curriculum. Regina enjoyed working and felt good about herself as an employee. Besides, they felt they could not possibly live on one income, with or without a baby.*

*The therapist asked Regina when the depression began and what kinds of thoughts and experiences seemed to be associated with the depressive feelings. Regina was able to pinpoint the onset of her depression as coinciding with the beginning of planning for a baby. Still, she was unable to understand why this planning would cause her to feel so overwhelmed and sad. The therapist asked Regina to keep a daily journal of her thoughts and feelings. Through this process and reflective listening on the part of the therapist, Regina discovered that the plans to have a baby had aroused great concern in her regarding whether she could possibly care for a child in addition to her work and family responsibilities. She began to notice that she felt angry and depressed about the inequity of the household responsibilities in their marriage, for example, when on Saturdays she cleaned the house while Thomas played golf, or when she cooked and cleaned the kitchen while Thomas read the paper. Yet, she also felt guilty about these feelings because Thomas was a very kind and caring husband.*

*Because Thomas was unwilling to come to therapy, Regina was the sole catalyst for change in the marriage. The therapist posited a frame that their difficulties were due to gender-role differences; Thomas was modeling after the other men in his family just as she was modeling her previous generation of women. The therapist helped Regina to clarify her thoughts and feelings, recognize that she and Thomas were assuming stereotypical gender roles that were not conducive to their contemporary dual career family lifestyle, communicate her needs by sending "I" statements, take care of her own needs by scheduling leisure time, distribute household responsibility by working out an equitable plan with Thomas, and determine how the plan was working through follow-up conversations with her husband.*

## Parenting

The conflict between family and work life often becomes most apparent in the area of parenting. Americans have placed a high value on caring for the next generation. Traditionally, this responsibility has fallen on women in the home. Long-standing parenting roles for men and women are now being challenged by current societal trends. The choice to parent adds another layer of responsibility and complexity to family life and stretches the boundary between work and family systems.

When a child is born, the entire family system changes, and the family must reorganize itself for the tasks of child care. At the same time, the financial burden of children makes work even more essential for the survival of the family. This challenge of balancing family and work responsibilities is fertile ground for parental conflict. Parents' experiences growing up, often quite divergent, lead to expectations about how their own children will be parented. Fathers who grew up with their mothers at home may prefer their children's mother to stay at home, reduce her work hours, or in other ways arrange her work to fit in with family needs. This preference may clash with the mother's expectations for what she believes to be an appropriate family–work balance. If she grew up with both parents working, or has invested much in terms of education or years on the job, she may not want to give up her work position. Parental conflicts typically surface around responsibilities for meeting children's needs and taking care of the home.

Fathers may find the birth of a child a new challenge to their role as a provider. Financial pressures at this time are common for men. By their own or others' expectations, they may feel some urgency not only in maintaining but often also in even enhancing their job roles, particularly if their spouses have reduced their work involvement. In the case of single fathers, they may hesitate to move so as to remain close to their children. In addition to the expectation that men meet their financial obligations to the family, many are increasing their share of domestic responsibilities.

Mothers may find the early childhood years particularly difficult. They may feel torn about whether to reduce their work hours or quit altogether to be with their children. In surveys of mothers' work preferences, women say that in the absence of financial necessity, they would choose to stay home (Evans, 1992; Louis Harris and Associates, 1981) or to work part time (Louis Harris and Associates, 1981). Women may feel guilty about whichever choice they make because they will either decrease their financial contributions to the family or leave their children in someone else's care to go to work. Women who reduce their work involvement or cycle in and out of the workplace may do so with regret about lost career momentum or professional satisfaction.

### CASE EXAMPLE: A DELICATE BALANCE

*Armando and Elena recently had their second baby. This event changed the work and family balance they had established. In addition to the usual trials of infant care, this child had some minor physical deformities and needed regular physical therapy. Elena was more educated and brought home a larger salary, but both saw Armando's work as more important. With the arrival of the baby, Elena used accrued vacation for maternity leave, then returned to work as they were dependent on both incomes. She began to resent his lesser-paying job and his seeming resistance to taking on child care and household tasks. She felt overwhelmed and wanted to stay home with the baby. Having agreed to help with the children, Armando did not understand her resentments; he had grown up in a family where his mother worked and reared her children without a father at home. Elena's mother worked too; in fact, so much so that Elena often felt neglected as a child.*

*One day her supervisor at work spoke with Elena about not meeting work demands as well as she had in the past. She complained about Elena's time away from the office for personal business and her personal use of the telephone on company time. Elena viewed her supervisor as not understanding the importance of her family and her new child-care responsibilities. She felt that her supervisor, a woman and mother herself, should be more sympathetic. She was angry when the supervisor recommended therapy. But with an uncaring supervisor and uncooperative husband, she knew she needed help. Besides, maybe the counselor would fix her husband.*

*The therapist taught the couple communication skills needed to directly express their thoughts and feelings to each other re-garding work and family disagreements. The therapist observed that the husband had most of the power in their decision making. Through exploration of his family genogram, Armando discovered that in his family of origin, little was expected of men, whereas they had most of the say in decision making. He confessed that he was intimidated by the special needs of their younger child. As the therapist provided a safe place for frank discussion, Armando was able to talk about his experienced loss of Elena as she focused so exclusively on their new child. Elena admitted she identified herself with this child because she felt that she had not received the love and affirmation she had needed growing up. Armando finally understood why she was so focused on this child and was more attentive to her needs for special attention. At the therapist's suggestion, they began to talk openly about how the new child had shifted the balance of power in their relationship.*

The compromise they finally reached was for Elena to negotiate part-time work for herself until the baby no longer needed special attention, a solution acceptable to her supervisor as well. In response to the therapist's questions about priorities for their lives, Armando began expressing his interest in spending more time with the children, even suggesting he work part time so Elena could go back to work full time. Reluctant at first to give up time with her children, Elena could see clear benefits to the children to having their father more involved in their lives. Fathers may find the birth of a child a new challenge to their role as a provider. Financial pressures at this time are common for men. By their own or others' expectations, they may feel some urgency not only in maintaining but often also in even enhancing their job roles, particularly if their spouses have reduced their work involvement. In the case of single fathers, they may hesitate to move so as to remain close to their children. In addition to the expectation that men meet their financial obligations to the family, many are increasing their share of domestic responsibilities.

## CASE EXAMPLE: A SINGLE FATHER'S DILEMMA

*Russell was so confused by his employer's offer for a promotion that he became paralyzed when faced with even the smallest decisions. He was referred for therapy by his family physician who had placed him on medication to help relieve his anxiety and to improve his concentration and sleep, which had become problematic after the job offer. In therapy, he explained in almost panicked tones that to accept the offer would mean a transfer to another part of the country. Russell was especially concerned about the effect of this change on his daughter, Robin, for whom he had primary custody. He felt guilty for even considering such a move because Robin had finally settled into a calmer period as she entered her senior year of high school. Russell and Robin's mother had divorced just a year and a half previously, and Robin had been quite depressed and angry, lost a lot of weight, and formed a questionable circle of friends. Robin cut classes and studied little, if at all. Much to her father's relief, she had a new boyfriend and was beginning to apply herself more and even talked about college.*

*The therapist hypothesized that Russell's indecisiveness was related to the dramatic crises and changes from which his family was not recovering. Through questions about his feelings of guilt and anguish regarding the current plan, Russell began to uncover the deeper roots of those feelings. Much to his regret now, he used to be what his former spouse called a "workaholic" during Robin's growing-up years. He had actually been afraid his boss was calling him in to tell him he was not performing up to par because he had been more involved in Robin's life this past year. But instead, his boss offered him the position he had always wanted. Now, he considered the move with mixed feelings. Through the therapist's direct questions about his reac-tions to his divorce, Russell began to realize that part of his paralysis was the anger and grief he had not had time to feel towards his estranged ex-wife. She had little contact with Robin now and even less with Russell since she had married the person she was seeing before their divorce.*

*In sessions with Robin, the therapist guided Russell in expressing his regret about the lost years when he was uninvolved in his daughter's life, and together they considered possible solutions to the current dilemma. It was decided that Robin, who wanted desperately to finish her senior year and stay near her boyfriend, would live with Russell's sister who lived in the same town. Using the genogram to explore the relationship of his current dilemma to his family history, Russell and his therapist uncovered reasons why letting people down, such as Robin or his boss, had become so paralyzing to him. Russell's parents had divorced when he was a teenager. His mother, with whom he lived, virtually dropped out of his life, at first to go to work, then to remarry. He realized that he often "overfunctioned" to keep the important people in his life needing him and felt guilty and fearful when he stopped trying so hard to please or perform. Through responses to questions asked by the therapist about how he would maintain a close father–daughter connection with Robin despite the physical distance, Russell recognized that he could continue to adequately parent his daughter by showing interest in her life through regular contact by telephone, mail, and visits.*

Families of origin usually have strong opinions on proper child care and may disapprove of some of the modern solutions to this problem. They may have strong reactions to decisions made by families who choose to combine parenting roles with work roles. Families of origin may be fearful their grandchildren will not have all of the advantages afforded by a mother's remaining at home. The reactions of families of origin may be quite intense, resulting in increased involvement with or withdrawal from their children's families. They may become intrusive in their attempts to influence their children's decisions, or they may express strong disapproval by withholding instrumental, financial, or emotional support related to parenting needs. Single parent families may be especially susceptible to intrusion and disapproval of their families of origin, depending on the circumstances surrounding their parenting status (e.g., because of death, divorce, or teenage parenting). The family–work roles of the traditional family may diverge so greatly from those of today's diverse lifestyles that families of origin have difficulty understanding or tolerating their children's decisions. Their children may also experience this "generation gap." For example, a woman's decision to divorce and to work may be met with disapproval and concerns for grandchildren by family members who disagree with both divorce and work for mothers. The woman may feel unsupported by her family or uncomfortable with her family's attempts to ameliorate her situation. Her family may feel burdened with requests for support or discounted when their attempts to help are rebuffed.

Finally, the children themselves may be caught in the middle of the changing balance between family and work. In divorcing families where the mother enters the workforce, children may be particularly distressed by this dual loss of their intact family and their mother leaving home to go to work (Ahrons & Rodgers, 1987). Children and teenagers may be required to assist with household chores or the care of elderly, young, or handicapped family members so that parents can spend more hours on the job. Some children may enjoy the independence and sense of competence these responsibilities engender; some may resent the added burdens and decreased time away from parents, studies, or friends. In the latter cases, children may develop symptoms such as school phobia or abdominal pain to bring their parents back home from work.

Parents who are extremely stressed by attempting to fulfill the multiple and often conflicting roles of work and family may unintentionally draw their children into their deliberations. For example, children may enter into parents' conflicts regarding household tasks, work, or child care responsibilities. Parents may attempt to involve a child in taking sides or accepting responsibilities that would otherwise fall to the parents so as to ease tension. Taken to the extreme, these dynamics can lead to spouse abuse with children as observers, or child abuse where parents project their anger at spouses onto their children.

As observers and participants in this changing work–family system, children contribute to the evolutionary process of role development. Teenagers who take on part-time jobs either to enhance their qualities of life or to help their families make ends meet will begin to form their opinions about the place of work in their lives. Female children may grow up expecting to participate in the workforce, or they may react against having less family involvement and commit to more time for their own families. Male children who have had their fathers very involved in their lives may choose to repeat this pattern, or on the other hand, realize the sacrifices their fathers made in their careers for the sake of family and choose to be more engaged in carrer.

## THE RESPONSE OF THE WORK SYSTEM

Like the family system, the work system has been both a barrier and a promoter of family–work societal trends. Although the workplace has tended to be dominated by men, often with traditional patriarchal values, it has also provided many opportunities for women to change their family status. Again, we will look at both reaction and evolution in the work system.

### Entrenched Attitudes in the Workplace

The workplace, like any system, has a set of norms and a history. When threatened by change, it is not unusual for the work system, like the family, to react strongly and demand that the deviants revert to the way things have always been done. A plea for loyalty, efficiency, or expediency is usually the rationale. However, unlike a family member, an employee who does not follow work traditions can be fired—ejected from the system. This vulnerability has made it particularly difficult for women to change their positions in the work system. The resulting perpetuation of traditional workplace norms can be seen in the form of entrenched negative attitudes toward any new family–work trends (Franklin & Sweeney, 1988).

New societal trends toward more women in the workplace, the evolution of family structures, and work environments that are more service-oriented and technologically based often clash with other vested interests in the workplace. As women struggle to define a satisfying place for themselves at work, men may perceive a threat to once well-established, secure positions. In addition, men who want to modify their career orientations to include more attention to their families may be penalized at work for less dedication to their careers. This clash of forces affects the individuals involved, the workplace, and the family.

Competition is a major value in most work settings. Often, men have been more socialized to cope with intense competition than women. Still, men may see competition with women as threatening, and women may perceive the normal competition of the workplace as nonsupportive, even devaluing. When the competitive atmosphere of work spills over into family life, spouses may compare their work successes. There is some evidence that men are particularly threatened by spouses who make more money or achieve greater success than they (Sekaran, 1986).

As men and women challenge traditional roles in the workplace, they may confront the same values that limited their roles in their family systems. Work for men has traditionally been viewed as primary, whereas work for women has often been seen as secondary and not comparable in value to that of men. Women have, therefore, had less success in securing higher-paying jobs traditionally reserved for men (Franklin & Sweeney, 1988) or have been unsuccessful in obtaining raises comparable to their male counterparts. Men may react with fear and anger to women now in competition for jobs and benefits, which sometimes results in a backlash toward women in the workplace. Men also oppose such traditional workplace attitudes at their own risk. Men who refuse to give careers priority over their families may be passed over for promotions or leadership positions and seen as less dedicated to their careers. In fact, researchers have found that if men raise parenting issues at work, they are seen as less serious about their careers (Gerson, 1993).

Regardless of their competence, women may receive little recognition or remuneration for their abilities or efforts. On average, in 1991 for men and women over age 25, women were paid seventy-three cents for every dollar paid a man (U.S. Bureau of the Census, 1992). Ambitious women often hit a "glass ceiling"—when they can rise only so far in the corporate world and no further. According to one study, even though single and childless women work longer hours, only in one profession (medicine) of three investigated (medicine, law, and engineering) did their increased work efforts yield higher incomes (Roskies & Carrier, 1992). Partners of these women may feel resentful of the time their mates spend in the workplace for relatively lower pay.

Job pressures resulting from a fluctuating economy and changes in gender-role expectations are intensifying for men and women. Men who have the financial pressures of supporting families or alimony payments may feel desperate to maintain their jobs in the face of a shifting economy. Women who are desperate for jobs as a result of divorce or other family demands may have overfunctioned in other aspects of their lives at first and may be eager to demonstrate their flexibility and hard work. Later, however, they may resent biased treatment or suffer from the stress of overwork.

Because of women's lack of power and authority in the workplace, both women and men are vulnerable. The more a woman needs a job and the fewer resources she has, the more exposed she is to exploitation. Women may be subjected to humiliation and even sexual harassment and may often feel they have little recourse in male-dominated businesses. As a result of incidents toward women in the workplace, men must be more cautious to avoid unintentionally offending women. At the same time, men may feel concerned that they are being unfairly scrutinized for infractions related to women.

Attitudes in the workplace about how male and female work roles should be prioritized can have an impact on the family system. If a husband's job is more valued at work, it can change the balance of power at home and lead the wife to be more willing to sacrifice her career for the family. Children easily pick up these messages about role behaviors and perpetuate them. Conversely, when the workplace starts to equally value the efforts of all its employees, then it will reinforce the family's adaptation to modern trends. It remains to be seen whether family or workplace will be the leader in this process.

*CASE EXAMPLE:*

*THE HARASSED FOREWOMAN*

*Angela is a 40-year-old forewoman in a manufacturing plant who presented in therapy with symptoms of anxiety and depression related to sexual harassment at work. She and her second husband had two children and enjoyed a good relationship. The strain in the marital relationship coincided with the difficulties Angela was having at work. The problem stemmed from a year of repeated abuses by her supervisor including lewd and demeaning remarks and continuous sexual advances. She reported distress, shame, and anger at facing daily intimidation by her supervisor and pressure by her female peers to seek redress. Angela felt shame and anger at being the subject of office scandal. The stress eroded her self-confidence and affected her sleep.*

*The strain from work spilled over into her home life. Aware and upset about taking out her anger on her children, she reported spanking them for minor infractions and feeling uncharacteristically rejecting of them. She felt angry and rejecting toward men in general, which led to a deterioration in her sexual relationship with her husband. As a result, Angela felt guilty and ashamed. Although her husband had been supportive and protective throughout most of this ordeal, he was beginning to feel neglected and angry because of Angela's preoccupation with her work problems.*

*In individual sessions the family psychologist validated Angela's intense feelings of devaluation and her lack of trust for the therapist whom she saw as an authority figure. The powerlessness she felt as a result of the lack of a resolute response to her accusations by supervisors at her workplace was a major focus of therapy.*

*To help the couple understand how Angela's experience had affected their relationship, conjoint marital therapy was begun. The therapist helped the couple better understand each other's distress by asking questions about how the incidents at work were affecting each of them, validating their feelings through empathic statements, and commenting how akin their feelings were to others who had similar experiences. In addition, "date nights" for the couple and more frequent family outings were suggested to relieve the couple's preoccupation with the workplace incident and feelings of alienation and rejection. Furthermore, the sessions were used to address ways to change the intolerable situation at work with her peers and supervisor. The couple explored the advantages and disadvantages of a number of alternative solutions, including filing suit against the supervisor, confronting Angela's peers with her need to cease discussing with them the incidents, and quitting her job. Finally, with increased communication and intimacy, the couple decided on a course of action and, in addition, developed a renewed interest in their sexual relationship.*

## The Bottom Line

In some ways, modern business is more flexible in the face of change than the family. After all, what fuels transformation of the work environment more than anything else is the bottom line. Many businesses, agencies, and institutions are realizing that the changes in family structures are here to stay and that they will fall short of their competition if they do not accommodate today's trends. In response to employees ranking family problems as the most difficult they face (Warshaw, 1990), organizations are beginning to strike a better balance related to family–work issues. Managers are receiving training in how to juggle nontraditional work schedules, managing people who work at home, or even filling in for employees who need leave time for family demands (Shellenberger, 1992). Many business organizations are building a management style that is more dedicated to enhancing the family lives of workers by experimenting with flexible schedules such as compressed work weeks, sabbaticals, and job-sharing programs (Towers Perrin & Hudson Institute, 1990). Such flexible schedules can make a significant difference in the family lives of workers. To illustrate, research findings of men and their participation in home life suggest that when work environments were more flexible in accommodating to family life, husbands were more likely to take equal responsibility in home life rather than aiding solely as their wives' helpers (Gerson, 1993).

Businesses are beginning to recognize the diversity and balance that different types of people can bring to the workplace. Men have long been recognized for their rationality, drive for achievement, and competitive spirit. Although many women possess these same qualities, some also bring to the workplace valuable skills often forged in their socialization as women, such as sensitivity to the needs of others and a collaborative orientation (Gilligan, 1982). These skills have been particularly valued in professions traditionally belonging to women, such as nursing, teaching, and social work, but have come to be seen as more widely applicable. The companionate and relational orientations of some women may foster group spirit and cooperation that, in turn, can enhance organizational loyalty. Businesses in today's growing service and information economy that are shifting away from authoritarian hierarchies and embracing more collaborative management styles may particularly value these relational skills (Franklin & Sweeney, 1988; Naisbitt & Auberdene, 1985). Similarly, in addition to the other skills and talents brought by minorities and ethnic groups to the workplace, these groups are increasingly recognized for their unique contributions that broaden the effectiveness of a company's services or products.

## FAMILY PSYCHOLOGISTS AND CHANGE: HARBINGERS OR MIDWIVES?

Family psychologists, as part of the smaller and larger systems we have described, respond and react to changing work–family trends. In our workplaces—family therapy and consultation rooms, research laboratories, classrooms, and community psychology settings—we encourage or discourage change. In our offices we see the constant struggle with role dilemmas and are drawn to take part in the ongoing societal trends. We have a choice to be part of the problem or part of the solution. We must be vigilant about the place of our own values as we join with other family systems. Many of us may have entered the field with a vision of doing things differently than our families of origin did—a force of reaction, encouraging reversals of tradition. However, in response to traditional attitudes from our families of origin or entrenched attitudes at our workplaces, we must also be watchful lest we settle into a state of equilibrium, unresponsive to the same forces of transformation propelling us to change.

Our role as therapist to families affords us the opportunity to help family members as they struggle to negotiate roles, values, and traditions that define them. We can help families understand how roles assigned by gender can contribute to the tension when choices different from their usual or traditional ones might succeed, and that asserting the importance of their family at work can make a difference in business and government (Bradt, 1989). Many among us are striving to develop new paradigms of family therapy. This process includes critiquing our long-standing systems theories for bias toward certain genders or classes and developing interventions that are sensitive to changing values in families and at work (Goldner, 1985; Hare-Mustin, 1978; Walters, Carter, Papp, & Silverstein, 1988).

As therapists, we can advocate for larger systems to be more responsive to work–family problems and dilemmas (Wiggins, 1992). For example, we can advocate for work settings to offer wellness centers and parenting classes for the purpose of preventing individual and family dysfunction. To address work–family problems, diagnostic classification systems that are sensitive to work and family issues have been proposed so that third-party payers will reimburse for therapeutic attention to work–family difficulties and individuals will not be stigmatized (Kaslow, 1993; Wiggins, 1992). We can advocate for employee assistance programs to continue their focus on family–work issues. Family psychologists are well-equipped to serve as both supervisors or providers in these programs.

In the research laboratory, family psychologists have opportunities to change traditional methods that look at one individual; one system; or one class, sex, or age category. It is important to attend to differences in the career status of, for example, dual-career versus dual-earner couples; traditional versus nontraditional value systems, economic, and educational levels; and cultural backgrounds of individuals or groups studied. We can move into uncharted or incomplete research territory, for example, to examine the effects on families when women become unemployed or retire or when men become househusbands or otherwise increase their involvement in child care, and the effects of fathers' employment on children, themselves, and their spouses (Bianchi & Spain, 1986; Pleck, 1983). Investigation into the effects of eldercare programs on employees' work and family lives is another example of an area ripe for family–work research (Scharlach, 1991).

Family psychologists have taken opportunities to teach employees about families and family-of-origin influences brought to the work setting. For example, didactic and experiential approaches have been used in seminars and workshops, one-on-one teaching, and peer groups to promote understanding of how systems function and the role of the family at work (McDaniel, Bank, Campbell, Mancini, & Shore, 1986; Shellenberger, Shurden, & Treadwell, 1988; Weinberg & Mauksch, 1991).

In consultation to work settings, family psychologists have used family systems frameworks to enhance many aspects of the workplace process and outcome. Contracting for such services have been health care institutions (Munson, 1986; Sluzki, 1986; Wellisch & Cohen, 1986), businesses (Borwick, 1986; Friedman, 1986), agencies and community service systems (Anderson & Goolishian, 1986; Fisher, 1986; Imber-Black, 1986; Weber & Wynn, 1986; Wynne & Wynne, 1986), and the military (Kaslow, 1986). Consultation goals have included improving individual functioning as a means of increasing productivity (Friedman, 1986), increasing group functioning as well as individual functioning (Kaslow, 1986), increasing productivity (Borwick, 1986), problem solving (Munson, 1986; Sluzki, 1986; Wellisch & Cohen, 1986), and assisting organizations to move forward from problematic points (Anderson &

Goolishian, 1986). Examples of approaches used to meet these goals include assisting individuals toward self-differentiation and avoidance of triangles as in Bowen family systems models (Friedman, 1986), overcoming impasses and blocks to effective functioning as in strategic-systemic models (Anderson & Goolishian, 1986), and assisting organizations in solving specific problems by the use of problem solving combined with systems models (Munson, 1986; Sluzki, 1986; Wellisch & Cohen, 1986).

Family psychologists, when consulting to work settings, have used family systems models or have combined family systems with organizational development–group relations models (McDaniel, Weber, & Wynn, 1986; Wynne, McDaniel, & Weber, 1986). Organizations most dramatically demonstrating the dilemma of whether family therapy approaches are necessary or sufficient in consultations are family-owned businesses (Kaslow & Kaslow, 1992; Kirschner, 1992; McClendon & Kadis, 1991; Whiteside & Brown, 1991). As usual, research lags behind our practice in terms of assessing the most efficacious models for enhancing the productivity or process of work settings.

Lastly, in the larger systems of work settings and at the government and policy-making levels, family psychologists can be advocates for promotion of family-centered work environments. This could be done through participation in community, state, and national boards and task forces, as well as by serving as elected or appointed officials.

## CONCLUSION

A major source of stress in our lives today has been the need for both the family and work systems to reorganize themselves in relation to new social trends. Of course, we could always return to the traditional solution of women remaining home during child-rearing years, possibly with government support. Because most families require more than one income to make ends meet, and many families have a single head of household, this solution seems highly unlikely (Moen, 1992). Advocates for change have proposed a number of solutions to ameliorate the situation: (a) husbands becoming more involved in family and home life, (b) workplaces becoming more accommodating, (c) technology advancing to assist in making housework more efficient (Moen, 1992), and (d) government taking a larger role in requiring the workplace to accommodate to family needs. These are examples of first-order systemic changes (Watzlawick, Weakland, & Fisch, 1974).

However, to reduce stress in our work–family systems may require a total reconfiguration of the entire structure of work and family life over the life cycle. Such fundamental, second-order changes (Watzlawick, Weakland, & Fisch, 1974), where norms of the current systems are altered, may radically change our current roles, values, and modes of operating. The shape of these changes can only be imagined at this point. Certainly, a new, more-equitable arrangement in gender relationships would be required, but beyond this, we can only speculate. Perhaps we would see new arrangements in the sequencing of periods of work and nonwork over the life span with parental leaves of absence and sabbaticals from work becoming common occurrences (Gerson, 1993; Moen, 1992). Or we may see grandparents, satisfied with their own histories of a comfortable work–family balance, choosing in larger numbers to devote energy in their later years to grandchildren so that parents may benefit from a more comfortable balance between their work and family lives. Finally, we may see the evolution of entirely new family structures, such as communal households where single working parents join together in the common task of raising children and sharing expenses. We look forward with great interest to how our society makes this radical transformation.

Family psychologists have much to contribute in this ongoing change process: by assisting families who struggle with questions of balance and change in their day-to-day lives, by investigating the various solutions that families use as they attempt to reduce their stress and find a satisfying work–family balance, and by consulting to businesses where managers are striving to create a more family-friendly work environment. With our ability to assess change from a systemic perspective, we are in a unique position to assist families as they struggle to cope with the necessary dislocations inherent in basic systemic transformation. This will take time. To put it in perspective, a recent study from the International Labour Organisation, a liaison office with the United Nations (Ducci, 1993), predicted it would take another 500 years before women finally reach economic and political equality in our global society. Family psychologists, there is no time like the present to begin.

## References

Ahrons, C. R., & Rodgers, R. H. (1987). *Divorced families: A multidisciplinary developmental view.* New York: Norton.

Anderson H., & Goolishian, H. (1986). Systems consultation with agencies dealing with domestic violence. In L. C. Wynne, S. H. McDaniel, & T. T. Weber (Eds.), *Systems consultation: A new perspective for family therapy* (pp. 284–299). New York: Guilford Press.

Bergman, B. R., & Roberts, M. D. (1987). Income for the single parent: Child support, work, and welfare. In C. Brown & J. A. Pechman (Eds.), *Gender in the workplace* (pp. 247–270). Washington, DC: Brookings Institution.

Bianchi, S. M., & Spain, D. (1986). *American women in transition.* New York: Russell Sage Foundation.

Birnbaum, J. A. (1971). Life patterns, personality style and self-esteem in gifted family-oriented and career-committed women. *Dissertation Abstracts International, 32,* 1834-B.

Borwick, I. (1986). The family therapist as business consultant. In L. C. Wynne, S. H. McDaniel, & T. T. Weber (Eds.), *Systems consultation: A new perspective for family therapy* (pp. 423–440). New York: Guilford Press.

Bradt, J. O. (1989). Becoming parents: Families of young children. In B. Carter & M. McGoldrick (Eds.), *The changing life cycle: A framework for family therapy* (pp. 235–254). Needham Heights, MA: Allyn & Bacon.

Burke, R. J., & Weir, T. (1976). Relationship of wives' employment status to husband, wife and pair satisfaction and performance. *Journal of Marriage and the Family, 38,* 279–287.

Busch, J. (1992). *Lifestyle stories of dual-career couples who commute.* Unpublished doctoral dissertation, California Graduate School of Family Psychology, Corte Madera.

The Conference Board. (1992). *Work–family roundtable: Elder care* (Vol. 3, no. 1). New York: Author.

Ducci, M. A. (1993, February). Women in authority: The ideal and the reality. *World of Work,* pp. 4–5.

Epstein, C. F. (1971). Law partners and marital partners. *Human Relations, 24,* 549–564.

Etaugh, C., & Nekolny, K. (1990). Effects of employment status and marital status on perceptions of mothers. *Sex Roles, 23,* 273–280.

Evans, S. (1992, December 7). For many mothers, home is where the office is. *Wall Street Journal,* pp. C1, C5.

Feld, S. (1963). Feelings of adjustment. In F. I. Nye & L. W. Hoffman (Eds.), *The employed mother in America* (pp. 331–352). Chicago: Rand McNally.

Fisher, L. (1986). Systems-based consultation with schools. In L. C. Wynne, S. H. McDaniel, & T. T. Weber (Eds.), *Systems consultation: A new perspective for family therapy* (pp. 342–356). New York: Guilford Press.

Franklin, D. W., & Sweeney, J. L. (1988). Women in corporate power. In E. Boneparth & E. Stoper (Eds.), *Women, power and policy: Toward the year 2000* (2nd ed., pp. 48–65). New York: Pergamon Press.

Friedman, E. H. (1986). Emotional process in the marketplace: The family therapist as consultant with work systems. In L. C. Wynne, S. H. McDaniel, & T. T. Weber (Eds.), *Systems consultation: A new perspective for family therapy* (pp. 398–422). New York: Guilford Press.

Gerson, K. (1993). *No man's land: Men's changing commitment to family and work.* New York: Basic Books.

Gilligan, C. (1982). *In a different voice.* Cambridge, MA: Harvard University Press.

Goldner, V. (1985). Feminism and family therapy. *Family Process, 24,* 31–47.

Goldscheider, F. K., & Waite, L. J. (1991). *New families, no families(?): The transformation of the American home.* Berkeley, CA: University of California Press.

Hare-Mustin, R. (1978). A feminist approach to family therapy. *Family Process, 17,* 181–194.

Hennig, M., & Jardim, A. (1977). *The managerial woman.* Garden City, NJ: Anchor/Doubleday.

Hochschild, A. (1989). *The second shift.* New York: Viking Press.

Hoffman, M. S., Foley, J., & McGuire, T. (Eds.). (1993). *The world almanac and book of facts 1993.* New York: St. Martin's Press.

Hopkins, J., & White, P. (1978). The dual-career couple: Constraints and supports. *The Family Coordinator, 27,* 253–259.

Imber-Black, E. (1986). The systemic consultant and human-service-provider systems. In L. C. Wynne, S. H. McDaniel, & T. T. Weber (Eds.), *Systems consultation: A new perspective for family therapy* (pp. 357–374). New York: Guilford Press.

Kaslow, F. W. (1986). Consultation with the military: A complex role. In L. C. Wynne, S. H. McDaniel, & T. T. Weber (Eds.), *Systems consultation: A new perspective for family therapy* (pp. 383–397). New York: Guilford Press.

Kaslow, F. (1993). Relational diagnosis: An idea whose time has come? *Family Process, 32,* 255–259.

Kaslow, F., & Kaslow, B. S. (1992). The family that works together: Special problems of family businesses. In S. Zedeck (Ed.), *Work, families and organizations* (pp. 312–351). San Francisco, CA: Jossey-Bass.

Kessler, R. C., & McRae, J. A., Jr. (1982). The effect of wives' employment on the mental health of married men and women. *American Sociological Review, 47,* 216–227.

Kirschner, S. (1992). The myth of the sacrifice of the daughter: Implications for family-owned businesses. *The American Journal of Family Therapy, 20*(1), 13–24.

Louis Harris & Associates, Inc. (1981). *Families at work: The General Mills American family report, 1980–1981.* Minneapolis, MN: General Mills.

Martin, T. C., & Bumpass, L. L. (1989). Recent trends in marital disruption. *Demography, 26,* 37–51.

McClendon, R., & Kadis, L. B. (1991). Family therapists and family business: A view of the future. *Contemporary Family Therapy, 13*(6), 641–651.

McDaniel, S. H., Bank, J., Campbell, T., Mancini, J., & Shore, B. (1986). Using a group as a consultant: A systems approach to medical care. In L. C. Wynne, S. H. McDaniel, & T. T. Weber (Eds.), *Systems consultation: A new perspective for family therapy* (pp. 181–198). New York: Guilford Press.

McDaniel, S. H., Weber, T. T., & Wynne, L. C (1986). Consultants at the crossroads: Problems and controversies in systems consultation. In L. C. Wynne, S. H. McDaniel, & T. T. Weber (Eds.), *Systems consultation: A new perspective for family therapy* (pp. 449–462). New York: Guilford Press.

Moen, P. (1992). *Women's two roles: A contemporary dilemma.* New York: Auburn House.

Moss, M. B., Lawton, M. P., Dean, J., Goodman, M., & Schneider, J. (1989). Satisfactions and burdens in caring for impaired elderly persons. *Journal of Gerontology, 44,* 181–189.

Munson, S. (1986). Family-oriented consultation in pediatrics. In L. C. Wynne, S. H. McDaniel, & T. T. Weber (Eds.), *Systems consultation: A new perspective for family therapy* (pp. 219–240). New York: Guilford Press.

Naisbitt, J., & Aburdene, P. (1985). *Re-inventing the corporation.* New York: Warner Books.

Ohlbaum, J. L. (1971). Self concepts, value characteristics and self-actualization of professional and non-professional women. *Dissertation Abstracts International, 32,* 1221B–1222B.

Orden, S. R., & Bradburn, N. M. (1969). Working wives and marital happiness. *American Journal of Sociology, 74,* 392–407.

Pleck, J. (1983). Husbands' paid work and family roles: Current research issues. In H. Z. Lopata & J. H. Pleck (Eds.), *Research in the interweave of social roles: Families and jobs* (pp. 251–233). Greenwich, CT: JAI Press.

Pleck, J., Staines, G., & Lang, L. (1980). Conflicts between work and family life. *Monthly Labor Review, 103,* 29–32.

Rapoport, R., & Rapoport, R. N. (1980). Three generations of dual-career family research. In F. Pepitone-Rockwell (Ed.), *Dual career couples* (pp. 23–48). Beverly Hills, CA: Sage.

Ratcliff, K. S., & Bogdan, J. (1988). Unemployed women: When "social support" is not supportive. *Social Problems, 35,* 54–63.

Rice, D. G. (1979). *Dual-career marriage: Conflict and treatment.* New York: Free Press.

Roskies, E., & Carrier, S. (1992). Marriage and children for professional women: Asset or liability? [Summary]. *Abstracts presented to the American Psychological Association and the National Institute for Occupational Safety and Health Conference,* Washington, DC.

Scharlach, A. E. (1991, July). *Elder care research and the worksite: Possibilities and problems.* Paper presented at the National Institute on Aging Research Conference on Employers, Eldercare, and the Worksite, New York.

Seidenberg, R. (1973). *Corporate wife—Corporate casualties.* New York: Anchor Press/Doubleday.

Sekaran, U. (1986). *Dual-career families: Contemporary organizational and counseling issues.* San Francisco: Jossey-Bass.

Shellenberger, S. (1992, December 7). Managers navigate uncharted waters trying to resolve work–family conflicts. *The Wall Street Journal,* pp. B1, B8.

Shellenberger, S., Shurden, K. W., & Treadwell, W. T., Jr. (1988). Faculty training seminars in family systems. *Family Medicine, 20*(3), 226–227.

Sluzki, C. E. (1986). Family consultation in family medicine: A case example. In L. C. Wynne, S. H. McDaniel, & T. T. Weber (Eds.), *Systems consultation: A new perspective for family therapy* (pp. 168–180). New York: Guilford Press.

Towers Perrin & Hudson Institute. (1992). *Workforce 2000 — Competing in a seller's market: Is corporate America prepared?* New York: Author.

U.S. Bureau of the Census. (1992). Number of workers with earnings and median earnings, by occupation of longest job held and sex: 1990. *Statistical Abstracts of the United States: 1992* (112th ed., p. 414). Washington, DC: U.S. Department of Commerce.

U.S. Department of Education, Office of Research & Improvement, National Center for Education Statistics. (1992). Earned degrees conferred by institutions of higher education, by level of degree and sex of student: 1869–70 to 1999–2000. *Digest of education statistics* (NCES-92-097, p. 241). Washington, DC: U.S. Government Printing Office.

U.S. Department of Labor, Bureau of Labor Statistics. (1989a). Employment status of civilian noninstitutional population 16 years and over by sex, 1948–88. *Handbook of labor statistics* (Bulletin 2340, pp. 10–12). Washington, DC: U.S. Government Printing Office.

U.S. Department of Labor, Bureau of Labor Statistics. (1989b). Number and age of children in families by type of family and labor force status of mother, March 1970–88. *Handbook of labor statistics* (Bulletin 2340, p. 248). Washington, DC: U.S. Government Printing Office.

U.S. Merit Systems Protection Board. (1991). *Balancing work responsibilities and family needs: The federal civil service response.* (ISBN 0-16-035918-X). Washington, DC: U.S. Government Printing Office.

Wagner, D. L. (1987). Corporate eldercare project: Survey findings. In M. Creedon (Ed.), *Issues for an aging America: Employees and eldercare.* Bridgeport, CT: Center for the Study of Aging, University of Bridgeport.

Walters, M., Carter, B., Papp, P., & Silverstein, O. (1988). *The invisible web: Gender patterns in family relationships.* New York: Guilford Press.

Warshaw, L. (1990). Stress, anxiety, and depression in the workplace. New York: New York Business Group on Health.

Watzlawick, P., Weakland, J., & Fisch, R. (1974). *Change: Principles of problem formation and problem resolution.* New York: Norton.

Weber, T. T., & Wynn, J. C. (1986). Consultation with the clergy: A systems approach. In L. C. Wynne, S. H. McDaniel, & T. T. Weber (Eds.), *Systems consultation: A new perspective for family therapy* (pp. 320–341). New York: Guilford Press.

Weinberg, R. B., & Mauksch, L. B. (1991). Examining family-of-origin influences in life at work. *Journal of Marital and Family Therapy, 17*(3), 233–242.

Weitzman, L. J. (1985). *The divorce revolution.* New York: Free Press.

Wellisch, D. K., & Cohen, M. M. (1986). The family therapist as systems consultant to medical oncology. In L. C. Wynne, S. H. McDaniel, & T. T. Weber (Eds.),

*Systems consultation: A new perspective for family therapy* (pp. 199–218). New York: Guilford Press.

Whiteside, M. F., & Brown, F. H. (1991). Drawbacks of a dual systems approach to family firms: Can we expand our thinking? *Family Business Review, 4*(4), 383–395.

Wiggins, J. G. (1992, November). *Occupational stress-related disorders.* Keynote address presented to the American Psychological Association and the National Institute for Occupational Safety and Health Conference, Washington, DC.

Wynne, L. C., McDaniel, S. H., & Weber, T. T. (1986). Editors' comments. In L. C. Wynne, S. H. McDaniel, & T. T. Weber (Eds.), *Systems consultation: A new perspective for family therapy* (pp. 441–446). New York: Guilford Press.

Wynne, A. R., & Wynne L. C. (1986). At the center of the cyclone: Family therapists as consultants with family and divorce courts. In L. C. Wynne, S. H. McDaniel, & T. T. Weber (Eds.), *Systems consultation: A new perspective for family therapy* (pp. 300–319). New York: Guilford Press.

# CHAPTER 27

# FAMILY–SCHOOL INTERVENTION

*Marvin J. Fine*

One could argue that the ecosystemic nature of human behavior is no better exemplified than in the arena of family–school intervention. Each child is a member of an immediate family that itself reflects a unique configuration of structure and relationships. The family, in turn, is embedded in its own cultural and social history. The child is simultaneously a member of a school classroom characterized by its particular structure, and that classroom again is embedded in a matrix of larger structures. These two major systems in the child's life interface in relation to the child and create a new *mesosystem* with its own characteristics (Bronfenbrenner, 1986).

It is against this background that the clinician, who may be a school employee, an agency representative, or a private practitioner, enters the scene. This person may be quite familiar with the child, family, and school or may enter with no prior connection.

Each system has its own unique structure, objectives, priorities, and regularities. They are very likely to differ in their emotional investments in the child. They may have historically interfaced in healthy, complementary ways or in antagonistic ways characterized by side taking and the triangulating of relationships. The identified child exists within and traverses these systems and is the main basis on which the two systems will connect. In some instances the child may have difficulties in only one setting, and in other instances the child may be a source of concern in both settings. How does the involved professional make sense out of all of this and develop a coherent intervention plan?

This chapter will explore family–school intervention from a broad ecosystemic perspective, one that allows for the confluence of both family systems and ecological theory and practice. A collaborative consultation framework will also be proposed as a service delivery model.

Any clinician attempting to bridge home and school must become familiar with the culture of the school, the way decisions are made, and the prerogatives of teachers. Therefore, this chapter will also incorporate discussion of some of the changes affecting schools and the treatment of students who experience major difficulties. There are some critical and extensive laws mandating educational planning for children with special needs and young at-risk children. These laws also stipulate how parents are to be involved. There is also a grassroots national movement, The Regular Education Initiative, that promotes a substantially greater inclusion of exceptional children in the regular classroom. Another significant factor is the growing emphasis on collaboration and team decision making, which is generated, in part, by the mandated provisions of services to exceptional and at-risk populations.

## ECOSYSTEMIC OVERVIEW

School–family interaction has been the subject of research and clinical intervention programs for some time (Aponte, 1976; Apter, 1982; Bronfenbrenner, 1979, 1986; Green, 1985; Hobbs, 1966, 1978; Tucker & Dyson, 1976). A number of family therapists have written from a more clinical perspective (Eno, 1985; Fisher, 1986; Lusterman, 1985; Okum,

1984; Rotheram, 1989). This literature has been complemented by the writings and research of professionals more closely aligned with education (Conoley & Haynes, 1992; Fine, 1992; Fine & Holt, 1983; Fish & Jain, 1985, 1988; Graden & Christenson, 1987).

The treatment orientation for children has shifted over the years from a primarily psychodynamic emphasis to one that is more systemic and ecological. The child may still be a major focus of treatment, but there is now a greater recognition of the importance of the settings and systems of which the child is a member. Hobbs (1978), in describing Project Re-ED, a nationally recognized program for helping emotionally disturbed children, explained how he and his colleagues were initially guided by the belief that the "problem" resided within the child. This belief led to an intervention model that proved ineffective. After becoming more aware of the reciprocal impact of the child with different persons and settings, Hobbs (1978) stated, "In time we came to define emotional disturbance in children as a symptom of acute imbalance, not in the child necessarily, but in the ecosystem that is defined by the child" (p. 760). Accordingly, he stressed the importance of facilitating "the coming together of child, school, family and community in the interest of restoring balance to the ecosystem" (p. 760). He pointed out the need for a consultant to bring the involved professionals together to coordinate their thinking and efforts. That person serves the role of maintaining communications as interventions are attempted, evaluated, and refined.

The role of the liaison facilitator might be described as a form of consultation. Fisher (1986) states:

> I will use the term "therapy" to apply only to family-based clinical situation. All other nonclinical intervention programs will be called "consultation." One does therapy with a family, but one consults with a school, even though similar principles of intervention may be utilized. (p. 344)

It is not always easy for parents and teacher to work together in a positive and productive fashion to resolve a school–family problem. The same observation holds true for community agencies. Professionals often act as if the client (whether it be an individual, couple, or family) exists only within the narrow spotlight of their agency's focus.

Either parents or school personnel may be defining the "problem" in a manner that unwittingly perpetuates it and thus precludes a successful collaboration. A negative history of past attempts to collaborate may also undermine current efforts. In such cases, an individual with an ecosystemic orientation who has legitimate entrée into the situation may undertake the liaison–consultant role. This person will assume responsibility for convening the representatives of the relevant settings and for assisting them in working out a viable plan.

The importance of the liaison role has also been recognized by others. According to Wynne, McDaniel, and Weber (1986),

> One very important task of the consultant is to convene the system in such a way that the different and often contradictory views of "reality" are allowed to merge into some integrated, working whole. Bringing the disparate parts into a whole not only fosters greater communication and efficiency, but also minimizes escalating battles and multiplies strengths. Convening members of the larger treatment system may be the consultant's most important task. (pp. 377–378)

This "coming together" or "convening" can take different formats. For example, a family–school interview (Aponte, 1976; Fine & Holt, 1983) could include the parents, the child, the teacher, other educational personnel, and the consultant (e.g. the school psychologist or the family therapist). In addition, the consultant might have telephone contacts or written correspondence with the parents and educational personnel. The consultant might also meet concomitantly with individuals or subsets of the involved persons and play out other roles such as therapist or mediator. As the family and school become better able to collaborate, the need for direct clinical treatment of the family will probably diminish.

The consultant will have to be sensitive to the predictable turf issues that exist in any professional setting. Attempts to orchestrate a coherent and systemically valid intervention that involves people from the different systems of which the child is a member require that the consultant demonstrate persistence, flexibility, strategic thinking, and effective interpersonal skills. For example, if the family's therapist takes on this role, the school may perceive him or her as the family's advocate, particularly if he or she seems unsympathetic to the efforts and concerns of teachers. When people feel blamed, a defense reaction may be expected.

The consultant will need to consider a number of questions. Who is concerned about the child and how is the "problem" being defined? Does the child's behavior vary across settings, and is the same behavior being defined differently in different settings? How is the family organized, and what is the child's place within the family? What are the similarities and differences of the family versus the school setting? What is the history of family–school interaction, and does the history reveal conflict or collaboration? Are there ethnic or cultural factors that play into the situation? Who are the not-so-obvious "players," for example extended family members, school administrators, or parents of classmates? What other agencies or services are in the picture, and how are they influencing the logistics of everyday life for the family?

A systems–ecological approach may also have implications beyond the immediate case and promote further change in the ecosystem. An example would be a teacher's increased readiness to work closely with parents. Indeed, increased parent–teacher cooperation has been found to correlate consistently with positive outcomes. These include a student's improved social and academic behavior, improved school morale, and greater community support (Christenson, Rounds, & Gorney, 1992; Epstein, 1991; Haynes, Comer, & Hamilton-Lee, 1989).

## COMPONENTS OF A SYSTEMS–ECOLOGICAL ORIENTATION

The terms *systems* and *ecological* may appear redundant, but they are combined to emphasize the im-

portance of the interactions of people, events, and settings, as well as to expand the possibilities for developing effective interventions. The reader should be aware that the two terms are used somewhat differently by different writers but are usually combined to project a broader ecosystemic picture of a situation than is captured by either term alone (Fine, 1992). Christenson and Cleary (1990) in their combining of the two terms drew primarily on general systems theory (von Bertalanffy, 1968) and ecological theory (Apter, 1982; Bronfenbrenner, 1979; Hobbs, 1982), with less input from the family therapy literature. Attempting to clarify distinctions between the two terms, Mannino and Shore (1984) stated,

> *Thinking "systems" and thinking "ecology" are not one in the same. The term ecology is broader and includes the concept of system; on the other hand, the concept of system does not necessarily include the concept of ecology. For example, from a systems perspective one can view the family as a group of individuals interacting within the context of a family. Here an individual's problem is seen as related to . . . the family relationship system. An ecological perspective broadens the context to include other relationship systems beyond the family, for example, school, workplace, hospital. (p. 75).*

Mannino and Shore (1984) also expressed concern that a family systems orientation alone might ignore the broader context within which a family operates and might lead to pathologizing the family through narrow concepts of dysfunctionality. Accordingly, the concepts to be discussed derive from a broad range of theories and therapeutic approaches, including general systems theory (Grinker, 1975; Guttman, 1991; von Bertalanffy, 1968), structural and strategic family therapy (Haley, 1976; Madanes, 1991; Minuchin & Fishman, 1981; Umbarger, 1983), and ecological theory (Apter, 1982; Bronfenbrenner, 1979, 1986; Conoley & Haynes, 1992; Hobbs, 1966, 1978, 1982; Rhodes, 1970; Rhodes & Paul, 1978). The first set of concepts relates to the contributions of systems theory to the understanding and treatment of larger systems.

## Selected Systems Concepts and Strategies

Most clinicians who identify with a family systems or ecological orientation are eclectic in their incorporation of various constructs into their interventions. Many of the concepts presented here have been treated extensively elsewhere in this book or may already be familiar to the reader. Thus, the reader shares in creatively integrating the concepts and formulations and in conceptualizing their applications to family–school intervention.

**Systems can be complex but have a discernible structure.** Relationships occur within a systemic context characterized by roles, boundaries, power differentials, and historical patterns of communication, decision making, and the expressing of affection. Each system will reflect its own unique configuration and have its own perceived history of evolution. A family will have its cultural, religious, ethnic, and socioeconomic identity and will be at a particular point in its developmental trajectory. The components of a system interconnect, and change in any part of a system is likely to affect other parts of the system. What happens to a child at school is likely to have some effect on the family, and the child's home experiences will influence his or her school adjustment.

Some systems may appear functional when life circumstances are without stress, but when stress is experienced the system cannot function effectively. Unsuccessful attempts to solve a problem may be rigidly applied even though they are not succeeding. An example would be frustrated parents who become progressively more punitive in their failing attempts to control a rebellious child.

Patterns of behavior cannot be separated from the interacting systems that support those patterns. A key objective of family–school intervention is to assist those systems to develop collaborative and problem-solving behaviors. This generally involves modifications or shifts in ways of thinking about the problem and in how people have been addressing the problem.

**People define themselves and can be understood in terms of their social interactions.** Simon, Stierlin, and Wynne (1985) describe *recursiveness* as follows:

> *In family systems in particular, the thoughts and feelings of each individual are embedded in the family context and sustained by the family rules. The reverse is also true: The patterns of each family member's thoughts and feelings maintain the status quo of the family rules. This represents a process of reciprocal stabilization.* (pp. 38–39)

An awareness of the recursive patterns that are characteristic of the subsystems larger-system interactions is essential for the consultant, as is the recognition that different participants hold different beliefs and have different perceptions. It is for this reason that the consultant should encourage the involvement of many mesosystem members, either in some group format or through separate interviews. By demonstrating an interest in understanding different viewpoints and learning about past efforts at intervention, the consultant models a valuing of people's ideas, a posture of neutrality, and a desire to build a "big picture" perspective. This process often reveals important data regarding alliances and triangulations, boundary issues, vested interests in defining the problem in a certain way, and the power hierarchy in terms of decision making.

**There is an interconnectedness among systems, and any individual is simultaneously a member of several systems.** Each system is embedded within or in other ways interconnected with a complex of systems. Bronfenbrenner (1979, 1986) describes the nesting of systems within systems. He begins with the microsystem (e.g., home and classroom) and then depicts a new system, the mesosystem, created by the interfacing of the two microsystems. These in turn relate to the larger exosystem (e.g., the community in which home and school coexist) and, ultimately, to the macrosystem (society at large). The consultant generally enters at the level of the mesosystem. For example, a nuclear family has an extended family and is concurrently connected through children to an educational system. Each system will possess sets of beliefs and attributions about itself, specific members, and the systems with which it interconnects. These beliefs will influence people's behavior and create confirming feedback loops.

A particular family may view academic success as the means to achieve upward mobility. In such a family, children will be exhorted to study, and the parents will work actively with their children to meet school demands. In another family, the schools might be seen as a hostile, negative force in the life of the family, where children are doomed to experience failure and parents will be blamed for their children's difficulties. Families that value education typically have higher achieving children with fewer problems than do families that are hostile toward the schools. In each instance, families will likely see their children's school experiences as confirmation of their beliefs.

The philosophy of a given school might emphasize the importance of positive family–school interaction. Under such a philosophy, parental input is valued and parents are encouraged to take an active partnership role with teachers in their children's education. This is a very different situation than one where parents are viewed as intrusive and a probable cause of their child's problem. In any school the philosophy of parental involvement and parental prerogatives is not likely to be restricted to only one teacher, although it is certainly possible. The philosophy is more likely to pervade the entire school and be reflected in printed documents, established procedures, and the explicit stance of the principal. Schools that develop a positive view of parents usually report more positive parent involvement.

### The microsystem can influence the individual.
The microsystem or behavioral setting can have a powerful influence on a student's behavior and how it is understood (Apter, 1982; Swap, 1984). Consider a situation in which the same child may be seen in a positive light in one setting and identified as a problem in another. This kind of contrast might exist between home and school or even between two classrooms. Behavior gets defined within settings by key

persons and in relation to the values of the persons or setting. A mismatch of child to setting can occur and is something that the consultant needs to consider.

> *CASE EXAMPLE*
> *Timmy, a somewhat impulsive and immature child, fit in well in a moderately structured first-grade classroom. The teacher understood and accepted the child's need for prompts, shorter assignments, and relatively immediate feedback and reinforcement. The second-grade teacher, on the other hand, expected students to be more self-managing and offered less structure and support. Timmy was easily distracted and frequently off-task. This led to conflict between the parents, who were accepting of Timmy's behavior, and the teacher, who defined Timmy as a behavior problem.*

**Causality is circular.** The reciprocal and bidirectional patterns of action and reaction make it impossible to clearly differentiate cause from effect. From a systemic perspective, causality is understood in a circular rather than linear fashion. Approaching causality from this circular and interactive posture avoids blaming one individual and instead encourages an examination of patterns of interaction among the involved persons.

When dealing with interacting systems, the consultant should be alert to simplistic and linear conceptualizations of the problem. Many teachers and parents have a tendency to engage in a linear, causal reductionism that, on the surface, seems to simplify matters. A teacher may believe that "Susie does poorly at school because she comes from a bad home." Such an explanation not only blames but also externalizes the responsibility for developing solutions. The consultant needs to listen to how attributions of responsibility get expressed. A person who holds others responsible for the problem or the solution may not be highly motivated to participate in problem solving.

**Behavior serves purposes within the system.** Just as a family therapist will speculate on the purpose of symptoms within a family, so should the consultant be prepared to explore what function the child's difficulties may be serving not only within the family or school but also in relation to the interfacing of these two systems. For example, Tommy may be acting in ways that reaffirm his group identity as the "bad kid," for which he receives reinforcing attention from his classmates. Tommy's misbehavior may also disguise his frustration and feelings of stupidity in relation to academic demands. In addition, his "bad" behavior may also serve to defuse some conflict between the parents as they now unite to address Tommy's difficulties. The stories that Tommy tells either the teacher or the parents may also serve to triangulate the home–school relationship and get the spotlight off his academic or behavioral problems.

By helping the group to examine how behavior may serve purposes both within and across systems, the consultant will elicit perceptions and beliefs from as many of the key players as possible. Unrevealed, such hidden agendas may undermine an intervention program.

### CASE EXAMPLE

*Consider the case of a teacher who, despite feeling overworked and unsupported by her principal, agreed to a course of action proposed by the consultant during a family–school meeting. The intervention plan required the teacher to send daily notes home to the parents and to increase positive reinforcement in the classroom. Even though some positive changes were occurring in the child's behavior, the teacher became erratic in sending the notes and finally stopped. The in-class plan also deteriorated. This was upsetting to the parents who confirmed their belief that the teacher did not like their child. A follow-up consultation revealed that the teacher felt that the onus of effort had been placed on her without adequate appreciation and support from others including the parents, the principal, and the consultant. When more attention and more explicit sharing of responsibility were forthcoming from others, she willingly reinstated the plan.*

**The concept of triangulation helps to explain conflicted relationships.** The triangulating of relationships may be reflective of a problem or at least interfere with problem resolution (Guerin & Katz, 1984; Umbarger, 1983). When parents and teacher are in conflict, the child may become triangulated. An example would be a teacher supporting a child against parents whom she believes hold unrealistic expectations about the child.

The child's way of portraying the teacher to the parents or the parents to the teacher can also contribute to triangulation process. As in any conflict situation, such side-taking tends to polarize the respective positions and to amplify the adversarial relationship. A consultant generally becomes involved when communication has broken down and the involved parties are already engaged in negative projecting about one another's motives.

When the consultant brings parents and teacher together, she may serve as a communication mediator. This may bring about a reduction of combativeness and lead to a better working relationship between home and school. The presence of the child at these meetings presents an occasion for an enactment of the triangulation and an opportunity for the consultant to intervene. By the same token, the consultant needs to guard against the danger that she may also be triangulated. This possibility especially exists as the consultant attempts to bridge both systems on behalf of the child.

**Joining the system creates strategic opportunities for the consultant.** As the consultant interacts with both systems, he or she will risk being seen initially as a representative or even an advocate of one of the systems by members of the other. Early in her involvement, the consultant needs to establish an image of respect for the integrity of both systems and concern with the best interests of the child. While individual therapists typically talk about establishing rapport and building a trusting relationship, family therapists more commonly talk about "joining the system." This concept embodies more than just developing a sense of trust. As Minuchin and Fishman (1981) stated, "joining a family is more an attitude than a technique, and is the umbrella under which all therapeutic transactions occur" (p. 31).

Joining a mesosystem requires that the consultant use tempo, choice of phrases, metaphors, and expressions of positive regard for each subsystem to encourage others to see him or her as an "insider" and not antagonistic to either system. Such joining puts the consultant in a more involved, activistic role, one very different from the traditional therapeutic posture of a more passive and emotionally detached person.

The active consultant may at times "play" with side-taking to strategically support an individual and in doing so should be alert to the risk of becoming triangulated. Nonetheless, the consultant must convey his or her underlying neutrality so that she continues to be seen as respectful of people's perceptions and ideas and intends to assist them to cope more effectively with the issues that brought them all together.

**Systems have a homeostatic quality that can result in resistance to change.** Human systems typically experience a natural tension between the pull to stay the same and the pull to change. Patterns of behavior get established over time through a kind of "process of complicity" by the members of that system. This usually means that key persons in the system may have a major investment in the status quo and in what might happen if and when change occurs. These observations are connected to earlier ones regarding the purposes of "symptoms" and the way that personal roles get established for people within a system and in relation to other people. As an example, a father already feeling inadequate because he cannot solve his child's problem may become threatened when his wife comes home from a school meeting with a new plan. He may openly denigrate the plan or find ways to sabotage its success. But at the same time he knows that something needs to change for the child to be helped. A similar plan made with the father present and with his ideas incorporated has a greater likelihood of success. His self-esteem as "man of the family" can be bolstered through his participation.

**Unbalancing a system can be a precursor to change.** Sometimes events occur that increase a person's level of concern and motivation to change.

When a system is in crisis, it is thrown off balance. It is this unbalancing that provides opportunities for new ways of thinking and relating.

*CASE EXAMPLE*

*Billy's parents had not been willing to confront their son about his marginal academic work. He had always managed to barely pass, and the parents did not feel it was worth the struggle to push him. In the current marking period they learned that he was failing three subjects and receiving warnings in two other subjects. Suddenly, they became extremely anxious and angry, and they both confronted their son in a united way. They asserted their parental authority more strongly than ever, insisted that things were going to change, and contacted the school counselor to arrange a meeting. At the subsequent meeting with the counselor—some teachers, their son, and themselves all present—they worked out a new set of expectations for their son regarding study time and turning in assignments. The teachers, who other than reporting grades had not made any concerted efforts to assist or motivate the student, now felt more personal accountability because of the parents' concern. The surprised parents reported that their son was complying with the new expectations and his school work was improving. They also now felt more comfortable and confident in continuing to closely monitor his academic performance.*

This example revealed how "natural" events unbalanced a system, leading to a positive restructuring. The parents' decision to take some initiative resulted in a strengthened parent subsystem, clearer hierarchical boundaries between the parent and child subsystems, the activation of school personnel, and the establishment of positive collaboration between the parents and teachers.

Because an unbalanced system is vulnerable to change, a family therapist may work to create such a state. The consultant may attempt to unbalance either or both of the family and the school microsystems to precipitate the restructuring of more functional relationships within and between the two systems.

The consultant can use a number of strategies to create an imbalance, including (a) helping family members or school personnel through logical means to see that current patterns of problem solving are not working; (b) encouraging people who have not been very active to voice an opinion and get more involved; (c) introducing new information that brings into question the procedures or patterns that have been followed unsuccessfully; and (d) reframing behavior or events so as to encourage people to see the reality of the situation differently.

**Relationships can be understood as existing on a continuum from enmeshment to disengagement.** The end positions on this continuum are often, but not always, reflective of dysfunctional relationships. The broad range of relationship configurations that can occupy the less extreme placements tend to depict healthier functioning. However, one needs to bear in mind that cultural and ethnic factors can influence family organization. To illustrate how enmeshment and disengagement can have an impact on family–school relationships, the two concepts will be discussed separately.

*Enmeshment.* In an enmeshed system a blurring of boundaries occurs. In some instances the parent–teacher alliance is so strong that there is not adequate differentiation between home and school in the life of the child. Parents and teacher come to perceive the child and define the problem in a similar but dysfunctional way.

> ### CASE EXAMPLE
>
> *A teacher convinced Mr. and Mrs. Mc-Neil that Robert needed to be punished at home for misbehaving at school. In this case the child was seemingly getting along well at home, and family life was satisfying. On the strength of the teacher's conviction, the parents agreed to ground the child over a weekend if he misbehaved at school. As this very critical teacher continued to find fault with the child and was not able to develop successful in-class interventions, the quality of home life, which had been excellent, began to deteriorate. The child felt that the teacher was wrong and that the parents were siding with her. The parents had in fact extended the reach of this inept teacher into the home, and they found themselves arguing over the appropriateness of the grounding. The teacher was an ineffective classroom manager who needed help to strengthen her skills. The parents, who had sought an outside consultation on the situation, gained a better sense of the teacher's legitimate responsibilities and were able to reestablish the positive home atmosphere. The consultant (in this case a private practitioner in the community) had met with the parents and child and had a separate meeting with the teacher and the school psychologist. From that meeting, the school psychologist and teacher agreed to meet to work on general classroom-management issues and to stop pressuring the parents. The parents continued to make their expectations clear to their child regarding good classroom behavior. A more appropriate differentiation of home and school had occurred.*

This example is consistent with Lusterman's description of his role in precipitating a disengagement of home from school when the intrusion of the school into the home gets out of control (Lusterman, 1985).

*Disengagement.* This concept refers to the extent of detachment either among persons within a system or between systems. Members of such systems feel emotionally isolated and unsupported. The consultant is faced with the challenge of assisting the two systems to come together in a more productive fashion so that the needs of both systems can be reasonably met and the child in question helped. This may require the consultant's assisting the family and teachers to appreciate their shared interests and to find ways to work together that respect appropriate boundaries between home and school.

*CASE EXAMPLE*

*Mr. and Mrs. Sanchez seemed reluctant to meet with a teacher who was concerned about their child's poor school performance. The parents found it difficult to agree on a meeting time and wondered if a phone conversation would suffice. The teacher believed that the parents did not really care about their child's school work and rather than continue pushing for a face-to-face meeting agreed to a phone conference. The teacher had already sent progress notes home in which it was recommended that the parents spend at least an hour each evening with the child on schoolwork. In fact, both parents worked long hours and were extremely stressed by a number of daily demands. The teacher's expectations that they work an hour each evening with their child was considered unreasonable and prompted feelings of guilt and anger. In this instance the teacher needed help in understanding that the parent's reluctance to work with the child did not mean that they were unconcerned, but rather that they were overwhelmed with other demands. The parents needed encouragement to meet with the teacher and the consultant to work out a more realistic plan that included learning about sources of help that were available in the community, such as an after-school tutorial program. When both teacher and parents saw progress in the child, a more cooperative relationship soon developed.*

## CURRENT EDUCATIONAL EVENTS INFLUENCING FAMILY–SCHOOL INTERVENTION

There are a number of important things happening in the public schools that can affect the nature of family–school intervention and about which some clinicians might be uninformed. A basic systems and ecological principle is to be reasonably informed about the system you will be entering. The topics to be briefly discussed include trends in the education of handicapped and at-risk children, teaming and collaborative decision making, and a rationale for collaborative consultation. A systems–ecological framework will be presented following this discussion.

## Trends in Special Services

Since 1975, with the passage of Pub. L. No. 94-142, the Education For All Handicapped Children Act, the implementation of special educational services has changed dramatically. The provisions of the act guarantee all handicapped children a free and appropriate education. However, to qualify a child has to meet the criteria for a specific handicap. In certain instances (e.g., a learning disability) the psychometric criteria can be set so as to preclude many children with milder learning problems and to include children with rather substantial problems. Another distinction has been made between emotionally disturbed and socially maladjusted children, with the latter excluded from the provisions of the act. Resources in the form of special teachers and facilities such as self-contained classrooms and resource rooms are only available to the properly identified students. The key issue is one of finances. Even though federal and state funds come to the local district, there are not enough funds to support the different programs if there is too liberal an inclusion policy.

Pub. L. No. 94-142 also stipulates that the identified children are to be educated in the least restrictive environment. This means, for example, that a given child may need the support of a special resource room two hours a day and spend the rest of the day in the regular classroom. In contrast, another child may have a severe enough problem to justify spending all day in a special class. Very few school systems can afford to have a full range of options. This has led to cooperative programming among school districts, a practice that sometimes leads to a less than optimal placement.

The likelihood is that, once evaluated, a child will receive a special education label and will not lose the label regardless of progress (Hobbs, 1975). Also, despite an apparent need for help, special-education services have produced mixed results. These observations have led the schools to institute requirements that every effort be made to educate the child in a regular class setting prior to the child being evaluated to determine special-education eligibility. These efforts not only include all kinds of in-class and in-school options but also very much argue for expanded efforts at parent involvement and greater family–school collaboration in the development of intervention programs.

The more recent Pub. L. No. 99-457 represents a downward extension age-wise to the earlier Pub. L. No. 94-142 and also has a much stronger family focus to service. Children from birth are entitled to special programs and services as their needs dictate. This law explicitly emphasizes the importance of parents and families in the life of the child with special needs and places additional requirements on professionals to consider family strengths and weaknesses and to involve the family in the big picture of intervention.

If a parent disagrees with any aspect of the plan and the differences cannot be worked out, the parent can request a due process hearing that would involve an outside hearing officer. The parents can also request an independent evaluation of the child if they remain dissatisfied with what has occurred in the schools. The identified child is also entitled to support services such as psychotherapy, if those services are deemed necessary for the child to benefit from the educational program. If the child is seen as learning adequately but having some emotional difficulties then the parents will probably be held financially responsible for the cost of treatment. Outside evaluations and due process hearings may be necessary on occasion to make the determination of the school's responsibilities.

A current movement has evolved that seems to be a reversal of the trend to develop special services and programs for children with special needs. The Regular Education Initiative (REI) encourages the education of most handicapped children in the regular classroom (Will, 1986). This movement has led to the widespread dissolution of special classes and other "separatist" educational structures and released a number of those teachers to work side by side with regular class teachers. This movement has oc-

curred to varying degrees across the country but is being strongly supported at the federal and state levels. Although likely to continue as an expanding educational philosophy, the movement is not without its problems and detractors. As with many trends in education, there is more rhetoric than data to support its implementation and anticipated outcomes.

Many parents are delighted to see their children back in the regular classroom, but other parents are fearful that these inclusionary efforts will be counterproductive and not beneficial to their children (Miller et al., 1992). Those concerns are not without some basis. Children with special needs have not fared all that well in terms of social acceptance when integrated into regular classrooms (Roberts & Zubrick, 1993). Many teachers are also concerned that with more children who have special needs entering their classrooms on a full-time basis that the demands on teachers will be excessive (Semmel, Abernathy, Butera, & Lesar, 1991). It is important to note that the REI has not replaced the public laws mandating appropriate services for all handicapped children. We can anticipate a number of legal decisions in the future as parents and child advocates take to the courts.

An outside consultant ought to have some familiarity with the laws affecting services to children with identified special needs but should also be aware that school districts may vary considerably in their interpretation of these laws. The consultant will appear a lot wiser and less intrusive if he or she queries the teacher on specific school policy and available educational resources rather than assuming what is supposed to exist. Even though the school district's plan to meet federal or state mandates has presumably been approved by the state educational agency, the consultant may wonder on occasion if the child is receiving appropriate services. Some consultant support for the parents to assertively explore available services with the school district may be appropriate as well as the consultant bringing up the subject during a school consultation or at a family–school meeting.

## Teaming and Collaborative Decision Making
The past several years have witnessed a remarkable growth in the concept of school faculty collaboration

and team decision making (Dettmer, Thurston, & Dyck, 1993; Morsink, Thomas, & Correa, 1991). The provisions of the laws regarding special education led to the establishment of multidisciplinary teams within the schools typically composed of teachers, administrators, school psychologists, special-education teachers, and parents. These team meetings focus on issues concerning the handicapped or suspected handicapped child, and the meetings are often in the form of staffings where a diagnosis can be agreed on or where an individual educational plan (IEP) is developed or monitored as required by law.

A number of school districts have organized teacher assistance teams that function within each school as a problem-solving and teacher support group (Chalfant & Pysh, 1989; Cosden & Semmel, 1992). These teams address many problem situations, and teachers can bring concerns about a child to a meeting. The contemporary emphasis on maintaining a wider range of children with special needs in the regular classroom has led to the expansion of such building-level resource teams. The team might include special personnel as needed, such as school psychologists, and serve to support the regular class as the setting in which the child is to be educated. The team is also a vehicle for greater parent involvement, and it would not be unusual for a parent to participate in the team meeting.

There has been an increased emphasis on educational personnel learning how to conduct themselves at these meetings in terms of a collaborative posture, consensus building, and decision making. A new educational industry has arisen in relation to people offering training workshops to educators on these topics. The clinician in a consultant role may end up meeting with such a team because the team has already become involved with the child's case. Although the team members may express some deference to the consultant because of his or her professional status, the team members are likely to be active participants in the session, ready to express their own ideas. The consultant who is unfamiliar with these trends may be surprised at the process and the teachers' skills in group problem solving.

These observations may be unduly optimistic, and the consultant may well enter a situation where such a process does not exist and where a meeting of the teachers, parents, and consultant would be considered a novelty. Outside consultants should also be aware that a common teacher complaint when a child is in a treatment situation has to do with the paucity of communication between the treatment agency and the schools. It may be a very new experience for the teachers to have a clinician actually come to the school to discuss a child. The school may also have a limited history of working with parents in a positive partnership fashion, and so to have a meeting that includes the clinician and the parent may be doubly unsettling for the teachers.

## A RATIONALE FOR COLLABORATIVE CONSULTATION

An intervention plan is at best a hypothesis about what might be helpful in a situation. Although the consultant may assist others to think through the nature of the problem and possible interventions, it will be the sustained involvement of family members and school personnel that will make the plan work. Any plan will probably require some modifications that speak to the importance of "staying power" by the involved individuals. The more that people feel invested in a plan, the more likely they are to exhibit the needed perseverance to make the plan work.

There are research findings indicating that teachers and parents often prefer being involved in collaborative decision making (Babcock & Pryzwansky, 1983; Kutsick, Gutkin, & Witt, 1991; Pryzwansky & White, 1983). A collaborative relationship among the professionals (educators and mental health consultants) and parents can result in a sense of shared ownership of the intervention plan. The consultant assuming a collaborative posture is a way to "join" with teachers and to support the parents in a participatory decision-making role.

The concept of collaboration may be alien to strategic therapists who commonly seek to influence clients through indirect means such as the use of paradoxical interventions. Strategic therapists generally identify with the proposition that as the experts their job is to bring about change in whatever ways will work (Haley, 1976). Consulting from a collaborative posture is considered appropriate if the consultant views problem solving as a shared enterprise among the involved persons (Fine & Gardner, 1994). Everyone has something to contribute, and everyone has something to learn from one another. Educators know the child within the school context and get to see him or her under circumstances very different from those experienced by the parents. But the parents also have a valid view of the child, a view developed within the family context and a view that includes the family's hopes and dreams. The consultant brings a frame of reference and a set of skills to the situation that allow him or her to be a catalyst for healthy change in ways that are respectful of the prerogatives of the family and the school.

Some clinicians, narrowly focused on mental health considerations, have discounted the legitimacy of the school's concerns with academic attainment and reasonably compliant pupil behavior. Clinicians have on occasion established goals of intervention from some theoretical conception of mental health that are antagonistic to family or school values. A collaborative posture to consultation has the consultant encouraging others to listen, share, and build on one another's ideas. The consultant needs to be ready to support the ideas and plans that develop from the interactions between family and school. The greater the comfort level and confidence that the family and teachers develop with one another, the better will they be able to work together successfully in the future.

## A SYSTEMS–ECOLOGICAL PERSPECTIVE ON INTERVENTION

Family systems concepts and interventions can blend in a complementary manner with ecological considerations. Together, these two themes can form a broad ecosystemic perspective that offers expanded and creative opportunities to professionals for effective family–school intervention. Each practitioner is likely to develop his or her own ecosystemic picture through a creative blending of concepts and techniques that derive from systems, ecological, and other complementary theories. The following are key elements that characterize this integration of viewpoints.

**A systems–ecological perspective is a frame-of-mind rather than a definitive methodology.** This perspective appreciates the systemic nature of relationships among people and the interfacing of persons and settings. The intervention process begins as the clinician enters the picture with a systems–ecological perspective. The observations that are made, the questions and kind of questions that get asked, and how the clinician presents himself or herself are all reflective of this perspective.

**The circular nature of causality encourages the examination of patterns and sequences of behavior as people act out their relationships.** This underscores the importance of observing and in other ways learning about the interactions of people with one another and within settings. Circular inquiries (Tomm, 1985) that prompt consideration of patterns and sequences (e.g., "what happens when he does that," or "who seems to be most concerned by the behavior") are more useful than static inquiries (e.g., "why did he do it," or "what do you think is his problem").

**Assessment is a dynamic and interactive process that can be concurrent with intervention.** This is different from a more traditional approach that precedes intervention with assessment. It certainly will be useful to the consultant to have access to any existing data pertaining to a child's academic performance, aptitude, and school social interactions. Questionnaires and rating scales can supplement existing data and also capture parents', teachers', and the child's perceptions of one another and of even the home and classroom environments. Multiple data sources help to round out a more complete and comprehensive picture and can be obtained as needed in the course of intervention.

An emphasis on objectification can lead some professionals away from appreciating the subjectivity of people's experiences and the reciprocal nature of interactions. The meaning that a child's behavior holds for the teacher and parents may say more about what is going on among all of the people in a situation than a purportedly objective analysis of the child's behavior alone.

By taking on a consultative role the clinician can explore the beliefs and behaviors of the involved people in face-to-face contacts. The consultative role becomes the vehicle for bringing together the parents, child, and teacher and facilitating greater family–school collaboration that in turn can lead to effective problem solving. The kinds of interactions that get orchestrated by the consultant during such meetings are a vital aspect of the intervention. During interviews or group meetings at which the child is present, the consultant can observe parent, teacher, and child interactions and can formulate hypotheses about the mesosystem. The consultant can also encourage an examination of the match of settings to child in relation to the appropriateness of the curricular organization, academic and behavioral expectations, and home–school attitudes and beliefs.

The consultant may need to assume an active and multifaceted role as he or she engages family members, educational personnel, the child, and others, often in a group context. A challenge for the consultant is to avoid being triangulated in relation to existing conflicts and being seen as adversarial by either the family or the school. Some awarenesses, concepts, and techniques that are associated with the family therapy literature may prove useful. Examples include joining, reframing, realigning alliances, modifying too rigid or blurred boundaries within or across systems, circular questioning, and using the power hierarchy within and across systems.

The consultant should be aware of the broader exosystem and macrosystem impact on the "problem" rather than thinking exclusively in a microsystemic or mesosystemic context. Cultural values, educational philosophy, and legal or economic considerations may all impinge to some extent on the current difficulties and on efforts to achieve a reasonable resolution. Sensitivity to these areas can influence the intervention plan and minimize the possibility of unforeseen negative consequences on the intervention.

The locus of intervention will vary with the situation and may include multiple objectives and intervention techniques. Swap (1984) described how there could be simultaneous interventions "directed at parents, teachers, and/or significant members of the child's community. Goals of these efforts might be to add to parents' or teachers' skills, or help them change their priorities or expectations, revise their perceptions, or acquire new resources" (pp. 109–110). The goals can include changes in individuals as a precursor to changes in a setting or a direct focus on changes in the settings. Also, the goals of an ecologically oriented intervention "are not reached through a new set of techniques or treatments but through a framework of using existing techniques in an ecological manner" (Conoley & Haynes, 1992, p. 180).

## CONCLUSION

The overall goals of a systems–ecological intervention are to support healthy family–school interaction, resolve the current concerns or issues, and serve the welfare of the child. Constructive solutions require the cooperation of all the involved people and should lead to a strengthened sense of collaboration between home and school. Furthermore, the systems–ecological nature of the consultative process assures an ecological validity to interventions. Changes or modifications occur as a result of the interplay of people and settings and are acceptable to all parties and most important, are consistent with the best interests of the child.

## References

Aponte, H. J. (1976). The family–school interview: An eco-structural approach. *Family Process, 15,* 303–311.

Apter, S. J. (1982). *Troubled children: Troubled systems.* Elmsford, NY: Pergamon.

Babcock, N. L., & Pryzwansky, W. B. (1983). Models of consultation: Preferences of educational professionals at five stages of service. *Journal of School Psychology, 21,* 359–366.

Bronfenbrenner, U. (1979). *The ecology of human development: Experiments by nature and design.* Cambridge, MA: Harvard University Press.

Bronfenbrenner, U. (1986). Ecology of the family as a context for human development: Research perspectives. *Developmental Psychology, 22,* 723–742.

Chalfant, J. C., & Pysh, M. V. (1989). Teacher assistance teams: Five descriptive studies on 96 teams. *Remedial and Special Education, 10,* 49–58.

Christenson, S. L., Rounds, T., & Gorney, D. (1992). Family factors and student achievement: An avenue to increase students' success. *School Psychology Quarterly, 7,* 178–206.

Christenson, S. L., & Cleary, M. (1990). Consultation and the parent-education partnership: A perspective. *Journal of Educational and Psychological Consultation, 1,* 219–241.

Conoley, J. C., & Haynes, G. (1992). An ecological approach to intervention. In R. C. D'Amato & B. A. Rothlisberg (Eds.), *Psychological perspectives on intervention* (pp. 176–189). New York: Longman.

Cosden, M. A., & Semmel, M. I. (1992). Teacher assistance teams: A conceptual and empirical review. *Special Services in the Schools, 6,* 5–25.

Dettmer, P., Thurston, L. P., & Dyck, N. (1993). *Consultation, collaboration, and teamwork.* Needham Heights, MA: Allyn & Bacon.

Eno, M. M. (1985). Children with school problems: A family therapy perspective. In R. L. Ziffen (Ed.), *Adjunctive techniques in family therapy* (pp. 151–180). New York: Grune & Stratton.

Epstein, J. L. (1991). Effects on student achievement of teachers' practices of parental involvement. In S. B. Silvern (Ed.), *Advances in reading/language research: Vol. 5. Literacy through family, community and school interaction* (pp. 261–276). Greenwich, CT: JAI Press.

Fine, M. J. (1992). A systems-ecological perspective on home-school intervention. In M. J. Fine & C. Carlson (Eds.), *The handbook of family-school intervention: A systems perspective* (pp. 1–17). Needham Heights, MA: Allyn and Bacon.

Fine, M. J., & Gardner, A. (1994). Collaborative consultation with families of children with special needs: Why bother? *Journal of Educational and Psychological Consultation, 5,* 283–308.

Fine, M. J., & Holt, P. (1983). Intervening with school problems: A family systems perspective. *Psychology in the Schools, 20,* 59–66.

Fish, M. C., & Jain, S. (1985). A systems approach in working with families of learning disabled children: Implications for the school. *Journal of Learning Disabilities, 18,* 592–595.

Fish, M. C., & Jain, S. (1988). Using systems theory for assessment and intervention: A structural model for school psychologists. *Professional School Psychology, 3,* 291–300.

Fisher, L. (1986). Systems-based consultation with schools. In L. Wynne, S. H. McDaniel, & T. T. Weber (Eds.), *Systems consultation: A new perspective for family therapy* (pp. 342–356). New York: Guilford.

Graden, J. L. & Christenson, S. L. (1987). Children and troubled families. In A. Thomas & J. Grimes (Eds.), *Children's needs: Psychological perspectives* (pp. 651–658). Washington, DC: The National Association of School Psychologists.

Green, B. (1985). Systems intervention in the schools. In M. P. Mirkin & S. L. Koman (Eds.), *Handbook of adolescents and family therapy* (pp. 193–206). New York: Gardner.

Grinker, R. R. (1975). The relevance of general systems theory to psychiatry. In D. A. Hamburg & H. K. Brody (Eds.), *American handbook of psychiatry* (2nd ed., Vol. 6, pp. 251–272). New York: Basic Books.

Guerin, P., & Katz, A. (1984). The theory in therapy of families with school related problems: Triangles and a hypothesis testing model. In B. F. Okun (Ed.), *Family therapy with school related problems* (pp. 28–45). Rockville, MD: Aspen.

Guttman, H. A. (1991). Systems theory: Cybernetics and epistemology. In A. S. Gurman & D. P. Kniskern (Eds.), *Handbook of family therapy* (Vol. 2, pp. 41–62). New York: Brunner/Mazel.

Haley, J. (1976). *Problem solving therapy.* San Francisco: Jossey-Bass.

Haynes, N. M., Comer, J. P., & Hamilton-Lee, M. (1989). School climate enhancement through parental involvement. *Journal of School Psychology, 27,* 87–90.

Hobbs, N. (1966). Helping disturbed children: Psychological and educational strategies. *American Psychologist, 21,* 1105–1115.

Hobbs, N. (1975). *The futures of children.* San Francisco: Jossey-Bass.

Hobbs, N. (1978). Families, schools, and communities: An ecosystem for children. *Teachers College Record, 79,* 756–766.

Hobbs, N. (1982). *The troubled and troubling child.* San Francisco: Jossey-Bass.

Kutsick, K. A., Gutkin, T. B., & Witt, J. C. (1991). The impact of treatment development process, intervention type, and problem severity on treatment acceptability as judged by teachers. *Psychology in the Schools, 28,* 325–331.

Lusterman, D. D. (1985). An ecosystemic approach to family-school problems. *The American Journal of Family Therapy, 13,* 22–30.

Madanes, C. (1991). Strategic family therapy. In A. S. Gurman & D. P. Kniskern (Eds.), *Handbook of family therapy,* (Vol. 2, pp. 396–416). New York: Brunner/Mazel.

Mannino, F. V., & Shore, M. F. (1984). An ecological perspective on family intervention. In W. A. O'Conner & B. Lubin (Eds.), *Ecological approaches to clinical and community psychology* (pp. 75–93). New York: Wiley.

Miller, L. J., Strain, P. S., Boyd, K., Hunsicker, S., McKinley, J., & Wu, A. (1992). Parental attitudes toward integration. *Topics in Early Childhood Special Education, 12*, 230–246.

Minuchin, S., & Fishman, H. C. (1981). *Family therapy techniques.* Cambridge, MA: Harvard University Press.

Morsink, C. V., Thomas, C. C., & Correa, V. I. (1991). *Interactive teaming: Consultation and collaboration in special programs.* Columbus, OH: Merrill.

Okum, B. F. (1984). *Family therapy with school related problems.* Rockville, MD: Aspen.

Pryzwansky, W. B., & White, G. W. (1983). The influence of consultee characteristics on preference for consultation approaches. *Professional Psychology: Research and Practice, 14*, 457–461.

Rhodes, W. C. (1970). *The emotionally disturbed child.* New York: Houghton Mifflin.

Rhodes, W. C., & Paul, J. L. (1978). *Emotionally disturbed and deviant children.* Englewood Cliffs, NJ: Prentice Hall.

Roberts, C., & Zubrick, S. (1993). Factors influencing the status of children with mild academic disabilities in the regular classroom. *Exceptional Children, 59*, 192–202.

Rotheram, M. J. (1989). The family and the school. In L. Combrinck-Graham (Ed.), *Children in family contexts: Perspectives on treatment* (pp. 347–368). New York: Guilford Press.

Semmel, M. I., Abernathy, T. V., Butera, G., & Lesar, S. (1991). Teacher perceptions of the regular education initiative. *Exceptional Children, 58*, 9–24.

Simon, F. B., Stierlin, H., & Wynne, L. C. (Eds.). (1985). *The language of family therapy: A systemic vocabulary and sourcebook.* New York: Family Process Books.

Swap, S. (1984). Ecological approaches to working with families of disturbing children. In W. A. O'Conner & B. Lubin (Eds.), *Ecological approaches to clinical and community psychology* (pp. 107–144). New York: Wiley.

Tomm, K. (1985). Circular interviewing: A multifaceted clinical tool. In D. Campbell & R. Draper (Eds.), *Applications of systemic family therapy: The Milan approach* (pp. 33–45). New York: Grune & Stratton.

Tucker, B. Z., & Dyson, E. (1976). The family and the school: Utilizing human resources to promote learning. *Family Process, 15*, 125–141.

Umbarger, C. C. (1983). *Structural family therapy.* New York: Grune & Stratton.

von Bertalanffy, L. (1968). *General systems theory: Foundations, development, applications.* New York: Braziller.

Will, M. (1986). *Educating students with learning problems: A shared responsibility.* Washington, DC: Office of Special Education and Rehabilitative Services, U.S. Department of Education.

Wynne, L. C., McDaniel, S. H., & Weber, T. T. (1986). *Systems consultation: A new perspective for family therapy.* New York: Guilford Press.

# PART VIII

# COERCION AND SUBSTANCE ABUSE

# Introduction

Perhaps the most striking element of problems involving coercion and substance abuse in families is their power to consume the family's energies. A family trapped in a cycle of coercion or substance abuse soon develops an identity that comes to be defined by the problem itself. It is as though the family had no past or future, only a present filled with struggle, misery, and despair. Therefore, a key element in working with families with these problems is to understand how the power of coercion and substance abuse often overrides other system variables and why these issues must be dealt with immediately in systems intervention.

In "Domestic Violence and Sexual Abuse: Multiple Systems Perspectives" (chap. 28), Robert Geffner, Mary Jo Barrett, and B. B. Robbie Rossman describe the controversies surrounding family therapy when violence occurs in the home. They stress the importance of ensuring that the preconditions providing for the safety of all family members are met before conjoint treatment is attempted. Using a multiple systems perspective, they describe generic issues in systems therapy for those involved in domestic violence and sexual abuse; stages of treatment in families experiencing these problems; and treatment models and techniques for individual adults, couples, children, and families.

As in the area of family violence, coercion by cults requires the systems therapist to have special knowledge and skills. In "Cults: Implications for Family Therapists" (chap. 29), Margaret Thaler Singer cautions therapists against assuming dysfunction in families with a cult member simply because the individual has been recruited into a cult. Stressing the need for therapists to be well informed about cult dynamics and to establish networks with cult experts before working with a family, she sees the role of the therapist as a consultant, educator, and network coordinator rather than a traditional family therapist. As families struggle to decide whether to try to extricate a family member from a cult, take action to do so, or attempt to reincorporate the cult member back into the family and community, she describes resources, information, and actions for the therapist.

In "Family Treatment of Alcohol and Drug Abuse" (chap. 30), M. Duncan Stanton and Anthony W. Heath review family patterns in addiction and provide an overview of the family therapy process with alcohol and other drug abusers and their families. They explain principles of treatment and the various systems involved at each of six phases of this process. The authors stress the need for the outpatient family therapist to work together with extended families, self-help programs, medical personnel, and significant others in the system in an inclusive, ecological process.

# CHAPTER 28

# DOMESTIC VIOLENCE AND SEXUAL ABUSE: MULTIPLE SYSTEMS PERSPECTIVES

*Robert Geffner, Mary Jo Barrett, and B. B. Robbie Rossman*

Domestic violence and sexual abuse are among the most distressing and controversial problems facing the professional therapeutic community and the community at large. Professionals are often appropriately cautious about doing family therapy with violent or abusive families. If proposing to do family therapy with such families means to require all family members to meet together, regardless of issues of revictimization and safety, then such a proposition should create serious concern for any clinician. At times, it is appropriate to include family members in conjoint therapy; at other times, this practice is counterproductive. If, however, by family therapy one means "that people are products of their social context, and that any attempts to understand them must include an appreciation of their families" (Nichols, 1984, p. 80), then most clinicians working with violent families probably would agree that a family approach is useful. Family therapy can be viewed as varying along a continuum from individual treatment, in which family influences (the implicit or internalized family) are considered, to conjoint family therapy, in which all family members are present (the explicit family). In this chapter, we will discuss various family techniques and issues that are helpful in working with violent and abusive families, the situations in which these may be used appropriately, and some of the controversies surrounding these views.

## FAMILY THERAPY: A CONTROVERSIAL OPTION

Although there continues to be controversy about the dangers of using various techniques in the treatment of violent families (e.g., symptom exaggeration or paradoxical intervention), two major issues emerge as one examines different approaches to conjoint family therapy. The first is an allegiance to the generally accepted principle of circular (systemic) causality, as opposed to linear (unilateral) causality of family violence or abuse (Dell, 1986; Imber Black, 1986). Although the traditional family systems approach accepts the assumption of circular causality, embedded in this assumption—as its critics point out—is the notion that victims share responsibility for their abuse. Circular causality views abuse and violence as signs of a boundary disturbance in the family system whereby victims and perpetrators are linked in a circular and reciprocal process (Lane & Russell, 1989; Larson & Maddock, 1986).

Although it may be argued that conjoint therapy does pose certain dangers, Trepper (1986) contends that systems therapists do view the abusing parent as responsible and nevertheless believe that conjoint therapy will have more impact than individual or other approaches because family structure often plays an important role in contributing to and maintaining the abuse. In sexual abuse, for example, different steps in treatment may be advocated—with individual therapy for mother, child, and perpetrator (if other than the mother) recommended as the first step, followed by counseling with the abusing parent, then marital counseling, and finally, conjoint family therapy if the abusing parent is willing to take responsibility for the abuse of the child (Giaretto, 1982; Porter, Blick, & Sgroi, 1982). Several adjunctive treatment modes, such as groups and support services for the spouse of the abuser, are also seen as useful (Furniss, 1983; Sgroi, 1982). Basically, however, staunch adherents of the circular causality model believe that the first treatment of choice is conjoint family therapy.

As a corollary to the controversy over circular versus linear causality, the second major issue is that of therapist neutrality versus advocacy for victims of domestic violence or sexual abuse (Henderson, 1990). Proponents of "advocacy" generally avoid conjoint family therapy; the family is not seen together because of the likelihood that such therapy may buttress or reinstate male dominance in the family and implicitly convey the message that the victims are somewhat to blame for their abuse. An advocacy approach includes the use of individual or supportive counseling for the spouse and child, groups involving other mothers or battered women, groups for child victims, and specialized individual counseling for the perpetrator.

Alternatively, therapist neutrality is a hallmark of the reconstructive approach. In this approach, the emphasis is more on the "cause" rather than "effect" of the abuse. Abuse is viewed as caused by both personal (linear) as well as family (circular) factors.

Our position in treating batterers, battered women, child sexual abuse victims, incest offenders, nonoffending parents, and child observers of abuses in the family represents a blend of the advocacy approach and the reconstructive approach. The advocacy approach is similar to many individual therapy approaches. It views the perpetrator as responsible for the abuse, assumes linear causality, and thus advocates "family-without-abuser" treatment (e.g., Zefran et al., 1982). The reconstructive approach includes conjoint family therapy when various prerequisites have been met, especially when there is good reason to believe that members of the family honestly want to work together in a nonabusive, noncoercive way. Furthermore, the victim should not take responsibility for the violence or abuse, and the therapist should not remain neutral on violence or abuse issues, just as therapists do not remain neutral on other issues of endangerment such as suicide, homicide, or child abuse. The safety of the victim is of paramount importance.

## PRECONDITIONS FOR CONJOINT FAMILY THERAPY

In order to ensure the psychological and physical safety of the children, battered women, and other victims in abusive families, many recommendations regarding preconditions to conjoint family therapy are summarized in Table 1 (e.g., Geffner, 1989b; Geffner & Pagelow, 1990b). Hodges (1991) and others warn that conjoint family therapy with divorcing families should be avoided "when custody is in question; when one parent is unavailable because of abandonment, prison, or heavy substance abuse; and when the danger of family violence exists" (Hodges, 1991, p. 328).

The Abusive Men Exploring New Directions (AMEND) policy (1990) regarding couples counseling with violent families recommends that it not occur until there have been no reports of violence for over 5 months, the perpetrator has accepted respon-

### TABLE 1

**Some Preconditions for Conjoint Family Therapy**

| Precondition | Reference |
| --- | --- |
| The victim and perpetrator desire this type of treatment. | Geffner, 1989b; AMEND, 1990 |
| The victim has a safety plan and understands the potential dangers. | Geffner & Pagelow, 1990b |
| An adult must accept responsibility if child abuse has occurred. | Wolfe, Wolfe, & Best, 1988; Trepper & Barrett, 1989 |
| There are no custody issues if the parents are divorcing. | Hodges, 1991 |
| Lethality evaluation suggests low probability of danger. | AMEND, 1990; Geffner et al., 1989 |
| The perpetrator does not harbor obsessional ideas toward the victim. | AMEND, 1990; Geffner et al., 1989 |
| Therapists are trained in both family therapy and domestic violence. | Geffner & Pagelow, 1990b |
| The patients are not currently abusing drugs or alcohol. | Geffner et al., 1989 |
| If there has been substance abuse, then treatment for this is required. | AMEND, 1990; Geffner et al., 1989 |
| Neither partner exhibits psychotic behavior. | AMEND, 1990; Geffner et al., 1989 |

sibility for his violent acts, and the clients have been able to cooperate and actively participate in treatment groups. This policy requires successful individual treatment prior to beginning family therapy, even if the clients continue to live together. Geffner, Mantooth, Franks, and Rao (1989) do not require a cessation of violence for 5 months, a lack of prior substance abuse problems, or completion of prior individual or group therapy as part of their criteria for conjoint treatment. Consistent with parts of the AMEND policy, though, they agree with most clinicians that treatment that brings abusers together with victims is not useful when the perpetrator has significant personality disorders such as an entrenched sociopathy, which is often the case when abusers repeatedly maltreat or are violent outside as well as inside the family (Geffner et al., 1989).

A formal assessment of risk and potential lethality should occur before any family approaches are used. Barnett, Pittman, Ragan, and Salus (1980) noted circumstances that heighten the risk of a battered woman's being abused again: when violence continues to recur or involves weapons, when one of the partners has been hospitalized due to injury during a violent episode, when children have been abused in the past or are exposed to danger during episodes of parental violence, or when separation is threatened or occurs. Other factors may also serve as warnings of lethality for individual families, and the clinician needs to develop an understanding of what they might be for each case.

Unfortunately, the prediction of future violent or abusive behavior is imprecise at best. Clinicians working with violent and abusive families need to make ongoing safety and lethality checks to prevent revictimization of family members. These checks involve gathering information about violence and abuse from all family members independently (e.g., Geffner et al., 1989) as well as from collateral sources (e.g., lawyers' descriptions of marital and family interactions; teacher reports about the child's behavior and communications; contact with neighbors, friends, extended family, or with other clinicians, agencies, and professionals who have worked with the family). Due to confidentiality requirements, releases of information must be obtained from all sources. The granting

of these releases may serve as one precondition for conjoint treatment.

The fact that endangered family members are residing in a shelter or crisis placement should not automatically be taken as either a guarantee of safety or as an exclusion from family treatment. In addition, hoped-for protections within the legal system, such as restraining orders, have had only variable success in protecting victims. The role of the clinician in protecting potential victims is an ethical and legal mandate for all professionals, as documented in *Tarasoff v. the Regents of the University of California* (1976).

It is important to recognize the numerous signs and symptoms of abuse that victims and offenders exhibit. These include low self-esteem, depression, feelings of helplessness or powerlessness, cognitive distortions, lack of effective or appropriate communication, low frustration tolerance, inability to manage stress effectively, excessive anger and hostility, lack of assertiveness, and inability to express feelings, let alone recognize them. Given the range of symptoms, all approaches should include safety and control plans, relapse prevention techniques, and empathy training for long-term effectiveness. Thus, for a family approach to be successful with violent or abusive families, it is helpful to have a blend of techniques that focus on both individual and family dynamics. Therapists need clinical training in family therapy and family violence; having expertise in only one of these areas is not sufficient if a family approach is to be used.

## GENERAL OR GENERIC ISSUES IN THE TREATMENT OF ABUSE: THE MULTIPLE SYSTEMS PERSPECTIVE

Violence and abuse in the family revolve around themes of power, control, and connection. The Multiple Systems Perspective (MSP), developed by Trepper and Barrett (1986, 1989), is an attempt to integrate the more salient features of perpetrator–victim models, family systems models, feminist theory, and ecosystemic approaches (Barrett, Trepper, & Stone Fish, 1990). If MSP is a responsible and viable option, it will invariably include all family members (if they agree to it and are able to participate), but it will also involve working intensively with individual family members, the parents' families of origin, and outside systems such as friends, attorneys, social service workers, schools, and shelters. The underlying premise is that treatment must intervene at each level of this complex of systems.

MSP treatment programs are divided into three stages and follow a general treatment protocol. This protocol allows family members, therapists, court personnel, caseworkers, and others to have a clear understanding of the treatment process. Therapists using MSP treatment also believe that change happens in stages, not as a "leap into health," but more as a methodical repetition so that change occurs in "bits and spurts."

The stages of this treatment are as follows:

1. Creating a context for change.
2. Challenging patterns and expanding realities.
3. Consolidation.

## Stage 1: Creating a Context for Change

The main purpose of the first stage is to establish a therapeutic context in which people affected by an abusive situation feel safe and more in control of their lives. This is especially important because they now feel that they have little control of their own destiny. The first stage of treatment is designed to be positive, to create the expectation that change can happen, and to respect the difficulty of change. Families in which there has been abuse perpetrated either by a family member or an entrusted other (e.g., clergy, family friend, babysitter, or teacher) enter treatment already feeling devastated. The therapeutic environment does not have to be punitive in order to produce change. The therapist communicates to each family member that the abuse and violence is abhorrent and unacceptable, but also that the therapist realizes that this is but one aspect of the family's experience and that, as a therapist, he or she can help them find strengths in other, more positive aspects of their lives.

In Stage 1, the therapist attempts to create a safe environment whereby both client and therapist experience some degree of power and control in the therapeutic process, which then enables them to estab-

lish a connection with each other. Power differentials are, unfortunately, a given between men and women, races, cultures, religions, and generations. Consequently, when humans feel powerless in their different environments, they fight (often literally) to regain control. At this stage of therapy, the therapist begins to create an environment in which family members experience a new relation to power—one of control and connection. There are three goals during the first stage of treatment.

The first goal is for the therapist to communicate clearly, from the beginning of treatment, that he or she may share information with other members of the family in order to provide safety to others and to the client. The therapist also urges clients to share secrets, because secrecy and lack of communication help perpetuate the problem of abuse. The therapist encourages offenders to report themselves if they engage in any further abuses. Self-reporting is potentially helpful to both abusers and victims because abusers can then feel in charge of their own recovery. The therapist actively creates the ethos that offenders must take responsibility for and accept the consequences of their behavior. If they do not self-report, then the therapist will do so—to safeguard the victims—and take steps that will entail social and legal consequences for the abuser.

The second goal is to assess the family (see also chap. 9 in this volume). To accomplish this, the therapist uses the vulnerability model (Trepper & Barrett, 1986, 1989). The concept of the general vulnerability model (Gottschalk, 1983; Zubin & Spring, 1977) suggests that assessment should not attempt to isolate one underlying cause of a problem. Rather, it should identify how the family system is vulnerable and how the presence or absence of many factors has contributed to the problem. Through a series of individual, family, and dyadic sessions—and sometimes psychometric measures—the therapist attempts to understand the interactional and intrapsychic nature of the individuals and the families. Based on this schema, both the family and therapist cocreate an understanding of how abuse happened in this particular family. The treatment plan and therapy goals are based directly on the resulting assessment.

The third goal is to understand the function of denial and help the family and external systems manage the inevitable denial that exists within each family member (Barrett, Sykes, & Byrnes, 1986; Barrett & Trepper, 1992a, 1992b). The goal is to help solve the problem of abuse or violence and all of its resulting symptoms, not to blame or to pathologize.

Examining the family's structure gives therapists an understanding about the family's interactions in the following areas: roles, rules, hierarchy, boundaries, cohesion, and adaptability (Minuchin, 1974; Olson, Russell, & Sprenkle, 1983). It is important to understand how power, control, and connection are experienced and acted out in each individual family. This information will help therapists understand the context that prevented the offender from exercising appropriate impulse control and from feeling empathetic and protective toward others.

Family communication needs to be evaluated for both strengths and weaknesses. Usually, affected families have very poor conflict resolution skills, a high degree of secrecy, are unable to listen or discuss feelings empathically, and repeatedly give confusing messages to one another.

Denial is often the individual's and family's natural protection from the painful realities of abuse and its disclosure. All members deny or minimize in order to maintain some sense of order and normalcy in their lives. If they acknowledged the facts and impact of the abuse, they would have a difficult time functioning, going to work, maintaining relationships, going to school, and so on. Also, there are severe negative consequences to acknowledging and admitting the abuse, including jail, foster home, divorce, economic loss, additional or more severe violence or abuse, outsiders' disbelief of the victim, anger, and betrayal. Denial is "safer" and more attractive than many of these options.

The offender must take responsibility for the abuse, and the clinician must always keep this goal in mind. However, the clinician should accept and expect denial early in treatment. The overall task of treatment is to help the family members find ways other than denial to protect themselves, ways that do not endanger their own or others' safety.

There are three strategies that can be helpful when dealing with denial:

1. **Normalization.** The therapist takes a supportive stand, that is, understands and accepts why the family needs to say that it did not happen, or that they cannot remember the details, or that it was not as bad as it sounds. At the same time, however, the therapist asserts his or her belief that abuse did occur and that the victim is credible. Then the therapist begins to help the clients understand that letting go of these protective stances will allow them and other family members to attain a more satisfactory, stable family life;

2. **Negative consequences of change** (Fisch, Weakland, & Segal, 1982). The therapist begins to explore with clients the positive emotional and psychological consequences of acknowledging their problems. Then the negative consequences (the fears, the realities, the loss) that may accompany positive growth and change are explored in depth. Equal time is spent exploring both sides of the ambivalence (Jenkins, 1990).

3. **Use of pretend techniques** (Madanes, 1981). We ask the client to pretend that he or she denied the violence, then owned up to its reality.

## Stage 2: Challenging Patterns and Expanding Realities

In Stage 2 of treatment, the therapist takes the dysfunctional behavioral patterns, belief systems, and interactional sequences, and designs interventions to interrupt them. Together, the family and therapists develop alternatives to those feelings and behaviors. The treatment is far more active in Stage 2 than in Stage 1, during which the therapist tries to avoid too many direct interpretations or challenging interventions. The focus of Stage 2 is to help individuals discover alternatives by broadening the interpretations. Usually, a more direct approach can be tolerated if the proper foundation has been created.

A variety of treatment modalities are used in Stage 2, and it is possible for different members of the family to be at different stages of treatment concurrently. Because the main purpose of family sessions in Stage 2 is to disrupt and change dysfunctional interactions and sequences, the therapist will also assess new behaviors and help the family manage problems that can be expected as a result of these changes.

A particularly important sequence that a clinician should identify and attempt to change with the clients is the "Victim-Survivor–Offender Cycle." The therapist discovers and highlights the behaviors and situations that trigger feelings of powerlessness, being out of control, and feeling disconnected (Barrett, 1992), as well as the experiences of "victimization." Then ways in which clients try to regain control or connection are explored. After exploring this internal sequence, the therapist examines how it is acted out by the family members. How does the way in which they protect themselves or regain control trigger a feeling of helplessness or powerlessness in others? For example, to an offending husband, one might say, "You said that when you feel powerless, you drink to gain strength, to be assertive, or to forget what has happened. How does your drinking affect your spouse? Do you become threatening?" Then this is discussed with the spouse along with ways she must take care of herself in order to regain control when feeling vulnerable: "How does his drinking make you feel vulnerable? How do the children get involved, and how does this affect other members of the family?" As patterns become clear, the clients will have a better understanding of why and how the escalation continues. Offenders need to learn that their patterns of abuse are attempts to take care of their own needs without regard for their impact on the family. The family's task then becomes to find alternative means for self-care that are not offending or threatening to one another.

## Stage 3: Consolidation

The therapist can recognize when the family has entered the final Consolidation stage, because meetings begin to seem more like reporting sessions than therapy sessions. The family members talk about issues and crises in terms of how they solved them rather than relying on a therapist's intervention. The family is more aware of what changes need to be made and has much clearer ideas of how to bring about those changes. Fine-tuning and relapse prevention often occur during this final stage, and the therapist is generally much more facilitative than directive.

This final stage "seals" changes that have taken place, explores potential problem areas in the future, and focuses on how the family will cope with and resolve those future situations. Interventions are designed for supporting the individual's and family's in-

dependence from therapy. The frequency of the sessions decreases, and, in the termination phase, clients may attend only monthly follow-up sessions. The valedictory message is that the clients may continue to have their struggles but that they also possess many new skills to resolve these problems. They can now think of therapy as a helpful resource rather than as a treatment they must undergo when they are in trouble emotionally or with the law.

## TREATMENT OF SPOUSE OR PARTNER ABUSE

Having discussed general issues in the assessment and treatment of abuse, we move now to a brief overview of specific programs and a discussion of various therapeutic configurations for the treatment of spouse abuse and child sexual abuse. Regarding spouse abuse, most of the programs initially developed for the treatment of family battering focused on anger control groups for men (Adams & McCormick, 1982; Saunders, 1982; Sonkin & Durphy, 1982). A few family approaches to reducing spouse or partner abuse were then developed in the mid-1980s (Deschner, 1984; Geffner, Franks, Patrick, & Mantooth, 1986; Geller & Wasserstrom, 1984; Neidig & Friedman, 1984). Even though some of these programs included couples, the focus was on anger control and in the context of a psychoeducational format (e.g., Deschner, 1984; Neidig & Friedman, 1984). Because research indicated that anger control was not sufficient to treat this complex problem (Gondolf & Russell, 1986), other programs developed more comprehensive approaches to work with the family (e.g., Cook & Frantz-Cook, 1984; Mantooth, Geffner, Franks, & Patrick, 1987).

There has been steady criticism concerning the use of conjoint therapy for the treatment of wife battering (e.g., Bograd, 1984; Stordeur & Stille, 1989), but research has not indicated that one particular approach works better than others for treatment of batterers (Geffner & Rosenbaum, 1990). Research is currently being conducted to compare techniques, but the results are not yet available. Therefore, the debate continues, often with strong emotional and "political" overtones. Jacobson (1993) observed that 20% of the husbands in a study of 60 violent couples who were monitored for physiological signs of arousal during conflict were devoid of any signs of anger or arousal. He points out that such a finding seriously challenges "anger management" training with these men and points instead to a deeper level of pathology for such batterers. Jacobson's results suggest, however, that family or conjoint approaches may be helpful with many other batterers because 80% of the violent men studied did not meet his criteria for the deeper pathology.

Clinicians working with couples report success equivalent to or better than those focusing only on men (e.g., Geffner, Kreager-Cook, Sharne, Crawford, & Persinger, 1987). The reported benefits of successful treatment for the family and the battered woman have much greater long-term potential because of the changes that occur in the relationship as well as in the reduction of violence (Geffner, 1989b; Geller, 1992). In addition, children who have observed the parental abuse are exposed to an appropriate modeling of communication and expression of feelings. Preconditions for this therapy are that the battered woman wants to be in such a program, wants to remain in the relationship, and is not being intimidated into making this choice. In addition, the level of prior violence is assessed, lethality is continually monitored and assessed, and the safety of the family is of prime importance. In some cases, treatment may occur while the woman and her children are housed in a shelter, with the therapy occurring elsewhere.

## Conjoint Therapy

We will now describe a conjoint therapy program for couples as an example of a family approach that has been successful (Mantooth et al., 1987). This treatment program relies heavily on techniques to improve communication, as well as on the management of violent and intimidating behavior (Geffner, 1993; Geffner, Mantooth, Patrick, & Franks, in press). It can be conducted with individual couples or with groups of couples, and the length of treatment is 26 weeks, plus follow-up sessions. The basic assumptions of this family approach are:

- Each person is responsible for his or her own behavior.

- Batterers have the ability to stop the abusiveness.
- Violence and intimidation are not acceptable behaviors.
- The clients have the resources to change their behavior and the relationship.
- The therapist can facilitate and motivate the clients in this process.

Blame is avoided, as is an emphasis on analyzing why the abuse occurred. It is assumed that the violence and intimidation must end and that both partners must also learn new skills to enhance their communication, self-esteem, assertiveness, and the relationship in general. It is made clear that the battered woman is not the cause of her partner's abusive behavior, regardless of any rationalizations. However, it is also clear that the relationship has become dysfunctional and that, for long-term success, both mates need help. The specific treatment is divided into four basic stages: foundations/brief interventions; communication/expression of feelings; self-management/assertiveness; and intimacy issues/relapse prevention.

This approach begins with plans for safety and control, contracts for nonviolence, basic anger management, behavioral controls, effective stress and anxiety management, and dealing with the social roots of aggression and alcoholism. The initial interventions are quite directive, behavioral, and psychoeducational. The therapists emphasize taking control of one's behavior and accepting responsibility for one's actions while diffusing emotional reactivity. Weekly monitoring of any aggressive or intimidating behavior is carried out, and specific safety plans are developed and completed for each client. It is very important in these initial sessions to balance any power issues and defuse attempts at intimidation. Normally, male and female cotherapists conduct the treatment. After behavioral control techniques have been learned through regular homework assignments, communication techniques then become the focus of therapy (Bach & Wyden, 1970; McKay, Davis, & Fanning, 1983; Satir, 1967).

The advantage of conjoint therapy is the opportunity for role playing between couples or between client and therapist in the presence of the partner. Role modeling is an important and beneficial component of this family approach because the couple can observe the therapist's interactions and assertiveness: Clients learn how to deal with feelings and begin to express them to each other without violence or intimidation. As anger and power issues begin to surface during these sessions, they can be discussed as well as understood, controlled, reframed, and altered in this new context.

Techniques to help the clients improve their own feelings of worthiness are then explored. Distorted beliefs and negative self-talk are examined so that they can begin to reframe their beliefs, focus on controlling anger better, and improve assertiveness skills. The support of others in couples groups helps improve their social skills, provides confrontation of distorted viewpoints (especially jealousy issues), and allows the couple to practice with each other while obtaining feedback from others and the therapists. Problem solving, decision making, and negotiation strategies are then included in the therapy. The couple must also deal with violent incidents in their past in order to better understand current power issues, to help the woman deal with the past intimidation and fear, and to help the man empathize with the pain he has caused. The couple is encouraged to express feelings in order to increase intimacy. They are pressed to deal directly with power issues, and role play is used to facilitate relapse prevention. This program not only encourages and produces individual changes in behavior but also helps change the dysfunctional system in which both partners had become trapped. It is therefore beneficial also to children growing up in these families.

## Mediation Issues

Before we change our focus to children who observe parental violence, it is important to mention another approach that has received increased attention by therapists, courts, and the media: family mediation. Mediation techniques (i.e., dispute resolution) have been recommended in recent years to help resolve marital conflicts and family disputes and for divorce and custody cases (e.g., Folberg & Milne, 1988; see also chap. 16 in this volume). Some states require mediation in divorce or custody cases (e.g., California). This technique has come under increasing attack, though, when violence and intimidation have

been occurring in the family. Some have argued, as have critics of conjoint therapy, that mediation should never be allowed when domestic violence has occurred. Others have argued that domestic violence is not a relevant issue for mediation. As noted earlier, our position is at neither extreme.

Mediation can be accomplished successfully under specific conditions for couples when battering has occurred (see Geffner, 1992; Geffner & Pagelow, 1990a). However, it is important for the mediator to be trained in both domestic violence issues and mediation so that he or she can ensure that the power is balanced and that the woman desires the mediation; battered women should never be required to participate in mediation. If the victim does choose mediation, the mediator can often model appropriate techniques in assertiveness, handle attempts at intimidation, and solve problems in ways that can be quite helpful to her. Thus family mediation not only empowers her but can enable her to learn new skills to deal with her husband or former husband in the future.

In the following sections, we will begin with a review of literature that deals with the effects of violence on children. We then explore various treatment issues and programs for children who have observed family violence. Next, we assess current views about broad treatment approaches to families in which children are the victims. Finally, we discuss the merits and applications of our conjoint therapy techniques for treating children.

## CHILDREN'S REACTIONS TO PARENTAL CONFLICT, ABUSE, AND VIOLENCE

Children react to traumatic and violent experiences in ways that reflect their developmentally different cognitive and emotional capabilities. Children as young as 12 to 28 months react to adult anger with concern and play disruptions (Cummings, Zahn-Waxler, & Radke-Yarro, 1981), avoidant reactions (Drell, Siegel, & Gaensbauer, in press), night terrors (Herzog, 1980), and regressive behaviors (Wallerstein & Kelly, 1975). Posttraumatic stress disorder (PTSD) symptoms in infants and toddlers can include hypervigilance, irritability, developmental regressions, sleep disorders, anxiety, withdrawal, and various dysregulations. Anecdotal reports from shelters for battered women and their children suggest that some infants and toddlers become irritable, disoriented, have trouble concentrating on play, have difficulty sleeping, or become quiet and withdrawn.

Cummings (1987), studying preschoolers, noted patterns of increased reassurance seeking, play disruption, increased aggression in play, and "freezing." Erickson, Egeland, and Pianta (1989) reported that physically maltreated preschoolers show anxious attachments, lower self-esteem, difficulties with hyperactivity, distractibility and persistence in tasks, and reduced self-control. Preschool child observers[1] of violence (Hughes & Barad, 1983) have been noted as exhibiting more severe reactions than older children. Younger children sense trouble but have difficulty understanding why something is wrong, and they have fewer cognitive and emotional resources to cope with confusing emotions than do older children.

Children of school age show reactions to adult anger, but the way in which they react is different than that shown by younger children (Cummings, Ballard, El-Sheikh, & Lake, 1991). PTSD symptoms in school-age victims of trauma have been noted in the work of Pynoos et al. (1987); Nader, Pynoos, Fairbanks, and Frederick (1990); Terr (1991); and others. Accumulating evidence suggests that these children may also show dissociative symptomatology in response to chronic trauma (Kluft, 1985; Putnam, 1991; Terr, 1991). School-age child observers of parental violence have been studied more extensively than any other age group, and the general conclusion is that they show difficulties in many areas, including school performance (Peplar & Moore, 1989); self-esteem (Hughes, 1988; Rossman & Rosenberg, 1992); anxiety (Hughes, 1988); social problem-solving skills (Rosenberg & Rossman, 1990); and both internalizing and externalizing problem behaviors (Jaffe, Wolfe, & Wilson, 1990).

The reactions of adolescent observers have not been studied sufficiently, but anecdotal reports of greater aggressiveness, delinquent behaviors, and victimization by others are common. In addition, adolescent observers appear more likely than younger observers to want to kill the perpetrator or to be injured or killed as they try to defend a battered mother. There are only a few studies of maltreated adolescents (Garbarino, 1989). Much more research needs to be done on the difficulties of adolescent victims. This should include study of the "conversion effect," often anecdotally reported by clinicians, which refers to the behavior of adolescents who have been exposed to parental violence for many years, especially during or subsequent to divorce, and begin acting like and taking on the characteristics of the perpetrator.

## TREATMENT ISSUES AND PROGRAMS FOR CHILDREN OBSERVING ABUSE

Children's reactions to adult anger, violence, and abuse, as reviewed previously, provide some guidance as to their multiple treatment needs. However, these children represent a heterogeneous group, and care in the assessment of the developmental level and needs of each child is critical (Jaffe, Sudermann, & Reitzel, 1992).

Hughes (1982) described a treatment plan, carried out in a battered women's shelter, which included several techniques requisite to the treatment of mothers and children. These include the enhancement of social and parenting skills and the improvement of mother–child relationships. Staff and clients confirmed the usefulness of the intervention, but it was not possible to assess separately the effectiveness of different components. Jaffe et al. (1990) used a 10-session peer group program with child observers aged 8 to 13. The goals included labeling feelings, dealing with anger, developing safety skills, improving social skills, and understanding the dynamics of family violence. They reported positive outcomes of these groups in terms of safety skills, child enjoyment, and some positive maternal perceptions. The family system is obviously involved by virtue of

---

[1] The term *child observers* will be used throughout this chapter to refer to children who grow up in violent families and who observed or were exposed to parental abuse and wife battering. The term *child witnesses* has often been used to describe these children, but Geffner (1989a; Geffner & Pagelow, 1990a) has argued that this is confusing because many professionals and others who work in the legal arena refer to child witnesses as those children who testify in court. Thus, a change in terminology was recommended to avoid confusion.

attention to all these goals, even though other family members were not active participants in this program.

Grusznski, Brink, and Edleson (1988) have reported positive outcomes for similar types of groups, as have Alessi and Hearn (1984). The use of parent–child groups in coordination with family members' individual treatment was noted by Gentry and Eaddy (1980), but intervention outcomes were not reported. Rossman and Rosenberg (1992) reinforce the importance of treatment goals emphasized by Jaffe et al. (1990), and they have added other components. They recommend assessing trauma symptoms, educational deficits, and health concerns; dealing with attachment and abandonment concerns; and managing aggression. It is clear that child observers, abused and nonabused, may need therapeutic attention for a variety of acute and chronic problems, and attention to any individual problems will likely have a positive effect on family functioning as a whole.

## An Overall Treatment Approach

There seems to be a consensus about what phases of treatment are needed for many kinds of victims, whether they are children, mothers, or even abusers (who are victims of their own behaviors). There is the need for crisis intervention and assessment, short-term intervention, and long-term therapy (e.g., Bell & Chance-Hill, 1991; Jaffe et al., 1992). These intervention phases have different goals and may use different treatment modalities. The goals of crisis intervention involve ensuring the safety of endangered family members, trauma symptom and distress assessment, information gathering about the history and nature of the abuse and violence, and the making of safety plans (Bell & Chance-Hill, 1991; Jaffe et al., 1990). It is important to help clients stabilize in a safe environment, begin to deal with changes in housing and other living circumstances, and enhance their competencies and self-esteem. These sessions may also focus on skill-learning goals, such as control of anger, conflict resolution, improved social skills, or anxiety management.

In shelters, these first two stages in treatment can involve individual work with children and mothers, mothers' groups, children's groups, and multifamily mother–child groups. As Bell and Chance-Hill

(1991) warn, every session must be treated as though it were the last one, because violent families often do not remain in contact with service providers for very long. Long-term therapy is sometimes provided by shelters and other community agencies as well as by private clinicians and may include a variety of goals in addition to ongoing safety assessment: work on personal growth goals, further understanding of family violence, and planning to avoid revictimization and violence.

## Techniques for Children Using Conjoint Family Therapy

Children from violent homes face the dilemma of their ultimate powerlessness in the family, coupled with their need to understand and remain in contact with all or part of their family. This situation dictates that, in considering conjoint family therapy, the child's clinician needs to ensure the child's safety and to examine how the treatment needs of the child mesh with parental needs.

The context for conjoint work can be encouraged by preparation sessions for children and parents. Parents need to understand developmentally appropriate expectations for their child's participation. We find that many parents in our population require training in effective parenting. Having parents, accompanied by an interpreting clinician, observe their child playing with a neutral adult can facilitate the development of appropriate expectations and interpretations (e.g., Lieberman, Weston, & Pawl, 1991), because abusive parents have been found to make limited and negative attributions about their children (Newberger & White, 1989).

Similarly, careful preparation needs to be carried out with the children prior to conjoint sessions. Children need help in learning to express their worries and fears, to anticipate their potential reactions, and to understand the family and their role in it. Children need help to develop safe, protective behaviors (which will be encouraged and respected during the sessions), such as the right not to respond to or feel that they are responsible for parental violence. The child's individual therapist may need to participate in conjoint sessions at times to facilitate the child's involvement and feelings of safety.

Children who have observed abuse are often isolated by fear and frequently feel the need to keep family secrets. Thus, they are likely to have fewer resources for sharing their reactions and confusions regarding joint sessions. It is particularly important for children to have sessions with their own therapist in which they have the opportunity to do some debriefing following the conjoint sessions. A variety of other techniques can translate sessions into concrete behaviors and reduce anxiety for a traumatized child. These are illustrated in Exhibit 1. If families use these kinds of props at home, they may become part of the family communication system and serve as constant reminders of the child's specific needs.

For child observers of abuse, it is important that the affective intensity of family interactions in and out of joint sessions be kept at a manageable level. Out-of-control affect is a major issue. Management will involve not only clinician planning, monitoring,

---

### EXHIBIT 1

**Strategies for Reducing Anxiety In Traumatized Children**

1. A clear statement is made of session rules that apply to all family members.
2. Dolls are used to allow younger children to show what happened.
3. Both dolls and props are used to help parents communicate with the child.
4. A flash pad or chalkboard is used to concretize narratives and/or the child can draw or assist the family therapist.
5. Traumagrams are used to examine family sequences of events (Figley, as cited in Markowitz, 1991).
6. Role play is facilitated.
7. Feelings cards are used to help older children express their feelings.
8. A feelings clock is used in the same way for younger children. This "clock" is similar to a regular clock, but the number positions are replaced with feeling faces, and the child points the clock hands to the feeling(s) he or she wishes to express.

---

and intervention within sessions, but also training the family in the use of such skills as relaxation, anger management, and humor. Belkap (1989) has designed relaxation exercises for children. Children also benefit from the development of family code words that can be interjected into intense situations to signal time-outs or remind family members of humorous or relaxing family incidents. It is also important that joint sessions not end with a child's feeling distressed or rejected. Fear, anger, attachment, and abandonment issues are especially difficult for traumatized children. A check on feelings at the end of joint sessions, and mood-changing procedures, such as having everyone share a good experience, may be useful.

## TREATMENT OF SEXUAL ABUSE

Sexual child abuse—a specific type of familial violence—causes enormous disruption and negative consequences to all involved. From both a legal and psychological standpoint, the pain, shame, guilt, and torment experienced by victim, nonoffending family members, and offender can be devastating. The extent of the problem necessitates that all clinicians understand the complex factors that contribute to family violence in general and to child sexual abuse specifically (see also chap. 6 in this volume). Therapists need a conceptual framework for understanding the problem and a therapeutic model for its treatment. Without a framework and model, the clinician will easily become lost in the emotional, familial, professional, and legal quagmire of child sexual abuse. The specific variables we believe contribute to the sexual abuse of children are (a) individual factors, (b) family factors, and (c) social/political/cultural factors. Techniques for obtaining the information in these three areas should be based on the style and experience of each individual therapist. Clinicians try to understand how past and present contexts of these family members influence their offending behaviors. This in no way implies that a child, or even a nonprotective parent, caused the abuse to occur or is to blame. The responsibility remains with the offender.

It is helpful to explore family beliefs regarding roles of men and women, division of labor, and rules about behavior in relationships. Research has indicated that 90% of incestuous fathers felt they had little or no caretaking involvement or relationship with their victims as infants (e.g., they did not change diapers or feed them; Trepper & Barrett, 1995). This resulted in a distancing that perhaps contributed to an inability to empathize with their victims. The incidence of sexual abuse or other childhood traumas in the parents' childhood is another variable that contributes to profound feelings of powerlessness and disconnection that many abusive parents and their spouses have experienced throughout their lives.

There are predominant styles of interaction in the family that are important to assess, such as (a) an inappropriate need for affection whereby children exist solely to meet the needs of the parents, (b) an eroticized style of interaction, (c) an aggressive and hostile style, or (d) violent rage (Larson & Maddock, 1986). These styles are indicative not of only the emotional environment in which the sexual abuse took place but also may infuse much of the family interaction.

## Stage 1: Individual Psychological Factors

Usually, in the first stage of treatment, the client does not discuss his or her sexual compulsions in detail. Therapists understand that many of the sex offender's personality characteristics may develop as a result of severe emotional deprivation or physical and sexual traumas in childhood. The parts of the personality that developed from this painful and deprived childhood are those characteristics that may later result in abuse. Therapists conceptualize this as an internal/intrapsychic cycle. As children, they were highly vulnerable and had little control of their own world. Consequently, as adults, they developed survival skills such as chemical dependencies, dissociation, aggression, sexual fantasies, self-absorption, and cognitive distortions. To protect themselves emotionally from the abuse and increase their sense of control, they learned offending behaviors as a form of self-protection. They did not have the opportunity to develop fully a sense of self-awareness that would include the capacity to monitor their feelings, thoughts, and behaviors. During Stage 1 of treatment, the therapist begins to understand and observe these intrapsychic patterns and explore "grooming patterns," that is, the interactions and attitudes of the

offenders that convince, manipulate, and build a relationship with the victim within which abuse may occur. The offender creates an environment in which he or she has access to the child and has also manipulated the situation so that the child does not feel safe enough to tell anyone about the abuse.

Exploration of the nonoffending parent's history of trauma and abuse is crucial. Their child's disclosure may have triggered their own traumatic memories and subsequent symptoms. Like the offender, they often have been victimized in one form or another as children and have learned survival skills that appear pathological to professionals (e.g., dissociation, mood swings, inability to trust, and substance abuse). They may present symptoms during treatment that are stimulated not only by the "terrible knowledge" (Stone Fish, 1991) about their child's abuse but also by the memory of their own abuses. Assessment of their situation physically, not just emotionally, is also important.

The child's symptoms must be assessed, and the clinician must remain aware of the possible function of such symptoms. These include depression, acting out, eating disorders, sexualized behavior, and social withdrawal. These symptoms serve to protect the child and to detour other family members and professionals away from acknowledging or exploring the sexual abuse. The child's relationships with other family members and their social network need to be assessed. It is also recommended that a substance abuse evaluation be conducted for all family members.

Stage 1 of treatment is concluded when early case management concerns are achieved, assessment of the factors contributing to the family's vulnerability is accomplished, reduction of initial denial occurs, the offender formally takes responsibility for the abuse, the family has agreed upon a treatment plan, and a trusting relationship and safe context is established between client and therapist. If the offender is not a family member but an entrusted other, therapists still explore and challenge any situations that may leave the victim vulnerable to further abuse. Sometimes the therapist will include the offender, depending on how involved he or she was in other aspects of the family's life, and on the family's progress in its own therapy.

Individual sessions for victim, offender, and non-offending parents are seen as an integral part of the MSP approach. There are many topics family members simply do not and should not talk about in the presence of others. Also, people behave differently in front of a group or with family members than one-on-one. Individual sessions allow the therapist to see many aspects of each client's personality. Safety and intimacy must be maintained between the client and therapist in order to help explore that person's history and to understand how abuse and trauma have contributed to shaping the person. Individual sessions also act as a metaphor for the individuation that is being encouraged in other parts of treatment. Individual sessions, however, are treated as part of the overall therapy and not as a replacement for family therapy sessions.

Therapists concentrate during the individual sessions on issues such as experiences and feelings of victimization, attempts at self-protection, and attempts to regain power and control. It is also important to examine sexual problems, arousal patterns, and attachment issues. The aim is to further the development of self-esteem, self-monitoring, and empathy.

## Stage 2: Group Therapy

Group therapy is often the most appropriate modality to address many of the issues involved in child sexual abuse. The members learn to interact differently in social encounters with nonfamily members. They also learn to understand better the universality of their feelings, motivations, and behaviors. They discuss previously unspeakable issues such as sexual attractions, fears, and fantasies.

**Subsystem sessions.** Child sexual abuse occurs in families with poor boundaries and a multitude of secrets. Often such families are socially isolated. For this reason, they especially benefit from work with and cooperation from all parties involved in the treatment. The sibling, extended family, social network, social service, and legal subsystems all may require therapeutic attention in Stage 2 of treatment.

Sibling sessions are used to allay children's fear, confusion, and anger about the molestation. Particularly if the offender was a sibling, it is important to help the family to establish behaviors among siblings that fit normal development levels. Nonabusing siblings experience guilt and remorse. This may include shame about their family, the offender sibling, or themselves, and sometimes even jealousy because the victim is being treated "specially." Many siblings are angry about the consequences of what happens to family members. Many times siblings will act out in attempts to distract or protect other family members from facing the terrible knowledge and pain of the abuse. Much of the same work that is done in family sessions is done in sibling sessions, emphasizing the specialness of their relationship and the importance of generational boundaries.

Members of the extended family are involved in numerous ways, and the sessions that include them help to change the transgenerational patterns that may have contributed to the abuse. These sessions must be handled with great caution and sensitivity as adult children speak, often for the first time, with their parents and confront them with the abuse. There is a great danger that old patterns of victimization will be rekindled, particularly where there is continuing and frequent familial contact. It is important to allow for enough sessions so that there is time for healing to occur.

The social service and legal systems should be continually informed of the progress of treatment. It may be continually necessary to reevaluate treatment goals and roles of the helping team. It is imperative that professionals maintain healthy functional relationships with the clients in order to prevent confusion and to model cooperative and adult interaction.

**Couple sessions.** Direct intervention for the couple system is another pivotal component of Stage 2. The adult couple sessions must focus on the following areas:

1. The nature and future of the relationship are discussed. In what form will the couple continue parenting together, making decisions together, and enforcing these decisions together? What will be the living arrangements? There are many practical issues that are explored.
2. Communication and conflict resolution are an ongoing struggle for the couple. How can they inter-

rupt and change the cycles of violence described earlier?

3. Discussions about sexuality and sexual problems help both parties explore their own needs for affection and sexual expression. Their fears of aggression, inhibited sexual desire, discrepancy in desire, and other problems are examined.

4. The link between each partner's family of origin and the couple's current situation must be examined. The role that each of the extended families is currently playing in a couple's life is examined.

## Stage 3: Final Stage of Treatment

In the final stage of treatment, the therapist should explore the question "What could make the sexual abuse happen again?" The offender is not the only one who should understand all the causative factors of the sexual abuse. Each family member should be encouraged to review the causative factors and to identify the behaviors, thoughts, and feelings that brought them into treatment, and how these have changed over time. This process helps prevent relapse.

## CONCLUSION

Domestic violence and sexual abuse are national epidemics that have devastating effects on the victims, nonoffending parents, and the offenders. It is imperative that long-term solutions be developed so that the ultimate goal can be achieved: that no woman, child, or man has to live with this kind of fear again. These societal and family problems are increasing in prevalence, and intergenerational cycles of abuse are still thriving. Family approaches have firm clinical and historical foundations. Therefore, these techniques should be considered as optional approaches in treating individuals or families whenever abuse occurs. Many victims and children who observe abuse are in a difficult position because the family system within which they were abused and powerless is likely to be the same system upon which they depend for protection, nurturance, and growth. There is an urgent need for treatment outcome research to evaluate the effectiveness of different types of interventions for these children, battered women, and offenders. Multiple systems approaches for work

with individuals and families trapped in a cycle of violence and abuse represent an excellent investment for ending intergenerational patterns of family violence and sexual abuse.

## References

Abusive Men Exploring New Directions. (1990). *AMEND's policy with regard to couples intervention and counseling.* Unpublished manuscript.

Adams, D. C., & McCormick, A. J. (1982). Men unlearning violence: A group approach based upon the collective model. In M. Roy (Ed.), *The abusing partner: An analysis of domestic battering* (pp. 170–197). New York: Van Nostrand.

Alessi, J. J., & Hearn, K. (1984). Group treatment of children in shelters for battered women. In A. R. Roberts (Ed.), *Battered women and their families: Intervention strategies and treatment programs* (pp. 49–62). New York: Springer.

Bach, G. R., & Wyden, P. (1970). *The intimate enemy.* New York: Avon Books.

Barnett, E. R., Pittman, C. B., Ragan, C. K., & Salus, M. K. (1980). *Family violence: Intervention strategies.* (DHHS Pub. No. 80-30258). Washington, DC: U.S. Department of HHS.

Barrett, M. J. (1992, October). *A delicate balance: Working systemically with incest.* Paper presented at annual conference of American Association of Marital and Family Therapy, Miami, FL.

Barrett, M. J., Sykes, C., & Byrnes, W. (1986). A systemic model for the treatment of intrafamily child sexual abuse. In T. Trepper & M. J. Barrett (Eds.), *Treating Incest: A Multiple Systems Perspective* (pp. 67–82). New York: Haworth.

Barrett, M. J., & Trepper, T. (1992a). Treatment of denial in families where there is child sexual abuse. In C. W. Le Croy (Ed.), *Case studies in social work practice* (pp. 57–68). Belmont, CA: Wadsworth Publishing.

Barrett, M. J., & Trepper, T. (1992b, May/June). Unmasking the incestuous family. *Family Therapy Networker,* 39–46.

Barrett, M. J., Trepper, T., & Stone Fish, L. (1990). Feminist informed family therapy for the treatment of intrafamily child sexual abuse. *Journal of Family Psychology, 4*(2), 151–165.

Belkap, M. (1989). *Taming your dragons.* East Aurora, NY: D.O.K. Publishers.

Bell, C. C., & Chance-Hill, G. (1991). Treatment of violent families. *Journal of the National Medical Association, 83,* 203–208.

Bograd, M. (1984). Family systems approaches to wife battering: A feminist critique. *American Journal of Orthopsychiatry, 54,* 558–568.

Cook, D., & Frantz-Cook, A. (1984). A systemic treatment approach to wife battering. *Journal of Marriage and Family Therapy, 10,* 83–93.

Cummings, E. M. (1987). Coping with background anger in early childhood. *Child Development, 58,* 976–984.

Cummings, E. M., Ballard, M., El-Sheikh, M., & Lake, M. (1991). Resolution and children's responses to expressions of anger and affection by others in the family. *Child Development, 52,* 1274–1282.

Cummings, E. M., Zahn-Waxler, C., & Radke-Yarro, M. (1981). Young children's responses to expressions of anger and affection by others in the family. *Child Development, 52,* 1274–1282.

Dell, P. F. (1986). In defense of "lineal causality". *Family Process, 25,* 513–521.

Deschner, J. P. (1984). *The hitting habit: Anger control for battering couples.* New York: Free Press.

Drell, M. J., Siegel, C. H., & Gaensbauer, T. J. (in press). Post-traumatic stress disorder. In C. Zeara (Ed.), *The handbook of infant mental health.* New York: Guilford Press.

Erickson, M. F., Egeland, B., & Pianta, R. (1989). The effects of maltreatment on the development of young children. In D. Cicchetti & V. Carlson (Eds.), *Child maltreatment: Theory and research on the causes and consequences of child abuse and neglect* (pp. 647–684). New York: Cambridge University Press.

Fisch, R., Weakland, J. H., & Segal, L. (1982). *The tactics of change: Doing therapy briefly.* San Francisco: Jossey-Bass.

Folberg, J., & Milne, A. (1988). *Divorce mediation: Theory and practice.* New York: Guilford Press.

Furniss, T. (1983). Mutual influence and interlocking professional family process in the treatment of child sexual abuse and incest. *Child Abuse and Neglect, 7,* 207–223.

Garbarino, J. (1989). Troubled youth, troubled families: The dynamics of adolescent maltreatment. In D. Cicchetti & V. Carlson (Eds.), *Child maltreatment: Theory and research on the causes and consequences of child sexual abuse and neglect* (pp. 685–706). Cambridge, England: Cambridge University Press.

Geffner, R. (1989a). Editor's comments. *Family violence Bulletin, 5,* 1.

Geffner, R. (1989b). Treating spouse abuse with conjoint marital therapy. *Family Therapy Today, 4,* 1–5.

Geffner, R. (1992). Guidelines for using mediation with abusive couples. *Psychotherapy in Private Practice, 10,* 77–92.

Geffner, R. (1993). *Domestic violence conjoint groups: A combined treatment program.* San Diego, CA: Family Advocacy Center, U.S. Navy.

Geffner, R., Franks, D., Patrick, J. R., & Mantooth, C. (1986, August). Reducing marital violence: A family therapy approach. In R. Geffner (Chair), *New treatment approaches for reducing family violence.* Symposium conducted at the annual convention of the American Psychological Association, Washington, DC.

Geffner, R., Kreager-Cook, S., Sharne, K., Crawford, C. M., & Persinger, A. (1987, August). Effectiveness of a couple therapy program for reducing marital violence. In R. Geffner (Chair), *Effectiveness of different treatment programs for reducing spouse abuse.* Symposium conducted at the annual convention of the American Psychological Association, New York, NY.

Geffner, R., Mantooth, C., Franks, D., & Rao, L. (1989). A psychoeducational, conjoint therapy approach to reducing family violence. In P. L. Caesar & L. K. Hamberger (Eds.), *Treating men who batter: Theory, practice, and programs* (pp. 103–133). New York: Springer.

Geffner, R., Mantooth, C., Patrick, J., & Franks, D. (in press). *Conjoint psychotherapy: A practical guide for reducing abuse in relationships.* New York: Springer.

Geffner, R., & Pagelow, M. D. (1990a). Mediation and child custody issues in abusive relationships. *Behavioral Sciences & The Law, 8,* 151–159.

Geffner, R., & Pagelow, M. D. (1990b). Victims of spouse abuse. In R. T. Ammerman & M. Hersen (Eds.), *Treatment of family violence: A sourcebook* (pp. 113–135). New York: Wiley.

Geffner, R., & Rosenbaum, A. (1990). Characteristics and treatment of batterers. *Behavioral Sciences & The Law, 8,* 131–140.

Geller, J. A. (1992). *Breaking destructive patterns: Multiple strategies for treating partner abuse.* New York: Free Press.

Geller, J. A., & Wasserstrom, J. (1984). Conjoint therapy for the treatment of domestic violence. In A. R. Roberts (Ed.), *Battered women and their families: Intervention strategies and treatment programs* (pp. 33–48). New York: Springer.

Gentry, C. E., & Eaddy, V. B. (1980). Treatment of children in spouse abusive families. *Victimology: An International Journal, 7,* 240–250.

Giaretto, H. (1982). *Integrated treatment of child sexual abuse: A treatment and training manual.* Palo Alto, CA: Science and Behavior Books.

Gondolf, E. W., & Russell, D. M. (1986). The case against anger control treatment programs for batterers. *Response, 9,* 2–5.

Gottschalk, L. A. (1983). Vulnerability to "stress." *American Journal of Psychotherapy, 37,* 5–23.

Grusznski, R. J., Brink, J. C., & Edleson, J. L. (1988). Support and education groups for children of battered women. *Child Welfare, LXVII*, 431–444.

Henderson, C. Y. (1990). *Presentation to the Colorado State Commission for the manual of treatment standards for domestic violence perpetrators.* Unpublished manuscript.

Herzog, J. M. (1980). Sleep disturbance and father hunger in 18- to 28-month-old boys: The Erlkoenig syndrome. *Psychoanalytic Study of the Child, 35*, 219–233.

Hodges, W. F. (1991). *Interventions for children of divorce: Custody, access, and psychotherapy.* New York: Wiley.

Hughes, H. M. (1982). Brief interventions with children in a battered women's shelter: A model preventive program. *Family Relations, 31*, 495–502.

Hughes, H. M. (1988). Psychological and behavioral correlates of family violence in child witnesses and victims. *American Journal of Orthopsychiatry, 58*, 77–90.

Hughes, H. M., & Barad, S. J. (1983). Psychological functioning of children in a battered women's shelter: A preliminary investigation. *American Journal of Orthopsychiatry, 53*, 525–531.

Imber-Black, E. (1986). Maybe "lineal causality" needs another defense lawyer: A feminist response to Dell. *Family Process, 25*, 523–525.

Jacobson, N. S. (1993, August). *Domestic violence: What are the marriages like?* Paper presented at the annual convention of the American Psychological Association, Toronto, Ontario, Canada.

Jaffe, P. G., Sudermann, M., & Reitzel, D. (1992). Child witnesses of marital violence. In R. T. Ammerman & M. Hersen (Eds.), *Assessment of family violence: A clinical and legal sourcebook* (pp. 313–331). New York: Wiley.

Jaffe, P. G., Wolfe, D. A., & Wilson, S. K. (1990). *Children of battered women.* Newbury Park, CA: Sage.

Jenkins, A. (1990). *Invitations to responsibility.* Adelaide, South Australia: Dulwich Centre Publications.

Kluft, R. P. (1985). *Childhood antecedents of multiple personality.* Washington, DC: American Psychiatric Press.

Lane, G., & Russell, T. (1989). Second-order systemic work with violent couples. In P. L. Caesar & L. K. Hamberger (Eds.), *Treating men who batter: Theory, practice, and programs* (pp. 134–162). New York: Springer.

Larson, N., & Maddock, J. (1986). Structural and functional variables in incest family systems: Implications for assessment and treatment. In T. Trepper & M. Barrett (Eds.), *Treating incest: A multiple systems perspective* (pp. 27–44). New York: Haworth.

Lieberman, A. F., Weston, D. R., & Pawl, J. H. (1991). Preventive interventions and outcome with anxiously attached dyads. *Child Development, 62*, 199–209.

Madanes, C. (1981). *Strategic family therapy.* San Francisco, CA: Jossey-Bass.

Mantooth, C. M., Geffner, R., Franks, D., & Patrick, J. (1987). *Family preservation: A treatment manual for reducing couple violence.* Tyler: University of Texas at Tyler Press.

Markowitz, L. M. (1991, November/December). After the trauma. *Networker*, 30–37.

McKay, M., Davis, M., & Fanning, P. (1983). *Messages: The communication book.* Oakland, CA: New Harbinger Publications.

Minuchin, S. (1974). *Families and family therapy.* Cambridge, MA: Harvard University Press.

Nader, K., Pynoos, R., Fairbanks, L., & Frederick, C. (1990). Children's PTSD reactions one year after a sniper attack at their school. *American Journal of Psychiatry, 147*, 1526–1530.

Neidig, P. H., & Friedman, D. H. (1984). *Spouse abuse: A treatment program for couples.* Champaign, IL: Research Press.

Newberger, C. M., & White, K. M. (1989). Cognitive foundations for parental care. In D. Cicchetti & V. Carlson (Eds.), *Child maltreatment: Theory and research on the causes and consequences of child abuse and neglect* (pp. 302–316). New York: Gardner Press.

Nichols, M. P. (1984). *Family therapy: Concepts and methods.* New York: Gardner Press.

Olson, D. H., Russell, C. S., & Sprenkle, D. H. (1983). Circumplex model for marital and family systems. *Family Process, 22*, 69–83.

Peplar, D. J., & Moore, T. E. (1989). Children exposed to family violence: Home environments and cognitive functioning. Paper presented at the meeting of the Society for Research in Child Development, Kansas City, MO.

Porter, F., Blick, L., & Sgroi, S. (1982). Treatment of the sexually abused child. In S. Sgroi (Ed.), *Handbook of clinical intervention in child sexual abuse* (pp. 109–146). Lexington, MA: Lexington Books.

Putnam, F. W. (1991). Dissociative disorders in children and adolescents: A developmental perspective. *Psychiatric Clinics of North America, 14*, 519–531.

Pynoos, R. S., Frederick, C., Nader, K., Arroyo, W., Steinberg, A., Eth, S., Nunez, F., & Fairbanks, L. (1987). Life threat and post-traumatic stress in school-age children. *Archives of General Psychiatry, 44*, 1057–1063.

Rosenberg, M. S., & Rossman, B. B. R. (1990). The child witnesses to marital violence. R. T. Ammerman & M. Hersen (Eds.), *Treatment of family violence: A sourcebook* (pp. 183–210). New York: Wiley.

Rossman, B. B. R., & Rosenberg, M. S. (1992). Family stress and functioning in children: The moderating effects of children's beliefs about their control over parental conflict. *Journal of Child Psychology and Psychiatry, 33,* 699–715.

Satir, V. (1967). *Conjoint family therapy* (rev. ed.). Cupertino, CA: Science and Behavior Books.

Saunders, D. G. (1982). Counseling the violent husband. In P. A. Keller & L. G. Ritt (Eds.), *Innovations in clinical practice: A sourcebook* (Vol. 1; pp. 16–29). Sarasota, FL: Professional Resource Exchange.

Sgroi, S. (1982). Family treatment of child sexual abuse. In J. Conte & D. Shore (Eds.), *Social work and child sexual abuse* (pp. 109–128). New York: Haworth.

Sonkin, D. J., & Durphy, M. (1982). *Learning to live without violence.* San Francisco: Volcano Press.

Stone Fish, L. (1991, October). Marital therapy with survivors of childhood sexual abuse. Paper presented at annual Midwest Conference on Sexual Abuse, Madison, WI.

Stordeur, R. A., & Stille, R. (1989). *Ending men's violence against their partners: One road to peace.* Newbury Park, CA: Sage.

Tarasoff v the Regents of the University of California, 17 Cal. 3d 425 (1976).

Terr, L. (1991). Child traumas: An outline and overview. *American Journal of Psychiatry, 148,* 10–20.

Trepper, T. (1986). The apology session. In T. Trepper & M. Barrett (Eds.), *Treating incest: A multiple systems perspective* (pp. 93–102). New York: Haworth.

Trepper, T., & Barrett, M. J. (1986). *Treating incest: A multiple systems perspective.* New York: Haworth.

Trepper, T., & Barrett, M. J. (1989). *Systemic treatment of incest: A therapeutic handbook.* New York: Brunner/Mazel.

Trepper, T., & Barrett, M. J. (1995). *Characteristics of intact sexually abusive families: An exploratory study.* Submitted for publication.

Wallerstein, J. S., & Kelly, J. B. (1975). The effects of parental divorce: Experiences of the child in early latency. *American Journal of Orthopsychiatry, 46,* 20–32.

Wolfe, D. A., Wolfe, V. V., & Best, C. L. (1988). Child victims of sexual abuse. In V. B. van Hasselt, R. L. Morrison, A. S. Bellack, & M. Hersen (Eds.), *Handbook of family violence.* New York: Plenum.

Zefran, J., Riley, H., Anderson, W., Curtis, J., Jackson, L., Kelly, P., McGury, E., & Suriano, M. (1982). Management and treatment of child sexual abuse cases in a juvenile court setting. In J. Conte & D. Shore (Eds.), *Social work and child sexual abuse* (pp. 155–170). New York: Haworth.

Zubin, J., & Spring, B. (1977). Vulnerability: A new view of schizophrenia. *Journal of Abnormal Psychology, 86,* 103–126.

# CHAPTER 29

# CULTS: IMPLICATIONS FOR FAMILY THERAPISTS

*Margaret Thaler Singer*

Involvement with cults presents a unique challenge for the family therapist. A family that contacts a mental health professional about a member who is in a cult is typically not in need of traditional family therapy, at least initially. Even though some families of cultists may present by saying, "Fix us because we caused our relative to depart" or "Diagnose our relative and help us find a way to help him or her," their actual needs are quite different, and it is up to the family therapist to indicate this to them. In the beginning, the family usually needs to gauge the reality of their concerns about a cult member, obtain information about cults in general and their member's cult in particular, and begin to assess their options.

Jean Merritt, a pioneer in working with families of cultists, noted, "Mental health professionals and the clergy are generally the worst people to talk to about cults" ("Experts Say," 1981, p. 3). She believed that such persons often had minimal knowledge about cults and other intense social influence programs. She spoke well over a decade ago. Knowledge about cults is much more widespread among mental health professionals, but there still is a great need for family therapists to gain knowledge and skill in working with cultists and their families. Fortunately, family therapists with a systems approach to working with clients are already primed to involve other systems in their interventions. In working with families of cultists, they may understand more readily than other therapists the necessity of involving a cult expert and other systems resources.

In consultation with cult experts, family therapists can be helpful to the families of cult members and the cult members themselves in at least four different ways, should the members leave the cult. First, family therapists can direct the family to sources of information and group support and can connect them with cult experts who can help them decide what actions are open to them. Second, family therapists can provide a holding environment for the family as they process their reactions to their family member's cult membership and decide what to do next. Third, once a member leaves a cult, family therapists can help the cultist design a post exit therapy plan that includes reintegration into the family, refer the cultist to appropriate sources of individual help, and then work with the individual and the family to achieve this reintegration. Fourth, and finally, if after all of these goals are achieved, the family evidences structural, communication, or other relationship difficulties, the family therapist can help in more traditional ways (i.e., family or couples therapy).

To instruct the therapist about the particulars of each of these roles is beyond the scope of this chapter. What I will do is present in some detail the initial phase of consultation, as this is the phase in which therapists who have not worked with cultists and their families often make the greatest mistakes. I then introduce some basic parameters of working during later phases, particularly after the family member has left the cult, and will refer the reader to selected resource agencies and suggested readings.

## CULTS: A BRIEF HISTORICAL OVERVIEW

The term *cult* is not necessarily pejorative, but it is descriptive, referring to the origins, social structure, and power structure of a group. However, the conduct of certain cults, especially groups that tend to exploit and abuse people and engage in deceptive, unethical, and illegal conduct, has resulted in the word having a largely negative connotation.

In the past two decades, 2,000 to 5,000 cultic groups have been identified in the United States. These groups vary in size from a dozen members to several million members worldwide. Adolescents and young adults are not the only people to be included in these numbers. Rudin (1984) estimated that there are thousands of small children in religious cults, with 5,000 small children in the European-based Children of God (also known as The Family) cult alone. Two hundred seventy-six of the 913 who died in Jonestown, Guyana in 1978 were children and teenagers (Wooden, 1981), some of whom were child wards of the state (e.g., California) who had been placed in foster care.

Middle-aged and older persons are also a significant proportion of those who join cults: For example, approximately one third of Jim Jones's followers who died in Guyana were older (Wooden, 1981). A former member of the Church Universal and Triumphant estimated that 15% of the members were over 50 years of age. Another estimated that 20% of members of The Walk were over 50 years old (Rudin, 1984). Reportedly, the Unification Church in the United States and England makes deliberate efforts to contact older persons. Former members of many other groups reported that they had been sent to recruit lonely, older persons with pensions and property; numerous adult children have reported losing a widowed parent to a cultic group that then alienated the parent from his or her relatives.

Cults can be formed around any ideology, worldview, or content area. They are organized around religious and spiritual beliefs, psychotherapy, unidentified flying objects, health fads, political beliefs, lifestyle, and other contents. Each has an ideology, a belief system, and a charismatic leader around which practices, lifestyles, and social rules develop. It is the process, rather than the particular content of cults, that distinguish them from other groups organized around a common interest. For example, cults often obtain control over the person's social and physical environment; instill a sense of powerlessness in the person; manipulate a system of rewards, punishments, and experiences that reinforce group conformity and place the group's welfare above that of the individual; and maintain a closed system of logic and an authoritarian structure (Singer & Ofshe, 1990).

Most contemporary cults originated in the United States and have become one of our least desirable exports. The decade of the 1970s was the era of youth cults, during which new members were recruited primarily from the 18- to 25-year-old age group. For this reason, many people in the 1980s continued to see the cult phenomenon as a youth issue, attributing cult membership to rebellion against parents and cultural mores (Levine, 1984, 1989). However, by 1980, families had begun to seek help in dealing with cults other than youth cults. Adult children were concerned about their parents and grandparents who joined closed, restrictive cultic groups that had gained control over their lifestyle and property and separated them from their offspring (Rudin, 1984; Singer, 1986). Additionally, grandparents, aunts, uncles, and older siblings sought legal and other counsel about young children who were being reared in cultic organizations (Greene, 1989; Kandel, 1988; Landa, 1989, 1991; Rudin, 1984; Singer, 1986). These relatives were often concerned about young children sent overseas, living under poor health and school conditions, being abused, or even being retained by the group while the child's parents were sent away (Landa, 1989, 1991; Singer, 1986).

The work of Enroth (1992), Halperin (1989), Landa (1989, 1991), Markowitz and Halperin (1984), McManus and Cooper (1976), Rudin (1984), and Wooden (1981) attests to the low status of children in certain cults; use of extreme forms of discipline; rearing of children by others than the parents; sheer neglect of children; lack of adequate medical, dental, and nutritional care; poor schooling; and the philosophical contents of the group with which both the parent(s) and children grapple after leaving some groups.[1]

In addition to the mistreatment or neglect of children, women in most cults are subjugated, denigrated, and abused. Marriage can be used to institutionalize the lower status of women as well as limit their freedom. Many groups that arrange marriages—not only the large, well-known Unification Church (i.e., the church of the Reverend Moon) but also smaller less well-known groups—emphasize conformity to the group over the sanctity of the marital relationship. Cult leaders often dictate who will have children and when, and occasionally specify who will father a particular woman's child (Hochman, 1984; Singer, Langone, & Temerlin, 1991). When one partner leaves and a spouse and children remain in the group, custody issues arise. These custody cases are growing in number (Greene, 1989; Kandel, 1988; Landa, 1991; Singer, 1986).

The documentation of life in various cults is growing. Ex-members have written memoirs, a professional journal devoted to cultic studies exists (*Cultic Studies Journal*), and there is a growing literature on influence, attitude changes, and the sequelae. In the 1990s, not only has the Waco incident heightened awareness but numerous other lesser known but alarmingly violent or harmful episodes are documented nearly weekly across the country. In November, 1994 in Quebec and Switzerland, 53 members of the Order of the Solar Temple were murdered or suicided and their buildings set afire by pre-planned wiring. In some cases, these reports have resulted in a growing awareness of the active processes used by cults to recruit, resocialize, and hold members.

As a result, public and professional understanding has shifted from the early view that cults were a youth phenomenon representing spiritual seeking, rebellion, or pathology in both the member and his or her family (Maron, 1988; Sirkin & Grellong, 1988) to the current view of cults as complex phenomena that can engage and influence normal individuals of all ages when they are in a vulnerable state.

## CULTS AND FAMILY THERAPY

Cults clearly have an intra- and intergenerational impact. Not only the cult member but the entire family is affected as well—parents, siblings, grandparents, and (adult) children. Before a family therapist can learn how to help families with a member who belongs to a cult, they must first learn to avoid the most common errors in dealing with these clients.

Among the most common errors is the assumption that there had to be something very wrong with the cult member and the family before cult membership or the cultist would never have joined in the first place. This is a variant of the "blaming the victim" stance often taken toward women who have been sexually assaulted. It reflects an oversimplification of cult phenomena. To commence individual or family therapy assuming that there is some inherent defect in the family or in the cultist is, unfortunately, a frequent practice.

Therapists espousing these views are largely unaware of the intense and often deceptive recruiting practices of cults. They have little or no understanding of the fearsome hold cult leaders—not just the famous ones such as Jim Jones and David Koresh but also "ordinary" ones in small groups—can have within their closed societies.

To summarize, in most cases, it is safest to assume that the cultist and family members were normal before the cult's recruitment efforts and that the family needs information, advice, and consultation, not necessarily treatment, so that they can make an informed choice among various options.

## LEARNING ABOUT CULTS

A consultative and educational approach in working with those who are involved in cults and their families is the initial method of choice. The professional who wants to work with families with a cult member needs considerable familiarity with social influence, cult dynamics, and cult content, especially the cult that a particular individual has joined.

[1] Landa (1989, 1991) documents the physical, sexual, and psychological abuse of children in cults.

## Resources

There are experts in cults who may be mental health practitioners, clergy, educators, lawyers, law enforcement agencies, experienced and ethical exit counselors, or former members of cults who live in the vicinity and are available to counsel with families based on their experience with the particular group.[2] Family therapists with a systems approach will be open to learning how ex-cultists and others can be of great service to them and to families of cultists.

## Basic Cultic Concepts and Processes

Two terms, *cultic relationships* and *thought reform programs,* are essential to understanding cult life. In a cultic relationship, one person intentionally induces another to become totally or nearly totally dependent on him or her for almost all major life decisions and inculcates in the follower a belief that he or she (the leader) has some special talent, gift, or knowledge (Singer, 1986).

The term *cultic relationship* conceptualizes a cult as characterized by a process in which power resides in the leader, who controls and shapes the ongoing, evolving relationships in the group through exploitative persuasion. It is the comprehensive, programmatic quality of cultic recruitment and maintenance of members that is noted by those who study the interactional processes of contemporary cults (Lifton, 1987; Ofshe & Singer, 1986; Singer, 1987).

*Thought reform* is the classic term for indoctrination and exploitative influence programs to recruit and maintain new members and to resocialize recruits to serve the group's goals (Lifton, 1961, 1989; Ofshe & Singer, 1986; Singer & Ofshe, 1990). Thought reform programs use well-known social and psychological influence techniques, not mysterious, esoteric methods.[3] Their tactics, maneuvers and strat-

egies rely on centuries-old human influence ploys (Singer, 1979b, 1987). The Wingspread Conference on Cults (West & Langone, 1986) called attention to the unethically manipulative techniques of persuasion and control used, such as isolation from former friends and family, special methods to heighten suggestibility and subservience, powerful group pressures to conform, information management, and suspension of individuality and critical judgment, combined with the promotion of total dependence on the group and fear of leaving it.

In short, cult leaders have refined the folk art of human influence, combined tactics and strategies of traditional thought control programs, and added a number of pop psychology techniques for manipulating guilt, fear, and defenses. The activities are intentional and aimed at gaining control over all or nearly all of a member's decision making. Attitudes and behavior are changed by the cult one step at a time, without the person's awareness that he or she is being changed for the benefit of the group or the leader (Ofshe & Singer, 1986; Singer, 1987; West, 1989). Other terms to describe such processes in the literature are *brainwashing* (Hyde, 1977; Verdier, 1977; Winn, 1983), *coercive persuasion* (Ofshe, 1992; Schein, 1961), *destructive persuasion* (Keiser & Keiser, 1987), *exploitative persuasion* (Singer & Addis, 1992), *systematic manipulation of psychological and social influence* (Singer & Addis, 1992), *coordinated programs of coercive influence and behavior control* (Ofshe & Singer, 1986), and even the less specific but widely used term *mind control* (Zimbardo, 1984).

## THE CONSULTATION PROCESS

Families usually consult therapists at certain turning points: (a) when a family member first joins a cult and/or when the person exhibits certain behavioral

---

[2] Three agencies that can provide information are Cult Awareness Network (CAN), 2421 West Pratt Blvd., Suite 1173, Chicago, IL 60645 (312) 267-777; American Family Foundation and *Cultic Studies Journal*, P.O. Box 2265, Bonita Springs, FL 33959-2265 (813) 495-3136; and Maynard Bernstein Resource Center on Cults, Commission on Cults and Missionaries, Jewish Federation Council. 6505 Wilshire Blvd., Los Angeles CA 90048 (213) 852-1234, Ext. 2813.

[3] For example, Winn (1983) reviewed the Chinese influence programs used in the revolutionary universities (Lifton, 1961, 1987) and with Korean War prisoners: "What was new was not method, but the manner of combining, in a systematic fashion, a variety of tried and tested methods."

or attitudinal changes that alarm the family, and (b) when the cultist has left the cult.[4]

## Pre-Exit Work With Families With a Cultic Member

The initial consultation should begin with a brief history of the family focused on the cultist and how the family sees the situation. Families of newly enrolled cultists often are alarmed and feel great pressure to "do something." Sometimes quick action is necessary because some groups send members abroad, move them far away in the same country, or roam nomadically. Whether this is, in fact, a risk is often the first information about the cult that should be sought, as noted earlier, and quick action with the help of a cult expert may need to be taken. In cases in which a significant geographical move is not imminent, it is often the first major task of the therapist to convince the family that a thoughtful, planned approach to the situation over several weeks is likely to be more effective than immediate crisis-driven action in the next few days.

Other families do not contact the therapist until the cultist has dropped family, friends, and career and displays attitudes and behavior that are out of character and appear self-destructive. They, too, may feel a great pressure to act. Unless the individual is in immediate danger of disappearing, however, this family, too, needs general information about cults, that the particular group that the family member has joined, and knowledge about influence programs.

Family therapists can also help by providing general support for feelings of self-blame that are often manifested at the time the family seeks consultation. Family members usually feel bereft, bewildered, alone, and humiliated. They may think that their behavior caused their relative to join a cult. They are usually unaware of the effectiveness of cult recruiting programs.

Helping to link families with a support group for families of cultists can also be useful at this point. Being with other people in similar situations can help family members realize that their distress and

responses to it are not signs of their abnormality but are, rather, common, normal responses to an abnormal situation. At this stage, as well as throughout his or her work with the family, the family therapist will be providing a holding environment as he or she helps the family develop and use cult expert resources. In this holding environment, the family feels neither blamed nor pressured to act.

## Exit Work

Later in the process, the family therapist can work with the cult expert to prepare the family for the time when the cultist (and perhaps spouse and children) leaves a cult. This can occur either as a "walk away" from the cult, initiated by the cultist, or as a result of family-instigated action. Families can be helped to anticipate that physical exit from the cult does not mean that the ex-cultist will immediately be able to resume his or her pre-cult life or identity. Family therapists can help them empathize with the kind of reentry stress that the ex-cultist immediately may experience and identify resources that might help the family member buffer this stress. One major resource is exit or reconsideration counseling, which usually is best provided by experienced ex-members of cults (Andres & Lane, 1988; Giambalvo, 1992; Hassan, 1988). Exit counselors provide the ex-cultist with information on the profound effect of social influence programs.

A person exiting a cult usually goes through three stages: reevaluation, readjustment and reacceptance (Andres & Lane, 1988; Ash, 1985; Giambalvo, 1992; Goldberg & Goldberg, 1988; Hassan, 1988; Martin, Langone, Dole, & Wiltrout, 1992; Singer, 1979a, 1986). Recovery time depends on the practices of the group and their interaction with the personality of the cultist, as well as the atmosphere into which the ex-cultist returns. Explaining these stages briefly can often provide the family with a useful structure for understanding what their family member is experiencing.

The reevaluation phase begins when the cultist walks away from the group or enters voluntary exit

---

[4] Three books are recommended to help guide the therapist and the family through the process of learning about specific cults, sorting through choices, and deciding how to proceed, including whether and how to communicate with cultists. These books are Andres and Lane (1988), Hassan (1988), and Giambalvo (1992).

reevaluation counseling with former members in conjunction with his or her family. The readjustment phase that follows varies in duration for each person. At this point, the ex-cultist will likely struggle with ambivalence about the cult, the self, and life goals. He or she may use therapy as a safe and nonjudgmental place to sort out these issues. The reacceptance phase is reached when there is commitment to remain outside the cult, and cult-induced symptoms have subsided.

During each stage of this process, the family therapist can help the family understand the issues with which the ex-cultist is struggling. A joint family meeting that includes an outside former cult member can be valuable in this regard. For example, the former cult member can explain problems that the ex-cultist may be experiencing, using his or her problems with concentration, memory, attention, relationships, and other aspects of life as examples. These temporary problems have often precluded the family's ex-cultist from returning immediately to college or to a previous career, and from functioning socially in family and other social situations. Moreover the family may fear that these are permanent effects of the cult experience. Seeing that the former cult member has overcome these problems provides needed reassurance both to families and to the ex-cultist that such problems eventually will recede.

## SEQUELAE TO CULT MEMBERSHIP AND THERAPEUTIC INTERVENTION

Mental health professionals have reported since the late 1970s that a significant portion of ex-cultists and their families first seek assistance immediately after the family member leaves a cult or soon thereafter (Clark, 1979; Singer, 1979a). Levine (1984), reporting on 800 former members of "new religions," found that more that 50% showed signs of emotional upheaval severe enough to warrant treatment during the first few months after their return. Levine (1989) reported that the vast majority of members have a difficult period after they exit but gradually reconstitute and reintegrate.

Others may experience more severe sequelae to cult life. Galanter (1983) found that 36% of a group

of former Unification Church members—71% of whom had left voluntarily—experienced serious emotional problems that continued for an average of 3.8 years after leaving. Swartling and Swartling (1992) in Sweden found that nearly half of 43 ex-members of the Word of Life that they studied had experienced psychosis-like symptoms, and one in four had attempted suicide. Singer and Ofshe (1990), reporting clinical observations from more than 3,000 ex-members of cults who were studied during the past 25 years, found periods of anomie present for varying periods in the vast majority. Often, symptoms that motivate the person or his or her family to seek therapy are the results of two main types of group practices: (a) those whose main effects are the production of intense aversive emotional arousal states; and (b) the use of meditation, trance states, and dissociative techniques. Two illustrative cases follow:

### CASE EXAMPLE ONE

*Jon's cult relied primarily on meditation and dissociative techniques. At age 17, he began to meditate twice a day in a guru-based meditation program. Soon Jon was sold advanced courses that were alleged to produce enlightenment, cure illness, teach levitation, and free a person of stress. He moved into a residence program where the twice daily brief meditation was replaced by more frequent and prolonged meditation, breathing techniques that produce states of hyperventilation and combined with yogic postures, and repetitive exposure to videos of the guru. Trainees were never to be alone and were assigned "buddies" to accompany them at all times. Banned were phone calls, reading newspapers or other printed materials, watching television, and listening to the radio. Jon reported that at this first residence course, he experienced states of euphoria punctuated by periods of dissociation as well as depersonalization, confusion, irritability, and memory difficulties. Along with the already instilled restrictions, he was now required to become a vegetarian and no longer talk with women.*

*Instead of becoming enlightened and free of stress and illness, he became depressed, chronically ill, and fatigued. When he left the group after a decade, he had difficulty reading. His memory and concentration were impaired, he felt dissociated, and he had involuntary shaking of his body.*

## CASE EXAMPLE TWO

*At age 18, Bryan joined a psychological cult that promised that he would attain communication skills and perfect mental and physical health, and that he would improve the planet. He was told to leave his family and college and live with the cult. His group used guided imagery under the direction of a personal guide who applied a device that was touted to be an infallible scientific instrument that could ascertain his truthfulness. The guide, using her instrument, verbally cued Bryan to create past lives and to experience intense emotional arousal while reliving them. These past lives were explored in increasingly expensive "courses," which he was led to purchase. He became like an "indentured serf" of the organization because he had to work for the cult at minimum wages to pay for the courses. Bryan was led by his guide to believe that in all his past lives, he had been a violent, child-murdering, law-breaking, guilt-ridden person. He became increasingly tense, unable to sleep, and chronically tired because of his emotional state and the long hours he worked to pay the cult for the courses, room, and board.*

*He reported that at the end of each guided imagery session, he was highly emotionally aroused and felt out of control. The guide prompted him to display a euphoria when he left his sessions to demonstrate to others nearby how exhilarated he felt. When alone, however, he was depressed, he ruminated about suicide, and he was immersed in feelings of guilt and anguish over*

*the "memories" that his "past lives" induced. Eventually, he obtained a gun to kill himself. A woman cult member called Bryan's parents, who rescued both of them.*

The first example illustrated primarily dissociative problems, and the second, high emotional arousal responses with accompanying feelings of guilt; both were engendered by the cult programs. However, no program relies solely on producing either of these two major responses. Each cult uses a variety of social and psychological techniques to produce desired effects that are then used as "proof" that the group has power and secret knowledge. The forms of dissociation, doubling, splitting, and related phenomena are central to producing some of the attitude and behavior changes reported in many cult members.

Some combination of individual, group, and family therapy may be useful when families seek help. An example of this combination approach is found in Martin (Martin et al., 1992), who has used an educational counseling and rehabilitation approach with many ex-cultists. Martin assists the ex-cultists and their families to understand cult dynamics and how the system of cult influence and control affected the person; to freely evaluate what happened; to recognize a cultic group in the future; and to see how identity, beliefs, and lifestyle were gradually changed during the cult process.

Some people request counseling after being in a cult for a long period of time, having left after years of disenchantment and broken promises from the leader. They still love their family and want to reconnect but may have a much more difficult time because of the guilt, fear, and sadness that have accumulated over time. The cult had forced them to sever family ties; write "disconnect" letters; and refuse presents, mail, and phone calls. Over the years changes have occurred in the family; parents have died, moved, or have been hurt so deeply that they avoid the cultist. Siblings may be especially angry at the cultist for hurting the family so much.

Families of long-term cult members also seek family therapy from a cult-knowledgeable family therapist in order to reintegrate an ex-cultist who continues to disconnect from the family or to work with another family member who refuses to accept the ex-cultist back into the family. Family therapists who are knowledgeable about cults have many skills to contribute in working with separated and polarized families during these difficult times.

## CONCLUSIONS

Working with ex-members of cults and their families can be rewarding and challenging. Families may reintegrate, and productive and satisfying lives may be restored. The therapist has the opportunity to utilize knowledge about social influence, group interaction, dissociative reactions, functionally impaired cognitive processes, and relaxation-induced anxiety, as well as learn about the social rules and practices of particular cults. This information can be useful with families dealing with other coercive processes, such as family violence. (See chap. 28 in this volume.)

If the destructive experience of cult involvement is to be prevented, families, therapists, and educators must come to understand the remarkable social and psychological influences used by cult leaders. Armed with this information, they can help prepare individuals and families to cope with cults. There needs to be further study of the coordinated programs of coercive influence and behavior control that cult leaders can wield over followers and the consequent impact on families.

## REFERENCES

Andres, R., & Lane, J. R. (1988). *Cults and consequences.* Los Angeles: Jewish Federation Council of Greater Los Angeles.

Ash, S. M. (1985). Cult-induced psychopathology, Part I: Clinical picture. *Cultic Studies Journal, 2,* 31–90.

Clark, J. G. (1979). Cults. *Journal of the American Medical Association, 242,* 179–181.

Enroth, R. M. (1992). *Churches that abuse.* Grand Rapids, MI: Zondervan.

Experts say education best way to limit cult influence. (1981, May 1). *Citizens Freedom Foundation News,* pp. 3–4.

Galanter, M. (1983). Unification Church ("Moonie") dropouts: Psychological adjustment after leaving a charismatic religious group. *American Journal of Psychiatry, 140,* 984–989.

Giambalvo, C. (1992). *Exit counseling: A family intervention.* Bonita Springs, FL: American Family Foundation.

Goldberg, L., & Goldberg, W. (1988). Psychotherapy with excultists: Four case studies and commentary. *Cultic Studies Journal, 5,* 193–210.

Greene, F. (1989). Litigating child custody with religious cults. *Cultic Studies Journal, 6,* 69–75.

Halperin, D. (1989). Families of cult members: Consultation and treatment. In M. Galanter (Ed.), *Cults and new religious movements* (pp. 109–126). Washington, DC: American Psychiatric Press.

Hassan, S. (1988). *Combatting cult mind control.* Rochester, VT: Park Street Press.

Hochman, J. (1984). Iatrogenic symptoms associated with a therapy cult: Examination of an extinct "new psychotherapy" with respect to psychiatric deterioration and "brainwashing." *Psychiatry, 47,* 366–377.

Hyde, M. O. (1977). *Brainwashing and other forms of mind control.* New York: McGraw-Hill.

Kandel, R. F. (1988). Litigating the cult-related child custody case. *Cultic Studies Journal, 5,* 122–131.

Keiser, T. W., & Keiser, J. L. (1987). *The anatomy of illusion.* Springfield, IL: Charles C Thomas.

Landa, S. (1989). Hidden terror: Child abuse in religious sects and cults. *Justice for Children, 1,* 2.

Landa. S. (1991). Children and cults: A practical guide. *Journal of Family Law, 29*(3), 591–634.

Levine, S. V. (1984). *Radical departures.* New York: Harcourt Brace Jovanovich.

Levine, S. V. (1989). Life in the cults. In M. Galanter, (Ed.), *Cults and new religious movements.* Washington, DC: American Psychiatric Press.

Lifton, R. J. (1961). *Thought reform and the psychology of totalism: A study of "brainwashing" in China.* New York: Norton.

Lifton, R. J. (1987). Cults: Religious totalism and civil liberties. In R. J. Lifton, *The future of immortality.* New York: Basic Books.

Lifton, R. J. (1989). *Thought reform and the psychology of totalism: A study of "brainwashing" in China* (Rev. ed.). Chapel Hill: University of North Carolina Press.

Markowitz, A., & Halperin, D. A. (1984). Cults and children: The abuse of the young. *Cultic Studies Journal, 1,* 143–155.

Maron, N. (1988). Family environment as a factor in vulnerability to cult involvement. *Cultic Studies Journal, 5*(1), 23–43.

Martin, P. R., Langone, M. D., Dole, A. A., & Wiltrout, J. (1992). An analysis of tests and interview data as measured by the MCMI before and after residential treatment. *Cultic Studies Journal, 9*(2), 219–250.

McManus, U., & Cooper, J. C. (1976). *Not for a million dollars.* Nashville, TN: Impact Books.

Ofshe, R. (1992). Coercive persuasion and attitude change. In E. F. Borgatta & M. L. Borgatta (Eds.), *Encyclopedia of sociology* (Vol. 1, pp. 212–224). New York: Macmillan.

Ofshe, R., & Singer, M. T. (1986). Attacks on peripheral versus central elements of self and the impact of thought reforming techniques: Review and analysis. *Cultic Studies Journal, 3,* 3–24.

Rudin, M. (1984). Women, elderly, and children in religious cults. *Cultic Studies Journal, 1,* 8–26.

Schein, E. H. (1961). *Coercive persuasion.* New York: Norton.

Singer, M. T. (1979a). Coming out of the cults. *Psychology Today, 12,* 72–82.

Singer, M. T. (1979b, May). Topics on target: Cults. *Forecast: Scholastic Magazine, 37.*

Singer, M. T. (1986). Consultation with families of cultists. In L. C. Wynne, S. H. McDaniel, & T. T. Weber (Eds.), *Systems consultation: A new persepective for family therapy* (pp. 270–283). New York: Guilford Press.

Singer, M. T. (1987). Group psychodynamics. In R. Berkow (Ed.), *The Merck manual* (15th ed., pp. 1467–1471). Rahway, NJ: Merck Sharp and Dohme Research Laboratories.

Singer, M. T., & Addis, M. E. (1992). Cults, coercion and contumely. In A. Kales, C. M. Pierce, & M. Greenblatt (Eds.), *The mosaic of contemporary psychiatry in perspective* (pp. 130–142). Zurich: Springer-Verlag.

Singer, M. T., Langone, M., & Temerlin, M. (1991). Psychotherapy cults. *Cultic Studies Journal, 7,* 101–125.

Singer, M. T., & Ofshe, R. (1990). Thought reform programs and the production of psychiatric casualties. *Psychiatric Annals, 20,* 188–193.

Sirkin, M. I., & Grellong, B. A. (1988). Cult vs. non-cult Jewish families: Factors influencing cult involvement. *Cultic Studies Journal, 5*(1), 2–22.

Swartling, G., & Swartling, P. G. (1992). Psychiatric problems in ex-members of Word of Life. *Cultic Studies Journal, 9,* 1–12.

Verdier, P. A. (1977). *Brainwashing and the cults.* Los Angeles: Wilshire Publishers.

West, L. J. (1989). Persuasive techniques in contemporary cults: A public health approach. In M. Galanter (Ed.), *Cults and new religious movements* (pp. 165–192). Washington, DC: American Psychiatric Press.

West, L. J., & Langone, M. D. (1986). Cultism: A conference for scholars and policy makers. *Cultic Studies Journal, 3,* 117–134.

Winn, D. (1983). *The manipulated mind: Brainwashing, conditioning and indoctrination.* London: Octagon Press.

Wooden, K. (1981). *The children of Jonestown.* New York: McGraw-Hill.

Zimbardo, P. G. (1984). Mind control: Political fiction and psychological reality. In P. Stansky (Ed.), *On nineteen eighty-four* (pp. 197–215). New York: Freeman Press.

# CHAPTER 30

# FAMILY TREATMENT OF ALCOHOL AND DRUG ABUSE

*M. Duncan Stanton and Anthony W. Heath*

When alcohol or drugs are abused, every member of the family suffers. Parents wait up nights, hoping that their abusing children will come home alive. They feel helpless, agonize in guilt, and beg for guidance. Spouses try to hide evidence of advancing drinking problems from their family, friends, neighbors, and employers as they struggle to maintain their illusions that the drinking is temporary. Children of alcoholics are consumed by the idea that they are to blame—feeling burdened with adult responsibilities at startlingly young ages, as they plead with their parents to come home without stopping to drink en route. Grown children of alcoholics may find themselves haunted by their past, despairing in relationships that inflict too much pain. Clearly, substance abuse affects every member of the family—for years, for decades, and perhaps, for generations.

For example, Rachel, 36 years old, walked into a therapist's office and complained of incapacitating anxiety. She could not understand this problem, she said. In the course of taking a family history, the therapist learned that Rachel's father had been an alcoholic until his death and that her brother still drank heavily. Rachel's mother had started drinking when Rachel's father died, and she often beat Rachel when she was a child. Rachel's son, age 17, had recently come home drunk. Her husband drank and used marijuana.

Rachel and her husband had sexual problems stemming, she believed, from the fact that she had been repeatedly raped as a child by her drunken father. Rachel and her husband did not talk about their problems. "I am afraid he'll get angry with me," she added.

Family therapy offers Rachel, her family, and others like them an opportunity to resolve the myriad of problems that plague the families of substance abusers. Family therapists believe that family treatment can help when any man, woman, or child has a complaint concerning alcohol or drug abuse, whether the individual is the abuser or the "abused." Family therapists serve many clients who present themselves for other reasons but also have concerns about substance abuse in their families, as well as "codependency" and physical or sexual abuse.

In this chapter, we will review the contributions made by family therapists to the treatment of families with alcohol and other drug abuse problems. We will begin with a brief examination of some of the many patterns that unite these families, and then turn to an exploration of the challenging process of family therapy conducted with families with drug and alcohol abuse. The chapter concludes with a discussion of issues that concern family therapists when they work with substance abusers and their families, plus a brief review of recent outcome studies on the ef-

This chapter is an expanded version of material that is covered in the chapter "Family Therapy" by A. W. Heath and M. D. Stanton in R. J. Frances and S. I. Miller (Eds.), *Clinical Textbook of Addictive Disorders* (pp. 406–430), 1991, New York: Guilford. Adapted with permission of the publisher.

fectiveness of family intervention with this
population.

## FAMILY PATTERNS IN ADDICTION

The importance of the family in the development,
maintenance, and alleviation of alcohol and other
drug abuse is well known. It is widely accepted that
addiction generally develops within a family context,
frequently reflects and promotes other family difficulties, and is usually maintained and exacerbated by
family interactive processes. Although genetic and
other biological components are important in the etiology of many alcohol and drug abuse cases, and
many other factors can also be critical (e.g., environmental, economic, and cultural), family variables
have achieved a position of salience in the conceptualization and treatment of addiction.

Twenty-six of 28 reports on family contacts of
drug abusers attest to the fact that they are commonly in close touch with their families of origin or
the people that raised them (Cervantes, Sorensen,
Wermuth, Fernandez, & Menicucci, 1988; Stanton,
1982, in press). This pattern extends to adult alcoholics, as many male alcoholics are in surprisingly
regular contact with a parent—usually the mother.
Clearly, these data suggest that addicted people are
often important in their families and that their families are important to them.

A number of additional characteristics distinguish
substance-abusing families from other seriously dysfunctional families (Stanton, Todd, & Associates,
1982). In brief, substance-abusing families exhibit:

- Higher frequency of multigenerational chemical
  dependency, particularly alcohol, plus a propen-
  sity for other addictive behaviors such as gam-
  bling. Such practices model behavior for children
  and can develop into family traditions.
- "Symbiotic" relationships are often observed between male addicts and their mothers, often lasting well into the addicts' adulthood
- More overt alliances, for example, between the
  addict and an overinvolved parent

- Parental behavior that does not mimic schizophrenia
- More primitive and direct expression of conflict
  in addictive families
- Drug-oriented peer group to which the addict re-
  treats following family conflict. This peer group
  gives the addict an illusion of independence.
- Preponderance of death themes and premature,
  unexpected, and untimely deaths in the addict's
  family
- "Pseudoindividuation" of the addict across several
  levels, from the individual–pharmacological level
  to that of the drug subculture[1]
- Frequent acculturation problems and parent–child
  cultural disparity within families of addicts

## CLINICAL INTERVENTION IN FAMILY THERAPY: PRELIMINARY CONSIDERATIONS

In this section, we will provide an overview of the
family therapy process with alcohol and other drug
abusers and their families.

Family therapists recognize that substance abusers
are not the family members most likely to seek the
services of a therapist. In fact, the most characteristic
feature of substance abuse may be the abuser's denial
that the use of the substance is a problem at all.
Similarly, it is almost universally accepted that substance abuse is often overlooked by family members;
it may even be overtly or covertly encouraged. Recognizing this fact, responsible family therapists offer
their services to *anyone* who wants to discuss the
substance abuse. Like Al-Anon and related self-help
programs, family therapists generally hold that every
family member can be helped to survive the abuse,
whether the substance abuser stops drinking or
"drugging" or not.

We believe that family therapy is appropriate and
helpful throughout the process of recovery: when the
problem is initially identified by a family member or
a therapist; when the family is mustering its forces to
convince the abuser of the extent of the problem and
the need for change; during any residential treatment

---

[1] This refers to the process whereby the chemical allows a compromise between being individuated (independent, responsible, competent) and
nonindividuated (dependent, infantile, incompetent).

for the substance abuse; and while the family learns new ways to go on in life without chemicals.

Indeed, we believe that a lack of some form of family-oriented services in substance abuse treatment may have calamitous consequences. According to Liepman, White, and Nirenberg (1986), "Without family therapy, most families would suffer serious 'side effects' if the alcoholic were to stop drinking" (p. 53). Without concurrent treatment for nonabusing members, families have been known to attempt to sabotage treatment efforts when those efforts begin to succeed (Stanton, 1979). Examples of this have been commonly reported in the literature; they range from the spouse who gives a bottle of liquor on a holiday to a recovering alcoholic, to the parents who refuse to work together in maintaining rules for their out-of-control adolescent. On the other hand, Steinglass, Bennett, Wolin, & Reiss (1987) have asserted, at least regarding alcohol treatment, that the evidence is compelling that "involvement of a nonalcoholic spouse in a treatment program significantly improves the likelihood that the alcoholic individual will participate in treatment as well" (pp. 331–332).

Families often have additional problems after residential treatment is completed if they have been left out of the treatment process. Sobriety for an individual can have difficult consequences for other family members, who may gain sudden awareness of their own problems or of other problems in their families. Divorce can be a consequence when adult substance abusers "dry out" or "clean up" (Stanton, 1985). Clearly, the family is crucial in determining whether someone remains addicted, and the social context of the abuser must be changed for the substance abuser's treatment to "take hold." Thus, responsibility is shared by both the abuser and the family members.

Families also can provide a significant positive influence in recovery. In a fascinating observational account of substance abuse among his contemporaries, Auerswald (1980) observed that significant improvements in substance abusers' interpersonal lives often led to a reduction—without professional intervention—in their use of intoxicants. Eldred and Washington (1976) found that heroin addicts rated their families of origin or their in-laws as most likely to be helpful to them in their attempts to give up drugs; their second choice was their opposite-sex partner.

Similarly, Levy (1972) found that in a 5-year follow-up of narcotics addicts, patients who successfully overcame drug abuse most often had family support. Family therapists enlist the inherent leverage offered by loving family members.

Family therapists, like other treatment professionals who have worked with substance-abusing families, know the difficulty involved in treating substance abuse. Only by collaborating with extended families, self-help programs, specialists in the field of chemical dependency, and physicians monitoring pharmacotherapy can substance abuse be controlled.

For therapy to succeed, professionals simply must work together. For example, we have found it helpful for outpatient family therapists to visit local treatment centers and become acquainted with the staff. This effort eases referrals to residential treatment and subsequent referral for continued therapy upon release. Staff members of Twelve-Step treatment programs often suspect, as do many Alcoholics Anonymous (AA) members, that all therapists harbor hostile and ignorant beliefs about addicts. Although few family therapists believe that attendance at AA, Al-Anon, or other self-help groups is necessary for healthy recovery in every case, many family therapists would agree with Davis (1987):

> As a therapist, I operate according to the same presuppositions that operate in self-help groups: that every patient/client already has the resources or the capacity to develop the resources needed, that experts don't have all the answers, and that we are ultimately responsible for our own behaviors. (pp. 138–139)

Furthermore, in those cases where substance abusers and their families are adamantly opposed to involvement in Twelve-Step groups, family therapy may offer a satisfactory alternative (Heath & Atkinson, 1988).

Many different modalities of family treatment have emerged, including marital therapy; group therapy for parents; concurrent parent and index patient therapy; therapy with individual families, both inpatient and outpatient; sibling-oriented therapy; multiple-family therapy; social network therapy; and family-systems-oriented therapy with one person.

Heath and Atkinson (1988) and Stanton (1988) provide extensive reviews of the full range of theoretical and clinical approaches within family therapy.

## STAGES OF FAMILY THERAPY

In this section, we will describe a selective, integrative model of the stages of family therapy (Heath, Stanton, & Atkinson, 1995) that synthesizes the literature on family therapy with alcoholic adults (e.g., Berenson, 1976a, 1976b, 1979, 1986; Davis, 1987; O'Farrell, 1989; Steinglass et al., 1987) and drug-abusing adolescents and young adults (e.g., Kosten, Jalali, & Kleber, 1982–1983; Piercy & Frankel, 1989; Stanton & Landau-Stanton, 1990; Stanton & Todd, 1992; Stanton et al., 1982), and emphasizes the relatively high degree of consensus among these authors. The literature cited in this discussion of stages offers a rich collection of clear and specific family therapy methods.

### Stage 1: Problem Definition and Contracting

Therapists must first convene enough of the family to gain adequate leverage to initiate change in family interaction. This may involve one, two, or dozens of family members and may even include nonfamily members of the substance abuser's social network. One generally starts by working with the most motivated family member or members, convening other family members when needed (Berenson, 1976a).

Family therapists next attempt to identify and define the problem. When substance abuse is suspected, many begin by asking simple questions, such as "Who drinks?" or "What medications are used in your family?" We ironically refer to these as "loaded" questions and ask them of all our clients as a matter of course. We do work hard, however, to avoid becoming involved in a debate over whether substance abuse is really "addiction" or "alcoholism" (e.g., Davis, 1987). Like Davis, we believe:

> This is not the time to fight over the presence of an "ism." It is enough to establish that there is a serious problem that needs treatment. The drinker and family members can make up their own minds after some success with AA and family therapy

> as to whether they have been dealing with alcoholism. (1987, p. 53)

Once the problem is defined, the therapist and family identify and prioritize their goals for treatment, starting with the primary goal of helping the substance abuser become "clean" or "sober" and directly relating each subsequent goal to this primary one. When family members bring up additional issues, the therapist may ask the family to justify them as relevant to the main goal of sobriety (Stanton & Todd, 1979).

Some other principles we find helpful are:

- **Establish alliances with senior family members.** In the case of an adolescent or very young adult, especially, treatment is unlikely to succeed or hold up unless parental figures and even grandparents are involved (Piercy & Frankel, 1989; Stanton et al., 1982).

- **Assume a nonblaming stance toward the entire family** (Stanton & Todd, 1992). Indeed, this tack should usually be taken even further, so as to "ascribe noble intentions" to family members' actions, such as pointing out how even misdirected "enabling" can come from a loving heart (Stanton & Todd, 1979).

- **The substance abuse should be labeled a *family* problem.** According to Steinglass et al. (1987), the therapist must, in the first session, "get across to the family that there is no issue more important at this stage of the work than the cessation of drinking, and that the family and the therapist must mobilize all resources toward that goal and that goal alone." (p. 354).

- **Use of a genetic, disease interpretation of addiction helps to reduce guilt, blame, and shame.** This explanation should, of course, be respected as such and not allowed—due to the immutability of genes—to immobilize the therapist and family. Instead, all participants need to understand that, through working together, the disease's symptoms can be overcome and that the ostensible "destiny" can be reversed so that people can lead chemical-free lives.

There are, of course, clients who reject the genetic and disease explanations for addiction. Indeed, there is no genetic evidence in the majority of alcoholics (Searles, 1991). But genetics or no genetics, addicted people can learn to live responsibly. They, too, can work together with their families to overcome their problems.

## Stage 2: Establishing the Context for a Chemical-Free Life

After substance abuse is defined as a problem, and a therapeutic contract is negotiated, family therapy enters a second stage in which a context for sobriety is established. Berenson (1976b) has stated that this stage involves "management of an ongoing, serious drinking problem and setting up a context so that the alcoholic will stop drinking" (p. 33).

Most family therapists consider the cessation of substance abuse to be a prerequisite for further treatment (e.g., Bepko & Krestan, 1985). Furthermore, many believe that therapists must consistently insist on abstinence over the course of therapy (e.g., Davis, 1987). In the words of Steinglass et al. (1987),

> *Meaningful therapy with an Alcoholic Family cannot proceed if the therapist adopts a laissez-faire attitude about drinking behavior and acquiesces in a decision to allow the identified alcoholic to continue drinking. The therapist must take a firm stand on this issue at the start of therapy, while at the same time acknowledging that it may not be an easy task and that there may be a number of slips before abstinence is achieved. (p. 343)*

In addition, some other principles for this stage are:

- **Refer family members to Twelve-Step programs** (e.g., Al-Anon, Nar-Anon, Cocaine Anonymous), and related self-help programs (Bepko & Krestan, 1985; Christopher, 1988; Davis, 1987).
- **With couples, use spouse support groups whenever possible** (Berenson, as cited in Stanton, 1981a).
- **Have no expectation that the change will occur.** The therapist must remain more "hopeless" than hopeful. This protects the therapist from pursuing family members unnecessarily and also

protects her or him from becoming too deeply inducted into the system (Berenson, 1976a).

- **Be prepared to deal with issues of unexpected deaths and unresolved losses at this stage** (Coleman, Kaplan, & Downing, 1986; Heard, 1982; Reilly, 1976; Rosenbaum & Richman, 1972; Stanton, 1977). If ignored, such issues can erode gains made with the presenting problem.

## Stage 3: Ceasing Substance Abuse

In the family therapy of alcohol and other drug abuse, there always comes a moment of truth. As a result of the changes in their family members' behavior and the firm position of the therapist, the abusers suddenly realize that they are going to have to choose between their families and their drugs. When consistently confronted (or abandoned) by parents, spouses, children, friends, employers, and perhaps even by recovering people in self-help groups or a therapist, substance abusers often "hit bottom." Sometimes they turn to the therapist for help in changing their lives.

There are basically three possible ways for therapists to proceed (Steinglass et al., 1987):

- **Arrange inpatient detoxification for the addicted substance abuser if this is indicated.** A therapist who knows there to be physical dependence on alcohol or drugs should refuse to continue therapy unless this option is selected, because without medical intervention, the addict's independent withdrawal is unlikely, if not dangerous.
- **Agree to let the family attempt detoxification with the abuser on an outpatient basis.** Proceed on the condition that if there has been no meaningful progress made toward detoxification within 2 weeks, then inpatient treatment will be pursued.
- **Allow outpatient recovery using the family as the "treatment team,"** if the physical complications from withdrawal are minimal or well controlled. This approach, labeled "home detoxification," had been developed by Scott and Van Deusen (1982) and Stanton and Todd (1982). It entails setting up a round-the-clock monitoring or "watch" schedule—involving as many adult family

members as possible—accompanied by therapeutic backup. Considerable effort is devoted ahead of time to anticipating slip-ups. A contract is also commonly negotiated to reiterate the process a second time, should the first attempt fail. Overall, the approach appears to be quite cost-effective (Stanton, Steier, Cook, & Todd, 1984).

Whichever course of action is selected, it is essential to keep all family members involved in the change process so that later they can accept some responsibility for the success of the treatment (Stanton, 1981b; Stanton & Todd, 1979). When treatment gets left to the "professionals," family members often fail to realize their responsibility for change. Then later, should the recovery process go awry, they may blame the setback on the treatment program. However, as noted earlier, blaming the family in such instances is rarely effective and usually results in their defecting from treatment.

## Stage 4: Managing the Crisis and Stabilizing the Family

Once the substance abuser becomes "clean and sober," family therapists are prepared for a new set of problems. Stunned by the unfamiliar behavior of the "new" family member and often terribly frightened, family members have been known to make seemingly irrational statements such as "I liked you better when you were drinking." One client we know actually gave a bottle of bourbon to her recently sober husband for his birthday. The potential for relapse is understandably high in this stage.

Steinglass et al. (1987) have described this phase of treatment as "the emotional desert." Families that have been organized around alcohol, especially over many years, experience a profound sense of emptiness when the drinking stops. These families "have the sensation of having been cut adrift, loosened from their familiar moorings, lost in a desert without any landmarks upon which to focus to regain their bearings" (Steinglass, 1987, p. 344). Instead of experiencing joy over the newfound sobriety, the family members feel empty and depressed. Thus the members of a family with a newly sober member tend to interact in more or less the same way that they did while that member was abusing drugs or alcohol.

Family therapists disagree over how quickly to move to resolve family problems in this stage. Berenson has suggested that it is usually advisable to begin this stage with a hiatus from therapy while things calm down, and thus he does not schedule regular appointments, but tells clients, 'Get back to me in a month or so' (Stanton, 1981a). Instead, he encourages his clients to continue their AA or Al-Anon activities, with the understanding that if this state of distress continues beyond 6 to 12 months, family therapy will resume on a more regular basis. After a period of sobriety, Berenson returns to a more orthodox therapy schedule. Others (e.g., Bepko & Krestan, 1985; Steinglass et al., 1987) believe that regularly scheduled family therapy sessions can be very helpful at these times, especially if they focus on solving the series of problems that hound the families and wear them down.

When a relapse into drinking or drug taking occurs, this question arises: "Who is responsible for the relapse?" Although conventional drug treatment programs and many therapists either thrust the responsibility on the substance abuser or accept it themselves, family therapists extend the responsibility to include the family. Stanton and Todd (1979) note that the addicted individual was raised by, and in most cases is still being maintained by, his or her family of origin. Thus the family shares the responsibility, and the therapist should help the family either to accept it or to *effectively* disengage from the addict so that he or she must accept it on his or her own.

## Stage 5: Family Reorganization and Recovery

Although some families restabilize before reaching this phase and remain organized around alcohol or drug issues (e.g., "dry alcoholic" families), for others, the previous stages of therapy culminate in a serious family crisis. This crisis then leads to disorganization and ultimately to a fundamentally different organizational pattern, which develops, albeit slowly, in Stage 5 of therapy.

In this stage, family therapists are concerned with helping families move away from interaction focused on substance abuse issues toward fundamentally better relationships. At this point, the substance abuser is stabilized and "clean and sober." The therapy now focuses on developing a better marriage, establishing more satisfactory parent–child relationships, and perhaps confronting long-standing family of origin and codependence issues. Steinglass et al. (1987) have called this process "family reorganization" (p. 344).

Bepko and Krestan (1985) have enumerated the following goals for their analogue for this stage, which they have termed "rebalancing" (pp. 135–136):

- **Shift extremes of reciprocal role behavior** from rigid complementarity to greater symmetry or more flexible complementarity.
- **Help the couple/family resolve issues of power and control.**
- **Directly address the pride structures of both partners** so that new forms of role behavior are permitted without the need for alcohol.
- **Help the couple achieve whatever level of closeness and intimacy is desirable for them.**

With young addicts, this stage of the therapy evolves beyond crisis management toward other issues, such as finding gainful employment and a place to live away from home (Stanton & Todd, 1979). Parents are often involved in these "launchings" so that they can feel part of the addict's eventual success. Over time, it becomes increasingly possible to shift the parents' attention to other siblings, grandchildren, or retirement planning, thereby allowing both the parents and the recovering addict to let go. When marital issues surface, as they often do, family therapists work to prevent addicts from getting involved in their parents' marriages.

## Stage 6: Ending Therapy

Ideally, treatment comes to an end when clients and therapist(s) mutually agree to stop meeting regularly (see chap. 4 in this volume). Family therapists agree to stop when they believe that serious structural and functional problems that have maintained substance abuse have been replaced with new family rules, roles, and interactional patterns. Optimally, substance abuse has not been replaced with other addictive behaviors; however, sometimes socially acceptable "addictions," (e.g., "workaholism") are tolerated by family therapists when they are tolerated by family members.

Therapy's length and the specific definition of successful treatment vary widely among models of therapy and among individual families. Stanton and Todd (1979), in describing their brief therapy model for treating drug addicts, have broadly stated that therapy is appropriately concluded when "adequate change has occurred and been maintained long enough for the family to feel a sense of real accomplishment" (p. 64). Adherents of other models would not attempt to reorganize family structure in the ways prescribed in our Stage 5. Instead, they may be content to conclude treatment when family members feel satisfied that their problems have been resolved (e.g., Heath, 1985; Heath & Ayers, 1991).

Therapy need not be thought of as an event or as a process with a distinct end point. In fact, clients often seek subsequent counsel from the same therapist on new, unrelated issues.

The six-stage model presented here is intentionally inclusive. We have made no effort to resolve differences among the models of family therapy or to examine the differences between treating alcohol or other drug abusers. Instead, we have sketched a viable course of treatment for the family with a substance-abusing member. Clinicians may wish to emphasize some stages of therapy more than others, depending on their preferred models of treatment.

## SPECIAL ISSUES IN FAMILY INTERVENTION WITH ALCOHOL AND OTHER DRUG ABUSE

Family therapists face a number of unique clinical issues when they work with substance abusers and their families. A discussion of several of the more salient issues follows.

## Convening Difficulties

Many therapists find it difficult to convene the whole family for therapy (Stanton, in press; Stanton & Todd, 1981). The families of addicts are particularly difficult to engage in treatment. Fathers of substance-abusing young people, in particular, often appear threatened by treatment and defensive about their contributions to the problem. Because many have drinking problems themselves, they may also fear being blamed for the problem or that their own addiction will be challenged.

Recognizing hesitancy to participate in therapy, family therapists reach out to recruit families into therapy. They do not ask other family members to do the recruiting, since this approach often fails. Instead, they extend personal invitations to the reluctant members. In less seriously disturbed families, one telephone call may enable a therapist to reassure family members that their contributions are important to the solution of the substance abuse. In more disturbed families, it may be necessary to meet family members on "neutral turf," like a restaurant, to write multiple letters, or even to pay family members for participation in treatment (Stanton & Todd, 1981).

## Management of Cases

To shift the responsibility for dealing with the substance abuser's problems to the family, a family therapist must have control of the case. Family therapists therefore wish to direct the overall case management, including the treatment plan, the use of medication and drug tests, and decisions about hospitalization. The family therapist being the primary therapist also helps to keep substance abusers from manipulating the relationships among a number of therapists.

Stanton et al. (1982) have estimated that approximately 50% of the effectiveness of treatment of drug addicts and their families depends on the efficiency and cohesiveness of the therapeutic system. If family members receive different advice from different professionals, they often end up arguing about the therapy rather than working toward recovery. Cohesion in the treatment system of substance abusers necessarily includes self-help programs used by their families. It is vital for therapists to know the local self-help groups and to work with them for the sake of their clients.

## Medication and Management

Therapists who work with substance abusers and their families must have at least a basic knowledge of psychopharmacology and the effects of illegal and misused prescription drugs. This information aids them during the detoxification process and reduces the tendency toward overcautiousness that sometimes occurs when a therapist is ignorant of drug effects.

In regard to the use of prescription drugs, it is vital that physicians, family therapists, and substance abuse counselors form a collaborative treatment team. Cooperation and open lines of communication are necessary to counteract the manipulative behaviors of many substance abusers. As a part of the team, the family therapist and physician can serve as allies in encouraging family compliance with prescribed medication and can provide each other with information on patient and family functioning (Woody, Carr, Stanton, & Hargrove, 1982).

Family therapists must have influence over the use of methadone in drug treatment. Families tend to believe that their recovering addicts are inherently helpless, fragile, handicapped people, and thus they forgive the most outrageous behavior. If family therapists argue that addicts can be competent and can function adequately without drugs, then they must assert that they are concerned with the addicts' detoxifying and getting off *all* drugs, including the opioid methadone. To encourage the cessation of methadone use, therapists and the family members must have significant input into how it is dispensed (Stanton & Todd, 1982; Woody et al., 1982).

## Involving Parents in Decisions

Parents must be involved in all decisions about treatment when a substance abuser is an adolescent or a young adult. Thus, parents should be involved in decisions about hospitalization, medication, and drug tests. A family therapist will go to some trouble to make the parents part of the treatment team, because it helps to get the couple working together and because a major part of the responsibility for the resolution of the problem is correctly theirs. When the parents of a young abuser are divorced or unmarried, the same holds true; adult caretakers must be encouraged to work together to help their children.

## Codependence

*Codependence* is a word that is often (and loosely) used to describe the process underlying many problems in the families of substance abusers. There is little consensus over how the term should be defined, but according to Schaef (1986), one of the chemical dependency field's most respected authors, codependence is a disease that parallels the alcoholic disease process and has specific and characteristic symptoms (e.g., external referencing, caretaking, self-centeredness, control issues, dishonesty, frozen feelings, perfectionism, and fear; Schaef, 1986). Codependence has generally replaced the concept of "enabling" and focused attention on the suffering of those who live with, or have lived with, a chemically dependent person.

Family therapists have learned a great deal about addiction and addiction treatment from Schaef (1986), Beattie (1987), and Wegscheider (1981), who have bridged the fields of family therapy and chemical dependency counseling. They have learned, for example, to address the individual fears and difficulties of the parents, spouses, children, and grown children of alcoholics. They have learned to recommend self-help groups and books on codependence for codependents. They have also learned to recognize addictive processes at work in families when individuals express any of the hallmark symptoms of codependence. They already know that the pain of addiction affects everyone in and around these families, often for generations.

We are cautious in the use of the term *codependence* because it has been disproportionately and pejoratively applied to women in our society. Clearly caretaking, supporting, and selflessness—often considered feminine characteristics or responsibilities—can be admirable and socially necessary. The word *codependence* must be applied to both sexes, linked to the underfunctioning that may describe other family members' behavior, and reserved for extreme and clearly harmful situations.

## Treatment Delivery Systems

A systemic view of alcohol and other drug abuse is often discordant with the traditional ways in which treatment has been administered. For example, a major residential treatment center for adolescent substance abusers in the Midwest offers two family sessions during a typical 28-day program, an intake staffing and a discharge staffing, both of which are informational in nature. The optional multiple-family group, which is attended by a minority of the parents of the center's patients, is used as a forum for psychoeducation on addiction and codependence. When the center's administrator was asked why the

center did not offer more family therapy, he said that many insurance companies did not consider it a part of necessary medical care and would therefore not pay for it.

At this writing, many insurance companies will not pay for outpatient family therapy when substance abuse is diagnosed. Instead, short-term, though more expensive, inpatient medical treatment services or intensive outpatient services provided by a state-licensed psychiatrist or psychologist are reimbursed. These reimbursement policies are already undergoing radical change in the United States, given government's and industry's commitment to reducing the cost of health care. Many major insurance companies now limit hospital stays for substance abusers to 14 days. There is a growing body of knowledge suggesting that there is no overall advantage for long-term, intensive, residential services for alcohol abuse (Miller & Hester, 1986). Clearly, the change has begun.

According to the 1989 accreditation standards of the Joint Commission on Accreditation for Healthcare Organizations, residential treatment programs for alcoholism and other drug dependencies must involve family members in the treatment process. This development is being echoed in the growing health care management industry, which is increasingly registering family therapists on its lists of reimbursable providers. In the difficult realm of substance abuse treatment, it seems both hopeful and logical to expect that eventually the entire treatment system will work to facilitate family treatment in every way possible, especially if family therapy proves cost-effective by shortening inpatient stays and reducing repeat admissions. However, it is important to acknowledge that family treatment for substance abuse remains at the mercy of the political system, which controls reimbursement policies.

## Confidentiality

When alcohol and other drug abuse, especially of the chronic variety, is seen as a family phenomenon, many of the existent regulations concerning confidentiality do not make much sense. Although there may be exceptions, such as in emergencies, some of the standing regulations on confidentiality may serve to perpetuate the problem. Shielding a person's drug or alcohol problem from his or her family may even be an exercise in self-delusion—the family members often already know about it—but at the very least, it results in "buying into" the family's denial. Thus, confidentiality provisions in law and ethical standards can give license to denial by sanctioning the identified patient as the problem and denying the importance of the family. For these reasons, we believe there is a need to change legal and ethical standards in order to distinguish between confidentiality within the family and confidentiality between the family and others, at least when there is evidence of substance abuse.

## Therapist Support

Family therapy with substance-abusing families can be grueling work. Therapists find it to be draining and occasionally find that the programs in which they work take on the characteristics of addictive family systems (e.g., "cross-generational" alliances, denial of problems, secrets, "wet" and "dry" behaviors). It is therefore vitally important, for the sake of therapists and clients alike, to establish and maintain healthy administrative policies and procedures that support frontline therapists.

The policies should include protection from unmanageable caseloads. In addition, treatment centers should make ample provision for supervision and consultation on all cases. When appropriate, consultants knowledgeable about family therapy and addiction should be retained. Similarly, continuing education should be made available in order to allow therapists to continue their learning while having time away from providing services. This process is essential in maintaining one's balance. (See chap. 33 in this volume.)

## RESEARCH AND EVALUATION

Research in the area of addiction treatment suffers from the usual difficulties of social science outcome research. It is hard to design, expensive to conduct, and sometimes difficult to interpret. Random assignment of subjects to treatment conditions is fraught with a variety of problems. Nevertheless, ever since the National Institute on Alcohol Abuse and Alcoholism recognized family therapy as "one of the outstanding current advances in the area of psycho-

therapy" for alcoholism (Keller, 1974, p. 116), the research has been, by and large, favorable. In this section we will present some of the highlights of this research and outline the recent findings emerging as this is written.

Several reviews have found "overwhelmingly favorable" (Steinglass et al., 1987, p. 331) evidence in support of the use of family therapy methods with alcohol problems (e.g., Janzen, 1977; Kaufman, 1985; O'Farrell, 1989; Steinglass, 1976). Furthermore, studies comparing the effectiveness of family and nonfamily treatments for alcoholism lend support to the argument that family therapy is more effective than nonfamily methods. The most current review of this research (O'Farrell, 1989) concluded that family treatment produces better marital and drinking outcomes than nonfamily methods.

Recently, Stanton and Shadish have reviewed the controlled studies of family treatment for drug abuse (Stanton, 1991; Stanton & Shadish, 1995). Fourteen studies were located that used random assignment to two or more treatment conditions; this was a fourfold increase in the number of such controlled studies since Kaufman's (1985) and Stanton's (1979) earlier reviews. In general, the quality of the studies was judged to be quite high, as determined by Gurman & Kniskern's (1978) 14-variable rating system of design quality.

Four of the studies were comparisons of two family-oriented treatments, rather than contrasts between family and nonfamily modes. Family therapy showed superiority to family psychoeducation in two of three studies, being equivalent in the third (Bernal et al., 1994), along with equal effectiveness compared to groups for relatives. In the fourth study, "one-person" family therapy was slightly more effective than conjoint family therapy, although it also required significantly more sessions (Szapocznik, Kurtines, Foote, Perez-Vidal, & Hervis, 1983, 1986).

Of the 10 studies that compared family therapy with nonfamily modalities—such as individual therapy or counseling and peer group therapy—eight showed superior results for family therapy. The remaining two yielded equal results for family therapy versus individual therapy or counseling, although in both of them, family treatment possessed advantages in terms of cost-effectiveness. A meta-analysis for family therapy versus these other modalities yielded an effect size of .52, which was significant at the .01 level.

A notable development in this area is the emergence of a number of studies with adolescent drug abusers (Henggeler et al., 1991; Joanning, Thomas, Quinn, & Mullen, 1992; Krinsley & Bry, in press; Lewis, Piercy, Sprinkle, & Trepper, 1990; Liddle et al., 1993; Szapocznik et al., 1983, 1986; Trepper, Piercy, Lewis, Volk, & Sprenkle, 1994). Whereas there does continue to be some activity in the family treatment of adult addicts (e.g., McLellan, Arndt, Metzger, Woody, & O'Brien, 1993), the spotlight has shifted a bit more toward younger patients. However, it should be noted that Stanton and Shadish's (in press) meta-analysis showed the family therapy effect sizes for adult and adolescent drug abusers to be equivalent.

In summary, research is increasingly demonstrating that family methods for substance abuse are both efficacious and cost-effective. The frequency with which they have been adopted (Coleman & Davis, 1978), therefore, seems adequately justified.

## CONCLUSION

Family therapy has established itself as an effective and efficient treatment means of breaking the vicious cycle of addiction in families. The integration of family therapy into the substance abuse treatment community has proven a challenging endeavor. With the notable exception of Alcoholics Anonymous and related groups, the treatment of substance abuse is generally performed in medical or paramedical environments. In such settings, "patients" are "diagnosed" and "treated" (individually and in groups) while their families sit in waiting rooms, waiting for doctors to report on the patients' progress. In this context, the doctors work, the patients receive, and the families spectate. In traditional substance abuse treatment programs, this paradigm prevails.

Family therapy is a more ecological, inclusive process; the therapists work, the substance abuser works, and the family works—together. Everyone is involved in change, and the change affects everyone. Now is the time for mental health and chemical dependency treatment professionals to work together to make family therapy available to families with problems in addiction.

## References

Auerswald, E. (1980). Drug use and families—In the context of twentieth century science. In B. Ellis (Ed.), *Drug abuse from the family perspective: Coping is a family affair* (DHHS Publication No. ADM 80-910, pp. 117–126). Washington, DC: U.S. Government Printing Office.

Beattie, M. (1987). *Codependent no more.* Center City, MN: Hazelden Educational Materials.

Bepko, C., & Krestan, J. (1985). *The responsibility trap.* New York: Free Press.

Berenson, D. (1976a). A family approach to alcoholism. *Psychiatric Opinion, 13,* 33–38.

Berenson, D. (1976b). Alcohol and the family system. In P. Guerin (Ed.), *Family therapy: Theory and practice* (pp. 284–297). New York: Gardner Press.

Berenson, D. (1979). The therapist's relationship with couples with an alcoholic member. In E. Kaufman & P. Kaufmann (Eds.), *The family therapy of drug and alcohol abuse* (pp. 233–242). New York: Gardner Press.

Berenson, D. (1986). The family treatment of alcoholism. *Family Therapy Today, 1,* 1–2, 6–7.

Bernal, G., Flores-Ortiz, Y., Sorensen, I. L., Miranda, J., Diamond, G., Bonilla, J. (1994). *Intergenerational family therapy with methadone maintenance patients: Findings of a clinical outcome study.* Manuscript submitted for publication.

Cervantes, O. F., Sorensen, J. L., Wermuth, L., Fernandez, L. & Menicucci, L. (1988). Family ties of drug abusers. *Psychology of Addictive Behaviors, 2*(1), 34–39.

Christopher, J. (1988). *How to stay sober: Recovery without religion.* Buffalo, NY: Prometheus Books.

Coleman, S., & Davis, D. (1978). Family therapy and drug abuse: A national survey. *Family Process, 17,* 21–29.

Coleman, S., Kaplan, J., & Downing, R. (1986). Life cycle and loss: The spiritual vacuum of heroin addiction. *Family Process, 25*(1), 5–23.

Davis, D. (1987). *Alcoholism treatment: An integrative family and individual approach.* New York: Gardner Press.

Eldred, C., & Washington, M. (1976). Interpersonal relationships in heroin use by men and women and their role in treatment outcome. *International Journal of the Addictions, 11,* 117–130.

Gurman, A. S., & Kniskern, D. P. (1978). Research on marital and family therapy: Progress, perspective and prospect. In S. L. Garfield & A. E. Bergin (Eds.),

*Handbook of psychotherapy and behavior change: An empirical analysis* (2nd ed.; pp. 817–901). New York: Wiley.

Heard, D. (1982). Death as a motivator: Using crisis induction to break through the denial system. In M. D. Stanton, T. C. Todd, & Associates, *The family therapy of drug abuse and addiction* (pp. 203–234). New York: Guilford Press.

Heath, A. (1985). Some new directions in ending family therapy. In D. Breunlin (Ed.), *Stages: Patterns of change over time* (pp. 33–40). Rockville, MD: Aspen Systems.

Heath, A., & Atkinson, B. (1988). Systemic treatment of substance abuse: A graduate course. *Journal of Marital and Family Therapy, 14,* 411–418.

Heath, A., & Ayers, T. (1991). MRI brief therapy with adolescent substance abusers. In T. Todd & M. Seleckman (Eds.), *Family therapy approaches with adolescent substance abusers* (pp. 49–69). Boston: Allyn & Bacon.

Heath, A., Stanton, M. D., & Atkinson, B. (1995). *Stages of family therapy in the treatment of substance abuse: An integrative model.* Manuscript submitted for publication.

Henggeler, S., Borduin, C., Melton, G., Mann, B., Smith, L., Hall, J., Cone, L., & Fucci, B. (1991). Effects of multisystemic therapy on drug use and abuse in serious juvenile offenders: A progress report from two outcome studies. *Family Dynamics of Addiction Quarterly, 1*(3), 40–51.

Janzen, C. (1977). Families in the treatment of alcoholism. *Journal of Studies on Alcohol, 38,* 114–130.

Joanning, H., Thomas, F., Quinn, W., & Mullen, R. (1992). Treating adolescent drug abuse: A comparison of family systems therapy, group therapy, and family drug education. *Journal of Marital and Family Therapy, 18*(4), 345–356.

Kaufman, E. (1985). Family systems and family therapy of substance abuse: An overview of two decades of research and clinical experience. *International Journal of the Addictions, 20,* 897–916.

Keller, M. (1974). Trends in the treatment of alcoholism. In M. Keller (Ed.), *Second special report to the U.S. Congress on alcohol and health* (DHEW Publication No. ADM 75-212; pp. 111–127). Washington, DC: U.S. Government Printing Office.

Kosten, T., Jalali, B., & Kleber, H. (1982–1983). Complementary marital roles of male heroin addicts: Evolution and intervention tactics. *American Journal of Drug and Alcohol Abuse, 9*(2), 155–169.

Krinsley, K. E., & Bry, B. H. (in press). Decreasing school failure and early substance use in high risk adolescents through coordinated behavioral family and school intervention. *Drug and Alcohol Dependence.*

Levy, B. (1972). Five years later: A follow-up of 50 narcotic addicts. *American Journal of Psychiatry, 7,* 102–106.

Lewis, R., Piercy, F., Sprenkle, D., & Trepper, T. (1990). Family-based interventions and community networking for helping drug abusing adolescents: The impact of near and far environments. *Journal of Adolescent Research, 5,* 82–95.

Liddle, H., Dakof, G., Parker, K., Diamond, G., Garcia, R., Barrett, K., & Hurwitz, S. (1993, June). *Effectiveness of family therapy versus multi-family therapy and group therapy: Results of the Adolescents and Families Project—a randomized clinical trial.* Paper presented at the Society of Psychotherapy Research Meeting, Pittsburgh, PA.

Liepman, M., White, W., & Nirenberg, T. (1986). Children of alcoholic families. In D. Lewis & C. Williams (Eds.), *Providing care for children of alcoholics: Clinical and research perspectives* (pp. 39–64). Pompano Beach, FL: Health Communications.

McLellan, A., Arndt, I., Metzger, D., Woody, G., & O'Brien, C. (1993). The effects of psychosocial services in substance abuse treatment. *Journal of the American Medical Association, 269*(15), 1953–1959.

Miller, W. R., & Hester, R. (1986). Inpatient alcoholism treatment: Who benefits? *American Psychologist, 41*(7), 794–805.

O'Farrell, T. (1989). Marital and family therapy in alcoholism treatment. *Journal of Substance Abuse Treatment, 6*(1), 23–29.

Piercy, F., & Frankel, B. (1989). The evolution of an integrative family therapy for substance-abusing adolescents: Toward the mutual enhancement of research and practice. *Journal of Family Psychology, 3,* 5–25.

Reilly, D. (1976). Family factors in the etiology and treatment of youthful drug abuse. *Family Therapy, 2,* 149–171.

Rosenbaum, M., & Richman, J. (1972). Family dynamics and drug overdoses. *Suicide and Life-Threatening Behavior, 2,* 19–25.

Schaef, A. (1986). *Codependence misunderstood/mistreated.* New York: Harper & Row.

Scott, S., & Van Deusen, J. (1982). Detoxification at home: A family approach. In M. D. Stanton, T. C. Todd, & Associates, *The family therapy of drug abuse and addiction* (pp. 310–334). New York: Guilford Press.

Searles, J. (1991). The genetics of alcoholism: Impact on family and sociological models of addiction. *Family Dynamics of Addiction Quarterly, 1,* 8–21.

Stanton, M. D. (1977). The addict as savior: Heroin, death and the family. *Family Process, 16,* 191–197.

Stanton, M. D. (1979). Family treatment approaches to drug abuse problems: A review. *Family Process, 18,* 251–280.

Stanton, M. D. (1981a). Strategic approaches to family therapy. In A. Gurman & D. Kniskern (Eds.), *Handbook of family therapy, Vol. 1* (pp. 361–402). New York: Brunner/Mazel.

Stanton, M. D. (1981b). Who should get credit for change which occurs in therapy? In A. S. Gurman (Ed.), *Questions and answers in the practice of family therapy* (pp. 519–522). New York: Brunner/Mazel.

Stanton, M. D. (1982). Appendix A: Review of reports on drug abusers' family living arrangements and frequency of family contact. In M. D. Stanton, T. C. Todd, & Associates, *The family therapy of drug abuse and addiction.* New York: Guilford Press.

Stanton, M. D. (1985). The family and drug abuse. In T. Bratter & G. Forrest (Eds.), *Alcoholism and substance abuse: Strategies for clinical intervention* (pp. 398–430). New York: Free Press.

Stanton, M. D. (1988). Coursework and self-study in the family treatment of alcohol and drug abuse: Expanding Heath and Atkinson's curriculum. *Journal of Marital and Family Therapy, 14*(4), 419–427.

Stanton, M. D. (1991). Effectiveness of family therapy: Recent outcome studies on family treatment of drug abuse [Summary]. In *conference highlights of the NIDA National Conference on Drug Abuse Research and Practice: An Alliance for the 21st Century* (DHHS Publication No. ADM 91-1818, pp. 31–32). Washington, DC: U.S. Government Printing Office.

Stanton, M. D. (in press). The role of family and significant others in the engagement and retention of drug dependent individuals. In L. S. Onken, J. D. Blaine, & J. J. Boren (Eds.), *Beyond the therapeutic alliance: Engagement and retention of drug abusers* [National Institute on Drug Abuse Research Monograph]. Washington, DC: U.S. Government Printing Office.

Stanton, M. D., & Landau-Stanton, J. (1990). Therapy with families of adolescent substance abusers. In H. Milkman & L. Sederer (Eds.), *Treatment choices in substance abuse* (pp. 329–339). Lexington, MA: Lexington Books.

Stanton, M. D., & Shadish, W. R. (1994). *Outcome for family treatment of drug abuse: A review of the controlled, comparative studies.* Manuscript submitted for publication.

Stanton, M. D., Steier, F., Cook, L., & Todd, T. E. (1984). *Narcotic detoxification in a family and home context: Final report 1980–1983* (Grant No. 5R01 DA 03097). Rockville, MD: National Institute on Drug Abuse, Treatment Research Branch.

Stanton, M. D., & Todd, T. C. (1979). Structural therapy with drug addicts. In E. Kaufman & P. Kaufmann, (Eds.), *Family therapy of drug and alcohol abuse* (pp. 55–69). New York: Gardner Press.

Stanton, M. D., & Todd, T. C. (1981). Engaging resistant families in treatment II: Principles and techniques in recruitment. *Family Process, 20*(3), 261–280.

Stanton, M. D., & Todd, T. C. (1982). The therapy model. In M. D. Stanton, T. C. Todd, & Associates, *The family therapy of drug abuse and addiction* (pp. 109–153). New York: Guilford Press.

Stanton, M. D., & Todd, T. C. (1992). Structural–strategic family therapy with drug addicts. In E. Kaufman & P. Kaufmann (Eds.), *Family therapy of drug and alcohol abuse* (2nd ed., pp. 46–62). Needham Heights, MA: Allyn & Bacon.

Stanton, M. D., Todd, T. C., & Associates. (1982). *The family therapy of drug abuse and addiction.* New York: Guilford Press.

Steinglass, P. (1976). Experimenting with family treatment approaches to alcoholism, 1950–1975: A review. *Family Process, 15,* 97–123.

Steinglass, P., Bennett, L., Wolin, S., & Reiss, D. (1987). *The alcoholic family.* New York: Basic Books.

Szapocznik, J., Kurtines, W., Foote, F., Perez-Vidal, A., & Hervis, O. (1983). Conjoint versus one-person family therapy: Some evidence for the effectiveness of conducting family therapy through one person. *Journal of Consulting and Clinical Psychology, 51*(6), 889–899.

Szapocznik, J., Kurtines, W., Foote, F., Perez-Vidal, A., & Hervis, O. (1986). Conjoint versus one-person family therapy: Further evidence for the effectiveness of conducting family therapy through one person with drug abusing adolescents. *Journal of Consulting and Clinical Psychology, 54*(3), 395–397.

Trepper, T., Piercy, F., Lewis, R., Volk, R. J., & Sprenkle, D. (1994). *Family therapy for drug abusing adolescents: A comparative study.* Manuscript submitted for publication.

Wegscheider, S. (1981). *Another chance: Hope and health for the alcoholic family.* Palo Alto, CA: Science and Behavior Books.

Woody, G., Carr, E., Stanton, M. D., & Hargrove, H. (1982). Program flexibility and support. In M. D. Stanton, T. C. Todd, & Associates, *The family therapy of drug abuse and addiction* (pp. 393–402). New York: Guilford Press.

# PART IX

# THE SELF OF THE SYSTEMS THERAPIST

# Introduction

It is well established that the self of the therapist is a major, if not *the* major factor in change in therapy. Conversely, conducting therapy changes the professional. In this section, we examine three areas in which the self of the systems therapist is tested and evolves: supervision, ethical issues involved in training, and exposure to traumatized families.

In "Family Therapy Supervision: Toward an Integrative Perspective," Douglas Breunlin, Cheryl Rampage, and Marina Eovaldi describe the therapist's career development as a "trajectory that passes through territories representing the many approaches constituting the vast field of psychotherapy." They describe the evolution of systems therapy over time and the convergence of the field into, it is hoped, a final stage of integration. The authors show how divergent theories of change can be bridged by two integrative models: integrative problem centered therapy and metaframeworks perspective. The special tasks of supervisors, which include managing complexity, helping the therapist work with each systems level, and fostering gender and culturally sensitive work with clients can be achieved through an integrative approach to supervision.

Michael Gottlieb, in "Ethical Dilemmas in Change of Format and Live Supervision," addresses two major issues that are particularly pertinent to systems therapy. In the course of treatment, systems therapists are likely to see individuals and subsystems of the family group, creating potential problems with confidentiality, roles, and iatrogenic effects. Live supervision, largely a province of family therapy, also has its own built-in ethical issues, such as professional responsibility, informed consent, and iatrogenic effects. The author provides a framework for the therapist to reduce ethical risks and unintended negative effects.

In an attempt to help family therapists avoid contracting traumatic stress disorders themselves when working with families experiencing traumatic stressors, Charles Figley in his chapter, "Systemic Traumatization: Secondary Traumatic Stress Disorder in Family Therapists," describes a model to understand, prevent, and treat the therapist's reactions. That therapists often experience symptoms similar to posttraumatic stress disorder (PTSD) in working with traumatized families is not widely discussed in the literature, according to Figley, and this lack of awareness may hinder therapists from understanding and taking action to protect themselves. This chapter presents concrete ways that the therapist can help him- or herself, describes how consultation can be of assistance, and urges education and training of family therapists about the secondary effects of client trauma on therapists and how to deal with them.

# CHAPTER 31

# FAMILY THERAPY SUPERVISION: TOWARD AN INTEGRATIVE PERSPECTIVE

*Douglas C. Breunlin, Cheryl Rampage, and Marina L. Eovaldi*

Therapists have unique careers that unfold over time through their work with diverse client systems. Over the life span of these careers, most therapists modify their beliefs about and practice of therapy in response to the demands of client systems, their clinical failures, changing interests, and the evolution of the field of psychotherapy itself. A career, then, is like a trajectory that passes through territories representing the many approaches that constitute the vast field of psychotherapy. The trajectory begins with a launching experience marked by formal training and is followed by a stage of consolidation during which the art and craft of therapy are refined and perfected. A third stage of independent practice involves maturing, development of style, and for some therapists, specialization.

At all points along the trajectory, therapists receive help to facilitate their development. This help can take the form of training, supervision, consultation, or some combination thereof. Training is the broadest form of help that includes protocols to impart the basic requirements for practice. Training always includes a supervisory component. Supervision guides the work of a therapist. It includes both the management of cases and clinician development. Supervisees are usually assigned a supervisor who retains legal culpability for cases. Consultation, on the other hand, is generally elected by experienced therapists. It is voluntary, and the consultant carries no culpability. These distinctions and others are complex and beyond the scope of this chapter. Our intent is to present a model for helping therapists develop and refine an integrative perspective. For conven-

ience, therefore, throughout this chapter we adopt the term *supervision* to refer to this helping process.

Supervision is most intense during the launching stage, when novice therapists learn their craft and rely on supervision to compensate for their lack of experience. New therapists, entering the stage of consolidation, receive supervision to bolster practice and complete credentialing requirements. In the stage of independent practice, therapists seek supervision to address difficult clinical situations and to refine practice needs.

We believe that the trajectories of most therapists eventually pass through the territories of both individual and family therapy. For example, VandenBos, Stapp, and Kilburg (1981) found that fewer than 1% of psychologists had formal training in family therapy, but more than 40% reported working with families and couples. Although the passage through one territory or the other can create strong preferences and loyalties, experienced therapists more often reconcile their beliefs about individual and family therapy and become comfortable practicing both. When most successful, this reconciliation produces therapists who practice an integrative perspective.

We believe that all forms of supervision at all points along a therapist's trajectory should be governed by the spirit of integration. Regrettably, this is often not the case because the field of psychotherapy is still divided into competing territories, with the advocates of each claiming the superiority and universality of their approach. As therapists move from one territory to another, therefore, they accumulate contradictions and confusion, which they must painfully sort out on their own. We believe therapists can be spared this pain if their supervision helps them build bridges between the approaches and points them toward solid integrative practice. This chapter, then, examines the supervision of family therapy from an integrative perspective.

Over the past four decades, the field of family therapy has evolved into a complex network of competing and often contradictory perspectives and models. One might conclude, therefore, that integration of family therapy models is impossible, let alone of family and individual therapy. In the past decade, however, significant trends have blurred the artificial boundaries marking these approaches and made possible a spirit of integration. Still, any therapist seeking family therapy supervision will encounter a myriad of choices. Selecting a family therapy supervisor from this maze is a daunting task. To do so, it is imperative to understand the contemporary scene in family therapy. Although not exhaustive, the following brief description of the context of family therapy is offered to educate therapists seeking supervision and to indicate how an integrative supervisor draws from the rich traditions of family therapy.

## THE CONTEXT OF FAMILY THERAPY

The history of family therapy can be summarized in four stages. The first stage involved the development of two tracks that have been characterized as *pure systems* and *psychoanalytic* (Group for the Advancement of Psychiatry, 1970). As these tracks matured, the second stage involved the delineation of specific models associated with each track. The third stage involved a period of reassessment and consolidation, and the fourth stage, which we believe the field is now entering, involves maturing and integration, affording not only bridges between the two tracks and their models but also between family therapy and other forms of therapy.

## The First Stage: The Evolution of Two Tracks

**The pure systems track.** Like all new therapies, family therapy initially struggled to establish itself. For several decades, the most vocal group of its pioneers championed the pure systems track. The pure

systems track was launched by the seminal publications of the Bateson research project, the writings of Don Jackson (Greenberg, 1977), and the early work of the Mental Research Institute (MRI; Watzlawick & Weakland, 1977). These pioneers purported that family therapy was a new paradigm that would revolutionize therapy and replace the supposedly ineffective therapy practices of the past. Adopting ideas borrowed from systems theory and cybernetics, these pioneers created what might be called an "equilibrium black box" approach to family therapy (Bruenlin, Schwartz, & Karrer, 1992). This approach asserted that problems were located not within the individual but within the family context and served the function of protecting the family's equilibrium (or homeostasis). Evoking cybernetic theory, the approach also asserted that only the system's inputs and outputs, that is, the family's observable interactions, were relevant; consequently, all mental process, including emotions and meaning, could be safely placed within the cybernetic black box and ignored. Family therapy based on this equilibrium black box approach was ahistoric and pragmatic, and geared to disrupt the family homeostasis by changing the action patterns of the family. Because it was a given that the family would resist change, only dramatic methods such as crisis induction and paradoxical interventions would be successful.

**The psychoanalytic track.** Another group of pioneers attempted to extend theories about individual functioning into the realm of the interpersonal. These pioneers also borrowed ideas from systems theory and cybernetics but incorporated them into existing neoanalytic theories such as object relations (Scharff & Scharff, 1987; Slipp 1991), self psychology (Kohut, 1971, 1977), and group analytic (Skynner, 1976). The psychoanalytic track moved beyond classical drive theory and postulated how psychic development involves interpersonal processes. Disturbances in these processes create arrests or fixations in individual development and limit a person's ability to relate interpersonally. For example, individuals may cope with intolerable affective states such as anger or anxiety by recruiting another family member to experience that state for them, using mechanisms such as splitting, projection, and projective identification. The result is detrimental to the individual, who pays a psychic price for disowning the state and for the relationship, which becomes distorted through the experience. Because these mechanisms occur outside of awareness, the psychoanalytic track continued to value unconscious process. Therapy, then, places a premium on internal process, using insight and interpretation to help family members understand how their internal states interfere with healthy relating.

## The Stage of Model Development

As family therapy matured in the decades of the 1960s and 1970s, the two tracks split further into therapy models, each espousing a particular focus. Pure systems models that espoused the equilibrium black box approach included structural family therapy developed by Minuchin and his colleagues (Minuchin, 1974; Minuchin & Fishman, 1981); the brief therapy model developed by Watzlawick, Weakland, & Fisch, and others at the MRI (Watzlawick, Weakling, & Fisch, 1974); Haley's problem-solving therapy (Haley, 1976); the solution-focused model first developed by De Shazer (1988) and colleagues; and Milan systemic therapy developed by Selvini-Palazzoli (1978) and colleagues. The psychoanalytic track also evolved models that included Boszormenyi-Nagy's (1987) contextual therapy, Skynner's (1976) group analytic family therapy, and object relations family therapy (Slipp, 1991). This stage was probably inevitable, as family therapy pioneers, overwhelmed by their first encounters with families, used each model's simplicity to manage the complexity of family life. Unfortunately, the models further fragmented the field and created a highly competitive environment that maximized differences and minimized the value of common denominators that existed among the models. Many family therapists trained during this stage became true believers of a specific model.

## The Stage of Questioning and Consolidation

By the end of the 1970s, family therapy completed its adolescence, and in the 1980s, several trends shook its essentialism and model purity, particularly that of the pure systems therapies. One trend questioned the quasiscientific metaphors of systems the-

ory and cybernetics on which the equilibrium black box family therapy was originally built (Hoffman, 1985). Homeostasis as an explanation for symptom maintenance was challenged (Dell, 1982), and the methods to disrupt it, crisis induction and paradox, fell out of favor as family therapy became gentler and more "user-friendly." Pure systems therapists opened the black box, paving the way for their rediscovery of the individual and the relevance of meaning and emotion in therapy. The narrative school of family therapy emphasizes meaning (Anderson & Goolishian, 1988; see chap. 2 in this volume; White & Epston, 1990), and even strategic therapists are beginning to write about emotion in therapy (Cade, 1993).

The two family therapy tracks now have much in common, as the sharp lines that once separated them continue to blur. If the tracks can transcend preferences for their own jargon, a new dialogue should be possible in which the common denominators become the three domains of human experience—action, meaning, and emotion—and how they interact to create and maintain problems (Greenberg & Safran, 1987).

Family therapy has also been influenced by postmodernism, thereby questioning the modernist belief in the universality of underlying principles (Doherty, 1991; see chap. 2 in this volume). The issue of gender has taken substance from the feminist critique of family therapy (Goldner, 1985; Goodrich, Rampage, Ellman, & Halstead, 1988), and multiculturalism has validated the "local knowledge" of the client system. Family therapy has also been forced to abandon its own brand of reductionism by looking beyond the family to include the larger system as part of the treatment unit (See chaps. 26 and 27 in this volume.)

Another trend was the inevitable sobering that occurs when therapy failures force an examination of the models' shortcomings and associated "blind spots." Additionally, the management of health care has influenced the growing importance of time-limited methods. Finally, the maturing of family therapy has also meant less a polemic and more genuine dialogue; consequently, the field is now less self-isolating and more open to influence from other therapies and other disciplines (McDaniel, Hepworth, & Doherty, 1992).

## Toward a Fourth Stage of Integration

The trends previously described are altering family therapy in several significant ways. Contemporary family therapists are adopting a biopsychosocial perspective in which biological, psychological, relational, community, and even societal processes are viewed as relevant to treatment. This perspective creates bridges between the tracks and their models and between family and individual therapy and social action. Contemporary family therapy, therefore, is less rigid and polarized in relation to the rest of the psychotherapy community. The term *family therapy* is even somewhat of a misnomer because today's family therapist is more of a systems therapist capable of understanding the interaction of several levels of a complex biopsychosocial client system. The distinguishing characteristic of such a therapist is not the unit of conceptualization or treatment but the belief in the recursiveness and relevance of several levels of process (Breunlin et al., 1992).

## SUPERVISION AND FAMILY THERAPY

The point of convergence for these trends is integration; consequently, we advocate supervisory experiences that facilitate the development and refinement of integrative practices at all points along a therapist's trajectory. However, just as therapy integration systematically combines several clinical perspectives, so also must the integrative supervisor choose from and sometimes modify the best supervisory practices from a range of available perspectives.

After four decades of growth, family therapy is populated by supervisory practices that are isomorphic with the associated therapy practices (Liddle, Breunlin, & Schwartz, 1988). The supervision of a pure systems or psychodynamic model differ markedly. Therapists seeking supervision should understand these differences and how they can be blended into an integrative perspective.

## Pure Systems Supervision

Pure systems supervision can feel like a conversion experience in which therapists must empty their clinical cup and refill it with the paradigm shift derived from systems theory and cybernetics. For therapists previously trained in individual therapy, having to relinquish access to internal process can be painful. Our own follow-up of therapists trained by us in our pure systems days, however, confirms that these therapists usually reincorporated individual therapy skill into their practices when family therapy failed. Today, we believe that becoming a family therapist does not require renouncing individual therapy skills.

We still recognize, however, how difficult it is to make the leap to systemic thinking, because most therapists are imbued with a nonsystemic Western thought process that encourages a reductionistic versus a holistic, and linear versus recursive understanding of the human condition. We have encountered many newly trained therapists who find it difficult to see the relevance of a biopsychosocial system because they are so enamored with individual psychology. We believe that family therapy supervisors should possess the enthusiasm with which the pure systems family therist views families, and we believe that it is possible to have this enthusiasm without eschewing the value of individuals in the system.

The supervisory methods most often associated with family therapy were developed by the pioneers and training centers of the pure systems family therapy models. Because these therapies eschewed the individual and focused exclusively on the family, the therapy became more public, paving the way for direct observation of therapy and the development of live and videotape supervision. These supervisory methods are consistent with the preference on the part of pure systems therapists for focusing on and changing observable interaction. In live supervision, the supervisor watches a session from behind a two-way mirror and offers suggestions that immediately impact what is happening in the therapy (Liddle & Schwartz, 1983; Schwartz, Liddle, & Breunlin, 1988; see chap. 33 in this volume). In videotape supervision, sessions are reviewed to identify repetitive patterns of interaction and to devise strategies to alter them (Breunlin, Karrer, McGuire, & Cimmarusti, 1988). The supervision is action-oriented and directive. It teaches therapists to become expert at observing, assessing, and changing patterns of interaction.

We believe that these supervisory experiences are indispensable to learning family therapy and that supervisors should have been trained to use these methods; that they themselves should have received supervision in them; and, of course, that they have access to the required equipment.

## Psychodynamic Supervision

Psychodynamic supervisors emphasize individual psychodynamics within an interpersonal context. The supervision will feel familiar to the supervision of individual therapy based on a model of internal process. Therapists are taught how individual family members use interpersonal processes such as splitting, projection, and projective identification to manage intolerable internal affective states, and how a system is created through the mutual interaction of these processes among several family members. Because the intolerable affective states have historical precursors thought to produce developmental arrests, a thorough knowledge of the psychodynamics is taught as therapists learn to value and access the past.

Supervisors also help therapists understand their own internal process, particularly the countertransference that activates emotional responses to the family. Therapists must learn to work with and tolerate the affect present in a therapy session, containing these emotions and helping family members deal with them differently. Like individual therapy, the therapeutic alliance is also viewed as central to the outcome of therapy; therefore, supervision focuses heavily on the development and maintenance of the alliance (Pinsof & Catherall, 1986).

The psychodynamic supervisor encourages therapists to undergo their own therapy, both to resolve conflicts that could interfere with their practice and to experience what their clients will undergo (Nichols, 1983). Some supervisors encourage therapists to enter individual therapy, whereas others prefer marital therapy or family of origin therapy. No matter what modality of therapy is chosen, the therapist's therapist is a powerful role model. The therapist as client brings a dual perspective to the therapy process, absorbing the manner, perspective, style, and theory of the therapist. As clients, therapists also experience what it feels like to struggle, learn, resist, and resolve issues. Many therapists cite their own personal therapy as the most profound influence on their style, as well as the best source of empathic connection to their clients.

Family of origin therapy, particularly that developed by Murray Bowen (1978), is a popular choice of family therapists in training who seek personal therapy. Bowen family systems therapy is well suited to this purpose, as it is an approach that is easily applied to a single person in treatment and directly addresses issues of individuation, autonomy, and connectedness, all concerns relevant to people in graduate school.

## Bridging Two Approaches to Supervision

The supervision literature often characterizes pure systems and psychodynamic supervision as diametrically opposite. For example, Haley (1976) referred to them as orientations A and Z, respectively, and biased his discussion to make pure systems supervision the obvious choice. Such polarizations were characteristic of the field's development at the time, but become counterproductive in today's era of integration. Unfortunately, the supervision literature usually lags behind the clinical and theoretical literature; therefore, there is far too little literature on the integration of supervisory practices (McDaniel, Weber, & McKeever, 1983).

We believe that there remain some real differences between pure systems and psychodynamic supervision. However, we see these differences as no longer mutually exclusive, but rather only emphasizing clinical material in different ways. We believe that pure systems supervision trains therapists to take action to change patterns of interaction, whereas psychodynamic supervision trains therapists to empathize with and alter emotional experience. The key distinction is between a supervision of *doing* and one of *being*. Once the pure systems therapies opened the black box, however, these distinctions became less clear. We propose that integrative therapy requires both being and doing and that integrative supervision helps therapists master both. The therapeutic skills of empathy, genuineness, and positive regard enable therapists to be with a family, but in such a way that families can still be encouraged to take action to do what is necessary to solve their problems.

## Model-Based Supervision

Most model-based supervisors have themselves been trained in the model. In the heyday of model-based training, students were heavily proselytized; consequently, many became true believers, and as supervisors, their fervor can exceed that of their teachers. This fervor can breed a narrow-mindedness that shields the supervisor from the blind spots present in the model, leaving him or her to insist that the model be used beyond its range of applicability.

Model-based supervision greatly reduces complexity because it affords straightforward and precise guidelines for the conduct of therapy. The ambiguity of therapy is minimized, affording therapists great confidence in the efficacy of the procedures. For example, a structural family therapy supervisor believes enactment is the principal intervention for changing interaction; consequently, he or she uses live supervision to help therapists perfect enactments. Using phone messages, the supervisor helps a therapist set up the enactment, keep the family focused on the issue being discussed, and assures that the intensity of the interaction is increased until a new pattern of interaction emerges (Colapinto, 1988). Inexperienced therapists often report that this level of certainty is comforting to them as they struggle with anxiety about therapy.

The downside of model-based supervision is that therapists can view the model as the essence of therapy and fail to see its limitations. We believe that supervision can school therapists in a model's assets, but we view these assets as relative to those of other models. For example, our supervisory methods for conducting enacements are similar to those of a structural family therapy supervisor, but we also stress that the enactment, while a good clinical decision at that moment, may or may not be sufficient to produce a successful outcome.

## INTEGRATIVE PSYCHOTHERAPY

An integrative perspective draws upon existing therapies in such a way that they can be practiced cohesively under one umbrella and can be modified and expanded to accommodate developments in the field. To succeed, a perspective must address several core concerns of integration. First, its presuppositions must constitute a unifying theoretical framework under which falls all clinical practice. Second, it must have rules specifying who should participate in therapy and in what order. Third, it must have rules determining the clinical orientation (e.g., behavioral, experiential, family of origin) to be practiced, and in what circumstances. Finally, it must postulate how problems can be generated and maintained through an interaction of several levels of a biopsychosocial system.

At the Family Institute in Chicago, we have adopted two integrative perspectives, integrative problem centered therapy (IPCT; Pinsof, 1983, 1994) and the metaframeworks perspective (Breunlin et al., 1992). The unifying theoretical framework for both is systems theory and second-order cybernetics, operationalized with six core domains of human functioning, which we call "metaframeworks": organization, sequences, development, culture, gender, and internal process (Breunlin et al., 1992). These domains bridge the pure systems and psychoanalytic tracks, encompass most of the essential features of the pure models, and incorporate the newer trends in the field, particularly, the emphasis on gender and multiculturalism.

Both perspectives are problem-oriented, and both operate on the principle of negative explanation (Bateson, 1972; White, 1986), which purports that problems are maintained by constraints that keep the system from solving the problem. By corollary, therapy enables clients to remove the constraints, providing access to resources needed to solve the problem. Constraints can exist at one or more levels of a biopsychosocial continuum, and, taken together, they constitute a web of constraints or what Pinsof has called a "problem maintenance structure" (Pinsof, 1983). Potentially, treatment could address the biological, psychological, relational, family, community, and societal constraints through the involvement of the family and the individual patient.

For example, many anorectics are constrained at all levels. They experience disturbances of biology as vital organ systems are adversely affected. At the individual level, they are constrained by beliefs about body image and by poor self-esteem and experience intense emotions relating to food. At the relational level, they often struggle with other overachieving siblings, or have parents whose marriage is distressed. At the family level, the constraints include overinvolvement, enmeshment, rigidity, and lack of conflict resolution (Minuchin, Rosman, & Baker, 1978). Anorectics most often come from upper middle-class communities where success is all-important. Finally, intense societal pressures link female success to appearance, thereby exacerbating the probability of eating disorders.

Our integrative perspectives dictate that hypothesizing about the nature of the problem maintenance structure or web of constraints should be no more complex than necessary to solve the problem. We also believe that the approach to solving the problem should be as simple and efficient as possible and should not incorporate complex and time-consuming procedures, unless necessary. Thus, the most accessible levels take priority over the less accessible, and direct and straightforward methods of intervention take precedence over those that are indirect or less straightforward.

We believe that problems are solved most directly when therapy mobilizes the family to use its resources to lift the constraints through action. Therapy, therefore, begins with the whole family's attempt to alter constraining patterns of interaction. The therapy at this stage resembles the pure systems track. For example, if a child is soiling himself, the first question is: What keeps the child from using the toilet? Having ruled out biologic explanations, initial hypothesizing focuses on family organization and interaction. The way that the family handles the soiling and its possible function for the family would be addressed.

If the family cannot solve the problem, then the therapist searches for other constraints, first looking at the beliefs and emotions that the family members have about the problem. Hence the question, What keeps the child from using the toilet? might focus on cultural beliefs about toilet training or fears of using it. If the problem still is not solved, then the focus would shift to intrapsychic blocks such as early trauma around toilet training, necessitating individual sessions with the child, at which point aspects of the

therapy would appear quite similar to the psychodynamic track.

With these perspectives, the distinction between individual and family therapy as distinct modalities disappears because each becomes the appropriate means to access a relevant level of the biopsychosocial continuum. Some cases require only family therapy, whereas others need both individual and family therapy. The course of therapy cannot be predicted a priori by the nature of the presenting problem or the presentation of the client system. Rather, the course of therapy is a function of the unique way that the therapist and family collaborate. We have successfully treated some cases that appeared to be very difficult by seeing only the whole family; alternatively, we have also treated some cases that had simple presentations but resulted in one or more family members' being seen individually.

## INTEGRATIVE SUPERVISION

Supervision of an integrative perspective requires supervisors not only to facilitate a therapist's work with individuals, families, and their larger system, but also how to move among these units and the various therapy orientations that apply to each. This supervision is, therefore, far more complex than pure model supervision. Integrative supervision has five components: management of complexity, work with families, work with individuals, focus on gender, and focus on culture.

### Managing Complexity

Supervisors are specialists whose expert knowledge is coveted by therapists; consequently, supervision often becomes microanalysis of a case centered on the supervisor's area of expertise. Intense scrutiny of one part of a system, however, can ignore other parts, thus breeding reductionism and making it difficult to see the system as a whole. We help therapists view all hypotheses as partial explanations, serving the immediate goals of therapy, but subject to revision in the face of new feedback or failure to solve the problem.

For example, a therapist presented a case involving an adolescent boy failing at school, ostensibly because of poor attendance. The goal was set for him to get to school, and the hypothesizing began with the question, What kept him from going? The therapist began treatment by seeing the family and reported to the supervisor a sequence in which the boy awoke many mornings with headaches and was unable to get up. The father would berate him, and the mother would become tearful. The supervisor and therapist decided to interrupt this sequence by getting the parents to adopt a consistent plan to deal with the morning routine. The plan was successful, and the relationship between the boy and his parents improved, but the headaches persisted. Puzzled, the supervisor wondered if awaking with headaches indicated a sleep disturbance. This was confirmed through a sleep study, and appropriate treatments eliminated the headaches, but the boy still had trouble getting up. Next, the supervisor suggested that the therapist see the boy alone for several sessions to better understand his beliefs and feelings about himself, his family, and school. He also suggested that the therapist visit the school to see whether conditions there kept the boy from attending. By considering the entire biopsychosocial continuum and resisting the temptation to microanalyze any one level, the supervisor was able to continue to further elaborate the constraints that kept the boy from doing well at school.

## Working With the Family Level

As integrative supervisors, our job is to get therapists interested and committed to beginning therapy by seeing the whole family if possible. This allows the therapist access to the greatest amount of data and, particularly, the action constraints that are the initial focus of therapy. When therapists present a new case, we insist that they have obtained as much information about the family as possible, and we plan with them how to get the whole family to attend the first session. It generally takes only a few successful experiences for therapists to become an advocate of this approach, and live supervision of first sessions can ensure a good outcome.

For example, a 10-year-old boy was referred for acting out at school. The therapist wanted to include the boy and his parents in the initial interview, but the supervisor convinced her to invite the boy's two younger brothers also. In the first session that was live-supervised, the mother reported that the boys refused to perform much of their own self-care, including brushing their teeth. The supervisor linked this information to the organization, sequences, and development metaframeworks and phoned the therapist to suggest that she ask the family to enact a teeth-brushing scene. It was hoped that if the mother could succeed in the enactment, she might also expect her son to behave at school. The therapist gave the mother two pencils to serve as tooth brushes and requested that the boys act like they do at home when they are asked to brush their teeth. The identified patient immediately complied, but the two younger brothers refused.

In the next supervision session, the supervisor played the videotape of the enactment and asked the therapist what had been gained by having the brothers attend the session. The therapist identified that she now had crucial information about the sibling subsystem, the organization of the family, and the competence of the identified patient. She was eager to include the brothers in subsequent sessions.

This example highlights how we first attempt to solve the problem by lifting action constraints according to the "Nike principle": Just do it. At this stage of the therapy, we encourage therapists to draw upon and use interventions from the action-oriented models of family therapy. However, we caution them to read the feedback carefully, because one or more family members may be constrained internally, thus having difficulty responding to direct requests to change behavior. Failure to read this feedback could threaten the therapeutic alliance with the family or with some members and make it more difficult to address internal constraints at a later stage of therapy.

When action constraints constitute only part of the web of constraints, we ask the therapist to hypothesize about constraints of meaning and emotion. For example, when the therapist prolonged the enactment, again asking the mother to get the younger boys to brush their teeth, the mother failed until she told the youngest he would go to bed if he refused, at which time he complied. As he rose to brush his teeth, the mother looked astonished and whispered to the father that she was amazed that what she had said produced the desired effect.

In supervision, the supervisor pointed out that this moment appeared to constitute an "Aha!" experience for the mother, in which she altered her beliefs about parenting so that she now believed that applying consequences for actions is effective. He also noted that the mother succeeded because nothing kept her from changing her beliefs about the use of consequences. He then asked the therapist to generate a list of constraints that might have kept another mother in a similar situation from succeeding. The therapist, still amazed that the mother had changed, noted that she might have been flooded with anxiety and unable to set limits. Prior to this, the mother might have believed that consequences would damage the boy, or her own abuse might have made any challenge of her children feel abusive. Such constraints could have defeated the mother.

We teach therapists to stay alert for such constraints of meaning and emotion and to relate empathically when family members begin to relate them. This ability to be empathic while collaborating with a family to initiate action is a core component of integrative therapy. Many therapists trained psychodynamically fear that requests for action will be experienced as judgmental or punitive, so they back away. On the other hand, therapists trained in a pure systems model can initiate change too eagerly and inadvertently wound family members. The balance between the two approaches is achieved when therapists learn to quickly establish an alliance but are also sensitive not to tear it too early in the therapy.

## The Individual in the System

We believe that internal process can contribute to the maintenance of problem, and we help therapists address individual dynamics when direct methods to solve the problem at the family level fail. Therapists trained in individual therapy, however, often use individual explanations of problem maintenance at the outset of a case, and, in doing so, obscure the relevance of other constraints. Unlike the pure systems family therapy supervisor, we do not demand that all theories about individual functioning be abandoned, but rather suggest that these theories be placed within the context of a biopsychosocial perspective. Internal constraints can then be assessed in relation to other constraints.

We first expect therapists to clarify their presuppositions about human nature, particularly how psychological problems are created and maintained by internal process. Therapists' presuppositions about psychopathology constitute one of the most complex and difficult issues. Those who view psychological problems as synonymous with psychopathology pose a particular challenge because they cannot see how to solve the problem without addressing the psychopathology that they believe causes it. Such a view creates a strong pull toward individual therapy and renders therapists ambivalent about the relevance of other constraints.

Family therapists have long known that deficit-based views of clients can constrain both therapist and clients from believing in and accessing the resources of the system. We prefer, therefore, not to look for pathology until forced to do so, electing instead to operate with a health premise that asserts that clients want to behave adaptively and fail only when they are constrained or blocked from so behaving (Breunlin et al., 1992; Pinsof, 1983; chap. 34 in this volume). This view enables therapists to enlist clients in a collaborative effort to identify blocks and constraints and to lift them so that the healthy faculties of people can then solve the problem.

The health premise is challenged when efforts to mobilize a client system to solve the problem fail and therapy reaches an impasse. Often, therapists want to attribute this failure to the existence of individual pathology. We believe that clients can be constrained internally in many ways that are not pathological. One alternative hypothesis is that the web of constraints within the biopsychosocial system is so powerful that it blocks necessary shifts in meaning and emotion essential to solve the problem. For example, in the course of marital therapy, a woman may express rage toward her husband. Efforts to improve the marriage may reach an impasse when the husband begins to abandon sexist attitudes and behaviors but the wife's rage persists. One hypothesis is that the woman's rage is pathological, but another hypothesis would draw upon both the internal process and gender metaframeworks, suggesting that her growing awareness of the accumulated experience of oppression fuels the rage that may actually get worse before it dissipates. The latter hypothesis would not pathologize the woman, but would instead suggest a plan that helps her manage rage and helps the husband to continue to abandon sexist behavior while he struggles to understand and tolerate her experience.

An integrative perspective must also reconcile various theories about human development and, particularly, the notions of fixation, developmental arrest, and regression. Some theories of internal process assume the presence of processes such as projective identification, indicate developmental arrest, and automatically indicate the need for intensive individual therapy. Other theories view such processes on a continuum and hypothesize that projective identification can be part of a normal process of relating or could indicate something more serious (Catherall, 1992). A key distinction is whether development is viewed as epigenetic, that is, whether failure to master a task at a certain time arrests a person at that stage of development. One corollary of the health premise is the plasticity of the human psyche. Applied to development, plasticity means that a person can experience difficulty at one developmental stage, but find multiple ways to compensate and catch up at a later stage. Historical information, therefore, is not sufficient to make a complete assessment; history must be weighed against current functioning that includes the plasticity and resiliency of the individual. In other words, at the outset of therapy, it is impossible to determine the extent of each family member's constraints.

The health premise does not preclude the existence of biological constraints. We believe that people do have manic episodes, chemically induced depressions, and hallucinations. When indicated, therefore, we may recommend a medication evaluation. In other cases, in which a family has struggled with a chronically mentally ill member, we recommend psychoeducational approaches (Anderson, Reiss, & Hogarty, 1986; Goldstein, 1981; chap. 10 in this volume).

Because our integrative perspective dictates that internal process becomes the focus only when it is necessary to solve the problem, we encourage therapists to select only that degree of complexity about internal process needed to solve our problem. We distinguish four degrees of complexity and begin a case with the simplest, moving to greater complexity only when necessary.

Because initial case discussion focuses on external constraints, a basic understanding of internal process suffices. We apply the communication axiom that behavior that is expressive for the individual is communicative for the group, and focus first on the communicative nature of interaction (Watzlawick & Weakland, 1967). For example, if the therapist reports that a wife appears sad, we would wonder what effect her sadness has on the marriage rather than whether the sadness is indicative of her depression. In the early stages of therapy, therefore, we essentially prefer the black box metaphor.

When thorough attempts to solve problems by changing interaction fail, we ask therapists to incorporate internal process into their hypothesizing, thereby taking into account both the interaction and the clients' experience of it. This opening of the black box constitutes the next level of complexity, which presupposes that thoughts and feelings that constrain the system are readily accessible. This level of complexity does not propose an intrapsychic explanation for the origin of thoughts and feeling, how they become constraining, or how they change.

The pure systems therapists first focused on constraining beliefs using interventions such as reframing and positive connotation (Watzlawick et al., 1974). More recently, the narrative therapies (Anderson & Goolishian, 1988; see chapter 2 in this volume; White & Epston, 1990) engage families in conversations with the intent of helping families author new and more workable stories about themselves. Still other approaches appropriate for this level of complexity are the cognitive and experiential therapies. All of these approaches can be used in an individual or a family context.

If internal process constraints cannot be lifted through direct focus on thoughts and feelings, then the next level of complexity is activated, which uses basic models of internal process such as transactional analysis (Harris, 1967), cast of character work (Watanabe, 1986), and the internal family system model (Schwartz, 1987). These models do not presuppose how the parts arrive at or change the thoughts and feelings over which they hold control. They use a layperson's language to explain how the mind works and are based on the multiplicity principle, which purports that the mental and emotional process consists of an internal dialogue between various parts of a person. When the parts disagree or become extreme or polarized, then the internal dialogue is constrained, making it difficult, if not impossible, for relevant thoughts and feelings to change. The goal of therapy is to assist the parts to reorganize so that thoughts and feelings can change, creating new experiences or opening pathways for new action. Using the language of parts with a family usually makes members less suspicious and more receptive to each other because each can see that just a part and not all of a person behaves, thinks, or feels a certain way. The work can involve the whole family, focus on one person's internal process in the presence of other family members, or be done individually.

If an individual remains constrained by internal process, the most complex view of internal process is evoked, which explains the origin and functioning of psychic mechanisms. Such views articulate how the self develops, how it can become disturbed, and how therapy is used to reconstruct the self so that it is capable of altering constraining thoughts and feelings. Models such as self psychology (Kohut, 1971, 1977) and object relations (Scharff & Scharff, 1987) explain extreme internal constraints and how to address them. At this point, the pace of the therapy may change as it addresses the extensive internal constraints of the participants. One characteristic of these models is a belief that seriously constrained individuals need a long-term therapeutic relationship to heal the self. This necessitates a decision either to begin individual therapy or to make a referral to another therapist for individual work.

## Gender-Sensitive Supervision

We believe integrative supervision should be gender-sensitive by incorporating the feminist critique of family therapy into our therapy and supervision. We invite therapists to examine and clarify how their beliefs about gender translate into their clinical practice (see chap. 17 in this volume). Many therapists have never done this; consequently, they are unaware of the way that their biases condone or impose gender inequities in their therapy. For example, many therapists are unaware of the patriarchal biases in their

views of family organization and development. These views lead them to accept uncritically family therapy theories that condone similar biases, for instance, the notion that families are equally benevolent for males and females.

Some family therapists trained in early versions of the pure systems track have beliefs about systems theory that conflict with a feminist-informed therapy. For example, they might believe that circularity means that each participant in an interaction always contributes equally to it. In the case of domestic violence, this view would hold the batterer and the battered equally responsible for an abusive sequence (see chap. 28 in this volume). Our supervision would point out that a battered woman may participate in an abusive cycle, but she generally cannot equally influence its outcome.

Gender raises many questions about therapist values and their place in therapy. We believe that therapists cannot *not* have values; consequently, their values are always present. The adage that to take no action is to take action applies equally well to therapy. To remain silent in the face of oppression is to condone the oppression. We do not advocate that every woman who enters therapy become a feminist, but rather that therapy should offer equal opportunities and access to resources for both men and women.

The application of a gender analysis to therapy has implications for men as well as women. Although sexism historically has privileged men, this privilege has come at a high cost. Emotional isolation, alienation, and coronary heart disease are just a few risks associated with the male role in a patriarchal culture. The therapist's awareness of the cost of sexism for men can be a crucial factor in maintaining a balanced alliance in marital therapy so that husbands do not see gender as "merely" a women's issue.

Gender-sensitive therapy directly affects clinical practice (see chapter 17 in this volume). For example, in the tooth-brushing example cited earlier, the supervisor asked the therapist why she had worked exclusively through the mother. The therapist answered that it was the mother who dealt with these transactions, so it seemed appropriate to ask her to make the changes. The supervisor then pointed out that therapists have often taken advantage of mothers, first using them to engage the family, then blaming them for the problem (for instance, characterizing them as overinvolved or enmeshed), and finally, asking them to be primarily responsible for solving the problem. The supervisor praised the therapist for her good work, but used the clinical material to indicate that in the future, she should work harder to involve the father.

We also spend time helping therapists understand their own gender and its impact on therapy. Depending on the circumstances, being a male therapist or a female therapist creates both opportunities and constraints in the clinical situation. Female therapists may overidentify with the oppression of women, whereas male therapists may become unhelpfully defensive. On the other hand, a male therapist may be able to use his alliance with a husband to challenge his sexist behavior more effectively than could a female colleague. Gender awareness, like personal awareness, is a process that must be woven into the fabric of supervision and addressed over a long period of time.

## Culturally Sensitive Supervision

The need for today's therapy and supervision to be culturally sensitive arises from the multicultural nature of America and the postmodern challenge to the universality of theory and the associated recognition of the value of clients' "local knowledge" (Amundson, Stewart, & LaNae, 1993; Doherty, 1991). We subscribe to Falicov's (1988) definition of culture: "those sets of shared world views and adaptive behaviors derived from simultaneous membership in a variety of contexts" (p. 336). Every individual, family, and group occupies a cultural niche that includes membership in several groups defined by religion, ethnicity, race, educational level, age, gender, geographic region, and politics (Breunlin et al., 1992; see chapters 19 and 20 in this volume). Within this niche, individuals and families must interface with a dominant culture, achieving a degree of fit with it that is more or less adaptive. For example, a Latino teenager can experience stress interfacing with the dominant culture in the high school, but may feel less stress than the parents, who cannot speak English. The fit can also shift in response to individual or

family migration or rate of acculturation. Culture, thus defined, creates both constraints and opportunities for individuals, families, and the various groups in which the individual and family hold membership.

We encourage therapists to assess and work with culture to identify constraints and to harness opportunities. For example, a therapist presented a case of a 17-year-old adolescent who was acting out and doing poorly in school. The therapist's initial hypothesis was based on the family's difficulty mourning the father's death the previous year. When the supervisor learned that the family was Mexican, he asked the therapist to recast the hypothesis in light of culture. In the next session, the family described how the son was struggling with his culture's expectation that he replace his father as "head of the household." Having lived in America for a decade, the son was torn between the expectations rooted in his Mexican heritage and his desire to be an American teenager. In subsequent sessions, the family's investment in therapy increased as they addressed the cultural constraints that kept the young man from negotiating the adolescent task of establishing his identity.

We help therapists understand their own cultural niche and recognize how it fits with each client system that they treat. This fit creates constraints and opportunities for the therapist. Alliances can be strengthened through a recognition that the therapist and family share membership in a particular group. Acknowledging differences can also minimize potential constraints. For example, we advise young therapists working with older parents not to act wiser about parenting than they are, and to appreciate the wisdom afforded by age.

## FINDING A SUPERVISOR

Our preference is clear: We believe that psychotherapy has evolved and will continue to evolve in the direction of integration; consequently, therapists should seek and integrative supervisor. Therapists having the luxury of choice should first interview supervisors, asking the following questions:

1. What is your theory of therapy, and how is it isomophically related to your supervision?

2. How has your therapy evolved over your career, and where do you think it is heading?
3. What recent trends in the field have you incorporated into your practice?
4. Have you been trained in individual and/or family therapy?
5. Do you identify yourself in the pure systems or a psychodynamic track?
6. Have you been trained in a pure model, and if so, how wedded to it are you?
7. What are your beliefs about psychotherapy integration?

Prospective supervisors lacking clear answers to these questions may not be able to help therapists come up with their own answers. We also believe that supervisors should receive training in their craft. This often is not the case, as many therapists become supervisors simply by virtue of extensive clinical experience. Therefore, we also recommend that therapists, where possible, select supervisors who have received training in supervision.

## CONCLUSION

We have been supervising for many years, during which time our clinical and supervisory trajectories have passed through both the pure systems and psychodynamic tracks and one or more of the models of family therapy. By evolving our own practice of supervision and remaining current with the evolution of the field of family therapy, we have come to believe that the integrative perspective is the trend of the future and one that serves therapists best.

Integrative perspectives and supervision, however, are still evolving, and they are not without problems. The major challenge is to provide focus for therapy amid the myriad set of hypotheses offered by the concept of the biopsychosocial continuum and to avoid paralysis in the face of the many clinical options made available by the integrative perspective.

The integrative perspective humbles us as we constantly confront the great complexity of human systems. We recognize that universal underlying theories of problem formation and maintenance give way to the complex web of constraints that are unique to each clinical situation. We are forced by this view to become collaborators with our therapists and the families they treat and to remain open to the many ways in which people use therapy successfully.

## References

Anderson, C., Reiss, D., & Hogarty, B. (1986). *Schizophrenia and the family*. New York: Guilford Press.

Anderson, H., & Goolishian, H. A. (1988). Human systems and linguistic systems: Preliminary and evolving ideas about the implications for clinical theory. *Family Process, 27*, 371–393.

Amundson, J., Stewart, K., & LaNae, V. (1993). Temptations of power and certainty. *Journal of Marital and Family Therapy, 19*, 111–123.

Bateson, G. (1972). *Steps to an ecology of mind*. New York: Ballantine.

Boszormenyi-Nagy, I. (1987). *Foundations of contextual therapy*. New York: Brunner/Mazel.

Bowen, M. (1978). *Family therapy in clinical practice*. New York: Aronson.

Breunlin, D. C., Karrer, B., McGuire, D., & Cimmarusti, R. (1988). Cybernetics of videotape supervision. In H. A. Liddle, D. C. Breunlin, & R. C. Schwartz, *Handbook of family therapy training and supervision* (pp. 194–206). New York: Guilford Press.

Breunlin, D. C., Schwartz, R. C., & Karrer, B. M. (1992). *Metaframeworks: Transcending the models of family therapy*. San Francisco: Jossey-Bass.

Cade, B., & O'Hanlon, W. H. (1993). *A brief guide to brief therapy*. New York: Norton.

Catherall, D. R. (1992). Working with projective identification in couples. *Family Process, 31*, 355–368.

Colapinto, J. (1988). Teaching the structural way. In H. A. Liddle, D. C. Breunlin, & R. C. Schwartz, *Handbook of family therapy training and supervision* (pp. 17–37). New York: Guilford Press.

De Shazer, S. (1988). *Clues: Investigating solutions in brief therapy*. New York: Norton.

Dell, P. F. (1982). Beyond homeostasis: Toward a concept of coherence. *Family Process, 25*, 21–42.

Doherty, W. (1991, Sept./Oct.). Family therapy goes postmodern. *Family Therapy Networker*, 37–42.

Falicov, C. J. (1988). Learning to think culturally. In H. A. Liddle, D. C. Breunlin, & R. C. Schwartz, *Handbook of family therapy training and supervision* (pp. 335–357). New York: Guilford Press.

Goldner, V. (1985). Feminism and family therapy. *Family Process, 24*, 31–47.

Goldstein, M. J. (Ed.). (1981). *New developments in interventions with families of schizophrenics*. San Francisco: Jossey-Bass.

Goodrich, T. J., Rampage, C., Ellman, B., & Halstead, K. (1988). *Feminist family therapy: A casebook.* New York: Norton.

Greenberg, G. S. (1977). The family interactional perspective: A study and examination of the work of Don D. Jackson. *Family Process, 16,* 385–412.

Greenberg, L., & Safran, J. (1987). Emotion, cognition, and behavior: An integration. In L. Greenberg & J. Safran (Eds.), *Emotion in psychotherapy* (pp. 144–167). New York: Guilford Press.

Group for the Advancement of Psychiatry. (1970, March). *The field of family therapy* (Report 78). Washington, DC: American Psychiatric Association.

Haley, J. (1976). *Problem-solving therapy.* San Francisco: Jossey-Bass.

Harris, T. A. (1967). *I'm OK—you're OK: A practical guide to transactional analysis.* New York: Harper & Row.

Hoffman, L. (1985). Beyond power and control: Toward a "second order" family systems therapy. *Family Systems Medicine, 3,* 381–394.

Kohut, H. (1971). *The analysis of the self.* New York: International Universities Press.

Kohut, H. (1977). *The restoration of the self.* New York: International Universities Press.

Liddle, H. A., Breunlin, D. C., & Schwartz, R. C. (1988). *Handbook of family therapy training and supervision.* New York: Guilford Press.

Liddle, H. A., & Schwartz, R. C. (1983). Live supervision /consultation: Conceptual and pragmatic guidelines for family therapy training. *Family Process, 22,* 477–490.

McDaniel, S. H., Hepworth, J., & Doherty, W. J. (1992). *Medical family therapy: A biopsychosocial approach to families with health problems.* New York: Basic Books.

McDaniel, S. H., Weber, T., & McKeever, J. (1983). Multiple theoretical approaches to supervision: Choices in family therapy training. *Family Process, 22,* 491–500.

Minuchin, S. (1974). *Families and family therapy.* Cambridge, MA: Harvard University Press.

Minuchin, S., & Fishman, H. C. (1981). *Family therapy techniques.* Cambridge, MA: Harvard University Press.

Minuchin, S., Rosman, B., & Baker, L. (1978). *Psychosomatic families: Anorexia nervosa in context.* Cambridge, MA: Harvard University Press.

Nichols, W. C. (1983). An integrative psychodynamic and systems approach. In H. A. Liddle, D. C. Breunlin, & R. C. Schwartz (Eds.), *Handbook of family therapy*

*training and supervision* (pp. 110–127). New York: Guilford Press.

Pinsof, W. (1983). Integrative problem centered therapy: Toward the synthesis of family and individual psychotherapies. *Journal of Marital and Family Therapy, 9,* 19–33.

Pinsof, W. (1994). An overview of Integrative Problem Centered Therapy: A synthesis of family and individual psychotherapies. *Journal of Family Therapy, 16,* 103–120.

Pinsof, W., & Catherall, D. (1986). The integrative psychotherapy alliance: Family, couple and individual therapy scales. *Journal of Marital and Family Therapy, 12,* 137–153.

Scharff, D., & Scharff, J. S. (1987). *Object relations family therapy.* New York: Jason Aronson.

Schwartz, R. C. (1987). Our multiple selves. *Family Therapy Networker, 11,* 23–31, 80–83.

Schwartz, R. C., Liddle, H. A., & Breunlin, D. C. (1988). Muddles in live supervision. In H. A. Liddle, D. C. Breunlin, & R. C. Schwartz, *Handbook of family therapy training and supervision* (pp. 183–193). New York: Guilford Press.

Selvini-Palazzoli, M., Cecchin, G., Prata, G., & Boscolo, L. (1978). *Paradox and counterparadox.* Northvale, NJ: Jason Aronson.

Slipp, S. (1991). *Object relations: A dynamic bridge between individual and family treatment.* Northvale, NJ: Jason Aronson.

Skynner, A. C. R. (1976). *Systems of family and marital psychotherapy.* New York: Brunner/Mazel.

VandenBos, G., Stapp, J., & Kilburg, R. (1981). Human service providers in psychology: Results of 1978 APA Human Resource Survey. *American Psychologist, 11,* 1395–1418.

Watanabe, S. (1986). Cast of characters work. *Contemporary Family Therapy, 8,* 75–83.

Watzlawick, P., & Weakland, J. H. (1967). *The interactional view.* New York: Norton.

Watzlawick, P., Weakland, J. H., & Fisch, R. (1974). *Change: Principles of problem formation and resolution.* New York: Norton.

White, M. (1986). Negative explanation, restraint, and double description: A template for family therapy. *Family Process, 25,* 169–184.

White, M., & Epston, D. (1990). *Narrative means to therapeutic ends.* New York: Norton.

# CHAPTER 32

# ETHICAL DILEMMAS IN CHANGE OF FORMAT AND LIVE SUPERVISION

*Michael C. Gottlieb*

Traditionally, psychotherapy was conducted on an individual basis, and ethical principles were written accordingly (Woody, 1990). The principles were relatively unambiguous and the lines of professional responsibility generally clear: A psychologist's primary obligation is to his or her client, whose autonomy and welfare he or she is expected to promote (American Psychological Association [APA], 1990).

Marital and family therapy has been practiced since the early 1950s (Hoffman, 1981) and has received much empirical support. Yet, perhaps due to its more complex nature, many years passed before scholarly articles began to appear regarding the ethical issues of this work (e.g., Boszormenyi-Nagy & Krasner, 1980; Grosser & Paul, 1964; Hines & Hare-Mustin, 1978; Karpel, 1980; Rinella & Goldstein, 1980). It was not until 1982 that two articles defined and organized the field (Margolin, 1982; O'Shea & Jessee, 1982), and it was another 10 years before psychology made its initial effort to address this work in its ethical principles (APA, 1992).

Margolin (1982) focused on four issues unique to treating couples and families. First, who is the client? Is it an individual, a particular dyad, or the family system? Second, if there is more than one client, how is the therapist to maintain a posture of therapeutic neutrality, and under what circumstances must this position be abandoned in favor of an individual family member? Third, how is confidentiality to be managed? Should the therapist keep some secrets from family members, keep none, or decide on a case-by-case basis? Finally, what is a therapist to do regarding matters of informed consent? For example,

when using strategic approaches, how much information should the therapist reveal, and how will the disclosure affect treatment? Iatrogenic risk, damage caused inadvertently in the course of treatment, is a problem usually associated with physical medicine. O'Shea and Jessee (1982) extended the concept to family therapy because "a previously asymptomatic family member may become symptomatic during or subsequent to therapy" (p. 15). How is a family therapist to manage treatment in the context of this potential problem?

Subsequent papers have explored additional ethical issues in family therapy (e.g., Margolin, 1986; Patten, Barnett, & Houlihan, 1991) and extended their scope to other areas of family practice, such as concurrent individual and family therapy sessions (Gottlieb & Cooper, 1990), working from a systemic perspective in hospitals (Gottlieb & Cooper, 1993), and treating families who have a member with a chronic physical illness (Gottlieb, 1995). Despite these advances, two important ethical issues have received no attention in the professional literature, in spite of the frequency with which they occur: change of format and live supervision.

Change of format was first mentioned by Margolin (1982) as an example of a frequently encountered problem of confidentiality in marital therapy. She noted that an ethical dilemma arose when a therapist who had been treating an individual changed the format to work conjointly with the individual and his or her spouse, or vice versa. However, she never precisely defined the problem, explored the issue, or made procedural recommendations for its management.

Live supervision is a commonly accepted method for training and treatment that may be practiced in a variety of ways. Essentially, the technique uses persons in addition to the therapist who become involved in treatment at the time that the family is seen. Other people may sit in the room with the therapist and family or observe through a one-way glass. They may speak with the therapist during or after the session with or without the family's knowledge of what is communicated. The others may serve in the capacity of supervisors, consultants, or cotherapists. Despite its popularity, the ethical questions this procedure raises have never been critically examined. The purpose of this chapter is to describe the ethical issues associated with each of these procedures and offer recommendations for both practitioners and trainers. The discussion that follows underscores the importance of approaching every case from a systemic perspective from the outset.

## CHANGE OF FORMAT

It is surprising that change of format has not been addressed earlier, because it occurs so often in a variety of professional contexts. For example, a clinical child psychologist changes format whenever he or she treats a child individually and then works on behavioral management issues with the child's parents. Family psychologists routinely change format, treating various subsystems within a family or seeing members of the extended family. In other situations, therapists may act as consultants to institutions or family businesses, where format may change frequently. Change of format was operationally defined as "a circumstance in which the formal definition of the client changes after the initiation of treatment such that the responsibility of the therapist is altered" (Gottlieb, 1986). Consider the following:

### CASE VIGNETTE

*A therapist is contacted by a woman because of marital difficulties. Based upon telephone screening, a recommendation is made that the couple attend the initial session together. At the appointed hour, the woman arrives alone. First, the therapist*

*explores why the husband did not come. It emerges that the husband is somewhat skittish about therapy, and the wife would like some individual sessions anyway. Together, the therapist and the woman agree to focus first on her individual issues. To keep the conjoint option open, the therapist asks to call the husband and garner his support for the plan. This accomplished, the woman and the therapist work together for six sessions before the husband joins them. Conjoint treatment then begins as originally planned. Later in treatment, the husband requests an individual session for himself.*

In change of format, three major ethical issues may arise: (a) confidentiality, (b) responsibility, and (c) specific iatrogenic risks.

## Confidentiality

A psychologist has an unambiguous obligation to keep confidential information that was revealed by his or her client (APA, 1992), except in cases of imminent danger to oneself or others (*Tarasoff v. Regents of the University of California*, 1975). Unfortunately, such principles are designed for the treatment of individuals and cannot be applied to treatment of multiple clients. With respect to the case vignette previously mentioned, how is the therapist to manage the information obtained during the first six sessions, when the woman was seen individually? The desirable course would be for the therapist to facilitate the wife's disclosure, but she may be reluctant or even unwilling to divulge certain information.

To comply with existing ethical guidelines, the therapist could have requested a release of information during the first individual session so that she or he could share information with the husband. Will the client remember all the information she has revealed? Would she have shared the information if she knew her husband would learn of it? To ensure that the release is fully informed, should the therapist take the responsibility of reminding the client of sensitive information she revealed but may have forgotten? If the client is not reminded, her release may not be fully informed and could be invalid.

A release could have been obtained at the outset of treatment. Had the client signed it, she might have retained vital information she did not wish divulged to her husband. By keeping information from the therapist, however, treatment efficacy could be reduced. These questions clearly demonstrate how treatment driven solely by current ethical guidelines may compromise the entire treatment process.

Alternatively, a client may refuse to sign the release of information and insist that confidentiality be maintained. Systems therapists typically would find it untenable to conduct conjoint therapy under such circumstances except for a circumscribed phase of therapy. Therefore, the therapist may elect to see the client individually or refer the couple to another therapist for marital therapy. However, the client should be informed that therapy will be delayed by the referral and that treatment effectiveness may be reduced if the information is not revealed.

Another possibility is that the client may release the therapist in general but request that specific information be kept confidential. In some cases, this request may pose no problem. For example, the wife may ask the therapist to keep from her husband the fact that she had a brief affair many years before. She may claim that revealing it would needlessly hurt him and that the experience only served to draw them closer together. The therapist may agree if he or she believes that the affair is a matter of personal privacy (Woody, 1990) or holds no systemic value (Gottlieb & Cooper, 1990). Unfortunately, such a decision could place the therapist in an ethical dilemma if he or she subsequently learns that the husband considered the information critical. The therapist's desire for a simple and straightforward solution may lead him or her to become triangulated by the wife's secret and potentially compromise treatment effectiveness (see chap. 14 in this volume).

On the other hand, what if a therapist is asked to keep a secret that he or she knows to be of vital importance to a client's spouse? Consider the following:

*CASE VIGNETTE*

*A family psychologist was consulted by a woman who presented with complaints regarding her sexual relationship with her husband. The psychologist recommended a conjoint session to further assess the problem, and she agreed, but at the appointed hour, the husband arrived without his wife. The psychologist, immediately aware of the potential conflict of interest that could arise if she saw him individually, prudently decided to explain the limits of confidentiality and her responsibility to his wife at the outset of the session as a matter of informed consent. Unfortunately, before she could do so, the husband blurted out that he was gay, had known this about himself before marrying, and continued to have frequent high-risk sexual liaisons. His wife knew none of this, and he acknowledged feeling horrible for deceiving her. He justified his decision to remain silent based upon the assumption that if she were to learn the truth, she would divorce him and try to keep him from their children. He desperately wanted to stay with his family and asked the psychologist to help him reveal the truth to her and end the deception.*

Briefly maintaining confidentiality and tolerating the conflict of interest may be indicated if the husband honestly wished to end the deception, because disclosure would benefit the wife. The therapist may, however, place a clear time limit on the husband's withholding of the information so that the therapist is not caught in the difficult situation—if the husband subsequently demurs—of keeping from her client information that would directly affect her well-being.

## Professional Responsibility

The Ethical Principles of Psychologists (APA, 1990) state that a psychologist's primary responsibility is to his or her client. However, the latest revision of this document notes that psychologists may "provide services to several persons who have a relationship, such as husband and wife or parents and children" (APA, 1992). It is the psychologist's responsibility to clarify from the outset the nature of the professional relationship with each of the persons involved. Systems-oriented therapists generally construe this to mean that they are responsible to all members of the family system equally.

Returning to the initial vignette, how is this responsibility to be managed when, after six sessions of individual therapy, a husband is to be incorporated into a conjoint treatment process with his wife? What risks are entailed in shifting from the previous position of exclusive responsibility to the wife to a new position of neutrality and equal responsibility to both? Might the wife feel betrayed by the therapist who used to be "on my side"? Conversely, will the husband be fearful of attack from his wife and the therapist whom he may assume is already aligned with her? How can the husband be persuaded of the therapist's neutrality? Furthermore, the family psychologist knows that he or she will have to devote a disproportionate amount of time at the outset to join with the husband in establishing a working relationship. How is this to be accomplished without alienating the wife in the process? The most straightforward solution is for the systems therapist to involve the husband in the second and all subsequent sessions. Otherwise, tremendous time and effort will be devoted to issues of change of format.

## Iatrogenic Effects

The third ethical issue that arises in change of format is of specific iatrogenic risks. Referring again to the initial example, one course of treatment may often be for couple and individual sessions to be balanced. If this is not done, then the wife may have improved over the six sessions of individual treatment, and the husband meanwhile may have deteriorated prior to his entering treatment.

An iatrogenic risk often noted is the deterioration of marriages when partners are seen individually. One that is seldom discussed among systemically oriented therapists is that of treating a couple conjointly when individual therapy is the treatment of choice. Although conjoint marital therapy and individual therapy with the same therapist is more complicated, it may be more desirable and can be an example of systems theory at its best.

## RECOMMENDATIONS FOR CHANGE OF FORMAT

The APA (1992) has formally endorsed the concept that a psychologist may have multiple clients from

the same family so long as lines of responsibility are clarified. Furthermore, changing format can be an ethical choice when clinically indicated (Kaslow & Racusin, 1990). When considering this option, the following recommendations may be helpful:

1. Each clinical situation must be evaluated on its own merit. At the very beginning, during the initial telephone call if possible, the therapist should start with a systems perspective and set up the initial meeting as a family session. As an alternative, immediately he or she should lay the groundwork for a future family session if one cannot be arranged first.

2. The therapist should frame the treatment so that personal information and secrets are viewed as clearly undesirable and ultimately not useful. If secrets do emerge, these should be clearly enumerated with the client(s) so that the therapist does not risk inadvertently revealing confidential information. If a secret is to be kept temporarily, the family psychologist should write a contract for the client to sign, including a specific deadline by which the information is to be shared. The document should include a provision that if the client fails to adhere to the agreement, treatment will be terminated and the client referred elsewhere or the secret revealed, especially when it may be eventually life-threatening (e.g., positive HIV status).

3. The therapist must also be aware of the responsibility he or she has toward the spouse who is joining the treatment. At the beginning of the first conjoint session, the therapist should review the agreement he or she has with the original client and determine whether the incoming spouse understands its provisions and the rules under which they will proceed. If these matters are understood and accepted, the family psychologist should take as much time as necessary to join with the incoming spouse in the treatment before proceeding with conjoint therapy.

4. Every effort should be made to encourage the original client to discuss transferential feelings before the arrival of the incoming spouse. The client should be informed of possible feelings of hostility, rejection, or abandonment whenever it is clin-

ically indicated. If the client has denied these feelings, it may not be possible to address them until the incoming spouse arrives. These complexities illustrate why it is better to start with a conjoint format and then evolve to individual sessions if indicated.

5. It is a family psychologist's ethical obligation to be familiar with the literature regarding the risks and benefits of individual, conjoint marital, and family therapy for the original client's presenting problem(s). No matter how devoted a systems therapist may be, proceeding conjointly is not necessarily the treatment of choice in all clinical situations.

6. Clients should be provided ample opportunity to discuss the risks and benefits of all treatment alternatives and time to think them through before a decision is made. This procedure begins a collaboration with the client in the decision-making process (Jensen, Josephson, & Frey, 1989).

## LIVE SUPERVISION

Live supervision has been an integral part of family therapy since its inception. Teams are seated behind a one-way glass and take an active role in the process. The supervisor, or other team members, may call into or enter the consultation room to make direct interventions in the session. In doing so, these team members become an integral part of the session itself.

Live supervision has numerous advantages in training, practice, and consulting. Some proponents believe treatment outcome may be both more effective and shorter because other professionals are involved in the treatment process. It is clear that live supervision can be a powerful treatment and training technique. However, important ethical concerns about this approach have not been critically evaluated heretofore. One way to think of this problem from an ethical perspective is to ask, "Who is the therapist?" or "Who is professionally responsible for the family?"

Originally, live supervision was practiced unobtrusively. The therapist was seated in the consulting room with the family, and the person behind the one-way glass acted as a consultant or supervisor for the therapist without interrupting the session. Shortly thereafter, telephones were installed to allow supervisors to call the therapist with their recommendations (Montalvo, 1973) with the understanding that they would only "call with reluctance" (Haley, 1976) to minimize disruption of the process. In subsequent models, the team called the therapist out of the session for consultation (e.g., Selvini-Palazzoli, Boscolo, Cecchin, & Prata, 1978) or communicated directly with both the therapist and the family (e.g., Papp, 1980). In other cases, a team member might enter the consulting room during the session to make an intervention and thus become part of the session itself (Minuchin & Montalvo, 1967).

These developments have created a situation in which a method of training has become a form of therapy in which families are no longer treated by an individual but by a group. Such a structure raises important ethical questions regarding (a) professional responsibility, (b) informed consent, and (c) specific iatrogenic risks.

### Professional Responsibility

It is a psychologist's ethical responsibility to clarify her or his professional role with clients and to accept appropriate professional responsibility for them (APA, 1992). How is this responsibility to be carried out when more than one person may be professionally responsible?

In so-called vertical models (e.g., Haley, 1976; Montalvo, 1973), the lines of responsibility are clear. Procedures are agreed upon in advance, and particular attention is paid to the roles of both trainee and supervisor, taking account of the power differential between them. Although the trainee is given wide latitude, the supervisor retains final authority, and this is explained to the family. In an alternative model, the team may interrupt with messages for the therapist, but the messages are strictly consultative. Therapists retain final authority over the treatment process (Watzlawick, Weakland, & Fisch, 1974).

Lines of responsibility are less clear in horizontal models. The Milan group (Selvini-Palazzoli et al., 1978) emphasizes the egalitarian nature of the team. A leader is assigned only to establish ground rules and facilitate the team's work in order to avoid the pitfalls of a leaderless group. Team members are equally responsible for the treatment, and all recommendations are made by consensus. A similar approach has been proposed by Heath (1982). The Ackerman Institute began with a vertical model (Papp, 1980), but more recently came to the position that all team members are equally responsible and are free to disagree with one another and inform the family of their disagreement if they choose to do so (P. Papp, personal communication; Mental Research Institute [MRI], 1986).

These horizontal models raise serious questions regarding procedure and lines of professional responsibility. In such cases, who is responsible for the family? Who is to be contacted in emergencies? How are decisions to be made if all team members are not present? May a trainee act independently, or must he or she first consult with the team? How is a team to proceed if it cannot reach consensus? If all are equally responsible, what is an individual team member to do if he or she disagrees with the majority's recommendation? If an adverse outcome occurs as a result of the recommendation, is that member less responsible than those who supported it?

## Informed Consent

A basic element of informed consent is that the client be given "significant information" regarding treatment procedures before their initiation (APA, 1992). Failing to provide such information may lead to misunderstanding and create a risk for treatment failure (e.g., Anonymous & Coleman, 1985). If the therapist has not been careful to fully inform the family and offer them other options for treatment, certain problems may arise. The family may feel tacitly coerced but reluctant to complain (Lefley, 1988). If they agree to the procedure, self-disclosure may be inhibited by the observation of others (Persaud, 1987). The treatment may be disrupted by the interruptions from the team (Smith, Smith, & Salts, 1991), and families may not develop confidence in a trainee who appears to require the supervision of an entire group (Bullock & Kobayashi, 1978).

Many of these problems converge when a "master practitioner" demonstrates his or her skills with a family in front of an audience. A family who is "stuck" in treatment may view the experience as an opportunity to help them move forward. However, if the family is satisfied with their progress, they may agree to this format only to please their therapist and then view the session more as a demonstration than therapy (Harari & Bloch, 1991). This arrangement may be fine if there is truly informed consent.

Without full consent, many questions arise, such as, What is the family told in advance about such encounters? Are they simply serving as props? Do they expect that the master will solve their problems in a single session? Finally, what message is indirectly sent to students and young colleagues about the thoroughness that is so necessary for effective clinical work?

A useful way of thinking about these issues is for therapists to ask how they would wish their own family to be treated. Under what circumstances would they be willing to experience live supervision themselves (Heatherington, 1990)? Would they not want to know about the process, its rationale, and how it might be helpful? Would they and their families also want to know about other treatment modalities that might be as effective and possibly take longer, but be less intrusive?

## Iatrogenic Risk

There is a particular iatrogenic risk in team treatment and live supervision that raises serious ethical questions not previously examined by systems therapists. Social psychologists have known for years that people will make more extreme or riskier decisions in groups, especially in groups of like-minded people, than they would have as individuals. This phenomenon is termed the *risky shift* (Hinsz & Davis, 1984).

The obvious implication of the risky shift is that the team may recommend more extreme measures than an individual therapist would in a similar situation. In doing so, they risk harming the family. This phenomenon is especially troublesome because the effect is enhanced in ambiguous situations (Elmes & Gemmill, 1990) and is contraindicated where convergence of thought may be better than divergence (Nemeth, Mosier, & Chiles, 1992). To compound the issue, social status plays an important role in the process, as low-status and inexperienced team members are more likely to defer to the differential power of the group (Schaller, 1992). Should this information change the way that one conducts live supervision? Is there a way of controlling the influence of the group? Proponents would argue that, in clinical situations that have been extremely resistant previously to more conventional interventions, a risky or radical intervention may be exactly what is appropriate. Alternatively, because the risky shift cannot be avoided, should the practice of team treatment be deemed too dangerous and discontinued?

## RECOMMENDATIONS FOR LIVE SUPERVISION

Presently, there are no ethical guidelines regarding the practice of live supervision (American Association of Marriage and Family Therapy [AAMFT], 1991; APA, 1992), and no consensus exists regarding which type of live supervision format is best for a particular clinical situation. However, it is important to emphasize that this lack of ethical guidelines and consensus exists for many other interventions. Therefore, practitioners, agency directors, and training supervisors who wish to employ this technique as part of a systems-oriented practice or training experience should proceed with caution. In this connection, the following recommendations may be helpful:

1. The practitioner or agency director should create a policy for live supervision consistent with his or her theoretical orientation, the policies of the agency, and the laws of the state. In addition to legal and agency requirements, the policy should include at least the following elements. The policy should explain the format of treatment and the purpose of the team. It should clearly explain to the family, therapist, and team members the lines of responsibility, specifying the authority of the therapist vis-à-vis the team in managing the case. In training situations, families should be informed regarding the training and experience of all those involved in their treatment.
2. Once the policy is established, it should be written and provided to incoming trainees, therapists, supervisors, and families. Therapists should discuss the policy with families at the outset of treatment as a matter of informed consent and allow them time to decide if they wish such treatment.
3. It is ironic that systems-oriented therapists have overlooked the influence of the group context in

team supervision. What is to be done about the risky shift and the converse need for "radical" interventions in certain previously "untreatable" cases? Certainly, it is vital that research efforts focus on the results of this phenomenon in therapeutic decision-making and treatment outcome. In the meantime, it is incumbent upon everyone who employs live supervision to be acutely aware of the risky shift. To increase awareness of the phenomenon, it should be taught to trainees. To sensitize them to it, they should be provided with the opportunity to observe and play the role of therapist, team member, and supervisor.
4. Team decisions should be reviewed by a supervisor or consultant who did not take part in the decision-making process. Like the individual therapist, the team, too, may become dysfunctional, and a colleague meta to the team is in the best position to prevent it from functioning in a harmful fashion.

## CONCLUSION

Because systems approaches to therapy enjoy great popularity, it is surprising that so little professional literature has been devoted to the ethical issues that they raise. This chapter has defined and discussed two ethical issues—change of format and live supervision—in systems therapy that have not been addressed previously. In examining these issues, it was not my intention to discourage the reader from working in these modes. Systemic thinking yields information that can have a powerful impact on families, and it is an approach worthy of the effort necessary to master it. Although no list of recommendations can apply to all clinical situations, I have provided suggestions as to how these problems can be managed in a sensitive, effective, and ethical manner.

This analysis of both change of format and live supervision underscores the need for the therapist to approach each treatment situation at the very beginning with a systemic framework. With adequate preparation of client systems for both change of format and live supervision, the systemic therapist may avoid a variety of potential problems. Treatment decisions cannot be totally driven by existing ethical principles; sound clinical judgment must also be exercised.

# References

American Association of Marriage and Family Therapy (1991). *AAMFT code of ethics.* Washington, DC: Author.

American Psychological Association. (1990). Ethical principles of psychologists (amended June 2, 1989). *American Psychologist, 45,* 390–395.

American Psychological Association. (1992). Ethical principles of psychologists and code of conduct. *American Psychologist, 47,* 1597–1611.

Anonymous & Coleman, S. B. (1985). We were somebody's failure. In S. B. Coleman (Ed.), *Failure in family therapy* (pp. 274–283). New York: Guilford Press.

Boszormenyi-Nagy, I., & Krasner, B. (1980). Trust-based therapy: A contextual approach. *American Journal of Psychiatry, 137,* 767–775.

Bullock, D., & Kobayashi, K. (1978). The use of live consultation in family therapy. *Family Therapy, 5,* 245–250.

Elmes, M. B., & Gemmill, G. (1990). The psychodynamics of mindlessness and dissent in small groups. *Small Group Research, 21,* 28–44.

Gottlieb, M. C. (1986, November). *Selected topics in the ethics of marital and family therapy.* Paper presented at the annual meeting of the Texas Psychological Association, Dallas.

Gottlieb, M. C. (1995). Some ethical issues in the treatment of families with chronically ill members. In S. McDaniel (Ed.), *Counseling families with chronic illness* (pp. 69–84). Alexandria, VA: American Counseling Association.

Gottlieb, M. C., & Cooper, C. C. (1990). Treating individuals and families together: Some ethical considerations. *The Family Psychologist, 6,* 10–26.

Gottlieb, M. C., & Cooper, C. C. (1993). Some ethical issues for family psychologists practicing in hospital settings. *Family Relations, 42,* 140–144.

Grosser, G., & Paul, N. (1964). Ethical issues in family group therapy. *American Journal of Orthopsychiatry, 34,* 875–884.

Haley, J. (1976). *Problem-solving therapy: New strategies for effective family therapy.* San Francisco: Jossey-Bass.

Harari, E., & Bloch, S. (1991). Potential perils of the demonstration–consultation interview in family therapy: A case study of contextual confusion. *Family Process, 30,* 363–371.

Heath, A. W. (1982). Team family therapy training: Conceptual and pragmatic considerations. *Family Process, 21,* 187–194.

Heatherington, L. (1990). Family therapy, control and controllingness. *Journal of Family Psychology, 4,* 132–150.

Hines, P., & Hare-Mustin, R. (1978). Ethical concerns in family therapy. *Professional Psychology: Research and Practice, 9,* 165–171.

Hinsz, V. B., & Davis, J. H. (1984). Persuasive arguments theory, group polarization and choice shifts. *Personality and Social Psychology Bulletin, 10,* 260–268.

Hoffman, L. (1981). *Foundations of family therapy.* New York: Basic Books.

Jensen, P. S., Josephson, A. M., & Frey, J. (1989). Informed consent as a framework for treatment: Ethical and therapeutic considerations. *American Journal of Psychotherapy, 43,* 378–385.

Karpel, M. (1980). Family secrets: I. Conceptual and ethical issues in the relational context. II. Ethical and practical considerations in therapeutic management. *Family Process, 19,* 295–306.

Kaslow, N. J., & Racusin, G. R. (1990). Family therapy or child therapy: An open or shut case. *Journal of Family Psychology, 3,* 273–289.

Lefley, H. P. (1988). Training professionals to work with families of chronic patients. *Community Mental Health Journal, 24,* 338–357.

Margolin, G. (1982). Ethical and legal considerations in marital and family therapy. *American Psychologist, 37,* 788–801.

Margolin, G. (1986). Ethical issues in marital therapy. In N. Jacobson & A. Gurman (Eds.), *Clinical handbook of marital therapy.* New York: Guilford Press.

Mental Research Institute. (1986). Newsletter.

Minuchin, S., & Montalvo, B. (1967). Techniques of working with disorganized and low socioeconomic families. *American Journal of Orthopsychiatry, 37,* 880–887.

Montalvo, B. (1973). Aspects of live supervision. *Family Process, 12,* 343–359.

Nemeth, C., Mosier, K., & Chiles, C. (1992). When convergent thought improves performance: Majority versus minority influence. *Personality and Social Psychology Bulletin, 18,* 139–144.

O'Shea, M., & Jessee, E. (1982). Ethical, value and professional conflicts in systems therapy. In J. C. Hansen (Ed.), *Values, ethics, legalities and the family therapist.* Rockville, MD: Aspen.

Papp, P. (1980). The Greek chorus and other techniques of paradoxical therapy. *Family Process, 19,* 45–57.

Patten, C., Barnett, T., & Houlihan, D. (1991). Ethics in marital and family therapy: A review of the literature. *Professional Psychology: Research and Practice, 22,* 171–175.

Persaud, R. D. (1987). Effects of the one-way mirror on family therapy. *Journal of Family Therapy, 9,* 75–79.

Rinella, V., & Goldstein, M. (1980). Family therapy with substance abusers: Legal considerations regarding confidentiality. *Journal of Marital and Family Therapy, 6,* 319–326.

Schaller, M. (1992). In-group favoritism and statistical reasoning in social influence: Implications for formation and maintenance of group stereotypes. *Journal of Personality and Social Psychology, 63,* 61–74.

Selvini-Palazzoli, M., Boscolo, L., Cecchin, G., & Prata, G. (1978). *Paradox and counterparadox: A new model for the family in schizophrenic transaction.* New York: Jason Aronson.

Smith, C. W., Smith, T. A., & Salts, C. J. (1991). The effects of supervisory interruptions on therapists and clients. *American Journal of Family Therapy, 19,* 250–255.

Tarasoff v. Regents of the University of California, 529 P.2d 553 (1975).

Watzlawick, P., Weakland, J., & Fisch, R. (1974). *Change: Principles of problem formation and problem resolution.* New York: Norton.

Woody, J. D. (1990). Resolving ethical concerns in clinical practice: Toward a pragmatic model. *Journal of Marital and Family Therapy, 16,* 133–150.

# CHAPTER 33

# SYSTEMIC TRAUMATIZATION: SECONDARY TRAUMATIC STRESS DISORDER IN FAMILY THERAPISTS

*Charles R. Figley*

Many talented therapists leave the profession because of job stress and burnout. The best therapists are sometimes the most vulnerable. Family therapists, because of the nature and context of their work, are perhaps, as a group, more likely to experience a special type of job-related stress, secondary traumatic stress disorder (STSD), which has much in common with posttraumatic stress disorder (PTSD).

PTSD (American Psychiatric Association, 1980, 1987, 1994) is an adjustment disorder that may develop as a result of exposure to an extraordinarily stressful event or series of events. These events could be one of a wide variety of traumatic stressors "outside the range of usual human experience and that would be markedly distressing to almost anyone" (APA, 1987) such as those associated with war, rape, the Holocaust, natural disasters, accidents, and the unexpected death of a loved one.

PTSD, according to the most recent version of the *Diagnostic and Statistical Manual of Mental Disorders* (*DSM-IV*; American Psychiatric Association, 1994) is characterized by a distinct set of symptoms that may include, but not be limited to, experiencing recurrent nightmares, intrusive thoughts, flashbacks of the traumatic event, phobic reactions, generalized apathy, hypervigilance, guilt, depression, and various symptoms of increased arousal. A cluster of symptoms that persist for at least a month merit the diagnosis of a stress disorder. Some PTSD clients experience bouts of amnesia surrounding the traumatizing experience. After an acute phase that includes exhibiting traumatic stress reactions, such as anxiety symptoms, PTSD clients also display symptoms of depression,

substance abuse, somatic problems, and, for some, antisocial or sociopathic tendencies. Others experience symptoms immediately following the event; then most or all of the symptoms disappear, only to reappear months, years, or even decades later (Figley, Scrignar, & Smith, 1992).

Most develop PTSD as a result of "being in harm's way." They were exposed to the traumatic event directly. Yet those who were not directly in harm's way are also vulnerable to what has been termed *secondary traumatic stress disorder* (Figley, 1995). STSD is an adjustment disorder that some people experience as a result of their involvement with someone who is experiencing traumatic stress. In other words, someone who has been exposed to "serious threat or harm to one's children, spouse, or other close relatives and friends" (American Psychiatric Association, 1987, p. 309.89A). Also included are professionals exposed in the line of duty to traumatized people. These professionals include emergency medical, fire, and safety personnel; child protection workers; disaster relief workers; and mental health professionals, including family therapists.

The symptoms and course of STSD are often identical to PTSD (see Table 1). The difference between PTSD and STSD is that the latter can be more directly tied to the adjustment and recovery of the traumatized person: As the sufferer improves, the supporter experiencing STSD improves. Of course, part of the consultation process with therapists experiencing STSD is to help them with differentiation in their relationship with their traumatized client. The therapist may need to recover well before the client does.

### CASE VIGNETTE

*Mary, a therapist specializing in work with victims of family abuse, suddenly found herself struggling personally, as well as professionally, with what a client was disclosing to her. The client was remember-*

*ing details of ritual abuse as a child. The case began to consume Mary:*

*"I felt that I was being confronted by evidence of an overwhelming evil. I was learning that the kinds of vile acts perpetrated by governments upon political prisoners and concentration camp inmates were being performed by adults upon small*

## TABLE 1

**Suggested Distinctions Between the Diagnostic Criteria for Primary and Secondary Traumatic Stress Disorder**

| Symptom type | Primary | Secondary |
|---|---|---|
| Stressor | Experienced an event outside the range of usual human experiences that would be markedly distressing to almost anyone, such as: | Helping victim who has experienced an event outside the range of usual human experiences that would be markedly distressing to almost anyone, such as: |
| | 1. Serious threat to self | 1. Serious threat to traumatized person (TP) |
| | 2. Sudden destruction of one's environment | 2. Sudden destruction of TP's environment |
| Reexperiencing trauma event | 1. Recollections of event | 1. Recollections of event/TP |
| | 2. Dreams of event | 2. Dreams of event/TP |
| | 3. Sudden reexperiencing of event | 3. Sudden reexperiencing of event/TP |
| | 4. Distress of reminders of event | 4. Reminders of TP/distressing event |
| Avoidance/numbing of reminders | 1. Efforts to avoid thoughts/feelings | 1. Efforts to avoid thoughts/feelings |
| | 2. Efforts to avoid activities/situations | 2. Efforts to avoid activities/situations |
| | 3. Psychogenic amnesia | 3. Psychogenic amnesia |
| | 4. Diminished interest in significant activities | 4. Diminished interest in significant activities |
| | 5. Detachment/estrangements | 5. Detachment/estrangements |
| | 6. Diminished affect | 6. Diminished affect |
| | 7. Sense of foreshortened future | 7. Sense of foreshortened future |
| Persistent arousal | 1. Difficulty falling/staying asleep | 1. Difficulty falling/staying asleep |
| | 2. Irritability or outbursts of anger | 2. Irritability or outbursts of anger |
| | 3. Difficulty concentrating | 3. Difficulty concentrating |
| | 4. Hypervigilance for self | 4. Hypervigilance for TP |
| | 5. Exaggerated startle response | 5. Exaggerated startle response |
| | 6. Physiologic reactivity to cues | 6. Physiologic reactivity to cues |

*Note:* Symptoms under one month duration are considered normal, acute, crisis-related reactions. Those not manifesting until 6 months or more following the event are delayed posttraumatic stress disorder or secondary traumatic stress disorder. From Figley (1995), p. 8. Copyright 1995 by Charles R. Figley. Reprinted with permission.

*children. I was forced to reevaluate my whole understanding of human nature and to acknowledge the monstrous depths to which human beings can sink. I believe that if some people can do these things, each of us, under some circumstances, must be capable of them. . . . My entire world went gray and I became somewhat obsessed with my client's account of her life and could not stop thinking about it."*

*Mary's preoccupations affected her work with other clients and her relationships with family and friends. When she learned that other professionals were also hearing such stories, she eagerly attending a conference on ritual abuse, but she found herself "physically too sick to sit through the lectures."*

*Fortunately, Mary's own marriage was stable and a steady source of support and affection. Another therapist provided some clarification and support in order for her to develop new patterns of emotional self-care. She also reached out to other therapists working with similar clients and formed a peer consultation group which now meets monthly. She reports the following:*

*"After about a year and a half, I felt recovered from that trauma and have since been able to work with other ritual abuse survivors without being overwhelmed or depressed. I have somehow managed to integrate that knowledge of evil into my world view and have still found enough innocence and beauty in the world to balance it. It was tough."*

*Mary was fortunate. She had the time, foresight, resources, and professional commitment both to recognize that she was traumatized and to take effective action. She sought help first, individually, from a therapist-colleague. Equally important, she empowered herself by forming a peer consultation group to maintain regular, personal support for her emotional reactions to her professional work. Many family thera-*

*pists with STSD eventually abandon their profession and seek administrative positions or leave the mental health fields entirely in an effort to seek relief (Figley, 1992c).*

Most systems-oriented family therapists are well aware of STSD (Figley, 1983;1992b). They understand that emotion not only resides in an individual but is a systemic issue as well. Emotions such as joy, pain, or irritability detected in one family member can "spread" and "infect" others in the family. Research on secondary traumatic stress reactions has revealed, for example, the transgenerational effects of the Holocaust on survivor children and spouses and the psychological trauma experienced by friends and family of victims of violent crime, former hostages, POWs, and war veterans. As family therapists become part of the family system, they, too, may be at risk of being traumatized by the stressors affecting the clients.

The purpose of this chapter is to alert therapists to the emotional pitfalls of working with traumatized people, including, but not limited to, experiencing secondary traumatic stress (STS) and STSD. STS is a normal and natural byproduct of working with traumatized people. Left unattended, however, STS can lead to STSD. By focusing on the process by which STS emerges and becomes STSD, I hope to help psychologists—both clinicians and researchers—avoid falling victim to STSD or, if stricken, enable themselves or their supporters to guide them back to a productive work as quickly as possible.

## HISTORICAL AND THEORETICAL FOUNDATIONS

Among the first efforts to recognize the role of the transmission of traumatic emotions from one family member to another was the classic study of World War II veteran families by Hill (1949, 1958). Hill originated the concept of family stress. He was the first to suggest that the system of the family is greatly affected by crisis events such as war and postwar reunion.

Traumatology, the study of traumatic stress, has literally been invented in the last decade. Even though the origin of the study of human reactions to traumatic events can be traced to the earliest medical writings in *Kunus Papyrus* published in 1900 B.C. in Egypt (Figley, 1989a, 1989b; Trimble, 1985; Veith, 1968), the justification for a field of study and treatment emerged only recently (Donovan, 1991; Figley, 1988).

Several factors suggest the need for systematic study and treatment of trauma and its sequelae. One factor is increased public and professional awareness of the frequency of traumatic events and their extraordinary impact on people. For example, *DSM-III* included the diagnosis of PTSD (American Psychiatric Association, 1980). Common symptoms experienced by a wide variety of traumatized persons are now viewed as a legitimate disorder that can be diagnosed and treated. The numbers of professionals working with traumatized people (including lawyers, therapists, emergency professionals, and researchers) has grown, as has the accumulation of empirical research that has validated the disorder.

The past 20 years have yielded research on the many types of traumatic events and the immediate and long-term consequences not only for those directly affected by the events (cf. Figley, 1978, 1982), but also for those indirectly affected as a result of knowing, living with, loving, or working with these "victims."[1] The new field of traumatology has recently made significant breakthroughs in understanding this process, evidenced by the establishment of the first world conference on traumatology (Figley, 1992a, 1992b, 1992c, 1995, Hobfoll, 1992). However, many family therapists may still not be aware that the same principles that would predict risk of trauma for a spouse or child of a traumatized person also apply to them.

## BURNOUT VERSUS STSD

The term *burnout* was coined by Freudenberger (1980). According to Pines and Aronson (1988),

burnout out is "a state of physical, emotional and mental exhaustion caused by long term involvement in emotionally demanding situations" (p. 9).

In contrast to burnout, which emerges gradually and is a result of emotional exhaustion (Cherniss, 1980; Rogers, 1987), STSD can emerge suddenly, without much warning. In addition to a faster onset of symptoms, Figley (1995) has noted that with STSD, in contrast to burnout, there is a sense of helplessness and confusion and a sense of isolation from supporters. Symptoms are often disconnected from real causes, and yet there is a faster rate of recovery from these symptoms (Kahill, 1988).

## TREATMENT OF PTSD AND STSD

Veterans—in particular, Vietnam War veterans—have fairly extensive treatment program information available (cf. Brende & Parson, 1987; Bondewyns, Hyer, Woods, Harrison, & McCramie, 1990; Kelly, 1985). Practice approaches and effectiveness in treating PTSD vary considerably. Some are more general and multiphasic. Treatment is based on the individual progress of each client, similar to programs that address and correct the compulsion to seek out life-threatening situations, known as "combat addiction."

Some programs focus more specifically, such as those that adopt a cognitive–behavioral approach, with direct exposure, implosion methods, various drug treatments, group psychotherapy, and hospital-based treatment. Other promising approaches provide even more specific procedures, such as a focus on ethnicity, dual diagnosis of substance abuse and PTSD (Black, 1987; Kuhne, Nohnber, & Baraga, 1986; Reaves & Maxwell, 1987; Moyer, 1988; Schnitt & Nocks, 1984), and differentiating secondary versus primary PTSD (Catherall, 1989; Figley, 1985a, 1993, 1995). Most recently, eye movement desensitization and reprocessing (EMDR), developed by Shapiro (1989), has gained an important following and early signs of success. The approach uses

---

[1] e.g., Burge, 1983; Cohen, 1988; Crenshaw, 1978; Feinauer, 1982; Figley, 1989a, 1989b; Figley & Sprenkle, 1978; Herndon & Law, 1985; Holstrom & Burgess, 1979; Remer & Elliot, 1988; Rodkin, Hunt, & Cowan, 1982; Silverman, 1978; White & Rollins, 1981.

procedures to access and alter traumatic memories associated with different types of traumatic incidents. Perhaps the most promising of all is Thought Field Therapy (TFT; Callahan & Callahan, in press), which uses the body's energy systems to eliminate perturbations associated with anxiety and other problems.

In addition to those traumatized in the line of military duty, others have been traumatized attempting to save lives. Some reports of effective treatment approaches have focused exclusively on medical personnel, such as Joinson (1992), who used the term *compassion fatigue* to describe this phenomenon. Most approaches, however, focus on other types of emergency personnel, such as police, firefighters, or flight crews. As an analogue, compassion stress experienced by family therapists is "the tension or demand associated with feeling compassion or sympathy" (Figley, 1993, p. 1).

There are growing reports of successful treatment of PTSD emergency workers, such as firefighters (Beaton & Murphy, 1995), police officers (Gersons, 1989), and medical personnel (McCammon & Allison, 1995; McCammon, Durham, Allison, & Williamson, 1988). In fact, the most widely adopted approach was developed initially by Mitchell (1986, 1988) in his efforts to work with firefighters. His Critical Incident Stress Debriefing (CISD) has been adopted internationally to aid groups of emergency personnel work through and process troublesome duty-related events. These CISD sessions typically involve a group meeting of emergency workers immediately following the critical incident. The focus of the meeting is psychoeducational. The goals are to educate workers about STS, to encourage group discussion regarding how the event affected each person personally, and to prevent STSD.

Mental health therapists experience STS in the course of their work and are also vulnerable to STS because of their role in providing direct services to people in crisis. McCann and Pearlman (1990) describe STSD as "vicarious traumatization," an accumulation of memories of clients' traumatic material that affects and is affected by the therapist's perspective of the world. They propose a team-oriented approach to both preventing and treating this special kind of stress.

## THE SPECIAL VULNERABILITY OF FAMILY THERAPISTS

Family therapists are immersed in the extreme intensity of family matters. No matter how hard they try to resist, family therapists are drawn into this intensity. Beyond this natural byproduct of therapeutic engagement, there are three additional reasons why family therapists are especially vulnerable to STSD. First, most traumatic experiences emerge within dysfunctional families. Because family therapists focus on the context of the family, the victim and the perpetrator tend to be from the same family. Therefore the expectations of confidentiality, neutrality, and assumptions of mutual social support by the therapist are especially challenging and stressful when dealing with perpetrators and victims in the same family.

Second, unresolved trauma in the therapist's life will be activated by reports of similar trauma in clients. Segal and Figley (1988) found that 80% of an undergraduate sample had already experienced some type of traumatic event so it can be deduced that a high percentage of therapists also have experienced trauma. Third, emergency workers report that they are most vulnerable to STSD when dealing with the pain of children (Reese, Horn, & Dunning, 1991). Because children are so often either the focus of family therapy, or at least important players, family therapists are more likely than other practitioners to be exposed to childhood trauma.

Although empathy is one of the key factors in the therapeutic process, it is a key factor in the cause of STSD. Thus, the process of empathizing with a traumatized person helps the therapist understand the person's experience of being traumatized, but, in the process, the therapist may be traumatized as well. This was illustrated by the case of Mary and her ritually abused client.

## HOW THE THERAPIST CAN AVOID STSD

The first strategy in avoiding STSD is to learn about it. The therapist should become familiar with burnout, traumatic stress, and work-related stress generally. Ideally, education about these topics and about the stress of family therapy practice should start in graduate school, especially for those who plan to work with traumatized populations. These programs should incorporate lessons on burnout and STSD as part of the overall orientation to the field and practice of psychotherapy. Continuing education programs—irrespective of the topic—should include information about the stress of practicing therapy and should provide education about how to cope. (Professional organizations that foster this kind of education are noted later in this chapter.)

Therapists should monitor their reactions to traumatized clients. Obviously, if any of the aforementioned observations applies to them, then they should be especially cautious about STSD. I have developed a quick, easy, and confidential method by which therapists can check their vulnerability to STSD. It is called *The Self-Test for Psychotherapists* (Figley, 1993, 1995) and is reprinted in Exhibit 1. It is composed of 40 items with Likert-type answer options. Scoring instructions allow the test taker to compute his or her score, which suggests the degree of risk of either being traumatized or burned out.

## THE TREATMENT OF STSD

Professional organizations play an important role in influencing practitioners. They sponsor conferences and publications and establish ethical principles and standards of practice. These organizations are an important part of professional socialization and therefore can significantly increase the quality of mental health services to traumatized people. There are several traditional, large professional associations, with family therapy members, who are interested in PTSD and STSD.[2] There are also three organizations that have emerged over the last decade whose mission centers on trauma.[3] These organizations account for nearly all of the professionals dedicated to studying and treating people exposed to highly stressful events.

Ultimately, the most effective remedy for STSD is the breadth and depth of the therapist's network of supportive relationships, combined with the setting of approximate limits. One can never overestimate the importance of the therapist's family in giving support. It is critical, however, to draw a very clear boundary between work and home and to have a crystal clear, almost contractural understanding with one's family about the traumatic nature of psychotherapy. As a first step, a therapist should seek out peer consultation with a trusted colleague. Participating in a peer consultation group is often an invaluable experience. As an additional step, the therapist could set up a formal supervision arrangement. Finally, personal therapy is an option.

Self-renewal, self-care, and sources of personal pleasure need to be expanded. Those concerned about others are drawn to the helping professions. It is necessary to recognize that therapy professionals can best help others and continue to do so by recognizing their own personal requirements that make possible their motivation to help others.

Therapists who are able to enjoy a long career generally free of STSD recognize the importance of setting realistic goals, limits, and boundaries in their work. They come to realize that life can be unfair and ugly at times; that clients with real and important therapy needs have existed, exist now, and will exist long after the therapist has retired; that there is only so much that any one person can do to help; and that the therapist must leave his or her work at the office in order to seek and secure sufficient renewal to be more effective and, ultimately, to be able to continue a career. Of course, this is more easily said than done.

## IMPLICATIONS FOR EDUCATION AND TRAINING FAMILY THERAPISTS

Faculty supervisors should have a heightened awareness of the emotional impact of psychotherapy work on the student therapist and of how individual cli-

[2] These include the American Association for Marriage and Family Therapy (1100 17th Street NW, 10th Floor, Washington, DC 20036, phone: 202-452-0109); the American Orthopsychiatric Association (19 West 44th Street, New York, NY 10036, phone: 212-354-5770); the American Psychological Association (750 First Street, NE, Washington, DC 20002-4242, phone: 202-336-5500); and the American Psychiatric Association (1400 K Street, NW, Washington, DC, phone: 202-682-6000).

[3] These include the International Critical Incident Stress Foundation (5018 Dorsey Hall Drive, Suite 104, Ellicott City, MD, 21042, phone: 410-730-4311); the International Society for Traumatic Stress Studies (435 North Michigan Avenue, Suite 1717, Chicago, IL 60611-4067, phone: 312-644-0828); and the National Organization for Victim Assistance (1757 Park Road, NW, Washington, DC 20036, phone: 202-232-6682).

## EXHIBIT 1

**Compassion Fatigue Self-Test for Psychotherapists**

Please describe yourself: ___ Male ___ Female; ___ years as therapist. Consider each of the following characteristics about you and your **current** situation. Write in the number of the best response. Use one of the following answers:

1 = Rarely/Never   2 = At Times   3 = Not Sure   4 = Often   5 = Very Often

Answer **all** items, even if not applicable. Then read the instructions to get your score.

Items About You:

1. ___ I force myself to avoid certain thoughts or feelings that remind me of a frightening experience.
2. ___ I find myself avoiding certain activities or situations because they remind me of a frightening experience.
3. ___ I have gaps in my memory about frightening events.
4. ___ I feel estranged from others.
5. ___ I have difficulty falling or staying asleep.
6. ___ I have outbursts of anger or irritability with little provocation.
7. ___ I startle easily.
8. ___ While working with a victim, I thought about violence against the perpetrator.
9. ___ I am a sensitive person.
10. ___ I have had flashbacks connected to my clients.
11. ___ I have had firsthand experience with traumatic events in my adult life.
12. ___ I have had firsthand experience with traumatic events in my childhood.
13. ___ I have thought that I need to "work through" a traumatic experience in my life.
14. ___ I have thought that I need more close friends.
15. ___ I have thought that there is no one to talk with about highly stressful experiences.

Again, please use one of the following answers:

1 = Rarely/Never   2 = At Times   3 = Not Sure   4 = Often   5 = Very Often

16. ___ I have concluded that I work too hard for my own good.

Items About Your Clients:

17. ___ I am frightened of things a client has said or done to me.
18. ___ I experience troubling dreams similar to a client of mine.
19. ___ I have experienced intrusive thoughts of sessions with especially difficult clients.
20. ___ I have suddenly and involuntarily recalled a frightening experience while working with a client.
21. ___ I am preoccupied with more than one client.
22. ___ I am losing sleep over a client's traumatic experiences.
23. ___ I have thought that I might have been "infected" by the traumatic stress of my clients.
24. ___ I remind myself to be less concerned about the well-being of my clients.
25. ___ I have felt trapped by my work as a therapist.
26. ___ I have felt a sense of hopelessness associated with working with clients.
27. ___ I have felt "on edge" about various things, and I attribute this to working with certain clients.
28. ___ I have wished that I could avoid working with some therapy clients.
29. ___ I have been in danger working with therapy clients.
30. ___ I have felt that my clients dislike me personally.

Items About Being a Psychotherapist and Your Work Environment:

31. ___ I have felt weak, tired, and rundown as a result of my work as a therapist.     *(continues)*

---

### EXHIBIT 1 (Continued)

32. ___ I have felt depressed as a result of my work as a therapist.
33. ___ I am unsuccessful at separating work from personal life.
34. ___ I feel little compassion toward most of my co-workers.
35. ___ I feel I am working more for the money than for personal fulfillment.

Again, please use one of the following answers:

1 = Rarely/Never   2 = At Times   3 = Not Sure   4 = Often   5 = Very Often

36. ___ I find it difficult separating my personal life from my work life.
37. ___ I have a sense of worthlessness/dissillusionment/resentment associated with my work.
38. ___ I have thoughts that I am a "failure" as a psychotherapist.
39. ___ I have thoughts that I am not succeeding at achieving my life goals.
40. ___ I have to deal with bureaucratic, unimportant tasks in my work life.

Scoring Instructions: (a) Be certain you **responded to all items.** (b) Circle the following 23 items: 1–8, 10–13, 17–26, and 29. (c) Add the numbers you wrote next to the item. (d) Note your risk of **compassion fatigue:** 23–40 or less = extremely low risk; 41–60 = moderate risk; 60–95 = high risk; 95–115 = extremely high risk. Then, (e) add the numbers you write next to the items not circled. (f) Note your risk of **burnout:** 17–36 = extremely low risk; 37–50 = moderate risk; 51–75 = high risk; 75–85 = extremely high risk.

*This instrument is under development. Please contact Charles R. Figley, PhD, Psychosocial Stress Research Program, Florida State University, MFT Center, Tallahassee, FL 32306-4097 (Phone: 904-644-1588; FAX: 904-644-4804). From Figley (1995) pp. 13–14. Copyright 1995 by Charles R. Figley. Reprinted with permission.*

ents and their stories, experiences, and reactions can be extremely provocative. A portion of each supervisory session, for example, should be devoted to the personal impact and feelings of the therapist. This would provide not only a useful learning experience that would improve the quality of psychotherapy, but it would also normalize the provocative nature of practicing psychotherapy. The opportunities for personal processing need to continue throughout the career of the psychotherapist.

Much more needs to be known about STSD—who gets it when and under what circumstances and how it can be treated and prevented. However, not enough is known to acknowledge generally that STSD is an occupational hazard of caring service providers. Recognizing this, family therapy educators have a special obligation to students and trainees to prepare them for these hazards. They can start by incorporating the topics of stress, burnout, and STSD into the curriculum and especially, into supervision in practica. They can use the relatively protected environment of educational centers and the clients that

seek help there as opportunities for discussing these issues. In addition to the fundamental principles for preventing STSD, training programs could (a) institute policies that require processing all clinical material that appears to be upsetting to *either* the therapist or a team member (including a supervisor); (b) recognize that upsetting clinical material is and should be discussed confidentially with a professional confidant (therapist or supervisor) who must agree to follow proscribed ethical procedures; and (c) experiment with various methods for avoiding STSD while maintaining clinical effectiveness.

## IMPLICATIONS FOR TREATING THERAPISTS

Given the nature of STSD and the context of the psychotherapy profession, it is not surprising that few therapists admit that they have a problem. When they do and seek help—either as a colleague or as a client—it is important first to dispel the myth that "If I have STSD as a therapist, it means that I am not meant for this type of work." My best guess is that only the *most effective therapists are most vulnerable to*

*STSD.* Compassion, sensitivity, empathy, and caring are the fundamental building blocks for establishing a therapeutic alliance between therapist and client. Under some conditions, however, these therapist features contribute to the therapist's becoming overly involved with the client's stressful experiences and reactions.

The next step is convincing the therapist with STSD to recognize that he or she requires the same kind of therapeutic attention as the victim clients who sought help from them. The same treatment procedures helpful in treating PTSD in victims are helpful in treating STSD in therapists.

Seven essential elements are critical in treating STSD (cf. Figley, 1992b). Only time and additional research will confirm their importance. An easy way to remember them is to think of the acronym RESPECT. (a) *Respect* the therapists who suffer from STSD, both for their courage in admitting it and for their dedication to others, which has contributed to their predicament; (b) *educate* them about the reactions and the causes and consequences of their compassion; (c) *stabilize* them so that they can become more functional for themselves, their supporters, and their clients; (d) *pamper* them and get them to pamper themselves, so that their life becomes more filled with fun and joy; (e) *empower* them to discover and take credit for relief of their fatigue and the solutions to their professional dilemmas; (f) *calm* them by helping them concentrate on hope and the road to recovery; and (g) *transfer* them to another person or support group for more lasting attention that will ensure that they can prevent fatigue in the future. In essence, the goal is to enable wounded healers to seek and secure their own survival strategies (Valent, 1995).

Returning to the case vignette, Mary is well on her way to recovery from her traumatic experiences in the practice of psychotherapy. She is fortunate. She had a stable personal and family situation, reached out to peers on an individual basis, and empowered herself by forming a peer consultation group. Her colleagues validated that nothing had changed in her life except exposure to her victim clients. They encouraged her to view herself as a victim who needed the same compassion and opportunities to heal as any other victim. She had the opportunity to make contact with other psychotherapists exposed to similar types of clients, and she recognized the resilience of a trauma survivor.

The difference between a survivor (someone who has endured a highly stressful event but is strengthened as a result) and a victim (someone who has been exposed to a highly stressful event but is weakened as a result) is a matter of shifting perspectives, of saying, "Of course I can do it because of what I have survived" rather than saying, "Of course I cannot do it because of how I have been victimized." The same principle can be applied to therapists (Figley, 1985b; Janoff-Bulman, 1985).

The challenge for traumatized therapists is to creatively transform the pain that they have absorbed from clients into a source of inspiration. They must find a way to recognize that their role is to help as many as possible, as much as possible; to recognize their limits; and to continue to improve to be even more effective in helping future clients, while taking care of themselves.

Society at large just cannot afford to lose these sensitive therapists, who at times because of their humanness and through their compassion, require help themselves. Not even one compassionate therapist should be lost to STSD.

## References

American Psychiatric Association. (1980). *Diagnostic and statistical manual of mental disorders* (3rd ed.). Washington, DC: Author.

American Psychiatric Association. (1987). *Diagnostic and statistical manual of mental disorders–revised* (3rd ed., rev.). Washington, DC: Author.

American Psychiatric Association. (1994). *Diagnostic and statistical manual of mental disorders* (4th ed.). Washington, DC: Author.

Beaton, R., & Murphy, S. (1995). Working with people in crisis. In C. R. Figley (Ed.), *Compassion fatigue: Secondary traumatic stress disorder in treating the traumatized* (pp. 51–81). New York: Brunner/Mazel.

Black, J. W. (1987). The libidinal cocoon: A nurturing retreat for the families of plane crash victims. *Hospital and Community Psychiatry*, 38(12), 345–346.

Brende, J. O., & Parson, E. R. (1987). Multiphasic treatment of the Vietnam veteran. *Psychotherapy in Private Practice*, 5(2), 51–62.

Boudewyns, P. A., Hyer, L., Woods, M. G., Harrison, W. R., & McCranie, E. (1990). PTSD among Vietnam veterans: An early look at treatment outcome using direct therapeutic exposure. *Journal of Traumatic Stress, 3*(3), 359–368.

Burge, S. K. (1983). Rape: Individual and family reactions. In C. R. Figley & H. I. McCubbin (Eds.), *Stress and the family: Volume II. Coping with catastrophe* (pp. 103–119). New York: Brunner/Mazel.

Callahan, R. J., & Callahan, J. (in press). Thought field therapy. In C. R. Figley & B. Bride (Eds.), *Death and trauma*. New York: Brunner/Mazel.

Catherall, D. R. (1989). Differentiating intervention strategies for primary and secondary trauma in PTSD: The example of Vietnam veterans. *Journal of Traumatic Stress, 2*(3), 289–304.

Cherniss, C. (1980). *Professional burnout in human service organizations*. New York: Praeger.

Cohen, C. J. (1988). Providing treatment and support for partners of sexual-assault survivors. *Psychotherapy, 25*(1), 94–98.

Crenshaw, T. L. (1978). Counseling the family and friends. In S. Halper (Ed.), *Rape: Helping the victim* (pp. 51–65). Oradell, NJ: Medical Economics.

Donovan, D. (1991). Traumatology: A field whose time has come. *Journal of Traumatic Stress, 4*(3), 433–436.

Feinauer, L. (1982). Rape: A family crisis. *American Journal of Family Therapy, 10*(4), 35–39.

Figley, C. R. (1978). *Stress disorders among Vietnam veterans: Theory, research, and treatment*. New York: Brunner/Mazel.

Figley, C. R. (1982, February). *Traumatization and comfort: Close relationships may be hazardous to your health*. Keynote presentation at a conference, "Families and Close Relationships: Individuals in Social Interaction," Texas Tech University, Lubbock, Texas.

Figley, C. R. (1983). Catastrophes: An overview of family reactions. In C. R. Figley & H. I. McCubbin (Eds.), *Stress and the family: Volume II. Coping with catastrophe* (pp. 3–20). New York: Brunner/Mazel.

Figley, C. R. (1985a). The role of the family: Both haven and headache. In M. Lystad (Ed.), *Role stressors and supports for emergency workers* (DHHS Publication No. Adm 85-1408; 84–94). Washington, DC: U.S. Government Printing Office.

Figley, C. R. (1985b). From victim to survivor: Social responsibility in the wake of catastrophe. In C. R. Figley (Ed.), *Trauma and its wake: The study and treatment of PTSD* (pp. 398–415). Brunner/Mazel: New York.

Figley, C. R. (1988). Toward a field of traumatic stress. *Journal of Traumatic Stress, 1*(1), 3–16.

Figley, C. R. (1989a). *Helping traumatized families*. San Francisco: Jossey-Bass.

Figley, C. R. (Ed). (1989b). *Treating stress in families*. New York: Brunner/Mazel.

Figley, C. R. (1992a). Posttraumatic stress disorder: Part II. Relationship with various traumatic events. *Violence Update, 2*(9), 1, 8–11.

Figley, C. R. (1992b). Posttraumatic stress disorder: Part III. Relationship with various traumatic events, continued. *Violence Update, 2*(10), 1, 8–11.

Figley, C. R. (1992c). Posttraumatic stress disorder: Part IV. Generic treatment approaches. *Violence Update, 3*(3), 1, 4, 7–8.

Figley, C. R. (1993, February). Compassion stress: Toward its measurement and management. *Family Therapy News*, pp. 1, 2.

Figley, C. R. (1995). Compassion fatigue as secondary traumatic stress disorder: An overview. In C. R. Figley (Ed.), *Compassion fatigue: Secondary traumatic stress disorder in treating the traumatized* (pp. 1–20). New York: Brunner/Mazel.

Figley, C. R., Scrignar, C. B., & Smith, W. H. (1992). PTSD: The after-shocks of trauma. *Patient Care, 22*, 111–127.

Figley, C. R., & Sprenkle, D. W. (1978). Delayed stress response syndrome: Family therapy indications. *Journal of Marriage and Family Counseling, 4*(1), 53–60.

Freudenberger, H. (1980). *Burnout*. New York: Bantam.

Gersons, B. P. R. (1989). Patterns of PTSD among police officers following shooting incidents: A two-dimensional model and treatment implications. *Journal of Traumatic Stress, 2*(3), 247–258.

Herndon, A. D., & Law, Jr., J. G. (1985). Post-traumatic stress and the family: A multi-method approach to counseling. In C. R. Figley (Ed.), *Trauma and its wake: Volume II. The study and treatment of PTSD* (pp. 264–280). New York: Brunner/Mazel.

Hill, R. (1949). *Families under stress*. New York: Harper & Row.

Hill, R. (1958). Generic features of families under stress. *Social Casework, 49*, 139–150.

Hobfoll, S. (1992, June). *Conservation of resources and loss*. Paper presented at the First World Conference of the International Society for Traumatic Stress Studies, Amsterdam.

Holstrom, L. L., & Burgess, A. W. (1979). Rape: The husband's and boyfriend's initial reactions. *The Family Coordinator, 28*, 321–330.

Janoff-Bulman, R. (1985). The aftermath of victimization: Rebuilding shattered assumptions. In C. R. Figley (Ed.), *Trauma and its wake: The study and treatment of PTSD*. New York: Brunner/Mazel.

Joinson, C. (1992). Coping with compassion fatigue. *Nursing, 22*(4), 116–122.

Kahill, S. (1988). Interventions for burnout in the helping professions: A review of the empirical evidence. *Canadian Journal of Counselling Review, 22*(3), 310–342.

Kelly, W. E. (Ed.). (1985). *Post-traumatic stress disorder and the war veteran patient.* New York: Brunner/Mazel.

Kuhne, A., Nohnber, W., & Baraga, E. (1986). Efficacy of chemical dependency treatment as a function of combat in Vietnam. *Journal of Substance Abuse Treatment, 3*(3), 191–194.

McCammon, S., & Allison, E. J. (1995). Debriefing and treating emergency workers. In C. R. Figley (Ed.), *Compassion fatigue: Secondary traumatic stress disorder in treating the traumatized* (pp. 115–130). New York: Brunner/Mazel.

McCammon, S., Durham, T. W., Allison, E. J., & Williamson, J. E. (1988). Emergency workers' cognitive appraisal and coping with traumatic events. *Journal of Traumatic Stress, 1*(3), 353–372.

McCann, L., & Pearlman, L. A. (1990). Vicarious traumatization: A framework for understanding the psychological effects of working with victims. *Journal of Traumatic Stress, 3*(1), 131–149.

Mitchell, J. T. (1986). Critical incident stress debriefing. *Response!,* pp. 24–25.

Mitchell, J. (1988). *Critical incident debriefing: A handbook.* Bowie, MD: Chevron Press.

Moyer, M. A. (1988). Achieving successful chemical dependency recovery in veteran survivors of traumatic stress. *Alcoholism Treatment Quarterly, 4*(4), 19–34.

Pines, A. M., & Aronson, E. (1988). *Career burnout: Causes and cures.* New York: Free Press.

Reaves, M. E., & Maxwell, M. J. (1987). The evolution of a therapy group for Vietnam veterans on a general psychiatry unit. *Journal of Contemporary Psychotherapy, 17*(1), 22–23.

Reese, J. T., Horn, J. M., & Dunning, C. (Eds.). (1991). *Critical incidents in policing.* Washington, DC: U.S. Department of Justice, Federal Bureau of Investigation.

Remer, R., & Elliot, J. (1988). Characteristics of secondary victims of sexual assault. *International Journal of Family Psychiatry, 9*(4), 373–387.

Rodkin, L. I., Hunt, E. J., & Cowan, S. D. (1982). A men's support group for significant others of rape victims. *Journal of Marital and Family Therapy, 8*(1), 91–97.

Rogers, E. R. (1987). Professional burnout: A review of a concept. *The Clinical Supervisor, 5*(3), 210–221.

Shapiro, F. (1989). Efficacy of the eye movement desensitization procedure in the treatment of traumatic memories. *Journal of Traumatic Stress, 2*(2), 199–224.

Schnitt, J. M., & Nocks, J. J. (1984). Alcoholism treatment of Vietnam veterans with PTSD. *Journal of Substance Abuse Treatment, 1*(3), 179–189.

Segal, S. A., & Figley, C. R. (1988). The prevalence of highly stressful events in a college population. *Hospital and Community Psychiatry, 39*(9), 998–999.

Silverman, D. C. (1978). Sharing the crisis of rape: Counseling the families of victims. *American Journal of Orthopsychiatry, 48*(1), 166–173.

Trimble, M. R. (1985). *Post-traumatic neurosis: From railway spine to the whiplash.* Chichester, UK: Wiley.

Valent, P. (1995). Survival strategies: Understanding secondary traumatic stress and coping in helpers. In C. R. Figley (Ed.), *Compassion fatigue: Secondary traumatic stress disorder in treating the traumatized* (pp. 21–50). New York: Brunner/Mazel.

Veith, I. (1968). *Hysteria: The history of a disease.* Chicago: University of Chicago Press.

White, P. N., & Rollins, J. C. (1981). Rape: A family crisis. *Family Relations, 30,* 103–109.

PART X

# FUTURE DIRECTIONS FOR FAMILY PSYCHOLOGY AND SYSTEMS THERAPY

# Introduction

Although many of the preceding chapters have described future directions for the field in areas in which families need help, this final section emphasizes healthy family functioning. This area of inquiry is newer than that of studying problems in families, but it offers insights for prevention as well as intervention in families and other larger systems.

In the final chapter, "From Family Damage to Family Challenge," Froma Walsh traces the evolution of research that moves away from family deficits and toward the competencies and resiliency of families in facing inevitable life challenges. Noting the growing awareness that general views of "normality" are socially constructed, she emphasizes that the field has progressed toward studying healthy family processes rather than particular family structures or forms. Walsh has organized her thinking about these processes into a family functioning assessment framework that comprises three domains of family functioning: family organizational patterns, family communication processes, and family development

and belief systems. Within each of these domains, there is empirical support for diversity in terms of what processes work. There is no "one-size-fits-all" when it comes to healthy functioning in any of these domains.

In describing challenges for family researchers, the author emphasizes multidisciplinary collaboration; a focus on stress, coping, and adaptation; and use of both quantitative and qualitative research methods. She notes that ways must be found of accommodating diverse family forms; address gender issues and combat sexism, racism, and ethnic bias; and take into consideration both the strengths and vulnerabilities related to culture, race, and class. Moreover, the researchers are challenged to make sense of the interaction of all of these variables as they study a particular family or subset of families. As family psychology and systems therapy continue to evolve in a more integrative way, a closer correspondence will occur between research and practice.

# CHAPTER 34

# FROM FAMILY DAMAGE TO FAMILY CHALLENGE

*Froma Walsh*

An important development in family therapy and family research has been the redirection from a pathology-based focus on family deficits to a normality-based orientation. This approach identifies and builds on family strengths and resources that enable mastery of life challenges and the healthy development of all family members. The purpose of this chapter is to further the understanding of normal family processes by examining constructions of family normality and recent advances in research on normal family functioning, drawing on conceptual and research contributions from the field of family therapy and the social sciences. First, I address problems in definition of family normality by clarifying four major perspectives. Next, I examine clinical views of normality, health, and dysfunction. The progress and challenges for family research, clinical training, and practice are then considered. Finally, emerging research findings are synthesized in an integrative framework that specifies key components of healthy family functioning in contrast to dysfunctional patterns of interaction.

## WHAT IS A NORMAL FAMILY?

### The Social Construction of Normality

Family systems therapists and researchers are becoming increasingly aware that all views of normality are socially constructed. Although some might argue that the subjectivity of any constructions of normality makes it impossible and unwise to address the topic at all, this very subjectivity makes it all the more imperative to examine the notions of normality that

powerfully influence all clinical theory and practice, family process research, and social policy. Researchers and clinicians need to be aware of the implicit assumptions about normality that they bring to their work that are embedded in their own worldview, including cultural standards, professional orientations, and personal experience. With recent theoretical contributions from constructivism and social constructionism (Gergan, 1985; Hoffman, 1990; see chap. 2 in this volume), it has become more apparent that clinicians—as well as researchers—co-construct the pathologies they "discover" in families. They also participate in the setting of therapeutic goals tied to family and therapist beliefs about family health. Therapists and researchers cannot avoid normative thinking at some level. This makes it imperative for them to be aware of their own assumptions about normality and more knowledgeable about research identifying key processes in healthy family functioning.

The very concept of family has been undergoing redefinition in the wake of major social changes in recent decades. The idealized norm of the modern nuclear family has given way to a multiplicity of family arrangements in the current postmodern era (Chilman, Nunnally, & Cox, 1988; Glick, 1992; Skolnick, 1991; Stacey, 1990), leaving many wary about defining *any* family pattern as normal. Moreover, the myth that one family model or form is essential for healthy family functioning and for the well-being and development of all members has stigmatized and pathologized those who do not conform to the ideal (Walsh, 1992).

The definition of family normality may refer to quite different concepts, depending on varying frames of reference. The label may hold quite different meanings to a clinician, to a researcher, or to a family concerned about its own normality. Our language confounds understanding, when such terms as *healthy, typical,* and *functional,* that hold a variety of meanings, are used interchangeably with the label *normal.* It is useful to distinguish among terms and concepts.

## Perspectives on Family Normality

To clarify constructs of family normality in the clinical field and the social sciences, four perspectives can usefully be distinguished (Walsh, 1982, 1993): (a) normal as asymptomatic, (b) normal as average, (c) normal as ideal or optimal, and (d) normal in relation to systemic transactional processes.

**Normal families as asymptomatic.** From this common clinical perspective grounded in the medical model, a family is regarded as normal—and healthy—if there are no symptoms of disorder in any family member. The judgment of normality is based on negative criteria: the absence of pathology. Families who are asymptomatic, manifesting no disturbances, are considered both normal and healthy.

This perspective is limited by its deficit-based skew and inattention to positive attributes of family well-being. Healthy family functioning involves more than the absence of problems and can be found in the midst of problems. As Minuchin (1974) has emphasized, no families are problem-free. The presence of a problem should not automatically be viewed as an indication of family pathology. Similarly, freedom from symptoms is rare: Kleinman (1988) has reported that at any given time, 75% of all people are "symptomatic," experiencing physical or psychological distress, yet most do not seek treatment but instead define it as part of normal life.

The common assumption that an individual disorder is invariably a symptom of family dysfunction is also faulty. There is no simple 1:1 correlation between individual and family health or dysfunction (Walsh & Olson, 1989). It is erroneous to presume that all individual problems are necessarily sympto-

matic of—and caused by—a dysfunctional family. Likewise, it cannot be assumed that a healthy individual has come from a healthy family. For example, Wolin's Challenge Model (Wolin & Wolin, 1993) grew out of a study of highly resilient individuals who successfully overcame the adversities of growing up in seriously troubled families.

Further problems arise when researchers define therapy as the marker for dysfunction, comparing clinical and nonclinical families as disturbed and normal samples (Riskin & Faunce, 1972). Therapy versus nontherapy should not be equated with assumptions of family pathology versus health. Simply because no family member is in treatment, it cannot be presumed that the family is either typical or healthy. Nonclinical families are a heterogeneous group, spanning the entire range of functioning. What is defined as a problem and whether help is sought vary with different family and cultural norms. A dysfunctional family may not seek therapy or may attempt to handle problems in other ways, as through kin support or religion. Conversely, as mental health professionals are the first to avow, seeking help can be a sign of health.

**Normal families as average.** This approach to normality seeks to identify typical patterns or traits. A family is viewed as normal if it fits a pattern that is common or prevalent in ordinary families. Thus, from this perspective, remarriage families, expected to become the predominant family form by the end of this decade, will become the norm—more common than intact first families.

This concept has been widely used by social scientists with statistical measures of frequency or central tendency. In the normal distribution (or bell-shaped curve), the middle range on a continuum is taken as normal and both extremes as deviant. Thus, by definition, families deviating from the norm are abnormal. Unfortunately, the negative connotations of deviance lead to the pathologizing of difference. Note that by this definition of "average," an optimally functioning family would be just as "abnormal" (i.e., atypical) as a severely dysfunctional family.

This perspective disengages the concepts of normality, health, and absence of symptoms. Family patterns that are common are not necessarily healthy and may even be destructive, such as problem drinking and violence. Moreover, because average families have occasional problems, the presence of a problem does not in itself signal family abnormality or pathology.

**Normal families as optimal.** This approach seeks to define a healthy family in terms of ideal traits or characteristics. Caution must be used in deriving standards of optimal family functioning from clinical theory and basing them on inference or extrapolation from disturbed cases. The pervasiveness of cultural ideals in defining family normality and health should also be considered. Social norms of the ideal family are culturally constructed values that prescribe how families ought to be. A certain range of conduct is deemed permissible, and particular family forms and traits are considered desirable according to prevailing standards in the dominant society. Ideals may vary in particular ethnic groups. Unconventional family arrangements that do not fit the standard deemed ideal may nevertheless be optimal for the functioning of a particular family.

It is crucial not to confound the concepts of normal as typical and normal as ideal. In the influential studies of the so-called normal family in the 1950s, Talcott Parsons made a theoretical leap from description of typical Caucasian, middle-class, suburban nuclear families to the prescription of those patterns and rigid gender roles as universal and essential for the proper development of offspring (Parsons & Bales, 1955). Lidz, a leading authority in psychiatry, extrapolated from this theory to contend that deviation from these roles is inherently pathogenic for children, even contributing to schizophrenia (Lidz, Fleck, & Cornelison, 1965). Such pathologizing of difference from the norm—both typical and ideal—continues to stigmatize families who do not conform to the invariant standard, such as dual-earner, single-parent, remarried, and gay and lesbian families.

**Normal family processes.** This fourth perspective, based on systems theory, considers both average and optimal functioning in terms of basic *processes* characteristic of human systems (Grinker, 1967). The transactional view is distinguished by its attention to

ongoing processes *over time*. In contrast, the perspectives described earlier have generally sought to identify fixed traits of a so-called normal family—thought of as a static, timeless entity or viewed cross-sectionally—at a single point in time. Normal functioning is conceptualized according to organizational principles governing interaction (Minuchin, 1974; Watzlawick, Beavin, & Jackson, 1967). Such processes support the integration and maintenance of the family unit and its ability to carry out essential tasks for the growth and well-being of its members, particularly the nurturance and protection of offspring, and care of older and disabled persons. Family operations are governed by a relatively small set of patterned and predictable rules that serve as norms.

A biopsychosocial systems orientation (see chaps. 21 and 25 in this volume) takes into account the multiple, recursive influences in individual and family functioning. From an ecosystemic perspective (Bronfenbrenner, 1979; see chap. 27 in this volume), each family's capabilities and unique coping style must be considered in relation to the attributes and needs of individual members and to the larger social systems in which the family is embedded. Successful family functioning is dependent on the *fit*, or compatibility, between the family, its individual members, and other social systems. Symptoms of dysfunction must be viewed in context: they may be generated by internal stressors, such as the strains of a serious illness, or triggered by external stressors, such as job pressures (Piotrkowski & Hughes, 1993) or poverty and racism (Boyd-Franklin, 1993; see chaps. 6 and 20 in this volume).

A family life cycle framework considers normal processes in the multigenerational system as it moves forward over time (Carter & McGoldrick, 1989; see chap. 5 in this volume). Normal family development is conceptualized in terms of adaptational processes that involve mastery of life stage tasks and transitional stress (Duvall, 1977; Hill & Rogers, 1964; McCubbin et al., 1980). The concept of normal as average can be used systemically to describe typical, expectable transactional processes over the course of the family life cycle. What is normal, in terms of optimal family functioning, will vary with different developmental demands and structural configurations.

For example, high cohesion is both expectable and optimal in families with small children, but becomes less typical and potentially dysfunctional in adolescents, who have demands for more separateness and autonomy (Combrinck-Graham, 1985; Olson, 1993).

Certain stressors are considered normative, that is, common and predictable. These accompany particular challenges of family life cycle phases and transitions. It is normal, and not necessarily indicative of family pathology, for disruption and distress to be experienced at such nodal points as the birth of the first child, divorce, or remarriage (Cowen & Hetherington, 1991; see chaps. 5, 7, and 15 in this volume). Nonnormative stressors, which are uncommon or unexpected, tend to be more traumatic for families (Neugarten, 1968), as in the untimely death of a child (Walsh & McGoldrick, 1991) or in the devastation of a hurricane, earthquake, or war (Figley, 1989). How the family responds as a functional unit is as critical for adaptation as the stress event itself. A number of adaptational routes are possible, with healthier families thought to use a larger variety of coping techniques, more effective problem-solving strategies, and more flexibility in dealing with internal and external life events. More recent work seeks to better understand key elements in family resilience and mastery (Walsh, in press).

The integration of systems and developmental perspectives forms an overarching framework for considering normality. The definition of average and optimal family processes is contingent on both social and developmental contexts. What is normal—either typical or optimal—varies with different internal and external demands that pose challenges for both continuity and change over the course of the family life cycle (Falicov, 1988a). This systems paradigm provides a common foundation for family therapy and for family process research.

It is important to clarify the terms *functional* and *dysfunctional,* which have become widely used in systems-based therapy and research, in place of the more value-laden labels of *normal* and *pathological. Functional* essentially means workable. It refers to the utility of a family pattern in achieving family goals. In addition to the instrumental criteria in judging a family functional (i.e., the family unit remains intact; it solves its problems), more recently, greater atten-

tion has been given to the subjective sense of well-being and connectedness among family members. Any judgment that processes are functional (or dysfunctional) is contingent on each family's aims—involving their own beliefs about normality and health—as well as situational and life-stage challenges, economic circumstances, and cultural imperatives.

*Dysfunctional* is also a descriptive term, referring to family patterns that are unworkable and associated with symptoms of distress—regardless of the origin of a problem. However, the term has assumed connotations of serious family disturbance and causal attributions that tend to overpathologize families and presume blame for individual and social problems. Popular self-help and recovery movements currently abound for "survivors." Because individual problems are not invariably caused by family pathology, caution is urged in use of the label "dysfunctional family," distinguishing those families with serious transactional disorders, abuse, and neglect from most families who are struggling with ordinary problems in living. It is preferable, and less stigmatizing, to identify particular family *patterns* or processes as dysfunctional (literally, "not working") or contributing to distress rather than to label the family.

When a family pattern is labeled functional, it is important to consider what is meant: functional to what end and for whom? A pattern that may be functional for one system level, or for a subsystem, may be dysfunctional for another. As a common clinical example, interactional rules that serve a function in stabilizing a fragile marriage may have dysfunctional consequences for a child. Assessment of family functioning must not be limited to the interior of the family but also evaluate available resources and the impact of other systems (see chap. 9 in this volume). For instance, social policies and workplace practices deemed necessary for a healthy economy and functional work system have in many ways been dysfunctional for families (Piotrkowski & Hughes, 1993). Traditional breadwinner role status and demands have kept fathers peripheral to family life and devalued the contributions of homemaker-mothers. Dual-earner and single-parent households experience tremendous role strain with the pressures of multiple, conflicting job and child care demands and inadequate supports. Many overburdened families break down, and many parents struggle to keep their families intact and children functional only at a high cost to their own well-being. Research, public policy, and larger system interventions are needed to support healthy family functioning and the active involvement of both men and women in family life.

## CLINICAL VIEWS OF FAMILY NORMALITY AND HEALTH

Constructions of family normality, health, and pathology underlie all clinical theory and practice. Traditionally, the mental health field, grounded in medical and psychoanalytic paradigms and concerned with understanding and treating psychopathology, has given insufficient attention to the definition or promotion of *health* (Masterpaqua, 1989). Consideration of the family in clinical theory and training—as well as in research funding priorities—has been focused on the diagnosis and treatment of negative family influences in the etiology of individual psychological disorders. The search for family deficits and conflicts has fostered a blindness to family strengths and a tendency to pathologize families to the extent that a normal family could be defined as one that has not yet been clinically assessed (Walsh, 1982).

Where family dysfunction is found, linear causal assumptions have attributed blame to the family—most often to the mother—as the source of a member's disturbance, failing to appreciate the reciprocal influence of that member's problems and associated stress on the functioning of the family (McGoldrick, Anderson, & Walsh, 1989; Walsh & Anderson, 1988). The development of a family systems perspective advanced the view of the multiple, recursive influences within and beyond the family that shape individual and family functioning. Yet, early family therapy theory and practice remained pathology-oriented, attending to family deficits and conflicts believed to contribute to the maintenance of symptoms, if not their origins (Walsh, 1982). Over the past decade, there has been a welcome shift in therapeutic focus and aims toward greater recognition and enhancement of family strengths and resources, al-

though these are generally not yet well defined. The generation of family therapists who have recently come to the fore over the past decade have brought increasing dialogue and integration of family therapy approaches (see chap. 31 in this volume) as well as more multidimensional views of family functioning (Breunlin, Schwartz, & MacKune-Karrer, 1992).

It is important to examine the basic premises about family normality, health, and dysfunction that are both explicit and implicit in the major approaches to family therapy, from the founding models to recent developments. Various aspects of family functioning are emphasized as they fit with different views of problem formation, therapeutic goals, and change processes. (See Walsh, 1993 for a survey of major models of family therapy.) These largely unexamined beliefs and assumptions exert a powerful influence in every assessment and intervention, belying the myth of therapeutic neutrality.

It is crucial for clinical training programs to examine social constructions of family normality and to explore how basic premises about normal family functioning influence family assessment and intervention (Walsh, 1987). In a survey of family therapists (Walsh, 1993), judgments of criteria for healthy family functioning varied widely, depending on a clinician's particular practice model. Psychodynamically oriented clinicians valued such qualities as empathy and absence of distorting projection processes; Bowen therapists emphasized differentiation; structural family therapists cited parental leadership and clear generational boundaries; behaviorally oriented therapists stressed communication and problem-solving skills. Notably, flexibility was a consistent value across therapeutic models.

Beliefs about family normality from clinicians' own life experiences also influence family evaluation and intervention goals. In the aforementioned survey, family therapists tended to rate as normal those interactional styles that were either similar to or opposite from their own family experience. Most interestingly, nearly half of the clinicians perceived their own family of origin as not having been normal. Yet, being abnormal held quite different meanings, corresponding to the different perspectives on normality identified earlier in this chapter. Some viewed their own families as very disturbed, or pathological. Others saw their families as *atypical,* such as having a "working" mother or divorced parents, not conforming to average families in their community. Still others felt their families were deficient in not living up to the *ideal* normal family, as portrayed in the TV images that were popular when they were growing up. Generally, family differences from either average or optimal norms were experienced as stigmatized deviance (bad or harmful) and as deficiencies in measuring up to a standard.

The experience of having been in therapy themselves also influenced clinicians' perceptions. Those who had received traditional psychodynamically oriented individual therapy tended to view their own families as more pathological—especially their mothers—and were more pessimistic about changing family patterns than those who had been in systems-oriented therapies, who were less blaming and more hopeful about change. Such experiences and beliefs profoundly influence clinical views of families in therapy and the possibilities for change.

The training of therapists profits immeasurably from exposure to nonclinical families. Because clinicians tend to notice what they are trained to see, they may be blind to strengths and too readily ascribe dysfunction. Interviews with nonclinical families are valuable experiences, attending to the diversity of family perspectives and experiences relative to life cycle phase, family form, gender position, and socioeconomic context (Walsh, 1987, 1993). Such contact and discussion of the range of normal families encountered provide an opportunity to deconstruct stereotyped images, myths, and assumptions and to construct new definitions of normality, encompassing a broad spectrum of families. Pathologizing tendencies inherent in the problem focus of clinical training are called into question. Students better appreciate that all families are challenged in one way or another and have some problematic areas of functioning. Guided to assess strengths and resources, as well as vulnerabilities, they gain awareness of family competencies. Multiple perspectives are afforded by having students conduct the interview in pairs or larger teams and discuss their observations and assessments, noting similarities and differences related to their own gender, ethnic background, and current family life cycle stage.

A multimodal family assessment can include the following: (a) interviews to gather different family member perspectives on shared (and nonshared) history, experience, and worldview; and (b) direct observation of family interaction on a structured task, such as planning an activity, discussing a topic on which they disagree, or joint storytelling. A family functioning assessment framework or rating scale, such as those developed by Beavers and Hampson (1990, 1993); Olson (1993; Olson, Russell, & Sprenkle, 1989); and Epstein and colleagues (Epstein, Bishop, & Levin, 1978; Epstein, Bishop, Ryan, Miller, & Keitner, 1993) can be used to describe and evaluate specific aspects of family interaction.

An important byproduct of the experience is the discovery that each clinician is part of the assessment system and influences what is observed, the information that emerges, the attribution of meanings, and the formulation of relational patterns as functional or dysfunctional. In expanding clinicians' perspectives on normality, the experience also depathologizes their views of clinical families. As clinicians increase knowledge about ordinary families and learn how families cope with and master their life challenges, their ability to be helpful to families in distress is enhanced and the process of therapy is humanized.

## Errors in Pathologizing Normal Processes

Two types of errors can be made in regard to questions of normality (Walsh, 1983). The first is to overpathologize families by mistakenly identifying a normal pattern as pathological or misconstruing difference (deviance) as abnormal (pathological). Certain family processes may be typical and expectable in particular family situations or under stressful circumstances. For instance, in cases of chronic mental or physical illness, family distress reactive to the demands of coping with a member's disabling condition can be misdiagnosed as family pathology and presumed to have played a causal role in the development of the disorder. In fact, the family may be coping as well as could be expected, given that patient's biological vulnerability and the family's depleted resources (Rolland, 1994; Walsh & Anderson, 1988).

A clinician may also err in confounding family style variance with pathology. A pattern that differs from norms—either typical or ideal—is not necessarily dysfunctional. For example, the pathologizing label "enmeshed family" is too readily applied to highly cohesive families. The value of independence and self-reliance in the dominant North American culture can lead to misdiagnosis of family pathology in families whose norms vary and to inappropriate therapeutic goals.

The overused label "enmeshment" carries connotations of pathology when high cohesion may be functional and even necessary in a family's life situation. Closeness in lesbian couples is commonly mislabeled as "fusion," with pathological implications (Laird, 1993; see chap. 18 in this volume). Zacks, Green, and Marrow (1988) found that on the cohesion scale of the Circumplex Model, lesbian couples scored in the high extreme, a pattern labeled enmeshment and considered dysfunctional. However, for the women in the relationship, this high cohesion was mutually satisfying and can be seen as a normal tendency in view of the high relational orientation prescribed in female socialization (Laird, 1993).

Any family typology that labels a family by a single trait or stylistic feature is spurious. Clinical assessments that reduce the richness of family interaction to a one-dimensional label too often stereotype families, are reductionistic, and are too readily confounded with pathology. As Lewis, Beavers, Gossett, and Phillips (1976) observed in their pioneering study of a wide range of families, "no single thread" distinguishes healthy from dysfunctional families. Rather, many strands are intertwined in family functioning, and families should be assessed on multiple system dimensions.

## Errors in Normalizing Dysfunction

The second type of error is to fail to recognize a dysfunctional family pattern by assuming it to be normal. Here, clinicians should be aware of their own value-laden assumptions and be knowledgeable about research on family functioning. For example, the myth that healthy families are conflict-free (Walsh, 1983, 1992) may lead to unquestioning acceptance of a couple's claims of perfect harmony. Conflict avoidance and denial of actual problems can be dysfunctional over time, contributing to symptomatic behavior and heightening the risk for marital failure (Gottman, 1993).

The aim of normalizing is to *depathologize* and *contextualize* family distress. It is not intended to reduce all problems and families to a common denominator and should not trivialize a family's experience. Care is needed not to oversimplify the complexity of contemporary family life nor to err in normalizing truly destructive family patterns. Violence and sexual abuse should never be normalized, even though they have become all too common in families as in the larger society. Likewise, acceptance of diversity is not the same as "anything goes," when family processes are destructive to any family member. Family psychologists are only beginning the most important dialogue in the field: examining the myth of therapeutic neutrality and sorting out serious ethical questions and therapeutic responsibility.

## FROM A DEFICIT TO A RESOURCE PERSPECTIVE: TOWARD A FAMILY RESILIENCE FRAMEWORK

As focus shifts to a competency-based, health-oriented paradigm, clinical assessment and intervention are directed to identify and amplify family strengths and resources. This positive, future-oriented stance shifts the emphasis of therapy from what went wrong to what can be done for enhanced functioning—imagining possible options appropriate to each family's situation and reachable through collaborative efforts.

Ordinary families in American society worry a good deal about their own normality (Walsh, 1983, 1992). In a culture that readily pathologizes families for any problem and touts the virtue of self-reliance, family members are likely to approach therapy feeling abnormal for having a problem and deficient for their inability to solve it on their own. Such feelings and beliefs are compounded by the overwhelming and confusing changes in contemporary family life, along with dwindling resources and a lack of relevant models for effective functioning. Further, referrals for family therapy are often based on the presumption that if an individual, especially a child, is showing a problem, the family must be the "real" problem and cause, or else must need the problem to serve a function for them. Much of what clinicians label as family "resistance" in therapy stems from the fear of being judged abnormal or deficient and blamed for their problems. Defensive reactions are too often taken as further evidence of their pathology.

It is crucial to appreciate the shaming and stigmatizing experience of families who have felt prejudged and blamed in contacts with mental health professionals, schools, courts, and public agencies. Such families are likely to expect a therapist to judge them negatively and may mistake a silent neutral stance as confirmation of that view. Clinicians should explore each family's beliefs about its own normality or deficiency and the models and myths that they hold as ideal. The rationale for family therapy should not be based on assumptions of pathology or family causality. Instead, family intervention is indicated to be responsive to family distress, to bolster family resources, and to involve the family as valued collaborators in problem resolution.

Social constructionist perspectives have heightened awareness that therapeutic constructions need to become more respectful of families (Hoffman 1990; see chap. 2 in this volume). The very language of therapy can pathologize the family. Attributions of blame, shame, and guilt are implicit in labels of "schizophrenogenic mother" or "schizophrenic family." Demeaning language and pejorative assumptions about dysfunctional families must be avoided (Anderson, 1986). Clinical training poses an adversarial struggle when therapist skills are taught as clever strategies to reduce family pathology and overcome family resistance. Implicit in such power-based hierarchical approaches has been an asymmetrical relationship between the expert helper-healer as normal or healthy and the patient or family who is pathological or deficient. Such models of family therapy are being eschewed in favor of more egalitarian and collaborative approaches. Rather than viewing the therapist as expert and powerful and the family as deficient, incompetent, and resistant, the therapist forms a partnership with the family, building on existing or potential systemic strengths and resources. Similarly, children's well-being is promoted by fostering parental competence and working within larger systems to empower family, friends, teachers, and supportive community services. Successful interventions rest as much on the resources of the family as on those of the therapist (Karpel, 1986).

A family challenge model is especially useful in work with multiproblem families (Walsh, in press). Treatment that is overly problem-focused can grimly replicate the joyless experience of family life, where problems are all-pervasive. Interventions aimed at enhancing positive interactions, supporting coping efforts, and building extrafamilial resources are more effective in reducing stress, enhancing pride and competence, and promoting more effective functioning. Considerable potential can be found in psycho-educational approaches, marital and family enrichment, and family consultation (Wynne, McDaniel, & Weber, 1986) to provide much needed information, skills, and support to families coping with serious and chronic disorders as well as to those in more normative transitional distress. Problem-solving communication skills training workshops are being designed to stabilize and strengthen families, such as divorce prevention programs for high-risk couples. Premarital inventories, such as Olson's Prepare (Fowers & Olson, 1986), can predict later marital satisfaction or divorce and target specific strengths and problem areas. We need to expand such approaches in the development of community-based programs, offering natural settings for valuable family-focused prevention and early intervention services.

Research on normal family processes has reoriented my own clinical approach toward a family resilience framework for understanding the strengths and vulnerabilities of families as they confront inevitable life challenges (Walsh, in press). This involves a shift in perspective from family damage to family challenge. A challenge model of family resilience corrects the tendency to think of family strengths and resources in a mythologized problem-free family. Instead, we need to understand how families can survive and regenerate even in the midst of overwhelming stress, adversity, or life-altering transition (Karpel, 1986).

This approach has much in common with emerging attempts to understand individual resiliency (Cohler, 1987; Masten & Garmezy, 1989; Rutter, 1987) and the concept of relational resilience (Jordan, 1992). In particular, Wolin's Challenge Model (Wolin & Wolin, 1993) identified the qualities of *healthy individuals* who showed resilience despite growing up in *troubled families*.

Research attention needs to be directed to healthy families who demonstrate resilience in response to adverse life challenges in order to identify the key transactional processes that enable mastery. It is important to understand the ingredients of family resilience: how it is possible for some families to emerge hardier from adversity—not in spite of, but actually strengthened through, their experience.

## PROGRESS AND CHALLENGES FOR FAMILY RESEARCH, TRAINING, AND PRACTICE

Family research and funding priorities must be rebalanced from psychopathology to health and prevention if the field is to move beyond the rhetoric of family strengths and resources to clearer delineation of the components of healthy family functioning and the necessary supportive interventions. Several pioneering family systems investigators have developed multidimensional empirically based models for the assessment of family functioning. The Beavers Systems Model (Beavers & Hampson, 1990, 1993), Olson's Circumplex Model (Olson, 1993; Olson et al., 1989; see chap. 12 in this volume), and the McMaster Model (Epstein et al., 1978; Epstein et al., 1993) have found wide application in family process research. Such models offer potential utility for intervention planning and outcome evaluation, enabling clinicians to assess a family's current functioning on key system dimensions and target focal priorities for specific change toward more optimal levels (Walsh & Olson, 1989).

## Areas of Research Challenge

As new concepts and methods are advanced, three areas of research challenge are particularly important to emphasize:

**Multidisciplinary collaboration.** Family studies are becoming increasingly multidisciplinary (Berardo, 1991). Yet the bridges between the social sciences and the clinical field need to be strengthened for mutual exchange of perspectives and approaches to understanding family functioning. Dialogue between clinicians and researchers should be encouraged in journals, conferences, training programs, and most critically, through collaborative projects.

**Stress, coping, and adaptation.** Stress research in the social sciences has long held promise for understanding individual and family coping and adaptation (Boss, 1987), as in the development of the Family Adjustment and Adaptation Response (FAAR) process model by McCubbin and Patterson (1983), evolved from earlier work. The cognitive appraisal model of stress and coping, advanced by Lazarus and Folkman (Lazarus, 1991; Lazarus & Folkman, 1984) offers a multilevel, multiprocess model for individual adaptation, with many parallels yet to be fully explored at the family system level.

A family life challenge framework can usefully guide inquiry with families undergoing stressful transitions, crises, and hardship, distinguishing the critical family processes and mediating variables that buffer stress and enable the family unit and its members to adapt. Much can be learned from resilient families, such as those who successfully navigate the disruptions and reorganizations in major losses and transitions, to inform interventions with families in distress.

**Quantitative and qualitative methods.** The contributions of both quantitative and qualitative methodologies to family process research are becoming increasingly valued. Quantitative research on family functioning has focused on organizational and communication patterns that can be measured through observation, rating scales, and self-report questionnaires. Qualitative methods, currently coming into greater use, hold potential for exploring meanings, perceptions, and other subjectivities concerning families (Gilgun, Daly, & Handel, 1993; Moon, Dillon, & Sprenkle, 1990; Rosenblatt & Fischer, 1993; Strauss & Corbin, 1990). Both insider and outsider perspectives yield important information (Olson, 1977).

Ethnographic methods and narrative accounts of experiences and their meanings for family members can be particularly valuable for understanding family development over time, as well as for the formation and transformation of shared family belief systems that both shape and reflect family organizational patterns and communication processes. Postpositivist research, currently coming to the fore, does not reject empirical research and the pursuit of knowledge but, rather, emphasizes the contextual and self-referential nature of the research process and findings (Doherty, Boss, LaRossa, Schumm, & Steinmetz, 1993). These approaches are finding application in phenomenologically based theories of the family and critical theories attending to sociocultural and political influences, particularly gender, race, and ethnicity.

## Challenges of Family Diversity

**Diverse family forms.** Family process research, clinical training, and public policy have not kept pace with the dramatic changes in family structure that have occurred over the past decades. The idealized 1950s model of the middle-class, intact nuclear family with traditional breadwinner–homemaker gender roles often subtly, yet powerfully, influences therapist views of families and of what should change (Walsh & Scheinkman, 1989). It must be made clear to families that varying family arrangements are not presumed to be inherently pathological or the likely cause of any presenting problems.

Beliefs and language can pathologize or distort family relationships. The label "latchkey child" attributes maternal neglect when parents must work. The term *single-parent family* can mask the important role of a noncustodial parent (Ahrons & Rogers, 1989; Walsh, 1991). A stepparent or adoptive parent relationship is viewed as inherently deficient when framed as not the "real" or "natural" parent. One judge denied a parental rights request by a lesbian woman who shared parenting for her partner's biological child on the grounds that it would be too confusing for a child to have two mothers. The same argument disenfranchises stepparents. Even when children are functioning well, the knowledge that they are living in a nonstandard family situation too often sets expectations by teachers or counselors that there must be underlying or latent damage that, like a time bomb, will sooner or later explode (Wallerstein & Blakeslee, 1989). It needs to be recognized that families in the past and in most other cultures have thrived with multiple and varied caregivers and that healthy family processes matter more than family form.

The wide spectrum of family configurations requires greater attention in family process research, clinical theory, and training. Of particular value is knowledge about the normative expectable challenges and tasks accompanying various family transitions and structural arrangements (Carter & McGoldrick, 1989; McGoldrick, Heiman, & Carter, 1993; Visher & Visher, 1993). Research on nonclinical families, particularly longitudinal studies, can enable clinicians to identify predictable strains and support adaptive family processes. For example, the impressive studies of Hetherington and colleagues (Hetherington, Law, & O'Connor, 1993), tracking family processes associated with successful (vs. dysfunctional) adjustment of children and their parents through divorce and later remarriage, illuminate an understanding of the process clinicians can promote to buffer the stresses and strengthen postdivorce functioning for all family members.

Attention should extend beyond members sharing a household to significant relational networks. The myth of the isolated nuclear family, intact and self-sufficient within the boundary of the white picket fence, belies the intimate and powerful connections among family members living separately and even at great distance. Such extended family bonds have enabled African-American and immigrant families to survive overwhelming conditions of poverty and discrimination (Billingsley, 1992; Boyd-Franklin, 1993; see chap. 20 in this volume). The significance of families of choice needs to be studied, especially the intimate partnerships and friendship networks formed in gay and lesbian communities. The strength and support of such networks in times of adversity, as in the AIDS crisis (Landau-Stanton, 1993; Walker, 1991), holds a model of community unknown to many families in the dominant culture.

**Gender and sexism.** Recent theoretical contributions on women's development (Jordan, Kaplan, Miller, Striver, & Surrey, 1991) have important implications for the understanding of gender-based roles and relationships in families, but lack, as yet, an integration with a systemic perspective. Feminist critique in family therapy has brought long overdue attention to the subordinated status of women in families, as in the larger society, and to gender blindness and bias in family theory and family therapy (see, for example, the collection of papers in Mc-Goldrick et al., 1989; see also chaps. 17, 24, and 31 in this volume). A therapeutic stance of neutrality and the tenet of circular influence can be seen to tacitly reinforce cultural biases and ignore the power differential that perpetuates inequity, violence, and sexual abuse of vulnerable women and children (see chap. 28 in this volume). Many therapists still tend to blame mothers for individual and family problems, pathologizing the traditional gender-role caretaking responsibility as enmeshment, or chiding working mothers for neglect. Although these issues have become more visible, they have yet to be taken into account in family process research, clinical training, and practice. For instance, gender-blind measures or mean scores of family adaptability may mask a skewed pattern of deference and accommodation by wives to husbands. Likewise, interventions and measures focused on communication need to address differential gender-based assumptions and behaviors that men and women, from their solicalization, bring to interactions and negotiation processes (Walsh, 1989b).

More recent exploration of men's gendered role expectations and experiences has focused on how the male model for rationality, competition, power, and instrumental success in the workplace has constrained family involvement, intimacy, and emotional expressiveness (Ellman & Taggart, 1993; Levant, 1992; see chap. 17 in this volume). Increased attention is needed to address the impact of gender socialization and sexism of larger systems and the media on family relations and child development.

**Culture, race, and class.** Family therapists are becoming more attuned to cultural diversity. Many ethnic scholars and practitioners, notably in the work of McGoldrick and her colleagues (McGoldrick, 1993; McGoldrick, Pearce, & Giordano, 1982; see chap. 19 in this volume); Falicov (1983b); Boyd-Franklin (1993; see chap. 20 in this volume), McAdoo (1985); Saba, Karrer, & Hardy (1989) have enriched an understanding of different cultural norms and experiences and have warned against pathologizing

differences that may be valued and, indeed, functional—or even necessary for survival. Yet, cross-cultural comparisons of family functioning have often erred in confounding the effects of social class and racism with ethnic differences. The debilitating family impact of poverty and discrimination demands far more research and practice attention.

**Diverse life cycle challenges.** Family process research and family therapy have tended to concentrate on families in the developmental stages of rearing children and adolescents. With the increasing diversity in pathways of individual and family development, greater attention is needed to the full and varied course of the life cycle (see chap. 5 in this volume), to normative (typical) developmental phases and transitions as well as the choices and challenges that make every individual and family unique. Some women and men become first-time parents at the age that others become grandparents; others forego marriage or child bearing altogether. We need to study the significant relationships and generative alternatives of single adults and couples who remain childless. New technologies enabling conception and others prolonging the dying process pose unprecedented family and clinical challenges (see chap. 24 in this volume). Family relationships in later life, a neglected area of clinical attention (Walsh, 1989a), should become an arena of research and training priority with the aging of the society, as serial monogamy and four- and five-generation families become more common and growing numbers of older persons require caregiving (see chap. 8 in this volume).

**Interactive effects.** Consideration of family diversity needs to be better integrated into research designs as well as into clinical training and practice approaches, and not marginalized as special issues (Falicov, 1988b). Attention must be given to the *interactions* of sexism, racism, heterosexism, ageism, classism, handicapping conditions, and other forms of discrimination and prejudice. Furthermore, systems therapists have an affirmative responsibility to advocate meaningful social change to benefit families. A narrow focus on immediate intrafamilial problem situations fails to address larger issues, such as gender bias and racism, that permeate society. The field of family therapy has only begun the critical dialogue to address serious ethical questions concerning responses and responsibilities toward achieving gender equality and social justice.

**Research dilemmas in addressing diversity.** Early research on family functioning centered on Caucasian, Protestant, middle-class, intact nuclear families, considered typical of the dominant culture in the United States and Canada, and, most often, in the life cycle stage of adolescence. Over the past decade, the data base has been extended to other groups and through comparison studies (e.g., Beavers & Hampson, 1990; Kazak, McCannell, Adkins, Himmelberg, & Grace, 1989; Vega, 1990; see chap. 12 in this volume). Yet, understanding the differences that make a difference has only just begun.

Many questions arise concerning the applicability to diverse families of questionnaire items and evaluation scales standardized on normative samples currently representing a narrow band on the spectrum. Families in other developmental stages, structural arrangements, or economic and cultural contexts still tend to be evaluated in comparison to that standard, with assessment instruments, categories, and norms of questionable relevance. The influences of cultural value biases and social desirability present a problem in some family assessment schemas, such as the Family Environment Scale (FES) by Moos and Moos (1976, 1986). Are families who differ from the norming standard pathologized? Are the constructs of health valid in different contexts? Are the questions and indicators relevant to various groups? Are different instruments and separate norms for various groups needed? Does that risk separatism and stereotyping, in overemphasizing differences among groups? Are they simply too many variables for any norms to be meaningful? These dilemmas must be addressed if a balance can be struck that allows key components of effective family functioning to be identified while taking differences into account.

In future research and theory construction, the challenges in defining family normality are twofold. First, the typical, or expectable processes for families of varying forms, social contexts, and life challenges need to be better understood. Second, key family process components and mediating variables for ef-

fective family functioning, successful adaptation, and the well-being of members need to be identified. To address both questions, constructs and methods must continue to be developed to fit the diversity of families that comprise the wide spectrum of family normality.

## TOWARD AN INTEGRATIVE FRAMEWORK: COMPONENTS OF HEALTHY FAMILY FUNCTIONING

The growing knowledge of normal family processes can enable clinicians to identify key components of family functioning and guide interventions to draw on, enlarge, and reinforce family strengths and resources (Walsh, in press). Diverse family challenges are not well served when therapy is driven by an invariant approach or a one-size-fits-all set of techniques for every family and problem. The recommendation of Gurman and Kniskern (1978) stands as a critical unmet challenge: A major task for family therapy and research is to determine which elements of intervention are most appropriate and effective with which presenting problems and with which elements of family functioning (see the Introduction to this volume). It is crucial to assess each family's strengths and vulnerabilities in relation to their particular social and developmental contexts in order to set appropriate intervention objectives. A family functioning assessment framework can guide more informed selection of relevant family variables to resolve problems while strengthening family functioning. Attention to components of effective family functioning offers a positive and pragmatic frame for intervention, generating optimism in the therapeutic process while grounding changes in specific reachable objectives.

In addition to the empirically based Beavers Systems Model, Olson Circumplex Model (see chap. 12 in this volume), and McMaster Model, a number of other family systems theorists have proposed a variety of conceptual schemas based on systems principles for mapping components of healthy family functioning (Kantor & Lehr, 1975; Moos & Moos, 1976; Skinner, Santa-Barbara, & Steinhauer, 1983; Schumm, 1985; Stinnett & deFrain, 1985). In delineating and organizing variables, all researchers and clinicians bring their own selective focus and interpretations, such that these models cannot be easily synthesized into a blueprint for a single unified model.

A quest for consensus is perhaps misguided, for the generalizability and appropriateness of any single model for health have come into question, considering the variety and complexity of contemporary family relationship patterns. Nevertheless, in surveying the major clinical and research-based models and despite selective emphasis of various aspects of family functioning and somewhat different definition of constructs, there is considerable overlap and agreement about key variables.

## Domains of Family Functioning

From this growing body of research, important components of family functioning can be identified and processes in healthy, well-functioning families distinguished from those in seriously dysfunctional families. For clinical training, family assessment, and treatment planning, I have found it useful to organize this information into a family functioning assessment framework (Walsh, in press). Three domains of family functioning (see also Sluzki, 1983) can usefully be described: (a) family organizational patterns, (b) family communication processes, and (c) family development and belief systems.

**I. Family organizational patterns.** The functioning of any family must be considered in terms of how effectively it organizes in relation to its structure and available resources. Different family configurations, such as an intact, two-parent family, a single-parent family, and a stepfamily, will have different challenges and organizational responses for optimal functioning. Likewise, dual-earner families must organize their household and family life quite differently from the traditional breadwinner–homemaker model. Athough family forms and resources vary, all families have to develop ways to meet certain basic structural demands, including the following:

*Family adaptability* is one of the core requisites for well-functioning families (Olson et al., 1989; Beavers & Hampson, 1990). Stability (homeostasis) and change (morphogenesis) are counterbalancing forces in family systems. To function well, a family needs continuity, clear leadership, and predictable, consistent rules and patterns of interaction. This stability must be balanced by the ability to adapt to changing external circumstances or internal, developmental imperatives as the family unit and its members co-evolve over the course of the life cycle. Lacking this adaptability, or flexible structure, clinical families at the dysfunctional extreme tend to be either overly rigid in roles and rules or chaotically disorganized and leaderless.

*Cohesion* is the other central dimension of family organization. Well-functioning families balance needs for closeness and connectedness with a tolerance for separateness and individual differences (Olson et al., 1989). In contrast, dysfunctional families tend toward extremes of enmeshment or disengagement. An enmeshed pattern sacrifices individual differences, privacy, and separation for unity and group survival. A disengaged family lacks mutual caring and support in its fragmentation and isolation of members. The functional balance of connectedness shifts as families move through the life cycle. Cultural norms also vary considerably in the value of cohesion. Clinicians must be cautious not to presume that a very highly cohesive pattern is necessarily dysfunctional.

Clarity of subsystems and boundaries is important for healthy functioning (Wood, 1985). Parental leadership and authority, whether a coparental or single-parent unit, need to be clear and firm across generational boundaries. A shared balance of power and authority between partners in a couple–parental unit tends to be found more in highly functional families, whereas skewed power relations predominate in more dysfunctional families (Beavers & Hampson, 1990). The complexity of divorced and remarried family configurations poses a challenge in forming workable parenting coalitions across households and involving biological and steprelations (Walsh, 1991). Gender-based, rigid role divisions and power differential (Goldner, 1988) negatively impact women in all measures of well-being.

Interpersonal boundaries define and separate members and promote their differentiation and autonomous functioning. Generational boundaries—the rules differentiating parent and child roles, rights, and obligations—maintain hierarchical organization in families. They are established by the parental subsystem, and, in turn, they reinforce the leadership and authority of the parental unit as well as the exclusivity of the couples relationship. In dysfunctional families, individual boundaries tend to be blurred, and generational boundaries may be breached by parentification of a child, who must sacrifice age-appropriate developmental needs, or by turning to the child as a mate, to the extreme of sexual abuse (Walsh, 1979; see chap. 28 in this volume).

Family–community boundaries are also important. Well-functioning families are characterized by a clear sense of the family as a unit, with permeable boundaries connecting the family to its community and social networks. In a closed system, family isolation and lack of social support contribute to dysfunction under stress and interfere with peer socialization and emancipation of offspring.

No structural form or style is inherently normal or abnormal. Any family evaluation should assess the *fit* of a family's organization with its functional demands in both developmental and social contexts. Family resilience requires clear yet flexible rules, subsystems, and boundaries to be able to mobilize alternative interactional patterns to meet life challenges.

## II. Family communication processes.

Communication processes are vital in facilitating the organization and functioning of a family system. Clarity of communication is important; messages—both verbal and nonverbal—need to be consistent and congruent for effective family functioning (Epstein et al., 1993). Relationship rules, both explicit and implicit, provide a set of expectations about roles, actions, and consequences in family life and define the role of each member in relation to all others, including gender-based assumptions of normative roles and behavior (Walsh, 1989b; see chap. 17 in the volume).

Functional families are able to establish a climate of mutual trust that encourages the open expression of a wide range of emotions, opinions, and responses that are caring, empathic, and tolerant of differences. Dysfunctional families, in contrast, tend to perpetuate a climate of mistrust, characterized by criticism, blame, and scapegoating. Communication tends to be blocked and secretive, with avoidance of sharing vulnerable, painful, or threatening feelings. Highly reactive emotional expression can fuel destructive cy-

cles of conflict and despair that may lead to violence or family dissolution.

Problem solving is perhaps the most critical process in families and is central to all approaches to family therapy. Well-functioning families are characterized not by the absence of problems but by their joint problem-solving ability. Epstein and his colleagues (1993) identify sequential steps in the problem-solving process, including: (a) identifying the problem; (b) communicating with appropriate people about it; (c) developing a set of possible solutions; (d) deciding on one alternative; (e) monitoring to ensure that it is carried out; and (f) evaluating the effectiveness of the problem-solving process. Negotiation and compromise are important, which can be hindered by competition and struggles over power and control. Mutual accommodation and reciprocity over time are crucial for long-term relationship balance (Walsh, 1989b).

Families need to develop effective strategies to resolve normal problems in daily living as well as nonnormative crises that may arise. How well the family, as a functional unit, masters these adaptational challenges carries reverberations throughout the system for the well-being of all members. Both instrumental and affective tasks must be addressed, such as household reorganization after death or divorce, as well as the resolution of grief associated with the loss (Walsh & McGoldrick, 1991). Gender-based socialization for men to carry instrumental tasks and women to be responsible for socio-emotional caretaking constrains family members from full expression and mutual support in this process (McGoldrick, Anderson, & Walsh, 1989; see chap. 17 in this volume).

## III. Family development and belief systems.

A family life cycle perspective considers family functioning in relation to the multigenerational relationship system that evolves over time. Healthy families are able to balance intergenerational continuity and change and to maintain links between their past, present, and future (Beavers & Hampson, 1990, 1993). In contrast, dysfunctional families tend to lack a perspective on time and the ebb and flow of the life cycle. Problems with current life cycle demands or resistance to change at developmental transitions may occur when families remain stuck in the past or cut off from it, or when catastrophic expectations fuel avoidance of a dreaded future moment. How well a family copes with any nodal event or transition depends on the convergence of developmental and multigenerational (historical) strains (Carter & McGoldrick, 1989). Although all normative change is to some degree stressful, when current stressors intersect vulnerable multigenerational issues, the family system becomes overloaded, increasing the risk of dysfunction and reactivation of unresolved conflicts and losses. Many families function effectively until they reach a critical point in the life cycle when complications arose a generation earlier (Walsh, 1983b). However, vulnerability from one's family of origin legacy may be offset by the spouse's successful past experience, in the context of a trusting couple's relationship.

The influences of multigenerational patterns in family functioning remain largely uncharted terrain in family process research because of their complexity. Significant events and relationship patterns can be tracked to understand family legacies and beliefs that guide action and response to life challenges. Clinically, attention to multigenerational family patterns has mainly focused on sources of dysfunction; the value in identifying sources of strengths and adaptive legacies, as well as potential resources, has not yet been fully realized (Walsh, 1993).

Families develop their own internal norms, expressed through relationship rules, both implicit and explicit. They organize family interaction and serve to maintain a stable yet flexible system by prescribing and limiting members' behavior. Family norms set expectations about roles, actions, and consequences that guide family life. Family belief systems, which are shared values and assumptions, provide meaning, organize experience, and guide action. Reiss (1981) found that all families construct their own family paradigm, an enduring structure of shared beliefs about the social world that are shaped by pivotal family experiences and, in turn, influence basic problem-solving styles and meanings attached to situations and relationships. Beavers and Hampson (1990, 1993) found that optimally functioning families tend to be bolstered by a transcendent moral or spiritual value orientation, a benign view of others, and an optimistic stance toward the future. A family's

beliefs about their competence to face and master life challenges is particularly crucial (Rolland, 1993). In this regard, a family's beliefs about what is normal and healthy are significant. Beliefs embedded in cultural myths that define health as "problem-free" or as requiring one particular family model can interfere with coping and adaptation by pathologizing and stigmatizing families with diverse structures, values, and challenges, who come to view themselves as deficient and deviant (Walsh, 1992, 1993).

Family beliefs and norms are transmitted across the generations and through the dominant culture and particular ethnic and religious traditions (McGoldrick, 1993; McGoldrick et al., 1984). Important stories, legends, and myths become encoded into family scripts that provide a blueprint—or taboo—for interaction. Belief systems may be empowering or debilitating, depending both on their underlying themes and their responsiveness to changing circumstances. Family rituals store and convey the family identity and beliefs, fostering stabilization and continuity over time and facilitating change and healing by marking significant transitions (Imber-Black, Roberts, & Whiting, 1988; Wolin & Bennett, 1984).

## Family Functioning Domains and Process Research

Earlier family process research paralleled developments in the field of family therapy in their focus on identification of key organizational and communication variables in the most proximate family unit. Concrete behaviors in current interactions could be operationally defined and specified. They could readily be observed by raters with relatively high degrees of reliability or reported by family members on easily administered questionnaires.

There is tremendous untapped potential in multigenerational family research. The schematic family genogram and timeline are useful tools in the assessment of relationship networks and the timing of critical events (McGoldrick & Gerson, 1985). Current efforts to computerize genogram data hold research potential for systematic assessment of within-family patterns and across-family comparisons. The recent burgeoning interest in qualitative methodologies, and developments in ethnographic and narrative approaches in particular, hold strong promise for the study of multigenerational life cycle patterns and belief systems in family functioning.

## Basic Elements of Healthy Family Functioning

At the risk of oversimplification in distilling a set of basic elements of healthy family functioning, a number of key family processes can usefully be identified (Walsh, 1993):

1. Connectedness and commitment of members as a caring, mutually supportive relationship unit ("We are family").

2. Respect for individual differences, autonomy, and separate needs, fostering the development and well-being of members of each generation, from the youngest to the oldest.

3. For couples, a relationship characterized by mutual respect, support, and equitable sharing of power and responsibilities.

4. For nurturance, protection, and socialization of children and caretaking of other vulnerable family members, effective parental/executive leadership and authority.

5. Adequate resources for basic economic security and psychosocial support in extended kin and friendship networks and in community and larger social systems.

6. Organizational stability, characterized by clarity, consistency, and predictability in patterns of interaction.

7. Adaptability: Flexibility to meet internal and external demands for change, to cope effectively with stress and problems that arise, and to master normative and nonnormative challenges and transitions across the life cycle.

8. Open communication characterized by clarity of rules and expectations, pleasurable interaction, and a range of emotional expression and empathic responsiveness.

9. Effective problem-solving and conflict-resolution processes.

10. A shared belief system that enables mutual trust, problem mastery, connectedness with past and future generations, ethical values, and concern for the larger human community.

Each process element reinforces other components. For instance, a core belief that problems can be mastered both furthers—and is reinforced by—effective problem-solving strategies. A counterbalance of processes is also important. For example, a balance between stability and flexibility is needed for both continuity and change. Likewise, needs for connectedness and togetherness must be balanced by tolerance for individual autonomy and separateness.

These basic components of family functioning may be organized and expressed in quite diverse ways and to different degrees as they fit different family configurations, resources and constraints, family and cultural values, and the life challenges unique to each family. For example, specific roles and rules and an optimal balance of connectedness–separateness will vary for a dual-earner family, a single-parent household with extended family involvement, a stepfamily spanning two or more households, heterosexual and gay or lesbian domestic partners, or a single adult caring for aging parents.

In assessing family processes, it is important to emphasize that whereas certain interactional dilemmas are expectable and certain strategies are likely to be more effective than others, each family is unique and should be encouraged to invent its own optimal solutions. Just as no single family type should be a model for all families to emulate, there are many pathways to healthy family functioning.

## SUMMARY

Although the research on normal family processes is still at a relatively early stage of development, recent efforts reflect a clear sense of excitement and potential in advancing new concepts and methods. Training programs and clinical practice can be greatly enriched by the perspectives and knowledge being gained. Normal family research has advanced from earlier attempts in the social sciences to define a "normal family" in terms of a singular family form or universal set of traits to an assessment of multidimensional processes that distinguish well-functioning from dysfunctional families. In conceptualizing and studying family normality, a distinction must be drawn between typical and optimal meanings of the term *normal,* and each must be addressed from a systemic perspective, in relation to social and developmental contexts. Efforts to investigate and conceptualize normal (typical) and healthy (optimal) family processes are producing better questions as efforts continue to understand family functioning. How do ordinary families cope with life challenges? What are the mediating variables in well-functioning families that facilitate successful mastery and adaptation? The most difficult challenge is to be aware of assumptions and biases and to attempt to be true to the complexity and diversity of contemporary family forms and processes. The challenge is two-fold: Key systemic processes that foster healthy family functioning need to be identified while family diversity in terms of definitions of health and multiple routes to achieving it is taken into account. A both/and position is needed in clinical theory, practice, and research.

In today's changing world, families are confused and concerned about their own normality and well-being as they question old myths and assumptions and experiment with new and complex family arrangements. More knowledge is needed about family functioning *in its diversity* if the broad spectrum of families in society is to be viewed sensitively and responsively.

# References

Ahrons, C., & Rogers, R. H. (1989). *Divorced families: Meeting the challenges of divorce and remarriage.* New York: Wiley.

Anderson, C. M. (1986). The all-too-short trip from positive to negative connotation. *Journal of Marital and Family Therapy, 12,* 351–354.

Beavers, W. R., & Hampson, R. B. (1990). *Successful families: Assessment and intervention.* New York: Norton.

Beavers, W. R., & Hampson, R. B. (1993). Measuring family competence: The Beavers Systems Model. In F. Walsh (Ed.), *Normal family processes* (2nd ed., pp. 73–103). New York: Guilford Press.

Berardo, F. (1991). Family research in the 1980s: Recent trends and future directions. In A. Booth (Ed.), *Contemporary families: Looking forward, looking back* (pp. 1–11). Minneapolis, NM: National Council on Family Relations.

Billingsley, A. (1992). *Climbing Jacob's ladder: The enduring legacy of African-American families.* New York: Simon & Schuster.

Breunlin, D., Schwartz, R., & MacKune-Karrer, B. (1992). *Metaframeworks.* San Francisco: Jossey-Bass.

Boss, P. (1987). Family stress. In M. B. Sussman & S. K. Steinmetz (Eds.), *Handbook of marriage and the family* (pp. 695–723). New York: Plenum.

Boyd-Franklin, N. (1993). Race, class, and poverty. In F. Walsh (Ed.), *Normal family processes* (2nd. ed., pp. 361–376). New York: Guilford Press.

Bronfenbrenner, U. (1979). *The ecology of human development.* Cambridge, MA: Harvard University Press.

Carter, B., & McGoldrick, M. (Eds.). (1989). *The changing family life cycle: Framework for family therapy.* Boston: Allyn & Bacon.

Chilman, C., Nunnally, E., & Cox, F. (1988). *Variant family forms.* Beverly Hills, CA: Sage.

Cohler, B. (1987). Adversity, resilience, and the study of lives. In E. J. Anthony & B. Cohler (Eds.), *The invulnerable child* (pp. 363–424). New York: Guilford Press.

Combrinck-Graham, L. (1985). A developmental model for family systems. *Family Process, 24,* 139–150.

Cowen, P., & Hetherington, M. (1991). *Family transitions.* Hillsdale, NJ: Erlbaum.

Doherty, W., Boss, P., LaRossa, R., Schumm, W., & Steinmetz, S. (1993). Family theory and methods: A contextual approach. In P. Boss, W. Doherty, W. LaRossa, W. Schumm, & S. Steinmetz (Eds.), *Sourcebook of family theories and methods* (pp. 3–30). New York: Plenum.

Duvall, E. (1977). *Marriage and family development* (15th ed.). Philadelphia: Lippincott.

Ellman, B., & Taggart, M. (1993). Changing gender norms. In F. Walsh (Ed.), *Normal family processes* (2nd ed., pp. 377–404). New York: Guilford Press.

Epstein, N., Bishop, D., & Levin, S. (1978). The McMaster Model of family functioning. *Journal of Marriage and Family Counseling, 4,* 19–31.

Epstein, N., Bishop, D., Ryan, C., Miller, I., & Keitner, G. (1993). The McMaster Model: View of healthy family functioning. In F. Walsh (Ed.), *Normal family processes* (pp. 138–160). New York: Guilford Press.

Falicov, C. (Ed.). (1988a). *Family transitions: Continuity and change over the life cycle.* New York: Guilford Press.

Falicov, C. (1988b). Learning to think culturally. In H. Liddle, D. Breunlin, & R. Schwartz (Eds.), *Handbook of family therapy training and supervision.* New York: Guilford Press.

Figley, C. (1989). *Helping traumatized families.* San Francisco: Jossey-Bass.

Fowers, B. J., & Olson, D. H. (1986). Predicting marital success with PREPARE. *Journal of Marital and Family Therapy, 12,* 403–413.

Furstenberg, F., & Cherlin, A. (1991). *Divided families.* Cambridge, MA: Harvard University Press.

Gergan, K. J. (1985). The social constructionist movement in modern psychology. *American Psychologist, 40,* 266–275.

Gilgun, J., Daly, K., & Handel, G. (Eds.). (1993). *Qualitative methods in family research.* Newbury Park, CA: Sage.

Glick, P. C. (1992). American families: The way they are and the way they were. In A. Skolnick & J. Skolnick (Eds.), *Family in transition* (pp. 82–111). New York: HarperCollins.

Goldner, V. (1988). Gender and generation: Normative and covert hierarchies. *Family Process, 27,* 31–48.

Gottman, J. (1993). A theory of marital dissolution and stability. *Journal of Family Psychology, 7,* 57–75.

Grinker, R. R. (1967). Normality viewed as a system. *Archives of General Psychiatry, 17,* 320–324.

Gurman, A., & Kniskern, D. (1978). Research on marital and family therapy: Progress, perspective, and prospect. In S. Garfield & A. Bergin (Eds.), *Handbook of psychotherapy and behavior change* (2nd ed. pp. 817–890). New York: Wiley.

Hetherington, M., Law, T., & O'Conner, T. (1993). Divorce: Challenge, changes, and new chances. In F. Walsh (Ed.), *Normal family processes* (2nd ed., pp. 208–234). New York: Guilford Press.

Hill, R., & Rogers, R. (1964). The developmental approach. In H. T. Christensen (Ed.), *Handbook of marriage and the family.* Chicago: Rand-McNally.

Hoffman, L. (1990). Constructing realities: An art of lenses. *Family Process, 29,* 1–12.

Imber-Black, E., Roberts, J., & Whiting, R. (Eds.). (1988). *Rituals in families and family therapy.* New York: Norton.

Jordan, J. (1992, April). *Relational resilience.* Paper presented at Stone Center Colloquium Series, Boston, MA.

Jordan, J., Kaplan, A., Miller, J. B., Striver, I., & Surrey, J. (1991). *Women's growth in connection.* New York: Guilford Press.

Kantor, D., & Lehr, W. (1975). *Inside the family: Toward a theory of family process.* San Francisco: Jossey-Bass.

Karpel, M. (1986). *Family resources: The hidden partner in family therapy.* New York: Guilford Press.

Kazak, A., McCannell, K., Adkins, E., Himmelberg, P., & Grace, J. (1989). Perception of normality in families. *Journal of Family Psychology, 2,* 277–291.

Kleinman, A. (1988). *The illness narratives: Suffering, healing, and the human condition.* New York: Basic Books.

Landau-Stanton, J. (1993). *AIDS, health, and mental health: A primary sourcebook.* New York: Brunner/Mazel.

Lazarus, A. (1991). *Emotion and adaptation.* Cambridge, England: Oxford University Press.

Lazarus, A., & Folkman, S. (1984). *Stress, appraisal, and coping.* New York: Springer.

Levant, R. (1992). Toward the reconstruction of masculinity. *Journal of Family Psychology, 5,* 379–399.

Laird, J. (1993). Lesbian and gay families. In F. Walsh (Ed.), *Normal family processes* (pp. 282–328). New York: Guilford Press.

Lewis, J., Beavers, W. R., Gossett, J., & Phillips, V. (1976). *No single thread: Psychological health in family systems.* New York: Brunner/Mazel.

Lidz, T., Fleck, S., & Cornelison, A. (1965). *Schizophrenia and the family.* New York: International Universities Press.

Masten, A. S., & Garmezy, N. (1989). Resilience in development: Implications of the study of successful adaptations for developmental psychopathology. In D. Cicchetti (Ed.), *The emergence of a discipline* (Vol. 1, pp. 261–294). Hillsdale, NJ: Erlbaum.

Masterpaqua, F. (1989). A competence paradigm for psychological practice. *American Psychologist, 44,* 1366–1371.

McAdoo, H. (Ed.). (1985). *Black families* (2nd. ed.). Newbury Park, CA: Sage.

McCubbin, H., Joy, C., Cauble, A., Comeau, J., Patterson, & Needle, R. (1980). Family stress and coping: A decade review. *Journal of Marriage and the Family, 42,* 855–871.

McCubbin, H., & Patterson, J. M. (1983). The family stress process: The Double ABCX model of adjustment and adaptation. In H. McCubbin, M. Sussman, & J. M. Patterson (Eds.), *Social stress and the family: Advances in family stress theory and research.* New York: Haworth.

McGoldrick, M. (1993). Ethnicity, cultural diversity, and normality. In F. Walsh (Ed.), *Normal family processes* (pp. 331–360). New York: Guilford Press.

McGoldrick, M., Anderson, C., & Walsh, F. (1989). *Women in families: A framework for family therapy.* New York: Norton.

McGoldrick, M., & Gerson, R. (1985). *Genograms in family assessment.* New York: Norton.

McGoldrick, M., Heiman, M., & Carter, B. (1993). The changing family life cycle: A perspective on normalcy. In F. Walsh (Ed.), *Normal family processes* (2nd ed., pp. 405–443). New York: Guilford Press.

McGoldrick, M., Pearce, J., & Giordano, J. (Eds.). (1984). *Ethnicity and family therapy.* New York: Guilford Press.

Meth, R., & Pasick, R. (1991). *Men in therapy: The Challenge of change.* New York: Guilford Press.

Minuchin, S. (1974). *Families and family therapy.* Cambridge, MA: Harvard University Press.

Moon, S., Dillon, B., & Sprenkle, D. (1990). Family therapy and qualitative research. *Journal of Marital and Family Therapy, 16,* 357–373.

Moos, R., & Moos, B. (1976). A typology of family social environments. *Family Process, 15,* 357–371.

Moos, R., & Moos, B. S. (1986). *Family environment scale manual* (2nd. ed.). Palo Alto, CA: Consulting Psychologists Press.

Neugarten, B. (1968). *Middle age and aging.* Chicago: University of Chicago Press.

Olson, D. H. (1977). Insider's and outsider's perspectives of relationships: Research strategies. In G. Levinger & H. Rausch (Eds.), *Close relationships* (pp. 115–135). Amherst, MA: University of Massachusetts Press.

Olson, D. H. (1993). Circumplex model of marital and family systems. In F. Walsh (Ed.), *Normal family processes* (pp. 104–137). New York: Guilford Press.

Olson, D. H., Russell, C. S., & Sprenkle, D. H. (1989). *Circumplex Model: Systemic assessment and treatment of families.* New York: Haworth.

Parsons, T., & Bales, R. F. (1955). *Family, socialization, and interaction processes.* Glencoe, IL: Free Press.

Piotrkowski, C., & Hughes, D. (1993). Dual-earner families in context: Managing family and work systems. In F. Walsh (Ed.), *Normal family processes* (pp. 185–207). New York: Guilford Press.

Reiss, D. (1981). *The family's construction of reality.* Cambridge, MA: Harvard University Press.

Riskin, J., & Faunce, E. (1972). An evaluative review of family interaction research. *Family Process, 11,* 365–455.

Rolland J. (1993). Mastering family challenges in serious illness and disability. In F. Walsh (Ed.), *Normal family processes* (pp. 444–473). New York: Guilford Press.

Rolland, J. (1994). *Families, illness, and disability: An integrative treatment model.* New York: Basic Books.

Rosenblatt, P., & Fisher, L. (1993). Qualitative family research. In P. Boss, W. Doherty, W. LaRossa, W. Schumm, & S. Steinmetz (Eds.), *Sourcebook on family theories and methods* (pp. 167–177). New York: Plenum.

Rutter, M. (1987). Psychosocial resilience and protective mechanisms. *American Journal of Orthopsychiatry, 57,* 316–331.

Saba, G., Karrer, B. M., & Hardy, K. (1989). *Minorities and family therapy.* New York: Haworth.

Schumm, W. (1985). Beyond relationship characteristics of strong families: Constructing a model of family strengths. *Family Perspective, 19,* 1–9.

Skinner, H., Santa-Barbara, J., & Steinhauer, P. (1983). The family assessment measure. *Canadian Journal of Community Mental Health, 2,* 91–105.

Skolnick, A. (1991). *Embattled paradise: The American family in an age of uncertainty.* New York: Basic Books.

Sluzki, C. (1983). Process, structure, and world views in family therapy: Toward an integration of systemic models. *Family Process, 22,* 469–476.

Stacey, J. (1990). *Brave new families: Stories of domestic upheaval in late twentieth century America.* New York: Basic Books.

Stinnett, N., & DeFrain, J. (1985). *Secrets of strong families.* Boston: Little, Brown.

Strauss, A., & Corbin, J. (1990). *Basics of qualitative research: Grounded theory procedures and techniques.* Newbury Park: Sage.

Vega, W. A. (1990). Hispanic families in the 1980s: A decade of research. *Journal of Marriage and the Family, 52,* 1015–1024.

Visher, E., & Visher, J. (1993). Remarriage families and stepparenting. In F. Walsh (Ed.), *Normal family processes* (2nd. ed., pp. 235–253). New York: Guilford Press.

Walker, G. (1991). *In the midst of winter.* New York: Norton.

Wallerstein, J., & Blakeslee, S. (1989). *Second chances: Men, women, and children a decade after divorce.* New York: Ticknor & Fields.

Walsh, F. (1979). Breaching family generational boundaries by schizophrenics, non-schizophrenics, and normals. *International Journal of Family Therapy, 1,* 254–275.

Walsh, F. (1982). Conceptualizations of normal family functioning. In F. Walsh (Ed.), *Normal family processes* (pp. 3–42). New York: Guilford Press.

Walsh, F. (1983). Normal family ideologies: Myths and realities. In C. Falicov (Ed.), *Cultural dimensions in family therapy* (pp. 3–69). Rockville, MD: Aspen.

Walsh, F. (1987). The clinical utility of normal family research. *Psychotherapy, 24,* 496–503.

Walsh, F. (1989a). The family in later life. In B. Carter & M. McGoldrick (Eds.), *The changing family life cycle* (pp. 311–332). Boston: Allyn & Bacon.

Walsh, F. (1989b). Reconsidering gender in the 'marital quid pro quo.' In M. McGoldrick, C. Anderson, & F.

Walsh (Eds.), *Women in families* (pp. 267–285). New York: Norton.

Walsh, F. (1989c). Perceptions of family normality: Refining our lenses. *Journal of Family Psychology, 3,* 303–306.

Walsh, F. (1991). Promoting healthy functioning in divorced and remarried families. In A. Gurman & D. Kniskern (Eds.), *Handbook of family therapy* (pp. 525–545). New York: Brunner/Mazel.

Walsh, F. (1992). *Beyond the myths of the normal family.* Plenary paper presented at the 50th annual meeting of the American Association of Marriage and Family Therapy (AAMFT). Monograph: Washington, DC: AAMFT.

Walsh, F. (1993). Conceptualization of normal family processes. In F. Walsh (Ed.), *Normal family processes* (pp. 3–69). New York: Guilford Press.

Walsh F. (in press). *Strengthening family resilience.* New York: Guilford Press.

Walsh, F., & Anderson, C. M. (1988). Chronic disorders and families: An overview. In F. Walsh & C. Anderson (Eds.), *Chronic disorders and the family* (pp. 3–18). New York: Haworth.

Walsh, F., & McGoldrick, M. (1991). Loss and the family: A systemic perspective. In F. Walsh & M. McGoldrick

(Eds.), *Living beyond loss: Death in the family* (pp. 1–29). New York: Norton.

Walsh, F., & Olson, D. H. (1989). Utility of the Circumplex Model with severely dysfunctional families. In D. Olson, D. Sprenkle, & C. Russell (Eds.), *The Circumplex Model: Systemic assessment and treatment of families* (pp. 51–78). New York: Haworth.

Walsh, F., & Scheinkman, M. (1989). (Fe)male: The hidden gender dimension in models of family therapy. In M. McGoldrick, C. Anderson, & F. Walsh (Eds.), *Women in families* (pp. 16–41). New York: Norton.

Watzlawick, P., Beavin, J., & Jackson, D. (1967). *Pragmatics of human communication.* New York: Norton.

White, M., & Epston, D. (1990). *Narrative means to therapeutic ends.* New York: Norton.

Wolin, S., & Wolin, S. (1993). *The resilient self: How survivors of troubled families rise above adversity.* New York: Villard.

Wood, B. (1985). Proximity and hierarchy: Orthogonal dimensions of family interconnectedness. *Family Process, 24,* 487–507.

Wynne, L., McDaniel, S., & Weber, T. (Eds.). (1986). *Family consultation.* New York: Guilford Press.

Zacks, E., Green, R. J., & Marrow, J. (1988). Comparing lesbian and heterosexual couples on the Circumplex model: An initial investigation. *Family Process, 27,* 471–484.

# Author Index

*Numbers in italics refer to listings in reference sections.*

Mangelsdorf, S. C., 441, *454*

Mangrum, L. F., 167, *181*

Mann, B., 539, *540*

Mann, L., 353, *356*

Mannino, F. V., 483, *494*

Manocherian, J. R., 108, *110*

Mantooth, C. M., 502, 503, 506, 507, *515, 516*

March, J., 263, *269*

Marchi, M., 416, *418*

Marcia, J., 130, *140*

Marecek, J., 222, *231*, 305, *324*

Margolin, G., 209, *214*, 561, *568*

Markman, H. J., 200, 201, 205, 209, *214*

Markowitz, A., 520, *526*

Markowitz, L. M., 511, *516*

Markowitz, M., 274, *282*

Marks, P. A., 328, *342*

Marks, T., 187, *195*

Marlow, L., 274, 276, *283*, 286, 287, 288, *293, 297*

Maron, N., 521, *526*

Marrow, J., 227, *233*, 336, *344*, 593, *606*

Martin, A., 338, *343*

Martin, C. E., 259, *269*

Martin, J., 114, *124*

Martin, P. R., 523, 525, *526*

Martin, T. C., 463, *477*

Mas, C. H., 207, 210, *212*

Mason, M. J., 241, *256*

Masten, A. S., 142, *158*, 200, *214*, 594, *604*

Masterpaqua, F., 591, *604*

Masters, W. H., 239, 243, 245, 249, *256*

Masterson, J., 439, *455*

Mastrioanni, L., 422, *435*

Mathy, R. M., 331, *344*

Mattessich, P., 172, *180*

Mattison, A. M., 328, 332, 333, *343*

Maturana, H. R., 29, *43*

Mauksch, L. B., 475, *478*

Maxwell, M. J., 574, *581*

May, P. R. A., 190, 191, *195*, 207, *213*

Mayol, A., 187, *195*

McAdoo, H. P., 359, *370*, 597, *604*

McAdoo, J. L., 359, *370*

McAvoy, P., 204, *213*

McCammon, S., 575, *581*

McCannell, K., 598, *604*

McClendon, R., 475, *477*

McCormick, A. J., 506, *514*

McCrae, R. R., 176, 177, *180*

McCranie, E., 574, *579*

McCubbin, H., 589, 595, *604*

McDanald, E., 28, *43*

McDaniel, S. H., 11, 16, 17, *24, 25, 26*, 45, 47, 52, 54, 60, 67, *71*, 142, 148, *157, 158*, 228, *233*, 377, 378, 379, 380, 382, 383, 384, 385, 386, *388*, 429, *435, 436*, 439, 454, *454*, 475, 477, 479, 482, *495*, 550, 551, *560*, 593, *606*

McFall, R. M., 208, *214*

McFarlane, W. R., 8, *25*

McGill, C. W., 190, 191, *194*, 207, *213*

McGoldrick, M., 6, 9, 10, 11, *23, 25, 26*, 74, *85*, 92, 93, 95, 99, 107, 108, 109, *109, 110*, 115, *121*, 126, *110*, 143, 144, 145, *157*, 174, 177, *180*, 308, 323, *324*, 341, *343*, 347, 350, *356*, 360, 363, *370, 371*, 424, 426, *434*, 439, *455*, 589, 590, 591, 596, 597, 600, 601, *603, 604*

McGrady, B. S., 206, *214*

McGrath, E., 307, 311, *324*

McGreen, P., 207, *213*

McGuire, D., 550, 556, *559*

McGuire, T., 461, *477*

McGury, E., 502, *517*

McKay, M., 507, *516*

McKeever, J. E., 16, *26*, 45, 52, 54, 58, 67, *71*, 551, *560*

McKinley, J., 490, *495*

McKnight-Erickson, M., 276, *282*

McLellan, A., 539, *540*

McManus, U., 520, *527*

McPherson, D., 338, *342*

McRae, J. A., Jr., 466, 467, *477*

McWhirter, D. P., 328, 332, 333, *343*

Meadows, L., 130, *140*

Meerman, R., 416, *418*

Melton, G. B., 207, *214*, 539, *540*

Mencher, J., 335, 337, 341, *342, 343, 344*

Menicucci, L., 530, *539*

Menning, B. E., 421, 422, *435*

Mermelstein, R., 177, *180*

Mesder, P., 377, *388*

Mesker-Niestan, J., 377, *388*

Messer, S. B., 30, *43*

Meth, R., 424, *435*

Metzger, D., 539, *540*

Meyer, C. J., 227, *232*

Meyers, S., 423, *435*

Meyerstein, I., 439, *455*

Mikesell, R. H., 82, *86*

Miklowitz, D. J., 184, 187, 188, 189, 191, 192, *194, 195, 196*

Miller, B. D., 439, 442, 444, *454, 455*

Miller, I. W., 220, 232, 592, *603*

Miller, J. B., 310, *324*, 596, *604*

Miller, L. J., 490, *495*

Miller, M. H., 271, *283*

Miller, W. R., 537, *540*

Milliones, J., 99, *110*

Millon, T., 177, *181*

Milne, A., 276, *282*, 508, *515*

Mintz, J., 187, 188, 189, *194, 195, 196*

Minuchin, P., 114, 121, 123, *124*

Minuchin, S., 6, 7, 8, *25*, 45, 46, 49, 70, 74, *86*, 117, 119, *124*, 363, *371*, 400, *402*, 408, 409, 412, 413, 414, 415, 416, *418*, 441, 447, *454, 455*, 483, 486, *495*, 505, *516*, 549, 553, *560*, 565, *568*, 588, 589, *605*

Minz, J., 187, *196*

Miranda, J., 538, *539*

Mirkin, M. P., 11, *25*

Mischel, W., 189, *196*

Mitchell, D., 423, *435*

Mitchell, J. E., 415, 417, *418*, 575, *581*

Moen, P., 462, 475, 476, *477*

Moklsink, H., 377, *388*

Montalvo, B., 565, *568*

Montemayor, R., 104, *110*

Montgomery, L. M., 200, 201, 204, 208, *215*

Moon, S., 595, *605*

Moore, L. J., 380, *388*

Moore, S. F., 108, *110*

Moore, T. E., 509, *516*

Moore Hines, P., 360, *370*

Moos, B. S., 177, *181*, 598, *605*

Moos, R. H., 177, *181*, 598, *605*

Morales, E., 328, 331, *343*

Morgan, L., 311, *324*

Morin, S. F., 336, *343*

Morrison, A., 177, *179*

Morsink, C. V., 491, *495*

Morton, D., 393, *402*

Morton, R. A., 392, 393, *402*

Mosier, K., 566, *568*

Mosniller, T., 311, *324*

Moss, H. B., 191, *194*, 207, *213*

Moss, M. B., 141, *157*, 463, *477*

Mott, F. J., 108, *110*

Moultrop, D., 16, *25*

Moya, G., 278, *283*

Moyer, M. A., 574, *581*

Moynihan, D. P., 358, 361, 362, *371*

Mullen, R., 207, *214*, 539, *540*

Munson, S., 475, *477*

Murphy, S., 575, *579*

# Subject Index

# Contributors

**James F. Alexander,** PhD, is Professor and Past Director of Clinical Training in the Department of Psychology, University of Utah. He is Past President of the Division of Family Psychology of the American Psychological Association (APA) and the author of numerous publications. He has been honored with the American Family Therapy Academy (AFTA) Distinguished Contribution to Family Therapy Research Award, has presented as a Master Therapist for the American Association for Marriage and Family Therapy (AAMFT), and is an AAMFT Approved Supervisor.

**Harlene Anderson,** PhD, founding member and Director of the Houston Galveston Institute, is Coeditor of the *Journal of Systemic Therapies* and is on the review boards of *Family Process, Journal of Marital and Family Therapy,* and *Zeitschrift für Systemische Therapie.* She serves on the Commission on Accreditation for Marriage and Family Therapy Education of the AAMFT.

**Mary Jo Barrett,** MSW, is the Director of Training at the Center for Contextual Change, Ltd., in Chicago. Barrett is also currently on the faculties of the Chicago Center for Family Health, the University of Chicago School of Social Service Administration, and the Institute for Juvenile Research. She has been working in the field of family violence, physical and sexual abuse of children, neglect, incest, and spouse abuse since 1974. She has coedited *Incest: A Multiple Systems Perspective* (1986) and coauthored *The Systemic Treatment of Incest: A Therapeutic Handbook* (1989).

**Cole Barton,** PhD, is Professor of Psychology at Davidson College. He has coauthored several book chapters and research articles about functional family therapy, and he did his clinical training with James Alexander at the University of Utah. He has studied families of missing children with Chris Hatcher and is currently investigating families of children with medical trauma. Cole also trains community clinicians in functional family therapy and in conducting clinical research.

**Stephen F. Beiner,** JD, is an attorney practicing family law through his offices in Boca Raton, FL, and New York City. A Law Review graduate of New York Law School, Beiner has written and lectured widely on topics including pre- and postnuptial agreements, custody, and interstate divorce and support proceedings. He is a cofounder and Codirector of the Center for Mediation in Boca Raton. He was the founder and Director of the Rockland County Center for Alternate Dispute Resolution and Crisis Intervention. Beiner holds degrees also from Yeshiva University and New York University.

**Nancy Boyd-Franklin,** PhD, is Professor and teacher of family therapy at Rutgers University Graduate School of Applied and Professional Psychology. She is the author of *Black Families in Therapy: A Multisystems Approach* (1989), and an editor of *Children, Families and HIV/AIDS: Psychosocial and Psychotherapeutic Issues* (with G. Steiner and M. Boland, 1995). She is the first recipient of the APA's Carolyn Attneave Award for Contributions to Diversity in Family Psychology.

**James H. Bray,** PhD, is Director of Family Psychology Programs and Associate Professor in the Department of Family Medicine at Baylor College of Medicine in Houston, TX. Bray is the 1995 President of the Division of Family Psychology of the APA and the Vice Chair of the APA Rural Health Task Force.

He is the Principal Investigator of the federally funded longitudinal study, Developmental Issues in Step Families Research Project.

**Douglas C. Breunlin,** MSSA, is Executive Vice President and Chief Operating Officer of The Family Institute in Chicago. He is also an Associate Professor in Counseling Psychology at Northwestern University. He is an Approved Supervisor and Fellow of the AAMFT, and serves on the Board of the AFTA.

**Gary R. Brooks,** PhD, is the Assistant Chief of Psychology Service at the O.E. Teague Veterans' Center in Temple, TX, and an Associate Professor in the Texas A&M Health Sciences Center. He writes, teaches, and conducts continuing education workshops on men's issues and psychotherapy. He is Co-chair of the Society for the Psychological Study of Men and Masculinity and a Board member of the National Organization of Men Against Sexism.

**Mary Ann Carini-Giordano,** MSW, is a trained psychoanalyst and family therapist in private practice in New York City and Westchester County. She specializes in women's issues.

**Timothy A. Cavell,** PhD, is Associate Professor in the Department of Psychology at Texas A&M University. He has been funded by the Hogg Foundation for Mental Health in Austin, TX, for his research on responsive parent training and psychological interventions with aggressive youth.

**William J. Doherty,** PhD, is Professor in the Department of Family Social Science at the University of Minnesota, where he is also Director of the Marriage and Family Therapy program. He has coauthored several books on family systems in health care, including *Medical Family Therapy* (1992), with Susan McDaniel and Jeri Hepworth. He is codirector of the Collaborative Family Health Care Coalition, and chair of the editorial board of the journal *Family Systems Medicine*. His most recent book is *Soul-Searching: Why Psychotherapy Must Promote Moral Responsibility* (1995).

**Natalie S. Eldridge,** PhD, is Psychologist and Clinical Supervisor with the Boston University Counseling Center and an Assistant Adjunct Clinical Professor in the Department of Developmental Studies and Counseling Psychology. Eldridge serves as a consulting editor to *Psychology of Women Quarterly* and as a member of the Lesbian Theory Group at the

Stone Center, Wellesley College. She is currently Co-chair of the Committee on Lesbian and Gay Family Issues of the Division of Family Psychology of the APA.

**Marina Eovaldi,** PhD, is Director of Postgraduate Education at the Family Institute in Chicago. She is an Approved Supervisor of the AAMFT and a member of the AFTA.

**Charles R. Figley,** PhD, is Professor and Director of the Family Therapy PhD Program, Director of the Center for Marriage and Family Therapy, and Director of the Psychosocial Stress Research Program at Florida State University. He is founding President of the International Society for Traumatic Stress Studies and founding editor of the *Journal of Psychotherapy and the Family* and the *Journal of Traumatic Stress*. He is a Fellow of the APA, the American Orthopsychology Association, and the AAMFT.

**Marvin J. Fine,** PhD, is Professor of Educational Psychology and Research and teaches in the School Psychology Program at the University of Kansas. He is a Fellow of the APA (School and Family), a clinical member of the AAMFT, and a Diplomate of the American Board of Professional Psychology (School). He also coordinates the Family–School Collaboration Project and has numerous publications on the family–school relationship.

**William N. Friedrich,** PhD, is Professor and Consultant, Mayo Medical School and Mayo Clinic, Rochester, MN. He is a Diplomate of the American Board of Professional Psychology (ABPP) in both Clinical and Family Psychology. He is the author, with M. P. P. Root and M. P. Fallon, of *Bulimia: A Systems Approach to Treatment* (1986), the author or editor of three books on the treatment of sexual abuse, and the author of approximately 90 articles and chapters in the areas of victimization, eating disorders, assessment, and family therapy. His clinical practice includes the family-based treatment of anorexia nervosa and bulimia nervosa.

**Robert Geffner,** PhD, ABPN, is founder and President of the Family Violence and Sexual Assault Institute in Tyler, TX; is Director of Counseling, Testing, and Psychiatric Services in Tyler; and is also director of a large private practice mental health clinic. He is editor of *Journal of Child Sexual Abuse, Aggression, Assault, and Abuse,* and *Family Violence &*

*Sexual Assault Bulletin.* Publications include treatment manuals, books, book chapters, and journal articles concerning family violence, sexual abuse, family and child psychology, and neuropsychology. He has served on national and state committees on family psychology, family violence, and child abuse.

**Randy Gerson,** PhD, is Director of Atlanta College for Systemic Thinking and Associate Professor in the Department of Psychiatry and Behavioral Science at Mercer University School of Medicine. He is coauthor (with Monica McGoldrick) of *Genograms in Family Assessment* and has written extensively on the use of genograms for understanding family patterns and the family life cycle. His research interests include the biographical analysis of famous families and developing computerized instruments for constructing genograms and analyzing family patterns.

**Joe Giordano,** MSW, is Director of Ethnicity and Mental Health Associates and has a family therapy practice in Bronxville, NY. He was formerly Director of the American Jewish Committee's Center on Ethnicity, Behavior and Communications, where he conducted pioneering studies on the psychological nature of ethnic identity and group behavior. He is coeditor of *Ethnicity and Family Therapy* and has written extensively on issues related to ethnicity in professional publications as well as in the popular press.

**Dean M. Gorall,** MS, is currently a doctoral student of Family Social Science at the University of Minnesota, specializing in Marriage and Family Therapy. He has a master's degree in Family Relations and Child Development, with specialization in Marriage and Family Therapy from Oklahoma State University. He has worked as a family preservation specialist doing in-home therapy with at-risk families.

**Michael C. Gottlieb,** PhD, ABPP, practices independently in Dallas. He is a Diplomate in Family Psychology; Fellow of the APA; and Past President of the Texas Psychological Association, the American Board of Family Psychology, and the Academy of Family Psychology.

**Anthony W. Heath,** PhD, is Director of the Division of Behavioral Sciences of the MacNeal Family Practice Residency Program in Berwyn, IL. Heath is a Fellow of the AAMFT and a member of the Society of Teachers of Family Medicine. He has served as

President of the Illinois Association for Marriage and Family Therapy and as editor of several publications.

**Robert W. Heffer,** PhD, is Assistant Professor and Director of the Psychology Clinic in the Department of Psychology at Texas A&M University. He previously served as Director of Psychology at Children's Hospital in New Orleans. Heffner has been funded for his research examining the effectiveness of a school reintegration program for chronically ill children.

**Jeri Hepworth,** PhD, is Associate Professor and Associate Residency Director in the Department of Family Medicine at the University of Connecticut School of Medicine. She is coauthor with Susan McDaniel and William Doherty of *Medical Family Therapy* (1992). She teaches, writes, and conducts workshops about collaborative care for families.

**Sandra S. Hoffman,** PhD, is a licensed psychologist in private practice at the Atlanta Network for Individual and Family Therapy in Atlanta, where she also serves as Administrative Director. She is an Approved Supervisor in the AAMFT. Hoffman was Georgia's representative to the APA Council of Representatives. She has served as President of the Georgia Psychological Association and on numerous psychology governance bodies.

**Susan H. Horwitz,** MS, is Assistant Professor of Psychiatry (Marital and Family Therapy), Division of Family Programs, University of Rochester Medical Center, Rochester, NY, and Approved Supervisor in the AAMFT. Her primary interests are in supervision and training; loss and bereavement; noncustodial divorced fathers; domestic violence; and larger systems consultation with businesses, schools, and agencies.

**Florence W. Kaslow,** PhD, is Director of the Florida Couples and Family Institute and President of Kaslow Associates, a private practice group. She is Visiting Professor of Medical Psychology in Psychiatry at Duke University Medical Center and Visiting Professor of Psychology at Florida Institute of Technology. She is a Past President and Fellow of APA Divisions of Family Psychology and Media Psychology and of the International Family Therapy Association. She has edited or coauthored 13 books and 115 articles.

**Deborah A. King,** PhD, is Associate Professor of Psychiatry and Psychology at the University of Rochester School of Medicine and Dentistry. She currently serves as Director of Training in Clinical Psychology and Director of Clinical Geriatric Training in the Department of Psychiatry. She also directs the Education and Training Core of the University of Rochester–National Institute of Mental Health (NIMH) Center for the Study of Psychopathology of the Elderly.

**Judith Landau-Stanton,** MB, ChB, DPM, family psychiatrist, is Professor of Psychiatry and Family Medicine, Director of the Division of Family Programs, Department of Psychiatry at the University of Rochester School of Medicine. A Fellow of the AAMFT, she is recognized for developing the Transitional Family Therapy approach and for her contributions to crosscultural studies and the study of HIV/AIDS. She is on the editorial boards of several journals and is coauthor of *AIDS, Health and Mental Health: A Primary Source Book* (1993).

**Jay L. Lebow,** PhD, is Director of Research at the Chicago Center for Family Health and Clinical Associate Professor of Psychology in the Department of Psychiatry of the University of Chicago. He is the author of numerous papers concerning the practice of integrative family therapy and the relationship between research and clinical practice. He is a member of the Board of Directors of the AFTA and an Approved Supervisor of the AAMFT.

**Felise B. Levine,** PhD, is cofounder of the Center for Family and Psychological Studies in San Diego and a psychology consultant to the Whittier Institute for Diabetes at Scripps Memorial Hospital in La Jolla. Levine has served on the faculties of University of Wisconsin–Madison, New York University, and Loyola Marymount University in Los Angeles. She currently teaches family therapy at the University for Humanistic Studies in Del Mar, CA.

**Don-David Lusterman,** PhD, ABPP, is in private practice in Baldwin, NY. He was the founding Executive Director of the American Board of Family Psychology, now one of the constituent boards of the ABPP. He is a Fellow of the APA and of the AAMFT, as well as a founding member of the AFTA. He serves as an editorial consultant for the *Journal of Family Psychology* and is on the editorial board of the *American Journal of Family Therapy*. He coauthored (with the late Jay M. Smith) *The Teacher as Learning*

*Facilitator: Psychology and the Educational Process* (1979) and is the author of numerous articles and book chapters.

**Laurel F. Mangrum,** MS, is a doctoral student in Clinical Psychology at Texas A&M University and a psychology intern at the University of Texas Health Science Center at San Antonio. Her research has emphasized conceptual and methodological issues in predicting couples' response to marital therapy.

**Susan H. McDaniel,** PhD, is Associate Professor of Psychiatry (Psychology) and Family Medicine at the University of Rochester School of Medicine and Dentistry and Highland Hospital in Rochester, NY. McDaniel is Associate Director of the Division of Family Programs in Psychiatry and Codirector of Psychosocial Education in Family Medicine. She is a Fellow of the APA and on the editorial boards of five journals. In addition to numerous journal articles in the areas of families and health, gender issues, and family therapy supervision, McDaniel is also coauthor of *Systems Consultation: A New Perspective for Family Therapy* (1986), *Family-Oriented Primary Care: A Manual for Medical Providers* (1990), *Medical Family Therapy: A Biopsychosocial Approach to Families with Health Problems* (1992), and *Counseling Families with Chronic Illness* (1995).

**Gail S. Meddoff,** JD, is an attorney practicing family and general law in Florida. Prior to obtaining her law degree, she served as Editor-in-Chief and Managing Editor of several national, business-oriented trade magazines.

**Richard H. Mikesell,** PhD, ABPP, is in private practice in Washington, DC, with a special interest in couples therapy, addictions, and health issues. He is a cofounder of the APA Division of Family Psychology, on the editorial board of three journals, a Diplomate in Family Psychology, and a Distinguished Practitioner in Psychology in the National Academies of Practice. The APA has honored him with several awards, including Family Psychologist of the Year (1984), Outstanding State Psychologist of the Year (1992), the Karl F. Heiser Presidential Award (1993), and Psychologist of the Year in Independent Practice (1994).

**Susan G. Mikesell,** PhD, is in private practice in Washington, DC, and is a consulting psychologist to the Montgomery Fertility Institute. She is a Clinical

Instructor in the Department of Obstetrics and Gynecology at Georgetown University School of Medicine and has served as the Chair of the Psychological Special Interest Group of the American Fertility Society. She is the author of numerous articles and has made a wide variety of presentations on infertility.

**David J. Miklowitz,** PhD, is Associate Professor of Psychology at the University of Colorado at Boulder. He received his Doctoral Degree from the University of California, Los Angeles (UCLA) in 1985. He has received Young Investigator awards from the National Alliance for Research on Schizophrenia and Depression and the International Congress on Schizophrenia Research. He is currently on the Board of Directors of the Society for Research in Psychopathology.

**Patricia Minuchin,** PhD, is Professor Emeritus of Temple University; Codirector of Family Studies, Inc., New York, NY; and Research Professor of Psychiatry at New York University Medical Center. She is a Fellow of the APA and the American Orthopsychiatric Association and a member of the Society for Research in Child Development.

**David H. Olson,** PhD, is Professor in Family Social Science at the University of Minnesota. He is a Fellow of the APA and the AAMFT. He was President of the National Council on Family Relations and the Upper Midwest Association for Marital and Family Therapy. He has written or edited more than 20 books and more than 100 articles on the theme of bridging research, theory, and practice. He and his colleagues have developed the Circumplex Model of Family System and numerous assessment tools for couples and families including FACES, PREPARE, ENRICH, PAIR, and AWARE.

**Carol L. Philpot,** PsyD, is Professor of Psychology and Associate Director of Clinical Training at the School of Psychology at Florida Institute of Technology, where she created and currently directs the Family Psychology Program. She is a member of the APA and has served as President of the Division of Family Psychology. She has presented and written in the areas of training and practice of family psychology, gender issues and gender-sensitive psychotherapy, and divorce. Philpot serves on the editorial board of the *Journal of Family Psychology* and *Contem-*

*porary Family Therapy* and is an AAMFT Approved Supervisor.

**Cheryl Rampage,** PhD, is Director of Graduate Education at the Family Institute in Chicago. She is also an Associate Professor in Counseling Psychology at Northwestern University. She is an Approved Supervisor of the AAMFT and serves on the Board of the AFTA.

**B. B. Robbie Rossman,** PhD, is Clinical and Research Associate and Senior Lecturer on the Child Clinical faculty in the Psychology Department at the University of Denver. She is a member of various professional societies and acts as a reviewer and Editorial Board member for several journals. Her research concerns children's reactions to stressful and traumatic experiences, and she has authored chapters and journal articles in this area. A forthcoming book will examine the topic of the multiple victimization of children.

**S. Richard Sauber,** PhD, ABPP (Clinical and Family), directs the Family Psychology Center for Therapy and Research, Inc., and codirects the Center for Mediation, Inc., in Boca Raton, FL. Sauber was on the founding Board of Directors of the Academy of Family Mediators and founding Board of *Mediation Quarterly*. Most recently, he has coauthored the *Handbook of Divorce Mediation* (1990) and the *Dictionary of Family Psychology and Family Therapy* (1993).

**David Schnarch,** PhD, is Director of the Marriage and Family Health Center, a treatment and training facility in Evergreen, CO. He is certified as a sex therapist and a sex therapy supervisor by the American Association of Sex Educators, Counselors, and Therapists and has been Chair of Professional Education for 8 years. He is a clinical member of the AAMFT and the author of the book *Constructing the Sexual Crucible* (1991). He has presented and published widely on the integration of sexual and marital therapy and serves on the editorial board of several professional journals.

**Roy Scrivner,** PhD, is a family psychologist at the Dallas Veterans Administration Medical Center, Dallas. He served as liaison between the APA Committee on Gay Concerns and the Texas Psychological Association (TPA) from 1984 to 1989. He established the TPA Lesbian and Gay Research Fund. He served in various elective positions in TPA from 1984 to 1993, including President. In 1993, he helped to found the APA Division of Family Psychology Committee on Lesbian and Gay Family Issues.

**David B. Seaburn,** MS, Assistant Professor of Psychiatry and Family Medicine at the University of Rochester School of Medicine and Dentistry, is Director of the Family Therapy Training Program in Psychiatry and teaches psychosocial medicine in the Family Medicine Residency Program of Highland Hospital. Seaburn also coordinates the Working Group for Family Therapists Practicing in Medical Settings. He has written (with S. McDaniel and T. Campbell) extensively, including a book, *Family-Oriented Primary Care* (1990). Seaburn currently is a department editor for the journal *Family Systems Medicine.*

**Sylvia Shellenberger,** PhD, is Professor of Family and Community Medicine at Mercer University School of Medicine in Macon, GA. She directs the Behavioral Science Program for the Family Medicine Residency at the Medical Center of Central Georgia. She has served on the Board of Directors of the APA's Division of Family Psychology for 4 years. She is on the editorial board of *Professional Psychology,* a journal published by the APA. Her research interests include the impact of family dynamics on health outcomes and interventions to enhance family and individual functioning.

**Cleveland G. Shields,** PhD, is Assistant Professor of Family Medicine and Psychiatry at the University of Rochester/Highland Hospital Department of Family Medicine in Rochester, NY. He is the Associate Director for Family Research in the Department of Family Medicine and 1995 President of the New York Association for Marriage and Family Therapy. He currently has a career development award from NIMH (K07; Mental Disorders in the Aging Branch), with which he is conducting research on the marital and family processes predictive of better functioning in later life couples coping with cancer, Alzheimer's disease, and depression.

**Margaret Thaler Singer,** PhD, is an Emeritus Adjunct Professor of Psychology at the University of California, Berkeley, and a former President of the American Psychosomatic Society. She has received research awards from the American Psychiatric Association, the American College of Psychiatrists, the Mental Health Association, the AFTA, and the AAMFT. She has also received the Leo J. Ryan Memorial Award for her work on cults, and an NIMH Research Scientist Award.

**Douglas K. Snyder,** PhD, is Professor and Director of Clinical Training in the Department of Psychology at Texas A&M University in College Station, TX. He is a Fellow of several APA Divisions and is also a Fellow of the Society for Personality Assessment. Snyder has been funded by NIMH for his research comparing alternative approaches to marital therapy. He is author of the *Marital Satisfaction Inventory* (1979), a widely used clinical and research measure, and serves as editor of the *Clinician's Research Digest.*

**M. Duncan Stanton,** PhD, is Professor of Psychiatry (Psychology) at the University of Rochester School of Medicine. A Fellow of the APA (four divisions) and the AAMFT, he is a Diplomate of the ABPP (Clinical, Family). A researcher in the addictions field for more than 25 years, he serves on seven journal editorial boards. From 1977 to 1980, he was the Family Consultant to the White House Office on Drug Abuse Policy.

**Margaret R. Stohner,** MSW, is in private practice in Washington, DC. She is a Board-Certified Diplomate in Clinical Social Work. She is a member of the AFTA, the Greater Washington Society of Clinical Social Work, and the Association of Oncology Social Work.

**Froma Walsh,** PhD, is a Professor at the University of Chicago, with joint appointments in the School of Social Service Administration and the Department of Psychiatry at the Pritzker School of Medicine. She is also founder and Codirector of the university-based Center for Family Health and its affiliated postgraduate family therapy training institute, the Chicago Center for Family Health. She is Past President of the AFTA and a Fellow of the Division of Family Psychology of the APA. She serves as Advisory Editor for several professional journals and has authored and edited numerous publications, including *Normal Family Processes* (1st and 2nd eds.; 1982, 1993), *Women in Families: Framework for Family Therapy* (1989), *Living Beyond Loss: Death in the Fam-*

*ily* (1991), and *Chronic Disorders and the Family* (1988).

**Timothy Weber,** PhD, is a senior faculty member and Director of the Systems Counseling Track at the Leadership Institute of Seattle/Bastyr University in Bellevue, WA. He is a clinical psychologist and an Approved Supervisor with the AAMFT. He coauthored (with L. Wynne and S. McDaniel) *Systems Consultation* (1986) and currently is working on a volume with J. Framo and F. Levine, *Coming Home Again,* which focuses on family of origin work.

**David Wellisch,** PhD, is Professor of Biobehavioral Sciences in the Department of Psychiatry at UCLA School of Medicine. He is Chief Psychologist of the Adult Division in his department. He has a long-term relationship with the American Cancer Society's Committee on Psychosocial Problems. He has been a consultant to the National Cancer Institute for policy and grant reviews.

**Beatrice L. Wood,** PhD, is Assistant Professor of Psychiatry and Neurology in the Division of Child and Adolescent Psychiatry at the University of Rochester School of Medicine and Dentistry. She currently serves as Director of the Project for the Biopsychosocial Study of Child and Adolescent Illness in the Child and Adolescent Psychiatry Clinic at the University of Rochester Medical Center.

**Lyman C. Wynne,** MD, PhD (in learning theory and social psychology), received his degrees from Harvard, with subsequent education in psychiatry and psychoanalysis. In the 1950s, he was one of the pioneers in the field of family therapy, working for 20 years at NIMH. In 1972, he became Professor and Chair of Psychiatry at the University of Rochester. Family communication patterns, gene/environment interaction in psychopathology, the epigenesis of relational systems, and family consultation are examples of his research and conceptual interests.

# About the Editors

**Richard H. Mikesell** is in private practice in Washington, DC, with a special interest in couples therapy, addictions, and health issues. He was elected President of the Academy of Family Psychology and then was a cofounder of the APA Division of Family Psychology. In addition, he has served as President of the District of Columbia Psychological Association, the APA Division of State Psychological Association Affairs, and the APA Division of Independent Practice. He holds the American Board of Professional Psychology (ABPP) Diplomate in Family Psychology, is a Fellow of APA Divisions, and is a Distinguished Practitioner in the National Academies of Practice. The APA has honored him with several awards, including Family Psychologist of the Year (1984), Outstanding State Psychologist of the Year (1992), the Karl F. Heiser Presidential Award (1993), and Psychologist of the Year in Independent Practice (1994). Mikesell is on the editorial boards of the *Journal of Family Psychology, American Journal of Family Therapy,* and *Professional Psychology.*

**Don-David Lusterman** is in private practice in Baldwin, NY. He founded the Program in Family Counseling at Hofstra University in 1973 and served as its coordinator until 1980. From 1983 to 1985 he served as the founding Executive Director of the American Board of Family Psychology (now part of ABPP) and holds the ABPP Diplomate in Family Psychology. Lusterman is a Fellow of the APA's Divisions of Family Psychology, Psychotherapy, and Independent Practice and is also a Fellow and an Approved Supervisor for the American Association for Marriage and Family Therapy. He is the coauthor of a book (with the late Jay Smith), *The Teacher as Learning Facilitator: Psychology and the Educational Process* (1979), and numerous articles and book chapters, many of which deal with aspects of family psychology and family–school issues. He is a consulting editor for the *Journal of Family Psychology* and a member of the editorial board of the *American Journal of Family Therapy.*

**Susan H. McDaniel,** Associate Professor of Psychiatry (Psychology) and Family Medicine at the University of Rochester School of Medicine and Dentistry and Highland Hospital in Rochester, NY, is known for her publications in the areas of family therapy supervision and consultation and family systems medicine. In addition to being the Associate Director of the Division of Family Programs, she codirects Psychosocial Education in the Department of Family Medicine and is a speaker at national and international meetings for both disciplines. She is on the editorial board of six journals and is the coeditor (with Thomas Campbell, MD) of *Families, Systems, and Health* (previously *Family Systems Medicine*). She is a Fellow in the Division of Family Psychology of the APA. She is editor of *Counseling Families with Chronic Illness* (1995); coeditor (with Lyman Wynne and Timothy Weber) of *Systems Consultation* (1986); and coauthor (with Thomas Campbell and David Seaburn) of *Family-Oriented Primary Care* (1990) and (with Jeri Hepworth and William Doherty) of *Medical Family Therapy* (1992).